Dictionary of Architecture and Building Construction

Dictionary of Architecture and Building Construction

Nikolas Davies and Erkki Jokiniemi

AMSTERDAM • BOSTON • HEIDELBERG • LONDON • NEW YORK • OXFORD
PARIS • SAN DIEGO • SAN FRANCISCO • SINGAPORE • SYDNEY • TOKYO

Architectural Press is an imprint of Elsevier

Architectural Press is an imprint of Elsevier
Linacre House, Jordan Hill, Oxford OX2 8DP, UK
30 Corporate Drive, Suite 400, Burlington, MA 01803, USA

First edition 2008

British Library Cataloguing-in-Publication Data
A catalogue record for this book is available from the British Library

Library of Congress Cataloging-in-Publication Data
A catalog record for this book is available from the Library of Congress

ISBN: 978-0-7506-8502-3

For information on all Architectural Press publications visit our website at www.books.elsevier.com

Typeset by Integra Software Services Pvt. Ltd, Pondicherry, India
www.integra-india.com

08 09 10 11 10 9 8 7 6 5 4 3 2 1

Contents

Contents

PREFACE

This book, which has been compiled by its authors over a 15 year period, is an illustrated dictionary of English language terms and concepts relating to architecture and building construction. While it is intended primarily for professional and academic use, it is also an invaluable resource for students and those otherwise interested in the subject.

The dictionary contains over 20 000 entries alphabetically arranged, each with a clear definition, synonyms and a reference to illustrations and tables, where applicable. There are over 260 illustrative plates arranged by subject, high-quality line drawings produced by the authors expressly for this book.

It encompasses all aspects of architecture and building construction from history and ornamentation to current modern technologies and professional project management, making it one of the most extensive and comprehensive books of its kind on the world market in terms of quality and content.

Content and layout

Subject areas covered by terminology can be roughly identified as follows:

- Building materials and methods: timber, metals, stone, plastics, ceramics, concrete, adhesives etc.
- Components and finishes: windows, doors, roofing, hardware
- Tools, trades and crafts, industrial production and fabrication
- Building construction and other technical aspects, building services, plumbing, acoustics
- Structural and civil engineering
- Landscape architecture
- Interior design, furnishing and decoration
- Town planning
- Traffic engineering: roads, bridges, traffic systems
- Building types (historical and contemporary)
- Conservation and restoration
- Architectural Styles
- History of architecture
- Ornamentation, art and sculpture
- Project management and professional practice: contract and site practice, regulations
- Basic concepts: units of measurement, chemical elements and compounds, perspective drawing

Part (i) is a glossary of 20 000 terms arranged in strict alphabetical order. Regardless of whether the entry is a single word, letter, compound word or abbreviation, it is arranged alphabetically as if hyphens, spaces or other punctuation were absent. Each entry contains the following components: a headword, possible synonyms, a definition, references to illustrations (where applicable), and a list of related subentries (where applicable). Part (ii) comprises the illustrative material, 260 pages of 130 full-page layouts arranged by subject. There are over 4000 line images produced especially for this book. Each illustrative page spread is devoted to a single subject, and all illustrations are logically arranged and located together rather than scattered randomly throughout the text, forming a 'book within a book', an illustrative guide to the diverse subject matter. By placing similar concepts on the same page we have achieved an accuracy of definition not possible with disparate images. When buildings or parts of buildings have been presented, we have tried to use existing, familiar and key buildings as examples, drawn to the indicated scale. Other information such as the name, architect, year of execution and location of the building has also been included for the added interest of the reader. Part (iii) includes the bibliography, tables, and a comprehensive list of names and locations of the buildings etc. appearing in the illustrations.

Scope

The original version of this book is a bilingual work in English and Finnish offering translations and definitions in both Finnish and English definitions. As a starting point, this aspect has had the effect of drawing on a wider base of concepts, and has helped greatly in clarifying their definitions.

Our aim in this English-language edition has been to cater for the international nature of the contemporary world-wide building and academic community and the modern construction industry. English is the world language of international communication, despite the fact that many architectural and building professionals and students involved use it as a second language. This book has been written with a clearness and simplicity with those in mind.

As with most works of this kind, a major dilemma is that, although English is also spoken as a first language by many hundreds of millions of people throughout the world, terminological and spelling conventions are in many cases localized so that there may be deviations in meaning and spelling in the specific language used. While this has not proved to be an insurmountable problem, certain decisions (often based on common sense) have had to be taken. We have thus adhered to the spelling conventions outlined in the Oxford English Dictionary (whilst including North American and other spellings where applicable), and tackled punctuation problems, especially the age-old three-pronged dilemma of the hyphen versus the compound word versus the space in a logical and consistent manner. Many capital letters have been dropped to reflect the common modern usage of terms such as nylon and other products.

The amount of synonyms in this book is also testament to the sheer number of terms existing for the same or similar concept world-wide.

There are many terms from non-English speaking cultures in this book, especially the historical terminology of Ancient Greece and Rome. By convention these entries would usually be in italics to indicate their foreign origin. Because of the diverse and specialist nature of terms within this book, and also the fact that many of these terms could be regarded as specialist English-language terms, we have dispensed with this procedure, indicating their origin with the abbreviations 'Lat.' or 'Gk'. instead. This frees us up to use italics for species of flora and fauna according to the Linnaeus classification, a surprising number of which make an appearance as entries.

This book is in essence descriptive rather than normative, which means that it relates to the wider use of words rather than to terms defined for use exclusively for norms, standards and committees. This makes it accessible to both the professional and layman alike, and promotes an understanding of the day-to-day aspects of buildings, as well as those relating to areas of specialist expertise. It also means that the book is unsuitable for use in cases where the strict definition of a term may be a subject of legal dispute. There are many works on the market intended expressly for this purpose.

One innovation of this book lies in the nature of its structure, that is to say, the way in which it has been compiled, collated and put together. We have attempted to produce a work of an encyclopaedic nature, an aid not only for the user who is looking for the meaning of a particular term, but also for those who know the vague area in which a term exists. Consequently many entries are referred to or listed under subject headings, called headwords; for example, different types of adhesive may be found listed under the headword 'adhesive', and so on. This concept is echoed in the illustrations, in which double-page spreads are arranged by subject, showing at a glance the comparative features of items within subject category. This duplicates the flexibility of electronic media by creating a series of links to equivalent or sub-entries, an essential aid in identifying the differences between otherwise similar concepts. A thorough and logical system of cross-referencing is essential for a book of this kind, making it more than just a list of words or set of illustrative plates.

Our book is aimed primarily at those working as professionals within the construction industry, and at academics and architectural historians: this includes those working in the fields of architecture, design and construction: architects and engineering, building services, landscaping and interior design consultants, builders and contractors, suppliers, product and component manufacturers, property and estates management professionals, town-planners, surveyors, craftsmen and those working with historical buildings, as well as officiating bodies. Because of the very wide scope of written material and selection of illustrations, our book also lends itself to use as a study aid. Finally, as a definitive work on building and buildings, its content has a household familiarity which appeals to the general consumer with a passing interest in DIY, building and buildings, interior design and decoration, architectural history, etc.

A note about the authors

Nikolas Davies and Erkki Jokiniemi are practising architects located in Helsinki. Together they have more than 50 year's experience in the private and public sector, and have been involved in the design of buildings of all shapes and sizes in places as diverse as Australia, Japan, Germany, Scandinavia and the UK. They teamed up in 1987 whilst working in the offices of Gullichsen Kairamo Vormala Architects in Helsinki, and as well sharing a fondness for buildings and books, soon discovered other common interests and pastimes of tennis, football, good beer and the music of a certain Mr Zimmerman.

Although for the most part the burden of work was shared evenly, each brought his own specialist skills and interests to the forum; the area of history, especially Roman architecture, was predominantly Erkki's domain, while Nikolas brought his passion for natural sciences to the project. It should also be mentioned that this has been in every sense an independent project, unaffiliated to any academic, commercial or industrial institution, and this has given the authors the freedom to manoeuvre the book in any direction they have seen fit, and full control over matters of style, content, structure and appearance.

Acknowledgements

Particular acknowledgements and thanks are given to all those who contributed time and support for the project over the last 15 years, especially our architect colleagues Timo Vormala, Kristian Gullichsen and Erkki Kairamo (who sadly passed away in 1994) and their staff;

thanks also to Timo Hirvonen and Vesa Huttunen for their invaluable input, and to the very many who have helped us out in some way, in particular Chris Bearman, Mikko Bonsdorff, Mikael Davies, Ville Hara, Vuokko Hosia, Timo Jokivaara, Jukka Jokilehto, Aulikki Korhonen, Sakari Laitinen, Jukka Laurila, Mikko Lindqvist, Matti Muonivaara, Meri Mäkipentti, Raili Pietilä, Anu Puustinen, Veikko Saarnio, Jyrki Sinkkilä, Matti Tapaninen, Kaisu Taskinen, Martti Tiula, Kati Winterhalten. A project of this sort is reliant on grants from private and public organizations for its survival, a debt of gratitude is therefore due to the following: the Kordelin Foundation, especially Esko Koivusalo, who was especially supportive of the project; the editor and linguist Kalevi Koukkunen who offered us insights into the mysteries of Greek and Latin; our English-language publisher The Architectural Press and its excellent staff and consultants; SAFA (the Finnish Association of Architects); the Finnish Cultural Foundation; the Wihuri Foundation, and the many other organizations whose backing has helped to transform an ambitious idea to the book you have in your hand.

A special mention should be given to Nigel Davies for reading an early version of the English manuscript and for many useful suggestions, and to Timo Hirvonen for reading the original Finnish manuscript (not published in this edition).

Finally, and most important of all, thanks to our partners Paula and Liisa, and all our wonderful children Eeva-Maija, Pauli, Maria, Sara, Robin and Samuel, whose patience in having to share their households with the spectre of the dictionary project for many years has been so magnificent.

Nikolas Davies
Erkki Jokiniemi

Part I

A

A0 a standard international paper size of 841 mm × 1189 mm (33" × 46¾"), whose measurements are derived from its area (1 m^2) and the ratio of the lengths of its sides (1:$\sqrt{2}$); smaller derivative sizes A1–A10 are half the area of the subsequent size with the same ratio of side lengths (A1 is 841 mm × 594 mm etc.); see B0, C0. →130, →Table 6

Aaron's rod architectural ornament depicting a rod with foliage, almonds and sometimes a serpent twined around it; from biblical episodes in which Aaron placed his staff before the tabernacle, after which it bloomed, and before the Pharaoh, at which it became a serpent; see also staff of Asclepius, Mercury. →120

abaciscus Lat.; diminutive form of the word abacus; a patterned tile or rectangular area in a mosaic.

abacus 1 Lat.; a flat squared slab at the very top of a classical column, the upper part of a capital above an echinus and below an entablature. →80, →81
see *classical orders* illustration. →78, →79
see *classical capitals* illustration. →81
see *caryatid* illustration. →76
see *Romanesque and Gothic capitals* illustration. →115
2 see abaciscus.

abatis see abattis. →104

abaton Gk; the sacred area in a classical Greek temple, to which public entry was forbidden.

abattis a number of sharpened stakes embedded into the ground in front of a fortification or castle to inhibit oncoming attackers; also written as abatis; see chevaux de frise, caltrap. →104

abattoir, slaughterhouse; a building in which animals are slaughtered for the production of meat and other products.

Abbasid architecture a classical phase in Islamic architecture, the time of the caliph dynasty who ruled Damascus and Baghdad from 750 to 1258 AD, characterized by lavish palaces and great mosques.
see *Abbasid spiral minaret* illustration. →67

abbey 1 a community of monks overseen by an abbot, or of nuns by an abbess; also the main buildings of this community.
see *Carolingian abbey* illustration. →98
2 see abbey church. →98

abbey church, abbey; the church of an abbey.
see *Carolingian abbey church* illustration. →98

abbozzo in painting, the sketching out of a composition in a single colour as a guide for a final work of art.

abele see white poplar.

aberration see chromatic aberration.

Abies spp. see fir.
Abies alba, see silver fir.
Abies balsamea, see balsam fir, Canada balsam.
Abies concolor, see white fir.
Abies sibirica, see Siberian fir.

ablution ritual cleaning of the body prior to religious activity; a room in a temple associated with this. →66

ablution fountain see wash fountain.

ablution trough see washing trough.

above ground see surface.

abraded finish see ground, honed, rubbed finish.

abrading the rubbing smooth or wearing down of a surface with an abrasive.

abrasion the act of being rubbed or worn down.

abrasion resistance the resistance of a surface, coating etc. to marking or scratching.

ABS acrylonitrile butadiene styrene.

abscissa in a system of coordinates, one of the two coordinates as a distance from an axis; usually the distance of a point from the Y-axis, measured parallel to the X-axis. →127

absidiole see apsidiole. →95, →98

absinthe green a shade of greyish green named after green absinthe liqueur, flavoured by the wormwood plant, *Artemisia absintium*.

absinthe yellow a shade of greyish yellow named after yellow absinthe liqueur; see also absinthe green.

absolute humidity the moisture content of air measured as the weight of water vapour per unit volume of air; SI units are kg/m^3.

absolute zero the lowest attainable temperature, equivalent to 0° C kelvin or −273.16° C.

absorber 1 in acoustics, any component, unit or surface treatment for absorbing sound in a space.
2 see resonator.

absorbing glass see tinted solar control glass.

absorption 1 a physical phenomenon, the soaking up of a liquid by a porous solid, a gas by a liquid, or energy in the form of sound, heat or light by matter.
2 see sound absorption.
3 see attenuation.

absorption coefficient 1 in room acoustics, a measure of the capacity of a material or construction to absorb sound of a given frequency incident upon it.
2 see sound absorption coefficient.

absorption unit see metric sabin.

absorptivity 1 a material property, the ability of a solid to absorb a liquid, radiation, energy etc.
2 thermal absorptivity.
3 see light absorptivity.

abstract art a branch of art which is non-representational or freely represents reality in the form of patterns and colours.

abutment 1 the meeting place, joint or lap of two adjacent components, parts of construction etc.
2 the planar joint formed by two surfaces or edges placed adjacent to or touching one another. →3
3 the meeting of the upper edge or verge of a pitched roof and a balustrade, parapet or upper wall surface; especially the vertical surface or structure which rises from this.
4 the part of a loadbearing system or member from which loads are supported.
5 walling or support on either side of the impost of an arch to prevent it from splaying outwards. →22
6 see bridge abutment. →31, →64
7 see end abutment.

abutment flashing in roof construction, a vertical sheetmetal flashing used with profiled sheet or interlocking tile roofing at an abutment. →56, →57

abutting tenon joint, butt tenon joint; a timber joint in which the grain ends of two tenons inserted in a common mortise from opposite sides abut each other. →5

abyss see fess point. →124

AC see alternating current.

acacia [*Acacia spp.*] a genus of bushes and hardwood trees from warm climates.
Acacia melanoxylon, see Australian blackwood.

academic relating to higher education or an academy; of art which follows the formal conventions of the era.

academy a place of higher education in the arts; a scientific or cultural society or institution.

acanthus Lat.; carved and decorative ornament found especially adorning classical Corinthian capitals, based on stylized leaves of the Mediterranean acanthus plant, Bear's breech or brank-ursine

[*Acanthus molla, Acanthus spinosa*]; akanthos in Greek. →81, →82, →121

Accadian period see Akkadian period.

accelerated curing see heat treatment.

accelerated set in concretework, an increase in the rate of stiffening during the setting of concrete.

accelerating admixture 1 see set accelerating admixture.
2 see strength accelerating admixture.

acceleration the progressive increase in velocity of a moving body, in units of m/s^2.

acceleration lane see merging lane.

accelerator 1 see set accelerating admixture.
2 see strength accelerating admixture.

accent lighting interior lighting designed to illuminate or accentuate features in a room, such as artwork, architectural details and furnishings.

acceptance in project administration, the agreeing by a client to a contractor's tender bid thereby creating a binding contract.

accepted risk, excepted risk; in project administration, known risks in construction such as uncertain ground conditions etc., referred to in the building contract, for which the client accepts liability.

acceptor a metal or extruded plastics product attached at the edge of a wall opening, to which a door or window frame can be easily attached.

access, 1 passage; internal or external circulation space leading to a building, opening or technical installation, or used as a route.
2 see entry.
3 see site access.
4 see vehicular access.
5 in computing, the means of getting to and handling information, often involving the use of codewords.

access balcony, walkway; a long approach balcony or external corridor providing access to the front doors of flats or other units of accommodation in an apartment block.
see *balcony-access flats* in residential building illustration. →61

access barrier see vehicular barrier.

access bridge see walkway.

access control any of a number of security systems using locks, surveillance equipment and card readers within buildings or restricted areas to allow the circulation of authorized persons but inhibit the passage of intruders.

access cover a covering hatch, plate or construction attached over an access opening in a drainage pipe, duct or vessel.

access door, access window, trapdoor; a removable panel in formwork which allows for internal inspection, cleaning etc.

access floor, 1 cavity floor, raised floor; flooring supported above a main floor structure to allow for the passage of electric and computer cables, ducts and other services beneath.
see *access floor* illustration. →44
2 raised access floor, see platform floor. →44

access gallery see access balcony.
see *gallery-access flats* in residential building illustration. →61

access gully a drainage gully with a rodding eye for cleaning.

accessibility 1 in town and traffic planning, a measure of how easily and by which mode of transport a particular area can be reached.
2 the ability of a component or construction to be easily accessed for maintenance, repair, replacement etc.

access ladder 1 a ladder attached to the external wall of a building to provide maintenance access to the roof; also called a roof access ladder.
2 see roof ladder.
3 see chimney ladder. →54
4 loft ladder, see disappearing stair.

access order in town planning and land management, an order issued by a local planning authority to ensure legal public access to private land for throughfare, recreation etc.

accessory any small components used to affix or supplement a construction, or fixings and trim supplied with a product, component or system.

access pipe a drainage pipe with an opening for cleaning.

access platform see gantry. →54, →61

access stair, service stair; a secondary stairway providing access to plant or other installations.

access time, search time; in computing, the time taken for a computer or search engine to find required data.

access window see access door.

accidental air see entrapped air.

accidental colours see afterimage.

accidental point in perspective drawing, any additional vanishing points not on the axes of the main points.

accommodation road a road through private land which another person or persons have the legal right to use, usually as a route to their own land, and often in return for land concessions.

accordion door a folding door with a number of hinged vertical panels which fold together when the door is open. →50

account 1 a written record showing financial transactions as tables of figures.
2 an arrangement with a bank or other financial establishment whereby money or assets are kept.
3 a personal arrangement with a supplier, shop or other commercial facility for the payment of goods, services etc.

accountancy, accounting, bookkeeping; the upkeep of the financial records of a company or organization.

accountants, bookkeepers; professionals employed to look after the books and accounts of a company.

accounting see accountancy.

accounting period a set period after which revenues and expenditures for a company are calculated.

accoupled in classical architecture, a description of columns or pilasters arranged in pairs, twinned or joined together.

Accrington brick a hard, dark red brick made of shale from East Lancashire in England, used for engineering and industrial purposes.

accuracy an expression of the range and magnitude of error in measurement, manufacture of products etc.

Acer spp. see maple.
Acer nigrum, see black maple, hard maple.
Acer pseudoplatanus, see sycamore.
Acer rubrum, see red maple, soft maple.
Acer saccharinum, see silver maple, soft maple.
Acer saccharum, see hard maple, sugar maple.

acetal see polyoxymethylene.

acetate a salt or ester of acetic acid, used for many plastic household products, as cellulose acetate for record discs and clear plastic sheet etc.; acetate compounds included as separate entries are listed below.
amyl acetate.
cellulose acetate, CA.
lead acetate.
polyacetate, see polyoxymethylene, POM.
polyvinyl acetate, PVA.

acetone a colourless, strong-smelling, volatile and flammable liquid distilled from organic compounds and used as a solvent.

acetylene black a form of the pigment carbon black made by cracking acetylene gas under heat.

Achaean art, Achaian art; art predating that of the Dorians, produced in Thessaly, ancient Greece, by the Achaean peoples from 2000 to 1100 BC.

Achaemenian art art with Assyrian influences predating the age of Alexander the Great, produced in Persia by the Achaemenid peoples from 559 to 330 BC.

Achaian art see Achaean art.

acheiropoeitos a sacred image in Byzantine art, not created (or thought not to have been created) by man; akheiropoeitos in Greek.

achromatic see colourless.

achromatic colour in colour science, a mixture of varying degrees of solely black and white.

acid a sour, alkali-neutralizing chemical substance capable of corroding metals.

acid cleaning a cleaning treatment for metals using sulphuric, phosphoric or citric acids in combination with surfactants to remove contaminants, rust and scale from the surface.

acid-curing lacquer a two-pack lacquer used on interior timber surfaces, based on urea or melamine formaldehyde resins; see next entry.

acid-curing paint a two-pack paint for interior use based on urea or melamine formaldehyde resins, with good surface hardness and long pot-life and which hardens by blending with an acid.

acid dew point the temperature at which combustion gases rich in sulphur and chlorine condense as liquid acid.

acidic rock, acid rock; types of igneous rock whose silica content is greater than 66%.

acidity, degree of acidity; the acid level of a soil, solution etc., as measured by obtaining its pH level.

acid rock see acidic rock.

acid wash a cleaning treatment for concrete and stonework by sponging with a solution of acid salts.

ACM see polyacrylate rubber.

acorn an ovoid finial resembling the fruiting body of an oak tree; used as an ornamental terminating element for a balustrade or pier etc., often unembellished; see pineapple, pine cone. →121

acorn nut see cap nut. →37

acoustic, acoustical; dealing with or based on sound, or the treatment of sound.

acoustic absorber see absorber, muffler.

acoustic absorption see sound absorption.

acoustic absorption coefficient see sound absorption coefficient.

acoustical see acoustic.

acoustical analysis a study of the sound insulating, absorbing and reflecting characteristics of a building or space, or a project at design stage.

acoustical design the design of a building or space with respect to absorption, insulation or enhancement of sound.

acoustical glass see sound control glass.

acoustical treatment see acoustic treatment.

acoustic attenuation see attenuation.

acoustic attenuator see muffler.

acoustic board softboard whose surface is shaped, perforated or machined to improve its properties of sound absorption.

acoustic ceiling a ceiling designed to provide sound insulation or absorption for a space.

acoustic consultant see acoustician.

acoustic control glass see sound control glass.

acoustic engineer see acoustician.

acoustic glass see sound control glass.

acoustician, acoustic engineer; an expert who provides professional consultancy on acoustic matters.

acoustic insulation see sound insulation.
see *soundproofing* in floors and flooring illustration. →44

acoustic intensity see sound intensity.

acoustic intensity level see sound intensity level.

acoustic isolation see sound insulation.

acoustic level see sound level.

acoustic level meter see sound level meter.

acoustic mortar see acoustic plaster.

acoustic panel a panel designed to absorb sound and thus regulate the acoustic quality of a space.

acoustic plaster plaster containing lightweight or other porous aggregates, used for its acoustic properties, especially sound absorption; also called acoustic mortar.

acoustic plasterwork plasterwork containing aggregate which has acoustic properties; finished work in acoustic plaster.

acoustic power see sound power.

acoustic power level see sound power level.

acoustic pressure see sound pressure.

acoustic pressure level see sound pressure level.

acoustic propagation see sound propagation.

acoustics 1 the study of sound and hearing.
2 the properties of a room pertaining to sound.
3 see acoustical treatment.
4 see room acoustics.

acoustic spectrum see audio spectrum.

acoustic treatment, acoustics; physical or spatial measures, materials or components added to affect the acoustic perception and performance in a space with respect to sound insulation, absorption and reflection.

acre an imperial unit of area equivalent to 4047 m^2.

acrolith in classical Greek architecture, a statue whose head, hands and feet are of marble fixed to a timber torso.

acropodium Lat.; in classical architecture, a pedestal or plinth for a statue; akropodion in Greek.

acropolis in classical Greek architecture, a city stronghold or fortress constructed on higher ground than surrounding urban fabric. →94

across the grain perpendicular to the general direction of the grain in timber.

acroter see acroterion. →78

acroterion, acroter; in classical architecture, a plinth or pedestal for statues, set at the apex or eaves of a temple; also often the statues or ornaments themselves; plural acroteria; Latin form is acroterium, Greek is akroterion. →78
see *acroterion* in classical temple illustration. →86

acroterium Latin form of acroterion. →78

acrylate adhesive acrylic-based polymer adhesive used for soft plastic seams and adhesive tapes.

acrylic a synthetic polymer resin used in plastics, paints, adhesives and textiles.

acrylic baking enamel see acrylic stoving enamel.

acrylic cellular sheet, cellular acrylic sheet; cellular sheet glazing or cladding manufactured from transparent acrylic resin.

acrylic coating see acrylic finish.

acrylic finish, acrylic coating; any surface covering or coating, such as tiling, boarding and paints, whose finish is acrylic.

acrylic flooring compound a hardwearing flooring for sports halls, corridors etc. laid over concrete floor slabs as a mixture of liquid acrylic, powdered hardener and fine aggregate.

acrylic paint emulsion paint based on a dispersion of acrylic in water.

acrylic polymer flooring see acrylic flooring compound.

acrylic powder coating, stoved acrylic; a hardwearing decorative coating whose binder is acrylic resin, applied to metal components as a powder and baked on.

acrylic primer acrylic paint used as a primer or undercoat.

acrylic rubber see polyacrylate rubber.

acrylic sealant an acrylic-based flexible sealant used for dry applications.

acrylic sheet strong translucent or opaque lightweight sheet of polymethyl methacrylate plastics used for glazing and cladding; marketed as Perspex and Plexiglas.

acrylic stoving enamel, acrylic baking enamel; a hardwearing paint coating used in the automotive industry, based on acrylic resin applied to metal surfaces as a liquid spray and baked on.

acrylonitrile butadiene styrene, ABS; a tough, strong thermoplastic used for waste pipes, garage doors, small vehicles and taxi-cab roofs.

actinium a radioactive, silver-white, metallic chemical element, **Ac**, which glows in the dark.

action area in town planning, a particular area designated by a planning authority to merit special change such as development, redevelopment or improvement.

activated carbon, activated charcoal; granular or powdered forms of porous carbon or charcoal processed to remove tarry components, used for adsorbing gases and odours from air, or dissolving contaminants from liquid solutions.

activated charcoal see activated carbon.

activated sludge organic mass produced from sewage aerated by blowing air through it, used in the treatment of waste water for the digestion of incoming sewage.

activated-sludge process the biological treatment of waste water using organisms in aerated sludge to digest the solid matter from incoming sewage.

active earth pressure the pressure of earth acting against the side of a wall and against which it provides resistance.

active fire protection mechanical or electronic control systems such as sprinklers, fire alarms etc. for indicating the presence of or extinguishing hazardous fires in buildings.

active leaf the door leaf in a double door usually used for throughfare. →50

activity analysis a study of the overall patterns of behaviour and activities of a particular user group such as inhabitants, consumers or occupants, used as a basis for the formulation of a design brief or town plan.

activity space, hobby room, recreation room; a space in a residential building or dwelling primarily used for leisure activities and hobbies.

act of God see force majeure.

actual size the size of an object as obtained by measurement; see also nominal dimension.

acute angle an angle of less than 90°.

acute arch see lancet arch. →24

Adam style a style in interior decoration in England from 1760 to 1770 named after the Adam brothers, John, Robert and James, and characterized by classical motifs and bold colours.

adapter see adaptor.

adaptive use in town planning, the change in use or function of a building from that for which it was originally designed.

adaptor, adapter; **1** a device for converting mains current to that suitable for operating electronic devices.

2 see plug adaptor.

3 see flue adaptor. →58

addendum a separate explanatory statement intended to clarify, amend or supplement a document, drawing etc.

addition 1 the process of adding numbers together to produce a sum.

2 an extension to an existing building.

additional work see extra work.

addition polymerization, polyaddition; the chemical joining together of two or more molecules of a compound such that the molecular weight of the polymer thus formed is a multiple of that of the original compound; the general form of polymerization.

additive a substance added to a material or process to modify its chemical or physical properties.

additive mixture in colour science, lighter colours formed when beams of coloured light are combined, thus adding spectral components together.

additive order the building of Romanesque and early Gothic churches with additional transepts, chapels and chancels. →97

addorsed a description of ornament or sculptured figures standing or situated back to back; see also affronted. →122

addressable system, intelligent fire alarm; an electronic installation for indicating the location and severity of an outbreak of hazardous fire in a building.

adhering knot see tight knot.

adhesion, bond; the action of sticking together; the strength of the attractive or fastening force evolved between a surface material or coating and its backing, or between two components which have been glued or bonded together.

adhesive a sticky solid or liquid bonding substance used for the firm sticking, surface joining and holding together of materials and components; the words adhesive and glue are generally synonymous, although adhesive is often applied to more technologically advanced products, while glues are often of plant or animal origin; a cement is an inorganic adhesive which sets in hard, brittle form; types of adhesive included as separate entries are listed below.

aerosol glue, see spray adhesive.
albumen glue.
anaerobic adhesive.
animal glue.
aqueous adhesive, see water-borne adhesive.
bituminous adhesive.
bone glue.
brushing adhesive.
casein glue.
cassava.
cellulose adhesive.
cold curing adhesive.
cold glue, see cold setting adhesive, cold curing adhesive.
cold setting adhesive.
collagen glue, see animal glue.
contact adhesive.
cyanoacrylate adhesive.
elastomeric adhesive.
emulsion glue, emulsion adhesive.
epoxide resin adhesive, see epoxy resin adhesive.
epoxy adhesive, see epoxy resin adhesive.
epoxy glue, see epoxy resin adhesive.
epoxy resin adhesive.
film adhesive, see film glue.
film glue.
fish glue.
gluten glue.
gun applied adhesive.
gunnable adhesive, see gun applied adhesive.
hide glue.
hot-melt adhesive, see thermoplastic adhesive.
hot-melt glue, see thermoplastic adhesive.
hot setting adhesive, see thermosetting adhesive.
hot setting glue, see thermosetting adhesive.
interior adhesive.
isinglass, see fish glue.
melamine formaldehyde glue.
moisture curing adhesive.
moisture resistant adhesive.
one-way stick adhesive.
phenol formaldehyde glue.
polymer adhesive, see polymerizing adhesive.
polymer glue, see polymerizing adhesive.
polymerizing adhesive.
polyvinyl acetate glue.
protein glue.

PVA glue, polyvinyl acetate glue.
resin adhesive, see synthetic resin adhesives.
resin glue.
resorcinol formaldehyde glue.
rubber adhesive, see elastomeric adhesive.
rubber glue, see elastomeric adhesive.
rubber solution.
Scotch glue.
single spread adhesive, see one-way stick adhesive.
solvent adhesive.
solvent-based adhesive, see solvent-borne adhesive.
Solvent-borne adhesive.
soya glue.
spray adhesive.
starch adhesive.
structural adhesive.
super glue, see cyanoacrylate adhesive.
synthetic resin adhesive.
synthetic rubber glue, see elastomeric adhesive.
thermoplastic adhesive.
thermoplastic glue, see thermoplastic adhesive.
thermosetting adhesive.
two pack adhesive, two component adhesive, two part adhesive.
two-way stick adhesive.
urea formaldehyde glue.
vegetable glue.
water-borne adhesive.
waterproof glue, see water-resistant adhesive.
waterproof adhesive, see water-resistant adhesive.
water-resistant adhesive.
water-based adhesive, see water-borne adhesive.
wood adhesive.
wood glue, see wood adhesive.

adhesive failure, bond failure; the failure of a glued joint due to a reduction in bonding between a glue or binder and glued parts.

adhesiveness the ability of a glue to provide a bond between two surfaces.

adhesive tape paper or plastics tape with adhesive on one or both sides and manufactured in rolls; used for fastening, fixing, masking, insulating etc.

adhocism a term coined by the architect Charles Jencks to describe modern eclectic styles of architecture which contain random references and historical motifs.

adiabatic referring to a thermodynamics process which occurs without the transfer of heat.

adit, aditus (Lat.); a passage or entranceway, especially one to a Roman building. →89, →90

aditus Latin form of adit. →89, →90

adjacent building a building on a site next to that of a proposed or existing building, such that there is space between the two.

adjoining building a building on a site next to that of a proposed or existing building, such that they are physically joined to one another.

adjustable the ability of a device, tool, machine, furnishing etc. to be able to be adjusted to suit the needs of the user or a process.

adjustable item an item in a bill of quantities for which provided information is insufficient and whose quantities are subject to reassessment.

adjustable prop see telescopic prop. →30

adjustable set square in technical drawing, a set square in which the angle of the hypotenuse can be adjusted by a sliding mechanism. →130

adjustable spanner a spanner with screw-adjustable jaws to suit a range of widths.

adjustable wrench see adjustable spanner.

adjustment see formula price adjustment.

adjustment screw in field surveying, a screw on an optical levelling instrument for making fine adjustments; a similar component on other devices.

administration, management; the overseeing, planning and direction of affairs and personnel in an organization.

administrative building a building connected to an institution, public building or industrial complex, from which it is governed.

admiralty brass an alloy of copper and zinc with additional tin to improve corrosion resistance and increase strength.

admixture a material added in small quantities to affect the properties of a concrete or mortar mix; types of admixture included as separate entries are listed below; see also agent.
accelerating admixture, see set accelerating admixture, strength accelerating admixture.
air-detraining admixture.
air-entraining admixture.
anti-foaming admixture.
antifreezing admixture.
bonding admixture.
colouring admixture.
corrosion inhibiting admixture.
expansion producing admixture.
flocculating admixture.
foam forming admixture.
fungicidal admixture.
gas forming admixture.
high range water-reducing admixture, see superplasticizing admixture.
mortar admixture.
permeability-reducing admixture, see pore filler.
plasticizing admixture.
set accelerating admixture.
set retarding admixture.
strength accelerating admixture.
superplasticizing admixture.
thickening admixture.
water-reducing admixture.
water-resisting admixture.
waterproofing admixture, see water-resisting admixture.

adobe **1** clay and unfired brick which has been baked in the sun; see mud brick.
2 forms of construction making use of this.

ADP acronym for automated data processing, see computing.

adsorption **1** the intake of a liquid or gas by a solid.
2 a water purification treatment in which water is percolated through solid granular material, to which impurities adhere.

adularia a transparent variety of the mineral orthoclase or potash feldspar found in the Alps. see moonstone.

aduton Greek form of adytum. →85

advance, advance payment, prepayment; a payment made prior to receipt of goods or services, such as that paid by a client to a contractor after the contract is signed but before the start of work.

advanced decay, typical decay; a late stage of decay in wood indicated by softening and loss of structural strength.

advanced work an outer defensive structure built close enough to main fortifications to gain covering fire from it; an outwork or first line of defence; also called a forework. →104
see *fortification* illustration. →104

advance payment see advance.

advent cross see tau cross. →117

adventure playground an area of landscaped ground, often with climbing frames etc., for children to play on.

advocacy planning in town planning, the preparation of plans or planning proposals on behalf of an organization, interest group or a community rather than by an official agency.

adyton see adytum. →85

adytum, sanctuary; Lat.; in classical architecture, the most sacred inner chamber of a Greek temple,

to which priests only were allowed access; the Greek form of the word is aduton or adyton.
see *adytum* in classical peristyle temple illustration. →85

adz see adze.

adze, adz; an axe-like hand tool for the rough shaping and smoothing of wood; it has a sharp curved steel blade whose cutting edge is perpendicular to the handle.

adze eye hammer a hammer whose head is fixed to the shaft by means of a sleeve at the base of the head.

aedicula Latin form of aedicule. →112

aedicule, aedicula (Lat.); in classical architecture, a niche, recess or pedimented structure, especially one housing a statue, surrounded by columns, pilasters or colonnettes. →112

Aegean art art from the bronze-age cultures of the Aegean Sea coasts from 2600 to 1500 BC, variously known as Minoan (Crete), Helladic (mainland) and Cycladic (islands) art.
see *Asian and Mediterranean columns and capitals* illustration. →69

aeolian deposit, wind deposit; any soil which has been deposited by the action of the wind.

Aeolic capital in classical architecture, a forerunner of the Ionic capital with a rectangular upper section supported by volutes divided by palmette decoration. →69

aerarium Lat.; in classical Roman architecture, the public treasury of a community, originally the treasury of the temple of Saturn.

aerated concrete, cellular concrete, porous concrete; various types of lightweight concrete for in-situ work and precast products with good thermal insulation, produced by the introduction of bubbles of gas into the mix, either by a foaming agent, by adding foam, by mechanical foaming or by adding a chemical which reacts with the concrete to produce gas bubbles; see also gas concrete, foamed concrete.

aeration the introduction of air into a material such as soil, water, concrete etc.; especially the introduction of oxygen into raw sewage to reduce the quantity of other dissolved gases.

aeration tank, oxidation tank; a tank in a waste water treatment plant in which raw sewage is treated by biological action initiated by the introduction of air.

aerator see tap aerator.

aerial, 1 antenna, (pl. antennae); a telecommunications receiver for airborne electromagnetic transmissions.
2 see satellite link aerial.

aerial amplifier an electronic device for increasing the strength of signals picked up by an antenna or aerial.

aerial perspective, 1 a perspective drawing in which the object or scene is viewed as from the air; usually a panoramic view.
2 atmospheric projection; a method of rendering a drawing to achieve the illusion of depth by drawing objects in the background less distinctly.

aerial photograph a photograph of a site, building or geographical feature taken from the air.

aerial ropeway a transportation system using ropes supported between towers to convey goods.

aerial survey the photographing of areas of land and coastline from the air for photogrammetrical map-making.

aerial view a presentation drawing, graphic visualization or photograph in which the subject or scene is viewed from above.

aerodrome see airfield.

aerodynamics a science which deals with gases in motion.

aerosol a suspension of fine particles of solid or liquid in a gas, usually air.

aerosol glue see spray adhesive.

aerosol spraying the spraying of a paint, varnish, glue or other liquid from a pressurized airtight container to form an aerosol; used for applying even coatings.

aerostatics a science which deals with the equilibrium and pressure of gases.

Aesculapian column see serpent column. →69

Aesculapius see staff of Asclepius. →120

Aesculus spp. see horse chestnut.
Aesculus hippocastanum, see European horse chestnut.

aesthete 1 a follower of the Aesthetic Movement in the 1800s.
2 any person who lives with a sense of artistic sensibility.

aesthetic pertaining to the visual nature of an object or work of art; visually and sensually pleasing, beautiful.

aesthetic control in town planning, the control of development with respect to its external appearance, massing, materials etc.

Aestheticism a theory of art developed by Immanuel Kant in the 1700s, based on the premise that art can be judged only within the bounds of an aesthetic philosophy.

Aesthetic Movement an artistic movement in England from the late 1800s promoting the idea of art for art's sake.

aesthetics the philosophy of beauty in art; the study of an object with regard to its visual and sensual impact.

aetoma see aetos. →86

aetos, aetoma; Gk; in classical Greek architecture, the tympanum of a pediment, usually ornamented with figures. →86

afara see limba.

afforestation, forestation; in landscaping and forestry, the planting of open land, mountainsides, recreation areas and derelict industrial areas with trees to form woodland or forest.

affronted a description of ornament or sculptured figures depicted facing towards the front or situated face to face; see also addorsed.

A-frame a simple triangulated framework of two leaning beams meeting at a ridge, connected by a stiffening collar.

African cherry see makore.

African ebony [*Diospyros crassiflora*, *Diospyros piscatoria*] a tropical African hardwood with especially heavy, dark timber.

African mahogany, khaya; [*Khaya ivorensis*, *Khaya spp.*] a group of West African hardwoods with relatively strong and durable orange-brown timber; used for interior joinery, furniture and boat-building.

africanum see opus africanum. →83

African walnut, alona, Congo wood; [Lovoa trichilioides, Lovoa klaineana] a West African hardwood with plain golden brown timber; used for furniture, panelling and veneers.

African whitewood see obeche.

afrormosia, kokrodua; [*Pericopsis elata*] a West African hardwood with rich yellow-brown timber used for internal and external joinery, furniture and as a substitute for teak.

afterimage, accidental colours; in colour physiology, an image which appears in complementary colours on a neutral or white background when the gaze is removed from a strong chromatic image.

afzelia, doussie; [*Afzelia spp.*] a group of African hardwoods with durable reddish brown timber; used for interior and external joinery and cladding.

against the grain in the milling of timber, the direction of cutting in which the grain of the piece is sloping upwards and into the milling edge.

agalma Gk; a work of art, votive sculpture etc. dedicated to a deity in a classical Greek temple. →84, →86

agate 1 a microcrystalline variety of the mineral chalcedony, of variable colour and pattern; used in technology, as gemstones and for decoration.
2 henna; a shade of reddish brown resembling the colour of the above, or the pigment prepared from the leaves of the tropical plant henna, Lawsonia inermis.

Agave sisalana see sisal.

agent 1 a material or substance used for its effect on another material or process; in concreting it is often called an admixture; types of agent included as separate entries are listed below.
air-detraining agent, see air-detraining admixture.
air-entraining agent, see air-entraining admixture.
alkaline cleaning agent.
binding agent, see binder.
bonding agent.
cleaning agent.
colouring agent, see colourant.
emulsifying agent, see emulsifier.
flocculating agent, see flocculating admixture.
foaming agent.
polishing agent, see polish.
release agent.
retarding agent, see retarder.
surface-acting agent.
suspension agent, see thickening admixture.
thickening agent, see thickening admixture.
2 one employed to organize matters on behalf of another.
see site agent.

agger Lat.; a Roman earthwork or rampart formed by heaping soil and other material from ditch excavation; the filling material of earth, sand, stone and wood therein. →104

agglomerated cork a light, porous, buoyant material manufactured by reconstituting granulated cork to form slabs and other products.

agglomeration the collecting together of very small particles in a suspension to form larger lumps which settle to the bottom.

aggregate inert granular material such as sand, gravel, crushed rock and clinker used as a main solid constituent in concrete, plaster, tarmacadam and asphalt; types of aggregate listed as separate entries are listed below.
angular aggregate.
blended aggregate.
coarse aggregate.
continuously graded aggregate.
crushed aggregate.
crusher-run aggregate.
cubical aggregate.
elongated aggregate.
expanded aggregate. →49
expanded clay aggregate, expanded shale aggregate, see expanded aggregate. →49
fine aggregate.
flaky aggregate.
flaky and elongated aggregate.
gap graded aggregate.
graded aggregate.
light expanded clay aggregate, see expanded aggregate.
lightweight aggregate.
manufactured aggregate.
natural aggregate.
rounded aggregate.
single sized aggregate.
sintered aggregate.
wood particle aggregate.

aggregate block same as aggregate concrete block. →30

aggregate/cement ratio the ratio of the mass of aggregate to that of cement in concrete or mortar.

aggregate concrete block see concrete block, usually refers to a lightweight aggregate concrete block. →30

aggregate exposure a finish treatment for a concrete surface in which water, or in some cases acid, is sprayed to wash away the surface layer of cement, revealing the coarse aggregate; the result is called exposed aggregate concrete.

aggregate impact value a measure of the resistance of aggregates used in road construction to fracture under impact, governed by the amount of debris resulting from repeated compactive testing.

aggressive water, corrosive water; piped supply water with dissolved carbon dioxide, acids or minerals which pose a corrosive hazard to copper pipework and equipment.

agitating lorry see agitating vehicle.

agitating vehicle, agitating lorry, truck mixer; a vehicle which both transports and mixes concrete.

Agnus Dei Latin for 'Lamb of God'; in religious symbolism, a representation of Christ as a lamb with a cross and chalice. →119

agora Gk; in classical architecture, a market or meeting place in a Greek city, the hub of public life where the most important public buildings were situated; cf. forum. →94

agreement 1 a binding decision made between two parties, a contract.
2 see articles of agreement.

agricultural drain see field drain.

agricultural land, farmland; in land use planning, any land used or designated to be used for agriculture.

agricultural unit an area of agricultural land and associated buildings farmed as a unit.

agriculture see farming.

Agromyza spp. see pith flecks.

A-hinge a hinge whose leaves are elongated and triangular, forming a lozenge shape when opened out; used for hanging wide or heavy doors. →38

AIA the American Institute of Architects, the national association of architects in the United States.

aid any substance added to a process to make it function more efficiently rather than affect the properties of the resulting product.

aile a wing or flank of a fortification.

aileron in church architecture, a gable with one vertical edge closing the end of an aisle; a half-gable. →113

aims of the competition the particular task for which entrants to an architectural or planning competition are to find suitable solutions.

air admittance valve a valve in a drainage system to permit the entrance of ventilating fresh air and to even out pressure differences.

airborne sound sound conveyed as pressure waves in air.

airborne sound transmission sound transmission through the air rather than the fabric of a building.

air brick, ventilating brick; a brick with regular round perforations from stretcher face to stretcher face, used to reduce the weight of walling construction and for ventilating cavity walls, basement spaces etc. →16

airbrushing a graphic technique employing paint sprayed with a special nozzle powered by compressed air.

air-change rate, ventilation rate; the specified number of times per hour that ventilating air in a room is completely renewed and old air extracted, expressed as the hourly volume of air provided to a space divided by the volume of the space.

air conditioning 1 a mechanical installation system providing warmed, cooled, clean and otherwise treated air into the habitable spaces of a building.
2 see central air conditioning.

air-conditioning duct an air duct used in an air-conditioning installation.
see *air-conditioning duct* in office building illustration. →60

air-conditioning unit, air-handling unit; a piece of mechanical services equipment for treating and conveying clean air into a space or building.

air content 1 the total amount of air in a substance, expressed as a percentage by volume.
2 in concreting, the total volume of air voids per unit volume in vibrated concrete, expressed as a percentage.

air-control tower see control tower.

air current the directional movement of heating and ventilation air within a space by convection.

air-detraining admixture, air-detraining agent; in concretework, an admixture included in the concrete mix to inhibit the inclusion of air.

air-detraining agent see air-detraining admixture.

air diffuser in air conditioning, an inlet grille which gives direction to supply air.

air diffusion see diffusion.

air distribution in air conditioning, the pumping of air via ducting to points of supply.

air-distribution system in air conditioning, an installation consisting of ducting and pumping plant for distributing treated air to outlets.

air dried, air seasoned; timber having reached equilibrium with outdoor atmospheric humidity, specified as 12% moisture content.

air duct 1 in air conditioning and mechanical ventilation, a long closed pipe or vessel of sheetmetal for conveying air to its points of use.
see *air duct* in office building illustration. →60
2 see ventilation duct. →60

air-entrained concrete a form of concrete with increased workability and resistance to weathering and frost, into which minute bubbles of air have been introduced using an air-entraining admixture.

air-entraining admixture, air-entraining agent; in concretework, an admixture included in the concrete mix to promote the inclusion of air.

air-entraining agent see air-entraining admixture.

air entrainment, entraining; the deliberate incorporation of tiny air bubbles into concrete to improve its workability and frost resistance.

airfield, aerodrome; a non-commercial area of land and associated buildings to accommodate the taking off, landing and administration of aircraft.

air filter in air conditioning, a porous barrier to collect impurities and particles from intake air.

air flow the directional movement of ventilation air within ductwork, usually induced by a fan.

air gap 1 in piped water supply, the vertical height between the outlet of a tap and rim of a sink, or ballvalve and overflow, a measure of the precaution against backsiphonage.
2 a narrow space between adjacent building components or materials allowed for in construction for the circulation of ventilating air, or for insulating purposes. →8

air-gap membrane a resilient membrane of high density polyethylene or similar polymer preformed with a grid of dimples or raised pattern, laid against foundation walls as tanking, also providing a small ventilating gap to allow moisture a passage out of the substructure; also called a cavity drainage membrane or tanking membrane. →29, →57, →59

air-handling luminaire a light fitting so designed that exhaust air from an air-conditioning or ventilation system is extracted through it.

air-handling plant room see ventilation plant room.

air-handling unit 1 see air-conditioning unit.
2 see fan unit.

airing cupboard, 1 wardrobe; a small ventilated room for the storage of clothes and household fabrics.
2 see drying cupboard.

air inlet 1 see fresh-air inlet. →58
2 see fresh-air vent. →58

air intake see return-air terminal unit.

air jet, airstream; the directed flow of ventilation and air-conditioning air produced by a supply air inlet.

airless spraying, hydraulic spraying; an industrial painting process employing a high pressure pistol with a fine nozzle to apply even coatings to building components and furniture.

air lock 1 an intermediate enclosed space or lobby between spaces with different environments or air conditions, affording access from one space to the other with minimal movement of air between the two.
2 an unwanted bubble of air trapped in pipework, inhibiting the flow of water or other fluids.

air outlet see supply air terminal unit. →60

air pocket see air void.

air pollution pollution caused by incomplete combustion of fossil fuels, emissions from various industrial processes, dust and grit from quarries and cement works, and the fumes from chemical works, oil refineries and motor vehicles.

airport see air terminal.

air-raid shelter see civil defence shelter. →61

air receiver see air vessel.

air release valve, bleed valve, pet-cock; a valve for releasing unwanted air or other gases from a system of pipes, cisterns etc.

air resistance the property of a pigment in paint to remain stable both in colour and structure when exposed to the effects of air and airborne pollutants.

air seasoned see air dried.

airstream see air jet.

airstrip, runway; a flat strip of land, nowadays paved with tarmac or concrete with systems of markings and guide lights, for aircraft to take off and land.

air-supported structure, pneumatic structure; any structure inflated with air as a means of structural support.

air terminal, airport; a complex with runways and associated buildings at which commercial aircraft land for loading and unloading of passengers and goods.

air terminal unit 1 in air conditioning and ventilation, any device, grille, diffuser etc. through which air is supplied to or extracted from a space.
2 see supply air terminal unit.
see *air terminal unit* in office building illustration. →60

air termination a component or system of vertical or horizontal metal rods located on a roof to intercept lightning strikes; part of a lightning protection installation for a building.

air test, pneumatic test; a test to inspect and locate leaks in pipework using compressed air which is introduced into the closed system and its pressure monitored over a period of time.

airtight, hermetic; furnished with seals, joints or mechanisms to prevent the flow of gas to or from an enclosed space; impermeable to air.

air-to-air heat transmission coefficient see U-value.

air treatment in air conditioning, the heating, cooling, purifying, filtering and humidifying or dehumidifying of air from the outside prior to distribution.

air vent a terminal device designed to allow the passage of fresh air to a space from the outside, or for release of stale air. →56

air vessel, air receiver; a pressurized vessel in an air compression system for the storage of compressed air for use while the pump is not in action.

air void, air pocket; in concretework, small spaces or voids in hardened concrete containing air and formed by air bubbles either intentionally introduced as entrapped air or unintentionally as entrapped air.

aisle 1 an open passageway in a building for circulation.

2 a longitudinal corridor flanking the nave of a church, basilica etc., bounded by an arcade or row of columns.
see *Roman basilica* illustration. →93
see *Early Christian church* illustration. →95
see *Byzantine domical church* illustration. →96
see *Carolingian abbey church* illustration. →98
see *Romanesque church* illustration. →99
see *Gothic cathedral* illustration. →100
see *Scandinavian hall church* illustration. →102
3 an open corridor running down the side of certain traditional timber-framed buildings, bounded by main posts and side walls.

aisled building a traditional timber-framed building type with rows of intermediate posts to support roof construction, thus forming side aisles in plan.

aisle post, arcade post; in traditional timber-framed building, one of a number of intermediate posts supporting a roof and forming an interior aisle or arcade.

akanthos Greek form of acanthus. →81, →82, →121

akheiropoeitos Greek form of acheiropoeitos.

Akkadian period, Accadian period; a naturalistic period in Mesopotamian art from the Akkadian age, 2470–2285 BC.

akropodion Greek form of acropodium.

akropolis Greek form of acropolis. →94

akroterion Greek form of acroterion. →78

ala 1 Lat., pl. alae; a small opening, alcove or room off the atrium in a Roman dwelling. →88
2 one of the side extensions of the rear wall of the cella of an Etruscan temple. →85
3 a side aisle in a basilica.

alabaster 1 a compact, fine-grained form of pure gypsum (calcium sulphate) with similar rocks such as calcareous sinter or onyx marble; easily worked, and used for interior decoration and sculptured ornament.
2 marble white, orange grey; a shade of light orange grey which takes its name from the above and some pale-coloured forms of marble.

alabastron an ancient Greek round-bottomed ceramic jug for containing ointment, perfume and oil; especially one made from alabaster.

alae plural form of ala. →85

alarm 1 any security or safety device which produces a signal in the form of a noise or light once triggered by a detector.
2 see fire alarm.

alarm bell a metal percussive device which produces a noise as an alarm sound.

alarm glass laminated glass whose interlayer is inlaid with fine electric wires connected to a circuit, which activate an alarm if broken.

alarm system 1 a system of warning bells, lights and other means which react to the presence of hazards in buildings such as fire, toxic gases and unauthorized entrants.
2 see intruder alarm system.

alarm thermometer a thermometer which sounds an alarm when a certain temperature has been reached.

alatorium Lat.; a wall-walk behind the battlements of a Roman fortification to enable defending soldiers to protect their position from above; an alure or parapet walk.

albarium opus Lat.; see opus albarium. →83

albedo see reflectance.

album Lat.; a tablet where announcements and messages were left, set in a public place in a Roman town.

albumen glue glue manufactured from egg protein.

albumen print a type of early photographic print, introduced in 1850, produced on paper coated with albumen (egg-white) and salt with silver nitrate.

alburnum see sapwood. →1

alcazar a Spanish fortified dwelling or palace, in particular a Moorish palace in an urban setting, inhabited by the regional military governor.

alcove 1 any recess formed in the thickness of, or bounded by, the wall of a room.
2 a similar recess to contain a bed.
3 see ala. →88

alder [*Alnus spp.*] a group of hardwoods with light, soft, fine-textured, non-durable, pinkish timber.
Alnus glutinosa, see common alder.
Alnus incana, see grey alder.
Alnus rubra, see red alder.

aleatorium Lat.; a room for playing dice games in a classical Roman building.

aleipterion Gk; see alipterion. →91

Aleurites spp. see tung oil.

Alexandrian blue see Egyptian blue.

alexandrinum see opus alexandrinum.

algebra a mathematical system of calculation and investigation in which numbers are substituted by symbols.

algorithm a set of rules or procedures for solving calculations, the basis of a computer program.

aliasing in computer graphics, imperfections in lower resolution graphics which make diagonal lines appear stepped.

alidade, diopter; a sighting device for a surveying level.

alien house a monastic settlement founded in England in the Middle Ages by monks from abroad, usually France.

alignment 1 the compositional lining up of a series of building masses or adjacent constructional surfaces, points and patterns.
2 a prehistoric straight row of standing stones, laid out for ceremonial, astronomical or symbolic purposes.

alipterion, unctuarium (Lat.); a room in a Roman bath house in which bathers were anointed with oils; alternative spelling is aleipterion (Gk). →91

alizarin 1 a red dye used by the ancients and produced by grinding the root of the common madder plant, [Rubia tinctorum]; after 1868 it has been manufactured artificially from anthraquinone.
2 alizarin colour; a range of dyestuffs manufactured in this way, with the addition of metal oxides to impart different shades of colour.

alizarin blue a range of artificial blue dyes used in printing inks; see alizarin.

alizarin brown, madder brown, brown madder; a brown form of the pigment alizarin crimson.

alizarin colour see alizarin.

alizarin crimson, alizarin lake, alizarin red, alizarin scarlet; an organic synthetic red pigment obtained from anthracene, a coal tar derivative, introduced in 1868 and used in water-based and oil paints.

alizarin lake see alizarin crimson.

alizarin red see alizarin crimson.

alizarin scarlet see alizarin crimson.

alizarin violet, violet madder lake; a clear transparent purple pigment manufactured from purpurin.

alizarin yellow a synthetic transparent dull yellow pigment; see alizarin.

alkali a water-soluble base or salt, especially hydroxide, which reacts with acids.

alkali-aggregate reaction, concrete cancer; an undesirable chemical reaction in concrete between alkalis contained in the Portland cement binder and some aggregates, causing internal swelling, rupture and scaling of the surface.

alkali feldspar a mineral, potassium feldspar or sodium-enriched plagioclase rock.

alkali metal one of a group of soft reactive metals from group Ia of the periodic table (lithium, sodium, potassium etc.) which form soluble hydroxides.

alkaline having the characteristics of an alkali; containing an alkali.

alkaline cleaning agent any highly effective metal cleaning product based on a solution of sodium hydroxide (caustic soda) or potassium hydroxide (NaOH, KOH), silicates, or phosphates, with a balanced amount of surfactants in water.

alkaline-earth metal one of a group of light volatile metal elements from group IIa of the periodic table (beryllium, calcium, strontium, magnesium, barium and radium), which form strong alkaline oxide.

alkalinity the ability of a water-based solution to react with hydrogen ions.

alkali-reactive referring to a chemical compound which reacts with an alkali.

alkali-resistant paint acrylic or resin paint with good resistance to alkali attack, suitable for use on concrete surfaces.

alkali-resistant primer primer used on concrete surfaces beneath other paints to protect them against alkali attack from the concrete.

alkali wash a treatment to remove grease and other impurities from metal surfaces with an alkaline solution containing a detergent and a surfactant before coating or painting.

alkyd baking enamel see alkyd stoving enamel.

alkyd paint an oil paint which contains alkyd resins, used externally as a coating and wood preservative; it is easy to brush, durable and quick drying.

alkyd putty a sealing and glazing compound with an alkyd resin binder.

alkyd resin a synthetic polyester resin used in the manufacture of paints, formed by combining an alcohol with an acid.

alkyd stoving enamel, alkyd baking enamel; a hardwearing paint coating used for metal components, based on a melamine or carbamine and alkyd resin binder, applied as a liquid spray and baked on.

alkyd varnish a varnish with alkyd resin as a binder, used as a protective coating for furniture, joinery and timber floors.

alla prima, au premier coup; a method of oil painting in which a single layer of pigment is applied to a white canvas without the use of a base, retouching, glazes or underpainting.

allegory art which seeks to convey an idea or feeling through the portrayal of a tale, event or situation.

allen head screw a screw with hexagonal recess in its head, turned using an allen key. →36

allen key a small L-shaped metal spanner, hexagonal in cross-section, for tightening bolts and screws with a suitably shaped sinking in their heads.

alley, close (Sc); a narrow external circulation space in an urban area, a road or path bounded on both sides by built form, intended for pedestrians and vehicles.

all-glass balustrade a simple balustrade which is a sheet of toughened and/or laminated glass, secured at its lower edge. →54

all-glass door a door whose leaf is an unframed sheet of structural glass, often tempered or laminated, to which hinges and door furniture are fixed. →51
see *types of door* illustration. →51
see *office building* illustration. →60

alligatoring see crocodiling.

allocation see appropriation.

allotment a small plot of usually public land, often in an urban setting, set aside for the cultivation of vegetables and other plants by local inhabitants.

allowance, 1 clearance, installation allowance; spaces left between adjacent components in design such as the space between a hinged door leaf or window casement and its frame, to allow for fitting, installation, manufacturing tolerances, expansion, workmanship and movement. →51
2 see rebate.

alloy 1 a composition of two or more chemical elements, one of which is always a metal, combined together to form a metal substance which benefits from their combined properties to provide improved strength, ductility, corrosion resistance etc.
2 the level of purity of a precious metal such as silver or gold, measured in carats.

alloy steel steel which contains over 5% carbon and other metals to improve its basic properties of strength, hardness and resistance to corrosion.

all-seeing eye see eye of God. →119

all-surface pencil a pencil with a special lead, often coloured, which can leave a line on any surface, including glass.

allure see alure. →103

alluvial deposit a soil type which has been deposited by the action of a river or stream.

almandine a reddish variety of the mineral garnet.

almary see aumbry.

almery see aumbry.

almond the mystical almond; see mandorla. →119

almond green a shade of dark green which takes its name from the underside of the leaves of the almond tree (*Amygdalus communis*, *Prunus dulcis*, *Prunus amygdalus*).

almond tree see almond green.

almonry a room or outbuilding in a church or monastery from which alms are distributed to the poor and needy.
see *almonry* in Carolingian monastery illustration. →97

almshouse a dwelling or group of dwellings traditionally provided for the poor and needy by private money or charity.

Alnus spp. see alder.
Alnus glutinosa, see common alder.
Alnus incana, see grey alder.
Alnus rubra, see red alder.

alona see African walnut.

along the grain parallel to the general direction of the grain in timber.

alpha and omega the first and last letters in the Greek alphabet, α and ω or A and Ω, signifying the eternity of God, without beginning or end, in religious symbolism. →119

alpha radiation penetrating electromagnetic radiation consisting of positively charged helium nuclei emitted from naturally radioactive elements.

altar 1 the focal point of worship in a church, temple or shrine.
see types of *altar* illustration. →116
see *Greek residential building* illustration. →87
see *Scandinavian church* illustration. →102
2 see sacrificial altar.
3 see thymele. →89
4 see high altar. →95
5 see side altar, by-altar. →96
6 see hestia. →87
7 see lararium. →88
8 see eschara. →87, →116
9 see bomos. →84, →92, →116

altar canopy in religious architecture, a canopy structure over an altar; a ciborium, baldachin or tabernacle. →95, →116

altare mobile Lat.; see portatile. →116

altare portatile Lat.; see portatile. →116

altar frontal 1 see antependium. →116
2 see antemensale. →116

altarpiece a work of art containing religious themes, placed behind an altar and often surrounded by a frame or portico.
see *altar* illustration. →116
see *Scandinavian hall church* illustration. →102

altar platform 1 see suppedaneum. →102, →116
2 see bema. →95, →96

altar rail, communion rail; in religious architecture, a rail or low balustrade in front of an altar which separates the altar and clergy from the

congregation, and at which communion is administered. →116
see *altar* illustration. →116
see *Scandinavian hall church* illustration. →102

altar screen 1 in religious architecture, a screen of wood or metal, often perforated or latticed, which separates the altar from the surrounding spaces; often a rood screen. →95, →98
2 see reredos.

altar table, mensa; the table on which the sacrament is administered by the clergy in a church. →116

altar tomb in church architecture, a tomb of a saint or martyr in the form of an altar with an effigy of the deceased lain on top. →116

alteration a minor change to a building, requiring construction work.

alternate bay construction see chequerboard construction, alternate lane construction.

alternate lane construction, alternate bay construction; a method of casting large areas of concrete floors etc. in which adjacent parallel areas are cast first and harden prior to casting of the remaining voids; see chequerboard construction.

alternating current, AC; electric current which reverses its direction of flow at a regular frequency.

alternating system of supports see alternation of support. →25, →100

alternating tread stair a stair with wedge-shaped steps arranged so that their wider edges alternate from side to side as the stair is ascended, used for steep stairs where space is limited. →45

alternation of support, alternating system of supports; a system of columnar supports for a Romanesque arcade or vaulting, in which alternating columns or piers have variations in column type, cross-section of shaft, embellishment etc. →25, →100

alternative another choice, possibility, offering or plan.

alternative escape route in planning for fire safety, a secondary specified escape route which may be used in the event that a main route cannot be reached.

alternative exit in planning for fire safety, a secondary specified exit from an escape route.

alternative offer in project administration, the offer by a tendering contractor to carry out work, or particular parts of it, in a manner differing to that outlined in contract documents.

altitude 1 the height of a specified point above sea level.
2 the perpendicular height of a triangle or a line defining it, measured from the apex to the base.
3 see solar altitude.

alto rilievo, high relief; sculptured relief ornament in which figures or elements are carved to such a depth as to appear separate from their background.

alum, potash alum; a sulphate salt of aluminium and potassium, white crystals used in the production of some glues and in the leather industry.

alum gypsum, marble gypsum; a mixture of plaster of Paris soaked with alum solution, burnt and finely ground, used as a high strength, hard plaster for tiles, boards, render and in-situ work.

alumina, aluminium oxide; a chemical compound, Al_2O_3, used in the manufacture of some types of brick, as an abrasive, and as a fireproof lining for ovens.
see corundum.

alumina hydrate an artificial form of aluminium hydroxide used as an inert base in oil paints.

aluminium, 1 aluminum (Am.); a pale, lightweight, ductile, common metal, **Al**, an important building material used for lightweight constructions, cladding and extrusions.
2 a shade of light grey named after the above.

aluminium alloy aluminium which contains other metals such as manganese, magnesium and silicon to improve strength.

aluminium brass an alloy of brass with added aluminium to improve strength, hardness and corrosion resistance.

aluminium bronze a bright golden-yellow alloy of copper and aluminium which is strong and corrosion resistant.

aluminium door any door manufactured primarily from aluminium parts.

aluminium-faced timber window see composite window. →53

aluminium fencing proprietary fencing whose structure and fabric are of aluminium.

aluminium foil aluminium produced in the form of very thin sheets.

aluminium-framed window see aluminium window. →53

aluminium hydroxide a non-toxic chemical alliance of aluminium with oxygen and hydrogen, **AlOH**, used as a white pigment.

aluminium mesh any mesh product manufactured primarily from aluminium.
see *wire mesh* illustrations. →34

aluminium oxide Al_2O_3, see alumina.
see corundum.

aluminium paint a metallic paint consisting of powdered aluminium and a vehicle such as oil.

aluminium plate aluminium or aluminium alloy supplied in the form of metal plate.
see *metal plate* illustration. →34
see chequerplate, checkerplate. →34

aluminium profile often synonymous with aluminium section, but usually more complex, thin-walled or hollow; used for patent glazing, door frames etc.
see *metal profiles* illustration. →34

aluminium roofing see aluminium sheet roofing.

aluminium section any thin length of aluminium steel which has been preformed by a process of welding, extrusion etc. into a uniform cross-section of certain shape and dimensions.
see *metal sections* illustration. →34

aluminium sheet aluminium rolled into sheets not more than 3 mm thick; used for exterior cladding etc.
see *sheetmetal* illustration. →34

aluminium sheet roofing profiled roofing of corrosion-free coated aluminium sheet used largely for industrial and low cost buildings.

aluminium window 1 a window whose frame is made primarily from coated aluminium; an aluminium-framed window. →53
2 aluminium-faced timber window, see composite window. →53

aluminium-zinc coating a protective galvanized surface coating for steel sheeting of hot-dip zinc with 55% aluminium and a small amount of silicon.

alumino-thermic welding see thermit welding.

aluminum see aluminium.

alur see alure. →103

alure a raised defensive walkway or gallery along the top of an external wall in a castle or fortification, often roofed and protected from enemy fire by battlements or a parapet; also called an alur, allure, rampart, parapet walk, bailey walk or wall-walk. →103

amalgam 1 a poisonous alloy of mercury and another metal.
2 any mixture of two or more substances.

amaranth, amaranth purple, amaranth rose; a shade of dark purple named after the colour of the leaves of the amaranth plant (*Amaranthus spp.*).

amaranth purple see amaranth.

amaranth rose see amaranth.

Amaranthus spp. see amaranth.

Amarna art and culture from the time of the ancient Egyptian Pharaoh Akhenaten (also known as Amenhotep IV, 1353–1336 BC), characterized by a new freedom in painting, natural realism and

reverence of the sun god; named after the Nile city established as the kingdom's capital.
amber, succinite; the fossilized resin from pine trees, a yellowish brown organic mineral; used as a gemstone, for decoration and as a raw material in some paints.
amber yellow a shade of greyish yellow which takes its name from the fossilized resin, amber.
ambient sound see background noise.
ambitus Lat.; in classical architecture, a niche in a tomb for a body or urn, or the area round the tomb.
ambo, 1 ambones (Lat.); a raised stone pulpit or dais in an Early Christian or Byzantine church, often surmounted by an altar at either side. →95
2 see epistle ambo. →95
3 see gospel ambo. →95
ambones Latin form of ambo.
ambrosia beetle [*Scotylidae*, *Platypodidae*] a number of species of insect which cause damage to unseasoned hardwood and softwood by burrowing.
ambrotype a pioneering photographic process patented in 1854, which utilized a bleached glass negative laid against a black background.
ambry see aumbry.
ambulatio Lat.; an open area or courtyard in a Roman bath house for taking exercise. →91
ambulatorium Latin form of ambulatory.
ambulatory 1 a place for walking in a cathedral or abbey church, a cloister, apse aisle etc.
2 a semicircular extension of side aisles of a church to form a walk behind the high altar and round the apse; any similar processional way in a church.
see *Late Antique church* illustration. →95
see *Romanesque church* illustration. →99
see *Gothic cathedral* illustration. →100
see *altar* illustration. →116
Amen see Amun. →74
amendment see revision.
amendment arrow see arrowhead. →130
amendment block see revision panel. →130
amendment cloud see revision cloud. →130
amenity grassland in town planning, an extensive area of grass, parkland etc. with functional or aesthetic value, designated for recreational use.
American ash [*Fraxinus spp.*] a common name for the green ash, *Fraxinus pennsylvanica*, and the white ash, *Fraxinus americana*, North American hardwoods with tough and flexible grey-brown timber used for furniture, interiors and tool handles.
American axe see felling axe.
American beech [*Fagus grandifolia*] a North American hardwood with whitish pink timber; used for interiors and furniture.
American bond see English garden-wall bond. →19
American caisson see box caisson.
American cherry, black cherry (Am.); [*Prunus serotina*] a North American hardwood with reddish brown timber; used for furniture.
American elm [*Ulmus americana*] a North American hardwood with strong, tough and flexible pale reddish brown timber; used for interior joinery, furniture and coffins.
American lime see basswood.
American mahogany see mahogany.
American plane, buttonwood, sycamore; [*Platanus occidentalis*] a North American hardwood with reddish brown timber, used for interiors and furniture.
American Standard Code for Information Interchange see ASCII.
American walnut, black walnut; [*Juglans nigra*] a North American hardwood with rich dark brown timber, valued for its decorative figure; used for furniture, panelling and veneers.
American white oak [*Quercus alba*] one of a number of similar species of North American hardwood used for flooring and other hardwearing applications.
American whitewood see tulipwood.
American with Flemish bond see Flemish stretcher bond. →18
americium a radioactive chemical element, **Am**.
amethyst 1 a form of purple or violet crystalline quartz, used mainly as gemstones and for decorative ornament.
2 amethyst violet; a shade of violet named after the above.
amethyst violet see amethyst.
aminobenzene see aniline.
amino-plastic a group of thermosetting resins formed by copolymerizing urea or melamine with an aldehyde, used for pressings, adhesives, coatings and laminates.
ammeter an electrical instrument for measuring the flow of current in an electrical circuit.
ammonia a colourless, water-soluble, gaseous, chemical compound, NH_3, which is strongly alkaline in solution and is corrosive to alloys of copper; used as a refrigerant and as a cleaning agent.
ammonium chloride, sal ammoniac; a white, crystalline, water-soluble, chemical compound, NH_4Cl, used in soldering flux, dry cells and in iron cement.
ammonium nitrate a white, crystalline, water-soluble, chemical compound, NH_4NO_3, used in explosives, fertilizers and freezing mixtures.
ammonium phosphate a chemical compound, $N_2H_9PO_4$, used as a fire retardant and in fertilizers.
Amon see Amun. →74
amoretto see cupid. →122
amorino see cupid. →122
amorphous referring to a material whose molecules and atoms do not form a crystalline structure, or one with no determinate shape or structure.
amortization the repayment of a debt in regular instalments.
amount a value defining how much or how many of a given substance or product there is.
amp see ampere.
ampere, amp; abb. **A**; SI unit of electrical current equal to a flow of one coulomb per second.
amphibole a black, dark green or brown rock-forming mineral with a double chain silicate structure, which increases the strength and toughness of the rocks in which it is found.
amphibolite a durable grey-green metamorphic rock formed from gabbro or basalt.
amphiprostyle in classical architecture, referring to a temple with rows of columns and a portico at each end but not along the sides; amphiprostylos in Greek. →84
amphiprostyle temple see above. →84
amphitheater see amphitheatre.
amphitheatre, 1 amphitheater (Am.); a classical arena for gladiatorial contests and spectacles consisting of an oval or round space surrounded by tiered seating for spectators; amphitheatron in Greek. →90
see *Roman amphitheatre* illustration. →90
2 any curved or tiered structure, such as a natural hollow in the landscape used as theatre seating, a large housing mass etc.
amplifier see aerial amplifier.
amplitude the depth of a wave, measured from its midpoint to its lowest point.
ampulla pl. ampullae; a small clay storage vessel or vase for oils and perfumes; in the Catholic church, a vessel containing oil used for religious rituals; also a similar ornamented orb used in regal coronations or a vessel used by Christian pilgrims etc. to contain ceremonial lamp-oil. →95
Amsterdam, School of a movement in Dutch architecture from the 1920s and 1930s

characterized by plastic forms in red brick, a contrast to the de Stijl movement.

Amun chief deity of the Theban triad (along with Mut and Khonsu) in Egyptian mythology, focus of cult worship in the New Kingdom at Karnak, Thebes; the 'unseen one' or 'lord of all gods', depicted as a human wearing ram's horns and the twin-feathered crown; also written as Amon, Amen. →74

amusement arcade a building or space for entertainment, often at an amusement park, housing various recreational facilities such as video games, slot machines etc.

amusement park, fairground, pleasure-ground; a recreational area containing carousels, arcades and sideshows etc.

amusement structure any of the recreational structures found at fairgrounds or amusement parks.

Amygdalus communis the almond tree; see almond green.

amyl acetate an organic chemical compound used as a solvent for nitrocellulose lacquers.

anactoron in classical Greek architecture, the sacred hall, shrine or building dedicated to the Mysteries; also anaktoron. →92

anaerobic adhesive an adhesive which sets by polymerization in the absence of oxygen.

anaerobic sealant a sealant which sets by polymerization in the absence of oxygen.

anaglyph referring to an ornament which has been embossed or sculpted in low relief.

anaglypta surface ornament sculpted or embossed in low relief.

anaktoron Greek form of anactoron. →92

analemma, iskhegaon; Gk; a retaining wall in ancient Greece and Rome, especially one supporting the side of a classical theatre. →89

analogous model see synthetic model.

analogue detector an electronic fire detector which sends warning signals to a central computer in the event of fire.

analytical statics a science which deals with the mathematical state of equilibrium.

anamorphosis a distorted projection or drawing of something which, through optical illusion, appears normal or recognizable when viewed from a particular point or with a particular mirror.

anastasis in Byzantine art, a depiction of the resurrection of the Old Testament saints.

anastylosis in building conservation, the process of reconstructing a historic building in such a way that new and added parts and materials are clearly differentiated from the original.

anathyrosis Gk; the dressing of stone joints at the surface of stonework to provide a neat fit, leaving concealed areas unworked or slightly rebated. →12

anchor 1 a metal fixing for connecting a structural member or secondary component firmly to a main structure or to fix something firmly in place; often called an anchorage; types of anchor included as separate entries are listed below.
anchor bolt. →36
concrete screw anchor. →36
door-frame anchor, jamb anchor. →50
ground anchor. →29
hollow-wall anchor. →37
rock anchor. →29
wedge anchor. →37
2 a barbed metal object on a length of rope or cable, designed for keeping ships and boats at mooring by affixing to the sea bed; symbolic representations of this in art and architectural ornament. →119

anchorage 1 a system of steel rods, guys, braces, bolts etc. for fixing a structure firmly to its base or to the ground; often synonymous with anchor, although anchorage is usually a construction, anchor a component. →54
see *anchorage* in suspension bridge illustration. →32
2 the process thus involved.
3 see anchor.
4 see end abutment.
5 see ground anchor. →29
6 see rock anchor. →29

anchor beam 1 in traditional timber frame construction, a beam whose end is anchored to a post by means of a tenon joint.
2 a timber tie beam fixed to the upper ends of parallel side walls of a building to prevent them from buckling outwards.

anchor bolt, foundation bolt, ragbolt; a bolt cast into concrete, whose threads are left protruding from the surface so that subsequent components can be attached. →36

anchor bracket a fixing for attaching a pipe to a wall surface so that linear movement of the pipe is restricted.

anchor cross a cross whose lower termination is shaped like a ship's anchor; also known as a crux dissimulata (Lat.). →117

anchored retaining wall a retaining wall restrained on the ground side by a series of ground, pile or rock anchors or a deadman. →29

anchor pile 1 see piled anchorage. →29
2 see tension pile.

anchor strap a perforated galvanized steel strip product used for tying adjacent components such as timber framing members, brick leafs etc. together. →22

ancient monument any ancient man-made structure such as a building or earthwork, which is of historical or cultural value and as such is protected by legislation.

ancient relic an archaeological finding, site or object which is a surviving memory of a previous culture.

ancient stronghold, prehistoric fortress; a castle, earthwork or fortification constructed in prehistoric times.

ancillary building, 1 auxiliary building; one of the buildings in a group or complex having a lesser function than a main building, or whose purpose is to serve it.
2 see outbuilding.

ancon see ancone.

ancona an early Italian altarpiece composed of a number of illustrated panels. →116

ancone, ancon; in classical architecture, a curved ornamental bracket or cornice for supporting a ledge, shelf, balcony, pediment or sculpture.

anda 'egg'; the massive solid dome of an Indian stupa, surmounted by a chattra. →68

andalusite a hard, yellowish, greenish or brownish aluminium silicate mineral used as gemstones and for decoration.

andesite a pale-coloured volcanic rock similar to basalt, used for road aggregates.

andradite a brownish black variety of the mineral garnet.

andron, 1 androne, andronitis; Gk; that part of an ancient Greek building used by men, especially a large formal dining or banqueting room with couches arranged on platforms around its periphery.
see *andron* in Greek residential building illustration. →87
2 a passage or corridor in a Roman dwelling.

androne see andron. →87

andronitis see andron. →87

androsphinx in Egyptian architecture, a sphinx with a human head or upper body, usually that of a male. →75

anechoic a description of a highly absorbent acoustic space with no echo, sound reflection or reverberation.

anechoic chamber an acoustic room with highly absorbing surfaces to reduce reverberation times to a minimum, used for testing and recording sound.

angel in religious symbolic ornamentation, a winged figure representing a messenger of God; attribute of the apostle Matthew. →119

angel light in Gothic church architecture, especially of the Perpendicular period, a small triangular light between the tracery of a window, panel, or between adjacent lancets. →109

angel roof in church architecture, a pitched timber roof decorated internally with carved angels.

Angevin Gothic a style of Gothic architecture characterized by drop arches and associated with the rule of the English Plantagenet kings in Aquitaine.

angiosperm a class of plants, including all flowering plants and hardwood trees, having seeds contained in an ovary.

angle 1 the spacing or rotational dimension between two lines that diverge.
2 see plane angle.
3 see angle profile.
4 an angle bead, see edge strip.
5 see steel angle.
6 a component of angled guttering used at the eaves of a hipped roof to convey water around a corner.

angle bar see steel angle.
see *angle profile* illustration. →34

angle bead, 1 corner bead; a strip of planed timber or other material used as trim to cover the corner joints between walls, floors, ceilings etc. →2
2 see edge strip. →2
3 see plasterwork angle bead.

angle bevelled halved joint, lateral bevelled halved joint; a timber angled halved joint in which the laps are bevelled for increased strength.

angle brace see angle tie.

angle branch a pipe fitting to connect a subsidiary pipe to a main pipe at an acute angle to the direction of flow.

angle brick any special brick whose end is formed at angles other than 90° to its stretcher face, used at a change of direction at corners and curves in brick walling. →16
1 see cant brick. →16
2 see squint brick. →16

angled cross see broken cross. →118

angle fillet, 1 arris fillet, cant strip; a horizontal timber strip, triangular in cross-section, laid at internal junctions in construction to round off sharp corners before the laying of membrane roofing, waterproofing etc. →49
2 a similar triangular strip of material included in formwork to provide a chamfer in cast concrete construction.

angle grinder a hand-held power tool with a rapidly rotating thin abrasive mineral disc, used for cutting metal sections and grinding stone and metals.

angle iron see steel angle.

angle joint, corner joint; a joint formed by members which are connected but do not lie in the same line, forming an angle with one another.

angle luminaire a luminaire which provides illumination whose light distribution is noticeably directional.

angle of attack see cutting angle.

angle of friction the angle between the perpendicular to a sloping planar surface and the resultant force of a body placed upon it, measured as the body begins to slide downwards.

angle of incidence the angle made by a ray of light meeting a surface and a line perpendicular to the surface.

angle of inclination the angle that a line or plane subtends with the horizontal.

angle of reflectance the angle made by a ray of light or other waveform with a reflecting surface.

angle of refraction the angle through which a ray of light bends on passing through a different medium.

angle of repose the angle which the side of a heap of loosely poured material naturally subtends with the horizontal.

angle parking, echelon parking; the layout of individual parking spaces in a sawtooth formation diagonal to a carriageway or pavement. →62

angle plane see corner scraper. →41

anglepoise lamp a worktop lamp with a screwed clamp fixing, pivoted supporting arms and a conical shade which can be moved into any position.

angle post in traditional timber construction, a corner post in the arcade of a timber-framed building.

angle profile, angle; any metal section whose uniform cross-section resembles the letter L; in aluminium these are formed by extrusion and in steel by bending or by cold or hot rolling; also called an L-profile or L-section; see also steel angle. →34
see equal angle. →34
see unequal angle. →34

angle rafter in timber roof construction, a diagonal rafter at the join of two sloping roof planes which meet at an angle; a hip rafter or valley rafter.

angle ridge see hip rafter.

anglesite a white, grey or black mineral, naturally occurring lead sulphate, $\mathbf{PbSO_4}$, used as a local ore of lead.

angle stair see quarter turn stair. →45

angle strut in traditional timber frame construction, a slanting compression member in the vertical plane used to brace and strengthen a corner joint. →4

angle tie, angle brace, diagonal brace, diagonal tie, dragon tie; in traditional timber frame construction, a diagonal member in the horizontal plane used to brace and tie together a corner joint; a similar brace in contemporary construction.

angle tile 1 in floor and wall tiling, a special L-shaped ceramic tile for covering an internal or external corner.
2 a similarly shaped exterior clay or concrete tile for tile hanging, covering the ridges and hips of tiled roofs etc.

angle trowel, corner trowel; **1** a plasterer's L-shaped trowel for smoothing inside and outside corners. →43
2 internal angle trowel, see twitcher trowel.
3 see external angle trowel.

Anglo-Norman architecture see Norman architecture. →109
see *medieval capitals* illustration. →115

Anglo-Saxon architecture, Saxon architecture; the church architecture or vernacular building of the Anglo-Saxons in England from the fifth century up to the Norman Conquest in 1066, characterized by simple forms and rough ornament.

angular relating to an object, form or building mass which is sharp-cornered.

angular aggregate coarse aggregate whose particles have sharp edges.

angular guilloche see meander. →124

angular hip tile a special L-shaped roof tile for covering the ridge formed by a hip.

angular momentum in dynamics, the momentum of a body rotating about a point or axis.

angular perspective see two-point perspective. →129

angular ridge tile an L-shaped ridge capping tile for covering a ridge.

angular speed see angular velocity.

angular unit any unit of measurement of an angle, a degree, radian, steradian.

angular velocity, angular speed; the speed at which a body rotates, measured in degrees per second.

anhydrite, 1 anhydrous calcium sulphate; natural mineral calcium sulphate, $CaSO_4$; used as a form of plaster and often produced by burning gypsum at high temperatures.
2 see synthetic anhydrite.

anhydrous calcium sulphate see anhydrite.

anhydrous lime see quicklime.

aniline, aminobenzene; a colourless oily liquid, originally produced by the distillation of the indigo plant [*Indigofera anil, Indigofera suffruticosa, Indigofera tinctoria*], now manufactured from nitrobenzene and used as a base in the production of dyes, drugs, plastics and rubber products.

aniline colour a group of synthetic organic pigments, distilled from coal tar and in use prior to the introduction of more permanent pigments.

animal capital see protome capital. →115
see bull capital. →69
see eagle capital.
see lion capital. →69

animal column, beast column; a decorative Romanesque stone column-type richly sculpted with intertwined animal figures. →114

animal fibre animal hair traditionally used as a building material by adding to a binder as reinforcement for plasters and mortars, or by pressing into slabs as insulation.

animal-fibre reinforced referring to composites of animal hair in a binder, traditionally used for cast and in-situ plasterwork, insulation, building boards and panels.

animal glue 1 glue made from collagen, a protein released by boiling the bones, hides and muscles of animals.
2 see bone glue.
3 see hide glue.

animal interlace, lacertine; any ornament which consists of stylized animal motifs.
see *decorative motifs* illustrations. →122
see *Christian symbols* illustrations. →119

animal ornamentation any ornamentation which features animals as decorative or symbolic motifs.
see *column styles in European architecture* illustration. →114
see *Romanesque and Gothic capitals* illustration. →115
see *decorative motifs* illustrations. →122
see *Christian symbols* illustrations. →119

animation 1 the running of a series of still images in quick succession to achieve the illusion of movement.
2 see computer animation.

anion, negative ion; a negatively charged chemical ion, one attracted to an anode.

anionic bitumen emulsion a dispersion of bitumen in water, with an emulsifying additive which coats the particles of bitumen with a negative ion, causing them to repel one another and to remain as separate droplets.

anisotropic referring to a material, object or construction which does not display the same properties in all directions; see also isotropic.

ankh, ansated cross, crux ansata (Lat.), Egyptian cross; a cross-like symbol whose upper limb is a loop, the symbol of life in ancient Egypt; also sometimes called the cross of Horus, handlebar cross, Coptic cross, key of life or key to the Nile. →74, →117

annealed glass ordinary untoughened glass that has been heated in an oven then cooled slowly to relieve internal stresses that would otherwise arise; cf. toughened glass. →53

annealed wire see binding wire.

annealing a heat treatment to soften steel and relieve internal stresses caused by work hardening or welding; the temperature is raised by heating right through to a certain level and then lowered slowly and evenly.

annex see annexe.

annexe, annex; a supplementary or subsidiary building constructed as an addition to a main building, but not necessarily attached to it physically.

annosus root rot, butt rot; [*Fomes annosus, Heterobasidion annosum*] a fungus which decays the roots of living trees of all ages, especially conifers, spreading into the lower part of the trunk and causing death of the tree.

annotation 1 written text or references which provide supplementary clarification about drawn objects in design drawings and documentation.
2 see lettering.

annual in landscaping, any non-woody, shallow-rooted plant grown from seed and which flowers, seeds and dies the same year.

annual report a document required by law to be produced on a yearly basis by the directors of a company for its shareholders to show the financial state of the company.

annual ring, growth ring; one of the ringed markings in the cross-section of a tree trunk, laid down annually as a new layer of timber is formed, appearing as a grain figure in converted timber. →1

annuity, instalment; a periodic payment made at regular intervals towards a loan, pension fund or other such financial agreement.

annuity system a method of repayment of a loan in instalments such that the size of instalment remains the same regardless of the proportion of interest.

annular in the shape of a ring or closed circle.

annular bit see hole saw. →42

annular nail, 1 improved nail, jagged-shank nail, ring-shanked nail; a nail, usually 19 mm–75 mm in length, with a series of ringed protrusions around its shaft to increase its fixing strength when driven into timber. →35
2 see plasterboard nail.

annular vault a barrel vault in the form of a ring or a hollow doughnut halved horizontally.

annulated column a Romanesque column type with a number of rings or annulets carved at intervals around its shaft; also called a banded or ringed column. →114

annulet, annulus (Lat.), shaft ring; a small semicircular or angular moulding carved round the shaft of a Doric column beneath the capital. →81

annuletted cross see cross annuletty. →118

annulus Lat.; see annulet. →81

annunciator see indicator panel.

Anobiidae see furniture beetle.

Anobium punctatum see common furniture beetle.

anode in electrochemical processes, a positive electrode or terminal to which anions or negatively charged ions are attracted.

anodic dip painting see electro-dip painting.

anodic oxide coating 1 a layer of aluminium oxide laid down as a protective coating during anodizing.
2 see anodizing.

anodization see anodizing.

anodized electrochemically coated with aluminium oxide.

anodizing, anodic oxide coating, anodization; the electrochemical application of a layer of coloured aluminium oxide as a corrosion-resistant and hardwearing protective surface coating for aluminium products and components.

anorthosite a variety of dark gabbro made up of spectral plagioclase or labradorite; see also Spectrolite.

Anpu see Anubis. →74

ansated cross see ankh. →117

anse de panier see three-centred arch. →24

answering machine, answerphone; an electronic apparatus which receives and stores telephone messages.

answerphone see answering machine.

anta Lat.; in classical architecture, a corner pier or pilaster which is of a different classical order than those in the rest of the building, most often an extension of the side walls of the main body of a temple; see antis temple, in antis; plural, antae. →84

antae Lat.; plural form of anta. →84

antarala in Hindu temple architecture, a vestibule leading to a shrine or sanctum. →68

anta temple 1 see antis temple. →84
2 see double antis temple. →84

antecella Lat.; a room, open vestibule etc. preceding a cella, especially in Roman architecture; called pronaos in Greek architecture.
see *Mesopotamian temple* illustration. →66
see *apteral temple* illustration. →84
see *peristyle temple* illustration. →85

antechamber see anteroom.
see *antechamber* in rock-cut tomb illustration. →74

antechurch, forechurch; a deep extension to the west end or front of a church, often a number of bays long and with a nave and aisles. →99

antefix see antefixa.

antefixa, plural antefixae; Lat.; in classical architecture, one of a number of decorative blocks placed at the eaves of a temple to cover the ends of roofing slabs or tiles. →47

antefixae plural form of antefixa. →47

antemensale 'in front of the table' (Lat.); a decorative panel or hanging for covering the front of a church altar; an altar frontal. →116

antenna 1 see aerial.
2 satellite antenna, see satellite link aerial.

antennae plural form of antenna.

antenna amplifier see aerial amplifier.

antepagment, antepagmentum (Lat.); in classical architecture, ornamental mouldings around a door or window opening which, according to Vitruvius, derived from the terracotta protective elements in archaic timber architecture and reappeared in stone as enrichment. →84

antepagmenta plural of antepagmentum. →84

antepagmentum Lat.; see antepagment. →84

antependium, altar frontal; 'suspended in front' (Lat.); a richly decorated metal, wood or textile ornamental covering, hanging or fixed at the front of an altar. →116

anteroom 1 a vestibule or transition space leading to a main room or hall; often a lobby, porch etc.
2 see prostas. →87
see *anteroom* in rock-cut tomb illustration. →74

anthemion 1 an ornamental motif found in classical architecture consisting of stylized honeysuckle foliage; the word derives from the Greek for flower, anthos. →82
2 see lotus anthemion. →82

anthemion and palmette an ornamental band motif found in the architecture of antiquity consisting of stylized honeysuckle leaves alternating with a palmette design.

Anthony's cross see tau cross. →117

anthracene a blue fluorescent crystalline material obtained from coal tar; used as a raw material in the production of some dyes.

anthracene oil an oil produced by the distillation of coal tar at above 270°C, used to produce anthracene.

anthracite, 1 anthracite coal, stone-coal; a hard, black, non-bituminous mineral consisting of over 94% carbon; used as high grade coal.
2 a shade of black named after the above.

anthracite coal see anthracite.

anthraquinoid red a transparent red organic pigment suitable for use in oil paints.

anthraquinone an organic compound derived from anthracene, used in the manufacture of a small group of synthetic dyestuffs.

anthropometric design the design of buildings, rooms etc. according to the relative proportions of measurements taken from the ideal human body, a practice originating during the Renaissance period. →106

anti-bandit laminated glass a class of security glass designed to resist breakage for a short length of time; 10 mm laminated glass is often used. →53

anti-capillary groove see capillary groove.

anticipatory cross see tau cross. →117

anticline in geology, an arched rock formation within the bedrock.

anti-dazzle screen, glare screen; in road design, a screen running between two carriageways conveying traffic moving in opposite directions, designed to reduce the glare from the headlights of oncoming cars.

anti-fading glass laminated glass containing a special interlayer to absorb 99% of ultraviolet light, used in display cases, shop windows etc. to protect coloured objects from fading.

anti-flooding gully a drainage gully containing a valve to prevent the backflow of water or other liquid.

anti-flooding intercepting trap a drainage trap containing a check valve, which prevents the passage of foul air from a sewer to a drain.

anti-flooding valve a valve which prevents a drain or sewer from flooding.

anti-foaming admixture in concretework, an admixture included in a concrete mix to inhibit the formation of air bubbles.

antifreeze see antifreezing admixture.

antifreezing admixture, antifreeze; in concretework, an admixture included in the concrete mix to raise its temperature and prevent it from freezing.

anti-intruder chain link fencing see woven wire fencing.

antimonite see stibnite.

antimony a brittle, metallic chemical element, **Sb**, used in a number of alloys; traditionally known as stibium.

antimony fahlerz see tetrahedrite.

antimony glance see stibnite.

antimony orange see antimony vermilion.

antimony trisulphide $\mathbf{Sb_2S_3}$, see stibnite, antimonite, antimony glance.

antimony vermilion, antimony orange; a range of bright poisonous red pigments based on antimony trisulphide; introduced in 1848, they have now largely been replaced by cadmium pigments.

antimony white a white pigment consisting of antimony oxide mixed with blanc fixe; used as titanium white and usually marketed under the name 'Timonox'.

antimony yellow see Naples yellow.

antiquarian a British standard paper size; 31" × 51", 787 mm × 1346 mm. →Table 6

antique glass glass with an uneven surface, hand blown in the traditional way or manufactured to appear that way.

Antique (the) see antiquity.

antiquity, the Antique; an age in architecture and art prior to the Middle Ages; especially Greek, Hellenistic and Roman architecture, whose principles enjoyed a rebirth during the Renaissance.

antiquum opus antiquum, see opus incertum. →83

antis see in antis.

antistatic referring to any device, product or surface treatment which counteracts the effects of static electricity.

antis temple, 1 anta temple, templum in antis; a classical temple type in which the frontal columns are in antis, bounded by extensions of the side walls. →84
2 see double antis temple. →84

anti-sun glass see solar control glass.

anti-thrust action a latch mechanism in a mechanical lock whose latch bolt cannot be retracted manually.

anti-vacuum valve, vacuum breaker; a valve in a system of pipework which can be opened to admit air as compensation for loss of pressure.

anti-vandal glass a class of special laminated glasses which are relatively resistant to vandalism. →53

anti-vibration cork a resilient cork product used as a damper under heavy vibrating plant etc.

Antrodia serialis see white spongy rot.

Antwerp blue, Haarlem blue; a pale blue pigment, Prussian blue reduced with 75% inert pigment, usually alumina hydrate.

Anubis in Egyptian mythology, the jackal-headed god of embalming, who guided the deceased through the court of Osiris to the Underworld; 'Anpu' in Egyptian, 'Anubis' in Greek. →74

anvil a heavy cast-iron bench on which a blacksmith or forge-worker hammers hot metals.

apadana in ancient Persian architecture, a columned hall surrounded by colonnades, used as an administrational and congregational space.
see *apadana column* illustration. →114

apartment see flat; types included as separate entries are listed below. →61
see *types of residential building* illustration. →61
bedsit, one-room flat.
corner apartment. →61
council flat.
maisonette, duplex apartment.
open-ended unit, through apartment. →61
two-roomed flat.

apartment block, block of flats, residential block; a multistorey building containing a number of separate apartments served by one or a number of stairs. →61

apartment building see apartment block. →61

apartment formwork, room formwork, tunnel formwork; proprietary formwork used for casting two concrete side walls and a horizontal slab spanning between them in one operation.

apartment house, mansion block; a residential building in a well-to-do urban area, containing a number of apartments on different levels, all accessed by the same entry and stair.

apatite a calcium phosphate mineral used as gemstones and as a raw material in the production of fertilizer.

Apennine culture the bronze-age culture of the Italian peninsula from c.1500 BC.

apex the highest point of a geometrical form such as a triangle or cone, or of a pitched or ridge roof.

apex stone see saddle stone.

apodyterion Gk; a dressing room in a classical Greek gymnasium or bath house. →91

apodyterium, pl. apodyteria; Lat.; a dressing room in a Roman bath house. →91

apophyge, apothesis; Gk; a slight curvature of the top of the shaft of a classical column where it meets the capital, and bottom where it meets the base. →80

apophysis see apophyge. →80

apostilb abb. **asb**; a unit of measurement of the luminance or brightness of a surface, equal to 1 lumen/m^2 of uniform radiation; see also lux.

apotheca Lat.; a store room on an upper floor of a Roman dwelling, usually for the keeping of wine.

apothecary a pharmaceutical chemist.

apothesis see apophyge. →80

apotropaic referring to an image, decoration, succession of spaces or sculptured ornament used in a building to prevent the influence of evil spirits; see next entry.

apotrope a symbolic statue, image or construction intended to provide protection against evil spirits. →75

apparatus see equipment.

appeal see planning appeal.

appearance see external appearance.

apple [*Malus spp.*] a genus of European hardwoods with fine-textured timber valued for its decorative grain; used for veneers and furniture.

apple green a shade of green which takes its name from the colour of the unripe fruit of the apple tree (*Malus spp.*).

appliance any mechanical device such as a shower, heater, fan etc. used for a specific task in a building or technical installation.

appliance flexible connection, flexible rubber hose; in gas installations, a length of resilient rubber hose for connecting the outlet of a gas pipe or riser to an appliance.

appliance governor in gas installations, a device which regulates the pressure and flow of gas to a particular appliance.

application 1 in computing, a series of interrelated software routines designed to perform a specific function.
2 a formal written request for an action to be undertaken, to order official services or permits, or for employment; see below.
planning application.
interim application.

application software in computing, software used for a specific useful function such as word processing or CAD.

applied art any art which is both functional and satisfies an aesthetic need (industrial design, furniture, architecture, graphics etc.).

applied column see engaged column. →13

applied sash glazing see secondary glazing.

appliqué ornamentation for fabrics and leatherwork with surface-applied rather than embroidered or embossed motifs.

apprentice a trainee who works under a tradesman or craftsman, filling out his training with courses at a technical college.

appropriation, allocation; in economics, a sum of money set aside within a budget for a particular purpose.

approval 1 the acceptance of a design or proposal by a client or local authority; generally an announcement to the effect that certain criteria have been satisfied.
2 see neighbours' consent.

Approved Document one of a number of documents approved by the Secretary of State in Britain, in which guidance and instructions for detailed design regarding structure, fire spread, site preparation, drainage, sound control, energy conservation etc., are given according to the Building Regulations; although they are not required to be followed by the letter, the relevant building regulation is deemed to be satisfied if they are.

approved school see community home.

approximation a quantity or estimate given as a close or rounded value, but not an exact one.

apricot, apricot yellow; a shade of yellow which takes its name from the colour of the ripened fruit of the apricot tree (*Prunus armeniaca*).

apricot yellow see apricot.

apron 1 see window apron.
2 see drop apron.
3 that part of a theatre stage in front of the curtain.
4 ramp; a strip of hard ground at an airport where an aeroplane is parked, refuelled or loaded with passengers and baggage.
5 see hearth apron. →56

apron eaves piece in sheet roofing, a T-shaped member used to support an eaves and provide a drip.

apron flashing a roofing flashing laid at the junction of the upper end of a pitched or flat roof and abutting wall or parapet; it is tucked into the wall with an upstand, and laid over the roofing. →56, →57

apsara a Buddhist or Hindu celestial winged female or animal figure.

apse 1 a semicircular or polygonal terminating space at or behind the high altar of a church or basilica, often roofed with a half-dome.
see *Early Christian and Late Antique church* illustration. →95
see *Byzantine domical church* illustration. →96
see *Carolingian abbey church* illustration. →98
see *Romanesque church* illustration. →99
see *altar* illustration. →116
2 see exedra. →93

apse aisle an aisle within the apse of a church; a deambulatory. →100

apsidal of a building form, relating to or in the form of an apse, semicircular or half-domed.

apsidiole, absidiole; in religious architecture, a secondary apse, semicircular niche or chapel which terminates a side aisle or is arranged around an apse. →95, →98

apsis Latin form of apse.

apteral temple see apteros. →84

apteros, apteral temple; 'wingless' (Gk); a classical temple with a colonnade at one or both ends only, not lining its sides.
see *apteral temple* illustration. →84

aquamanile a traditional water vessel used for washing hands; frequently of bronze or pottery and in the shape of an animal or bird.

aquamarine 1 a pale blue variety of beryl, a semi-precious beryllium aluminium silicate mineral, used as a gemstone.
2 a shade of light blue which takes its name from the colour of the above.

aquarelle a general name for watercolour paints which are transparent as opposed to gouache and casein paints which are relatively opaque.

aquarelle paper see watercolour paper.

aquatic plant any species of landscaping plant which usually grows in or under water.

aquatint 1 a method of making subtle and delicate graphic prints using a resin-coated plate partially etched away with acid in the desired pattern.
2 the print thus formed.

aqueduct a bridge or other structure designed to convey fresh water, usually a canal or river supported by piers and arches, or a tunnel; from the Latin, aquae ductus, 'conveyance of water'.
see *Roman structures* illustration. →93
see *Roman thermae* illustration. →91

aqueous see water based.

aqueous adhesive see water-borne adhesive.

ara Lat.; a classical Roman altar for a deity. →116

arabesque intricate decoration based on Moorish and Arabic antecedents, combining a complexity of flowing lines with geometrical and symmetrical patterns.
see *arabesque* in symbols and ornaments illustration. →120
see *arabesque capital* in medieval capitals illustration. →115

Arabic arch see horseshoe arch. →24

araeostyle 'lightly columned'; in classical architecture, the spacing between adjacent rowed columns, known as intercolumniation, at a distance of over three column diameters, also written as areostyle. →77

Aralia papyrifera see rice paper.

aramid fibre a group of very strong, tough and stiff synthetic fibres used in the manufacture of radial tyres, fibre-reinforced composites, heat-resistant fabrics and bulletproof vests; one of these is commercially marketed as Kevlar.

Araucaria angustifolia see Parana pine.

arbalestina see balistraria. →103

arbitration an accepted procedure for settling disputes, outside the courts but with legal force, using independent persons acceptable to both parties in dispute.

arboriculture the planting and cultivation of trees individually or in woodland.

arborvitae see thuja.

arcade 1 a passage or open walk, often lined with columns carrying arches, and roofed with a vaulted ceiling.
see *Byzantine domical church* illustration. →96
2 a row of columns surmounted by a series of arches.
see *Gothic cathedral* illustration. →100
3 an intermediate row of posts in an aisled building.
4 see amusement arcade.
5 see shopping arcade.

arcade plate in traditional timber frame construction, a horizontal member joining the tops of aisle posts and supporting rafters.

arcade post see aisle post.

arcading a row or series of arches.

arc doubleau see transverse rib. →101

arch 1 a two-dimensionally curved beam construction for supporting loads between two points of support over an opening; traditional masonry arches were constructed from wedge-shaped stones locked together by loading from above; types of arch included as separate entries are listed below. →24
2 a pattern or motif consisting of this.
see *true arches* illustration. →24
see *flat, false and decorative arches* illustration. →23
see *arched and vaulted construction* illustration. →22
acute arch, see lancet arch. →24
Arabic arch, see horseshoe arch. →24
arcuated lintel, see Syrian arch. →24
basket arch, see three-centred arch. →24
bell arch. →23, →24
blind arch.
brick arch. →23
cambered arch.
chancel arch. →99
cinquefoil arch. →24
cinquefoliated arch. →23
circular arch. →24
corbelled arch, corbel arch. →23
corbelled lintel. →23
crossette, see joggled arch. →23
depressed arch, see drop arch. →24
depressed ogee arch, see two-centred ogee arch. →24
depressed three-centred arch.
discharging arch, see relieving arch. →23
draped arch. →24
drop arch. →24
Dutch arch. →23
elliptical arch. →24
equilateral arch. →24
false arch. →23
fan arch. →123
five-centred arch. →24
flat arch. →23
Florentine arch. →23
foliated arch, see cinquefoliated, multifoliated, trifoliated arches. →23
four-centred arch, see Tudor arch. →24
four-centred pointed arch, see Tudor arch. →24
French arch, see Dutch arch. →23
gauged arch. →22, →23
Gothic arch, see pointed arch. →24
horseshoe arch. →24
inflected arch, see ogee arch. →24
inverted arch. →24
Italian arch. →23
Italian pointed arch. →23
Italian round arch, see Florentine arch. →23
jack arch, see flat arch. →23
joggled arch. →23
keel arch. →24

lancet arch. →24
masonry arch. →22, →23, →24
Moorish arch, see horseshoe arch. →24
multifoil arch. →24
multifoliated arch. →23
Norman arch.
ogee arch. →24
parabolic arch. →24
pointed arch. →24
pointed cinquefoil arch. →24
pointed cinquefoliated arch. →23
pointed equilateral arch, see equilateral arch. →24
pointed horseshoe arch. →24
pointed multifoliated arch. →23
pointed Saracenic arch.
pointed segmental arch. →24
pointed trefoil arch. →24
pointed trifoliated arch. →23
principal arch. →25
pseudo four-centred arch.
pseudo three-centred arch. →23
quadrifrontal arch. →93
quatrefoil arch.
Queen Anne arch.
raking arch, see rampant arch. →24
rampant arch. →24
relieving arch. →23
reverse ogee arch. →24
Roman arch. →22, →24
Romanesque arch.
rood arch.
rough brick arch, rough arch. →22, →23
round arch, see circular arch. →24
round cinquefoliated arch. →23
round horseshoe arch, see horseshoe arch. →24
round multifoliated arch. →23
round trefoil arch. →24
round trifoliated arch. →23, →110
Saracenic pointed arch, see pointed Saracenic arch.
segmental arch, segmented arch. →22, →24
semi-arch.
semicircular arch. →22, →24
skew arch.
squinch arch, see squinch. →26
stilted arch.
stilted pointed arch, see pointed Saracenic arch.
stilted semicircular arch.
straight arch, see flat arch. →23
strainer arch. →23
straining arch.
structural arch, see arched structure.
Syrian arch. →24
tented arch, see draped arch. →24
three-centred arch. →24
three-pointed arch, see equilateral arch. →24
three-hinged arch, three-pinned arch.
transverse arch. →25
trefoil arch. →24
triangular arch. →23
tribunal arch. →99
trifoliated arch. →23, →110
triumphal arch. →93
true arch. →24
Tudor arch. →24
two-centred ogee arch. →24
Venetian arch. →23

archaeology the study of human history and culture based on the findings from excavations and from ancient artifacts.

archaic referring to art which is ancient, outdated, old fashioned or at a primitive stage of development.

Archaic period the time of the first and third dynasties in Egyptian culture from 3200 to 2680 BC, and that in Greece between the bronze-age Helladic and Classic periods from 1150 to 480 BC.
see *Doric capital from the Archaic period* illustration. →81

archaic solution in classical architecture, the spacing of columns beneath an entablature evenly, so that, for each triglyph to be centrally above a column, the corner triglyphs are further apart than the others; see classical solution. →77

archaism the deliberate imitation of something ancient or prehistoric in art or architecture.

archaistic that which imitates ancient art, especially the Archaic art of the classical Hellenists and Romans.

arch beam see cambered beam. →30

arch brace, concave brace; in traditional timber frame construction, a naturally curved timber member for bracing the junction between a post and beam, trussed rafters etc.

arch braced roof truss in traditional timber roof construction, a simple roof truss with sloping rafters braced at the eaves with arch braces.

arch brick see radial brick. →16

arch bridge, arched bridge; a bridge whose main supporting construction is an arch. →32
see cambered bridge. →32

arched beam see cambered beam. →30

arched bridge see arch bridge. →32

arched construction see arch, arched structure.

arched head, arcuated head; the curved uppermost member of an arched window. →111

arched structure, structural arch; a simple convex beam structure, used for vaulting large spaces, in which all points along the structure are in compression.

arched truss see trussed arch. →33

arched window see arch window. →111

archetype a basic form, model, pattern or specimen from which variations are derived.

Archimedean spiral, logarithmic spiral, equiangular spiral; a geometrical spiral constructed mathematically such that the angle between the tangent and radius vector is the same for all points on the spiral.

archipelago a distinct and extensive group of islands in a particular region of the sea.

architect a qualified professional or organization who designs buildings and supervises their construction.

architectonic having the spatial qualities, properties and language special to architecture.

architect's office, architectural practice; a private company, owned or run by one or a number of architects for the professional practising of architecture.

architectural pertaining to architecture; relating to, involving, in the manner of architecture.

architectural competition an ideas or design competition in which the purpose is to find outline or detailed solutions for the design of a building or buildings.

architectural design that part of the design of a building produced by an architect, which encompasses technical, structural, aesthetic and financial aspects.

architectural drawing a drawing produced by an architect as part of design documentation for a building project.

architectural language, vocabulary; the architectural elements, form, detailing, technical and functional solutions of a building, the expression, symbolism and meaning contained therein.

architectural practice see architect's office.

Architectural style, Second Pompeian style, Illusionistic style; a style of interior wall decoration popular from 80 BC to c.100 AD in Roman Pompeii, in which principal motifs are pilasters and entablatures with pastoral perspective scenes between.
see *Pompeian styles* illustration. →126

architecture 1 the art and science of producing built form, the product and study of this.
2 in computing, the specification of the contents and functioning of a particular computer system or network.

architrave 1 a strip or moulding used around a door frame to cover the joint between the door and the surrounding construction.
2 epistyle; in classical architecture, the lower horizontal band of an entablature, supported by columns.
see *architrave* in classical orders illustrations. →78, →79, →80
3 a beam dividing aisles in a basilica.

archive see tablinum. →88

archivolt arcus volutus (Lat.); a decorated band above or on the soffit of the intrados in an arch.

arch truss see trussed arch. →33

archway an arched construction, often an open door or gateway, with a path, corridor or throughfare passing through it.

arch window a window whose upper edge is in the form of an arch. →111

arcology a term coined by the Italian architect Paolo Soleri to define an ecological architecture of future urban settlements involving minimal use of land and natural resources.

arcosolium a niche, arched recess or sepulchral cell housing a tomb in an Early Christian church or late Roman catacomb.

arc pattern a paving pattern of small stones or cobbles laid in a series of parallel rows. →15

arcuated of a construction or pattern which features arches as a main structural device or motif, or is bowed in shape.

arcuated head see arched head. →111

arcuated lintel a beam over an opening, whose underside is concave to form an arch; often used as a decorative motif, see Syrian arch. →24

arcus Lat.; a classical Roman arch, especially a triumphal arch.

arcus triumphalis see triumphal arch. →93

arcus volutus Lat.; see archivolt.

arc welding a method of fusion welding in which the metals to be joined are melted together by an electric arc.

ardhamandapa 'half mandapa'; the portico or entrance porch of a Hindu temple.

are abb. **a**; a unit of area equal to 10 m × 10 m = 100 m^2.

area 1 a contained or defined part of the earth's or some other surface, often with a specific function, characteristic or ownership; a district, sector or zone.
2 see surface area.
3 see basement area.

area lighting, floodlighting; the illumination of large external areas such as sports venues, industrial sites, airports, storage depots etc.

area of archaeological interest see prehistoric site.

area of historical interest see historic site.

area of outstanding natural beauty an area of countryside with fine landscapes etc. protected by legislation to control development because of its national value.

arena 1 the main central space of a Roman amphitheatre or circus, or of a bullring, often sanded.
see *arena* in amphitheatre illustration. →90
2 a modern sports or entertainment venue, often along the lines of the above, a stadium.
3 see stadium.

arenaceous, sandy; pertaining to types of soil, rock or landscape composed of or containing a large proportion of sand.

arenaceous rock, arenite; referring to sandstone or other sedimentary rock composed from sandy grains.

arenite see arenaceous rock.

areostyle see araeostyle. →77

argentite, silver glance; a lead grey to black metallic mineral, naturally occurring silver sulphide, **AgS**, an important ore of silver.

argillaceous rock, claystone; rock which contains an abundance of clay materials.

argon a gaseous chemical element, **Ar**, used in fluorescent and incandescent lamps.

arithmetic the science of numbers and calculation thereby.

arithmetic mean in statistics and calculation, an average value given by the sum of a group of numbers divided by the amount in the group.

arkose a form of reddish sandstone with a high content of feldspar.

arma Lat.; the front portion of a Roman contubernium, a military tent or barrack, where personal equipment and arms were stored.

armamentarium Lat.; a Roman weapons store, armoury or arsenal for hand weapons used by gladiators in an amphitheatre, or legionaries in a fortified encampment.

armarium Lat.; a cupboard or niche recessed into a church wall beside an altar, containing vessels and utensils relating to the liturgy; an aumbry.

armature in sculpting, a shaped framework used to support plaster, clay etc. in the building up of models.

armorial porcelain a Chinese porcelain artifact decorated with a European heraldic emblem or coat of arms.

armour see pitching.

armouring metal covering for an electric cable to afford protection against external forces, abrasion etc.

armour-plated glass see bullet-resistant laminated glass. →53

armoury a room or space for the storage of weaponry and armour in a castle or barracks.
see armamentarium.

Arnaudon's green an obsolete variety of the pigment chromium oxide green.

aromatic referring to a chemical compound whose molecule has a ringed structure, such as benzene.

aromatic cedar [*Juniperus virginiana*], see eastern red cedar.

arrangement drawing see general arrangement drawing.

arras a rich patterned textile, often used as a tapestry, developed in the French town of Arras.

arrester bed in traffic planning, a strip of soft material beside a carriageway, usually on a downhill slope, designed to slow down vehicles which have veered off the carriageway.

arricciato see arriccio.

arriccio, arricciato; in fresco painting, the coarse middle of three coats of plasterwork, between the trullisatio and intonaco, on which the design is sketched out.

arris 1 a corner or meeting of two planar sides of an object such as a piece of timber, masonry unit etc.
see *arris* in conversion of timber illustration. →2
see *arris* in brickwork illustration. →21
2 eased arris, see pencil round. →14

arris fillet see angle fillet. →49

arris gutter in roof construction, a V-shaped gutter, often constructed as a raised strip of roofing protruding directly from the roof plane.

arris knot a knot in seasoned timber which appears on the longitudinal corner of a sawn plank. →1

arrissed edge see pencil round. →14

arrow 1 see arrow-headed bastion. →104
2 see arrowhead.
3 egg and arrow, see egg and dart. →82
4 arrow of Jupiter, arrow of Zeus, see thunderbolt. →120

arrow cross see cross barbée. →117

arrowhead 1 in the dimensioning and annotation of drawings etc., a notation for indicating where a dimension begins and terminates.
2 a similar triangular marking for drawing attention to recent revisions made to a drawing. →130

arrow-headed bastion a bastion shaped in plan like an arrow, with a narrow way or gorge leading to the main rampart; also called an arrow. →104

arrow loop 1 a narrow vertical opening in the external wall of a castle or fortification for archers to fire arrows at potential attackers; also known as an arrow slit, loophole, loop or loup, and sometimes as oeillet, oilet, oillet, eyelet or oylet, though these often refer to the round enlargements at either extremity. →103
2 see balistraria. →103

arrow of Jupiter see thunderbolt. →120

arrow of Zeus see thunderbolt. →120

arrow slit see arrow loop. →103

arsenal a building or factory for the manufacture and storage of weapons and ammunition.

arsenic a grey, poisonous, chemical element, **As**, used in the preservation of wood and as an insecticide.

arsenic sulphide silver arsenic sulphide, see proustite.

arsenic trioxide a poisonous, white, chemical compound, As_2O_3, used in the manufacture of pigments, glass and insecticides.

arsenic trisulphide a yellow or red chemical compound, As_2S_3, used as the pigment king's yellow. see orpiment.

arsenic yellow see king's yellow.

arsenopyrite a grey, metallic, crystalline mineral, **FeAsS**, from which arsenic is extracted.

arshin a Russian and Turkish unit of length equivalent to 71.12 cm.

art creative aesthetic action and its product.

Art Deco, Style Moderne; a style in architecture and interiors (originating from the Exposition de Arts Décoratif in Paris in 1925) in Europe and America in the 1920s and 1930s, characterized by Art Nouveau and Modernist influences, playful forms and abstract decoration.

artefact, artifact; in general, a man-made object; also often used in a derogatory sense to refer to a shallow or characterless work of art.

Artemisia absintium see absinthe green.

Arte Povera a form of minimalist art, originating in the 1960s, which utilizes humble, cheap and waste products, materials and methods.

artesando in Spanish architecture, an intricately carved wooden ceiling of Moorish influence.

artesian groundwater groundwater contained in saturated rockbeds or aquifers which, when drilled, will rise to the surface under its own pressure.

artesian well a well consisting of a bored hole in the ground through which water below the local water table will be conveyed to the surface by pressure.

art for art's sake, l'art pour l'art; a concept according to which the value of a work of art is based purely on its aesthetic rather than political or symbolic content.

art gallery, art museum; a building, group of buildings or part of a building in which visual art and sculpture are on display.

articles of agreement in project administration, the document in which parties to a contract undersign as confirmation of their agreement.

artifact see artefact.

artificial cementing, grouting, injection; a method of strengthening, stabilizing and waterproofing weak or porous soils or rock by injecting concrete into the voids therein.

artificial fibre, synthetic fibre; any fibre of polymer, carbon, glass, ceramic or metal which is man-made; see also natural fibre.

artificial intelligence computer hardware and software intended to imitate human decision-making processes or the intelligence of living creatures.

artificial light light produced by means other than by the sun.

artificial lighting, 1 illumination; lighting for a space provided by lamps, luminaires or means other than by daylighting.
2 see permanent artificial lighting.

artificial stone see cast stone.

artificial ultramarine, French blue, French ultramarine, Gmellin's blue; an artificial blue pigment made by heating clay, soda, sulphur and coal, with the same colour and chemical properties as genuine ultramarine produced from lapis lazuli.

artist one who practises art.

artistic pertaining to the arts; having a particular persuasion or skill for artistic work.

art mobilier any small movable objects, statuettes, vases etc., used as decorative ornament or interior decoration.

art museum see art gallery.

Art Nouveau a movement in art and architecture in Europe from 1890 to 1910 characterized by the use of flowing naturalistic ornament and informal compositions of plan and elevation; see also Jugendstil, Modern Style, Stile Liberty.
see *Art Nouveau portal* illustration. →113

Arts and Crafts a movement in architecture and design from England, initiated by William Morris in 1867 to counteract industrialism; it is characterized by an interest in the handcrafted, and uses motifs from nature and the Gothic Revival.

arts centre see cultural centre.

artwork drawings, photographs and graphics in such a form as to be of use in printing and reproduction.

Arundo phragmites common reed, see best reed, Norfolk reed.

arx Lat.; a Roman name for an acropolis or citadel.

arylide yellow, Hansa yellow; a range of slightly poisonous synthetic organic transparent yellow pigments which have good weatherability, light, acid and alkali resistance.

Asar see Osiris. →74

asbestos a mineral, magnesium silicate, occurring naturally as a glassy rock which can be split into small fibres; formerly used as reinforcement and fireproofing, it is hazardous to health and rarely used nowadays in new construction.

asbestos board any building or insulation board consisting of asbestos fibres in a binder; these products are no longer in general use due to their toxic nature.

asbestos cement a material consisting of asbestos fibres bonded with Portland cement; formerly used for a range of durable and fireproof cast products.

asbestos cement pipe asbestos cement pressed into tough, durable and waterproof drainage and sewer pipes; now withdrawn and widely regarded as a health hazard.

asbestos cement sheet asbestos cement pressed into sheet form; formerly used as tough, durable, fireproof building board but has since been replaced with less hazardous fibre cement board.

asbestos cement slate a tough, durable asbestos cement roofing tile resembling a roofing slate; now withdrawn due to health hazards.

asbestos fibre fibres manufactured from asbestos, formerly used as reinforcement and fireproofing in many products but extremely hazardous to health if not part of a solid matrix.

asbestos fibre reinforced composite any composite consisting of asbestos fibres in a binder (cement, lime, plastics, bitumen); formerly used as asbestos cement, vinyl floor tiles and bitumen felts.

asbestos-free slate a roofing tile resembling a roofing slate, consisting of fibres of a material other than asbestos, and cement.

asbestos removal, asbestos work; the specialist work involving the dismantling of hazardous asbestos construction and its transport, safely packed, to a place of disposal.

asbestos work see asbestos removal.

Ascension in religious art and ornamentation, a representation of the soul and body of Christ ascending to heaven forty days after the Resurrection.

ASCII in computing, a standard representation of letters, numbers, symbols and punctuation in binary code; an acronym for American Standard Code for Information Interchange.

Asclepian column see serpent column. →69

Asclepius see staff of Asclepius. →120

Asian architecture see *Asian temples* illustration. →68
see *Asian and Mediterranean columns and capitals* illustration. →69

Asiatic base, Ephesian base; a classical Ionic column base which evolved in Asia Minor, consisting of a drum with scotia mouldings surmounted by a reeded torus moulding. →69, →81

ash 1 [*Fraxinus spp.*] a pale hardwood valued for its toughness and flexibility; see European ash, American ash; see ***Fraxinus spp.*** for full list of species of ash included in this work.
2 a deposit or residue that remains after the combustion of organic material.
3 see ash grey.

ash blonde a shade of grey used for hair colour: blonde with a hint of grey.

ashcan see refuse bin.

ash grey, ash, cendre; a shade of grey which takes its name from the colour of slightly yellow ashes.

ashlar, 1 ashlar masonry; masonry blocks or facing stone which has been dimensioned, squarely dressed and laid in bonded courses with narrow joints. →12
2 a single block of squared and dressed stone used in masonry. →12
see coursed ashlar. →11
see dimension stone. →12
see dry ashlar walling.
see natural stone block. →12
see range work.
see rusticated ashlar, rustic ashlar. →12
see uncoursed ashlar, random ashlar. →11

ashlar facing stone facing for rough or rubble masonry or concrete which consists of thin dimensioned and dressed stones; used to provide a fine finish at a lower cost than ashlar masonry.

ashlaring, ashlering; in traditional timber pitched roof construction, short vertical timber members for concealing the internal triangular gap between external joists, wall plate and rafters and to brace the eaves, often lined with board or infilled with blockwork.

ashlar masonry see ashlar. →12

ashlar post in traditional timber roof construction, a short post running from a wall plate to a principal rafter as part of ashlaring. →33

ashlering see ashlaring.

ash pan a vessel or pit inside a fireplace or solid-fuel appliance, located beneath the grate to collect ash and other debris from burnt material. →56

ash pan door a hatch in the front of a fireplace or solid-fuel appliance from which the ash can be removed. →56

aspen [*Populus tremula*, *Populus tremuloides*] hardwoods from Europe and North America respectively with soft, porous, straight-grained, pale-coloured timber; used as boards for cladding and for plywood and matches.

asphalt a mixture of bitumen and an aggregate such as sand used as a hardwearing surface in road construction and external paved areas.

asphaltic concrete a mixture of asphalt and concrete used in road production to provide a strong, stiff, structural surface.

asphalt oil see road oil.

asphalt roofing roofing of molten asphalt laid in successive layers.

asphalt shingles see strip slates. →49

asphalt surfacing see asphalt topping.

asphalt topping, asphalt surfacing; asphalt laid as a final durable and flexible surface for roads, pavements etc.

asphaltum a mixture of asphalt and turpentine used as a blackish-brown colouring agent.

assembly 1 the putting together of prefabricated parts of a component, construction or installation on site.
2 a range of components which functions together to form a whole, as in a doorset.
see automatic-closing fire assembly.
door assembly, see doorset.
see fire assembly.
see window assembly.

assembly drawing a detailed drawing which shows how a component, joint or construction is assembled or put together on site; a construction drawing.

assembly hall 1 a large main congregational hall in a building, especially an establishment such as a school.
2 see lesche. →92

assembly room, 1 meeting room, conference room, committee room; a large room with associated facilities used for official meetings.
2 a building for social or societal functions.

asser Lat., pl. asseres; a common rafter in Roman timber roof construction. →47

asseres Lat.; plural form of asser.

assessor, judge; a person who has been selected to judge an architectural or town planning competition and whose decision on the submitted designs is regarded as final.

assets any property or items of value owned by a person or company.

assignment model in traffic planning, a transportation model which determines the most likely route taken in travelling from a particular place to a chosen destination.

assistant one who lends aid, gives advice and generally helps out in various tasks, especially in a design office.

assisted area in town planning, a region, which may be deprived, suffering local recession or financial hardship, designated by an authority for receipt of aid to stimulate development and stabilization.

association of architects, institute of architects; a professional body to further the interests and rights of its architect members; see also AIA, RIBA, UIA.

as specified referring to stipulations in regulations, standards, designs, contract documents etc.

Assumption in religious art and ornamentation, a representation of the Virgin's soul and body being taken up to heaven three days after her death.

Assyrian architecture the Middle Eastern architecture of the organized society in the area now known as Iraq, at its height around 800 BC, characterized by single-storey dwellings in mud brick and expansive palaces and temples.
see *Assyrian ziggurat* illustration. →67
see *Asian and Mediterranean columns and capitals* illustration. →69

Assyrian period an era from c.1200 to 625 BC during the Babylonian period in Mesopotamian art.

astatine a non-metallic, radioactive element, **At**, used as an additive in steel.

astragal 1 'knuckle-bone' (astragalos, Gk); in classical architecture, a small circular moulding between the shaft and capital of a column or pilaster, in the

Doric order typically between the trachelion and hypotrachelion. →81
2 baguette moulding; an ornamental moulding consisting of a small semicircular projection in cross-section, often incorporating other motifs such as bead and reel. →14, →82
3 a small dividing glazing bar in a window. →111
4 a vertical strip attached to the edge of a door leaf or window frame to close the gap between it and the frame.

astroturf see synthetic grass.
astwerk see branch tracery.
astylar referring to architecture, usually classical, which does not contain columns or pilasters.
asymmetrical referring to a figure which has no symmetry; not symmetrical.
asymmetrical glazing unit, asymmetrical hermetically sealed double glazing unit; a glazed unit with two panes of glass of unequal thickness or consistency sealed around an edging strip with a gap usually filled with an inert gas.
asymmetrical hermetically sealed double glazing unit see asymmetrical glazing unit.
asymmetry see asymmetrical.
asymptote in mathematics, a straight line which is continually approached by a given curve but does not meet it within a finite distance.
atelier see studio.
Aten the ancient Egyptian solar disc, the chief deity during the reign of Amenhotep IV (Akhenaten) in 1340 BC; one of the many forms of the sun god Ra (Re), depicted as the sun at midday at its hottest and brightest, with radiating beams terminating in life-giving hands; also written as Aton. →74
at grade double mini-roundabout see mini-roundabout. →62
at grade junction a road junction in which all roads involved meet at the same level. →62, →63
see *at grade junctions* illustration. →62
athenaeum, 1 the Athenaeum; originally the temple of Athena in classical Athens.
2 subsequently a place where professors, orators and poets gathered to teach and present their works.
3 athenaeum; a literary or scientific institution, reading room or library.
atheneum see athenaeum.
Athens Charter a manifesto published by CIAM in 1933 which proposed solutions to the problems of modern urban dwelling, recreation, work, transport and historic buildings.
athletic field see playing field.
atlantes the plural form of atlas. →76
Atlantis cross a cross-like design of concentric circles, according to Plato symbolizing the town plan of the mythical city of Basilaea, in the lost land of Atlantis. →123
atlas, telamon (Gk); pl. atlantes; in classical architecture, a massive carved statuesque stooping male figure, often serving as a columnar support for a pediment. →76
Atlas cedar [*Cedrus atlantica*] a species of cedar tree from North Africa.
atmospheric burner see natural draught burner.
atmospheric projection see aerial perspective.
atmospheric pressure see barometric pressure.
atom the basic unit of chemistry; each element has its own atom consisting of a positively charged nucleus orbited by negatively charged electrons.
atomic power station see nuclear power station.
atomic weight see relative atomic mass.
atomizing oil burner a burner in an oil heating system in which oil is dispersed into small droplets and mixed with air prior to combustion.
Aton see Aten. →74
atramentum Lat.; a Roman name for pigments and inks made from carbon.
atrium 1 Lat.; an open central courtyard in a Roman dwelling, surrounded by the habitable spaces of the building; an aula in Greek architecture. →88
see *atrium* in Roman residential buildings illustration. →88
2 atrium paradisus; a forecourt, often colonnaded, in front of the vestibule of an Early Christian or Romanesque church.
see *Early Christian church* illustration. →95
see *Byzantine domical church* illustration. →96
see *Carolingian church* illustration. →98
3 a large space which functions as a transition space into more important rooms.
4 a large central space or court with a glazed roof.
5 the glazed roof for such a space.
atrium corinthium, Corinthian hall; Lat.; a Roman atrium dwelling type with a large central opening whose edges are supported by rows of columns on all sides.
atrium displuviatum Lat.; see displuviatum.
atrium house 1 a Roman dwelling type in which the building mass surrounds a main central space, the atrium, open to the sky. →88
2 patio house; a modern dwelling type planned with rooms arranged around facing an open central space; sometimes constructed with similar buildings in an adjoined row. →61
atrium paradisus Lat.; see atrium. →95, →96, →98
atrium testudinatum Lat.; see testudinate.
atrium tetrastylum Lat.; see tetrastyle.
atrium tuscanicum Lat.; see tuscanicum.
attached column see engaged column. →13
attached pier a pier structurally connected to or built into a wall to provide lateral stability.
attack 1 see corrosion.
2 see fungal attack.
attenuation, 1 absorption, loss; the reduction in strength of a signal in a telecommunications or sound system with distance from its source.
2 see sound attenuation.
attenuator see muffler.
attic 1 an upper room or space contained within the pitched roofspace of a residential building; see also garret.
2 a blindstory raised above the eaves or entablature line of a classical building to conceal the roof.
Attic base the most common classical column base consisting of an upper and lower torus and scotia separated by a fillet, primarily found with the Ionic order. →81
attic storey 1 the uppermost storey beneath the pitched roof of a residential building, containing storage or habitable space.
2 a storey above the entablature or cornice of a classical building, in strict proportion with lower elements.
attic truss a roof truss designed so as to allow for the construction of habitable roof space between its structural members. →33
atto- abb. **a**; a prefix for units of measurement or quantity to denote a factor of 10^{-18} (a million million millionth). →Table 1
attorney see letter of attorney.
attribute 1 an object or element used by convention in a work of art, especially painting, to symbolize a deity, saint or mythological figure.
2 in computer-aided design, a characteristic which defines the significance of a graphic object or group.
Atum one of the many forms of the ancient Egyptian sun god Re (Ra), depicted as the setting sun; according to Egyptian mythology he was the first god on earth, born of the primeval watery chaos, who created all things by spitting or by masturbation; also written as Tum; see also Aten, Khepri. →74
aubergine, eggplant; a shade of purple brown which takes its name from the colour of the edible fruit of the eggplant [*Solanum melongena*].

Aubusson a tapestry or carpet originating in the French town of the same name in the 1600s.

Aucoumea klaineana see gaboon.

audience hall see apadana.

audio spectrum, acoustic spectrum, sound spectrum; in acoustics, the range of frequencies and intensities of sound emitted from a source or sources at any given time; the measurable make-up of a sound source.

audio-frequency a frequency of sound within the audible range; frequencies of any oscillations within this range.

audit the legally required annual inspection of the accounts of a company.

auditor a professional accountant whose task is to examine the accounts of a company.

auditorium 1 that part of a theatre, concert hall etc. in which the audience is seated.
2 loosely, any building containing the above.

Auditor's report a document containing the written details of an official inspection of the final accounts of a company.

auditory church a spartan church type appearing in England in the 1600s after the Reformation, based rather on preaching from a pulpit or lectern than worship at an altar; a religious auditorium.

auger a corkscrew-like tool or drill bit used for boring round holes in solid material such as wood or stone.

auger bit a spiral drill bit in the shape of an auger, used for drilling long large-bore holes, circular housings etc. →42

augered pile in foundation technology, a form of bored pile in which the hole is cut with an auger. →29

augite a dark, crystalline form of the mineral pyroxene, occurring in volcanic and metamorphic rocks.

aula 1 the surrounded courtyard of an ancient Greek dwelling, an atrium in Roman architecture.
2 an assembly room in a German school or university.

aulaeum Lat.; the curtain of a classical theatre, raised through a slot at the front of the stage. →89

aumbry, ambry, almary, almery; a small lockable cupboard or niche in a church where the communion chalice and other sacred utensils were stored; an armarium.

aume a traditional English unit of measurement for liquid capacity, especially wine, equal to 40 gallons (approximately 150 l).

au premier coup see alla prima.

aureole, glory, halo, nimbus; in painting and religious symbolism, light or radiance which surrounds a saint or sacred person; when limited to the head, it is called a nimbus, when surrounding the whole body, an aureole. →119

aureolin see cobalt yellow.

auricular ornament, lobate ornament; decorative ornament, foliage and volutes, resembling parts of the human ear, found in early Baroque architecture in northern Europe in the late 1500s and early 1600s. →122

auripigmentum see king's yellow.

aurora, aurora red, aurora orange, dawn, rose dawn; a shade of pink which takes its name from the colour of the sky at sunrise.

aurora orange see aurora.

aurora red see aurora.

aurora yellow see cadmium yellow.

aurum mussivum see mosaic gold.

austenite a solution of carbon and other materials appearing in gamma iron, formed when iron is heated over 910°C; found in some stainless steels used for cutlery.

austenitic stainless steel stainless steel which contains 16–19% chromium and 4–6% nickel.

Australian blackwood, black wattle (Aust.); [*Acacia melanoxylon*] an eastern Australian hardwood with strong, flexible, golden brown timber; used for furniture, interior joinery and woodwind instruments.

authoritarian planning town planning which emphasizes the power of the state over its inhabitants, characterized by the use of a grand scale for governmental buildings, axial streets terminated with patriotic monuments, and spartan uniformity of layout and form for residential buildings.

autoclave a sealed pressure vessel which contains steam at high temperatures, used for curing concrete and calcium silicate bricks.

autoclave curing see autoclaving.

autoclaved aerated concrete a form of aerated concrete often containing aluminium or zinc powder as a foaming agent, which has been steam cured in an autoclave to control the aerating process.

autoclaving, high pressure steam curing, autoclave curing; a method of curing concrete, usually lightweight concrete, by exposing it to high pressure superheated steam in a sealed vessel for a given time in order to increase dry shrinkage and speed up hardening.

autodestructivism a term coined for certain types of artworks of the 1960s and 1970s which are designed ultimately to destroy themselves.

autodidact one who is self-taught.

autogenous shrinkage, hardening shrinkage; in concretework, a reduction in size caused by further hydration of cement during final hardening, much less than during initial drying.

autograph 1 in the arts, a term sometimes used for an unsigned work of art of a known artist, to which the author can be attributed.
2 see signature.

automat an automatic machine from which a service such as parking tickets, telephone calls and goods can be bought by pushing money or a credit card into a slot.

automated data processing, ADP; see computing.

automatic-closing fire assembly a motorized fire door, shutter etc., normally kept in an open position, which closes automatically in the event of fire; an automatic fire door.

automatic door a motorized door controlled by an optical or motion sensor, which operates door gear and opens and closes it automatically.

automatic door gear the range of mechanisms and equipment for controlling the opening and closing of an automatic sliding or swinging door, operated by signals from detector devices, remote controls etc.

automatic door operator a motorized device which controls the opening and closing of a door leaf.

automatic fire door see automatic-closing fire assembly.

automatic fire extinguisher a fire extinguisher operated automatically by detectors in the event of outbreak of fire.

automatic fire-extinguishing system, auto-suppression system; any system for detecting a building fire by means of light, heat or smoke sensors and for extinguishing it using an automated system such as a sprinkler system.

automatic fire valve see fire valve.

automatic lighting controller see photoelectric lighting controller.

automatic lock see coin operated lock.

automatic writing see Automatism.

automation 1 the functioning of a process, installation or system without the use of continuous human input.
2 door automation, see automatic door gear.

Automatism, automatic writing; spontaneous activity or art related to surrealism in which conscious will and thought are eliminated.

automobile, passenger car, motor car, car; a four-wheeled motor vehicle, often privately owned, for carrying a small number of passengers.

auto-suppression system see automatic fire-extinguishing system.

autoxidation the spontaneous oxidation of a material caused by the presence of oxygen; weathering and deterioration of materials due to this.

auxiliary building see ancillary building.

auxiliary circuit an electric circuit used as part of an installation for powering auxiliary devices such as compressors, fans, transformers etc.

auxiliary pigment a substance used in paints as a filler, to improve opacity and to strengthen the paint film.

availability the ability of a product or service to be easily obtained.

avant-garde 1 innovative and groundbreaking work in the arts.
2 the practitioners of the above.

avant-gardism the practice and principles of the avant-garde.

avatar in Hindu religious culture and ornament, the manifestation of a god in human form, a statue representational of this.

avelane see cross avellane. →118

Avellane cross see cross avellane. →118

avenue 1 a wide, straight street in an urban context lined with broad-leaved trees.
2 a prehistoric double row of standing stones believed to form a ceremonial way to a major monument or cult centre.

average see mean.

aviary, bird house; a building or structure, often of mesh or netting for the keeping of birds.

Avillan cross see cross avellane. →118

award, prize; a merit, medal, sum of money etc. awarded to successful entrants of architectural and design competitions, outstanding buildings etc.

awl see bradawl. →42

awning, shade; a framed textile external shading apparatus which can be extended over and in front of windows to exclude direct sunlight from interiors.

awning window see top-hung casement window. →52

axe a hand tool with a handle and sharpened steel head for felling trees, shaping and chopping wood and stone etc.; types of axe included as separate entries are listed below.
American axe, see felling axe.
brick axe, see bricklayer's hammer. →40
chop axe. →40
double axe, double headed axe, see labrys. →122
felling axe.
hand axe.
hatchet.
hewing axe. →6
mason's axe, see masonry axe. →40
masonry axe. →40
patent axe. →40
pickaxe, see pick. →40
rock axe, see masonry axe. →40
stone axe, see masonry axe. →40
stonemason's axe, see masonry axe. →40
trimming axe, see masonry axe. →40
wood axe, see felling axe.

axed finish a rough stonework finish produced by dressing with an axe, pick or bush hammer.

axes plural of axis, see coordinate axes.

axial church see longitudinal church. →102

axial composition, symmetrical composition; artistic composition balanced around a main axis.

axial-flow fan in mechanical ventilation systems, a high efficiency fan which pumps air through the main axis of its rotors, installed along a line of ducting.

axiom, postulate; in mathematics and logic, an accepted and generally accepted principle.

axis an imaginary line denoting symmetry of an object, direction, point of rotation etc.; see also coordinate axes.

axis of sight see central axis of vision. →128

axis of vision see central axis of vision. →128

Axminster carpet a form of carpet with a soft tufted cut pile woven into a base layer; originating in the English village of Axminster, Devon.

axonometric pertaining to axonometry; usually the drawing resulting from an axonometric projection.

axonometric cube see coordinate cube. →127

axonometric perspective an outdated name for axonometric projection. →127

axonometric projection 1 a form of projection drawing depicting three dimensions with coordinate planes inclined, using parallel projectors perpendicular to the plane of projection. →127
2 a generic name for true isometric, dimetric and trimetric projections, in full orthographic axonometric projection.
3 an oblique projection based on a true plan of a subject laid obliquely to the horizontal, usually 45° and 45° or 30° and 60°; verticals are drawn to the same scale as the plan and the lines in each dimension are drawn parallel; more accurately called a military or planometric projection.

axonometry, parallel projection; a method of drawing in which the object is pictured in three dimensions such that all lines in each of the three major axes are parallel; especially pertaining to isometric, dimetric and trimetric projections, though usually used for all parallel projections depicting three dimensions on a flat plane. →127
see *axonometry* illustration. →127

ayaka a circumferential columned platform near the base of the dome of a Buddhist stupa. →68

ayous see obeche.

azelejo in Spanish, Portuguese and Latin American architecture and ornament, a glazed pottery floor or external wall tile with floral designs.

azimuth see solar azimuth.

azimuthal projection, zenithal projection; in geometry, especially cartography, a projection of part of the surface of a sphere, usually the earth, as a flattened disc.

azo dye one of the largest classes of synthetic dyes comprising over half the commercial dyes, manufactured from various coloured organic compounds containing nitrogen and used for colouring fabrics.

Aztec architecture the architecture of the Aztec Indians in Mexico from c.1350 to 1500, characterized by monumental cities on a gridiron plan, teocallis and zoomorphic ornament.
see *Aztec pyramid temple* illustration. →67

azure blue 1 an early name for smalt.
2 a general name given to shades of sky blue, regardless of the composition of the base pigment.

azure cobalt see cobalt blue.

azurite, azzura della magna, blue malachite, mineral blue, mountain blue; a mineral form of basic copper carbonate $Cu_3(OH)2(CO_3)_2$, used as a clear deep permanent water-based blue pigment since Roman times, and occasionally as a gemstone.

azzura della magna see azurite.

azzuro oltremarino see lapis lazuli.

B

B0 a standard international paper size of 1000 mm × 1414 mm (39" × 55"), used for posters and card; successive smaller sizes B1–B10 are derived by halving the area of the next size up; see A0, C0. Table 6

baby blue a shade of pale greyish blue which takes its name from the colour of the clothes of infant boys.

Babylonian period a period in Mesopotamian art from the time of the Kassite invasion in c.1800 BC culminating with the onset of Persian rule in 539 BC.

Bacchus, staff of see thursus. →120

back 1 the reverse, inferior or secondary face of a piece, component, building etc.
2 worse face; the surface of a timber board to the reverse side of the outer, usually finished surface.
3 the edge of a sawtooth adjacent to its cutting edge.
4 see window back.

back bed in glazing, bedding compound or a proprietary product applied to a rebate in a window frame, against which a pane is fixed.

back boiler 1 in a heating system, a boiler fitted to the rear of a solid fuel heater, which provides the thermal energy for water heating.
2 see high output back boiler.

back clearance in glazing, the horizontal distance between the inner face of the pane or glazing unit and its supporting frame.

back cut veneer decorative veneer formed by peeling the inner side of a half log or flitch off-centre on a lathe. →10

backdraught, smoke explosion; a rush of air into a room containing smouldering contents due to the opening of a door during a hazardous building fire, causing spontaneous ignition.

backer see back-up material.

backfill, fill; in sitework, earth replaced and compacted into an excavation to cover subsoil foundations and services once they have been laid.

backflap hinge a hinge whose leaves are long rather than tall, used for applications such as furnishings and table flaps where a butt hinge is insufficient. →38

backflow a phenomenon in which liquid flows along a pipe or channel in the reverse direction to that intended, caused by pressure or a partial vacuum; see also backsiphonage.

backflow prevention device a device for inhibiting the backflow of water in a drainage or sanitary installation.

backflow valve, 1 back-siphonage preventer, backwater valve, back-pressure valve; a check valve in a water system which allows water in a pipeline to flow in one direction only.
2 see pipe interrupter.

back form in concreting, formwork or formwork surfaces used in locations which remain hidden in the final structure; back formwork, in full.

back gutter in roof construction, a channel or gutter formed at the junction of a pitched roof and abutment wall, or behind a parapet or chimney to convey water away. →56

background see plastering background.

background noise, ambient sound; in acoustics, general noise present in an environment.

background noise level in acoustics, the level of background noise in a space.

back hearth the lowest masonry construction on which combustion takes place beneath a flue in a fireplace or fireplace recess; the floor of an open fireplace. →55

backing 1 a structural base such as concrete, masonry or a framework onto which cladding is fixed.
2 see back-up material.

backing coat see plaster undercoat.

backing strip see back-up material.

backings see plastering background.

backland open or bounded land to the rear of existing buildings as viewed from a road or street.

backnut 1 a nut at a threaded pipework joint which is tightened to secure the joint between two fittings.
2 see stop nut.

backplane see motherboard.

back-pressure valve see backflow valve.

back putty, bed putty; in glazing, a fillet of putty applied to a rebate in a window frame, against which a pane is bedded.

backsaw a handsaw with a rectangular blade whose back is reinforced with a metal strip to inhibit bending; used for carpenter's benchwork.

backset the horizontal distance from the face of the forend of a lock to the centre of the keyhole.

backsiphonage backflow of a liquid in pipework caused by siphonage; see also backflow.

back-siphonage preventer see backflow valve.

back sliced veneer decorative veneer sliced from the heart side of a half log or flitch. →10

Backsteingotik see brick Gothic.

back-to-back housing a form of basic urban housing in Britain from the late 1800s and early 1900s consisting of rows of terraced or attached houses constructed with frontages to streets in opposite directions and sharing common party walls on either side and to the rear. →61

back to wall pertaining to a soil appliance such as a bidet or WC which is connected to a wall or vertical surface, through which all pipes, drains and outlets etc. are connected.

backup a failsafe copy of a file or program.

back-up material, backer, backing; material such as foam rubber strip placed into a construction joint to limit the depth of overlaid sealant. →53

backwater valve see backflow valve.

back yard an enclosed yard or garden to the rear of a building as viewed from the street.

badia an Italian abbey, a monastery or monastic church headed by an abbot.

baffle a strip of material applied into construction joints between components or materials as weather or soundproofing.

bagasse board a building board manufactured from the waste fibres from sugar cane processing.

baguette moulding see astragal. →14

Bahia rosewood [*Dalbergia nigra*] a Brazilian tropical hardwood with yellowish brown streaked timber; used in veneers and for interiors.

bail 1 see shackle. →39
2 see bailey. →103

bailey, 1 bailey wall; the fortified outer wall of a castle, its first line of defence; often known as a curtain wall. →103
2 ward; the open area of land, yard or court enclosed by a castle fortification wall, between the keep and curtain wall. →103
bail and bayle (trad.) are synonymous with both meanings of bailey.
3 see enceinte. →103
4 see curtain wall. →103

Bailey bridge a prefabricated trussed steel bridge used by the military and constructed in small sections to allow for speedy assembly and dismantling.

bailey castle 1 see keep and bailey castle. →103
2 see motte and bailey.
bailey walk see alure. →103
bailey wall see bailey. →103
baked see stove enamelled.
baked enamel, stoving enamel; any hardwearing protective polymeric coating for metal components, building boards etc. which requires elevated temperatures to activate a curing process; also known as baking enamel, baking finish, stoved enamel, stoved finish; see also powder coating.
baked finish see baked enamel.
bakelite see phenol formaldehyde.
baking see stove enamelling.
baking enamel 1 see baked enamel.
2 see acrylic stoving enamel.
3 see alkyd stoving enamel.
baking finish see baked enamel.
balance bridge see bascule bridge. →64
balanced construction the pairing of matched layers in plywood or composite boards around either side of the central layer to form a symmetrical construction and prevent warping. →9
balanced door an automatic door assembly in which the counterbalanced leaf swings open around an eccentrically placed pivot. →50
balanced pressure tap a mixer tap, usually of stainless steel, fitted with a regulating device which produces equal pressures of hot and cold water drawn from it.
balanced seat see self-raising seat.
balanced step see dancing step. →45
balance sheet in business management, a document which shows all the credits and debits, and their difference, of a company or organization and thus its financial situation.
balaneion Gk; see balneum.
balbides Gk; the starting line or place for contests in an ancient Greek stadium. →89
balcony an accessible outdoor or glazed and balustraded platform projecting from the external face of a building, often for recreational use. →54
see *balcony* illustration. →54
see *balcony* in residential building illustration. →61
see *internal balcony* in office building illustration. →60
balcony-access flats see gallery-access block. →61
balcony deck the structural floor of a balcony; see also balcony slab. →54
balcony drain see balcony outlet. →54
balcony glazing a proprietary or specially designed openable glazing assembly which provides shelter from the elements by closing off the front and sides of a balcony above its balustrade. →54
balcony outlet, balcony drain; a fitting in an exposed balcony through which rainwater and melted snow from a balcony floor or deck is conveyed to a downpipe or other drainage system. →54
balcony slab the structural concrete or stone floor of a balcony. →54
baldacchino see baldachin. →112
baldachin, baldacchino, baldaquin; an ornamental canopy of or representing fabric over an altar, throne, bed or doorway; see ciborium. →112
baldachin altar a church altar situated beneath a highly ornate canopy supported by columns, an altar type typical in Baroque church architecture, see also ciborium altar.
baldaquin see baldachin. →112
balection moulding see bolection moulding.
balineum Lat.; see balneum. →88
balistraria a narrow cross-shaped opening in the external wall of a castle or fortification for crossbow archers (balisters) to fire arrows at potential attackers; also known as an arbalestina; see also arrow loop. →103
balk see baulk. →2
Balkanization in town planning, the natural fragmentation of groups according to social, religious or ethnic background, forming areas of distinctive quality and often interrelated conflicts.
ball and flower, ballflower; an ovular decorative motif found in the church architecture of the early 1300s, a stylized three-petalled flower enclosing a small globule. →123
ballast 1 material such as gravel, concrete slabs or cast concrete laid above an insulating layer on roofs and walkways to provide weight and prevent its removal and deterioration by the forces of weather and wind.
2 an electronic component for maintaining a constant current applied to a discharge or fluorescent lamp.
ball-bearing a construction or component consisting of a number of steel spheres arranged in a ring and cased, providing a frictionless support for a rotating attachment. →38
ball-bearing butt hinge see ball-bearing hinge. →38
ball-bearing hinge, ball-bearing butt hinge; a hinge with a ball-bearing incorporated between adjacent knuckles to reduce friction between them. →38
ball catch, bullet catch; a catch which holds a door closed by means of a sprung ball in a casing, fixed into the edge of the door leaf; see also roller catch. →39
ball clay a fine textured, plastic, adhesive natural clay used in the manufacture of earthenware and firebricks.
ballcock see ballvalve.
ballflower see ball and flower. →123
ball hinge a hinge whose pins rotate upon a ball-bearing to reduce friction in turning. →38
ballium 1 Lat.; the enclosed courtyard of a medieval castle; a bailey.
2 see bailey. →103
balloon see wire balloon.
balloon frame a form of timber frame construction in which vertical studs rise from sole plate to header plate through two or more stories; intermediate floors are carried on wall plates nailed to the inside face of the studs. →57
ball peen hammer a hammer whose peen is hemispherical. →40
ball pen, ball point pen; an ink pen having a small metal ball at its point, which regulates the flow of ink through rolled contact with the paper or base.
ball point pen see ball pen.
ballroom a large main hall in a mansion, institute or public building, often used for celebratory functions, especially dances.
ballvalve, 1 ballcock, floatvalve, float operated valve; a valve in the flushing cistern of a soil appliance which controls the level of water therein with the aid of a float; a flushing valve.
2 in plumbing pipework, a valve containing a perforated ball, which can be turned to align with ports in the casing and allow liquid to pass through.
balm see balsam.
balneolum Lat.; see balneum.
balneum, 1 balineum (Lat.), balneolum, balaneion (Gk); Lat., plural balneae; in Roman architecture, a small public or private bath house, suite of rooms etc.; see also thermae. →88
2 a bathing pool in a Roman bath house or dwelling. →91
balsam a fragrant and medicinal resinous exudation from certain conifers; see oleoresin.
balsam fir [*Abies balsamea*] a Canadian softwood whose cream-coloured timber is used for construction work and packaging.
balsam poplar [*Populus balsamifera*, *Populus tacamahaca*] a North American hardwood with pale brown timber; used in plywood, as sawn boards and for furniture.

balsa wood [*Ochroma spp.*] a group of South American tropical hardwoods with soft and extremely light timber; used for modelmaking, floating construction and lightweight insulating coreboards.

balteus, 'belt'; (Lat.); **1** a wide horizontal gangway step in a Roman theatre or amphitheatre, providing a circulation route for spectators; forms the praecinctio or diazoma. →90
2 the carved swelling in the bolster side of an Ionic capital, which appears to hold it together. →80

baluster 1 one of a series of vertical members, often ornate and carved from stone, which fill the space between the floor or ground level and handrail or coping of a balustrade. →24
2 a similar slender element of timber or metal in a lightweight balustrade; also called a standard or upright. →54

baluster column any column whose shaft is short and thick, resembling a baluster, especially those in ancient Assyrian architecture, whose carved upper capital, lower base and cylindrical shaft form a symmetrical whole. →69

balustrade 1 any waist-high barrier, open or closed, designed to provide protection from falling at the edge of a change in level.
see *balustrade* illustration. →54
2 an ornate equivalent of the above, consisting of a series of ornate vertical members or balusters of stone or wood, often carved, supporting a coping. →24
3 the side barrier of an escalator or similar device, most often a glass sheet with a moving rubber handrail.
4 see stair balustrade. →45
5 see bridge parapet. →31

balustrade height the total height of a balustrade measured from finished floor level to top of handrail; in a stair this is measured vertically from the line of nosings. →45, →54

bamboo 1 [*Bambusa spp.*, esp. *Bambusa arundinacea*] a group of giant hollow-stemmed grasses used as a basic structural building material in tropical countries.
2 blonde, flax; a shade of yellowish grey which takes its name from the colour of dried stems of the above.

Bambusa spp. see bamboo.

banana, Chinese yellow; a shade of dark yellow which takes its name from the colour of the peel of the ripe fruit of the banana tree (*Musa sapientum*); the colour of traditional gowns in China.

band 1 in acoustics and electronics, a range of frequencies between two defined limits.
2 see moulding.

band and hook hinge see hook and band hinge. →38

band course, string course; in masonry, a projecting course, decorative moulding, row of bricks etc. set into an elevation, often at storey level, to throw off rainwater and as decoration.
see *Pompeian styles* illustration. →126

banded column 1 see annulated column. →114
2 see rusticated column. →13, →114

banderole, bannerol; in architectural decoration and ornament, the depiction of an inscribed banner or scroll. →123

banding 1 in decorative veneerwork and similar crafts, strips of material arranged around central panels to form a border.
2 a horizontal protrusion round the circumference of the shaft of a column. →114

bandsaw a mechanical saw whose blade is a toothed steel belt which revolves between two powered wheels.

bandsawing the longitudinal sawing of timber with a bandsaw.

bandsawn a description of timber which has been resawn with a bandsaw.

bandstand a raised structure, often covered and located in a park, upon which an orchestra or band can play.

banister 1 a light balustrade for a stair comprising a handrail supported on closely spaced balusters.
2 one of the balusters in such a stair balustrade.

bank 1 a building or establishment for financial transactions and various dealings in money.
2 see embankment. →31

banker 1 a timber workbench on which traditional stonework is carried out.
2 a rough box, platform or bench in which small batches of concrete, plaster or mortar are mixed by hand.

banking 1 a sloping mass of earth, an embankment.
2 see superelevation.

bankruptcy a financial situation in which a company is unable to pay its debts, and whose assets are seized and distributed to benefit its creditors.

bank seat in bridge construction, a foundation at a bridge abutment.

bank transfer, transfer; a document authorizing the transfer of funds from an account.

bannerol see banderole. →123

banqueting hall 1 a large main hall in a mansion, institute or public building, often used for celebratory functions, especially dinners.
2 see estiatorion. →92

banquette a raised step or platform along the inside of a rampart of a castle or fortification, from which defending soldiers may give fire over a high parapet. →103

baptismal font see font.

baptistery, baptistry; a space, area or separate building of a church or cathedral, containing a font where baptism takes place.
see *Byzantine domical church* illustration. →96
see *Carolingian abbey church* illustration. →98
see *Romanesque church* illustration. →99

baptistry see baptistery. →96, →98, →99

bar 1 any longitudinal solid length of material with a uniform cross-section, usually metal; called a section when thin flanged or hollow; types included as separate entries are listed below.
see *metal bars* illustration. →34
angle bar, see steel angle.
crow bar.
deformed bar.
flat bar, see flat. →34
glazing bar. →111
hexagonal bar. →34
locking bar.
panic bar.
reinforcing bar. →27
round bar. →34
square bar. →34
T-bar, see T-section. →34
threaded bar, see threaded rod. →36
water bar.
2 in heraldry, a narrow fess. →125
3 a small establishment where drinks are sold, see public house.
4 the counter in a bar or restaurant, from which food and drinks may be served.

barbacan see barbican.

barbe see barbette. →103

barbecue, grill; an outdoor fireplace on which food may be cooked, often a metal grille placed over an open fire or a proprietary apparatus fuelled by charcoal.

barbed cross 1 see cross cramponée. →118
2 see cross barbée. →117

barbed moulding a decorative moulding with a series of hooked motifs joined end on end; primarily found in heraldic designs. →125

barbed wire a steel wire product wound with a series of sharp protrusions; used for security fencing.

barbed-wire fence security fencing made from or topped with barbed wire.

barbée see cross barbée. →117

bar bender 1 a manual or powered device used for bending reinforcement bars into the desired shapes for reinforced concrete.
2 see bending tool.
3 see bar bending machine.

bar bending machine, power bender; a powered device for bending reinforcement bars.

barbet see barbette. →103

barbette a mounting place or platform for guns and cannon to fire over a parapet; also written as barbe, barbet or barquette. →103

barbican, barbacan; an outer defensive watch-tower or fortification for the entrance or gateway to a castle or fortified town; a fortified gatehouse.

barbkin see barmkin.

barby see cross barbée. →117

bar cramp see joiner's cramp.

bar cropper, bar cutter; in reinforced concretework, a machine or tool used for cutting reinforcing bars to their desired lengths.

bar cutter see bar cropper.

barefaced tenon joint a mortise and tenon joint in which the tenon is cut to one side of the end of a member. →5

barefaced tongued and grooved joint a timber butt joint in which the grain end has been rebated forming a tongue which is housed in a groove in the receiving piece.

barge couple, cantilever rafter; in timber roof construction, one of the short end rafters which projects beyond the end of a gable wall and onto which barge boards are fixed.

barge stone in masonry construction, one of a series of stones, often projecting, laid along the upper edge of a stone gable.

bargeboard, gableboard, timberboard, vergeboard; in timber roof construction, a board at a gable end or verge of a pitched roof which covers the joint between wall and roof.

barite see barytes.

barium a whitish, malleable metallic chemical element, **Ba**.

barium chromate a yellow chemical compound, the basic ingredient of the pigment barium yellow.

barium sulphate a chemical compound, $\mathbf{BaSO_4}$, see barytes, blanc fixe.

barium yellow, lemon yellow, permanent yellow, ultramarine yellow, yellow ultramarine; a pale yellow pigment, now obsolete, consisting of barium chromate; used formerly in oil paints.

bark 1 the exterior protective layer of tissue on a tree. →1
2 see birch bark.

bark beetle [*Scotylidae*] a family of insects which damage hardwood trees and their unseasoned timber by burrowing beneath the bark.

bark borer [*Ernobius mollis*] an insect whose larvae burrow under the bark of dry softwood logs.

bark pocket see inbark.

bark-thatched roof a traditional roof in colder climates, whose waterproof consists of overlapping strips of bark peeled from birch or other trees, laid as tiles and often covered with boards or turf. →48

bark-ringed knot see encased knot. →1

barking chisel, peeling chisel, peeling iron; a wide-bladed chisel or similar implement for peeling or stripping bark from boles.

barley-sugar column see spiral column. →114

barmkin, barbkin; a fortified enclosure round a Scottish castle or tower house for the protection of livestock; in Ireland it is known as a bawn.

barn, 1 cowshed; an agricultural outbuilding for the housing of livestock, their feed etc.
2 a similar structure for the storage of grain, hay, agricultural implements etc.

barometer an instrument for measuring the pressure of surrounding air or that in the atmosphere.

barometric damper see draught diverter. →56

barometric pressure, atmospheric pressure; the pressure of the air in the atmosphere.

baronial style a romantic architectural style in Great Britain from the 1800s and early 1900s characterized by medieval motifs such as turrets and gatehouses, and used mainly for private castles, country houses, hotels and other buildings of significance; see also Scottish baronial.

Baroque an architectural style originating from southern Europe in the 1600s and 1700s, characterized by classical motifs used in a dramatic and theatrical manner, lavish ornamentation and integration of art and sculpture; phases of Baroque architecture included as separate entries are listed below.
see *Baroque window* illustration. →111
see *Baroque portal* illustration. →113
see *column styles in European architecture* illustration. →114
early Baroque.
high Baroque.
late Baroque.

Baroque classicism see Louis XIV style.

barque sanctuary a room or building within an ancient Egyptian temple complex in which the solar barque of the Pharaoh or deity, or its image, was revered. →72

barquette 'tray' Fr.; see barbette. →103

barrack 1 temporary accommodation or a hut for workmen, soldiers etc.; often used in the plural.
2 soldiers' communal accommodation; also known as a billet. →104

barred window a window with a protective or security grille affixed over its exterior face.

barrel a unit of capacity of both wet and dry goods, especially oil and foodstuffs: for oil and associated products this has been fixed by standard at 35 imperial gallons, 42 US gallons or approximately 159 l.

barrel bolt 1 a simple fastener for a door or gate consisting of a round metal bar which moves in a tube or ring, fixed to the door, and engages in a hole in a jamb or gate post. →39
2 see foot bolt. →39
3 see flush slide.

barrel nipple, shoulder fitting (Am.); in pipework, a short connecting pipe which is externally threaded at either end, and which often has a cast nut in between for tightening with a spanner.

barrel vault, 1 cradle vault, cylindrical vault, tunnel vault, wagon vault, wagonhead vault; a masonry or concrete roof vault which is semicircular in cross-section, especially used in early churches. →25
2 see pointed barrel vault. →25

barrel vaulted roof any roof structure which is semicircular in section and in the shape of an elongated semicircular arch.

barrier a physical obstacle, rail etc. designed to prevent access or penetration; types included as separate entries are listed below.
access barrier, see vehicular barrier.
boom. →64
cavity barrier, see fire barrier.
crash barrier, see vehicle safety barrier.
fire barrier.
noise barrier.
plenum barrier.
safety barrier, see vehicle safety barrier.
snow barrier.
traffic barrier, see vehicular barrier.
vapour barrier. →8
vehicle safety barrier.
vehicular barrier.

barrow, **1** long barrow, tumulus; a prehistoric round or longitudinal mound of earth or stones, often surrounded by a ditch, usually used to cover a burial chamber or chambered tomb.
2 see wheelbarrow.

bar schedule, bending schedule, reinforcement schedule; in the design of reinforced concrete, a document providing dimensions, bending patterns and arrangement of all reinforcements in a component.

bar stop in ornamentation, the termination of a chamfered moulding or carving with a protruding carved perpendicular bar.

bar tendon in prestressed concrete, a single reinforcing bar which acts as a prestressing tendon.

bartisan see bartizan.

bartizan, bartisan; an overhanging corner turret in a medieval castle, palace or fortification, used for defence; often applied as ornament in later romantic revival styles.

bar tracery a range of types of Gothic tracery originating in the late 1200s, formed by vertical window mullions which interlink to form intricate patterns in the pointed window head.

baryta green see manganese green.

baryta paper paper coated with baryta sulphate gelatine, used for text impressions on photocomposing machines.

baryta white see blanc fixe.

barytes, barite, heavy spar; a pale-coloured mineral, barium sulphate, $\mathbf{BaSO_4}$, used as a raw material in some white paints, for increasing the specific gravity of drilling fluids and for providing protection against radiation.
see Bologna stone.
see heavy spar.

basal till a soil type consisting of compressed mineral deposits laid down by the base of a glacier.

basalt a blue-grey, brownish or black, fine-grained, dense igneous rock, often used for paving; the earth's most abundant volcanic rock type.

bascule bridge, balance bridge, counterpoise bridge, counterbalanced bridge; a bridge with a motorized hinged and counterbalanced deck which can be raised to allow vehicles or vessels to pass under; earlier versions were manually operated. →64

base 1 the lowest, thickened section of a column, pedestal etc. beneath its shaft, often decorated, which transfers loading onto a plinth or to a foundation.
see *base* in caryatid illustration. →76
2 see classical base. →76, →78, →81
see *column base* in classical orders illustrations. →78, →79, →80
see *column styles in European architecture* illustration. →114
see *Asian and Mediterranean columns and capitals* illustration. →69
3 a substance which may chemically combine with an acid to form a salt.
4 see substrate. →20
5 the lower portion or lower third part of a heraldic shield. →124

baseboard 1 see skirting board. →2, →44
2 see gypsum baseboard.

base coat, 1 brown coat, browning coat, floating coat, key coat; in plastering and rendering, a roughly finished layer or layers of mortar applied to masonry to provide a key or even surface for a finish coat. →83
2 see *base coat* in Roman walling illustration. →83

base course, 1 roadbase; in road construction, a surfacing layer of material directly beneath and supporting the wearing course. →62
2 the lowest course of stones, bricks or blocks in masonry walling.
3 the lowest layer of logs in horizontal log construction.

base cruck truss in traditional timber frame construction, a simple principal truss of curved timber members or crucks which meet at a collar, supporting the purlins onto which rafters are laid.

base floor, bottom floor; the lowest constructed floor level of a building, that adjacent to the ground; it may be at basement or ground floor level. →28

base floor construction the horizontal layers of construction which make up a base or bottom floor. →59
see *base floor construction* in brick house illustration. →59

basement the usable area of a building that is situated partly or entirely below ground level and may contain habitable rooms; in North America it is less than halfway below ground level. →61

basement area, dry area, area; in town houses, an unroofed narrow external space below street level to provide light, air and often access to rooms in a basement, and to separate external basement walls from the surrounding ground to prevent entry of water.

basement floor see basement storey. →61

basement parking an area of parking located in the basement of a building. →62

basement storey, basement floor; a storey below the ground floor of a building, which may contain habitable rooms, utility or storage spaces. →61

base moulding a decorative moulding at the lower end of the shaft of a column. →80

base plate see sole plate. →8, →57, →58

base ring, base unit; in drainage, a suitably shaped precast concrete, ceramic or plastics component used as the base for an inspection chamber or well, around which it is constructed.

base rock see bedrock.

base sheet, 1 reference drawing, underlay; a drawing or graphic image whose information is used, often by tracing through, in the production of a drawing.
2 first layer felt; in built-up roofing, the lowest layer of bitumen felt, often bonded to the underlying structure and intermediate sheet above.

base unit see base unit.

base wall see wall base.
see *Roman walling* illustration. →83
see *concrete frame* illustration. →28
see *timber-framed building* illustration. →57

basic lead carbonate a form of the pigment white lead.

basic rock types of igneous rock whose silica content is between 45% and 52%.

basic wage the normal amount paid to an employee on a regular basis, before the inclusion of deductions, bonuses or additional payments.

basilica 1 a Roman building type, rectangular in shape with an apse at either end, used as a court of justice and an exchange. →93
see *Roman basilica* illustration. →93
2 a building type consisting of a clerestoried nave, side aisles and terminated with a rounded apse containing an altar; adopted by the Early Christian church from Greek and Roman precedents.
see *Early Christian basilica* illustration. →95
3 see basilica church. →99

basilica church a church type based on a basilica antecedent, usually with a rectangular plan divided by colonnades into a nave and aisles, with an apse or apses at one end. →99
see *basilica church* in Romanesque church illustration. →99

basilica discoperta a basilica church whose nave has no roof.

basilisk, cockatrice; in medieval ornament and depiction, a mythical reptile born of a serpent from a cock's egg, whose breath or gaze was believed to be fatal. →122

basin 1 an open-topped vessel, often of ceramics and built into a worktop, designed to hold water for washing and other purposes.
2 see handrinse basin.
3 a widened area of docks or bounded area within a harbour.

basin mixer a mixer tap which can be fitted for use with a basin.

basin tap any tap which can be fitted for use with a basin.

basket arch see three-centred arch. →24

basket capital a capital found in Byzantine architecture, consisting of a splayed upside-down pyramid or cone-shaped block with intricate carvings. →115

basketweave pattern 1 a paving pattern resembling woven strands, in which rectangular pavers are laid in twos or threes side by side, forming a series of squares at right angles to one another; similar patterns in tiling. →15
2 see half-basketweave pattern. →15
3 a veneering and parquetry grid pattern in which alternate squares of even size are laid with their direction of grain running perpendicular to one another, forming a chequerboard appearance. →10

bas-relief see basso rilievo.

basso rilievo, bas-relief, low relief; a form of sculptured relief ornament in which figures or elements are carved so as to project half their depth from a surface or background.

basswood, American lime; [*Tilia americana*] a hardwood from North America; see also lime.

Bast see Bastet. →74

bastard grain grain that forms an angle of 30–60° with the face of a piece of sawn timber.

bastard sawing see through and through sawing. →2

bastel house see bastle house.

Bastet the ancient Egyptian feline goddess, daughter of the sun god Re; originally associated with the destructive force of the sun (see Sekhmet), later portrayed as a cat with a brood of kittens, protector of joy, music and dancing; also written as Bast. →74

bastide a fortified town built mainly during the twelfth to fourteenth centuries in England, Wales and France, whose task was to strengthen the hold of a ruler over a particular region.

bastile see bastille.

bastille, bastile; a medieval French fortification or fortified tower often used as a prison; originally a fortified siege structure whose flanking towers were at the same height as the curtain wall which joined them.

bastille house see bastle house.

bastion a polygonal structure projecting from the main fortified wall of a town or castle, with two or more long faces meeting at an angle, used for siting cannon and other weaponry to afford clear fire in a number of directions outside the main line of defence; types included as separate entries are listed below. →103, →104
arrow-headed bastion. →104
demi-bastion. →104
double bastion, see cavalier. →104
half bastion, see demi-bastion. →104
inner bastion, see cavalier. →104

bastioned trace see bastion trace. →104

bastion face see face. →104

bastion flank see flank. →104

bastion front see bastion trace. →104

bastion line see bastion trace. →104

bastion trace a fortified front consisting of a number of bastions connected by a curtain wall; a polygonal fortification, also called a bastion front, bastion line or bastioned trace. →104

bastle house, bastel house, bastille house; a traditional dwelling from the border area of England and Scotland, whose lowest storey is fortified against assault.

bat, 1 brickbat; a full brick cut down to size in order to act as a space filler in bonded brickwork; often larger than a quarter brick; types included as separate entries are listed below. →21
halved three quarter bat. →21
half bat. →21
quarter bat.
three quarter bat. →21
2 mineral wool and other insulating products manufactured into thick slabs for ease of storage and installation. →59

batardeau a wall built across a fortification ditch or moat to regulate the amount of water therein, constructed with a sharp ridge to prevent its use by attacking troops.

batch 1 a portion of material or goods mixed for use, packed for delivery etc. at any particular time.
2 see concrete batch.
3 see plaster batch.

batch mixer in the production of concrete, a mixer which produces a set amount of concrete at any one time; see also continuous mixer.

batch production the manufacturing or processing of a product or material in a series of predetermined quantity rather than in a continuous run.

batching see proportioning.

batching and mixing plant see batching plant.

batching plant, batching and mixing plant; an industrial assembly for mixing concrete to be used on site.

bath, bathtub; a large vessel connected to a water supply and a drain, in which a person can be fully immersed in water while washing; types included as separate entries are listed below.
footbath.
hip bath.
jacuzzi.
plunge bath.
treatment bath.
whirlpool bath.

bath house 1 a public or private establishment for personal cleaning, swimming and relaxation.
2 see thermae. →91
3 see balneum. →88

bathroom 1 a room for personal cleaning, containing a bath or shower and other sanitary appliances. →57, →59
2 see balneum. →88

bathroom lock a lock designed for use principally with the doors of bathrooms, toilet cubicles etc., containing a latch with handles, and a dead bolt operable from the inside only; the dead bolt is connected to an indicator panel to show whether the room is occupied or not. →39

baths 1 a public or private establishment for personal cleaning, swimming and relaxation.
2 see thermae. →91, →94
3 see balneum. →88
4 see loutron. →91

bathtub 1 see bath.
2 see loutron. →91

batik an originally Malayan method of making graphic prints on cloth by masking patterned areas with wax; the dyed cloth is then boiled to melt the wax, leaving a design of undyed marks.

bat's wing an arched decorative motif with lines or flutes radiating from a central point, resembling the outstretched wings of a bat. →123

batted finish, broad tooled finish; a stonework finish with a series of parallel cut grooves produced by dressing with a batting tool. →12

batten 1 one of a number of strips of timber laid at regular spacing as a base onto which cladding, sheet materials and tiles may be fixed; types included as separate entries are listed below. →57
counterbatten.
flooring batten. →44

tiling batten. →59
roof batten. →58
2 any sawn timber section with cross-sectional dimensions of less than 25 mm thick and 25 mm–50 mm wide. →2
3 in timber classification, a sawn softwood section with cross-sectional dimensions of 44 mm–100 mm thick and 100 mm–200 mm wide; always considerably wider than thick.
4 parquet batten, see parquet block. →44
5 screed batten.

battenboard a timber building board formed by gluing veneers on either side of a core of solid wood strips with a width greater than 30 mm; the grain of the veneers runs at 90° to that of the core. →9

battened stanchion a composite steel lattice column or stanchion in which vertical rolled steel sections are joined together with stiff horizontal members.

battening 1 timber strips attached to the frame of a roof or wall as a base to receive a finish such as tiling, boarding or cladding, or to support a construction etc. →8, →44, →57
2 in particular, spaced battens laid as a nailing base for tiling or cladding. →8
3 a series of shallow timber battens fixed to floor substructure, onto which wooden flooring or a floating floor is fixed. →44, →57
4 the job of laying such battens.

batten roll joint see roll joint. →49

batter, 1 rake; a slope in the face of any wall.
2 in particular, the outwardly sloping base of a defensive wall in a castle or fortification, used for stability and to throw off missiles which have been dropped from the battlements; also called battering or a talus. →103

battered referring to a massive wall, especially a retaining or fortification wall, the front face of which is sloping.

battering see batter. →103

batter pile see raking pile. →29

battery, 1 cell; a portable device for producing and storing electricity via chemical reaction, used as an energy source in applications where mains supply is unavailable or impractical.
2 platform, terreplein; a level mounting place for guns and cannon, an emplacement. →103
3 see heating battery.
4 see lift battery.

battery mould one of a number of formwork panels used in series for casting in-situ concrete.

batting tool, broad tool; a broad-faced masonry chisel used for dressing stone with a batted or fluted finish. →41

battlement, embattlement; a crenellated parapet and walkway in a castle or fortified wall, used for the purposes of defence; see also crenellation. →103
see *battlement* illustration. →103

battlemented see castellated.

battlemented moulding see crenellated moulding. →124, →125

Battle of the Styles a period in English architectural development from the mid-1800s centring on which revival style, especially Gothic and classical, was suitable for use in public buildings.

baud in computing and telecommunications, a unit of transmission speed equal to one information unit or bit per second.

Bauhaus a school and movement in modernist architecture, design and craft founded by Walter Gropius in Weimar in 1919, which functioned until 1933 in Dessau.

bauk see baulk. →2

baulk a piece of sawn timber with cross-sectional dimensions of 100 mm × 100 mm or larger; in traditional timber construction, it may be a squared log; any heavy log or timber; also variously written as bauk, balk or bawk. →2

bauxite a white or reddish sedimentary rock, a dense and earthy clayish mineral which contains a high proportion of aluminium and is thus used as its principal ore.

bawk see baulk. →2

bawn see barmkin.

bay, 1 trave; a division in a ceiling or roof marked out by adjacent vaults, beams or arches, especially in stone vaulted architecture. →25, →101
2 the division of a space defined by the spacing of roof trusses, partitions or columns.
3 an area of natural water, sea or a lake surrounded by land on three sides.
4 see loading bay.
5 see parking space.
6 see bus bay.

bayle see bailey. →103

bay-leaf garland an ornamental motif found in classical and Renaissance architecture consisting of a mesh of lines which intertwine to form openings in the shape of eyes or bay-leaves. →82

bayonet cap a lamp cap which connects to a holder by means of transverse pins in its side.

bayonet saw see jigsaw.

bay window a window set into a protrusion from the elevational plane of a building.

bazaar an oriental covered market or arcade of shops.

beach an area of coast or shoreline, often with sand or shingle, used for recreation, swimming and sunbathing.

beaching small stones of 70 mm–200 mm used as revetment for embankments.

bead, 1 beading; a thin strip of planed timber or other material used for covering joints, fixing of glazing or panelling in frames and as surface decoration.
see *timber trim* illustration. →2
2 see glazing bead. →2, →53
3 see bead moulding.
4 see beaded moulding.

bead and quirk moulding see quirk bead moulding. →14

bead and reel, reel and bead; a decorative moulding consisting of a series of small round beads, elongated hemispheres or half-cylinders alternating with pairs of flattened discs. →80, →82, →124

bead boarding decorative timber cladding boards whose surface is planed with a series of convex mouldings or reeds: also called reeded or moulded boarding. →8

bead saw a small fine-toothed saw, 100 mm–250 mm long, with a reinforced back and turned handle, used for fine work.

beaded joint a brickwork mortar joint in which the mortar is laid flush with the brick surface then scored with a special tool to form an inset convex shape or bead. →16

beaded moulding, 1 paternoster, pearl moulding; an ornamental motif or moulding consisting of a row of beads or small hemispheres; also loosely known as a bead moulding. →124
2 see bead and reel. →80, →82

bead edged boarding decorative timber cladding boards whose edge has been planed with a bead. →8

beading see bead.

bead moulding, 1 roundel; a slender decorative moulding, semicircular in cross-section; when found in classical architecture it is called an astragal. →14, →126
2 see beaded moulding. →124
3 see pellet moulding. →124

bead polystyrene see expanded polystyrene.

beakhead see beak moulding. →122

beak moulding, 1 beakhead; a decorative moulding of Norman origin formed with pointed projections resembling the head of a man, bird or mythical beast with a protruding beak or lip. →122

2 bird's beak moulding; a decorative quadrant moulding with a concave underside. →14
3 see cock beak moulding. →14

beam 1 a horizontal structural member which transfers loading from above to its bearing points; types included as separate entries are listed below.
anchor beam.
arch beam, arched beam, see cambered beam. →30
architrave.
binder.
box beam.
brick beam, see reinforced brick lintel. →22
built-up beam. →7
cambered beam. →7
cantilever beam. →7
collar beam. →33
composite beam. →7
concrete beam. →60
continuous beam. →7
corrugated ply-web beam. →7
cross beam.
double tee beam. →27
downstand beam.
dragon beam, dragging beam.
edge beam.
epistyle, see architrave.
filigree beam.
fish-bellied beam. →30
flanged beam.
framed beam, see trussed beam. →33
girder.
glued and laminated beam, glulam beam, see laminated timber beam. →7
ground beam, grade beam. →29
hammer beam. →33
haunched beam.
hollow composite beam.
hollow-core beam. →27, →28
I-beam. →30
in-situ concrete beam. →27, →60
inverted beam.
joggle beam. →7
L-beam. →30
laminated timber beam. →7
laminated web beam.
lattice beam, see trussed beam. →33
lintel. →22, →23, →57
longitudinal beam.
main beam, see principal beam.
pitched beam. →30
plywood box beam, see box beam. →7
plywood web beam, ply-web beam. →7
precast beam. →28
prestressed concrete beam.
principal beam, primary beam.
ridge beam. →33
rood beam.
roof beam. →48, →59
secondary beam.
solid timber beam. →7
spine beam, see mono-carriage. →45
steel beam.
stiffening beam. →32
straining beam. →33
strut beam, see collar beam. →33
summer beam, see summer.
T-beam, tee beam. →30
tie beam. →33
timber beam.
trabs, trabes. →47
transverse beam, see cross beam.
trimmed beam. →4
trimmer beam, see trimmer. →4
trussed beam. →33
universal beam, see I-section. →34
upstand beam.
wind beam, see collar beam. →33
2 a narrow ray of light or other radiation.

beam block bond-beam block, see channel block. →30

beam box, beam form; formwork for a reinforced concrete beam.

beam brick see lintel brick. →16

beam bridge see continuous beam bridge. →32

beam compass, trammel; a compass for the drawing and marking out of large circles, whose centre pin and scribing device are along the length of a rod or beam.

beam form see beam box.

beam reinforcement steel reinforcement for a reinforced concrete beam. →27

beam spread in artificial lighting, the angle over which a spotlight or floodlight directs the major quantity of its light output.

beam unit see precast beam. →28

beam vibrator in the compaction of fresh concrete, a surface vibrator in the shape of a beam.

bearer any device or construction for holding a component in place.
see ceiling bearer. →60
see gutter bearer. →46
see soffit bearer.

bearing a structural device which transfers load from a moving, movable, slipping or rotating part to a fixed support.
see ball-bearing. →38
see bridge bearing.
see roller bearing.
see sliding bearing.

bearing capacity, loadbearing capacity, loading capacity; the amount of force, pressure, weight or stress that a material, soil, foundations or a structure can safely withstand without failure.

bearing pile, foundation pile; in foundation technology, a pile which transmits vertical rather than earth-pressure loads to the ground or hard subsoil. →29
see **types of pile** in foundation drawing, and list of common pile types under 'pile'. →29

bearing seat see bridge cap. →31

bearing surface any surface which bears the thrust of a structural component.

bearing wall see loadbearing wall. →28

bearing wall system see loadbearing wall construction. →28

beast column see animal column. →114

beauty parlour commercial premises for preserving or improving the aesthetic value of the face or body.

Beaux Arts an architectural style originating from France at the école de Beaux Arts in the 1800s, characterized by monumental forms and eclectic decoration.

beaver a shade of dark brown which takes its name from the colour of the pelt of the beaver (*Castor fiber*).

becquerel Bq the SI unit of radioactivity, equal to one disintegration per second.

bed 1 the lower horizontal surface of a brick as laid in masonry. →21
2 bedding; a layer of material, often mortar, in which a brick, block or stone is laid.
3 bedding; the horizontal joint thus formed; a bed joint.
4 floor bed, see ground supported floor.
5 the lower surface of a roofing slate.
6 stratum; in geology, a layer of sedimentary rock and the natural plane in which it lies in the ground.
7 a piece of furniture designed for sleeping in.

bed chamber 1 a bedroom.
2 see cubiculum. →88

bedding 1 in masonry construction, the laying of a brick, block or stone into mortar or another cementitious material, and tapping it into the correct position.
2 see bed.
3 see glazing bedding.

4 see sand bedding. →15
5 see mortar bedding.
6 see edge bedding. →21
7 see face bedding.

bedding compound 1 a compound applied beneath materials as bedding.
2 a compound applied to joints between components.

bedding mortar 1 coarse cement consisting of a binder (lime, cement etc.), fine aggregate and water used in masonrywork as a jointing material onto which successive courses are laid; also called masonry mortar.
2 see tiling mortar. →59

bedding plane in geology, the surface between two layers or beds of sedimentary rock.

bedding plant in landscaping, any plant, usually flowering, seasonally planted in ornamental flower beds.

bedehouse a medieval almshouse or dwelling provided by charity, for which the occupant was obliged to offer prayers for the provider.

bed height the natural height of a layer of sedimentary rock as found in the ground.

bed joint, horizontal joint; a horizontal joint between two courses of stones, bricks or blocks laid in masonry. →20
see *reinforced bed joint* in arched and vaulted construction illustration. →22

bed mould 1 in classical architecture, the flat fascia course directly beneath a cornice; also called a bed moulding. →78, →79
2 the lowest moulding in any band of mouldings.

bed moulding see bed mould. →78, →79

bedpan washer a soil appliance in which bed pans, urine bottles etc. undergo thorough cleaning and sterilization in hospitals and other care establishments.

bed putty see back putty.

bedrock, base rock; the solid layer of rock beneath loose soil, sand or silt in the earth's crust, which may be used as a firm base for bearing foundations.

bedrock foundation a foundation which transmits building load directly to the underlying bedrock. →29

bedrock map, solid map; a geological map showing formations of solid rock, often with different rock types in different colours.

bedroom 1 a private room in a dwelling or accommodation building used primarily for sleeping. →57, →59
2 see dormitory.
3 see cubiculum. →88

bedsit, one-room flat; a dwelling or apartment containing one room and an adjoining kitchen or kitchenette; sometimes also called a studio apartment.

bedstone, foundation stone; a large flat boulder used as a foundation, usually for a temporary or traditional timber building. →6

beech [*Fagus spp.*] a group of hardwoods from Europe, Asia Minor, Japan and North America whose heavy, strong, hard, tough, pale pink timber has flecked markings; used for flooring, interiors and furniture; see ***Fagus spp.*** for full list of beech included in this work.

beehive cell, clochan; an Early Christian drystone dwelling used by monks in Ireland and the Scottish Western Isles, constructed in the shape of a beehive with corbelled vaulting.

beehive tomb see tholos. →65

beeswax wax produced by bees, applied with a solvent to finished joinery and polished as a surface treatment.

beetle, 1 maul; a sledgehammer with a wooden head, used for driving in pegs, wedges and staves.
2 any hard-shelled insects of the order Coleoptera, many of which cause damage to trees, timber, and timberwork in buildings; species included as separate entries are listed below.
ambrosia beetle, [*Scotylidae, Platypodidae*].
bark beetle, [*Scotylidae*].
common furniture beetle, [*Anobium punctatum*].
death-watch beetle, [*Xestobium rufovillosum*].
furniture beetle.
house longhorn beetle, [*Hylotrupes bajulus*].
longhorn beetle, [*Cerambycidae*].
lymexylid beetle.
sawyer beetle, [*Monochamus*].
spruce beetle, [*Tetropium spp.*].
woodworm, see furniture beetle.
3 dung-beetle ornament; see scarab. →75
see Khepri. →75

beetroot purple a shade of purple which takes its name from the colour of the root of the beetroot (*Beta vulgaris*).

beige, ecru, flaxen, light blonde; a general name for shades of greyish yellow similar to the colour of unbleached and uncoloured wool, and the colour of the ripened flax plant.

Belfast truss a roof truss composed of a curved upper chord and flat lower chord braced by diagonals; a bowstring truss. →33

belfry, belltower; a structure for housing bells, surmounting the roof of a church or cathedral, or freestanding.
see *belfry* in Scandinavian hall church illustration. →102

Belgian truss see fink truss. →33

bell 1 the bulging part of a hammerhead which bears the striking face, opposite the peen. →40
2 see socket.
3 see church bell.
4 see doorbell. →51
5 see campanula. →78
6 see calathus. →81

bell-and-spigot joint see spigot-and-socket joint.

bell arch 1 a round arch supported on corbels with rounded undersides, often in a different stone. →23
2 see reverse ogee arch. →24

bell capital, 1 blossom capital, campaniform, open capital; an Egyptian capital carved in the form of an upside-down bell in stylized imitation of an open papyrus or lotus flower. →73
see papyrus capital. →73
2 a medieval capital type with a central conical drum terminated at upper and lower edges by rings, discs or annulets. →115
3 see trumpet capital. →115

bell cast in renderwork, the thickening of the lower edge of a laid render coat to act as a drip.

bellcot see bellcote.

bellcote, bellcot, bell gable; a small belfry which surmounts the ridge of the roof of a church or public building.

belled pile see under-reamed pile. →29

bell face hammer a hammer whose striking face is rounded so as to avoid damaging the surrounding surface when driving nails. →40

bell gable see bellcote.

bell pavilion a structure housing a large bell, used in ritual cleansing ceremonies in Japanese Buddhist and Shinto temples. →68

bell pliers large pliers with notched jaws, side cutters and a notched depression; used for gripping and cutting wire.

belltower a church or other tower containing bells in an open or louvred chamber near the top; see belfry.
see *Early Christian church* illustration. →95
see *Byzantine domical church* illustration. →96
see campanile. →96

belt a longitudinal area of landscaped greenery; greenbelt.
see balteus. →90

belt conveyor mesh see conveyor belt mesh. →34

belt sander a hand-held power sanding tool with a motor-driven belt of sandpaper or abrasive cloth.

beltway see ring road.

belvedere, gazebo; any building or structure of recreation from which fine views are afforded; often a glazed rooftop turret, terrace or a pavilion set in parkland.

bema 1 Gk; an orator's platform in Greek architecture, and in a synagogue. →92
see *Greek and Roman public buildings* illustration. →92
2 in Early Christian architecture, a raised platform in the vicinity of the altar for seating of the clergy.
see *Early Christian and Late Antique church* illustration. →95
see *Byzantine domical church* illustration. →96

benben an ancient Egyptian short, slender obelisk with a polygonal cross-section, symbolic of the rising sun and regeneration of life, often a cult object of sun-worship in a sun temple. →73

bench 1 a hard seat of stone, timber, metal or plastics for a number of people, with or without a back.
2 see sauna bench.
3 see workbench.

bench chisel a traditionally wooden-handled chisel used for general woodwork. →41

bench end an intricately carved wooden panel fixed to the ends of a pew in a church.

bench grinder, grinder, grinding wheel; a bench-top power tool with a rigid rotating disc of abrasive material, used for sharpening tools and grinding metal surfaces.

benching 1 a horizontal ledge in an embankment or other earthwork.
2 the addition of concrete to support and reinforce an embankment.
3 sloping side construction in the base of a drainage manhole to control the flow of water and provide a base to stand on.

benchmark 1 in engineering, computing and technology, a predefined standard or set of operations against which to test systems under trial.
2 in surveying, a fixed point of known position and altitude, used as a datum from which other measurements can be referred.

bench plane a flat-bottomed wooden or metal plane used for reducing, levelling and smoothing wood; a generic term for all flat and wide-bottomed planes.

bench saw, joiner saw; a cross between a handsaw and a spineless backsaw.

bench vice, carpenter's vice; a vice used by a carpenter, fixed or incorporated into a workbench to hold pieces in place while they are being worked.

bend 1 a curved pipe fitting to change direction of flow in a pipeline or duct; types included as separate entries are listed below.
bent ferrule.
branch bend.
elbow.
fire bend.
knee, see elbow.
knuckle bend.
long radius bend.
machine bend.
pulled bend.
reducing bend.
2 a diagonal band, strip or line across the face of a heraldic shield, often dividing areas of different colours. →125

bending 1 in structures, the bowing deformation of a beam or other member under load.
2 the forming of materials or components such as metal pipes and profiles with bends.

bending moment, moment of deflection; the total bending effect at any section of a loaded beam caused by the turning effect of remote force upon a point; units are Nm.

bending radius in the bending of pipes and other metalwork, the radius of curvature of a bend.

bending schedule see bar schedule.

bending strength, flexural strength; the ability of a beam or other structural element to resist forces in bending.

bending stress in structures, the stress, usually in a beam, caused by a bending moment.

bending tool, hickey (Am.), hicky (Am.); a hand tool used for bending reinforcement bars, pipes etc. into their desired shapes.

bendlet in heraldry, a narrow diagonal stripe; see bend; also called a garter. →125

Benedictine church a church of the monasterial order named after and following the principles of St Benedict (c.480–574), which valued obedience, moderation and humility and the integration of prayer, manual labour and study into the daily routine.
see *Carolingian abbey church* illustration. →98

bensine see benzine.

bent pertaining to pipes, glass, timber and metals which have been curved using a special tool, pressure or casting process.

bent ferrule, bend; in water and gas pipework, a pipe fitting with a 90° bend.

bent glass, curved glass; glass that has been reheated and curved in a kiln for use in special glazing applications.

bentonite a form of clay which undergoes great expansion with increase of water content; used diluted in drilling fluids, rubber compounds and synthetic resins.

bentonite suspension a thixotropic drilling fluid consisting of bentonite and water.

bent plywood plywood which has been bent using jigs during the gluing stage of production; used for specially shaped interior panels and furniture. →9

bent pyramid, rhomboid pyramid; an Egyptian pyramid type in which each triangular planar surface changes direction as it approaches the top, as in a mansard roof; sometimes also called a blunt or false pyramid. →70

bent-up bar in reinforced concrete slabs and beams, a tensile reinforcing bar in a beam which has been bent to provide shear reinforcement.

benzine, bensine; a strong-smelling volatile liquid obtained by distilling coal tar and petroleum; used as a solvent and as fuel.

benzol black see carbon black.

berkelium an unstable, short-lived transuranic chemical element, **Bk**.

Berlin blue a name for the pigment Prussian blue used especially in France.

berm the level part of an earthwork in a castle or fortification, a ledge in the wall of a ditch, behind a rampart; see covered way. →104

berth a sleeping place in a cabin or ship.

beryl a colourless or variously coloured mineral used as ornamentation and gemstones (emerald, aquamarine) and as an ore for the extraction of beryllium.
see aquamarine.
see chrysoberyl.
see emerald.
see heliodor.
see morganite.

beryllium a hard, light, metallic chemical element, **Be**, used as an alloy to reduce fatigue in copper.

bessalis Lat.; a Roman triangular or square brick of which two adjacent sides are two thirds of a Roman foot (197 mm) in length; see also bipedalis. →83

Bessemer process a steelmaking process in which hot air is blown through molten pig iron in a converter to reduce the quantities of undesirable elements such as phosphorus and silicon.

Bessemer steel high grade steel manufactured in a converter using the Bessemer process.

best reed, Norfolk reed; unbroken stalks of the water or common reed [*Arundo phragmites*, *Phragmites australis*] dried and used as thatched roofing, mainly in marshy areas of England, especially East Anglia.

beta radiation penetrating electromagnetic radiation consisting of negatively charged electrons emitted from naturally radioactive elements.

Beta vulgaris the beetroot, see beetroot purple.

beton brut an untreated in-situ concrete finish which bears the indentations and markings of the sawn boards into which it was cast.

better face see face side.

betterment a real increase in the value of land or property as a result of planning schemes, policy or permission for a local area, occasionally reimbursable as a payment by the owner to a local authority.

betterment levy the monetary charge by a local authority for a betterment.

Betula spp. birch.
Betula alleghaniensis, yellow birch.
Betula papyrifera, paper birch.
Betula pendula, silver birch.
Betula pubescens, downy birch.

bevel, 1 chamfer, splay; the blunting with a slanting edge of a right-angled or sharp corner. →14
2 see bevel moulding. →14
3 a slanting planar surface in a piece of glass, usually formed by grinding an edge.
4 see grinding bevel. →41
5 see honing bevel. →41
6 see bevel square.

Bevel-edge chisel see bevelled-edge chisel. →41

bevelled corner joint, splayed corner joint; a timber corner joint in which the halved ends of members are bevelled for increased strength and convenience. →4

bevelled-edge chisel, bevel-edge chisel; a sturdy chisel whose blade is bevelled on both long edges as well as its end, used for the cleaning of edges, rebates and mortises in woodwork. →41

bevelled halved joint, splayed halved joint; a timber halved joint whose laps are bevelled for increased strength. →4

bevelled housed joint in timber frame construction, a joint in which one member is received into an angled recess or housing in another.

bevelled moulding see bevel moulding. →14

bevelled scarf joint, longitudinal bevelled halved joint, straight bevelled halved joint; a timber lengthening joint in which the halved ends are bevelled to fit together. →3

bevel moulding a decorative moulding whose cross-section is that of a fillet splayed to the vertical; also known as a chamfered or splayed moulding. →14

bevel square, bevel; a measuring tool with a hinged metal blade or two jointed legs used for measuring, checking and marking out angles.

biacca an alternative name for white lead.

bianco sangiovanni, St John's white, lime white; a white pigment consisting of a mixture of calcium hydroxide and calcium carbonate used in fresco painting.

bibcock see bib tap.

bible paper very thin, opaque, tough paper used for weighty books such as bibles, prayer books, dictionaries etc.

bib tap, bibcock; a simple water tap for filling or emptying vessels etc. whose nozzle is bent downwards.

bice a variety of Bremen blue pigment.

biclinium Lat.; a Roman dining room with dining couches seating two.

bicycle lane see cycle lane.

bicycle shelter, bike shed, cycle shelter; an exterior canopy or similar construction under which bicycles can be stored for protection from the elements.

bicycle store a room or internal space within a building used as a temporary store for the occupants' bicycles.

bid, offer; an offer of a sum of money for goods or a price for the gaining of a contract, usually in competition with others for the same item; see tender.

bidet a seated sanitary appliance for washing the private parts, consisting of a bowl connected to a water supply and drain.

bidet shower a shower hose and head assembly in proximity to a WC suite and connected to a water outlet.

Biedermaier see Biedermeier.

Biedermeier, Biedermaier, Biedermeyer; a straightforward style in interior design and furniture from 1815 to 1848 in Germany, named after a fictional satirical character and supposedly representing middle-class vulgarity.

Biedermeyer see Biedermeier.

biennial any species of plant planted as a seed one year and which flowers, seeds and dies the following.

bifurcated cross see swallowtailed cross. →117

bi-fold door a horizontally folding door with two leaves, hinged in the middle. →50

BIIR see bromine butyl rubber.

bike shed see bicycle shelter.

bile yellow a shade of yellow green which takes its name from the colour of the bitter liquid, bile, stored in the human gall bladder.

bill 1 a written document stating money owed for goods and services; see invoice.
2 see bill of quantities.

billet, 1 billet moulding; a decorative moulding, found especially in Romanesque architecture, consisting of a series of recessed cylinders or rectangles arranged in a chequered pattern. →124
see round billet, roll billet. →124
see square billet. →124
2 temporary lodging for soldiers, workmen etc.

billet moulding see billet. →124

billety cross billety, see cross potent. →117

billion, 1 milliard; a thousand million (10^9), general usage.
2 trillion (Am.); a million million (10^{12}), popular usage.

bill of materials see bill of quantities.

bill of quantities, bill of materials (Am.); a written contract document produced by a quantity surveyor containing an itemized list of all materials, methods and workmanship for a particular construction project; see priced bill of quantities.

bill of sale a receipt.

bin see refuse bin.

binary number a value defined in terms of ones and zeros in a binary system.

binary system a system of numbers which uses the digits one and zero to define powers of two added together; the decimal system uses the number 10 as its basic unit.

bin chamber see bin store.

binder, 1 binding agent, cementitious material; any material, usually a liquid which hardens, used in mortar, concrete, paints, plaster etc. for bonding a mass of solid particles together.
2 see paint binder.
3 in timber frame construction, any horizontal timber member used for holding together a series of components, studs, rafters etc. of a timber frame. →57
4 binding beam, binding joist, bridging joist; in traditional timber frame construction, a heavy main beam or joist which gives intermediate support to floor or roof joists.
5 see bridging joist.
6 a timber tie beam for connecting the upper ends of parallel side walls to prevent them from splaying outwards.
7 see stirrup. →27

binding agent see binder.

binding beam see binder.

binding course in stone and brick masonry, a row of through stones or bricks laid crosswise to internally stabilize a wall, join two leaves together etc. →20

binding joist see binder.

binding wire, annealed wire, iron wire, tying wire; in reinforced concrete, soft iron wire for tying reinforcing bars together before the casting of concrete.

bindweed ancient Egyptian and heraldic ornament depicting the stylized twining stems and bell-flowers of plants of the family *Convolvulaceae*. →121

binocular having two eyes with which to see.

binomial in mathematics, an expression which contains the sum or difference of two parts.

bin shelter, bin store; an external shelter in which waste bins are stored.

bin store, 1 bin chamber, refuse store; in waste management, a space, building or shelter for the housing of waste bins or other receptacles for refuse.
2 a bin shelter.

biodegradable waste see organic waste.

biogenic see organic.

biosystem the interaction of the living organisms, flora and fauna in any particular place; part of an ecosystem.

biotechnic according to Mumford's classification of the evolution of urban civilization, an era in which biological sciences have become intertwined with technology, and ecological aspects have become of importance in economical and political spheres.

biotite a form of dark brown, green or black mica, a soft potassium iron magnesium silicate mineral.
see black mica.
see glauconite.

bi-part folding door a vertical folding door leaf of two horizontally hinged panels, which lie in a horizontal plane above the doorway when the door is fully open. →50

bi-parting door see centre-opening door. →50

bipedalis Lat.; a Roman triangular or square brick of which two adjacent sides are two Roman feet (592 mm) in length; see also bessalis. →83

birch [*Betula spp.*] a group of hardwoods from the northern hemisphere with hard, pale timber; used for furniture, interior joinery, pulp and plywood; see ***Betula spp.*** for full list of birch species included in this work.

birch bark 1 the pinkish white exterior protective layer of tissue on a birch tree [*Betula spp.*], traditionally peeled and used as waterproofing for roofing in areas where it is abundant.
2 a shade of pale orange grey which takes its name from the colour of the above.

birch grey a shade of orange grey which takes its name from the colour of the bark of the inner birch tree [*Betula spp.*].

birch plywood plywood in which all or face plies are of birch veneer.

bird box a wooden box, hollowed out log or other construction for birds to build their nest in.

bird cherry [*Prunus padus*] a European hardwood with bitter scented, hard and tough timber.

bird house see aviary.

bird-pecked finish see sparrowpecked finish.

bird sanctuary an area of countryside with restricted access during the breeding season, designated as an area for indigenous and threatened bird species to nest in their natural habitat.

bird's beak moulding see beak moulding. →122

bird's eye in woodwork and joinery, pertaining to certain cuts of the sugar maple with small circular markings on the wood surface, valued for their decorative appearance.

bird's eye maple see bird's eye.

bird's-eye perspective a bird's-eye view constructed as a perspective projection.

bird's-eye view a view or visualization of a scene or object from above.

bird's head sculpted band ornament with a row of bird heads as if hung downwards, found especially in English Norman architecture. →122

birdsmouth, sally; in timber frame construction, a notch cut into the end of an inclined timber to receive a horizontal timber running perpendicular to it; used for the housing of rafters. →4

birdsmouth brick a special brick manufactured with an indented end, designed for use in decorative brickwork and at an internal obtuse corner in a brick wall. →16

birdsmouth joint, birdsmouthed notched joint; in timber roof construction, a joint formed by notching the extremity of a rafter with a birdsmouth and fastening it to a wall plate; any joint similar to this. →4

birdsmouthed notched joint see birdsmouth joint. →4

Birmingham wire gauge, Stub's wire gauge; abb. BWG; a classification of thicknesses for wire and steel sheet, based on imperial units.

birth-house see mammisi. →72

biscuit referring to ceramic products which have been fired but have not undergone further treatment such as glazing.

bisector in geometry, a line drawn from an apex which divides an angle into two equal parts.

bishop's palace a lavish residence constructed by the powerful bishops of the Middle Ages.

bishop's throne see cathedra. →95

bishopric the official seat or diocese of a bishop.

bismuth a grey, metallic chemical element, **Bi**, used in alloys and medicine.

bismuth glance see bismuthite.

bismuthite, bismuth glance; a white or yellow-grey mineral, naturally occurring bismuth sulphide, $\mathbf{Bi_2S_3}$, an important ore of bismuth.

bismuth sulphide a chemical compound, $\mathbf{Bi_2S_3}$, found naturally as bismuthite, an important ore of bismuth.

bismuth white, Bougival white; a white pigment consisting of bismuth nitrate, used in the early 1900s and now largely replaced by zinc white.

bister see bistre.

bistre, bister, brown lampblack; a yellowish brown pigment consisting of soot containing tar from the charring of beech wood; used as a watercolour wash.

bit 1 a unit of information in a binary system.
2 a replaceable rotating blade for use with a power tool.
3 see cutter.
4 see drill bit. →42
5 see screwdriver bit.

bit hilani a palatial building type originating in Syria in 1200 BC, based on a four-roomed scheme and an attached temple with a columned portico, long reception room and an adjoining staircase.

bitmac see bitumen macadam.

bitmap in computing, a graphic representation made up of pixels.

bitter spar 1 see magnesite.
2 see dolomite.

bitumen a solid or viscous black tarry liquid found naturally or produced from the distillation of petroleum, used as a binder, an adhesive and for waterproofing membranes.

bitumen-based coating material see bituminous paint.

bitumen-coated chipboard chipboard which has been precoated with bitumen.

bitumen emulsion a dispersion of bitumen in water with an emulsifying additive; used in construction for the bonding of overlapping membranes and general waterproofing.

bitumen felt, bituminous felt, roofing felt; a waterproofing membrane consisting of a thin fibrous mat of polyester or glass fibres saturated with bitumen or a bitumen-polymer; used for roofing, tanking etc.

bitumen felt roofing 1 see built-up roofing. →49
2 see roll-jointed roofing. →49
3 see lap-jointed roofing. →49
4 bitumen shingles, see strip slates. →49

bitumen impregnated softboard a low density fibreboard impregnated with 10–30% bitumen as water resistance.

bitumen macadam, bitmac; a temporary or base surfacing for roads, coarser than asphalt, consisting of graded aggregate coated with bitumen to provide adhesion.

bitumen paint see bituminous paint.

bitumen-polymer membrane bitumen-polymer sheet used as tanking or roofing.

bitumen-polymer sheet a form of bituminous felt which contains a polymer modifier and is reinforced with a layer of fibreglass or other mesh.

bitumen primer in bituminous roofing, a bituminous liquid applied as a waterproofing coating and to glue down successive layers of roofing felt.

bitumen roofing 1 see bitumen felt roofing. →49
2 see bituminous roofing.

bitumen shingles see strip slates. →49

bitumen solution a viscous liquid consisting of bitumen and a solvent, used for masonry tanking, waterproofing layers, coating steelwork and the underbodies of cars etc.

bituminous pertaining to a material or product which contains bitumen, tar or pitch.

bituminous adhesive any adhesive based on bitumen or coal tar used for bonding sheet materials such as roofing felt and linoleum.

bituminous binder a bituminous material that has adhesive and waterproofing properties.

bituminous coating a thin layer of bitumen, applied hot by mopping, used in tanking and roofing etc.

bituminous felt see bitumen felt.

bituminous felt roofing 1 roofing or layers of laid bituminous felt, either glued on flat roofs using bituminous solutions or tacked on pitched roofs using clout nails. →49
2 see built-up roofing. →49
3 see roll-jointed roofing. →49
4 see lap-jointed roofing. →49
5 bitumen shingles, see strip slates. →49

bituminous membrane a general name for bitumen felt and other similar products.

bituminous paint, bitumen paint, bitumen-based coating material; paint or a thin coating consisting of asphalt or bitumen in a solvent or emulsion, used for protecting ferrous metals.

bituminous putty in glazing, a kind of putty which consists of bituminous products and elastomers.

bituminous roofing 1 any waterproof roofing which is bitumen based; often bituminous felt roofing.
2 see bituminous felt roofing. →49
3 see built-up roofing. →49

bivallate describing a fortification, especially a hillfort, which is surrounded by two concentric ditches and ramparts.

black a general name for achromatic shades of colour which reflect very little light and are at the dark end of the grey scale; see below for list of black pigments.
acetylene black.
benzol black, see carbon black.
black lead, see graphite.
black oxide of cobalt.
black oxide of iron, see Mars black.
black oxide of manganese.
blue black, see vine black.
bone black.
carbon black.
cobalt black, see black oxide of cobalt.
coke black, see vine black.
cork black, see vine black.
Davy's grey.
diamond black, see carbon black.
drop black.
Frankfurt black.
gas black.
German black, see vine black.
grape black, see vine black.
graphite.
ivory black.
kernel black, see vine black.
lampblack.
manganese black.
Mars black.
oil black.
Paris black.
pine soot black.
slate black.
vine black.
yeast black.

black alder see common alder.

black and white work traditional English and central European half-timbered wall construction in which the exposed timber frame is blackened and the wattle and daub infill is rendered white. →7

blackbutt [*Eucalyptus pilularis*] an Australian hardwood with brown, heavy timber; used in construction for sheathing, flooring and for furniture.

black cherry see American cherry.

black cottonwood [*Populus trichocarpa*] a North American hardwood whose pale brown timber is used as sawn boards and for plywood, packing and furniture.

black gum see tupelo.

black iron oxide see iron oxide.

black lead see graphite.

black locust an alternative name for timber from the robinia tree.

black maple [*Acer nigrum*] a North American hardwood; a hard maple used for furniture and panelling.

black medic see shamrock. →121

black mica a black or dark-coloured form of biotite mineral.

black oxide of cobalt, cobalt black; cobalt oxide, Co_3O_4, similar in properties to Mars black or black oxide of iron, used as a black pigment.

black oxide of iron see Mars black.

black oxide of manganese natural manganese dioxide formerly used as a black pigment; see manganese black.

black pigments see 'black' for list of black pigments.

black poplar [*Populus nigra, Populus spp.*] a group of hardwoods, especially from Europe with soft, pale timber; used for plywood.

blacksmith's hammer a traditional name for an engineer's hammer. →40

black spruce [*Picea mariana*]; a softwood marketed as Canadian spruce.

black spruce beetle [*Tetropium castaneum*], see spruce beetle.

black walnut see American walnut.

black wattle see Australian blackwood.

blackwood see Australian blackwood, [*Acacia melanoxylon*].

blade 1 the metal cutting edge of a knife, plane, saw or any other cutting tool.
2 see plane iron.
3 see chisel blade. →41

blade set, sawing pattern; in the conversion or manufacture of timber, the setting of the cutting edges so as to achieve the least waste from the original log, plank or piece.

blanc fixe, baryta white, constant white, enamel white, permanent white; a form of artificial barium sulphate, $BaSO_4$, used as a base and inert pigment in paints.

blanc titane see titanium white.
blank 1 in mass-produced manufacturing, a piece of material (metal, timber or plastics), which has been roughly shaped or moulded before working into a finished state.
2 a preform.
3 see blind.
blank cap see end cap.
blank tracery see blind tracery. →109
blank window a window opening which has been walled up; often the same as a false window.
blast cleaning a method of cleaning large masonry and concrete surfaces by projecting a gas, usually air, a liquid, usually water, or an abrasive through a nozzle at high velocity.
blast furnace a large industrial vessel where iron is smelted from iron ore by mixing it with limestone and coke and heating at 1100°C.
blast-furnace cement, blast-furnace slag cement; a blended cement composed of ground blast-furnace slag mixed with a hydraulic binder such as Portland cement.
blast-furnace concrete see slag concrete.
blast-furnace slag, slag; a clinker composed mainly of calcium, magnesium and alumino-silicates, a by-product of steel production used as a binder and aggregate in concrete.
blast-furnace slag cement see blast-furnace cement.
blasting, shot firing; the removal of rock from the ground, either for commercial use or during excavation, using explosives.
blasting treatment the high velocity projection of a gas, liquid or granular solid as a cleaning treatment and for producing a finish on stone, concrete etc.
blast-resistant laminated glass glass specially manufactured with interlayers to have anti-bandit and bullet-resistant properties.
blast venting panel, blast wall; a panel wall designed to give way in the event of an explosion, thus absorbing some of its energy.
blast wall 1 a structural wall designed to afford protection from an explosion.
2 see blast venting panel.
bleb see blow-hole.
bleeding, 1 bleed-through; a discolouring defect in a paint finish appearing where pigment or other material has diffused into the paint film from below.
2 see concrete bleeding.
bleeding Stereum [*Stereum sanguinolentum*] a fungus which attacks wood in exterior timberwork and in storage.
bleed valve see air release valve.
bleed-through see bleeding.
blemish an undesirable feature, stain etc. that depreciates the visual appearance of a product, surface or finish, but has no effect on its quality.
blend see mixture.
blende see zinc-blende.
blended aggregate a mix of more than one type of aggregate in concrete.
blended cement, blended hydraulic cement; a cement composed of a latent hydraulic binder such as ground blast-furnace slag, pozzolana or fuel-ash mixed with ordinary Portland cement; the mix produces a chemical reaction which improves the properties of the cement.
blended hydraulic cement see blended cement.
blending see mixing.
bleu-ciel see sky blue.
blight see planning blight.
blind 1 a retractable shading device for a window or other glazed opening, often of textile or slatted construction.
2 see venetian blind.
3 see roller blind.
4 blank; referring to an opening in construction which has been walled up, or a decorative panel on a wall which imitates a window, door, tracery or some other opening.
blind alley, dead end; an alley closed off at one end; a cul-de-sac.
blind arcade 1 an arcade whose arches have been blocked up with masonry infill. →100
2 a similar decorative effect formed by a series of arches on a solid wall.
blind arch an arch which is blocked up, or appears as decoration on the surface of a solid masonry wall.
blind door see false door.
blind dovetail joint see lapped dovetail joint. →5
blind hinge see concealed hinge.
blinding a layer of lean concrete 50 mm–100 mm thick laid over soil to seal the ground and provide a clean bed for further construction work.
blinding concrete concrete suitable for use as a blinding over soil to seal it and provide a clean bed for subsequent construction work.
blinding course in road construction, a layer of concrete, crushed rock, gravel or sand laid to protect the surfacing from moisture rising up from the underlying ground.
blind mortise see stopped mortise.
blind nailing see secret nailing. →3
blindstory 1 a portion of the external wall of a building one storey high with no openings; often a full storey parapet wall above roof level.
2 in church architecture, a triforium with a blind arcade. →100
blind tracery, blank tracery; Gothic tracery carved onto masonry wall surfaces and timber panelling as relief ornament. →109
blind window see false window.
blister 1 an imperfection in glass consisting of a trapped bubble of gas.
2 blistering; a defect in a plaster finish consisting of a local swelling which may cause the plaster to peel away from its base.
3 blistering; a defect in a paintwork finish consisting of trapped air bubbles caused by the evaporation of moisture or other substances beneath the paint surface.
blister figure a decorative mottled figure in veneers cut from timber with irregular grain, resembling blisters in the surface.
blistering see blister.
block, 1 building block, masonry block; a rectangular unit, solid, perforated or otherwise shaped, used in masonry construction; it may be made of clay, concrete or other mineral composition and is usually larger than a brick.
see concrete block.
see hollow clay block. →16
see glass block.
paving block, see concrete block paver. →15
2 any small solid piece of material such as stone, metal, wood, plastics etc., often a squared lump used in construction as a spacing, filling or packing piece.
see location block.
see parquet block. →44
3 an urban plot of densely built form bounded by three or four intersecting streets.
4 a building with a number of floors; see multistorey building.
see apartment block.
5 see blockage.
6 see title block.
7 see sketchpad, sketchbook.
blockage, block; **1** in pipework, trapped solid matter which inhibits the flow of a liquid or gas.
2 the resulting problem caused by this.
block altar an altar which is a single monolithic unembellished or carved block of stone. →116
blockboard a timber building board formed by gluing veneers on either side of a core of solid wood strips

with a width of between 7 mm and 30 mm; the grain of the veneers runs at 90° to that of the core. →9

block capital a common Romanesque capital whose roughly cubic form has a rounded undersurface; also called a cushion capital or cubic capital. →115

block diagram a graphical representation of units of information linked by a series of connecting lines, indicating how a process, device or system functions.

block end ridge tile, ridge end; a ridge capping roof tile specially formed with one closed end to cover the end of a ridge.

block flooring see end-grain wood block flooring. →44

block foundation see concrete block foundation. →57, →58

block of flats see apartment block. →61

blockout see box out.

block paver see concrete block paver. →15

block paving see concrete block paving. →15

block pillar in log construction, a hollow pier of notched logs, square in plan, which functions as a buttress in long or high log walls. →102

block plan, location plan; a drawing or vignette on a drawing which shows the location in plan of a site with respect to other parts of an area, or the location of part of a building with regard to the whole, usually drawn as simple outlines or blocks. →130

block plane a small one-handed plane for smoothing and finishing small pieces, especially useful for working the end grain of wood.

block stone a large block of stone roughly squared at a quarry, ready for use as building stone.

block wall any wall laid from blocks.

blockwork **1** walling construction in laid blocks, or the result of this process.
see *inner leaf blockwork* in brick house illustration. →59
2 see horizontal log construction. →6

blonde see bamboo.

Blondin see cableway.

blood red, bronze red, brownish red, Orient red, Turkey red, Turkish red; a shade of red which takes its name from the colour of blood; Turkey red refers to the colour of Turkish dyed linens.

bloodstone **1** a form of the mineral haematite, a dense red iron ore, used as a gemstone.
2 see heliotrope.

bloom see efflorescence.

blossom various forms of Egyptian, Greek etc. ornament depicting open flowers. →82
blossom and pine cone. →82
see bud and blossom. →82
see anthemion. →82
see floriated ornament, floral decoration. →82, →121
see hom. →82

blossom capital see bell capital. →73

blotting paper a very porous, unsized paper used for absorbing excess ink or paint to prevent smearing while writing or drawing.

blow see throw.

blower **1** see fan.
2 see fan unit.

blow forming a method of forming thermoplastics moulded products by fastening a heated sheet around its edges and blowing it like a bubble; may or may not be blown against a mould.

blow-hole, bleb, bug hole; in concretework, a pitted defect in a hardened concrete surface caused by air pockets released from the concrete and becoming trapped against the formwork.

blowlamp, blowtorch; a portable burner with a hot and accurate flame, produced by the forcing of liquid fuel through a nozzle which is ignited on mixing with air; used for various jobs on site such as warming, melting, cutting etc.

blow moulding a method of forming hollow thermoplastics products by blowing air into a heated mould; sheet material is thus forced against both halves of the mould.

blown bitumen, oxidized bitumen; bitumen through which air has been blown to improve its elasticity and raise its softening temperature.

blown glass **1** any glass traditionally produced by manual blowing.
2 see blown sheet glass.
3 see crown glass.

blown linseed oil see blown oil.

blown oil, blown linseed oil; refined linseed oil which has had air blown through it to promote oxidation and thickening; used as a vehicle in paints.

blown sheet glass traditional sheet glass formed by blowing glass into cylindrical moulds, allowing it to cool and then cutting, reheating and flattening it.

blown vinyl relief wallcovering wallcovering whose face surface has been rendered with a raised pattern, formed by foaming a layer of polymer such as PVC.

blow out in concretework, the removal of unwanted material, debris etc. from inside formwork with compressed air before casting of concrete.

blowtorch see blowlamp.

blue a general name for shades of blue light, with an electromagnetic wavelength in the range 440–480 μm; blue pigments listed below.
Alexandrian blue, see Egyptian blue.
alizarin blue.
Antwerp blue.
artificial ultramarine.
azure blue.
azure cobalt, see cobalt blue.
azurite.
azzura della magna, see azurite.
azzuro oltremarino, see lapis lazuli.
Berlin blue.
bice.
blue ashes.
blue bice.
blue celeste, see cerulean blue.
blue malachite, see azurite.
blue verditer.
Bremen blue.
bronze blue.
Brunswick blue.
caeruleum, see cerulean blue.
celestial blue.
cerulean blue.
chessylite, see azurite.
Chinese blue.
cobalt blue.
cobalt ultramarine.
coelin, see cerulean blue.
coeruleum, see cerulean blue.
copper blue, copper green.
corruleum blue, see cerulean blue.
cyanine blue.
Egyptian blue.
eschel.
French blue, French ultramarine, see artificial ultramarine.
Gahn's blue.
Gmellin's blue, see artificial ultramarine.
green ultramarine, see ultramarine, ultramarine green.
Haarlem blue, see Antwerp blue.
Indian blue, see indigo.
Italian blue, see Egyptian blue.
indanthrone blue.
indigo.
intense blue, see phthalocyanine blue.

iron blue, see Prussian blue.
king's blue.
lapis lazuli.
lazuline blue, see lapis lazuli.
Leithner blue.
Leyden blue.
lime blue.
manganese blue.
Milori blue, see Prussian blue.
mineral blue, see azurite.
Monastral blue, see phthalocyanine blue.
mountain blue, see azurite, Bremen blue.
Paris blue, see Prussian blue.
paste blue, see Prussian blue.
phthalocyanine blue.
Pompeian blue, see Egyptian blue.
Pozzuoli blue, see Egyptian blue.
Prussian blue.
Saxon blue, see smalt.
sky blue.
smalt.
soluble blue.
steel blue, see Prussian blue.
thalo blue, see phthalocyanine blue.
Thénard's blue, see cobalt blue.
ultramarine, ultramarine blue.
Vestorian blue.
Vienna blue.
woad.
zaffer, zaffre.

blue ashes a variety of Bremen blue pigment.

blue bice a variety of Bremen blue pigment.

blue black see vine black.

blue brick see Staffordshire Blue brick.

blue celeste see cerulean blue.

blue fungus see blue stain.

blue john, fluorite; a violet form of fluorite found in deposits in Derbyshire, England.

blue lily see blue lotus. →82, →121

blue lotus the sharp-petalled blue water lily, *Nymphaea caerulea*; see lotus. →82, →121

blue malachite see azurite.

blue pigments see list of blue pigments under 'blue'.

blue stain, blue fungus; a fungus which leaves an unsightly blue tinge on wood, but does not affect its strength or other physical properties; see also following entry.

blue stain fungus fungal micro-organisms such as *Ophiostoma minus*, which produce unsightly but structurally harmless blue stain in timber.

blue verditer a variety of Bremen blue pigment.

blunt pyramid see bent pyramid. →70

blushing a defect in a transparent lacquer or varnish finish consisting of a milkiness caused by moisture or cold.

bms see building management system.

board 1 any rigid sheet material of wood, plaster, plastics etc. used in construction for cladding and bracing a frame; a building board.
2 in the conversion of timber, a piece of sawn timber with cross-sectional dimensions of less than 38 mm thick and greater than 75 mm wide. →2
3 a planed section of timber of similar dimensions used in finished flooring, external cladding, linings etc.
4 thin, stiff, wood or paper-based sheet used in drawing, painting and modelmaking.
5 board of directors; a number of people chosen by shareholders to run the affairs and administration of a company or institution as its decision-making body.

board and batten cladding a form of board on board cladding in which the joints between laid vertical boards are covered externally with thin strips of timber. →8

board cladding see timber cladding, weather-boarding. →8, →58

boarded ceiling a ceiling comprising dressed timber boards laid side by side.

boarded roof rudimentary roofing of sawn timber boards laid lengthways from ridge to eaves, or overlapping and parallel to the ridge. →48

board finish plaster, board plaster; hemihydrate plaster used as a finish for even surfaces such as gypsum plasterboard and other relatively smooth building boards.

board flooring 1 flooring composed of dressed wooden boards laid side by side, either laid over joists or on battens over a concrete slab.
2 see wood board flooring.

board formwork 1 formwork in which the concrete is placed against an assembly of sawn timber boards.
2 similar formwork using plywood or other building boards.

boarding, 1 sheathing; the cladding of a building frame in building board as stiffening, weatherproofing, lining etc.
2 the boards thus fixed.
3 sawn or planed timber boards or planks laid side by side as cladding or lining for a frame.
4 see roof boarding. →48
5 floorboarding, see floorboards.
6 see weatherboarding, siding. →8

boarding school a school with living accommodation provided for pupils or scholars.

board-marked finish a finish for concrete in which the pattern of the boards used as formwork are evident in the surface.

board of assessors, jury, competition jury, panel of judges; a committee whose task is to assess the merits of entries to an architectural or planning competition, and choose a winning proposal.

board of directors see board.

board on board cladding, staggered siding; external timber cladding of boards laid vertically in two layers so that the outer layer covers the gaps between boards in the layer below. →8, →57

board on board roofing a traditional form of timber roofing in which boards are laid in the direction of the slope; a second layer of boards is then laid in the same direction over the gaps between the lower boards.

board plaster see board finish plaster.

board sawn timber timber which has been converted into boards.

boardwalk a pedestrian recreational walkway, often found at coastal resorts, consisting of a raised timber platform in proximity to the sea.

boaster, drover; a broad-faced masonry chisel for working stone to a relatively smooth surface. →41

boat grave, boat pit; ancient Egyptian sea-going vessels buried in pits at the foot of the great pyramid at Giza, believed to be for transporting the entombed Pharaoh to his final resting place. →71

boat pit see boat grave. →71

bodhi tree see tree of Buddha. →121

body 1 the main volume of a church. →99, →100
2 see cylinder body. →39
3 Platonic body, see Platonic solid.
4 see rigid body.

Body Art, Living Sculpture; a form of modern performance art in which the living human body is the mode of expression or part of the work of art.

body-tinted glass glass to which a tint has been added throughout its thickness, usually for the control of solar radiation.
see smoked glass.
see tinted solar control glass.

bog a natural habitat of wet or waterlogged land on acid soil.

bog oak ordinary oak which has been immersed in ponds, rivers, wet land etc. for up to a hundred years, whose wood has a blackish hue and is valued in turnery.

bog plant in landscaping, any species of plant which usually grows in marshy areas, where the acid soil is always wet.

Bohemian garnet see pyrope.

boiled linseed oil quick-drying raw linseed oil with added chemical lead or manganese-based accelerators or driers, originally cooked to induce polymerization, used as a varnish for wood finishing, or in paints and other varnishes.

boiler, furnace (Am.); a water heater which heats water to below boiling point for domestic or other use; types included as separate entries are listed below.
back boiler.
central heating boiler. →56
electric boiler.
electric water heater.
gravity boiler.
high output back boiler.

boiler house a building or part of a larger building complex in which boiler plant is housed.

boiler plant, 1 water-heating plant; mechanical plant consisting of boilers, pipework, flues etc. for producing hot water for a building.
2 see heating plant.

boiler room plant room that houses boiler plant.

boiling oil hole see murder hole. →103

boiling point in the heating of water and some other liquids, the temperature at which vaporization occurs; for water this is 100°C.

bois de rose see rosewood.

boiserie decorative timber wall panelling which is elaborately carved.

bold roll tile see double roll tile. →47

bole 1 the trunk of a tree especially when used for conversion into timber.
2 types of fine compact clay usually containing iron oxide, used as pigments.
3 gold size; a mixture of clay and rabbit skin or hide glue applied to the surface of an object being prepared for gilding.

bolection moulding, balection moulding, raised moulding; a moulding used to cover the joint between two flat surfaces which do not lie in the same plane, such as for the joint between a timber panel and its frame.

bollard a low sturdy cast-iron or stone post around which a rope can be tied when mooring a boat or ship, or one of concrete, steel or other construction designed to prevent the passage of vehicular traffic.

Bologna chalk calcium carbonate sulphate used as a filler in gesso for frescos.

Bologna stone the mineral heavy spar found near Bologna in Italy.

bolster, 1 headtree, saddle; in traditional timber frame construction, a horizontal timber piece fixed to the top of a post to spread the load of a beam supported by it. →4
2 a wide masonry chisel used for cutting bricks and blocks. →41
3 the thickening of the neck of a chisel and similar tools to prevent the blade being forced into the handle when it is struck with a mallet. →41

bolt 1 a flat-ended fastener with a helically threaded shank whose head has a hexagonal, octagonal or square projection allowing it to be tightened to a nut using a spanner; types included as separate entries are listed below. →37
see *screws and bolts* illustration. →36
anchor bolt. →36
carriage bolt, see coach bolt. →36
coach bolt. →36
countersunk head bolt. →36
cremone bolt, cremona bolt, cremorne bolt. →50
expanding bolt, expansion bolt.
foundation bolt, see anchor bolt. →36
handrail bolt, see joint bolt.
joint bolt.
hexagonal bolt, hex-head bolt. →36
king bolt.
lag bolt, lag screw, see coach screw. →36
machine bolt. →36
ragbolt, see anchor bolt. →36
rail bolt, see joint bolt.
rock bolt.
roofing bolt. →36
toggle bolt. →37
2 any fastening or catch for a door which involves a sliding bar which engages in a housing in a jamb, the most common of which is a barrel bolt.
barrel bolt. →39
dog bolt, see hinge bolt. →38
fire-exit bolt, see panic bolt.
flush bolt, see flush slide.
foot bolt. →39
hinge bolt. →38
panic bolt.
security bolt, see hinge bolt. →38
slide bolt. →39
tower bolt.
3 draw bolt, lock bolt; that part of a latch or lock which engages with a striking plate in the frame to hold the door in a closed position. →39
catch bolt, see return latch. →39
claw bolt. →39
dead bolt. →39
hook bolt. →39
indicating bolt. →39
latch bolt, see return latch. →39
slide bolt, snib bolt.
4 see thunderbolt. →120
5 see veneer bolt. →10

bolt croppers, bolt cutters; a long scissor-like tool with long handles and powerful jaws for shearing thicker metal objects such as bolts and screws.

bolt cutters see bolt croppers.

bolted joint a joint fixed with a bolt or bolts. →3, →34

boltel see bowtell. →14

bolt-through fixing a fixing for components and fittings in which a bolt is passed through the supporting construction and fastened on the reverse side with a nut.

bomb shelter see civil defence shelter. →61

bomos 1 Gk; a stone altar situated at or near the entrance to a Greek temple, on which offerings were made to a deity. →84, →92, →116
2 see eschara.

bond 1 the fixing or securing force provided by mortar, adhesives, coatings etc.; see adhesion.
2 see brickwork bond. →18
3 see concrete bond.
4 in project management, a sum of money or securities placed by a building contractor with a client or third party as a guarantee of completion of construction work.

bond-beam block see channel block. →30

bond breaker see separating layer.

bonder, bondstone, bonding brick; a brick or stone laid crosswise into a wall to tie surface masonry to the rest of the wall.

bond failure see adhesive failure.

bonding admixture in concretework, a latex admixture included in the mix to improve tensile and bond strength.

bonding agent, bonding primer; a chemical substance applied in liquid form to a hardened substrate to improve the bond of subsequent layers or coatings.

bonding brick 1 any brick which has been cut or manufactured to non-standard size or shape in order to fill space at the edges and corners of a brickwork bond; often a cut brick or bat. →21
2 see bonder.

bonding compound, hot bonding compound, hot stuff (Am.); in bituminous roofing, molten oxidized bitumen applied to bond successive layers of bitumen felt together.

bonding plaster plaster used for undercoats in circumstances where the base has little key or adhesion.

bonding primer see bonding agent.

bond line see bond plane.

bond plane, bond line; the surface of adhesion or bonding in a joint.

bondstone see bonder.

bond strength 1 the strength of the adhesive bond created by glue between two glued or bonded elements, or between a coating and its substrate.
2 in reinforced concrete, the strength of the bond between reinforcing bars and the surrounding concrete, measured at the point of failure of the bond.

bond stress in reinforced concrete, stress which occurs between the surface of reinforcement and the surrounding concrete in a member under load.

bond timber, chain timber; in traditional construction, a timber laid horizontally in a solid masonry wall to provide bracing and reinforcement.

bone black a strong black pigment consisting of impure carbon obtained from burnt and ground bones; see also ivory black.

bone china white porcelain fired with bone ash to a translucent state before a glaze is applied, when it is fired at a lower temperature; developed in the late 1700s by Josiah Spode to provide a competitor for imported oriental porcelain.

bone glue a form of animal glue, traditionally used for furniture-making, bookbinding and gums, manufactured by boiling the bones of animals.

bonnet see chimney cap.

bonnet hip tile, granny bonnet; a special roof tile formed into a convex shape to cover a hip; its open end is usually filled with mortar once laid.

bonus, 1 bonus payment; a payment given as a result of the completion of a building in advance of its agreed completion date, increased or improved performance and production.
2 a periodic reduction in insurance payments for long-term and trustworthy customers.

bonus payment see bonus.

bookcase a shelf unit for the storage of books.

bookkeepers see accountants.

bookkeeping see accountancy.

book match see bookmatching. →10

bookmatching 1 a veneering pattern in which successive sheets cut from a log are laid side by side as mirror images of one another, resembling an open book, also called book match. →10
2 see vertical butt and horizontal bookmatching. →10

book value in economics, the value of an asset as shown in the accounts of a firm.

Boolean operations in computer-aided design, a solids modelling technique which combines two simple solids to produce something more complex.

boom, 1 barrier; a light barrier across a road or waterway, a hinged bar or pole which can be lifted to allow traffic to pass underneath. →64
2 see jib.
3 see chord.

booster 1 see booster pump.
2 see fire booster.

booster pump, booster; a pump for increasing the local pressure in a water supply pipeline.

boot 1 in computing, starting a computer program to make it run.
2 see warm boot.

booth, 1 stall, stand; a small temporary shelter used for selling tickets, trinkets and other merchandise, often at a fair or event; see kiosk.
2 see cabin.
3 a telephone booth; see telephone box.

boot lintel an L-beam supporting overhead external wall construction above a strip window. →30

borax sodium borate in natural form, used in soldering and as a detergent.

Bordeaux (red) see wine red.

border 1 the dividing line between two politically or administrationally independent areas.
2 in landscaping, a strip of planting used at the edge of a building or pathway.
3 a decorative edging band for a panel or area of wall.
4 an inset line demarking the edge of a drawing on all four sides. →130

bored pile in foundation technology, a pile placed using excavations or boring into the ground; most often a cast-in-place pile. →29
see augered pile. →29
see cast-in-place pile. →29
see large diameter pile.
see percussive bored pile.

bore dust fine powdered wood, the product of the burrowing of wood boring insects.

borehole see wormhole.

boric acid a chemical compound, H_3BO_3, used in the manufacture of ceramics, cements and glass.

boring see drilling.

Borneo camphorwood see kapur.

bornite a reddish mineral, naturally occurring copper iron sulphide, Cu_5FeS_4, an important ore of copper.

borocarbon see boron carbide.

boron a chemical element, **B**, used in metal alloys, abrasives, nuclear reactors and as boric acid in the manufacture of enamel.

boron carbide, borocarbon; a chemical compound, B_4C, used as a hard abrasive.

borosilicate glass, Pyrex; a fire-resisting glass which softens at high temperatures but does not crack.

borough a town with a municipal corporation, previously one with privileges granted royal charter.

borrowed light a glazed panel incorporated into an internal wall or partition; an internal window between two spaces.

Borstal a community home for young offenders.

boss 1 a decorative ovular protrusion, knob or node, found as a centrepiece in domes and ceilings, at the meeting of ribs in a vault, and as a terminating element for mouldings. →101
2 see knot.
3 a protruding spout in a sanitary appliance or pipe to which a pipe fitting can be attached.
4 see screwed boss.

bossage in stonework, projecting stones which have been left untreated either as rustication or awaiting further tooling. →12

Bos taurus see bull. →119

bothie, bothy; a rough shack or shelter in Scotland, inhabited by shepherds and labourers.

bothy see bothie.

botony see cross botonée. →117

bottega 1 a Renaissance workshop in which an Italian master artist practised with his apprentices under his guidance.
2 a work of art, a shop picture, undertaken by one of these apprentices under the auspices of the master.

bottle bank in waste management, a storage vessel located in a public place, in which glass and bottles are collected to be recycled.

bottled gas combustible hydrocarbon fuel such as butane or propane gas, stored in metal cylinders under compression in liquid form.

bottle green a shade of dark green which takes its name from the colour of glass used for bottles.

bottle trap a drainage trap with a water-filled vessel divided by a baffle or interior pipe to form a lock, and a removable base to facilitate cleaning.

bottom bead the lowest glazing bead in a window, which fixes the lower edge of a pane or unit into a frame.

bottom chord see lower chord. →33

bottom floor see base floor. →28

bottom floor construction see base floor construction. →59
see *bottom floor construction* in brick house illustration. →59

bottomgrate, 1 grate; a metal grille in a coal or wood fire on which the combustible material rests and under which air is free to circulate during combustion; most often of cast iron construction. →56
2 see stool bottomgrate.

bottom hung referring to a window, casement or hatch whose opening leaf is hinged at its lower edge.

bottom-hung casement window a window type whose opening casement is hinged at its lower edge. →52

bottom rail the lowest horizontal member in a framed door leaf or window sash. →51, →52, →111

bottom raker in temporary sitework, the lowest slanting prop in a raking shore.

bottom reinforcement in reinforced concrete, longitudinal reinforcement placed near the base of a cast beam or slab to resist tensile forces. →27

bottony see cross botonée. →117

bouchard a hand-held bush hammer. →40

boucharde alternative spelling of bouchard. →40

bouclé 1 a form of looped yarn with a knotted appearance.
2 the fabric woven from this.

boudoir a small living room for ladies in a large dwelling or palace.

Bougival white a form of the white pigment bismuth white.

boukranion Greek form of bucranium. →122

boulangerite a grey black mineral, occasionally used as an ore of lead.

boulder, 1 rock; a large naturally occurring lump of stone in or at the surface of the ground, by classification over 200 mm in size; sometimes laid as cobbled paving.
2 see *boulder* in paving illustration. →15

boulder clay, glacial till, till; a soil type laid down by glacial action, consisting of unstratified sharpened mineral deposits representing a range of grain sizes from boulders down to clay.

bouleterion see bouleuterion. →92

bouleuterion Gk; an ancient Greek council chamber with rows of stepped benches surrounding a central platform; sometimes also written as bouleterion or buleuterion, or in Latin form as bouleuterium, buleuterium. →92, →94

bouleuterium see bouleuterion. →92, →94

boulevard a wide avenue-like thoroughfare in an urban context, often with a central reservation planted with trees; originally the upper surfaces of city ramparts which became grassed promenades when these had fallen into disuse.

boultine see bowtell. →14

boundary 1 the edge of a specified area, building site or officially registered tract of land.
2 see site boundary.
3 in computer-aided design, the geometrical perimeter of an area.

boundary fencing, perimeter fencing; any fencing for a site boundary.

boundary representations, Brep, B-rep; in computer-aided design, a method of representing a solid by its spatial boundaries.

boundary wall see perimeter wall. →70, →102

bourdonee cross bourdonee, see cross potent. →117

bournonite, wheel ore; a grey to black mineral, a locally important ore of lead and copper.

boutell see bowtell. →14

bow, camber; the warping of improperly seasoned timber boards evident as longitudinal curvature along the flat faces. →1

bowed bridge see cambered bridge. →32

Bowen knot, true-lover's knot, tristram, St Han's cross; a decorative motif or simple heraldic device with a cord arranged in a square formation, looped at each corner. →123

Bowen cross a Bowen knot on its side with its loops made angular; see cross of infinity. →118

bow handle an arched or U-shaped pull handle fixed to a door leaf by both ends.

bowl urinal, pod urinal; an individual wall-mounted urinal.

bow saw, continental bow saw, scroll bow-saw; a versatile saw with an interchangeable blade held in tension by its curved metal frame.

bowstring bridge a bridge supported by an arch or arches tied by the bridge deck, or by beams at the same level; a bridge supported by a bowstring truss. →32

bowstring truss a trussed beam in which the lower chord is flat and the upper chord is curved with its apex in the middle, forming a braced upside-down U shape. →33

bow window a bay window, curved in plan.

bowtel see bowtell. →14

bowtell, boltel, boultine, boutell, bowtel, edge roll; a decorative moulding whose cross-section is a three-quarter segment of a circle. →14

box 1 a private viewing enclosure at a theatre or stadium with its own entrance; see also loge.
2 see cabin.
3 see boxwood.

box beam a compound beam formed of an upper and lower chord of timber with plywood or other sheet webbing fixed to either side, thus forming a hollow box in cross-section; also similar construction in steel, when it is also known as a box girder.
see *plywood box beam* illustration. →7

box caisson, American caisson, stranded caisson; a reinforced concrete caisson constructed in such a way that it is open at the top and closed at the base, forming a part of the final foundation construction.

box corner joint a many-tenoned corner joint used in cabinetmaking for joining boards and sheets at right angles; sometimes called a finger joint or combed joint. →5

box dovetail joint a many-tenoned dovetailed corner joint used in cabinetmaking for joining boards and sheets at right angles. →5

boxed lap notch in log construction, a log joint in which square notches are made in the upper and lower ends of logs to fit with corresponding notches in perpendicular logs. →6

box frame see cased frame.

box frame construction a form of timber frame construction in which the vertical members (posts or studs), horizontal members (plates) and bracing form a rigid box; the roof structure is then placed or built on top.

box girder a box beam which consists of a welded rectangular tube of steel plate.

box girder bridge a bridge whose main supporting construction is a box girder.

box gutter, 1 rectangular gutter; in roof construction, any rainwater gutter which is rectangular in cross-section.
2 roof channel; a large gutter set below the level of roof planes, usually rectangular in section; used to drain in flat or butterfly roof forms, at valleys, behind parapets etc.
see *box gutter* in office building illustration. →60

boxing in timber construction, the casing of a timber frame with boards.

box match 1 a veneering pattern in which four triangular pieces of straight-grained veneer are laid in a rectangular arrangement with diagonal joints, forming a series of diamond shapes by the direction of grain. →10
2 see reverse box match. →10

box out, blockout (Am.), core, former, pocket; a formwork mould for creating an opening in concrete, or the opening so formed.

box pew in church architecture, a waist-high pew with doors at either end to protect against draughts, thus forming compartments.
see *box pew* in Scandinavian hall church illustration. →102

box pile in foundation engineering, a pile which is a square hollow tube of welded or rolled steel; a square pipe pile. →29

box spreader a machine with a hopper which spreads concrete to the required thicknesses between forms to produce a concrete road surface.

box staple, keep, staple; a metal hood attached to the side of a door frame into which the latch of a rim lock engages. →39

box strike a metal component fitted into a mortise in a door jamb to receive a deadbolt and protect it from being tampered with when the door is closed. →39

boxwood, box; [*Buxus sempervirens*] a hardwood from Europe, North Africa and the Middle East with pale yellow and very hard timber; used for turned work, inlay, chisel handles, chessmen and dressers.

BR butadiene rubber.

brace 1 a hand tool with a crank and handle for boring holes; a large manual drill with a kinked shaft.
2 in frame structures, any structural element which stiffens and reinforces the angle between two members. →4
3 a diagonal structural member, strut or rod providing rigidity to a frame, see also cross brace, diagonal. →33
4 see braces.

braced stanchion see lattice stanchion.

brace moulding, bracket moulding, double ogee moulding; a projecting decorative moulding formed by two back to back ogees, their convex ends together; see keel moulding. →14

braces mathematical enclosure symbols { and }.

bracing 1 any system of structural members designed to maintain the rigidity of a structure, frame etc.
2 the application of such a system.
3 see cross-bracing.
4 see frame bracing.

bracing panel a sheet component fixed over a frame in order to provide rigidity. →57

bracken green a shade of green which takes its name from the colour of the upper surface of fern fronds, especially that of *Pteridium aquilinum*.

bracket 1 a secondary projecting fixing component from which other components are supported, suspended or hung from a structure.
2 a projecting construction in masonry architecture to support pediments over doorways, balconies, ornamentation etc.
3 see parentheses.

bracket fungus see conk.

bracketing in ornamental plastering, a series of timber brackets constructed to support lathing when casting a cornice.

bracket moulding see brace moulding. →46

bracket saw see fretsaw.

brad, 1 oval brad head nail; a slender shanked nail with a small bullet-shaped head, used for interior finishing work and locations where a concealed fixing is desirable.
2 a flat L-shaped nail cut and bent from steel strip.
3 see glazing sprig.

bradawl, awl; a pointed tool used for piercing holes in thin wood or board, or for making starter holes for screws. →42

bradder a small nail gun for light nails up to lengths of 75 mm; used for fixing boarding and cladding.

brad hammer see tack hammer. →40

brad point drill, dowel bit; a drill bit with a sharp point at the drilling end for accurate centring, used for the drilling of holes in wood. →42

brake in lift machinery, an electro-mechanical safety device for stopping the lift car if the electrical supply fails or is switched off.

branch 1 a secondary connection from a main to a point of use in pipework, ductwork, wiring installations etc.
2 see branch fitting.
3 see branch discharge pipe.
4 one of the woody stems of a tree which spread outwards from the main trunk, from which leaves etc. grow, and which appear as knots in sawn timber. →1
5 see branch office.

branch bend a curved branch fitting for changing the direction of flow in a drainage pipeline.

branch discharge pipe a drainage pipe into which waste from one or a number of appliances on the same floor of a building is conveyed into a discharge stack.

branched knot, winged knot; a knot in seasoned timber formed by two or more branches in close proximity cut at the same point. →1

branch fitting, branch; in a system of sanitary pipework, a T-shaped piece of drainage pipe, pipe fitting etc. for making the connection of a secondary pipe to a main.

branch office in commerce and business, a local office of a large organization, whose headquarters are located elsewhere.

branch tracery, astwerk; the tracery found in German Gothic churches of the 1400s and 1500s, with trees and branch motifs.

branch vent see branch ventilating pipe.

branch ventilating pipe, branch vent; a drainage pipe connected to a ventilation stack, providing ventilation and balancing pressure fluctuations in a branch discharge pipe.

brand see trade mark.

brashing in landscaping and forestry, the removal of dead branches and twigs from trees, the woodland floor etc.

brashy, short grained; a description of defective timber which is brittle and snaps cleanly under lateral loading, either due to fungal attack or natural causes.

brass 1 a strong, corrosion-resistant, yellowish alloy containing mainly copper and zinc, often with traces of lead, tin, aluminium, manganese, iron and nickel; used as sheetmetal and for pipes, castings and forgings.
2 see brazen yellow.
3 a brass plate fixed over a tomb or grave in the floor of a church, and incised with an inscription and a pictorial representation of the deceased.

brattice a timber construction, walkway or tower in a castle or fortification; most often a wooden gallery built out from the parapet of a castle, used during a siege; also written as brattish, bretessé, bretêche or brettice. →103

brattish see brattice. →103

brazen yellow, brass; a shade of golden yellow which takes its name from the colour of the alloy brass.

Brazilian rosewood [*Dalbergia spruceana*] a tropical hardwood from the Amazon basin with red or violet streaked timber; used for furniture and interiors.

brazing, hard soldering; a form of soldering which employs alloys (often of copper, zinc and silver) which melt at a much higher temperature than normal soft solder; the joints are thus stronger.

brazing solder see hard solder.

breach of contract, violation of agreement; a situation arising when a party who has signed a contract, or made an agreement, fails to keep to the conditions or terms of that agreement.

breadth the width of an object. →2
break-glass unit a manual fire indicating device with an alarm switch set behind a glass panel, which must be broken in order to set off the alarm.
breaking joint in masonry bonding, the overlapping of bricks in alternate courses so as to avoid continuous vertical joints.
breaking strength see ultimate strength.
breakwater a masonry or concrete structure constructed at the mouth of a harbour or similar place to protect the coastline from the erosive wave action of the sea. →64
breast see chimney breast. →55
breast drill a drill with an attachment which is pressed against the chest to provide additional force in drilling.
breast lining joinery panelling, boarding etc. for the portion of the internal surface of a wall between window sill and floor.
breastsummer, bressummer, brestsummmer; in traditional timber-framed building, a timber beam which carries a load over an opening.
breather paper, building paper; in timber frame construction, thick water-resistant paper used in the thickness of wall construction, which allows for ventilation but acts as a barrier against the effects of driving rain and wind pressure.
breccia any rock consisting of angular fragments of stone solidified in a finer matrix such as limestone or clay; some marbles with this composition are used for decorative stone cladding.
breech fitting, 1 breeching; a Y-shaped pipe fitting used to converge two parallel pipelines.
2 see group connector.
breeching see breech fitting.
Bremen blue, mountain blue, mountain green; a poisonous blue pigment consisting of copper hydroxide and copper carbonate, produced in various shades.
Brep, B-rep see boundary representations.
bressummer see breastsummer.
brestsummer see breastsummer.
Bretêche see brattice. →103
Bretessé see brattice. →103
brettice see brattice. →103
brick, building brick; a rectangular block made of fired clay, burnt mud, concrete or other mineral material, used for building walls, paving and other constructions; its size is usually no larger than 338 mm × 225 mm × 113 mm, so it can be held in one hand for ease of laying; types included as separate entries are listed below.
see *brick* illustrations. →16, →17, →18, →19, →20, →21
Accrington brick.
air brick. →16
angle brick. →16
arch brick, see radial brick. →16
beam brick, see lintel brick. →16
birdsmouth brick. →16
blue brick, see Staffordshire Blue brick.
bonder.
bonding brick. →21
building brick, see brick. →16
bullhead brick, see cownose brick. →16
bullnose brick. →16
burnt brick, see fired brick. →16
calcium silicate brick.
cant brick. →16
capping brick. →16
cavity brick, see hollow brick. →16
channel brick, see lintel brick. →16
clay brick. →16
common brick. →16
concrete brick. →30
coping brick. →16
cored brick, see perforated brick. →16
cove brick. →16
cownose brick. →16
cuboid brick. →16
cut brick. →21
dogleg brick.
engineering brick.
facing brick, face brick.
firebrick. →56
fired brick. →16
fireproof brick, see flue block, firebrick. →16, →55, →56
flared brick.
flint-lime brick.
flue brick, see flue block. →16
frogged brick. →16
full brick. →21
glass brick, see glass block. →30, →53
glazed brick.
great brick.
green brick.
handmade brick.
hollow brick. →16
imperial standard brick. →16
later. →83
lintel brick. →16
metric brick, see modular standard brick. →16
metric modular brick, see modular standard brick. →16
metric standard brick. →16
modular brick. →16
modular standard brick. →16
mud brick.
paving brick, paviour brick. →15
perforated brick. →16
plinth brick. →16
pre-chased brick. →16
pressed brick.
purpose made brick. →16
radial brick. →16
red brick.
refractory brick, see firebrick. →56
Roman brick. →83
rusticated brick, rustic brick.
saddleback capping brick. →16
saddleback coping brick. →16
sand-faced brick.
sand-lime brick, see calcium silicate brick.
solid brick. →16
special brick, special shape brick. →16
split face brick.
squint brick. →16
Staffordshire blue brick.
standard brick. →16
standard modular brick, see metric brick. →16
standard special brick, see special brick.
sun-baked brick, sun-dried brick, see mud brick.
tax brick.
three quarter brick, see king closer. →21
US standard brick. →16
ventilating brick, see air brick. →16
whole brick, see full brick. →21
wirecut brick.
wooden brick, see nog.
brick-and-a-half wall, one-and-a-half brick wall; a solid bonded brick wall whose width is the sum of the length and width of one standard brick plus one intermediate joint, 13" or 327 mm. →21
brick arch 1 any masonry arch laid with bricks. →23
2 see rough brick arch. →23
3 see gauged arch. →23
see *true arches* illustration. →24
see *flat, false and decorative arches* illustration. →23
see *arched and vaulted construction* illustration. →22
brick architecture architecture in which unrendered brickwork is the principal structural, expressive or decorative material.
brick axe see bricklayer's hammer. →40
brickbat see bat. →21
brick beam see reinforced brick lintel. →22
brick bond see brickwork bond.

brick capping 1 the uppermost protective course of capping bricks in a freestanding wall or parapet. →16
2 see capping brick. →16

brick coping 1 the uppermost protective course of coping bricks in a freestanding wall or parapet. →16
2 see coping brick. →16

brick clay see brick earth.

brick column a structural column laid in bonded brickwork. →21

brick course a single row of bricks forming a horizontal band in a wall. →20

brick earth, brick clay; clay suitable for use in the manufacture of bricks.

brick facing, brick veneer; a skin of non-structural brickwork attached to a structural base such as concrete, masonry or, in some cases, studwork.

brick factory see brickworks.

brick Gothic, Backsteingotik; Gothic architecture in northern Germany and the Baltic states in the 1400s, with the slender stone forms of western and central European Gothic interpreted in simplified form in the local material, brick.
see *medieval capitals* illustration. →115

brick hammer see bricklayer's hammer. →40

brickie a colloquial name for a bricklayer.

brick joint 1 any joint between adjacent bricks in masonry. →20
2 the final shaped mortar in horizontal bed and vertical joints after the bricks have been laid; see *types of brickwork joint* illustration. →16

bricklayer, brickie; a tradesman or skilled worker who lays bricks and blocks on a construction site.

bricklayer's hammer, brick axe, brick hammer; a light hammer used in bricklaying for shaping and chipping bricks and concrete blocks; its head has one chiselled end for cutting and one flat face or peen for tapping into place. →40

bricklayer's line, builder's line, stringline; a length of fine cord strung between two points on a building site to establish the line and level of prospective construction, as an aid in bricklaying and setting out etc.

bricklayer's trowel, brick trowel, mason's trowel, masonry trowel; a steel-bladed hand tool used in bricklaying for applying and smoothing bedding and jointing mortar. →43

brick lintel see reinforced brick lintel.

brick nogging in traditional half-timbered construction, brick infill for the timber frame.

brick on bed see brick on flat. →20

brick on edge in brickwork, a brick laid on its side so as to leave either its shorter edge or its bed showing in the masonry surface; either a rowlock or shiner. →20

brick-on-edge coping coping for a freestanding wall formed from a row of bricks laid on edge, usually across the thickness of the wall as rowlocks.

brick-on-edge paving see brick paving. →15

brick on end in brickwork, a brick laid on its end, either to leave the longer edge or the bed showing vertically; see soldier, sailor. →20

brick-on-end paving see brick paving. →15

brick on flat, brick on bed; a brick laid on its largest side, in the way intended. →20

brick paving 1 bricks laid side by side in a horizontal plane as a hardwearing external paved surface. →15
2 brick-on-edge paving paving of bricks laid in series with sides upwards. →15
3 brick-on-end paving paving of bricks laid in series with ends upwards. →15

brick pier 1 a bonded vertical projection or thickening in a long or high brick wall to provide support and stability. →21
2 see brick column. →21

brick pillar see brick column. →21

brick red, terracotta, tile red; a shade of reddish brown which takes its name from the colour of burnt clay which contains iron oxide.

brick sizes see standard brick. →16

brick slip a thin cladding brick or brick-shaped tile of the same material and finish as the surrounding brick masonry, used for facing lintels, beams etc.; often a brick cladding tile.
see *brickwork* illustration. →21
see *arched construction* illustration. →22

brick tile a clay wall tile used as a facing for concrete and other materials in imitation of brick. →21

brick trowel see bricklayer's trowel. →43

brick veneer see brick facing.

brick wall a wall laid from bricks bedded in mortar, or one having the appearance of this.
see *Roman walling* illustration. →83
see *brickwork* illustrations. →20, →21

brickwork any construction in bricks laid with a binder such as mortar; types included as separate entries are listed below. →20
see *brickwork* illustrations. →20, →21
see *outer leaf brickwork* in brick house illustration. →59
carved brickwork.
chequered brickwork.
coloured brickwork, see polychrome brickwork.
dogtooth brickwork. →20
fair-face brickwork.
gauged brickwork.
herringbone brickwork. →17
honeycomb brickwork. →17
houndstooth brickwork, see dogtooth brickwork. →20
loadbearing brickwork.
moulded brickwork.
mousetooth brickwork, see dogtooth brickwork. →20
ornamental brickwork, see decorative masonry.
patterned brickwork.
polychrome brickwork.
rendered brickwork.
rubbed brickwork, see gauged brickwork.
structural brickwork.

brickwork bond the overlapping and interlocking of bricks laid in mortar in successive courses to provide strength and for decorative effects.
1 see various types of *brickwork bond* illustration. →17
2 see variations of *Flemish bond* illustration. →18
3 see variations of *English and Flemish double-stretcher bond* illustration. →19

brickwork joint see brick joint. →20

brickworks an industrial plant for the production and firing of bricks.

brickwork weathering, exfoliation, flaking; the degradation and scaling of a brickwork surface over time due to exposure to the elements and chemical reaction with the cement, causing internal swelling and rupture.

Bride's cross St Bride's cross, see St Bridget's cross. →117

bridge a construction built between two points of support over an obstacle or ravine to enable passage of a road, railway or pathway; types included as separate entries are listed below.
see *bridge types* illustrations. →32, →64
access bridge, see walkway.
arch bridge, arched bridge. →32
Bailey bridge.
bascule bridge, balance bridge. →64
beam bridge, see continuous beam bridge. →32
bowed bridge, see cambered bridge. →32
bowstring bridge. →32
box girder bridge.
cable-stayed bridge.
cambered bridge. →32
cantilever bridge.
chain bridge.
closed spandrel bridge, see solid spandrel bridge. →32
continuous bridge, see continuous span bridge. →32
counterbalanced bridge, counterpoise bridge, see bascule bridge. →64
curved bridge. →64
drawbridge. →103

ferry bridge. →64
floating bridge.
footbridge. →64
frame bridge, see portal frame bridge. →32
girder bridge.
horizontal bridge. →32
humpback bridge, hump bridge. →32
Irish bridge.
king post bridge. →32
lattice girder bridge.
lift bridge. →64
link bridge.
movable bridge. →64
multiple span bridge. →32
open spandrel bridge. →32
overbridge. →64
pedestrian bridge, see footbridge. →64
pivot bridge, see swing bridge. →64
pontoon bridge, see floating bridge.
portal frame bridge, portal bridge. →32
queen post bridge. →32
railway bridge, rail bridge. →64
retractable bridge. →64
rigid frame bridge, see portal frame bridge. →32
road bridge. →64
rope bridge.
single span bridge, simple span bridge. →32
skew bridge. →64
slab bridge. →32
sloping bridge. →32
solid spandrel bridge. →32
span bridge, see single span bridge. →32
spandrel braced arch bridge. →32
stayed bridge, see cable-stayed bridge. →32
straight bridge. →64
suspension bridge.
swing bridge, swivel bridge.
through bridge.
traversing bridge, see retractable bridge. →64
trussed arch bridge. →32
trussed bridge.
turn bridge, see swing bridge. →64
underbridge. →64
viaduct. →32
waterway bridge. →64

bridge abutment in bridge construction, a retaining mass of earth or masonry to provide support for the extremities of a bridge at either end, and on which a ramp is often constructed. →31, →64

bridge balustrade see bridge parapet. →31

bridge bearing in bridge construction, a structural component which transfers the loading of a superstructure or deck onto vertical supports such as foundations, piers, piles or supports, allowing for movement, expansion etc. →31

bridge cap in bridge construction, the upper surface of a pier or abutment, on which bearings supporting the deck superstructure are located; also called a bridge seat, bearing seat or bridge pad. →31

bridge deck in bridge construction, the structural slab-like base or flooring superstructure which supports traffic and transfers loads to the substructure. →31, →32

bridge pad see bridge cap. →31

bridge parapet in bridge construction, a low wall, railing or protective fence for the deck of a bridge. →31

bridge pier in bridge construction, a vertical intermediate support for the spans of a bridge. →31

bridge pylon see pylon. →32

bridge seat see bridge cap. →31

bridge structure the various parts and systems which serve to support a bridge.
see *bridge structure* illustration. →31

bridge substructure that part of the structure of a bridge below the bridge deck, which supports it. →32

bridge superstructure the structural parts of a bridge supported by its piers and buttresses. →31, →32

bridge suspender in bridge construction, one of a number of vertical supporting cables in a suspension bridge, also called a hanger. →32

Bridget cross see St Bridget's cross. →117

bridge tower see pylon. →32

bridge type the classification of bridges according to structural system, material, mode of transport, form, use etc.
see *bridge types by structure* illustration. →32
see *bridge types by function* illustration. →64

bridging joist, binder; a main spanning beam in a timber floor, which supports floor joists.

bridled scarf joint a timber lengthening joint formed by cutting a tenon at the end of one member; this sits in a bridle or open housing or slot cut into the end of the other. →3

bridle joint a timber angle joint in which the end of one timber is cut with a groove or slot to fit into a suitably shaped cutting in the side of another; sometimes called an open tenon joint if at a corner. →5
see double tenon joint. →5

bridle path a bridleway.

bridle road a bridleway.

bridleway, bridle path, bridle road, driftway, droveway, packway; a rural or outlying route, road or track used by horses, people and agricultural vehicles.

brief, 1 programme; in the commissioning of a building project, a statement of the client's requirements which includes the scope of works, usage, number and floor area of spaces and functional requirements.
2 competition brief.

brightness in colour theory, an objective measure of the apparent luminance of a colour; pure white is the brightest, pure black the least bright.

bright timber commercial sawn timber with no defects in colouration or from staining.

brilliant a finely cut diamond.

brilliant green a strong, clear shade of the colour green.

brilliant yellow see Naples yellow.

brise soleil a window louvre.

bristle one of the hairs, fine strands or wires in a brush.

Bristol board smooth paper-faced card available in a range of thicknesses, used in printing, drawing and modelmaking.

British Columbia cedar [*Thuja plicata*] see western red cedar.

British Columbian pine see Douglas fir.

British Standard Whitworth thread see Whitworth thread.

British thermal unit an imperial unit of energy, 1 Btu is equal to 1055.06 joules.

British zonal system, BZ system; in lighting design, a system for classifying luminaires according to their luminous intensity distribution.

brittleness the property of a material or object to break suddenly under loading without appreciable deformation.

brittle point the highest temperature at which a rubber material or elastomer loses its elasticity and will fracture under sudden impact.

broach a narrow-bladed masonry chisel used for working stone surfaces. →41

broached hip see half hipped end.

broach stop, pyramid stop; in ornamentation, the termination of a chamfered moulding or carving with a protruding half-pyramid.

broadfoot a cross with a thickening at the base of its vertical shaft.

broad-leaf any non-coniferous tree, which may be deciduous or evergreen, from which hardwood is obtained; a member of the angiosperm group; see **hardwood** for a list of tropical and European hardwood trees.

broad tool see batting tool. →41

broad tooled finish see batted finish. →12

broadside a sheet of paper printed on one side only.

broch a prehistoric Scottish fortified tower dwelling, round in plan and with a tapering profile, constructed of drystone masonry in cellular construction; alternative spellings are brough and brugh. →65

broken-apex pediment see open pediment. →112

broken-bed pediment see broken pediment. →112

broken colour in paint and colour science, a base colour to which a small amount of another colour has been mixed to add subtlety.

broken cross a leaning Latin cross motif whose lower limb is broken, symbolic of the death of Christ; also known as an angle cross, chevron cross, cross of suffering. →118

broken curtain a curtain wall linking two bastions in a fortification, and formed of two sections of walling at an angle to one another. →103

broken line see dashed line.

broken pediment, 1 broken-bed pediment, open-bed pediment; in Neoclassical and Baroque architecture, a pediment in which the base has a central opening. →112

2 a broken-apex pediment, see open pediment. →112

3 see broken segmental pediment. →112

broken segmental pediment a segmental pediment whose base has a central opening. →112

broken white see off-white.

brominated anthranthrone a bright semi-transparent yellow pigment used in the automotive industry.

bromine a dark reddish toxic chemical element, **Br**, used in the manufacture of dyes, synthetic rubbers etc.

bromine butyl rubber, BIIR; a tough synthetic rubber, butyl with a halogen, used for car tyres, seals and hoses, cured more easily and readily than butyl, and thus more suitable for use with other rubbers.

bronze 1 a hard, dark brown alloy of copper and tin which is resistant to corrosion; copper alloys with other metals, such as aluminium, magnesium and silicon are also given the name bronze.

2 see tin bronze.

3 bronze brown; a shade of dark brown which takes its name from the above.

Bronze Age a period in the ancient and prehistoric cultures of the Near East and Europe from 3500 to 800 BC during which forging technology for rudimentary implements etc. in bronze was first developed, running concurrently with the Stone Age.

bronze blue Prussian blue pigment which has a bronze sheen.

bronze brown see bronze.

bronze green a shade of dark grey green which takes its name from the colour of tarnished or oxidized bronze.

bronze plating see bronzing.

bronze red see blood red.

bronzing, 1 bronze plating; the application of a protective or decorative coating of bronze to metals.

2 the treatment of a copper surface with chemicals to alter its colour.

broom dyer's broom, see genet.

broom cupboard, cleaning cupboard; a closet, cupboard unit or small room in which cleaning equipment such as vacuum cleaners, mops etc. is kept.

broomed finish see brushed finish.

brooming see brushing.

brotch, spar, spick, spike, staple; a fastener for bundles of thatched roofing made of a willow or hazel branch bent into a hook-shape and pushed into underlying construction. →48

brough see broch. →65

brown a general name for shades of darkened yellow and dusky orange colour, not evident in the visible spectrum; see list of brown pigments below.

alizarin brown.
asphaltum.
bistre, bister.
brown lampblack, see bistre.
brown madder, see alizarin brown.
brown ochre.
burnt sienna.
Cassel earth.
Cologne earth, see Cassel earth.
Egyptian brown, see mummy.
iron brown, see Prussian brown.
madder brown, see alizarin brown.
Mars brown.
mummy.
Prussian brown.
Rubens brown.
sepia.
sienna.
umber, umbre.
Vandyke brown.

brown cement see Roman cement.

brown coal see lignite.

brown coat see base coat.

browning coat originally plaster which is brown in colour, see base coat, browning plaster.

browning plaster plaster used for undercoats, made from gypsum and sand and used in instances where the base has a good key and adhesion.

brownish red see blood red.

brown iron ore see limonite.

brown iron oxide see burnt sienna.

brown lampblack see bistre.

brown madder see alizarin brown.

brown millerite mineral oxides of calcium, iron and aluminium oxides found in sulphate-resistant cements.

brown ochre a dull brownish yellow form of the native pigment ochre.

brown pigments see list of brown pigments under 'brown'.

brown rot a general term for fungal decay which attacks cellulose in timber leaving a brown powdery residue.

brown rot fungus a large group of fungi which attack the cellulose of dead wood to leave the brown lignin, causing serious decay and weakening of timber construction.

brown spruce longhorn [*Tetropium fuscum*], see spruce beetle.

brugh see broch. →65

bruised lath in ornamental plasterwork, timber laths which have been softened, or whose surface has been broken by striking with a hammer to provide a key for a plaster coating.

Brunswick blue a form of the blue pigment Prussian blue to which barytes has been added.

brush 1 a sweeping, cleaning and scouring implement consisting of a number of stiff fibrous bristles fixed into a head.

2 a similar implement with a clump of soft fibres or hairs bound to a wooden or plastic handle, used for applying paint, glue and other liquids to a surface.

3 see *paintbrushes* entry (for list of brushes) and illustration. →43

brushed finish, broomed finish; a decorative or non-slip finish texture produced by scouring or scrubbing the surface of fresh concrete or plaster with a stiff broom.

brushing, 1 brooming; a surface treatment for fresh concrete and plaster produced by scoring with a stiff brush, either as decoration or to provide a rough finish.

2 the application of paints, coatings, adhesives etc. manually, with a brush.

brushing adhesive types of adhesive which can be applied in liquid form with a brush.

brushwood in landscaping, dried branches which have fallen or been pruned from trees.

Brutalism, 1 New Brutalism; a modern architectural style in Europe from the 1950s and 1960s, characterized by lack of decoration, expression of structure, and use of modern materials such as glass, steel and board-marked concrete.

2 see futurism.

bruzz chisel, corner chisel, dogleg chisel, parting chisel; a woodcarving chisel whose blade is V-shaped in section. →41

BSW thread acronym for British Standard Whitworth thread; see Whitworth thread.

bubble, bubbling; a defect in a paint finish consisting of trapped bubbles of gas in the hardened paint film, often caused by careless application or by the use of volatile solvents in the paint mix.

bubbling see bubble.

buck a fixing member at the side of a doorway or window opening to receive a door or window and fasten it in place. →6

door buck, see door lining.

bucket-handled joint see keyed joint. →16

bucket sink, cleaner's sink; a wide low-level sink used by a cleaner for emptying and filling buckets, rinsing cleaning implements etc.

buckling 1 in structures, the sudden creasing failure by crumpling of a longitudinal structural member loaded eccentrically with a compressive force.

2 the creasing of sheetmetal and other sheet products due to lateral forces, defects, impact etc.

buckling load the compressive load at which a column or strut begins to buckle.

bucrane see bucranium. →122

bucranium, bucrane; Lat.; carved decorative motif depicting the skull of a bull, found in classical architecture; Greek form is boukranion. →122

bud a common motif in ancient ornamentation, a stylized depiction of a closed flower bud. →82

bud and blossom Egyptian painted ornamental banding depicting stylized open flowers alternating with closed flower buds. →82

bud capital, closed bud capital, closed capital; an Egyptian capital carved in stylized imitation of the closed flower of the lotus or papyrus plant. →73

see papyrus capital. →73

Buddha's navel a Buddhist symbol of the universe, an omphalos or tomoye. →120

Buddhist temple see *Japanese temple precinct* illustration. →68

budget 1 a sum of money allocated for a particular purpose.

2 a financial plan presented as itemized sums of money.

buffer 1 any device that cushions the effect of an impact or provides protection from the collision of moving objects, as installed on vehicle loading bays, trains, lifts and behind heavy doors.

see door buffer. →51

see car buffer.

see fender.

2 in computing, a temporary information storage area or intermediate memory used during data transfers between devices that are working at different speeds.

3 a machine tool with a rotating disc of wool or cotton fabric, used for polishing floors and other surfaces.

buffet see sideboard.

bug in computing, an error in a computer program which may cause it to continually misfunction.

bug hole see blow-hole.

bugle head screw a screw with a trumpet-shaped head containing a cross, allen or torx slot in its flat end. →36

buildability the ability of a construction to be assembled on site without undue difficulty.

builder see contractor.

builder's see building firm.

builder's lift a temporary lift used on a building site, consisting of a moving cage in which workmen, goods etc. can pass rapidly between levels of a building under construction or repair.

builder's line see bricklayer's line.

builder's pencil see carpenter's pencil. →130

building 1 any permanent structure which provides shelter, encloses space and can be occupied by people, animals, goods or services.

2 the process or product of assembly of elements, components, materials and finishes on a building site; also generally known as construction, building development or building construction to differentiate it from other forms of construction.

building and loan association a building society.

building automation see building management system.

building ban a local authority notice preventing the construction of a building or buildings on a particular site.

building block 1 any mineral-based unit designed for use in construction; larger than a brick; usually simply called a block.

2 see concrete block. →30

3 see hollow clay block. →16

4 see glass block.

5 paving block, see concrete block paver. →15

building board any rigid sheet material of timber, mineral fibre, plastics, gypsum etc. used in construction for cladding and lining frames as a surface for a finish, as insulation or as bracing. →9, →59

see *timber-based building boards* illustration. →9

building brick see brick. →16

building by-laws locally varying regulations controlling the construction and erection of buildings administered by local authorities on the basis of model by-laws provided by government.

building code see building regulations.

building codes of practice legal documentation setting out requirements to protect public health and safety, and outlining standards of good practice with regard to the construction and occupancy of buildings.

building component a prefabricated assemblage of parts or product such as a door or window assembly, technical utility etc. supplied ready for installation on site.

building conservation see conservation.

building construction the discipline, process etc. of constructing buildings; matters pertaining to this.

building contract an agreement by which a building contractor is committed to construct a building, carry out building works etc. for a certain price within a certain time and to documented designs.

building contractor see contractor.

building control, building inspection; the process of inspection, issuing permits, granting approval etc. pertaining to buildings under construction and repair, administered by a local authority to ensure that they are properly constructed.

building control officer, building inspector; a person, often employed by a local authority, who inspects designs and constructions to ensure they comply with standards and regulations.

building cost, construction cost; a cost incurred as a result of building development, usually plural.

building development see development.

building element any major functioning part of, or structural assembly in, a building, such as roof, floor, walls, beams, slabs or foundations; often made up of building components. →28

building envelope, external envelope, envelope; the external roof and wall components and constructions of a building which protect the interior from the effects of temperature and the weather.

building firm, builder's; a private firm which provides a building service; usually a small or family business.

building floodlighting the aesthetic use of electric lighting to highlight external features of buildings and their elevations in the dark.

building frame 1 the loadbearing elements, columns, slabs, beams, walls and foundations in a building; often simply referred to as a frame.
2 see timber frame. →57
3 see steel frame.
4 see concrete frame. →28, →60

building group, complex, scheme; a cluster of linked or physically attached buildings serving an associated function.

building industry, construction industry; the industry of manufacturing, production, design, administration and construction involved in the erection of buildings.

building inspection 1 a periodic checking on site by a local authority official to ensure that parts of a building have been constructed according to regulations, by-laws etc.
2 the detailed surveying of a building in use to ascertain its general condition, whether it has any particular faults and is in need of remedial work.
3 see building control.

building inspector see building control officer.

building line an agreed-upon boundary line for the area occupied by a proposed building or indicating how close to a site boundary, public land etc. a building may be constructed, usually determined by the local authority.

building maintenance the act of looking after, servicing and cleaning property regularly.

building maintenance company a firm responsible for building maintenance.

building management system, building automation, bms; an automated computer-based system for controlling the mechanical services and security installations in a building.

building material any basic substance, raw or manufactured material, product etc. used in the construction of buildings.

building moisture extraneous water which builds up within the construction and structure of a building due to occupation or faulty design and construction.

building owner a person or organization which owns the title to a building.

building paper, 1 kraft paper; thick paper or card laminated with an infill of waterproofing material such as bitumen, used in the construction of roofs, floors and walls as a moisture barrier. →8
2 see breather paper.

building permission see planning permission.

building permit formal approval in written form by a local authority to an application for planning permission.

building preservation an action by a planning authority to maintain a building of certain historical or cultural value in its current state, preventing alteration or demolition.

building product any item used in construction which has been manufactured in a factory prior to delivery on site.

building project, development; the preliminary arrangements, administration, funding and construction work undertaken during the realization of a particular building or structure, viewed as a whole.

building regulation a statutory code which regulates the construction, alteration, maintenance, repair, and demolition of buildings and structures.

building regulations a series of laws which control the layout, safety, health, materials and fire regulations in buildings; in Britain called the Building Regulations, in the US and Australia the Uniform Building Code.

building sealant see sealant. →53

building site, construction site, site; the area of land on which excavation work, building construction, storage of materials and plant etc. for a particular building project take place.

building society, building and loan association; a financial association or establishment which grants long-term loans for building or buying property by using the property as security.

building stock the existing buildings and structures in a particular area or ownership.

building stone natural stone used in building construction for walling, cladding, paving etc.

building survey an inspection of a property, usually undertaken by a professional prior to being bought or sold, to ascertain its general condition and prospective repair work.

building surveyor a professional who inspects and reports on the condition of existing buildings and carries out building surveys.

building technology see construction technology.

building type the categorization of buildings according to any of a range of criteria such as function, type of heating system, number of stories etc.

building volume see gross building volume.

built environment, environment; an urban or rural milieu, structured or produced by built form; that part of the surroundings relating to buildings, structures and civil engineering works.

built-in cupboard, closet; a cupboard fixed in place so as to appear or function as an integral part of a space. →57

built-up area in town planning, a relatively densely populated area occupied by buildings, in which street lighting and other municipal services are required.

built-up beam in timber construction, a beam made from more than one timber fixed together by bolts or splices to provide greater bearing capacity. →7

built-up column a column or post made up of more than one vertical member fixed together for improved strength.

built-up felt roofing see built-up roofing. →49

built-up roofing, built-up felt roofing; roofing constructed of a number of layers of bitumen felt, laid in succession with overlapping joints, usually used for flat roofs. →49

bulb 1 that part of an electric lamp, usually of thin transparent or translucent glass, which contains the gas, vapour or filament from which light is emitted.
2 see lightbulb.

bulbous dome see onion dome. →26

buleuterion see bouleuterion. →92

buleuterium Lat.; see bouleuterion. →92

bulk density the weight per unit volume of a loose material, measured in kg/m^3; usually used in conjunction with non-homogeneous materials such as concrete or piled timber which contain voids or water pockets.

bulk heater a device in an oil heating installation for warming oil to reduce viscosity prior to use.

bulk zoning a method of subdividing a city or town into districts where specified uses are authorized and bulk requirements are imposed.

bull, ox; a male bovine animal (*Bos taurus*), depicted in symbolic art and ornament to represent patience and good will; when shown with wings it is the attribute of St Luke. →119

bull capital an ornamental stone capital carved with a paired bull's head motif, especially found in the apadanas of ancient Persian architecture. →69

bulldog plate see toothed plate connector. →35

bullet catch see ball catch. →39

bullet-head nail see lost-head nail. →35
bullet-resistant laminated glass, armour-plated glass; glass that can withstand the penetration of gunfire, usually formed from several sheets of glass laminated together with resin. →53
bull-faced finish hammer-dressed finish. →12
bull header see rowlock. →20
bull header course see rowlock course. →20
bullion, 1 bullion glass, bull's-eye glass; a traditional form of glass with a central circular bulge, formed by rotating a clod of molten glass via its centre.
2 the central bulge so formed.
bullion glass see bullion.
bullhead brick see cownose brick. →16
bullnose a rounded external edge. →14
bullnose brick 1 any special brick with one or more rounded edges; used for decorative brickwork, paving etc. →16
2 see cownose brick. →16
bullseye 1 a small traditional round window or light glazed with crown or bullion glass.
2 any small round window in general.
bull's-eye glass see bullion.
bull stretcher see shiner. →20
bull stretcher course see shiner course. →20
Bulnesia arborea see verawood.
bulwark a low defensive rampart or fortification in a castle, especially an earthwork in polygonal or semicircular plan; originally one of logs. →103
bumper door bumper, see door stop. →51
bunch, shove; a bundle of Norfolk reed used as a basic roofing material in thatching; see also nitch.
bunched cabling electric or telecommunications cables installed together in tied groups.
bundle see bundled bars.
bundle column 1 a group of Egyptian column types with shafts carved to resemble bunches of tied plant stems, named according to the plant in question. →73
see papyrus column. →73
2 a stone column type in Gothic, Romanesque and Renaissance architecture with a shaft carved into a number of stems, as if of separate smaller columns, terminating at a capital; modern equivalents of this. →114
3 see compound pier. →13, →101
bundled bars, bundle; in reinforced concretework, a group of reinforcing bars tied together in a bundle with wire, which act as one larger bar.
bundle pier a Gothic compound pier with a large number of shafts. →13, →101
bundling in reinforced concrete, the placing of a number of reinforcing bars tied side by side with wire to act as a larger bar.
bungalow any one-storey detached dwelling house, originally a Hindi dwelling in Bengal, India. →61
bunk, cot; a rudimentary bed, bench, hammock or other platform for sleeping on.
bunker a fortified construction, usually underground, for the protection of people and equipment during conflict.
buon affresco see buon fresco.
buon fresco, true fresco, buon affresco; a form of mural painting in which mineral or earth pigments are applied to lime or gypsum plaster while it is still wet; see in reference to fresco secco.
buoyancy 1 the tendency of a body immersed in a denser liquid to float.
2 the force thus exerted, which moves the body towards the surface and causing it to float.
buprestid beetle see metallic wood borer.
Buprestis spp. see metallic wood borer.
bureau a piece of furniture with a folding down lid and set of drawers, used as a writing table.
bureaucracy a central, hierarchical, public administrative organization.
burg a medieval fortress town.
burgh, burh; a town in Scotland which holds a charter, a borough.
burglary the unlawful breaking into premises with intent to commit theft.
Burgundy a shade of dark red which takes its name from the colour of wines produced in the Burgundy district of France.
Burgundy cross a cross formed by two overlapping diagonal branch motifs. →118
Burgundy violet see manganese violet.
burgus Lat.; a Roman watchtower connected to a defensive wall. →104
burh see burgh.
burial chamber, funerary chamber, tomb; a prehistoric or ancient funerary chamber in which the dead were interred, often containing collective graves and the symbolic effects of the deceased.
see *prehistoric structures* illustration. →65
see *mastaba and pyramid* illustration. →70
see *altar* illustration. →116
see *Egyptian rock-cut tomb* illustration. →74
burial chapel a funerary chapel, usually an ancient or historical one. →102
burial ground any area for the burial of the dead, a graveyard.
burial mound, grave mound; a prehistoric mound or hillock constructed over a burial place as an indication of the site of an interment; a barrow or tumulus. →65
burial place see burial site.
burial site, burial place; a place containing a grave, tomb or funerary remains.
burial tower see tower tomb. →93
burial urn see cinerary urn.
burin, graver; a small wooden-handled implement for making intricate cuts on wood or metal consisting of a metal shaft with a sharp pyramid-pointed end.
burl, burr, knur, knurl; a growth deformity in a tree which, when cut as timber, is valued for its decorative figure in veneer, furniture and turnery.
burlap see hessian.
burlesque a form of humorous, mock-serious or derisive art, theatre or literary work.
burl veneer, burr veneer; decorative veneer with mottled or wavy figure, cut from the burl of a tree.
burner a device or chamber where the oil or gas fuel for a heating or lighting system is burned.
burning off in landscaping and forestry, the destruction of surface growth with fire to encourage new growth, kill weeds and unwanted roots etc.
burnishing the polishing of a metal surface by rubbing.
burnt brick see fired brick. →16
burnt carmine see roasted carmine.
burnt lime see quicklime.
burnt sienna, Italian earth, natural brown iron oxide; a rich orange-brown native pigment, sienna, crushed and calcined in a furnace; one of the most used pigments.
burnt umber, 1 jacaranda brown, mineral brown, Spanish brown; raw umber heated in a kiln to form an orange-brown native pigment.
2 see Vandyke brown.
burr see burl.
see grinding burr. →42
burr veneer see burl veneer.
bursting see rock burst.
bus in traffic planning, a motor vehicle capable of conveying a large number of people, often on prescribed routes, with designated stopping places.
bus bay in traffic planning, a short splayed widening in a road for buses to pull into from the main carriageway to pick up and unload passengers. →63
bush 1 in drainage and plumbing, a short piece of pipe or pipe fitting for joining lengths of pipe with

different diameters, threaded internally at one end and externally at the other.
2 reducing bush, see socket reducer.

bushel, 1 imperial bushel; a traditional measure of dry and liquid capacity in Britain equal to 8 imperial gallons or 36.4 litres.
2 Winchester bushel; a measure of dry capacity in the US which derives from an ancient English equivalent, equal to 4 pecks, 32 dry quarts or 35.2 litres.

bush hammer a machine or hand tool for producing a textured finish on the surface of stonework and hardened concrete; a hand-held bush hammer is often called a bouchard or boucharde. →40

bush-hammered a relatively even pitted finish for concrete or stone in which the surface has been worked with a bush hammer. →12

business see company.

business centre see commercial centre.

businessman a person who is involved in commercial enterprise, a trader, entrepreneur or self-employed person; more correctly called a businessperson.

business park a group of buildings with parking, set in parkland or on another designated area, for business and the manufacture of products.

busk a plastering hand tool consisting of a flexible steel sheet, used for removing excess hardened plaster.

bus lane a lane in a vehicular road reserved for the permanent or occasional use of bus traffic.

bus station, bus terminal; a building or complex where buses stop, begin and end their journeys.

bus stop, coach stop; a marked area of road, often inset from the main carriageway and with a shelter, at which buses and coaches make predesignated timetabled stops.

busta plural form of bustum (Lat.).

bus terminal see bus station.

bustum, plural busta; Lat.; a Roman wall enclosing an area used for cremations and the storage of cinerary urns.

butadiene rubber, BR, polybutadiene; a synthetic resilient rubber with many uses, including car tyres, made from butadiene, a gaseous unsaturated hydrocarbon.

butane see commercial butane.

butsuden see kondo. →68

butt chisel, pocket chisel, sash chisel; a chisel with a short, wide blade. →41

butt-edged boarding see square-edged boarding. →8

butter yellow a shade of pale yellow which takes its name from the colour of butter, especially that churned in the summer months.

buttercup yellow, 1 sunflower (yellow); a shade of bright yellow which takes its name from the blossom of the buttercup (*Ranunculus spp.*) or that of the sunflower (*Helianthus annuus*).
2 see zinc yellow.

butterfly blue a shade of pale blue which takes its name from the coloured wings of certain butterflies [*Plebejus argus*, *Polyommatus amandus*].

butterfly damper a flue damper with paired winged flaps which are folded back in their normal open position, and spring flat to close off a duct or flue.

butterfly head screw see one-way head screw. →36

butterfly hinge a hinge with two decorative leaves fixed to a central knuckle, resembling a butterfly or bow-tie when opened out. →38

butterfly nut see wing nut. →37

butterfly roof, Y-form roof; a roof form in which two sloping planes rise outwards and upwards from a central gutter. →46

butterfly tie see butterfly wall tie. →22

butterfly toggle see spring toggle. →37

butterfly wall tie a galvanized steel wire wall tie twisted into a figure '8' shape. →22

buttering 1 the smearing of mortar onto the underside and end of a brick or block before laying into masonry.
2 mortar smeared especially on the header of a brick before laying, which forms a vertical joint or perpend in the finished wall.

butternut, white walnut; [*Juglans cinerea*] a North American hardwood with pale brown timber; used for decorative veneers.

butt gauge see marking gauge.

butt hinge a hinge with two rectangular metal leaves and a central joining pin, usually inset into the edge of a door leaf and its frame; types included as separate entries are listed below. →38
ball-bearing hinge, ball-bearing butt hinge. →38
falling-butt hinge. →38
lift-off butt hinge, lift-off hinge. →38
loose butt hinge, see lift-off butt hinge. →38
loose pin butt hinge, loose pin hinge. →38
loose-joint hinge, loose-joint butt hinge.
non-mortised hinge, non-mortised butt hinge. →38
hinge, see loose pin butt hinge. →38
rising hinge, rising-butt hinge. →38

butt joint, 1 the joint or seam made by the edges of two components or sheets situated side by side without overlapping.
2 end joint; a weak joint between two long members joined end on end without lapping or interlocking. →3

butt match 1 a bookmatched veneering pattern in which adjacent sheets are mirrored vertically. →10
2 see vertical butt and horizontal bookmatching. →10

button, 1 turn button; a simple catch consisting of a piece of stiff material fixed with a pivot to the inside of a door or exterior door frame, and which rotates to keep the door closed.
2 see push button.

buttonwood see American plane.

butt purlin, tenon purlin, tenoned purlin; in timber roof construction, a purlin that is tenoned into the side of principal rafters.

buttress 1 a vertical rib or mass of masonry, concrete etc. to provide lateral support and stability to a wall, tower etc.; sometimes called a counterfort.
see *ziggurat* illustration. →67
see *Gothic cathedral* illustration. →100
see *Scandinavian hall church* illustration. →102
2 see block pillar. →102
3 see flying buttress. →100
4 see counterfort.
5 see pier. →21

buttress wall see counterfort wall. →29

butt rot see annosus root rot.

butt tenon joint see abutting tenon joint. →5

butt veneer a decorative veneer with a distorted figure, cut from the stump of a tree.

butt weld a welded joint between abutting metal components. →34

butt welding, resistance butt welding; a method of resistance welding metal bars, wire or rods end to end by pressing them together and passing a current through them.

butyl 1 an isomeric form of the chemical butylene; a tough synthetic rubber used for sealing, roofing and in paints.
2 see bromine butyl rubber.

Buxus sempervirens see boxwood.

buzzer see door transmitter.

by-altar see side altar. →95, →96, →98, →99

by-law see building by-laws.

byobu a folding screen used as a room divider in Japanese architecture.

bypass a road designed to divert through traffic round a congested or built-up area.

by-product any substance, often useful waste, detritus, sediment etc., which occurs as a result of a manufacturing or production process.

byre a traditional cowshed.

byte in computing, a series of eight binary digits, ones and zeros, treated as a unit.

Byzantine architecture, Italian Romanesque; architecture of Byzantium or the Eastern Roman Empire originating in c.400 AD, characterized by the round arch, the circle in plan, the dome and work in mosaic.
see *Byzantine centralized church* illustration. →95
see *Byzantine domical church* illustration. →96
see *column styles in European architecture* illustration. →114
see *medieval capitals* illustration. →115

Byzantine purple see Byzantium purple.

Byzantine revival a revival style in church architecture from the late 1800s and early 1900s, characterized by the use of domes, round arches, mosaics, campaniles and the basilica plan.

Byzantium purple, Byzantine purple; a bluish shade of Tyrian purple pigment used by the Romans for the robes of dignitaries.

BZ system see British zonal system.

C

C0 a standard international paper size of 917 mm × 1297 mm, used for envelopes; successive smaller sizes C1–C7 are derived by halving the area of the next size up; see A0, B0. →Table 6

CA cellulose acetate.

CAB cellulose acetate butyrate.

cabaret a restaurant or space in which a programme of entertainment is provided; the entertainment therein.

cabin 1 a small dwelling, hut or house, usually of log or timber frame construction.
2 booth, box, shelter; a small, often temporary compartment or structure for workmen, watchmen etc. to provide shelter from the weather.
3 a room or compartment on a ship or train.

cabinet a piece of furniture, often freestanding and ornamented, containing shelves, drawers or doors and used for displaying or storing objects of value, drawings, documents etc.

cabinet hinge, furnishing hinge; traditionally any small hinge used for cupboard doors etc., nowadays any one of a wide range of patented mechanized hinges, often with spring mechanisms and specialized fixings. →38

cabinet lock, furniture lock; a small lock fitted to the doors, drawers, chest lids etc. of furnishings. →39

cabinetmaker a craftsman who makes fine furnishings, joinery and veneerwork.
see *timber mortise and tenon joints* illustration. →5

cabinetmaker's tenon joint see keyed tenon joint. →5

cabinet projection a form of oblique projection in which the Y and Z axes are in plan and the X axis is at 45° upward and to the right, with scaling of lines parallel to it at half that of the others; see cavalier, military projections. →127

cabinet saw a timber-framed bow saw like a turning saw, but with a wider blade.

cabinet scraper, spokeshave scraper; a woodworking tool used for smoothing and scraping; a scraper mounted in a spokeshave.

cabinetwork the trade of making fine furnishings, joinery and veneerwork; the furnishings thus produced.
see *timber mortise and tenon joints* illustration. →5

cabin hook a large hook and eye, in which the hook and ring are attached to backplates, not screw fittings.

cable, 1 steel cable, wire rope; a structural steel product consisting of steel wire wound round a central steel core, very strong in tension and used for guys, stays, fastening and bracing.
2 see suspension bridge cable.
3 see electric cable.
4 see cable moulding. →125
5 see cable length.

cable balustrade, wire balustrade, wire-rope balustrade; a balustrade with a number of parallel lengths of stainless steel wire rope strung between uprights. →54

cable car a high-level transportation system with cabins carried on cables which move on rollers supported on towers, pylons or abutments.

cable channel a channel on cable television.

cable clamp see wire-rope clamp. →37

cable duct, pipe duct; a pipe buried in the ground, under concrete floors etc. to provide a protected route for electric cables.

cable ferry a ferry bridge guided and propelled across a river or other narrow waterway by means of cables connected to both shores between fixed landing stages. →64

cable ladder a series of interlinked structural brackets for supporting a group of parallel electric cables at or adjacent to a wall surface or slab soffit.

cable length, cable; an imperial unit of length equal to 200 yards.

cable lift a lift system in which the car and counterweight are hung from a series of steel cables over a sheave.

cable manhole a manhole in which maintenance work can be carried out on subterranean cables; sometimes called a junction chamber.

cable moulding, cabling, rope moulding; a decorative moulding representing the twisting coils of a rope. →125

cable radio a radio system whereby signals are sent by cable, usually to paying customers.

cable-stayed bridge, stayed bridge; a bridge whose deck is supported by a series of inclined cables or rods strung from one or a number of pylons or towers.
see *cable-stayed bridge* illustration. →32

cable-stayed structure any structure supported and braced by a system of diagonal cables or rods.

cable-supported structure any structure supported by a system of cables in tension.

cable television a television system whereby signals are sent by cable, usually to paying customers.

cable thimble see wire-rope thimble. →37

cable tray a pressed sheetmetal bracket for supporting a group of parallel electric cables, often at high level or in a ceiling void.

cableway, Blondin; an aerial transportation system for people or goods, consisting of cabins or cages hung on moving cables strung between a series of pylons.

cabling see cable moulding. →125

cabmen's shelter a rudimentary timber structure found in Victorian England to provide shelter for the drivers of horse-drawn cabs.

cacao see cocoa.

cache in computing, an area of high speed memory situated between a processor and a main memory, in which the computer temporarily stores usable data.

cactus (green) a shade of dark green which takes its name from the colour of certain cacti (e.g. *Epiphyllum hybridum*).

CAD acronym for computer-aided design.

cadet blue, Royal Air Force blue; a shade of grey blue which takes its name from the colour of uniforms of certain officers' training schools.

cadmium a soft bluish-white metal, **Cd**, whose uses in construction include corrosion-resistant protective surface coating for iron and steel.

cadmium plating the protective treatment, rustproofing etc. of a metal surface by application of a thin layer of cadmium.

cadmium red, selenium red; a lightfast and alkali-resistant inorganic red pigment mixed from cadmium sulphide and cadmium selenide, in wide use since 1910, opaque, quick drying and suitable for use in all types of paint.

cadmium yellow, 1 aurora yellow; a range of yellow pigments manufactured from cadmium sulphide with good hiding power and performance.
2 see flame yellow.

caduceus, staff of Hermes, staff of Mercury; Lat.; a short rod entwined by two snakes and topped by a pair of wings, the magic wand of the Greek god Hermes, Roman Mercury, messenger of the gods; called a kerykeion in Greek. →120

caementicium see opus caementicium. →83
caementum see opus caementicium. →83
caeruleum see cerulean blue.
Caesar's gate porta Caesarea, see Imperial gate. →96
caesium, cesium (Am.); a soft, pale-coloured, highly radioactive chemical element, **Cs**.
café, coffee shop, coffee room, tearoom; a building or part of a building in which refreshments and pastries are sold for consumption on the premises; also written as cafe.
café-au-lait a shade of light grey brown which takes its name from the colour of coffee with milk.
cafeteria a self-service café, especially one serving food and refreshments within a public building or workplace.
cage a three-dimensional assembly of reinforcing bars for a reinforced concrete beam or column, often prefabricated. →30
see beam reinforcement. →27
see column reinforcement. →27
caher see cashel.
cairn 1 a prehistoric landmark for burial grounds and symbolic places, consisting of a simple pile of rough stones.
2 see chambered cairn.
caisson 1 a hollow foundation system, impervious to water, which is fabricated, sunk into the ground and emptied of soil and water to allow construction work within.
2 see coffer. →86
calathus Lat.; the main basket-like body of a Corinthian capital, surrounded by acanthus leaves, sometimes called a bell; Greek form is kalathos. →81
calcareous, calcarious; pertaining to a mineral or substance which contains a relatively high proportion of calcium carbonate, $\mathbf{CaCO_3}$.
calcareous rock types of sedimentary rock which contain considerable amounts of calcium carbonate, such as limestone, sinter and chalk.
calcareous tufa a form of highly porous, pure limestone or calcareous sinter, used traditionally as building stone for arches, and burnt to produce lime.
calcarious see calcareous.
calcic pertaining to a substance which contains calcium.
calcining the heating of ores and minerals to drive off water and carbon dioxide.
calcite, calc-spar; a crystalline, white or coloured mineral form of calcium carbonate found in limestone, marble and chalk; used in the production of Portland cement, in the chemical, glass and cellulose industry, and in the smelting of iron ores.
calcium a chemical element, **Ca**, found naturally as a carbonate in building stones such as limestone and marble, and used in compound form in the manufacture of cement; see following entries.
calcium aluminate cement see high alumina cement.
calcium carbonate a chemical compound, $\mathbf{CaCO_3}$, the chemical form of chalk, limestone and marble; used also as a white pigment in paint.
see calcite.
see chalk.
see dolomite, bitter spar (calcium magnesium carbonate).
see limestone.
see marl.
see quicklime.
see whiting.
calcium chloride a chemical compound, $\mathbf{CaCl_2}$, used as an accelerator in concrete and mortar.
calcium hydroxide a chemical compound, $\mathbf{Ca(OH)_2}$, calcium oxide mixed with water, used in cements and mortars as a binder; the chemical form of slaked or hydrated lime. →Table 5
calcium magnesium carbonate a chemical compound, $\mathbf{CaMg(CO_3)_2}$, see dolomite, bitter spar.
calcium oxide a chemical compound, **CaO,** otherwise known as quicklime, made from heating limestone or marble; forms lime putty when mixed with water. →Table 5
calcium silicate one of a number of chemical salts of silicon and oxygen combined with calcium, manufactured by heating lime with silica sand and used as a binder in concrete and in the manufacture of calcium silicate bricks and blocks.
calcium silicate block a building block of similar constitution to a calcium silicate brick, but of a considerably larger size.
calcium silicate board an incombustible and chemical-resistant fibre cement board used for fireproofing applications and as a general weatherproof building board.
calcium silicate brick a light grey or white brick made by pressing a mixture of slaked lime mixed with sand (sand-lime brick) or crushed flint (flint-lime brick) and heating in a steam autoclave.
calcium sulphate a chemical compound $\mathbf{CaSO_4}$; see anhydrite.
$\mathbf{CaSO_4.2H_2O}$, see gypsum.
calc-spar calcite.
calculation, 1 computation; the process of mathematical or arithmetical reckoning.
2 a singular piece or instance of this.
calculator, 1 electronic calculator; any electronic device with a keyboard and display, used for carrying out calculations.
2 pocket calculator; a small flat hand-held version usually operated by batteries.
caldarium, calidarium (Lat.); pl. calidaria; a hot room in a Roman bath house, containing warm baths. →91
Caledonian brown poor quality burnt sienna.
Caledonian white a white pigment no longer in general use, made from lead chloro-sulphite.
calefactorium Latin form of calefactory. →97
calefactory a warm room in a monastery or medieval castle used by inhabitants as a sitting room, heated by warm air channels within walls and floors; calefactorium in Latin. →97
calendar month the time span between the same dates in successive months of the year.
calendered polymeric roofing roofing membrane of compressed layers of bitumen polymer and fibre reinforcement, manufactured by controlled rolling processes.
calendering a method of forming thin thermoplastics sheet, laminate or backed sheet by feeding molten material between hot rollers and cooling rollers in succession.
calf's-tongue moulding see calves'-tongue moulding. →124
calibration the adjustment of measuring equipment and devices with a known constant to give correct readings.
calida lavatio Lat.; a warm bath in a Roman bath house. →91
calidarium Lat.; see caldarium. →91
caliduct a pipe or duct in classical and medieval buildings to convey warm water, air or steam for space heating.
californium a chemical element, **Cf**.
caliper see calliper.
call box see telephone box.
call for bids see invitation to tender.
calligraphy the art of lettering or decorative writing, especially as practised with brush and ink in China and Japan.
calliper, 1 caliper; an instrument with two hinged legs for measuring the diameter or thickness of bodies; also called callipers.
2 see vernier callipers.
calliper gauge see vernier callipers.
Callitris quadrivalvis the gum juniper tree, see sandarac.
call point any kind of manually operated fire alarm switch such as a break-glass unit.

callus new tissue that has grown over an old wound in a living tree.

Calocedrus decurrens see incense cedar.

calorie, calory; abb. **cal**; a unit of energy equal to 4.19 joules; equivalent to the amount of energy required to raise one gramme of water by 1°C.
Calorie; see kilocalory (1000 calories).

calorific value, heating value; the amount of heat generated by the combustion of a unit weight of specified material; its units are kJ/kg.

calorifier, heat exchanger; a water heater used in district heating systems etc. which heats domestic water via a heating battery containing piped hot water from a central heating plant.

calory see calorie.

calotte a dome which is less than a hemisphere in shape, a shallow dome. →26

caltrap, **1** caltrop; an iron ball or construction with spikes pointing outwards, placed on the ground in front of fortifications to ensnare the feet of cavalry horses. →104
2 a decorative motif based on the above, consisting of a pointed star with limbs rendered as if bevelled. →117

caltrop see caltrap. →104, →117

Calvary cross, cross calvary; a Latin cross which surmounts a base of three pyramidical steps; sometimes also called cross of Calvary, Passion cross, graded cross, cross of Golgotha or holy cross. →117

calves'-tongue moulding, calf's-tongue moulding; a decorative moulding with a series of small recessed pointed arches, taking its name from the row of intermediate sharp elements which resemble the tongues of young cows or deer. →124

Calypso bulbosa the fairyslipper orchid, see calypso (red).

calypso (red) a shade of bright red used for the colouring of textiles and cosmetics; the same colour as scarlet and China red, it has taken its name from the colour of the flowers of an orchid [*Cytherea* (or *Calypso*) bulbosa].

calyx classical ornament depicting leaf and plant motifs in a realistic fashion, as in a Corinthian capital. →81

camber 1 a slight convex curvature in an otherwise horizontal line or surface as with the convex cross-sectional curvature of a road.
2 see hog.
3 see bow. →1

cambered arch a brickwork arch with a flat extrados and a curved intrados, often used to relieve the illusion of sagging.

cambered beam, arched beam; a beam with upper, lower or both surfaces curved to form an arch.
see *traditional cambered beam* illustration. →7
see *concrete cambered beam* illustration. →30

cambered bridge a bridge which is slightly convex in elevation, lending arched support to its span. →32

cambered vault see segmental barrel vault. →25

camber piece see turning piece. →22

camber slip see turning piece. →22

cambium the thin layer of living cells in a tree between the bark and wood, responsible for the growth.

came see lead came.

camel a shade of grey brown which takes its name from the colour of hair from the camel [*Camelus bactrianus*].

camera 1 Lat.; a vaulted roof or ceiling in Roman architecture.
2 a chamber or space thus enclosed.
3 an optical instrument for taking photographs, either on film or as digital data.
4 see surveillance camera.

camera obscura a darkened room with a small hole in the wall for the projection of an image of an exterior view onto a wall or screen, developed during the Renaissance.

camera surveillance, video surveillance; intruder security provided by banks of cameras installed at key points in and around a building, linked to a central monitoring point.

camera survey closed circuit television survey.

camp Roman military camp, see castrum. →104

campaniform 'bell-shaped'; see bell capital. →73

campanile an Italianate bell tower, freestanding or attached to a building.
see *campanile* in Byzantine domical church illustration. →96

campanula 1 a shade of pale grey blue which takes its name from the colour of the flowers of the harebell (Campanula rotundifolia).
2 occasional name for gutta; 'bell' in Latin. →78

camping ground see camp-site.

Camponutus herculeanus see carpenter ant.

camposanto an Italian cemetery, as the one in Pisa, surrounded by a colonnade.

camp-site, camping ground; an area of land, often provided with rudimentary toilet and cooking facilities, on which people, usually tourists, can pitch their tents for overnight stay.

campus the land and buildings that make up a university, college, or other large higher education establishment.

Canada balsam an oleoresin exuded from the balsam fir [*Abies balsamea*], used as a medium in paints, varnishes and adhesives.

Canadian spruce [*Picea mariann*, *Picea glauca*] a collective name for the black and white spruces, common North American softwoods with stiff, resilient, pale yellow timber; used widely in building construction and joinery.

canal, channel; a man-made waterway, similar in form to a river, for the transport of goods and people between towns and cities; often part of a network.

canalis Lat.; in classical architecture, a fluting or hollow between volutes in an Ionic capital. →80

canary wood see tulipwood.

canary yellow a shade of greyish yellow which takes its name from the colour of the canary bird [*Serinus canarius*].

cancelli, choir screen; a decorated timber latticed screen separating the choir from the main body of a church.
see *Early Christian church* illustration. →95
see *Carolingian abbey church* illustration. →98

candela abb. **cd**; the SI unit of luminous intensity.

candelabra pl. of candelabrum.

candelabrum, pl. candelabra; **1** Lat.; a large branched candleholder which supports a number of candles or lights, often hung from the ceiling.
2 in Roman architecture, a decorative motif based on the above.
3 see menorah. →123
4 see chanuk(k)iah. →123

candelabrum column highly ornate columns in Renaissance and Baroque architecture, with decoration resembling that on candlesticks; also called a candlestick column. →114

candle a wax or tallow stick with a centre wick of natural fibre, lit with a flame to produce light; symbolic of Christ, life and immortality when used in religious art.

candleholder 1 a fitting for holding burning candles; it may be a candlestick or a sconce.
2 see candlestick. →116
3 see sconce. →116
4 see candelabrum.

candle lamp a decorative tapered lightbulb whose upper end terminates in a point, reminiscent of the flame of a candle.

candlepower distribution curve see light distribution curve.

candlestick a frame for holding a candle, usually not fixed to building fabric. →116

candlestick column see candelabrum column. →114
cane 1 see caravansary.
2 see rattan.
canephora, canephore, canephorum, kanephoros (Gk); 'basket-carrying' (Lat.); in classical architecture, a carved statuesque column of a draped female figure, a caryatid, carrying a basket, or with a basket on her head. →76
canephore see canephora. →76
canephorum see canephora. →76
Canis vulpes see fox.
canker rot see red ring rot.
Cannabis sativa see hemp.
cannel see grinding bevel. →41
canon an overriding principle or fundamental set of rules.
see *canon of proportion* illustration. →106
canopy 1 any overhanging roof, shelter or ceiling providing cover or shelter. →54
2 an open ornamental shelter or covering, especially for an altar, tomb or throne; a baldachin.
3 hood; the upper construction in a fireplace, which directs smoke up a chimney. →55
cant see superelevation.
cant brick, angle brick; a special brick manufactured with one or two corners chamfered, used in decorative and angled brickwork. →16
cant chisel see framing chisel.
canteen a space or spaces in an institution or workplace in which food is prepared, served and consumed.
cantharus, kantharos (Gk); a fountain or pool located in the courtyard of an Early Christian church and used for baptizing.
see *cantharus* in Byzantine domical church illustration. →96
cantherii plural form of cantherius. →47
cantherius, pl. cantherii; Lat.; a principal rafter in Roman timber roof construction; see also asser. →47
cantilever 1 a horizontal structural member supported at one end only.
2 the structural configuration thus created.
cantilever balcony a balcony which is attached as a cantilever, without supporting tie rods or columns. →60
cantilever beam a beam of which part or all is a cantilever, and on which loads are supported. →7
cantilever bridge a bridge whose main supporting construction is a cantilever.
cantilevered balcony see cantilever balcony. →60
cantilevered stair, 1 flying stairs; a stair in which each step is cantilevered out from a wall or central newel. →45
2 see double cantilevered stair.
cantilever rafter see barge couple.
cantilever retaining wall see cantilever wall. →29
cantilever slab a concrete slab which extends beyond its points of support forming a cantilever, as in a balcony.
cantilever wall an L-shaped retaining wall which resists lateral pressure by the weight of earth resting on its flat protruding footing. →29
cantledge see kentledge.
canton in heraldry, the rectangular portion in the upper right corner of a shield, as worn. →124
cantoria see singers' gallery. →98
cantorum see schola cantorum. →95
cant strip see angle fillet. →49
caoutchouc, indiarubber; unvulcanized natural rubber, an elastic and waterproof material tapped from certain tropical trees.
cap an upper terminating fitting or one designed to cover or seal an opening; types included as separate entries are listed below.
see bayonet cap.
blank cap, see end cap.
bridge cap. →31
chimney cap.
Edison screw cap, see screw cap.
end cap.
flue cap. →56, →58
inspection cap.
lamp cap.
pile cap.
rain cap. →56, →58
ridgecap, see ridge capping.
screw cap.
wall cap, see coping.
capacitance 1 the ability of an electrical component or system to store electrical energy.
2 the amount of electric charge that can be stored by an electrical component per unit change in electric potential.
capacitor an electrical component for storing charge.
capacity 1 a measure of the internal volume of any vessel.
2 the volume of liquid that a storage tank, cistern etc. is designed to hold.
3 the ability of a system, workforce etc., to cope with the demands of a certain task.
4 the quantifiable ability of a machine, vehicle or other conveyor to move people, products and goods from one place to another.
capacity restrained assignment model modelling used in traffic planning for simulating speed/flow relationships in modern road systems in order to ascertain travel times and shortest paths for vehicles.
cape see headland.
capella imperialis Lat.; see Imperial chapel. →98, →99
Cape ruby see pyrope.
capillarity, capillary action; the rise of liquid in a fine bore tube or dry porous material due to surface tension.
capillary, capillary tube; a narrow vessel or pore narrow enough for capillary action to occur.
capillary action see capillarity.
capillary fringe an area of ground above the water table containing water held by capillary action.
capillary groove, anti-capillary groove; in window and roof construction etc., a groove cut in a sill or overhang to prevent the backflow of water into adjacent construction.
capillary space in concretework, microscopic interlinked spaces or voids in hardened concrete containing water drawn through by capillary action; see water void.
capillary tube see capillary.
capillary water groundwater suspended above the water table through capillary action.
capital 1 a separate block or a thickening at the top of a column or pilaster, used to spread the load of a beam, or as decoration; types included as separate entries are listed below.
Aeolic capital. →69
animal capital, see protome capital. →115
basket capital. →115
bell capital. →73
block capital. →115
blossom capital, see bell capital. →73
bud capital. →73
bull capital. →69
classical capital. →81
closed bud capital, see bud capital. →73
closed capital, see bud capital. →73
Composite capital. →81
Corinthian capital. →81
crocket capital. →115
cubic capital, see block capital. →115
cushion capital. →115
Doric capital. →78, →81
double scallop capital. →115
eagle capital.
Egyptian capital. →73
figured capital. →115

foliated capital.
Hathor capital. →73
historiated capital, see figured capital. →115
Ionic capital. →80, →81
lily capital. →73
lion capital. →69
lotus capital. →73
moulded capital, see bell capital. →115
open capital, see bell capital. →73
palm capital. →73
palmette capital. →73
papyrus capital. →73
plume capital, see palm capital. →73
protome capital. →115
scallop capital, scalloped cushion capital. →115
stalactite capital. →115
stiff-leaf capital. →115
supercapital, see dosseret. →115
tent-pole capital. →73
trumpet capital. →115
Tuscan capital. →81
vine leaf capital. →82, →115
volute capital. →69
waterleaf capital. →115
see *classical capitals and bases* illustrations. →78, →79, →80, →81
see *Asian and Mediterranean columns and capitals* illustration. →69
see *types of Egyptian capital* illustration. →73
see *Romanesque and Gothic capitals* illustration. →115
2 money and property owned by a business, or money used to start a business.
3 see capital city.
4 see cross capital. →117

capital city, capital; a city which is generally the seat of government for a country or state.

cap nut, acorn nut, dome nut; a nut with a domed covering over its hexagonal base. →37

capoc see kapok.

caponier a covered vaulted passage over a ditch or other work in a castle or fortification, projecting outwards from the main work to provide defending soldiers with the possibility of giving flanking fire. →104

Cappagh brown poor quality umber pigment.

cappellaccio locally obtained tufa used by the Romans as stone in the construction of monumental buildings from c.700 BC.

capping 1 any long timber, plastics or metal product used to cover a joint, welt or seam. →2
2 see coping.
3 see glazing capping.
4 see capping brick. →16

capping block a coping block. →30

capping brick 1 a special brick designed as the uppermost protective course in a freestanding wall or parapet; usually the same length as the width of the walling. →16
2 see saddleback capping brick. →16
3 see coping brick. →16

capping tile 1 ridge capping tile, see ridge tile.
2 see imbrex. →47
3 see kalypter. →47

capreoli plural form of capreolus. →47

capreolus, pl. capreoli; Lat.; one of the members in ancient timber roofwork, especially the struts or braces in a Roman timber roof. →47

Capri blue a shade of turquoise, the colour of the pigment named after the tone of the walls of the Blue Grotto on the Isle of Capri near Naples.

cap sheet in built-up roofing, the uppermost layer of bitumen felt, bonded to the underlying intermediate sheet and often coated with chippings or foil and fibre reinforced.

capsicum red, paprika (red), pepper red; a shade of bright red which takes its name from the colour of the fruit of the plant *Capsicum spp.*

capstone a large horizontal stone, often dressed or ornamented, surmounting two standing stones in a prehistorical portal tomb, or covering a passage or chamber; see dolmen.

captivity in transport planning, a situation in which alternative forms of transport offered to the inhabitants of a particular area are diminished as a result of inadequate initial design.

caput mortuum a reddish-violet pigment formed from iron oxide with clays and gypsums.

car 1 see automobile.
2 see lift car.

caramel (brown) a shade of orange brown which takes its name from the colour of melted brown sugar.

carat 1 a measure of the purity of gold, given as a proportional scale of 1 to 24; pure gold is 24 carat.
2 metric carat; abb. **mct**; a measure of the weight of gemstones, 1 metric carat is equal to 0.02 g.

caravan, mobile home, trailer; a lightweight wheeled dwelling unit, which can be towed by a motor vehicle, providing temporary or permanent living accommodation.

caravan park see mobile home park.

caravansary, cane, caravanserai, han, khan, serai; an oriental or Arabic inn consisting of a large quadrangular building enclosing a court to accommodate travelling caravans, livestock etc.

caravanserai see caravansary.

caravan site, trailer park (Am.); an area of land, often provided with power points, water and other facilities, designated for the siting of caravans or trailers for short periods or holiday use; cf. mobile home park.

carbide any of a number of chemical compounds of carbon with a metallic or semi-metallic element; see tungsten carbide, calcium carbide.

carbide hydrate see hydrated high calcium by-product lime.

carbohydrate one of a wide range of organic compounds, including sugars and starches, which contain water and hydrogen.

carbolic acid see phenol.

carbolic oil an oily substance produced by the fractional distillation of coal tar at 170–230°C, containing naphthalene, phenols and also other alkaline compounds; used in the chemical, dye, food flavouring and cosmetic industries; also called middle oil because of its distillation sequence.

carbon a chemical element, **C**, found in many inorganic and organic compounds, and in natural form as graphite and diamond.
see activated carbon.
see anthracite.
see diamond.
see graphite, plumbago.

carbonation the combination of calcium oxide or calcium hydroxide with carbon dioxide, responsible for the hardening of plasters and cements.

carbon black, 1 benzol black, diamond black; a very fine, opaque black pigment, pure carbon, with high staining power.
2 a shade of black which takes its name from the colour of coal.

carbon dioxide a chemical compound, CO_2, a colourless, odourless gas, found naturally in the atmosphere and used as dry ice and an extinguishant in fire extinguishers.

carbon dioxide fire extinguisher a fire extinguisher used for industrial and service spaces, which functions by increasing the percentage of carbon dioxide gas in air to such a degree as to make combustion impossible.

carbon disulphide a chemical compound, CS_2, a pungent, poisonous, clear, flammable liquid used as a solvent and in the manufacture of cellophane.

carbon fibre a lightweight thread of pure carbon used for reinforcing polymers and metals.

carbon-fibre reinforced a description of plastics, mineral and metal products toughened with strengthening fibres of carbon; CRP is an acronym for carbon-fibre reinforced plastics.

carbon monoxide a chemical compound, **CO**, a poisonous, odourless, colourless gas formed as a result of carbon burning in insufficient oxygen.

carbon paper thin paper coated on one side with a pigment mixed with wax, previously used for making written or typed duplicate copies of documents.

carbon silicide see silicon carbide.

carbon steel 1 steel containing carbon, which may also contain small amounts of silicon, manganese and copper according to specification; usually refers to high carbon steel.
2 see low carbon steel.
3 see medium carbon steel.
4 see high carbon steel.

carborundum silicon carbide used as an abrasive.

carborundum saw a circular saw whose blade is edged with carborundum.

car buffer a resilient sprung or oil-loaded construction at the base of a lift shaft to cushion the fall of the lift car in the event of failure of the lift mechanism, cabling etc.

carbuncle see escarbuncle. →123

carburizing, cementation; a surface-hardening process for steel by heating it with charcoal and coke in a carbonaceous environment for a number of hours, during which carbon diffuses into the surface.

carcase see carcass.

carcass, carcase; the frame of a building excluding wall and roof cladding, services, fittings and finishes; the term usually refers to timber-framed construction.

carceres Lat., pl.; a starting gate in a Greek hippodrome or Roman circus. →89

carcinogen a material or substance believed or proven to cause cancer.

card 1 see cardboard.
2 see expansion board.

cardboard, pasteboard, card, paperboard; stiff board manufactured by gluing sheets of paper together; available in a wide range of thicknesses and grades and used for printing, drawing, modelling, packaging etc.

carded yarn a yarn spun from fibres of short-stapled wool which have been combed.

cardinal (red), strawberry, fez; a shade of deep red which takes its name from the hat worn by cardinals and Moroccans; also the colour of the ripe fruit of the strawberry plant [*Fragaria ananassa*].

cardinal point any one of the four main points of the compass, north, east, south and west.

cardinal virtue a decorative motif dating from antiquity, originally one of the four allegorical female figurines, Justice, Prudence, Temperance and Fortitude, to which Faith, Hope and Love were added during the Middle Ages.

cardo Lat.; the shorter main axis or street in a typical Roman city, town or military encampment (castrum), running north to south and crossing the principal street or decumanus nearer one end; in a castrum, it is called the via principalis and is not necessarily aligned north–south. →104

card reader in security and access control systems, an electronic device, often used in conjunction with a motor-locked door, through which an encoded card is passed to permit access.

Carelianism see Karelianism.

carell see carrel.

caretaker, janitor, property manager; a person employed to see that a building is properly maintained, kept clean and serviced.

car heating point see vehicle heating point.

caricature a humorous or satirical rendering of a portrait with prominent features or exaggerated manner.

carmine, 1 Munich lake, nacarat carmine, Vienna lake; a red pigment made from cochineal.
2 crimson; a shade of bright red, the colour of the above.

carnarium Lat.; a Roman abattoir, refuse pit, charnel house or other establishment concerned with the disposal of animal or human remains.

carnauba wax a hard wax used as a vehicle in paints and varnishes, obtained from the leaves of the Brazilian palm *Copernicia cerifera* (sometimes referred to as the tree of life); often added to beeswax to provide hardness.

carnelian see cornelian.

carnonite a yellow or greenish yellow mineral, naturally occurring vanadate of potassium and uranium, an important ore of vanadium and uranium.

carol a partitioned area of the cloister of a church for private study and solitude.

Carolingian pertaining to the pre- and early Romanesque art and Byzantine-influenced architecture in France during the dynasty of the Frankish kings (768–843) founded by Charlemagne.
see *Carolingian abbey church* illustration. →98
see *Carolingian monastery* illustration. →97
see *Carolingian volute capital* illustration. →115

car park, 1 parking lot (Am.); a multistorey structure or designated area of ground where motor vehicles may be parked when not in use.
2 see parking garage. →62

carpenter, wright; a craftsman or tradesman who works on site in structural and framing timber; in North America this also includes one who works in joinery.

carpenter and joiner a tradesman responsible for the woodwork in a building.

carpenter ant [*Camponutus herculeanus*] a species of insect which burrows and nests in dead hardwoods and softwoods.

Carpenter's Gothic a decorative Gothic Revival style in English and American timber domestic architecture from the 1800s.

carpenter's joint see framing joint. →4
see *types of timber framing joint* illustration. →4

carpenter's mallet a small wooden hammer or mallet used by woodworkers for applying blows to chisels etc. →40

carpenter's pencil a sturdy pencil with a thick lead and rectangular cross-section to avoid rolling when put down, used by a carpenter for marking of cuts, levels etc. on wood and other materials; sometimes known as a builder's pencil. →130

carpenter's square see framing square.

carpenter's vice see bench vice.

carpentry construction work in timber; in North America this also includes joinery.

carpet 1 a thick floor covering woven from fibres, supplied in rolls and usually laid as fitted carpet; types included as separate entries are listed below.
Axminster carpet.
cork carpet. →44
cut pile carpet.
fitted carpet. →44
flocked carpet.
looped pile carpet.
needle-punch carpet.
tufted carpet.
velvet carpet.
wall-to-wall carpet, see fitted carpet. →44
Wilton carpet.
woven carpet.
2 see wearing course. →62

carpet strip a strip of metal, timber or plastics used to hold down the edge of a carpet or other sheet flooring. →2, →44

carpet tile a soft flooring consisting of prefabricated rectangular sheets of carpet which can be laid as tiles.

Carpinus betulus see hornbeam.

carport a covered space, canopy or shelter, open on at least one side, under which one or a number of vehicles may be parked; see also garage. →61

Carrara marble a high quality, hard, white and durable form of marble, quarried in Carrara in Italy; polished and used as an external and internal finish.

carrel, carell; a small niche, recess or cubicle in a library or cloister for private study; see carol.

carriage, centre string; **1** a sloping beam which supports the treads of a wide stair in the middle between the strings.
2 see mono-carriage.

carriage bolt see coach bolt. →36

carriageway, roadway; that part of a road used by vehicular traffic. →62, →63

carrier the inert liquid medium in which the adhesive material, pigment etc. in adhesives and paints is suspended or dissolved.

carrot red a shade of orange which takes its name from the colour of the edible root of the carrot [*Daucus carota*].

cartel a group of businesses which formulate an agreement to limit competition by fixing prices or production levels.

Cartesian coordinate system a system of coordinates with two or three straight parallel axes, X and Y in two dimensions, or X, Y and Z in three, perpendicular to one another. →127

carthame see safflower.

Carthamus tinctorius see safflower.

cartography the presentation of geographical information in the form of maps and charts; the production of these.

cartoon 1 a full size sketch on paper for a larger artwork, especially a tapestry, mural or mosaic.
2 a humorous drawing, often satirical or political, published in a newspaper or magazine.
3 a sequence of drawings which tell a story.
4 a humorous film using drawn or animation techniques.

cartouche a decorative tablet in the shape of an open scroll, often inscribed and carved with ornament; in ancient Egyptian carvings it is a rectangular tablet with rounded corners, inscribed with the hieroglyphs of a king or deity. →74, →123

cartridge a British standard paper size; 12" × 26", 305 mm × 660 mm. →Table 6

cartridge paper thick, rough-surfaced paper used for printing and drawing, wrapping, envelopes and book jackets; originally used for holding gunpowder in cartridges.

carved brickwork laid brickwork carved with a pattern or relief.

carver's mallet a mallet used by a stone or wood carver. →40

carving chisel see woodcarving chisel. →41

carving knife a small hand tool with a short, shaped blade used for decorative woodcarving.

Carya spp. see hickory.

caryatid in classical architecture, a carved statue of a draped female figure which functions as a column. →76

Casali's green a form of viridian pigment.

case 1 see casing.
2 see lock case. →39

cased frame, box frame; the hollow frame in a sash window, which contains the mechanisms such as a rope or cable and a counterweight.

casehardening a condition in improperly seasoned timber where the outer layers of the wood have been dried too rapidly resulting in internal tensions.

casein a phosphorous protein found in the milk of mammals; used in glues and paints.

casein glue a glue made from casein, more water resistant than fish or animal glue.

casein paint paint supplied as a water-soluble powder, whose binder is a mixture of casein and lime; often applied as a finish to sawn exterior timber, plaster, murals etc.

casein painting a quick-drying, matt painting technique, using casein paints for murals etc.

casemate a vaulted chamber contained in the thickness of an exterior wall of a castle or fortification for the storage of artillery, or as a firing position for cannon. →103

casement an openable, framed, glazed and hinged light in a window unit. →52

casement door, French door, French window; a fully glazed panelled door, usually paired, which opens onto a terrace, balcony or adjacent room.

casement frame a fully glazed panelled door, usually paired, which opens onto a terrace, balcony or adjacent room. →53

casement handle a device or fitting used for opening a casement. →52

casement hinge a hinge used in a side or top hung casement window. →52, →53

casement stay any device for regulating and inhibiting the opening of a window casement.

casement vent a small hinged casement in a window unit, openable for ventilation.

casement window a window with one or more hinged sashes or casements. →52
see top-hung casement window, awning window. →52
see side-hung casement window. →52
see bottom-hinged casement window, hopper light. →52

case mould in ornamental plastering, a flexible mould formed by pouring moulding compound into the void between the object to be modelled and a surrounding plaster case.

casework see casing.

cash discount a discount on the price of building materials from a supplier to a contractor for prompt payment, regular custom etc.

cashel, caher; a ringfort in Ireland from the Iron Age to the Middle Ages, constructed of drystone masonry.

casing, 1 casework, encasing; any material, product, boarding etc. used as a covering for a structural member or service to conceal unsightly construction or as fireproofing.
2 case, cover; a protective outer layer for an appliance, component or device.
3 see formwork.
4 see pile casing.
5 see concrete casing.

casino a summer pavilion used for entertainment and dancing, or a building dedicated to gambling.

cassava a starch glue made from tapioca, the starch flour obtained from the tuberous root of the tropical cassava plants (Manihot esculenta, Manihot dulce).

Cassel earth, Cologne earth; a form of the brown earth pigment Vandyke brown.

Cassel green see manganese green.

cassiterite, tin-stone; a brownish mineral, naturally occurring tin dioxide, SnO_2, the most important ore for the extraction of tin.

cassolette a vessel in which essence is burnt, or a decorative motif representing such a vessel.

cast see fibrous plaster cast.

Castanea sativa see sweet chestnut.

castelet, castlet; a small castle or fortification. →103

castella plural form of castellum.

castellated 1 constructed in the form of a castle, with fortifications, turrets and battlements.
2 describing a pattern, component etc. which is rendered with a series of indents or rectilinear undulations, as with battlements; also called crenellated, embattled or battlemented.

castellated moulding see crenellated moulding. →124, →125

castellated nut, castle nut; a nut whose outer edge is formed with a series of stepped slots to fit with a cotter pin through threaded shafts to secure the bolted joint. →37

castellation see crenellation. →125

castellum, pl. castella, Lat.; **1** a Roman castle or fortress.
2 in Roman architecture, a reservoir in which water conveyed by an aqueduct was collected prior to distribution for use.

cast glass, **1** roughcast glass; traditional flat glass, often with an uneven surface, manufactured by casting on a bed of sand.
2 see plate glass.

casting the shaping of material such as concrete, metal or plastics by pouring them in liquid form (molten for metals) into suitably shaped moulds and allowing it to harden.

casting plaster a grade of plaster suitable for casting in moulds for ornament and mouldings.

cast-in-place see in situ.

cast-in-place concrete see in-situ concrete.

cast-in-place pile, bored pile, cast-in-situ pile, in-situ pile; in foundation engineering, a concrete pile constructed by placing reinforcement and concrete into a preformed borehole or driven casing tube. →29

cast-in-situ see in situ.

cast-in-situ concrete see in-situ concrete.
see *in-situ concrete frame* in office building illustration. →60

cast-in-situ pile see cast-in-place pile. →29

cast iron a hard alloy of iron, carbon and silicon cast when molten into a mould, then often machined; written cast-iron in adjectival form.

cast-iron stove a solid-fuel room heater of cast-iron construction. →56

castle a fortified military or residential building or group of buildings with defensive exterior walls to provide protection against attack; types included as separate entries are listed below. →103
see *medieval castle* illustration. →103
castelet. →103
castrum. →104
citadel.
cliff castle.
contour fort.
fort, fortress.
hillfort.
keep and bailey castle. →103
military fort, see castrum. →104
motte and bailey.
plantation castle.
promontory fort, see cliff castle.
ringfort, rath.
Roman fort, see castrum. →104
stronghold.

castle nut see castellated nut. →37

castlet see castelet. →103

castle wall 1 see curtain wall. →103
2 see bailey. →103
3 see enceinte. →103

Castor fiber see beaver.

castrum Lat.; a Roman encampment or military fortress based on a standard model whose principles were also used for the layout of cities; any town in Britain whose name has the suffix 'chester' or 'cester' is a site of a Roman castrum; the word is later used for medieval castles. →104

cast steel, crucible steel; steel been cast from molten material, and not worked thereafter.

cast stone, artificial stone, patent stone, reconstructed stone; a reconstituted stone product used in place of natural stone, manufactured from stone fragments in a cement binder.

cast tile a tile manufactured by casting ceramic material in a mould then firing it. →20

cat see Bastet. →74

catabasion a vault beneath the altar of a Greek Orthodox church. →116

catacomb a series of subterranean vaulted spaces with niches and recesses, used as a cemetery.

catafalco see catafalque. →116

catafalque, catafalco; an ornamental platform in a church on which a coffin or effigy is placed during a funeral. →116

catagogion, katagogion; an ancient Greek lodge for pilgrims near a temple, along sacred routes etc.

catalogue a written list of products and associated information produced by a manufacturer.

catalyst, promoter; a substance which increases the rate of a chemical reaction without itself being consumed.

cataphoresis see electrophoresis.

catch any device used for the fastening of a gate, door or hatch in a certain position. →39
ball catch, bullet catch. →39
magnetic catch.
turning catch, see turning latch.
roller catch. →39

catch bolt see return latch. →39

catchment area 1 a discrete geographical area, often hilly, from which precipitation drains to the same waterway, river, canal, or reservoir.
2 in town planning, an area whose inhabitants will use a particular service, such as that from which a shopping centre will draw its customers.

catenary a geometrical curve as formed by a heavy string or chain hanging between two points.

catenary cable see suspension bridge cable. →32

cathedra, bishop's throne, tribune; Lat.; the throne of the presiding bishop in an Early Christian church, raised and set behind the high altar; Greek form is kathedra.
see *Early Christian and Late Antique church* illustration. →95
see *Romanesque church* illustration. →99
see *altar* illustration. →116

cathedral a large and principal church of a diocese, the seat of a bishop.

cathedral glass a strong roughcast coloured glass, often with lead cames in imitation of stained glass.

Catherine wheel a decorative motif consisting of a spiked or burning wheel with radiating spokes, an instrument of torture, the symbol of Saint Catherine of Alexandria, to which she was bound. →122

Catherine wheel window, wheel window; a round window with a series of glazing bars radiating out from the centre. →109

cathode a negatively charged electrode, to which positive chemical ions (cations) are attracted.

cathodic dip painting see electro-dip painting.

cation a positively charged ion.

cationic bitumen emulsion a dispersion of bitumen in water, with an emulsifying additive which coats the particles of bitumen with a positive ion, causing them to repel one another and to remain as separate droplets.

cat's eye 1 see pin knot. →1
2 see reflecting road stud.

cat's head, catshead; an ornamental motif or moulding, similar to a beakhead, consisting of a series of stylized heads resembling those of cats. →122

catslide roof a pitched roof which continues in the same plane on one side beyond the main eaves to the roof of an adjacent structure, or in which the eaves is lower on one side than the other. →46

cat's paw see nail claw.

cattle creep a tunnel constructed beneath a rural road, through which livestock and cattle can be driven.

cattle station a cattle farm in Australia and New Zealand.

catwalk, roofway, walkway; a long platform or access bridge on a roof, often with a balustrade, providing maintenance access to rooftop services and other fittings. →46

caulcole see caulicole. →81

caulicole, caulcole, cauliculus; the spiral stalks which carry leaves and volutes at the corners of a Corinthian capital. →81

cauliculus Latin form of caulicole. →81

caulking, 1 stopping; the filling of joints and gaps in construction with flexible material as weatherproofing and windproofing.
2 stopping; the sealing substance or product thus used.
3 a product and process in which fibrous material such as old rope, hemp or rags are forced into the gaps in a timber boarded structure as jointing; see oakum.

caulking chisel, caulking iron; a metal implement with a wide, blunt blade used for caulking joints.

caulking ferrule a screwed sleeve for an opening in a pipe, sealed by caulking.

caulking gun, extrusion gun, pressure gun; a simple mechanical device for applying prepacked sealant into joints, using hand pressure on a trigger.

caulking iron see caulking chisel.

causeway 1 a raised road, carriageway or path which provides a route across marshy land, waterways or land likely to be submerged by tides or floods.
2 see pyramid causeway. →71

causewayed camp a North European prehistoric defensive enclosure dating from c.4000–2000 BC, consisting of a series of radial causeways intersected by a ring of concentric ditches and ramparts.

causeway sett see sett.

caustic lime see quicklime.

caustic soda see sodium hydroxide.

cavaedium see cavum aedium.

cavalier a raised platform usually situated on a bastion or fortified wall, on which artillery was mounted to command the surrounding area, and as a look-out; an inner or double bastion. →104

cavalier projection in technical drawing, an oblique projection in which the Y and Z axes are in plan and the X axis is at 45° upward and to the right; all scales are the same; see cabinet, military projections. →127

cavea Lat.; the semicircular banked stand of stepped seating in a Roman theatre or circus; the auditorium seats. →89, →90

cave painting prehistoric depictions of animals, hunting scenes and rites from the palaeolithic periods, as first discovered adorning cave walls in Southern Europe.

cave temple see rock-cut temple. →68

cavetto 1 a decorative concave moulding which is roughly a quarter of a circle in profile; when appearing in a cornice, concave side down, it may be called a cove. →14
2 see scotia. →14, →80

cavitation the formation of gas bubbles in flowing liquids due to the turbulent action of a pump or propeller, which, in water supply installations, may lead to corrosive oxidation of metal parts.

cavity 1 a void within a component to reduce weight such as in a hollow core slab, or in construction between two components for insulation, such as between the leaves of a cavity wall.
2 see gap. →8

cavity absorber, Helmholtz resonator; in acoustics, a construction consisting of bottle-like cavities containing air which absorbs sound of a narrow band of frequencies by sympathetic resonance.

cavity barrier see fire barrier.

cavity block see cellular block. →30

cavity bond, hollow wall bond; any true masonry bond in which bricks or blocks are stacked in such a way as to leave a cavity in the centre of the wall; see rat-trap bond, Dearne's bond. →17

cavity brick see hollow brick. →16

cavity closer in cavity wall or prefabricated concrete panel construction, a piece of timber or other rigid material placed in the cavity at an edge or opening to provide a thermal break and onto which window and door frames may be attached; also called a closure piece. →28

cavity drainage membrane see air-gap membrane. →29, →57, →59

cavity floor see access floor. →44

cavity gas the inert gas between two sheets of glass in a sealed glazing unit.

cavity membrane see air-gap membrane. →29, →57

cavity tie see wall tie. →22, →59
see *types of cavity tie* illustration. →22
see *cavity tie* in brick house illustration. →59

cavity wall, hollow masonry wall, hollow wall; a common exterior wall construction, often of masonry, composed of two adjacent walls or leaves tied together at intervals with an air space between, often partially or wholly filled with ventilated insulation. →21
see *cavity wall* in brick house illustration. →59

cavity wall tie see wall tie. →22, →59

cavo-relievo see sunk relief.

cavo-rilievo see sunk relief.

cavum aedium, cavaedium; Lat.; according to Vitruvius, a hall in the great houses of the Great Republic and Early Empire of Roman development.

C-clamp see gee-clamp.

CCTV closed circuit television.

CCTV survey closed circuit television survey.

CD compact disc.

CD-ROM compact disc read-only memory.

cedar [*Cedrus spp.*] a group of softwoods with strongly scented and extremely durable timber; used for joinery, fencing and interior panelling; others such as the western red cedar, eastern red cedar, incense cedar, yellow cedar, white cedar are not true cedars; see ***Cedrus spp.*** for full list of species of cedar included in this work.

Cedar of Lebanon [*Cedrus libani*] a softwood from the mountainous regions of the Near East and Syria with a distinctive smell, used locally for building construction.

Cedrus spp. see cedar.
Cedrus atlantica, see Atlas cedar.
Cedrus deodara, see deodar.
Cedrus libani, see Cedar of Lebanon.

ceiba 1 [*Ceiba pentandra*] a tropical African and Asian hardwood with extremely light timber; used for furniture.
2 see kapok.

Ceiba pentandra see ceiba.

ceiling the upper horizontal construction or surface in an interior space; usually either suspended or the soffit of the overlying construction; types included as separate entries are listed below.
see *brick house* illustration. →59
see *office building* illustration. →60
acoustic ceiling.
boarded ceiling.
coffered ceiling. →93
drop ceiling, false ceiling.
illuminated ceiling, luminous ceiling.
suspended ceiling.

ceiling bearer a primary profile or beam in a suspended ceiling system, from which ceiling runners are suspended. →60

ceiling board 1 any board products such as plasterboard, plywood etc. fastened to a frame or soffit to make up a fixed ceiling.
2 one of a number of machined timber boards used as a ceiling. →57, →59

ceiling boarding the task and result of laying ceiling boards. →57, →59

ceiling component any component or product, a panel, hanger, runner etc. used to form a suspended ceiling.

ceiling construction the materials, components and structure which comprise a ceiling.

ceiling fan a large-bladed rotating fan attached to a ceiling soffit to provide circulation of air within a space.

ceiling hanger, ceiling strap; one of a number of metal components attached to the soffit or frame of the floor above from which a suspended ceiling is hung. →60

ceiling heating radiant space heating provided by electric cables, steam or hot water pipework incorporated into ceiling panels.

ceiling height, floor-to-ceiling height, headroom, room height; the vertical height of an internal space, measured from floor level to ceiling soffit.

ceiling joist in timber roof construction, one of a number of horizontal members to which ceiling boards, panels etc. are fixed. →33
see *rafter and purlin roof* illustration. →33
see *holiday home and sauna* illustration. →58

ceiling linear strip see exposed runner.

ceiling luminaire a light fitting designed to be attached to a ceiling soffit.

ceiling-mounted shower any shower whose outlet is fixed permanently to a ceiling.

ceiling painting see plafond.

ceiling panel 1 a removable sheet product of gypsum board, plastics, mesh or sheetmetal, suspended on a system of rails and hangers to make up a suspended ceiling. →60
2 see metal pan, metal tray. →60

ceiling rose see centrepiece.

ceiling runner a metal profile supported by ceiling hangers, which forms the basis of the frame into which ceiling panels are laid in a suspended ceiling. →60

ceiling strap see ceiling hanger. →60

ceiling strip a horizontal moulding or cover strip at the junction of an internal wall and ceiling; see also cornice.

ceiling surface the lower visible surface of a ceiling.

ceiling suspension system the frame of hangers and profiles by which panels in a suspended ceiling are supported.
see *ceiling suspension system* illustration. →60

ceiling tile a rectangular tile of plastics, laminates or ceramics used in series to form a ceiling surface.

ceiling trim see perimeter trim. →60

ceiling void the space between a false or suspended ceiling construction and the soffit of the overlying construction, usually taken up with services and ducts. →60

ceiling work construction work involved with the installation of ceiling components and panels.

ceilure see celure.

celadon green see lavender green.

celestial blue a form of the pigment Prussian blue similar to Brunswick blue.

cell 1 one of the curved vaulting panels or surfaces between the ribs in a rib vault; the curved or planar surface of a vault; also called a severy or web. →25, →101
2 see monastic cell.
3 see beehive cell.
4 prison cell; a lockable room for the forced detainment of a person or people.
5 see dungeon. →103
6 see oubliette. →103
7 see solar cell.
8 see photoelectric cell.
9 a normally non-rechargeable battery for a small appliance such as a radio or torch; see battery.
10 fire cell, see fire compartment.

cella, 1 pl. cellae; Lat.; in classical architecture, the central sanctuary space in a Roman temple containing a cult image; a naos in Greek architecture; cella is often used for all enclosed shrine-like spaces.
2 the main body of a peristyle temple, including the pronaos and opisthodomos.
see *cella* in Mesopotamian temple illustration. →66
see *cella* in classical apteral and peristyle temple illustrations. →84, →85

cellae plural of cella.

cellar a basement or part of a basement used for storage, heating plant and for purposes other than habitation; a cellar in a castle or palace is often called a vault.

cellar rot [*Coniophora cerebella*, *Coniophora puteana*] a fungus which attacks timber in constantly damp conditions.

cell ceiling, egg-crate ceiling, open cell ceiling; a suspended ceiling system formed from rectangular or polygonal grids of baffles, slats etc. with openings to allow for the passage of air and light from services located in the ceiling void.

cellophane a transparent plastics material made from viscose and used for wrapping.

cellular a description of a material, construction layout or structural configuration of a number of open cells, voids etc., such as honeycomb.

cellular acrylic sheet see acrylic cellular sheet.

cellular board, cellular plywood; a building board of one or more veneers glued to either side of a cellular construction. →9

cellular block a concrete building block with voids incorporated in its thickness during manufacture, to reduce weight and improve thermal and sometimes acoustic performance; variously known as a cavity block or hollow concrete block. →30

cellular brick 1 a perforated brick whose cavities are large in proportion to its volume, or of a particular shape. →16
2 see perforated brick, cored brick. →16
3 see air brick, ventilating brick. →16
4 see hollow brick, cavity brick. →16

cellular concrete see aerated concrete.

cellular concrete block see cellular block. →30

cellular glass, foam glass; a glass product manufactured by heating pulverized glass with carbon to form a strong, lightweight, fireproof and water-resistant solid foam, used as an insulating material; also known as expanded glass.

cellular glazing see cellular sheet.

cellular growth in town planning, urban expansion in rough repetition of existing units of city structure.

cellular paver, crib paver; a concrete paving block with small holes, filled with earth and sown with seed when laid in series, forming a hardwearing grassy surface. →15

cellular paving, grass paving, crib paving; paving of concrete units precast with patterns of holes; once laid these are filled with earth and seed compound for grass to grow, providing a soft but hardwearing paved surface. →15

cellular phone system see wireless communication network.

cellular plastic a generic name for both expanded plastics and foamed plastics. →59

cellular plywood see cellular board.

cellular polycarbonate see polycarbonate cellular sheet.

cellular raft a concrete raft foundation whose beams and crosswalls form a grid structure in plan.

cellular rubber a generic term for both foam rubber and expanded rubber.

cellular sheet, extruded cellular sheet; an insulating transparent polycarbonate or acrylic sheet product of two thin sheets around a hollow cellular core, used for lightweight glazing and roofing.

celluloid a thermoplastic made from cellulose nitrate, camphor and alcohol; traditionally used for cinema film.

cellulose a major constituent of dried wood and plant matter which, when extracted as pulp, is processed for use in the manufacture of a wide range of synthetic products including papers, fibres, plastics, paints and adhesives.

cellulose acetate, CA; a tough thermoplastic used as a binder in emulsion paints, for light fittings and door furniture.

cellulose acetate butyrate, CAB; a tough thermoplastic used for coatings and illuminated signs.

cellulose adhesive any adhesive such as wallpaper paste, which contains cellulose.

cellulose lacquer, cellulose varnish; a quick drying varnish, used mainly on wooden surfaces, based on nitrocellulose compounds in a solvent-based medium, which dries by the evaporation of the solvent.

cellulose loose-fill insulation loose-fill insulation prepared from shredded waste paper, cardboard etc., treated with water and insect repellent.

cellulose nitrate, CN; a flammable thermoplastic used for paint finishes and in the manufacture of celluloid.

cellulose paint a solvent-based paint, similar to cellulose lacquer, containing compounds of nitrocellulose and usually applied by spraying.

cellulose plastics thermoplastics such as acetate and celluloid which are manufactured from cellulose.

cellulose varnish see cellulose lacquer.

cellure see celure.

Celsius see degree Celsius.

Celtic architecture the domestic, ceremonial and defensive architecture of the Celtic peoples of present-day Scotland, Wales and Brittany from 700 BC to 1100 AD, including hillforts, ceremonial Celtic crosses, standing stones and domestic dwellings; often ornamented with interlace.

Celtic circle see Celtic love knot. →108

Celtic cross 1 a Latin cross whose crossing is superscribed with a circle; a symbol of ancient Celtic culture; also called a ring or Ionic cross. →117
2 see high cross. →118

Celtic love knot simple knotwork ornament of Celtic origin, with interlaced heart motifs; often called a Celtic circle if in round format. →108

Celtic Revival an architectural style in Ireland from the late 1800s and early 1900s, characterized by the use of the Celtic cross, Celtic ornament and other motifs from Hiberno-Romanesque architecture.

celure, ceilure, cellure; in church architecture, a decorated panelled ceiling over a chancel or altar.

cembra pine see Siberian yellow pine.

cement 1 a powdered mineral substance, usually containing lime or gypsum, mixed with water to form a paste which will set to form a hard, brittle material; used as a binder in concrete, mortars, plasters etc.; types included as separate entries are listed below.
asbestos cement.
blast-furnace cement, blast-furnace slag cement.
blended cement, blended hydraulic cement.
brown cement, see Roman cement.
calcium aluminate cement, see high alumina cement.
coloured (Portland) cement.
composite cement, see fillerized cement.
corrugated asbestos cement.
expanding cement.
extra rapid-hardening Portland cement.
Ferrari cement.
fibre-reinforced cement, fibre cement, FRC.
fillerized cement, filler cement.
fuel-ash cement, see Portland pulverized fuel-ash cement.
glassfibre-reinforced cement, GRC.
high alumina cement.
high-early-strength cement, see rapid-hardening Portland cement.
hot cement.
hydraulic cement.
hydrophobic cement.
lap cement, see sealing compound.
lime cement.
low heat cement, see low heat Portland cement.
low heat Portland blast-furnace cement.
magnesite cement, see oxychloride cement.
masonry cement.
ordinary (Portland) cement.
oxychloride cement.
Parker's cement, see Roman cement.
Portland blast-furnace cement.
Portland cement.
Portland pozzolana cement.
Portland pulverized fuel-ash cement.
pozzolanic cement.
quick-setting Portland cement.
rapid-hardening Portland cement.
Roman cement.
soil cement.
sorel cement, see oxychloride cement.
sulphate-resistant cement, see sulphate-resisting Portland cement.
supersulphated cement.
white (Portland) cement.
2 any liquid substance used for sticking things together, usually an inorganic adhesive.
3 a shade of grey which takes its name from the colour of Portland cement.

cementation 1 see carburizing.
2 see grouting.

cementation process in ground engineering, a process whereby cement grout is injected into underlying soil or rock in order to support and strengthen it.

cement bonded chipboard see wood cement chipboard.

cement clinker partially fused incombustible residue from a kiln created under high temperatures, ground and used as cement in concrete.

cement content in concreting, the amount of hydraulic binder per unit volume or mass of mix.

cement fillet see mortar fillet.

cement fixing see mortar fixing. →11

cement flooring see cement rubber latex flooring.

cement gel in concretework, the cohesive mass of microscopic calcium silicate hydrate crystals in cement.

cement gun a pipe and nozzle used with sprayed concrete and operated by compressed air.

cement grout see neat grout.

cementite, iron carbide; a white, brittle compound, Fe_3C, found in white cast iron.

cementitious material see binder.

cementitious matrix in fibre-reinforced products, the medium of resin, polymer or cement into which fibres are dispersed as reinforcement.

cement lime mortar see composition mortar.

cement lime plaster see composition mortar.

cement lime render see composition render.

cement mixer a small portable concrete mixer with a rotating ovular vessel which is pivoted in order to empty out its contents.

cement mortar, compo; mortar which contains a cement binder as well as sand and water.
see masonry cement mortar.

cement paint an absorbent water-based paint in which the binder is Portland cement, often with added pigment to provide colour.

cement paste cement powder and water mixed to form a thick smooth paste.

cement plaster 1 see cement render.
2 see Portland cement plaster.

cement render, cement plaster; cement mortar used as render for external walls.

cement rubber latex flooring durable flooring of a mixture of cement, rubber latex and aggregates of stone, woodchips etc., laid in situ over a concrete slab and ground to form a smooth surface.

cement screed see screed. →44

cement slurry a liquid mix of cement paste used in grouting and rough render for masonry wall surfaces.

cement tile see concrete tile. →44

cement/water ratio in mixes of concrete, mortar or grout, the ratio of the mass of cement to contained water, the reciprocal of water/cement ratio.

cemetery a graveyard, usually one on public land, or one not within a churchyard.
see *cemetery* in Carolingian monastery illustration. →97

cemetery chapel a funerary chapel at a cemetery.

cenacle, cenaculum; a dining room, especially of a Roman dwelling; later the upstairs rooms in general.

cenaculum Latin form of cenacle.

cenatio see coenatio. →88

cendre see ash grey.

cenobium see coenobium.

cenotaph a memorial tablet or monument for the dead who are buried elsewhere.

cental a unit of weight of 100 lb or 45.36 kg.

centaur a mythological Greek figure with a human torso and head attached to the body of a horse, often found as a decorative motif adorning the metopes of classical temples. →122

Centaurea cyanus see cornflower blue.

centering, centres; a temporary curved frame of wood or other material for supporting a masonry arch while it is being constructed. →22
see *arched and vaulted construction* illustration. →22

centi- abb. **c**; a prefix for units of measurement or quantity to denote a factor of 10^{-2} (one hundredth). →Table 1

centigrade see degree Celsius.

centner see hundredweight.

central air conditioning an air conditioning installation in which air treatment plant, fans etc. are located in one place, from which conditioned air is distributed throughout a building.

Central American mahogany see Honduras mahogany.

central area see inner city.

central axis of vision in perspective projection, an imaginary sight-line perpendicular to the picture plane, the central line of the cone of vision; variously known as the direction of view, central ray, visual ray or axis of sight. →128

central core building 1 see point-access block. →61
2 see high-rise block.

central corridor block a multistorey residential building type in which apartments are arranged with their entrance doors on either side of a central spinal corridor on each floor; also called a double-loaded corridor block. →61

central energy station, power plant; in a district heating system, a building or group of buildings where water is heated, and from where it is distributed.

central fan system see central plant system.

central hall a semi-public space in a large building, providing access and circulation to surrounding rooms; often a high space or atrium. →66, →91

central heating a heating system for a building or group of buildings in which a centrally located boiler heats water which is then circulated as hot water or steam to radiators and storage tanks; see district heating.

central heating boiler a boiler which provides heated water for a central heating network. →56

central heating installation the appliances and devices that make up a central heating system: a centralized boiler and pipework to provide heat in the form of hot water throughout a building.

centralized boiler system see centralized hot water supply.

centralized church see centrally planned church. →95

centralized hot water supply, centralized boiler system; a large-scale hot water heating system for industrial premises, schools, apartment blocks etc. in which water is heated, stored, and distributed throughout from a central location.

central locking a system by which all locks in a building or secure area can be operated from the same central lock.

centrally planned building a square, circular, or polygonal building with an open space at the centre, around which other spaces are arranged.

centrally planned church, centralized church; a church type in which all spaces are arranged around a centrally located altar.
see *centralized church* in Late Antique architecture illustration. →95

central perspective see one-point perspective.

central place in town planning, the source of goods and services for surroundings beyond its own area.

central plant system, central fan system; an air-conditioning system in which air is treated in a centralized plant and ducted to the various spaces in a building.

central ply, core ply; the central layer or ply around which the other plies in plywood are glued. →9

central processing unit, CPU; the main body of a personal computer, a cased unit containing processors, drives and other electronics to which a keyboard, mouse, monitor and auxiliary devices are connected.

central ray see central axis of vision. →128

central reservation see central reserve. →63

central reserve, central reservation, median; the central marked or raised area of a road to provide clear separation of traffic moving in opposite directions. →63

centre 1 in geometry, the point around which an arc is defined.
2 the midpoint of a linear object, arc etc.; the distance between the supports of an arch.
centre to centre, see centres.
mass centre, see centre of gravity.
3 a facility where activities of a certain nature are concentrated; see following list of examples.
business centre, see commercial centre.
city centre.
civic centre.
commercial centre.
community centre.
conference centre, congress centre.
cultural centre.
day care centre, see nursery.
district centre.
exhibition centre.
health centre.
leisure centre.
local centre, see district centre.
mass centre, see centre of gravity.
municipal centre, see civic centre.
neighbourhood centre, see district centre.
parish centre, parochial centre.
rehabilitation centre.
shopping centre.
sports centre.
television centre.
town centre.
training centre.
youth centre, see youth club.

centre bit a flat-ended drill bit with a centring spike for drilling holes or circular depressions in wood. →42

centre boards in the conversion of timber, boards sawn longitudinally from the middle of a log, with the end grain forming a series of concentric circles. →2

centre gutter a flat-bottomed gutter between two inwardly sloping pitched roofs.

centre hinge see centre pivot hinge.

centre line in road design, a theoretical line which marks out the centre of a carriageway.

centre match a variation of the bookmatched veneering pattern in which an even number of pieces of veneer are mirrored across the centre line of a panel to form a symmetrical image on the other half. →10

centre of curvature in geometry, the point from which an arc is generated.

centre of gravity, centre of mass, mass centre; the theoretical point within a body about which it will balance, and to which external forces impinge.

centre of mass see centre of gravity.

centre of projection see station point. →128

centre of vision in perspective projection, the point of intersection of the central axis of vision and the picture plane; sometimes called the principal point or centre point. →128

centre-opening door, bi-parting door; a double sliding door in which both leaves slide away from the middle of the opening; lift doors are typical examples. →50

centrepiece, rose, ceiling rose; a decorative central feature in a ceiling, from which light fittings are often suspended.

centre point see centre of vision. →128

centre pivot hinge, centre hinge, centres; the pivoted fastening on which a pivot window rotates.

centre punch, punch; a tool for marking points or making starter drill holes in metal.

centres, 1 centre to centre, spacing; abb. ccs; in dimensioning and general construction, a notation expressing the distance between the centres of adjacent objects such as rafters, columns, studs, beams, battens etc. in an equally spaced series.
2 see centre pivot hinge.
3 see centering. →22

centre string see carriage.

centre to centre see centres.

centrifugal fan a fan used in air conditioning installations, in which air is sucked in perpendicular to the rotor blades and blown out radially.

centrifugal force the physical tendency of a revolving body to move away from the centre of revolution.

centrifuge a rotating apparatus which utilizes centrifugal force to separate mixtures of liquids of different densities etc.

centripetal force the physical force acting on a revolving body, directed at the centre of rotation, which keeps it in circular motion.

Cerambycidae see longhorn beetle.

ceramic pertaining to products manufactured from fired or burnt clay such as pipes, tiles, bricks, terracotta and pottery.

ceramic fibre an artificial fired clay thread used in bulk in fireproofing products.

ceramic glaze see glaze.

ceramics 1 any products made from a mixture of mineral substance and a clay binder fired to produce a hard insoluble material.
2 the field of practice and production in fired clay.

ceramic tile a thin, durable clay tile, pressed and fired at a high temperature; usually used for cladding floors and walls.
see *tiling patterns* in paving illustration. →15
see *ceramic tile* shapes illustration. →20
see *ceramic tiling* in brick house illustration. →59

ceramic tiled paving see tiled paving.

ceremonial court a large courtyard within the walls of a castle, palace, temple used for parades and other ceremonies; in ancient Egypt the courtyards laid out for the Sed festival of the Pharaoh. →70, →72

ceremonial gate see porta pompae. →90

ceremonial stair a grand stair within or leading to the main entrance of a palace, castle, temple etc. for use of the most revered guests and dignitaries. →66

cereography see encaustic.

cerium a grey, metallic chemical element, **Ce**.

ceroplastics modelling in wax.

certificate 1 a legal document issued as proof of something attained, origin of goods, standard of work, evidence of quality etc.
2 see completion certificate.

certificate of deposit a written document stating that a sum of money or valuables have been deposited by a bank.

cerulean blue, blue celeste, caeruleum, coelin, coeruleum, corruleum blue; a bright, opaque, blue pigment used in artist's paints and ceramics, consisting of cobaltous stannate, a compound of oxides of cobalt and tin.

ceruse an old name for the pigment white lead.

cerussite, white lead ore; a grey or brownish mineral, natural lead carbonate, $\mathbf{PbCO_3}$, an important local lead ore in places where it is found.

cesium see caesium.

cesspit see cesspool.

cesspool, cesspit, sewage tank; in the treatment of waste water, an underground storage container, emptied at regular intervals, for sewage which cannot be piped away for treatment.

Ceylon ebony [*Diospyros ebenum*] a hardwood from tropical India and Sri Lanka; its timber is very heavy and dark brown or black.

Ceylon satinwood, East Indian satinwood; [*Chloroxylon swietenia*] a tropical hardwood from India and Sri Lanka with very heavy timber.

chain 1 a fastening or connecting rope-like structure formed of a number of interlocking metal loops.
2 an ornamental motif representing the linked loops of a chain. →125
3 an imperial unit of length equal to $^1/_{80}$ mile, 22 yards or 20.12 m.
4 see door chain. →51

chain bridge a suspension bridge supported by forged chain cables.

chained library a medieval library whose books are fixed to their shelves with chains.

chain ferry a ferry bridge guided by chains anchored on either side of a river or narrow waterway. →64

chain line, dot-dash line; in technical drawing, a line consisting of alternating dashes and dots, usually representing centre or symmetry lines, lines of reference and cutting planes.

chain link fence fencing constructed from a mesh of interwoven wires, chain link mesh, supported between spaced posts or uprights.

chain link mesh wire mesh made from a series of wires interwoven in a zigzag pattern to form diamond-shaped openings; most often galvanized or organically coated and used as fencing material. →34

chain moulding an ornamental moulding representing the linked loops of a chain. →125

chain pipe wrench, chain tongs, chain vice; a tool for gripping and rotating objects such as pipes or tight bolts, consisting of a lever attached to a short length of chain which tightens around the object to be gripped.

chainsaw a hand-held motor-driven saw with a cutting chain, used for logging and rough work; see saw chain.

chain sling a crane sling.

chain timber see bond timber.

chain tongs see chain pipe wrench.

chain vice see chain pipe wrench.

chair 1 a seat for one person, usually with a backrest. →9
2 a construction of bent bars for supporting the uppermost layer of reinforcement in horizontal concrete slabs, beams etc. while concrete is being placed.

chair rail, dado rail; an interior horizontal moulding at approximately waist height as an upper termination for wainscotting or to prevent the backs of chairs from scraping the wall surface.

chaitya a Buddhist temple or the meeting room of a monastery in India.

chajja an overhanging eaves or cornice in a Hindu temple or other Indian building to provide shelter from sun and rain.

chalcedony a blue-grey form of microcrystalline quartz, used for its decorative quality; also a general name for agate, onyx, cornelian and crysophrase.
see agate.
see cornelian, carnelian.
see heliotrope.
see jasper.
see sard.

chalcidicum **1** Lat.; in Roman architecture, a monumental vestibule, portico or porch which functions as the main entrance and frontispiece of a building.
see *chalcidicum* in Roman basilica illustration. →93
2 in Roman architecture, an administrative building or one used as a court of law.
3 in Early Christian architecture, the narthex of a basilica.

chalcocite, chalcosine, copper glance; a lead-grey mineral and naturally occurring sulphide of copper, Cu_2S, an important ore of copper.

chalcolithic period see Copper Age.

chalcopyrite, copper pyrites; a greenish brass-coloured copper mineral, $CuFeS_2$; an important ore of copper.

chalcosine see chalcocite.

chalet **1** a small dwelling or holiday home, most often of log or light timber construction.
2 see Swiss chalet.

chalk **1** a form of soft, pale or white coloured, porous limestone used in the manufacture for drawing or writing chalks, and burnt to produce lime. →Table 5
2 artificial calcium carbonate used as a bright white pigment in water-based paints and a ground in oil paints.

chalking a defect in an exterior paint finish consisting of the deposition of pigment in a chalky layer on the surface due to decomposition of the binder.

chalk lime quicklime produced by heating chalk.

chalk line, snap line, snapping line; a long thread covered in chalk or coloured powder, used to mark and set out long lines of proposed construction on a building site.

chalky, lily white, snow white; a shade of white which takes its name from the colour of chalk, snow and the flowers of the lily (Lilium spp.).

Chamaecyparis lawsoniana see Lawson's cypress.
Chamaecyparis nootkatensis, see yellow cedar.

chamber **1** a small private bedroom, living space or guest room in a rudimentary dwelling, palace etc.
see *chamber* in prehistoric structures illustration. →65
2 antechamber, see anteroom.
3 bed chamber, see bedroom.
4 bin chamber, see bin store.
5 see waste storage chamber.
6 a darkened or enclosed space used for a specific purpose such as a monk's cell or torture chamber.
7 see burial chamber. →65, →70
8 womb chamber, see garbha-griha.
9 a large meeting room used by a court or a decision-making body.
10 any sealed space or housing within a technical installation in which a particular function, action or process occurs.
11 see anechoic chamber.
12 combustion chamber, see firebox.
13 see smoke chamber.
14 see inspection chamber, manhole.

chambered cairn a prehistoric chambered tomb covered with stones rather than earth. →65

chambered tomb a prehistoric burial chamber consisting of a mound of earth or stones surmounting one or more subterranean chambers for the interment of the dead. →65

Chambord style a style in French architecture with both Gothic and Renaissance elements and named after Chambord Palace in central France.

chamfer, 1 bevel; the splayed surface formed when a corner is removed from an acute or right angle, usually at 45°.
2 see chamfered moulding. →14

chamfer stop in ornamentation, the terminating device for a chamfered moulding or carving.

chamfered moulding a decorative moulding or trim in which any edge has been cut or formed with a chamfer. →14

chamois, 1 see chamois leather.
2 chamois yellow; a shade of brownish yellow which takes its name from the colour of the hide of the chamois antelope and cleaning leathers made from similar materials.
3 an obsolete name for the pigment yellow ochre.

chamois leather, chamois; soft leather used for polishing, originally obtained from a species of European antelope with the same name [*Rupicapra rupicapra*], nowadays from livestock.

chamois yellow see chamois.

chamotte see grog.

Champagne a shade of greyish yellow which takes its name from the colour of the sparkling wine produced in the Champagne region of France.

Champagne chalk a high quality grade of chalk, originally found in deposits in Champagne, France.

chancel **1** the area to the east end of the crossing of a church, containing an altar, and often a choir and an apse.
see *Carolingian monastery* illustration. →97
see *Romanesque church* illustration. →99
see *Gothic cathedral* illustration. →100
see *altar* illustration. →116
2 see east chancel. →97
3 see west chancel. →97

chancel aisle an aisle at the side of a chancel of a large church. →99, →100

chancel arch a major transverse arch supporting the roof or tower of a church at the intersection of the chancel and transept. →99

chancellery see chancery.

chancelry see chancery.

chancery, chancellery, chancelry; a building or part of a building which is the administrative section of an embassy.

change see variation.

changing room **1** a room in which clothes are removed and others put on, usually for a specific activity such as sport.
2 see *changing room* in sauna illustration. →58

channel, 1 channel iron, channel section; a structural steel section formed by rolling, whose uniform cross-section resembles the letter C or U. →34
2 a watercourse, often excavated, connecting one body of water with another.
3 see canal.
4 drainage channel; any open watercourse for the conveyance or drainage of water.
5 see floor channel. →58
6 roof channel; see box gutter. →60
7 in telecommunications, a range or band of wavelengths designated for the sending of signals.
8 see canalis. →80

channel block a concrete block which is U shaped in cross-section; designed for use with reinforcing bars and in-situ concrete as a beam or lintel over a window or door opening; also called a lintel or bond-beam block. →30

channel brick see lintel brick. →16

channel glass, profile glass, glass plank; a glass product manufactured with a U-shaped section by rolling or casting; a number of these, when placed vertically together, form a glazed screen. →53

channel grating a longitudinal grating over a drainage channel.

channel iron see channel. →34

channel section see channel. →34

chantry a privately owned chapel within a church, where prayers are devoted to the donor or one of his or her choosing. →99

chanuk(k)iah a Jewish candelabrum with nine branches, the symbol of the Jewish festival of Chanukkah (Hanukkah); the festival of lights; also written hanukkiah, hanukiah. →123

chaos theory a theory, often linked to deconstructivist architecture, which deals with the outcome of a complex chain of events governed by laws but which is so unpredictable as to appear random.

chapel a small space within a church or temple, or a separate building, for private worship; types included as separate entries are listed below. →100
see *chapel of Anubis* in Egyptian temples illustration. →72
burial chapel. →102
capella imperialis, see Imperial chapel. →98, →99
cemetery chapel.
chapel of ease.
cult chapel. →70
funeral chapel, funerary chapel. →102
Imperial chapel. →98, →99
Lady chapel. →100
meeting house.
palace chapel. →66
parecclesion, parekklesion. →96
retrochoir. →116
sacrificial chapel.
side chapel.
shrine.

chapel of ease a chapel or church for the use of more outlying parishioners, which has its own minister but remains under the jurisdiction of a larger church.

chapter house 1 a space within a church or monastery used by church governors or monks for administration, discussion and meetings.
2 a separate building used for similar duties by church governors.

character 1 the special collective qualities of a material, place, space or building.
2 in computing, a single letter or symbol.

characteristic the distinguishing or typical feature, property, function etc. particular to something.

characteristic strength in structural engineering, the theoretical strength of a material gained from tests and research under normal conditions of loading, used as a base for structural calculations.

character printer a printer which prints one character at a time; see line printer, page printer.

character set a set of mathematical or scientific symbols, letters or characters of an alphabet and numbers, especially that recognized by a computer or printer.

charcoal 1 porous pieces of partially carbonized wood, used as a fuel and in rod form (originally willow or vine twigs) as drawing implements; see stick charcoal, compressed charcoal.
2 see activated carbon.

charcoal paper soft, coarse, opaque paper suitable for drawing in charcoal, pencil, pastel and crayon.

charge 1 the amount or accumulation of energy in a system, especially electricity in a battery.
2 see electric charge.
3 debit; a sum of money demanded as payment for goods and services.

chargehand, leading hand; a tradesman who is head of a team of tradesmen and labourers on site.

chariot see quadriga. →89

charnel house a building or space within a building for storage of bones or bodies of the dead; also an ossuary.

chart, 1 hydrographical map, sea chart; a map of a sea or major waterway indicating water depths and other features.
2 see diagram.

chartered engineer, professional engineer; a qualified engineer who, as well as having a university degree in engineering, has met the requirements of an engineering institute.

Chartreuse a shade of dull yellow which takes its name from the colour of the liqueur produced at the monastery of Chartreuse in France.

chase 1 in general construction, a shallow channel cut into a solid wall, floor or ceiling for the location of electrical servicing or pipework, usually subsequently filled.
2 in joinery or carpentry, a long groove cut into a piece of timber to receive another piece; a housing or dado. →5

chattering undesirable vibration of tools which cause ripples in the finished surface of a plasterwork moulding, certain extruded products, machined timber etc.

chattra 'the royal parasol'; stone ornament placed atop a Buddhist stupa, a number of diminishing umbrella-like discs on a central stem (the yasti) representing Buddhism. →68

chauntry see chantry.

check 1 a split in an improperly seasoned timber piece which appears as a result of uneven shrinkage; a seasoning shake. →1
2 a heart check, see heartshake. →1
3 see surface checks. →1
4 in masonry, a rebate in the face of a brick, block or stone.
5 see cost check.
6 door check, see door closer. →51
7 vapour check, see vapour barrier. →8, →59
8 see water check.

checkerboard plan see grid plan. →94

checkered alternative spelling of chequered.

checkered pattern see square pattern. →15

checkerplate see chequerplate. →34

checkerwork see chequerwork. →124

checking a defect in a paint finish caused by a fine mesh of surface cracks caused by shrinkage or uneven drying.

check lock see snib. →39

check valve, 1 clack valve, valve, non-return valve, reflux valve; a valve which allows for flow in a pipeline in one direction only.
2 see backflow valve.
3 see pipe interrupter.

cheek 1 in timber jointing, the side of a tenon, mortise or recess. →5
2 the triangular side wall of a dormer window or similar construction.
3 the flat side surface of a hammerhead. →40

chemical cleaning the treatment of a surface or object by the application of a chemical to clean it.

chemical closet a WC in which stored soil waste is broken down and neutralized by chemical action to form a harmless product.

chemical compound a substance consisting of two or more elements which are chemically bound together.

chemical element see element.

chemical plating, electroless plating; the application of protective or decorative metal coatings to plastics or ceramic products by immersion into various chemical solutions, during which deposition occurs by chemical reaction without the use of electricity.

chemical reaction the chemical binding together of two or more substances to form a new substance which may have different properties from its constituents.

chemical resistance the ability of a material or finish to withstand chemical attack or reaction.

chemical shrinkage in concretework, a reduction in size caused by chemical changes during setting and final hardening.

chemically strengthened glass a toughened glass used for optical lenses and lamps, whose surface is hardened against abrasion by heating with salts to encourage replacement of ions.

chemist a commercial outlet for the preparation and sale of medicines and drugs; variously known as an apothecary, pharmacy or dispensary, or, in the US, a drugstore (Am.).

chemistry a branch of science which deals with the study of the structure of matter as atoms and molecules.

chequerboard construction, alternate bay construction, hit and miss construction; in concretework, a method of construction of casting large areas of deck, floor, paving etc. to reduce cracking from drying shrinkage; diagonally adjacent areas or bays are cast then allowed to harden, after which the remaining voids are filled using the existing concrete as support.

chequerboard pattern 1 see square pattern. →15
2 see basketweave pattern. →10

chequerboard plan see grid plan. →94

chequered brickwork decorative brickwork based on a repeated grid pattern as a result of the use of occasional coloured bricks, added stone or the arrangement of bricks of varying colour into squares or rectangles.

chequered pattern see square pattern. →15

chequerplate, checkerplate, raised pattern plate, tread plate; hot-rolled steel plate treated with a raised surface pattern, used as durable cladding, industrial flooring to provide grip etc. →34

chequerwork, checkerwork; decoration based on the use of a squared grid in which alternate squares are rendered in a second colour, relief or manner. →124

cherry 1 [*Prunus spp.*] a number of species of European hardwood with deep red-brown, dense and fine-grained timber; used for flooring, joinery and furniture; see ***Prunus spp.*** for full list of related species included in this work.
2 currant red, Post Office red; a shade of red which takes its name from the ripe fruit of the cherry tree (*Prunus cerasus*) and the redcurrant bush (*Riber rubrum*).

cherry mahogany see makore.

chert, hornstone; a dense, fine-grained sedimentary rock composed mainly of cryptocrystalline silica; difficult to work but used, like flint, for stone facing; also a general name for all horn-like rocks.

chessboard plan see grid plan. →94

chessylite see azurite.

chest altar a church altar table with a large ornamented or panelled base for the storage of sacramental vessels. →116

chester a walled town based on a previous Roman settlement or castrum; a common suffix for place names in England, sites of Roman forts.

chest freezer a large commercial and domestic freezing appliance for storage of foodstuffs etc., often accessible from above and sometimes with an upwardly opening door.

chest of drawers a piece of furniture containing a number of sliding storage drawers.

chestnut, sweet chestnut, horse chestnut; **1** any nut-producing hardwood from the genus *Castanea*, found in temperate regions of the Northern hemisphere; see sweet chestnut; many other unrelated species from other parts of the world are also known as chestnuts.
2 see sweet chestnut.
3 see horse chestnut.
4 a shade of brown which takes its name from the colour of the shelled fruit (conker) of the horse chestnut tree; also known as chestnut brown.

chestnut brown an alternative name for the pigment raw umber.

cheval see chevaux de frise. →104

chevaux de frise 1 a number of obstacles, often sharp stones, stakes, iron spikes or barbed wire, placed on or embedded into the ground in front of a fortification or castle to inhibit oncoming attackers; singular is cheval de frise. →104
2 see abattis. →104
3 see caltrap. →104, →117

chevet in church or cathedral architecture, an apse with projecting radiating chapels or niches. →100

chevron Romanesque ornament consisting of a series of parallel zigzag lines. →124

chevron cross see broken cross. →118

chevron match see V-match. →10

chevron moulding see chevron. →124

chiaroscuro in painting, the technique of contrasting light and shadow for the dramatic expression of form; developed by Leonardo, Rembrandt and Caravaggio.

Chicago School a school and movement in architecture in the American mid-west in the late 1800s, characterized by innovative steel-framed high-rise commercial buildings.

chicken wire a wire netting of thin galvanized wire with hexagonal openings; also known as hexagonal mesh. →34

chickrassy, Chittagong wood; [Chukrasia tabularis] a southern Asian hardwood whose reddish brown heartwood is used in furniture.

chief the upper portion or upper third of a heraldic shield. →124

children's home an establishment, building or part of a building, for the care of children on a full-time basis.

children's playground see playground.

chiller see refrigeration unit.

chilling see refrigeration.

chimaira see chimera. →122

chimera a mythical fire-breathing monster with a lion's head, goat's body and serpent's tail, symbolic of the forces of darkness and compulsion; alternative spelling is chimaira. →122

chimney 1 a vertical structure which contains one or more flues to extract waste gases and smoke from a building, boiler or other apparatus.
2 see flue. →55, →56
3 see chimney stack. →56
see *chimney and flue system* illustration. →56
see *fireplace* illustration. →55
see *balcony and balustrade* illustration. →54
see *sauna* illustration. →58

chimney block see flue block. →16

chimney bond, column bond; brickwork bonds used for slender constructions such as brick chimneys, piers and columns. →21

chimney breast a thickening or recess in a masonry wall containing space for a fireplace and flue constructions. →55

chimney cap, 1 bonnet; a device attached to the outlet in the top of a flue or chimney which rotates in the wind and improves draught within the flue.
2 see flue cap, rain cap. →56, →58

chimney-corner see inglenook.

chimney cricket see chimney saddle.

chimney crown the masonry or concrete construction at the top of a brick or stone chimney stack, often overhanging or weathered, to provide protection from rain, snow etc. →56

chimney flashing a layer of felt or other sheet membrane laid around the base of a chimney or flue at the point at which it penetrates the roof structure to prevent the passage of water. →58

chimney gutter a back gutter on the upward side of the junction between a chimney and a sloping roof to convey rainwater from behind the chimney. →56

chimney ladder an external ladder attached to the side of a chimney or flue for use during maintenance. →54, →61

chimney-nook see inglenook.

chimney saddle, chimney cricket (Am.), cricket (Am.); in roofing, a shaped piece of impervious sheet material, laid under roof tiles and other roofing behind a chimney to protect the junction of chimney and roof plane.

chimney shaft a large, usually industrial, freestanding chimney, containing a large flue.

chimney stack 1 the structure or constructional surround for a chimney or flue. →56
2 the part of a chimney exposed above the upper surface of a roof.

chimney-sweeping the manual cleaning of soot from the inside surfaces of flues by the insertion of long brushes.

Chimú culture the culture of the Indians of north-west Peru c.1300–1400 after the Mochica and predating the Inca civilization.

china 1 see bone china.
2 see vitreous china.

china clay, Devonshire clay; an impure variety of kaolin, hydrated aluminium silicate, a fine white mineral powder used for making chinaware and as an inert pigment in paints.

Chinagraph pencil a pencil with a white, waxy lead used for writing on glass and ceramics; instead of being encased in wood it is wound within a spiral tube of paper.

China red, Chinese red, Chinese rouge; a shade of bright red often associated with the colour of the pigments chrome red and oxide red; the same colour as calypso and scarlet.

China wood oil see tung oil.

Chinese architecture the architecture of China, characterized by fine timber frames and pagodas with ornate decoration, coloured glazed ceramic tiles etc.

Chinese blue a form of high quality Prussian blue pigment.

Chinese bond see rat-trap bond. →17

Chinese red 1 see China red.
2 see chrome red.

Chinese rouge see China red.

Chinese vermilion a red pigment, genuine vermilion, manufactured in China; also the name of a shade of red which takes its name from this.

Chinese white zinc white pigment prepared for use as a watercolour.

Chinese yellow 1 a name applied to a number of yellow pigments, especially king's yellow.
2 see banana.

Ching, Ch'ing, Qing, Tsing; a period in Chinese cultural history during the time of the Manchu or Ching dynasty from 1644 to 1911.

chink gap in horizontal log construction, the gap between the long groove and the log course below, filled with insulating material. →6

chinoiserie decorative Rococo ornament and style in Europe from the 1700s which arose as a result of trade with China; it is characterized by a fascination with Chinese painting, wallpaper, vases and pagodas.

chip angle see cutting angle.

chipboard, wood chipboard; a building board formed from chipped fibrous material, usually woodchips, bonded together with resin then pressed into sheets; types included as separate entries are listed below. →9, →59
see *particleboard* illustration. →9
bitumen-coated chipboard.
extruded particleboard. →9
graded density chipboard. →9
laminated chipboard.
melamine faced chipboard.
multilayer chipboard. →9
oriented strand board. →9
platen-pressed chipboard. →9
primed and filled chipboard.
sanded chipboard.
single layer chipboard. →9
tongued and grooved chipboard.
veneered chipboard.
wood cement chipboard.

chipboard flooring flooring, underflooring or decking consisting of abutted or tongued and grooved chipboard.

chipped grain a timber machining defect in which small chips are torn from the wood by blunt or worn cutting tools, leaving an undesirable pitted surface. →1

Chippendale a decorative style in furniture named after the carpenter Thomas Chippendale (1718–1779), which was influenced by Rococo, Gothic, Queen Anne and chinoiserie.

chippings crushed rock aggregate between 3 mm and 20 mm used in road surfacing, roofing, render etc.

chippy a slang term for a carpenter.

chips, woodchips; in the conversion and machining of timber, waste wood, rough sawdust and shavings reused in the manufacture of wood-based products.

Chi-Rho see Christ monogram. →119

chisel a hand tool whose metal blade is sharpened at one end, used for cutting and shaping timber and stone; types included as separate entries are listed below. →41
see *types of chisel* illustration. →41
barking chisel.
batting tool. →41
bench chisel. →41
bevelled-edge chisel, bevel edge chisel. →41
boaster. →41
bolster. →41
broach. →41
bruzz chisel. →41
butt chisel. →41
cant chisel, see framing chisel.
carving chisel, see woodcarving chisel. →41
caulking chisel, caulking iron.
claw chisel, claw tool. →41
clourer. →41
cold chisel. →41
corner chisel, see bruzz chisel. →41
dogleg chisel, see bruzz chisel. →41
drawer lock chisel.
driver. →41
fantail tool, see fishtail chisel. →41
fillet chisel. →41
firmer chisel. →41
fishtail chisel, fishtail tool. →41
floor chisel.
framing chisel.
gouge. →41
hammer-headed chisel. →41
heading chisel, see mortise chisel. →41
hinge chisel.
joiner's chisel, see paring chisel. →41
jumper. →41
lock chisel.
long-cornered chisel, see skew chisel. →41
mallet-headed chisel. →41
masonry chisel, mason's chisel; see entry for full list of masonry chisels. →41
mortise lock chisel. →41
mortising chisel, mortise chisel. →41
nicker, see splitter.
paring chisel. →41
parting chisel, parting tool.
patent claw chisel. →41
peeling chisel, peeling iron, see barking chisel.
pitching tool, pincher, pitcher. →41
pocket chisel, see butt chisel. →41
point tool. →41
punch. →41
quirking tool. →41
registered chisel.
ripping chisel. →41
sash chisel, see butt chisel. →41
scraping tool, scraper. →41
sculptor's point. →41
skew chisel. →41
spindle, see fillet chisel. →41
splitter.

stonecarving chisel, stone chisel, stonemason's chisel, see masonry chisel. →41
swan-neck chisel, see mortise lock chisel. →41
tooth tool, see patent claw chisel.
tracer.
turning chisel. →41
turning gouge. →41
waster. →41
woodcarving chisel. →41
woodworking chisel; see entry for full list of woodcarving chisels. →41

chisel blade the longitudinal steel part of a chisel, sharpened for cutting and shaping wood. →41

chisel handle the handle to which a blade of a chisel is attached, usually of plastic or a hardwood such as beech, and often with metal ferrules at one or both ends to prevent splitting when struck with a mallet. →41

Chittagong wood see chickrassy.

chlorinated rubber paint a hard, water and chemical resistant paint which contains a binder consisting of rubber treated with chlorine.

chlorinated rubber varnish a varnish in which the binder is natural rubber treated with chlorine.

chlorine a heavy, greenish, poisonous, gaseous chemical element, **Cl**, used as a disinfectant and in bleaching.

chlorite a greenish magnesium, iron alumino-silicate crystalline composite mineral.

Chlorophora excelsa see iroko.

chloroprene rubber, polychloroprene; the chemical name for the synthetic rubber neoprene.

Chloroxylon swietenia see Ceylon satinwood.

chocolate (brown) a shade of dark brown which takes its name from the colour of plain chocolate.

choir, quire; **1** the area in a church or cathedral where the choir sits, situated to the east of the crossing in the chancel.
see *Late Antique church* illustration. →95
see *Carolingian church* illustration. →98
see *Scandinavian hall church* illustration. →102
2 see schola cantorum. →95

choir aisle an aisle in a large church alongside the choir.

choir screen 1 a decorative screen which separates the choir from the nave and other spaces in a church; often a rood screen. →99, →100
2 see cancelli. →95, →98

choir stalls bench seating for the choir in a church, often in ornately carved wood.
see *Romanesque church* illustration. →99
see *Gothic cathedral* illustration. →100

choker ring in foundation construction, the lower, wider edge of a caisson, used for cutting its housing in the ground.

Chola architecture also spelled Cola; the architecture and art of the Chola dynasty in Sri Lanka and southern India from 900 to 1300 AD.

chop axe 1 a heavy mason's axe for evening off a stone surface before dressing. →40
2 see felling axe.

chopin an old measure of liquid capacity equal to approximately one English quart.

chopped strand glass reinforcement for fibreglass consisting of short lengths of glass fibre arranged in overlapping random fashion.

choragic monument khoros (Gk) = 'choir'; a small decorative tripod structure erected in ancient Greece to commemorate the victory of the leader of a chorus or theatrical group in competitions during the feasts of Dionysus.

chord, 1 boom; an upper or lower horizontal member in a trussed beam.
2 see upper chord, top chord. →33
3 see lower chord, bottom chord. →33
4 in applied mathematics, a straight line drawn between two points.
5 in pure mathematics, a straight line joining two points on a curve or arc.

Chou see Zhou.

chresmographeion a hall or room for the oracle in a Greek temple; also written cresmographeion.

Chrismon see Christ monogram. →119

Christian IV pertaining to the Dutch-influenced Renaissance architecture in Denmark during the reign of Christian IV (1577–1648), himself an amateur architect.

Christian VIII pertaining to the classicist and Rococo styles of furniture and interiors in Denmark from 1825 to 1855.

Christian antiquity referring to art and decoration from the early centuries of the Christian church that bears classical influences.

Christ monogram a common decorative motif in Christian religious art and architecture, formed of the letters X (Greek letter chi) and P (Greek letter rho), Christ's initials in Greek; also called the monogram of Christ, Christogram, Chi-Rho, Chrismon, Constantine's cross; see also labarum. →119

Christogram see Christ monogram. →119

chroma see colour saturation.

chromatic aberration an optical phenomenon, the blurring of colours at the edge of an image due to the inability of a lens to focus all colours to the same point.

chromatic colour, spectral colour; any colour contained in the spectrum of visible light.

chromatic pigment a pigment which consists of colours other than simply black, white or grey.

chrome see chromium.

chrome green a range of green pigments formed by mixing blue pigments, especially Prussian blue, and chrome yellow pigments; this range includes leaf green, leek green, moss green, myrtle green, Royal green, zinnober green.

chrome orange an opaque poisonous orange pigment which consists of lead chromate; used in oil paints and glues.

chrome plated referring to metals which have been treated with a thin protective coat of chrome; as an adjective it is written chrome-plated.

chrome plating see chromium plating.

chrome red, Chinese red, Derby red; an opaque poisonous red pigment which consists of lead chromate; used in oil paints and glues.

chrome steel, chromium steel; a hard and fine-grained alloy of steel containing significant quantities of chromium.

chrome yellow, Leipzig yellow, Paris yellow; an opaque yellow pigment consisting of lead chromate, used in large quantities in cheap paints.

chroming see chromium plating.

chromite a black, dully glossy, greasy mineral, $\mathbf{FeCr_2O_4}$, naturally occurring iron or magnesium chromate, the principal ore for the extraction of chromium.

chromium, chrome; an extremely hard metal, **Cr**, used as an alloy in the manufacture of stainless steel, and as a corrosion-resistant coating for steel.

chromium oxide green, 1 oxide of chromium, Schnitzer's green; an opaque pale green inorganic pigment consisting of calcined chromium oxide; used in oil and watercolour paints despite its low tinting power.
2 see viridian.

chromium plating, chrome plating, chroming; the electrochemical application of a thin protective layer of chromium to metals.

chromium steel see chrome steel.

chromo-paper paper used in lithography, heavily coated with casein or glue mixed with starch and china clay.

chromophore in chemical science, that part of a molecule which gives a substance its colour.

Chrozophora tinctoria see folium.

chrysoberyl a yellowish, greenish or brownish mineral used for ornament, as a gemstone (emerald, aquamarine) and as raw material in the extraction of beryllium.

chrysolite see olivine.

CHS see circular hollow section. →34

chuck an adjustable device for holding a drill bit in a drill, or wood on a lathe.

chumon the inner gateway of a Japanese temple. →68

Chukrasia tabularis see chickrassy.

church a building or consecrated space for the practice of Christian worship; types included as separate entries are listed below.
see *Early Christian basilica* illustration. →95
see *church of Late Antiquity* illustration. →95
see *Carolingian abbey church* illustration. →98
see *Romanesque church* illustration. →99
see *Gothic cathedral* illustration. →100
see *Scandinavian hall church* illustration. →102
see *log church* illustration. →102
abbey church.
auditory church.
axial church, see longitudinal church. →102
basilica church. →99
Benedictine church.
centralized church, see centrally planned church. →95
collegiate church.
convent church.
cross church, see cruciform church. →98
cross-domed church. →95
cruciform church. →98
domical church. →95, →96
double chancel church. →97
double cruciform church.
double-ended church, see double chancel church. →97
five-aisled church. →100
five-domed church, see cross-domed church. →95
fortress church.
Franciscan church.
friary church.
hall church.
longitudinal church. →102
mast church, see stave church.
monastic church.
nave-and-chancel church. →98
pilgrimage church.
priory church.
pseudo cruciform church. →102
quatrefoil church, see tetraconch church.
quincunx church, see cross-domed church. →95
Romanesque church. →99
round church.
Scandinavian church illustration. →102
stave church.
tetraconch church.
three-aisled church. →102
three-apsed church, see triconch church. →99
title church, see titular church. →95
titular church. →95
town church.
triconch church. →99
wooden church. →102

church bell a large bell in a church tower or belfry, rung on occasion for calling worshippers to services etc.

church hall, parish hall; a building in the ownership of a church, used for congregational meetings, gatherings and receptions, but not usually religious services.

church tower a tower often at the crossing or west end of a church, sometimes capped with a spire and containing bells.
see *church tower* illustration. →26
see *Scandinavian hall church* illustration. →102

churchyard the area of enclosed land surrounding a church, usually a graveyard. →102

Churrigueresque highly embellished Baroque architecture in Spain and Mexico in the 1600s and 1700s with plateresque influences, which takes its name from the Spanish architect José Churriguera (1650–1723).

chute, 1 shaft; a vertical void or sealed hollow structure through a building through which goods, laundry and refuse are thrown, to be collected at a lower level.
2 see concrete chute.

CIAM, Congrès internationaux d'Architecture moderne; a community of modernist architects founded in 1928 by Helene de Mandrot and revolving around le Corbusier and Siegried Giedon, who championed functionalist ideas and were responsible for the Weissenhof housing exhibition; also the International Congresses of Modern Architecture.

CIRPAC, Commité internationale pour la résolution des problèmes del'architecture contemporaine; the administrative organ of CIAM.

ciborium Lat.; in Early Christian and Byzantine churches, a canopy mounted on four posts over an altar, shrine or the tomb of a martyr; a baldachin; the original Greek form is kiborion.
see *ciborium* in Early Christian and Late Antique church illustration. →95
see *ciborium* in altar illustration. →116

ciborium altar a church altar surrounded or surmounted by a masonry vaulted canopy supported by columns, an altar-type typical in Early Christian or Byzantine church architecture; see also baldachin altar. →116

cicada a Mediterranean large-winged jumping or hopping insect of the family [*Cicadoidea*], a common motif in ancient Greek ornament where it is the attribute of the tireless poet and muse; in Chinese decoration symbolic of immortality. →120

Cicadidea see cicada. →120

cill see sill.

cill plate see sill plate. →57

cimier see crest. →124

cinema, movie house (Am.), movie theater (Am.), picture house; a building containing an auditorium and screen for showing films.

cinerarium Lat.; a room or vessel containing the ashes of the deceased.

cinerary urn, burial urn, funerary urn; a small clay or wooden vessel for containing the cremated remains of a deceased person.

cinnabar 1 red native mercury sulphide in ore form, used since early times to make the red pigment vermilion.
2 a shade of bright red which takes its name from the above; an old name for the colours scarlet and vermilion.

cinnamon (brown) a shade of brown which takes its name from a common spice ground from the inner bark of the cinnamon tree [*Cinnamomum spp.*].

cinnamon stone hessonite.

cinquecento the classical high Renaissance style of art and architecture in Italy from the late 1400s and 1500s.

cinquefoil 1 a decorative and ornamental device consisting of five leaf motifs radiating out from a point. →108, →109
2 see pointed cinquefoil. →108

cinquefoil arch a decorative arch with five lobes or foils in a cloverleaf arrangement. →24

cinquefoliated arch 1 a decorative arch whose intrados is composed of five lobes or foils in a cloverleaf arrangement, and whose extrados is a round or pointed arch; especially found in Gothic architecture. →23
2 see round cinquefoliated arch. →23
3 see pointed cinquefoliated arch. →23

cipolin see cipollino.

cipollino, cipolin; a metamorphic rock originating from Italy, marble patterned with folded stripes; used in building as decorative stone.

cippus Lat.; a low inscribed stone pillar used by the Romans as a border or mileage stone, road sign, landmark or gravestone.
circle 1 a round planar geometrical figure described through 360° around a single point, whose radius is a constant. →108
2 Celtic circle, see Celtic love knot. →108
circle-end clamp see gee-clamp.
circle template in technical drawing, a template for drawing circles, perforated with round holes of varying diameters. →130
circline lamp see circular fluorescent tube.
circlip, retaining ring, lock ring; a flat sprung steel ring with a break at one point for prising open so that it can be passed over an axle, shaft or spindle and fitted into an annular recess, providing a collar to prevent bearings and other components from moving.
circuit see auxiliary circuit.
see control circuit.
see electrical circuit.
see final circuit.
see pipe circuit.
see radial circuit.
see ring circuit.
see short circuit.
circuit board in electronic equipment, a specially formed sheet of insulating material onto which electrical components can be soldered.
circuit breaker, cutout, trip switch; a device which automatically stops the flow of current when an electric circuit is overloaded or otherwise in danger; once the circuit has been rectified it can be reset.
circuit diagram a diagrammatic design drawing showing the layout and connections of the various components in an electrical circuit.
circuit efficacy, luminous efficacy, efficacy; in lighting design, the ratio of the amount of light, luminous flux, emitted by a light source compared to how much power it and its circuitry and control equipment use; its unit is the lumen/watt.
circular, round; in the shape of a circle.
circular arch, round arch; any arch composed of a segment of a circle, usually a semicircle; see also segmental arch, horseshoe arch and semicircular arch. →24
circular column, round column; a column whose shaft is circular in cross-section. →13
circular fluorescent tube, circline lamp; a doughnut-shaped fluorescent tube.
circular hollow section, round tube, steel pipe; a circular hollow steel section formed by rolling and welding steel plate, used for structural purposes such as columns, posts etc. →34
circular measure a form of angular measurement in radians, in which the length of an arc is equal to its radius.
circular pattern a paving pattern of small stones or cobbles laid in a series of concentric circles with infill between; also called concentric pattern. →15
circular plane see compass plane.
circular road, ring road; an urban road which runs circumferential to a town centre, alleviating congestion and linking outer suburbs and radial arteries.
circular saw a power saw with a rotating steel cutting disc whose teeth are often shaped or tipped with abrasive; may be hand-held, mounted in a bench, or part of a larger industrial installation such as a sawmill.
circular stair 1 any stair whose treads are arranged radially about a central newel. →45
2 see spiral stair. →45
circular temple see round temple. →85
circulating water the heating water conveyed in sealed pipework to provide warmth to radiators etc. in a central heating installation.
circulation 1 in the internal planning of a building, the system of prescribed routes, including stairs, lifts and corridors used frequently by its occupants.
2 see vertical circulation.
circulation pump, circulator; a pump used to provide pressure in the hot and cold water systems of a building.
circulation space a stair, corridor or gangway space within a building along which people, goods etc. can move or be moved from place to place.
circulator see circulation pump.
circumference 1 the length of the perimeter of a circle.
2 the perimeter of a circle itself.
circumscribed angle in geometry, an angle between two lines which are tangents of an arc.
circus 1 Lat.; in Roman architecture, a long U-shaped or enclosed arena for chariot racing; a hippodrome. →89
2 a circular open space, place, roundabout etc. in an urban setting.
3 a formal urban street and buildings laid out in the form of a circle or oval.
cist a prehistoric grave of flat slabs of stone forming a burial chest, either covered with a mound or exposed.
cistern 1 an open vessel for storing water at atmospheric pressure in a water supply system; a storage tank. →91
see expansion cistern.
2 a storage tank containing water for flushing a WC or other sanitary appliance; a flushing cistern.
see dual-flush cistern.
see flushing cistern.
see high-level cistern.
trough cistern, see flushing trough.
citadel 1 a fortified military castle or fortress, in which a garrison of soldiers are stationed, overlooking or guarding a city; also the inner fortified stronghold of a fortified complex.
2 see acropolis. →94
citizen participation see public participation.
citrine a yellowish variety of quartz, used as a gemstone; often misleadingly called topaz.
citron yellow 1 a form of zinc yellow pigment.
2 any shade of pale yellow, especially lemon yellow.
Citrus limon see lemon yellow, citron yellow.
Citrus maxima, see grapefruit.
Citrus reticulata, see mandarin orange.
Citrus sinensis, orange, see mandarin orange.
city 1 a large town, especially one which has been created by charter.
2 a town containing a cathedral.
see *city in antiquity* illustration. →94
city centre, commercial centre, downtown (Am.); the central commercial and civic area of a town, containing shops and businesses.
city council see council.
city hall a building or group of buildings for municipal administration, the seat of the city council.
city park see urban park.
city planning, town planning, urban planning, planning; the legislative process of land-use planning, layouts etc. for an urban area, designed to regulate development and provide a healthy environment for its inhabitants, taking into account various socio-economic, aesthetic, industrial, and recreational factors.
civic architecture, civic design; architecture and built form of a quality and suitability for an urban setting.
civic centre, municipal centre; **1** the administrative hub of a town, city or district, containing public buildings such as council and local authority premises, public works departments and sometimes libraries, law courts etc.
2 a building complex which houses similar functions.
3 see county hall.
civic design 1 in town planning, the provision of colour, visual interest and texture to the urban fabric.
2 see civic architecture.
civil defence shelter a subterranean shelter, often hewn out of the bedrock, to provide safety for

inhabitants of a building or area in the event of attack by air bombings, radiation or poisonous gases; also called an air-raid shelter or bomb shelter. →61

civil engineer a qualified professional who designs public utilities, roads, bridges and sewers, and supervises their construction and maintenance.

civil engineering the construction of roads, waterways, bridges, excavations, earthworks and other structures, rather than buildings; also civil engineering works.

civitas 'nation, state' (Lat.); a Roman territory occupied by a conquered tribe, a Roman administrative district.

clachan a small scattered village or hamlet in the Scottish Highlands.

clack valve see check valve.

cladding, facing; **1** any non-loadbearing system of boards, prefabricated components, stone, brick, sheeting etc. attached to a building frame as weatherproofing or as an exterior or interior finish; types included as separate entries are listed below.
2 the action of producing the above, the work thus involved.
external cladding. →8
metal cladding.
natural stone cladding. →11
stone cladding, see stone facing, natural stone cladding.
tile cladding.
tiling.
timber cladding. →8
wall cladding.

cladding cleat see holdfast. →11

cladding component see cladding unit.

cladding glass, spandrel glass; opaque float glass that has been fired on one surface with a non-transparent coloured ceramic enamel, used for external wall panels, blind windows etc. in curtain walling.

cladding panel see cladding unit; types included as separate entries are listed below.
ceiling panel. →60
cladding glass.
concrete panel, see precast concrete panel.
external wall panel.
insulated infill panel.
precast concrete panel.
sheetmetal cladding panel. →60

cladding rail one of a series of lightweight metal profiles fixed at regular spacing to a structural base as a means of fixing external cladding panels, components, boards etc. →11

cladding stone see stone facing. →11

cladding unit, cladding panel, cladding component; a prefabricated weatherproofing component of metal, concrete or composite material for cladding the exterior surface, frame etc. of a building; types included as separate entries are listed below.
see *pressed metal cladding panel* in office building illustration. →60
ceiling panel. →60
concrete panel, see precast concrete panel.
external wall panel.
see insulated infill panel.
precast concrete panel.
sheetmetal cladding panel. →60

Cladium mariscus see sedge.

claim 1 in contract management, a demand by one party for additional payment to which he is entitled under the contract, or for damages for breach of contract due to faulty workmanship, failure to supply goods on time etc.
see contractual claim.
see extra-contractual claim, ex-contractual claim.
ex-gratia claim, see ex-gratia application.
2 an application to an insurance company for reimbursement due to damage or loss to insured goods or property.

clamp 1 see cramp.
2 see wire rope clamp. →37

clamping ring a fitting for securing the joint between a flue and the outlet pipe of a gas, oil or solid fuel appliance.

clapboard roof traditional roof construction whose roofing is of overlapping boards laid horizontally, parallel to eaves and ridge; see next entry. →48

clapboard roofing traditional pitched roof covering of boards laid horizontally, parallel to ridge and eaves, each overlapping the board below as with roof tiles. →48

clapboarding, colonial siding; external timber wall cladding boards laid horizontally so that each board overlaps the one below. →8

clarifier see sedimentation tank.

claret see wine red.

clasp knife see penknife.

clasped purlin, trapped purlin; in traditional timber frame construction, a purlin held at the angle of a principal rafter and collar.

clasped purlin collar rafter roof in traditional timber roof construction, a rafter roof with a collar supporting a clasped purlin.

class see grade.

classic of a work of art or architecture, of such quality as to stand the test of time and retain its relevancy.

classical 1 pertaining to a period in history when a culture flourishes or produces its culminating or most typifying works; especially classical Greece between the Archaic and Hellenistic periods c.480–323 BC, Rome during the time of Augustus c.63 BC–14 AD, but also Mayan architecture from 250 to 1000 BC, Islamic Abbasid architecture from 750 to 1250 AD, the Renaissance in Italy, and France during the reigns of Henry IV and Louis XIII and XIV (1589–1715).
see *Doric capital* of Classical period illustration. →81
2 Classical; referring to the architecture and art of classical Greece and Rome, or any architecture which follows the same principles and ideas, such as Renaissance, neoclassical or revival styles; see classicism.
see Greek architecture. →78, →80, →81, →84, →85, →111
see Roman architecture. →79, →81, →111
3 referring to physical theories and principles of pre-quantum mechanics.

classical base a base on which a column of any of the classical Greek and Roman orders is placed, carved according to set patterns and proportions. →81
see *classical base* illustrations. →81
see *column base* in classical orders illustrations. →78, →79, →80

classical capital a capital surmounting a column of any of the classical Greek and Roman orders, carved according to set patterns and proportions. →81
see *classical capital* illustrations. →81
see *capital* in classical orders illustrations. →78, →79, →80

classical column a column of the classical Greek and Roman orders, carved according to set patterns and proportions. →78, →79
see Doric column. →78
see Ionic column. →78, →80
see Corinthian column. →78
see Composite column. →79
see Tuscan column. →79

classical column base see classical base. →81

classical Greek orders see Greek orders and *Classical Greek orders* illustration. →78, →80, →81

classical maze see Cretan maze. →123

classical mouldings the series of mouldings as found in a classical entablature. →80

classical orders the Doric, Ionic and Corinthian orders of ancient Greek classical architecture, and the Tuscan and Composite orders of Rome. →78
see *classical orders* in Roman amphitheatre illustration. →90

classical portico see *classical portico* illustration. →86

classical Roman orders see Roman orders and *classical Roman orders* illustration. →79

classical solution in classical architecture, the spacing of triglyphs in an entablature evenly, so that, for each triglyph to be centrally above a column, the corner columns are nearer to one another than the others; see archaic solution, corner contraction. →77

classical temple see *classical temple* illustration; types included as separate entries are listed below. →86
amphiprostyle temple. →84
antis temple. →84
apteral temple, apteros. →84
circular temple, see round temple. →85
double antis temple. →84
double temple. →85
Etruscan temple. →84
Greek temple, see *apteral and peristyle temple* illustrations. →84, →85
megaron temple. →84
monopteros. →85, →94
monostyle temple. →84
peripteral temple, see peripteros. →85
peristyle temple.
prostyle temple. →84
Roman temple, see *apteral and peristyle temple* illustrations. →84, →85
round temple. →66, →85

classical theatre see theatrum. →89

classicism 1 architecture and arts which follow the ideas and styles of classical Greek and Roman precedents.
2 see neoclassicism.
3 Baroque classicism, see Louis XIV style.

Classic revival an architectural style, neoclassicism, in Europe from the early 1800s, characterized by strict adherence to classical principles of Greek and Roman architecture; see Greek Revival.

classification, grade, grading; the division of a mass of data, information, or products and materials into categories; the resulting scheme.

classification of soils see soil classification.

classroom a room in a school or educational institution used for group academic or technical instruction.

clastic sedimentary rock sedimentary rock which has formed as a result of the fusion of particles from older, weathered and broken down rocks.

clavicula a defended passage in front of the gates of a Roman military camp.

claw bolt the bolt for a sliding door lock or latch, with two sprung hook-shaped pieces which grasp a striking plate attached to the door frame. →39

claw chisel a toothed hand chisel used for dressing stonework; also called a claw tool. →41

claw chiselling in stonework, the final dressing of a surface with a claw chisel.

claw hammer a hammer with a fork or claw opposite the striking face for extracting nails. →40

claw tool see claw chisel. →41

clay 1 a range of fine plastic soils or rocks containing a high proportion of water; flowing saturated clay is called mud.
2 a shade of yellowish brown which takes its name from the general colour of the above.

clay block see hollow clay block. →16

clay block paving see brick paving. →15

clay brick 1 the most common type of brick, made or manufactured from moulded clay, hardened by firing in a kiln or baking in the sun. →16
2 see fired brick. →16
3 see mud brick.

clay cob see cob.

clay roof tile any roof tile manufactured from fired clay. see *roof tile* illustration. →47

clayslate, killas; a greenish or dark grey sedimentary rock with excellent cleavage, used as building stone for roof and wall tiles, and for insulating slabs.

claystone argillaceous rock.

clay tile 1 any tile manufactured from fired clay. →20
2 see clay roof tile. →47

cleanout see cleanout trap.

cleanout trap, cleanout; a removable panel at lower level in formwork, from which rubbish and other unwanted material can be removed prior to casting or placing concrete.

clean room, sterile room; a space in a research facility or hospital in which levels of contamination, temperature and humidity are carefully controlled.

cleaner one employed to clean surfaces, polish floors, empty waste vessels etc. in a building.

cleaner's sink, bucket sink; a wide sink fixed at waist height for use by a cleaner to empty and fill buckets, clean mops etc.

cleaning, 1 wash; the removal of dirt, scale, impurities and other unwanted surface material using chemical treatments, processes or agents.
2 the clearing up of rubbish, washing of surfaces and other activities on a building site after construction is complete or as maintenance of a building.

cleaning agent any chemical substance used for removing unwanted dirt, scale and impurities from a surface.

cleaning cupboard see broom cupboard.

cleaning eye, inspection eye, rodding eye; a small covered opening to provide access to a pipeline for cleaning and clearing by rodding.

cleaning hinge see easy-clean hinge. →38

clear, 1 colourless; a description of glass products, liquids, sealants etc. which are uncoloured.
2 see transparent.
3 in artificial lighting, the classification of a lamp whose bulb is of transparent glass; cf. pearl, opal.

clearance 1 a space between two adjacent components for fitting, access, circulation etc.
2 the narrow gap between a hinged door leaf or window casement and its frame which allows it to open.
3 see back clearance, front clearance.
4 see allowance. →51
5 see door clearance. →51
6 see headroom.
7 see stair headroom. →45
8 see clearing.

clear felling in landscaping and forestry, the cutting down of all trees from an area.

clear float glass float glass which is transparent.

clearing, 1 clearance, site clearing; the removal of trees, stumps, vegetation, rubbish, stones and other unwanted debris from a building site prior to the commencement of construction.
2 an open area of natural land surrounded by trees or woodland.

clear plate glass ground cast glass or float glass.

clear sheet glass, flat drawn glass; glass formed by a process of drawing sheets of glass upwards from a reservoir of molten material to a tower where they are cut into suitable lengths.

clear span the open horizontal distance between adjacent abutments of supporting construction for a beam, truss, arch etc.
see *clear span* in bridge structure illustration. →31

clearstory see clerestory. →100

clearstory window see clerestory window.

clear timber timber with no visual defects.

clear-water reservoir see service reservoir.

clearway a busy road or urban motorway on which vehicles are not permitted to stop.

clear width see stair clear width. →45

cleat 1 any light secondary fixing for attaching components in place, preventing lateral movement of sheet cladding etc.
2 see sheetmetal cleat.
3 see glazing cleat.

cleavage plane, cutting way, quartering way; in geology, the natural plane or direction along which some rocks split easily and neatly.

Clechée see cross clechée. →118

cleft stone any building stone shaped by cleaving rather than by sawing or hewing.

clematis blue a shade of deep violet which takes its name from the colour of the flowers of the clematis plant [*Clematis spp.*].

clenching see clinching. →3

Cleopatra's needle one of four obelisks originally from Egypt, subsequently situated in London, Paris, Rome and New York; the term is occasionally synonymous with obelisk. →73

clerestory, clearstory; the upper part of the side walls in the main body of a Romanesque or Gothic church, often with large windows to allow light into the space. →100

clerestory lighting natural lighting for large high spaces provided by windows at high level or near the roof line.

clerestory roof see split-level roof. →46

clerestory window, clearstory window; a window at or near the top of an internal wall, found in basilicas, Romanesque and Gothic churches and in some modern factory buildings, halls, gymnasia etc. for top lighting.
see *clerestory window* in Roman basilica illustration. →93

clerk of works, project representative; a qualified professional employed by the client to carry out periodical inspections of a building under construction and ensure that work is carried out according to the terms of the contract.

clevis a metal fastener for chains etc. consisting of a U-shaped metal whose ends are closed off with a threaded bolt or cotter. →37

client a person or organization which commissions a building or construction.

client's representative see project manager.

cliff castle, promontory fort; a coastal fortification from the Iron Age, using natural coastline and cliffs as defensive elements.

climate the conditions of temperature, weather, wind, rainfall, sunshine, frost etc. for a particular region.

climber, 1 climbing plant; any species of landscaping plant which requires a supporting structure to grow upwards.
2 see bindweed. →121

climbing formwork wall formwork raised and supported on previously casted concrete once this has hardened.

climbing frame a recreational structure for climbing, usually provided in a children's playground.

climbing lane, crawler lane; a lane provided on an uphill stretch of a road for the use of slower and heavier traffic.

climbing plant see climber.

clinching, clenching; the hammering or bending over of the exposed ends of driven nails or bolts on the reverse side of construction to prevent the joints from working loose. →3

clinic 1 a building or part of a building in which medical specialists give treatment or advice to non-resident patients.
2 see dental clinic.
3 see maternity clinic.

clink see double welt. →49

clinker partially fused incombustible mineral material such as blast-furnace slag and fused ash created under high temperatures, used as a lightweight aggregate and in ground form in concrete.

clip 1 any small metal fastener which holds a component in place by a clamping action; examples included as separate entries are listed below.
2 tie, tingle; a narrow strip of metal or cleat used for securing roll joints and standing seams in sheet roofing.
circlip.
glazing clip.
insulation clip. →22
paper clip.
pipe clip, see saddle clip.
resilient clip.
saddle clip.
spring clip.
tile clip.
union clip.
wire-rope clip, see wire rope clamp. →37

clipeus Lat.; a decorative motif consisting of a medallion containing the portrait of an ancestor, found in Roman ornamentation.

clipped gable roof see half-hipped roof. →46

cloaked verge tile a special roof tile designed to cover the edge of a verge.

cloakroom 1 a room or space, especially in a public building in which outer clothing, such as headgear and overcoats, may be temporarily stored.
2 see toilet.

clochan see beehive cell.

clock rate in computing, the rate at which the processor sends out signals, a measure of its performance, in MHz.

clocktower a tower with a clock or clocks situated near its summit, usually situated in an urban environment or as part of a building.

cloison in decorative enamelling, surface panels or cells formed by bent wire or solder fixed to the metal base to separate areas of colour in the enamelling process; a similar use of clay ridges in glazing ceramics.

cloisonné in coloured enamelwork or pottery, the use of cloisons to separate areas of colour.

cloisonné masonry decorative masonry in which small stone blocks or panels are framed by bricks placed vertically and horizontally in single or double courses.

cloister a covered walkway or ambulatory around an open quadrangle in a monastery, college, or monastic cathedral, previously used as a link, and for discussion and pensive thought.
see *Early Christian church* illustration. →95
see *Byzantine domical church* illustration. →96
see *Carolingian abbey church* illustration. →98
see *Carolingian monastery* illustration. →97

cloister vault, domical vault; a domelike vault constructed over a square or polygonal base, from which curved segments rise to a central point. →25, →26

close 1 a short cul-de-sac in an urban or suburban residential area.
2 a walled precinct round a cathedral or abbey, see alley.

close boarding boarding laid side by side so that there are no gaps between adjacent boards. →57

close couple rafter roof see close couple roof. →33

close couple roof, close couple rafter roof, span roof; a couple roof tied by a ceiling joist or ties at the base of its rafters; a simple triangular roof truss. →33

close coupled WC pan a WC whose cistern is connected directly with the top of the pan.

closed assembly time the period of time during which parts of a glued joint may still be repositioned before the adhesive sets.

closed bud capital see bud capital. →73

closed capital see bud capital. →73

closed circuit television, CCTV; a security system of television cameras and monitors used for surveillance and observation of a building or premises.

closed circuit television camera see surveillance camera.

closed circuit television survey, camera survey, CCTV survey; the inspection of drains and sewers using remote video cameras to check for corrosion, blockages and cracks.

closed cruck truss, full cruck truss; in traditional timber-framed construction, a cruck truss tied with a collar beam.

closed eaves an overhanging eaves whose lower horizontal edge is closed with soffit boards.

closed face see tight side. →10
closed riser stair a stair in which the space between alternate treads is filled with a riser. →45
closed side see tight side. →10
closed spandrel bridge see solid spandrel bridge. →32
Closed style see Ornamental style.
see *Pompeian styles* illustration. →126
close grained, close grown, dense grained, fine grained, fine grown, narrow grained, narrow ringed, slow grown; a description of slowly grown wood having densely spaced growth rings.
close grown see close grained.
closer 1 the last brick in a brick course at a stopped end or corner, often manufactured to a non-standard large or small size to make up space in a brickwork bond. →21
2 a brick which exposes a half-header or header in brickwork, usually used to make up space in the brick bond. →21
see queen closer. →21
see king closer. →21
3 see cavity closer. →28
4 a device for closing a door, window or hatch automatically; see door closer. →51
closet 1 a cupboard located in a recess in a wall or constructed as part of the building fabric. →57
see *brick house* illustration. →59
see *timber-framed house* illustration. →57
2 see built-in cupboard.
3 see toilet.
closing face the face of a hinged door leaf, hatch or casement which closes against its frame. →50, →51
closing jamb see shutting jamb. →50, →51
closing stile see shutting stile. →50, →51
closure a thin brick used to bond inner and outer leaves of masonry in early forms of cavity wall construction.
closure piece see cavity closer. →28
cloth 1 see fabric.
2 see mesh.
clothes hook a hook or set of hooks fixed to a wall for hanging items of clothing on.
clothes line see washing line.
cloud see revision cloud. →130
cloured finish hammer-dressed finish. →12
clourer a pointed masonry chisel, used for the initial rough shaping of stone surfaces; also called a point. →41
clout, clout nail, felt nail; a short galvanized nail with a large flat head, used for fixing down roofing felt and thin boarding. →35
clout nail see clout. →35
clove a traditional unit of weight in Britain and America, equivalent to 8 lb or 3.6 kg.
see oil of cloves.
clove oil see oil of cloves.
cloven finish see riven finish.
cloverleaf a decorative motif derived from the leaves of some plant species of the pea family which have three lobes, Trifolium spp., symbolic of the Holy Trinity; cf. shamrock. →121
cloverleaf interchange see cloverleaf junction. →63
cloverleaf junction 1 any grade-separated junction in which flow of traffic is controlled by looped ramps resembling a cloverleaf; generally a full cloverleaf. →63
2 see full cloverleaf junction. →63
3 see partial cloverleaf junction. →63
cloverleaf moulding see trefoil moulding. →125
club hammer, lump hammer, mash hammer; an iron-headed mallet or sledgehammer small enough to be held in one hand. →40
clubhouse a building used by a sporting club or other community for functions and associated activities.
club-room a space in a residential or communal building for activities, games and hobbies.
clustered housing housing built in close-knit groups, either detached or linked with common facilities, courtyards, foundations etc. →61
clustered pier see compound pier. →13, →101
clutch eraser see clutch rubber.
clutch head screw see one-way head screw. →36
clutch pencil, lead holder; a pencil whose lead is held in a jaw mechanism so that it may be retracted when not in use and extended when it wears down. →130
clutch rubber a device consisting of a stick of erasing material which works in much the same way as a clutch pencil; used for rubbing out marks in lead pencil.
CN cellulose nitrate.
coach in traffic planning, a motor vehicle, a bus, used for long-distance transportation of passengers.
coach bolt, carriage bolt; a bolt with a dome-shaped head cast with a square protrusion on its underside which locks into a timber surface or shaped housing when tightened with a nut. →36
coach screw, lag bolt (Am.), lag screw (Am.); a heavy screw whose head is hexagonal and can be turned with a spanner. →36
coach station a building where coaches stop, begin and end their journeys.
coach stop a bus stop for long-distance buses.
coagulation in water purification, a process of treating waste water with flocculating chemicals which adhere to impurities and encourage their removal from the water.
coal 1 a black carboniferous mineral substance, mined and burnt as fuel to produce energy and heat.
see anthracite.
2 a shade of dark grey which takes its name from the colour of porous coal after it has been heated to release gases and tar.
coal bunker a cellar in which coal for domestic use is stored.
coal gas combustible gas manufactured from the distillation of coal and burnt to produce energy for domestic and industrial use; now largely superseded by natural gas.
coal shed an outhouse in which coal for domestic use is stored.
coal tar a dark viscous liquid formed as a result of the distillation of coal; used as a preservative and in the chemical industry.
coal-fired referring to a heating system utilizing coal as its combustible fuel.
coal-fired power station a plant for generating electricity with turbines fuelled by coal.
coal-tar pitch a black aromatic resinous residue left over in the distillation of coal tar, used as road tar.
coarse aggregate aggregate which consists largely of particles over 5 mm in diameter; types included as separate entries are listed below.
angular aggregate.
cubical aggregate.
elongated aggregate.
flaky aggregate.
flaky and elongated aggregate.
rounded aggregate.
coarse grained, 1 granular; a description of a soil which contains a substantial proportion of sand or gravel.
2 see coarse textured.
coarse gravel in soil classification, a range of particles of mineral soil which vary in size from 20 mm to 60 mm.
coarse mortar mortar whose aggregate is coarse sand; see coarse stuff.
coarse plaster see coarse stuff.
coarse sand in soil classification, a range of particles of mineral soil which vary in size from 0.6 mm to 2 mm.
coarse silt in soil classification, a range of particles of mineral soil which vary in size from 0.02 mm to 0.06 mm.

coarse soil see granular soil.
coarse stuff **1** plaster, used for undercoats, produced from lime putty and coarse sand.
2 simple lime sand mortar used in bricklaying.
coarse textured, open grained, coarse grained; a description of wood with large pores or largely spaced growth rings.
coastline the meeting, and border area thus formed, of a sea or large lake and land.
coat **1** a single continuous layer of material applied to a surface as protection, decoration or to provide a treatment.
2 a single applied layer of paint; cf. film.
3 see plaster coat.
4 see thatch coat.
coated chippings, coated grit; aggregate between 3 mm and 20 mm in size range with a coating of a binder such as tar or bitumen, used in road construction.
coated felt see mineral granule surfaced bitumen felt.
coated float glass see surface coated float glass.
coated grit see coated chippings.
coated macadam see tarmacadam.
coated paper, surfaced paper; paper coated with a mineral such as china clay or enamel on one or both sides to improve the quality of images printed on it, increase glossiness etc.
coated plywood plywood manufactured or pretreated with a thin protective or sealing surface coat of material such as polyester, urethane, epoxy etc.
coated wallpaper a wallcovering surface treated with a thin layer of polyvinyl acetate or similar flexible material.
coating, 1 finish; a protective or decorative layer or coat of material such as paint, plastics, zinc etc. applied to a surface.
2 the surface application of one or a number of layers of protective material to provide a finish.
coating material a material applied in a layer to provide a finish or protection for a surface.
coating system a number of layers or coats of material applied to a surface in the correct order to provide a finish.
coat of arms the official graphical emblem of a society, institution, family, district or company, usually a heraldic shield with various motifs. →124
coaxial cable in telecommunications, a transmission cable consisting of a conductor shielded by two intertwined tubes of metal wire, designed to have low radiation losses and high resistance to external interference.
cob a traditional walling material of unburnt clay mixed with sand and straw, laid in situ and left to harden.
cobalt a silvery white metal, **Co**, used as an alloy in steel, in pigments and as an oxide in the manufacture of blue glass.
cobalt arsenide $CoAs_3$, see skutterudite, smaltite.
cobalt black see black oxide of cobalt.
cobalt blue, 1 azure cobalt, Thénard's blue, king's blue, Vienna blue; a permanent, opaque, blue pigment consisting of a compound of cobalt and aluminium oxide with varying degrees of zinc.
2 a shade of blue which takes its name from the above.
cobalt glance see cobaltite.
cobalt green, Gellert green, Rinman's green, Swedish green, zinc green; a bright green inorganic pigment consisting of a compound of cobalt zincate and zinc oxide; developed in 1780 and suitable for use in oil, watercolour and acrylic paints.
cobalt oxide see black oxide of cobalt.
cobalt ultramarine a violet form of the blue pigment cobalt blue made without phosphoric acid.
cobalt violet, cobalt violet phosphate; an inorganic clear semi-opaque violet pigment originally used in fresco painting, initially made from a rare ore of cobalt and now manufactured artificially.
cobalt violet phosphate see cobalt violet.
cobalt yellow, aureolin; a toxic bright transparent yellow pigment used in watercolour, tempera and oil paints.
cobaltine see cobaltite.
cobaltite, cobalt glance, cobaltine; a red-tinged silvery white mineral, naturally occurring cobalt arsenosulphide, **CoAsS**, an important ore of cobalt.
cobble, cobblestone; **1** a naturally occurring lump of stone, by classification from 60 mm to 200 mm in size.
2 one of a series of small roughly squared pieces of natural stone laid in sand or mortar as road surfacing or paving; sometimes called a cube. →15
3 see pebble. →15
4 see sett. →15
5 see cube. →15
6 see boulder. →15
cobbled paving paving laid in natural stone cobbles. →15
cobblestone see cobble. →15
cobblestone wall, cobble wall; a rough masonry wall constructed of rounded stones or cobbles laid in mortar. →11
cobble wall see cobblestone wall. →11
cobra see Wadjet. →74
see uraeus. →74
cob wall see cob.
cobwork see horizontal log construction. →6
coccolite a white or green form of the mineral pyroxene, a silicate of lime, magnesium or manganese; used as building stone at the beginning of the 1900s.
Coccus ilicis kermes insect, see cochineal.
Coccus lacca, see lake red.
cochineal a red dyestuff produced from the Central American insects *Dactylopius coccus* (a red scale insect that feeds on cacti) and the kermes insect; used in the manufacture of carmine.
cock 1 any simple tap from which piped fluid or gas can be drawn off for use, or supply cut off to particular appliances.
2 plug tap, plug cock, plug valve; in water installations, a tap or stopvalve containing a cone-shaped plug perforated with a hole, set in a housing and turned with a lever through 90° to cut off flow.
3 see draw-off tap.
cockatrice see basilisk. →122
cock beak moulding a decorative moulding whose cross-section is that of a shallow convex surface with a flat underside, used in edging for boards and tables; cf. thumbnail. →14
cock comb see cock's comb.
cocking piece see sprocket.
cock's comb red see cock's comb.
cock's comb, cock comb, coxcomb; **1** a hand-held serrated metal plate drawn across a surface to produce a grooved finish in stonework; a toothed drag.
2 a shade of red which takes its name from the colour of the comb of a cock [*Gallus gallus*].
cocoa, cacao, leather, tan; a shade of brown which takes its name from the colour of the crushed seeds of the cocoa tree [*Theobroma cacao*], or the colour of ox hide tanned with oak bark.
coconut fibre see coir.
coctus Lat.; Roman fired clay products, bricks etc.
code building code, see building regulations.
code of professional conduct a set of standards of integrity, ethics, guidance and procedure drawn up by a professional body, to which their members are expected to adhere.
codes of practice see building codes of practice.
coefficient a numeric factor which defines the property of a substance or process, used as a multiplier in calculations; examples included as separate entries are listed below.
absorption coefficient.

acoustic absorption coefficient, see sound absorption coefficient.
air-to-air heat transmission coefficient, see U-value.
coefficient of diffusion, see diffusion coefficient.
coefficient of heat transfer, see U-value.
coefficient of thermal conductance, see C-value.
coefficient of thermal conductivity, see k-value.
coefficient of thermal resistance, see R-value.
coefficient of thermal transmittance, see U-value.
C-value.
differential coefficient, see derivative.
diffusion coefficient.
external surface resistance value, see RSO-value.
heat transmission value, see k-value.
internal surface resistance value, see RSI-value.
iodine value.
k-value.
Los Angeles coefficient.
noise reduction coefficient.
RSI-value.
RSO-value.
R-value.
sound absorption coefficient.
surface coefficient.
U-value.

coefficient of diffusion see diffusion coefficient.

coefficient of heat transfer see U-value.

coefficient of thermal conductance see C-value.

coefficient of thermal conductivity see k-value.

coefficient of thermal resistance see R-value.

coefficient of thermal transmittance see U-value.

coelin see cerulean blue.

coenatio, cenatio; Lat.; a roofed dining room in a Roman dwelling, adjoining a garden or courtyard. →88

coenobium, cenobium; Lat.; in the Early Christian architecture of Asia Minor, a monastic convent in which monks lived and prayed together.

coeruleum see cerulean blue.

coeur see fess point. →124

coffee a shade of dark brown which takes its name from the ground beans of the coffee plant [*Coffea arabica*].

coffee room see café.

coffee shop see café.

coffer, caisson; one of a number of recessed polygonal panels in a decorative or structural ceiling. →86

coffered ceiling 1 a decorated or structural ceiling relieved with a series of polygonal recessed panels, cassettes or coffers. →86
see *classical temples* illustration. →86
see *Roman basilica* illustration. →93
2 see lacunar. →86

coffered slab see waffle slab. →27

coffering the decorative relieving of a ceiling or soffit with coffers.

cog 1 in timber jointing, a square cut made into a member received by another member to prevent movement within the joint. →4
2 in log construction, a cutting along the lower edge of a log, interlocking with a recess in the lower log, designed to prevent lateral movement. →6
3 see nib.

cogged corner joint a timber bevelled corner joint in which the halved ends of one member is cut with a cog for increased strength. →4

cogged halved joint a timber halving joint in which a cog or recess is cut into the halved surface to provide a lock for the joint. →4

cogged joint 1 a timber framing joint in which the end of one member is cut with a square notch or cog to fit into another shaped member.
2 see double cogged joint. →4

cogging see notching.

cognac a shade of orange brown which takes its name from the brandy produced in the Cognac region of France.

cohesion the sticking together of particles of the same substance.

cohesion pile in foundation technology, a pile, similar in action to a friction pile, which transmits forces to surrounding ground around its circumference, through cohesive forces. →29

cohesiveness the ability of the particles in a material such as concrete, or an assembly of components, to remain united with another.

cohesive soil a soil whose particles adhere to form hard lumps due to its high content of fine particles.

coign see quoin. →12

coil 1 in heating and refrigeration technology, helical piping through which chilled or hot liquid is passed to alter the temperature of surrounding liquid, air etc.
2 windings of copper wire in an electric motor, transformer, electromagnet etc.
3 in the hot-rolling of steel, the product of a strip mill, subsequently decoiled and flattened to produce steel strip.
4 any ornament with spiral motifs; see continuous coil spiral, volute, helix. →125

coil coating, prepaint process; a continuous automated industrial process for coating sheetmetal before fabrication into panels and other components, in which a coil of metal is unwound and cleaned, chemically treated, primed and given a baked or painted coating and rewound ready for supply to a manufacturer.

coin see quoin. →12

coincidence in acoustics, a resonance-like phenomenon in which skin structures such as double glazing or panelled frames experience a loss in sound-insulating properties at certain frequencies.

coin flooring see studded rubber flooring. →44

coin operated lock, 1 automatic lock; a lock for public conveniences etc. which releases its bolt on insertion of a coin.
2 a lock used for storage lockers in public spaces, changing rooms etc. which releases a key on insertion of a coin.

coin-pattern flooring see studded rubber flooring. →44

coir, coconut fibre; the fibre from the outer husks of coconuts, used for making rope and matting.

coir matting a rough-textured floor covering woven from coconut fibres, used for doormats, and for corridors, foyers etc.

coke a solid fuel manufactured from the carbonization of coal.

coke black see vine black.

Cola see Chola architecture.

colcothar an obsolete variety of red iron oxide pigment, formed by the distillation of sulphuric acid from iron sulphate.

cold bridge, heat bridge, thermal bridge; a conductive path in construction between interior and exterior for the easy passage of heat from inside to outside, usually causing problems with heat loss, thermal discomfort and condensation.

cold chisel a heavy duty steel-handled chisel used with a mallet for the chipping, cutting and shaping of masonry. →41
see *cold chisels* illustration. →41

cold curing adhesive any adhesive that sets without the application of heat.

cold drawing, wire drawing; the production of high strength metal wires by extruding cold material through a series of dies.

cold drawn wire steel wire that has been cold drawn to improve its strength; used as concrete reinforcement and for nails.

cold feed pipe a pipe that conveys cold water from a cistern to a water heater.

cold formed section a lightweight structural steel section, often formed into an open profile by bending, or rolled into various cross-sectional forms while cold. →34
see *cold formed steel beam* in metal profiles illustration. →34

cold forming, cold rolling; the process of forming light steel sections, profiles etc. by bending steel plate with a series of rollers.

cold galvanization see zinc-rich paint; the result of this process.

cold glue see cold setting adhesive, cold curing adhesive.

cold oil ring main oil heating pipework in which oil is supplied to a burner unheated, and any unused fuel returned to the storage tank.

cold-pressed paper, not-pressed paper; an open-textured paper used for watercolour painting.

cold pressing a method of producing high quality linseed oil, used as a vehicle in paints, by extraction under low pressure without heat.

cold radiation the apparent cooling sensation produced by cold objects, the night sky, areas of glazing etc. caused by the absence of heat radiation.

cold rolling see cold forming.

cold roof pitched roof construction in which insulation is situated between or directly above horizontal ceiling joists, creating an uninsulated roof void or attic space above.

cold room a thermally insulated and mechanically cooled storeroom used for storing commodities such as foods and medicine at lower than normal temperatures.

cold setting adhesive, cold glue; any adhesive that will set at temperatures below 23°C.

cold start lamp see instant start lamp.

cold twisted bar in reinforced concrete, a reinforcing bar, square in profile, which has been twisted to improve its strength and bonding with the concrete. →27

cold water pipe, cold water supply pipe; a pipe within a building which distributes cold water supply to cisterns, heaters, appliances and taps.

cold water supply pipe see cold water pipe.

cold-weather bricklaying see winter bricklaying.

cold-weather concreting see winter concreting.

cold welding a welding process in which soft metals are joined together by the application of pressure through hammering.

cold worked deformed bar in reinforced concrete, a deformed bar which has been cold worked to improve its properties.

cold working the process of working metal when cold, as in cold drawing and cold rolling, so as to increase hardness; see hot working.

colisaeum see colosseum.

coliseum see colosseum.

collage a work of art which makes use of glued pieces of paper, cloth, photograph, newspaper and other materials as its medium.

collagen glue see animal glue.

collapsible formwork formwork with telescopic or hinged parts that can be easily dismounted when striking.

collapsible gate, scissor gate; a side-opening shutter for goods lifts and service areas, consisting of a latticework of pivoted steel slats which enable the door to be folded to one side.

collar 1 any fixing or restraining component which fits over and is tightened to a cylindrical member.
2 see loose socket.
3 see collar beam. →33

collar and tie beam truss in timber frame construction, a roof truss of slanting rafters, a horizontal tie beam joining their lower edges and a collar beam situated between tie beam and ridge. →33

collar beam, collar, collar piece, strut beam, wind beam; in timber frame construction, a transverse beam between eaves level and ridge connecting two principal rafters. →33

collarino see trachelion. →81

collar piece see collar beam. →33

collar plate see collar purlin.

collar purlin, collar plate; in traditional timber roof construction, a longitudinal horizontal purlin carried on a crown post or by other means, and supporting the collars between pairs of rafters. →33

collar rafter roof see collar roof. →33

collar roof, collar rafter roof; a form of simple timber roof construction with each pair of rafters tied between eaves and ridge by a horizontal collar beam. →33

collar screed a specially shaped screed rail used in the plastering of concrete or masonry columns.

collateral see security.

colleague a fellow worker in an office or similar workplace.

collector see solar collector.

college a building for further professional or vocational education or training.

collegiate church a church, similar in origin to the cathedral, but usually considerably smaller, staffed by a college of clergymen.

collision load a temporary dynamic load imposed on a structure by the collision of a vehicle or some other moving object.

colloid a substance consisting of ultramicroscopic solid particles suspended in a liquid or gas.

colluvarium in classical Roman architecture, a ventilating opening in an aqueduct.

colluvial deposit soil and loose rock fragments deposited at the base of mountainous slopes by the action of erosion and rain.

Cologne earth see Cassel earth.

colonia Lat.; a Roman settlement of retired legionaries, given a pension and plot of land to work in a colonized country.

colonial architecture any architecture, especially from 1600 to 1900, which is heavily influenced by that of its colonial settlers.

colonial siding see clapboarding. →8

colonial style classical architecture of the 1600s and 1700s in North America, which reflects that of the colonists' European homelands, often English Georgian or timber-framed buildings.

colonnade 1 a series of columns which support a beam, roof or, in classical architecture, an entablature.
see *Egyptian mortuary temple* illustration. →72
see *classical temple* illustration. →86
see *Asian temples* illustration. →68
2 see pteron. →85

colonnaded court 1 a courtyard bounded on all sides by a colonnade, often carrying a roof, canopy etc.; a peristyle. →88
2 see stoa. →92, →94

colonnette a small column often adorning windows, niches etc. and carrying a pediment or arch. →99

colony a settlement of people in a foreign country, ruled from their mother country.

colophony see rosin.

color see colour.

colorant see colourant, colouring admixture.

coloring agent see colourant.

colorism see colourism.

colossal order, giant order; in classical architecture, a column which extends in height through two or more storeys of the building.

colosseum, coliseum, colisaeum; originally the Flavian Amphitheatre, begun by Vespasian in Rome (the Colosseum), which took its name from the adjacent monumental statue of Nero; in general, a large arena or amphitheatre used for sporting events and contests. →90

colossus a gigantic statue, building or object.

colour, color (Am.); **1** the visual sensation of rays, transmittance and reflectance of light from one or a mixture of parts of the visible spectrum on the human eye.
2 that particular shade or hue of a surface produced by certain wavelengths of light.

colourant, 1 colorant (Am.), colouring agent; any substance used as a physical means of adding colour to a material or surface; a stain, dye or pigment.
2 see colouring admixture.

colour chart, 1 colour schedule; a design document containing samples to show the range of colours, and often materials and finishes in a building or space.
2 printed matter reproduced as small patches indicating the range of standard colours produced by a particular paint manufacturer.

colour circle see colour wheel.

colour coding any signing system which uses colour to indicate use or action of a device, escape route etc.

coloured brickwork see polychrome brickwork.

coloured cement see coloured Portland cement.

coloured concrete concrete containing cement to which permanent, inert pigments have been added, imparting a colour to the finished surface.

coloured mortar mortar to which a coloured pigment or aggregate has been added.

coloured opaque glass non-transparent glass body tinted, laminated or coated with coloured material, used for work surfaces, cladding and bathroom finishes.
see cladding glass, spandrel glass.

coloured pencil, crayon; a pencil with coloured lead made from a mixture of pigment, filler, lubricant and binder, which may or may not be water soluble; used for drawing and marking.

coloured Portland cement ordinary or white Portland cement to which inert pigments have been added to provide colour.

coloured rendering rendering in which coloured mortar has been used.

colour fastness the ability of a material or pigment to retain its colour over a period of time, or when exposed to the weather or treatment etc.

colour filter see filter.

colouring admixture, colorant, colourant; in concretework, an admixture or pigment included in the mix to add colour.

colouring agent see colourant.

colouring pigment see stainer.

colour intensity in colour science and painting, the measure of purity and brightness of a hue, its saturation.

colourism, colorism; a branch of visual art in which colour is used as the primary mode of expression.

colourist an artist or painter who uses colour as the main mode of expression.

colourless, 1 clear; of a transparent material such as glass or liquids, without colour.
2 achromatic, neutral; referring to a shade of colour composed entirely of black, white and grey, without spectral colour.

colour perspective the portrayal of apparent distance in landscape painting and architectural renderings using warmer tones in the foreground and bluer shades in the distance.

colour purity in colour science, the physical equivalent of colour intensity, the property of a hue which reflects light of single wavelengths and is not mixed with black or white.

colour rendering in lighting design, the variation in appearance of colours under different lighting conditions.

colour rendering index in lighting design, a measure of how much a colour changes under different lighting conditions; the degree to which it is rendered by different wavelengths of light, compared to a reference.

colour sample in design, a patch of colour or coloured material to display the final colour intended for a particular surface.

colour saturation, 1 chroma, tone; in colour science, the degree of purity of a colour, how much white, grey or black has been added to a hue.
2 the point at which the addition of pigment will no longer change the appearance of a particular colour.

colour schedule see colour chart.

colours in oil see oil paste.

colour system in colour and paint science, any system by which colours are arranged and classified in a logical manner.

colour temperature in lighting and colour science, the temperature at which a black body emits light (or radiation) of a certain colour.

colour wheel, colour circle; in colour theory, a circular diagram of the colours of the spectrum arranged around the circumference with complementary colours opposite one another.

Columba livia see pigeon blue.

columbarium 1 a recess left in a masonry wall as a housing for a timber joist or beam.
2 a storage place for cinerary urns, originally a Roman memorial chamber with vaulted niches containing cinerary urns of the dead. →93
3 see dovecote.

Columbidae see dove. →122
see pigeon blue.

columbium a rare name for the metallic chemical element niobium, **Nb**.

columen a wooden beam high up in a Roman sloping roof; a Roman ridge piece or collar beam. →47

column a structural shaft of concrete, masonry, metal or timber which transfers applied vertical loads through its length to its base; see also pillar; types included as separate entries are listed below.
see *traditional masonry column types* illustration. →13
see types of *Egyptian columns and capitals* illustration. →73
see *Asian and Mediterranean columns and capitals* illustration. →69
see *figured column* illustration. →76
see *classical Greek columns* illustrations. →78, →80
see *classical Roman columns* illustration. →79
see *column styles in European architecture* illustration. →114
Aesculapian column, Asclepian column, see serpent column. →69
animal column, beast column.
annulated column. →114
applied column, attached column, engaged column. →13
baluster column. →69
banded column, see annulated column. →114
barley-sugar column, spiral column. →114
brick column. →21
built-up column.
bundle column. →73
candelabrum column, candlestick column. →114
circular column, round column. →13
classical column. →78, →79
columna. →47
composite column, complex column (historical). →73
composite stanchion (modern).
concrete column.
Corinthian column. →78
corner column, edge column. →80
coupled columns. →13, →114
Cretan column, Minoan column. →69
demi-column, half-column. →13
detached column. →13
Djed column. →74
Doric column. →78
edge column. →80
edge-rolled column. →13
Egyptian column. →73
engaged column. →13
figured column. →76
filleted column.
fluted column. →13, →73
freestanding column.
Greek column, see classical column. →78
half-column, see demi-column. →13
Hathor column. →73, →76
inserted column, see engaged column. →13
see Ionic column. →78, →80

see knotted column. →114
lighting column, see lighting post.
lotus column, lotiform column. →73
Minoan column. →69
Mycenaean column, see Minoan column. →69
Osiris column. →73, →76
palm column. →73
papyrus column, papyrus-bundle column. →73
post.
precast column. →28
proto-Doric column. →73
rectangular column. →13
recessed column. →13
reinforced concrete column, see concrete column.
reverse taper column, see Minoan column. →69
ringed column, see annulated column. →114
Roman column, see classical column. →79
rostral column, see columna rostrata. →69
round column, see circular column. →13
rusticated column. →13, →114
salomonica, see spiral column. →114
serpent column. →69
spiral column, Solomonic column. →114
square column. →13
stanchion, steel column.
stone column, see vibroreplacement.
tent-pole column. →73
thermal column, convection column.
Tuscan column. →79
twinned columns, see coupled columns. →13, →114
twisted column, see spiral column. →114
universal column, see H-section.
ventilating column.
wreathed column, see spiral column. →114

columna 1 a post or column in Roman construction; a timber king post in a Roman roof. →47
2 see columna rostrata, rostral column. →69
3 see columna caelata.

columna caelata Lat.; a Roman carved column.

column and beam construction see post and beam construction. →27, →28

column and slab construction a structural system in which the floors in a building are supported by a series of columns; the external walls are usually non-loadbearing. →27, →28

columna rostrata, rostral column; Lat.; in classical Roman architecture, a freestanding pillar with maritime ornament, constructed in commemoration of naval success in battle. →69

column base 1 see base. →76
2 classical column base, see classical base. →81
see *classical column base* illustrations. →81
see *classical orders* illustrations. →78, →79, →80

column block a concrete block designed for use as a reinforced or plain concrete column or pilaster when laid in a vertical stack; also called a pilaster block. →30

column bond see chimney bond. →21

column figure carved slender figures of saints and noblemen adorning the recesses of a medieval church portal; see jamb figure, trumeau figure. →113

column footing see pad foundation. →29

column foundation see pad foundation. →29

columniation the proportioned lining up of or grouping columns in classical architecture; see also intercolumniation. →77

column radiator in hot-water heating, a radiator with a number of interlinked vertical chambers of steel tube or cast iron, in which heating water circulates.

column reinforcement steel reinforcement for a reinforced concrete column. →27

column shaft see shaft. →76, →78, →79, →80

column strip in concretework, the linear zone of a reinforced concrete slab that links the upper ends of supporting columns and oversails the column width in the spanning direction of the slab. →27

column unit see precast column.

comb 1 see scratcher.
2 see drag. →43
3 see cock's comb.
4 see roof comb. →67

combed joint a joinery corner joint for drawers and boxes in which pieces are cut with a series of square notches to fit each other, also called a comb joint, finger joint or boxed corner joint. →5

combed plasterwork see comb-finish rendering.

combed yarn see worsted yarn.

comb-finished rendering, combed plasterwork, dragged plasterwork; rendering whose wet surface has been worked with a serrated tool to produce striations in its surface.

combination drill bit a drill bit which drills a hole and countersink for a screw head at the same time. →42

combination lock a lock whose mechanism can be opened by dialling or tapping out a numerical or alphabetical code.

combination plane, universal plane; a versatile hand-held plane with adjustable and removable blades used for a variety of smoothing applications.

combination pliers see footprints.

combination sink a domestic sink with a drainer cast or pressed in one piece.

combination square see try and mitre square.

combined crown, double crown; the dual head-dress of the united kingdoms of ancient Egypt, made up of the red and white crowns of Lower and Upper Egypt respectively. →74

combined drainage see combined system.

combined extract and input system see mechanical input and extract ventilation.

combined sewerage see combined system.

combined system a system of drainage or sewerage in which both foul water and surface water are conveyed in the same pipelines.

comb joint see combed joint. →5

combustible referring to a material which will ignite and burn.

combustion air the air used up in combustion of fuel in a fireplace, burner, hazardous fire etc.

combustion chamber see firebox. →56

combustion gas colourless and poisonous gases given off burning matter before the emission of smoke; combustion gases include carbon monoxide, carbon dioxide, hydrogen chloride and hydrogen cyanide.

combustion gas detector a fire detector which reacts to the presence of smoke and other combustion gases from hazardous building fires.

combustion rate, rate of combustion; the speed at which the mass of a material or component will decrease during burning.

comfort see thermal comfort.

comitium Lat.; a Roman public building in which local officials were elected; also part of a building used for other political purposes.

command in computing, a coded instruction to the computer to perform a function.

commencement notice in contract administration, a written announcement to local authority building control informing of starting dates of construction work.

commerce, trade; the buying and selling of merchandise and services.

commercial building a building for the practice of business.

commercial butane organic gas fuel, C_4H_{10}, stored and transported in compressed form as liquids.

commercial centre, 1 business centre; an urban area, group of buildings or complex devoted to commerce.
2 see city centre.

commercial enterprise a business, project or venture set up with the intention of providing goods and services to make a profit.

commercial grade the standard state in which a product is sold or supplied.

commercial premises buildings or spaces within a building designated by planning authorities for the practice of business.

commercial propane colourless and odourless flammable gas fuel, $CH_3CH_2CH_3$, stored and transported in compressed form as liquids.

commercial timber timber of value in the construction, joinery and furniture industries etc., often sold outside its country of origin.

commercial-utilitarian planning see utilitarian planning.

commercial waste, trade waste; material waste from a commercial process such as shops, offices etc.

commission an order from a client to an architect for the design of a building.

commissioning 1 the scope of decisions and actions by an owner or client in having a building built.
2 the testing, adjusting and running in of a technical or mechanical services installation prior to handover.

committee a body of persons appointed to represent a larger group to make official decisions, discuss regulatory and legislative matters etc.

committee room see assembly room.

commodity any service or product which is of use or value, especially with regard to commerce.

common see common brick. →16

common alder, black alder; [*Alnus glutinosa*] a European hardwood with light, soft, pale brown timber; used for joinery and plywood.

common bond 1 see English garden-wall bond. →19
2 see Flemish stretcher bond. →18

common brick, common; a standard general-purpose rectangular mass-produced brick with untreated faces; not generally used for special applications or visual quality. →16

common furniture beetle [*Anobium punctatum*] a species of insect whose larvae cause damage to furniture and other timber by burrowing.

common grounds see grounds. →44

common joist in timber frame construction, a basic floor or ceiling joist.

common madder [*Rubia tinctorum*]; see madder red, see alizarin.

common method the simplest method of constructing a two-point perspective using a series of radiating lines from a station point onto a plan of the object and vanishing points projected on the horizon at an angle of 90°; heights are taken from an elevation drawing; also known as the direct plan projection method. →129

common oak see pedunculate oak.

common purlin, horizontal rafter; in timber roof construction, one of a series of horizontal members parallel with a ridge or eaves, carried on principal rafters or trusses and onto which roof boarding may be nailed.

common purlin roof, horizontal rafter roof; timber roof construction in which roof trusses support a series of horizontal rafters, onto which the roof boarding or roofing material is attached.

common rafter 1 in timber roof construction, a secondary rafter, one which does not carry purlins, supporting roof covering. →33
2 see asser. →47

common reed [*Arundo phragmites*, *Phragmites australis*]; see best reed, Norfolk reed.

common room a communal room in an academic or residential building for leisure activities and discussion.

common wall see separating wall.

common willow see white willow.

communication the transmission of information.

communication pipe that part of the service pipe of a water or gas supply system, outside a site boundary and thus maintained by the supplier, which connects a building to the supply main.

communion bench a low platform in front of an altar rail on which parishioners kneel while taking communion. →116

communion rail see altar rail. →116

communion table in church architecture, a table or altar of wood or stone often covered with a cloth, at which communion is taken. →116

community a group of people who may be regarded as a distinct unit due to their common dwelling place or common pattern of living.

community centre a social and recreational meeting place for the inhabitants of a neighbourhood regardless of social, religious, and political backgrounds.

community facilities, community services; in town planning, any facility for the good of the community provided by public funding: schools, police and fire stations, libraries, health centres, water supply, sewers, refuse disposal and other utilities.

community forum, public participation; in town planning, an assembly of interest groups such as the local public, inhabitants, occupants, designers, developers and planners to discuss matters concerning a particular planned area.

community home, approved school, reformatory (Am.), Borstal, reform school; an institution which provides care and education for young offenders and other juveniles with difficulties or in custodial care.

community project an experimental development project in which new ideal ways of living are implemented with respect to social, ecological and technological aspects.

community services see community facilities.

commuting the process of travelling between homes in one district or town to places of work in another.

compact disk, compact disc, CD; in computing, a plastic disc on which digital data is stored, for retrieval by a suitable laser device.

compact disk read-only memory, CD-ROM; in computing, a compact disc furnished with a read-only memory, often containing software.

compact fluorescent lamp a small fluorescent lamp with good efficiency and long service life, with bayonet or screw caps and single or double U-shaped tube, often used as a replacement for incandescent lamps.

compaction 1 see concrete compaction.
2 see ground compaction.

compactor see waste compactor.

company, business, firm; an organization or group of people involved in the production of goods and services to make money; see partnership.

comparison the inspection of matters or material and their differences.

compartment 1 any subdivision of a space bounded by screens, partitions or furnishing groups.
2 a cabin in a railway carriage.
3 a subdivision of a shelf, drawer or storage furnishings.
4 see fire compartment.

compartmentation see fire compartmentation.

compartment wall see fire wall.

compass, 1 pair of compasses; a two legged instrument with a marker which revolves around a fixed point; used for drawing circles.
see beam compass.
see dividers.
trammel.
see wing compass.
2 a navigational instrument for indicating the direction of magnetic north and bearings from it.

compass plane, circular plane, roundsil (Sc.); a plane with a convex curved base for planing curved surfaces.

compass saw a small saw with a narrow tapering blade used for cutting curves or holes.

compatibility the design of devices, systems or components, especially computer hardware and software, to function together, fit or complement one another without modification.

compatible referring to components, devices, computer programs and systems which will function with other systems without modification.

compensation an award, usually a sum of money, paid out for injury or loss or damage to property.

competition **1** an arrangement by which parties contend with one another to offer the most suitable solution to an aim with a given set of criteria.
2 see architectural competition.
3 see design competition.
4 see ideas competition.
5 in economics, a market situation in which all traders in a certain product or service strive for custom and to maximize profits; see perfect market.

competition area the specific area for which proposals for an architectural or planning competition should be produced.

competition brief a programme of intent drawn up by the organizers of an architectural or planning competition stating the aims of the competition and other necessary information.

competition entry, proposal; a design submitted for assessment to an architectural or town planning competition.

competition jury see board of assessors.

competitiveness the ability to survive in economic competition.

competitive tendering a procedure for awarding a contract by choosing the most reasonable offer from a number of bidders.

complementary, complementary colour, complementary hue; in colour science, colours that are diametrically opposite one another on the colour circle; a colour opposite.

complementary colour see complementary.

complementary hue see complementary.

completion, 1 realization; the finishing of all or parts of construction on a building site; the stage at which a building is ready to be occupied.
2 practical completion; the state of readiness for occupation of the whole works, although some minor work may be outstanding.
3 partial completion, see partial handover.

completion certificate in contract management, a document issued to the contractor that certifies completion of specific areas of work, which have been approved by building control.

completion date, handover date; the date on which work on a building under construction or repair is due to be completed, as written in the building contract.

completion of defects certificate in contract management, a document issued at the end of the defects liability period certifying that all defects have been made good or repaired.

complex 1 any group of related and interconnected buildings or industrial installations.
2 see building group.
3 see pyramid complex. →70, →71

complex column see composite column. →73

complexity richness, variation and layering of space, form, material, colour and detail in architecture.

complex number in mathematics, a number or figure which contains both a real component and the square root of a negative quantity.

compluvium Lat.; the central opening in the roof of the atrium space of a Roman dwelling, through which rainwater drained into a central pool, the impluvium. →88

compo 1 see composition mortar.
2 compo render, see composition render.
3 see cement mortar.

component 1 one of a number of items, substances, parts etc. which, when assembled or blended together in an appropriate way, form a different and more complex item.
2 see building component.
3 one of a number of different semi-liquid compounds mixed together to form a substance which sets, such as an adhesive, paint or sealant.
4 in mechanics, that part of a force expressed as a vector in a particular direction.

component drawing a contract drawing showing the dimensions and construction of a component such as a door or window.

component range drawing a design or contract drawing outlining the quantity, sizes, treatments and specifications for components of a similar type in a building project.

compo render see composition render.

composite any product or construction made up of a number of different materials or technologies; usually a laminated material or one of plastic, concrete or cement reinforced with fibres of glass, mineral, metals or polymers.

composite beam 1 any beam constructed of a number of different structural materials or using a variety of loadbearing methods.
2 see hollow composite beam.
3 see filigree beam.
see *traditional composite beam* illustration. →7

composite board a building board formed by gluing veneers on either side of a core of material other than timber, such as cardboard. →9

Composite capital 1 a capital at the top of a column of the classical Roman Composite order, carved both with lavish acanthus foliage and leafy volutes, surmounted by a flat abacus. →81
2 composite capital; an ancient Egyptian capital combining various different motifs and styles.

composite cement see fillerized cement.

composite column, 1 complex column; an ancient Egyptian column type combining various different motifs and styles. →73
2 Composite column; a column of the classical Roman Composite order. →79
3 see composite stanchion.

composite construction the acting together of two or more materials, such as steel and concrete, to form a construction with improved properties of strength, durability etc.

composite floor slab, composite slab, steel deck floor; structural floor construction of profiled steel sheeting onto which concrete is cast; the steel acts as a permanent shuttering and resists tensile forces in bending.

Composite order a classical Roman order, a hybrid of Ionian and Corinthian, with fluted columns, a capital with both volutes and acanthus leaves, a base and an entablature with dentils. →79
see *Composite order* in Roman amphitheatre illustration. →90

composite pile in foundation technology, any pile which makes use of a number of different methods of piling to fulfil its purpose.

composite slab see composite floor slab.

composite stanchion, composite column; a steel and concrete column consisting either of a hollow steel stanchion filled with concrete or a steel profile cased in concrete; used to minimize the amount of steel and for fire safety.

composite truss a truss in which the main spanning members or rafters are of timber and the other members, struts, infill etc. are of steel.

composite window 1 a window assembly whose frame and casements are manufactured from different materials, often timber window frames with outer casements in aluminium; also known as a compound window. →53
2 two or more windows joined to fill an opening.

composition 1 the various component parts of which a substance is mixed or made up; the proportion of parts therein.
2 the deliberated arrangement of elements, forms and massing in a building, painting, sculpture etc. to create a desired aesthetic effect.

composition mortar, compo, cement lime mortar; slow setting mortar consisting of proportioned amounts of cement, lime and sand, with good resistance to cracking, used for bricklaying and rendering.

composition render composition mortar used as exterior-grade plaster or render; usually called compo render, properly known as cement lime render.

composition shingles see strip slates.

compost organic matter, rich in nutrients, used as fertilizer and created by the biodegrading of household and garden waste; also the structure for its production.

compost bin see composter.

composter, compost bin; a specially designed vessel, often with a heater, for producing compost from organic waste material.

composting in waste management, the action of producing fertilizer by the biodegrading of organic waste.

composting closet, composting toilet; a toilet in which waste products are converted to compost in a ventilated chamber.

composting toilet see composting closet.

compound 1 a union or mixture of separate substances combined for increased or enhanced properties; examples included as separate entries are listed below.
acrylic flooring compound.
bedding compound.
bonding compound.
chemical compound.
curing compound.
dressing compound, see levelling compound.
elastic glazing compound.
flexible moulding compound.
flooring compound, see acrylic flooring compound.
foam compound, see foaming agent.
glazing compound.
hot bonding compound, see bonding compound.
jointing compound.
levelling compound.
non-setting glazing compound.
parting compound, see release agent.
pointing compound.
sealing compound, sealant. →53
smoothing compound.
2 a bounded or fenced area of land, an enclosure.

compound column see compound pier. →13

compound pier, clustered pier, compound column; in Gothic architecture, a heavy column carved with a number of vertical cuttings to appear as if it were formed from a number of round shafts of lesser diameter; each shaft rises to form the various ribs of the vaulted ceiling; see also bundle pier, bundle column. →13, →101

compound window see composite window. →53

comprehensive development the development of a sizeable area of land with buildings or built form with associated roads, lighting and other infrastructure, usually as a phased operation.

comprehensive redevelopment, urban redevelopment; the rebuilding and modernization of a large urban area, often of derelict, redundant or unsuitable buildings, in accordance with a plan.

compressed air air produced or stored at higher than atmospheric pressure, used as a source of energy for powering tools, spraying and blast cleaning.

compressed air caisson, pneumatic caisson; a caisson whose air pressure is kept above atmospheric level to prevent the infiltration of surrounding water and allow for dry working conditions inside.

compressed charcoal charcoal sticks used by artists manufactured from ground charcoal compressed with binding agents; less fragile but more abrasive than stick charcoal.

compressed straw slab see strawboard.

compressibility the ability of a material to undergo compression and a corresponding reduction in size without fracture, rupture or damage.

compression 1 a pressing force which acts along the axis of a member or inwards on a body.
2 the act, result and state of being pressed or squeezed with this force.
3 see packing.

compression failure, cross break; failure of the fibres in a piece of structural timber due to excessive longitudinal compression or bending.

compression fitting a pipe fitting whose joint is secured by compressing the pipe end with a threaded nut or other clamping device.

compression moulding a method of forming thermoplastics products by placing material powder into a mould then applying heat and pressure.

compression reinforcement in reinforced concrete, reinforcement which has been designed to withstand compressive loading.

compression wood wood sawn from the undersides of branches and leaning trees with uneven growth rings and low strength; reaction wood in softwood. →1

compressive strength the property of a material or component which has good resistance to forces in compression without fracture.

compressive strength test in concretework, a test to determine the compressive strength of concrete, either by cube testing or cylinder testing.

compressive washer see spring lock washer. →37

compressor a device for producing compressed air (or other gas) for plant, tools and cooling equipment.

compulsory acquisition see compulsory purchase.

compulsory purchase, compulsory acquisition, condemnation (Am.), involuntary condemnation proceeding; in town planning, the obligation of a landowner to sell land and property on which public development such as road building has been planned to a local authority.

compulsory purchase power, eminent domain (Am.); the right of an authority to force landowners to sell land and property for public use.

computation see calculation.

computer an electronic device which processes data, performs calculations and runs programs.

computer-aided design, CAD; the design and drawing of a system, building, component or object using a computer.

computer animation, animation; a computer generated film used in architectural design for exploring, in three dimensions, the spacial relationships in and around buildings.

computer graphics the generation of a graphic representation, animation or drawing with a computer.

computer model see model.

computer modelling see modelling.

computer program, program; in computing, a set of instructions combined to perform a specific function.

computer software see software; see hardware.

computing, ADP, EDP (outdated); the electronic processing of data using a computer; using a microcomputer for doing clerical and design jobs, calculations etc.

concave brace 1 in traditional timber frame construction, an inwardly curved brace between two perpendicular members to stiffen the frame.
2 see arch brace.

concave joint see keyed joint.

concave moulding 1 see cavetto, congé, cove. →14
2 see scotia, gorge, trochilus. →14
3 see hollow moulding. →14

concealed door closer a door closer mounted within the thickness of a door leaf or threshold.

concealed dovetail joint see lapped dovetail joint. →5

concealed fixing see secret fixing.

concealed hinge, blind hinge; a special hinge used for high quality joinery, visible only when the door it supports is open.

concealed nailing see secret nailing. →3
concealed system a suspended ceiling system whose supporting profiles are not visible in the finished ceiling surface, usually provided by slotting joints or by fixing to the rear of the ceiling panels.
concentrate a concentrated or undiluted form of a mixture of chemicals or other constituents in a liquid-based solution.
concentrated load see point load.
concentration the proportion of a substance suspended or diluted in a liquid or gas.
concentric in geometry, a description of arcs or circles constructed from the same centre point.
concentric pattern see circular pattern. →15
concentric plan a town plan type in which main roads and activities are planned in a pattern of concentric rings around a central area, connected by radial streets.
concentric taper in drainage and plumbing, a short piece of conical pipe or similar fitting for joining two pipes of different diameters so that their centres lie along the same line.
concept 1 a general abstract notion; a principle or central idea relating to a certain range of things.
2 the underlying or generating thought, idea, philosophy, method or process for a design proposal or scheme.
Concept Art see Conceptual Art.
Conceptual Art, Concept Art; a form of art originating during the 1960s in which the inherent idea, language or symbolism is central to the work of art itself.
concert hall 1 a large auditorium designed for the performance of music, with seats and a stage.
2 a building in which music is performed to an audience.
concertina blind, folding blind; a pleated window blind of sheet material such as paper or cloth, which folds up or down with a concertina action.
concertina door see sliding folding door. →50
concetto in Renaissance philosophy of art, a mental image or concept as opposed to a drawing.
conch, 1 concha (Lat.); a half dome used to roof semicircular apses in some churches. →26, →116
2 ornamental carving or decoration in the form of a stylized conch shell. →123
concha Latin form of conch. →26, →116
concourse 1 a large public space within a public building, railway station, airport etc.
2 a public open place where people gather in front of a large building, at a university campus etc.
concrete a mixture of sand, aggregate, cement and water, often including admixtures, which sets to form a hard, versatile building material, mainly used for its structural properties; types included as separate entries are listed below.
see *concrete* illustrations. →27, →28, →30, →83
aerated concrete.
air-entrained concrete.
asphaltic concrete.
autoclaved aerated concrete.
blast-furnace concrete, see slag concrete.
blinding concrete.
cast-in-place concrete, cast-in-situ concrete, see in-situ concrete.
cellular concrete, see aerated concrete.
coloured concrete.
cyclopean concrete.
dry packed concrete.
expanded aggregate concrete.
exposed aggregate concrete.
exposed concrete.
extruded concrete.
facing concrete.
fairfaced concrete.
fat concrete, see rich concrete.
ferroconcrete, see reinforced concrete.
fibre concrete, fibrous concrete, see fibre-reinforced concrete.
flowable concrete, see self-placing concrete.
flowing concrete.
foam concrete, see foamed concrete.
fresh concrete.
gas concrete.
glass concrete.
glassfibre-reinforced polymer/concrete, glassfibre-reinforced cement.
green concrete.
grouted aggregate concrete, see grouted concrete.
hardened concrete.
heavy concrete.
high alumina cement concrete.
high strength concrete.
high density concrete, see heavy concrete.
in-situ concrete.
insulating concrete.
insulating lightweight concrete, see insulating concrete.
intrusion concrete, see grouted concrete.
lean concrete.
lightweight aggregate concrete.
lightweight concrete.
low heat concrete.
luminescent concrete.
mass concrete.
mixed concrete.
monolithic concrete.
no-fines concrete.
non-vibration concrete, see self-placing concrete.
no-slump concrete.
pavement concrete.
plain concrete.
plasticized concrete.
pneumatically applied concrete, see sprayed concrete.
polymer concrete.
polymer fibre-reinforced concrete.
polymer impregnated concrete.
polymer modified concrete.
polymer Portland cement concrete, see polymer concrete.
porous concrete, see aerated concrete.
Portland cement concrete.
post-tensioned concrete.
precast concrete.
pre-packed concrete, see grouted concrete.
preplaced concrete, see grouted concrete.
prestressed concrete.
pretensioned concrete.
pumpable concrete.
ready-mixed concrete, readymix concrete.
refractory concrete.
reinforced concrete.
resin concrete, see polymer concrete.
retarded concrete.
rich concrete.
roller-compacted concrete, rolled concrete.
Roman concrete.
rubble concrete.
sawdust concrete, see wood-cement concrete.
self-placing concrete, self-consolidating concrete, self-compactable concrete.
site concrete, see mixed concrete.
site mixed concrete.
slag concrete.
spaded concrete, see tamped concrete.
sprayed concrete.
steel concrete, see reinforced concrete.
steel-fibre reinforced concrete.
stiffened concrete.
structural concrete.
superplasticized concrete.
tamped concrete.
terrazzo concrete, see terrazzo.
tremie concrete.

underwater concrete.
unreinforced concrete, see plain concrete.
vacuum dewatered concrete, vacuum concrete.
vibrated concrete.
white concrete.
wood-cement concrete.

concrete admixture a substance added to a concrete mix with the aim of changing its properties of drying, setting, workability etc., see list of concrete admixtures under **admixture**.

concrete aggregate see aggregate.

Concrete Art a form of abstract art consisting of non-representational forms and the 'concrete' implements of the artist such as line and colour.

concrete batch in concretework, an amount of concrete mixed for use at any one time.

concrete beam 1 any beam of cast in-situ or prefabricated concrete, often prestressed or reinforced with steel. →60
2 see concrete lintel. →22
3 see in-situ concrete beam. →27, →60
4 see precast beam. →28
see types of *concrete beam* illustration. →30

concrete bit see masonry drill. →42

concrete bleeding, water gain; in concretework, the seeping out of excess water not taken up by the hydration of cement.

concrete block a masonry block manufactured from precast concrete, usually of cellular or aggregate construction; types included as separate entries are listed below. →30
see *concrete block* illustration. →30
beam block, see channel block. →30
bond-beam block, see channel block. →30
capping block, see coping block. →30
cavity block, see cellular block. →30
cellular block. →30
channel block. →30
column block. →30
coping block. →30
hollow block, see cellular block. →30
insulated block. →30
lightweight concrete block.
lintel block, see channel block. →30
partition block. →30
pilaster block, see column block. →30
radial block. →30
sill block. →30

concrete block foundation a foundation laid entirely from concrete blocks with reinforced bedding joints, used primarily for lightweight or temporary buildings. →57, →58

concrete block paver a precast rectangular or interlocking concrete paving stone; also called a unit paver, paving block; types included as separate entries are listed below, see also next entry.
see *concrete block paving* illustration. →15
cellular paver, crib paver. →15
hexagonal paver. →15
interlocking paver, interpaver. →15
interweave paver. →15
key paver. →15
pattern paver. →15
wavy paver. →15

concrete block paving an external paved surface made up of evenly sized concrete units, laid on sand or a concrete bed; also called unit paving.
see *concrete block paving* illustration. →15

concrete bond in concretework, the bond caused by friction and adhesion between the concrete and steel reinforcement.

concrete brick an unfired brick made from concrete rather than clay. →30

concrete building block see concrete block. →30

concrete cancer see alkali-aggregate reaction.

concrete casing concrete used as a fireproof covering for structural steel.

concrete chute in the production of concrete, an inclined open steel channel along which concrete is transferred from a mixer into formwork.

concrete compaction in concreting, the manipulating of freshly placed concrete by tamping or vibration to release air voids and settle the mass.

concrete column 1 a column cast from reinforced concrete, with cage reinforcement.
2 see precast column. →28
3 see in-situ concrete column. →27

concrete construction 1 building activity in which the principal material is concrete for foundation, framing, wall, floor or roof construction, cladding products etc.
see *in-situ concrete construction* illustration. →27
2 see precast construction.
see *precast concrete construction* illustration. →28

concrete cover, cover; in reinforced concrete, the thickness of protective concrete between a reinforcing bar and the exterior surface of the concrete.

concrete cracking see cracking.

concrete cube see test cube.

concrete culvert 1 a length of large bore concrete pipe, often used to form a bridge where a road or railway crosses a stream, drain or ditch.
2 see precast concrete ring.

concrete curing, curing; the treatment of hardening concrete by covering, wetting, or steam treatment to maintain its temperature and moisture level in order to provide water for hydration, prevent cracking and improve the quality of the concrete.

concrete cylinder see test cylinder.

concrete drill see masonry drill. →42

concrete flag see concrete paving slab. →15

concrete flow a measure of the workability of fresh concrete; see next entry.

concrete flow test in concretework, a test to determine the consistency and degree of segregation of fresh concrete by subjection to repeated jolting.

concrete footing see in-situ concrete footing. →27

concrete formwork see formwork. →30

concrete frame 1 any building frame of prefabricated or cast-in-situ concrete beams, columns, walls, slabs etc., onto which cladding components, flooring, roofing etc. are fixed.
see *concrete frame* in stone cladding illustration. →11
2 see precast concrete frame. →28
see *precast concrete frame* illustration. →28
see *in-situ concrete frame* illustration. →27
see *in-situ concrete frame* in office building illustration. →60

concrete grade see grade of concrete.

concrete ground slab see ground supported floor. →57

concrete inner leaf the inner loadbearing wall in prefabricated concrete construction, from which external panels are suspended. →28

concrete lintel an in-situ or precast reinforced concrete beam component used over openings in brick and block walls. →22

concrete maturity in concretework, a measurement of the strength of hardening concrete as a function of time and temperature, in units of degree day or degree hour.

concrete mesh reinforcement see fabric reinforcement.

concrete mix the component parts of concrete such as sand, aggregate, cement, water and admixtures combined in an appropriate ratio.

concrete mixer 1 in the production of concrete, a machine for mixing the various constituents to form a homogeneous concrete mix.
2 see cement mixer.

concrete nail see masonry nail. →35

concrete outer leaf the outer loadbearing leaf in prefabricated concrete construction, usually hung from the structural inner leaf. →28

concrete panel see precast concrete panel.
see drop panel.
see edge panel.
see external wall panel.
see precast concrete panel.
see precast concrete unit.
see sandwich panel. →28
see wall panel. →28
see window panel.

concrete patching in concretework, the filling of surface holes and voids and repairing of defects in the cast surface with mortar after the concrete has set.

concrete pavement 1 see concrete paving.
2 see prestressed concrete pavement.
3 see continuously reinforced concrete pavement.

concrete paver 1 a precast concrete unit or slab laid in series to form hardwearing external paved areas.
see concrete block paver. →15
see concrete paving slab. →15
2 a machine which runs on rails and produces concrete pavement.

concrete paving 1 precast concrete units or paving slabs laid horizontally as a hardwearing external surface.
see concrete block paving. →15
2 concrete pavement; a layer of reinforced concrete laid as a hardwearing surface on roads, pavements and pedestrian areas.

concrete paving block see concrete block paver. →15

concrete paving slab, precast concrete flag; a large rectangular concrete slab used for paving external surfaces such as pedestrian areas. →15

concrete pile in foundation technology, a reinforced concrete pile, either precast and driven in, or cast in-situ in a prebored excavation; types included as separate entries are listed below. →29
see **types of pile** in foundation drawing. →29
augered pile. →29
bored pile, see cast-in-place pile. →29
cast-in-place pile. →29
in-situ pile, see cast-in-place pile. →29
precast pile. →29

concrete pipe any of a number of hollow precast concrete products of various sizes, used as drains, culverts, tunnelling etc.

concrete placer see pneumatic concrete placer.

concrete placing, placement; the laying, pouring or pumping of fresh concrete into formwork, moulds, excavations etc. to attain its final shape.

concrete plank 1 a precast concrete flooring unit laid in series to span between beams or crosswalls and provide a floor structure.
2 see hollow-core beam. →28

concrete pump a machine for pumping concrete from a mixer or storage vehicle into formwork, excavations etc.

concrete reinforcement 1 steel rods, deformed bars, meshes and other steel products incorporated into reinforced concrete to withstand tensile forces; types included as separate entries are listed below.
see *concrete reinforcement* illustration. →27
beam reinforcement. →27
binder, see stirrup. →27
bottom reinforcement. →27
cage.
column reinforcement. →27
compression reinforcement.
concrete mesh reinforcement, see fabric.
concrete reinforcement.
fabric reinforcement.
foundation reinforcement. →27
helical reinforcement.
lateral reinforcement. →27
ligature, see stirrup. →27
link, see stirrup. →27
longitudinal reinforcement. →27, →57
main reinforcement. →27
mesh reinforcement, see fabric reinforcement.
principal reinforcement, see main reinforcement. →27
secondary reinforcement.
shear reinforcement.
slab reinforcement. →27
steel reinforcement, see concrete reinforcement.
stirrup. →27
tension reinforcement, tensile reinforcement.
top reinforcement. →27
transverse reinforcement, see lateral reinforcement. →27
two-way reinforcement.
wall reinforcement. →27
web reinforcement, see shear reinforcement.
wire-mesh reinforcement, see fabric reinforcement.
2 see reinforcing bar. →27

concrete ring see precast concrete ring.

concrete roof structure roof structure of a precast, prestressed or in-situ concrete slab. →28

concrete roof tile any roof tile manufactured from concrete.
see *roof tile* illustration. →47

concrete saw a large powered circular saw used for cutting openings in hardened concrete.

concrete screed see screed. →44

concrete screw, masonry screw; any hard-metal screw for fixing to hard porous surfaces such as concrete or masonry. →36

concrete screw anchor a double-helical screw for fixing components such as door frames, pipe hangers etc. directly to a concrete or masonry surface into predrilled holes. →36

concrete segregation a defect in concreting caused by the separating out of constituent parts, especially coarse aggregate, from the mix.

concrete skip a container for transporting and holding mixed concrete.

concrete slab any relatively thin planar area of reinforced concrete, usually a structural floor or roof slab; types included as separate entries are listed below. →60
see *concrete slab structures* illustration. →27
coffered slab, see waffle slab. →27
column and beam construction, see post and beam construction. →27, →28
column and slab construction. →27, →28
concrete paving slab. →15
flat slab, see mushroom slab. →27
folded plate, folded slab. →27
hollow-core beam, hollow-core slab, hollow-core plank. →28
honeycomb slab, see waffle slab. →27
mushroom slab. →27
post and beam construction. →27, →28
waffle slab. →27

concrete slab unit see precast slab unit. →28

concrete slump the degree of collapse of a sample of fresh concrete as measured in a slump test.

concrete slump test a standard on-site test to ascertain the consistency of fresh concrete by measuring the degree of collapse of a cone-shaped sample.

concrete spraying, spraying, pneumatic concreting, shotcreting; the application of sprayed concrete.

concrete stair a stair whose flights are made of reinforced concrete; see precast stair unit. →45

concrete stair unit see precast stair unit.

concrete structure 1 see reinforced-concrete structure.
2 see concrete frame.
3 see opus caementicium, opus concretum. →83

concrete T-beam a concrete flanged beam, T-shaped in cross-section. →30

concrete testing see below for types included as separate entries.
see compressive strength test.
concrete flow test.
concrete slump test.
consistometer test, see VB-consistometer test.
core test.
cube test.
cylinder test.
flow test, see concrete flow test.
slump test.
strength test, see compressive strength test.
VB-consistometer test.
Vebe test, see VB-consistometer test.
works cube test.

concrete tile 1 a floor or wall tile of pressed, extruded or wet-moulded concrete, usually less than 300 mm × 300 mm in size; also called a cement tile, depending on the aggregates used. →44
2 see concrete roof tile. →47

concrete topping a layer of concrete or mortar, usually 50 mm thick, laid as a smooth hardwearing finish for a cast concrete floor slab, deck or other construction. →49

concrete unit 1 see precast concrete unit.
2 see precast slab unit.
3 see precast stair unit.
4 see prefabricated unit.
5 see concrete block paver. →15
6 see precast concrete panel.

concrete vibrator in the production of concrete, a mechanical device for compacting concrete by vibration.

concrete yield, volume yield; the volume of concrete produced by a given amount of cement aggregate and water, measured by weight.

concrete wall 1 a wall of in-situ concrete cast into formwork, or one of precast panels assembled on site, most often with integral steel reinforcement.
2 see *Roman concrete wall* illustration.
3 see in-situ concrete wall. →27

concretework 1 any sitework relating to the casting, erection and finishing of concrete construction; also the result of this.
2 see precast concretework.
see *precast concrete frame* illustration. →28

concreting working with fresh concrete, especially concrete placing.

concretum see opus caementicium.

condemnation see compulsory purchase.

condensates pan, condensation pan; in an air-conditioning system, a vessel beneath a chilling coil in a condenser to collect water.

condensation 1 the process of water vapour or steam cooling to water on contact with a surface below its dewpoint.
2 the resulting droplets of water thus formed; surface condensation.
3 see flue condensation.
4 see polycondensation.

condensation pan see condensates pan.

condensation point see dewpoint.

condensation polymerization see polycondensation.

condenser that part of an air-conditioning and refrigeration system in which refrigerant vapour is condensed, producing heat which is either reused or released to the outside.

condition 1 a proviso for an action such as a planning application, which should be fulfilled in order to gain approval.
2 see planning condition.

conditional planning permission planning permission granted on the grounds that certain local authority conditions are fulfilled; see reserved matter.

conditions of contract, 1 terms of agreement; in contract administration, the terms describing the rights and obligations of a contractor to which he or she must adhere for the contract to remain valid.
2 terms of contract; a contract document outlining contractual obligations, rights of both parties and general practical matters used in a particular contract.
3 general conditions of contract; a similar standard document prepared by a professional advisory body, government department or other authority for use in all contracts.

conduct see code of professional conduct.

conductance 1 the property of a material or substance through which energy can freely flow, usually relating to heat or electricity.
2 see thermal conductance.
3 see electrical conductance.

conductance see electrical conductance.

conduction see thermal conduction.

conductivity 1 see thermal conductivity.
2 see electrical conductivity.

conductor 1 any material, component or construction through which electricity or heat can pass with minimum resistance, and for which it is made use of.
2 that part of an electric cable through which the electricity flows.
3 see electrical conductor.
4 see lightning conductor.

conductor header see rainwater head.

conduit 1 a closed housing within a construction to conceal or provide a passage for pipework and wiring.
2 see electrical conduit.
3 see pipe duct.

cone 1 a solid shape whose surface is formed by joining the points of a circle to a single point not on the plane of the circle.
2 see double cone moulding. →124
3 see pine cone. →121

cone of vision in perspective projection, the cone-shaped field of vision radiating out from the station point or observer; also called the visual cone.

cone penetration testing, deep penetration testing; in soil investigation, penetration testing in which a cone-shaped testing implement is pushed with a steady force into the soil to measure its bearing capacity.

conference see meeting.

conference centre, congress centre; a building which provides specialist facilities for meetings and conferences.

conference room 1 see meeting room. →60
2 see assembly room.

confessio, confession; **1** Lat.; a tomb in which a martyr is buried, often elaborately decorated and surmounted with an ornamental structure, often beneath or near a high altar in a church; a precursor to a crypt. →116
2 the structure or altar surmounting such a burial site.

confession see confessio. →116

confessional in the Roman Catholic church, a wooden stall or box in which the priest sits, unseen, to witness confessions.

configuration 1 in computing, the installation of software programs so that they are compatible with the operating system and hardware.
2 see harp configuration. →32
3 see fan configuration. →32
4 see radial configuration. →32

configuration file in computing, programming which loads initial settings for software.

confirmation of order a written receipt which records the placing of an order for goods or services.

confrontation a hostile opposition or attitude towards local authorities, ethnic or social groups etc. in a multiracial or socially separated area.

congé a concave decorative moulding; a cavetto or cove surmounting a vertical surface. →14

congestion in traffic planning, a build-up of traffic to a level which causes delays and traffic jams.

conglomerate, puddingstone; rock consisting of rounded stones or pebbles embedded in a finer material such as limestone.
Congo wood see African walnut.
congress centre see conference centre.
conical roll joint see roll joint. →49
conical roof a roof form in the shape of a cone.
conical vault 1 a masonry vault, or part of a vault, in the form of a segment of a cone.
2 expanding vault; a barrel vault whose diameter gradually increases along its length, used over splayed corridors and other spaces with funnel-shaped plans. →25
conic section any planar figure formed from the cross-sectional cutting of a cone (examples of these are circle and ellipse).
conifer any cone-bearing evergreen tree with needle-like leaves, from which softwood is obtained; a member of the gymnosperm group which includes pines, firs, spruces, larches etc.
see list of species of tree from which softwood is obtained under **softwood**.
Coniophora cerebella see cellar rot.
Coniophora puteana see cellar rot.
conisterium Lat.; in Greek and Roman recreational architecture, a space where wrestlers were sprinkled with dust or sand before a contest; Greek form is konisterion. →91
conk, bracket fungus, shelf fungus, polypore; [Polyporaceae] a group of fungi which attack timber and produce hard fruiting bodies protruding from the trunks of trees and logs.
connecting, 1 connection; the linking of a building, appliance etc. to a gas, electricity, water or some other supply or installation.
2 the joining of two or more components together.
connecting point see connection.
connection, 1 joint; the meeting point of two components such as pipes or structural members which are fixed together; the joint thus formed.
2 connecting point; the point at which a building is connected to the mains water supply, or to a public sewer.
3 in telecommunications and networks, physical access to a phone line or network which allows for communication.
4 see telephone connection.
5 see connecting.
connector any accessory for fixing two components, members, pipe fittings etc. together; examples included as separate entries are listed below.
electrical connector.
flue connector. →56
group connector.
pipe fitting.
shear plate connector. →35
split ring connector. →35
toothed plate connector. →35
union.
consecration cross a circular emblem enclosing a cross motif; originally the symbol with which the walls of new churches were marked on consecration. →118
consent 1 see planning consent.
2 see neighbours' consent.
conservation 1 the maintenance, rehabilitation and protection of old buildings and structures in their original state using traditional and authentic materials and methods.
2 see physical conservation.
3 the wise use and management of resources to meet future needs.
conservation area an area of urban or rural land designated as being of special architectural or historical significance and protected by legislation to control development.
conservator a person employed by a museum to ensure the preservation of its artifacts.
conservatory, 1 sun lounge; a glazed room attached to a dwelling, used for relaxation and the cultivation of exotic plants. →57
2 winter garden; a building or room within a building, often with large areas of glass, in which plants are cultivated or displayed in a heated environment.
consignatorium Lat.; an apsed anteroom in an Early Christian basilica in which parishioners received a blessing before their first communion.
consistency the firmness or cohesiveness of thick liquid suspensions and pastes such as concrete.
consistometer an apparatus for measuring the firmness or cohesiveness of suspensions and thick liquids such as concrete, mortar, grouts and cement pastes.
consistometer test see VB-consistometer test.
console 1 a classical masonry bracket or corbelled stone for supporting overhangs, pediments, balconies and shelves, often ornate and decorated with volutes.
2 see monitor.
3 an operating station for electronic or automated equipment consisting of a monitor and keyboard, mouse, joystick etc.
consolidation 1 the compressing of soil due to the weight of overlying structures bearing down on it.
2 see dynamic consolidation.
constant a value which always remains the same in a mathematical or numerical function.
Constantine's cross see Christ monogram. →119
constant white see blanc fixe.
construction 1 an assembly of materials or components which function together to make up part of a building; examples included as separate entries are listed below.
2 whole structural or building systems based on this.
3 see structure.
4 see building, building construction.
5 the setting out of technical drawings and constructing of geometrical forms such as perspectives with guide lines and other points of reference.
see *construction of brick house* illustration. →59
see *construction of office building* illustration. →60
alternate bay construction, see chequerboard construction, alternate lane construction.
arched construction, see arch, arched structure.
balanced construction. →9
box frame construction.
building construction.
ceiling construction.
chequerboard construction.
column and slab construction. →27, →28
column and beam construction, see post and beam construction. →27, →28
composite construction.
concrete construction.
crosswall construction. →28
cruck construction. →7
deconstruction, see deconstructivism.
discontinuous construction.
floor construction.
Greek construction, see graecorum structura. →83
half-timbered construction.
hit and miss construction, see chequerboard construction.
horizontal log construction. →6
isodomic construction.
large-panel construction.
lift slab construction.
loadbearing wall construction. →28
log construction. →6
muntin and plank construction. →7
offshore construction.
panel construction.
plank construction. →7
post and beam construction, post and lintel construction. →27, →28
precast concrete construction.

prefabricated construction, see prefabrication.
rammed earth construction, see pisé.
reconstruction.
road construction.
roof construction.
shell construction.
stave construction.
steel construction.
stressed skin construction.
timber construction.
trabeated construction, see post and beam construction. →27, →28
truss plate construction.
trussed construction.
upper floor construction, see intermediate floor construction. →59
vaulted construction, see *arched and vaulted construction* illustration. →22
window construction.

construction cost see building cost.

construction drawing a drawing showing how parts of a building are to be constructed on site, usually produced at a large scale (1:10, 1:20), often wall sections, junctions etc.

construction engineering a discipline dealing with the structural frames and constructional technology of buildings and structures.

construction fund a fund set up by a housing company or business to finance the construction of new buildings or renovation work and repairs to existing ones.

construction industry see building industry.

construction joint in concreting, a joint between adjacent layers or areas of concrete that have been cast at different times.

construction line see reference line.

construction manager a contractor's employee responsible for managing and supervising work on a large site or several small ones; a senior site manager.

construction moisture water in laid concrete, mortar, or other wet trades, which evaporates away during the construction period.

construction sequence, sequencing of operations; in project planning, the stages in which construction proceeds, dictating the order in which materials and components arrive on site.

construction site see building site.

construction technology, building technology, building science; a branch of technology dealing with the erection and assembly of buildings, their components and structure.

construction time 1 the contract time or time for completion of a building as specified in a contract.
2 the period of time during which a building is under construction.

construction waste any material such as rubble, earth or remnants left over from construction or demolition work whose disposal is the responsibility of the contractor.

construction work any work pertaining to building construction; the various operations involved in assembling the foundations, frame, fabric and finishes for a building; types included as separate entries are listed below.
additional work, see extra work.
asbestos work, see asbestos removal.
blockwork.
brickwork. →20
cabinetwork.
casework, see casing.
ceiling work.
cobwork, see horizontal log construction. →6
concretework.
cribwork, see cribbing. →29
daywork.
earthwork.
electrical work, see electrical installation work.
extra work.
facework, see fair-face brickwork.
falsework.
formwork.
framework.
groundwork.
landscape work, see landscaping.
lathwork, see lathing.
measured work.
network.
paintwork.
panelwork, see panelling.
parquet work, see parquetry.
pipework.
plasterwork.
ragwork. →11
range work.
remedial work, see renovation.
repair work, see renovation.
sheetmetal work.
shift work.
specialized work.
steelwork.
stonework.
studwork.
tabernacle-work.
telework.
timberwork.
veneerwork, see veneering. →10
westwork.

construction works that body of work on a building site concerned with the actual assembling of a building, as opposed to temporary work, ground work etc.

constructivism 1 any architecture, art or sculpture based on a manifestation of structure or geometric construction.
2 Russian constructivism; an architectural and artistic movement originating from Soviet Russia in the early 1900s, characterized by dynamic constructions and expression of movement.

constructivist 1 one who advocates or practises constructivism.
2 pertaining to or taking motifs from constructivism.

consultant a qualified person or professional body employed by an organization to give professional advice, liaise or produce specialist designs for various aspects of a construction project.

consulting room a private room in which advice and treatment, usually of a medical nature, are given.

consumer price index a set of figures which shows the variation in retail prices of basic goods and services bought by the public over a stated period of time.

consumption see electricity consumption.

contact see electrical contact.

contact adhesive an adhesive applied in liquid form to surfaces to be joined, then allowed to partially dry before components are pressed together, resulting in instantaneous adhesion.

contact metamorphic rock a name for types of metamorphic rock which have formed under high temperatures caused by magmatic intrusion; hornfels.

container a large standardized box manufactured from steel plate for the transportation of freight.

containment 1 see fire containment.
2 the prevention of escape of radiation from a nuclear reactor.

contamination poisonous or polluting substances entering a system, water course etc., rendering it unusable.

conté crayon a hard, coloured pastel used for drawing and sketching.

content the relative amount of one substance in another, expressed as a percentage or ratio.

continental bow-saw see bow saw.

contingency see contingency sum.

contingency sum, contingency; money set aside within a building contract to be used to cover the cost of unforeseen or unplannable items or events.

continuous bar balustrade a balustrade constructed from horizontal bars supported by uprights at regular intervals. →54
continuous beam a single beam which spans over more than two points of support, so that loading one section will affect conditions over the other spans. →7
continuous beam bridge a continuous span bridge supported on a central beam or girder. →32
continuous bridge see continuous span bridge. →32
continuous coil spiral an ornamental motif consisting of a pattern of curving lines which meet in spirals. →125
continuous hinge see piano hinge. →38
continuous line in technical drawing, an unbroken line, usually representing visible and cut forms and dimension lines.
continuously graded aggregate in concretework, graded aggregate which contains all grain sizes within a particular range.
continuously moving form see slipform.
continuously reinforced concrete pavement, CRCP; road construction in which the main structural base is a reinforced concrete slab with no transverse movement joints.
continuous mixer in the production of concrete, a concrete mixer which produces a continuous flow of concrete.
continuous moulding any decorative moulding whose cross-sectional profile is uniform along its length. →14
continuous slab bridge a continuous span bridge supported by a central slab. →32
continuous span bridge a bridge whose deck is supported by a continuous beam or slab, with intermediate supporting piers; variously called a continuous slab or continuous beam bridge depending on the mode of support. →32
continuum in physics, a continuous series of component parts that merge into one another; an unbroken mass or course of events.
contorta pine see lodgepole pine.
contour 1 see contour line.
2 see topography.
contour fort a hillfort bounded on one or more sides by substantial banks or natural ramparts.
contour line a line on a topographical map which represents all points at a given height above sea level.
contract, 1 contractual agreement; a legally enforcing agreement between two or more parties regarding provision of goods, work or services, the scope of work included therein.
2 see building contract.
contract document any written, drawn or computerized document that forms part of a package on which a contract is based.
contract drawing any drawing which forms part of a package on which a contract is based.
contraction the reduction of the physical dimensions or area of a body.
contraction joint, shrinkage joint; in monolithic concrete or masonry construction, a joint which allows for the shrinkage of materials on drying, often filled after the material has hardened.
contractor, builder, building contractor; a person or organization which carries out building work according to a contract or agreement; types included as separate entries are listed below.
electrical works contractor.
main contractor.
management contractor.
nominated subcontractor.
specialized contractor.
subcontractor.
contract period a period stipulated in the contract for the execution of work, during which the contract is valid.
contract price see contract sum.
contracts manager a contractor's representative responsible for managing contractual aspects of construction projects, usually large-scale ones.
contract sum, contract price; the sum of money payable by a client to a contractor for the execution of work outlined in the building contract.
contract time, construction time, time for completion; the time specified for the prospective completion of a construction job or building, measured from an agreed starting date to handover or another specified juncture.
contractual agreement see contract.
contractual claim a claim that can be settled within the terms of the contract without recourse to legal proceedings.
contrapposto in painting and sculpture, the asymmetrical compositional balance of a human torso around a central vertical axis.
contrast tension formed by opposites of form, size and colour in architectural composition.
control see building control.
control circuit an electric circuit by which mechanical equipment is controlled.
control device, regulator; a device for operating motors, actuators etc. to control automated and mechanical installations.
control point in surveying, a fixed point of known position (both horizontally and vertically) used as a reference for all measurements.
control tower a structure at an airport or airfield containing equipment and personnel to monitor and give instructions to arriving and departing air traffic; air-control tower, in full.
control valve, discharge valve, regulating valve; a valve for regulating the rate of flow and preventing backsiphonage of liquid in a pipeline.
controversy of triglyphs see corner contraction. →77
contubernium Lat.; a Roman military tent or room in a barrack block for eight legionaries.
conurbation, metropolitan region; an extensive urban area, often the merging of adjacent urban settlements as they expand, or the built-up areas surrounding a major urban centre.
convection 1 the transfer of heat or electrical charge via thermal currents in a gas or liquid.
2 see thermal convection.
3 see free convection.
convection column see thermal column.
convection heater see convector.
convector 1 a space heater which provides warmth by the movement of air over a hot surface, to be conveyed into the surrounding air by convection.
2 see fan convector.
convenience see toilet, public convenience.
convent see nunnery.
convent church a church belonging to a convent or nunnery.
convergence 1 the meeting of a number of lines at a point.
2 in perspective, the apparent radiation of parallel lines from a point an infinite distance away.
conversion 1 the sawing of logs into large timber sections, profiles and mouldings for use in building. →2
see *conversion of timber* illustration. →2
2 in computing, the transmutation of a computer program or file to make it usable by another computer system.
conversion defect defects in sawn timber sections which occur as a result of improper machining, blunt or poorly adjusted tools etc. →1
see *conversion defects* illustration. →1
conversion methods the various ways in which a log or flitch may be sawn into timber sections to take advantage of section sizes, grain pattern etc. →2
see *conversion of timber* illustration. →2
converter 1 a large industrial vessel in which steel is produced from pig iron.

2 an electronic device which converts direct current to alternating current.
convex brace in traditional timber frame construction, an outwardly curving timber for stiffening the angle between two perpendicular members.
convex head roofing nail, nipple head nail, springhead roofing nail; a nail for fixing corrugated roofing with an inverted cup-shaped addition beneath its head to cover the curved space between nail head and crest of sheeting.
convex joint see extruded joint. →16
convex plane see round plane.
conveyancing legal work and documentation undertaken in the transfer of ownership of property.
conventional system see low velocity system.
conveyor 1 a mechanical device, usually part of a manufacturing process or plant, for moving goods and parts from one area to another.
2 passenger conveyor.
conveyor belt mesh woven wire mesh with a weave permitting pivoting along its length; used for industrial conveyor belts, and as a cladding material for elevations, ceilings etc. →34
cooker, stove; **1** a gas-fuelled or electrical appliance with an oven and hotplates for cooking food.
2 see electric cooker.
3 see gas cooker.
cooktop see hob.
cool colour in colour theory, a colour dominated by green, blue or violet, which produces a subjective feeling of cold.
cooler unit see unit air-conditioner.
cooling 1 the reducing in temperature of an object, gas, room etc.
2 in air-conditioning, those measures designed to produce thermal comfort by introducing cool air to a space.
3 see cooling period.
cooling coil in air-conditioning, a unit containing copper tubes supplied with chilled water or other liquid to cool supply air to a desired temperature.
cooling period in the steam curing of concrete, the period during which heat is no longer applied and the concrete slowly cools.
cooling tower 1 in air conditioning, an externally mounted device for cooling warmed water from the system by spraying it over a system of ventilated baffles, causing partial evaporation and resultant cooling.
2 a wide hollow concrete chimney in which water vapour from power stations etc. is cooled.
cooperative, co-operative; a business association owned and run by its members, who share the profits.
coordinate, co-ordinate; in geometry, a point defined in space measured as a distance or value from one of the coordinate axes.
coordinate axes three perpendicular reference lines, usually designated as X, Y and Z which meet at an origin and are used to set out the basic structure of a drawing, graph, geometrical figure etc. →127
coordinate cube the basic volume unit or cube marked out by the three mutually perpendicular, gradated coordinate planes in an axonometric or oblique projection; sometimes called an axonometric cube. →127
coordinate plane 1 a two-dimensional geometric plane formed by the area scribed by two coordinate axes. →127
2 see vertical plane, front plane. →127
3 see profile plane, side plane. →127
4 see horizontal plane, ground plane. →127
coordinate system, 1 system of coordinates; a system of usually perpendicular graded axes which define space as a series of distances from these axes. →127
2 see Cartesian coordinate system. →127
3 see polar coordinates.
coordination the combining of people, systems or services so as to function together in an efficient and harmonious way.
coordinator see door co-ordinator.
copaiba balsam an oleoresin exuded from some species of South American tree [*Copaifera spp.*], used with a solvent as a cleaner or isolation varnish in oil-painting.
Copaifera see copaiba balsam.
cope see long groove. →6
Copernicia cerifera the carnauba palm, see carnauba wax.
coping, 1 capping, wall cap; a construction of brick, block, stone or sheetmetal on top of a free-standing wall or parapet to shed off and prevent infiltration of rainwater; types included as separate entries are listed below.
coping brick. →16
featheredged coping. →16
pressed metal coping.
saddleback coping. →16
segmental coping. →16
2 the cutting of stone slabs by making a groove on either face with a saw and then giving blows to the groove until the stone cracks.
coping block 1 a concrete block with a sloping upper surface, designed for use as a coping for a freestanding wall. →30
2 see masonry capping.
coping brick a special capping brick designed to be wider than the freestanding wall or parapet which it protects, with throated overhangs on one or both sides. →16
see saddleback coping brick. →16
see featheredged coping. →16
coping saw, scribing saw; a fine-toothed bow saw whose blade is held in tension in a deep metal frame; used for cutting out patterns and curves in board.
coping stone see masonry capping.
see featheredged coping. →16
copolymer in the chemistry of plastics, a polymer formed from more than one type of chained monomer; see homopolymer.
copper 1 a soft and malleable metal, **Cu**, which has good resistance to corrosion, is a good conductor of heat and electricity, and which can be used as an alloy with other metals; used for wires, pipework and sheetmetal cladding.
2 a shade of orange brown which takes its name from the colour of untarnished copper metal.
Copper Age, chalcolithic period; a short prehistoric period after the Stone Age in the Near East during which copper but not bronze was used for implements.
copper alloy tube see copper pipe.
copper blue a form of the pigment Bremen blue.
copper carbonate see azurite, see malachite.
copper glance see chalcocite.
copper green, **1** a form of the pigment Bremen blue.
2 copper rust, malachite green; a shade of green which takes its name from the colour of the patina which occurs on weathered copper; also the colour of the mineral malachite.
coppering see copper plating.
copper iron sulphide a chemical compound, Cu_5FeS_4, see bornite, an important ore of copper.
copper mesh any mesh product manufactured primarily from copper.
see *wire mesh* illustrations. →34
copper nail a round-shafted nail fabricated from copper, often for decorative use.
copper oxide Cu_2O, see cuprite, red copper ore.
copper pipe, copper alloy tube; narrow-bore pipes of copper alloy used in water and gas installation pipework.

copper plate a copper mill product of flat plate over 10 mm thick, usually manufactured from a copper alloy.
see *metal plate* illustration. →34

copper plating, 1 coppering; the coating of an object with a thin layer of copper as corrosion resistance or decoration.
2 the layer thus formed.

copper pyrites see chalcopyrite.

copper rust see copper green.

copper sheet copper rolled into sheets not more than 3 mm thick; used for patinated exterior cladding etc.
see *sheetmetal* illustration. →34

copper sulphide Cu_2S, see chalcocite.

CuS, see covellite.

Coptic cross 1 Egyptian cross, see ankh. →117
2 a cross with a nail or tack situated at the angle between each limb; sometimes called an Ethiopian cross. →118

copy, 1 print; a reproduction of a drawing, print or artwork using a reprographic or other process.
2 see duplicate.
3 see photocopy.

copy paper any paper suitable for use in photocopiers and other printing machines, usually A4 or A3 size and of thicknesses from 80–120 kg/m^2.

copy protection a mechanism inbuilt to certain computer programs to prevent them from being unlawfully copied.

copyright the legal protection of creative work such that certain rights of use, making duplicate copies etc., are restricted by patent or assigned to a particular party, usually the author.

copy shop see print shop.

coqueliquot, red lead, ponceau, poppy (red); a shade of red which is the same as the colour of the pigment red lead, and that of the blossom of the poppy [*Papaver rhoeas*].

coquillage Rococo decoration based on stylized shell forms.

coral (red), jasper (red); a shade of red which takes its name from a coral formed by the coral polyp *Anthozoa*, or the colour of the mineral jasper.

corbel a masonry bracket projecting from the face of a building surface to provide support for an overhanging object or member. →23

corbel arch see corbelled arch. →23

corbelled arch, corbel arch; a false arch composed of a series of stones corbelled out from either side to meet in the middle; not a true arch. →23

corbelled lintel a lintel whose span is reduced by the use of corbel stones on either side of an opening; usually found in stone architecture. →23

corbelled vault a masonry vault constructed by overlapping successive courses of stone to meet at the highest point; not a true vault. →65

corbelling a method of constructing a masonry overhang by projecting each successive edge course slightly outward. →26

corbel table an ornamental banded motif consisting of a series of arches which project from a wall surface; often found beneath the parapet in Romanesque architecture. →124

corbie gable see crow steps.

corbie steps see crow steps.

Corchorus capsularis see jute.

cord, string; a thin rope-like product of wound fibres of natural or artificial material used for tying, binding and tensile applications; also a length of this.

cordierite, dichroite, iotite; a blue or brown magnesium aluminium silicate mineral used as a raw material in the ceramic industry and as decorative stone.

cordon 1 a masonry course, often projecting, at the foot of battlements in a wall of a castle or fortification, or along the upper surface of a ditch.
2 in walling, a projecting band course of masonry or brickwork, often rounded in cross-section.

corduroy work a surface treatment for ashlar stonework consisting of narrow vertical reeding.

core 1 the central layer of material in components such as certain forms of composite construction, building boards, composite constructions or steel cables.
see *concrete core* in Roman walling illustration. →83
2 the internal filling of lower grade wood in a timber-based board, covered by veneers. →9
3 see door core. →50
4 see test core.
5 see box out.

coreboard any timber building board manufactured by gluing veneers to either side of a solid timber core, to which the grain of the veneers runs at 90°; types included as separate entries are listed below. →9
battenboard. →9
blockboard. →9
cellular board. →9
composite board. →9
laminboard. →9

cored brick see perforated brick. →16

core drilling in soil investigation, drilling into the ground with special apparatus to obtain core samples for testing.

core form a mould introduced into the formwork for creating an opening in cast concrete.

core ply see central ply. →9

core plywood plywood in which the core is considerably thicker than the face plies; see coreboard. →9

core roll in sheet roofing, a timber fillet around which roofing material is dressed at joints and corners.

core stiffening the fixing of intermediate floors of a building to a central core, often a lift shaft, stair or services block to provide vertical stability.

core strength the compressive strength of a concrete core sample, taken from a cast or existing concrete member.

core test in concreting, a test to measure the compressive strength of a concrete core sample, drilled from a cast concrete member.

Corinthian pertaining to the Corinthian order; see following entries.

Corinthian capital a capital at the top of a column of the classical Greek Corinthian order, lavishly carved with acanthus foliage surmounted by a flat abacus. →81

Corinthian column a slender column of the classical Greek Corinthian order. →78

Corinthian hall see atrium corinthium.

Corinthian order the youngest of the three classical Greek orders, characterized by slender fluted columns, an ornate capital decorated with acanthus motifs, a base and an entablature with dentils. →78
see *classical Greek orders* illustration. →78
see *Corinthian order* in Roman amphitheatre illustration. →90
see *Corinthian order* in superimposed orders illustration. →114

Corinthian roofing the antique term for classical roof tiling of clay pan-and-roll tiles, laid with flat, lipped tiles capped with rows of V-shaped tiles, often terminating with antifixae at the eaves. →47

cork the bark of the cork oak [*Quercus suber*], used in construction for its buoyancy, lightness, insulating and resilient properties.

cork black see vine black.

corkboard a building board made from granulated cork pressed together with a binder.

cork carpet, cork matting; a flooring product in sheet form manufactured from granulated cork, mineral fibre and a binder of resin or oil attached to a backing sheet, often with a surface coating of plastic. →44

cork ceiling tile a ceiling tile made from reconstituted expanded granulated cork; often used for its acoustic properties.

cork floor tile a hardwearing and warm flooring product consisting of rectangular sheets of cork carpet laid as tiles.

cork linoleum a hardwearing flooring product in sheet or tile form consisting of ground cork and polymerized linseed oil on a hessian backing. →44

cork matting see cork carpet. →44

cork oak [*Quercus suber*] a Mediterranean hardwood whose outer bark, cork, is used for thermal insulation, buoyancy aids, bottle corks, gaskets and vibration control.

cork powder in the manufacture of cork products, granules less than 0.25 mm in diameter.

corkscrew stair see spiral stair. →45

cork tile a hardwearing rectangular floor or wall tile which consists of granulated cork and a binder such as oil or resin attached to a backing sheet.

cork wall tile a rectangular soft wall tile made from sheets of granulated cork in a binder.

cork wallpaper cork paper manufactured with a backing and used as a wallcovering.

corkwood in the manufacture of cork products, the material obtained after the initial treatment of cork bark.

corn see golden wheat.

cornel see dogwood.

cornelian a reddish-brown microcrystalline variety of the mineral chalcedony, used as gemstones and for decorative ornament; alternative spelling is carnelian.

corner 1 the meeting point of two lines or planes.
2 the meeting of two members, components, elements etc. at an angle.
3 see inside corner. →14
4 see outside corner. →14
5 see arris.

corner apartment an apartment situated at the external corner of a slab block, with windows on two adjacent walls. →61

corner bead 1 see angle bead. →2
2 see edge strip. →2

corner board in timber-clad construction, vertical boards nailed over the cladding at corners as protection.

corner chisel see bruzz chisel. →41

corner column see edge column. →80

corner contraction a visual refinement in the classical Doric frieze, as found in the Parthenon, in which the spacing of end columns in the row are reduced to maintain the impression that every other triglyph is centred over a column; this variation in spacing of triglyphs vs columns is called the controversy of triglyphs; see archaic solution, classical solution. →77

corner cramp, picture frame cramp, mitre cramp; a cramp used for holding and pressing corners of a rectangular wooden frame in place while it is being glued.

corner fillet a timber finishing strip used to cover the internal corner joint between two perpendicular surfaces.

corner fireplace a two-faced fireplace located at the meeting of two walls at right angles to one another. →55

corner half lap joint a timber halved joint in which one member is perpendicular to another, forming the outside corner of a frame.

corner joint any joint in which the members to be connected are not in a straight line, or in the same plane; see below for list.
angle joint.
bevelled corner joint. →4
box corner joint. →5
box dovetail joint. →5
cogged corner joint. →4
corner half lap joint.
notch (log construction). →6

corner post in traditional timber frame construction, a sturdy post at the meeting of two exterior walls.

corner scraper, angle plane, French plane; a bladed hand tool used in plastering for removing excess plaster from internal corners. →41

corner tile see inside corner tile. →20

corner trowel see angle trowel. →43

corner unit see corner apartment. →61

cornerstone, foundation stone; a block of masonry cast or laid into foundations as a memorial of the commencement of construction of a building, usually inscribed with information about the client, contractor and the occasion at which it was laid.

cornflower blue a shade of blue which takes its name from the colour of the blossom of the cornflower [*Centaurea cyanus*].

cornice, 1 ceiling strip; a decorative horizontal moulding at the meeting of internal wall and ceiling.
2 in classical architecture, the horizontal overhanging upper band of an entablature above a frieze, made up of a cymatium, corona and other mouldings. →80
see *classical orders* illustrations. →78, →79, →80
see *caryatid* illustration. →76
see *Pompeian styles* illustration. →126
3 in masonry, a large projecting moulding, often classical, at the top of an exterior wall.

cornucopia see horn of plenty. →121

Cornus florida see dogwood.

corollary in mathematics, a proposition which can be proved as a result of something already proven.

corona 1 Lat.; the lower moulding in a classical cornice, a projecting element with a vertical face beneath the cymatium; often called a geison in Greek temples. →78, →79, →86
2 see corona moulding. →14
3 a circular side chapel in a church or cathedral.

corona moulding a protruding horizontal moulding whose lower surface is profiled to form a drip. →14

corona podii the low marble wall or parapet between the podium and arena of a Roman amphitheatre. →90

coronata opera coronata, see crownwork. →104

coroplastics the use of relief ornament and sculpture in terracotta work.

corporal 'corpus' (Lat.) = body; a square of white cloth placed on a church altar, on which the chalice and paten are placed during the Mass, to catch particles falling from the vessels.

corporation see limited company.

correction the action of altering or amending an item such as settings on an appliance so that it functions properly, or amendments to a document so as to be accurate.

corridor 1 a narrow longitudinal circulation space within a building providing internal access to rooms or other spaces.
see *brick house* illustration. →59
see *office building* illustration. →60
2 fire corridor, see fire break.

corridor block 1 a multistorey residential building type in which apartments are arranged with their entrance doors accessed via a corridor running down the length of the building. →61
2 see central corridor block. →61
3 see single-loaded corridor block. →61

corrosion, attack; the wearing away, destruction or decay of a material, especially a metal, due to chemical or electrochemical reaction with its surroundings; types included as separate entries are listed below.
crevice corrosion.
deposit corrosion.
electrochemical corrosion.
erosion corrosion.

microbiological corrosion.
pit corrosion.
stress corrosion.

corrosion fatigue fatigue in steel caused by corrosion in members subjected to repeated changing stresses in a corrosive environment.

corrosion inhibiting, rust inhibiting; the painting and other coating treatments of metal, usually steel and cast-iron components, with compounds to inhibit corrosion.

corrosion inhibiting admixture in concretework, an admixture included in a concrete mix to inhibit the corrosion of reinforcement.

corrosion inhibitor a surface treatment, alloyed substance etc. used with metals to prevent oxidation.

corrosion resistance the ability of a metal to withstand chemical corrosion, oxidation, weathering etc.

corrosive the property of a liquid or gas to gradually wear away another material or surface through chemical action.

corrosive water see aggressive water.

corrugated asbestos cement asbestos cement which has been pressed into corrugated sheets; formerly used as a tough and durable roofing material.

corrugated cardboard a sheet product of thin card formed into a wavy shape and often laminated between two flat sheets; used for padding and packing. →59

corrugated fastener, wiggle nail, mitre brad; a short piece of corrugated steel with sharpened edges, hammered into a timber butt joint to secure it. →35

corrugated glass rough cast glass sheeting manufactured with corrugations and used for glazed roofing.

corrugated iron a steel product of sheetmetal preformed in a wavy cross-section to provide longitudinal stiffening.

corrugated ply-web beam a plywood web beam whose vertical web is wavy in plan to increase transverse buckling strength. →7

corrugated sheeting 1 a metal or plastics sheeting product preformed in a wavy cross-section to provide longitudinal stiffening. →49
2 see corrugated iron, corrugated sheetmetal.

corrugated sheetmetal a product of steel, zinc, aluminium etc. sheetmetal preformed in a wavy cross-section to provide longitudinal stiffening.

corrugated sheet roofing profiled sheet roofing which has been formed with a wavy profile in cross-section. →49

corrugated shell a tunnel, bridge, conduit etc. structure of corrugated sheet steel.

corrugation filler in profiled sheet roofing, a component fitted beneath sheeting at eaves, ridge or other edges to block up the gaps formed beneath the corrugations.

corruleum blue see cerulean blue.

Corsican pine [*Pinus nigra*] a softwood from Europe with light yellowish brown timber; used for joinery.

Cor-ten a proprietary weathering steel with a high copper content whose surface rusts evenly to form a weather-resistant orange-brown coating on exposure to the elements; used for external cladding.

cortile the inner courtyard of an Italian palace or building, often lined with arcades.

cortina see curtain wall. →103

corundum a hard mineral form of aluminium oxide, Al_2O_3, used as gemstones (ruby, sapphire) and as a grinding and polishing agent; see also emery.
see ruby.
see sapphire.

Corvus corax see raven.

coryceum Lat.; see korykeion. →91

Corylus avellana see hazel.

cosine a trigonometric function; in a right-angled triangle, the length of the side adjacent to an angle divided by the length of the hypotenuse is the cosine of that angle.

Cosmati a group of architects, sculptors and decorative artists who worked in the same style in marble and mosaic in the 1100s–1300s in Rome and Naples.

Cosmati work geometrical mosaic work in coloured marble, glass and stone, usually religious work for choir screens, pulpits, floors and walls; see above. →123

cosmogram an Indian and Tibetan mandala, representative of the universe in triangles, squares and circles. →120

cost 1 an amount of money outlaid or to be paid for a product, service or completed work.
2 a sum of money spent on running a business.

cost accounting the financial accounting of all the costs arising from running a business.

cost analysis a costing technique for tendering or physical construction using estimated or costed parts of construction work distributed between cost headings, allowing for easy and efficient comparison.

cost appraisal the weighing up of potential costs for a project to ascertain methods of construction, materials, funding and scheduling etc.

cost benefit analysis a method of comparing costs and resources needed for a particular project with advantages and profits from that project.

cost check a periodical financial assessment at any stage of a building project against a preplanned budget.

cost comparison the process of comparing alternative systems, solutions and components for use in a building project with regard to cost.

cost control the task of continuous monitoring of costs incurred and available finances for a building project.

cost estimate an estimation of the cost of a construction project based on designs, often undertaken by a quantity surveyor at an early stage in design work.

cost in use a comprehensive cost estimate of a design, component or product, measured by adding together capital expenses and costs incurred subsequently by maintenance and operation.

cost index a figure expressing the change in value of products or services in relation to time.

costing the calculation of prospective costs for a development.

cost limit the sum of money with which the client requires a project or part of a project to be constructed.

costly see expensive.

cost of living index a published list which indicates variation in retail prices of basic goods and services over a stated period of time.

cost per square metre, unit cost; a measure of the potential or final relative cost of a building calculated by dividing the construction costs by built gross or net area of the building.

cost plan a document outlining the estimated costs for a construction project according to cost headings for major areas of work.

cost reduction, cost saving; reducing the cost of a construction project at design stage by making design alterations.

cost-reimbursement contract, do-and-charge work; a form of building contract in which the contractor bills for costs expended, usually taking a percentage of the total or fixed sum as payment for overheads and profit.

cost saving see cost reduction.

cot 1 see bunk.
2 see bothie.

cotangent a trigonometric function; in a right-angled triangle, the tangent of the acute angle opposite to an angle, its complement.

coticed cross see cross cotised. →118

cottage a small country dwelling for permanent habitation or in use as a holiday home, often of stone construction.

cottage industry, handicraft; the manufacture of artifacts by hand, usually within the home environment.

cottage orné a style in English and French domestic architecture from the late 1700s and early 1800s, characterized by the use of vernacular motifs in a romantic fashion.

cotter pin a removable split wire fixing inserted into a hole in a housed component to secure it in place.

cottise see cross cotised. →118

cotton oil see cottonseed oil.

cottonseed oil, cotton oil; a semi-drying oil used as a medium in some oil paints, produced from the seeds of the cotton plant, *Gossypium spp.*

cottonwood [*Populus spp.*] a group of hardwoods from North America with soft, pale timber; used for furniture, panelling and plywood; see ***Populus spp.*** for full list of related species included in this work.

coulomb abb. **C**; SI unit of electric charge, the quantity of energy transported by a current of 1 amp in 1 second.

coumarone indene, coumarone resin; a thermoplastic resin made from coumarone, C_8H_6O, present in coal tar, used as a medium in paints, a binder in floor tiles, in the rubber industry etc.

coumarone resin see coumarone indene.

council, 1 city council, town council; the local elected administrative body of an urban area.
2 see local government.

council chamber see bouleuterion. →92, →94

council estate a housing area consisting of properties owned and rented by the council.

council flat an apartment or flat owned and rented by a local authority.

council house a dwelling or block of dwellings owned and rented by a local authority.

council housing see public housing.

counter a table surface for the service of customers in a shop or commercial establishment.

counterbalanced bridge see bascule bridge. →64

counterbatten in tiled roof construction, battens laid above the roofing membrane onto which horizontal tiling battens are laid.

counterbattening in timber frame construction, secondary battening nailed across studs, rafters or primary battens to allow for ventilation and water run off within construction.

counter flashing see cover flashing.

counterfort a vertical rib, projection, buttress or thickening in a wall to provide strength and stability; in retaining walls it is built into the side of the wall facing the ground and thus works in tension.
see *retaining wall* illustration. →29
see *Scandinavian hall church* illustration. →102

counterfort wall, buttress wall; a cantilever retaining wall ribbed with a number of spaced buttresses to reinforce the junction between wall and footing. →29

counterguard a narrow rampart or projecting outwork in a fortification, often triangular in plan and open at the rear, constructed as protection in front of a major work such as a bastion, ravelin etc. →104

counterpoise bridge see bascule bridge. →64

counterscarp the outer slope of the surrounding ditch of a fortification, opposite the scarp, and facing inwards. →104

countersignature a second signature on a document as affirmation, witness or guarantee.

countersink 1 a drill bit with a cutting edge for making a cone-shaped depression around the rim of a hole drilled for a countersunk screw. →42
2 the widening cut thus made.

countersunk head bolt a bolt with a conical countersunk head, tightened with a screwdriver or driver bit. →36

countersunk head screw, countersunk screw, flat head screw; a screw whose head is cone-shaped so that it can be housed in a sinking, flush with a finished surface. →36

countersunk screw see countersunk head screw. →36

countersunk washer see recessed screw cup. →36

counter top basin see vanity basin.

counterweight a weight attached with cables over a series of pulleys from a lift car to counterbalance its weight.

country cottage see summer residence. →58

country house a rural retreat, mansion or residence, the home of a country gentleman.

country of origin the country in which a product is manufactured, produced or processed.

country planning see rural planning.

countryside see open country.

county 1 a division of land and population in Great Britain which has its own local government.
2 see municipality.

county council see local government.

county hall, civic centre; a building in which county administrative departments are located.

coupled, twinned; a description of pillars, pilasters or columns, grouped or joined together in pairs. →114

coupled columns, twinned columns; a pair of columns linked or grouped together for visual effect, or used in place of a single stouter column. →13, →114

coupled door a door which has two door leaves, one behind the other, hinged on the same side and linked so that they open as one. →50

coupled light an openable component in a window consisting of two sashes, one interior and the other exterior, hinged separately but linked so they open as one.

coupled rafter roof see couple roof. →33

coupled rafters, couple truss; in timber roof construction, a truss consisting simply of two rafters which meet at a ridge; see couple roof. →33

coupled window a double-glazed window whose openable part is a coupled light.

coupler 1 a fitting for joining members in tubular scaffolding.
2 see pipe fitting.

couple roof, coupled rafter roof; the simplest form of pitched roof structure of pairs of slanting rafters meeting at a ridge. →33

couple truss see coupled rafters. →33

coupling a pipe fitting for making a connection between two pipes in a pipeline.

cour d'honneur in some French Renaissance castles, a major enclosed courtyard in front of a main entrance gateway.

course 1 a row of bricks, stones or blocks which form a horizontal band in masonry walling construction, either one brick or stone high, or of uniform height. →20
2 in horizontal log construction, a single layer of logs laid as walling.

coursed ashlar 1 ashlar masonry which has been laid in courses of equal height. →11
2 ashlar masonry which has been laid in courses of varying height. →11

coursed rubble masonry walling of unsquared stones laid in rough courses; may be of squared or unsquared stones. →11

coursed squared rubble masonry roughly squared pieces of stone laid as masonry in courses. →11

coursed stonework any masonry laid in courses with continuous horizontal joints. →11

court 1 an external area bounded by walls, buildings or rooms on four sides; a courtyard.
see *prehistoric structures* illustration. →65

see *Egyptian pyramid complex* illustration. →70
see *Greek residential building* illustration. →87
2 see peristyle. →87
3 an enclosed area with a flat, hard surface for playing ball games such as tennis, basketball etc.

court cairn a prehistoric chambered tomb with a small forecourt before the actual burial chamber, of Irish origin.

court-house see law courts.

courting chair see love seat.

courtyard, 1 court; an open area of land surrounded or enclosed by buildings or built form, often private or semi-public.
see *prehistoric structures* illustration. →65
see *Mesopotamian temple* illustration. →66
see *Greek residential buildings* illustration. →87
see *Roman residential buildings* illustration. →88
2 see inner courtyard. →103
3 see peristyle. →87
4 see atrium. →88
5 see quadrangle.

courtyard house 1 a prehistoric dwelling from Iron Age Britain and northern Europe, with a series of chambers entered via a central area. →65
2 see atrium house.

cove, 1 a curved underside or soffit.
2 coving; a concave moulding of plaster, timber or plastics, fixed as a decorative covering at the meeting of ceiling and wall; any meeting of ceiling and wall treated in this way.
3 see cavetto. →14
4 see cove tile.
5 a group of prehistoric standing stones laid out in a U shape to form a tall unroofed box, open at the top and one side.

cove brick a special brick with a concave indentation running along one of its upper edges; used in decorative features, or at the meeting of a wall and brick paving etc. →16

coved skirting tile a cove tile used as a skirting. →20

coved tile see cove tile. →20

coved vault a masonry vault composed of four coves meeting at a central point, the reverse of a groined vault; a cloister vault. →25

cove lighting luminaires concealed behind a cove, directing light against a ceiling to provide indirect lighting for a space.

covellite a blue-black mineral, naturally occurring copper sulphide, **CuS**, an important ore of copper.

cover 1 the thickness of a protective layer of covering material, such as earth for a pipe, concrete over reinforcement.
2 see concrete cover.
3 see nominal cover.
4 see casing.

cover block see spacer.

cover board in board on board cladding, one of the surface boards nailed over the base cladding to cover the vertical gaps.

covered causeway see pyramid causeway. →71

covered market, indoor market, market hall; a large covered space with stalls for selling of goods and produce.

covered way, 1 link; a roofed external corridor space or passage connecting two buildings.
2 a sunken path for troop communication and the placement of battery around the outside edge of a ditch surrounding a fortification or castle, protected by a parapet or earthwork; also called covert way. →104

cover fillet a strip of material, trim etc. used in construction to cover a joint or seam. →2

cover flashing, counter flashing; in roofing, a flashing laid against of an abutment to cover an upstand flashing.

cover meter a device for measuring the depth of concrete over reinforcement, or concrete cover.

cover soaker see pipe flashing.

cover strip, 1 joint strip; any strip of material, product etc. used to cover a joint in construction.
2 capping; any similar product used to conceal unsightly construction or fixings beneath. →2
3 see architrave.

cover tile see capping tile.

covert way see covered way. →104

cove tile a curved ceramic tile fitting for creating a smooth, concave join between adjacent perpendicular wall, floor or ceiling surfaces. →20
see coved skirting tile. →20
see inside corner tile. →20

coving see cove.

cow see Hathor. →74

cowl a device attached to the upper outlet of a flue to improve draught and provide protection from the elements. →58

cownose brick, bullhead brick; any special brick with one header rounded into a semicircle, used for wall ends, decorative banding etc. →16

cow plane see roughing plane.

cowshed see barn.

coxcomb see cock's comb.

C-profile see C-section, channel. →34

CPU see central processing unit.

CR chloroprene rubber.

crack a visible defect caused by linear failure in a brittle material such as metal, stone, masonry, render or plastics.

cracking, 1 concrete cracking; a defect evident in the surface of set concrete caused by stresses induced by shrinkage, loading or chemical reaction.
2 a defect in a dry paint finish, usually caused by internal stress, poor adhesion or ageing; various types of cracking are crazing and checking.

crackle see crazing.

cradle 1 a specially designed fitting to provide support for a length of curved plumbing and drainage pipe or any other vessel with a curving base.
2 a decorative representation of a small child's bed, the letter 'C' lying on its back, symbolic of motherly love and early childhood. →123

cradle vault see barrel vault. →25

craft knife, 1 modelling knife; a knife with a small sharp interchangeable blade used in modelling and graphics.
2 see scalpel. →130

craft operative see skilled labourer.

cramp, 1 clamp; a simple frame tightened with screws or wedges for holding pieces in place and applying pressure during gluing and working.
2 see dog. →3

crampon see dog. →3

cramponée see cross cramponée. →118

crane tall freestanding mechanical plant used on site for hoisting materials and lifting components into position, allowing for movement in three dimensions.

crane skip a container lifted by a hoist or crane, used for carrying loose material such as sand, concrete, hardcore and builder's waste on site; a number of different types are available dependent on use.

crane sling, chain sling; a length of chain by which skips and other vessels are carried by a crane.

cranked brace, elbow brace; in traditional timber frame construction, a naturally bent brace at the angle between two members.

cranked handle see cranked pull handle. →51

cranked hinge a hinge in which one or both leaves is bent along their length, allowing movement of a door through 180°. →38

cranked pull handle, offset handle; a pull handle for a door, whose grip is offset from its points of fixing. →51

cranked ridge sheet a longitudinal profiled sheet roofing component used at a ridge as capping.

cranked sheet a profiled sheeting component bent across its profile ribs, designed for use at an angle.

crank gouge a gouge whose neck is kinked to allow for it to be driven along deep grooves.

crannog a prehistoric lake dwelling found primarily in Ireland, constructed on a foundation of timber piles driven into the bed of a lake, onto which a structure of clay, brushwood and stones was assembled.
craquelure crazing in the glaze of old pottery.
crash barrier see vehicle safety barrier.
crashing in computing, the failing of programs and hardware with loss of data due to a system error, after which the computer should be restarted.
Crataegus spp. see hawthorn.
crate a rough packing case of open construction made from timber slats.
craticium see opus craticium. →83
crawler lane a climbing lane.
crawlway a space within floor construction or beneath a building, high enough to be crawled through, providing access to services.
crayon any coloured drawing stick consisting of a pigment held together by a binder such as wax; see also coloured pencil, wax crayon, oil pastel.
crazing, 1 map cracking; fine widespread defective cracking of a surface layer of concrete, plasterwork, ceramic glazes or paint.
2 crackle, craquelure; in old paintings and glazed ceramics, a mesh of hairline cracks which forms on the glaze due to shrinkage of the base.
crazy paving see ragwork. →15
CRCP continuously reinforced concrete pavement.
cream a shade of pale yellow which takes its name from the colour of cream.
cream of lime see lime white.
crêche a facility which provides day care for very young children and babies.
credit, 1 rebate, refund; money returned when paid-for goods and services do not live up to expectation, are cheaper than expected, are supplied late etc.
2 the provision of goods or services in such a way that they can be received immediately and paid for later.
credit memorandum see credit note.
credit note, credit memorandum (Am.); a written acknowledgement by a supplier that a customer is due money for goods and services which are lower in value than those paid for.
creep the physical property of a material to undergo gradual permanent deformation under continual stress.
creep settlement in foundation technology, the steady downward movement of a building which occurs after immediate settlement on certain soil types due to deformation or slipping of the underlying soil without appreciable increase in loading.
crematorium, pl. crematoria; a building containing facilities for the burning of corpses.
Cremnitz white, Krems white; highly corroded white lead pigment made in the 1900s, using litharge instead of the metal lead.
cremona bolt see cremone bolt. →50
cremone bolt, cremona bolt, cremorne bolt; a long mechanical fastener for holding double doors, with a paired bolt running the whole vertical height of the door, which, when activated by turning a handle, pushes out through the top and bottom of the door to engage in holes in the floor and frame; see espagnolette. →50
cremorne bolt see cremone bolt. →50
crenel see crenelle. →103
crenelation see crenellation. →103
crenellated 1 referring to an ornamental motif, parapet etc. which is toothed in some way or represents a battlement.
2 see castellated.
crenellated moulding, 1 embattled moulding; a decorative moulding rendered with the rectilinear undulations of a battlement. →124, →125
2 see indented embattled moulding. →125
crenelet a small crenelle.
crenellation, crenelation; the indented upper line of a battlement parapet, with merlons providing shelter from attackers and crenelles providing openings for archers and marksmen. →103
crenelle, crenel, kernel; openings or indentations in the parapet of a battlement, between merlons, to allow archers and artillery to defend a fortification; an embrasure. →103
creosote, creosote oil; a dark brown, strong smelling oil distilled from coal tar at 230–340°C, used as a cheap preservative for exterior woodwork and timber fencing.
creosote oil see creosote.
crepidoma in classical architecture, the stepped base or plinth on which a temple stands. →86
crescent 1 the scythe shape which remains when one circle is cut out of the side of another one. →120
see decrescent. →120
see increscent. →120
see star and crescent. →120
2 a formal urban street and buildings laid out in the form of an arc.
cresmographeion see chresmographeion.
crest 1 a heraldic embellishment of feathers etc. set above a crown in a coat of arms. →124
2 the upper part of the profile of a roof tile or profiled sheet.
3 see cresting.
cresting, crest; raised and often perforated ornamentation along the ridge of a roof or top of a wall or screen.
Cretan column see Minoan column. →69
Cretan maze an ancient symbolic design depicting a labyrinth with only one entrance and one exit, found as decoration on walls, stamped on coins, rendered in manuscripts, woven into baskets and laid out with stones on the ground, found as far afield as North America, Scandinavia, Italy, India and Egypt; sometimes called a classical maze, Troytown, Jericho or Jerusalem. →123
crevice corrosion a localized form of corrosion which occurs in a stagnant environment in tight spaces or crevices under gaskets, washers, insulation material, fastener heads, surface deposits, and coatings etc., initiated by changes in local chemistry within the crevice.
crib 1 a framework of crossed timbers or structural members used as a buttress, to line a shaft, as a container, or as steel reinforcement in a foundation.
2 a log crib; see timber foundation grillage. →29
3 see cradle. →123
cribbing, cribwork; a series of hollowed concrete blocks, interlocking or filled with earth, used as a banked retaining wall for earth embankments. →29
crib paver see cellular paver. →15
crib paving see cellular paving. →15
cribwork see cribbing. →29
cricket see chimney saddle.
crimped mesh see crimped wire mesh. →34
crimped wire in pretensioned concretework, reinforcing wire which is wavy along its length for improved bonding.
crimped wire mesh a mesh product manufactured from two sets of parallel metal wires woven or welded against one another with locking crimps to maintain rigidity. →34
crimson see carmine.
crinkling see wrinkle.
criosphinx in Egyptian architecture, a sphinx which has a ram's head. →75
cripple stud 1 in timber frame construction, a stud which has been trimmed for use over an opening or under a window.
2 see jamb post.
crippling load, buckling load; the load at which a column begins to buckle.
crocket Gothic ornament based on a stylized florid motif, found adorning pinnacles, capitals and spires. →109
crocket capital a capital found in Norman architecture, consisting of a block carved with a number of crockets. →115

crocks see crucks. →7

crocodile see Sobek. →74

crocodiling, alligatoring; a defect in a paint finish consisting of a network of cracks or splits which resemble crocodile skin, caused by shrinkage.

crocoite, red lead ore; a shiny yellowish red mineral, natural lead chromate, $PbCrO_4$, of little economic importance.

Crocus sativa see saffron.

croft 1 a modest rural smallholding or the main house therein, found in the Highlands and Western Isles of Scotland.
2 see crypt. →99

cromlech see dolmen.

crook, 1 spring; a form of warp resulting in bending along the edge of an improperly seasoned timber board. →1
2 a long steel nail used in thatched roofing for fastening down reed thatch.
3 see crucks. →28
4 a common motif in ancient Egyptian decoration, symbolic of Royal authority, a loop-headed staff often depicted crossed over the chest of a ruler; similar motifs in religious art and decoration, symbolic of the holy shepherd. →74

crooks see crucks. →28

cropping 1 the removal of the unwanted projecting ends of bolts, reinforcing bars, timbers or similar components in construction.
2 in graphic design and photography, the cutting down to size of a picture to enhance composition or omit unwanted elements.

croquis, sketch; in drawing, a rapid study made of a live model or the first sketch of a composition.

cross 1 an ancient symbolic figure consisting of two bars which cross each other, often at right angles; it appears as a religious motif and ornament in many different forms.
see *cross* illustrations. →117, →118
2 a cross-shaped pipe fitting for making the connection between two secondary pipes and a main pipe at right angles.
3 see high cross.

cross annuletty, annuletted cross; a cross whose limbs are terminated with a ring motif. →118

cross avellane, Avellane cross; a cross with four perpendicular flower or filbert motifs radiating from a point; also written avelane, Avillan. →118

crossbanding the laying of alternate plies in the thickness of plywood perpendicular to one another for increased strength. →9

cross barbée, cross barby, arrow cross; a cross in which each limb terminates in an arrow-shaped head. →117

cross barby see cross barbée. →117

cross beam, transverse beam; a beam perpendicular to the main axis of a space, which runs between two cross walls, or is perpendicular to other beams.

cross billety see cross potent. →117

cross bond any of a number of brickwork bonds with alternating courses laid so that the joints form distinct cross motifs in the surface brickwork.
see English cross bond. →19
see Flemish cross bond. →18
St Andrew's cross bond, see English cross bond. →19

cross botonée, botony, bottony; a cross in which the extremity of each limb is terminated with a round trefoil; also known as the cross of Lazarus, threefoil or trefoil cross. →117

cross bourdonee see cross potent. →117

cross brace one of a pair of intersecting diagonal braces used to stiffen and strengthen a frame.

cross-bracing a method of stiffening a frame using diagonal tension members which cross one another.

cross break see compression failure.

cross bridging see herringbone strutting. →4

cross calvary see Calvary cross. →117

cross capital a cross in which the extremity of each limb is chamfered outwards; also called a Templar or teutonic cross. →117

cross church see cruciform church. →98

cross cotised a heraldic cross with a distinct border around its edge, or one surrounded by another larger cross, as with the German iron cross; also written as cotice, cottise, custere. →118

cross clechée 1 a heraldic cross whose limbs spread out gradually towards their extremities, ending in arrowheads. →118
2 see key cross. →118

cross couped a heraldic cross whose limbs do not extend to the edge of a shield; sometimes called a cross humetty. →118

cross cramponée a cross whose limbs are terminated by a hook or one-sided barb. →118

cross crosslet 1 a cross whose limbs are crossed with perpendicular bars. →117
2 see crossed square. →118

cross-cut saw any saw with teeth adapted for cutting across the grain of wood; see rip saw.

cross cutting sawing across the grain of timber, perpendicular to the longitudinal axis of its fibres.

cross degraded a cross whose limbs are terminated with a stepped attachment. →117

cross-domed church a common Byzantine church type with five domes arranged over the extremities and centre of its cross-shaped plan; also called a quincunx church or five-domed church. →95

crossed cross see cross crosslet. →117

crossed square a square emblem with a small cross protruding from each side; a cross crosslet whose limbs are small crosses. →118

crossed slot the cross-shaped indentation in the head of a cross-slot screw.

cross engrailed, engrailed cross; a cross whose limbs are formed from a series of convex curves with sharp joins. →118

crossette see joggled arch. →23

crossfall in road engineering, the slope across a width of carriageway.

cross fimbriated a heraldic cross circumscribed with a line. →118

crossfire, cross talk; in telecommunications, interference caused by the presence of unwanted signals from another source, an adjacent cable or channel.

cross fitched see fitched cross. →117

cross fitchee see fitched cross. →117

cross fitchy see fitched cross. →117

cross fleurettée, fleury, flory; a cross with an ornamental fleur-de-lis termination at the end of each limb. →117

cross formée see cross patée. →118

crossform roof a pitched hip and valley roof for a building which is cross shaped in plan, with four valleys and four gabled or hipped ends. →46

cross fourchée, forked cross, fourchée cross; a cross in which each limb terminates in an open V-shaped fork; also called a miller's cross. →117

cross grain grain at an angle to the edge of a board cut from compression wood, making it difficult to work and season properly.

cross-grained float a flat-bladed wooden plastering float whose grain runs perpendicular to its length.

cross-grained plywood plywood in which the grain of the outer ply is approximately parallel to that of the lateral or shorter edge of the piece.

cross gringoly a cross which has representations of snake heads at the termination of its limbs.

cross half lap joint, crosslap joint, halved crossing joint; a timber halved joint in which both face sides of crossing members are cut away to receive each other. →4

cross humetty see cross couped. →118

cross indented, indented cross; a cross whose limbs are terminated with a series of sawtooth cuttings. →118

crossing 1 the area where the transepts, chancel and nave in a church or cathedral intersect, often surmounted by a tower.
see *Carolingian abbey church* illustration. →98
see *Romanesque church* illustration. →99
see *Gothic cathedral* illustration. →100
2 a meeting and crossing of roads and railways, other roads etc. at the same level.
see *road junction* illustration. →62

crossing joint, cross joint; any joint in which two members are fixed across one another; see also cross half lap joint. →4

cross invected, invected cross; a cross whose limbs are formed from a series of concave curves with sharp joins. →118

cross joint, 1 transverse joint; a construction joint perpendicular to the general plane of a surface. →20
2 see perpend. →20
3 see crossing joint. →4

crosslap joint see cross half lap joint. →4

crosslet cross see cross crosslet. →117

cross-link system see metropolitan railway.

cross-linked polyethylene, PEX, XLPE; a tough thermosetting plastic used for electric-cable insulation, hot-water pipes, films and durable sections.

cross-linking a chemical reaction which occurs in the hardening of some thermosetting plastics and films, in which polymeric molecules form a network of links.

cross moline a cross whose arms terminate in widened, split and curved back ends; sometimes also known as a cross recercelée or cross sarcelly. →117

cross moulding a decorative moulding of intertwined cross motifs; particular to heraldry. →125

cross nogging see herringbone strutting. →4

cross nowy see nowy cross. →117

cross of Calvary see Calvary cross. →117

cross of Christ see Latin cross. →117

cross of Constantine see Christ monogram. →119

cross of Golgotha 1 see Calvary cross. →117
2 see Coptic cross. →118

cross of Horus see ankh. →117

cross of infinity a motif drawn with a single interlaced line to form a cross whose limbs are triangles, their apexes formed inwards; also known as a Bowen or knotwork cross. →118

cross of life see Latin cross. →117

cross of Lazarus see cross botonée. →117

cross of Lorraine see Lorraine cross. →117

cross of Pisa see key cross. →118

cross of promise see Maltese cross. →118

cross of Palestine see Jerusalem cross. →118

cross of St James a cross moline with a pointed base, symbol of some Iberian orders of knighthood; also known as Santiago cross or cruz espada. →117

cross of St Julian a saltire or oblique cross whose ends are crossed. →117

cross of Toulouse a voided key cross with beads at each extremity. →118

cross of suffering see broken cross. →118

cross of the Evangelists a Calvary cross with four underlying steps, representing Matthew, Mark, Luke and John. →117

cross of the Fathers see Russian cross. →117

crossover a bridge which carries a road over another road or obstacle at right angles to it. →64

cross patée, 1 cross formée, formy, paty, pattée; a cross whose limbs are wedge shaped, getting wider towards their extremities. →118
2 one with concave wedge-shaped limbs inscribed in a circle.

cross patonce a cross whose four wedge-shaped limbs have doubly indented ends, each ending in three points; sometimes called a cross griffee-de-loup or 'wolf-clawed' cross. →118

cross peen hammer, Warrington hammer; a hammer whose peen is a sharp wedge of steel with its ridge perpendicular to the hammer shaft. →40

cross pillar, cross slab; a standing stone carved with ornamentation and crosses originating in Scotland and Ireland in c.700 AD. →118

cross pointed see pointed cross. →117

cross pommelé, cross, pomée, pomy or pommy; a cross with a ball, roundel or knob at the termination of each limb. →117

cross potent a cross whose arms terminate in the shape of a letter T; occasionally called a cross bourdonee, cross billety or crutch cross. →117

cross quadrate see quadrant cross. →118

cross raguly 1 a cross whose limbs are ragged as if of sawn-off branches. →118
2 see Burgundy cross. →118

cross recercelée a cross whose limbs are split at the ends and turned back on each other, a cross moline. →117

crossroads a meeting and crossing of two roads at the same level, a road junction of two roads which cross each other, most often at right angles. →62

cross sarcelly see cross moline. →117

cross-section see section. →130

cross shakes see thunder shakes.

cross slab see cross pillar. →118

cross-slot screw any screw with a cross-shaped indentation in its head for turning with a special screwdriver or bit. →36

cross spar, pattern spar; a decorative fastener or brotch laid visible at the ridge of a thatched roof. →48

cross-street a minor urban road running perpendicular to a main street.

cross talk see crossfire.

cross urdy, pointed cross; a cross whose limbs have pointed ends. →117

cross vault see groin vault. →25

cross voided see voided cross. →118

crosswalk a pedestrian crossing in the US and Australia.

crosswall construction a structural system in which the floors of a building are spanned across a series of transverse loadbearing walls. →28

cross-welt 1 in sheetmetal roofing, a horizontal joint in which two adjacent sheets are bent over each other then hammered down; these are usually staggered and run parallel to the eaves. →49
2 see single-lock welt. →49
3 see double welt. →49

cross wheel see wheel cross. →118

crow bar a toughened steel implement, a bar with forked ends for prizing, wedging and extracting nails.

crown 1 the highest point or apex of an arch. →22
2 the highest point in the cambered cross-section of a road, usually in the centre.
3 head; in landscaping and forestry, the part of a tree above the trunk, containing branches and leaves. →1
4 see chimney crown. →56
5 a British standard paper size; 15" × 20", 318 mm × 508 mm. →Table 6
see double crown. →Table 6
see quad crown. →Table 6
see quad double crown. →Table 6
6 a ring-like metal head-dress with a circle of upturned spines, often lavishly decorated and ornamented with gems, symbolic in decorative art of power and ruling, or regal status. →122
see combined crown. →74
see crown-of-thorns.
double crown, see combined crown. →74
see red crown. →74
see white crown. →74

crown course in profiled sheet roofing, a longitudinal piece used at a ridge as ridge capping.
crown glass glass made traditionally by the cutting of a hollow blown glass sphere which is spun flat into a nearly circular sheet.
crown land any land which belongs to the ruling or governing body of a country.
crown-of-thorns, thorny crown; a decorative depiction of the thorny head-dress forced on Christ while carrying the cross, symbolic of suffering and humiliation. →119
crown post in traditional timber roof construction, a vertical strut between tie beam and collar beam, supporting a collar purlin. →33
crown post and collar purlin roof see crown post rafter roof. →33
crown post rafter roof, crown post and collar purlin roof, crown post roof; in traditional timber roof construction, a collar roof with a purlin which runs beneath the collars and is supported on crown posts. →33
crown post roof see crown post rafter roof. →33
crown saw see hole saw. →42
crown silvered lamp, silvered-bowl lamp; a lightbulb whose bulbous end is internally coated with reflective material to direct light inwards and produce indirect lighting.
crownwork a powerfully fortified outwork of two or more bastions connected by curtain walls to demibastions; also known as opera coronata. →104
crow steps, corbie steps, stepped gable; in traditional masonry construction, a decorative gable parapet whose upper edge is a series of steps.
CRP carbon-fibre reinforced plastic.
crucible steel see cast steel.
crucifix 1 a statue, carving or other effigy representing Christ on the cross. →117
2 see rood. →117
cruciform in the shape of or resembling a cross.
cruciform church, cross church; a church whose ground plan is in the shape of a cross, in which the transepts are its limbs. →98
cruciform plan the ground plan of any building, especially a church, whose outline is cross shaped.
cruck blade in traditional timber frame construction, one roughly hewn timber from a pair of crucks.
cruck construction traditional timber frame construction whose main supporting elements are heavy curved timbers, called crucks. →7
crucks in traditional timber frame construction, a pair of heavy curved timbers which lean together forming an inverted V-frame as the basis for a building frame; also variously known as crooks, crocks, crutches, forks or siles. →7
cruck truss a rudimentary traditional timber frame construction consisting of a rigid frame or truss made from crucks tied together with a tie and/or collar beam.
crude oil see petroleum.
crude sewage see raw sewage.
crudus Lat.; Roman unfired clay products, sun-dried mud bricks etc.
crusaders' cross see Jerusalem cross. →118
crushed aggregate aggregate produced by crushing rocks and mineral materials.
crushed brick broken and powdered clay products used as a surface material for sports venues, as hardcore etc.
crushed gravel fines fine aggregate produced by crushing gravel.
crushed rock coarse aggregate produced by the crushing of rocks and minerals.
crushed rock fines fine aggregate produced by crushing rock.
crusher-run aggregate an aggregate made up of ungraded crushed rock.
crutch cross see cross potent. →117
crutches see crucks. →7
crux ansata Lat.; see ankh. →117
crux capitata Lat.; see Latin cross. →117
crux decussata Lat.; see St Andrew's cross. →118
crux dissimulata Lat.; see anchor cross. →117
crux gammata Lat.; see gammadion, swastika. →118
crux gemmata Lat.; an ornate cross decorated with gold and gems. →121
crux immissa Lat.; see Latin cross. →117
crux quadrata Lat.; see Greek cross. →118
crux stellata Lat.; see four-pointed star. →118
cruz espada see cross of St James. →117
crypt crypta (Lat.), krypte (Gk.); a vaulted basement or undercroft in a church or cathedral, often containing a chapel and tombs or graves; sometimes called a shroud or croft.
see *Romanesque church* illustration. →99
see *altar* illustration. →116
cryptoportico in Roman architecture, a roofed corridor or passage which has side walls with openings; used as a shaded walk or store and often partly or fully below ground level; also written as cryptoporticus (Lat.). →91
cryptoporticus Latin form of cryptoportico. →91
crystal 1 a mass of chemically uniform material with atoms, molecules or particles arranged in regular structure, often with plane faces or a polygonal arrangement.
2 cut glass; decorated glass which has been cut with facets and polished.
crystal glass see lead glass.
crystal lattice the three-dimensional systematic and repeated arrangement of atoms and molecules in a crystalline substance.
crystalline schist a coarse-grained metamorphic rock with a structure of long sheetlike crystals.
crystallography a branch of science dealing with the structure and properties of crystals.
C-section 1 a cold-formed structural steel profile which has the cross-sectional shape of a squared letter 'C'.
2 other metal profiles with the same shape; see channel. →34
Cuba a certain shade of dark brown.
Cuban mahogany see mahogany.
cube, 1 a solid three-dimensional shape whose surface is composed of six squares at right angles to one another.
2 cobble; a small square sett or concrete paver, used for paving roads, driveways etc. →15
3 see test cube.
cube root in mathematics, a value the third power of which gives that number; the third root of a number.
cube strength in concretework, the compressive strength of a concrete test cube as measured in a cube test.
cube test in concretework, a compressive strength test carried out by crushing a sample cube of concrete to be used in construction.
cubical aggregate coarse aggregate whose particles are almost cubical in shape.
cubic capital see block capital. →115
cubic centimetre abb. **cc**; the SI unit of capacity equal to 10 mm × 10 mm × 10 mm.
cubic foot abb. **cu.ft**; an imperial unit of volume equivalent to 28.32 m^3.
cubic inch abb. **cu.in.**; an imperial unit of volume equivalent to 16.39 mm^3.
cubicle 1 an area of space partitioned off to provide temporary privacy for an individual.
2 see shower unit.
cubic metre abb. $\mathbf{m^3}$; SI basic unit of volume.
cubic millimetre abb. $\mathbf{mm^3}$; SI basic unit of volume.
cubic yard abb. **cu.yd**; imperial unit of volume equivalent to 0.765 m^3.
cubiculum Lat., pl. cubicula; a bed chamber in a Roman dwelling. →88
cubism an abstract movement in art initiated by Picasso and Braque at the beginning of the 1900s,

in which objects are depicted as three-dimensional angular forms.

cubit 1 an archaic unit of length equal to that of the forearm. →107
2 see royal cubit. →106

cuboid brick any mass-produced rectangular brick with a square cross-section, often a modular brick. →16

Cufic see Kufic.

cul-de-lampe a decorative console or support for a candle or light in the shape of an inverted cone.

cul-de-sac a street closed at one end to which access is gained from one end only; in residential areas it is called a close.

culina Lat.; a kitchen in a Roman dwelling. →88

culmen Lat.; the highest part or apex, especially the ridge of a roof in Roman architecture.

cult chapel a suite of rooms within a temple, or separate shrine for the worship of images of a particular deity. →70

cult image an image or sculpture of a deity, sometimes made of precious metals, located in temple shrines as the principal object of worship and veneration.

cult statue any statue which is an object of worship in a temple. →68

cult room a room within a temple or shrine for the worship of images of a particular deity. →66

cult temple a temple or shrine containing images of a particular deity, or for its worship. →66

cultural centre any public building or complex which contains recreational facilities such as libraries, auditoria for music, theatre and the arts.

cultural history the historical development of a particular culture.

cultural layer a stratum in the earth containing archaeological effects and findings from a distinct era or culture of human civilization.

culture the spiritual, material products and achievements of a community, their customs and way of life.

culvert 1 a large rigid pipe, often of plastics, concrete or metal plate which conveys water underneath a road or other obstacle.
2 see concrete culvert.

culvert header, tapered stretcher; a special brick, wedged shaped in section so that its long faces are not oblong, used as a header in a barrel vault. →16

culvert stretcher, tapered header; a special brick, wedged shaped in section so that its short faces are not oblong, used as a stretcher in a barrel vault. →16

cunei plural form of cuneus. →89, →90

cuneus 'wedge' (Lat.), plural cunei; a sector or wedge-shaped area of stone seating between radiating entrance gangways in a Roman theatre or amphitheatre; called kerkis in a Greek theatre. →89, →90

cup, 1 transverse warping; a form of warp resulting in cross-sectional curvature in an improperly seasoned timber board. →1
2 see screw cup. →36
3 see grinding cup. →42

cupboard 1 a freestanding piece of storage furniture with closable doors and shelves.
2 a storage space with a closable door, built in to a recess.

cup hook a screw hook with a collar above the threaded shank to restrict its screw-in depth and cover the edges of the hole. →36
see square cup hook. →36

cupid, amoretto, amorino; a classical statue or depiction of the god of love, Amor or Cupid in Rome and Eros in Greece, represented as a young winged boy with a bow and arrow. →122

cupola 1 the central dome of an interior space. →26
2 domed vaulting or a dome-shaped recess in a ceiling.
3 a small dome adorning a roof. →26

Cupressus spp. see cypress.
Cupressus nootkatensis, see yellow cedar.

cuprite, red copper ore; a reddish mineral, naturally occurring copper oxide, $\mathbf{Cu_2O}$, a locally important ore of copper.

cupro-solvency the dissolving of copper in copper and brass pipework caused by high flow rates, turbulent flow and air or particles in the water.

cup shake, ring failure, ring shake, shell shake; a shake or cracking occurring between the annual rings of a piece of timber; see also wind shake. →1

cupstone a stone hewn with cup-shaped markings, used as an altar, sacrificial stone or in other ritual practices in various ancient cultures. →116

curb see kerb. →15, →62

curb parking see street parking. →62

curb roof, double pitched roof, knee roof; any pitched roof that slopes away from the main ridge in two successive planes at different angles with a ridge between; see gambrel roof, mansard roof.

curbstone see kerbstone. →62

Curculionidae see weevil.

curia Lat.; the meeting place of the senate or council of an ancient Italian or Roman town.

curing 1 the hardening and gaining strength of a paint, glue, concrete or other similar material after it has set.
2 see concrete curing.

curing compound in concretework, any material placed over fresh concrete to inhibit evaporation of water.

curing cycle the time taken for the complete process of steam curing of concrete, including heating and cooling periods.

curium a synthetic radioactive chemical element, **Cm**.

curl 1 see wavy grain.
2 see knuckle. →38

currant red see cherry (red).

currency money in the form of coins and banknotes of a particular country or community.

current 1 see electric current.
2 see air current.

curriculum vitae abb. **CV**; a written document containing personal information about a prospective employee, date of birth, academic and professional qualifications, work history, awards and merits etc., sent in along with a job application.

curry yellow, dark yellow; a shade of yellow which takes its name from the oriental powdered spice.

cursor a small character for locating and directing position on a computer screen.

curtain 1 a domestic textile furnishing hung above a window on a sliding track to provide shade and privacy; see also blind.
2 see fire curtain.
3 see shower curtain.
4 see sag.
5 see curtain wall. →103, →104
6 see broken curtain. →103

curtaining see sag.

curtain rail a rail above a window which supports a curtain, usually attached to it by means of sliding fixings.

curtain rod a rod above a window which supports a curtain, usually attached to it by means of curtain rings.

curtain wall 1 in modern construction, a lightweight exterior walling system of metal framing members and infill panels of glass, ceramics and sheetmetal for a building structure or frame; the processes involved in this.
2 curtain; the surrounding outer wall of a castle or fortification between towers, battlements and bastions; also called a curtain, cortina, bail or bailey wall in a medieval castle. →103, →104

see enceinte. →103
see bailey. →103
see broken curtain. →103

curtainwalling see curtain wall.

curtilage the land between a building and the boundary of the plot of land on which it stands; the plot on which a building is situated.

curvature deviation from a straight line to form part of the circumference of a circle.

curve 1 any line or form of which no part is straight; an implement, gauge, component etc. shaped like this.
see flexible curve. →130
see French curve. →130
2 a line defining a mathematical function, data on a graph etc.
candlepower distribution curve, see light distribution curve.
see deflection curve.
elastic curve, see deflection curve.
see grading curve.
see light distribution curve.
polar curve, see light distribution curve.

curved bridge a bridge type whose deck is curved in plan projection. →64

curved glass see bent glass.

curved triangle see reuleaux triangle. →108

Curvilinear style a late development of the Decorated style of English Gothic architecture in the late 1300s, characterized by a flamboyance and richness of motif not encountered in the Geometric style.

curvilinear tracery see flowing tracery. →110

curving stair a stair which is curved in plan. →45

cushion capital 1 a capital found in Norman architecture, consisting of a squared block with its four lower corners rounded off; also called a block or cubic capital. →115
2 any other wide capitals, especially one surmounting Minoan or other Aegean column types. →69

cushioning see padding.

cusp in Gothic tracery and vaulting, the decorated intersection of two arcs, forming an ornamented point. →108

custere see cross cotised. →118

customer parking an area of parking designed for the use of the customers of a commercial facility.

customized section a non-standard metal profile which has been specially formed to a design specification.

cut 1 a physical division made by the action of cutting a material, product or surface.
2 see section. →130

cut-away front seat see open front seat.

cut back bitumen bitumen to which a volatile oil is added to reduce its viscosity.

cut brick a brick shaped by cutting, sawing or breaking on site, most often used for making up space in brickwork bonds. →21

cut glass see crystal.

cut length in steel manufacture, steel strip that has been cut to predetermined lengths from decoiled and flattened coil.

cut nail a nail whose shaft is rectangular in cross-section, manufactured by slicing from heated steel strip. →35

cut pile carpet a carpet manufactured by cutting woven loops to form a surface layer of upright strands.

cut stone see dimension stone. →12

cutout 1 see circuit breaker.
2 see fuse.

cutter, 1 bit; the revolving cutting blade or knife of a planer.
2 machine bit; a hard metal blade or bit for a router or milling machine for cutting profiles in wood, metal and plastics.

cutting 1 the process of splitting, sawing, or dividing parts of an object using a machine or hand tool, flame, axe, laser etc.
2 see veneer cutting. →10

cutting angle, angle of attack, chip angle, hook angle, rake angle; in the slicing of veneers, the angle between the face of a cutting edge and a plane perpendicular to its cutting direction.

cutting edge the sharpened edge or tip of a sawtooth, chisel blade or plane iron, honed for cutting. →41

cutting gauge a device used for cutting parallel to an edge of wood; a marking gauge with a blade instead of a spike.

cutting plane the apparent plane through which a building or component is cut in a sectional drawing.

cutting way see cleavage plane.

cutwater see starling. →31

CV see curriculum vitae.

C-value, coefficient of thermal conductance; a theoretical measure of how well a given construction will conduct heat, whose units are $W/m^{2\circ}C$; used in heat loss calculations and taken as the amount of energy passing through a unit area of construction for unit temperature difference on either side of the construction; equal to k-value divided by thickness of construction; see also U-value.

cyanine blue a blue pigment formed by mixing the pigments cobalt blue and Prussian blue.

cyanoacrylate adhesive, super glue; an adhesive containing a compound which polymerizes instantaneously when in contact with atmospheric moisture to form strong bonding without the need for heating and clamping.

Cycladic pertaining to the prehistoric art and architecture of the bronze-age peoples of the Cyclades, islands in the Aegean Sea, from 2800 to 2250 BC.

cyclamen a shade of red which takes its name from the colour of the blossom of the Alpine violet (Cyclamen europaeum, Cyclamen persicum).

cycle crossing in road design, a marked area on a carriageway at which it is safe for cyclists to cross.

cycle lane, bicycle lane; a lane incorporated within or alongside a vehicular road for the sole use of bicycle traffic.

cycle path, cycle track, cycleway; a narrow carriageway or marked area of a footpath for the use of bicycle traffic only. →63

cycle shelter see bicycle shelter.

cycle track see cycle path. →63

cycleway see cycle path. →63

cyclic rotating or oscillating in a circling motion; occurring in cycles or repeated periods.

cycloid in geometry, a curve traced by a point on the surface of a rolling circle.

cyclopean concrete a form of concrete which contains large pieces of broken stone and boulders as a filler.

cyclopean masonry 1 masonry construction for massive walls, especially from ancient Mycenae, consisting of large roughly hewn irregular blocks of stone packed with clay and small stones; also called Pelasgic masonry; generally known nowadays as polygonal masonry. →11
2 see polygonal masonry. →11

cylinder 1 a solid shape whose surface is composed of a circle extruded through a straight line perpendicular to its plane.
2 that component part of a cylinder lock, including tumblers and a cylinder plug, into which the key is inserted, which transmits its turning motion to operate a bolt. →39
3 see storage cylinder.
4 see test cylinder, concrete cylinder.
5 see gas cylinder.

cylinder body the external casing of a lock cylinder. →39

cylinder caisson see open caisson.

cylinder collar see cylinder guard. →39

cylinder guard, cylinder collar; a metal ring-shaped component which is fitted around the keyhole of a cylinder lock to protect it and prevent forcing. →39

cylinder hinge a form of invisible hinge consisting of two jointed cylinders recessed into hinged components, commonly used for kitchen unit doors. →38

cylinder lock a door lock in which the key-operated mechanism is contained in a cylinder located separate from the bolting mechanism. →39
see *cylinder lock* illustration. →39

cylinder strength in concretework, the compressive strength of a concrete cylinder tested to ascertain its suitability as structural concrete.

cylinder test in concretework, a test to determine the compressive strength of a sample cylinder of concrete to be used in construction.

cylindrical vault see barrel vault. →25

cyma 1 Lat. (Gk kuma); a doubly curved S-shaped moulding composed of alternating concave and convex segments in profile, as found in classical architecture; an ogee moulding, see cyma recta, cyma reversa. →82
2 see Lesbian cyma. →82
3 see Doric cyma. →82
4 see Ionic cyma. →82

cyma recta 1 Lat.; a doubly curved cyma or S-shaped moulding with its concave part uppermost. →80, →82
2 see Doric cyma. →82

cyma reversa 1 Lat.; a doubly curved cyma or S-shaped moulding with a convex part uppermost; a reverse ogee moulding. →80, →82
2 see Lesbian cyma. →82

cymatium, sima; the uppermost member of a classical cornice, convex in cross-section; Greek form is kymation. →78, →79

Cyperus papyrus, see papyrus.

cypress [*Cupressus spp., Chamaecyparis spp.*] a group of softwoods found in temperate regions, whose timber is pale pink, durable and used for external construction and joinery; see ***Cupressus spp.***, ***Chamaecyparis spp.*** for full list of species of cypress included in this work.

Cytherea bulbosa the fairyslipper orchid, see calypso (red).

cyzicenus Lat.; the name given by Vitruvius to a large recreational hall used by the Greeks, decorated with sculptures and provided with a view over gardens.

D

dabbed finish, dabbled finish; an even stonework finish produced by dressing with a point; a fine sparrow pecked finish.

dabbled finish see dabbed finish.

dabs see plaster dots.

dacite a grey volcanic rock, rich in silica, used in building construction for aggregates, chippings and as decorative stone.

Dacron see polyethylene terephthalate.

Dactylopius coccus red scale insect, see cochineal.

dado 1 in joinery, a long groove machined into a board to house another board, a chase or housing. →5

2 die, tympanum; the unadorned rectangular or cylindrical central portion of a classical pedestal, on which a column is supported. →76, →80

3 the portion of an internal wall up to waist height when faced or painted differently to the upper part.

dado joint see housed joint. →5

dado plane a plane for cutting a groove across the grain in wood.

dado rail see chair rail.

dagger 1 a typical pointed tracery motif formed by intersecting glazing bars in the Gothic Decorated style. →110

2 see mouchette. →110

dagoba a Buddhist dome-shaped stupa containing a chamber with sacred relics.

dais see podium.

Dalbergia spp. see rosewood.

Dalbergia latifolia, see Indian rosewood.

Dalbergia nigra, see Bahia rosewood.

Dalbergia spruceana, see Brazilian rosewood.

dam a structure designed to hold back and control the flow of a stream, often to create a reservoir or to provide hydroelectric power.

Dama dama fallow deer, see fawn (brown).

damar, damar resin; a soft natural resin gathered from the forest trees of Malaya, Borneo, Java and Sumatra; mixed with a solvent such as turpentine and used as a varnish.

damar resin see damar.

damp see dampness.

damp course see damp proof course. →29

damper 1 see smoke damper.

2 see flue damper.

3 see fire damper.

4 see muffler.

5 see vibration insulator.

damper opening see throat. →55

dampness, damp; undesirable moisture within layers of construction, rooms etc. from the ground, rainwater or as a result of poor ventilation.

damp proof, moisture resistant; a description of a material, product or construction designed to withstand or inhibit the presence of moisture.

damp proof course, damp course, dpc; a horizontal layer of impervious material laid in a masonry or concrete wall above ground level to prevent the vertical passage of moisture. →29

damp proofing the treatment of a surface or construction to inhibit the passage of moisture; also the result of this process.

damp proof membrane, dpm; **1** any impervious layer included in construction to prevent the passage of moisture.

2 a layer of plastics sheet material or mastic asphalt laid in base floor construction to prevent the passage of ground moisture upwards.

damp resisting plaster plaster or render containing an admixture which inhibits the penetration of water, sometimes called waterproof plaster or render.

Dance of Death, danse macabre; in medieval painting and the arts, an allegorical depiction of the living dancing with the dead.

dancetty banded ornament consisting of a zigzag line, a chevron or zigzag; primarily in heraldic motifs. →124

dancing step, balanced step, French flier; one of a series of tapered steps in a curving or spiral stair which do not radiate from the same point. →45

danger area internal space or external areas where a possible hazard to people or property has been identified.

danse macabre see the Dance of Death.

danske the toilet or garderobe overhanging the exterior walls of a castle; originally one constructed by the Teutonic knights. →103

darby, Darby float, derby; a long metal rule or board with handles, used for levelling fresh plasterwork on walls and ceilings. →43

Darby float see darby. →43

dark in colour perception, describing shades of colour which contain little white, or have black added.

dark-red silver ore see pyrargyrite.

dark room a room used for processing photographic material.

dark yellow see curry yellow.

dart a decorative motif in the form of a sharp triangle, arrowhead or wedge-shaped design; see egg and dart, leaf and dart.

dash a masonry or concrete finish in which a render coat is thrown on; this may then be left as a final coat or rendered (wet dash), or coated with aggregate (dry dash).

see spatterdash.

dashed finish see wet dash.

dashed line, broken line; in technical drawing, a line of intermittent strokes end-on-end, usually made use of to represent hidden outlines and edges.

data information in digital form used and processed by a computer or other collating system.

data communications the transmission and receiving of digital information via electronic devices and networks.

data processing the collection, storage and editing of information.

data transfer the transmission and receiving of digital information as signals on an electronic or telecommunications system.

data transfer rate in computing, the speed at which information is transmitted from one device to another, measured in bauds (bits per second).

database in computing and other information systems, a collection of interrelated information stored together.

datum in measuring and setting out, a point or level from which all subsequent measurements or levels are taken.

datum height see datum level.

datum level, datum height, datum plane; in measuring and setting out, a level from which all subsequent vertical measurements or levels are taken.

datum line in measuring and setting out, a line from which all subsequent measurements are taken.

datum plane see datum level.

daub see wattle and daub.

daubing, rendering; the rough application of mortar to a wall as a rendered finish, either by hand with a trowel or with an applicator.

Daucus carota the carrot plant, see carrot red.
Davy's grey powdered slate used as a pigment; see slate black.
dawn see aurora.
dawn grey a shade of grey which takes its name from the colour of an overcast sky at daybreak.
day abb. **d**; a measure of time equal to 24 hours or 86 400 s.
day care centre see nursery.
day joint see stop end form.
daylight in lighting design, all solar radiation, direct and indirect, that reaches the ground.
daylight lamp see neodymium oxide lamp.
daylight size see sight size. →52
daywork in contract management, a method of payment for additional construction work on the basis of hourly rates of labour, materials and plant.
DC direct current.
dead in room acoustics, referring to a space which has poor reverberance and little reflected sound.
dead bolt a rectangular lock bolt operable by the turning of a key only. →39
dead end see blind alley.
dead knot a knot in seasoned timber which can be easily knocked out, not intergrown with the surrounding wood. →1
dead leg in pipework for domestic water supply, a length of pipe extending from a circuit, whose end is fitted with a tap or appliance.
deadlight see fixed light.
dead load, permanent load; the structural load in a building due to the weight of the structure and other unchanging factors; see live load.
deadlock a lock which can be operated with a key only, but from both sides of a door. →39
deadman a buried concrete slab attached with ties to the rear of a retaining wall to provide a restraining anchorage. →29
dead shore, vertical shore; a heavy timber post used as support for the underside of construction under repair, during underpinning, excavation work etc.
dead-soft temper one of the annealed conditions and states of hardness in which copper is supplied; others are hard and half hard.
deal 1 commercial timber from the Scots pine tree, *Pinus sylvestris*.
2 a piece of sawn softwood with cross-sectional dimensions of 47 mm–100 mm thick and 225 mm–275 mm wide. →2
deal yard blue see yard blue.
deambulatory an aisle within the apse of a church; see ambulatory; deambulatorium in Latin. →99, →100
Dearne's bond, Dearne's hollow wall; a brickwork bond in which courses of headers are laid with alternate courses of stretchers on edge to form 9" brick wall with cavities. →17
Dearne's hollow wall see Dearne's bond. →17
death-watch beetle [*Xestobium rufovillosum*] a beetle whose larvae cause damage to old wood and hardwood furniture by burrowing; it makes a ticking sound when moving, which was popularly believed to be an omen of imminent death.
debit 1 an expense or outlay of money in accountancy.
2 a charge by a supplier of materials or services.
debt, liability; money owed, especially that which cannot be paid back immediately.
debtor one who is in debt to another.
deburring the removal of unwanted sharp edges from a treated or milled metal or plastics surface.
deca- abb. **da**; a prefix for units of measurement or quantity to denote a factor of ten. →Table 1
decadentism a movement in art in France from the 1880s dealing with the peculiarities and decline of art and society; in architecture the term characterizes the decline in the development of an architectural style.
decagon a planar regular or irregular ten-sided figure. →108
decahedron a solid shape whose surface is composed of ten planar faces.
decastyle in classical architecture, a portico supported by a row of ten columns. →77
decay 1 fungal decay, see rot.
2 see dote.
decayed knot see unsound knot. →1
decay rate in acoustics, the rate of decrease in sound pressure level of a sound with respect to time; the slower the decay rate, the longer the reverberation time.
deceleration lane see diverging lane.
decentralization in town planning, the movement of the centre of gravity of a city away from its traditional centre due to dispersal and suburban expansion.
deci- abb. **d**; a prefix for units of measurement or quantity to denote a factor of 10^{-1} (one tenth). →Table 1
decibel abb. **dB**; the basic unit of sound pressure level.
deciduous tree any species of tree which loses its leaves annually, often (but not always) one from which hardwood is obtained; see **hardwood** for list of tropical and European hardwood trees.
decimal fraction in mathematics, a fraction expressed as a series of numbers written after a decimal point.
decimal place in mathematics, the position of a digit after the decimal point.
decimal point a point which distinguishes a whole number and a fraction of 1 in a numerical value.
deck 1 a loadbearing raised slab or horizontal composite construction supporting a floor, roof or external area.
2 see bridge deck. →32
decking 1 prefabricated components, boarding or other sheet material used to provide the structure of a floor, roof or deck as a base for surface materials.
2 spaced boarding laid as flooring for a veranda, or as a platform, duckboards etc. →58
3 see roof decking. →59
4 see soffit formwork.
deck parking an area of parking on one of a number of concrete decks, usually the lower floors of a building, a multistorey car park etc. →62
declination 1 in surveying, the angle that any given plane makes with true vertical.
2 see solar declination.
declivity a downwards-sloping embankment, called a glacis when situated in front of a castle.
deconstruction see deconstructivism.
deconstructivism, deconstruction; an architectural movement in the late 1980s and early 1990s, which sought to expose hitherto unquestioned assumptions and was manifested by dislocation and distortion of built form.
decor see interior design.
Decorated style an architectural style in England from 1289 to 1400, the second of three phases of English Gothic architecture, characterized by rich decoration and tracery, lavish rib vaults and ogee arches; see also Geometric, Curvilinear.
decorated tracery tracery of the Decorated style; see flowing tracery. →110
decoration, 1 ornament, embellishment; adornment, pattern, carvings, sculpture etc. for a surface or space.
see *continuous mouldings* illustration. →14
see *floriated and foliated ornament* illustration. →82
see *repeated mouldings* illustration. →124
see *fret and heraldic mouldings* illustration. →125
see *geometrical figures* illustration. →108
see *symbols and ornamental motifs* illustration. →119, →120, →121, →122, →123
see *cross* illustration. →117, →118
2 surface patterning or removable objects of art for walls, ceilings, theatre sets etc.
3 see decorative work.
decorative art 1 art and design in the form of decorative prints, sculpture, furniture etc. intended to enhance the interior decoration of a space.

2 enrichment; applied decoration for parts and surfaces of buildings and objects.
3 see decorative work.

decorative brickwork see below for list.
carved brickwork.
chequered brickwork.
decorative masonry.
diaper. →19
gauged brickwork.
herringbone brickwork. →17
lacing course.
moulded brickwork.
patterned brickwork.
polychrome brickwork.
rubbed brickwork, see gauged brickwork.

decorative inlay inlay.

decorative masonry, decorative brickwork; masonry which makes use of different coloured, glazed bricks, carved stones etc. laid in patterns and banding as decoration for wall surfaces.

decorative motif see ornamental motif. →14

decorative painting ornamental painting, murals etc. applied to the surfaces of a building.

decorative tile see ornamental tile.

decorative veneer a thin sheet of high quality wood used for its decorative value, quality of grain figure etc. as a facing for lower quality timber, board or plywood.

decorative work the preparation of any decoration, ornamentation, painting, carving, printing etc. for a building; variations included as separate entries are listed below.
artwork.
black and white work. →7
checkerwork, see chequerwork. →124
corduroy work.
Cosmati work. →123
diamond work. →19
fanwork, see fan tracery.
fretwork, fret ornament; see fret. →125
honeycomb work, see stalactite work. →115
knotwork. →108, →118, →125
leafwork, see foliated ornament. →82, →121
long and short work. →12
poker-work.
stalactite work. →115
strapwork. →122

decrescent a crescent shape which has its concave side facing to the right of the viewer, the symbol of a waning moon.

decumana 1 see porta decumana. →104
2 see via decumana. →104

decumanus Lat.; the principal straight axis or street of a Roman town, encampment etc., generally running east–west and crossed towards one end by the cardo; in a castrum it is the via decumana and via praetoria. →104

deduction see tax deduction.

deep compaction, sand piling; a method of ground stabilization in which pits or holes are made into soft ground, then filled with compacted sand or gravel to increase the bearing capacity of the ground; see also dynamic consolidation, vibrocompaction.

deep foundation any foundation which requires a deep excavation for reasons of ground, groundwater or frost conditions. →29

deep freeze see freezer.

deep freeze store a cold room maintained at a temperature substantially lower than the freezing point of its contents.

deep penetration testing see cone penetration testing.

deep seated rock see plutonic rock.

deep yellow see flame yellow.

deer house a structure or shelter to protect deer and other semi-wild animals from the elements; usually situated in parkland or a deer-park on large estates.

default in computing and other electronic control systems, an initial value or setting used if no other is offered.

defect, 1 fault; an imperfection which lowers the quality of a material, product or construction and may spoil it both physically and visually.
2 see structural defect.
3 see growth defect. →1
4 see seasoning defect. →1
5 see conversion defect. →1
6 see sawing defect. →1

defective referring to a material or object which is of a lower standard than required by a specification, is unserviceable or does not function properly.

defects liability period, maintenance period; the agreed period from completion of a building during which the contractor has an obligation to repair any faults and shortcomings in the construction work, performance of components and materials covered by the contract.

defects schedule see schedule of defects.

deficit in accountancy, the amount by which expenditure exceeds income for a particular period of time.

deflection, deflexion; elastic deformation of a member under load, often the downward movement of the mid-span of a loaded beam.

deflection curve, elastic curve; in structural design, the curve of the main axis of a beam or other laterally stressed member under loading.

deflexion see deflection.

deformation in structures, the change in shape of a member or other component under loading; see also elastic deformation, plastic deformation.

deformed bar in reinforced concrete, a reinforcing bar whose surface is textured with a series of transverse parallel ridges to provide better bonding with the concrete; sometimes called a ribbed bar. →27

deformed wire steel wire, used as concrete reinforcement, which has a textured surface to improve its bonding with the concrete matrix.

degreasing the removal of grease or oily material from a surface, product or component prior to further treatment or use.

degree abb. °; **1** the angular unit of measurement of a plane angle, equal to the rotation round $^1/_{360}$ of a circle.
2 the unit of measurement of temperature, see degree Celsius, degree Fahrenheit.

degree Celsius, degree centigrade; abb. **°C**; SI unit of measurement of temperature based on the thermometric scale in which the freezing point of water is taken as 0°C, its boiling point as 100°C, and the interval divided into one hundred degrees.

degree centigrade see degree Celsius.

degree day in concreting, a measure of the curing time, and thus strength or maturity of cast concrete based on local statistical coldness conditions.

degree Fahrenheit imperial unit of measurement of temperature based on the thermometric scale in which the freezing point of water is 32°F and its boiling point 212°F under standard conditions.

degree hour in concreting, a measure of the strength or maturity of concrete.

degree Kelvin abb. **°K**; SI unit of temperature whose magnitude unit is the same as that in the Celsius scale, but in which 0°K is absolute zero, equivalent to −278°C.

degree of acidity see acidity.

dehumidifier an appliance which decreases the relative humidity of air, making conditions more comfortable in spaces whose air contains too much moisture.

del., delin., delineavit; in graphic prints, a suffix to a signature which denotes the name of the designer, as opposed to the engraver of the print.

delamination in plywood or a veneered surface, adhesive failure resulting in the separation of adjacent plies; similar separation of adjacent layers in laminated construction due to poor bonding.

delay penalty see liquidated damages.

Delft blue, Turkey blue, Turkish blue; a shade of grey blue which takes its name from the colour of pottery from Delft, Holland, originally copied from oriental porcelain.

delin. see del.

delineavit Lat.; see del.

deliquiae Lat., plural form; a term used by Vitruvius to describe roof boards or gutters.

delivery charge, transportation charge; a charge made for the transport of goods; see also freight.

delivery time the time elapsing between the ordering of goods or services and their arrival.

Delphinidae see dolphin. →119

delphinium (blue) a shade of blue which takes its name from the colour of the blossom of the larkspur [*Delphinium cultorum*].

Delrin see polyoximethylene.

delta Nile delta, see Lower Egypt. →74

delta connection an electric point with three holes designed to receive a plug from a three-phase power supply.

demand consumer desire for a particular product or service.

demesne, grounds; an area of land, gardens or an estate for a building in Ireland.

demi-bastion a half bastion in a fortification, consisting of a face with one flank. →104

demi-column, half-column; a decorative semicircular protrusion in a wall resembling a column which has been sunk into the wall surface, found in classical architecture. →13

demilune a semicircular outwork in a castle wall or fortification to provide protection for an entrance to the castle; a semicircular ravelin; also known as a mezzaluna or half moon. →104

demirelief see mezzo rilievo.

demography the branch of statistics which deals with the movement, migration, social and economic status, density and distribution of human populations in order to gain knowledge about the condition of communities.

demolition the destruction or dismantling and removal of old and unserviceable buildings or dysfunctional parts of construction, often prior to redevelopment or further construction work.

demolition ban a local authority notice preventing the demolition of a building or parts of a building.

demolition order a local authority notice requiring the demolition of a building or parts of a building.

demolition permit a permit issued in certain circumstances by a local authority prior to the demolition of a building or parts of a building, especially one which is the subject of protective legislation.

demountable partition, relocatable partition; a freestanding partition held in place with mechanical fixings, which can be erected and taken down without the need for refurbishment or construction work.

denier a unit of fineness of fabric yarns taken as the weight in grams of a 9000 m length of yarn.

dense grained see close grained.

densifier see plasticizing admixture.

density mass per unit volume.
see bulk density.
see fire-load density.
flux density, see magnetic induction.
see mass density.
see snow density.

dental clinic a medical establishment in which dental care is provided, often as part of a health centre.

dental cuspidor a sanitary appliance designed to flush away mouthwashing water from dental operations and procedures.

dentil an ornamental motif consisting of a series of square plates in relief. →124

dentilation **1** masonry walling decoration consisting of a horizontal protruding toothed course of bricks or dressed stone. →21
2 dentil moulding. →80, →124

dentil frieze see dentil moulding. →126

dentil moulding **1** an ornamental moulding consisting of a row of spaced rectangular recesses or projections; called a dentil frieze if below a cornice. →80, →124, →126
2 see Venetian dentil moulding. →124

deodar [*Cedrus deodara*] a softwood from the Himalayan mountains with pale brown timber; used for interiors.

deoxidized copper a grade of copper which can be easily soldered or brazed; used, among other things, for domestic plumbing.

department of architecture a municipal or educational department for the practice or teaching of architecture.

department store a large shop with a number of departments selling different categories of merchandise.

deposit the placing of money or valuables for safekeeping and to gain interest in an account or the vaults of a financial institution.

deposit corrosion, under-deposit corrosion, poultice corrosion; a form of crevice corrosion occurring under or around a hole, crack or break in a protective deposited coating on a metallic surface.

depressed arch see drop arch. →24

depressed ogee arch see two-centred ogee arch. →24

depressed three-centred arch a flat three-centred arch.

depth **1** the measure of an object from the upper surface downwards, from the outer surface inwards or from front to back.
2 see excavation depth.
3 see foundation depth.

depth sounding **1** see echo-sounding.
2 see sounding.

derby see darby. →43

Derby red see chrome red.

derelict land vacant land which is so damaged or contaminated by a previous use so that it cannot be beneficially used without treatment.

derivative, differential coefficient; in mathematics, an expression which represents the instantaneous rate of change of a function with respect to an independent variable.

desalination in the treatment of waste water, the removal of salt.

descriptive geometry a branch of mathematics which deals with the description and representation of three-dimensional objects in two dimensions; the science of projections.

descriptive specification a concise specification outlining the characteristics of a product, process or design, usually including design and constructional details with sizes, basic technical data and colour and material composition.

desiccant a substance incorporated into some products, processes or sealed components to absorb unwanted moisture.

design **1** the process or formulating, creating and planning a functional, graphic or mass produced object such as a building, furnishing or fitting.
2 scheme; the representation, usually as a series of sketches, documents, drawings, models or computer generations, of a building, built area, structure or object.
3 see interior design.
4 see motif.

design and build contract see design and construct contract.

design and construct contract, design and build contract, package deal, turnkey contract; a form of building contract based on a brief provided by the client in which a developer organization has full responsibility for the design and construction of a project.

designated fabric in reinforced concrete, fabric reinforcement which can be defined by a coded fabric reference, negating the need for a design drawing or schedule.

design competition an architectural competition whose aim is to generate solutions which form the basis of designs for a building.

designer a person or organization responsible for designing parts of a building, artifact etc.

design guideline information providing a specialist designer with assistance concerning design matters from the point of view of regulations, good practice, user and client requirements etc.

design life the minimum length of time for which a component has been designed to correctly carry out its specified function.

design load in structural design, the maximum load for which a particular structure or structural member is designed.

design philosophy the principles, thought processes and decisions behind a particular design or scheme.

design programme a plan drawn up by clients and designers indicating the scope, stages and timing of design work for a particular building project.

design project, design scheme; a particular building or development at design stage.

design scheme see design project.

design stage the pre-contract stage of a building project, from initiation up to tendering, when most or all of the design work is being carried out.

design theory a series of principles or methodology, often based on exact sciences or sociopolitical research, used as a basis for design.

desk 1 a worktop or counter for the service of customers in an office or shop.

2 a piece of furniture with a sloping or horizontal surface, a table for reading and writing.

desktop publishing the use of a personal computer or program to collect and assimilate text, data and graphics for presentation or publication.

desornamentado austere and ascetic Renaissance architecture in Spain during the reign of Philip II (1556–1598).

dessiatine, desyatin; a Russian measure of area equivalent to 1.1 hectares or 2.7 acres.

destrictarium Lat.; a room in a Roman bath house or gymnasium next to the palaestra, in which sand and oil were scraped off the skin of wrestlers by slaves, using strigils. →91

destructive testing the physical and chemical testing of samples of materials and components in such a way that they are damaged, crushed or changed during testing.

desulpho gypsum the mineral gypsum produced as a by-product of the purification of sulphurous flue gases produced during the combustion of fossil fuels.

desyatin see dessiatine.

detached column a column adjacent to a wall, but not physically attached to it, often a decorative column on a pedestal or plinth. →13

detached house a single-family house surrounded by space on all sides; any such building which contains one dwelling, rather than one split into a semi-detached or terraced house; a freestanding dwelling. →61

see bungalow. →61

detail in design and construction, a solution to a small scale issue such as a construction joint or the meeting of adjacent components in such a manner as to be both functional and aesthetically pleasing.

detail drawing a drawing showing a constructional detail at small scale, usually drawn as a section through the part.

detailed fabric in reinforced concrete, fabric reinforcement whose arrangement is such that it requires a detailed drawing.

detection device, detector, sensor; a device which produces a signal in the presence of smoke, heat, water or movement and triggers an alarm.

detector 1 see detection device.

2 see heat detector.

3 see combustion gas detector.

4 see smoke detector.

5 see flame detector, radiation detector.

detensioning, transfer; in the making of prestressed concrete, the transfer of stresses from the tendons and prestressing bed to the concrete.

determination in contract administration, bringing a building contract to an end before completion, under conditions specified in the contract or at common law.

detonation in the outbreak of fire, a sudden chemical explosion of gaseous material in which the energy waves travel faster than the speed of sound.

detritus fine powdered material found in some stone; remnants of broken rock.

deuterium, heavy hydrogen; an isotope of hydrogen, whose mass is approximately double that of ordinary hydrogen.

develop and construct contract a form of building contract based on a scheme design prepared by the client, for which a contractor produces production drawings and carries out construction works.

developer a building firm which develops urban or greenfield sites with buildings, housing estates etc.; often a speculative builder.

development, 1 the process of constructing buildings or other structures.

2 project; a new building under design or construction.

3 see urban development.

4 see building project.

5 see fire development.

development control see planning control.

development corporation in urban planning, a group constituted to undertake development of land for a new town, enterprise zone or urban renewal area.

development plan proposals prepared by a local authority in the form of written documents, maps and diagrams relating to housing, schools, industry, shopping, and roads.

development with deemed consent in building control, building development that does not require formal planning permission.

deviation 1 in quality control, the difference in size (or some other measurable property) from a sample or delivered component to that which has been specified.

2 in statistics, the amount by which a single measurement or statistic differs from the mean or average.

3 see mean deviation.

device see peripheral.

device driver see driver.

devil see scraper. →41

devil float see nail float. →43

Devonshire clay see china clay.

dewatering, 1 groundwater lowering; the artificial lowering of groundwater in a particular location or construction site using excavations and other means.

2 measures such as pumping and drainage to reduce the amount of water around foundations below the water table.

3 drying; reducing the water level in a subterranean structure or the water content of a saturated material.

dewpoint, condensation point, saturation point; the lowest temperature at which the contained water vapour in air of a given humidity condenses; relative humidity at this point is 100%.

dexter in heraldry, the part of a shield to the right of the wearer or bearer; to the left as viewed by the spectator. →124

dexter chief in heraldry, the point in the upper right corner of a shield, as worn. →124

dextrin gum produced from starch, used as a binder in watercolours and paste.

dezincification the slow disappearance or seepage of the zinc in brass due to electrolytic action when in contact with water; brass pipes are corroded as porous copper is laid down.

dharma chakra, dharma wheel, wheel of law; an eight-spoked wheel, the symbol of Buddha's suffering and rebirth, each spoke representing one of the tenets of Buddhist belief, a typical motif in eastern art and decoration. →120

dharma wheel see dharma chakra. →120

diabase, traprock; a dark igneous rock used as building stone, similar to basalt but with a larger grain structure.

diaconicon a room or space on the south side of the sanctuary (to the right of the altar) in an Orthodox or Early Christian church for the keeping of garments and vessels; Greek form is diakonikon; Latin form is diaconicum.
see *Late Antique church* illustration. →95
see *Byzantine domical church* illustration. →96

diaconicum Latin form of diaconicon.

diaeta Lat., Greek form of diaita; a living or summer recreation room in a Roman dwelling; a Roman summer home.

diagonal 1 in geometry, a line which is not parallel or perpendicular to a main axis, usually from corner to corner of a rectangle.
2 see oblique.
3 a diagonal strut or tie in a trussed beam or space frame. →33
4 see brace.
5 see diagonal brace. →57

diagonal boarding, diagonal sheathing; boarding nailed diagonally to clad a building frame as bracing and for decorative effect. →8

diagonal bond 1 see Flemish diagonal bond. →19
2 see diagonal pattern. →15
3 diagonal Flemish double stretcher bond, see Flemish double stretcher bond. →19

diagonal brace any member set diagonally from corner to corner of a frame to stiffen it. →57
see angle tie.

diagonal grain see sloping grain. →1

diagonal pattern a paving pattern in which rows of pavers are laid with joints oblique to a main axis, often forming a lozenge pattern; also called diagonal bond; similar patterns in parquetry, tiling and veneering. →15

diagonal point see diagonal vanishing point. →128

diagonal rib, ogive, groin rib; a rib in a rib vault which runs diagonally from corner to corner of the bay. →101

diagonal sheathing see diagonal boarding. →8

diagonals, method of see method of diagonals. →128

diagonal tie see angle tie.

diagonal vanishing point, diagonal point, distance point; in perspective drawing, a vanishing point for lines which recede at 45° to the picture plane. →128

diagram 1 a simplified graphical representation or chart showing how a system or process works, often not drawn to any scale.
2 see circuit diagram.

diaita Greek form is diaeta.

diakonikon Greek form of diaconicon. →95

dial-a-bus a bus transport system in which the desired pick-up points and destinations of passengers are phoned in to the system controller, and a central computerized exchange timetables buses accordingly.

dial gauge an instrument for measuring very small dimensions, consisting of a needle plunger configured to a dial or meter.

diameter 1 in geometry, the dimension measured across a circle through its centre; also the distance thus defined.
2 the transverse dimension of any polygonal object.

diamond a very hard crystalline form of carbon, usually transparent, used as a gemstone and produced industrially for drilling, cutting and grinding tools.

diamond black see carbon black.

diamond fret, lozenge fret; an ornamental motif consisting of fillets which join together forming a series of diamond shapes. →124

diamonding a form of warp which results in improperly seasoned square timber sections becoming diamond shaped. →1

diamond interchange see diamond junction. →63

diamond junction a road junction in which a minor road passes under a dual carriageway and has four straight slip roads in a diamond formation, providing access and exit. →63

diamond match 1 a veneering pattern in which four rectangular pieces of straight-grained veneer are laid together with their individual grain at an angle to one another, forming a series of diamond shapes. →10
2 see reverse diamond match. →10

diamond moulding see diamond fret. →124

diamond saw a power saw whose blade is tipped with industrial diamonds, used for cutting masonry or concrete.

diamond work decorative masonrywork formed with a repeated lozenge motif. →19

diaper 1 decoration consisting of a grid of elaborated or ornamented squares or lozenges. →124
2 a diamond pattern in brickwork created with the use of bricks in various colours and surface textures, coloured mortar etc. →19

diastyle 'wide columned'; in classical architecture, the spacing of rowed columns in a portico at the centres of three column diameters. →77

diathermal in thermodynamics, referring to a process which occurs with the transfer of heat.

diazoma Lat.; in ancient Greek architecture, a horizontal gangway between rows of seats in the auditorium of a theatre, semicircular in plan; called a praecinctio in a Roman theatre. →89

dicasterium Latin form of dikasterion.

dichroic mirror lamp a halogen lamp whose rear mirror reflector, often honeycombed, reflects light but not infrared energy, producing a cool beam.

dichroism an optical phenomenon in which an object appears to be coloured differently under different circumstances.

dichroite see cordierite.

die 1 a hard metal implement formed with an inside-threaded hole of a certain gauge, used for cutting threads into round metal rods by rotation.
2 see dado. →76, →80

diesel see diesel oil.

diesel oil, diesel; a form of distilled petroleum used as fuel in diesel engines.

differential in mathematics, relating to infinitesimal differences.

differential coefficient see derivative.

differential detector see thermo-differential detector.

differential equation in mathematics, an equation involving derivatives.

diffracted sound in acoustics, sound which reaches the listener as a result of being bent round obstacles by diffraction.

diffraction 1 the bending of light or sound waves when they come into close proximity to an opaque edge.
2 effects of light or sound caused by this phenomenon.

diffused glass see diffuse reflection glass.
see obscured glass.

diffused illumination see diffused lighting.

diffused lighting space lighting which does not have a directional quality and provides a uniform degree of illuminance.

diffuse light light or illumination without noticeable direction, such as that from a cloudy sky.

diffuse porous wood hardwood with evenly sized and distributed pores.

diffuser 1 in an air-conditioning or mechanical ventilation system, an outlet or air terminal unit which directs supply of air in the desired manner.
2 the translucent or slatted construction in a luminaire designed to scatter light and prevent glare.

diffuse reflection glass translucent glass one face of which is textured to diffuse light passing through. see obscured glass.

diffusion 1 the movement of molecules or suspended substances in a gas from an area of high concentration to one of lower concentration.
2 in mechanical ventilation and air-conditioning systems, the distribution of air within a space in the required manner by a terminal device.

diffusion bonding a method of welding specialized metal parts by pressing together under high temperatures, during which adjacent surfaces are fused together by atomic bonding caused by diffusion.

diffusion coefficient, coefficient of diffusion; a measure of the movement of water vapour through the thickness of a wall, floor and roof construction when the vapour pressure is higher on one side than the other.

diffusion resistance a physical property, with units of measurement m^2sPa/kg, which determines how well a material can inhibit the transmission of water vapour.

digestion the process of chemically breaking down a substance with heat or a solvent.

digger see excavator.

digging in construction work, landscaping and forestry, the manual turning over of topsoil, loosening of ground, or making of excavations in situations where mechanical plant cannot be used.

digit 1 any one of the numbers from zero to nine.
2 see finger. →106

digital 1 based on numbers or digits.
2 referring to electronic systems in which information is coded in numerical units.

digital display a device for showing numbers, usually readings in electronic instruments.

digitizer in computing and electronics, a device for converting analogue information into digital form.

diglyph in Renaissance architectural ornamentation, a decorative projecting element with two vertical grooves.

dikasterion Gk, an ancient Greek court of justice; Latin form is dicasterium.

dike see dyke.

dilapidated in poor condition or falling apart.

dilettante one who practises the arts as a hobby or in an amateurish or frivolous fashion.

diluent see thinner.

dilution 1 the thinning of a concentrated liquid such as a paint by a solvent or diluent liquid.
2 the ratio of concentrate to thinner.

dimension 1 a mode of linear extension in measurable space; length, breadth and height; see below.
2 the measurement of a distance between two points to indicate size, as marked on drawings etc.; see below.
actual size.
daylight size, see sight size. →52
dressed size, dressed dimension.
external dimension.
finished size.
full size, see tight size. →52
glass size, glazing size, see pane size.
measurement.
modular size, modular dimension.
neat size, see dressed size.
nominal dimension, nominal size.
overall dimension, overall size.
span dimension.
pane size.
sight size. →52
tight size. →52

dimensional coordination the dimensioning of prefabricated components and fittings such that they will comply with a modular building system.

dimensional stability the ability to retain shape and size under conditions of changing moisture and temperature.

dimensioned drawing a drawing to scale, usually of a floor plan, annotated with dimensions.

dimensioning 1 in design, the adding of annotated dimensions on a drawing.
2 the dimensions themselves.

dimension line a straight line along which incremental dimensions are added in a dimensioned drawing.

dimension stock a piece of accurately sawn timber with non-standard cross-sectional dimensions for a particular purpose.

dimension stone, natural stone block, cut stone; a piece of natural stone which has been cut into rectangular blocks for use in ashlar masonry. →12

dimetric projection 1 'two measurements'; in general, any axonometric or oblique projection drawing in which lines parallel to two of the three main axes are drawn to the same relative scale, with lines on the third at a different scale; scales and angles are chosen to produce the most realistic depictions. →127
2 in particular, an axonometric projection in which the projection of the X axis is 40° 31′ above the horizontal, the Y axis is 7° above the horizontal, Z is vertical, and the X axis is foreshortened using a different scale; many standardized variations of this orthographic dimetric projection are in use. →127

dimmer, dimmer switch; in lighting, a device to vary the amount of illumination given out by a luminaire.

dimmer switch see dimmer.

dinette, dining recess; a space or part of a room in a dwelling, usually adjoining a kitchen, in which meals are taken.

Dingler's green a variety of chromium oxide green pigment.

dining area a space in a residential building in which meals are taken. →59

dining hall 1 a large room in a grand dwelling, residential building or community in which meals are taken.
2 see refectory. →97

dining kitchen a space in a dwelling, often part of a living area, in which food is both prepared and eaten.

dining recess see dinette.

dining room 1 a room in which meals are served and eaten. →57
2 see andron. →87
3 see oecus. →88
4 see dining area, dinette. →59
5 see dining hall.
6 see dining kitchen.
7 see refectory. →97
8 see triclinium. →88
9 see coenatio. →88

Dionysus, staff of see thursus. →120

diopside a usually greenish glassy mineral, polished for decorative inlay and as gemstones.

dioptase a glossy transparent emerald-green silicate mineral used in ornament and as a gemstone.

diopter 1 see alidade.
2 an ancient instrument for measuring angles and altitudes.

diorite a dark grey or greenish even-grained igneous rock, similar in appearance to granite; used as building stone.
see quartz diorite.
Diospyros spp. see ebony.
Diospyros celebica, see Macassar ebony.
Diospyros crassiflora, see African ebony.
Diospyros ebenum, see Ceylon ebony.
Diospyros piscatoria, see African ebony.
dioxazine purple a transparent bluish-purple organic pigment used in oil, watercolour and acrylic paints.
dioxide an oxide with two atoms of oxygen in its chemical formula.
see carbon dioxide.
silicon dioxide, see silica.
see sulphur dioxide.
see titanium dioxide.
dip in geology, the inclination of a layer or bed of sedimentary rock to the horizontal.
dip painting, 1 dipping; a method of applying paint to objects by immersing them in a vessel of paint.
2 see electro-dip painting.
dip pen an ink pen whose nib is repeatedly dipped into ink to replenish it.
dipping 1 see dip painting.
2 see hot-dipping.
dipteral in classical architecture, referring to a temple surrounded by a double row of columns. →85
dipteros Gk; a dipteral temple. →85
diptych a decorative hinged panel with two leaves, often used as an altarpiece at a secondary altar; see also triptych.
diptych altar a winged altar whose altarpiece consists of two decorated panels hinged together.
direct costs costs such as material or labour outlays incurred as a direct result of making a product or producing a service.
direct current, DC; electricity which flows in one direction only.
direct glare in lighting design, glare caused by light from a direct source.
direct glazed light fixed glazing fitted directly to the main frame of a window.
direct heating 1 any heating systems in which thermal comfort is produced directly from the combustion of fuels or electricity as with stoves, bar-heaters etc.
2 any heating systems in which heating energy is produced within the building in which it is distributed.
direct hot water supply system a system of pipes and heating vessels to provide a hot water supply, heated by a direct source of energy.
direct–indirect lighting artificial lighting in which luminaires distribute an approximately equal amount of the emitted light upwards and downwards, and in which there is minimal horizontal illumination.
direction 1 the position, course or line of an object in relation to points of a compass, a map etc.
2 see orientation.
directional lighting space or task lighting designed to be beamed predominantly onto a certain area or feature.
directional T junction a grade-separated T junction where one major road meets another at right angles, with two loop ramps and slip roads permitting free flow of traffic on and off all carriageways; a special variation on the trumpet junction. →63
direction of view see central axis of vision. →128
direct lighting lighting for a space or task provided by a visible source of illumination; see also indirect lighting.
Directoire pertaining to an extravagant style in the arts and fashion from 1790 to 1805 in France at the time of the revolution; in architecture it is French neoclassicism.
directory in computing, an ordered filing system or archive in which files or programs may be stored and from which they can be retrieved.
direct plan projection method see common method. →129
direct projection method see visual ray method. →128
direct solar radiation see sunlight.
direct sound in acoustics, sound which reaches the listener directly from a source, without reflection.
diribitorium Lat.; a Roman public building in which votes were counted by election officials.
disability glare in lighting design, glare which makes seeing difficult without causing physical discomfort.
disabled referring to a person or persons with physical disability, for whom special provisions may have to be made in design and construction.
disabled parking see parking for the disabled. →62
disappearing stair, loft ladder; a retractable stepladder providing access to a roof space, either sprung-hinged or telescopic to fold away when not in use.
disc see disk.
disc grinder see angle grinder.
discharge 1 see emission.
2 fluid waste from a cooling or manufacturing process, drainage system etc.
3 flow rate; the rate of flow of a liquid in a pipeline, channel or waterway, measured in litres per second.
discharge lamp an electric lamp consisting of a glass tube containing an inert gas or metal vapour; light is produced by electrical discharge which excites the gas or vapour.
discharge pipe, drain, drainline, drain run, drain pipe; a succession of pipes joined end to end to convey waste water away from its point of use. →58
discharge stack in drainage, a vertical pipe into which a number of sanitary appliances, branch pipes etc. on successive storeys of a building may discharge waste material.
discharge valve see control valve.
discharging arch see relieving arch. →23
discoloration a material defect, the loss or change in original colour, staining or an undesired colour phenomenon; also spelled discolouration.
discomfort glare in lighting design, glare which causes physical discomfort without making it difficult to see.
discontinuous construction in acoustics, types of construction for walls and floors etc. in which no direct path is provided for structure-borne transmission of sound.
discount 1 see rebate.
2 see trade discount.
disc tumbler one of a number of pivoted discs in a lock mechanism which serve to hold the bolt fast until activated with a suitable key.
disc vent a round outlet device attached to a wall or ceiling surface, through which stale air passes out of a space. →56
dish aerial, dish antenna, satellite dish; in communications, a concave, dish-shaped aerial for receiving satellite transmissions; see satellite antenna.
dish antenna see dish aerial.
disharmony aesthetic incongruence produced by effects of colour, form, material or proportion.
dishwasher a domestic or industrial appliance for washing kitchen utensils, crockery etc.
disk, disc; in computing, the general name for a magnetized spinning disc-shaped storage unit: a hard disk, floppy disk or compact disc.
disk drive 1 in computing, a device for rotating a storage disk, and a read-write facility to access information.
2 a port into which floppy disks are inserted and read by the computer.

diskette, floppy disk, microdisk, microfloppy, minidisk; a small portable magnetized disk in a plastic case on which digitized information can be stored.

disk memory in computing, memory units contained on magnetic disks.

dismantleability the property of a component, construction or installation which can be easily and efficiently dismantled.

dispensary see chemist.

dispersal 1 in town planning, the migration of population and industry outwards from the inner areas and traditional centres of cities to smaller towns and outlying areas.
2 the encouragement of smoke flow to the outside along predesigned routes or ducts during a building fire.

dispersion the mixture of one substance in another in the form of fine droplets, as in an emulsion paint, aerosol etc.

dispersion paint a paint containing droplets of pigment or latex in a non-dissolving liquid such as water.

dispersivity see light dispersivity.

displacement in design and construction, the relocation of an object and the distance between its old position and new.

displacer see plum.

display, display unit; in computing, a visual interface, the screen on which information is presented.

display case, vitrine; a glazed cabinet for the display of objects or ware.

display control unit, graphic accelerator; in computing, hardware which controls the performance of a display unit.

display unit, visual display unit, VDU; in computing, the device on which data, information and graphics are visually displayed.

display window, shop window; a window at ground level in a commercial building for the display of products, wares or advertising.

displuviate court see displuviatum.

displuviatum, displuviate court; Lat.; according to Vitruvius, an atrium in a Roman dwelling which has surrounding roofs sloping downwards and outwards on all sides.

disruption in contract administration, events or stoppages outside the contractor's control that slow down the progress of the work on site and may justify additional payments.

dissolvent see solvent.

distance 1 the measure of linear extension between two points.
2 in perspective, the perpendicular measurement from the station point to the picture plane. →128

distance point see diagonal vanishing point. →128

distemper a traditional water-based paint consisting of pigment and chalk or clay bound together with glue.

distemper brush, flat brush; a large brush traditionally used for painting and decorating large internal surfaces such as ceilings or walls. →43

disthene see kyanite.

distortion a perceived breaking up of sound caused by alteration or interference of waveforms in an electronic audio system, rendering signals incomprehensible or unrecognizable.

distributed load a structural load which acts evenly along the length of a beam, or over the surface area of a slab.

distributing pipe, distribution pipe; a pipe that conveys water, fuel etc. from a cistern, tank or main to an appliance.

distribution 1 the conveying of goods, materials, energy or water from a centre of manufacture or supply to its various consumer outlets.
2 see heat distribution.
3 see air distribution.

distribution bars secondary reinforcement at right angles to the main reinforcement in a reinforced concrete slab or wall, designed to spread a concentrated load and as support during concreting.

distribution network see gas distribution network.

distribution pattern in air conditioning and ventilation, a graphic representation of the spread of air from a supply air inlet, part of its technical specification.

distribution pipe see distributing pipe.

distribution reservoir see service reservoir.

distributor road an urban road primarily used to distribute local traffic from a main road to a final destination such as a residential area.

district, 1 region; an area of land with certain distinguishing characteristics, geographical features, local culture or livelihood.
2 an area of a town or city with its own character, cultural and commercial activity, administrative body etc. which can be perceived as a unit.

district centre, local centre, neighbourhood centre; an area of shops and services which serves the day to day needs of an urban or suburban area outside a city or town centre.

district heating a system of heating for an area or district, usually residential, in which heated water is piped to a number of buildings from a central heating plant.

district heating pipeline, heating main; in a district heating system, a supply pipeline consisting of pipe-in-pipe, valves and other control devices.

disturbed sample see remoulded sample.

distyle in classical architecture, a portico which has two supporting columns. →77

distyle in antis in classical architecture, a portico which has two columns between the antae, or side wall extensions or pilasters. →84

ditch, 1 drainage ditch, land drain; an open trench dug for the drainage of surface water.
2 a long excavation made outside a major fortified wall, rampart etc. to provide a line of defence; see moat. →104
3 see trench.
4 see fossa. →104
5 see moat. →103

ditching 1 in landscaping and forestry, the digging, cleaning out or widening of ditches.
2 see land drainage.

ditriglyph in classical architecture, a column spacing spanned on the entablature by two triglyphs and three metopes instead of the usual one and two.

divan, 1 diwan; a room in an oriental dwelling, furnished with a low couch and open to one side.
2 a sofa or couch without sides, handrests or a headrest.

divan-i-am, diwan-i-am; a public audience hall in Persian or Indian architecture.

divan-i-kas, diwan-i-kas; a private audience hall in Persian or Indian architecture.

diverging lane, deceleration lane; in road design, a lane which provides an exit from a major road to a minor road or intersection, on which traffic reduces speed.

divergent perspective the practice of depicting scenes using lines of view which diverge rather than converge as in true perspective, producing unnatural distortion; found particularly in Byzantine and Russian iconic art.

diversion a road or route, often temporary, providing an alternative to one which is congested or obstructed by roadworks.

diversity richness and variation of species and habitats in the natural environment.

diversity factor in pipework and electrical installations, a design factor to determine the maximum rate of flow of water or electricity in a system based on the various appliances connected to the system and their requirements.

divided carriageway see dual carriageway. →63

dividend in economics, an amount of money paid periodically to a shareholder based on company performance and number of shares held.

dividers a pair of compasses with points at the end of each leg; used for measuring, transferring dimensions and scribing arcs.
wing dividers, see wing compass.

dividing strip 1 in floor construction, a strip of flexible material used to divide a monolithic floor into discrete areas to allow for movement.
2 verge, margin, median; in traffic planning, a strip of planted land to provide separation between a pedestrian path and a carriageway.

division in mathematics, the number of times in which one value fits exactly into another.

division bar see glazing bar. →111

Divisionism a painting technique invented by the impressionists, in which small points of pure colour are painted to give the impression of a far greater range of colours; synonymous with pointillism.

division wall see fire wall.

diwan see divan.

diwan-i-am see divan-i-am.

diwan-i-kas see divan-i-kas.

DIY see self-build.

Djed column in ancient Egyptian mythology and decoration, a pillar motif with four discs around its upper end, symbolic of steadfastness and stability; also written as Djet. →74

Djehuty see Thoth. →74

Djet alternative spelling of Djed. →74

do-and-charge work see cost-reimbursement contract.

dock a basin or stretch of water between two wharves in a harbour which provides a mooring for a boat.

dockland a waterside or harbour area of a town with docks and berths for mooring, loading and unloading freightships.

dockyard see shipyard.

document an official or unofficial written text, computer file, drawing etc. produced for a particular purpose of information, intent, instruction or evidence.

documentation 1 the preparation of working drawings, specifications and other documents for a construction project to form the basis of a building contract.
2 the collection of photographic and other documentary evidence of buildings for an inquiry, building survey, conservation project etc.

dodecagon a planar regular or irregular twelve-sided figure. →108

dodecahedron a solid shape whose surface is composed of twelve pentagonal faces.

dodecastyle in classical architecture, a portico supported by a row of twelve columns. →77

dog, cramp, crampon, dog iron; a large steel or iron U-shaped fastener hammered into a timber joint to strengthen it and hold it together. →3

dog bolt see hinge bolt. →38

dog iron see dog. →3

dogleg brick a kinked brick used at the join of two wall planes meeting at an obtuse angle.

dogleg chisel see bruzz chisel. →41

dog-legged stair see dogleg stair. →45

dogleg stair, dog-legged stair, return stair; a stair with two parallel flights side by side, joined by a single intermediate landing at half-storey height. →45

dogmatic referring to a work of art which follows a creed, fashion, theory or style in a pedantic way.

dogtooth, 1 tooth ornament; a decorative moulding found in Norman architecture, consisting of a series of raised lozenge shapes with a carving resembling the imprint of a tooth set into each. →122
2 see dogtooth brickwork. →124

dogtooth brickwork, houndstooth brickwork, mousetooth brickwork (Am.); decorative brickwork in which a course or courses of bricks are laid diagonally so as to expose a horizontal sawtooth edge in a wall surface. →20

dogtooth moulding, houndstooth moulding, mousetooth moulding; a decorative sculptured band with a series of protruding notched carvings, resembling fluting in which the arcs are made into V shapes. →124

dogwood, cornel (Am.); [*Cornus florida*] a hardwood from North America with pinkish non-splintering timber, traditionally used for small objects such as spindles for the textile industry.

do-it-yourself see self-build.

dolerite a coarse-grained igneous rock, a form of young basalt.

dolly in piledriving, relatively soft material such as a piece of hardwood or log placed over the top of the pile as protection from impact damage during driving.

dolmen, cromlech, portal tomb, quoit; a prehistoric tomb structure consisting of a large flattish stone resting on a number of other upright stones.

dolomite, 1 bitter spar; crystalline calcium magnesium carbonate, **$CaMg(CO_3)_2$**, in mineral form found in some limestones; used for its fire-resistant properties.
2 dolostone; limestone containing a high proportion of the above.

dolomitic lime, high magnesium lime; quicklime made from dolomite high in magnesium oxide, a mixture of calcium oxide and magnesium oxide in the ratio 1:1.

dolomitic limestone limestone with a high content of the mineral dolomite.

dolostone see dolomite.

dolphin 1 one of a group of piles or a similar construction sunk into the bed of a lake or the sea bed as a mooring for boats and buoys, to mark out zones and to afford protection to a dock or bridge. →64
2 an ornamental representation of a toothed whale from the family *Delphinidae*, symbolic of an ancient sea god and the bearer of the dead to their final resting place, a common decorative motif found in Mediterranean architecture. →119

doma Gk, Latin is domus; the central room of a Mycenaean megaron dwelling, containing a hearth. →87

dome 1 a hollow, flattened or raised hemispherical roof structure, often of masonry, which rests on a circular, square or polygonal base; see below. →26
see *types of dome* illustration. →26
see *classical temple* illustration. →86
bulbous dome, see onion dome. →26
drum dome.
glass dome.
half dome. →26
melon dome, see umbrella dome. →26
onion dome. →26
parachute dome, see umbrella dome. →26
pendentive dome. →26
pumpkin dome, see umbrella dome. →26
sail dome, sail vault. →26
saucer dome. →26
semi-dome, see half dome. →26
umbrella dome. →26
2 see domelight.

domed basilica a basilica church roofed with one or a number of domes.

domed roof, 1 domical roof; a roof in the form of a dome.
2 one made up of a number of domes.

dome head referring to a screw or rivet whose head is hemispherical.

dome head screw, round head screw; a screw with a hemispherical head which protrudes above the surface into which it is fixed. →36

domelight, dome rooflight; a rooflight of moulded polycarbonate plastics or shaped glass, usually dome shaped but often square, mono-pitched, barrel vaulted or a pyramid, and often functioning as a smoke vent.

dome nut see cap nut. →37

dome rooflight see domelight.

domestic refuse, household waste; waste material produced by the inhabitants of dwellings and other residential establishments, usually food-stuffs, packaging etc.

domestic sauna a sauna facility within a dwelling or block of flats.

domestic solid fuel appliance see room heater.

domestic water heater a water heater intended for a small central heating system, for one household or a small building.

domical church a centralized church type capped by a dome, typical in Byzantine architecture. →95, →96 see *Byzantine domical church* illustration. →96

domical grating in drainage installations, a removable dome-shaped grating to protect the outlet of a drain from blockage by leaves, gravel etc.

domical roof see domed roof.

domical vault see cloister vault. →25, →26

dominant wavelength in colour theory, for any sample of colour, the corresponding wavelength of visible light.

domino a shade of black which takes its name from the colour of a black clerical robe.

domus Lat.; a Roman dwelling type for the well-to-do in which rooms were arranged round a colonnaded hall without an atrium.

donjon 1 see dungeon. →103
2 see keep. →103

donkey saw see mill saw.

door 1 an opening in a wall with a hinged or sliding partition to allow access from one space to another. →50, →51
2 the partition itself, see door leaf.
3 the partition and its associated frame, see doorset. →50
4 see doorway.
see *door* illustration, and below for list of types of door. →50, →51
access door.
accordion door. →50
all-glass door. →51
aluminium door.
ash pan door. →56
automatic door.
automatic fire door, see automatic-closing fire assembly.
balanced door. →50
bi-fold door. →50
bi-part folding door. →50
bi-parting door, see centre-opening door. →50
blind door, see false door.
casement door.
centre-opening door. →50
concertina door, see sliding folding door. →50
coupled door. →50
double door. →50
double sliding door. →50
exit door.
external door. →51
false door.
fire door.
firebox door. →56
firebreak door, see fire door.
fireplace door. →56
flush door. →51
folding door. →50
framed and ledged door.
framed door. →51
framed, ledged and braced door.
frameless glass door, see all-glass door. →60
French door, see casement door.
front door, see main entrance.
glass door, all-glass door. →60
glazed door. →51
glazed metal door. →51
glazed timber door. →51
hinged door. →50
hollow-core door. →51
inspection door.
internal door.
landing door.
ledged and braced door. →51
ledged door. →51
lift car door.
louvred door. →51
matchboard door.
metal door. →51
metal glazed door, see glazed metal door. →51
multi-folding door.
overhead door. →50
panelled door, panel door. →51
pass door, see wicket door.
plastics door.
rebated door. →51
revolving door. →50
roller door, see roller shutter. →50
Royal door, see porta regia. →89
sectional overhead door. →50
side-hung door. →50, →51
side-opening door. →50
single door. →50
sliding door. →50
sliding folding door. →50
smoke door, smoke control door.
soot door. →56
stable door. →50
steel door.
strongroom door, see vault door.
swing door. →50
timber door. →51
timber glazed door, see glazed timber door. →51
trapdoor.
unframed door.
unglazed door. →51
up-and-over door. →50
vault door.
vertical folding door. →50
wicket door.
wooden door, see timber door. →51

door acceptor see acceptor.

door assembly see doorset. →50

door automation see automatic door gear.

doorbell a sounding device attached to or near a door to attract the attention of occupants. →51

door buck see door lining.
see buck. →6

door buffer 1 a piece or strip of resilient material set in the rebate of a door jamb to reduce noise from the door leaf slamming.
2 see door stop. →51

door bumper see door stop. →51

door buzzer see door transmitter.

door casing see door lining.

door chain, door limiter; a security door fitting for inhibiting the opening of an entry door to its full extent, consisting of a short length of chain attached to the inside face of a door leaf and the locking jamb. →51

door check see door closer.

door clearance 1 the horizontal or vertical open dimension between the members of a door frame. →51
2 the small gap between door leaf and its frame, which allows it freedom of movement in opening and closing.
3 the installation gap between a door frame and surrounding fabric to allow for manufacturing tolerances and workmanship. →51

door closer, **1** door check; a sprung or hydraulic device for closing a door automatically and keeping it closed until manually opened; used for fire doors and external doors. →51

2 see concealed door closer.
3 see jamb mounted door closer.
4 see overhead door closer.
5 see surface-mounted door closer.
6 see door spring.

door co-ordinator a device fitted in conjunction with a door closer in a set of double fire doors to ensure that the leaves close in the correct order and that rebated edges and locks function properly.

door core the filling material for a composite door leaf, usually of foamed plastics, timber-based material or honeycomb construction. →50

door face 1 the external planar surface of a door leaf. →50
2 see opening face. →50, →51
3 see closing face. →50, →51
4 door facing; the surface covering for a door leaf.

door facing see door face.

door fittings see door furniture. →51

door former formwork to create an opening for a door in a concrete wall.

door frame the structural surround for a door leaf, in which it is hung. →50, →51

door-frame anchor a short length of metal strip for fixing a door frame to surrounding construction. →50

door furniture, door ironmongery, door hardware; any fittings such as hinges, door handles and closers for the operation and functioning of a door. →51

door gear 1 see automatic door gear.
2 see sliding door gear.
3 see swing-door operator.

door handle a device or fitting used for manually opening a door by grasping with the hand and pulling; types included as separate entries are listed below. →50, →51
flush handle.
lever handle. →50, →51
pull handle. →51
sliding door handle.
trapdoor handle.

door hardware see door furniture. →51

door head, 1 door soffit; the horizontal flat underside of a door opening.
2 the upper horizontal member in a door frame or door lining. →50, →51

door hinge 1 a hinge designed for hanging a door leaf. →38
2 gravity door hinge, see rising hinge. →38
3 swing door hinge, see double-acting hinge.

door holder a door fitting designed to hold a door in an open position, usually a hook or catch attached to a floor or adjacent wall. →51

door ironmongery see door furniture. →51

door jamb 1 one of the vertical members of a door frame. →50
2 see door reveal.

door knob a rounded or oval door handle. →39

door knocker a hinged device attached to a door leaf for tapping against the door leaf to attract the attention of the occupants of a building from outside. →51

door leaf 1 the openable part of a door, usually a hinged or sliding planar construction. →50
2 see active leaf. →50
3 see inactive leaf. →50

door limiter see door chain. →51

door lining, door casing, door buck; boarding etc. to cover the joint between a door frame and surrounding construction at a door reveal.

door lock any lock specially designed for securing a door, operated with a removable key. →51

doormat a mat placed in front of a door for the wiping of feet.

door opening see doorway. →28, →51

door operator 1 see automatic door operator.
2 see swing-door operator.

door panel one of the non-structural infills in a panelled door. →51

door phone see telephone entry system.

door plate 1 see kicking plate. →51
2 see push plate. →51

door post in timber-framed construction, a vertical member at the edge of a door opening onto which the door frame is fixed.

door reveal, door jamb; the vertical flat side of a doorway, perpendicular or skew to the main wall surface.

door schedule a contract document listing types of door, their ironmongery, fire rating and other specifications for a project.

door scope, door viewer, peephole; a security door fitting with a wide-angle lens, through which occupants can view visitors etc. before opening the door. →51

door seal, door strip; a draught excluder for a door.

doorset, door assembly, door unit, door; a manufactured unit consisting of door frame, door leaf, door trim and associated ironmongery. →50

door sill 1 the lowest horizontal member in a door frame; a threshold.
2 the framing member at the base of a door opening of a traditional timber framed building.

door soffit see door head.

door spring a simple door-closing mechanism consisting of a steel spring attached to the door leaf and frame on the hinged side.

door stay see door stop. →51

doorstep the small platform or short stair in front of the external door to a building, making the transition between floor level and external ground level. →28

door stile 1 one of the vertical framing members in a panelled door leaf. →50
2 see shutting stile, closing stile, lock stile. →50

door stop, 1 a rebate or abutment in a door frame against which the door leaf closes. →50
2 door stay, door buffer, door bumper; a fitting set into a wall or floor beside a door to prevent the door leaf or handle from striking the adjacent wall on opening; often a rubber stud or a metal pin with a rubber surround. →51

door strip see door seal.

door swing the curve traced by the edge of a door leaf as it opens, as marked on plan drawings. →50

door transmitter, door buzzer; an electronic doorbell device for an apartment block, often with microphones for inhabitants to communicate with visitors outside the main door.

doortree a door post, or vertical member of a door frame.

door trim a strip of rigid material fixed around a door to cover the joint between door frame and the surrounding construction; an architrave.

door type a door as classified by material, function, opening mechanism or manner etc.; see *door type* illustration. →50, →51

door unit see doorset. →50

door viewer see door scope. →51

doorway, 1 door opening; the opening formed by a door in a wall, into which the door frame is fitted. →28, →51
2 door opening; the open space between the jambs of a door frame and the threshold and door head, in which the door leaf is fitted. →50, →51
see *historical styles of doorway* illustration. →113

Doppler effect in acoustics, an apparent change in pitch of sound as the listener moves towards or away from the source.

Doric pertaining to the architecture of the Doric order; see following entries.

Doric capital a capital at the top of a column of the classical Greek Doric order, consisting simply of a swelling or echinus surmounted by a rectangle. →78, →81

Doric column 1 a column of the classical Greek Doric order, with pronounced entasis, fluting, a

simple capital and no base; considerably sturdier than those of other classical orders. →78
2 see proto-Doric column. →73

Doric cyma an ornamental cyma recta moulding double curved in cross-section, concave at its outer edge and convex at its inner edge; in classical architecture originally rendered with a rectangular version of egg and dart embellishment. →82

Doric entablature see Doric order. →78

Doric order 1 the oldest classical Greek order, originating in Dorian Greece, characterized by fluted columns, a simple capital, no base and an entablature with triglyphs and metopes. →78
2 see Roman Doric order. →79
see *classical Greek orders* illustration. →78
see *Doric order* in Roman amphitheatre illustration. →90
see *Doric order* in superimposed orders illustration. →114

Doric portal see *historical styles of portal* illustration. →113

Doric Roman order see Roman Doric order. →79

dorm shortened form of dormitory.

dormant, dormant tree, dormant; in traditional timber frame construction, an old term for a timber beam or purlin which carries secondary beams.

dormant tree see dormant.

dorment see dormant.

dormer see dormer window.

dormer vault a secondary transverse vault in the side of a larger vault to make an opening for a semicircular or arched window. →25

dormer window a projecting vertical window and surrounding construction located on a pitched roof, usually to afford light to an attic or upper storey space.

dormitorium see dorter, dormitory.

dormitory 1 any communal room primarily for sleeping in.
2 the sleeping quarters of the occupants of a community, especially of students or monks.
3 see dorter.
see *dorter, dormitory* in Carolingian monastery illustration. →97

dormitory area a district whose inhabitants work primarily in another locality.

dormitory suburb a suburban residential area inhabited largely by people who travel to work in a neighbouring city or city centre.

dorsal see dossal. →99

dorter, dormitorium; a dormitory in a monastery. →97

dossal 1 an ornamental cloth for covering the backrest of a seat such as a choir stall, also called a dorsal or dosser. →99
2 an ornamental cloth hung behind an altar or at the sides of the chancel of a church.

dosser see dossal. →99

dosseret an additional block of stone sometimes placed above the capital of Byzantine and Romanesque columns; also called a pulvin, impost block or supercapital. →115

dot matrix in computing, a rectangular area of points which, in various combinations, forms a range of characters on a display or printout.

dot matrix printer see matrix printer.

dot-dash line see chain line.

dote, incipient decay, hardrot; fungal decay which attacks the heartwood of living trees.

dots see plaster dots.

dotted line in technical drawing, a line made up of dots.

double-acting hinge, swing door hinge; a hinge containing a mechanism which allows a swing door to open in either direction.

double-acting spring hinge a double-acting hinge which contains a spring mechanism which automatically returns the door leaf to its closed position.

double antis temple a classical temple type in which frontal columns at both ends are in antis, bounded by extensions of the side walls. →84

double axe see labrys. →122

double bastion see cavalier. →104

double-bay system, engaged system; a pattern of columns to support vaulting in Romanesque basilicas where the side aisles are half the width of the nave, requiring columns for aisle vaulting at half-bay widths along the sides of the nave. →25

double cantilevered spiral stair a spiral stair with treads supported from their midpoints on a helical beam.

double cantilevered stair a stair in which each step is supported only at its midpoint by a sloping beam, and thus cantilevers out sideways in both directions. →45

double chancel church a Carolingian and Romanesque church type which has a chancel at both east and west ends; also called a double-ended church. →97

double-clawed hammer an unusual claw hammer with two sets of claws, one above the other, used for retrieving long nails from wood. →40

double-coated adhesive tape see double-sided adhesive tape.

double cogged joint a timber crossing joint in which a small notch is cut into one member to receive a sunken cog in the other. →4

double cone moulding an ornamental moulding with a series of raised cone motifs joined together, apex to apex, and base to base. →124

double cross 1 see Lorraine cross. →117
2 doubled cross, see patriarchal cross. →117

double crown 1 a British standard paper size; 20" × 30", 508 mm × 762 mm. →Table 6
2 see combined crown. →74

double C-scroll a decorative motif composed of two C-shaped scrolls joined at their tails, in mirror image of one another. →108

double cruciform church any church whose plan is that of a cross intersected by a square.

doubled cross see patriarchal cross. →117

double digging in excavation and landscaping, manual digging to twice the depth of a spade's blade.

double door 1 a door with a pair of leaves meeting in the middle, hung on either jamb of the same frame. →50
2 a door with a pair of leaves hung on the same jamb, opening successively; used for applications with demanding acoustic and thermal requirements. →50
see coupled door. →50
see stable door. →50
see double sliding door. →50

double eagle, double headed eagle; a decorative motif originating in Mesopotamia and often used in heraldry, consisting of a stylized eagle with heads facing in either direction and wings outspread. →122

double elephant a British standard paper size; 27" × 40", 686 mm × 1016 mm. →Table 6

double enceinte a double line of fortification for a castle or town.

double-ended church see double chancel church. →97

double-entry bookkeeping bookkeeping in which each expense or revenue is shown as having an effect on both credits and debits.

double face hammer a small sledgehammer with a face on both ends of the head. →40

double Flemish bond a brickwork bond laid with Flemish bond showing on both inner and outer faces of a solid brick wall more than 9" thick.

double foolscap a British standard paper size; 17" × 27", 432 mm × 686 mm. →Table 6

double gable roof see M-roof. →46

double-glazed unit, double-glazing component, hermetically sealed double-glazed unit; a glazed unit with two panes of glass sealed around an edging strip with a gap between; the gap is usually filled with an inert gas.

double-glazed window a window with two parallel panes of glass with an air space between for improved thermal and sound insulation.

double glazing glazing in which two parallel layers of glass, with a gap between them, separate the inside and outside of a building.
see *glazing* illustration. →53

double-glazing component see double-glazed unit.

double hammer beam truss in traditional timber roof construction, a roof truss with two pairs of hammer beams, one resting on the other.

double headed axe see labrys. →122

double headed eagle see double eagle. →122

double headed nail, duplex nail, scaffold nail, form nail; a nail with two heads on the same shank, one above the other; used in temporary fixings and easily withdrawn with the claw of a hammer. →35

double header bond see Flemish double header bond.

double hipped roof a roof form consisting of two hipped roofs, side by side with a gutter in between, and a common eaves.

double-hung sash window see sash window. →52

double lap joint a timber joint in which two members in the same direction form a lap joint on either side of another timber; used in truss construction.

double lean-to roof a V-shaped roof formed by two lean-to roofs which slope towards each other with a gutter in between. →46

double-loaded corridor block see central corridor block. →61

double-lock welt see double welt. →49

double mini-roundabout an urban road junction in which traffic flow is organized by consecutive mini roundabouts linked by a short stretch of roadway. →62

double monastery a monastery with separate and independently functioning buildings and facilities for both monks and nuns.

double notched joint a timber crossing joint in which the face of both members are cut with notches to receive each other. →4

double ogee moulding see brace moulding. →14

double orientation referring to an apartment or dwelling unit with windows on two external walls, opening out in different directions; a corner or open-ended apartment. →61

double pantile, double S-tile; a wide pantile which has two troughs instead of one. →47

double pipe ring in pipework, a tightenable bracket for fixing two parallel pipes to a wall surface or ceiling soffit.

double pitched roof see curb roof.

double-quirked bead moulding see flush bead moulding. →14

double return stair an ornamental staircase with one flight leading to an intermediate landing, and two flights leading in the return direction from that landing. →45

double roll tile, bold roll tile; a double pantile or double Roman tile. →47

double Roman tile a wide single-lap roof tile with two waterways or channels interspersed with convex projections. →47

double roof see purlin roof. →33

double sash window a window composed of two single glazed windows hung in the same window frame, forming a kind of double glazing; if the two sashes act as one, it is called a coupled window.

double scallop capital a Romanesque scallop capital with only two convex undulations at the underside of each face. →115

double-sided adhesive tape, double-coated adhesive tape, double-side tape; adhesive tape which has an adhesive coating on both sides.

double-side tape see double-sided adhesive tape.

double-skin facade modern facade construction methods making use of an extra cladding of glass attached separately to the external wall surface to utilize effects of cooling and warming of air within the cavity space.

double-skin roof covering roofing construction with waterproofing provided by both a profiled sheeting and an underlying weatherproof membrane.

double sliding door a sliding door with two leaves, either a centre-opening or side-opening door. →50

double spiral screwdriver see spiral ratchet screwdriver.

double S-tile see double pantile. →47

double stretcher bond see monk bond. →18, →191

double tee beam, double tee slab, double T plank; a precast reinforced or prestressed concrete beam component laid in series to form long-span concrete slabs; it is shaped like two adjoining tees in cross-section with an upper flat slab or table and two parallel protrusions or stalks. →27

double tee slab see double tee beam. →27

double temple a classical temple type which has two cellae, each with its own entrance, for the worship of two deities. →85

double tenon joint a strong timber joint in which the end of one member is cut with two tenons to fit into a housing or mortise in another; sometimes called a twin tenon joint or, in varied form, a bridle joint. →5

double T plank see double tee beam. →27

double triangle tie a galvanized steel wire wall tie, in which each end is bent back on itself to form a pair of triangular shapes, also called a twin triangle wall tie. →22

double trumpet junction a flyover road junction in which two major roads cross each other, consisting of two trumpet junctions on opposite sides of one of the roads; traffic flow is ideal for stationing of tollbooths serving a tollroad. →63

double welt, clink, double-lock welt; in sheetmetal roofing, a joint in which two adjacent sheets are doubly bent over each other then hammered down. →49

double window a window which has two lights side by side, separated by a mullion, in the same frame.
see coupled window.
see double glazed window. →53
double-hung sash window, see sash window. →52

doubling piece, tilting fillet, eaves board; in timber roof construction, a timber strip, wedge shaped in cross-section, used to raise the outer edge or the row of tiles or slates at an eaves.

Douglas fir, Oregon pine, British Columbian pine; [*Pseudotsuga menziesii, Pseudotsuga douglasii, Pseudotsuga taxifolia*] a North American softwood with strong reddish timber; the most important structural timber in North America.

doussie see afzelia.

dove any of the small pigeons of the family *Columbidae*, a much used decorative motif, the universal symbol of peace and reconciliation, representative of the Holy Ghost and gentleness in Christian symbolism. →122

dovecote, columbarium, pigeon house; a building or structure with niches and nesting boxes for the keeping of pigeons.

dovetail pertaining to a rhomboid or wedge-shaped form.

dovetail corner joint see box dovetail joint. →5

dovetailed housing see dovetail housed joint. →5

dovetailed joint see dovetail joint. →5

dovetailed notch in log construction, a flush log joint in which the ends of corresponding logs are dovetailed to form a tight interlocking joint. →6
locked dovetailed notch, see locked lap notch. →6

dovetail halved joint, dovetail lap joint; a timber tee half-lap joint in which one halved timber is cut into a dovetail on one or both sides. →4

dovetail housed joint in timber frame construction, a joint in which the member to be housed is dovetailed into a recess; also called a dovetail housing. →4, →5

dovetail housing see dovetail housed joint. →4, →5

dovetail joint any timber joint in which a tenon or lap is splayed to form a wedge-shaped dovetail to fit into a reciprocal housing; also called a dovetailed joint; types included as separate entries are listed below.
box dovetail joint. →5
dovetail corner joint, see box dovetail joint. →5
dovetail halved joint. →4
dovetail housed joint.
dovetail lap joint, see dovetail halved joint. →4
dovetail scarf joint. →3
dovetail tenon joint. →5

dovetail lap joint see dovetail halved joint. →4

dovetail marker see dovetailing template.

dovetail moulding a decorative moulding carved or rendered with a series of rhomboids. →124

dovetail nailing see skew nailing. →3

dovetail saw a medium-sized backsaw or small bow saw whose blade is 200 mm–250 mm long, used for fine work and cutting dovetails and tenons.

dovetail scarf joint a timber lengthening joint in which the halved ends of both timbers are cut with a dovetailed tenon to fit into a corresponding slot. →3

dovetail tenon joint in joinery, a mortise and tenon joint in which the tenon is dovetailed; a wedge or key is driven in to tighten the joint. →5

dovetailing template, dovetail marker; a tool or stencil for marking out dovetail joints.

dowel 1 a piece of joinery timber milled so that it is round in cross-section. →2
2 a small round wooden pin or peg used for fastening joints in timber. →5
3 see wood key. →6
4 see dowel bar.

dowel bar, dowel; in reinforced concrete, a short reinforcing bar which protrudes from the surface of cast concrete, extends across a joint, or onto which a fixing may be attached.

dowel bit see brad point drill. →42

dowel joint any timber joint in which wooden dowels are glued into receiving holes in the members to be connected. →5

dowel nail a wire nail with points at either end, used for fastening secret joints. →35

dowel screw a screw fixing with threads at either end and no head, used for fastening concealed joints in timber. →36

dowel sharpener a sharpened hollow drill bit for chamfering the rims of dowels used in fastening wood joints. →42

dower house a traditional dwelling built on the grounds of a larger house or landed estate as the residence of the landowner's widow, thus making it possible for the following generation to occupy the main buildings.

down conductor in lightning protection for a building, a conductive path to convey current from a lightning strike safely to earth.

down-draught cold, downwardly moving air from the outside, inside a flue or flue system, which restricts its efficiency functioning.

downlight, downlighter; a luminaire which produces a concentrated downward beam of light, used for illuminating high spaces from the ceiling to avoid glare.

downlighter see downlight.

downpipe a vertical water pipe directing rainwater from a roof or roof guttering to the ground or to a drain. →46

downstairs, lower floor; the storey at ground level in a building with two or more stories.
see *downstairs* in brick house illustration. →59

downstand beam a beam which protrudes from the lower surface of a concrete slab.

downtown see city centre.

downy birch see European birch; [*Betula pubescens*].

dpc see damp proof course. →29

dpm see damp proof membrane.

drab see mouse grey.

drachm see dram.

drachma a traditional unit of weight in Scandinavia, Greece, France, Germany and Holland, varying from country to country from 3 to 4 grams.

draft 1 see preliminary.
2 the North American spelling of draught.
3 see drafted margin. →12

draft damper see draught diverter. →56

drafted margin, marginal draft; in the cutting and dressing of stone, an area around the edge of a block of stone dressed initially to facilitate its further squaring and smoothing.

draft excluder see draught excluder.

draft flue system see natural draught flue system.

drafting see draughting. →130

drafting equipment see drawing instruments. →130

drafting film see drawing film.

drafting instruments see drawing instruments. →130

drafting fountain pen see Graphos.

drafting machine see draughting machine. →130

drafting paper see drawing paper.

drafting pen see draughting pen. →130

drafting table see drawing table.

drafting tape see draughting tape.

draft lobby see draught lobby. →59

draftsman see draughtsman.

draftsmanship see draughtsmanship.

draft stabilizer see draught diverter. →56

draft strip see weatherstrip. →52

draft stop a fire-resistant partition in an attic or above a suspended ceiling to prevent the spread of a building fire within ceiling and roof voids.

drag, 1 comb; an implement with a serrated steel blade used in plastering for spreading and evening out plaster surfaces, for removing excess plaster, spreading tiling mortar etc. →43
2 see scratcher.
3 comb; a hand-held metal toothed or serrated plate drawn across the surface of masonrywork to produce a striated finish.

dragged plasterwork see comb-finish rendering.

dragger see flogger. →43

dragging beam see dragon beam.

dragline excavator a crane-like vehicle with a large bucket used for excavating soil and rock below the level at which it is stationed.

dragon a mythical fire-breathing, lizard-like creature with a long tail and often more than one head, often found as a decorative and ornamental motif, symbolic of evil, destruction or the devil. →122

dragon beam, dragging beam; in traditional timber frame construction, a horizontal strengthening roof beam which projects outwards from a corner at 45° and receives the thrust of a hip rafter, also a similar beam in timber floor structures.

dragon's eye an ancient Germanic and Nordic decorative motif consisting of an equilateral triangle divided through its centre by three lines into three equally sized triangles; symbolic of the balance of love, power and wisdom. →123

dragon tie see angle tie.

drain a channel, pipe or system of pipework to convey foul water, surface water, rainwater etc. from buildings within a private boundary; types included as separate entries are listed below.
see *drain* in sauna illustration. →58
agricultural drain, see field drain.
balcony drain, see balcony outlet. →54
discharge pipe. →58
ditch.
filter drain, see field drain.

floor drain. →58
foul water drain, foul drain.
French drain, see field drain.
gravity drain.
gully.
irrigation drain, see subsoil drain.
land drain, see ditch, field drain.
outlet.
rainwater outlet.
sand drain.
sewer.
soil water drain, soil drain.
storm drain.
subsoil drain, subsurface drain. →59
vertical sand drain, see sand drain.

drainage **1** the removal of excess water from a building or construction.
2 the runoff of surface and rainwater from a building or built area into a system of drains.
3 see surface-water drainage.
4 the use of drain systems to remove excess water from building surfaces; see drainage system.
see *drainage* in sauna illustration. →58

drainage channel **1** any large open watercourse for the conveyance, irrigation or drainage of water.
2 a small concave component or recess in a floor or paving etc. for conveying surface water into a gulley or drain. →58

drainage ditch a longitudinal excavation dug into agricultural and forest land to collect suspended groundwater and dry out soil.

drainage gully see gully.

drainage layer that layer of inert granular material in landscaped planting, green roofs etc. beneath the growing medium, which allows water to drain away. →48

drainage membrane see air-gap membrane. →29, →51, →59

drainage pipe a drain pipe or discharge pipe. →58

drainage system a system of drains to convey waste and surface water away from a building to a soakaway, sewer or septic tank.
see *drainage system* in sauna illustration. →58

drain cock in water supply, hot-water heating, air conditioning etc., a tap at the lower end of a system of pipework for emptying the installation of liquid, condensation etc.

drainer a preformed stainless steel kitchen worktop with an integral sink and perforated for the fitting of taps etc., from which water can drain back into the sink.

draining cupboard see drying cupboard.

draining rack, plate rack; a freestanding wire or wooden grill in which crockery is placed after washing, and in which it dries.

drainline see discharge pipe. →58

drain pipe **1** a length of pipe, usually a proprietary component with suitably formed ends, joined in series to form a drain. →58
2 see discharge pipe. →58
3 perforated pipe; a proprietary product consisting of a length of plastic pipe with regular holes or slots, used in a field drain. →59

drain plug in heating, air conditioning and other piped systems, a plug which can be extracted for removal of excess condensation and other liquids.

drain run see discharge pipe. →58

drain valve a valve used to drain water or other liquid from a pipework installation, cistern etc.

Dralon a proprietary name for synthetic fibres of polyacronitrile.

dram, 1 drachm; an avoirdupois weight of $^1/_6$ ounce or 1.77 g.
2 fluid drachm, fluid dram, fluidrachm, fluidram; a unit of liquid volume, in the UK equal to $^1/_8$ fluid ounce, 0.217 cu.in. or 3.56 cc; in the USA equal to 0.225 cu.in. or 3.69 cc.

draped arch, tented arch; an ornamental arch whose intrados has convex haunches, as if draped with hanging fabric. →24

drapery **1** see linenfold. →123
2 see lambrequin. →112

draught, 1 draft (Am.); an upward current of warm air in a flue or chimney which carries smoke and other products of combustion out of a building.
2 the feeling of discomfort arising from the movement of cool air in a space, often from gaps in construction or excess ventilation.
3 a slope given to surfaces of a concrete, plaster etc. mould to aid the release of a cast from it; also called draw.
4 see fibrous plaster draught.
5 draft, see preliminary.

draught diverter, barometric damper (Am.), draught stabilizer; a mechanism for reducing excessive draught in a flue by automatically introducing cold air from the outside into the flue. →56

draughted margin see drafted margin. →12

draught excluder, seal, wind stop, weatherstrip; a strip of flexible material applied into joints between a door or window casement and its frame to prevent the passage of air. →53
see *draught excluder* in window illustration. →53

draught flue system see natural draught flue system.

draughting the profession of producing accurate line drawings of a product, component, building etc., showing various standard annotated views by which it can be presented or constructed; written as drafting in North America. →130

draughting equipment see drawing instruments. →130

draughting film see drawing film.

draughting fountain pen see Graphos.

draughting instruments see drawing instruments. →130

draughting machine, drafting machine; in technical drawing, a device attached to a drawing board, consisting of two rulers hinged and adjustable, used as guides for draughting. →130

draughting paper see drawing paper.

draughting pen a specialized ink pen whose nib consists of a thin metal tube with a wire inside, capable of drawing a line of very exact thickness, used in draughting and technical drawing; also called a stylo pen, drawing or technical pen. →130

draughting table see drawing table.

draughting tape, drafting tape; adhesive paper tape used in draughting for holding down drawings.

draught lobby a small enclosed space immediately after an external door whose purpose is to prevent the movement of cold air, rain or snow into the building. →57, →59

draughtsman, draftsman; a person employed in a design office to carry out technical drawing and draughting.

draughtsmanship, draftsmanship; the art of draughting or technical drawing.

draught stabilizer see draught diverter.

draught strip see weatherstrip. →52

dravida a style in Hindu temple architecture from medieval South India.

draw, draught; in concretework, a slight inclination of the face of formwork to make striking easier.

draw bolt see bolt. →39

drawboring in traditional timber pegged jointing, the practice of drilling holes slightly offset from one another so that when pegs are hammered in, the pieces are pulled together and the joint thus tightened.

drawbridge a hinged bridge lifted by ropes or wires to allow vessels to pass under, traditionally used over a moat for closing off the main gate of a castle or walled town. →103

drawer a rectangular sliding storage box contained in a chest or cabinet and pulled horizontally to open.

drawer lock chisel a chisel with an L-shaped blade for cutting hidden mortises for locks.

drawer unit a standard factory-made furnishing unit consisting of a series of sliding drawers; see chest of drawers.

draw-in see lay-by.

drawing 1 a two-dimensional representation of an area, building, technical installation, component or detail; usually annotated and set out on a sheet of paper, card or film, or produced from a computer file; a drawing containing information for construction is often called a plan; types included as separate entries are listed below.
architectural drawing.
arrangement drawing, see general arrangement drawing.
assembly drawing.
block plan.
component drawing.
component range drawing.
construction drawing.
contract drawing.
detail drawing.
dimensioned drawing.
earthworks plan.
elevation.
fixed furnishings drawing.
floor plan.
foundation drawing.
freehand drawing.
furnishings drawing, see fixed furnishings drawing.
furniture drawing.
general arrangement drawing, general location drawing.
layout drawing.
layout plan, see site layout plan.
line drawing.
location drawing.
location plan, see block plan.
measured drawing.
mounted drawing, see mounting.
outline drawing, see sketch drawing.
paraline drawing.
part plan.
pastel drawing.
pencil drawing.
perspective drawing.
preliminary drawing, see sketch drawing.
production drawing.
projection drawing.
record drawing.
reference drawing, see base sheet.
revised drawing, see revision.
roof plan. →130
sectional drawing, see section.
site plan.
sketch drawing.
structural drawing.
survey drawing, see record drawing.
working drawing.
2 the act of producing the above.
3 see draughting. →130
4 see drawing-in.

drawing board a flat work surface, which may or may not have its own supports, used as a base for draughting and designing. →130

drawing cabinet see drawing chest.

drawing chest, drawing cabinet; a furnishing, often wood or metal, with a number of shallow sliding drawers used for the storage of drawings.

drawing file in computer-aided design, a computer file containing a design or drawings.

drawing film, draughting film, drafting film; transparent or semi-transparent plastic sheet on which ink drawings are produced, used in the design office.

drawing-in, drawing; the installation of electrical cables and wiring into protective conduit by pulling them through.

drawing ink water-based ink used especially for technical drawing and draughting rather than for writing.

drawing instruments the draughting pens, compasses, ink, rubbers, stencils, set squares, rulers etc. required to produce a technical drawing. →130
see *drawing instruments* illustration. →130

drawing knife, draw knife, draw shave, shaving knife; a two-handled, bladed tool used for the removal of excess wood and bark from timber.

drawing office a space within the design department of an establishment or firm in which draughting and designing is practised.

drawing paper, draughting paper, drafting paper; paper on which drawings are produced.

drawing pen see draughting pen. →130

drawing pencil a lead pencil used for drawing; the leads come in a range of degrees of hardness from 6B to 9H; HB is the standard grade.

drawing pin, thumbtack; a pin with a large flat head which can be pushed in by hand to fix paper on board.

drawing plane in perspective and other projection drawing, the plane on which construction lines, vanishing points and the construction itself are drawn.

drawing room a room in a formal dwelling in which guests can be received and to which they can retire for relaxation after dinners etc., a sitting room.

drawings schedule, schedule of drawings; a written tabulated document with a list of project drawings, their content and dates of amendment.

drawing table, draughting table, drafting table (Am.); a drawing board which has been mounted horizontally on supports.

drawing up in drawing and draughting, the making of the final drawing from sketches, underlays and reference drawings.

draw knife see drawing knife.

drawn glass see sheet glass.

drawn sheet glass see sheet glass.

draw-off pipe in pipework, a length of pipe to which a tap, valve or appliance is fitted.

draw-off tap, cock; a tap fitted to piped water supply from which water can be drawn off for use.

draw shave see drawing knife.

dredging excavation work carried out from below a body of water such as a lake, river or the sea, by a special rig mounted on a floating deck.

drench shower a shower device designed to provide a rapid soaking for contents and surfaces in a building in the event of fire.

dressed, surfaced, wrot, planed; referring to sawn timber which has been smoothed with a plane or planer on one or more surfaces. →2

dressed dimension see dressed size.

dressed finish any kind of worked finish to a stonework surface.

dressed size, dressed dimension, neat size; in milled timber, the finished dimension after planing converted timber, slightly smaller than the sawn size.

dressed timber a range of readily available timber sections whose surfaces have been machined smoothed with a plane. →2

dressing, 1 planing, surfacing; the smoothing or finishing of a timber surface with a plane or planer.
2 the surface smoothing of rough timbers with an adze.
3 the working of stone with tools to provide a finished surface.
4 see top dressing.

dressing compound see levelling compound.

dressing room a changing room, especially at a theatre, residential building, retail establishment etc.

dressing up in ornamental plasterwork, the fixing of plaster castings in place, and the associated finishing work.

drier, 1 an agent or compound designed to speed up the drying process of paints and varnishes by oxidation of oils.
2 siccative; metallic salts (oxides of manganese, lead or cobalt), combined with oils, resins and

solvents and mixed with paints and varnishes to accelerate drying.
3 see hardener.
4 see hand drier.
5 see tumble drier.
6 see drying fan.

driftway see bridleway.

drill 1 a tool or machine for drilling or boring a hole.
2 see drill bit. →42
see *types of drill bit* illustration; types included as separate entries are listed below. →42
brad point drill. →42
breast drill.
concrete drill, see masonry drill. →42
electric drill, see power drill.
flat spade drill. →42
glass drill. →42
hammer drill.
hand drill.
masonry drill. →42
metal drill. →42
power drill.
twist drill. →42
wood drill. →42

drill bit a sharpened metal blade for boring holes, often helically shaped, attached to and rotated by the chuck of a brace or drill. →42
see *types of drill bit* illustration; types included as separate entries are listed below. →42
auger bit. →42
brad point drill, dowel bit. →42
centre bit. →42
combination drill bit. →42
countersink. →42
dowel sharpener. →42
expansive bit, expansion bit. →42
flat spade drill. →42
Forstner bit. →42
glass drill. →42
grinding burr. →42
hole saw, tubular saw, hole cutter, annular bit, crown saw. →42
Jennings pattern bit. →42
masonry drill, concrete drill. →42
metal drill. →42
plug cutter. →42
reamer. →42
twist drill. →42
wood drill. →42

drilling, boring; the making of a hole in a material, component or the ground, using a rotating blade or similar device.

drilling hammer a heavy hammer or maul used for striking with cold chisels to drill or punch holes in stone and metal. →40

drill press a power drill vertically mounted in a rigid frame, used for heavy duty drilling and accurate work.

drill stop a circular ring attached to a drill bit to regulate depth of drilling.

drinking fountain an appliance, often found in public places, schools and institutions, consisting of a basin from which a jet of clean drinking water can be discharged.

drinking water see potable water.

drip, throat, throating; in building construction, a slot in the undersurface of a protruding external component such as a sill to prevent water running back to the surface of the building.

drip edge see drop apron.

drip sink a small sink located under a water tap to drain away flow and dripping rather than to contain water.

dripstone see hood-mould. →110

drive-in any commercial facility in which customers can be served or entertained while remaining in their cars.

driven pile in foundation technology, any type of pile placed by driving it into the ground. →29

driver 1 a flat-bladed masonry chisel for dressing stone to a smooth surface. →41
2 device driver; in computing, software or programming which operates a device such as a disk drive or printer.

drive screw see screw nail. →35

driveway a private road leading from a public road up to a building.

driving 1 in foundation construction, the repeated hammering of certain types of pile into the ground using a pile driver or similar apparatus.
2 see piledriving.

driving shoe in foundation construction, a pointed component attached to the lower end of a pile to enable it to be driven more easily into the ground.

drôlerie see drollery.

drollery, drôlerie; grotesque or humorous medieval decorative designs used in carved ornament and for illustrating manuscripts.

dromos 1 Gk; a passage, route or corridor in an ancient building. →65, →91
2 an entrance corridor or ceremonial passageway leading to a domed Greek tomb or tholos. →65

drop 1 see drop panel.
2 see gutta. →78

drop apron, drip edge; in sheet roofing, a flashing laid vertically at an eaves or verge to provide a drip and protect the edge.

drop arch, depressed arch; a form of pointed arch composed of segments whose radii are less than the span of the arch. →24

drop black a variety of vine black pigment.

drop box see murder hole. →103

drop ceiling see false ceiling.

drop chute, rubble chute; a temporary chute with a number of interlocking plastic conical pieces, assembled on site and used for the removal of builder's waste from an upper level in a building during refurbishment or demolition work.

drop hammer, ram; in piledriving or drop-forging, a rig consisting of a heavy steel cylindrical weight known as a monkey, which is hoisted up and then repeatedly dropped from a controlled height to apply percussive force.

droplet see gutta. →78

droplight see pendant luminaire.

drop panel a thickening in a flat slab or mushroom slab floor at a column head to spread the load from the slab and reinforce the joint; also called a drop.

drover see boaster. →41

droveway see bridleway.

drugstore see chemist.

drum see tambour. →26

drum dome a dome which sits atop a cylindrical wall structure or tambour.

drum tower a cylindrical tower, often in a castle or palace. →103

drunken saw, wobble saw; a circular saw set so that it does not rotate in one plane; used to cut a groove or kerf.

dry see shake.

dry area 1 an area in a building in which the air is free of moisture, or which is not used for washing or other activities involving water.
see *dry area flooring* illustration. →44
2 see basement area.

dry ashlar walling ashlar masonry which has been laid without mortar to bond the joints.

dry brush technique in painting, the use of stiff pigment brushed on to textured paper such that it clings to raised areas only.

dry-bulb temperature the temperature of air as indicated by an ordinary thermometer.

dry cleaning powder in draughting in ink, a non-abrasive powder sprinkled over draughting film to keep the surface clean and grease free.

dry closet a toilet in which flushing liquid is not used.

dry dash a hardwearing finish for concrete or masonry in which the surface has been treated with a coating of mortar to which aggregate is then applied; see also pebbledash, shingle dash, spar dash.

dry fresco see fresco secco.

dry glazing glazing in which preformed polymeric seals and gaskets are used for fixing the glass in its frames rather than liquid sealants, putty etc. →52

dry hydrate a white powder, calcium hydroxide, $Ca(OH)_2$, manufactured by the controlled addition of water to quicklime, calcium oxide, **CaO**; see also slaked lime, hydrated lime.

drying 1 the evaporation of water from a material.
2 the transformation of a coat of paint, coating etc. from liquid to solid state.
3 see forced drying.
4 see seasoning. →1
5 see dewatering.

drying cupboard, 1 airing cupboard; a warm ventilated cupboard for the drying and storage of laundered and wet linen and garments.
2 draining cupboard; a kitchen unit, situated over a drainer or sink unit, with a perforated rack in which crockery is placed after it has been washed.

drying fan, drier; any fan which blows out a stream of warm air, used for drying of work on site, laundry etc.

drying oil any oil used in paints as a vehicle which then dries by oxidation or absorption of air to form a tough adhesive film.

drying rack a fixed or loose furnishing on which objects, textiles etc. may be left to dry.

drying rail see towel rail.

drying room a room often adjoining a wash-room for drying laundry.

drying shrinkage see dry shrinkage.

dry joint a masonry joint without mortar.

dry kiln a large oven for seasoning converted timber.

drylining see plasterboard drylining.

dry main see dry standpipe.

dry mix 1 dry mix plaster; see preblended plaster.
2 see dry mix concrete.

dry mix concrete dry mix cement with aggregate added, delivered to site where water is added to form concrete.

dry mix mortar see preblended mortar.

dry mix plaster see preblended plaster.

dry-mix process a sprayed concrete process in which damp aggregate and dry cement are mixed with water in the nozzle of a pump prior to being projected at high velocity; see wet-mix process.

Dryobalanops spp. see kapur.

dry packed concrete concrete which has a low water content when fresh, and is compacted by ramming.

dry packing, dry-tamp process; the placing of concrete which is damp and stiff rather than wet, into existing hollows and joints where it is tamped with a suitable tool.

dry-pipe system a sprinkler installation used for subzero applications, whose pipes are connected to a permanent supply of water, but under normal conditions are full of air under pressure; in the event of a fire the air draws water from a main into the system.

drypoint a technique of making graphic prints in which an image is scribed into a metal printing plate using a sharp pointed tool, forming small furrowed channels which collect ink for printing.

dry powder non-conducting, non-toxic, water repellent fine powder used in some fire extinguishers to smother flames and cool outbreaks of fire.

dry-powder extinguisher a fire extinguisher used for putting out fires caused by electrical faults and burning liquids; it is operated by exuding dry inflammable powder, see above.

dry pressing, semi-dry pressing; a method of producing clay bricks and other ceramic products by the mechanical compressing of clay powder with a water content of 6–10% into suitable shapes.

dry ridge tile a special roof tile formed to cover a ridge, fixed with a clip without mortar bedding.

dry rot, tear fungus; [*Serpula lacrymans*], [*Merulius lacrymans*] a fungal decay which attacks damp timber in unventilated spaces; also a general name for similar fungi.

dry shrinkage, drying shrinkage; in concretework, a reduction in physical size on hardening due to the evaporation of water.

dry standpipe, dry main; an empty vertical water pipe running the full height of a building, to which a fire hydrant or pumper vehicle can be connected to provide water for firefighting at each floor of the building.

dry-stone wall a freestanding masonry wall used for boundary fencing of stacked stones without mortar; see next entry.

dry-stone walling the technique of constructing walls using unworked or roughly tooled stones stacked without the use of mortar.

dry-tamp process see dry packing.

dry to handle a stage in the drying of paint at which paintwork will not be damaged by handling.

dry to touch see touch dry.

dry walling any masonry walling laid without the use of bonding mortar.

drywall see plasterboard drylining.

drywall screw, plasterboard screw; a self-tapping screw with a thin shank, fine threads and flat wide head, used for fixing plasterboard to studwork. →36

dual carriageway, divided carriageway; a road consisting of two carriageways containing traffic moving in opposite directions, separated by a central reservation. →63

dual duct system an air-conditioning system in which hot and cold air are provided in separate ducts and mixed locally according to a thermostat.

dual duct terminal unit, mixing box; a component in a dual duct air-conditioning system in which hot and cold air are blended according to strictly controlled conditions before being released to a space.

dual-flush cistern a water-saving WC-flushing cistern which provides the user with the alternative of flushing with two different amounts of water.

dubbing the application of a first layer of plaster to level off recesses and gaps in a plastering background such as lathing, masonry etc., also called dubbing out.

dubbing out see dubbing.

ducento the 1200s in Italian art.

duckstone see pebble. →15

duct 1 any sealed channel in a building for the passage of air, waste gases, electric cables and other services.
2 see air duct.
3 see cable duct.

ducted flue a flue system in which intake and outlets are in the same duct or flue.

ductility the property of a material, particularly a metal, to be able to undergo plastic deformation without fracturing.

due date, payment date; the date by which a payment or monetary instalment should be made towards a loan, fees etc.

dumb scraper see scraper. →41

dumb waiter a small service lift designed for use in restaurants to transfer food between a kitchen and dining hall on different levels.

dumbell interchange see dumb-bell junction. →63

dumb-bell junction a road junction in which a major road is overpassed by a minor road whose slip roads are linked with a pair of mini roundabouts; also written as dumbell junction or interchange. →63

dummy a hammer whose head is of a soft metal such as zinc or lead, used for striking wooden headed chisels. →40

dummy furniture any fittings for a door or window which have no function other than decoration.

dummy joint, groove joint; in concretework, a longitudinal groove cast in the surface of concrete designed to provide a natural line for inevitable cracking during drying and expansion.

dump see rubbish dump.

dump bucket concreting a method of placing concrete by lowering batches by crane in a closed container, from where it is discharged via a hatch into formwork or excavations.

dumper a small steerable motor vehicle with four rubber-tyred wheels and a tippable hopper or skip for moving earth and other materials on site.

dumpling a mass of unexcavated soil left as excavation work is carried out initially at the edges, removed from the site as the work nears its end.

dun a circular fortified settlement from Iron Age Scotland and Ireland.

dung-beetle see scarab. →75

dungeon, donjon; a strongroom, usually in the basement of a castle or fortification, for the enforced confinement of people. →103

duofaced hardboard hardboard which is smooth on both surfaces.

duomo an Italian cathedral.

duopitch roof see saddleback roof. →46

duplex apartment see maisonette.

duplex house see semi-detached house. →61

duplex nail see double headed nail. →35

duplex stainless steel a chemically resistant, strong and hardwearing stainless steel developed in the 1950s, containing 25% chromium and small percentages of nickel, copper and molybdenum.

duplicate, copy; an exact copy of something such as a key, photograph, receipt, artwork, moulded object etc.

durability the property of a material or component to be longlasting, especially in terms of repeated use under force, other changing circumstances, the weathering of the elements etc.

durable concrete concrete that withstands the purpose and lifespan for which it was designed.

duramen see heartwood. →1

durbar the reception rooms in a Persian or Indian palace.

durmast oak, sessile oak; [*Quercus petraea*]; a species of European oak tree with heavy, hard and strong pale brown timber marketed as European or English oak.

dust a shade of grey which takes its name from the colour of earth dust.

dust dry, dust free; a stage in the drying of paint at which airborne dust will no longer stick to the surface.

dust free see dust dry.

dusting brush a handled brush with soft bristles, used in printing and graphic work for sweeping dust, dirt and erasing residue from artwork, drawings and prints. →43

dust-pressed tile a tile manufactured by pressing into shape from semi-dry granulated clay then fired.

dustproof relating to a construction or mechanism which is protected by casing etc. so that the accumulation of dust does not affect its performance.

dust tightness a material or spatial property, the ability to prevent the flow of particles of dust from one space into another.

dust-tight referring to a component or construction which is sealed so as to prevent the entry of dust.

dustbin see refuse bin.

dustbin lorry see waste collection vehicle.

dustcart see waste collection vehicle.

Dutch arch, French arch; an arch in brick formed by leaning rectangular-shaped pieces whose intrados is horizontal and nearly straight. →23

Dutch bond, 1 staggered Flemish bond (Am.); a brickwork bond in which each course consists of alternating headers and stretchers, with headers in consecutive header courses laid with a half-header overlap. →18
2 see Dutch paving. →15

Dutch paving paving in different sized square pavers and slabs, laid in a diagonal interlocking pattern, a type of herringbone pattern. →15

Dutch white a form of the pigment white lead made by an old Dutch process.

dwarf gallery a low arcade with small arches supported on colonnettes with a passage behind, often a feature in the exterior wall of a tower, cathedral etc., and bound by string courses. →99

dwarf wall a low masonry or brick wall.

dwelling a permanent residential unit usually containing sleeping, cooking and sanitary facilities; the collective name for a house, flat, home etc.
see *types of residential building* illustration. →61

dwelling house see residential building.

dwelling type a dwelling as categorized by its layout of spaces, number of levels or whether or not it is part of a larger building.

dwelling unit a single fully functioning unit of accommodation in a larger building or complex; a flat or house. →61
see *dwelling unit* in residential buildings illustration. →61

dye, dye-stuff; a colourant which, unlike a pigment, is soluble in a liquid; used for colouring fabrics.

dyer's broom see genet.

dyer's rocket Reseda luteola, see weld.

dye-stuff see dye.

dyke, 1 dike; a low wall or causeway of turf or stone built as a boundary marker, division or enclosure in post-Roman Britain.
2 a wall construction built along the coastline of low-lying countries to protect land against flooding.

dyke rock see hypabyssal rock.

dynametropolis in town planning theory, a chain of dynapolises or settlements designed in such a manner as to accommodate future development and growth.

dynamic referring to a work of art or aesthetic composition which, through use of line, colour and form, expresses tension or the idea of movement.

dynamic art art or composition characterized by movement, direction and rhythmical elements and the contrasts of form and colour.

dynamic compaction a method of consolidating granular soils prior to construction by the repeated dropping of a heavy weight over areas of the soil.

dynamic consolidation, ground bashing, heavy tamping; in groundwork, the strengthening of poor soils by repeatedly dropping a heavy ram at intervals to form pits which are then filled with sand and compacted; also known as ground compaction or ground compression.

dynamic load any structural load which includes a moving element or impact such as the loads on a floor caused by the walking of occupants.

dynamic penetration testing in soil investigation, penetration testing in which the testing implement is hammered with percussive force into the soil.

dynamics, kinetics; the branch of mechanics which deals with forces acting on bodies to produce a change in motion.

dynamism see futurism.

dynamite a powerful high explosive made from nitroglycerine, nitrocellulose and ammonium nitrate, used in blasting.

dynapolis in town planning, an orderly planned and rapidly growing city which expands around an inner city area along traffic arteries.

dysprosium a radioactive chemical element, **Dy**, used in nuclear reactors.

E

eachea in classical architecture, clay or bronze urns built into masonry to improve the acoustics of theatres.

eagle depictions of the great bird of prey, *Aquila spp.,* the 'king of the birds'; in architectural ornament symbolizing the heavens, sun, gods and kings, power and majesty in general; attribute of the apostle John. →119

eagle capital a Romanesque column carved with four eagle motifs.

ear see sheetmetal cleat.

early Baroque the early stage in Baroque architecture c.1580–1620.

Early Christian architecture church architecture from the first few centuries of Christianity in Europe during the late Roman period from 200 to 600 AD.
see *Early Christian basilica* illustration. →95

Early English style an architectural style in England from 1150 to 1280; the first of three phases of English Gothic based on Norman and French models and characterized by sparse decoration and no tracery.

early Gothic 1 the first period in the development of Gothic architecture in France from 1140 to 1200, in England represented by the Early English style, and elsewhere in Europe from 1150 to 1300.
see *early Gothic window* illustration. →111
see *Romanesque and Gothic capitals* illustration. →115
2 see Early English style.

early Renaissance Renaissance architecture from the early period, quattrocento in Italy, c.1420–1490.
see *early Renaissance window* illustration. →111

early stiffening see false set; an outdated term.

earlywood, springwood; the portion of the annual ring of a tree which forms first and has large, low density cells.

earth 1 material excavated from the upper layers of the ground, fine mineral material or topsoil.
2 ground (Am.); the mass of conductive earth whose potential is zero, to which cables in a low voltage electrical system are also connected.

earth colour, earth pigment, natural pigment; any of a number of natural pigments such as ochre, umber and chalk made from coloured mineral earth; see below for list of earth colours and mineral pigments; types included as separate entries are listed below.
bole.
brown ochre.
burnt sienna.
brown iron oxide, see burnt sienna.
burnt umber.
Caledonian brown, burnt sienna.
Cappagh brown, umber.
caput mortuum.
chestnut brown, raw umber.
colcothar.
glauconite, see green earth.
gold ochre.
green earth.
Indian red, see oxide red.
Italian earth, see burnt sienna.
iron yellow, see Mars yellow.
jacaranda brown, see burnt umber.
Mars yellow, Mars orange.
mineral brown, see burnt umber.
natural brown iron oxide, see burnt sienna.
ochre, ocher.
oxide red.
Persian red, see oxide red.
raw sienna, see sienna.
raw umber.
red ochre, see red oxide paint.
red oxide paint.
reddle, see red oxide paint.
Roman ochre, yellow ochre.
ruddle, see red oxide paint.
Sicilian brown, see raw umber.
Siena, see sienna.
sienna.
sil, yellow ochre.
Spanish brown, see burnt umber.
terra alba.
terra di Siena, see sienna.
terra ombre, see raw umber.
terra rossa, see red oxide paint.
Terra Sienna, see sienna.
terra verde, see green earth.
umber, umbre.
Venetian red, see oxide red.
yellow ochre.
yellow oxide of iron, see Mars yellow.

earth-coloured, mould; a shade of dark greyish brown which takes its name from the colour of dry earth or mould.

earth electrode an electrical conductor such as a cable or metal pipe buried in the ground, making an earth connection for a building's electrical installation with it.

earthenware a ceramic material which contains a relatively high proportion of limestone and is used for wall tiles and ordinary quality china crockery.

earthing the connection of an electrical supply to the ground, or the result of this.

earth-moving in building construction, any operation such as excavation or backfilling prior to laying foundations which involves movement of earth.

earthquake a natural catastrophic movement, cracking, upheaval and shaking of the earth's crust caused by the release of interior geological forces and by volcanic action.

earthquake load structural loads on a building imposed by the sporadic occurrence of an earthquake, taken account of in structural calculations in regions where one is liable to occur.

earthquake resistance the ability of the structure of a building to withstand the effects of an earthquake.

earth pigment see earth colour.

earth pressure in geotechnical engineering, the pressure exerted by a mass of ground on a retaining wall or similar construction (see active earth pressure) or the exertion required to deform a mass of earth (see passive earth pressure).

earth termination the lowest component in a lightning protection installation, any metal constructions providing a low resistance path to earth for surges of electrical current from lightning strikes.

earthwork 1 any work on a construction site involving digging, moving, filling and levelling earth; sometimes called groundwork.
2 see groundwork.
3 rampart; any artificial mound of earth, ditch or embankment used as a defensive fortification; see work, outwork.
see *fortification* illustration. →104
4 see agger. →104
5 see outwork. →104

earthworks plan a drawing to show the scope of excavations, ground levels, areas of fill for a construction project.

eased arris see pencil round. →14

eased edge see pencil round. →14

easement a legal right of use of part of a private area of land, such as a path, drain or waterway running through it, by a party which does not own the land.

east one of the points of the compass, the direction from which the sun rises and lies in the Northern hemisphere at six o'clock in the morning.

east chancel a choir at the east end of a medieval choir, usually the main choir or chancel. →97

east end the end section of a church containing the main altar, traditionally facing east in Early Christian and medieval architecture. →116

eastern hemlock, hemlock spruce (Am.); [*Tsuga canadensis*] a North American softwood with soft, pale brown timber; used for interior work and fencing.

eastern larch see tamarack.

eastern red cedar, aromatic cedar; [*Juniperus virginiana*] a North American softwood with white streaked red and highly aromatic timber; used for fence posts, shingles and mothproof closet linings.

eastern cross see Russian cross. →117

Easter sepulchre see sepulchre. →116

East Indian rosewood see Indian rosewood.

East Indian satinwood see Ceylon satinwood.

easy-clean hinge, cleaning hinge; a hinge for a side or top hung casement window, whose pin is projected outward from the plane of the leaves, thus making it easier to clean the windows. →38

eaves the junction of the roof and wall of a building.
see sectional drawing of **eaves**. →46
see **eaves** in timber-framed building. →57

eaves board 1 a timber board laid across rafters at an eaves to raise the lower edge of the bottom row of tiles in a tiled roof to the same angle as the other tiles; same as a doubling piece.
2 see fascia board. →48

eaves closure piece a component fitted beneath the sheeting at the eaves to block up the corrugations in profiled sheet roofing.

eaves course the lowest course of roof tiles laid as roofing; if a double course is used, the upper of the two.

eaves flashing, pressed metal flashing, sheetmetal flashing; preformed sheetmetal or other sheeting product to convey rainwater away from adjacent eaves construction, or to rainproof an eaves. →49

eaves gutter a channel at eaves level to collect rainwater from the roof of a building and convey it to a downpipe. →46

eaves height the vertical height of the meeting of elevation and roof line in a building, measured from ground level.

eaves soffit see soffit board. →46

eaves tile a special roof tile which is shorter than other tiles, used for the lowest or eaves course in roofing.

eaves ventilator a device or component for providing an unobstructed ventilation path into roof space or roof construction at an eaves.

ebb tide the local periodical lowering of the sea level at coastlines due to the action of the moon, see also low tide.

ebonite, vulcanite; a form of fully vulcanized hard rubber.

ebony 1 [*Diospyros spp.*] hardwoods from South and Central America, Africa, South-East Asia and Australia with black, hard, strong and durable timber; used for carving and ornamental cabinetwork; see ***Diospyros spp.*** for full list of related species included in this work.
2 a shade of black which takes its name from the colour of ebony heartwood.

eccentric referring to something which is off-centre; eccentric motion occurs when a circle is rotated about a point other than its centre.

ecclesiasterion, 1 ekklesiasterion (Gk); a building or place for performing and dance, and for large public political gatherings in ancient Greek colonial architecture. →92
2 a meeting room in early Christian architecture.
3 any hall for religious meetings.

Eckhart method see method of intersections. →127

echelon parking see angle parking. →62

echinus 1 in classical architecture, a ring-shaped moulding carved around the lower part of a Doric capital or above the head of a caryatid, making the transition from the abacus to the column shaft; ekhinos in Greek. →81
see *classical orders* illustrations. →78, →79
see *classical capital* illustration. →81
see *caryatid* illustration. →76
2 a decorated moulding beneath the cushion of an Ionic capital. →80

echinus and astragal see egg and dart. →82

echo in acoustics, sound reflected with such intensity as to be perceived as a distinct sound.

echoing a description of a device or space in which echoes are produced, or in which they naturally occur.

echo-sounding, depth sounding; the surveying of depth and measuring of the profile of the sea bed etc. using a device which operates using reflected ultrasound.

eclectic an artist who produces work which combines elements from a number of styles, movements or theories.

Eclecticism a name given to a style of European and American architecture from the 1800s, characterized by the use of decorative motifs from a range of different styles.

Eclectic style see Fantastic style.
see *Pompeian styles* illustration. →126

eclogite a mottled metamorphic rock which contains a large proportion of a red variety of the mineral garnet; used locally for aggregates and decorative slabs.

e-coating see electro-dip painting.

ecological architecture architecture and construction whose philosophy is based on the use of energy-saving materials, methods and systems and makes use of ecological methodology.

ecological study in town planning, the environmental study of forests, surface and subsurface water, marshlands, features of unique visual quality etc. and the natural processes they support.

ecology a branch of science which deals with the relations between living organisms and their environment.

economic pertaining to the management of finances and resources.

economical reasonably priced, efficient or using little energy.

economic study in town planning, the analysis of systems of production, distribution, and consumption, including manufacture, agriculture, extraction, trade, finance, transport, government etc.

economizer a subsidiary water heater for preheating water conveyed to a boiler by passing it over tubes containing hot combustion gases.

economy, 1 the management of material resources for a particular area or community.
2 efficiency; the use of material resources, energy, finances etc. in a sparing way, or in a way such as to maximize output.

ecosystem the interaction of the living organisms and their natural environment in any particular place.

ecotone in landscape architecture, the area where two different environments or ecosystems merge.

ecru see beige.

eddy a small vortex in a liquid, gas or electrical field.

eddy flow see turbulent flow.

edge 1 the extremity, side, boundary or arris of an object, surface or area.
2 the sharp boundary line between two perpendicular planes, as with adjacent sides of a block etc.; an arris. see *edge* in brickwork illustration. →21
3 radial surface; the narrower side of a piece of sawn timber, which, if converted in the traditional manner, has growth rings running approximately radially in relation to the original log from which it was cut. →2

edge bead see edge strip. →2

edge beam in structures, a beam which bears the outer edge of a slab, floor or roof construction, from which exterior non-loadbearing walling or cladding is often supported.

edge bedding the laying of a brick or stone in masonrywork with its natural bedding plane vertical and perpendicular to the plane of the wall rather than the usual horizontal; used with stones laid in arches, soldier courses and copings. →21

edge column, corner column; a column at the termination of a colonnade, especially one in a classical Ionic peristyle temple where the volutes of the capital are evident on two adjacent sides. →80

edged, squared; a description of sawn timber in which the wane has been trimmed off to produce a rectangular section.

edge form, side form; formwork used for casting the edge of a concrete slab.

edge grain the surface of a piece of sawn timber which has been roughly radial in the original log.

edge grained see quartersawn.

edge-halved tenon joint a mortise and tenon joint in which the tenon is cut to one edge of the end of a member. →5

edge knot a knot at the edge of a piece of timber.

edge panel in concretework, a precast concrete wall panel designed for use at an external corner.

edge roll see bowtell. →14

edge-rolled column a square column whose arrises are embellished with round mouldings. →13

edge straightness the specification of timber boards, tiles etc. to be supplied with edges straight and true.

edge strip, edging, edge bead; **1** a length of timber, plastics or metal trim to cover the edge of a panel, component or joint. →2, →14
2 angle bead, corner bead, L-profile; a milled timber profile which is L shaped in cross-section; see above.

edging 1 in the primary conversion of timber, the removal of one or two curved edges from a log to provide a flat edge prior to through and through sawing. →2
2 the removal of wane from sawn boards. →15
3 see edge strip. →2
4 in landscape design, a border strip for a carriageway, path, area of planting etc. →15

edict pillar smooth-shafted freestanding ceremonial columns originally erected by the Indian ruler Asoka (273–232 BC); capped with lotus capitals carved with animal motifs, expounding Buddhist teachings; also called edict column. →69

edifice a building or structure, often large or imposing.

Edison screw cap see screw cap.

EDP acronym for electronic data processing, see computing.

educational building any building offering taught instruction including nursery and elementary schools, secondary and specialized schools, colleges and universities.

educational park a number of schools or educational units situated in a park and grouped round a central core which provides shared facilities.

Edwardian period an architectural style in England during the reign of Edward VII (1901–1910); it is characterized by the use of Baroque elements in public buildings, and a romance for the past in domestic architecture.

effect 1 the result of a certain set of actions or plan.
2 in architecture and the arts, the outward appearance or impression caused by use of a certain material, form or other device.

efficacy see circuit efficacy.

efficiency 1 the management of a system and machine with minimum loss of energy, time etc.
2 see economy.

effigy mound a large-scale prehistoric earthwork found in American Indian culture, depicting a snake, bird or other animal.

efflorescence, 1 bloom; an often temporary defect in clay brickwork caused by soluble salts which are leached from new bricks and deposited as white crystals on the surface.
2 a defect in paintwork caused by condensation and resulting in a surface deposition of crystals of soluble salts which have migrated to the surface of the dry paint film.

effluent the liquid component of pretreated or untreated sewage conveyed to a waste water treatment plant.

effusion the passage of water vapour in circumstances when the size of pores in building construction is smaller than the average distance between adjacent water molecules.

effusive rock see volcanic rock.

egg and anchor see egg and dart. →82

egg and arrow see egg and dart. →82

egg and dart, egg and anchor, egg and arrow, egg and tongue, echinus and astragal; a classical Ionic decorative motif consisting of a series of carved ovular protrusions alternating with sharp dart-shaped infill; see also Ionic cyma. →80, →82

egg and tongue see egg and dart. →82

egg-crate ceiling see cell ceiling.

eggplant see aubergine.

eggshell a general word to describe a grade of glossiness in a dry paint surface, that between gloss and flat; in the USA, the second of four grades of glossiness, slightly more reflective than flat.

eggshell flat, low sheen, silk; the second of five grades of glossiness in a dry paint surface, characterized by little sheen from oblique angles.

eggshell gloss, low gloss, satin; the middle of five grades of glossiness in a dry paint surface, midway between gloss and matt.

egress see means of egress.

Egyptian architecture architecture in ancient Egypt from c.2850 BC to the Roman conquest in 30 BC; it is characterized by stone burial tombs, massive pylons and geometrical structures, the use of beam and post construction, and elegantly carved and coloured religious and mythical motifs. →70, →71, →73
see *Egyptian burial monuments* illustration. →70
see *Egyptian pyramid complex* illustration. →71
see *Egyptian temples* illustration. →72
see types of *Egyptian column* illustration. →73
see *Egyptian systems of proportion* illustration. →106
see *Egyptian rock-cut tomb* illustration. →74
see *Egyptian mythology* illustration. →74
see Old Kingdom. →70
see Middle Kingdom. →72
see New Kingdom.

Egyptian blue, Alexandrian blue, Italian blue, Pompeian blue, Pozzuoli blue; a blue pigment consisting of a mixture of copper silicates used by the ancients in ceramics and fresco painting; one of the earliest artificial pigments.

Egyptian brown see mummy.

Egyptian capital capitals adorning ancient Egyptian columns, often richly carved with plant motifs such

as lotus and papyrus, or with the heads of deities such as Osiris and Hathor. →73
see types of *Egyptian capital* illustration. →73

Egyptian column stone columns in ancient Egyptian architecture, often carved as in the form of stems of plants or deities. →73
see types of *Egyptian column* illustration. →73

Egyptian cross 1 see ankh. →117
2 see tau cross. →117

Egyptian crown see white crown. →74
see red crown. →74
see combined crown. →74

Egyptian green a green variety of Egyptian blue pigment.

Egyptian hall a secular function hall with a peristyle or internal row of columns dividing the space into aisles, as described by Vitruvius and favoured in buildings of the Palladian style.

Egyptian heraldic pillar ancient Egyptian free-standing granite pillars carved with the emblems of Upper and Lower Egypt, lily (or lotus) and papyrus respectively; found in pairs and symbolic of the unification of the two kingdoms. →73

Egyptian lotus see blue lotus. →82, →121

Egyptian portal see *historical styles of portal* illustration. →113

Egyptian pyramid 1 great burial structures erected by the Pharaohs of Egypt, notably at Giza, usually, but not always, consisting of four sloping triangular sides culminating at an apex. →71
2 see step pyramid. →70
3 see bent pyramid. →70
4 see Nubian pyramid. →70

Egyptian rock-cut tomb see rock-cut tomb, *Egyptian rock-cut tomb* illustration. →74

Egyptian temple see below for list of types of temple.
cave temple, see rock-cut temple. →68
funerary temple, see mortuary temple. →70, →72
mortuary temple. →70, →72
pylon temple. →72
pyramid temple. →70, →71
rock-cut temple. →68, →72
sun temple. →72
terraced temple. →72
valley temple. →71

eight-pointed star a star with eight radiating limbs. →123
mullet of eight points. →123
see octagram. →108

einsteinium an unstable chemical element, **Es**.

ekhinos Greek form of echinus. →81

ekistics the name given by Constantinos A. Doxiadis in 1944 to the science of human settlements embracing architecture, town planning, economics, politics, anthropology and history.

ekklesiasterion Gk; see ecclesiasterion. →92

elaeothesium Lat.; a room in an ancient Greek bath house or gymnasium in which bathers were anointed with oils; Greek form is elaiothesion. →91

elaiothesion Greek form of elaeothesium. →91

elastic compression see immediate settlement.

elastic curve see deflection curve.

elastic deformation, elastic strain; in structures, the change in dimension of a member under load within a range over which it will resume its original form when the load is released.

elastic glazing compound an elastic sealant used as a glazing compound.

elasticity the ability of a material or structural member to recover its original form after loading forces on it are released.

elastic limit the point at which a material under continuously increasing loading begins to undergo plastic deformation and will not return to its original shape.

elastic modulus see modulus of elasticity.

elastic sealant a flexible sealant which responds to movement between jointed components or materials by stretching or compressing accordingly.

elastic strain see elastic deformation.

elastomer an elastic material containing modified natural or synthetic rubber, which can be stretched and will return to its original form once stresses on it are released.

elastomeric adhesive, synthetic rubber glue; a rubber-like glue manufactured by a chemical process from polymers such as acrylic; used for gluing and sealing a wide range of materials.

elastomeric sealant a sealant applied as liquid or paste which cures to form a flexible solid.

elbow, knee; a piece of curved pipe or pipe fitting to form a sharp acute bend in a pipeline; see bend.

elbow board see window board. →53

elbow brace see cranked brace.

electric referring to a device or system which consumes, produces or contains electricity.

electrical operated by or concerned with electricity; see also electric.

electrical appliance any device or appliance which is powered by electricity.

electrical cabinet, electrical cupboard; a built-in cupboard or proprietary storage unit containing control equipment and meters serving the electrical installation of a building.

electrical circuit an arrangement of wires and electronic components around which electricity flows to perform a function.

electrical conductance the ability of a given object to transmit or conduct electricity, the inverse of resistance, measured as current divided by voltage; its unit is the siemen.

electrical conductivity the measure of how well a given material will conduct electrical current, the inverse of resistivity, measured as conductance per unit volume.

electrical conductor 1 any material, object or component through which electricity flows freely.
2 a component specifically designed to conduct electricity.

electrical conduit small diameter plastic or metal piping laid in construction to contain a building's electrical installation wiring; sometimes known as pipe duct.

electrical connector an electric point with holes or protrusions designed to connect two parts of an installation circuit together.

electrical contact that part of an electric circuit or device by which a connection can be made.

electrical contract see electrical works contract.

electrical contractor see electrical works contractor.

electrical cupboard see electrical cabinet.

electrical energy, electric power; energy created by electromagnetic activity.

electrical engineer a qualified consultant who designs the electrical installations for a building, oversees their installation etc.

electrical engineering a discipline which deals with the technology of electricity and its use for servicing buildings and installations.

electrical installation 1 the circuitry, wiring, control gear and fixed appliances for providing and maintaining an electricity supply within a building.
2 the job of work involved in attaching and connecting the above; also called electrical installation work.

electrical installation contract see electrical works contract.

electrical installation contractor see electrical works contractor.

electrical insulation in electrical installations, non-conductive coatings for components and conductors.

electrical lock see electric lock.

electrically wired hinge see electric hinge.
electrical power generation the generation of electricity for supply to a community or area-wide network.
electrical power transmission the distribution of electricity from a power station via substations to places of consumption.
electrical resistance, resistance; the opposition to flow of electricity in a conductor, measured as amps per volt, whose basic unit is the ohm, Ω.
electrical resistor, resistor; a device for inhibiting the flow of electricity in a circuit and converting it into heat.
electrical work see electrical installation work.
electrical works contract, electrical installation contract, electrical contract; a contract for the electrical installation work in a building project.
electrical works contractor, electrical installation contractor, electrical contractor; a specialized contractor, reputable firm etc. which carries out electrical installation work in a building project.
electric boiler a domestic water heater powered by electricity.
electric cable an insulated metal wire or bundle of wires, part of an electrical installation for conveying electricity.
electric charge the amount of electrical energy in a body, component, system etc.
electric cooker, electric stove; an electrical appliance with an oven and hotplates for cooking food.
electric current the rate of flow of electric charge whose SI unit is the ampere (A).
electric drill see power drill.
electric eraser in technical drawing, an eraser powered by a small motor which produces a spinning action.
electric fan heater see fan heater.
electric field an area around charged particles which exerts forces on other charged matter.
electric heater a heating device which converts electrical energy into useful heat.
electric fan heater, see fan heater.
see electric water heater.
electric heating space and other heating for a building for which the energy source is electricity.
electric hinge, electrically wired hinge; a hinge which allows for the passage of electrical wires from electric fittings and locks in a door leaf to a door frame.
electrician a tradesman or skilled worker who is responsible for the installation and repair of electrical services.
electricity a form of energy resulting from the existence of charged subatomic particles such as the electron and proton.
electricity board, power generating board; a company which provides, monitors and maintains an electricity supply service.
electricity consumption 1 the amount of electrical energy used by a device, household, community etc.
2 the using of this energy.
electricity meter, electric meter; a meter for measuring and recording the flow and consumption of electricity.
electricity supply 1 the supply of electricity by a generation or distribution company to buildings.
2 the provision and continuous distribution of electricity to an area or building.
electricity supply grid, power supply network; an area-wide distribution network of cables, substations and other equipment to provide a supply of electricity.
electric lamp a device for converting electrical energy into useful light.
electric lead a cable with a plug for connecting an electric appliance to an electricity supply.
electric light 1 light produced by electrical means.
2 a light, lamp or luminaire powered by electricity.
electric light fitting a light fitting powered by electricity.
electric lighting artificial lighting powered by electricity.
electric load the power required by an electric appliance.
electric lock, electrical lock; a lock which is fastened or whose bolt is operated by electrical power; see electromagnetic lock, solenoid lock, electromechanical lock.
electric lock control the provision of building security with electric locks operated by timers, remote or access control etc. to control the latches of doors.
electric meter see electricity meter.
electric plug in electric installations, a suitably formed coupling with metal pins, attached via a cable to an appliance, which fits in a socket outlet at a power point.
electric point, power point; in electric installations, a point from which electricity can be drawn for appliances.
electric power see electrical energy.
electric sauna heater a sauna heater powered by electricity and which requires no flue.
electric shock the sudden hazardous flowing of electric current through the human body.
electric stove 1 see electric cooker.
2 see electric heater.
3 see electric sauna heater.
electric transmission line see power line.
electric water heater, boiler, immersion heater; a domestic water-heating appliance containing heating electrodes or elements powered by electricity.
electrification the conversion or adaptation of an appliance or building for use with electricity.
electro-acoustics the process of converting sound energy into electrical form or electrical energy into sound.
electrochemical pertaining to or aided by electrochemistry.
electrochemical coating, electroplating, electrodeposition; the application of thin corrosion-resistant and protective coatings of oxides, zinc etc. on metals by electron transfer using electrical current.
electrochemical corrosion, galvanic corrosion; corrosion which takes place when two dissimilar metals are in direct contact in the presence of an electrolyte, setting off an electrochemical reaction which corrodes one of the metals.
electrochemistry a branch of chemistry which deals with the use of electricity to affect chemical reactions, and the chemical production of electricity.
electrocoating see electro-dip painting.
electrode a terminal through which electricity is conducted to a liquid, gas or other medium.
electrodeposition see electrochemical coating.
electro-dip painting, cathodic dip painting, anodic dip painting, e-coating; an industrial painting process developed originally for the automotive industry, in which aluminium, zinc, brass, steel etc. parts to be coated are dipped into acrylic paint and an electrical field applied between them and an electrode, depositing an extremely uniform paint film; also known as electrocoating, electronic coating, electronic painting, electrophoretic coating.
electrodynamics the science of electricity in motion.
electroless plating see chemical plating.
electrolysis chemical decomposition produced by the passing of an electric current through a liquid, usually a solution of salts; used for the electrolytic deposition of metal coatings and responsible for some forms of corrosion.

electrolyte a chemical solution broken down by electricity during electrolysis.

electrolytic zinc coating, zinc electroplating; the application of a protective layer of zinc to steel components by electrolysis.

electromagnet a device consisting of a conductive coil wound around an iron core which, when supplied with an electric current, becomes magnetic.

electromagnetic based on or concerning electromagnets.

electromagnetic lock, magnetic lock; an electric lock which holds a door in the closed position by means of a powerful electromagnet; see also electromechanical lock.

electromagnetism magnetism caused by or which is a product of electrical current.

electromechanical lock, motor lock; a versatile electric lock used for security and access controlled applications, whose bolt is operated by a remotely controlled electric motor; see electromagnetic lock.

electromechanical lock control the provision of building security with electromechanical locks operated by timers, remote or access control etc. to control the action of doors such that, when activated, they may be pushed open, otherwise a key must be used.

electron a subatomic, negatively charged particle, which normally orbits the nucleus of an atom.

electron-beam welding a form of accurate welding making use of a dense stream of electrons converted to heat upon impact, usually carried out in a vacuum.

electronic calculator see calculator.

electronic coating see electro-dip painting.

electronic data processing, EDP; see computing.

electronic mail see e-mail.

electronic painting see electro-dip painting.

electronic shielding glass glass designed to reduce the transmission of electromagnetic radiation, used for the protection of computer and other electronically or magnetically sensitive systems.

electro-osmosis in geotechnical engineering, a method of lowering the amount of groundwater in silty soils by passing a current through the ground to induce electrolytic movement, and pumping away excess water which gathers at the cathodes.

electrophoresis, cataphoresis; the movement of electrically charged particles through a liquid under the influence of an electric field, used in the deposition of some industrial coatings.

electrophoretic coating see electro-dip painting.

electroplating 1 a process whereby a layer of metal is deposited on a surface in a solution of metal salts through electrochemical action; electrochemical coating.
2 see electrolytic zinc coating.

electroslag welding a method of fusion welding for thick steel plates using a consumable electrode immersed in molten slag.

electrostatic based on or dealing with electrostatics.

electrostatic deposition, elpo priming; the process of applying liquid or powder coatings by charging them so that they are attracted to and deposited on the surface to be coated.

electrostatics a branch of physics that deals with electric charge at rest.

electrotechnical pertaining to the technological aspects of electricity.

electrum 1 an alloy of gold and silver used as a decorative coating in ancient times.
2 gold found naturally which contains some silver.
3 see German silver.

element, 1 chemical element; a basic substance which cannot be broken down into a simpler form by chemical reaction. →Table 4
2 see building element. →28
3 see motif.

elementarism a term coined by Theo van Doesburg to describe the constructive use of line, plane, mass and colour not only as the primary means of expression but as an end in itself, a movement in architecture following on from neoplasticism.

elephant skin, metal grey; a shade of grey which takes its name from the colour of the skin of the Indian or Asian elephant (*Elephas maximus*), and from a number of metals.

elevation 1 one of the exterior vertical planar surfaces of a building. →130
see end elevation.
see frontage.
see frontispiece. →12
see main elevation. →130
see rear elevation. →130
side elevation, see end elevation.
2 a drawing or planar projection showing a representation of the outside face or facade of a building, viewed theoretically from infinity and at right angles to the face. →130
3 the height of a particular point in a building or landscape above sea level.

elevator North American word for lift.

Elizabethan architecture architecture in England during the reign of Elizabeth I (1558–1603), principally evident in secular palaces and country houses, and characterized by the use of Renaissance elements.

elk fence, moose fence; in roads in northern Europe and North America, a fence by the side of the carriageway designed to prevent elk and other mammals from running across the path of traffic.

ellipse an oval planar figure described by a line around two points or foci; the total distance from one focus to a point on the ellipse to the other focus is the same for all points on the ellipse. →108

ellipsograph in technical drawing, a device for constructing and drawing ellipses of varying sizes.

elliptical arch an arch composed of half an ellipse; see also five-centred arch. →24

elm [*Ulmus spp.*] a group of hardwoods found in temperate climates in the northern hemisphere, whose timber is hard and tough and used for interior joinery and furniture; see ***Ulmus spp.*** for full list of species of elm included in this work.

elongated aggregate coarse aggregate with longish particles.

elpo priming see electrostatic deposition.

e-mail, electronic mail; the sending, reception and storage of messages including images, computer files and software in real time via computers, networks and telecommunications systems.

embankment, 1 bank; a sloping earthwork at the side of a river, road, cutting or change of level to restrain water, retain earth pressure, support a road etc.
see *embankment* in bridge structure illustration. →31
2 see agger. →104

embassy a public building which serves as the diplomatic representation of a state abroad.

embattled see castellated.

embattled moulding 1 see crenellated moulding. →124, →125
2 see indented embattled moulding. →125

embattlement see battlement. →103

embellishment see decoration.

emblema, pl. emblemata; in Roman mosaic or carving, an inlaid decorative or symbolic embellishment for a floor, panel or other surface.

embossing a form of imprinting in which lettering or a pattern is raised above the surface of paper, metal plate, plastic sheet, leather etc. using dies.

embrasure, 1 embrazure; a splayed opening in the parapet of a fortified wall, through which a gun could be fired at a range of angles, while giving cover to the marksman; a crenelle or loop. →103

2 the recess of a window in a wall, between the reveals.

embrazure see embrasure. →103

emerald a green variety of the mineral beryl, used as a gemstone.

emerald chromium oxide see viridian.

emerald green, 1 Imperial green, Schweinfurt green; a very poisonous, brilliant green pigment consisting of copper aceto-arsenate now used only in artist's colours.

2 Paris green; a shade of light green which takes its name from the colour of the precious emerald stone.

emeraulde green see viridian.

emergence hole, exit hole, flight hole; in timber which has been infested by insects, a hole from which the insect leaves the timber.

emergency gas control a valve in a gas-heating system designed to automatically close off supply in the event of an emergency.

emergency handset a remote telephone handset for alerting a central exchange of a building in the event of an emergency; also known as emergency telephone.

emergency lighting see safety lighting.

emergency services a public service establishment consisting of fire, ambulance and rescue services which provide aid in the event of an emergency such as a fire, accident etc.

emergency stair see escape stair.

emergency telephone see emergency handset.

emery a naturally occurring mixture of corundum and iron oxide ground and used as an abrasive.

emery cloth 1 stiff cloth used for sanding by virtue of an abrasive coating of powdered mineral or hard metal.

2 a similar product coated with emery.

emery paper see sandpaper. →41

emery wheel a rotating wheel of emery for sharpening metal tools, grinding etc.

emigration the movement of people or populations from one country to settle in another.

eminent domain see compulsory purchase power.

emission, 1 discharge; pollution and waste material released into the environment as gases and noise by motor vehicles, industry etc.

2 radioactivity or electromagnetic radiation given off by a source.

emissivity the property of a surface to emit heat, measured as the rate at which it does so compared to that of a black body of the same temperature.

Empire style an architectural style in France from 1804 to 1815, coinciding with Napoleon's First French Empire, characterized by the use of neoclassical elements; also Russian neoclassical architecture of the same epoch. →12

see *Empire style* facade in stone finishes illustration. →12

empore a columned gallery above the aisles of some Early Christian, Byzantine, Romanesque and Gothic churches, above the arcade and opening out onto the nave. →98, →100

emporion Gk; a market place or commercial centre in ancient Greece; Latin form is emporium.

emplacement, platform, terreplein; a level mounting place for guns and cannon, a battery. →103

emplecton ancient Greek and Roman walling masonry of external leaves of ashlar filled with rubble and cement; same as opus antiquum; Greek form is emplekton. →83

employee parking an area of parking reserved for the use of the employees of an adjacent facility.

employer a person or company who has people paid to work under agreement, directly in their service.

emulator programming for a computer to enable it to behave like another device.

emulsifier, emulsifying agent; a chemical agent used to promote the formation of an emulsion in liquids such as paint.

emulsifying agent see emulsifier.

emulsion the suspension of one liquid in another as a dispersion of tiny droplets.

emulsion adhesive, emulsion glue; a cold setting adhesive consisting of an emulsion of synthetic polymer in a liquid carrier, which dries by evaporation so that the droplets coalesce.

emulsion cleaning the precleaning of a surface using an organic solvent suspended in water to remove oils and other contaminants prior to painting.

emulsion glue see emulsion adhesive.

emulsion paint, plastic paint; a range of paints in which a dispersion of small drops of polymer such as acrylic are suspended in water; the paint dries by the evaporation of the water.

enamel, vitreous enamel; a hardwearing opaque glassy material fused at high temperatures as a protective coating for ceramics, metal and other hard materials.

enameling see enamelling.

enamelling, 1 enameling (Am.); the process of applying an enamel glaze to a ceramic or metal surface.

2 see stove enamelling.

enamel white see blanc fixe.

encampment Roman military encampment, see castrum. →104

encarpus Lat.; in classical sculptured ornament, a festoon of foliage, fruit and flowers; Greek form is enkarpos. →121

encased knot, bark-ringed knot; a knot surrounded by bark in the face of a timber board. →1

encasing 1 in building construction, cladding to cover or encase unsightly structure or services, as fireproofing etc.

2 see casing.

encaustic, 1 cereography; a method of painting, used since ancient times, which employs pigments mixed with a binder of hot wax.

2 in ceramics, the use of inlaid clay decoration of a different colour to that of the base.

enceinte a fortified wall for a medieval castle, town or fortification, and the area it surrounds; often synonymous with bailey. →103

enclosure 1 an area surrounded by a fence, hedge or wall.

2 see compound.

3 see building envelope.

end 1 the smallest side of any long object such as a masonry unit, timber section or building, at which it terminates.

2 the smallest side of a brick, shown as a header face when exposed in a brick wall. →21

3 see stopped end. →21

4 see east end.

5 see gable end.

end abutment, anchorage; that part of a pre-tensioning rig to which the ends of the tendons are anchored during prestressing.

end-bearing pile, point-bearing pile; in foundation construction, a pile which transmits forces to solid ground at its base, through compression. →29

end cap, blank cap; in plumbing and pipework, a cup-shaped fitting which is threaded internally and attached to a pipe to close off an open end.

end cruck, hip cruck, hip post; in traditional timber frame construction, a cruck blade placed at the end of a frame at right angles to the other crucks, used for forming a hip roof.

end elevation, side elevation; one of the shorter or subsidiary elevations of a building.

end grain grain whose fibres run perpendicular to the surface of a piece of timber, showing as growth rings in a log or timber section cut across its length. →2

end-grain wood block flooring, wood block flooring; hardwearing timber flooring, used in workshops and laboratories, in which the end grain of inlaid blocks of wood form the floor surface. →44

end joint a butt joint formed by two timbers or long members fixed end on end. →3

endoscope an optical device with a rigid or flexible shaft, used for remote surveys of the interior cavities of closed bodies such as pipework, pumps or valves, or for inspecting cavities in building construction for damp problems etc.
see fibrescope.
see videoscope.

endurance limit in the fatigue testing of materials and components, the maximum stress which will not cause damage despite repeated loading and unloading.

end view the projected view of the shorter side of a building or object. →127

end wall the shorter external wall at the side or end of a building, block, or terraced row.

energy a physical quantity of power to perform mechanical work, whose SI unit is the joule; varieties of this in readily usable form.

energy balance the calculation or equilibrium of the energy input and output of a technical installation or other system.

energy-saving measures taken in the design of devices, appliances or systems to reduce the amount of energy they consume.

en face of a portrait or sculpture, facing straight ahead.

enfilade the vista caused through aligned doorways in a succession of rooms.

enforcement notice in building control, a notice served by a planning authority that requires a contravention of planning control to be remedied before it can be approved.

engaged of pillars, piers or columns, joined to or part of an adjacent wall; see engaged column. →13

engaged column, attached column, engaged pier, applied column, inserted column; a column built into, adjacent or physically attached to a wall, either for structural stability or for decorative effect. →13

engaged pier see engaged column. →13

engaged system see double-bay system. →25

Engelmann spruce [*Picea engelmannii*] a softwood marketed as Canadian spruce.

engine house a building designed to contain machinery which serves a main factory or industrial complex.

engineer 1 a qualified professional who designs structures, technical services or public utilities and supervises their construction and maintenance.
2 see chartered engineer.

engineered log see milled log.

engineering a branch of science which deals largely with producing alterations, designs and structures through the use of technology; see below for list of engineering disciplines.
civil engineering.
construction engineering.
electrical engineering.
fire engineering.
geotechnical engineering.
ground engineering, see geotechnical engineering.
mechanical services engineering.
precision engineering.
social engineering.
structural engineering.
traffic engineering.
water engineering.

engineering brick a dense, evenly sized, high quality brick with high crushing strength and low porosity used for foundation and basement walls, civil engineering projects etc.

engineer's hammer a small cross peen sledgehammer as used for striking implements and work in a metalwork shop. →40

engineer's sledge a large two-handed engineer's hammer, also called a peen sledge. →40

English ash see European ash.

English Baroque a classical architectural style in England from the end of the 1600s to 1730; a restrained version of continental Baroque.

English bond a brickwork bond consisting of alternating courses of headers and stretchers; see variations below and in *English bonds* illustration. →19
American bond, see English garden-wall bond. →19
common bond, see English garden-wall bond. →19
English cross bond. →19
English garden-wall bond. →19
Liverpool bond, see English garden-wall bond. →19
St Andrew's cross bond, see English cross bond. →19

English cross bond, St Andrew's cross bond; a brickwork bond with alternating courses of headers and stretchers, laid with a half-brick overlap between alternating stretcher courses to produce an interlocking cross pattern in the wall surface. →19

English elm [*Ulmus procera*] a European hardwood with tough, strong, dull brown timber; used for cladding, furniture and panelling.

English garden-wall bond, American bond (Am.), common bond (Am.), Liverpool bond (Am.); a brickwork bond with one course of headers alternating with three or five courses of stretchers. →19

English Gothic an architectural style in England from 1150 to 1550, comprising three phases: Early English, Decorated and Perpendicular; characterized by use of the pointed arch and medieval decoration.

English landscape garden see landscape garden.

English oak see European oak.

English vermilion genuine vermilion pigment made in England.

English walnut see European walnut.

English white see whiting.

engobe, slip; in coloured plasterwork and pottery, a cream-coloured clay dilution applied to cover the original colour of the surface.

engrailed cross see cross engrailed. →118

engrailed moulding a decorative moulding consisting of a row of arched forms joined at sharp points. →124

engraving a method of making graphic prints by cutting lines into a wooden block or linoleum, or by etching metal; a general name for woodcut, wood engraving, linocut and etching.

enkarpos Greek form of encarpus. →121

enkoimeterion a portico outside a classical Greek temple for the sick to gather while waiting for divine provision of healing.

enlarged base pile a foundation pile with a widening at its base to spread its load over a wider area. →29

enlarging in design and graphics, the changing in scale of an object such that it appears larger; in general, increasing the size of something.

enneagram a star-shaped figure composed of three interlocking equilateral triangles; in Christian art, a symbol of the nine spiritual gifts of love, joy, peace, patience, gentleness, goodness, faith, obedience and temperance. →108

enneastyle in classical architecture, a portico supported by a row of nine columns. →77

en profil, profile; of a portrait or sculpture, facing to the side.

enrichment, 1 ornamentation; decoration, pattern or artwork which embellishes a surface or space.
2 see plasterwork enrichment.

entablature in classical architecture, a thick horizontal band or beam member supported by columns in a portico, consisting typically of three sections, the architrave, frieze and cornice. →80
see *classical temple* illustration. →86
see *classical orders* illustrations. →78, →79, →80
see *caryatid* illustration. →76

Entandrophragma angolense see Gedu nohor.
Entandrophragma candollei, see omu.
Entandrophragma cylindricum, see sapele.
Entandrophragma utile, see utile.

entasis Gk; in classical architecture, the slight vertical convex curvature in the length of a column shaft to give it the appearance of straightness under load. →78, →79

enterprise 1 see commercial enterprise.
2 see private enterprise.

enterprise zone in town planning, an urban area in which building control is relaxed and restrictions eased to stimulate industrial and commercial activity etc.

entersole see mezzanine.

enthalpy in thermodynamics, the total internal energy of a system added to the product of its pressure and volume.

entropy-maximizing model in traffic planning, a trip distribution model based on concepts derived from statistical mechanics.

entrained air in concretework, microscopic spherical bubbles of air which have been deliberately introduced into the mix, usually by an air-entraining admixture, to improve workability and frost resistance.

entraining see air entrainment.

entrance 1 a door, gate, portal etc. by which a building or area can be entered; the area or space in its immediate vicinity.
see *prehistoric structures* illustration. →65
see *rock-cut tomb* illustration. →74
see *residential buildings* illustration. →61
2 see main entrance, principal entrance. →113

entrance floor, entrance level; the storey of a multistorey building, usually at ground level, at which it can be entered from the outside.

entrance hall, 1 hall; interior circulation space adjacent to the front door of a dwelling or main entrance of a building, giving access to other spaces.
see *timber-framed house* illustration. →57
see *brick house* illustration. →59
2 the main circulation space at the entrance of a prolific, large or public building, a foyer or lobby.
see *Egyptian pyramid* illustration. →70
3 see vestibule.
4 see porch.

entrance level see entrance floor.

entrance passage 1 see entranceway.
2 see fauces. →88
3 see thyrorion. →87

entrance ramp a ramp leading to the main entrance of a building to negotiate a change in level between outside and in. →66

entranceway, passageway; an open entrance passage through a building, linking a courtyard with the street.

entrapped air, accidental air; in concretework, small unintentional air pockets in hardened concrete which occur during mixing and remain after compaction.

entrelace see interlace, knotwork. →108, →125

entrepreneur a person who initiates a business activity and is responsible for its funding.

entresol see mezzanine.

entry, 1 access; a point at which a building or site can be entered.
2 see competition entry.

entry-phone system a door control system for flats etc. by which communication via intercom is possible and the door can be opened by a remote switch; see also door transmitter.

envelope see building envelope.

environment, 1 milieu; all physical, social and dwelling conditions for a particular external or internal area of habitation.
2 see built environment.

environmental art a movement in art originating in the 1950s, which seeks to enhance a particular outdoor place with structures, colours, forms or lighting.

environmental impact assessment a detailed evaluation of the potential environmental and social effects of a major development project.

environmental pollution contaminating the environment, air, waterways, agricultural and building land etc., by the harmful introduction of industrial waste.

enzyme a protein used as a catalyst in biochemical reactions.

eolithic period a prehistoric period predating the palaeolithic stone age, during which rudimentary-shaped flint tools were in use.

eopolis according to Mumford's classification of city growth, the initial stage, the prototype of a city, an agricultural village settlement.

eotechnic a term coined by Patrick Geddes and Lewis Mumford to describe the period from the thirteenth century to the industrial revolution, seen as a preparation for industrialism, during which the main sources of energy were wind, water and timber, also the most important building material; see also neotechnic and paleotechnic.

EP epoxide resin.

EPDM ethylene propylene diene rubber.

EPDM gasket a preformed seal of ethylene propylene diene rubber, used in proprietary dry window and door glazing systems.

ephebeion, ephebeum (Lat.); Gk; in classical architecture, a main room in a bath house or gymnasium for recreation, relaxation, gymnastics and exercise. →91

ephebeum Latin form of ephebeion. →91

Ephesian base, see Asiatic base. →69, →81

epicranitis, epikranitis (Gk); a decorative moulding in the wall surface of a classical building, above the capitals of a row of pilasters or columns. →93

epidote, pistacite; a glassy, greenish complex silicate mineral, occasionally used in jewellery.

epikranitis Greek form of epicranitis. →93

epinaos Gk; see opisthodomos. →84

Epiphyllum hybridum the orchid cactus, see cactus (green).

episcaenium Lat.; see episcenium. →89

episcenium, episkenion (Gk), episcaenium (Lat.); the upper storey of the stage building in a classical theatre. →89

episcope a device for projecting the image of a drawing onto a screen such that it can be copied to an exact scale.

episkenion Gk; see episcenium. →89

epistle ambo in Early Christian architecture, a lectern or space to the south of the altar from which the epistle texts were delivered; see also gospel ambo. →95

epistle side in church architecture, the right side of an altar or chancel as viewed from the congregation, from which the epistular texts were traditionally read; generally reserved for men; see gospel side. →95

epistylium Latin form of epistyle; see architrave. →78, →79, →80

epistyle see architrave. →78, →79, →80

epitaph a memorial tablet, painting or icon in an Orthodox church.

epithedes Gk; the upper decorated moulding or cymatium, along the upper edge of a classical entablature or cornice.

E-plan the generic plan of a building resembling the shape of the letter 'E', especially as made use of in Elizabethan architecture for country mansions, formed of a main body with perpendicular wings at each end and an entrance porch in the middle.

epoxide resin, epoxy resin, EP; a tough, stable thermosetting resin, usually supplied in two mixable component parts, used for in-situ flooring, paints, adhesives and varnishes.

epoxide resin adhesive see epoxy resin adhesive.

epoxy adhesive see epoxy resin adhesive.

epoxy coating a two-component epoxy resin finish for metal structures such as bridges and pipes in contact with water and subject to corrosion.

epoxy ester paint special epoxy paint used for its properties of water, acid or alkali resistance; usually a gloss paint.

epoxy glue see epoxy resin adhesive.

epoxy paint a tough, chemical- and solvent-resistant paint containing a two component epoxy resin binder which, on hardening, forms a thermosetting plastic coating, used for floors and hardwearing interior surfaces.

epoxy powder coating a tough, corrosion- and chemical-resistant polymeric powder coating whose binder is epoxy resin.

epoxy resin see epoxide resin.

epoxy resin adhesive, epoxide resin adhesive, epoxy glue; an adhesive, usually supplied in two components, consisting of a synthetic thermosetting resin which produces a tough, hard chemical bond.

EPS expanded polystyrene.

equal angle an angle profile of steel or other metal whose flanges are of equal length. →34

equation in mathematics, a function containing two algebraic expressions which are equal to one another.

equiangular in geometry, referring to a polygonal figure whose internal angles are all of equal size. →108

equiangular spiral see Archimedean spiral.

equilateral in geometry, describing a polygon whose sides are of equal length. →108

equilateral arch, pointed equilateral arch, three-pointed arch; a pointed arch form whose two radii of curvature are identical, and equal to the distance between the imposts. →24

equilateral triangle a planar three-sided figure in which all sides are of equal length and each internal angle is 60°. →108

equilibrium, state of equilibrium; a state of a body which is at rest or balance due to the counteracting action of forces which counteract each other.

equilibrium moisture content in the natural seasoning of timber, the point at which the moisture content of the dried timber is the same as that of its surroundings, and drying ceases.

equipment, apparatus, plant, gear; the functioning collection of machinery or devices in a building services installation for performing a mechanical, electrical or communications task.

equivalent weight the weight of a chemical element which has the same displacing power as one gram of hydrogen.

eraser, rubber; a small piece of rubber, vinyl or other abrasive material used for rubbing out marks in drawings and designs; types included as separate entries are listed below. →130
clutch rubber.
indiarubber, see caoutchouc.
kneaded rubber, see putty rubber.
ink rubber, see ink eraser.
putty rubber.

eraser pencil a pencil which has a thin rod of eraser as its core. →130

eraser shield see erasing shield. →130

erasing shield a thin template or stencil of stainless steel perforated with various shaped openings, used to protect surrounding pencilwork when rubbing out particular areas; also called an eraser shield. →130

erbium a chemical element, **Er**.

erection 1 the construction or assembly of a building frame or similar component, usually prefabricated, on site.
2 see formwork erection.

eremotes weevil [*Eremotes spp.*] a group of species of long-snouted insects which infest dead softwood.

ergastulum Lat.; in Roman architecture, a workhouse or prison for slaves, prisoners of war and debtors.

Ernobius mollis see bark borer.

Eros the Greek god of love; see cupid. →122

erosion 1 the wearing away of surface layers of ground, facing materials or shoreline due to action of flowing water or wind.
2 see scour.

erosion corrosion an accelerated rate of corrosive attack in metal pipework due to the relative motion of a flowing corrosive fluid.

eruptive rock see igneous rock.

escalator, moving staircase, moving stairway; a motorized staircase used as a means of automated vertical circulation, in which treads fixed to a circulating belt move up or down in the plane of the stair.

escallop see scallop. →123

escape see means of egress.

escape ladder see fire escape ladder.

escape lighting safety lighting required by law to illuminate an escape route and its signs in the event of a building fire or other emergency.

escape route 1 a designated route along which occupants can get to a safe place in the event of a fire or other emergency in a building.
2 see means of egress.

escape stair, fire escape, fire stair, emergency stair; a protected or outdoor stair which is part of an escape route for use in the event of a fire or other emergency in a building.

escarbuncle a heraldic symbol shown as eight sceptres radiating from a central annulet, originating from the iron bands used to strengthen a shield; a representation of a precious stone, symbolic of supremacy. →123

escarp see scarp. →104

escarpe see scarp. →104

escarpment see scarp. →104

eschara, eskhara (Gk); Lat.; an ancient Greek hearth altar for burnt offerings. →87, →116

eschel a variety of smalt.

esconson see scuntion.

escutcheon, 1 scutcheon, escutcheon plate; any metal protective plate for a door or window, often ornate.
2 key plate, scutcheon; a metal plate which surrounds a keyhole and protects a door surface when a key is inserted. →39, →51
3 an inscribed or decorated plate, especially one in the shape of a shield bearing arms.
4 see shield. →122

escutcheon pin a short pin, usually brass, used for attaching ironmongery to joinery; it may be decorative. →35

escutcheon plate see escutcheon. →39, →51

Eset see Isis. →74

eskhara see eschara. →116

esonarthex that part of a church between the exonarthex and nave.
see *esonarthex* in Byzantine domical church illustration. →96

espagnolette a fastener for holding double windows or shutters closed, consisting of a long mechanism which runs the whole vertical height of the window, and when activated, pushes hooks out through the sides of or ends of the casement to engage in holes in an adjacent window or frame; see cremone bolt.

esplanade 1 an area of level open ground surrounding a castle or fortification overlooking a town, whose use for construction land was restricted due to reasons of security.
2 a long open level area or roadway, often planted with trees or along the sea front, for taking walks and recreation.

essential oil, volatile oil; an oil extracted from plants and seeds, used as a vehicle for some paints, varnishes and other substances, based on alcohol, which evaporates on drying of the substance.

establishment, plant; an organization, commercial enterprise of industrial complex providing a public service such as power generation or water purification.

estate an extensive area of land including dwellings and other associated buildings.

estate clerk of works a qualified professional employed on a large public property to ensure it is maintained.

estates management see property management.

ester one of a number of organic chemical compounds formed by the reaction between an alcohol and an acid with the release of a molecule of water.

estiatorion Gk; a room or building intended for dining and banqueting in ancient Greece. →92

estimate see cost estimate.

estoile in decorative ornamentation, a star of five or six flame motifs radiating out from a point. →123

estrade a raised area of floor beneath a throne, altar etc. to emphasize its importance. →116

etching, 1 frosting; the treatment of a glass or metallic surface with an acid or electrochemical means to roughen it or produce a matt finish.
2 a form of printmaking in which acid is used to etch a design or pattern into the surface of a metal plate, from which prints are taken.
3 the resulting print thus produced.

Ethiopian cross see Coptic cross. →118

ethylene propylene diene rubber, EPDM; a tough, durable, weather- and acid-resistant synthetic rubber used for flexible seals and gaskets, cable insulation, hoses and roofing membranes.

Etruscan architecture the architecture of pre-Roman central Italy from c.700 BC to around the beginning of the first century.

Etruscan hall see tuscanicum.

Etruscan order see Tuscan order. →79, →114

Etruscan temple a temple reminiscent of a Greek Doric temple, often of timber and clay, with terracotta embellishment emphasis on the front elevation, which often included a deep porch and three separate cellae or cult rooms. →84

eucalyptus [*Eucalyptus spp.*] a wide-ranging genus of Australian evergreen hardwood trees, some species of which are used in the construction and timber industries; often tough and resistant to termites and insect attack, used in framing, as building timber, in joinery and as wood fibres.
Eucalyptus diversicolor, see karri.
Eucalyptus marginata, see jarrah.
Eucalyptus microcorys, see tallowwood.
Eucalyptus pilularis, see blackbutt.

Eugenia caryophyllata see oil of cloves.

eurhythmy, eurythmy; harmonious proportions, regularity and symmetry in architecture and built form.

eurythmy see eurhythmy.

European ash, English ash; [*Fraxinus excelsior*] a European hardwood with flexible white to light brown timber; used for making tool handles, furniture and trim.

European beech [*Fagus sylvatica*] a European hardwood with pinkish, mottled timber; used for flooring, interiors and furniture; often simply called beech.

European birch, silver birch, downy birch; [*Betula pendula, Betula pubescens*] species of European hardwood with hard, strong, white to pale brown, uniform timber; used for making furniture and plywood and whose burr is often used in decorative veneers.

European hop-hornbeam [*Ostrya carpinifolia*] a southern European and south-west Asian hardwood with very heavy timber.

European horse chestnut [*Aesculus hippocastanum*] a European hardwood with soft whitish timber.

European lime, linden; [*Tilia europaea, Tilia vulgaris*] a European hardwood with fine-grained, light, soft, weak, pale yellowish timber; used for carving, turnery and plywood.

European oak, English oak; [*Quercus robur, Quercus petraea*] species of European hardwood with heavy, hard and strong pale brown timber; used in traditional timber construction as framing, nowadays for joinery, flooring and furniture.

European plane [*Platanus hybrida, Platanus acerifolia*] European hardwoods with warm, light-brown rayed timber; used for interiors, decorative work and veneer.

European redwood see Scots pine.

European walnut, English walnut, Persian walnut; [*Juglans regia*] a southern European hardwood with grey streaked timber; valued for its decorative figure, used for panelling and veneers.

europium a metallic chemical element, **Eu**.

eustyle 'well columned'; the spacing of rowed columns in classical architecture at a distance of two and a quarter column diameters between the centres of adjacent columns. →77

euthynteria Gk; the foundation structure or lower step of a Greek temple, on which it is constructed to provide a level base on uneven land. →86

Evangelists see cross of the Evangelists. →117

evaporation the change of state of a material from a liquid into a vapour.

evaporation point in the heating of a solid or liquid, the temperature at which it will turn into a vapour.

evaporator, expansion coil; that part of an air-conditioning and refrigeration system in which coolant or refrigerant is vaporized, binding latent heat and thus producing a cooling effect.

even of a planar surface, without wrinkles or irregularities.

even grained, even textured; a description of timber which has a uniform structure throughout the growth ring.

even textured see even grained.

evergreen any species of tree which maintains its leaves, needles etc. throughout the year.

evolute in mathematics, designating a curve which is the locus of curvature of a given curve.

exa- abb. **E**; a prefix for units of measurement or quantity to denote a factor of 10^{18} (a million million million). →Table 1

excavation 1 any work on a construction site involving digging, blasting and removing material from the ground.
2 the result of this.
3 pit; a hole, trench etc. dug into the ground on a building site for the location of foundations, drainage services and other subterranean constructions.

excavation depth the depth to which an excavation is to be made, the lowest point in the construction of a building.

excavation shoring temporary construction works to give support for the sides of an excavation.

excavator, 1 digger; a motor vehicle used on a construction site for making excavations, often a tractor, crane or bulldozer.
2 see dragline excavator.

excepted risk see accepted risk.

exchange see telecommunications exchange.

exchange value the price or value of goods when they are exchanged for other goods or money.

ex-contractual claim see extra-contractual claim.

executive a North American standard paper size; 7.5" × 10", 190 mm × 254 mm. →Table 6

exedra, exhedra; **1** Gk; a semicircular recess or apse, often with a structural function and containing a raised seat.
2 in Greek and Roman architecture, a recess or room, often in the thickness of a wall, used for relaxation, contemplation and conversation. →88
see *Roman residential buildings* illustration. →88

see *classical temple* illustration. →86
see *Roman basilica* illustration. →93
see *Roman thermae* illustration. →91

exfoliation **1** the natural and chemical scaling of a masonry surface due to the action of the elements.
2 see brickwork weathering.

ex-gratia application, ex-gratia claim; in contract management, a request by a contractor for payment in circumstances where he has no legal right to reimbursement.

ex-gratia claim see ex-gratia application.

exhaust in heating and ventilation, the removal of used air from a space, gases up a flue etc. to the outside.

exhaust air in mechanical ventilation and air-conditioning systems, stale air which has been extracted from spaces and released to the outside.

exhaust duct see return-air duct.

exhaust fumes see exhaust gas.

exhaust gas waste gases produced by combustion or similar processes.

exhaust outlet an opening through which exhaust air from an air-conditioning system is conveyed to the outside. →58

exhaust vent **1** in ventilation, a grille or other device to allow the passage of stale air from a room to the outside. →58
2 see exhaust outlet. →58

exhedra see exedra. →88

exhibition a display, usually for the general public, of works of art, museum artifacts, industrial systems and processes or commercial products.

exhibition centre a building or complex for the display or presentation of products, services and activities.

exhibition hall a building in which exhibitions and displays of various kinds are organized.

exit that portion of a fire escape route which is surrounded by fire-resistant construction and leads to the outside.

exit corridor in fire safety, a passageway surrounded by fire-resistant construction, part of an escape route.

exit door, final exit; in fire safety, an external door leading from an escape route to the outside.

exit hole see emergence hole.

exit lighting in fire safety, an electric lighted sign which draws attention to the presence of a fire exit.

exit stairway in fire safety, a fire-resistant stairway leading to the outdoors.

exonarthex the outer vestibule of an Orthodox or Early Christian church, that adjacent to the entrance.
see *Early Christian church* illustration. →95
see *Byzantine domical church* illustration. →96

expanded aggregate, expanded shale aggregate, expanded clay aggregate, light expanded clay aggregate, Leca; a lightweight aggregate used in concrete, blocks etc., consisting of clay, shale or other mineral which has been heated so that it expands to form a porous structure; used also as thermal insulation for floors and flat roofs. →49

expanded aggregate concrete lightweight concrete whose coarse aggregate is expanded clay or shale, or perlite.

expanded clay aggregate see expanded aggregate. →49

expanded glass **1** see foam glass.
2 see cellular glass.

expanded granulated cork in the manufacture of cork products, granulated cork which has been expanded by heating.

expanded metal a metal mesh product manufactured from slitted metal plate or sheet which is stretched to form lozenge-shaped perforations. →34

expanded metal flooring metal flooring for walkways, service gangways, access platforms etc. fabricated from heavy-gauge expanded metal sheet in a steel frame.

expanded metal lathing a base for renderwork manufactured from metal sheet which has been perforated.
see ribbed expanded metal lathing, rib lathing.

expanded plastics any lightweight plastics material which has been chemically changed by the introduction of an additive which evolves gas; a cellular plastic.

expanded polystyrene, EPS, foamed polystyrene, bead polystyrene; a lightweight plastics material consisting of a foamed structure of beads, used as boards for insulation.
see *expanded polystyrene insulation* in flooring illustration. →44
see *expanded polystyrene insulation* in brick house illustration. →59
see extruded polystyrene.

expanded rubber cellular rubber containing a network of gas bubbles which are closed and not interconnected, used for seals.

expanded shale aggregate see expanded aggregate.

expanding bolt, expansion bolt; a fastener used for anchoring components to concrete or masonry, consisting of a bolt which mechanically expands when its head is turned, tight against the sides of the hole in which it is fixed.

expanding cement cement which expands on setting.

expanding vault see conical vault. →25

expansibility **1** the ability of a material, installation etc. to increase in size.
2 see ductility.

expansion see thermal expansion.

expansion bit see expansive bit. →42

expansion board, card; a piece of computing hardware, a printed circuit board which provides the computer with extended functions such as network, graphic and fax facilities.

expansion bolt **1** see expanding bolt.
2 see wedge anchor. →37

expansion cistern a cistern for a hot water supply system which accommodates expansion in the heated water.

expansion coil see evaporator.

expansion joint a joint in monolithic concrete, masonry or other forms of mass construction which allows for the expansion of materials during an increase in temperature.

expansion producing admixture in concretework, an admixture included in the mix to produce a controlled expansion.

expansion slot in computing, a port or slotted housing inside a computer to which an expansion board may be connected.

expansion tank, 1 expansion vessel, sealed expansion vessel; a reservoir to compensate for variations in volume and to contain excess liquid on expansion in a system of closed pipework with pressure and temperature differences.
2 an open vessel which allows for an increase in volume of water on heating in a hot-water heating system.

expansion vessel see expansion tank.

expansive bit, expansion bit; a drill bit with a blade which can be adjusted to a range of diameters for the drilling of different sized holes. →42

expected life the predicted service life of a material, product or installation, calculated from tests.

expense an outlay of money.

expensive, costly; referring to a commodity or service which is not cheap.

experimental art a general name for pioneering and groundbreaking forms in art.

experimental building a building in which new technical, ideological and structural ideas are tested.

experimental project, pilot project; any design or construction project in which new methods and solutions are tried out.

explementary angle in geometry, one of a pair of angles whose sum is 360°.
explosion a sudden and violent release of energy.
explosive 1 the ability of a substance to produce an explosion, its volatility with respect to this.
2 any highly unstable substance which will cause an explosion when activated or ignited, used in blast excavating.
explosive welding the welding of metal plates by bringing them together at high velocity using a controlled explosion which fuses the pieces together at the join.
exponent in mathematics, a number or symbol signifying a power.
exponential function a mathematical function defining a quantity whose rate of increase is a constant.
export the taking or sending of goods for sale outside the country of manufacture or production.
exposed aggregate concrete concrete whose coarse aggregate has been exposed as a surface finish; see following entry.
exposed aggregate finish a hardwearing, decorative concrete surface finish or thin finish facing for precast units in which coarse aggregate in the concrete is exposed by brushing or spraying with water.
exposed aggregate plaster a mineral plaster or render with a facing quality aggregate, which is exposed in the surface by washing, scouring or sandblasting, producing a finish not unlike dry dash.
exposed concrete concrete whose exterior surface as cast is its finished state, unfaced in the final structure; special care is usually taken with its components, surface texture etc.
exposed rock see outcrop.
exposed runner, ceiling linear strip; in a suspended ceiling system, a profiled section which remains visible in the finished ceiling surface.
exposed system a suspended ceiling system whose supporting profiles are visible in the finished ceiling surface, usually of hung inverted T-shaped profiles which support ceiling panels.
expression in mathematics, a series of symbols or functions which express a quantity.
expressionism art or architecture which expresses the subjective experience or emotions of its author.
expressive of architecture or art, visually flamboyant, bold, evoking an emotion, making a statement.
expressway an urban or suburban road for fast through traffic, often linking parts of a town and usually accessed via an interchange or roundabout.
expropriation 1 the dispossession of an owner of his property for a public development or the implementation of planning or transportation schemes by an authority.
2 see compulsory purchase.
extender, 1 filler, inert pigment; a white mineral pigment added to paints to increase volume, reduce cost or to modify the finished paint surface.
2 any of a number of fine inert granular substances added to glues to increase volume and spreading capacity.
extending the diluting of paints, glues etc. with fillers, usually translucent white pigments for paints, to increase their volume.
extension, 1 lengthening piece; an addition to any member to increase its length.
2 addition; a building or part of a building constructed as an enlargement, annexe etc. for an existing building.
3 see log extension. →6
4 see extension of time.
5 see prolongation.
extension line, leader line; in measured drawing, one of a number of straight lines projected out from the key points on a dimensioned object, at right angles to a dimension line, defining the extremities of dimensions thereon.
extension of time in contract administration, the allowance of extra time for completion due to delays outside a contractor's control.
extent, scope, scale; the full quantity or amount of construction works or any other development.
extent of contract see scope of contract.
exterior 1 space which is outside and open to the elements, usually in close proximity to a building.
2 the surface of a building, component etc. facing outwards.
3 see outer surface.
exterior boarding see weatherboarding. →8
exterior cladding see external cladding. →8
exterior exit a fire exit door leading to the outside at ground level.
exterior facing see external cladding. →8
exterior luminaire a weatherproof luminaire designed for use outside.
exterior paint, external paint; any paint suitable for use outside and which can withstand moisture and frost.
exterior perspective a perspective drawing of the exterior of a building.
exterior plywood plywood for external use glued with adhesives which are moisture and frost resistant.
exterior wall see external wall.
exterior woodstain woodstain used for external applications.
external air see outside air.
external angle see outside corner. →14
external angle trowel, outside corner trowel; a plasterer's hand tool for smoothing external corners in plasterwork with a handled blade of bent steel sheet. →43
external appearance the visual impact of a building produced by the colours, materials and massing of its external surfaces.
external boarding see weatherboarding. →8
external cladding, 1 facing; any non-loadbearing material such as boards, tiles, sheetmetal pans, concrete panels etc. for covering the wall surfaces of a building and forming their external finished surface. →8
2 see weatherboarding. →8
external corner see outside corner. →14
external dimension, overall dimension; in dimensioning and setting out, the dimension of the external outline of a building in plan, measured along one of its main axes.
external door any door of which at least one face is exposed to the outside of a building. →51
external envelope see building envelope.
external facing see external cladding. →8
external force a force on a member or structure produced by external action.
external glazing glazing in which at least one glass surface is exposed to the outside of a building; the outermost panes of glass in a double-glazed unit. →52, →60
external grille a grille fixed over an outlet on the exterior face of a building, usually allowing for ventilation to the interior or structure.
external leaf, outer leaf; the leaf of a cavity wall which is exposed to the elements. →59
external paint see exterior paint.
external stair any stair situated outside, either linking external areas at different levels or an approach to the entrance of a building.
external surface 1 the surface of a wall or building component facing towards the outside.
2 see outer surface.
external surface resistance value see RSO-value.
external tooth washer a tooth washer with serrations along its outer edge. →37
external vibrating, form vibrating; a method of compacting concrete using a vibrator attached to the external surface of formwork.

external vibrator, form vibrator; a machine attached to the outside of formwork for compacting in-situ concrete by vibration.

external wall one of the walls forming the external envelope of a building and exposed to the elements. see *external wall* in concrete frame illustration. →28 see *external wall construction* in brick house illustration. →59

external wall panel a prefabricated external wall unit attached between vertical or horizontal structural frame members of a building.

external works 1 the scope of work for a building project which lies outside a building; the landscaping, hardstanding, drainage, fences and walls etc.
2 see landscaping.

extinguishant see extinguishing medium.

extinguisher see fire extinguisher.

extinguishing see fire-fighting.

extinguishing foam see foam.

extinguishing medium, extinguishant; any non-combustible material used to extinguish a fire in a building: water, inert gas, vaporizing liquid, dry powder, foam.

extra see extra work.

extra-contractual claim, ex-contractual claim; in contract administration, a claim for damages not covering matters included under terms of the contract.

extract 1 the removal of stale air from spaces within a building via ducting or vents using a fan.
2 see mechanical extract.

extract air see return air.

extract duct see return-air duct.

extract fan see smoke extract fan.

extractive industry in land use planning, types of industry which involve extraction of raw material from the earth such as mining and quarrying.

extractor see roof extractor.

extractor hood, hood; a metal appliance with grease filters and a fan, suspended above a stove or similar appliance to convey steam and other unwanted fumes away into an air duct.

extract unit see return-air terminal unit.

extract ventilation, negative pressure ventilation; a system of mechanical ventilation which functions by extraction of the air in spaces, thus causing negative pressure which sucks in fresh air.

extrados the upper line of the voussoirs in an arch. →22

extra-low voltage electrical supply of less than 50 V.

extra-low voltage lighting electric lighting which runs off a low voltage, less than 50 V.

extra rapid-hardening Portland cement Portland cement which hardens more quickly than rapid-hardening Portland cement.

extra work, extra, additional work; in contract administration, construction work ordered by the client after the contract has been awarded, not included in the contract and for which the contractor is paid separately.

extruded cellular sheet see cellular sheet.

extruded chipboard see extruded particleboard. →9

extruded concrete concrete preformed into profiled or cellular slabs by a process of extrusion.

extruded joint, convex joint; a brickwork mortar joint with mortar shaped with a tool to form a longitudinal convex bulge protruding beyond the brickwork plane. →16

extruded particleboard, extruded chipboard; chipboard manufactured by a process of extrusion, with particles arranged perpendicular to the plane of the board. →9

extruded polycarbonate sheet see polycarbonate cellular sheet.

extruded polystyrene, XPS, styrofoam, polystyrene foam board; expanded polystyrene whose structure contains small closed bubbles of gas rather than a mass of lightweight beads, used for thermal insulation.

extruded tile a tile formed by a process of extrusion.

extruding see extrusion.

extrusion 1 a method of forming thermoplastic, aluminium and ceramic products such as pipes, profiles, bricks etc. by forcing hot or cold material through a die into the required cross-sectional shape.
2 extruding; a process of making precast concrete units by extruding the material through a die into the required shape then vibrating.

extrusion gun see caulking gun.

extrusive rock see volcanic rock.

eye 1 a hole formed through the head of a hammer, axe or similar hand tool, by which it is connected to the shaft. →40
2 see hook and eye. →36
3 see screw eye. →36
4 see padlock eye. →39
5 see dragon's eye. →123
6 see eye of Horus. →75
7 see eye of God. →119

eye blue a shade of blue which takes its name from the colour of the human iris.

eye brown a shade of brown which takes its name from the colour of the human iris.

eye grey a shade of grey which takes its name from the colour of the human iris.

eye of Horus, Wadjet eye; a common Egyptian decorative motif symbolizing both the vengeful eye of the sun god and the eye of the god Horus. →75

eye of God religious decoration consisting of an eye motif within a radiating triangle, symbolic of God's presence throughout; also known as the all-seeing eye. →119

eye point see station point. →128

eye wash fountain a clinical sanitary appliance designed for rinsing the eyes with a mild jet of warm water.

eyelet 1 see oeillet. →103
2 see roundel.

eyvan see iwan.

F

fabric, 1 cloth; a textile material woven or otherwise fused from natural, mineral or synthetic fibres.
2 see welded mesh.
3 see fabric reinforcement.
4 the main constructional mass of a building, its frame, structure, walling, roofing and floors.
fabric reference in the design of reinforced concrete, a standard defining the size and spacing of bars used in fabric reinforcement.
fabric reinforcement, mesh reinforcement, wire-mesh reinforcement, welded fabric; reinforcement for concrete slabs or walls of steel bars or wires welded or woven into a preformed mesh or grid.
facade, 1 façade; a grand or imposing elevation or outside face of a building.
See *Baroque façade* illustration. →113
2 see elevation. →130
face 1 the external or visible planar surface of an object.
2 see door face. →50
3 the wider side of a piece of sawn timber, whose growth rings run approximately tangentially in relation to the original log from which it was cut.
4 the exposed surface of a brick, block or stone in masonry; see side. →21
5 see stretcher face. →20
6 see header face. →20
7 the vertical side, facing outwards, of a laid brick.
8 the striking surface of a hammer, axe etc. →40
9 the front cutting surface of a sawtooth.
10 the long sides of a fortified bastion which meet at a point, the salient angle. →104
face bedding the laying of a stone or brick in masonry with its natural bedding plane upright rather than the usual horizontal; used with cladding, voussoirs etc.
face brick see facing brick.
face coat see final plaster coat. →83
face contact material in concreting, any material included in the formwork, usually sheeting or boarding in direct contact with the cast concrete, providing its surface with support and shape.
faced wall a clad or composite wall whose component parts function together structurally.
face grain the surface of a piece of sawn timber which has been roughly tangential in the original log.
face joint a mortar joint visible in the surface of brickwork masonry, often finished by pointing.
face knot a knot in the face of a piece of timber.
faceplate see forend. →39
face ply the outer layer of veneer in plywood, often of a higher grade or quality timber than the inner plies. →9
face putty see putty fronting.
face side, better face, work face; the face of a piece of sawn timber which is regarded as superior in quality and to which a finish is applied.
face value the value or quantity shown on the face of a coin, printed banknote or other financial document.
face veneer a decorative veneer used for the surfacing of furniture, joinery and interior work. →9
face wall a bastion face, see face. →104
face width in tongued and grooved or rebated boarding, the width of a board exposed on laying.
facet a slanting face in the surface of cut glass.
facework see fair-face brickwork.
facilities see community facilities.
facing 1 the covering of a product, surface or frame with a decorative or protective finish material.
2 a layer of stone, brick, timber boarding, tiling etc. applied to the face of a wall as cladding.
3 see facing brick.
4 the surface application of one or a number of layers of protective material to provide a finish.
5 see coating.
6 see cladding.
see ashlar facing.
see brick facing, brick veneer.
door facing, see door face.
exterior facing, see external cladding. →8
see natural stone facing. →11
see rubble facing.
timber facing, see timber cladding. →8
facing brick, face brick (Am.); any fairly durable brick used for its appearance in external walls.
facing concrete a layer of concrete placed over cast concrete as a finish.
facing stone high quality dressed natural stone or similar products used for facing the external wall of a building.
facsimile a detailed copy of a work.
factor of safety, safety factor; in structural engineering, a design coefficient utilized to ensure that structural members are never overloaded, calculated as the maximum stress that an element can withstand divided by the calculated design stress.
factory a building or complex for the manufacture of products.
factory finish a finish coating applied to a component at manufacturing stage.
factory glazed window a window whose glazing is installed at the manufacturing stage, prior to its arrival on site.
factory-made see prefabricated.
fading a minor defect, the paling of surface colour in a paint, plastic or other coloured finish exposed to sunlight or chemical attack.
Fagus spp. see beech.
Fagus grandifolia, American beech.
Fagus sylvatica, European beech.
Fahrenheit see degree Fahrenheit.
faience a tin-glazed or decorated form of terracotta originating in the village of Faenza, Italy.
faience blue a shade of blue which takes its name from the colour of the porcelain of the same name.
failure the breakdown in performance of a material or component due to overloading, wear, defect, deterioration or corrosion.
fair see market.
fair-face brickwork, facework; brickwork of sufficient quality that it requires no applied finish.
fair-face casting the casting of concrete to provide a finish which requires no further coating, tooling or facing.
fair-faced 1 referring to brickwork or blockwork laid in a neat fashion without the need for further covering or applied finish.
2 describing a fine finish in cast concrete which requires no further treatment.
fairfaced concrete concrete which has been cast to provide a finish requiring no further coating, tooling or facing.
fairground see amusement park.
fair-trading, department of, trading standards department; an authority responsible for legislation protecting the rights of the consumer, ensuring that trading competition is carried out within the law.
falcon 1 see Horus. →74
2 see Sokar.

fall the angle of a slope, line, road or river to the horizontal, measured as a difference in height per length or as a percentage.

falling-butt hinge a hinge whose cylindrical pin housings or knuckle are cut with a helix so that the door leaf drops slightly when opened and swings open under the force of gravity. →38

fallow deer see fawn (brown).

fallow land in landscaping and forestry, land which has not been used for cultivating plants for over a year.

fall trap see murder hole. →103

false acacia see robinia.

false arch types of arch such as triangular or corbelled arches which do not utilize masonry voussoirs to provide support over an opening. →23
see *flat, false and decorative arches* illustration. →23

false bond in brickwork, the laying of bricks without overlap on successive courses such that there is no structural bonding between adjacent bricks other than that provided by the mortar. →17

false ceiling, drop ceiling; a ceiling which is lower than the soffit of the floor slab above to make a hidden space for services and ductwork, or to cover up unsightly overhead construction; it may be a suspended ceiling or simply attached to the underside of ceiling joists.

false door, blind door; a decorative element in a building elevation, which mimics a door, but does not function as such.

false front see screen façade.

false hammer beam in traditional timber roof construction, a hammer beam with no hammer post.

false jetty, hewn jetty; in traditional timber frame construction, a jetty made by the increased dimension of posts at the jetty level rather than making use of cantilevering beams.

false pyramid see bent pyramid. →70

false set, early stiffening, hesitation set, premature stiffening, rubber set; in concreting, the unusually rapid setting of cement which can be unhardened by further mixing.

false tinder fungus [*Phellinus ignarius, Fomes ignarius*] fungal decay found in living hardwoods, especially aspen.

false window, blind window; a decorative element in a building elevation, which mimics a window, but does not function as such.

falsework in construction work, any temporary structure for supporting unfinished structures, construction, masonry etc.

family see family unit.

family of gases in gas heating, a group of gases used for combustion which comply with certain standards of heat output; see Wobbe number.

family unit, family, household; traditionally the smallest unit of a society, a group of people living together, usually adults living with their children.

famn an old Scandinavian unit of length equivalent to 1.78 m; see also fathom.

fan, 1 blower; a device for propelling a stream of air through an air-conditioning or ventilation system.
2 any mechanical device, often portable, for bringing about air circulation within a space.
3 see ceiling fan.
4 see flue fan.

fan arch a decorative design with a fan motif under an arch, often with a figure at the centre. →123

fan circulated flue system see fanned draught flue system.

fan coil system a localized air-conditioning system consisting of a series of fan coil units.

fan coil unit a localized air-conditioning unit in which air is blown into a room using an in-built fan over coils to heat or cool it.

fan configuration the arrangement of cables in a cable-stayed bridge so that all cables fan out from a series of points located down the side of supporting pylons; see radial configuration, harp configuration. →32

fan convector an electric room heater which sucks in cold air, passes it over a heating element and blows it out using a fan.

fan heater, 1 electric fan heater; a portable heater containing a fan which blows out a stream of warm air over a heated coil.
2 see warm-air heater.

fan heating see warm-air heating.

fanlight, 1 transom light, transom window; any window or glazed panel above a door, often fitted in the same frame.
2 a fan-shaped window with radiating glazing bars above a door. →111

fanned draught flue system, fan circulated flue system; a flue system in which draught is provided by a fan.

fan pattern see fantail pattern. →15

fantail tool see fishtail chisel. →41

fantail pattern a traditional paving pattern of small stones or cobbles forming radiating areas resembling a fan or the tail feathers of a bird; originating from the area that could be paved by hand by one man without moving from his place; also called peacock tail or fan pattern. →15

Fantastic style, Fourth Pompeian style, Eclectic style; a style of Roman mural painting from Roman Pompeii depicting historical events, pastoral scenes or mythical images; this final Pompeian style was prevalent as a result of repairs to many buildings after earthquake damage; see Pompeian style.
see *Pompeian styles* illustration. →126

fan tracery, fanwork; Gothic blind tracery found on the surface of fan vaulting.

fan truss a triangular roof truss whose diagonals fan out from a single point, usually the ridge. →33

fanum Lat.; a Roman sacred place or sanctuary, surrounded by a profanum.

fan unit, air-handling unit, blower; that part of a mechanical ventilation or air-conditioning system which blows air along ductwork.

fan vault intricate Gothic vaulting from the late 1400s and early 1500s with stone ribs fanning out from each column and a flat diamond-shaped area at the apex of each vaulted bay. →101

fanwork see fan tracery.

farad the basic unit of capacitance, one farad is equal to one coulomb per volt.

farm an establishment for the independent practice of agriculture.

farmhouse the main residence or dwelling of a farm.

farming, agriculture; the raising of cattle and crops on agricultural land for a living.

farmland see agricultural land.

farmstead, grange; a farm and its farmhouse, including ancillary buildings and land.

fasces Lat.; a Roman emblem of magistrates' power and unity, characterized by a bundle of rods tied together with an axe, a common motif in Roman decoration. →122

fascia 1 see fascia board. →48, →58
2 one of a number of undecorated flat horizontal bands in a classical architrave, a fascia moulding; a fillet. →14, →78
see *Greek orders* illustration. →78
see *Ionic order* illustration. →80

fascia board, fascia; in roof construction, a horizontal board attached vertically to the ends of joists or rafters at eaves level. →48, →58

fascia bracket in roofing, a support for fixing an eaves gutter to a fascia board.

fascia gutter in roofing, a gutter fixed to the fascia board of an eaves.

fascia moulding an ornamental moulding consisting of a slightly projecting flat band, wider than a fillet; a fascia. →14

Fascist classicism eclectic architecture from Italy and Germany in the 1930s during the time of the Fascist dictators, characterized by monumental classical forms interpreted in such a way as to symbolize power and military might.

fastener 1 any device or construction for fixing or holding a component in place; may be a fixing, fastening or latch.
2 see corrugated fastener. →35
3 see push-pull fastener.
4 toothed plate fastener, see nail plate. →35

fastening see fixing.

fastigium Lat.; a ridge or pedimented gable end of a building, especially in Roman architecture. →86

fast-pin hinge, tight-pin hinge; a hinge whose pin is fixed in place and cannot be withdrawn, or one whose pin is integral with the lower hinge leaf. →38

fat concrete see rich concrete.

fathom 1 an imperial unit of length equal to 6 feet or 1.83 m, used in measuring the depth of the sea.
2 see famn.

fatigue the permanent weakening or depreciation of the strength of a material or component, often a moving part, due to its repeated loading and unloading.

fatigue failure the physical failing of a material or component due to fatigue.

Fatima, hand of see hand of Fatima. →120

Fatimid architecture Islamic architecture from 909 to 1171 in Egypt, Syria and other parts of North Africa, characterized by great mosques and palaces; it takes its name from Fatima (or Fatimah), the daughter of the prophet Muhammad.

fat lime, rich lime; high quality hydrated lime produced from pure limestone, which in lime putty can be spread evenly and has good properties of plasticity and setting.

fat mix see rich mix.

fatness see plasticity.

fatty oil, fixed oil; neutral organic hydrocarbon liquid compounds from animal or vegetable sources, oils which are viscous at normal temperatures and become fluid on heating, traditionally used in paints, varnishes and other finishes; see also mineral oil, essential oil.

fauces Lat.; a narrow passageway leading from the street to the atrium of a Roman dwelling, or from the atrium to the peristyle. →88

faucet see water tap.

fault see defect.

faun a Roman satyr with goat's legs and horns; plural is fauni. →122

fauni plural form of faun. →122

faunus Latin form of faun. →122

faux blanc see off-white.

fawn (brown) a light shade of brown which takes its name from the colour of the hide of a fallow deer (*Dama dama*).

fax see telefax.

feasibility the analysis of costs, scheduling, funding, planning, ground conditions and resources in the planning stages of a construction project to ascertain its practicability.

feasibility study in information technology, the assessment by a systems analyst of the prospective advantages and disadvantages of a potential computer system.

feasible, viable; of a building or development project, planning process etc., that which is possible to undertake or bring to completion.

feather, 1 plume; a common ornamental device in Egyptian, Arabic, pre-Columbian and classical architecture, attribute of deities and rulers. →120
2 see spline. →5, →8
3 see plug and feathers.

featherboarding see featheredged boarding. →8

feather crotch see feather grain.

feather curl see feather grain.

featheredged board 1 a timber exterior cladding board, wedge shaped in cross-section, laid horizontally with the thicker edge of one board laid downwards and overlapping the thinner edge of the one below. →8
2 see rebated featheredged board. →8

featheredged boarding, featherboarding; exterior timber wall cladding in featheredged boards. →8

featheredged coping a coping stone or special brick which is wedge shaped in cross-section to encourage rainwater to run off to one side. →16

feather grain, feather curl, feather crotch; a decorative timber figure in the form of a sweeping curve, found in curl veneer.

feather joint see spline joint.

feather-jointed boarding see spline-jointed boarding. →8

Federal style neoclassical architecture in North America after the War of Independence from 1789 to 1830.

fee, payment; a sum of money paid in return for services.

feed, input; the supply of a liquid to a source, water to a boiler or gas or oil to a burner.

feed pipe see cold feed pipe.

feed-roller marks defective indentations along the edge of sawn timber boards caused by mechanical feed rollers during automated conversion. →1

feeler gauge a simple device with a number of calibrated thin blades used for measuring a narrow gap between two components.

fee scale a scale of standard charges for the services of professional consultants, local authorities etc.

feint, set; the slight bend along the edges of sheetmetal cappings and flashings to provide rigidity and strength.

feldspar, felspar; a common white or reddish, structurally brittle, alumino-silicate mineral.
see alkali feldspar.
Labrador feldspar, see labradorite.
see potash feldspar.

felling in landscaping and forestry, the cutting down of trees; see also harvesting.

felling axe, American axe, wood axe; a large long-handled axe with a wedge-shaped blade, used for felling and woodcutting.

felling saw, two-man cross cut saw; a large handsaw with a handle at either end of a usually curved blade; used by two men in the felling of trees.

felspar see feldspar.

felt an unwoven fabric of fibres matted together using heat, pressure or mechanical action.
see roofing felt.
see bitumen felt.

felt nail see clout. →35

felt pen, felt-tipped pen; a pen in which spirit-based ink is transferred from an internal reservoir to the paper via a small tip of felt-like material. →130

felt roofing 1 see bituminous felt roofing. →49
2 see built-up roofing. →49
3 see roll-jointed roofing. →49
4 see lap-jointed roofing. →49

felt shingles see strip slates. →49

felt tiles see strip slates. →49

felt-tipped pen see felt pen. →130

felt underlay bitumen felt used beneath tiled, slate or sheet roofing; often reinforced felt. →57

femto- abb. **f**; a prefix for units of measurement or quantity to denote a factor of 10^{-15} (a thousand million millionth). →Table 1

fence a barrier or screen used for dividing or enclosing an area of land.

fencing 1 the material or components from which a fence is made, a length of fence.
2 the construction of fences.

fender a flexible structure such as a large timber baulk, piece of rubber or matting fixed to the side of a dock as protection for and from mooring vessels.

fenestration **1** the multitude and arrangement of windows, glazed panels etc. in a building elevation.
2 the arrangement of glazing bars in a single window or glazed panel.

fer de moline see millrind. →123

fermium an unstable synthetic chemical element, **Fm**.

feroher a symbol of the sun deity found adorning Mesopotamian temples, the Mesopotamian version of the winged sun disc, representative of the Assyrian god Ashur. →75

Ferrari cement an alternative name for sulphate-resistant cement, named after its inventor.

ferric oxide see iron oxide.

Ferris wheel a revolving fairground structure, a large vertical wheel hinged at its centre with seating hung along its circumference.

ferrite a sintered ceramic material with magnetic properties, consisting of a mixture of iron and other metal oxides.

ferritic stainless steel a form of stainless steel containing 17% chromium.

ferroconcrete see reinforced concrete.

ferrous pertaining to a substance containing iron, especially an alloy or ore with a significant quantity of it.

ferrous ferric oxide see iron oxide.

ferrous metal any metal whose major constituent is iron.

ferrous oxide see iron oxide.

ferrule, 1 sleeve; a metal sleeve which attaches the head to the handle or shaft of a brush, chisel or similar implement.
2 a small metal ring fitted around one or both ends of the handle of a chisel or other hand tool to prevent splitting when struck with a mallet. →41

ferry 1 a waterborne vessel for transporting passengers and vehicles across a stretch of water.
2 see cable ferry. →64
3 see chain ferry. →64

ferryboat a ferry controlled from within the vessel rather than operated from the shore.

ferry bridge 1 a moving floating bridge for carrying vehicles across a river, guided by cables or chains anchored on either side. →64
2 see cable ferry. →64
3 see chain ferry. →64

fertility, natality; in town planning, the calculating of birth rate for the population of a specified area.

fertilizing in landscaping and forestry, the addition of chemicals into the soil to enhance plant growth.

fess a horizontal band, strip or line down the middle of a heraldic shield, often dividing areas of different colours; also written as fesse. →125

fesse see fess. →125

fess point the point in the very centre of a heraldic shield; also called a coeur, abyss or heart point. →124

festoon, garland, swag; a decorative motif consisting of a hanging representation of flowers, foliage, fruit or fabric carved as if suspended between two points. →121

fez see cardinal (red).

FFL see finished floor level.

fiber see fibre.

Fibonacci series a number series in which each number is the sum of the previous two (2, 3, 5, 8, 13, 21 etc.), which bears the name of the Tuscan mathematician Leonardo Fibonacci (c.1170–1230), who observed that, as the series progresses, the ratio of each successive pair approaches the golden section (1:1.618). →106

Fibonacci spiral a spiral constructed by a series of quadrants which increase in size according to numbers in the Fibonacci series. →106

fibre, fiber (Am.); a very thin filament or thread of material.

fibreboard, 1 fibre building board; a building board manufactured from wood fibres mixed with water and compressed; see hardboard, MDF, softboard. →9
2 see hardboard. →9
3 see MDF, medium density fibreboard.
4 see softboard, insulation board.

fibre building board see fibreboard. →9

fibre cement see fibre-reinforced cement.

fibre cement board see fibre cement sheet.

fibre cement sheet, fibre cement board; a non-toxic, durable, fireproof and resilient sheet material consisting of cement, cellulose and mineral filling; a replacement for asbestos products used for cladding and encasing.

fibre cement slate a rectangular or shaped roofing tile manufactured from Portland cement pressed together with natural or synthetic fibres.

fibre concrete see fibre-reinforced concrete.

fibred plaster see fibrous plaster.

fibreglass a strong lightweight material consisting of fine filaments of glass woven into a mat or matrix and embedded in a plastic or resin.

fibre optics a branch of telecommunications using a carrier beam of light to transmit signals along fine fibres of glass.

fibre-reinforced cement, fibre cement; a fibre-reinforced composite consisting of fibres in a Portland cement matrix, used for building boards and wall panels; often abbreviated to FRC.

fibre-reinforced composite any composite material which consists of a dispersal of reinforcing fibres in cement, concrete, plastics etc.; often abbreviated to FRC.

fibre-reinforced concrete, fibre concrete, fibrous concrete; concrete containing fibres of glass, steel etc. to reduce weight and increase tensile strength; often abbreviated to FRC.

fibre-reinforced plaster see fibrous plaster.

fibre-reinforced plastic, reinforced plastic; a light composite material consisting of reinforcing fibres of glass, steel or plastics in a synthetic resin matrix, usually polyester; used for structural applications, car bodies, mouldings, sheets, roofing slates and drainage fittings; often abbreviated to FRP.

fibre-reinforced render special render with added polymer fibres, which mesh together in the applied product to form a flexible and impact-resistant surface.

fibre reinforcement natural, artificial or glass fibres used as reinforcement in composite materials such as concrete, plaster, resins, plastics etc.

fibre saturation point, saturation point; in the seasoning of timber, the point at which all free moisture has evaporated, leaving only the water in the cell walls of the wood.

fibrescope an endoscope with a long flexible tube, illuminated by fibre-optics.

fibre tip, fibre-tipped pen; a pen in which spirit-based ink is transferred from an internal reservoir to the paper via a small tip of hard fibrous material; similar to a felt pen.

fibre-tipped pen see fibre tip.

fibrous concrete see fibre-reinforced concrete.

fibrous plaster, fibred plaster; gypsum plaster used for casting ornaments and mouldings, often strengthened with glass fibres, lathing or textile.

fibrous plaster case in ornamental and fibrous plastering, a cast for supporting a mould.

fibrous plaster cast a cast ornament in fibrous plasterwork.

fibrous plaster draught in plaster casting, a slope given to surfaces of a mould to aid the release of a cast from it.

fibrous plastering the process of working in fibrous plaster.

fibrous plastering model an existing object, sculpted ornament etc. from which a cast is taken to create a plastering mould.

fibrous plastering mould, plaster mould; in ornamental plasterwork, a mould, usually made from a thermoplastic material, used for the casting of repeated plaster objects.

fibrous plaster moulding a plasterwork decorative moulding containing fibrous reinforcement and produced with a template when wet.

fibrous plaster rope a strip of plaster-soaked canvas used as reinforcement in casting of fibrous plastering.

fibrous plasterwork, ornamental plasterwork; any finishing work done in fibrous plaster.

fibula Lat.; a Classic decorative motif representing a brooch or clasp. →125

Ficus religiosa the sacred fig tree, see tree of Buddha. →121

fiddleback grain, fiddleback mottle; a decorative grain pattern found in certain hardwoods with curly figure; traditionally used for the backs of violins.

fiddleback mottle see fiddleback grain.

field 1 in computing, a set of one or more characters that is the smallest unit of data and represents a single item of information.
2 the area of action of a magnet, electromagnet or gravitational system.

field drain, agricultural drain, filter drain, French drain, land drain; a drain for drying out damp or saturated ground consisting of a backfilled trench containing a length of perforated pipe; in building construction most often referred to as a land drain.

field drainage see land drainage.

field surveying see land surveying.

fig tree see tree of Buddha. →121

figure the pattern caused by grain on a wooden surface.

figured capital, historiated capital; a Romanesque capital decorated with figures of animals, birds, humans with or without foliage, often symbolic or part of a narrative sequence. →115

figured column any decorative column carved or shaped in the form of a human figure; a caryatid, canephora, atlas etc. →76
see *figured column* illustration. →76

filament a thin wire of tungsten inside an incandescent lamp, which glows white hot when electricity is passed through it, giving off light.

filament yarn in textile manufacture, a number of synthetic fibres bundled together and loosely wound.

file 1 a hand tool whose steel blade is roughened with a series of serrations, used for sharpening cutting tools and shaping metal.
2 in computing, a set of related data, a document etc. stored, used or edited as a discrete entity.

fill 1 in sitework, earth or other material such as hardcore used to raise or level the existing ground or to make an embankment.
2 earthmoving and similar operations for the above.
3 see backfill.
4 material used to fill a void in construction, as packing etc.
see *fill* in Egyptian burial monuments illustration. →70

filler 1 a substance added to plastics, paints and some adhesives to improve their properties and reduce cost by bulking; also known as an extender.
2 surface filler; in finishing walls and ceilings, a paste applied over a surface to fill in any irregularities and, when hard, provide a smooth surface for painting, also called stopping or spackling.
3 a fine material such as fine aggregate used to stiffen a bituminous binder.
see corrugation filler.
see jamb filler.
see joint filler. →53
see lintel filler.
see pore filler.

filler cement see fillerized cement.

fillerized cement, composite cement, filler cement; ordinary Portland cement to which an inert material or filler of finely ground limestone has been added to increase its volume.

fillet, 1 list; a thin straight raised or sunk horizontal decorative moulding. →14
see raised fillet, square fillet. →14
see sunk fillet. →14
2 see moulding.
3 see fascia, fascia moulding. →14, →80
4 a thin strip of material.
see angle fillet. →49
see mortar fillet.
see tile fillet.

fillet chisel, spindle; a narrow-bladed masonry chisel used for carving details and ornament in stonework. →41

filleted column, filleted pier; a Gothic column carved in such a way as to appear to be formed from small round columns joined together.

filleted pier see filleted column.

fillet raised moulding a decorative moulding consisting of a small rectangular projection in cross-section.

fillet saw a fine saw for cutting fillets and other details in stonework, or one for cutting mouldings in joinery.

fillet sunk moulding a decorative moulding consisting of a groove, rectangular in cross-section.

fillet weld a V-shaped butt weld in which abutting metal components have been chamfered, stronger than a normal butt weld. →34

filigree glass decorative glass with internal coloured threads or strands embedded within.

filigree beam a composite beam whose steel formwork shell is filled with concrete and acts as tension reinforcement once the concrete has set.

filling station see petrol station.

fillister head screw a screw with a raised cylindrical head whose upper surface is convex. →36

film 1 the thin layer formed from one or a number of coats of hardened paint or varnish.
2 any thin flexible plastic sheet product, often transparent and used for packing.
3 see drawing film.
4 a thin sheet of plastic with a light-sensitive coating, on which photographic and cinematic images are reproduced.

film adhesive see film glue.

film-faced plywood plywood which has been faced with resin impregnated film; has good resistance to moisture and is thus used for shuttering.

film glue solid phenol formaldehyde resin used in thin layers for gluing expensive veneers to a backing by hot pressing.

film studio a building or complex where films are made and produced.

filter 1 a cleaning or purifying apparatus for the separation of unwanted particles of solid material, gas, liquid, radiation or sound from a medium.
2 colour filter, light filter; a piece of coloured translucent material placed in front of a light source to change its colour and composition.
3 a device for eliminating electromagnetic output of selected wavelengths.
4 see strainer.

filter cloth see filter fabric. →44

filter drain see field drain.

filter fabric strong fibrous sheet used in concrete construction paving, planted areas etc. to prevent layers of construction mixing with one another, to provide stability and to prevent the penetration of roots, while allowing drainage through; also called filter cloth. →44

filter mat a sheeting component included as a layer in landscaping, green roofs etc. to prevent fine material being drained away, while allowing for water to pass through; see also filter fabric. →48

filter paper very absorbent unsized paper used for filtering suspended solids out of liquids.

filtration the cleansing of a liquid or gas of impurities by passing it through a filter or other screening device.
fimbriated cross see cross fimbriated. →118
fin 1 see flash line.
2 see flash.
final account in contract management, a document stating the cost of all work undertaken and the total payment to be paid, as accepted by all parties involved.
final certificate in contract management, a document that authorizes payment to the contractor of the final account, an approval that the terms of the contract have been met.
final circuit an electric circuit between an electric point and an appliance.
final coat, finish coat, finishing coat; in painting and plastering, the uppermost coat applied to a surface as a finish.
final exit see exit door.
final inspection a building inspection held after all work by the contractor has been completed to a reasonable degree, prior to handover and concurrent with official approval.
see period of final inspection.
final plaster coat, 1 face coat, finishing coat, setting coat, skimming coat; in plastering, any coat of plaster laid as a finished surface. →83
2 see *final plaster coat* in Roman walling illustration. →83
final set the later period of setting of cement or concrete, as measured by standard tests.
final sum the cost of all works as mentioned in the final account.
financial statement see statement.
financial year, fiscal year; in accountancy, a year in the economic life of a company; often measured from 1st April to 31st March.
financing, funding; **1** the provision of money for a particular purpose such as a construction project.
2 the money thus provided.
financing plan a plan indicating how a development or project is to be financed.
fin de siècle the decadent taste typical of artistic and literary circles in the 1890s.
fine see penalty.
fine aggregate aggregate consisting largely of particles with a size range of 75 μm–5 mm.
fine-aggregate asphalt rolled asphalt road surfacing with a high proportion of sand or other fine aggregate.
fine art a Renaissance concept of architecture, sculpture, painting, music and dance as distinguishable from applied art, science and crafts.
fine grained 1 referring to very cohesive types of clay or silty soil which contain little or no coarse materials larger than 0.02 mm and are highly compressible and impermeable.
2 see close grained.
fine-grained soil see previous entry.
fine gravel in soil classification, a range of particles of mineral soil which vary in size from 2 mm to 6 mm.
fine grown see close grained.
fine mortar mortar whose aggregate is coarse sand; see coarse stuff; see also finish stuff.
fineness modulus in aggregate grading, a measure of the fineness of an aggregate obtained by passing a sample through a standard set of sieves and dividing the sum of percentages of each size by 100.
fines in soil classification, material whose particles will pass through a 0.06 mm sieve.
fine sand in soil classification, a range of particles of mineral soil which vary in size from 0.06 mm to 0.2 mm.
fine silt in soil classification, a range of particles of mineral soil which vary in size from 0.002 mm to 0.006 mm.
fine stuff see finish plaster.
finger 'yeba'; an ancient Egyptian unit of measurement equal to one twenty eighth part of a royal cubit, or one quarter of a palm, approximately 19 mm; also called a finger-width or digit. →106
finger joint 1 a timber lengthening joint formed by cutting or machining deep zigzags into the ends of two timbers to be joined, then gluing them together; used especially in laminated timber products and factory-made assemblies. →3
2 see box corner joint, combed joint. →5
finger-jointed plywood plywood which has been increased in dimension using finger joints.
finger plate see push plate. →51
finger-width see finger. →106
finial florid Gothic decoration for the top of a gable, spire or pinnacle. →100, →109
finish 1 the final surface treatment for an object or component produced by the application of a coating or facing, by machining or mechanical or chemical processes.
2 a final covering, facing, treatment or coating for a surface or component.
3 see coating.
4 see surface treatment.
5 see finishing.
6 see stonework finish. →12
finish carpentry see joinery.
finish coat see final coat.
finished floor level, FFL; the floor level of flooring, screeds etc. above the structural floor, usually excluding thin floor coverings, from which all vertical measurements and levels are taken in a room or storey.
finished size the size of a piece of machined timber, subject to machining tolerances.
finishing, 1 finish; a final treatment, layer of material or coating for a surface or component.
2 the act of producing a finish.
finishing coat 1 see final plaster coat. →83
2 see final coat.
finishing nail see lost-head nail. →35
finishings 1 the final coverings, facings, treatments or coatings for surfaces and components.
2 see paint finishing.
finishing trowel, smoothing trowel; a plasterer's trowel used for the application and smoothing of a final coat of plaster. →43
finish plaster 1 fine grade plaster used as a coating for undercoat plaster, providing a finish.
2 fine stuff; hard lightweight plaster used as a finish.
finish washer see screw cup. →36
Fink truss, Belgian truss, French truss; a diagonally braced pitched roof truss without vertical strutting, whose diagonals form a W-shaped pattern; developed by the German engineer Albert Fink in America in the 1800s. →33
Finnish Association of Architects, SAFA; a professional body to further the interests and rights of its architect members in Finland.
fir 1 [*Abies spp.*] a group of common softwoods from the northern hemisphere with pale, lightweight, straight-grained timber which is prone to fungal attack; used in construction work, packaging and for pulp; see ***Abies spp.*** for full list of species of fir included in this work, see also Douglas fir.
2 fir green, pine needle, spruce green; a shade of green which takes its name from the colour of the needles of the fir (*Abies spp.*), pine (*Pinus spp.*) and spruce (*Picea spp.*) trees.
3 see fir tree moulding. →125
4 see fir twig moulding. →125
fire 1 any heater or other appliance in which material is burned and has a live flame.
2 the destructive burning of a building or part of a building.

fire alarm 1 a device which emits a sound on detection of the presence or outbreak of fire in a building to draw attention to a possible fire hazard.
2 the sound made by this device.

fire alarm indicator an electronic control panel which indicates the location of fire alarms which have been triggered by a fire.

fire alarm system a fire safety system which will sound an alarm or alarms in the presence of a building fire, triggered by a fire-detection system.

fire area in planning for fire safety, a discrete area, rooms or spaces etc. of a building bounded by fire-resistant construction to prevent the spread of fire; the area within a fire compartment.

fire assembly any assembly of materials, construction or component which has fire-resistant properties; usually refers to a rated fire door, window or hatch with fittings.

fireback a shaped unit or laid masonry of refractory brick forming the rear and side walls of a fireplace. →55

fire barrier in fire protection, an area of non-combustible sheet material attached to components, across cavities within construction etc. to inhibit the spread of fire.

fire behaviour see fire performance.

fire bend a bend in metal pipework made by softening the pipe with a blowtorch and bending; see also pulled bend.

fire block a fire barrier for preventing the spread of fire through or within timber elements such as walls or floors.

fire booster an automatic water pump used during fire-fighting to increase the pressure of water in a main for drenching water and sprinkler installations.

firebox, combustion chamber; the closed compartment of a solid fuel appliance, gas stove, burner or fireplace in which combustion takes place. →56

firebox door a small hinged front-opening hatch to close off the firebox of a fireplace, stove etc. →56

fire break 1 construction in a building to inhibit the spread of fire from one compartment to another.
2 open space left between rows of housing or adjacent buildings to curtail the spread of fire in a built-up area.
3 fire corridor; a linear zone of agricultural or forest land cleared to soil level of trees, plants, crops etc. to prevent the spread of fire.

firebreak door see fire door.

firebreak floor see fire floor.

firebreak wall see fire wall.

firebrick, refractory brick; a brick of special composition capable of withstanding high temperatures without melting or fusion, used for masonry chimneys, flue linings, kilns and fireboxes. →56
see *firebrick lining* in fireplace illustration. →55

fire brigade, fire department, fire services; a local authority or voluntary organization whose task is to put out building and other fires in a particular district.

fire calculations mathematical modelling for analysing the functioning of a building in the event of fire.

fire cell see fire compartment.

fire certificate in planning for fire, a document, issued by the fire brigade following an inspection, specifying means of escape, alarms, extinguishers, signage and other fire precautions.

fireclay a simple ceramic material with high kaolin content used for firebricks.

fire containment 1 measures in building design to restrict the spread of fire by inclusion of fire compartments, non-combustible construction, extinguishing systems and procedures, and smoke venting routes.
2 the restriction of smoke flow and spread of flame by firefighters during a hazardous building fire.

fire corridor see fire break.

fire compartment, fire cell, compartment; a subdivision of a building into an isolated unit surrounded by fire walls and floors to inhibit the spread of fire.

fire compartmentation in planning for fire safety, the division of a building or part of a building into discrete fire compartments.

fire curtain, safety curtain; in theatre design, a fireproof curtain which can be lowered to isolate the stage area from the main body of the auditorium in the event of a fire.

fire damper, fire shutter; a shut-off valve in an air-handling system for preventing the flow of smoke and combustion gases through a duct.

fired brick, burnt brick; any clay brick which has been fired in a kiln; cf. mud brick. →16

fire department see fire brigade.

fire-detection system a system of fire safety sensors which react to the presence of heat, smoke or flame and set off fire prevention measures.

fire detector in planning for fire safety, an electric sensor which reacts to the presence of excess heat, smoke and flame; it may trigger alarms, sprinklers, alert the fire brigade and set off other methods of inhibiting the spread of fire.

fire development the way in which a hazardous building fire spreads from an outbreak into a full blaze; see also ignition, combustion, flashover.

fire door, 1 firebreak door; a specially designed and approved door assembly rated to contain the spread of a building fire for a specified time.
2 see fireproof hatch.

fire engineering the discipline of planning for fire in a building using calculation and testing.

fire escape see escape stair.

fire escape ladder, escape ladder; an external ladder for providing escape from a rooftop or balcony in the event of a fire or other emergency.

fire-exit bolt see panic bolt.

fire exit sign any sign in a building designed to indicate the location of fire escape routes and emergency exits.

fire extinguisher a portable apparatus for putting out a small fire.
see carbon dioxide fire extinguisher.
see dry-powder extinguisher.
see fire extinguishing system.
see foam extinguisher.

fire extinguishing see fire-fighting.

fire extinguishing system, fire suppression system; an integrated system of piped extinguishant such as a non-combustible liquid, gas, vapour or foam released in the event of a fire; types included as separate entries are listed below.
automatic fire extinguisher.
carbon dioxide fire extinguisher.
dry-powder extinguisher.
foam extinguisher.
fire extinguisher.
halon fire-extinguishing system.
sprinkler system.

fire-fighting, extinguishing; actions by occupants of a building or a fire brigade to put out or contain hazardous and dangerous fires and limit their damage to a minimum using specialized equipment.

fire-fighting equipment fire hoses, blankets, portable extinguishers, fixed systems and other apparatus used in the event of a fire breaking out.

fire floor, firebreak floor, party floor; the upper or lower protective construction of a fire compartment, a floor or ceiling slab which forms its fireproof boundary.

firefront, fret; the front of an open fire. →55

fire glass see fire resisting glass.

fire grading see fire-resistance grading.

fire hazard any combustible material, assembly or situation which poses a threat to fire safety in a building and increases the risk of spread of fire.

fire hose a hose of approved and tested material, construction and dimension used in fire-fighting.

fire-hose reel, hose reel; a fire hose coiled and placed in a designated cabinet at a fire point with a connection to a main, used by occupants of the building in the event of a fire.

fire hydrant an outlet from a fire main from which a supply of extinguishant water can be used for fire-fighting in the event of a building fire.

fire inspection an official inspection of a building by a fire-prevention officer prior to the issue of a fire certificate.

fire insulation see fireproofing.
sprayed mineral insulation, see firespraying.

fire insurance insurance taken to cover damages caused by building fires.

fire load a measure of the combustibility of the contents of a space in a building, given as the total energy in megajoules given out when its entire contents burn, used to calculate fire severity.

fire-load density a measure of the potential relative severity of fire within a space, given as fire load per unit floor area, measured in units of MJ/m^2.

fire loading see fire load.

fire main in fire-fighting, a mains water pipe used by firemen to extinguish a fire.

fire modelling in planning for fire control, a computer analysis of the performance of a building in the event of a potential fire.

fire officer, fire-prevention officer; a person, often in the employ of the local fire brigade, who inspects designs, constructions and site procedures to ensure they comply with safety standards and regulations with regard to fire.

fire performance, fire behaviour; a description of the combustibility, smoke release, toxicity etc. of a particular material or component with regard to fire and fire safety.

fire-performance plasterboard plasterboard graded according to its properties of fire resistance.

fireplace a domestic masonry construction, recess or proprietary metal appliance, usually open or with glazed doors at the front and fitted to a flue, in which solid fuel is burnt to provide heating and atmosphere to a room; types included as separate entries are listed below. →55
see *fireplace* illustration. →55
freestanding fireplace. →55
masonry fireplace. →55
open fireplace, see open fire. →55
see-through fireplace. →55
three-faced fireplace. →55
two-faced fireplace. →55

fireplace canopy see canopy. →55

fireplace door a hinged door, often glazed, to close off the front of a fireplace, keeping heat and smoke inside. →56

fireplace hood see canopy. →55

fireplace recess a recess made in a wall to house a fireplace. →55

fireplace surround a decorative surround for an open fireplace; often called a mantelpiece. →55

fire point a clearly marked designated place within a building where fire-extinguishing equipment is located for use in the event of a fire.

fire precautions measures taken in a building and on a building site to inhibit the ignition of a fire and to protect people and property in the event of a fire.

fire prevention measures taken in a building to reduce the risk of outbreak of fire.

fire-prevention officer see fire officer.

fireproof, fire resistant; a general term for a material or component with good fire resistance; in North America a material or component which can safely withstand the burning of the whole building.

fireproof brick 1 see flue block. →16
2 see firebrick. →55, →56

fireproofing, fire protection; material or treatment added to construction to increase its resistance to fire.
sprayed mineral insulation, see firespraying.

fireproofing paint see intumescent paint.

fireproof hatch, fire door; an access hatch which has a fire rating.

fireproof lining, refractory lining; non-combustible material added to a surface as fireproofing. →56
see *firebrick lining* in fireplace illustration. →55

fireproof mortar see refractory mortar.

fireproof plaster see fire-retardant plaster.

fire protection 1 see fireproofing.
2 see active fire protection.
3 see passive fire protection.

fire pump a water pump which maintains pressure in sprinkler systems in the event of a fire.

fire rating see fire-resistance grading.

fire red, flame red, flame scarlet; a shade of orange red which takes its name from the colour of red in fire.

fire reserve water for use in fire-fighting stored in tanks in the basements and roof spaces of buildings.

fire resistance the relative non-combustibility of a material or component which restricts the spread of fire or maintains its structural properties in the event of a fire.

fire-resistance grading, fire grading, fire rating, fire-resistance rating; a system of grading materials and components according to the results of laboratory tests carried out to ascertain their fire-resisting properties.

fire-resistance rating see fire-resistance grading.

fire resistant see fireproof.

fire-resistant gasket in glazing, a strip of fire-resistant material fixed around the external edges of a pane of glass to provide a seal.

fire-resistant glass see fire-resisting glass.

fire-resisting glass, 1 fire glass, fire-resistant glass; glass of special construction or constituency, used where a certain degree of fire protection is required.
2 see laminated intumescent glass.

fire retardant a chemical treatment applied to materials and components, fabrics etc. designed to inhibit their combustion; especially one applied by impregnation as protection for timber.

fire retardant board a grade of chipboard or other wood-based panel product whose surface is faced or treated with fire retardant material; suitable for use as a lining and cladding in situations such as fire escapes where the spread of fire is to be avoided.

fire retardant plaster types of plaster used to increase the level of fire protection; see also perlite plaster, vermiculite plaster; sometimes called fireproof plaster.

fire safety measures taken to reduce the risk of fire and to inhibit damage to the occupants, property and construction of a building in the event of a fire.

fire safety sign 1 any sign in a building designed to provide information about the location of fire escape routes, emergency exits, firefighting equipment, smoke vents etc.
2 see fire exit sign.

fire separation fire-resistant construction such as a bounding wall, floor or roof with the appropriate properties to contain a fire within a compartment for a specified amount of time.

fire service access see vehicle access route.

fire services see fire brigade.

fire severity a measure of the combustibility of the contents and surface finishes in a fire compartment used in design for fire safety.

fire shutter 1 a large sliding, folding or rolling door to prevent the spread of fire in a building, often operated automatically.
2 see fire damper.

firespraying, sprayed mineral insulation; the sprayed application of mineral-based covering to improve the fire resistance and insulating properties of a structure or component.

fire stair see escape stair.

fire station the headquarters of a fire brigade with vehicles, buildings and fire-fighting equipment.

fire stop, fire stopping; a thin strip of non-combustible material inserted into joints to prevent the spread of fire through gaps such as joints between components, and where pipes and cables pass through construction.

fire stop sleeve, pipe closer; a pipe fitting used as fire protection for plastic pipe crossing from one fire compartment to another; if this melts during a building fire it expands to fill the gap, preventing the spread of fire.

fire stopping see fire stop.

fire suppression system see fire extinguishing system.

fire test the controlled burning of a material, construction or component under laboratory conditions to ascertain its fire rating.

fire valve a valve to automatically close off the supply of gas or oil in the event of a building fire.

fire vent, smoke outlet, smoke vent; an openable or fusible vent, window or hatch opened automatically, manually or by melting in the event of a building fire to allow the release of combustion fumes and smoke to the outside.

fire venting, smoke venting; in fire control, the expelling of combustion gases and smoke from a building through specially designed ducts and hatches.

fire venting installation **1** measures such as shafts, mechanical apparatus, vents etc. within a building to facilitate the extraction of smoke in the event of a fire.
2 mechanical smoke extraction system; mechanical plant for removing smoke in the event of a fire.

fire wall, compartment wall, firebreak wall, division wall; **1** a wall or partition in a building designed to prevent the spread of fire between compartments.
2 a continuous fire-rated wall running from foundation to roof level to provide subdivision of a building or fire separation from adjoining buildings.
3 see separating wall.

fire window a window assembly which has a specified fire resistance and approved construction for its use.

fir green see fir.

firkin an archaic unit of measurement of liquid capacity, half a kilderkin; 1 kilderkin is equal to half a barrel, 16 or 18 gallons.

firm **1** a usually small privately owned professionally based commercial organization involved in the provision of goods and services.
2 see company.

firmer chisel a sturdy chisel whose blade is rectangular in section, used with a mallet for general rough work, removing of wood and initial smoothing. →41

firmer gouge a gouge whose blade is sharpened on its convex edge, used for cutting shallow depressions in wood; see also scribing gouge. →41

firm price contract a form of building contract in which the price cannot be amended regardless of changes in economic conditions.

firring, furring; thin strips or pieces of timber or other material laid or fixed to a structure or frame to raise the level of a surface cladding or to make it even, to provide falls etc. →8

firring piece, furring piece; a piece of timber nailed to the upper surface of roof joists to provide a slope for a flat roof.

first angle projection a standard draughtsman's method of arranging the six planar orthographic projection drawings of main views of a building or object in relation to one another, as if unfolding the hinged sides of an imaginary cube onto which the projections have been made; also called a first quadrant projection, it is widely favoured in Great Britain; see also third angle. →127

first coat see first plaster undercoat.

first family gas in gas heating, a gas used for combustion which has a Wobbe number of 24.4–28.8 MJ/m^3.

first floor the storey above the ground floor in the UK; in continental Europe and USA this is the second floor.
see *first floor* in brick house illustration. →59
see ground floor.

first layer felt see base sheet.

first moment of area see static moment.

first plaster undercoat, 1 floating coat, pricking-up coat, render coat, scratch coat, straightening coat; in plastering, the first coat of plaster, applied directly to lathing or onto another background; see two coat, three coat plastering. →83
2 see *first plaster coat* in Roman walling illustration. →83
3 see base coat. →83

first quadrant projection see first angle projection. →127

first refusal see refusal.

First Pompeian style see Incrustation style.
see *Pompeian styles* illustration. →126

fir tree moulding a decorative moulding of stylized intertwined conifer motifs; particular to Finnish heraldry. →125

fir twig moulding a decorative moulding of stylized intertwined conifer frond or twig motifs; particular to Finnish heraldry. →125

fiscal year see financial year.

fish an ancient symbol of life and fertility; ikhthus in Greek, piscis in Latin. →119, →123

fish and anchor a Christian symbol representative of faith, redemption and hope. →119

fish-bellied beam a concrete or steel beam whose underside is curved downwards towards the middle, forming a U shape. →30

fish-bellied truss a trussed beam in which the upper chord is flat and the lower chord is curved, forming a braced U shape. →33

fish bladder see vesica piscis. →108

fish glue, isinglass; glue made by boiling up the swim bladders and skins of fish.

fish joint see spliced joint. →3

fish piece see fish plate. →3

fish plate, fish piece, splice plate; a plate fixed to either side of a lengthening joint to fix two members rigidly together. →3

fish plate joint see spliced joint. →3

fish tenon joint see free tenon joint. →5

fishtail chisel, fishtail tool, fantail tool; a chisel with a wedge-shaped blade splayed outwards towards its cutting edge. →41

fishtail tie see fishtail wall tie. →22

fishtail tool see fishtail chisel. →41

fishtail wall tie a wall tie formed from metal strip with split and forked ends to provide a better bond with masonry. →22

fistuca Lat.; a Roman tamping implement or piledriver.

fitched cross, pointed cross; any cross whose lowest limb is terminated with a point or sharpened end; variously known as cross fitched, fitchy or fitchee. →117

fitment, fitting; a fixed component such as a hook, door handle etc. that is not part of the building fabric.

fitness club see health club.

fitted carpet, wall-to-wall carpet; a carpet fixed in place at its extremities which extends over the whole floor area of a space. →44

fitted cupboard a cupboard unit such as a kitchen unit fitted permanently in a space against a wall.

fitter a skilled workman who installs and assembles system products such as suspended ceilings,

fixed furnishings and technical installations on a building site.
fitting 1 a piece of hardware for a door, window or hatch.
2 any fixed accessory such as a kitchen cupboard or basin which can be removed without damage to the building fabric.
3 the fastening in place of fixed furnishings, technical appliances and installations.
4 see installation.
5 see mounting.
6 see fitment.
7 see water fitting.
8 see pipe fitting.
9 light fitting, see luminaire. →60
10 door fittings, see door furniture. →51
fitting-out the installation of fixed furnishings, fitted cupboards and joinery, finishings and carpets etc. for a building project.
fittings 1 see fixed furnishings.
2 see rainwater goods.
3 door fittings, see door furniture. →51
five-aisled church a basilica church type in which four colonnades divide the main body of the church into four aisles and a central nave. →100
five-centred arch an arch whose intrados is constructed from five centres of curvature, an approximation of a true elliptical arch. →24
five-domed church see cross-domed church. →95
fivefold cross a cross with small crosses situated at the four angles between the limbs; a Jerusalem cross. →118
five-pointed star a star motif with five radiating limbs. →108, →123
see mullet. →123
see pentagram. →108
see spur rowel. →108
five pound maul a heavy one-handed hammer with a steel head; used for striking chisels and other implements. →40
fixative, fixer; a sealing chemical substance with which chalk, charcoal and lead pencil drawings are treated to make them permanent and prevent smudging.
fixed cost in business management, an overhead or necessary cost such as rent, which does not vary and is always payable.
fixed furnishings, fittings; any built-in furnishings for a project, included in the contract documents.
see *fixed furnishing unit* in office building illustration. →60
fixed furnishings drawing a contract document which indicates the fixed furnishings, their quantity, type, location and finishes, sometimes including details, for a particular building.
fixed light, deadlight, fixed sash; a glazed area of a window which is not openable, or a window whose glass is fixed directly to the frame.
fixed luminaire a luminaire fixed permanently to a wall, floor or other surface.
fixed oil see fatty oil.
fixed price contract a contract in which the contract sum is given in a tender or is based on a schedule of rates; this sum may be exceptionally amended due to a change in economic conditions.
fixed sash see fixed light.
fixed shower any shower fixed permanently to a ceiling or wall, as opposed to one held by hand.
fixer a chemical with which photographic images are treated during developing to make them permanent; also known as fixative.
fixing, 1 fastening; the connecting of two components together or the attachment of one to another.
2 any hardware such as nails, screws, bolts etc. used to attach components in place or connect them together, also called a fastener.
3 the laying of tiles, fine stone, ashlar etc. into mortar with fine joints; see bedding.
4 see pipe fixing.
5 see holdfast. →11
fixing block see nog.
fixing mortar 1 fine mortar, lime putty, stone dust or cement used for bedding stonework with fine joints. →11
2 see tiling mortar. →59
fixture 1 any fitting or furnishing built in to the fabric of a building.
2 light fixture, see luminaire. →60
fixtures the furnishings, appliances and installations which are built in or firmly attached to the fabric of a building.
flag 1 see slab.
2 see natural stone paver, also flag.
3 see concrete paving slab. →15
flag of victory see labarum. →119
flag-pole, flagstaff; a pole, either freestanding or fixed to a wall, to which a flag, banner or pennant is fixed.
flagstaff a traditional name for a flag-pole.
flagstone a heavy paving stone, see natural stone paver, also flag.
flail a common motif in ancient Egyptian decoration, symbolic of Royal authority, a thonged whip often depicted crossed over the chest of a ruler; also known as a scourge. →74
flakeboard particleboard manufactured from flat chips or flakes of wood bonded together with resin and pressed into sheets. →9
flake white, Flemish white, French white; white lead pigment in flake form.
flaking 1 a defect in a paint, plaster or other finish involving the separation in flakes of a coat from its underlying surface.
2 wattle, withe braiding; in thatched roofing and similar traditional construction, a layer of woven reed or thin twigs of hazel or willow laid as a base for thatch, daub etc.
3 see brickwork weathering.
flaky aggregate coarse aggregate with flattish particles.
flaky and elongated aggregate coarse aggregate whose particles are long and flat.
Flamboyant style the later phase of French Gothic architecture from the late 1400s, characterized by flowing and flamelike tracery.
flamboyant tracery tracery of the Flamboyant style; see flowing tracery. →110
flame cutting the cutting of metals by local melting using an intense flame of gas such as oxyacetylene.
flame detector, radiation detector; a fire detector which reacts to the presence of flickering ultraviolet or infrared light, present in many types of flame.
flamed finish, thermal finish; a rough-textured non-slip stone surface treatment produced by using high intensity flamers to crack surface crystals in the stone; often used for granite flooring and facing. →12
flame red see fire red.
flame-retardant paint see intumescent paint.
flame scarlet see fire red.
flame-spread rating a fire safety classification which determines the surface spread of flame across an interior finish.
flame yellow, cadmium yellow, deep yellow, saffron yellow; a shade of strong orange yellow; the colour of saffron or cadmium yellow pigment.
flamingo a shade of pink which takes its name from the colour of the flamingo bird (*Phoenicopterus roseus*).
flammability the measure of how well a material or component will burn with a flame.
flammable a description of a material which will readily burn with a flame.
flammable liquid any volatile liquid which will burn with ease, including liquid fuels and thinners.

flammable material any materials, especially plastics and fabrics, which will burn with ease.

flange any flat protruding part of a component, such as the flattened end which encircles a pipe as a fixing or the upper and lower flat protrusions in an I-beam.

flanged beam a beam whose upper or compression surface is increased by widening; in a steel beam this may be the upper or lower flange, in concrete it may be a floor slab.

flange joint a pipework joint made by bolting together the flanges at the ends of consecutive pipes.

flank the sides of a fortification to the rear of a bastion, connecting the faces to a curtain wall. →104

flanking path in acoustics, an undesired route for the transmission of sound from one space to another via voids, cavities, ducting, pipework etc.

flanking sound see flanking transmission.

flanking transmission, flanking sound; in acoustics, the transmission of sound from one space to another through openings in partitions, usually ductwork or piping.

flanking window, wing light; a full-length window beside an external door.

flap hinge see strap hinge. →38

flare the widening of a lane or carriageway on the approach to a road junction to enable uncongested flow and good visibility of traffic. →63

flared brick a brick which, after firing, is darker at one end, and is used as a header in patterned brickwork; similar decorative bricks with a darker or discoloured surface.

flash see flash line.

flash butt welding see flash welding.

flashing 1 a strip of impervious sheet material or preformed profile laid in construction to protect a joint from the passage of rainwater; types included as separate entries are listed below.
abutment flashing. →56
apron flashing. →56
chimney flashing. →58
cover flashing.
eaves flashing. →49
head flashing.
raking flashing.
sheetmetal flashing.
stepped flashing.
upstand flashing. →56
2 a defect in painting consisting of glossier patches in the paintwork caused by paint drying while the surface is being painted.

flash line, 1 fin, mould mark; a visible raised line evident in the surface of cast products such as fibrous plaster, concrete or plastics, caused by the seepage of cast material into joints between adjacent parts of a mould.
2 linear protrusions occurring in a finished concrete surface due to joints in adjacent formwork boards.

flashover, ignition; in the development of a fire within a building, the point at which the heat reaches such a level that a large part of the contents of a space ignite, causing a small explosion.

flashpoint the lowest temperature at which enough vapour from a volatile liquid will evaporate to burn in the presence of a flame.

flash welding, flash butt welding, resistance flash welding; a method of resistance welding rails end to end by passing a large current between to form an arc and thus melt the ends before pressing together.

flat 1 a rectangular metal bar formed by rolling, whose uniform cross-section is wider than thick, but whose thickness exceeds one tenth of its width; uses in construction include braces, brackets, frames, base plates, ornamental work etc. →34
2 matt, matte; the lowest of five grades of glossiness in a dry paint surface, characterized by little or no sheen, even from oblique angles.
3 apartment; a single (or double) storey dwelling within a multistorey residential building; some types of flat listed below. →61
bedsit, one-room flat.
corner apartment. →61
council flat.
maisonette, duplex apartment.
open-ended unit, through apartment. →61
two-roomed flat.

flat angle, straight angle; in geometry, an angle of 180°, a straight line.

flat arch, jack arch, straight arch; a masonry arch formed of wedge-shaped pieces, whose intrados is horizontal and nearly straight. →23
see *flat, false and decorative arches* illustration. →23

flat bar see flat. →34

flat brush 1 any paintbrush with bristles held by a flattened ferrule, forming a rectangular bristle-head; the most basic form of paintbrush, available in a range of widths and bristle types; also called a flat wall brush, or flat varnish brush, depending on use.→43
2 see distemper brush. →43

flat cutting, flatting, ripping, rip-sawing; the resawing of converted timber into planks or timber sections along the grain.

flat cut veneer a decorative veneer produced by the through slicing of a log or flitch; also variously known as flat sliced, plain cut, straight cut. →10

flat drawn glass see clear sheet glass.

flat glass any glass manufactured in flat sheets.

flat grain see plain sawn.

flat head screw any screw in which the upper surface of the head is flat; often a countersunk head screw. →36

flat joint see flush joint. →16

flatlet a small flat, a bedsit.

flat nose pliers pliers which have flat, wide jaws.

flat plate synonymous with metal plate, especially that made from steel. →34

flat roof, platform roof (Scot.); a roof which has a slope of less than 10°.

flatsawing see through and through sawing. →2

flat sawn see plain sawn.

flat slab see mushroom slab. →27

flat sliced veneer see flat cut veneer. →10

flat spade drill a drill bit with a flat, sharpened cutting edge and centre spur for drilling holes in non-metallic materials such as wood. →42

flat stop in ornamentation, the termination of a chamfered moulding or carving with a perpendicular triangle.

flatted factory a multistorey building containing a number of industrial concerns or factory premises on different floors, making use of common technical installations and waste disposal.

flatting see flat cutting.

flatting down, rubbing; the scouring of a primed surface with a fine abrasive to remove irregularities prior to painting.

flat top truss a steel or timber long-span lattice girder whose upper chord is parallel or nearly parallel to the lower chord. →33

flat truss see flat top truss. →33

flat varnish brush a flat brush whose bristles are designed for the application of varnish. →43

flat wall brush see flat brush. →43

flat washer, plain washer; an ordinary flat circular washer with a hole in the centre; if the hole is small compared to the washer's surface area, it is called a penny washer. →37

flax a blue-flowered plant, *Linum usitatissimum*, whose dried stem fibres are woven into linen (in use as early as 2500 BC by the Egyptians for wrapping their mummies), pressed into flaxboard etc., and whose seeds are pressed for linseed oil.
see bamboo.

see beige.
see linseed oil.

flaxboard particleboard manufactured from the stem fibres of the flax plant, or other similar plants, bonded together with resin then pressed into sheets. →9

flaxen see beige.

fleak a rough hewn timber used in scaffolding.

fleam in the sharpening of a saw, the angle between the cutting edge of the tooth and the plane of the saw blade.

Flemish bond 1 a brickwork bond in which each course consists of alternating headers and stretchers, laid so that each header is centred over a joint in the course below. →18
2 any of a number of brickwork bonds based on this pattern; see illustration and below. →18
American with Flemish bond, see Flemish stretcher bond. →18
common bond, see Flemish stretcher bond. →18
Dutch bond. →18
Flemish cross bond. →18
Flemish double header bond. →18
Flemish double stretcher bond, see monk bond. →18, →19
Flemish garden-wall bond. →18
Flemish header bond. →18
Flemish stretcher bond. →18
flying bond, see monk bond. →18
monk bond. →18
raking Flemish bond. →18
Silesian bond, see Flemish garden-wall bond. →18
staggered Flemish bond, see Dutch bond. →18
Sussex bond, see Flemish garden-wall bond. →18
Yorkshire bond, see monk bond. →18

Flemish cross bond a brickwork bond in which courses of alternating headers and stretchers are interspersed with courses of stretchers, laid so that the joints form distinct cross motifs; a form of Flemish stretcher bond. →18

Flemish double header bond a brickwork bond in which each course consists of stretchers alternating with two headers. →18

Flemish diagonal bond variations of Flemish stretcher and Flemish double stretcher bond in which brickwork joints create a pattern of interlocking diamond shapes. →19

Flemish double stretcher bond 1 a brickwork bond in which each course consists of a repeated series of one header and two stretchers; see also monk bond; see variations in illustrations. →18, →19
2 staggered Flemish double stretcher bond. →19
3 diagonal Flemish double stretcher bond. →19
4 raking Flemish double stretcher bond. →19

Flemish garden-wall bond, Sussex bond, Silesian bond; a brickwork bond in which each course consists of a repeated series of one header and three stretchers; alternate courses are laid symmetrical about the header. →18

Flemish header bond 1 a brickwork bond in which courses of alternating headers and stretchers are interspersed with courses of headers, and in which the stretchers are always laid in the same vertical line. →18
2 see Flemish double header bond. →18

Flemish stretcher bond, 1 American with Flemish bond (Am.), common bond; a brickwork bond in which one course of alternating headers and stretchers alternates between one and six courses of stretchers. →18
2 Flemish double stretcher bond, see monk bond. →18

Flemish white see flake white.

flesh a shade of pale reddish grey which takes its name from the colour of the skin of Caucasian peoples.

fleur-de-lis, French lily; a decorative motif of three stylized lily petals tied near their base, especially used in ornament and heraldry by the French. →121

fleuron decoration consisting of a carved flower or leaf motif. →81, →121, →123

fleury see cross fleurettée. →117

fleury moulding a decorative moulding with a series of fleur-de-lis motifs joined end on end; primarily found in heraldic designs; also called flory moulding. →125

flexibility the ability of a material to bend, twist or stretch without failure under loading; the opposite of brittleness.

flexible curve a rod of soft, malleable metal coated in plastic used in technical drawing as a ruler for drawing curves of varying radii. →130

flexible metal roofing see supported sheetmetal roofing. →57

flexible mould a mould of a non-rigid material for taking ornamental plaster casts from difficult or intricate situations.

flexible moulding compound in ornamental plastering, a flexible material used for making moulds for casting.

flexible pavement a road construction made up of a base layer of aggregate surfaced with bituminous material.

flexible pipe, hose; metal or plastics pipe which can be deformed by hand or with pipe benders etc. without fracturing.

flexible rubber hose see appliance flexible connection.

flexible saw see saw chain.

flexible steel tape measure, tape measure; a device consisting of a scaled sprung roll of steel tape used for measuring distance.

flexible tube any tube, conduit, pipe etc., often spiral wound or segmented, which can easily be bent by hand.

flexural strength see bending strength.

flier, 1 flyer, parallel tread; a flat rectangular step in a normal staircase. →45
2 see flying shore.

flight, stair flight; **1** a number of steps in continuous series between two landings or levels; a straight section of a stair between two landings. →45, →61
2 see precast stair unit, prefabricated stair unit.

flight hole see emergence hole.

flint a dense, siliceous rock type found as distinct round lumps in chalky ground; it is difficult to work but traditionally used in England for stone facing and paving.

flint-lime brick a light, weak brick made from a mix of lime and crushed flint as opposed to clay; see calcium silicate brick.

flint nogging in traditional timber frame construction, flint infill for a timber stud frame.

flitch 1 a large rough timber sawn from a log or the trunk of a tree. →2
2 a log or piece of timber from which veneer is peeled or sliced.
3 veneer flitch, see veneer bolt. →10

flitch sawing in the primary conversion of timber, the through and through sawing of a log into timber pieces of even dimension after two opposite curved edges have been removed. →2

float, 1 floater (Am.), plasterer's float, plastering float; a hand tool for compacting and smoothing plaster surfaces, a flat steel blade with a handle on its reverse; types included as separate entries are listed below. →43
cross-grained float.
darby, Darby float, derby. →43
devil float, see nail float. →43
nail float. →43
plastering float, plasterer's float. →43
power float, rotary float.
skimming float.
sponge float. →43
straight-grained float.
wood float. →43

2 any material or component designed to provide buoyancy; see pontoon. →64
floated coat see float-finished rendering.
floated finish a smooth finish for concrete or plaster formed with a wooden or steel float.
floater see float. →43
float-finished rendering, floated coat; rendering whose wet surface has been worked with a hand-held float, producing a smooth but rather uneven finish.
float-finishing the smoothing of a concrete or plaster finish with a float in a circular action; also called floating or scouring.
float glass 1 transparent sheet glass with an exceptionally smooth and even surface, manufactured by pouring molten glass onto a bed of molten tin on which it floats.
2 see clear float glass.
see *glazing* illustration. →53
floating 1 see flooding.
2 see float-finishing.
floating bridge, 1 pontoon bridge; a bridge supported on floats or pontoons over water.
2 see ferry bridge. →64
floating coat 1 see first plaster undercoat.
2 see second plaster undercoat. →83
3 see base coat.
floating floor the upper layer of floor construction supported on battens, mountings or a resilient sheet membrane of damping material such as expanded polystyrene or mineral wool to provide acoustic isolation.
see *floating floor* illustration. →44
floating rule a rule used in plastering for levelling a plaster surface.
floating screed concrete floor construction separated by layers of resilient material from its base and side walls to provide acoustic isolation. →44
float operated valve see ballvalve.
floatvalve see ballvalve.
flocculating admixture, flocculating agent; in concretework, an admixture included in the mix to increase cohesion.
flocculating agent see flocculating admixture.
flocculation 1 a process of treating waste water with chemicals to form flaky solids which adhere to impurities and encourage removal from the water.
2 the tendency of the particles in some paints in storage to combine, gel or settle into distinct clumps.
flocked carpet carpet manufactured by electrostatic projection of polymer fibres against an adhesive-coated or surface-melted backing.
flocked wallcovering a wallcovering treated with a layer of textile fibres standing perpendicular to its surface.
flogger a paintbrush with a long head of bristles, dragged or slapped over wet paint or glaze to apply surface texture or pattern, especially used to mimic the background grain figure of woods such as mahogany, walnut, rosewood and cedar; sometimes also called a dragger. →43
flood, flood-tide; the local periodical increasing of the sea level at coastlines due to the action of the moon; see also high tide.
flooding, floating; the separating out of pigments in a paint film such that one comes to the surface; may be a defect or deliberately caused for effect.
floodlight a powerful external luminaire used for area and building lighting.
floodlighting 1 see area lighting.
2 see building floodlighting.
flood-tide see flood.
floor 1 the horizontal lower surface of a room or interior space and its supporting construction; see also flooring, floor covering, floor construction; types included as separate entries are listed below.
access floor.
base floor. →28
bottom floor, see base floor. →28
cavity floor, see access floor. →44
fire floor, firebreak floor.
floating floor.
glazed floor, glass floor. →60
ground supported floor. →57, →59
honeycomb floor, see waffle floor.
in-situ concrete floor. →44
intermediate floor. →28
modular floor, palette floor, see platform floor. →44
plate floor.
platform floor, raised access floor. →44
raised floor.
ramped floor.
rectangular grid floor, see waffle floor.
solid floor. →44
steel deck floor, see composite floor slab.
structural floor. →44
subfloor. →44, →57, →59
suspended base floor.
suspended floor.
timber floor. →44
timber upper floor.
waffle floor.
2 any level in a building, between two successive floors' constructions; see storey. →61
basement floor, see basement storey. →61
entrance floor.
first floor.
ground floor. →61
lower floor, see downstairs.
top floor.
upper floor.
floor area 1 see gross floor area.
2 see net floor area.
floor base material which supports a flooring sub-base or flooring. →44
floor bed see ground supported floor. →59
floorboard a timber board used as flooring.
floorboarding see floorboards.
floorboards, floorboarding; flooring of timber boards laid side by side over joists, battens etc.
see *timber cladding boards* illustration. →8
see *holiday home and sauna* illustration. →58
floor channel a long recess in the floor of wet spaces, garages etc. for conveying waste and surface liquids into a drain. →58
floor chisel a long sturdy chisel used for prising up floorboards.
floor construction 1 the component parts or layers of the horizontal levels in a building, including structure, insulation and floor covering.
2 see upper floor construction, intermediate floor construction.
see *intermediate floor construction* in brick house illustration. →59
3 see base floor construction, bottom floor construction.
see *base floor construction* in brick house illustration. →59
floor covering thin sheet material such as linoleum, carpet or plastics matting used for providing a finish to a floor; see also **matting** and **flooring** for lists of types of floorcovering. →44
floor drain, floor gully; a trapped outlet fitting for the floor of a wet area, garage etc., through which waste water and other fluids are conveyed into a drain. →58
floor finish, floor finishing; material laid above a concrete or timber floor structure or subfloor to provide a hardwearing walking surface.
floor finishing see floor finish.
floor framing the timber frame of joists, trimming pieces and strutting etc. which supports a boarded floor.
floor grating a framework of metal slats immediately outside external doors, often in a mat well, to collect dirt from footwear.

floor gully see floor drain. →58
floor heating see underfloor heating.
floor height, floor-to-floor height, storey height; the height between successive storeys of a multistorey building, as measured from floor level to adjacent floor level.
flooring any material used for surfacing a floor or providing a floor finish.
see *flooring* illustration; types included as separate entries are listed below. →44
acrylic polymer flooring, see acrylic flooring compound.
block flooring, see end-grain wood block flooring. →44
board flooring.
cement rubber latex flooring, cement flooring.
chipboard flooring.
coin flooring, coin-pattern flooring, see studded rubber flooring. →44
studded rubber flooring. →44
end-grain wood block flooring. →44
expanded metal flooring.
floor covering.
latex cement flooring, see cement rubber latex flooring.
metal flooring, see open metal flooring.
natural stone flooring, see stone flooring.
open bar metal flooring.
open metal flooring.
overlay flooring. →59
parquet flooring. →44
pattern flooring, see studded rubber flooring. →44
plank flooring, see wide plank flooring. →44
plywood flooring. →44
puncheon flooring.
raised-pattern flooring, see studded rubber flooring. →44
rubber flooring.
rubber latex cement flooring, see cement rubber latex flooring.
sheet flooring.
solid timber flooring. →60
stone flooring.
strip flooring, see wood strip flooring. →44
studded rubber flooring. →44
tiled flooring, see tile flooring. →44, →59
timber flooring.
wide plank flooring. →44
wide strip flooring, see wide plank flooring. →44
wood block flooring, see end-grain wood block flooring. →44
wood board flooring. →44
wood flooring.
wood strip flooring. →8, →44
flooring batten one of a series of timber strips fixed to a structural floor as a base for decking or floorboards. →44
flooring bead a strip of planed timber or other material for concealing the edge of laid flooring. →2, →44
flooring board see floorboard.
flooring component a prefabricated component used to form a base on which a floor surface is laid.
flooring compound see acrylic flooring compound.
flooring saw, inside start saw; a handsaw with teeth on both sides of the blade and a rounded end, enabling cuts to be started in the middle of a piece of wood; used for cutting holes in boards.
flooring strip see flooring bead. →2, →44
flooring sub-base that part of floor construction which provides a base for the flooring material. →44, →59
flooring tile see floor tile. →20
flooring underlay a sheet product designed for use as resilient underlay for matting, parquet etc.; see underlay.
floor joist in frame construction, one of a series of beams or joists which carry flooring.
see *timber cladding boards* illustration. →8
see *timber floor* illustration. →44
see *timber frame* illustration. →57
see *sauna and holiday home* illustration. →58
see *brick house* illustration. →59
floor lamp, standard lamp; a freestanding movable lamp consisting of a light source at the top of a pole which is fixed to a base.
floor-mounted closer see floor spring.
floor outlet see floor drain. →58
floor paint tough paint based on epoxy or acrylic resin, used as a sealant or decoration for concrete or timber floors.
floor plan a schematic drawing showing the entire spatial layout, structure and components of a building in horizontal projection. →130
floor quarry see quarry tile. →44
floor sander a machine tool containing a dust bag and revolving sanding head used for smoothing and sanding a timber floor.
floor saw a machine tool for cutting openings in concrete floors with a diamond-tipped circular saw.
floor sealant a polyurethane-based treatment for a timber floor to increase durability and seal the pores in the wood.
floor slab 1 a horizontal suspended construction of concrete or similar material which provides the structure for a floor.
2 see solid floor. →44
3 see composite floor slab.
4 see in-situ floor slab. →27, →60
floor space standard, floor space factor; a standard measure of the floor space per person required for buildings of different functions, used in space planning and fire safety calculations.
floor space factor see floor space standard.
floor spring, floor-mounted closer; a door closer incorporated into a pivot mechanism recessed into floor construction, on which the leaf of a pivot door turns.
floor square see parquet floor square. →44
floor strip 1 a thin strip of material such as plastics, timber or metal, used to cover the join between floor and wall, or adjacent areas of floor. →44
2 see flooring bead. →2, →44
3 see carpet strip. →2, →44
4 see skirting. →2, →44
floor structure 1 loadbearing construction which supports a floor surface, often a concrete slab or a timber, steel or composite frame.
2 upper floor structure, intermediate floor structure.
3 base floor structure.
floor surface the upper surface of a floor, in contact with the occupants of a building.
floor tile, flooring tile; one of a number of tiles of ceramic, concrete, cork, stone or plastics material, laid as a durable floor surface. →20, →59
floor tiling 1 the laying of floor tiles.
2 the product of this process. →59
floor-to-ceiling height see ceiling height.
floor-to-floor height see floor height.
floppy disk 1 in computing, a forerunner of the diskette, a 5.25" magnetized storage disk in a protective cardboard case; no longer in general use.
2 see diskette.
floral decoration see floriated ornament. →82, →121
Florentine arch, Italian round arch; a round arch whose extrados and intrados do not spring from the same point, and which is fatter at the apex than at the sides. →23
Florentine mosaic, pietre dure; inlaid mosaic work in coloured semi-precious stones, found in palaces, churches and table tops especially in Florence.
floriated carved or rendered with decorative flower motifs; see also foliated.

floriated ornament decorative ornament of stylized flower motifs. →82, →121
flory see cross fleurettée. →117
flory moulding see fleury moulding. →125
flotation a process of mechanically treating waste water with bubbled gas so that impurities rise to the surface and can be removed.
flow 1 see flow water.
2 see concrete flow.
3 see heat flow.
4 see air flow.
5 see backflow.
6 see overflow.
7 see turbulent flow, eddy flow.
8 see streamline flow, laminar flow.
9 plastic flow, see plastic deformation.
flowable concrete see self-placing concrete.
flower decoration see floriated ornament. →82, →121
flowing concrete concrete whose consistency is such that it flows easily when wet, achieved by adding a small percentage of superplasticizer.
see self-placing concrete.
flowing tracery, curvilinear tracery, undulating tracery; tracery found in churches of the late 1200s and 1300s (Decorated and Flamboyant styles), characterized by free-flowing patterns and ogees. →110
flow pipe in hot-water heating and similar installations, a pipe from a boiler or hot water storage vessel to radiators, outlets etc.; cf. return pipe.
flow main in a district heating system, a pipeline which conveys water to a place of use from its heating plant.
flow rate see discharge.
flow rock see igneous rock.
flow test see concrete flow test.
flow water hot water distributed for use in a central or district heating system.
fluctuation in contract management, an increase or decrease in the prices of labour, materials or plant from those specified in the tender, allowed for in the building contract.
flue, 1 smoke pipe, chimney; a vertical pipe or duct to remove smoke, combustion gases and other gaseous products from a fireplace, boiler or other heating device to the outside of a building; a chimney. →55, →56
2 any vertical sealed channel for conveying ventilation air, usually out of a building.
3 see insulated flue. →58
4 see ducted flue.
flue adaptor a fitting for connecting a solid-fuel stove or other appliance to a flue. →58
flue block, chimney block, flue brick; **1** a specially formed solid or hollow brick or block which is of modular size to enable it to be laid uncut for flues and chimneys. →16
2 a fireproof brick or block used to line a flue.
flue brick see flue block. →16
flue cap a flue terminal or rain cap, fitted to the upper outlet of a flue to prevent the passage of rainwater and improve draught. →56, →58
flue condensation condensation which occurs in a flue as a result of flue gases being too cool.
flue connector that part of a fireplace, stove or other flued appliance, or a separate component, by which it is connected to a flue. →55, →56
flue damper an adjustable pivoting sheetmetal plate for controlling the flow of air in an air-conditioning or mechanical ventilation system.
flue fan a fan connected to a flue to aid and improve natural draught.
flue gas any gas produced as a result of combustion within an appliance or installation, including soot and particles in suspension, which passes up through a flue.
flue gas analysis a study of the composition of gases given off by a particular burner or fire to define its combustion characteristics, whether it is functioning correctly etc.
flue ladder see chimney ladder. →54, →61
flue lining fire-resistant surface material of plaster, refractory brick for the inside of a flue or chimney. →55, →56
flue pipe a flue or part of a flue constructed or assembled from metal tube. →56
flue system an assembly of fittings for a working flue or group of flues, the means by which waste gases from a building are discharged. →56
flue terminal a protective device fitted to the upper outlet of a flue to prevent the passage of rainwater and snow, and to reduce or utilize the effects of wind.
flueway the inner open space of a flue, through which combustion gases are conveyed to the outside. →56
fluid a generic term for both liquids and gases, not solids, composed of particles which are able to move freely relative to one another.
fluid drachm see dram.
fluid dram see dram.
fluid mechanics a branch of science dealing with liquids and gases in motion and equilibrium.
fluid ounce 1 a unit of liquid capacity in Britain equal to one twentieth of an imperial pint, equivalent to 1.734 cu.in. or 28.4 cc; in US = $^1/_{16}$ US pint = 1.804 cu.in. = 29.6 cc.
2 fluidounce (Am.); a unit of liquid capacity in North America equal to one sixteenth of a US pint, equivalent to 1.804 cu.in or 29.6 cc.
fluidounce see fluid ounce.
fluidrachm see dram.
fluidram see dram.
fluorescent lamp, fluorescent tube; an electric discharge lamp with a phosphor-coated glass tube containing argon and a mercury vapour, producing light by excitation of the layers of phosphor.
fluorescent luminaire a luminaire containing fluorescent tubes and associated starting and control devices.
fluorescent reflector lamp a fluorescent lamp with an internally silvered inner surface to reflect light outwards in a certain direction.
fluorescent tube see fluorescent lamp.
fluorine a pale yellow, poisonous, gaseous chemical element, **F**.
fluorite, fluorspar, blue john; a coloured, crystalline mineral used as a flux in the metal industry and in the production of hydrochloric acid.
fluorspar see fluorite.
flush 1 a description of a surface, joint or other construction which is smooth and in a continuous plane.
2 a description of a component or fitting assembled with its outer surface at the same level as adjacent surfaces in which it is housed.
flush bead moulding, double-quirked bead moulding, recessed bead moulding; a decorative moulding cut with two parallel quirks or notches on either side to form a bead which is flush with the surface; a variety of quirk bead moulding. →14
flush bolt see flush slide.
flush door a door whose leaf has flat, unprofiled or unrebated surfaces on both sides. →51
flush eaves an eaves in which the roof terminates at or close to the outer wall.
flush fireplace a fireplace whose front face is flush with the wall into which it is recessed. →55
flush grated waste a plug-hole fitting for a basin or sink connected to a discharge pipe, which contains a grating to collect solid waste.
flush handle a handle for a door, window or hatch which is flush with the surface into which it is housed.

flushing rinsing in a sudden rush of moving water.
flushing cistern a cistern containing stored water for flushing a soil appliance.
flushing mechanism a device for producing a specified amount of flushing water for a WC in a specified time, usually by manual operation of a ballvalve.
flushing trough, trough cistern; a cistern for the periodic flushing of a number of soil appliances such as a row of urinals.
flushing valve, flush valve, flushometer valve (Am.); a valve for delivering a regulated amount of flushing water to a soil appliance.
flush joint, flat joint, plain cut joint; a brickwork mortar joint in which the mortar is laid at the level of the brickwork surface, or set slightly behind it. →16
flush lift a recessed handle for trapdoors, crates etc. used to facilitate lifting and opening.
flush mounting, recessed fixing; a description of a fitting such as a luminaire or electrical point installed so that its visible parts are flush with the surface in which it has been fitted.
flushometer valve see flushing valve.
flush pipe a pipe which conveys flushing water from a cistern or tank to a soil appliance.
flush pointing in brickwork, pointing in the same plane as the brick surface, forming a smooth surface.
flush pull a metal or plastics fitting housed in the leaf of a sliding door, which provides a finger recess by which the door can be opened or closed.
flush rodded joint a masonry flush joint tooled with a longitudinal concave depression when the masonry is wet. →16
flush slide, flush bolt; a small mechanical door bolt, often incorporated into the thickness of the door, to engage with the floor.
flush valve see flushing valve.
flute in classical architecture, one of a series of shallow concave grooves cut along the length of a column, pilaster or moulding. →80
fluted referring to a surface that has been cut or formed with a series of parallel concave grooves; see also reeded. →14, →114
fluted column any column inscribed with decorative vertical concave indentations along the length of its shaft, originating in the masonry columns of the Greek Doric order and those of the Egyptian Old Kingdom (proto-Doric). →73, →114
fluted moulding any horizontal flat or torus moulding scored with a series of parallel concave indentations. →14
fluted torus moulding a semicircular decorative moulding carved with flutes or parallel concave indentations; especially found on some classical column bases. →81
fluting surface decoration of longitudinal concave grooves (flutes) for classical columns and other objects. →14, →81
flutter see flutter echo.
flutter echo, flutter; in acoustics, a series of echoes in rapid succession resulting from reflection between two parallel surfaces such as walls in a corridor.
flux 1 in ceramics, a chemical applied to fired clay to aid the fusing of a subsequent glaze.
2 see magnetic flux.
3 see luminous flux.
flux density see magnetic induction.
fly-ash see pulverized fuel-ash.
flyer see flier. →45
flying bond see monk bond. →18
flying buttress in Gothic church architecture, a stone buttress designed to take the lateral thrust of a roof, vault, or wall; it consists of a slender bar of masonry which transmits loading to a heavy pier on an outer wall. →100
flying shore, flier, horizontal shore; horizontal props to provide temporary support for the external wall of a building, sides of an excavation etc. from an adjacent vertical structure or abutment.
flying stairs see cantilevered stair. →45
flyover, 1 overpass; a modern road bridge for an urban expressway etc. which passes over another road, railway or other obstacle. →63
2 see grade-separated junction. →63
flyway see log extension. →6
fly wire see insect screen.
foam, 1 any lightweight solid or liquid with considerable quantities of small entrained bubbles of gas.
2 extinguishing foam; a fire-extinguishing medium consisting of small bubbles of non-combustible material which smother, wet and cool down a fire.
foam compound see foaming agent.
foam concrete see foamed concrete.
foamed concrete, foam concrete; aerated concrete made by the addition of a foaming agent.
foamed glass see foam glass.
foamed plastics any lightweight plastics material which has been aerated to introduce gas bubbles; a cellular plastic.
foamed polystyrene see expanded polystyrene.
foamed polyurethane polyurethane to which a foaming agent has been added; used for injected cavity insulation and as a sealant.
foam extinguisher a fire extinguisher containing liquid which, on release, expands into a foam which is sprayed onto a fire.
foam forming admixture in concretework, an admixture included in the mix to promote the formation of air bubbles.
foam glass, 1 foamed glass, expanded glass; low density glass with entrained bubbles of gas used for thermal and acoustic applications.
2 see cellular glass.
foaming agent, 1 foam compound; a liquid used in fire-fighting and as fireproofing which becomes a non-combustible foam when released or activated.
2 various substances added to some plastics, rubbers or concrete to promote the formation of tiny gas bubbles within the material and improve properties of thermal insulation, fireproofing and to reduce weight.
foam rubber, sponge rubber, latex foam; a form of cellular rubber containing a network of gas bubbles which are open and interconnected; used for packing and padding.
focus 1 in mathematics, one of a number of points from which an ellipse or parabola is defined.
2 the point at which an optical lens or mirror converges rays of light to a point.
3 Lat.; a bowl, basin or recess in or on the upper surface of a Roman altar, into which offerings of wine, oil or blood were poured, or offerings burnt. →116
focusing effect in acoustics, the usually undesirable effect of concave walls, domes, vaults etc. in a space to locally reinforce sound levels by focusing reflected sound to a point.
fog a shade of grey which takes its name from the colour of fog seen against a light background.
fog blue a shade of grey which takes its name from the colour of fog seen against a dark background.
fogou, souterrain, weem; a prehistoric subterranean passage and chamber, used for storage or as a means of escape from a ringfort or other settlement.
foil 1 any metal produced in very thin sheets less than 0.15–0.25 mm thick; actual thickness varies with national specification and type of metal. →34
see aluminium foil.
gold foil, see gold leaf.
2 a decorative motif representing a stylized leaf.
see trefoil. →108
see quatrefoil. →108, →110
see cinquefoil. →108
see sexfoil.
see multifoil. →108, →110

foil-faced plywood plywood which has been faced with metal foil.

foil moulding a decorative moulding with a series of pointed leaf motifs joined end on end; primarily found in heraldic designs. →125

foil wallcovering see metal foil wallcovering.

folded plate a reinforced concrete shell structure used for long span roofs, consisting of a number of thin cast slabs at a vertical angle to one another, forming a zigzag pattern in cross-section; also called a folded slab or polygonal shell. →27
see *folded plate and shell structures* illustration. →27

folded slab see folded plate. →27

folding blind see concertina blind.

folding casements a pair of hinged window casements, hung in either side of a frame, which do not have a mullion or frame member between them.

folding door 1 a door hinged at one edge which folds with a concertina action along the line of a threshold. →50
2 see sliding folding door. →50
3 see bi-part folding door. →50
4 see bi-fold door. →50

folding rule a traditional measuring stick, a rule jointed at fixed intervals for convenience in carrying.

folding wedges in timber jointing, paired timber wedges driven into a joint during or after assembly to tighten it. →3

folding window see sliding folding window. →52

foliage 1 the leaves and branches of a tree or plant.
2 an ornamental representation of this.

foliage green, leaf green; a shade of green which takes its name from the colour of chlorophyll pigment in growing plants.

foliated having been carved or rendered with decorative leaf motifs; see also floriated.

foliated arch see cinquefoliated arch. →23
see multifoliated arch. →23
see trifoliated arch. →23, →110

foliated capital any ornamental capital carved with leaf-like decoration.
see *medieval capitals* illustration. →115
see Corinthian capital. →81
see stiff-leaf capital. →115
see crocket capital. →115
see water leaf capital. →115
see vine leaf capital. →115

foliated cross a cross with leaves growing from it, a Christian version of the Scandinavian Tree of Life.

foliated gneiss see gneissose micaschist.

foliated ornament decorative ornament of stylized leaf motifs, also known as foliation or leafwork; see also festoon, foliage, leaf scroll. →82, →121

Foliated style a form of English Geometric Gothic architecture characterized by the use of carved leaf motifs.

foliate head, green man; a traditional decorative round semi-human face motif of plant and foliage forms representing the force of nature merging with humanity.
see *ornamentation* illustration. →122
see *medieval capitals* illustration. →115

foliation see foliated ornament. →82, →121

folium a traditional dark violet pigment made from the seeds of the turnsole plant (*Chrozophora tinctoria*), used originally for inscriptions.

folk art traditional or vernacular art, decoration and ornamentation for household utensils and homesteads.

folly a purely decorative building or structure, often a fake ruin, tower or statue, located in parkland.

Fomes annosus see annosus root rot.

Fomes ignarius see false tinder fungus.

Fomes pini see red ring rot.

fons a small water-bearing vessel or pool in Roman architecture; a spring. →88

font, 1 baptismal font; a vessel in a church containing holy water used in baptism.
2 a typeface as used in computing and graphics.

foolscap a British standard paper size, 13½" × 17", 343 mm × 432 mm; also a size for writing paper of 13" × 8". →Table 6

foot abb. **ft** or ′; imperial unit of length equal to 12 inches or 30.48 cm.

footbath a shallow hygienic bath designed for rinsing, disinfecting or washing the feet.

foot bolt a barrel bolt set vertically at the foot of a door to hold it shut by engaging with a housing in floor construction. →39

foot brace in traditional timber frame construction, a down brace between a post and sole plate, used to stiffen the lower corner. →4

footbridge, walkway, pedestrian bridge, overpass; a bridge to ensure the safe passage of pedestrians and light traffic over a busy road or railway. →64

footing 1 a foundation slab beneath a column or wall. →28, →29, →57
2 strip footing, see strip foundation. →29
3 column or isolated footing, see pad foundation. →29
4 see wall base.

footing block a dense concrete block specially manufactured to serve as a foundation or footing slab when laid in series. →30
see *concrete block* illustration. →30
see *holiday home* illustration. →58

footing unit 1 see precast foundation.
2 see footing block.

footlights theatre lights incorporated into the front of a stage floor.

footpath 1 see footway.
2 see public footpath.

footprints, combination pliers, pipe tongs; long-handled pliers or tongs with adjustable pivoted and serrated jaws, used by a pipe fitter for gripping pipes and other cylindrical objects.

footstreet a vehicular road in an urban area that has been changed to a pedestrian precinct or area.

footway, 1 footpath, path, pavement, pedestrian way; sidewalk (Am.); a raised path or way along the side of a road, street or carriageway for use by pedestrians. →62
2 walkway; an elevated pedestrian corridor or pathway. →64

force a physical quantity which causes a change of movement in a body, or stress in a stationary body; its SI unit is the newton (N).

forced draught burner in gas heating, a gas burning appliance whose burner is provided with air under pressure.

forced drying a mild form of baking in air at temperatures of 30–60°C for coatings and paints to greatly reduce their drying time.

forced ventilation see mechanical ventilation.

force majeure, act of God; in contract law, an unforeseeable event such as an earthquake or the outbreak of war that is outside the influence of parties to a contract and prevents a contractor from fulfilling his obligations either in part or in full.

ford, watersplash; a low lying area of a road at which it is crossed by a shallow stream, and through which vehicles can normally pass.

forechurch see antechurch. →99

forecourt an external courtyard, area of hardstanding or driveway in front of a building.
see *Mesopotamian temple* illustration. →66
see *Egyptian temple* illustration. →72

foreman the contractor's representative responsible for supervising work on a building site.
see general foreman.
see section foreman.
see trades foreman.

forend, lock faceplate, lock front; the outer plate of a mortise lock, visible in the narrow edge of a door, which has holes for screws, a bolt, and any secondary bolts or latches. →39

foreshortening in perspective and axonometric drawing, the shortening of oblique or converging lines perpendicular or skew to the picture plane, to produce the illusion of three dimensionality; in dimetric and trimetric projections this is often constructed by convention.

foreshortening factor the ratio by which dimensions along one or two of the oblique axes are arithmetically reduced in an axonometric, dimetric or trimetric projection. →127

forest an area of land with primarily trees growing on it; the environment thus formed; forest is usually a large or cultivated tract of land in relation to woodland, although the terms are often synonymous.
ancient woodland, high forest.
mixed forest.
see woodland.

forestation see afforestation.

forester's saw see tubular bow saw.

forestry the planting, managing and felling of forests to produce timber and improve the environment.

forework see advanced work. →104

forge 1 in manual metalworking, a hearth or fireplace, usually with bellows or a fan to increase heat, used for heating metals to make them workable.
2 see smithy.

forged nail a traditional nail which has been fashioned by heating and hammering into shape; also called wrought nail. →35

forge welding, smith welding; the simple joining of metals by hammering them together when red hot.

forging the shaping of metal by hammering, either manually or with heavy machinery, while red hot.

forked cross, 1 furca; a cross in the shape of the letter Y; also variously known as a ypsilon cross, Y-cross, robbers' or thief's cross. →117
2 see cross fourchée. →117

forked junction see fork junction. →62

fork interchange see grade-separated fork junction. →63

fork junction 1 a road junction in which one road meets another obliquely at the same level. →62
2 see grade-separated fork junction. →63

forks see crucks. →7

forkstaff plane a plane for carving out and smoothing convex surfaces in wood.

form 1 the state in which something, such as a building contract, is arranged.
2 see shape.
3 see formwork.
4 an official piece of printed documentation to be filled in when ordering a product or service, making a declaration or claim etc.

formaldehyde, methanal; a poisonous, colourless, pungent gas, **HCHO**, used in the production of resins, adhesives etc.
see melamine formaldehyde, melamine, MF.
see phenol formaldehyde, phenolic resin, PF.
see urea formaldehyde, UF.

formalin a solution of formaldehyde in water; used as a disinfectant and preservative.

formalism any art or style which adheres strictly to stylistic or philosophical dogma.

format 1 the basic state of the operating system of a computer, which defines all programs and files used on it.
2 the size and shape of a drawing or print.

formation see foundation. →15, →29, →62

formée see cross patée. →118

former see box out.

forming, shaping; in manufacturing, the pressing, extruding or moulding of a plastic material into a predesigned shape; see thermo-forming, vacuum forming.

form lining see formwork lining.

form nail see double headed nail. →35

form oil see mould oil.

formply plywood used as shuttering, usually waterproofed with film or resin impregnated paper.

form stop see stop end form.

form tie see formwork tie.

formula price adjustment in contract management, a method of calculating the amount to be added to or deducted from a contract sum due to changes in the costs of labour, plant and materials during construction using a price variation formula.

formula variation of price contract a variation of price contract in which prices are amended according to previously agreed terms.

form vibrating see external vibrating.

form vibrator see external vibrator.

formwork, 1 casing, mould, shuttering; concreting moulds of boarding, sheet material or specialized construction to give temporary support for in-situ concrete while it hardens.
see *formwork* illustration; types included as separate entries are listed below. →30
apartment formwork.
board formwork.
climbing formwork.
collapsible formwork.
lost formwork.
permanent formwork.
quick strip formwork.
reusable formwork.
room formwork, see apartment formwork.
soffit formwork.
table formwork.
tilt-up formwork.
top formwork.
tunnel formwork, see apartment formwork.
2 the on-site work involved in building and installing these; formwork erection.

formwork erection the construction or assembling of formwork prior to casting in-situ concrete.

formwork lining, form lining; sheet material included in formwork to give a particular surface texture to the concrete.

formwork nail see double headed nail. →35

formwork panel reusable framed sheet material against which concrete is cast in formwork; see shuttering.

formwork sheeting see sheeting.

formwork striking see striking.

formwork tie, form tie; one of a number of small steel tension members used to hold formwork accurately in place once concrete is placed.

formy see cross patée. →118

fornices plural of fornix. →93

fornix, plural fornices; 'arch, vault' (Lat.); in classical architecture, originally a triumphal arch in the Roman republic, subsequently any arch supporting an entablature. →93

Forstner bit a patent drill bit for drilling flat-bottomed holes or round sinkings in wood. →42

fort 1 a construction, often with surrounding ditches and ramparts and a body of troops, used as a place of defence; frequently a small fortress without a surrounding town.
2 see castelet. →103
3 see castle. →103
4 see stronghold.
5 see citadel.
6 see castrum. →104

fortification 1 a structure consisting of walls and battlements constructed for defence.
2 part of a defensive structure, a fortifying component such as a battlement or tower, a work.
see *fortification* illustration. →104

fortlet a small fort.

fortress 1 a strongly fortified military castle or walled town, the home of a large garrison.
2 a large fort.
3 see castle. →103
4 see stronghold.
5 see citadel.
6 see bastide.

fortress church a church built in such a way so that it may be used for defensive purposes in times of strife.

fortress town a town which has evolved from a fortress, is surrounded by a wall for protection or is strongly fortified.

fort temple prehistorical and historical temple types constructed also with defence in mind; especially those in southern India built on hilltops and crags, reminiscent of castles. →66

forum 1 Lat.; in classical architecture, a civic square in a Roman city, used as a meeting or market place, and for public events; cf. agora. →104
2 any meeting place for events, discussion or commerce.

fossa Lat.; a ditch, moat or excavation outside a Roman town wall or military encampment, for purposes of defence. →104

fosse a prehistoric or medieval ditch, constructed for drainage or to mark a boundary; often usage is the same as fossa.

fossil, petrifaction; the stony remains of prehistoric organisms found in certain sedimentary rocks.

fossil resin a natural resin extracted from the earth, the fossilized resin of prehistoric trees.

foul drain see foul water drain.

foul water in drainage and waste water treatment, a mixture of soil water and waste water conveyed to a sewer.

foul water drain, foul drain; in drainage and waste water treatment, a horizontal pipe, most often buried beneath the ground, for leading soil and waste water from a building to a private or public sewer.

foundation 1 a subterranean structure designed to transmit the structural loading of a building to the ground. →29
see *foundation types* illustration. →29
see *strip foundation* in brick house illustration. →59
see *concrete block foundation* in holiday home illustration. →58
2 see spread foundation. →29
3 see piled foundation. →29
4 see stereobate. →86
5 see footing. →28, →29, →57
6 formation, subgrade, subsoil, ground; the bearing layer of soil or rock below the substructure of a building or other construction. →15, →29, →62
7 an organization which maintains and distributes funding for the arts, research, scholarships etc.

foundation block see precast foundation.
see footing block. →30, →58

foundation bolt see anchor bolt. →36

foundation depth the distance between ground level and the lowest point of foundation construction.

foundation drawing, foundation plan; a drawing produced by a structural engineer showing the layout and type of foundations for a building or structure.

foundation grillage 1 see grillage.
2 see timber foundation grillage. →29

foundation pile see bearing pile. →29
see **types of pile** in foundation drawing, and list of common pile types under 'pile'. →29

foundation plan see foundation drawing.

foundation reinforcement steel reinforcement for a reinforced concrete foundation. →27

foundation stone 1 see bedstone. →6
2 see cornerstone.

foundation type the chosen method by which loads from a building are transmitted to the ground below. →29

foundation unit see precast foundation.

foundation wall 1 that part of the external wall of a basement which is below ground level and transmits loading to the foundations or ground below. →28, →29
2 see wall base. →28, →29, →57

fountain an ornamental structure, usually situated in a pool, which projects water up into the air; in historical architecture it often refers to a well or spring.

fountain pen an ink pen which contains a built-in rubber reservoir which can be refilled with ink by suction.

fountain pump a mechanical device for pumping water in a fountain.

four-centred arch 1 see Tudor arch. →24
2 see pseudo four-centred arch.

four-centred pointed arch see Tudor arch. →24

fourchée cross see cross fourchée. →117

four-pointed star, star sun; a decorative motif of a star with four pointed limbs radiating out from a central point at equal intervals; in Christian symbolism it is known as the crux stellata (Lat.), stellar, stellated or star cross. →123

Fourth Pompeian style see Fantastic style.
see *Pompeian styles* illustration. →126

fox a shade of reddish brown which takes its name from the colour of the fur of the fox (*Vulpes vulpes* or *Canis vulpes*).

fox wedge, secret wedge; in timber mortise and tenon jointing, one of two wedges placed into cuts made in the base of the tenon to tighten the joint on assembly.

fox-wedged joint any timber tenon joint which has been fastened and tightened with a fox wedge. →5

foyer, 1 lobby, entrance hall; a main entrance hall at ground level in a public building, hotel or large office building.
2 lobby; a main open space in a theatre or concert hall, in which the audience may gather before a performance or during the intervals.

fraction in mathematics, the ratio of two proper numbers.

fracture line a line along which a structural member or surface treatment has cracked or failed structurally.

Fragaria ananassa the strawberry plant, see cardinal red.

Fragaria vesca the wild strawberry, see fraise.

fraise a shade of bluish red which takes its name from the colour of the fruit of the wild strawberry (*Fragaria vesca*).

frame, 1 framework; a rigid structure of slender loadbearing members joined together, for attaching and supporting cladding, infill and other components; examples included as separate entries are listed below.
2 skeleton; the loadbearing elements of a building, erected first, onto which cladding and other components are fixed.
3 see building frame (types of building frame listed there).
4 the surrounding construction of members onto which a door leaf or window casement is hinged.
5 framing; the peripheral members which form the structure of a window sash or casement, or a panelled or glazed door leaf.
6 see door frame. →50, →51
7 see window frame. →52, →53
box frame, see cased frame.
casement frame. →53
climbing frame.
hyperstatic frame, see statically indeterminate frame.
isostatic frame, see statically determinate frame.
loadbearing frame, structural frame.
mainframe.
mat well frame.
perfect frame, see statically determinate frame.
piling frame, see pile driver.

plane frame.
portal frame, rigid frame. →33
redundant frame, see statically indeterminate frame.
statically determinate frame.
statically indeterminate frame.
space frame.
subframe. →53

frame anchor see door-frame anchor. →50

frame bracing, frame stiffening; any elements such as cross walls, diagonals etc. to provide stiffening to a building frame.

frame bridge see portal frame bridge. →32

framed and ledged door a door in which the leaf is formed of a rigid frame with a middle rail or ledge as stiffening; boarding is then attached to this.

framed beam see trussed beam. →33

framed building 1 any building or structure in which loading is transmitted to the foundations via a framework rather than massive construction.
2 see timber-framed building.

framed door 1 any door whose leaf is supported by a frame; may be a glazed door or panelled door. →51
2 see panelled door. →51
3 see glazed timber door. →51
4 see glazed metal door. →51

framed, ledged and braced door a framed and ledged door with diagonal bracing between the horizontal members.

frameless glass door see all-glass door. →60

frameless glazing 1 glazing for facades, partitions, balustrades etc. of glass panels with primarily sealed butt joints, drilled proprietary fixings, not installed in fixed framing.
see *frameless glazed partition* in office building illustration. →60
2 see structural glazing. →53

frame member, glazing bar; part of a window frame between two openable sashes or casements; see mullion, transom.

frame saw 1 see gang saw.
2 see mill saw.

frame stiffening see frame bracing.

frame structure a construction method whereby loads are transmitted to the foundations via a frame rather than by loadbearing walls.

framework 1 any basic secondary structural rails, battens or other structure fixed to a building frame as a base for cladding.
2 a surrounding, supporting or loadbearing structure of members for a construction.
3 see frame.

framing see frame.

framing chisel, cant chisel; a heavy chisel with a reinforced, rounded or canted back for heavy carpentry and framing.

framing gun a robust nail gun for nails up to 100 mm long, used for fixing timber flooring and in framing work; sometimes called a stud gun; see also nail gun.

framing hammer a large nail hammer used by construction workers. →40

framing joint any joint between two timbers used in timber frame construction, fashioned by a carpenter on site. →4
see *types of framing joint* illustration. →4

framing square, carpenter's square; a large steel try square with many scales and gradations used for marking and measuring 90° angles in building work; see square.

Franciscan church a church of the monasterial order founded by St Francis of Assisi (c.1181–1226) in c.1209, which renounced earthly possessions and devoted its life to preaching and providing aid to the poor and sick.

francigenum opus francigenum, see opus modernum.

francium a radioactive chemical element, **Fr**.

Frankfurt black a brownish black pigment made by grinding up burnt grapevines and other waste products of the wine industry.

Franki pile in foundation technology, a patented driven cast-in-place pile consisting of a metal pipe driven into the ground and then filled with concrete.

Frankish art art from northern France and the Rhine valley from 450 to 750 AD.

frater a dining hall or refectory in a monastery. →97

Fraxinus spp. see ash.
Fraxinus americana, see white ash.
Fraxinus excelsior, see European ash.
Fraxinus pennsylvanica, see green ash.

FRC see fibre-reinforced concrete.
see fibre-reinforced cement.
see fibre-reinforced composite.

free bed in geology and quarrying, loose stone material occurring naturally between solid layers of stone.

free convection, natural convection, self convection; the transfer of heat within a fluid or gas by movement induced by temperature and density differences within it.

freehand drawing any drawing done without the aid of technical drawing instruments or construction lines.

free match in decorative wallpapering, a description of patterned wallpaper which does not have to be hung in a specific sequence for the overall pattern to be evident.

free port a harbour in which goods can be loaded and unloaded without having to pay duty.

freestanding column 1 a column which does not carry structure, essentially for decorative or monumental purposes.
2 a rostral column, see columna rostrata. →69
3 see serpent column. →69

freestanding dwelling see detached house. →61

freestanding fireplace a centrally located fireplace which is open or glazed on all sides and whose flue is not integrated into a wall. →55

freestanding wall any wall which has no support at its upper edge.

free tenon joint, fish tenon joint, slip tenon joint; a timber mortise and tenon joint in which a mortise is cut into both members and the tenon is a separate piece. →5

freeway see motorway. →63

freezer, 1 deep freeze; a domestic or industrial appliance for freezing foods or foodstuffs etc., usually to below −18°C.
2 see chest freezer.
3 see upright freezer.

freezing compartment, icebox; an upper space in a fridge for frozen goods.

freezing point the temperature, 0°C at which water turns into ice.

freight 1 the transport of goods, especially by sea or air; also the goods themselves.
2 a charge made for the transport of goods, especially by sea or air; see delivery charge.

freight terminal, goods depot; a storage and administrative complex for goods conveyed as freight by train, plane or other forms of transport.

French arch see Dutch arch. →23

French blue see artificial ultramarine.

French chalk, steatite, soapstone; ground magnesium silicate used as a dusting powder, in dry cleaning etc.; another name for talc as sold in North America and Great Britain.

French curve in technical drawing, a template of transparent plastic used for drawing a number of curves of varying radii. →130

French door see casement door.

French drain see field drain.

French flier see dancing step. →45

French lily see fleur-de-lis. →121

French nail see round wire nail.

French plane see corner scraper. →41

French polish a mixture of shellac and a solvent such as methylated spirit rubbed with a rotary motion into a smooth untreated joinery surface as a fine but non-resistant finish.

French polishing, polishing; the art and craft of applying French polish to wooden artifacts, fine joinery etc.

French Regency style see Regency style.

French Rococo see rocaille.

French truss see fink truss. →33

French ultramarine see artificial ultramarine.

French white see flake white.

French window see casement door.

frequency the rate of repetition of an event, especially the speed of variation of electromagnetic waves in cycles per second, whose SI unit is the hertz (Hz).

fresco 1 mural painting in mineral or earth pigments applied to lime or gypsum plaster while it is still wet; otherwise known as buon fresco; see also fresco secco.
2 see buon fresco.
3 see fresco secco.
see *fresco* in Roman walling illustration. →83

fresco secco, dry fresco, secco; decorating painting on dry plaster or subsequent touching up for true fresco, undertaken once the plaster surface has dried.

fresh air 1 air from the outside, drawn into a ventilation or air-conditioning system to replace stale air in a building.
2 see supply air.

fresh-air inlet 1 an opening in an outside wall to allow the passage of fresh ventilation air into a space. →58
2 an opening to allow the entrance of fresh air to a drainage system.

fresh-air vent in natural and mechanical ventilation systems, a component containing a grille and filter, installed in an opening in an external wall, through which fresh air is introduced; often referred to simply as an inlet or vent. →58

fresh concrete concrete that has not yet begun to set and is still in a workable condition.

freshwater naturally occurring water containing no salt.

fret 1 banded running ornament of lines or fillets linked or interlinked to form a continuous motif; often called a key pattern, which always has orthogonal geometry. →125
see key pattern. →125
see meander, labyrinth fret. →125
see Greek key. →125
see guilloche. →125
see diamond fret. →124
see Vitruvian scroll. →125
see potenty moulding. →125
2 see firefront. →55

fretsaw, bracket saw, jigsaw, scroll saw; a fine-toothed saw whose narrow blade is held in tension in a very deep frame, used for cutting small openings and curves in boards.

fretwork fret ornament; see fret. →125

friability the ability of a material or construction to be broken down into fragments.

friary a monastery inhabited by monks, especially of the mendicant orders (Augustinian or Austin friars, Carmelites or White Friars, Dominicans or Black Friars, Franciscans or Grey Friars), receiving alms and having good links with the local community.

friary church the church of a friary.

friction joint any joint or connection which remains fast due to the action of friction.

friction pile in foundation technology, any pile which transmits forces to surrounding ground around its circumference, through friction. →29

friction welding a specialized method of welding in which heat is generated by the high speed rotation of one component while pressed to the other.

fridge see refrigerator.

frieze 1 a decorated horizontal band adorning the elevation or interior wall of a building below a cornice, eaves or ceiling line.
2 in classical architecture, the middle band of an entablature, often decorated with sculpture. →78, →80
see *apteral temple* illustration. →84
see *classical orders* illustration. →78, →79, →80
see *caryatid* illustration. →76
see *Pompeian styles* illustration. →126

frigidarium Lat.; a cool room in a Roman bath house, with cold baths in which bathers could relax after sweating in the caldarium and sudatorium. →91

fringe see outskirts.

frit a blue ceramic glaze known to the Egyptians, made by melting siliceous materials with copper, lead and other metallic salts, then cooling and grinding.

fritting a protective or decorative treatment for a ceramic or glass surface consisting of granular mineral material, often powdered glass or sand, which is baked on.

frog an indentation in the upper, lower or both large surfaces of a brick, made in order to reduce weight. →21

frogged brick a common clay brick with a depression or frog in its upper (and sometimes lower) face to save on weight and material, and to provide improved bonding with mortar. →16

front bastion front, see bastion trace. →104
false front, see screen façade.
see firefront.
lock front, see forend. →39
wave front.

frontage 1 the main or front elevation, usually imposing, of a building.
see *classical frontage* illustration. →86
see *Baroque frontage* illustration. →113
2 street frontage; that part of a building or site facing a street.

frontal 1 of an elevation of a building, sculpture or figure, facing towards the front.
2 altar frontal, see antependium, antemensale. →116

frontality the portrayal of scenes, figures and sculptures from the front with minimal perspective effects; a technique in art used from earliest times up to the Renaissance.

front bent gouge see spoon gouge. →41

front clearance in glazing, the horizontal distance between the outer face of the pane or glazing unit and its glazing bead.

front door see main entrance.

front garden a bounded external area between a domestic dwelling and a public road, often planted or landscaped.

fronting in glazing, a fillet of soft material, putty etc., triangular in section, applied to the external edges of a window pane to hold it in place in its frame.

frontispiece the main or monumental elevation, bay or entrance of a building. →12

fronton see pediment. →112

front plane see vertical plane. →127, →128

front putty see putty fronting.

front view in projection drawing, the orthographic planar projection made of an object or building on the vertical plane, as if viewed from the front. →127

frost 1 the state or weather condition of being below the freezing point of water, 0°C.
2 frozen ground; the freezing of water in or on the surface layer of ground, freshly laid concrete or surface water during cold weather.

frost action detrimental effects caused by the build-up of ice in and around construction, beneath foundations etc. due to contained water freezing in very cold weather.

frost attack see frost damage.

frost boil in soil engineering, the softening of soil after it has thawed after a period of frost or being in a frozen state.

frost cleft see frost crack.

frost crack, frost cleft; cracking in wood due to damage caused to the living tree by the freezing of water in the sapwood.

frost damage 1 damage which occurs to building fabric because of subzero weather, often due to the expansion of trapped water on freezing.
2 frost attack; the pitting and spalling of a hardened concrete surface due to the expansion of water held in pores during freezing weather.

frosted see pearl.

frost heave the rising up of the surface of ground during freezing weather due to trapped groundwater expanding as it freezes.

frosting 1 a defect in a gloss paint finish consisting of a matt or textured surface.
2 see etching.

frost insulation in-ground insulation laid beside foundations and external foundation walls in cold climates to prevent freezing. →59

frostline the maximum depth to which ground will freeze solid during an average winter.

frost protection measures taken in construction, the use of insulation in foundations, careful detailing etc. to prevent damage caused by freezing.

frost resistance the ability of a material or construction to withstand subzero temperatures without adverse effects on performance.

frottage, rubbing; the production of an image by laying paper or cloth over an embossed, indented, textured or inscribed surface and rubbing with a chalk or crayon, as with brass rubbing.

frozen ground see frost.

FRP see fibre-reinforced plastic.

fuel any solid, liquid or gaseous material that can be burned or otherwise chemically treated to produce energy.

fuel-ash see pulverized fuel-ash.

fuel-ash cement see Portland pulverized fuel-ash cement.

fuel gas, gas fuel; any combustible gas burned as an energy source.

fuel oil blended oil heated for use in atomizing burners and other heating apparatus.

fugitive referring to a pigment which will not retain its colour in the prolonged presence of light.

full brick, whole brick; a brick in brick masonry which has not been cut or shaped to fit in with bonded brickwork. →21

full cloverleaf junction a grade-separated junction in which the flow of traffic is controlled by four looped ramps within a diamond arrangement of four slip roads; see partial cloverleaf. →63

full cruck truss see closed cruck truss.

full gloss, high gloss; the highest of five grades of glossiness in a dry paint surface, characterized by a smooth mirror-like finish.

full overtaking sight distance in road design, the minimum specified sight distance over which a vehicle can safely overtake without exceeding the speed limit.

full size see tight size. →52

full-spectrum lamp see neodymium oxide lamp.

full-turn stairs see one-turn stairs. →45

fume cupboard a laboratory furnishing with an extractor hood connected to a flue, used for tasks which involve release of unwanted gases.

function 1 a mathematical expression containing more than one variable, in which a variation in one will effect change in others.
2 in design and planning, the purpose for which a space, structural element, material or component has been designed; its performance as regards the whole.

functionalism a Modernist architectural and design movement in Europe and America from the 1920s and 1930s, characterized by a concentration on the functional aspect of buildings and objects and an interest in structure and material rather than decoration.
see *functionalist portal* illustration. →113

function room a room in a restaurant or hotel for private parties or other functions.

fund in finance, money or property set aside or collected for a particular purpose.

funding see financing.

funeral chapel see funerary chapel. →102

funerary chamber see burial chamber. →65, →116

funerary chapel, burial chapel, funeral chapel; a chapel in which a funeral service or ceremony is administered; often located at a cemetery or graveyard. →102

funerary temple see mortuary temple. →70, →72

funerary urn see cinerary urn.

fungal attack see rot; see list of wood-attacking fungi under **fungi**.

fungal decay see rot; see list of wood-attacking fungi under **fungi**.

fungi simple forms of microscopic plant whose parasitic attack of wood may cause surface staining, mould or decay; plural form of fungus; species included as separate entries are listed below.
annosus root rot [*Fomes annosus, Heterobasidion annosum*].
bleeding Stereum [*Stereum sanguinolentum*].
blue stain, blue fungus, deal yard blue, log blue, sap-stain.
blue stain fungus [*Ophiostoma minus*].
bracket fungus, see conk.
brown rot fungus.
canker rot, see red ring rot.
cellar rot [*Coniophora cerebella, Coniophora puteana*].
conk [*Polyporaceae*].
dote.
dry rot [*Serpula lacrymans, Merulius lacrymans*].
false tinder fungus [*Phellinus ignarius, Fomes ignarius*].
hardrot, see dote.
heartwood rot.
honeycomb rot, see red ring rot.
incipient decay, see dote.
mould.
pith flecks [*Agromyza*].
pocket rot.
polypore, see conk.
red ring rot [*Phellinus pini, Fomes pini, Trametes pini*].
ring scale fungus, see red ring rot.
roll-rim [*Paxillus panuoides*].
root rot, see annosus root rot.
sap-stain.
sapwood rot.
scaly cap fungus [*Lentinus lepideus*].
shelf fungus, see conk.
slash conk [*Gloephyllum separium, Lenzites separia*].
spalt.
tear fungus, see dry rot.
white pitted rot, white pocket rot, see red ring rot.
white rot.
white rot fungus.
white spongy rot [*Antrodia serialis*].

fungicidal admixture in concretework, an admixture included in the mix to inhibit attack from fungi.

fungicide, 1 preservative; a substance, usually in liquid form, used for the treatment of timber against fungal attack.
2 see fungicidal admixture.

fungistat a substance which prevents the growth of mould and fungi, used in wood preservative and foodstuffs.

fungus the singular form of fungi.

funicular polygon the polygonal shape assumed by a chord suspended at both ends which has a number of loads hung from it at intervals.

funicular railway a cable-drawn hillside or mountain railway with counterbalanced carriages moving concurrently upwards and downwards.

funnel in road design, a wedge-shaped area of carriageway caused by the merging of a traffic lane with one adjacent to it. →63

funt a traditional Russian unit of weight equal to 409.1 g.

furan any of a number of colourless organic compounds with a chemical ring structure, used in plastic form for chemical-resistant adhesives, varnishes etc.

furca 'fork' (Lat.); originally the Y-shaped timber frame to which criminals were tied by the Romans as punishment; symbolic images of this; see forked cross. →117

furfural see furfuraldehyde.

furfuraldehyde, furfural; a colourless liquid, originally obtained from distilling bran or corn cobs, used to produce polycondensate plastics for use in laminates.

furlong an imperial unit of length, equal to one eighth of an English mile, 220 yards or 201.17 m.

furnace see boiler.

furnishing the design and process of assembling, mounting and arranging furniture, furnishings and loose fittings in a space.

furnishing hinge see cabinet hinge. →38

furnishings 1 the non-fixed items of furniture and fabrics in a building.
2 the above when regarded as a whole.

furnishings drawing see fixed furnishings drawing.

furnishing textile a general name for curtains, drapery, carpets, mats, upholstery and other fabric products used in interior decoration.

furniture 1 any non-fixed fittings in a building such as chairs, tables, curtains etc.
2 see piece of furniture.
3 see door furniture.

furniture beetle, 1 woodworm; [*Anobiidae*] a family of insects whose larvae cause damage to furniture and timber by burrowing.
2 see common furniture beetle [*Anobium punctatum*].

furniture designer a specialist designer of pieces of furniture, often an interior designer who also produces furnishing layouts.

furniture drawing a design drawing from which a specific piece of furniture can be constructed.

furniture lock see cabinet lock. →39

furring 1 see scale.
2 see firring. →8

furring piece see firring piece.

furrowed referring to a surface that has been cut or shaped with a series of fine parallel grooves.

fuse, cutout; an electric component which melts in the event of a flow of excess current, breaking the circuit.

fused silica glass, quartz glass; glass produced from 99% silica or quartz, expensive to manufacture and used for special applications such as laboratory equipment.

fusible link a jointing component for holding a damper or fire door open, which melts at a relatively low temperature (68°C) to release the mechanism in the event of fire.

fusion rock see igneous rock.

fusion welding a method of welding in which the metals to be joined are melted together as in gas or arc welding, often with a filler rod to provide additional material.

futurism a movement in the arts from Italy in 1909, known also as brutalism or dynamism, which attempted to break free from historical precedent and is characterized by the expression of movement and energy.

fuzzy grain, woolly grain; in the conversion or manufacture of timber, a machining defect resulting in wood fibres frayed loose at the surface after cutting. →1

fylfot see swastika. →118

G

gabbro a very dark, coarse-grained plutonic rock composed of pyroxene and plagioclase, used as a building stone.

gabion, rubble basket; a stackable component of loose stones or boulders in a rectangular cage of galvanized mesh or welded reinforcing bars, used for road embankments, retaining walls, erosion control etc. →29

gabion wall a retaining wall of loosely stacked or tied gabions, used to restrain earth embankments at roadsides or in landscaping. →29

gable 1 the triangular upper portion of wall at the end of a double pitched roof.
2 see pignon.
3 see fastigium. →86

gableboard see bargeboard.

gabled mansard roof, gambrel roof (Am.); a double pitched roof with a gable at either end. →46

gable dormer a dormer window with a pitched roof and gablet over the glazed area.

gabled roof see gable roof. →46

gable end an exterior elevation or end of a building containing a gable.

gable roof, gabled roof; a roof with two sloping planes which meet at a central ridge and a gable at one or both ends. →46

gablet a small gable, as found in a dormer window.

gablet roof see gambrel roof.

gable wall any wall which contains a gable.

gaboon, okoume; [*Aucoumea klaineana*] a West African hardwood with brown, featureless timber; used for interiors and plywood, rarely as solid wood.

gadolinium a rare chemical element, **Gd**.

gadroon, godroon, knulled ornament, lobe ornament, nulled ornament, thumb moulding; ornament made up of a number of protruding parallel convex mouldings, lumps or carvings. →124

gadrooned decorated with a series of longitudinal convex protrusions. →124

gage see gauge.

Gahn's blue a variety of cobalt ultramarine pigment.

gain see planning gain.

gain and loss account see profit and loss account.

galena, lead glance; a dark grey, metallic lead mineral, **PbS**, the most common and important lead ore mineral.

Galfan a high quality zinc coating consisting of zinc with 5% aluminium and 1% misch metal.

galilee a porch or chapel situated at the west end of a church; Latin form is galilea. →95, →99

gall see rind gall.

galleria a shopping arcade in Italy.

gallery 1 an upper space, bounded by a balustrade, opening out to a larger space.
2 an upper storey of a church, cathedral or other large hall, which opens out into the main space, often for seating.
see *Late Antique church* illustration. →95
see *Carolingian abbey church* illustration. →98
see *Gothic cathedral* illustration. →100
3 see empore. →100
4 see art gallery.
5 access gallery, see access balcony.
6 a small boutique for the sale of art and for exhibitions.

gallery-access block, balcony-access flats; a multistorey residential building type in which entry to all flats is via long external walkways at storey level, each joined to a central stairway. →61

gallery flats see gallery-access block. →61

gallery grave, chambered tomb; a prehistoric chambered tomb found in the British Isles, in which burial chambers are arranged on either side of a corridor or gallery.

giallolino, giallorino; an obsolete synthetic inorganic yellow mineral pigment used in Italy, a basic antimoniate of lead with good qualities of opacity; the same as Naples yellow.

gallicum opus gallicum, see murus gallicus. →83

Gallic wall see murus gallicus. →83

gallium a grey, metallic chemical element, **Ga**, used in high temperature thermometers.

gallon, 1 imperial gallon; a unit of liquid volume and dry capacity in use in the British Isles equal to 8 pints, 4 quarts (277.42 cu.in.) or 4.55 l.
2 US gallon, petroleum gallon; a unit of liquid volume equal to 8 pints, 4 quarts (231 cu.in.) or 3.79 l.

Gallus gallus cock, see cock's comb.

galvanic corrosion see electrochemical corrosion.

galvanic couple, voltaic couple; the phenomenon of electricity produced by chemical reaction between two dissimilar conductors in contact with one another, often leading to accelerated corrosion of exposed metal components in buildings; see electrochemical corrosion.

galvanization the deposition of a metal coating onto a material by electrolysis or hot dipping, in construction usually the coating of steel with a layer of zinc as corrosion resistance.

galvanized referring to a steel product which has been coated with a protective layer of zinc; see also above.

galvanized iron see galvanized steel.

galvanized steel, galvanized iron, zinc coated steel; steel treated with a thin protective coating of zinc either by electrolysis or by dipping in baths of molten zinc.

gamboge a natural yellow gum from Thailand used as a transparent pigment.

gambrel roof, 1 gablet roof; a roof having a gablet near the ridge and the lower part hipped. →46
2 see gabled mansard roof. →46

game reserve an area of protected countryside where animals live and breed freely in a natural habitat, and in which hunting is strictly controlled.

gamma cross see gammadion. →118

gammadion 1 a cross formed from varying combinations of the Greek letter gamma, Γ; often a hollow Greek cross or a swastika; also known as crux gammata. →118
2 see hollow Greek cross. →118

gamma iron see austenite.

gamma radiation penetrating electromagnetic emission consisting of short wave, high energy photons emitted from naturally radioactive elements.

gammata crux gammata, see gammadion. →118

ganged form, gang form; a number of prefabricated formwork panels attached together in situ for casting large concrete elements.

ganger a workman who is in charge of, and works with, a number of labourers on site.

gang form see ganged form.

gang nail see nail plate. →35

gang saw, 1 frame saw; a group of parallel saws which cut a log lengthways into boards simultaneously.
2 see mill saw.

gangway a narrow interior circulation space between furnishings, rows of seats, machinery or other equipment to provide access.

gantry, access platform, walkway; a lightweight platform used to give access to high levels for maintenance, and often to provide support for service installations, often with a railing. →54, →61

gaol see prison.

gap 1 see air gap, cavity. →8
2 see ventilation gap. →59
3 installation gap, see allowance. →51

gap graded aggregate graded aggregate without particles of a certain size.

gapped boarding see spaced boarding. →8, →57, →58

garage, 1 repair shop; an establishment or workshop for mending motor vehicles.
2 an enclosed space or shelter used for the parking or storage of a vehicle or vehicles; see also carport.
see *residential buildings* illustration. →61
see *brick house* illustration. →59
3 see parking garage. →62

garage gully a deep gully containing a sediment bucket to collect small amounts of waste oil and petrol in places where motor vehicles are stored or maintained.

garance a reddish dyestuff produced by treating the madder root with sulphuric acid.

garbage solid waste material from food preparation; see also domestic refuse.
see rubbish.

garbha-griha, womb chamber; the most sacred chamber in a Hindu temple, a centrally situated windowless room in which the deity and linga were located. →68

garden 1 a planted recreational yard or area of landscaped ground often linked to buildings.
2 see back garden.

garden black ant [*Lasius niger*] a species of insect which infests cladding boards, logs and wood-based insulation by burrowing and building its nest within the wood.

garden bond 1 see mixed garden bond.
2 see English garden-wall bond. →19
3 see Flemish garden-wall bond. →18

garden city in town planning, an independent urban entity with its own social, manufacturing and cultural infrastructure, characterized by airy low-rise layouts, widespread parkland and other green or planted areas. →105

garden fence a fence of timber or wire mesh but not masonry, surrounding a garden or yard, or serving as a screen or barrier therein.

garden furniture, outdoor furniture; any furniture, benches, tables, seats and sunshades intended for external use, usually of weatherproof materials such as treated wood, plastics and metal.

gardens extensive land planted with trees and shrubs for recreational use by the occupants of an attached building or the public.

garden suburb in town planning, an outlying residential area of a city designed on the principles of garden city planning and which makes use of natural rural features.

garden wall a freestanding wall surrounding a garden or yard, or constructed therein as a screen or barrier.

garden-wall bond 1 see English garden-wall bond. →19
2 see Flemish garden-wall bond. →18

garderobe, necessarium, privy; an external toilet structure overhanging the exterior wall of a castle, monastery or fortification, with openings in the floor to release waste. →103

gargoyle 1 a projecting stone water spout at the eaves or parapet of a building which has been carved into the form of a grotesque animal or head. →100
2 see rainwater spout.

garland see festoon. →121

garnet 1 a silicate mineral which occurs in many different types of rock and is evident in a number of colours, especially deep red; used as a grinding agent and as gemstones; various forms of garnet are listed below.
see almandine.
see andradite.
see grossular, grossular garnet or grossularite.
see hessonite, cinnamon stone.
see pyrope, Bohemian garnet, Cape ruby.
see spessartine.
see uvarovite.
2 a shade of dark red which takes its name from the colour of the above.

garnet brown a shade of reddish brown which takes its name from the colour of the mineral garnet.

garnierite a yellow-green or blue-green mineral, naturally occurring silicates of magnesium and nickel, an important ore of nickel.

garret, 1 loft; a habitable room, dwelling or apartment in the attic space of a building.
2 see attic.

garrison a major building or group of buildings located in a town, used by a body of soldiers for defence or as a permanent base.

garrison town a town containing a permanently stationed body of troops or other military establishment.

garter see bendlet. →125

garth open space in a monastery such as a cloister or yard, used for recreation by the occupants.
see *garth in Carolingian monastery* illustration. →97

gas 1 a state of matter where the atoms or molecules are widely spaced (see solid, liquid), and whose volume varies widely with temperature and pressure.
2 a combustible gaseous fuel burned to provide heat and other services for buildings; see natural gas, manufactured gas.

gas appliance an appliance such as an oven, fire or lamp which runs on natural or bottled gas.

gas black a black pigment, carbon formed as soot from the chemical industry.

gas bottle see gas cylinder.

gas concrete aerated concrete made by the addition of a foaming agent.

gas cooker, gas hob, gas stove; a cooker which runs on gas.

gas cylinder, gas bottle; a portable metal pressure vessel designed to store combustible gas in liquid form.

gas detector see combustion gas detector.

gas distribution network, gas supply network; the pipework and other appliances for providing a mains supply of natural gas to buildings in a community.

gas fire a gas-fuelled room heater whose flames are visible, often for decorative effect.

gas-fired referring to a heating system which uses gas as its combustible fuel.

gas-fired furnace a furnace fuelled by gas to produce high temperatures for industrial processes of heating, drying, baking etc.

gas-fired central heating, gas heating; central heating in which water etc. is heated by the combustion of gas in boilers.

gas fitter a tradesman skilled in the fitting of gas pipework and appliances.

gas forming admixture in concretework, an admixture included in the mix to promote the formation of bubbles of gas.

gas fuel see fuel gas.

gas governor in gas heating, a device for regulating the flow of gas in a pipeline and for converting mains pressure to that suitable for domestic use.

gas group in gas heating, a subdivision of a family of gases used for combustion which comply to certain standards of heat output.

gas heater, gas stove; any heating device fuelled by gas.

gas heating see gas-fired central heating.

gas hob see gas cooker.
gasholder see gasometer.
gas installation pipework any pipework, meters and associated apparatus which convey gas fuel to its outlets and appliances for use.
gas installation riser see installation riser.
gasket, 1 seal; a preformed strip of flexible sheet material of variable cross-section included to form a compression seal at a butt joint or convey water out of construction joints.
2 see glazing gasket. →53
gas main a principal gas supply pipe to which individual users or buildings can be connected.
gas mantle, mantle; in gas lighting, a perforated or woven hood of metal, ceramics etc. over the outlet of a luminaire, which glows on ignition of the gas to produce incandescent light.
gas metal-arc welding see GMA welding.
gas meter a meter for measuring and recording the flow and consumption of gas supplied to an installation.
gas oil distilled oil which is thicker and with a higher boiling point than kerosene, used as a fuel in atomizing burners.
gasolene see petrol.
gasoline see petrol.
gasometer, gasholder; a large hollow cylindrical structure with a telescopic action for storing combustible gas at an even pressure.
gas oven a domestic or industrial oven in which heat is produced by the combustion of gas, used for the preparation of food and drying.
gas pipe any sealed tube through which gas is conveyed from a place of storage or manufacture to a point of use.
gas point a point in a gas installation from which gas can be extracted or to which an appliance can be connected.
gas service riser a length of supply and distribution pipe installed vertically in a gas installation.
gas-shielded metal-arc welding see GMA welding.
gas-shielded welding one of a number of welding processes in which an inert gas is used to protect the metal being welded from reaction with the surrounding air.
gas soundness test in gas heating, a test for leakage of gas pipework and appliances.
gas stove 1 see gas cooker.
2 see gas heater.
gas supply the supply of gas for a building from a main.
gas supply network see gas distribution network.
gas tank a fixed or portable storage vessel for gas, usually under pressure.
gas tungsten arc welding see TIG welding.
gas welding a skilled method of fusion welding in which the metals to be joined are melted together using a blowtorch burning oxyacetylene, propane or oxyhydrogen.
gasworks a factory for the manufacture of gas from coal or oil.
gate 1 a hinged barrier, door or hatch in a wall or fence which can be opened to allow thoroughfare.
see collapsible gate.
lich gate, see lych gate. →102
lift gate, see lift car door.
see lock gate.
see lych gate. →102
scissor gate, see collapsible gate.
starting gate, see carceres. →89
2 see shutter.
see roller shutter.
3 an opening in a fortified wall, the entrance to a castle or walled town; a gateway.
Caesar's gate, porta Caesarea, see Imperial gate. →96
ceremonial gate, see porta pompae. →90
see Imperial gate. →96
see porta. →89, →104
triumphal gate, see porta triumphalis.
gatehouse 1 a security building or construction at the entrance to a castle, building complex or estate to control entry and exit. →92, →103
2 see barbican.
3 see propylaeum. →92
gate tower a tower which functions as a gateway to a fortress or other construction.
gateway 1 the structural or ornate surround for an entrance opening in a wall or building; a portal. →113
see *gateway in Asian temples* illustration. →68
2 see torii. →120
3 see postern. →102
gather, gathering; the narrowing of the top of a fireplace to meet a flue. →55
gathering see gather. →55
gauge, gage; **1** meter; any instrument designed to measure a varying dimension or quantity, displaying the measured value numerically.
2 an instrument, tool or apparatus used for measuring whether a component or material conforms to a standard or designed measurement.
3 a measure of the thickness of thin sheet objects.
4 a mason's tool used for marking out parallel lines when setting out a piece of work.
5 honing guide.
types of gauge included as separate entries are listed below.
Birmingham wire gauge.
cutting gauge.
dial gauge.
feeler gauge.
marking gauge.
mortise gauge.
micrometer.
plug gauge.
pressure gauge.
thread gauge.
vernier callipers.
wire gauge.
gauge board a board on which mixed plaster stands while awaiting use.
gauged arch a brick arch in which all the voussoirs are wedge shaped. →22, →23
gauged brickwork, rubbed brickwork; decorative and relief effects produced in facing brickwork by laying soft bricks rubbed to exact dimensions in thin mortar joints.
gauged coarse stuff plaster used for undercoats, produced from lime putty and sand mixed with Portland cement or gypsum plaster; see coarse stuff.
gauged lime plaster see gauged stuff.
gauged setting stuff finishing plaster produced from lime putty and sand mixed with gypsum plaster; cf. setting stuff.
gauged stuff, gauged lime plaster; traditional plaster consisting of lime putty mixed with either gypsum plaster or cement to reduce setting time.
gauge rod, storey rod; a vertical timber batten used in the setting out of brickwork, onto which the levels of brick courses, sill heights etc. are marked.
gauging trowel a plasterer's trowel with a triangular metal blade used for applying small amounts of plaster. →43
Gaussian distribution see normal distribution.
gazebo see belvedere.
G-clamp see gee-clamp.
gear in building installations, the mechanical apparatus for operating doors, shutters and other automated systems.
Geb in ancient Egyptian mythology, the primeval deity of earth, created by the sun god Atum, forming the cosmos together with Nut: the heavens, Shu: air, and Tefnut: moisture. →74
Gedu nohor [*Entandrophragma angolense*] a tropical West African hardwood sold as mahogany; it has

pale reddish brown timber and is used for plywood, veneered furniture and interiors.

gee-clamp, G-clamp, C-clamp, circle-end clamp; a cramp consisting of a U-shaped piece of cast metal with a screw for clamping objects.

geison Gk; a corona in a classical Greek cornice; see corona. →78

gel 1 any semi-solid jelly-like mass which consists of a finely divided solid dispersed in a liquid.
2 see cement gel.

gelatin, gelatine; a white or yellowish adhesive substance, brittle when dry, obtained from boiling animal sinews, bones and hides, which, when mixed with water, sets to form a jellyish solid; used in food preparation, photographic processes and some glues.

gelatine see gelatin.

Gellert green a variety of cobalt green pigment.

gem, gemstone; any precious or semi-precious stone which may be used in ornamentation and jewellery.

gemmology the science of precious stones.

gemstone 1 see gem.
2 see precious stone.

genera plural form of genus.

general arrangement drawing, general location drawing; a type of design drawing, usually a plan, showing the layout of construction works, how they are located in relation to one another, door and furnishing codes, and other references to detail and assembly drawings.

general conditions of contract see conditions of contract.

general contractor see main contractor.

general diffuse lighting artificial lighting in which luminaires distribute 40–60% of the emitted light downwards or to the area to be illuminated.

general foreman, foreman; the contractor's employee responsible for supervising all work on site.

general lighting lighting of a space whose task is to provide a uniform light level, as opposed to highlighting certain areas.

general lighting service lamp, GLS lamp; a standard incandescent 25–2000 W lamp running off 220–240 V, with a clear, opal or pearl bulb and a screw or bayonet lamp cap.

general location drawing see general arrangement drawing.

general partner one of the members of a partnership who is legally liable for an agreed share of the potential debts of the company.

general partnership, partnership; a company formed by two or more people who are personally liable for its potential debts.

general purpose knife see trimming knife.

general purpose mortar common and versatile mortars which can be used for masonry bedding, tile fixing, cement render patching etc.

general purpose screw a steel or brass screw for fixing to wood, timber-based boards, plastic etc. →36

general surround lighting lighting designed to provide a general lighting level in a space, without regard for the illumination of special features or exits etc.

generation see electrical power generation.

generator 1 any device for producing electrical energy from motion or mechanical energy.
2 especially a petrol-fuelled machine for generating electricity on a building site.

genet, dyer's broom; a shade of yellow which takes its name from the colour of the blossom of the broom shrub [*Genista tinctoria*].

Genista tinctoria see genet.

genius loci see sense of place.

genre in painting, art from Holland in the 1600s displaying scenes from everyday life.

gentian blue a shade of blue which takes its name from the colour of the flowers of certain Alpine plants [*Gentiana acaulis, Gentiana clusii*].

genus, plural genera; in the classification of flora and fauna, a group of species differentiated from all others by certain common characteristics.

geodesy see land surveying.

geodisist see land surveyor.

geogrid a synthetic sheet product with large perforations, incorporated into groundworks as soil stabilization.

geological map a map which presents the distribution of underlying rock, mineral and soil types for a district, with different types usually shown in different colours.

geology the branch of science that deals with the structure of the earth and the formation of rocks.

geomembrane in geotechnical engineering, an impermeable membrane, often of sheet plastics, incorporated in the ground to inhibit penetrations of liquids and gases.

geometrical acoustics, ray acoustics; a method of analysing acoustical effects as lines of disturbance and wavefronts, used for large spaces where the wavelengths of sound are small compared with the dimensions of the space.

geometrical stair a stair cantilevered out from a wall. →45

geometrical tracery see geometric tracery. →110

geometric determinism a theory by which nature and natural phenomena are based on and governed by mathematical principles, in practice used as a basis for design in defining architectural form and proportion.

geometric mean in mathematics, the average or mean value of a number of quantities calculated by multiplying the quantities together and finding the nth root of their product.

geometric planning a form of town planning in which streets are arranged orthogonally, usually with little regard for topographical or climatic conditions, to produce a mechanical grid of streets.

Geometric style 1 a decorative style from Archaic Greece (900–750 BC) with regular geometrical patterns such as keys and frets, especially used for vase painting.
2 an early development of the Decorated style of English Gothic architecture in England in the early 1300s, characterized by geometrical patterns and forms in tracery and other decorated elements.

geometric tile specially shaped ceramic tiles designed to be laid with other similar tiles and form a geometric pattern on the tiled surface; see hexagonal tile. →20

geometric tracery tracery found in Gothic churches of the late 1200s, with slender vertical bars supporting a pattern of foils and circles; also called geometrical tracery. →109, →110

geometry 1 the study and graphical representation of points, lines, two- and three-dimensional forms and their associated properties.
2 see plane geometry.
3 see descriptive geometry.

Georgian architecture an architectural style in England during the consecutive reigns of Georges I–IV (1714–1830), characterized by the use of purist classical elements in public buildings and urban dwellings.

Georgian wired glass wired glass with a 13 mm steel mesh.

geosynthetic referring to any synthetic product, including geomembranes and geotextiles, incorporated into the ground for soil drainage, sealing or reinforcing.

geosystem the inorganic system encompassing the geological, chemical and mechanical aspects of the earth's crust.

geotechnical engineering, ground engineering; a branch of engineering whose task is to investigate and improve the ground on which a building or structure is to be constructed.

geotechnical investigation see geotechnical survey.

geotechnical survey, geotechnical investigation, ground investigation; in geotechnical engineering, investigation of the soil and foundation conditions of a particular site.

geotextile a durable woven plastics mat incorporated into the ground to inhibit erosion and as stabilization against shear or slip.

geothermal energy heat stored naturally in underground rock formations, utilized as a heating source for buildings by drilling deep boreholes.

geranium (red) a shade of red which takes its name from the colour of the flowers of the geranium plant [*Geranium sanguineum*].

German black see vine black.

germanium a hard, grey, metallic chemical element, **Ge**, used as a semiconductor.

German silver, electrum, nickel brass; a silverish alloy of brass, containing zinc, nickel and copper.

gesso a mixture of gypsum, a glue and linseed oil used as a base in painting and for cast plaster decoration.

getee see jetty.

gettiez see jetty.

ghetto originally that part of the city in which Jews were required to live, in modern usage applied to any area or quarter which a minority or often deprived social group inhabits.

ghost island in road design, a marked area of carriageway designed to direct or divert traffic, usually at a road junction.

giant arborvitae [*Thuja plicata*] see western red cedar.

giant cedar [*Thuja plicata*] see western red cedar.

giant order see colossal order.

Gibbs surround an ornamental masonry surround for a doorway or window with alternately projecting blocks.

giga- abb. **G**; a prefix for units of measurement or quantity to denote a factor of 10^9 (a thousand million). →Table 1

gilded, gilt; coated with a layer of gold leaf or painted with gold paint.

gilder's cushion, gilder's pad; a small oblong board or frame covered with calfskin stretched over two or three layers of thick soft material, used by a gilder for cutting and preparing gold leaf.

gilder's liquor a mixture of water and alcohol used in gilding to activate the dried glue present on the surface onto which gold leaf is applied.

gilder's pad see gilder's cushion.

gilding the art and craft of providing a decorative surface coating with a thin layer of gold leaf.

gilding size see gold size.

gilding primer in gilding, a compound or filler used to smooth and seal a surface prior to sticking down gold leaf.

gill, 1 a unit of liquid volume or dry capacity equal to ¼ of a pint.

2 imperial gill; a unit of liquid volume in use in the British Isles equal to 5 fluid ounces, 8.67 cu.in. or 0.14 l.

3 US gill; a unit of liquid volume in North America equal to 7.22 cu.in. or 0.12 l.

gilt see gilded.

gilt leather embossed leather with ornament in gold leaf, especially popular in the 1800s, used for tapestries and decorated artifacts.

gimlet, twist gimlet, wimble; a pointed hand tool for making starter holes in wood for nails or screws. →42

gimp pin a small brass panel pin for upholstery, whose shaft is 10–19 mm in length.

girder a large main steel beam with upper and lower chords separated by a web; a lattice beam, truss or universal beam.

girder bridge a bridge whose main structural elements are steel girders.
see box girder bridge.
see lattice girder bridge.

glacial till see boulder clay.

glacis an artificial downwards-sloping embankment or declivity in front of a fortification to provide protection in the event of attack; especially the outward sloping rampart exterior to the covered way, kept clear of obstacles to enable clear views. →104

glance one of a number of dark, soft, glossy, metal sulphide ores.

glare in lighting design, a condition of poor light distribution in which the ability of the human eye to see is impaired due to excessive contrasts.

glare screen see anti-dazzle screen.

glass a hard, impermeable, transparent material formed from sand, soda ash, limestone and dolomite; used for many applications especially window glazing.
see *glass and glazing* illustration; types included as separate entries are listed below. →53
absorbing glass, see tinted solar control glass.
acoustical glass, acoustic control glass, see sound control glass.
alarm glass.
annealed glass. →53
anti-bandit laminated glass.
anti-fading glass.
anti-sun glass, see solar control glass.
anti-vandal glass.
antique glass.
armour-plated glass, see bullet-resistant laminated glass.
bent glass.
blast-resistant laminated glass.
blown glass.
blown sheet glass.
body-tinted glass.
borosilicate glass.
bull's-eye glass, see bullion.
bullet-resistant laminated glass.
bullion, bullion glass.
cast glass.
cathedral glass.
cellular glass.
channel glass. →53
chemically strengthened glass.
cladding glass.
clear float glass.
clear plate glass.
clear sheet glass.
coated float glass, see surface coated float glass.
coloured opaque glass.
corrugated glass.
crown glass.
crystal glass, see lead glass.
curved glass, see bent glass.
cut glass, see crystal.
diffuse reflection glass, diffused glass.
drawn sheet glass, drawn glass, see sheet glass.
electronic shielding glass.
expanded glass, see foam glass, cellular glass.
fibreglass, fiberglass.
filigree glass.
fire-resisting glass, fire-resistant glass, fire glass.
flat drawn glass, see clear sheet glass.
flat glass.
float glass.
foam glass, foamed glass.
fused silica glass.
Georgian wired glass.
heat-absorbing glass, see tinted solar control glass.
heat-resisting glass.
heat-soaked glass.
insulation glass, see sealed glazed unit. →53
intumescent glass, see laminated intumescent glass.

laminated glass. →53
laminated intumescent glass.
laminated safety glass.
laminated solar control glass.
laminated sound control glass.
laminated ultraviolet light control glass.
lead glass.
lead X-ray glass.
leaded glass, see leaded light.
low emissivity glass.
milk glass.
mirror glass, mirrored glass.
noise control glass, noise reduction glass, see sound control glass.
obscured glass.
one-way glass.
opal glass, opalescent glass.
opaque glass.
patterned glass.
plate glass, polished plate glass.
potash water glass.
profile glass, see channel glass. →53
Pyrex, see borosilicate glass.
quartz glass, see fused silica glass.
radiation-shielding glass.
reeded glass.
reflective float glass, see surface coated float glass.
reflective glass.
rolled glass.
roughcast glass.
safety glass.
security glass.
sheet glass.
shielding glass, see radiation-shielding glass.
silica glass, see fused silica glass.
silk-screened glass, silkscreen glass.
smoked glass.
soda-lime glass.
solar control glass.
sound control glass, sound insulation glass, sound reduction glass.
spandrel glass, see cladding glass.
special glass.
surface coated float glass.
surface-modified tinted float glass.
tempered glass, see toughened glass. →53
tessera.
tinted glass.
tinted solar control glass.
toughened glass. →53
translucent glass, see diffuse reflection glass.
transparent mirror glass.
ultraviolet control glass, see laminated ultraviolet light control glass.
Venetian mirror glass.
volcanic glass.
water glass, see sodium silicate.
window glass.
wired glass, wired cast glass.
X-ray resistant glass, see lead X-ray glass.

glass balustrade 1 see all-glass balustrade. →54
2 see glazed balustrade. →54

glass bit see glass drill. →42

glass block, glass brick, hollow glass block; a rectangular hollow block made from two moulded glass units fused together, whose surfaces may be clear, coloured or textured; used to form glass screens and external translucent glazing. →30
see *types of glass block* illustration. →30
see *glass block walling* illustration. →53

glass brick see glass block. →30, →53

glass concrete solid glass blocks bonded with reinforced concrete, used to form a wall, screen or surface.

glass cutter a small tool with a longitudinal handle and sharpened rotating wheel used by a glazier for cutting glass; a scored line is made on the glass surface, along which it will naturally snap.

glass dome a prefabricated glass hemisphere or dome used for rooflighting.

glass door 1 see glazed door. →51
2 see all-glass door. →60
3 see casement door, French door.

glass drill, glass bit; a drill bit for boring holes in sheets of glass, usually tipped with a cutting plate of hard metal. →42

glass fibre fibres manufactured from glass, used widely as reinforcement in compound products.

glassfibre-base bitumen felt bitumen felt whose supporting fibrous mat is mainly of glass fibres.

glassfibre cloth, woven roving; reinforcement for fibreglass and composite materials consisting of rovings which have been woven into a mesh.

glassfibre mat a reinforcing mat of chopped strand used in fibreglass and other composite materials.

glassfibre reinforced referring to composite products and materials which consist of glass fibres in a matrix of cement, concrete, plastics etc., also called glass reinforced.

glassfibre-reinforced cement, glassfibre-reinforced concrete, GRC; a fibre-reinforced composite consisting of glass fibres containing zirconium in a Portland cement matrix; used for thin-walled panels and street furniture.

glassfibre-reinforced concrete 1 see glassfibre-reinforced polymer/concrete.
2 see glassfibre-reinforced cement.

glassfibre-reinforced gypsum, glass-reinforced gypsum, GRG; a tough, non-combustible composite consisting of glass fibres in a gypsum matrix; used for making fire-resisting building boards and panels.

glassfibre-reinforced plaster see glass-reinforced plaster.

glassfibre-reinforced plastics any products consisting of glass fibres which have been impregnated with synthetic resin, usually polyester; used for mouldings, sheets, roofing slates and drainage fittings.

glassfibre-reinforced polymer/concrete, glassfibre-reinforced concrete, GRPC; a polyester resin-bound concrete which contains glass fibres; less dense than ordinary concrete and with a higher tensile strength.

glass floor see glazed floor. →60

glasshouse see greenhouse.

glass lens see lens.

glass mosaic one of a number of small, flat pieces or blocks of glass supplied on a paper backing, used as tiled floor and wall covering and for decorative effects.

glasspaper fine sanding paper whose abrasive is powdered glass, used for smoothing and polishing. →41

glasspaper block, sandpaper block; a small pad to which a number of sheets of abrasive paper have been attached; used for sharpening lead pencils and charcoals.

glass partition see glazed partition.

glass plank see channel glass. →53

glass/polyester base bitumen felt bitumen felt whose reinforcing fibrous mat is mainly of glass and polyester fibres.

glass reinforced see glassfibre reinforced.

glass-reinforced gypsum glassfibre-reinforced gypsum.

glass-reinforced plaster plaster which contains glass fibres for added reinforcement, used for ornamental pillars, pilasters, cornices etc.; abb. GRP; often glassfibre-reinforced gypsum.

glass-reinforced polyester, GRP; a product consisting of glass fibres which have been impregnated with polyester resin; used for mouldings, sheets, roofing slates and drainage fittings.

glass roof see glazed roof. →60

glass sheet a flat piece of manufactured glass.

glass silk see glass wool.

glass size see pane size.

glass tile, glass slate; a roofing tile made of glass, used to allow light into a roofspace and laid with normal roofing tiles.

glass unit see sealed glazed unit. →53

glass wool, glass silk; an insulating material produced from fine glass fibres which have been sprayed with a binder and formed into random masses.

Glauber salt hydrated sodium sulphate used in the manufacture of dyes and in some heat storage systems.

glauconite 1 a dark green form of the mineral biotite, an iron silicate mineral found in the sea bed.
2 see green earth.

glaze, glazing; a hardwearing glossy impenetrable finish for tiles and other ceramic products achieved by vitrification of the surface and of a surface coating such as ash, enamel etc.

glazed 1 referring to an opening, frame or partition into which glazing has been fitted.
2 referring to ceramic products which have been fired with a glaze.

glazed balustrade a balustrade with an infill of glass in a timber, steel or aluminium frame. →54

glazed brick a brick of which at least one end and one face have been glazed during firing.

glazed door 1 a door whose leaf is glazed, particularly one with glazed panels in a frame. →51
2 see all-glass door. →51, →60
3 see casement door, French door.

glazed floor, glass floor; a transparent or translucent floor of specially strengthened glass panels held in frames. →60

glazed metal door, metal glazed door; a steel or aluminium framed door with one or more glazed panels. →51

glazed partition, glass partition; an interior dividing screen which consists of framed or structural glass.

glazed roof, glass roof; a roof or part of a roof constructed of glass panels in a timber, steel or aluminium frame.
see *glazed roof* in office building illustration. →60

glazed tile a ceramic tile which has been treated with an earthenware or enamel glaze before firing to provide a shiny impenetrable surface. →20

glazed timber door, timber glazed door; a timber framed door with one or more glazed panels. →51

glazed unit 1 see double glazed unit.
2 see sealed glazed unit. →53
3 see triple glazed unit.

glazed wall see window wall.

glazier a tradesman or skilled worker responsible for the installation and replacement of windows and glazing.

glazier's hammer a hammer with an angled oblong head used in framing and the pinning of glazing beads; also any small hammers used for this purpose. →40

glazier's point see glazing sprig.

glazier's putty see putty.

glazing 1 the installation of glass, glass panels or products into frames or other supporting systems.
see *glazing* in office building illustration. →60
2 the resulting glass panels and windows thus installed.
see *glazing* illustration, and below for list of types of glazing. →53
applied sash glazing, see secondary glazing.
balcony glazing. →54
cellular glazing, see cellular sheet.
double glazing.
dry glazing. →52
external glazing. →52, →60
frameless glazing.
inside glazing.
internal glazing, interior glazing. →52, →60
intruder glazing.
lead glazing, see leaded light.
outer glazing, see external glazing. →52
outside glazing.
patent glazing. →53
planar glazing, see structural glazing. →53
polycarbonate cellular glazing, see polycarbonate cellular sheet.
roof glazing, see glazed roof, rooflight. →60
safety glazing.
secondary glazing.
security glazing.
single glazing.
structural glazing. →53
subsidiary glazing.
system glazing, see patent glazing. →53
triple glazing.
upper glazing, see top light. →60, →111
3 the application of a glaze to ceramic products.
see salt glazing.

glazing bar, 1 division bar, window bar; a framing member to which glazing is fixed; part of a timber window frame or metal patent glazing etc. →111
2 see frame member.

glazing bead, glazing fillet; a strip of timber, metal or other material used to fasten glazing in a frame.
see *timber trim* illustration. →2
see *glazing* illustration. →53

glazing bedding in glazing, a bedding compound such as putty applied around the rebate in a window frame prior to the fitting of a pane of glass.

glazing block, setting block; in glazing, a packing piece set beneath or beside the glass to keep it in position in its frame while it is being fixed with putty or beads. →53

glazing capping 1 a profile fixed to the outside of glazing bars to protect and conceal the joint between it and the glazing.
2 especially one of extruded aluminium or metal clipped on over glazing bars of a patent glazing system.

glazing cleat a small angled stainless steel or aluminium metal jointing component fixed to a frame to hold a pane in position.

glazing clip in glazing, a small non-corrodible metal jointing component inserted into a hole in a metal window frame to hold a pane in position.

glazing compound in glazing, resilient material applied in semi-liquid form, putty or sealant which sets to form a seal between a glass pane and its frame.
see elastic glazing compound.
see non-setting glazing compound.
see putty.

glazing fillet see glazing bead. →2

glazing gasket, seal; a strip of flexible material such as neoprene fixed around the external edges of a pane of glass to provide a weathertight seal between it and its framing member. →53

glazing peg in metal framed glazing, one of a number of pieces holding the glass pane or panel in its frame.

glazing putty see putty.

glazing rebate a rebate in a glazing bar or frame against which glazing is fitted.

glazing sealant see glazing compound.

glazing size see pane size.

glazing sprig, brad, glazier's point; in glazing, a small headless nail used to hold a pane of glass in a timber frame while the putty hardens, or to fasten a glazing bead.

glazing system see patent glazing. →53

glazing tape adhesive tape used as weatherproofing for a window.

glazing unit see sealed glazed unit. →53

glazing unit spacer see spacer. →53

global system for mobile communications see GSM.

globe a spherical or ovoid translucent diffuser or shade for a luminaire.

globe valve in water supply pipework, a screwdown valve with a spherical body.

Gloephyllum sepiarium see slash conk.

glory see aureole. →119

gloss 1 reflectance or shininess in a surface such as paint, varnish, ceramics or other planar material.
2 the degree of reflection of light from a dry paint surface; in Britain graded into 5 degrees: flat, eggshell flat, eggshell gloss, semi-gloss, full gloss; in the US there are only 4, with eggshell covering both eggshell flat and eggshell gloss.
3 a vague word to describe grades of glossiness in a dry paint surface, characterized by a high reflectance of light.

gloss paint any paint such as alkyd paint which has a high gloss finish, used on wood and metal surfaces.

GLS lamp see general lighting service lamp.

glue any adhesive manufactured from boiling up animal and fish remains, or one that sets without applied heat; in general use glue is synonymous with adhesive, although adhesive is the preferred term in construction; see **adhesive** for types of glues; see also cement.

glue block, see angle block.

glued and laminated beam see laminated timber beam. →7

glued joint a joint in which glue is used as the fastening medium.

glue gun an electrically heated device for applying lines of hot melt glue to parts to be joined together, seams of vinyl matting etc.

glue-laminated log see laminated log.

glue laminated timber, glulam, laminated wood; a structural wood product composed of lengths of timber glued together longitudinally in strips to form a larger piece; this reduces the effects of defects in individual strips.
see laminated timber beam. →7
see laminated log.

glue line the thin gap or seam between two abutting glued surfaces, filled with adhesive.

glue size 1 a weak water-based glue solution for sealing plaster and other porous surfaces onto which further decoration may be applied.
2 a similar solution used also to stiffen paper, card and cloth and for gluing light papers and metal foils to a base.

glue spreader a simple rubber or plastic implement with a straight or serrated blade for applying glue to large surfaces. →43

glulam see glue laminated timber.

glulam beam see laminated timber beam. →7

gluten glue starch glue made from gluten, a mixture of proteins present in wheat flour.

glyph in classical architecture, a vertical decorative groove or channel found in threes making up triglyphs in an entablature. →78

glyptotheca Lat.; a building designed to house sculpture.

Gmellin's blue see artificial ultramarine.

GMA welding, gas metal-arc welding, gas-shielded metal-arc welding; a method of welding metals in which the arc is shielded with an active gas such as carbon dioxide or oxygen, an inert gas such as argon, or a mixture of the two; a generic name for MIG, MAG and TIG welding.

gneiss a dark, banded, coarse-grained metamorphic rock composed of quartz, feldspar and mica, formed under intense conditions of heat and pressure.
see gneissose micaschist, foliated gneiss.
see granite-gneiss.

gneissose micaschist, foliated gneiss; a dark grey or black, layered, metamorphic rock containing a high proportion of mica; a variety of gneiss, it is cleaved for use in construction as paving and tiles.

gnomonic projection in cartography, a projection of part of the surface of a sphere, usually the earth, viewed from its centre as a flattened disc, a form of azimuthal projection.

goal formulating, goal setting; in plan preparation, the establishment of goals, objectives, and policies to be achieved in the plan.

goal setting see goal formulating.

gobelin 1 high quality woven decorative fabric from a state-owned French carpet factory named after its founder family which supplied to the court from Arras in Flanders in the 1400s.
2 any tapestry of a similar type or weave.

God, eye of see eye of God. →119

God, hand of see hand of God. →119

godroon see gadroon. →124

goice an archaic form of the word joist.

going, 1 run; the horizontal dimension of a step as measured in plan, perpendicular to its front face. →45
2 see total going. →45

gold a yellowish, heavy, soft and malleable metal, **Au**, which is an excellent conductor of electricity; a much sought after commodity also used in the form of leaf as a decorative finish and in industrial products such as thin conducting coatings for glass.

golden section, sectio aurea (Lat.); a division of a line or value into two parts such that the ratio of the length of the longer part to the whole is equal to that of the length of the shorter part to the longer part (about 1:1.618); designs made on this basis are considered to have good composition. →107

golden wheat, corn, wheat; a shade of yellow which takes its name from the colour of wheat [*Triticum vulgare*] ready for harvesting.

Golden Hall see kondo.

gold foil see gold leaf.

gold ground in medieval religious art, a method of painting in which colours are applied to a background of gesso covered with gold leaf, thus emphasizing celestial glory.

gold leaf, gold foil; fine sheet of gold as thin as 0.0001 mm, used for the ornamental covering of embellishment, plaster casts, and for illuminating manuscripts.

gold ochre a cleaned and crushed warm brownish variety of yellow ochre pigment.

gold size 1 an oleoresinous varnish used for sticking down gold leaf and for making fillers; also called gilding size.
2 see bole.

Golgotha cross 1 see Calvary cross. →117
2 see Coptic cross. →118

Gonystylus spp. see ramin.

goods depot see freight terminal.

goods lift a large robust lift designed to carry goods and people.

goods yard in railway architecture, an area of interlinking tracks, sheds and platforms at which freight is loaded and unloaded and wagons are stored.

goose turd a shade of dark grey green which takes its name from the colour of the excrement of a goose or duck.

gopura a southern Indian stepped tower or pyramid over a gateway to a shrine; also written as gopuram. →68

gopuram see gopura. →68

Gordian knot Roman and Romanesque ornament based on an ancient and complex mythological knot of thongs of cornel bark, reputedly tied by Midas at the acropolis and eventually untied by Alexander the Great. →123

gorge 1 a narrow structure or neck in a castle leading to a bastion, or the rear entrance to any other fortification.
2 see trochilus. →14
3 see scotia. →14, →80

gorgerin see hypotrachelion. →81

gorgon Gk; an ornamentation motif of a horrifying mythological female figure such as Medusa, with snakes for hair and grotesque teeth, whose gaze was reputed to turn an onlooker into stone. →122

gospel ambo in Early Christian architecture, a lectern or space to the north side of the altar or choir from which the gospel texts were delivered; see also epistle ambo. →95

gospel side in church architecture, the left side of an altar or chancel as viewed from the congregation, from which the gospel was traditionally read as if preaching, facing north, to the heathens; see also epistle side. →95

Gothic arch see pointed arch. →24

Gothic architecture, pointed architecture; religious architecture in Europe in the Middle Ages, originating from France in the 1200s, characterized by use of the pointed arch, verticality of decoration, rib vaults and richly carved ornament; styles of Gothic architecture included as separate entries are listed below.
see *Gothic cathedral* illustration. →100
see *Gothic columns* illustration. →114
see *Gothic rib vault* illustration. →101
see *types of Gothic tracery* illustration. →110
see *Romanesque and Gothic capitals* illustration. →115
Angevin Gothic.
brick Gothic.
early Gothic. →100
Curvilinear style.
Decorated style.
Early English style.
English Gothic.
Flamboyant style.
Foliated style.
Geometric style.
Gothic revival.
high Gothic. →100
international Gothic.
Jagiello, Jagello.
late Gothic.
neo-Gothic architecture.
Perpendicular style, Rectilinear style.
ogival.
Steamboat Gothic.
Venetian Gothic.

Gothick see Gothic revival.

Gothic naturalism art and ornament in Gothic churches with representations of human and natural subjects, rather than religious or metaphysical.

Gothic revival, Gothick; an architectural style in Europe from the 1700s and 1800s characterized by a renewed interest in Gothic forms and decoration.

Gothic survival a term describing European architecture of the true Gothic style which was built during the advent of the Renaissance period (1600s and 1700s).

Gothic tracery see tracery. →110

Gothic vault 1 light and decorative vaulting, often very intricate, for roofing the nave and aisles of Gothic churches. →101
see *Gothic rib vault* illustration. →101
2 see pointed barrel vault. →25

gouache 1 a quick-drying opaque watercolour paint with a gum binder and filler of opaque white.
2 a method or technique of painting with gouache paints.

gouge a concave chisel used for cutting rounded grooves in wood; types included as separate entries are listed below. →41
crank gouge.
firmer gouge. →41
front bent gouge, see spoon gouge. →41
spoon gouge. →41
turning gouge. →41

government land see crown land.

governor see gas governor, appliance governor.

Gowering lock a vertical air lock that has separate chambers for materials and personnel.

grade 1 see gradient.
2 the ground level of final excavations and earthworks in a building site.
3 see quality.
4 see classification.
5 class; the classification of a material, product, system or piece of work regarding quality.
6 see grade of concrete.
7 see commercial grade.

grade beam see ground beam. →29

grade crossing see level crossing.

graded aggregate 1 aggregate which has been sorted into particles of a particular range of sizes; see also continuously graded aggregate, gap graded aggregate.
2 see continuously graded aggregate.

graded cross see Calvary cross. →117

graded density chipboard chipboard manufactured with woodchips of various sizes, graded from finer on the surface to coarser towards the core. →9

graded interchange see grade-separated junction. →63

grade of concrete, concrete grade; for concrete, the specified characteristic cube strength expressed in N/mm^2.

grade-separated fork junction a road junction in which a side road meets a major road and allows for flow of traffic in one direction only; also called a fork interchange. →63

grade-separated junction, flyover, graded interchange (Am.); a road junction or interchange in which roads meet at different levels and pass over or under one another, with slip roads for traffic to change from one road to another; see interchange, road junction. →63

grade-separated roundabout junction a road junction or interchange with slip roads leading from a major road to a roundabout constructed above it, from which traffic is distributed to minor roads. →63

gradient, grade, slope; the degree of slope of an inclined plane, track or pipeline relative to the horizontal, expressed as a percentage or given as a ratio of the level difference to horizontal travel.

grading 1 the breakdown of percentages by weight of different sized particles in a granular material such as soil or aggregate.
2 see sieving.
3 see classification.
4 in siteworks, the formation of masses of earth into the required contoured shape with bulldozers and other mechanical plant, into embankments etc.

grading curve a graphical representation of the range of grain sizes of particles in a granular material such as soil or concrete.

gradus 'step' (Lat.); a row of seats in the cuneus of a Roman theatre or circus. →89, →90

graecorum structura 'Greek construction' (Lat.); the term given by Vitruvius when referring to Greek emplecton masonry in hard stone such as flint, bonded with staggered vertical joints. →83

graecostasis Lat.; a place in the Roman forum from where Greek ambassadors and other foreign dignitaries were permitted to stand and listen to the debates.

graffiti 1 plural form of graffito.
2 unwanted writings or drawings on building surfaces in spray paints, felt pen etc.

graffito, pl. graffiti; **1** writing inscribed or written on a wall, especially in ancient times.
2 a marble tablet onto which carved decoration making use of shadows is inscribed.
3 see sgraffito.

grain 1 abb. **gr**; an old unit of weight, one seven-thousandth part of a pound avoirdupois, equivalent to 0.065 g, deriving from the weight of one grain of wheat.

2 the arrangement and direction of the fibres in wood.

grainer any paintbrush used for imitating the grain effects of wood and marble on wall surfaces as decoration.

graining a decorative surface treatment made by painting or otherwise imitating the figure of wood or marble.

grain of the ply referring to the direction and form of the grain in plywood veneers.

grain size a property of the coarseness of a granular material, the relative size of its constituent granules.

gram, gramme; SI unit of mass, abb. **g**.

gram-equivalent the combining power of a chemical element equivalent to 8 grams of oxygen, expressed in grams; see valence.

Gramineae see grass.

gramme see gram.

granary an agricultural building, structure or part of a building in which grain is stored.

grandiose of a building or style of architecture, extravagant, overscaled, pompous.

grand master key a key which fits all the locks in a number of suites of locks, each of which has a master key.

grand stair a lavish or ceremonial stair within or leading to the main entrance of a palace, castle, temple etc. →67

grandstand a permanent covered stand with tiered seating for spectators.

grange, farmstead; a farming establishment or rural residence attached to a farm.

granite a very durable igneous rock type whose basic constituents are alkali feldspars and quartz, much used in construction as cladding, masonry and paving.

granite-gneiss a composite metamorphic rock, gneiss, which occurs in abundance with granite.

granny bonnet see bonnet hip tile.

granny's tooth see router plane.

granodiorite a granite-like igneous rock used in building for cobblestones, kerbstones, flooring and cladding.

grant financial support given for a particular purpose or project.

granular 1 referring to a material which is composed of discrete pellets or grains, or whose structure is such.
2 see coarse grained.

granular backfill, gravel fill; granular mineral material used for backfilling excavations, providing a stable and permeable covering for foundations and footings. →29, →59

granular soil, coarse soil; non-cohesive soil composed of particles of sand, gravel etc. over 0.06 mm in size.

granulate particles or grains of plastic, often from a recycling process, used as a raw material in the manufacture of cast and pressed plastics products.

granulated blast-furnace slag blast-furnace slag, a by-product of steel making, cooled in water to form granules; it is used, ground, as a binder in cement.

granulated cork corkwood, usually offcuts from a conversion or manufacturing process, which is ground and used as loose thermal insulation.
see *granulated cork underlay* in brick house illustration.

granulation the tendency of coarse particles in some watercolour paints to settle out and produce a grain-like surface effect or texture.

granulite a banded metamorphic rock which contains quartz and feldspar, similar to gneiss but without mica.

grape an ornamental motif consisting of a series of tear-shaped forms. →115

grape black see vine black.

grapefruit a shade of dark yellow which takes its name from the colour of ripe grapefruit [*Citrus maxima*].

graph see nomogram.

graphic pertaining to representation by graphs, diagrams, digital means or by a printing process; see also graphics.

graphic accelerator see display control unit.

graphic art see graphics.

graphic ore see sylvanite.

graphical statics a branch of statics represented diagrammatically.

graphic card in computing, a circuit board, often added separately, containing a display processing unit.

graphic data in computing, information in graphic form, either as geometric shapes such as vectors, lines, arcs etc., or as a series of pixels.

graphics 1 pictorial matter produced by digital, printed or other repetitive means.
2 see computer graphics.
3 graphic art; art produced by a repeatable process of printmaking such as woodcut, linocut, engraving and silk screen printing; prints are limited to a certain number and each is produced by the artist himself.

graphite, plumbago; **1** a naturally occurring form of grey carbon used as pencil lead, as a lubricant and for its properties of electrical conductivity.
2 black lead; the above used as a greyish black pigment.

graphite pencil see lead pencil.

Graphos the trade name for a draughting fountain pen used by architects, draughtsmen and engineers before the introduction of technical pens.

graph paper paper marked out with a scaled grid, subgrids etc. used for drawing scaled designs and graphs.

grass any of a large number of species of hardy plant from the family *Gramineae* or *Poaceae* used in landscaping for covering areas of parkland, fields and lawn.

grass green a shade of green which takes its name from the colour of ordinary green grasses.

grass paving see cellular paving. →15

grass roof 1 see turf roof. →48
2 see green roof. →48

grate 1 see bottomgrate. →56
2 see grating.

grated channel a drainage channel with a grating housed in its upper surface; used for external paved areas, garages etc. where continuity of surface is desirable; often a rebated block channel.

grating, 1 grate, grille; a metal barred or perforated component over an opening in construction to provide protection while allowing for the passage of air, water etc.
2 see inlet grating.
3 see channel grating.
4 see outlet grating.
5 see domical grating.

grave 1 an excavation, room, space or structure for the interment of the dead.
2 see tomb.

gravel, shingle; a classification of granular mineral material, broken stone composed of particles from 2 mm to 60 mm in size; see also fine, medium, coarse gravel.
see *gravel* fill in foundation illustration. →29

gravel board, gravel plank; a horizontal board fixed on edge to the base of the vertical slats in a close boarded fence to prevent them from decay when in contact with the ground.

gravel fill see granular backfill.
see *foundation* illustration. →29
see *brick house* illustration. →59

gravel pit a designated area from which gravel can be or has been taken for construction and other uses.

gravel plank see gravel board.

grave mound see burial mound. →65

graver see burin.
gravestone, tombstone; an inscribed slab or other ornamental commemorative stone article placed above or beside a grave.
graveyard, 1 cemetery; an organized burial area for the dead, often with tombs, headstones and monuments, either on public or church land.
see *graveyard in church* illustration. →102
2 see churchyard.
3 see burial ground.
gravitational force see gravity.
gravity, gravitational force; the force which causes a body to move towards the centre of the earth or towards another heavenly body.
gravity boiler a heating appliance from which hot water or steam is circulated for use via convection, without the need for pumps, based on the fact that hot water in flow pipework will rise when balanced by cooler water in return pipework.
gravity door hinge see rising hinge. →38
gravity drain a drainpipe in which waste and soil water is conveyed by the force of gravity rather than by pumping.
gravity model in traffic planning, a synthetic trip distribution model based on the idea that any particular destination has a certain notional attractive gravity which will diminish with distance from that place.
gravity retaining wall a retaining wall which resists horizontal forces by virtue of its weight alone. →29
gravity toggle a toggle bolt with a locking 'job' hinged off-centre so that it swings into a vertical position once inserted into a bored hole, and clamps against the rear of construction. →37
gravity wall see gravity retaining wall. →29
gravure a method of making graphic prints by etching a pattern into a metal plate; ink is then applied to the plate and wiped clean leaving ink in the etched areas, which is then transferred to paper.
gray 1 abb. **Gy**; the SI unit of radiation dosage equal to 1 joule of energy imparted by the absorbed radiation per kilogram of absorbing matter.
2 see grey.
GRC glassfibre-reinforced cement.
grease interceptor see grease trap.
grease trap, grease interceptor; in the drainage of industrial kitchens and restaurants, a chamber in a drain which separates grease or oil from the waste water to prevent the clogging of pipes.
great brick a large, thin brick used in medieval England to avoid paying excessive brick tax.
see tax brick.
great hall a large main hall in a historical building, castle or mansion, especially medieval.
see *great hall in Mesopotamian temple* illustration. →66
Great Monad in Greek philosophy, the basic unit, one, unity, the Deity, God; often manifested by a symbol resembling the yin-yang or omphalos. →120
Grecian purple see Tyrian purple.
Greek architecture the architecture of ancient Greece from c.3000 BC to the Roman period, characterized by temples, use of proportions and orders; roughly divided into the Geometrical, Archaic, Classic and Hellenistic periods. →78, →80, →81, →84, →85, →111
see *Greek residential buildings* illustration. →87
see *apteral temple* illustration. →84
see *peristyle temple* illustration. →85
see *classical temples* illustration. →86
see *classical public and commercial buildings* illustration. →92
see *classical stages and spectator structures* illustration. →89
see *gymnasium* illustration. →91, →94
see *Asian and Mediterranean columns and capitals* illustration. →69
see *classical Greek orders* illustration. →78
see *classical capital and bases* illustrations. →81
see Aegean art.
see Helladic.
see Hellenistic.
see Mycenaean architecture. →113
see Minoan architecture.
Greek column see classical column. →78
see Doric column. →78
see Ionic column. →78
see Corinthian column. →78
see *classical Greek columns* illustration. →78
Greek construction see graecorum structura. →83
Greek cross, 1 crux quadrata (Lat.), quadratic cross; a cross with four perpendicular limbs of equal length. →118
2 see hollow Greek cross. →118
Greek Doric order see Doric order. →79
Greek Ionic order see Ionic order. →79
Greek key classical two-tone banded ornament using a fret or meander pattern. →124
Greek orders the three orders of classical Greek architecture, Doric, Ionic and Corinthian; see Greek architecture entry. →78, →80, →81
Greek orthodox cross see Russian cross. →117
Greek pitch see rosin.
Greek residential buildings the residential masonry building types of ancient Greece; see megaron, prostas, pastas and peristyle houses; see *also Greek residential building* illustration. →87
Greek Revival an architectural style in England from the 1700s and 1800s, characterized by an interest in forms and decoration from classical Greek architecture.
Greek temple see apteral and peristyle temple illustrations. →84, →85
Greek walling see opus and *Greek walling* illustration. →83
green 1 a description of timber that is freshly cut and unseasoned, with a moisture content above saturation point.
2 see green concrete.
3 a general name for shades of colour in the visible spectrum between blue and yellow, covering the range of electromagnetic wavelengths 480–560 μm; see **green pigments** for full list.
green ash see American ash, [*Fraxinus pennsylvanica*].
greenbelt in town planning, an area of open country, parkland, woodland etc. within or surrounding a built-up area, left unbuilt to prevent the spread of urban development and provide amenity for the local inhabitants.
greenbelt town a North American town planning ideology of providing low rent housing based on relative self-containment, isolation of pedestrian and vehicular traffic, and unpierced residential superblock districts.
green brick a clay brick pressed into shape but not dried or fired.
green concrete a description of concrete that has set but not yet hardened.
green earth, glauconite, terra verde; a group of greenish mineral clays or earths containing iron hydroxide, used in the manufacture of earth pigments.
greenfield site a site of rural or parkland character targeted for development, often at the periphery of a built-up area, on which there are not, nor have ever been, existing buildings.
green gold, nickel azo yellow; a slightly poisonous greenish-yellow pigment used in oil and watercolours.
greenhouse, glasshouse; a light domestic or agricultural building made of glass or other transparent sheet material, used for the cultivation of plants.
greenhouse effect the gradual heating up of the lower atmosphere by heat from the sun retained as infrared radiation emitted from the earth's surface.

green man see foliate head. →115, →122
green manuring in landscaping, the improvement of the quality and drainage of soil by the addition of organic plant material.
green of Greece, verdigris, Spanish green; a shade of grey green which takes its name from the colour of the pigment known in France as vert de gris.
green pigments see below.
Arnaudon's green.
baryta green, see manganese green.
Casali's green, viridian.
Cassel green, see manganese green.
chrome green.
chromium oxide green.
cobalt green.
Dingler's green, chromium oxide green.
emerald chromium oxide, see viridian.
emerald green.
emeraulde green, see viridian.
Gellert green, cobalt green.
green gold.
Guinet's green, see viridian.
Hungarian green, see malachite.
Imperial green.
leaf green, see chrome green.
leek green, see chrome green.
malachite.
manganese green.
mineral green, see malachite.
Mittler's green, viridian.
Monastral green, see phthalocyanine green.
moss green, see chrome green.
mountain green.
native green, chrome oxide.
nickel azo yellow, see green gold.
nitrate green, chrome green.
oil green.
oxide of chromium, see chromium oxide green.
Pannetier's green, see viridian.
phthalocyanine green.
Plessey's green, chromium oxide green.
Rinman's green, see cobalt green.
Rosenstiehl's green, see manganese green.
Royal green, see chrome green.
Schnitzer's green, see chromium oxide green.
Schweinfurt green, see emerald green.
smaragd green, see viridian.
Swedish green, see cobalt green.
thalo green, see phthalocyanine green.
transparent oxide of chromium, see viridian.
vert emeraude, see viridian.
viridian.
zinc green, see cobalt green.
green roof 1 roof construction comprising growing plant material laid in soil over a drainage layer and waterproofing membrane; the soil layer provides insulation and protection from the elements. →48
2 see turf roof, grass roof. →48
greenstone a dark green igneous rock type, diabase, containing feldspar and hornblende.
green timber timber which is unseasoned.
green ultramarine see ultramarine, ultramarine green.
green wedge in town planning, a belt of woodland or parkland extending from country areas into a city or urban area for recreation, cemeteries, parks etc.
grey, gray (Am.); a general name for shades of achromatic colour containing only black and white.
grey alder, white alder (Am.); [*Alnus incana*] a European hardwood with light, soft, dull brown timber; used for plywood.
grey cast iron, grey iron; non-ductile cast iron which contains carbon in flake form.
grey iron see grey cast iron.
grey lime quicklime produced by heating grey-coloured chalk.
grey poplar [*Populus canescens*] a hardwood from the British Isles.
grey scale in colour theory, a scale of achromatic colours, ranging from white to black, used to define the greyness of a colour.
greywacke a grey or grey-green, fine-grained sandstone used locally for aggregates and chippings.
grey water waste water from domestic use, which does not contain soil from toilets and other soil appliances.
GRG glassfibre-reinforced gypsum.
gribble, marine crustacean; [*Limnoria spp.*] any of a number of marine organisms which cause damage to wood submerged in seawater by boring.
grid, 1 structural grid, modular grid; a regular framework of reference lines to which the dimensions of major structural components of the plan of a building are fixed.
2 in town planning, a chequerboard network of intersecting streets and avenues forming the basic layout of a city or town.
3 see electricity supply grid.
gridiron plan see grid plan. →94
grid line one of the lines demarking a structural, modular or layout grid of a building, to which dimensions are coordinated.
grid plan an urban plan type in which streets are laid out in an orthogonal network, forming a pattern of approximately rectangular blocks; also called a chequerboard plan, checkerboard plan, chessboard plan or gridiron plan. →94
see *Hippodamian system* illustration. →94
griffe see spur. →115
griffin, gryphon; a decorative motif of a mythological beast with a lion's body and the head of an eagle, used especially in Romanesque times, but known from Mesopotamia, Egypt and Greece. →122
grill 1 see grille.
2 see barbecue.
grillage, grillage foundation; **1** a foundation construction for a column or concentrated load consisting of a series of layered beams laid at right angles to one another.
2 see timber foundation grillage. →29
grillage foundation see grillage.
grille, 1 grill; an open grating or screen to allow for the passage of air, as a security measure, to enclose space etc.
2 in ventilation and air conditioning, a protective cover for an air terminal unit with openings, baffles etc. for air to pass through.
3 see window grille.
4 see window louvre.
grinder 1 a machine tool with a rotating mineral disc for shaping and smoothing hard materials such as stone, concrete and metals.
2 see bench grinder.
3 see angle grinder.
grinding the removal of excess material on a rough stone or metal surface to produce a fine finish using an abrasive.
grinding bevel, cannel, ground bevel; the splayed end or edge surface of the blade of a chisel or other cutting tool, honed to provide a cutting edge. →41
grinding burr a round, conical, disc-shaped etc. drill bit of mineral material, used in specialist stone- and metalwork for smoothing and cleaning irregular surfaces. →42
grinding cup a metal disc attachment for a rotary stone grinder, with a raised circumferential edge coated or faced with abrasive material. →42
grinding disc a replaceable thin rotating disc of abrasive material as used in an angle grinder, used for cutting and grinding. →42
grinding wheel 1 a stiff rotating disc of abrasive material used for honing tools, grinding and sanding. →42
2 see bench grinder.

grindstone an even block or spinning wheel of mineral material used for sharpening the blades of tools and grinding stone surfaces. →41

grinning see grinning through.

grinning through, grinning; a defect in a paint or plaster finish in which the colour or a pattern from an underlying layer or coat is clearly visible.

grip a sheath of rubber, plastic, leather or other material for the handle of a door or hand tool such as a hammer or chisel. →40

grisaille painting in tones of grey, often with the addition of gold, a method used in glass and altar painting by Cistercian monks in the 1100s.

grit coarse angular aggregate used as an abrasive surface in road construction.

grocery store a shop which sells foods and household provisions.

grog, chamotte; a ceramic material used for making firebricks and terracotta, consisting of fresh clay mixed with crushed fired clay.

groin the curved edge formed by the intersection of two masonry vaults. →101

groined vault see groin vault. →25

groin rib see diagonal rib. →101

groin vault, cross vault, groined vault, intersecting barrel vault; a vault formed by the perpendicular intersection of two barrel vaults, found especially in early masonry churches. →25

groove 1 any slot-like cutting or relief in construction.
2 the recess in one side of a tongue and groove joint. →2
3 see long groove. →6

groove joint see dummy joint.

grooving saw, notching saw, stairbuilder's saw, trenching saw; a saw which resembles a plane, having a saw blade embedded in the base of the stock; used for cutting grooves in wood.

gross the full quantity of a weight, measure, payment etc. before deductions such as weight of packaging, planing or finishing, taxes etc. are made.

gross building volume in measurement and surveying, the volume of a building, measured to the external surface of external walls, and often disregarding unheated attic spaces.

gross external area 1 the floor area of a building measured to the external surface of the external walls, including all stairs, wells, internal walls etc.
2 the same when regarding only a single storey of a building.

gross floor area the total floor area of a building including the thickness of the exterior walls.

gross internal area the floor area of a building measured to the internal surface of the external walls, including all stairs, wells, internal walls etc.; used by quantity surveyors in estimating construction costs.

gross price the whole price of something excluding reductions.

grossular a greenish variety of the mineral garnet; also known as grossular garnet or grossularite.
see hessonite, cinnamon stone.

grossularite see grossular.

grotesque, grottesco; a decorative artwork or carving which makes use of vines embellished with interwoven animals, plants and fruit. →122

grottesco see grotesque. →122

grotto in Renaissance, Baroque and Romantic parkland and palace architecture, a naturally picturesque or decorated cave or subterranean space decorated to resemble a cave.

ground 1 material at or under the surface of the earth.
2 an area or plot of the earth's surface, land.
3 see foundation.
4 one of a number of timber strips fixed at regular spacing to masonry as a nailing base for finishing boards. →57
5 the treated opaque surface in painting which provides a base for the application of paint.
6 see substrate. →20
7 see earth.
8 a description of a concrete, masonry, metal etc. finish produced by smoothing with abrasives; see honed, rubbed finish.

ground anchor, ground anchorage; a system of steel rods, bolts, guys or braces for fixing a structure firmly to its base, to a foundation or to the ground. →29

ground anchorage see ground anchor.

ground bashing see dynamic consolidation.

ground beam, 1 grade beam (Am.); in concrete construction, a beam which transmits the weight of walls to a foundation structure, or is itself a foundation. →29
2 tie beam; in piled foundation construction, a concrete beam which connects a number of piles or pile caps and transmits the loading from walls etc. down to the piles.
3 in timber-framed construction, the lowest structural timber beam which transmits loading from walls to a foundation.

ground bevel see grinding bevel. →41

ground coat in paintwork, a matt base coat of pigment over which a glaze coat is applied.

ground compaction 1 the reduction of the air and water content of the underlying soil by mechanical vibrating, rolling and by various forms of draining.
2 see dynamic consolidation.

ground compression see dynamic consolidation.

ground engineering see geotechnical engineering.

ground finish see ground.

ground floor 1 a lower storey in a building that provides principal access at or near ground level; in the USA and continental Europe this is known as the first floor. →61
see *ground floor in brick house* illustration. →59
2 see base floor.
see *ground floor construction in brick house* illustration. →59

ground improvement see soil reinforcement.

ground investigation see geotechnical survey.

ground line in perspective and other projections, a horizontal line representing the ground; the meeting of ground plane and picture plane. →128

ground plane in perspective and other projections, a horizontal plane from which vertical measurements can be taken; usually represents the ground on which the object is placed; also known as the horizontal plane. →127, →128

ground plate, ground sill; the lowest horizontal frame member in traditional timber-framed or log construction, to which other structural components such as floor joists and posts are fixed. →6

ground profile see topography.

grounds, 1 groundwork; timber battens attached to a masonry or other wall surface as a base for a lining such as wallboard. →57
2 common grounds, rough grounds; narrow timber pieces set into or attached to masonry as nailing strips for a lining, battening or trim.
3 an area of surrounding land, gardens or an estate attached to a building; see also policies, demesne.

ground sill see ground plate.

ground slab see ground supported floor. →57, →59

ground supported floor, ground slab, slab-on-grade (Am.), floor bed; reinforced concrete floor construction cast directly onto the underlying ground so that loads from the floor are transmitted evenly to the ground below. →57, →59

groundwater water, usually clear and bacteria free, found in saturated ground below the water table.

groundwater level see water table.

groundwater lowering see dewatering.

groundwater table see water table.

groundwork 1 in the construction of a building, the initial stage of construction, making and filling

excavations, laying drains and dealing with groundwater; also called earthwork.
2 see grounds. →57

group 1 a small collection of people, objects, buildings etc. which form a unit.
2 syndicate; a number of companies working together on a large project or initiative.
3 an agglomeration of companies owned by a holding company.

group connector, breech fitting; a drain fitting with a number of inlets connected to a gully.

group heating a system of heating for a complex or housing estate, smaller than district heating, in which heated water is piped to a number of buildings from a central heating plant.

grout 1 a liquid mixture of cement and water used for filling cracks, joints and voids in masonry and concrete construction, and for cementing components in place.
2 a soft flowing slurry of cement, sand and water injected into voids in unstable ground to provide support and reinforcement.
3 see injection mortar.
4 see tile grout.

grout concreting work in grouted concrete.

grouted aggregate concrete see grouted concrete.

grouted concrete, grouted aggregate concrete, intrusion concrete, pre-packed concrete, preplaced concrete; concrete made by placing coarse aggregate in a mould or form and then grouting or injecting with a binding mortar; used for special cases and underwater work.

grouted macadam in road construction, a structural surfacing formed by pouring a mortar of cement or bitumen and sand over a layer of compacted aggregate.

grouting, 1 cementation, injection; the strengthening and support of unstable or loose soils and rock, and in some cases old masonry, concretework etc. by the injection of cement grout into prebored holes and small voids.
2 see pressure grouting.
3 see artificial cementing.

grouting concrete concrete used to fill voids and cracks in existing concrete construction.

grout rake see raker.

growing medium the uppermost layer of nutritious soil laid in landscaping and green roofs etc. for plants to grow in; also called a growth medium. →48

growing season in landscape design, the warmer parts of the year during which new growth appears on plants.

growth area in town planning, an area with potential for prosperity, in which development occurs.

growth defect any timber defect arising from the irregular growth of the tree from which wood has been cut. →1

growth-factor method in traffic planning, a trip distribution method based on multiplying the number of trips at present by a factor to take future expansion and changing methods of travel into account; see synthetic model.

growth medium see growing medium. →48

growth rate, rate of growth; in forestry and landscape design, the rate of increase in tree girth, expressed as rings/inch or rings/cm.

growth ring see annual ring. →1

GRP glass-reinforced polyester.
see glass-reinforced plaster.

GRPC glassfibre-reinforced polymer/concrete.

grubbing, grubbing out, stump grubbing; in site clearance, landscaping and forestry, the removal of unwanted tree stumps and roots etc. prior to further work.

grubbing out see grubbing.

gryphon an archaic form of the word griffin. →122

GSM, global system for mobile communications; a network for mobile telephones with agreed protocol which allows for communication across national boundaries.

GTA welding see TIG welding.

Guaiacum spp. see lignum vitae.

guarantee, 1 guaranty, warranty; a written agreement covering repair or replacement of defects or faults in products or workmanship within a set period of time.
2 see security.

guaranty see guarantee.

guard rail a lightweight metal protective fence, railing or balustrade to provide protection against falling over an edge at a difference in level, to bound off a secure area, to separate a footway from a carriageway etc.

guest bedroom, guest room; a room in a dwelling intended for the use of visitors.

guest room see guest bedroom.

guideline see design guideline.

guildhall 1 a medieval building where the trade guilds met to discuss related affairs.
2 a municipal building in which the commercial interests of the city are dealt with.
3 see scuola.

guilloche 1 a decorative motif consisting of interwoven curving bands surrounding a series of circles, usually applied to a moulding; a curving fret motif. →82, →125
2 angular guilloche, see meander. →124
3 see wave pattern. →15

guillotine a device for cropping paper and sheet material, consisting of a base with a sharp hinged blade.

Guinet's green see viridian.

gullet the measured length from one point of a sawtooth to the adjacent trough in the blade of a saw.

gulley see gully.

gully, drain, gulley, trapped gully; **1** an outlet fitting for a drain, most often trapped, into which rainwater, surface water, waste water and other fluids are conveyed.
2 see floor drain. →58

gum, 1 sweetgum; [*Liquidambar styraciflua*] a valuable tropical hardwood from south-west USA with pinkish grey heartwood used for furniture, posts and packaging.
2 black gum, see tupelo.
3 a local name for some species of eucalyptus tree.
4 latex; the water-soluble resinous secretion of some tropical hardwood trees and shrubs which hardens on drying; also a corresponding synthetic product, used as a base for rubber.
5 see gutta-percha.
6 see gamboge.
7 any sticky liquid exuded from plants which may be used as a weak adhesive; any materials similar to this.
8 see paste.

gum acacia see gum arabic.

gum arabic, gum acacia; a water soluble gum from some species of acacia [*Acacia spp.*] used in the manufacture of certain glues.

gum juniper see sandarac.

gum sandarac see sandarac.

gum strip paper tape with a layer of adhesive on one side which becomes sticky when wetted.

gun 1 see caulking gun.
2 see cement gun.
3 see nail gun.
4 see framing gun.
5 see glue gun.
6 see paint spray gun.
7 see plaster spray gun.
8 see staple gun.

gun applied adhesive, gunnable adhesive; adhesive supplied in prepacked tubes, suitable for application with a caulking gun.

gunite sprayed concrete containing aggregate smaller than 10 mm in size, placed by projecting it against a surface using pneumatic pressure.
gunnable adhesive see gun applied adhesive.
gun platform 1 see emplacement, terreplein. →103
2 see cavalier. →104
3 see barbette. →103
gunstock see jowl.
gusset, gusset plate; in timber roof construction, a piece of timber board or plywood for fastening together members in a planar truss with nails; a timber nail plate.
gusset plate see gusset.
Gustav III referring to a neoclassical architectural style in Sweden and Finland from 1770 to 1795, similar to that of Louis XVI in France, named after the reigning monarch, Gustav III.
gutta, drop; pl. guttae; Lat.; in classical architecture, one of a series of carved droplet projections beneath the regula and metopes in the Doric entablature; occasionally also called campanulae, lachrymae or trunnels. →78
see gutta-percha.
see gamboge.
guttae plural form of gutta. →78
guttae band see regula. →78
gutta-percha the dried resinous sap or latex from the Malayan gutta-percha tree, *Isonandra gutta*, used as electrical insulation and in dentistry.
gutter a channel to collect water and lead it away from a surface; types included as separate entries are listed below. →62
arris gutter.
box gutter. →60
centre gutter.
chimney gutter. →56
eaves gutter. →46
fascia gutter.
half round gutter.
hung gutter.
rainwater gutter. →46
secret gutter.
valley gutter.
gutter bearer any device or framework for supporting or fixing a gutter in place. →46
gutter bracket a steel strip or proprietary accessory bent into the shape of a hook, used for carrying a gutter. →46
gutter end see stop end. →46
gutter plane see round plane.
gutter stop see stop end. →46
guy, guy rope, stay; a diagonal tension cable, wire or rope anchored to the ground or an abutment to stabilize a mast structure, suspension bridge or tent structure.
guy rope see guy.
gym see gymnasium.
gymnasion Greek form of gymnasium. →91, →94
gymnasium, pl. gymnasia; **1** Lat.; an ancient Greek centre for sports, with buildings, playing areas and baths; also written in Greek form as gymnasion. →91, →94
2 gym; a building or part of a building in which gymnastics are practised.
gymnosperm one of the two main classes of plant to which conifers or softwoods belong, with woody stems and seeds unprotected by fruit.
gynaeceum, gyneceum; Lat.; chambers or an apartment for women in an ancient Greek or Roman dwelling; Greek form is gynaikeion.
gyneceum see gynaeceum.
gypsum 1 a white or coloured mineral, hydrated calcium sulphate, $\mathbf{CaSO_4.2H_2O}$, used as a building material in plasters etc. and as a raw material in the ceramics industry.
2 natural calcium sulphate used as an inert pigment and an adulterer in paints.
see gypsum rock.
see phospho gypsum.
see selenite.
see synthetic anhydrite.
see terra alba.
see titano gypsum.
gypsum adhesive see gypsum-based adhesive.
gypsum baseboard plasterboard manufactured to receive a surface coating of plaster.
gypsum-based adhesive an adhesive whose main constituent is gypsum binder.
gypsum board see plasterboard. →57
gypsum cove, plasterwork cove; a preformed plaster component for covering the internal junction between ceiling and wall, with a similar construction to that of plasterboard.
gypsum-perlite plaster see perlite plaster.
gypsum plank, plasterboard plank; a plasterboard cladding product formed in thick, narrow boards.
gypsum plaster a quick-setting plaster consisting of gypsum and water, used for plaster casts and rendering.
gypsum plasterboard see plasterboard. →57, →59
gypsum plasterboard composite a laminated building board of which at least one layer is plasterboard.
gypsum rock 1 rock which contains a high proportion of gypsum.
2 see natural gypsum.
gypsum-vermiculite plaster see vermiculite plaster.
gypsum wallboard thin plasterboard, 9.5 mm thick, suitable for receiving a finish on at least one face, used for lining partitions and internal walls.
gypsum wallboard panel see prefabricated gypsum wallboard panel.
gyratory system a traffic system which makes use of roundabouts, priority routing and traffic signals to organize and maintain the flow of traffic.

H

Haarlem blue see Antwerp blue.
habitability a measure of the quality of an area, building or dwelling with regard to its suitability for human occupation.
habitable room any room for living in, not usually including kitchens, toilets, bathrooms and other service spaces. →57
habitat the natural environment in which a species or group of species exist or can be expected to.
habitation 1 the action and conditions of living, the occupation of a building for living in.
2 the dwelling place so occupied.
3 see settlement.
hacking in concretework, the working at a hardened concrete surface with hand tool and mallet; see tooling.
hacksaw a bow saw with a fine blade held in tension in a metal frame, used for cutting metal and plastics.
haematite, hematite; a grey-black or red-brown mineral, a natural oxide of iron, Fe_2O_3, used in various forms for pigments and jewellery; also a very important iron ore.
see bloodstone.
see also iron oxide.
hafnium a poisonous chemical element, **Hf**.
haft the handle or shaft of a hand tool.
hag's tooth see router plane.
hagioscope see squint.
hair brown a certain shade of dark brown.
hair cracking see hairline crack.
hairline crack, hair cracking; a defect in a concrete, plaster or paint finish, a very fine surface crack.
half-basketweave pattern a paving pattern resembling basketweave pattern, but with arrangements of stones forming rectangular areas; similar patterns in parquetry and tiling. →15
half bastion see demi-bastion. →104
half bat, snap header; in brickwork bonding, the squared remains of a brick which has been cut in half, and which shows in a masonry wall as a header. →21
half-brick wall a solid brick wall whose thickness is that of the short side of a brick. →21
half cloverleaf junction see partial cloverleaf junction. →63
half-column see demi-column. →13
half dome, semi-dome; a vaulted roof of half a hemisphere used for covering a semicircular space, as found in religious architecture over apses; see also conch. →26
half drop see offset match.
half hipped end, broached hip; the trapezoidal sloping roof plane at one or both ends of a half hipped roof, capped by a gable or gablet.
half-hipped roof, jerkinhead roof, hipped gable roof, shread head roof, clipped gable roof; a roof, often a mansard roof, which is hipped from the ridge halfway down to the eaves and gabled from there down; the opposite of a gambrel roof. →46
half landing, half space landing; a landing between two flights of stairs parallel to one another, between two adjacent storey levels. →45
half lap joint see halved joint. →4
half mandapa see ardhamandapa.
half moon see demilune. →104
halfpace stair, half-space stairs; a stair which turns through 180° on its ascent, consisting of two parallel flights with a half-height landing at one end, with or without a stairwell; a halfpace stair without a well is known as a dogleg stair. →45
half relief see mezzo rilievo.
half round 1 a milled joinery profile which is semicircular in cross-section. →2
2 an ornamental moulding which is semicircular in cross-section. →14
half round capping a half round coping brick whose length matches the width of the wall on which it is laid, without overhangs on either side. →16
half round channel a drainage channel which is semicircular in cross-section.
half round coping a special coping brick or block whose upper surface is semicircular, wider than the wall for which it is designed, and with throated overhangs on either side, used as an upper termination for freestanding walls and parapets. →16
half round gutter, rhone; a rainwater gutter which is semicircular in cross-section.
half round moulding see half round. →14
half round veneer a decorative veneer formed by peeling the outer side of a half log or flitch off-centre on a lathe. →10
half-space landing see half landing. →45
half-space stairs see halfpace stair. →45
half span roof see lean-to roof. →46
half tile a special roof tile which is half the width of other tiles in the same roof, used at edges and junctions.
half timber in the conversion of timber, a baulk cut longitudinally in half.
half-timbered building a traditional timber-framed building whose structural timbers are blackened and exposed in the external faces of the walls. →7
half-timbered construction a traditional form of timber frame construction in which timber cross members form a lattice of panels filled with a non-loadbearing material or nogging of brick, clay or plaster; the frame is often exposed on the outside of the building.
half truss in traditional timber frame construction, half a roof truss placed perpendicular to the other trusses at the end of a building to form a hip; also modern equivalents.
half turn circular stair a circular stair which occupies a semicircular shaft, turning through 180° on its ascent. →45
half turn stair 1 any stair which turns through 180° on its ascent around an open well or lift shaft, with stair flights on three sides. →45
2 see halfpace stair. →45
3 see dogleg stair. →45
halite, rock salt, salt stone; a colourless or pale-coloured mineral, natural sodium chloride, **NaCl**, with cubic crystals; used as culinary salt and in the chemical industry for the production or extraction of chlorine, sodium and hydrochloric acid; rock salt also refers to a sedimentary rock whose main constituent is halite.
hall 1 a building containing a large open space for events or gatherings.
2 any large high space within a building for gatherings.
3 a large main space in a public building for functions and assemblies.
4 a space within a building which leads to other spaces.
5 see hallway.
6 see entrance hall. →59
hall church a Romanesque or Gothic church type which, regardless of whether it is aisled or not, has a single high roof of relatively uniform height.
see Scandinavian hall church. →102

hall crypt a large church crypt or undercroft beneath the main altar of even height, subdivided by a grid of columns into a nave and aisles.

hall of residence see student hostel.

hallway, hall; a corridor or passageway.

halo 1 see aureole. →119
2 three-rayed nimbus, see triradiant halo. →119

halogen a collective name for the group of gases, fluorine, chlorine, bromine, iodine and astatine, which react well with most metals and many non-metals.

halogen lamp, tungsten-halogen lamp; an electric incandescent lamp which produces light by means of a heated tungsten filament suspended in a glass tube filled with low pressure bromine or iodine vapour.

halon any compound of carbon and bromine or fluorine with other halogens, often used in fire extinguishers but damaging to the ozone layer.

halon fire-extinguishing system a fire-extinguishing system used for technical spaces such as computer rooms and electronic archives, which operates by releasing halon gas to choke a building fire.

halved and tabled scarf joint, indented scarf joint; in timber frame construction, a lengthening joint in which the ends of the timbers are cut with cogs to fit each other.

halved and tenoned scarf joint a timber lengthening joint in which the halved ends of both timbers are cut with a protruding tenon to fit into a corresponding slot. →3

halved crossing joint see cross half lap joint. →4

halved joint, half lap joint, halving joint; a timber joint in which both pieces have been cut away or halved at the joint to receive the other. →4

halved scarf joint a timber lengthening joint in which the ends of the timbers are halved to receive one another. →3

halved tenon joint a timber joint in which two tenons inserted in a common mortise from opposite sides are cut in half so that they fit side by side. →5

halved three quarter bat, queen closer; a three quarter bat cut in half for use in brickwork bonding. →21

halving the notching and rebating of the ends of timber members to be jointed in order to form a timber halved joint.

halving joint see halved joint. →4

hamlet a small rural settlement or group of buildings, often without a church or commercial facilities, smaller than a village.

hammam, hummum; in Islamic architecture, a bathing establishment, often in proximity to a mosque, for taking Turkish baths and recreation.

hammer 1 a hand tool with a shaft and heavy metal head for striking, breaking or driving nails. →40
see *types of hammer* illustration; types included as separate entries are listed below. →40
adze eye hammer.
ball peen hammer. →40
beetle.
bell face hammer. →40
blacksmith's hammer. →40
bouchard. →40
brad hammer, see tack hammer. →40
bricklayer's hammer, brick hammer, brick axe. →40
bush hammer. →40
carpenter's mallet. →40
claw hammer. →40
club hammer. →40
cross peen hammer. →40
double-clawed hammer. →40
double face hammer. →40
drilling hammer. →40
drop hammer, ram.
dummy. →40
engineer's hammer. →40
engineer's sledge. →40
five pound maul. →40
framing hammer. →40
glazier's hammer. →40
jack hammer.
joiner's hammer. →40
lump hammer, see club hammer. →40
machinist's hammer, peen. →40
mallet. →40
mash hammer, see club hammer. →40
maul, mall. →40
nail hammer. →40
peen, see machinist's hammer. →40
peen hammer. →40
peen sledge, see engineer's sledge. →40
pick hammer. →40
pin hammer, see tack hammer. →40
pitching hammer. →40
riveting hammer.
rock pick. →40
saddler's hammer. →40
scabbling hammer, scabbler. →40
scaling hammer. →40
scutch hammer, scutch. →40
sledgehammer, sledge. →40
smith's hammer, see blacksmith's hammer. →40
soft face hammer. →40
spall hammer, spalling hammer. →40
splitting hammer. →40
straight peen hammer. →40
striking hammer. →40
tack hammer. →40
tinner's hammer. →40
trimmer's hammer. →40
upholsterer's hammer. →40
veneer hammer, veneering hammer. →40
Warrington hammer, see cross peen hammer. →40
2 see water hammer.

hammer beam in traditional timber roof construction, a short horizontal member cantilevered out from a wall top, brace or purlin, supported on an arch brace and carrying a hammer post which gives support to a primary rafter. →33

hammer-beam roof a roof whose rafters are given additional support by hammer beams, as with many timber roofed medieval halls. →33

hammer-beam roof truss in traditional timber roof construction, a roof truss whose rafters are given additional support by hammer beams, hammer posts and arch braces. →33
see double hammer beam truss.

hammer-dressed finish, bull-faced finish, cloured finish, hammer-faced finish; a rough stonework finish produced with a hammer; also called a quarry finish when machined on commercial stone. →12

hammer drill a drill for boring a hole in masonry and concrete with a drill bit which oscillates back and forth with a chattering action.

hammer-faced finish see hammer-dressed finish. →12

hammerhead the metal striking component of a hammer, fixed to its shaft. →40

hammer-headed chisel a solid steel masonry chisel with a flat end shaped so as to take striking with a lump hammer; cf. mallet-headed chisel. →41

hammer post in traditional timber roof construction, a post resting on a hammer beam and supporting a principal rafter. →33

han 1 see caravansary.
2 see Han period.

hance see haunch. →22

hand axe a small axe used for construction and in the workshop.

handbasin see handrinse basin.

hand drier a wall-mounted electrical sanitary appliance which pumps warm air for hand drying.

hand drill a hand tool for boring holes.

handed 1 referring to the side of a door or window casement which bears hinges.
2 referring to hand tools etc. supplied as mirror-image products for right-handed and left-handed users.
handicraft 1 artifacts manufactured by hand, usually with natural or organic materials and unmechanized methods.
2 see cottage industry.
handing a term describing which direction a hinged door or window opens and the side on which it is hinged, affecting its hardware specification, denoted as right handed or left handed; there is no universal rule about which is which, and definition of handing varies from country to country; according to the Scandinavian classification, a left-hand door which opens outwards has its hinges on the left, and so on; in Britain and North America this is most often called a right-hand door, but not always. →50
handle 1 a construction or fitting grasped by the hand for opening, closing or moving a component.
2 see pull handle.
3 see door handle. →50
4 see casement handle. →52
5 that part of a hand tool by which it is held, its grip. →40, →41
6 the long part by which a hammer or axe is held, traditionally of wood, its shaft. →40
7 see chisel handle. →41
handlebar cross see ankh. →117
handmade brick a brick, usually uneven in shape, which has been manually moulded using a timber mould.
handmade paper paper made from linen or cotton rag pulp pressed by hand in a mould.
hand mixing the mixing of small batches of concrete using hand tools rather than mixing plant.
hand-plastering plasterwork which is carried out manually, using hand tools; sometimes called trowelled plastering.
hand of Fatima, khamsa, xomsa; a decorative motif of the outstretched palm of a hand with two thumbs, depicting that of the prophet Mohammed's favourite daughter Fatima (or Fatimah), a symbol of fortune in Muslim art; khamsa or xomsa is the number 'five' in Arabic. →120
hand of God Christian ornament consisting of a hand motif within a circle or cloud. →119
handover 1 the legal process by which the contractor hands back the site and completed building to the client at the end of construction.
2 see partial handover.
handover date see completion date.
handpull a handle, inset etc. for opening and closing a sliding panel, door or partition.
handrail 1 a rail for support or protection at approximately waist height above a balustrade, or fixed to a wall by a stair. →54
2 see stair rail. →45
handrail bolt see joint bolt.
handrinse basin, washbasin, handbasin; a small basin mounted at waist height and connected to a water supply and drain, designed for washing the hands.
handsaw any hand-held saw with a wide, tapering blade.
handset 1 a hand-held shower head connected to a water source by a length of flexible pipe.
2 see telephone set.
hand shears see tin snips.
handstop a hand-operated valve or apparatus for inhibiting the flow of water in a channel.
hangar a large building for the storage and maintenance of aircraft and spacecraft.
hanger 1 in timber roof construction, a vertical timber hung from a ridge, rafter or purlin, which gives support to ceiling joists.
2 a similar timber member in a log building.
3 any strap or component for fixing cabling, ceilings, pipes, ducts etc. to walls and soffits.
4 one of a series of vertical cables or rods supported at their upper ends by a suspension bridge cable, from which the bridge deck is hung; also called a suspender. →32
5 see tie rod. →54
6 see pipe hanger.
7 see ceiling hanger. →60
8 see joist hanger. →4, →44
hanging jamb the vertical frame member to which a window casement or door leaf is attached with hinges. →50, →51
hanging knee in traditional timber frame construction, a knee fixed in an upper corner of a frame.
hanging sash window see sash window. →52
hanging stile the vertical side member of a window casement or framed door leaf from which it is attached with hinges to a frame. →51
Han period a period in Chinese cultural history, either that of the Western Han dynasty during 206 BC–25 AD, or the Eastern Han dynasty during 25–220 AD.
Hansa yellow see arylide yellow.
hanse see haunch. →22
hanuk(k)iah see chanuk(k)iah. →123
Hapi ancient Egyptian deity of the Nile in flood, depicted with a blue-green body and a female breast, depicted as uniting Upper and Lower Egypt by binding together or wearing a crown of lotus and papyrus, the heraldic plants of Upper and Lower Egypt respectively. →74
Harappan civilization one of the earliest and most important urban cultures of the Indus valley, from c.2500 to 1700 BC, situated in the Punjab around the city of Harappa in what is now Pakistan, characterized by hilltop fortresses surrounded by grid plan towns constructed in brick.
harbour 1 a safe coastal haven for the mooring of boats and ships for maintenance, unloading and loading.
2 see port.
hard anodizing a tin-based anodic coating for aluminium which produces shades of bronze formed during the coating process.
hardboard a dense fibreboard formed into thin sheets with a density of over 800 kg/m^3; used for lining and casing, thus one side is usually smooth and the other embossed. →9
hardboard pin a small nail 13–38 mm in length used for fixing hardboard, softboard and thin ply, often with a square sectioned shank. →35
hardcore small chunks of stone, broken brick, concrete and other minerals used as inorganic fill beneath foundations and roads.
see *hardcore* in foundation illustration. →29
hard disk a revolving magnetized disc in a computer on which information such as programs and files are stored.
hard drawn wire steel wire formed by pulling through a die at normal temperature, used as reinforcing bars.
hard dry a stage in the drying of paint at which the surface has hardened and cannot be easily marked.
hardened concrete concrete which has attained a major part of its final strength, usually at least 28 days after placing.
hardened verge in road construction, a grassed area next to the carriageway on which vehicles may stop in an emergency.
hardener, drier; a catalyst or other substance added to paints, varnishes, glues, concretes and plasters to increase their speed of drying.
hardening 1 the gain in strength of concrete after the initial setting of the cement.
2 a heat treatment to increase the hardness of steel by heating it to a certain temperature and then rapidly cooling in water, brine or oil.
3 see surface hardening.

hardening shrinkage autogenous shrinkage.
hard manganese ore see psilomelane.
hard maple [*Acer saccharum, Acer nigrum*] a collective name for timber of the sugar maple and black maple of North America.
hardness 1 the property of a material to resist permanent change in form as a result of attempted abrasion, penetration or indentation.
2 a measure of the content of mineral salts in water, measurable with a pH test.
hardness number a value obtained by impact and compressive testing to measure the hardness, scratch resistance and resistance to deformation of a material.
hard rock, hard stone; according to a classification of hardness of rocks used by stone masons and construction technicians, rock which has a compressive strength above 1800 kg/cm^2; this class including igneous rocks, quartz and gneiss.
hardrot see dote.
hard shoulder a surfaced strip next to the carriageway of a large road or motorway for the use of vehicles in an emergency or during roadworks. →63
hard solder, brazing solder; a form of solder which contains copper, usually an alloy of copper, zinc or silver used in brazing.
hard soldering see brazing.
hard stone see hard rock.
hard strip in road design, a narrow hard shoulder adjacent to the carriageway.
hard temper one of the annealed conditions of copper and states of hardness in which it is supplied; others are half hard and dead-soft.
hardware, 1 ironmongery; any of the metal fittings such as hinges, locks and latches or other equipment for a door, window or hatch. →51
door hardware, see door furniture. →51
2 a general term for computers and other associated electronic devices as opposed to software or computer programs.
hardware schedule see ironmongery schedule.
hard water piped water containing dissolved mineral salts of calcium or magnesium, which react unfavourably with soaps and cause build-up of scale in hot water vessels.
hardwood the wood from a broad leaved tree in the botanical group angiosperm, in general denser and harder than softwood, but not necessarily so; listed below are species of European and North American hardwood tree, followed by a list of tropical hardwoods and eucalypts; see also softwoods.
temperate climates (European and North America).
acacia, *Acacia spp.*
alder, see *Alnus spp.*
apple, *Malus sylvestris.*
ash, see *Fraxinus spp.*
aspen, *poplars, Populus spp.*
beech, see *Fagus spp.*
birch, see *Betula spp.*
boxwood, *Buxus sempervirens.*
cherry, see *Prunus spp.*
chestnut, *Castanea spp., Aesculus spp.*
dogwood, *Cornus florida.*
elm, see *Ulmus spp.*
hawthorn, *Crataegus spp.*
hazel, *Corylus avellana.*
hickory, *Carya spp.*
hop-hornbeam, *Ostrya carpinifolia.*
hornbeam, *Carpinus betulus.*
horse chestnut, *Aesculus spp.*
lime, see *Tilia spp.*
maples and sycamores, see *Acer spp.*
oak, see *Quercus spp.*
pear, *Pyrus communis.*
plane, see *Platanus spp.*
poplars, aspen, see *Populus spp.*
robinia, *Robinia pseudoacacia.*
rowan, mountain ash, *Sorbus aucuparia.*
sweet chestnut, *Castanea sativa.*
tulipwood, *Liriodendron tulipifera.*
walnut, see *Juglans spp.*
willow, *Salix spp.*
tropical climates (Africa and Asia)
African mahogany [*Khaya ivorensis*].
African walnut [*Lovoa trichilioides, Lovoa klaineana*].
afrormosia [*Pericopsis elata*].
balsa wood, *Ochroma spp.*
ceiba [*Ceiba pentandra*].
Ceylon satinwood [*Chloroxylon swietenia*].
chickrassy, Chittagong wood [*Chukrasia tabularis*].
ebony, *Diospyros spp.*
eucalyptus, jarrah, karri etc. see *eucalyptus spp.*
gaboon, okoume [*Aucoumea klaineana*].
Gedu nohor [*Entandrophragma angolense*].
gum [*Liquidambar styraciflua*].
idigbo, limba, *Terminalia spp.*
iroko [*Chlorophora excelsa*].
kapur [*Dryobalanops spp.*].
lignum vitae [*Guaiacum spp.*].
mahogany, *Swietenia spp.*
makore [*Mimusops heckelii, Tieghemella heckelii*].
obeche [*Triplochiton scleroxylon*].
padauk, *Pterocarpus spp.*
ramin, *Gonystylus spp.*
rosewood, palisander, see *Dalbergia spp.*
sandalwood, *Santalum spp.*
satinwood [*Chloroxylon swietenia*].
teak [*Tectona grandis*].
tupelo, *Nyssa spp.*
verawood, Maracaibo lignum vitae [*Bulnesia arborea*].
wenge [*Millettia laurentii*].
hardwood board a piece of sawn hardwood with a thickness less than 50 mm. →2
hardwood plank a piece of sawn hardwood with a thickness greater than 50 mm. →2
hardwood plywood plywood whose face veneers are of hardwood; used for decorative purposes. →9
hardwood scantling a piece of sawn hardwood with non-standard cross-sectional dimensions. →2
hardwood strip a piece of sawn hardwood with cross-sectional dimensions of less than 50 mm thick and 50–140 mm wide.
harem the private living quarters of women in an Islamic dwelling.
harewood see sycamore.
harl see wet dash.
harmika in Indian architecture, a symbolic railed structure in stone, the 'world mountain' surmounting a stupa, enclosing the spire. →68
harmonic see well proportioned.
harmonic mean in mathematics, the reciprocal average or mean value of a series of reciprocals.
harmony 1 a combination of component parts in agreement and accord.
2 in architectural composition, the grouping of elements together in such a way so as to be in balance and without contradiction.
see *harmony of classical proportion* illustration. →79
harp configuration the arrangement of series of oblique cables in a cable-stayed bridge so that all cables to one side of a pylon are parallel; see radial configuration, fan configuration. →32
harsh a description of a fresh concrete mix that is difficult to work and place due to its consistency.
harvesting the felling of planted woodland and forest to provide commercial timber.
hasp 1 any simple fastener for a door, gate or other hinged component.
2 the hinged metal plate in a hasp and staple.
hasp and staple a fastener for a door, gate or casket with a slotted hinged plate attached to the leaf, fitting over a ring attached to the jamb; the assembly is usually made fast with a padlock through the ring.
hatch 1 a small hinged door in a roof, wall or floor.
2 see roof hatch.
3 see sliding hatch.
4 see inspection hatch.

hatchet a small short-handled axe often with a hammer-head poll or claw opposite the blade.

hatching in drawings, graphical shading and fill using a series of parallel lines, crossed parallel lines or other repeated lined pattern.

hatchment a decorated heraldic memorial plate or escutcheon applied to a tomb or building.

Hathor the ancient Egyptian cow-goddess, nursemaid to Horus; attribute of gold and turquoise, music and revelry, giver of milk, symbolic of childbirth and caring; depicted as a woman with a cow's head or ears and a head-dress with the solar disc surrounded by cow's horns. →74

Hathor capital an ancient Egyptian capital on which two or four sides are carved the face of the goddess Hathor. →73

Hathor column an Egyptian column with a capital decorated with the head of the goddess Hathor. →73, →76

haunch the curved part of an arch between the crown and springing; sometimes written as hance or hanse (trad.). →22, →101

haunched beam a beam with a downward thickening at its bearing points.

haunched tenon joint a joinery mortise and tenon joint with an L-shaped tenon flush with both edges of the member at its stem, then stepped back on one side towards its end. →5

Havana (brown), tobacco (brown), snuff (brown); a shade of dark brown which takes its name from the colour of the dried leaves of the tobacco plant [*Nicotiana tabacum*].

haven an area of coastline with quays and jetties for the mooring of boats; a harbour or marina.

hawk, mortar board; a board with a straight handle fixed to its underside for carrying plaster and mortar on site, and from which it is applied with a trowel to a surface, to bricks and block etc. →43

hawthorn [*Crataegus spp.*] a hardwood tree or shrub with dense, fine-grained timber; used mainly for the decorative value of its grain in veneers and quality furniture.

hayloft the upper part of a stable or barn used for the storage of hay.

hazardous waste, problem waste; waste material from a process considered potentially dangerous, poisonous or pollutant, whose disposal is governed by regulations.

hazel, 1 [*Corylus avellana*] a deciduous hardwood from the northern hemisphere with pale red-brown or green-brown resilient timber.

2 rust, rust brown; a shade of brown which takes its name from the colour of the shells of ripe nuts from the hazel tree; also the colour of oxidation on iron.

hazelnut oil a fatty oil produced by pressing the nuts from the hazel tree.

HD polythene high density polythene.

HDPE high density polythene.

head 1 the highest part of a construction.

2 the upper horizontal member in a door or window frame.

3 see door head. →50

4 see window head. →52

5 see soffit.

6 see crown. →1

7 see shower head.

8 see sprinkler head.

9 see rainwater head. →46

10 the upper end of a roof tile or slate as laid. →47

11 the metal striking or cutting component of a hammer, axe or other similar hand tool, fixed to its shaft.

12 see hammerhead. →40

13 the enlarged part of a screw, nail or other fixing, by which it is attached or driven in; a nailhead or screw head. →35, →36

header 1 a brick or stone laid with its short side or end exposed in a masonry surface. →20

2 plinth header, see header plinth. →16

3 see radial header. →16

4 tapered header, see culvert stretcher. →16

5 bull header, see rowlock. →20

6 see head plate. →57, →58

7 a heavy beam over a window in traditional timber construction. →6

8 rainwater header, see rainwater head. →46

header bond, 1 heading bond; a brickwork bond in which each course is a series of headers; alternate courses are laid with a half header overlap. →17

2 see Flemish header bond. →18

header course, 1 heading course; in brickwork, a course of bricks with only their short sides showing in the wall. →20

2 the uppermost layer of logs in horizontal log construction.

header face the visible side of a brick when laid in masonry as a header. →20

header joint see perpend. →20

header plate see head plate. →57, →58

header plinth, plinth header; a special brick whose upper arris has been chamfered along one of its short sides for use as a header in a brick coping or above a projection. →16

head flashing a flashing used over an opening to direct water outwards and waterproof the lintel.

heading bond see header bond. →17

heading chisel see mortise chisel. →41

heading course see header course.

head joint see perpend. →20

headland, cape, peninsula; an area of land which projects out into the sea or other body of water.

headlap the overlap of adjacent parts of roofing material such as tiles or roof sheeting in a line parallel to the slope of the roof.

head office see headquarters.

head piece see head plate. →57, →58

head plate, head piece; the upper horizontal framing member in a timber-framed wall or partition, or stud wall. →57, →58

headquarters, 1 head office; the main administrative centre of a large industrial or commercial enterprise.

2 see principia. →104

headroom, 1 clearance, overhead clearance; the free height between a floor and overhead obstacle such as a door head, beam etc.

2 see stair headroom. →45

3 see ceiling height.

headstone 1 a stone slab laid over the entrance to a prehistoric burial chamber or similar tomb.

2 the vertical stone memorial slab at the head of a grave.

headtree see bolster. →4

health centre a building or part of a building in which primary medical treatment or advice is given to non-resident patients.

health club, fitness club; a club with gymnasia and other apparatus for the improvement of personal fitness.

health insurance insurance taken by a party against loss of income and welfare costs due to ill health.

health resort, spa, kursaal; a commercial establishment containing steam rooms, exercise facilities and baths for recreation and relaxation.

hearing human physiological and psychological processes which produce the perceived sensation of sound.

heart see fess point. →124

heart and dart see leaf and dart. →82

heart check see heartshake. →1

hearth 1 a large and often rudimentary fireplace, used for food preparation and heating in a traditional dwelling.

see *hearth* in Greek residential building illustration. →87

2 the base or floor of a fireplace, on which combustion takes place. →55
see *hearth* in fireplace illustration. →55
3 see eschara.

hearth altar 1 see hestia. →87
2 see eschara. →87, →116

hearth apron a metal or tiled plate covering the floor in front of a fireplace or solid-fuel stove to prevent the flooring from catching fire from flying sparks. →56

hearth shrine an ancient Babylonian temple type from c.2500 BC, a small shrine with a long cult room. →66

hearth temple see hearth shrine. →66

heart moulding 1 an ornamental nebule moulding consisting of a raised undulating line with a sunken lower edge, with upper and lower extremities resembling heart motifs. →124
2 heart and dart, see leaf and dart. →82

heart-palmette see palmette heart. →121

heart point see fess point. →124

heartshake, heart check, rift crack, star shake; a radial crack near the centre of a tree trunk, apparent in timber cut from it. →1

heartwood, duramen; the central core of wood in a tree, whose timber is often of a different colour to the sapwood. →1

heartwood rot fungal decay in the heartwood of timber.

heat the property of warmth, caused by the movement of atoms and molecules excited by energy; its unit is the joule.

heat-absorbing glass see tinted solar control glass.

heat balance 1 the result of subtracting heat losses from heat gains for a space, building or installation.
2 thermodynamic equilibrium; the stable temperature state of equilibrium produced by this.

heat bridge see cold bridge.

heat capacity see thermal capacity.

heat detector, detector; a fire detector which reacts to the presence of heat and triggers an alarm signal at a certain temperature.

heat differential detector see thermo-differential detector.

heat distribution the distribution of heat throughout a building in the form of hot water or steam from a centralized boiler or district heating plant.

heated space any space within a building containing a heating appliance and which is kept relatively warm.

heater 1 see heating appliance; types of heater are listed below.
2 that part of an air-conditioning system which transfers heat to the supply air.
bulk heater, outflow heater.
convection heater, see convector.
domestic water heater.
electric heater.
electric fan heater, see fan heater.
electric water heater.
fan heater.
gas heater.
immersion heater, see electric water heater.
outflow heater.
pressure water heater.
radiant heater.
radiator.
room heater. →56
sauna heater. →58
solid-fuel heater, see solid-fuel stove. →56
storage heater.
thermal storage heater, see storage heater.
warm-air heater.
water heater.

heat exchanger 1 a device which transfers thermal energy from one installation to another without the direct flowing of material between the systems.
2 in an air-conditioning system, a device for transferring heat to or from air passing over it, usually via heated or cooled liquid-filled coils, metal baffles etc.
3 see calorifier.

heat exchange plant room a plant room containing calorifiers and control equipment for transferring heat from a district heating main to water for domestic use.

heat exchange station that part of a district heating system in which energy is transferred from heated water and distributed at a lower temperature for use in buildings.

heat flow the rate of transfer of heat energy in watts, joules per second.

heath an area of open rural land with low vegetation such as heather.

heath plant any species of low lying plant such as heather which usually grows on heathland.

heating, 1 space heating; the provision of heat to spaces of a building by appliances and mechanical installations to provide a level of thermal comfort.
2 see heating period.
see *heating* in sauna illustration. →58

heating and ventilation see mechanical services.

heating and ventilation engineer a person who is responsible for designing technical services, and supervising their construction and maintenance.

heating appliance, heater; a device or apparatus located within a space for providing warmth, either fuelled directly by electricity, gas, oil or solid fuel, or fed with warm air or water from a centralized plant.

heating battery 1 in air-conditioning, coiled piping in which hot water is circulated, used for heating air to the desired temperature.
2 in district heating and other indirect hot-water heating systems, a unit of pipework or a coil inside a cistern, through which hot water circulates to heat up water within the cistern.

heating cable an electric cable embedded in floor construction, under pavements etc., which provides heat for underfloor heating and similar installations when electricity is passed through it.

heating installation, heating system; the means, devices and apparatus to provide warmth for a building.

heating main see district heating pipeline.

heating period, heating; in steam curing of concrete, the period for which heat is applied so that the concrete heats up slowly.

heating pipework pipework carrying hot water in a heating installation.

heating plant, boiler plant; in heating and hot-water systems, the installation producing thermal energy for heating, transferred and distributed by water, steam, air etc.

heating point see vehicle heating point.

heating season that period in the year during which the heating system of a building is required to be in use.

heating stove see room heater. →56

heating system see heating installation.

heating value see calorific value.

heating, ventilation and air conditioning see HEVAC.

heat insulation see thermal insulation. →59

heat load the amount of excess heat within a space that has to be transferred by an air-conditioning system.

heat loss the transfer of heat from a body or building to the outside, usually as waste energy.

heat of hydration a rise in temperature produced during the setting of concrete and cements due to the chemical reaction of the cement with water.

heat-proof see heat resistant.

heat pump a device, used in refrigeration, geothermal and some solar heating systems, in which a gas is compressed or expanded to raise or lower its temperature.

heat recovery in air-conditioning, a process whereby heat from exhaust air is transferred using a heat exchanger to fresh input air.

heat recovery unit, thermal wheel; in air-conditioning, a heat exchanger for transferring thermal energy and sometimes moisture from the return air to the supply air.

heat resistance the ability of a surface or construction to withstand heat.

heat resistant, heat-proof; relating to a material or surface which has the ability to withstand high temperatures.

heat resisting glass types of glass such as fire glasses or borosilicate glass which can withstand high temperatures without shattering.

heat-soaked glass toughened glass used for external wall systems and roofs, re-treated to remove imperfections and overcome the problems of spontaneous fracture.

heat transfer the movement of heat energy from one place or medium to another by conduction, convection, evaporation or radiation.

heat transmission value see k-value.

heat-treated wood, heat-treated timber; sawn timber sections of pine, spruce, birch and aspen processed into an ecological wood product by baking at temperatures of 200°C or more to break up sugars inside the wood into a form unusable by rot fungi.

heat treatment, 1 accelerated curing; a method of curing concrete using hot water or steam to speed up hardening; it may reduce the final strength of the concrete.
2 the modification of the mechanical properties of steel by its controlled heating and cooling; heat treatments include hardening, tempering, annealing and normalizing.

heat welding a method of joining plastics components by pressing together and briefly heating by either high frequency electric current, friction, a hot-knife or by ultrasonic means.

heavy clay a soil type material that contains more than 60% clay, tough and plastic when wet, hard and uncrumbling when dry.

heavy concrete, high density concrete; concrete which contains heavy aggregate such as iron ore, scrap iron, or barium sulphate; it weighs between 2800 and 5000 kg/m^3 and is used for radiative shields.

heavy duty wallcovering wallcovering designed to be durable and easily cleanable.

heavy hydrogen see deuterium.

heavy industry large-scale industry concerned with the manufacture of heavy goods, materials and mass products, refining etc.

heavy plate see quarto plate.

heavy spar a naturally occurring form of the mineral barytes, see Bologna stone.

heavy tamping see dynamic consolidation.

hecatompedon a vague term designating a Greek temple whose naos is 100 Attic feet (approx. 31 m) long, or whose porch is 100 Attic feet wide; Greek form is hekatompedon. →84

hectare abb. **ha**; a unit of area of 10 000 m^2, 100 m × 100 m.

hecto- abb. **h**; a prefix for units of measurement or quantity to denote a factor of 10^2 (one hundred). →Table 1

Hedera helix the ivy plant; see ivy green, ivy leaf.

hedge a landscaped barrier of shrubs grown closely together as a wall and periodically trimmed.

heel gable a gable at the outside corner of two gable roofs which meet at right angles. →46

height 1 the vertical dimension of an object.
2 see mounting height.

height in storeys the height of a multistorey building given as the number of floors.

height zoning in town planning, the regulating of the maximum height for buildings in particular areas of a city.

hekatompedon see hecatompedon. →84

***Helianthus annuus* 1** see sunflower.
2 see sunflower seed oil.

helical ramp, spiral ramp; a ramp, circular in plan, which connects adjacent levels in a building, especially found in multistorey car parks. →67

helical reinforcement concrete column reinforcement which is spiral or helical in shape, binding the main reinforcement within the column to form a three-dimensional cage.

helical stair see spiral stair. →45

helices plural form of helix.

helicopter see power trowel.

heliocaminus Lat.; a room in a Roman baths or other building in which benefit is taken from the sun's heat; a solar-heated or sunny room; Greek form is heliokaminos. →91

heliodor a light yellow variety of the mineral beryl, used as a gemstone.

heliotrope, 1 bloodstone; a dark green microcrystalline variety of the mineral chalcedony speckled with red streaks of jasper; used for decorative ornament and as gemstones.
2 a shade of violet which takes its name from the colour of the flowers of the heliotrope plant.

helium a light inert gaseous chemical element, **He**, used in airships.

helix, 1 pl. helices; any spiral shape, especially ornament as found in a classical building.
2 Lat.; one of the spirals or volutes beneath the abacus in a classical Corinthian capital; often used in the plural, helices. →81
3 see volute.

Helladic pertaining to prehistoric bronze-age cultures on mainland Greece from 2800 to 1500 BC; later Helladic culture (1570–1150 BC) is known as Mycenaean.

Hellenistic the last phase of ancient Greek culture (323–30 BC) from the death of Alexander the Great to the Roman Imperial age, characterized by influences from the east.

helm a helmet, especially one enclosing the entire head and reaching down to the shoulders. →122, →124

helmet, helm; a heraldic and ornamental motif based on the hard protective headgear of a soldier, symbolic of security and invulnerability; when used in a coat of arms, it is usually called a helm, and denotes the rank of the wearer. →122, →124

Helmholtz resonator see cavity absorber.

helm roof a hipped roof constructed diagonal to the rectilinear geometry of a building thus producing gables on all four sides; usually used for spires.

helve the handle or shaft of a tool, especially an axe.

hematite see haematite.

hemihydrate gypsum plaster see hemihydrate plaster.

hemihydrate plaster, hemihydrate gypsum plaster, plaster of Paris, stucco; plaster whose binder is calcium sulphate hemihydrate.

hemisphere a solid shape whose surface is formed by the rotation of a semicircle through 180°; half a sphere.

hemitriglyph, (Gr hemitriglyphos, Lat. hemitriglyphus); half a triglyph.

hemlock 1 [*Tsuga spp.*] a genus of North American softwood trees with soft, light, pale brown timber.
2 see eastern hemlock.
3 see western hemlock.

hemlock spruce see eastern hemlock.

hemp 1 an Indian plant [*Cannabis sativa*] and the fibres obtained from it, used for making ropes and rough fabric.
2 see Manila hemp.

hempseed oil a drying oil used as a vehicle in paints, pressed from the seeds of the hemp plant.

henna 1 a tropical plant, *Lawsonia inermis*, whose powdered leaves and shoots are prepared to produce a reddish-yellow colourant, principally used as a hair dye.
2 see agate.

henostyle, henostyle in antis; in classical architecture, a portico which has one central supporting column between projecting side walls or antae. →77, →84

henostyle in antis see henostyle. →77

henry abb. **H**; the SI unit of inductance in a circuit in which an electromotive force of one volt is produced by a changing current of one ampere per second.

Henry II pertaining to early French Renaissance architecture during the reign of Henry II, 1547–1559.

heptagon a planar regular or irregular seven-sided geometrical figure. →108

heptagram a star-shaped figure with seven points, constructed using a single unbroken line; a mystical symbol relating to the number seven, including phenomena such as the planets, days of the week etc. →108

heptahedron a solid shape whose surface is composed of seven planar faces.

heptastyle in classical architecture, a portico supported by a row of seven columns. →77

heraldic pillar see Egyptian heraldic pillar. →73

herald's staff the recognized classical symbol of a divine messenger (keryx in Greek), a winged staff entwined with foliage, ribbons, serpents etc.; see Aaron's rod, staff of Asclepius, Bacchus, Hermes, Mercury and Dionysus. →120
see caduceus. →120
see kerykeion. →120

heraldry the study of historical coats of arms or shields. →124, →125

herati Persian rosette ornament of regular interwoven geometric and foliated motifs, taking its name from Herat in present-day Afghanistan. →120

herb in landscaping, a class of flowering plants whose stem is never woody.

herbage low ground-covering plant growth in landscaping.

heredium 1 Lat.; a Roman unit of land area measure equivalent to 1.246 acres or 5060 m^2.
2 a Roman vegetable garden or plot, originally the inheritable portion of a property.

herm, herma, plural hermae; in classical architecture, a square tapered column capped with the carved head, bust or torso of a figure, usually Hermes; originally used by the Greeks as a boundary marker, later as decoration. →76

herma see herm. →76

hermae plural of herma. →76

Hermes, staff of see caduceus. →120

hermeneutics the study and interpretation of works of art.

hermetic see airtight.

hermetically sealed double glazed unit see double glazed unit.

hermetically sealed multiple glazed unit see sealed glazed unit. →53

hermit colony a loose community of early Christian devouts, retired from society at large, usually to the wilderness, and dwelling in solitary spartan cells or caves.

heroon, heroum (Lat.); Gk; a Greek shrine or monument dedicated to a hero, often constructed at his presumed burial place; now a small temple-like monument. →85, →94

heroum Latin form of heroon. →85, →94

herringbone a decorative pattern in which stones, bricks, tiles or lines are arranged diagonally to interlink with one another so that each successive course points in the opposite direction; see also herringbone pattern. →124
see herringbone pattern, herringbone match. →10
see herringbone brickwork, herringbone bond. →17

herringbone bond see herringbone brickwork. →17

herringbone brickwork, 1 herringbone bond; decorative brickwork in which bricks are laid at a slant with alternate bricks at right angles. →17
2 Roman herringbone brickwork, see opus spicatum. →83

herringbone match see herringbone pattern. →10

herringbone panelling in traditional timber frame construction, the filling of the half-timbered panels in a framed wall by diagonally laid timbers or bricks.

herringbone parquet mosaic parquet flooring laid in a herringbone pattern by gluing or nailing. →44

herringbone pattern a veneering pattern in which veneers with slanting grain are glued side by side in mirror image along a centre line, resembling the bones of a fish attached to its spine; a similar pattern in tiling, paving and parquetry. →10

herringbone paving paving laid in a herringbone pattern. →15
see Dutch paving. →15

herringbone strutting, cross bridging, cross noggin; short timber diagonal members used to cross brace and stiffen the joists in a timber joist floor laterally. →4

hertz the SI unit of frequency or cycles per second, abb. **Hz**.

hesitation set an outdated term meaning false set.

hessian, burlap (Am.), sackcloth; a roughly woven fabric made of natural fibres such as hemp or jute, often used in construction for reinforcing plasterwork.

hessonite, cinnamon stone; a brownish orange variety of the mineral garnet, a form of grossular.

hestia Gk; a domestic altar to Hestia, the Greek goddess of the hearth, on which offerings were burnt. →87

Heterobasidion annosum see annosus root rot.

HEVAC acronym of HEating, Ventilation and Air Conditioning, also shortened to HVAC; the discipline which deals with the design and installation of heating, ventilation and air-conditioning services for a building; also called mechanical services engineering or mechanical engineering.

hewing axe a wide-bladed axe used for shaping logs into roughly square timbers; especially of use in log construction. →6

hewn jetty see false jetty.

hexadecimal a number system consisting of 16 digits, in which numbers 10 to 15 are replaced with the letter symbols A to F.

hexagon 1 a planar regular or irregular six-sided geometrical figure. →108
2 regular hexagon; a planar six-sided figure with six equal sides and six equal internal angles of 120°. →108

hexagonal bar a manufactured metal bar, hexagonal in cross-section; when of steel it is used in welded construction for tie rods, detail work etc. →34

hexagonal bolt, hex-head bolt; a bolt with a hexagonal head which can be tightened with a spanner. →36

hexagonal mesh see chicken wire. →34

hexagonal nipple a short connecting pipe fitting externally threaded at either end, whose middle section is hexagonal in section so that it can be tightened with a spanner.

hexagonal nut, hex nut; a nut which is a regular hexagon in section so that it can be tightened with a spanner. →37

hexagonal paver a concrete paving unit which is hexagonal, laid in a honeycomb pattern. →15

hexagonal tile a ceramic floor tile which is hexagonal, laid in a honeycomb pattern. →15, →20

hexagram a six-pointed star created by the overlapping of two equilateral triangles; called the Star of David when associated with the Jewish faith. →108

hexahedron a solid geometrical shape whose surface is composed of six planar faces.
hexapartite vault see sexpartite vault. →26
hexastyle in classical architecture, a portico supported by a row of six columns. →77
hex-head bolt see hexagonal bolt. →36
hex nut see hexagonal nut. →37
H-hinge see parliament hinge. →38
Hiberno-Romanesque architecture, 1 Hiberno-Saxon; religious architecture from Ireland in the early 11th century, characterized by sparing use of detail, bulky forms and the round arch; Romanesque architecture in Ireland; see also Insular art.
2 see Insular art. →97
Hiberno-Saxon architecture see Hiberno-Romanesque architecture.
hickey see bending tool.
hickory [*Carya spp.*] a North American hardwood with hard and strong pinkish brown timber; used for tool handles, ladder rungs, furniture and sports equipment.
hicky see bending tool.
hidden file in computing, a file which does not appear in typical file listings and directories.
hidden line in computer-aided design, a line in a three-dimensional object which remains unseen in certain projections of the object.
hidden line image in computer-aided design, a visualization of a three-dimensional computer model in which any lines which lie behind elements in the foreground are not shown.
hide glue animal glue made from collagen, a protein released by boiling the hides of animals.
hiding power, see opacity;
hieracosphinx a sphinx with the head of a hawk. →75
hieron Gk; in classical architecture, a sacred area or shrine, or the area surrounding a temple.
high altar the main altar of a church or cathedral.
see *Early Christian and Late Antique church* illustration. →95
see *Byzantine domical church* illustration. →96
see *Romanesque church* illustration. →99
see *Gothic cathedral* illustration. →100
high alumina cement, calcium aluminate cement; a cement produced by grinding the clinker formed by burning calcareous and aluminous materials in a kiln; an active hydraulic binder.
high alumina cement clinker, high alumina clinker; a clinker formed by burning calcareous and aluminous materials in a kiln; composed mainly of alumina (aluminium oxide) and oxides, hydroxides or carbonates of calcium.
high alumina cement concrete concrete made with high alumina cement.
high alumina clinker see high alumina cement clinker.
high Baroque the middle phase of Baroque architecture, c.1620–1670.
high carbon steel tough steel which has a carbon content of 0.5–1.5%; used for casting and cutting tools.
high cross, Celtic cross; a carved decorative stone cross with a circle springing from the crossing, evolving in Ireland in the 900s and originally erected in public places to illustrate biblical events; see market cross.
high density concrete see heavy concrete.
high density polythene, HD polythene, HDPE; a hard and rigid form of polythene used for plastics sheet, containers and pipes.
high early-strength cement see rapid-hardening Portland cement.
high forest forest made up solely of maiden trees.
high gloss see full gloss.
high Gothic 1 the middle phase of Gothic architecture in France in the 1200s (see Rayonnant) and elsewhere in Europe in the 1300s (see Decorated). →100
see *high Gothic window* illustration. →111
2 see Rayonnant style.
3 see Decorated style.
4 see Geometric style.
5 see Curvilinear style.
high-level cistern a WC flushing cistern set high up on a wall above the pan to provide water pressure for flushing.
highlighting see spotlighting.
high magnesium lime see dolomitic lime.
high output back boiler a boiler fitted to the rear of a solid fuel heater which provides water for domestic use and space heating.
high performance referring to materials, products or components of reputed high quality, strength, durability or special properties; see also standard.
high pressure sodium lamp a sodium lamp capable of producing a wider spectrum of coloured light than normal sodium lamps, used for external and garden lighting.
high pressure system see high velocity system.
high pressure steam curing see autoclaving.
high range water-reducing admixture see superplasticizing admixture.
high red see signal red.
high relief see alto rilievo.
high Renaissance the middle phase of Renaissance architecture, cinquecento in Italy, from c.1480 to 1535.
see *high Renaissance window* illustration. →111
high-rise block, high-rise building; a tall freestanding apartment building with separate flats usually arranged around a single main stair. →61
high-rise building see high-rise block. →61
high strength concrete concrete that has a cube strength at 28 days of at least 50 N/mm^2.
High Tech an architectural style originating from England in the 1970s and 1980s, characterized by use of modern technology in design solutions and in the outward mechanistic expression of buildings.
high tensile brass see manganese bronze.
high tensile steel structural steel with a carbon content of up to 3% and which may contain significant proportions of other metals.
high tension steel cable one of a number of cables which give a post-stressed concrete member its structural strength.
high tide the occasion, usually occurring twice daily, when the sea level is at its highest, measured at a point on a coastline; see also flood, spring tide.
high velocity system, high pressure system; an air-conditioning system in which air is forced through ductwork at 5–20 m/s using a powerful fan, enabling use of smaller duct sizes.
high voltage a voltage greater than 1000 V in an electric circuit.
highway 1 a road, route or path which is open to the public, usually one for vehicular use.
2 (Am.), a major traffic road or motorway in North America.
hiking route a rural track designated as a right of way across private land and national parks for ramblers and walkers.
hillfort an ancient form of defensive structure with a system of concentric ditches and ramparts constructed around a hill; see univallate, bivallate, multivallate.
hill town a rural town built on the crown or slopes of a hill for reasons of climate, religion or defence.
hilani see bit hilani.
hinge a pivoting mechanism to provide a fixing and rotating action to framed door leaves, window casements etc. →38
see *hinge* illustration; types included as separate entries are listed below. →52
A-hinge. →38
backflap hinge. →38

ball-bearing hinge, ball-bearing butt hinge. →38
ball hinge. →38
band and hook hinge, see hook and band hinge. →38
blind hinge, see concealed hinge.
butt hinge. →38
butterfly hinge. →38
cabinet hinge. →38
casement hinge. →52, →53
centre pivot hinge, centre hinge.
cleaning hinge, see easy-clean hinge. →38
concealed hinge.
continuous hinge, see piano hinge. →38
cranked hinge. →38
cylinder hinge. →38
door hinge. →38
double-acting hinge.
double-acting spring hinge.
easy-clean hinge. →38
electric hinge, electrically wired hinge.
falling-butt hinge. →38
fast-pin hinge. →38
flap hinge, see strap hinge. →38
furnishing hinge, see cabinet hinge. →38
gravity door hinge, see rising hinge. →38
H-hinge, see parliament hinge. →38
hook and band hinge. →38
invisible hinge.
lift-off butt hinge, lift-off hinge. →38
loose butt hinge, see lift-off butt hinge. →38
loose pin butt hinge, loose pin hinge. →38
loose-joint hinge, loose-joint butt hinge.
non-mortised hinge, non-mortised butt hinge. →38
parliament hinge. →38
piano hinge. →38
pin hinge, see loose pin butt hinge. →38
rising hinge, rising-butt hinge. →38
rule joint hinge. →38
screw hook and eye hinge, screw hinge. →38
secret hinge, see invisible hinge.
spring hinge.
strap hinge. →38
surface hinge.
surface-fixed hinge, see non-mortised hinge. →38
swing door hinge, see double-acting hinge.
tee hinge, T-hinge. →38
rule joint hinge, see table hinge. →38
tight-pin hinge, see fast-pin hinge. →38
weld-on hinge. →38
window hinge. →52, →53

hinge bolt, dog bolt, security bolt; a metal security lug fitted to and projecting sideways from the hinge stile of a door leaf, which fits in a housing in the jamb when the door is shut and prevents it from being forced open. →38

hinge chisel a thin chisel with a serrated cutting edge, used for making thin mortises for concealed hinges.

hinged door 1 a door whose leaf is hinged on one side so that it opens by turning. →50
2 see swing door. →50
3 see double door. →50
4 see single door. →50
5 see trapdoor.

hinge joint see pin joint. →33

hinge leaf one of the metal flaps by which a hinge is fixed to the edge of a door and its frame. →38

hinge mortise, hinge rebate; a shallow depression cut into a door frame and the edge of a door leaf to receive the leaves of a hinge and ensure flush installation. →38

hinge pin that part of a hinge around which the leaves rotate; either retractable or permanently fixed to one of the leaves; a hinge pin in a lift-off hinge is often called a pintle. →38

hinge rebate see hinge mortise. →38

hip, 1 hip end, hipped end; the sloping triangle of a roof plane at one or both ends of a hipped roof.
2 piend; the sloping ridge formed by two pitched roofs which meet at an outside corner. →46

hip and valley roof a pitched roof constructed with both hips and valleys, as with an L-shaped building. →46

hip bath, sitz bath; a short bathtub with a shelf for a person to sit upright.

hip cruck see end cruck.

hip end see hip. →46

hipped end see hip. →46

hipped gable roof see half-hipped roof. →46

hipped mansard roof, mansard roof (Am.); a hip roof in which all four roof surfaces are doubly pitched. →46

hipped roof see hip roof. →46

Hippodamian system a rectilinear town layout in which blocks of dwellings are divided up by narrow side streets linked together by wider main roads, developed by the Ionian Hippodamus of Miletus in the 5th century BC. →94
see *Hippodamian system* illustration. →94

hippodrome, hippodromos (Gk); an open or roofed track or arena for chariot and horse racing in ancient Greece and Rome; a Roman circus. →89

hippodromos Greek form of hippodrome. →89

hip post see end cruck.

hip rafter, angle ridge; in timber roof construction, a diagonal rafter at a junction or hip formed by two sloping roofs in different planes.

hip roof, hipped roof; a pitched roof with slopes on all four sides which meet at the corners to form hips; it may or may not have a ridge. →46

hip tile a roof tile which is specially formed to cover a hip.
see angular hip tile.
see bonnet hip tile, granny bonnet.

historiated capital see figured capital. →115

historical monument any building or structure of historical interest, usually protected by legislation.

historicism an eclectic movement in art in the 19th century; architecture making use of motifs and styles from an earlier age.

historic site, area of historical interest; an area of land of cultural and historical value by virtue of a structure thereon, or as the site of an important historical event, often protected by legislation.

history painting a painting which depicts real, fictitious or legendary historical events in an exaggerated manner.

hit and miss construction see chequerboard construction.

hoard see hoarding. →103

hoarding 1 in site works, a fence enclosing a construction site.
2 a large freestanding screen designed to carry adverts.
3 a covered overhanging wooden gallery built next to the parapet of a fortified wall or tower to allow defenders to drop missiles on assailants below; also known as a hoard or hourd; see brattice; machicolation. →103

hob 1 the rings and plates on the upper surface of a coal, gas, wood or electric cooker, through which heat is transferred to cooking utensils.
gas hob, see gas cooker.
2 hob unit, cooktop; an appliance containing a series of heatable cooking rings sunk into a worktop.

hobby room see activity space.

hob unit see hob.

hockey stick a strip of planed timber which is L-shaped or rebated in cross-section, used as trim to cover the corners or edge joints of partitions, panels etc.; an edge strip with one limb longer than the other. →2

hod a three-sided wooden or plastic box supported on a short pole, used on a building site for carrying bricks, blocks or mortar to their place of use.

hoeing in landscaping and forestry, the breaking up of clods of soil with a hoe.

hog, camber, hogging; the built-in upward bowing of a prestressed or other beam, which then becomes straight on loading.

hogging see hog.

hoist 1 apparatus for lifting and lowering components and equipment on site.
2 see winch. →64

hoisting plant see lifting equipment.

hoistway see lift well.

holder 1 see lampholder.
2 see door holder. →51

holdfast a metal fixing or cleat used for fastening stone cladding to a structural frame. →11

hole a small opening.

hole cutter see hole saw. →42

hole gauge see plug gauge.

hole saw, tubular saw, hole cutter, annular bit, crown saw; a drill bit for drilling large bore circular holes in board, by means of a blade which is a short length of tube with a serrated edge. →42

holiday see miss.

holiday home see summer residence. →58

holing in slate roofing, the making of a hole in a roof slate for fixing with a nail.

hollow see hollow moulding. →14

hollow bedding the laying of blocks in masonry in such a way that mortar is applied only to the edges and sides to protect the blocks against cracking during movement.

hollow block see cellular block. →30

hollow brick, 1 cavity block; a brick manufactured with a large hole or holes through it, forming cavities within the thickness of a brick wall to reduce weight and to house wiring and pipe installations etc. →16
2 a general name for all types of perforated brick. →16

hollow-chisel mortiser a drill or drill bit with a square casing around a helical bit, used for cutting rectangular mortises in wood.

hollow clay block a lightweight clay building block extruded with internal voids. →16

hollow composite beam a patented hollow perforated steel beam site-grouted with concrete, used for the support of precast floor slabs and planks.

hollow concrete block see cellular block. →30

hollow-core beam a precast and pretensioned concrete slab unit with longitudinal voids, used as rapidly laid structural floor and roof components to span between main beams; also called a hollow-core slab or concrete plank. →27, →28

hollow-core door a door whose leaf is of light cellular cardboard construction with veneers or laminate sheets bonded to either side. →51

hollow-core slab see hollow-core beam. →28

hollow cross 1 see voided cross. →118
2 see hollow Greek cross. →118

hollow glass block see glass block. →30, →53

hollow Greek cross a Greek cross formed from L-shaped pieces arranged around a cross-shaped void; a gammadion. →118

hollow masonry wall see cavity wall. →21

hollow moulding 1 a decorative moulding composed of a curved segmental or three-quarter circular recess, used at the inner junction of perpendicular surfaces such as ceilings and walls. →14
2 see trochilus. →14
3 see scotia. →14, →80

hollow plane a woodworking plane with a concave base and blade used for cutting convex shapes; usually sold as a pair with a round plane.

hollow roll joint a bitumen sheet or sheetmetal roofing joint in which two adjacent sheets are intertwined along their edges without a core roll. →49

hollow section, tubular section; a round or rectangular hollow steel section formed by rolling and welding steel plate, used for structural purposes. →34
see circular hollow section. →34
see rectangular hollow section. →34
see square hollow section. →34

hollow wall see cavity wall. →21
see *hollow wall* in brick house illustration. →59

hollow-wall anchor, molly, toggle; a metal threaded fastener for fixing to plasterboard hollow wall surfaces inserted into a drilled hole and secured by means of a sleeve which is retracted to clamp tight against the reverse side of construction when the screw is turned. →37

hollow-wall bond see cavity bond. →17
see Dearne's bond. →17
see rat-trap bond. →17

hollow-wall plug, 1 molly, toggle; a nylon version of a hollow-wall anchor, used for fixing lighter objects. →37
2 see legs anchor. →37

holmium a rare chemical element, **Ho**.

holy cross 1 see Calvary cross. →117
2 see Roman holy cross. →117

Holy Ghost the third member, together with the Father and Son, of the Christian Holy Trinity, often depicted in religious decoration and ornament as a dove. →122

holy of holies 1 the innermost shrine or chamber of a temple or place of worship, especially a Jewish temple, to which access was denied to all but those of highest priesthood; a cella or naos. →72, →85
2 see sanctuary.
3 see adytum. →85
4 see anactoron. →92
5 see garbha-griha. →68

Holy Trinity various three-part, triangular or trefoil motifs in Christian symbolic ornament depicting the Father, Son and Holy Ghost; 'trinitas' in Latin. →119

hom stylized fan-like flower ornament with seven petals, originating from ancient Syria. →82, →121

home 1 the permanent dwelling place of a person, persons or family.
2 see dwelling.
3 institution; a residential establishment which provides care for long-term medical patients, drug abusers, the aged or other groups in need.

home-based trip in traffic planning, any trip from which the home is a starting point.

homelessness the state of being without a permanent home or dwelling place.

homelift a lift designed for domestic use by the elderly and disabled.

homestead a unit of occupied rural land with dwellings and associated buildings.

homo mensura (Lat.) 'Man is the measure of all things'; (Gk = metron anthropos); the concept in architectural theory that the basic measurements of the human frame and existence are reflected in the built environment, based on the teachings of the Greek philosopher Protagoras (454–410 BC).

homogeneous referring to a material or substance which is of uniform composition.

homogeneous plywood plywood in which all the veneers are of the same species of wood.

homopolymer in the chemistry of plastics, a polymer formed from one type of repeated monomer; see copolymer.

Honduras mahogany, Central American mahogany; [*Swietenia macrophylla*] a Central American tropical hardwood with red or golden brown timber; used for interior and exterior joinery, flooring, furniture and boat-building.

hone, whetstone; a fine-grained grindstone used for sharpening the blades of tools and polishing stone surfaces.

honed 1 a description of a smooth, lightly polished, matt finish in stonework, produced by treatment with a fine abrasive; the same as a polished finish, but without the final shine. →12
2 see rubbed finish.

honey yellow a shade of greenish yellow which takes its name from the colour of honey.

honeycomb brickwork brickwork laid with staggered openings between adjacent bricks for decoration or to permit ventilation through the wall. →17

honeycomb floor see waffle floor.

honeycomb rot see red ring rot.

honeycomb slab see waffle slab. →27

honeycomb work see stalactite work. →115

honeycombing, rock pocket (Am.); voids in faulty concrete caused by a lack of fine aggregate or insufficient compaction.

honeysuckle see anthemion. →82

honing the sharpening of the tip of a metal blade of a hand tool or the production of a matt surface on stonework using a fine grindstone or hone.

honing bevel the very tip of the bevelled blade of a chisel or other cutting tool, ground or sharpened to provide a cutting edge. →41

honing guide, gauge; a device for holding the blade of a tool such as a chisel at the correct angle while it is being sharpened.

honourable mention a special mention given to proposals for an architectural competition, which are outside the group of those awarded but of particular merit.

honour point the point immediately above the centre of a heraldic shield. →124

hood 1 see extractor hood.
2 see canopy. →55

hood-mould, dripstone, label; a raised protruding moulding above a masonry arch or opening to throw off rainwater. →110

hook 1 in reinforced concrete, a reinforcing bar whose end has been bent back on itself around a thick pin in order to provide anchorage.
2 see screw hook. →36

hook and band hinge, band and hook hinge; a hinge consisting of a flap which fits over a pin attached to a back plate, bolt or lug; used for cupboard doors. →38

hook and eye a simple fastener for a window or door consisting of a pivoted hook, attached to the leaf, and a ring, attached to the frame, into which the hook fits. →36

hook angle see cutting angle.

hook bolt 1 a lock bolt which is hook shaped or curved, used for fastening sliding doors. →39
2 a metal fastening consisting of a bolt whose end is bent over, used for fixing profiled sheet roofing to a steel frame.

hooked scarf joint 1 see tabled scarf joint. →3
2 see splayed and tabled scarf joint.

hook pin in traditional timber frame construction, an iron peg hammered into a joint as a temporary fixing, replaced with a wooden peg at a later stage.

hook screw see screw hook. →36

hop-hornbeam see European hop-hornbeam.

hopper head see rainwater head.

hopper light a bottom-hinged window casement which opens inwards, often a small vent window beneath a larger fixed light. →52

horizon 1 the line delineating the point at which the sky appears to meet land or built form in the horizontal distance.
2 see skyline.
3 see horizon line. →128

horizon blue, pale turquoise; a shade of blue which takes its name from the colour of the sky viewed at about 5° to the horizon.

horizon line, horizon; in perspective drawing, the horizontal line formed by the meeting of the horizon plane and the picture plane, most often at the level of the station point. →128

horizon plane in perspective drawing, a horizontal plane at the level of the observer's eye or station point, on which the perceived horizon lies. →128

horizontal parallel to the surface of still water or theoretical horizon; perpendicular to the vertical.

horizontal boarding timber cladding boards laid horizontally on a frame as interior boarding, weatherboarding, clapboarding or shiplap boarding. →8

horizontal bridge any bridge the upper surface of whose deck is horizontal. →32

horizontal glazing bar see lay bar. →111

horizontal joint 1 any construction joint which runs horizontally.
2 see bed joint.

horizontal log construction, blockwork, cobwork; a form of construction using solid logs laid horizontally and interlocking at the corners. →6
see *log construction* illustration. →6

horizontal pivot window, tip-up window; a window with an opening light hung centrally on pins on either side of the frame, about which it opens. →52

horizontal plane in parallel and perspective projection, the coordinate plane which is perpendicular to the vertical or front plane and the side or profile plane, on which points are defined by x and y coordinates; often the same as the ground plane. →127, →128

horizontal rafter see common purlin.

horizontal rafter roof see common purlin roof.

horizontal section a drawing representing a horizontal cut through a site, building or object; a plan view.

horizontal shore see flying shore.

horizontal sliding window see sliding window. →52

hornbeam [*Carpinus betulus*] a European hardwood with extremely hard, heavy, dense and durable white timber which turns and machines well; used where toughness and durability are essential.

hornblende a dark brown, black or green mineral containing silicates of iron, magnesium and calcium; found in granite and many other rocks.

hornfels 1 a collective name for types of fine-grained metamorphic rock which have formed under high temperatures, often dark grey or greenish and very weather resistant.
2 see contact metamorphic rock.
3 see crystalline schist.

horn of plenty, cornucopia; a classical ornamental motif depicting a curved animal horn filled with fruit and foliage, symbolic of fertility, prosperity and happiness, emblem of Bacchus, Hercules etc. →121

horntail see woodwasp.

hornwork the outwork of a castle or fortification consisting of a curtain wall flanked by two demi-bastions. →104

horreum Lat., pl. horrea; a storage building or granary in antiquity. →104

horse chestnut [*Aesculus spp.*] a genus of hardwood trees from the northern hemisphere, the most common of which is the European horse chestnut, *Aesculus hippocastanum*.

horsed moulding see run moulding.

horse mould see running mould. →14

horsepower abb. **hp**; imperial unit of power equal to 746 W.

horseshoe arch, 1 Arabic arch, Moorish arch, round horseshoe arch; an arch composed of a segment of a circle which subtends an angle of more than 180°, often stilted. →24
2 see pointed horseshoe arch. →24

hortus Lat., pl. horti; a garden or park for a Roman dwelling.

Horus the sky and solar god of the ancient Egyptian Nile valley, depicted as a man with the head of a falcon; mythological son of Osiris and Isis, avenger of his father's murder at the hands of Seth; often seen in the form of Ra-Horakte. →74

Horus, eye of see eye of Horus. →75

hose a flexible pipe, especially one for conveying a liquid or gas.

hose reel see fire-hose reel.

hospice a building in which residential or day care is provided for the terminally ill.

hospital 1 an establishment for treatment of the sick and injured, with accommodation for overnight or longer-term patients.
2 see infirmary. →97
3 see valetudinarium. →104
4 a charitable establishment for housing the aged and destitute.

hospital bed lift a lift for hospitals and health centres which is large enough to incorporate a hospital bed and accompanying staff.

hospitales see portae hospitales. →89

hostel, 1 hostelry; an establishment which provides cheap lodging and food for travellers, a place of residence for students etc.; see also inn.
2 see lodging house.
3 see youth hostel.

hostelry see hostel.

hot-air dried see kiln dried.

hot-air stripping in painting and decorating, renovation work etc., the softening of old paint prior to removal using an appliance which provides a blast of hot air.

hot bonding compound see bonding compound.

hot cement cement at an undesirably high temperature at its time of use, usually caused by inadequate cooling after manufacture.

hot-dipping, hot-dip zinc coating; the application of a protective layer of zinc to steel components by immersion in a bath of molten zinc; a form of galvanizing.

hot-dip zinc coating see hot-dipping.

hotel an establishment providing temporary residential accommodation and communal facilities, primarily for travellers, tourists and those on holiday or business.

hot forming see hot working.

hot-melt adhesive see thermoplastic adhesive.

hot-melt glue see thermoplastic adhesive.

hotplate a heated metal plate in the hob of a cooker or range, through which heat is transferred to cooking utensils.

hot-pressed paper handmade paper with a smooth glazed texture, made by pressing with heated metal plates.

hot pressing the production of linseed oil for paints and finishes by extraction under extreme pressure and heat.

hot-rolled deformed bar a deformed bar produced by a hot rolling process, used as concrete reinforcement.

hot-rolled steel section a structural steel section formed by a process of hot rolling. →34

hot rolling the most common process of forming steel sections by passing hot steel through a series of heavy rollers.

hot setting adhesive see thermosetting adhesive.

hot setting glue see thermosetting adhesive.

hot stuff see bonding compound.

hot water water heated by gas, electricity, oil or steam to no more than 65°C for use in a domestic supply.

hot water central heating a central heating system in which piped hot water is circulated from a boiler or storage cylinder to radiators etc.

hot water heating a heating system in which the heating medium is circulated hot water.

hot water storage heater see storage heater.

hot water supply system a system of pipes and heating vessels for the provision and distribution of hot water to spaces in a building.
see indirect hot water supply system.
see direct hot water supply system.

hot water system hot water supply system.

hot working, hot forming; the process of shaping metal when hot by forging and hot rolling etc. to prevent brittleness in the final products; see also cold working.

houndstooth brickwork see dogtooth brickwork. →20

houndstooth moulding see dogtooth brickwork. →124

hour abb. **h**; a unit of time, one 24th part of a day, equal to 60 minutes or 3600 seconds; not an SI unit.

hourd see hoarding. →103

hourly rate, 1 hourly wage; money paid to employees or workers per hour of work done.
2 work charged per hour of labour.

hourly wage hourly rate.

house 1 a freestanding dwelling with living space for one family unit; in classification terms called a one-family house or single-family house. →61
2 in town planning, a building for human habitation, usually a self-contained unit such as a detached house.
3 see detached house. →61
4 see private house.
5 see dwelling.
6 see residential building.
7 see split-level house. →61

houseboat a boat or barge, usually permanently moored, which serves as a dwelling.

housebuilding see housing production.

housed joint, 1 housing joint; any timber joint in which the end of one member is held in a depression or housing in another.
2 a timber joint in which the end or side of one piece is housed in a longitudinal cutting or groove in another; also called a dado joint or housing joint. →5

housed scarf joint, shouldered scarf joint; a timber scarf joint in which the ends of both timbers are cut with a stepped halving to interlock with one another and provide added bending strength. →3

household, family unit; a basic unit of the community in statistics and town planning etc., the people living in one dwelling who act domestically and economically as a whole.

household waste see domestic refuse.

house longhorn beetle [*Hylotrupes bajulus*] a large insect which causes damage to dry softwood in buildings by burrowing.

house tomb, house-type tomb; an ancient Egyptian tomb reminiscent of a house replete with interior decoration and furnishing, a 'house for the dead'.

house-type tomb see house tomb.

housing 1 a cutting or recess in one member to receive another.
2 in joinery, a long groove machined into a board to house another member; a chase or dado; in framing construction this may be called a let-in. →5
3 in log construction, a longitudinal groove made in the underside of logs to incorporate the upper face of the underlying log; this is usually filled with caulking.
4 policies, regulations, development and other matters relating to residential buildings, when viewed as a whole.
5 a general term for a group of dwellings; a housing development.
6 see housing production.

housing area see residential area.

housing benefit state-provided welfare payments intended to go towards rent and other living expenses.

housing development, housing scheme, residential development; an area of new housing functioning as a unit, either a design scheme or as completed.

housing estate, residential development; a distinct area of dwellings of a similar character, usually all constructed at one time and for a particular socio-economic group.

housing federation see International Federation for Housing and Planning.

housing joint see housed joint. →5

housing policy sociopolitical measures to provide new dwellings and improve existing housing stock for a particular region.

housing problem in town planning, a local social problem caused by a housing shortage or lack of appropriate dwelling types.

housing production, housebuilding; that area of design, development and construction relating to residential buildings.

housing project 1 see residential development.
2 see public housing.

housing scheme 1 see housing development.
2 see residential scheme.

housing shortage in town planning, a lack of dwellings in relation to demand.

housing stock the number of existing dwellings or buildings intended as dwellings in a particular area.

hovel a rough shelter or miserable dwelling.

hovertrain a metropolitan railway system in which vehicles move on a bed of pressurized air.

Howe truss a form of lattice beam or triangular truss patented by the American William Howe in 1840, in which, by virtue of the layout of its web members, all diagonals are in compression and all verticals in tension, the opposite of those in a Pratt truss; diagonals in the triangular version form a V-pattern and in flat trusses an A-pattern; see Pratt truss, Vierendeel truss, Warren truss. →33

H-pile any steel pile whose main shaft is an H-section. →29

H-section, **1** UC section, universal column; a structural steel stanchion section, formed by rolling, whose uniform cross-section resembles the letter H in which the width of flanges is approximately equal to the height of the web.→34
2 similarly shaped non-structural sections in other metals and materials.

hue in colour science, that aspect of a colour which defines its actual colour (as opposed to brightness or saturation), caused by a specific wavelength or wavelengths of light.

human scale a concept whereby the dimensions of a built environment and its components take into account the physical and psychological well-being of its inhabitants. →107

humidifier an appliance which increases the relative humidity of air, making conditions more comfortable in spaces whose air is too dry.

humidifying in air-conditioning, the introduction of water vapour to dry air.

humidity 1 water vapour suspended in air
2 a measurement of the water content of air.
3 see relative humidity.

hummum see hammam.

hump see road hump.

humpback bridge, hump bridge; a traditional bridge, usually of stone, which steeply arches over a stream, railway line or other obstacle. →32

hump bridge see humpback bridge. →32

humus highly organic soil formed by the decomposition of vegetable matter.

hundredweight, abb. **cwt**. **1** centner (Ger.), metric hundredweight, Zentner (Ger.); a metric weight of 50 kg or 110.2 lb.
2 long hundredweight; an avoirdupois unit of weight, 112 lb or 50.802 kg.
3 short hundredweight; a unit of weight in North America equal to 100 lb or 45.36 kg.

hung ceiling see suspended ceiling. →60

hung gutter a gutter at eaves level, separate from the fascia, hung on gutter brackets.

Hungarian green see malachite.

hunting lodge a small building in a rural or wilderness setting used as temporary accommodation during hunting trips.

hut 1 a small dwelling, usually of log or timber frame construction.
2 a movable or permanent rudimentary building providing shelter.

HVAC see HEVAC.

hyacinth blue a shade of blue which takes its name from the colour of the flower of the hyacinth plant [*Hyacinthus orientalis*].

hybrid a description of a construction or component based on unusual combinations of products or non-standard or one-off solutions.

hydrant 1 an outlet point through which water can be drawn from a mains water supply.
2 see fire hydrant.

hydrant box a covering construction for a hydrant, usually some sort of cupboard.

hydrated high calcium by-product lime, carbide hydrate; a white powder whose main constituent is calcium hydroxide, **$CaOH_2$**; a by-product of the manufacture of acetylene gas used as hydrated lime.

hydrated lime, lime hydrate; quicklime to which water has been added, either supplied in powdered form as dry hydrate or in liquid form as slaked lime. →Table 5

hydration 1 the chemical alliance of a substance with water.
2 the reaction of the silicates and aluminates in cement with water to form a hard mass.

hydraulic binder a cement binder which sets by chemical reaction with water, as opposed to evaporation of water, and will thus harden under water.

hydraulic cement a binder for concrete which will set under water, produced by the grinding of clinker.

hydraulic lift a lift with a lift drive powered by piped liquid under pressure to raise a piston, plunger or ram on which the lift car is located.

hydraulic lime quicklime in which the amount of silica and aluminates is sufficient for it to set in contact with water, or under water.

hydraulic lime mortar a versatile mortar made from hydraulic lime; it has good properties of elasticity, permeability and resistance to weather, fungal growth etc., and is used for general plastering, rendering and renovation work on traditional and vernacular buildings.

hydraulic spraying see airless spraying.

hydraulic test see water test.

hydraulics the science of fluids in motion and at rest, especially that of fluids in pipes.

hydro-electric power station a power station in which electricity is produced by a mass of moving water flowing under gravity through generating turbines.

hydrocarbon any chemical compound containing hydrogen and carbon.

hydrochloric acid a corrosive solution of hydrogen chloride, **HCl**, in water, used in galvanizing, steel pickling and the electronics industry.

hydrodynamics the science of fluids in motion.

hydrogen the most common chemical element, **H**, a colourless, odourless gas which burns explosively in the presence of oxygen to form water.

hydrogen chloride a corrosive, gaseous chemical compound, **HCl**, which, when mixed with water, becomes hydrochloric acid.

hydrogen peroxide a chemical compound, **H_2O_2**; an oxidizing, antiseptic and bleaching agent.

hydrogen sulphide a poisonous, pungent, gaseous chemical compound, **H_2S**, used in metallurgy and in the manufacture of chemicals.

hydrographical map see chart.

hydrography the scientific charting and survey of seas and inland waterways to survey depths, tides and their suitability for navigation.

hydrology the science of water and its properties; especially as applied to its circulation in nature.

hydrolysis a chemical reaction of water with a substance to form more new substances.

hydrometer a device for measuring the specific gravity of a liquid.

hydrophilic attracted to or having a tendency to absorb water.

hydrophobic having a tendency to repel water.

hydrophobic cement, water-repellent cement; a form of Portland cement whose particles are protected with a water-repellant treatment such as wax, worn off during mixing, which prevents it from setting during storage or transport.

hydrostatic head, hydrostatic pressure; the pressure of a liquid measured at any point; it is the depth of the liquid multiplied by its density.

hydrostatic level see water level.

hydrostatic pressure see hydrostatic head.

hydrostatics the science of fluids at rest.

hydroxide a chemical compound containing a negatively charged OH ion.
see aluminium hydroxide.
see sodium hydroxide.

hygrometer, moisture meter; a device for measuring the relative humidity of air.

hygroscopic a description of a solid with the tendency to absorb water from air containing water vapour.

hygroscopic moisture the adsorbed or capillary moisture in a substance such as soil when in contact with air.

Hyksos period a period in ancient Egyptian history encompassing the 13th to 17th dynasties from c.1720 to 1567 BC.

Hylotrupes bajulus see house longhorn beetle.

hypabyssal rock, dyke rock, transitional igneous rock; types of igneous rock formed from magma hardening in channels and vents in the earth's crust; their use in the building industry is minimal due to the relatively small size of deposits.

hypaethral, hypethral; in classical architecture, referring to a building which is fully or partly open to the sky. →85, →86

hyperbola a mathematical curve generated from two points such that the difference in distance from any point on the line to the two foci is a constant.

hyperbolic paraboloid roof a shell roof shaped like a butterfly in profile, formed from the three-dimensional curvature of a hyperbolic parabola.

hypermedia computer data structured with interconnected links to simplify access, cross-reference and use.

Hyper Realism see Super Realism.

hyperstatic frame see statically indeterminate frame.

hypertext in information technology, text in hypermedia files which can be activated to provide an electronic link to associated computer files.

hyperthyrum in Greek architecture, a decorative cornice or lintel over an opening such as a window or doorway.

hypethral see hypaethral. →86

Hypnum triquetrum see moss green.

hypocaust in classical Roman architecture, an underfloor room heating system using voids or channels through which hot air is introduced from a central furnace; also the underfloor space itself.

hypogaion Gk; see hypogeum. →90

hypogaeum Lat.; see hypogeum. →90

hypogeum, hypogaeum; a subterranean structure hewn out of rock; an underground mine, room, crypt, basement or burial chamber; Greek form is hypogaion. →90

hyposcaenium Latin form of hyposkenion (Gk). →89

hyposcenium see hyposkenion. →89

hyposkenion, hyposcaenium (Lat.), hyposcenium; Gk; in classical architecture, a low wall in front of the stage in a theatre. →89

hypostyle hall a hall in an Egyptian temple whose roof is supported by a dense grid of thick columns. →72

hypotenuse in geometry, the longest side of a right-angled triangle.

hypotrachelion see hypotrachelium. →81

hypotrachelium Lat.; the upper part or groove in the shaft of a Doric column beneath the trachelion; Greek form is hypotrakhelion. →81

I

ianua Lat.; the exterior door of a Roman dwelling.

I-beam any steel, concrete or timber beam with an upper and lower flange connected to a central web, I shaped in cross-section. →30
see I-section. →34

ibis see Thoth. →74

ice blue a shade of greenish blue which takes its name from the colour of the feathers of the kingfisher bird (Alcedo atthis).

ice rink, skating rink; **1** an open-air artificial area of ice for skating and other winter sports.
2 a building containing an area of ice for skating and spectator seating.

icebox see freezing compartment.

icon 1 a Greek or Russian Orthodox religious painting on metal or wooden panels, of traditionally predefined subject matter and style.
see *icon in Byzantine domical church* illustration. →96
2 in computer graphics and multimedia, a hypermedia symbol representing a program or file.

Iconoclasm a religious dispute over the holiness of religious icons and images used in worship, culminating in their destruction and prohibition by the Byzantine emperor Leo III in 730 AD.

iconodule a person who opposes Iconoclasm and venerates religious images or icons.

iconography in painting, the study of portraits and investigation of symbolic subject matter.

iconology the interpretation of the subject matter of a work of art with respect to its wider cultural and historical background.

iconostasis in Byzantine and Russian and Greek orthodox church architecture, an ornate painted screen containing icons, dividing the altar from the nave; a wall of icons. →96

icosahedron a solid shape whose surface is composed of twenty planar faces.

ichthys Latin form of the Greek word ikhthus, see fish. →119, →123

ideal city a working city model based on utopian and ideal socio-political values, taking into account the zoning of industry, traffic, parks, workplaces and residential areas for the benefit of its inhabitants. →105
see *ideal city* illustration. →105

ideal gas, perfect gas; a hypothetical model of a gas obeying simple physical laws but without cohesion between particles in the gas.

idealism in aesthetics and the arts, the concept of a perfect or ideal set of circumstances.

ideal point the point at which parallel lines in a parallel projection or axonometric drawing theoretically meet, at an infinite distance away from the observer.

ideas competition an architectural or town planning competition in which the aim is to develop outline solutions which can be used as a base for a more specific design.

idigbo [*Terminalia ivorensis*] a hardwood from the West African rainforests with yellow to yellow-brown timber; used for its attractive appearance in joinery and floors.

idyll a typical theme in painting from the late 1700s, the depiction of idealized rustic and pastoral scenes.

IFHP International Federation for Housing and Planning.

igneous rock, magmatic rock, pyrogenic rock, fusion rock, flow rock, massive rock, eruptive rock; types of rock which have formed from the solidification of volcanic magma, including plutonic, hypabyssal and volcanic rocks; types included as separate entries are listed below.
acidic rock, acid rock.
andesite.
basalt.
basic rock.
diabase, traprock.
diorite.
dolerite.
dyke rock, see hypabyssal rock.
effusive rock, volcanic rock.
extrusive rock, volcanic rock.
gabbro.
granite.
granodiorite.
greenstone.
hypabyssal rock, dyke rock, transitional igneous rock.
intermediate rock.
lava rock.
pegmatite.
peridotite.
plutonic rock, plutonite.
porphyry.
pyroxenite.
quartz diorite.
syenite.
transitional igneous rock, see hypabyssal rock.
ultrabasic rock.
volcanic rock, vulcanite, effusive rock, extrusive rock.

ignimbrite, welded tuff; a brown volcanic rock originally formed from fused deposits of glowing hot clouds; used locally as building stone.

ignitability in fire testing, the property of the surface of a sheet or slab material to catch light in the presence of a naked flame.

ignition 1 in the outbreak of a building fire, the initial stage of combustion, catching fire or beginning to burn.
2 see flashover.
3 see ignition point.

ignition point, ignition; in the development of a fire, the lowest temperature at which a material will burst into flame due to spontaneous combustion and continue burning without extra external heat.

ikhthus Gk; see fish. →119, →123

ikria Gk; a wooden grandstand or seating for spectators in an ancient Greek theatre or other event.

ill-proportioned a description of a building or composition without visual or spatial harmony, one out of scale.

illuminance in lighting design, the ratio of luminous flux per area falling on a surface, measured in lux.

illuminated ceiling see luminous ceiling.

illuminated sign any sign to guide traffic, give information or advertise merchandise, incorporating lighting so that it can be seen in the dark.

illumination 1 see lighting.
2 see artificial lighting.
3 the art of decorating manuscripts with ornament, gold leaf, colours etc.; especially those often complex and colourful designs hand-painted by monks for decorating the initial letter of a page. →97

illusionism, trompe l'oeil; in visual art, the use of devices such as perspective which create an illusion of space, depth or reality.

Illusionistic style see Architectural style.
see *Pompeian styles* illustration. →126

illustration a drawn or graphic visualization of a building, depiction of events in a text etc.

ilmenite a violet-black mineral, naturally occurring iron titanite, $FeTiO_3$, an important raw material in the production of titanium.

ima cavea see maenianum primum.
image a two-dimensional graphic or visual representation of something.
image plane see picture plane. →128
image processing software computer programs for displaying, editing, manipulating and enhancing graphic images such as photographs and designs.
image transmission in telecommunications, computer and security installations etc., the transfer of graphic images and film in digital format from one system to another, or from a remote camera to a monitor.
imaginary number in mathematics, a number which is a function of a root of a negative quantity.
imbrex, pl. imbrices; Lat.; a U-shaped roofing tile used in conjunction with a tegula in Italian and Roman tiling, often capped with antefixae at eaves and ridge. →47
imbrices Lat.; plural form of imbrex. →47
immediate settlement, elastic compression, initial settlement; in foundation technology, the slight downward movement of a building which occurs during and immediately after construction, caused by compression of soil grains and gas pockets in the underlying ground due to the weight of the building.
immersion heater see electric water heater.
immersion treatment the preservation of timber by immersing it in a solution of preservative for a specified time.
immersion vibration, poker vibration; the compaction of fresh concrete using an immersion vibrator.
immersion vibrator, internal vibrator, poker vibrator; a vibrating probe fully immersed in fresh concrete to provide compaction through gentle agitation, provided by means of an eccentrically rotating mechanism; see surface vibrator.
immigration the movement of people or populations into a nation from abroad.
impact driver see impact screwdriver.
impact insulation class a measure of the sound caused by impacts such as walking etc. transmitted between adjacent rooms.
impact noise see impact sound.
impact printer a computer printer which imparts images and text on paper by metal hammers or pins pressing against an inked ribbon, as in a typewriter or dot-matrix printer.
impact resistance see impact strength.
impact screwdriver, impact driver; a heavy-duty cast steel hand tool for opening tight screws and bolts by striking with a mallet to produce a turning action.
impact sound, impact noise; in acoustics, sound which arises as the result of an impact on building fabric, such as that of footsteps or a door closing.
impact sound isolation a thin layer of fibrous or porous sheet material laid under hard flooring to prevent vibration, walking impacts etc. being transferred to the floor structure, and to spaces below. →59
impact strength the property of a material which is able to resist forces on impact without permanent deformation or rupture; impact resistance.
impasto in painting, a technique or phenomenon in which the thickness of applied paint creates a textural surface of ridges and depressions; see pastose.
impedance the effective electrical resistance of a component in a circuit at a given frequency of current.
imperfection a feature that depreciates the appearance or lowers the quality of an item, product, surface or finish; a defect.
imperfect manufacture a defect in a piece of timber due to conversion or machining processes.
imperfect market an economic situation in which a single or small number of businesses affect or define the price of goods or services.
imperial referring to a non-metric system of standard weights and measures used by Great Britain and the Commonwealth.
imperial bushel see bushel.
Imperial chapel, capella imperialis (Lat.); a balconied space to the west end of a Carolingian or Romanesque church in which a ruler took part in religious services; a similar space is also found in Byzantine centralized churches; sometimes called a solarium. →98, →99
imperial gallon see gallon.
Imperial gate, porta Caesarea; a ceremonial doorway reserved for the use of the Caesar and his entourage, especially the central entrance doorway of certain types of Byzantine church. →96
imperial gill see gill.
Imperial green, emerald green; a variety of emerald green pigment which has been reduced with an inert pigment.
imperial pint see pint.
imperial standard brick a standard size of brick previously in use in Great Britain with regular dimensions of $8^5/_8" \times 4^1/_8" \times 2^5/_8"$ (219 mm × 104.8 mm × 66.8 mm). →16
implement 1 any tool or simple device used for a particular trade or purpose.
2 see drawing instruments. →130
implementation in town planning, the putting into action of a town plan after all elements have been formulated.
impluvium Lat.; a basin or vessel in the atrium of a Roman dwelling, for collecting rainwater from the inwardly sloping roof surfaces. →88
impost a stone, block, brick or masonry from which the voussoirs of an arch are supported. →22
impost block see dosseret. →115
a corbelled stone at the impost of a masonry arch, on which its voussoirs are supported.
impregnated timber see pressure impregnated timber.
impregnation a process by which timber is saturated with a wood preservative or flame retardant.
imprimatura in painting, a transparent glaze or base tone used over a white canvas before paint is applied.
improved nail see annular nail. →35
improved wood timber whose pores are impregnated with synthetic resins, heated and subjected to pressure, used for floorings and exterior work.
inactive leaf the leaf in a double door which is usually kept locked, against which the active leaf is latched. →50
in-and-out screwdriver see spiral ratchet screwdriver.
in antis 1 Lat.; in classical architecture, a description of a temple whose frontal columns are bounded at either side by extensions of the side walls; see also antis temple. →84
2 henostyle in antis, see henostyle. →77
3 see distyle in antis. →84
inbark, bark pocket, ingrown bark; bark around branches and knots which has become embedded in wood as the tree grows.
inbond a Scottish word for a header or bonder in stonework and brickwork masonry. →20
Inc. abbreviation of incorporated company, see limited company.
Inca architecture the architecture of Aztec cultures in the Peruvian Andes from c.1200 to 1500 AD, highly developed both in organization and technology and characterized by planned walled cities, massive buildings with ground stone joints and ziggurats.
incandescence the emission of light by a heated object or body.

incandescent lamp an electric lamp which produces light by means of a heated tungsten filament suspended in a glass tube in a vacuum or filled with an inert gas.

incense cedar [*Calocedrus decurrens*] a softwood from western USA whose close-grained timber has a fragrant resinous odour and is highly resistant to moisture; used as sawn boards.

incertum see opus incertum. →83

inch 1 abb. **in.** or **"**; an imperial unit of length equal to 25.4 mm.
2 see thumb.

incinerator in waste management, a furnace in which solid waste is disposed of by burning.

incipient decay see dote.

inclination the angle of a slope or line to the horizontal.

inclined, sloping; of a roof, ramp, channel or other planar surface, at an angle to the horizontal.

inclined pile see raking pile. →29

income any money received as salary, sales or other payments by a person or firm.

income tax taxation on earnings from employment and investments.

incorporated company abb. **Inc.**, see limited company.

increscent a crescent shape whose concave side is facing to the left of the viewer, the symbol of a waxing moon prior to a full moon.

Incrustation style, First Pompeian style, Masonry style; a style in decorative stucco wall surfaces from Roman Pompeii, c.200–80 BC, painted in imitation of marble-faced pilasterwork and panelwork.
see *Pompeian styles* illustration. →126

indanthrene a proprietary name for a number of commercial pigments based on anthraquinone and related compounds, especially indanthrone blue and indanthrene yellow, which has replaced traditional Indian yellow.

indanthrene yellow see indanthrene.

indanthrone blue a synthetic organic blue pigment used in oil paints and acrylics for internal use.

indanthrone pigment a group of pigments manufactured from anthraquinone, used for dying fabrics.

indentation see indents. →21

indented cross see cross indented. →118

indented embattled moulding an embattled moulding whose upper protrusions have V-shaped indentations. →125

indented moulding, 1 sawtooth moulding; a decorative moulding consisting of a series of triangular indentations. →124
2 see indented embattled moulding. →125

indented scarf joint see halved and tabled scarf joint.

indented wire steel wire used as reinforcement, with surface indentations to improve its bonding in concrete.

indenting see indents. →21

indents recesses left during masonry construction into which later work, including perpendicular walls, ornament etc. can be bonded; often called reverse toothing. →21

index a table or list of contents of a document, computer file etc., used to determine their location.

index of plasticity see plasticity index.

index of refraction see refractive index.

indiarubber see caoutchouc.

Indian architecture the Hindu, Buddhist, Islamic and Jainist architecture of the Indian subcontinent subsequent to the Indus valley cultures, characterized by walling in mud brick and timber, and lavishly adorned with decorated temples.
see *Asian temples* illustration. →68
see *Asian and Mediterranean columns and capitals* illustration. →69

Indian blue see indigo.

Indian ink a black drawing ink originally made from lampblack and animal glue in China and Japan, used in watercolour painting and calligraphy.

Indian oak see teak.

Indian red see oxide red.

Indian rosewood, East Indian rosewood; [*Dalbergia latifolia*] a reddish violet tropical hardwood with streaked timber; used for high class furniture.

Indian yellow, puree, pwree; a yellow pigment used in the 1900s, originally produced in India by heating the urine of cows fed on mango leaves.

indicating bolt, snib latch; a lock for a WC or bathroom incorporating a dial indicating by colour or words whether the room is occupied. →39

indicator panel, annunciator; any electronic panel with a number of warning lights or LCDs to display the running of a system, activated alarms etc.

indigenous plant, native plant; any species of plant which grows naturally in a locality.

indigo, 1 Indian blue; a deep blue pigment originally extracted from the Indian indigo plant [*Indigofera tinctoria*, *Indigofera anil*] but since made synthetically from coal tar; used mainly as a dyestuff.
2 indigo blue; a shade of blue which takes its name from the colour of the above.
3 see aniline.

indigo blue see indigo.

Indigofera spp. the indigo plant, see indigo, aniline.

indirect cost see overhead.

indirect hot water supply system a hot water system in which hot water is provided by an indirect cylinder or calorifier rather than a boiler.

indirect lighting illumination or task lighting provided by light reflected, refracted or diffused by surfaces; see also direct lighting.

indirect solar radiation see skylight.

indium a soft, white, rare, metallic chemical element, **In**.

indoor market see covered market.

indoor swimming pool see swimming baths.

induced siphonage the sucking out of a water seal in a trap by siphonage caused by pressure differences in a drain, allowing foul air to escape into a room.

inductance 1 the magnitude of electromotive force produced by a change in electrical current in a circuit or conductor.
2 see magnetic induction.

induction hardening a surface-hardening treatment for steel by briefly heating it with a high frequency electrical current and then immediately quenching in water.

induction loop see inductive loop.

inductive loop an aerial wrapped around a building or embedded in construction, which receives electromagnetic signals from a portable transmitter; used in telecommunications and remote control doors etc.; also called an induction loop.

induction convector system, induction unit system; an air-conditioning system in which the temperature of ducted air is regulated locally by hot and cold water pipes.

induction unit a localized air-conditioning unit in which ducted air is blown into a room over coils to heat or cool it; cf. fan coil unit.

induction unit system see induction convector system.

Indus civilization the prehistoric urban culture of the peoples of the Indus valley, India, from 2500 BC up until the Aryan invasion in 1500 BC.

industrial belonging to, concerned with or produced by an industry, factory or plant.

industrial building a building for the production or manufacture of materials, goods and products.

industrial design the design of industrial or consumer artifacts.

industrial effluent liquid waste discharged as waste from an industrial plant, often as environmental pollution.

industrial estate an area of urban land where various types of industry are concentrated; see also industrial park.

industrialized building the construction of buildings using prefabrication, specialized building components and factory-made units to increase site efficiency and speed up construction.

industrial park an industrial estate, usually for manufactured goods of light industry, in which industrial units in an arranged layout are rented out to companies.

industrial suburb see satellite town.

industrial town a town in which the main source of income and jobs is based around a particular industry or industries.

industrial waste solid or liquid waste material left over from an industrial process.

industry large-scale production or manufacture of goods or services.

inert gas see noble gas.

inertia 1 the tendency of a material or body to resist change.

2 the property of a body to remain at rest or move in a straight line at a uniform velocity in the absence of external forces.

3 see law of inertia.

inertia block a thick layer of heavy material onto which mechanical equipment is placed to reduce its resonant frequency and absorb vibration caused by moving or oscillating parts.

inert pigment see extender.

infill, 1 infilling; material used to fill in the spaces in a building frame, such as panels of glass or sheet material held in curtainwalling profiles.

2 the part of a balustrade between the handrail and floor level, which is filled with solid material, glass or obstructing wires or rods to afford protection. →54

infilling see infill.

infiltration 1 the seepage of fresh air into a building through open vents, cracks and construction joints around windows and doors etc. as ventilation.

2 the undesirable leakage of air into construction and spaces.

3 air introduced in such a way, often causing draughts and discomfort.

infiltration rate a measure of the seepage of fresh air into a building, given as m^3/h or litres per second (l/s).

infinite in mathematics, a value which is greater than any possible value, endlessly large.

infirmarium the buildings or spaces in a medieval monastery where the sick and elderly were cared for; an infirmary. →97

infirmary 1 buildings or spaces where the sick and injured of a communal establishment such as a monastery or school are cared for; a hospital; see also infirmarium.

see *infirmary in Carolingian monastery* illustration. →97

2 see valetudinarium. →104

inflammable same as flammable; often confused with its opposite, non-flammable.

inflected arch see ogee arch. →24

inflection point, inflexion point, point of inflection; the point at which a mathematical or geometrical curve changes direction.

inflexion point see inflection point.

influence line in the theory of structures, a graph plotted to show loading at various points along a beam.

information technology the storage, processing and manipulation of information on computer systems.

infrared lamp an electric lamp which produces light and heat from the invisible infrared end of the spectrum.

infrared radiation electromagnetic radiation of a longer wavelength than that of the visible spectrum.

infrared radiator a heater which produces heat by the emission of infrared radiation.

infrasound sound with a frequency below that which can be heard by the human ear, less than about 15–30 Hz.

infrastructure the basic public installations, utilities and facilities, housing, roads, sewers and power, which form the physical foundation of an urban community.

inglenook, chimney-corner, chimney-nook; a seat, seating place or bench integrated into a large traditional open fireplace.

ingot 1 a lump of cast metal prior to manufacture into products and profiles by recasting, rolling, forging or extruding.

2 see steel ingot.

ingrain wallcovering see woodchip wallpaper.

ingrown bark see inbark.

inhabitant one who lives in a dwelling, town, region or country.

inhibitor a substance which slows down a chemical process.

initialization in computing, the setting up of a basic program variable before use.

initial prestress, initial stress; in prestressed concrete, the stretching force applied to prestressing tendons, which is then imparted to the concrete as compressive stress.

initial settlement see immediate settlement.

initial stress see initial prestress.

injection 1 see artificial cementing.

2 see grouting.

injection mortar a wet mix of mortar used for grouting; grout.

injection moulding a method of forming thermoplastics and thermosetting plastics products by heating granulated material and injecting it into a mould.

ink 1 a coloured fluid, often black or dark blue but available in other colours, used in printing and for writing and draughting.

2 see Indian ink.

3 see drawing ink.

ink black a shade of black which takes its name from the colour of black Indian ink.

ink blue a shade of dark blue which takes its name from the colour of blue-coloured ink.

ink eraser, ink rubber; an eraser used for rubbing out ink on draughting film or acetate.

ink-jet printer a printer in which ink is applied to paper in small sprayed jets from continually moving ink heads.

ink pen see pen.

ink rubber see ink eraser.

inland waterway a route for waterbound traffic in a lake, river or canal.

inlay flush decoration made by gluing or casting material of another colour, composition or pattern into surface depressions.

inlet 1 see fresh-air inlet. →58

2 see fresh-air vent. →58

inlet grating the perforated or slatted lid for a gully, through which surface water passes to a drain.

inn, 1 hostel; a public house which provides lodging and food for travellers.

2 see public house.

3 see taberna. →88, →91

inner bark see phloem. →1

inner bastion see cavalier. →104

inner city, central area; the area of a city including and immediately surrounding the city centre.

inner courtyard an enclosed courtyard surrounded by built form such as a residential block, castle or monastery; in a castle it is sometimes called an inner ward. →103

inner leaf the skin of brickwork, blockwork, stonework or concrete cavity wall construction which faces the interior of a building; in concrete construction it is usually loadbearing.
see *concrete inner leaf in concrete frame* illustration. →28
see *inner leaf blockwork in brick house* illustration. →59

inner ply one of the layers or veneers in plywood which are not on the surface. →9

inner sash the sash in a coupled window which faces the interior of a room. →52

inner ward the inner courtyard of a castle or keep. →103

innovation the making of something new, an improvement on or addition to an established process, product or idea, or the commercial realization of an invention.

inorganic referring to a substance which is not found in or derived from living organisms, or one of mineral origin.

inorganic pigment, mineral pigment; a pigment which is either a synthetic metal salt such as zinc oxide, or a treated native earth such as burnt sienna.

inorganic polymer any polymer which does not contain carbon.

input 1 in computing, any information fed into a computer.
2 something introduced for the purpose of effecting a system, such as a business, industry or process.
3 see feed.

input air see supply air.

input device see supply air terminal unit.

input ventilation, pressure ventilation; mechanical ventilation by pumping fresh air into spaces, thus causing internal pressure which forces out stale air.

insanitary a description of a construction or space contaminated by biological pollutants such as bacteria and living microbes which may be a liability to the health of occupants.

inscribed angle in geometry, an angle between two lines whose meeting point is on an arc and which are chords on that arc.

insect mesh see insect screen.

insect screen, fly wire; a fine mesh of metal wire or plastics fixed to a frame to prevent insects from entering a building via windows, doors, eaves etc.; the mesh itself is called insect mesh.

insert see patch.

inserted column see engaged column. →13

inserted plywood plywood in which defects in the surface plies have been repaired with patches of veneer.

inset screw cup see recessed screw cup. →36

inset seat, pad seat; a WC seat with two pads of impervious material fitted to a WC pan.

inside calliper a measuring tool with a pair of curved hinged legs, used for measuring the inside diameter of pipes and other hollow objects.

inside corner the meeting of two perpendicular walls, vertical surfaces etc. which form an angle less than 180°; also called an internal corner or internal angle. →14

inside corner tile a ceramic tile designed for use at the lowest edge of a tiled wall, where it meets the floor. →20

inside corner trowel see internal angle trowel. →43

inside face the face of a piece of sawn timber which is nearest the heart when cut from a log. →2

inside glazing glass or other glazing material that has been added to the inner side of external glazing.

inside start saw see flooring saw.

in situ, cast-in-place (Am.), cast-in-situ; referring to concrete and other similar materials which have been cast fresh on site as opposed to being prefabricated; written in-situ when used as an adjective.

in-situ casting the process of casting materials such as concrete, plaster and flooring compounds in their final place rather than using prefabricated products.

in-situ concrete, cast-in-place concrete (Am.), cast-in-situ concrete; concrete placed on site in formwork rather than having been precast as units.
see *in-situ concrete construction* illustration. →27
see *in-situ concrete floor in floors and flooring* illustration. →44
see *in-situ concrete frame in office building* illustration. →60

in-situ concrete beam a concrete beam which is cast in situ. →27, →60

in-situ concrete column a concrete column which is cast in situ. →27

in-situ concrete floor a floor whose structural concrete slab has been cast in situ. →44

in-situ concrete footing a concrete foundation which is cast in situ. →27

in-situ concrete slab 1 a structural concrete floor slab which has been cast in situ. →44
2 see in-situ floor slab. →27, →60

in-situ concrete wall a concrete wall which is cast in situ. →27

in-situ floor see in-situ concrete floor. →44

in-situ flooring floor surfacing laid or cast in situ.

in-situ floor slab a concrete floor which is cast in situ. →27, →60

in-situ pile see cast-in place pile. →29

in-situ plastering, solid plastering; the process of working with in-situ plasterwork.

in-situ plasterwork, solid plasterwork; ornamental plasterwork cast or laid in its final position, as opposed to being precast and fitted.

in-situ slab see in-situ concrete slab. →44

inspection a periodic survey or check of work at key stages in construction, undertaken on site by a qualified person such as a local authority official, clerk of works or architect to ensure that it meets with building regulations and norms, and is in accordance with the designs; examples included as separate entries are listed below.
building inspection.
final inspection.
fire inspection.
investigation.
property survey.
reinspection.
site inspection.
survey.

inspection cap an end cap for the open end of a drainage pipe, which can be removed for inspection.

inspection chamber, manhole; a subterranean chamber with a removable cover at ground level, usually located outside a building to provide open access for inspection and maintenance of a drainage or sewerage system.

inspection cover an openable cover for an inspection chamber.

inspection door an inspection hatch in a flue.

inspection eye see cleaning eye.

inspection hatch, inspection door; a door or hatch in a casing or ductwork which can be opened for inspection, cleaning, maintenance etc. of a concealed device or construction.

inspector 1 see building control officer.
2 see fire officer.

installation 1 a fixed assembly of appliances, components and fittings which provides a mechanical or electrical service for a building or construction.

2 fitting; the fixing of prefabricated components or services in place and subsidiary work to affect their performance.

3 the fastening in place and connection to a supply of technical appliances and plant.

installation allowance see allowance. →51

installation gap see allowance. →51

installation riser any vertical gas pipe within a building.

installation tolerance the amount, specified in documentation, by which the installation of a component may deviate from that shown in drawings.

instalment see annuity.

instant start lamp, cold start lamp; a fluorescent lamp which lights up immediately after being switched on.

instant tack the spontaneous sticking together of surfaces coated with wet contact adhesive as they are brought together to form a joint.

institute of architects see association of architects.

institute of higher education see university.

institute of technology see polytechnic.

institution see home.

instructions to tenderers in tendering for building work, the requirements and conditions covering the preparation and submission of a tender.

instrument see drawing instruments. →130

insula Lat.; a Roman masonry and concrete tenement block for the labouring classes, often a multistorey structure with commercial premises and workshops (tabernae) at street level; originally the plot of land bounded by urban streets, on which one was built. →88

insulant see insulating material. →44

Insular art the art and culture of the Celtic peoples of Ireland and Britain from 400 to 900 AD, especially illumination of scripts, lettering and calligraphy; characterized by the use of complex intertwined ornament and figures; see also Hiberno-Romanesque architecture. →97

insulated block a lightweight concrete block with an interlayer or core of polystyrene incorporated as thermal insulation during manufacture. →30

insulated flue a prefabricated flue of metal twin-wall construction with fireproof insulation between the inner steel tube and outer sheetmetal sheathing. →56, →58

insulated glazing unit see sealed glazed unit. →53

insulated infill panel opaque infill panels for glazing and curtainwalling systems, containing thermal insulation.

insulated render proprietary rendering systems in which render is applied to wire mesh lathing attached directly to a layer of thermal insulation.

insulating, non-conductive; the property of thermally, acoustically or electrically isolating with a barrier of suitable material to inhibit the flow of heat, sound or electricity.

insulating concrete, insulating lightweight concrete; concrete with a low thermal conductivity and good insulating properties.

insulating glass unit see sealed glazed unit. →53

insulating lightweight concrete see insulating concrete.

insulating material, insulation, insulant; any material used as thermal, electrical or sound insulation. →44

insulation the laying or installation of thermal or acoustic insulation; the insulating layer thus formed; types included as separate entries are listed below.

acoustic insulation, see sound insulation.
electrical insulation.
fire insulation, see fireproofing.
frost insulation. →59
heat insulation, see thermal insulation. →59
insulating material. →44
sound insulation.
thermal insulation. →59
vibration insulation.

insulation bat a preformed panel of thermal insulation such as mineral wool and wood wool slabs.

insulation board see softboard.

insulation clip a thin plastic accessory attached along the length of a wall tie to hold insulation bats in their correct position in a masonry cavity wall; also called an insulation retainer. →22

insulation glass 1 see sealed glazed unit. →53

2 sound insulation glass, see sound control glass.

insulation retainer see insulation clip. →22

insurance 1 financial protection against damage, destruction, injury, theft or loss in the form of regular payments to an insurance company, which will pay compensation in the event of these happening.

2 see fire insurance.

insurance premium a payment made towards an insurance policy or agreement.

INT interior adhesive.

intaglio a method of making graphic prints by etching or engraving a pattern into a metal plate, which is then inked, excess ink wiped clean and a print taken from ink that has remained in the depressions.

intaglio rilevato see sunk relief.

intarsia, tarsia; decorative inlaid work in mosaic of various colours and materials, especially wooden inlay from the Italian Renaissance; see marquetry.

integer in mathematics, a whole number from one to nine and from minus one to minus nine.

integral in mathematics, a function which satisfies a given differential equation.

integrated services digital network see ISDN.

integrated system an air-conditioning or mechanical ventilation system using in-built ducting, air-handling luminaires etc.

integrity 1 see soundness.

2 in computer-aided design, the quality of a group whose geometry is shared among all unchanged copies of a group.

intelligent fire alarm see addressable system.

intense blue see phthalocyanine blue.

intensity 1 the force with which a phenomenon occurs.

2 see colour intensity.

3 see sound intensity.

intensity level see sound intensity level.

intent see letter of intent.

interactive referring to a computerized system in which there is a two-way flow of information so the user can actively participate in events.

intercepting trap, 1 interceptor, interceptor trap; a drainage fitting or construction which inhibits the passage of unwanted gravel, silt, oil etc. in the waste water to a drainage system.

2 see petrol intercepting trap.

interceptor 1 see intercepting trap.

2 see oil interceptor.

3 see petrol interceptor.

interceptor trap see intercepting trap.

interchange a major road junction in which traffic can flow freely from one road or motorway to another without stopping or slowing down; most often a grade-separated junction with a number of ramps leading from carriageway to carriageway; types included as separate entries are listed below. →63

cloverleaf junction. →63
diamond junction. →63
grade-separated fork junction. →63
roundabout interchange, see roundabout junction. →63
trumpet junction. →63

intercolumnation see intercolumniation. →77

intercolumniation (Lat. intercolumnium); in classical architecture, the systematic spacing of columns expressed as multiples of column diameters; see araeostyle, diastyle, eustyle, pycnostyle and systyle; also written as intercolumnation. →77

intercom see internal telephone system.

interest a sum of money charged for money borrowed or paid for money invested, primarily stated as a percentage of the whole.

interface 1 in computing, hardware and software which enables functioning of associated devices.
2 see user interface.

interference 1 in wave physics, the phenomenon in which two waves will combine to reinforce or lessen their effects.
2 see noise.

intergrown knot, 1 live knot; a knot in seasoned timber whose grain is intergrown with the surrounding wood. →1
2 see red knot. →1

interim application in contract administration, a document drawn up periodically by a contractor requesting fees owed for work carried out.

interim payment in contract administration, a payment made at any given stage in construction for work carried out up to that point.

interior 1 the inside of a building, space, component, installation etc.
2 that part of a building bounded by internal walls, ceilings and floors.
3 see interior design.
4 see interior architecture.

interior adhesive, INT; adhesive intended primarily for interior use, unresistant to prolonged damp, the weather and boiling water.

interior architecture architectural design relating to the volumes, colours, details, materials and spaces within a building.

interior decoration see interior design.

interior design 1 the discipline and profession of designing interior spaces, including the planning of layouts and design and choice of surface finishes and furnishings.
2 decor, interior, interior decoration; the wall and floor finishes, surfaces, materials and treatments, colour scheme, layouts and furnishing of a building or space.

interior designer a trained person or professional consultant responsible for designing and specifying decor and furnishings for the interior of a building.

interior glazing see internal glazing. →52, →60

interior luminaire a non-weatherproof luminaire designed only for use within a building.

interior paint, internal paint; paint suitable for interior use only; often emulsion paint.

interior perspective a perspective drawing of the interior of a building or space.

interior plaster plaster suitable for use on interior walls.

interior plywood plywood intended for interior use, glued with adhesives which have low resistance to humidity.

interior view a photograph, drawing or computer rendering of the interior space of a building.

interior wall, partition; a wall inside a building, neither of whose faces are open to the outside.

interlace, 1 entrelace; decorative ornament of complex intertwined bands or lines. →125
2 see knotwork. →108

interlaced arches, interlacing arches, laced arches; a series of round arches or arched shapes in which adjacent arches overlap one half-arch width. →124

interlacing arches see interlaced arches. →124

interlocked grain, interlocking grain, twisting fibres; timber grain produced in alternate groups of growth rings forming spirals in reverse directions round the tree trunk; it is generally difficult to work and used in decorative veneers.

interlocking grain see interlocked grain.

interlocking paver, interpaver; a proprietary concrete paving product preformed in a variety of shapes and laid in groups to form patterned surfaces; sometimes called a key or interweave paver, depending on its profile. →15

interlocking tile a clay or concrete roof tile whose edges are moulded with a series of grooves to fit into corresponding mouldings in adjacent tiles. →47

intermediate floor, upper floor; the horizontal construction between two stories of a building. →28

intermediate floor construction, upper floor construction; the horizontal layers of construction which make up an intermediate floor. →59
see *intermediate floor construction in brick house* illustration. →59

intermediate landing, stair landing; a horizontal platform between two flights of stairs, or at the top of a stair between two floors. →45, →61

intermediate rail 1 a rail between the top and bottom rails of a panelled door to provide added stiffness. →51
2 a horizontal rail fixed to balusters or verticals between floor level and the handrail of a balustrade. →54

intermediate rock types of igneous rock whose silica content is between 52% and 66%.

intermediate sash the middle of three window sashes in a triply glazed window unit. →52

intermediate sheet in built-up roofing, a smooth middle layer of bitumen felt bonded to the underlying base sheet and cap sheet above.

intermodulation interference in an electronic or communications system caused by the transmittance of signals of different frequencies travelling in the same media.

internal angle see inside corner. →14

internal angle trowel, inside corner trowel; a plasterer's trowel for smoothing internal corners in plasterwork with a handled blade of bent steel sheet. →43

internal corner see inside corner. →14

internal door a door between two adjacent spaces in a building, neither face of which is exposed to the outside.

internal force a force occurring within and restrained by a structural member, material, component etc.

internal friction see viscosity.

internal glazing glazing not exposed to the outside; a window or glass screen in an internal partition. →52, →60

internal paint see interior paint.

internal plaster see interior plaster.

internal surface the surface of a wall or building component facing towards the inside.

internal surface resistance value see RSI-value.

internal telephone system, intercom; an electrical communications system for use within a building or complex.

internal tooth washer a tooth washer with serrations along its inner circumference. →37

internal vibrator see immersion vibrator.

internal wall see partition. →28

International Federation for Housing and Planning, IFHP; an international organization founded in 1913 and based on the ideals of Ebenezer Howard, to provide professional advice and education on housing and town planning matters in certain UN organizations.

international Gothic, international style; a style of naturalistic, mostly secular painting and decorative art originating in France and Burgundy towards the end of the 1300s and spreading quickly to Italy and Germany.

International Organization for Standardization, ISO; an organization which aims to unify units of weights and measures, to carry out research on measurement technology and to approve and recommend units for the SI.

international style 1 an architectural style in Western Europe and America from the early 1900s based on the functionalist non-vernacular ideal, and making use of modern materials such as concrete, steel, glass and render.

2 see international Gothic.

International System of Units, SI, Système Internationale d'Unites; an internationally accepted series of measures of basic quantities and units such as mass (kilogram, kg), distance (metre, m), time (second, s), temperature (kelvin, K), electrical current (ampere, A), light intensity (candela, cd). →Table 2, →Table 3

interpaver see interlocking paver. →15

interrasile see opus interrasile.

interrupter see pipe interrupter.

intersecting barrel vault see groin vault. →25

intersecting tracery Gothic tracery in which parallel mullions are bent over at their upper ends to form a series of interlaced pointed arches. →110

intersections, method of see method of intersections. →127

intersole see mezzanine.

interspace the gas-filled cavity between adjacent sheets of glass in a sealed glazed unit.

intervallum road see via sagularis. →104

interview room a private room in which consultation or interviews are undertaken.

interweave paver a specially shaped concrete paving unit which is laid to create a regular undulating pattern. →15

interzonal in traffic planning, relating to movement between two different zones.

intonaco the smooth uppermost coat of three layers of plaster, onto which a fresco is painted.

intrados the lower line, underside, soffit or face of an arch. →22

intrazonal in traffic planning, relating to movement within a single zone.

intruder alarm system a warning system of bells, lights and other means which react to the presence of unauthorized entrants to a building.

intruder glazing glazing designed to prevent the forced entrance of intruders to a building via its windows; types are listed below.

see alarm glass.

anti-bandit laminated glass.

anti-vandal glass.

armour-plated glass, see bullet-resistant laminated glass.

blast-resistant laminated glass.

security glass.

security glazing.

toughened glass. →53

intrusion the forceful and undesired entry of a person or persons into an area or building.

intrusion concrete see grouted concrete.

intrusive rock see plutonic rock.

intumescent glass see laminated intumescent glass.

intumescent paint, flame-retardant paint; a surface coating for metals which changes into a fire-resisting and insulating foam in the event of excess heat from a fire.

invected cross see cross invected. →118

invected moulding see scallop moulding. →124

inverse see reciprocal.

invert, invert level; the level of the lowest part of the inside of a channel, pipeline or other vessel in a drainage system.

inverted arch an arch constructed upside down, usually for structural reasons. →24

inverted beam a beam which protrudes above the plane of the surface which it supports, so that its soffit is at the same level as the soffit of the floor or roof construction.

inverted cross, 1 any cross motif rendered upside down.

2 reversed cross, St Peter's cross; a Latin cross whose upper limb is longest of all, supposedly symbolizing the cross on which Peter was crucified upside down.

inverted roof see upside down roof.

inverted siphon see sag pipe.

invert level see invert.

investigation, 1 survey; the inspection, measuring and researching of ground conditions, condition of repair of existing structures etc. prior to sale, construction, design etc.

2 see geotechnical survey.

3 see site investigation.

investment the placing of funds, shares or property in enterprises with the expectation that they produce a profit or gather interest.

invisible hinge, secret hinge; a hinge which is not visible when the door to which it is fixed is both open or closed; see also concealed hinge.

invitation to tender, call for bids (Am.); in project management, an invitation to selected firms to submit tenders, or an announcement that tenders are invited to carry out certain work.

invited competition an architectural or planning competition in which participation is restricted to those invited by the organizer; see also open competition.

invoice, itemized bill; a document or bill listing goods and services provided, and stating money owed for them.

involuntary condemnation proceeding see compulsory purchase.

inward opening referring to a window casement or door which opens inwards with respect to the exterior of a building.

iodine a black, solid chemical element, **I**, which turns directly to a purple gas when heated.

iodine number see iodine value.

iodine value, iodine number; in chemistry, a measure of the degree of unsaturation of an oily substance, defined by the mass of iodine taken up by 100 grams of the substance.

ion in chemistry, an atom or molecule which has an electric charge; see anion, cation.

ion exchange a chemical process of purifying and softening water in which an additive (zeolite) is introduced to exchange pollutant dissolved salts with less harmful ones.

Ionic pertaining to the Ionic order. →80

Ionic base 1 a column base used with the classical Ionic order, usually differentiated as an Attic base or a Samian base. →80, →81

2 see Attic base. →81

3 see Samian base. →81

Ionic capital a capital surmounting a column of the classical Ionic order, with characteristic paired volutes over an egg and dart moulding. →80, →81

Ionic column a column of the classical Greek Ionic order, with fluting, a voluted capital and Ionic base; considerably more slender than those of the Doric order. →78, →80

Ionic cross see Celtic cross. →117

Ionic cyma in classical ornamentation, a cyma moulding enriched with egg and dart ornament. →82

Ionic order a classical Greek order originating in Ionian Greece, characterized by fluted columns, a voluted capital, a base and an entablature with dentils. →78, →79

see *Ionic order* illustration. →80

see *classical Greek orders* illustration. →78

see Roman Ionic order. →79

see *Roman amphitheatre* illustration. →90

see *superimposed orders* illustration. →114

Ionic portal see *historical styles of portal* illustration. →113

ionization chamber smoke detector a smoke detector which reacts to a voltage difference between two ionization chambers, occurring in the presence of combustion gases.

iotite see cordierite.

IR isoprene rubber.

iridium a white metal, **Ir**, used in hard metal alloys.

Irish bridge in traffic engineering, a paved ford in mountainous areas with a culvert or pipes to carry water and sewage beneath the roadway at low flow levels, which overflows during heavy rainfall.

iroko [*Chlorophora excelsa*] a tropical African hardwood whose yellow-brown to dark brown timber is strong and highly durable; used as a substitute for teak.

iron 1 a common, pale-coloured, strong metal, **Fe**, used primarily as a basic ingredient of steel, alloyed with carbon to improve its hardness and corrosion resistance.
2 see plane iron.

Iron Age a prehistorical or historical period, running concurrent with the Bronze Age from c.1200 BC to 1 AD, during which implements were forged from iron.

iron arsenide see löllingite, **$FeAs_2$**.

iron blue see Prussian blue.

iron brown see Prussian brown.

iron carbide see cementite.

iron carbonate $FeCO_3$, see siderite, iron spar, sparry ironstone.

iron disulphide see iron pyrites.
see marcasite.

ironmongery 1 see hardware.
2 door ironmongery, see door furniture. →51

ironmongery schedule, hardware schedule; a design and contract document listing and specifying metal fittings, hardware and components for doors and windows in a construction project.

iron nickel sulphide see pentlandite.

iron oxide, 1 ferrous oxide; a dark greenish black chemical compound, **FeO**, used as a pigment in glasses.
2 ferric oxide, red iron oxide, haematite; a red chemical compound, **Fe_2O_3**, used as a polishing agent and as a red pigment.
see limonite, brown iron ore, **$Fe_2O_3.nH_2O$**.
see haematite, hematite, **Fe_2O_3**.
3 ferrous ferric oxide, black iron oxide; a black chemical compound, **Fe_3O_4**, used as pigment, polishing agent and in magnetic coatings for computer disks and tapes.
see magnetite, black iron oxide, magnetic iron ore: **Fe_3O_4**.
4 brown iron oxide, see burnt sienna.

iron pyrites, pyrite, sulphur-ore; a brassy yellow mineral, natural iron disulphide, **FeS_2**, an important source of sulphur, sulphuric acid and iron sulphide, and also gold and copper, which it contains in small quantities.

iron spar see siderite.

iron sulphide FeS, see pyrrhotite, pyrrhotine.

iron titanite $FeTiO_3$, see ilmenite.

ironworks a factory where iron or iron goods are produced.

iron wire see binding wire.

iron yellow see Mars yellow.

irrational number in mathematics, a number, such as pi, which cannot be expressed exactly with a finite series of digits.

irregular bond, random bond; a brickwork bond in which bricks in consecutive courses overlap, but with no regular repeating pattern. →17

irregular grain grain in a piece of timber which is not straight due to natural abnormalities in the wood.

irregular polygon a planar many-sided figure whose sides are not of equal length.

irrigation the introduction of piped, channelled or sprinkled water to agricultural land and arid landscaping.

irrigation channel an open waterway for the irrigation of agricultural land.

irrigation drain see subsoil drain.

irritation causing the ability of a material or substance to cause a rash and other physical irritation.

Isatis tinctoria see woad.

ISDN, integrated services digital network; a telecommunications network making use of optical fibres for the simultaneous transmission of carrying voice, text and video.

I-section, 1 I-beam, UB section, universal beam, joist; a structural steel beam section formed by rolling, whose uniform cross-section resembles the letter I and whose height is over 1.2 times its width. →34
2 similarly shaped non-structural sections in other metals. →34

Ishtar, star of see star of Ishtar. →120

isinglass 1 mica, especially that found in thin sheets.
2 see fish glue.

Isis in ancient Egyptian mythology, consort and sister of Osiris, mother of Horus, daughter of Nut and Geb, depicted with a head-dress of the solar disc surrounded by cow's horns; symbolic as the divine Mother, and, by extension, of all women, motherhood, purity and sexuality; 'Eset' in Egyptian, 'Isis' in Greek. →74

iskhegaon Gk; see analemma. →89

Islamic architecture, Moslem architecture, Muslim architecture, Saracenic architecture; sacred architecture from Islam at the time of the crusades, characterized by use of polychromy and rich ornament combined with local motifs.
see *Abbasid spiral minaret* illustration. →67

island see refuge.

ISO International Organization for Standardization.

isocephaly in painting, especially that of the classical and Renaissance periods, the composition of human figures in such a way that their heads are all at the same height, regardless of posture.

isocyanurate see polyisocyanurate.

isodomic construction masonry laid in courses of equal height.
see *Pompeian styles* illustration. →126

isodomum see opus isodomum. →83

isolated footing see pad foundation. →29

isolating membrane see separating layer.

isolating varnish a general name for thin varnishes sprayed on to recently dried paint to provide a base for overpainting or correction.

isolation mount see vibration insulator.

isomer in chemistry, an atom which has the same atomic weight as another atom, but different radioactive properties.

isometric 1 relating to isometry, of equal measurement.
2 in geometrical projection, drawing and draughting, a system of representation of three-dimensional objects in two dimensions using three axes which are 120° apart and in which all measurements are to the same scale.

isometric projection 1 'of equal measurement'; in general, any axonometric or oblique projection drawing in which all lines parallel to the three main axes are drawn to the same relative scale. →127
2 in particular a conventional axonometric drawing constructed by extending a plan drawn on axes skewed to 30° on either side of the vertical to a dimensioned height, with all lines parallel to the three main axes, which are 120° apart, drawn to the same scale; the most common form, properly classified as an orthographic isometric projection. →127

Isonandra gutta see gutta-percha.

isophot see isophote.

isophote, isophot; in lighting design, one of a number of theoretical lines or contours on a drawing representing points of equal light intensity.

isoprene rubber, IR; a synthetic rubber, similar to natural rubber, often found in conjunction with other polymers such as isobutene in butyl, used for inner tubes and gaskets.

Isoptera spp. see termite.

isosceles referring to a triangle or trapezoid which has two mirrored sides of equal length.

isosceles trapezoid a planar four-sided figure in which no sides are parallel and two opposite sides are of equal length.

isosceles triangle a triangle in which two sides are of the same length. →108

isostatic frame see statically determinate frame.

isotope in chemistry, an atom of a particular element which has a different atomic weight but similar chemical properties.

isotropic referring to a material or substance which displays the same properties in all directions.

isotropic slab concrete floor slab construction whose inlaid reinforcement is of the same magnitude in both directions.

Italian arch a round or pointed arch whose intrados and extrados are constructed from different centres so that the archivolt is thicker at the apex than at the base; see Italian pointed arch, Florentine arch. →23

Italianate referring to any architecture or ornamentation which adopts the styling and motifs of the Italian Renaissance.

Italian blue see Egyptian blue.

Italian earth see burnt sienna.

Italian pointed arch a pointed arch whose intrados and extrados are constructed from different centres so that the archivolt is thicker at the apex than at the base. →23

Italian Renaissance **1** see quattrocento, Italian early Renaissance.
2 see cinquecento, Italian high Renaissance.
3 see Mannerism.

Italian Romanesque see Byzantine architecture.

Italian round arch see Florentine arch. →23

Italian tiling, pan and roll tiles; roof tiling in which the gaps in a lower course of flat tiles with side lips (tegula) are covered with a course of U-shaped tiles (imbrex), laid with concave side down. →47

italicum see opus italicum.

itemized bill see invoice.

iteration in mathematics, the process of using a function or formula repeatedly to achieve a closer approximation to an answer.

itinera versurarum the side doors leading from the wings of a Roman theatre to the stage area; see parados. →89

ivory, natural, platinum blonde, sand; a shade of yellowish grey which takes its name from the colour of material from the tusks of an elephant.

ivory black a strong black pigment consisting of impure carbon obtained from burnt and ground bones, originally the tusks of elephants; synonymous with bone black.

ivy green a shade of dark green which takes its name from the colour of the leaves of the ivy plant [*Hedera helix*].

ivy leaf a Gothic decorative motif based on the leaf of the climbing plant ivy, *Hedera helix*.

iwan, eyvan; in Parthian, Sassanid and Islamic architecture, a three-sided barrel-vaulted hall whose fourth side is open and arched.

J

Jacaranda [*Jacaranda spp.*] a group of South American tropical hardwood shrubs and trees with hard and dark timber.
jacaranda brown see burnt umber.
jack see jacking device.
jackal see Anubis. →74
jack arch see flat arch. →23
jacked pile in underpinning work, any pile forced into the ground in sections using the weight of the overlying building.
jack hammer a large hand-operated percussive implement powered by compressed air, used for breaking, demolishing and the digging of stone.
jacking device, jack; in concretework, a hydraulic or screw device attached to slipform to raise it at regular intervals.
jack knife see penknife.
jack plane a standard sized bench plane (320 mm–360 mm long).
jack rafter in timber roof construction, a shortened rafter running between eaves and hip or valley and ridge.
jack shore a slanting member of a raking shore which supports a riding shore.
Jacobean architecture a late Renaissance architectural style in England during the reign of James I (1603–1625); found primarily in secular palaces and country houses, and characterized by the use of classical elements, Dutch gables and roof turrets.
Jacobethan a term used loosely to describe a fusion of the Jacobean and Elizabethan style in English architecture.
jacuzzi a recreational or treatment bath designed for more than one person, incorporating water jets for massage etc.; see also whirlpool bath.
jade a hard, green, blue or white sodium aluminium silicate mineral used principally for ornament and as jewellery; a general name for the minerals jadeite and nephrite.
see nephrite.
see jadeite.
jade green a shade of green which takes its name from the colour of jade.
jadeite a hard greenish mineral, often cut for decoration as jade.
Jagello see Jagiello.
jagged-shank nail see annular nail. →35
Jagiello, Jagello; Polish late Gothic architecture from the 1400s, which takes its name from Wladyslaw II Jagiello, king of Poland 1386–1434.
jail see prison.
jailhouse see prison.
jamb 1 a vertical abutment on either side of a door or window opening. →51, →111
2 see reveal.
3 the vertical side member of a door or window frame.
closing jamb, see shutting jamb. →50, →51
door jamb. →50, →51
window jamb. →52, →111
hanging jamb. →50, →51
shutting jamb, closing jamb. →50, →51
4 a vertical timber at the edge of an opening in log or traditional timber frame construction, to which a door or window frame is fixed.
jamb anchor a metal strip used to fix a door or window frame to surrounding construction.
jamb filler a preformed flashing of sheetmetal, used at the side of a door or window opening to cast out water.
jamb figure a carved column figure decorating the jamb columns or recesses in the main portal of a medieval church; also called a jamb statue. →113
jamb lining a timber board used to cover the jamb of an opening.
jamb mounted door closer a door closer mounted to the door jamb and hinged edge of the door leaf.
jamb post, cripple stud; in timber frame construction, a post which supports a lintel over an opening.
jamb statue see jamb figure. →113
janitor see caretaker.
Japanese architecture the traditional architecture of Japan from 500 AD, characterized by temples, pavilions and dwellings with fine crafted timberwork and intricate jointing.
see *Asian temples* illustration. →68
Japanese larch [*Larix kaempferi, Larix leptolepis*] a hardy softwood found in Japan and the British Isles, whose timber is used for sawn boards.
Japanese mon see mon. →120
Japanese oak [*Quercus mongolica*] an Asian hardwood with relatively durable pale yellow timber; used in construction, for furniture and in boat-building.
Japanese paper 1 thin, tough, absorbent, silky paper used in printing.
2 a machine-made equivalent of China paper.
Japan scraper one of a set of simple steel-bladed spatulas with rounded corners and plastic or wooden handles, designed to apply and shape plaster and putty, remove paint etc. →41
jaquemart a decorative mechanical bellringing figure in a medieval clocktower.
jarrah [*Eucalyptus marginata*] a durable and resistant Australian hardwood with pink to dark red timber, used for heavy constructional work, flooring, panelling and veneers.
jasper 1 a microcrystalline variety of the mineral chalcedony, varying in colour and pattern, used as gemstones and for ornament.
2 jasper (red); see coral red.
jaune brilliant see Naples yellow.
jaune d'antimoine see Naples yellow.
Java cotton see kapok.
Jennings pattern bit an auger bit with a double helically shaped shank for drilling deep accurate holes in wood. →42
jenny leg calliper, odd leg caliper; a calliper with one leg ending in a point and the other turned in at its base, used for scribing lines parallel to a surface.
Jericho see Cretan maze. →123
jerkinhead roof see half-hipped roof. →46
Jerusalem see Cretan maze. →123
see road of Jerusalem. →123
Jerusalem cross a cross potent which has a small cross situated at the angle between each limb; also known as the crusaders' cross, cross of Palestine or fivefold cross. →118
Jesse window a church window whose tracery and stained glass bear motifs from the Tree of Jesse, symbolizing the family tree of Christ.
Jesuit architecture Baroque church architecture in Europe from 1580 to 1670; also decorative Baroque in Mexico and Latin America.
Jesus monogram in religious art and architecture, the symbolic monogram IHS, IHC or JHS, standing for 'In hoc signo (vinces)' (in this sign (you shall conquer); Lat.), 'Iesus hominum salvator' (Jesus saviour of mankind), 'In hoc (cruce) salus' (in this (cross)

salvation), or 'Jesus Christos Soter' (Jesus Christ Saviour); I H and S are also the first three letters (iota, eta, sigma) of the Greek spelling of Jesus. →119

jet see jet inlet.

jet inlet, jet, nozzle; in mechanical ventilation, a small-bore terminal device which produces a stream of air in a particular direction.

jetting the cleaning of a pipeline by forcing a high pressure stream of water through it.

jetty, 1 getee, gettiez, jutty; a projection of a traditional timber frame building outwards at first floor level.
2 a structure which projects into the sea or natural body of water, to which boats can be moored.

jib, boom; a main horizontal or slanting beam attached to the vertical mast of a crane or lifting device, from which loads are carried.

jig a device used to guide the blade of a machine tool when cutting repetitive patterns or milling; any similar implement for a specific job of work.

jigsaw, 1 bayonet saw, sabre saw; a power operated saw with an oscillating blade for cutting curves and openings in board.
2 see fretsaw.

job 1 a design or building project, the work involved therein.
2 see jobbing order.

jobbing order, job; small and relatively basic building works which involve simple agreements and minimal site administration and organization.

job card, production card; in stonework, a card which lists the type of masonry, scope of work, size and shape of stones etc. for any particular job.

job description a statement of the tasks, skills and responsibilities involved in a particular position of employment.

joggle 1 in oblique timber jointing, a shaped abutment in one piece which bears the thrust of another.
2 see joggle piece. →3

joggle beam a built-up timber beam in which the timbers are held in place with joggles or cogged pieces. →7

joggled arch, crossette; a masonry arch in which adjacent voussoirs are cut with rebates and interlocked. →23

joggle piece, joggle; an extra cogged piece sometimes added to tie a timber scarf joint or built-up beam together. →3

joggle post see king post. →33

joggle-spliced scarf joint a timber lengthening joint which makes use of a joggle piece to fix the pieces together. →3

joggle tenon joint see stub tenon joint. →5

joggle truss a timber truss in which the chord or tie beam is above a vertical joggle post; the end of the post is triangulated with the ends of the chord by diagonal braces.

John see eagle. →119

joiner a tradesman responsible for the non-structural timberwork such as furniture, interiors and panelling in a building.

joiner saw see bench saw.

joiner's chisel see paring chisel. →41

joiner's cramp, bar cramp, sash cramp; a large cramp with a long bar along which adjustable stops can be placed, used for holding large objects in compression while they are being glued.

joiner's hammer a medium sized hammer with an octagonal or bell head and claw or wedge-shaped peen, used by a joiner. →40

joinery, finish carpentry (Am.); fine woodwork such as doors, window frames, trim and panelling in a building.

joinery joints see mortise and tenon joint. →5

joinery moulding see timber trim. →2
see *joinery mouldings* illustration. →2

joinery profile see timber trim. →2
see *joinery profiles* illustration. →2

joint 1 the meeting of two components or materials in construction.
2 the formation and sealing material placed there.
3 see connection.
4 see brick joint. →16, →20
5 see sand joint. →15
6 see construction joint.
7 see knuckle. →38
8 see timber joint. →3, →4, →5

joint bolt, handrail bolt, rail bolt; a threaded shaft to which nuts can be screwed, used as a concealed connector in butt jointed wooden components such as handrails.

jointer 1 any tool for shaping and smoothing mortar jointing and pointing in brickwork. →43
2 see saw jointer.

jointer plane, trying plane; a long plane 500 mm–750 mm in length traditionally used for dressing long timber boards.

joint filler 1 any compound or substance applied as filling for joints between adjacent components or materials; called jointing compound if an organic sealant. →53
2 see jointing strip. →53

jointing 1 the making or filling of construction joints.
2 the binding of bricks together using mortar, same as bedding.
3 the tidying up and smoothing of excess wet mortar from a brickwork joint, and shaping it into the desired form; see *types of brickwork joint* illustration. →16
4 the result of the above actions.

jointing bead see jointing strip. →53

jointing compound a compound applied to joints between components or materials as bedding, weatherproofing, finishing or as an adhesive.

jointing mortar mortar used for jointing in masonrywork and tiling. →11

jointing strip, joint strip, jointing bead, sealant strip; preformed foam, mastic or elastic strip pushed into the gaps or open joints between adjacent components or elements to form a base for applied sealant. →53

jointing tape various types of adhesive tape used for joining sheet materials such as bitumen felt and carpet together and for closing seams and sealing pipe fittings etc.

jointing tool a mason's trowel with a bent round or hemispherical steel rod which is run along mortar joints to form a keyed joint. →43

jointing trowel a very thin-bladed bricklayer's trowel for shaping and smoothing masonry joints. →43

joint method see method of joints.

joint sanding, sand jointing; the spreading or brushing of sand over freshly laid external paving to fill the joints between alternate paving stones or slabs. →15

joint sealant see sealant. →11, →53

joint strip 1 see cover strip.
2 see jointing strip. →53

joint venture a grouping of two or more organizations to carry out work in cooperation, with each liable for the actions of the other.

joist one of a series of spaced beams used to support a floor or roof; types included as separate entries are listed below. →4
binding joist, see binder.
bridging joist.
ceiling joist. →33
common joist.
floor joist. →8, →44, →58, →59
rolled steel joist, rsj: see I-section. →34
roof joist. →58
steel joist, see I-section. →34
timber joist.
trimmed joist, see trimmed beam. →4
trimmer joist. →4
trimming joist. →4

joist hanger a metal fixing component for attaching the ends of joists and other horizontal timber members at right angles to other construction. →4
see *timber floor construction* illustration. →44
see *brick house construction* illustration. →59

joist spacing the distance, centre to centre, between alternate joists in a floor or roof structure.

joule, newton-metre; abb. **J**; SI unit of energy or work equal to that required for a current of 1 amp to operate against a resistance of 1 ohm, or that required to move 1 metre against a force of 1 newton.

jowl, gunstock; in traditional timber frame construction, the thickening at the top of a post or column to receive another member.

joyce in traditional timber frame construction, a joist.

jubilee court see ceremonial court. →70, →72

judge see assessor.

juffer in traditional timber frame construction, a square timber 4–5 inches in dimension.

jugend see Jugendstil.

Jugendstil, jugend; a northern European version of the Art Nouveau style in decorative art and architecture.
see *Jugendstil portal* illustration. →113

Juglans spp. see walnut.
Juglans cinerea, see butternut.
Juglans nigra, see American walnut.
Juglans regia, see European walnut.

Julian cross see cross of St Julian. →117

jumper 1 in brick or stonework walling, a long vertical or horizontal stone which overlaps two or more smaller stones.
2 a pointed masonry chisel for making holes in stone. →41

junction 1 the meeting or joining place of two parts of construction such as that formed by a roof and wall.
2 a length of pipe for attaching a subsidiary pipe to a main pipeline.
3 see road junction. →62
4 see at grade junction. →62
5 see grade-separated junction. →63
6 see interchange. →63

junction box a casing for connections or junctions in an electrical installation.

junction chamber see cable manhole.

jungle green a shade of green which takes its name from the colour of impenetrable jungle.

juniper [*Juniperus communis*] a softwood whose brownish aromatic timber contains numerous solid knots.

Juniperus communis see juniper.
Juniperus virginiana, see eastern red cedar.

Junk Art a form of art, especially sculpture, which makes use of the waste products from modern industrial and consumer society.

Jupiter, arrow of see thunderbolt. →120

jury see board of assessors.

jute fibres from the inner bark of the jute plant from India [*Corchorus capsularis*], used for making ropes and rough fabric, canvas, sackcloth etc.

jutty see jetty.

K

Kalathos Greek form of calathus. →81
kali soda ash, potash, oxide of potassium.
kallaite see turquoise.
kalypter Gk; an ancient Greek clay capping roof tile, equivalent to a Roman imbrex, used for covering the gaps between adjacent rows of flat or concave tiles; cf. stegaster. →47
kanephoros Greek form of canephora. →76
kantharos Gk; see cantharus. →96
kaolin a form of pure clay produced from the decomposition of feldspar, hydrated aluminium silicate, used as a filler and white pigment in latex and emulsion paints; often the same as China clay.
kapok, ceiba, capoc, Java cotton, silk cotton; a water-resistant wool product formed from the seed fibres of the tropical ceiba tree [*Ceiba pentandra*]; used for stuffing mattresses and furniture.
kappland a traditional Swedish unit of area equal to 154.26 m^2.
kapur, Borneo camphorwood; [*Dryobalanops spp.*] a hardwood from Malaysia and Indonesia with coarse, heavy, reddish brown timber; used for outdoor furniture and joinery.
Karelianism, Carelianism; National Romantic architecture in Finland from the late 1800s which contains naturalistic motifs inspired by the national epic poem, the Kalevala.
karri [*Eucalyptus diversicolor*] a durable and resistant Western Australian hardwood with reddish brown timber, used for heavy constructional work.
Kassler yellow see Turner's yellow.
katabasion Gk; see catabasion. →116
katagogion Gk; see catagogion.
kathedra Greek form of cathedra.
keel arch a decorative pointed arch with two mirrored S shapes which meet at the apex; a pointed reverse ogee arch. →24
keel moulding an ornamental projecting moulding whose section is roughly in the shape of a pointed arch, formed by two ogees with their concave ends together. →14
keep, 1 donjon; the central masonry tower, stronghold or building of a medieval castle, a place of residence and refuge in times of siege; also known as a donjon, later corrupted into dungeon, as prisoners were often held here. →103
2 see shell keep. →103
3 see box staple.
keep and bailey castle a common medieval castle type with a central masonry stronghold or keep surrounded by a fortified wall, leaving an open space, the bailey, with ancillary buildings between. →103
keeper see striking plate.
klimakes the stepped aisles between wedges of seating in a Greek theatre building. →89
Kelvin see degree Kelvin.
Kentish tracery Gothic tracery found in some English churches of the Perpendicular style, characterized by use of foils and barbs.
kentledge, cantledge; temporary weight added to test or provide stability to a structure.
kepos Gk; an ancient Greek vegetable garden or cultivated park.
kerb, curb (Am.); in road and street construction, the raised edge of the carriageway where it adjoins a footpath, often formed by a row of cut stones or concrete units. →15, →62
kerb parking see street parking. →62
kerbstone one of a number of cut or dressed stones or specially cast concrete units laid to form a kerb at the edge of a carriageway; written curbstone in USA. →62
kerf the groove made by a saw when cutting timber.
kerkides Gk; plural form of kerkis. →89
kerkis Gk; pl. kerkides; a sector or wedge-shaped area of stone seating between radiating entrance gangways in a Greek theatre or amphitheatre; called cuneus in a Roman theatre. →89
kermes a dark red dyestuff made from the bodies of adult females of the insect *Kermes ilicis.*
Kermes ilicis kermes insect, see cochineal.
kernel see crenelle. →103
kernel black see vine black.
kerosene see paraffin.
kerykeion Greek form of caduceus. →120
Kevlar see aramid fibre.
key 1 any roughness in a surface designed to encourage the bonding of a successive layer of material.
2 see keystone. →22
3 a small portable implement by which a lock can be operated. →39
4 one of the buttons on a computer keyboard which represent symbols when written.
5 in computing, a group of characters used to identify an item or record within a file.
6 see key pattern, Greek key. →124
7 key of life, key to the Nile, see ankh. →74, →117
8 see wood key. →6
key block see keystone. →22
keyboard a manual device for writing instructions and commands to a computer.
key coat, 1 primary coat; a coating or layer of material such as plaster, paint etc. applied to a surface to promote the adhesion of further coats.
2 see base coat. →83
key cross, cross of Pisa; a heraldic cross whose limbs spread out gradually towards their extremities, ending in points. →118
key drop, keyhole cover; a pivoted metal flap which covers a keyhole.
keyed alike a description and the associated programming of a number of locks within a building such that they are operable with the same key.
keyed joint, 1 any timber joint tightened with a wedge or peg.
2 bucket-handled joint, concave joint, rodded joint; in brickwork, a recessed concave mortar joint either as a key for receiving a finish or as a decorative treatment. →16
3 see raked joint. →16
keyed lock one of the locks belonging to a suite of locks.
keyed scarf joint, wedged scarf joint; a timber lengthening joint tightened by driving a pair of folded wedges into a notch cut into the splayed ends. →3
keyed, splayed and tabled scarf joint in timber frame construction, a splayed lengthening joint hewn so as to be tightened with a peg or pair of folding wedges after assembly; a keyed scarf joint. →3
keyed tenon joint, pinned tenon joint, cabinetmaker's tenon joint; any through timber mortise and tenon joint which has been fastened with a transverse wedge, peg or pin on the reverse side of the mortised piece. →5
keyhole a hole or shaped orifice which receives a key into a lock.
keyhole cover see key drop.
keyhole saw, lock saw, pad saw; a compass saw whose tapering flexible blade and handle are aligned, used for cutting the apertures for locks in doors.

keying the physical programming of locks within a suite to enable or restrict passage for various combinations of keyholders.

key of life see ankh. →74, →117

key pattern 1 classical banded running ornamentation made up of horizontal and vertical lines or fillets which interlink to form a geometrical pattern; often synonymous with fret. →124
2 angular guilloche, see meander. →124
3 see potenty moulding. →125
4 see Greek key. →125

key paver a concrete paving unit which is shaped to create a patterned paved surface of similar interlocking blocks; also called an interlocking paver or interpaver. →15

key plate see escutcheon. →39

keystone, key, key block; the highest wedge-shaped piece in a masonry arch, often decorated, which locks the voussoirs in position. →22

key to the Nile see ankh. →74, →117

khaki a shade of dirty yellow which takes its name from the colour of uniforms used by the Anglo-Indian army.

khamsa see hand of Fatima. →120

khan see caravansary.

khaya see African mahogany.

Khaya ivorensis see African mahogany.

kheker frieze a decorative frieze of bundles of stylized plant ornament adorning the top of ancient Egyptian walls. →82

Khepri one of the many forms of the ancient Egyptian sun god Re (Ra), depicted as a beetle, the rising sun, symbol of regeneration; also written as Kheperi, Kheper. →75

Khnum the ram-headed creator god of ancient Upper Egypt, who moulded man on a potter's wheel; guardian of the first cataract of the River Nile at Aswan. →74

Khonsu the son of the ancient Egyptian deities Amun and Mut; 'the traveller' who crossed the night sky as the moon, depicted in mummy-dress with the head of a boy or falcon; also written as Khons. →74

khora Gk; the land that surrounded and supported an ancient Greek city, urban centre or temple area.

kiblah, qibla, qiblah; the prime orientation in Islamic architecture, the direction of Mecca.

kiborion Greek form of ciborium.

kicker in concretework, a small raised area of a cast concrete slab which provides a location for wall or column formwork.

kicking plate, door plate, kick plate; a protective plate, usually of metal or plastics, fitted to the lower part of a door leaf to prevent wear. →51

kick plate see kicking plate. →51

kilderkin a unit of measurement of liquid capacity, approximately equal to 16 or 18 gallons.

killas see clayslate.

killed steel in steel processing, steel which has been well deoxidized when being poured into ingots, showing no evolution of gas as it solidifies.

kiln see dry kiln.

kiln dried, hot-air dried, kiln seasoned; a description of timber which has been dried in a kiln to assure controlled seasoning and minimize warpage.

kiln seasoned see kiln dried.

kilo- abb. **k**; a prefix for units of measurement or quantity to denote a factor of 10^3 (one thousand). →Table 1

kilobit, abb. **Kb**; in computing, a unit of memory equal to 1024 bits.

kilobyte, abb. **kB**; in computing, a unit of memory equal to 1024 bytes.

kilocalory, Calorie; abb. **Cal**; a unit of energy = 4190 joules; the energy required to raise one kilogram of water by 1°C.

kilogram, kilogramme; abb. **kg**; SI basic unit of mass.

kilogram of force see kilopond.

kilogramme see kilogram.

kilometre abb. **km**; the SI unit of length equal to one thousand metres.

kilopond, kilogram of force; the gravitational force of the earth on a mass of one kilogram, equal to 9.806 newtons.

kilowatt abb. **kW**; the SI unit of power equal to one thousand watts.

kindergarten see nursery.

kinematic pair any mechanical device for transmitting kinetic energy through a system, with at least two components in contact, and at least one axis of relative motion, such as a pair of cogs, or a belt and pulley.

kinematics a branch of physics which deals purely with motion, disregarding the forces which cause it.

kinetic art a form of art which expresses movement through images or colour, or is composed of moving bodies.

kinetics see dynamics.

king block in traditional timber roof construction, a timber at which principal rafters or blades form an apex, often carrying a ridge purlin.

king bolt, king rod; in traditional timber roof construction, a vertical wrought iron rod replacing a king post in a king post roof truss.

king closer, three quarter brick; a three quarter length brick or bat with one splayed corner to give the appearance of a closer in brickwork; also misleadingly called a three quarter brick due to the three out of four faces which can still be used as exterior edges. →21

king piece see king post. →33

king post, 1 king piece, joggle post; in traditional timber roof construction, a central vertical strut rising from a tie beam and carrying a ridge purlin. →33
2 see columna. →47

king post bridge a bridge whose main support is a framework in the shape of a king post truss. →32

king post roof in traditional timber roof construction, a roof truss with a tie beam, coupled rafters and a king post. →33

king post roof truss in traditional timber roof construction, a roof truss with a tie beam, coupled rafters and a king post. →33

king post truss see king post roof truss. →33

king rod see king bolt.

king's blue a variety of cobalt blue pigment.

king strut in traditional timber roof construction, a central vertical strut rising from a tie beam but not carrying a ridge purlin.

king strut roof truss in traditional timber roof construction, a roof truss with a tie beam, coupled rafters and a king strut.

king's yellow, arsenic yellow, auripigmentum, orpiment, Royal yellow; a very poisonous bright opaque yellow pigment consisting of artificial arsenic trisulphide, no longer in use since the introduction of cadmium yellow.

king tie, upper king post; in traditional timber roof construction, a short central vertical member rising from a collar and carrying a ridge purlin in a timber truss.

kink a localized warp in a timber board caused by the presence of a knot or other weak spot. →1

kiosk 1 a small permanent or movable hut or similar construction designed for the sale of merchandise; a booth or stall.
2 a small ornamental pavilion originating in Asia Minor, used as a shelter or bandstand in parkland.
3 a freestanding stone canopy structure supported by columns in Egyptian architecture. →72

kirk the term for church in Scotland.

kit building a prefabricated building assembled from a set of standard prefabricated parts.

kitchen 1 a space within a dwelling or establishment where food is prepared and cooked. →57, →59
see *brick house* illustration. →59
see *Greek residential building* illustration. →87
2 see culina, a kitchen in a Roman dwelling. →88

kitchenette a small open kitchen space adjoining a living space.

kite step, kite winder; a triangular or wedge-shaped step in a turning or circular stair. →45

kite winder see kite step. →45

kleros Gk; an allotment of cultivatable land distributed to habitants or Spartans in an ancient Greek colony.

kneaded rubber see putty rubber.

knee 1 in traditional timber frame construction, a timber block fixed at the meeting of two framing members to stiffen the joint.
2 see elbow.

knee brace in traditional timber frame construction, a short up brace.

knee roof see curb roof.

knife a tool with a sharpened steel cutting blade and longitudinal handle.

knife cut veneer see sliced veneer.

knife-edge load, line load; a structural load imposed along the length of a thin line; see distributed load, point load.

knob 1 an ovoid handle for a drawer, door etc.
2 see door knob. →39
3 a decorative carved boss, a knot.

knocker see door knocker. →51

knocking up see retempering.

knop a round decorative element, a boss or knot.

knosp, knot; a boss carved in the shape of a bud.

knot 1 an imperial unit of velocity used in sea and air travel, equivalent to one nautical mile per hour or 1.85 km/h.
2 a hard, ovoid or swirling growth evident in the surface of sawn timber, a branch stem in the original tree cut through its width. →1
see *knots in timber* illustration. →1
3 boss, knosp, knop, knob; a carved decorative terminating element representing knotted twine or foliage located at the meeting of ribs in a vault or at other similar locations.
4 see Gordian knot. →123
5 see Celtic love knot. →108
6 see Bowen knot, true-lover's knot. →123

knot cluster a group of knots appearing in the surface grain pattern of seasoned timber. →1

knot hole a hole in a piece of machined timber left by the removal or separation of a knot. →1

knot sealer see knotting.

knotted column a Romanesque stone column or coupled columns whose compound shafts are carved as if knotted together in the middle; also known as a knotted pillar. →114

knotting 1 a transparent liquid consisting of shellac dissolved in methylated spirits, used as a sealer to inhibit the bleeding through of surface resin from knots in timber before the application of paint.
2 the application of the above.

knotwork, entrelace, interlace; in the early architecture and art of northern Europe, especially that of Christian Ireland, decorative ornamentation representing intertwined, overlapping and knotted bands. →108, →118, →125

knotwork cross see cross of infinity. →118

know-how technical expertise or practical knowledge.

knuckle the joining tube of a hinge, in which the pin rotates and around which the leaves pivot, sometimes known as a loop, joint or curl. →38

knuckle bend a curved pipe fitting with a small radius of curvature; designed for use at a sharp change of direction in a pipeline.

knulled ornament see gadroon. →124

knur see burl.

knurl see burl.

koilon Gk; the semicircular banked auditorium of the Greek theatre.

kokoshnik in Russian medieval church architecture, a succession of corbelled arches for supporting either a dome or cupola drum, or as a decorative element.

kokrodua see afrormosia.

kondo, Golden Hall; in Japanese temple architecture, a central hall containing sculptures and used for worship; also called a butsuden. →68

konisterion Greek form of conisterium. →91

kore 1 a classical statue of a young draped female figure, a canephora or caryatid. →76
2 see caryatid. →76
3 see canephora. →76

korykeion a space in a Greek gymnasium or palaestra with the korykos (punch or sand bags) and other equipment for boxers to practise; a coryceum in Roman buildings. →91

kouros Gk; an ancient Greek statue of a naked or draped male figure; in architecture an atlas or telamon. →76
see *atlas* in caryatid illustration. →76

kraft paper 1 strong brown paper made from sulphate pulp.
2 see building paper. →8

kremlin a castle or fortified area within an old Russian town, surrounded by walls or earthworks.

Krems white see Cremnitz white.

krypton an inert gaseous chemical element, **Kr**.

Kufic, Cufic; a decorative and jagged Arabic script from the ancient city of Kufa, often used to embellish Islamic architecture.

kuma Greek form of cyma. →82

kumimono see masugumi. →68

kursaal see health resort.

k-value, coefficient of thermal conductivity, heat transmission value; a theoretical measure of how well a material or construction of unit thickness will conduct heat, whose units are W/m°C; calculated as the amount of energy passing through a unit area of one metre thick construction for unit temperature difference on either side of the construction (the C-value is obtained by multiplying by thickness of construction, see also U-value).

kyanite, disthene; a hard, bluish, crystalline aluminium silicate mineral with a high melting point; used for heat-resistant materials and as jewellery.

kymation Greek form of cymatium. →78, →79

L

labarum Lat.; a Roman military standard consisting of a vertical staff with a horizontal transom or crossbar from which purple flags were tied, later adopted by Emperors as the Imperial Standard, and to which the Roman Emperor Constantine the Great added the monogram of Christ; a symbol for which men live and die. →119

label see hood-mould. →110

labile, unstable; referring to a body which is unstable and liable to physical or chemical change under a small force or action.

labor American English spelling of labour.

laboratory a building or part of a building for scientific research, testing and study.

labour 1 manual work involved in building; that part of a cost incurred by this.
2 see workforce.

labour cost, labor cost (Am.); a building cost incurred by human work rather than by materials, products, spare parts, sales or transportation.

labourer a person employed on a construction site to carry out manual or unskilled work.

labour force see workforce.

labour-only contract a building contract covering the supply of labour only.

Labrador a trade name for larvikite.

Labrador feldspar see labradorite.

labradorite, Labrador feldspar; a highly coloured and specular variety of the mineral plagioclase, polished and used in ornamental masonry, or carved for decoration.

labrum Lat.; pl. labri; a cold water bath in a Roman bath house.

labrys, double axe, double headed axe; Gk; a decorative motif originating in ancient Minoan architecture, a sacred two-headed axe symbolizing the mother god; also appearing in Norse, African and Greek ornamentation. →122

labyrinth 1 a complex pattern of lines marking out a route (unicursal) to its centre, with one entrance and exit; cf. maze. →123
2 a covered or roofed structure with a number of meandering corridors leading to chambers, in which orientation is difficult and exits and entries minimalized.
3 see stone labyrinth. →123
4 see road of Jerusalem. →123
5 see Classical maze, Cretan maze. →123

labyrinth fret see meander. →124

laced arches see interlaced arches. →124

laced stanchion a composite steel lattice column or stanchion in which vertical rolled steel sections are joined together with stiff diagonal members.

lacertine see animal interlace.

lacing 1 see lacing course.
2 laced arches, see interlaced arches. →124

lacing course a course or courses of bricks or finer material used as decoration or reinforcement in a rough stone or rubble wall.

lachryma occasional name for gutta; 'tear' in Latin. →78

Laconian roof tiling the antique term for classical clay roof tiling of under-and-over tiles; nowadays also known as mission or Spanish tiling. →47

laconicum Lat.; the sweating room in a Roman bath house, one with low moisture; a sudatorium. →91

lacquer see cellulose lacquer.

Lactuca sativa see lettuce green.

lacunar Lat.; in classical architecture, a decorated ceiling relieved with a series of polygonal recessed panels or coffers; a coffered ceiling. →86

ladder a freestanding or fixed frame to provide temporary or permanent vertical access, consisting of two vertical side rails with horizontal rungs or steps in between; types included as separate entries are listed below. →54, →61
access ladder. →45
cable ladder.
chimney ladder. →54, →61,
escape ladder, see fire escape ladder.
fire escape ladder.
flue ladder, see chimney ladder. →54, →61
loft ladder, see disappearing stair.
roof access ladder, see access ladder.
roof ladder.
stepladder.

ladder stair see open riser stair. →45

Lady chapel a chapel in a church or cathedral dedicated to the Virgin Mary, usually situated at the east end. →100

lag bolt see coach screw. →36

lagging thermal insulation of mineral wool or foamed plastics for boilers and pipes.

lag screw see coach screw. →36

laid on purlin see through purlin.

laid paper paper marked with a series of parallel lines by smoothing rollers in the manufacturing process.

laissez-faire 'allow to do'; lack of government interference in economic life; in town planning the permitting of development to go ahead without planning constraint and intervention, governed solely by commercial interest.

lake any pigment formed by the addition of an organic dye to a metal oxide, hydroxide or salt to render it insoluble.

lake asphalt a naturally occurring viscous liquid asphalt which, when added to distilled bitumen, increases the hardness and durability of a road surface without detracting from flexibility; see also natural rock asphalt.

lake dwelling see pile dwelling.

lake red a shade of red which takes its name from the colour of dye made in India from the secretion of the insect *Coccus lacca*.

lake settlement see lake village.

lake village, lake settlement; a prehistoric homestead consisting of a group of dwellings constructed on piles in a lake.

lamassu large stone colossi, winged bulls or lions, guarding a gateway or portal in ancient Assyrian monumental architecture. →75

Lamb of God see Agnus Dei. →119

lambrequin 1 a short drapery fringe above a window etc.; ornament representing this. →112
2 see mantling. →124

lamé a fabric of silk or other yarns interwoven with metallic threads.

laminar flow see streamline flow.

laminate, plastics laminate; hardwearing or decorative sheet material produced by bonding thin sheets of thermosetting plastics such as melamine, urea or phenol formaldehyde resins together.

laminated referring to a material or composite product made up of thin layers of material bonded together for added strength.

laminated beam see laminated timber beam. →7

laminated chipboard a building board used for hardwearing interior working surfaces, cupboard doors etc., made from chipboard with plastics laminate bonded to its surface.

laminated glass glass which has been manufactured with a core of plastic sheet to provide resistance

against impact; types included as separate entries are listed below. →53
alarm glass.
anti-bandit laminated glass.
anti-fading glass.
coloured opaque glass.
intumescent glass, see laminated intumescent glass.
laminated intumescent glass.
laminated safety glass.
laminated solar control glass.
laminated sound control glass.
laminated ultraviolet light control glass.
safety glass.
security glass.
ultraviolet control glass, see laminated ultraviolet light control glass.

laminated intumescent glass a fire-resisting glass with a layer of intumescent material which expands to a foam on heating and becomes opaque and fire resisting.

laminated log, glue-laminated log, lam-log, structural log; an industrial timber product of uniform rectangular or round cross-section and cogged ends, glue-laminated and machined from a number of strips of wood and used in the construction of system-built and off-the-shelf log buildings.

laminated safety glass safety glass whose strength is provided by laminating two or more sheets of glass around plastic interlayers.

laminated solar control glass laminated glass with a tinted interlayer between the two sheets, or in which one of the sheets is solar control glass.

laminated sound control glass laminated glass in which the plastic interlayer and thickness of the glass used make it useful for improving sound insulation.

laminated timber beam, glulam beam, glued and laminated beam; a beam consisting of timber strips glued one on top of the other for added strength. →7
see corrugated ply-web beam. →7
see laminated web beam.
plywood box beam, see box beam. →7
see plywood web beam, ply-web beam. →7

laminated timber board 1 a general term for timber boards such as plywood or blockboard made of timber strips, sheets or pieces glued together side by side.
2 a timber product used for shelves and worktops, made from strips of solid wood glued together side by side under pressure, then planed.

laminated ultraviolet light control glass, ultraviolet control glass; special glass laminated with an interlayer capable of reflecting up to 98% of harmful ultraviolet radiation from the sun.

laminated veneered board any building board to which a surface layer of plastics laminate has been bonded for decoration or protection.

laminated web beam a laminated timber beam consisting of plywood or similar thin timber pieces glued side by side.

laminated wood see glue laminated timber.

lamination the bonding of two or more sheets of material such as paper, timber or fabric together with a polymer, resin or glue to form a composite sheet.

laminboard a timber building board manufactured by gluing veneers on either side of a core of solid wood strips with a width less than 7 mm; the grain of the veneers runs at 90° to that of the core. →9

lam-log see laminated log.

lamp 1 a component powered by electricity, oil, gas or other fuel to produce light.
2 the replaceable part of a luminaire from which light is emitted; a lightbulb; types included as separate entries are listed below.
candle lamp.
circular fluorescent tube, circline lamp.
cold start lamp, see instant start lamp.
compact fluorescent lamp.
crown silvered lamp.
daylight lamp, see neodymium oxide lamp.
dichroic mirror lamp.
discharge lamp.
electric lamp.
fluorescent lamp.
fluorescent reflector lamp.
full-spectrum lamp, see neodymium oxide lamp.
general lighting service lamp, GLS lamp.
halogen lamp.
high pressure sodium lamp.
incandescent lamp.
infrared lamp.
instant start lamp.
mercury vapour lamp, mercury lamp.
metal halide lamp, metallic-additive lamp.
neodymium oxide lamp.
reflector lamp.
silvered-bowl lamp, see crown silvered lamp.
sodium lamp, sodium-vapour lamp.
spot lamp, see reflector lamp.
standard lamp, see floor lamp.
tri-phosphor lamp.
tungsten-halogen lamp, see halogen lamp.
ultraviolet lamp.
3 see luminaire.
4 a luminaire such as a table or floor lamp which can be moved while in use; a non-fixed luminaire, see below.
anglepoise lamp.
blowlamp.
floor lamp.
streetlamp, see streetlight.

lamp base 1 see lamp cap.
2 see lamp stand.

lampblack pure carbon powder originally collected from the combustion of burning oils, used since prehistoric times as a black pigment; a form of carbon black.

lamp cap, lamp base; the metal part of an electric lamp by which it is connected to an electricity supply and fixed to a holder.
see bayonet cap.
Edison screw cap, see screw cap.

lampholder a device from which an electric lamp is supported, and by which a contact is made with an electricity supply.

lamp post a tall concrete or metal post supporting a streetlight.

lampshade, shade; a shading or diffusing component placed in front of or over a lamp to prevent glare and produce scattered or directional light.

lamp stand, lamp base; the base and shaft of a table or floor lamp.

lamp starter an electronic component for providing a momentary increase in voltage required to excite the gas, vapour etc. in a discharge lamp and provide light.

lancet see ogival.

lancet arch, acute arch; a sharply pointed arch. →24

lancet window a slender sharp-pointed arched Gothic window.

land an area or plot of ground on the earth's surface.

land capability classification one of a number of soil classifications made primarily for the agricultural industry and farming.

land drain 1 see ditch.
2 see field drain.

land drainage, **1** ditching, subsoil drainage, field drainage; the digging of networks of ditches to drain areas of land, usually to improve ground for agriculture, forestry and construction.
2 the control of external water around the foundations of a building or structure using a system of drains, channels and walls.

landed property, real estate; a term which includes any immovable development on the land, see real property.

landing 1 a horizontal platform or level area at the top of a flight of stairs, which may have another flight leading from it. →45, →61
2 see intermediate landing. →45, →61
3 see storey landing. →45, →61
4 see landing stage. →64
5 see lift landing.

landing door the outer door of a lift, which opens out onto a landing and does not move with the lift car.

landing plate a level metal platform at either end of an escalator or similar device, from which passengers step on and off.

landing stage a floating or fixed structure over water from which boats can be moored for storage, loading and unloading etc.; a wharf. →64

landing valve a water outlet located at each level in a building, connected to a fire riser, and used by firemen in the event of a fire.

landmark a building, structure or natural protrusion in the landscape which may act as a symbol for a particular area or as a navigational aid.

land register an official archive containing details of land and buildings thereon regarding ownership, size and specification.

land registration the listing of land and property in an official register.

land restoration work to prepare an area of land for development or other use after it has been damaged by mineral extraction or industrial processes.

landscape 1 a natural, man-made or planted exterior environment and its visual and sensual impact.
2 a view, painting etc. of an external scene.

landscape architect, landscape designer; a qualified professional or organization responsible for designing gardens, parks and external environments.

landscape architecture 1 the design and planning of external areas, gardens and parkland, especially those in proximity to built form, to provide a pleasing, safe and healthy environment.
2 the particular design of parks, gardens and public open spaces from an aesthetic and functional perspective.

landscape design 1 the discipline of planning the external areas, hard surfaces, planting and roads surrounding a new or existing building.
2 landscaping; a design or designs thus produced.

landscape designer see landscape architect.

landscape garden, English landscape garden; an informal planned garden or park surrounding a country house or mansion, fashionable in England in the 1700s.

landscape painting a form of painting originating in the 1300s portraying landscapes and scenes from nature.

landscape preservation the maintenance and protection of landscapes with historical, aesthetic or cultural value.

landscape work see landscaping.

landscaping, 1 landscape work; construction work to provide a functional and amenable external environment around a building using earthworks, structures, hardy materials and planting.
2 see landscape design.

land survey, survey; the measuring and inspection of land prior to design and construction.

land surveying, 1 field surveying, surveying; the physical measuring of the dimensions and topography of a particular site or area of land.
2 geodesy; the science of measuring and presenting the form and size of tracts of land.

land surveyor, geodisist; a qualified professional who measures the topography of an area of land or site and produces a map or survey from the results.

land use the use of land for a specific purpose as designated by a town or area plan.

land use study in town planning, an analysis of potential of a large area or small site for development according to its physical attributes including land value, previous use, geology and local climate.

land value a measure of the quality of land based on its location, terrain and features, natural resources and potential, especially in terms of commercial gain or monetary and taxable value.

lane 1 a narrow or small road.
2 see walk.
3 a marked strip of roadway reserved for a single line of vehicles moving in the same direction; a traffic lane; types included as separate entries are listed below. →63
acceleration lane, see merging lane.
bicycle lane, see cycle lane.
bus lane.
climbing lane.
crawler lane, see climbing lane.
cycle lane.
deceleration lane, see diverging lane.
diverging lane.
merging lane.
overtaking lane.
taxi lane.
4 see sea lane. →64

language see architectural language.

lantern the upper part of a church or other tower which is glazed to allow light in; see also lantern light. →26

lantern light, lantern; a glazed turret or other construction on the roof of a building or construction to allow daylight into a space beneath, often of ornamental nature.

lanthanide any of a series of chemical elements having an atomic number from 57 to 71, a transition metal.

lanthanum a metallic chemical element, **La**.

lap, 1 lapping, overlap; the covering of one another by two laid adjacent materials or products such as jointed timbers, sheets, tiles, bricks etc.; the distance, dimension or amount of this. →3
2 in brickwork, the surface formed by two bricks in adjacent courses which overlap to form a bond.
3 lap length; in reinforced concrete, the overlap of two longitudinal reinforcing bars to form one longer bar.

lap cement see sealing compound.

lapis see lapis lazuli.

lapis albanus Lat.; see peperino.

lapis lazuli, 1 lazurite, lapis; a semi-precious blue mineral consisting of silicates of aluminium, lime and soda, found in Iran, Afghanistan, China and Chile and used for mosaics and as a pigment.
2 azzuro oltremarino, lazuline blue; a rich blue pigment formed by grinding the precious stone of the same name and refining the product, used since ancient times as ultramarine, now largely replaced with artificial ultramarine.

Lapith, pl. Lapithae; a decorative motif found in classical architecture representing a mythological Thessalonian who waged war on the centaurs.

lap joint, lapped joint; **1** the joining of two members, components, sheets etc. so that they overlap. →3
see *lap joint* in sheetmetal roofing illustration. →49
2 any timber joint in which the face sides of two members are joined together, often rebated or half lapped. →3, →4

lap-jointed roofing felt roofing in which seams running parallel to the ridge and eaves are formed by overlapping the roll of felt above and nailing through. →49

lap length see lap.

lap notch see boxed lap notch. →6
see locked lap notch. →6

lapped corner joint a corner joint used in cabinetmaking for joining boards and sheets at right angles, in which the end of one piece is halved along its edge to receive the other abutting edge. →5

lapped dovetail joint a cabinetmaking joint in which dovetailing shows on one side of the joint only; may also be called a blind, concealed, secret or stopped dovetail joint. →5

lapped joint see lap joint. →3

lapping see lap. →3

laptop computer, portable computer; a small mobile computer with a rechargeable battery, incorporated mouse, keyboard and foldable screen lid.

lap weld a welded joint between overlapping metal components. →34

lararium Lat.; an altar, shrine or chapel to household gods in a Roman dwelling. →88

larch [*Larix spp.*] a deciduous softwood of northern climates with tough, dense, durable timber which has good resistance to rot; see ***Larix spp***. for full list of species of larch included in this work.

larder a ventilated and often cool room or closet for the storage of food.

large diameter pile in foundation technology, a bored pile which has a diameter of greater than 600 mm; usually a steel pile.

large-panel construction industrialized building using precast concrete panels for structural frame and cladding of buildings, involving careful design to ensure that components fit together on site, but saving time and expense at construction stage.

Larix spp. see larch.
Larix kaempferi, see Japanese larch.
Larix laricina, see tamarack.
Larix leptolepis, see Japanese larch.
Larix occidentalis, see western larch.
Larix russica, see Siberian larch.
Larix sibirica, see Siberian larch.

larvikite a bluish grey or dark green variety of syenite containing colourful feldspar, found in Larvik, Norway; used for decorative floors, as cladding and for ornamental stone, and often sold under the trade name Labrador.

l'art pour l'art see art for art's sake.

laser a device which produces a narrow, powerful beam of monochromatic light.

laser cutting a method of cutting metals using a jet of gas which has been heated with a powerful laser beam.

laser printer a high definition printer in which text and graphics are formed as black or coloured images on a light-sensitive drum with the aid of a laser, and printed from this.

laser welding a method of fusion welding in which heat is produced by a powerful focused laser beam.

Lasius niger see garden black ant.

last a unit of measurement of a ship's cargo equal to two tons.

latch any lock-like fastening mechanism for a door or gate, in which a handle rather than a key is pushed or turned to disengage a bolt; types included as separate entries are listed below.
mortise latch.
panic latch.
return latch.
rim latch.
snib latch, see indicating bolt. →39
spring latch, see return latch. →39
turning latch.

latch bolt see return latch. →39

latchet see sheetmetal cleat.

latchset a set of door fittings comprising a latch, two door handles, two roses, two cover plates and a spindle.

Late Antiquity the final period of Greek and Roman art and architecture from 250 to 600 AD, especially used in reference to the art of the Roman empire.
see *church of Late Antiquity* illustration. →95

late Baroque Baroque architecture in Europe c.1670–1710.

late Gothic 1 Gothic architecture in Europe from c.1400 to 1500, the Flamboyant style in France and the Perpendicular in England.
see *late Gothic window* illustration. →111
2 see Flamboyant style.
3 see Perpendicular style, Rectilinear style.

later, pl. lateres; Lat.; in Roman construction, a brick which has either been fired (called 'later coctus' or 'later testaceus') or sun-dried (called 'later crudus'). →83

lateral see long groove. →6

lateral bevelled halved joint see angle bevelled halved joint.

lateral bracing the stiffening of a structure or building frame perpendicular to its main axis using cross walls etc.

lateral groove see long groove. →6

lateral reinforcement, transverse reinforcement; secondary concrete reinforcement linked and placed at right angles to the main reinforcement to provide stiffening and resistance against shear forces. →27

later coctus, pl. lateres cocti; Lat.; a Roman brick of fired clay; see later. →83

later crudus, pl. lateres crudi; Lat.; a sun-dried Roman clay brick; see later. →83

late Renaissance the latter stage in Renaissance architecture, c.1530–1580.
see *late Renaissance window* illustration. →111

lateres Lat.; plural form of later. →83

latericium see opus latericium. →83

lateritium see opus latericium. →83

latewood, summerwood; the portion of the growth ring of a tree with small, dense cells, formed after earlywood during periods of slower growth.

latex 1 the milky sap of the rubber tree or a similar synthetic liquid consisting of a polymer dispersed in a water-based vehicle.
2 see gum.

latex cement flooring see cement rubber latex flooring.

latex foam see foam rubber.

latex paint an easily brushable and rapidly drying emulsion paint with a latex binder in water, which evaporates off during drying, leaving a film of latex, pigment and additives.

lath 1 a thin strip of wood, often formed by cleaving, used in basketwork, making fences and lattices.
2 a split timber batten fixed to a base in rows as a base for plaster; see lathing.
see bruised lath.
3 a piece of sawn timber with cross-sectional dimensions of 6 mm–17 mm thick and 22 mm–36 mm wide.

lathe a powered machine on which wood or metal is shaped into cylindrical or round forms by cutting blades while being fixed to a rapidly spinning chuck.

lathing, lathwork; any surface of timber battens, expanded metal or mesh fixed to a wall surface to provide a mechanical key for plasterwork; lathwork most often refers to timber lathing; types included as separate entries are listed below.
bruised lath.
expanded metal lathing.
mesh lathing, see wire lathing.
metal lathing.
ribbed expanded metal lathing, rib lathing.
timber lath.
timber lathing.
wire lathing, wire-mesh lathing.

lathwork see lathing.

Latin cross, crux immissa (Lat.); a cross with four perpendicular limbs of which three are of equal length and the fourth, the lower, is longer; an ancient symbol of divinity found in China, Greece and Egypt, later the symbol of Christ's suffering and Christianity; variously known as the cross of life, cross of Christ, Passion cross, crux capitata (Lat.) or long cross. →117
see *Latin cross* illustration. →117

latrina Lat.; a private or communal lavatory in a classical or medieval dwelling, monastery etc.
see *latrina* in Carolingian monastery illustration. →97

latrine 1 a building, block or room containing toilets, especially of a monastic community, camp etc.
see *Mesopotamian temple* illustration. →66
see *Carolingian monastery* illustration. →97
2 see outhouse.
3 see latrina. →97

lattice beam see trussed beam. →33

lattice girder bridge a bridge whose main structural elements are lattice girders or trusses.

lattice stanchion, braced stanchion; a composite steel column or stanchion with a number of vertical rolled steel sections braced at intervals with diagonal or horizontal struts, or a combination of both.

lattice structure see truss.

laundrette a commercial laundry whose facilities are operated by the customers themselves.

laundry 1 premises or rooms containing washing machines for domestic, commercial or public use.
2 see wash-house.

laundry chute a chute leading to a laundry or collecting point in an establishment such as a hospital or hotel, down which clothing and fabrics to be washed can be thrown.

laundry room a room or space in a building used for the cleaning and maintenance of clothes and fabrics.

LA unit see Los Angeles coefficient.

laura, lavra; a Greek Orthodox monastery in which monks lived in isolation in separate cells.

laurel wreath a classical and Christian ornamental motif depicting a head-dress of interwoven laurel leaves, symbolic of victory and sainthood. →121

lavabo see lavatorium.

lava rock types of igneous rock which are ejected from the earth's crust as lava and solidify rapidly in air.

lavatorium, lavabo; Lat.; a washing place in a monastery.

lavatory 1 see toilet.
2 see washroom.

lavatory bowl see water closet pan.

lavatrina Lat.; a private washroom in a Roman dwelling; often the same as latrina. →88

lavender blue, lavender grey; a shade of grey blue which takes its name from the colour of the flowers of the lavender plant [*Lavandula spica, Lavandula officinalis*].

lavender green, celadon green; a shade of grey green which takes its name from the colour of the leaves of the lavender plant [*Lavandula spica* or *Lavandula officinalis*].

lavender grey see lavender (blue).

lavender oil see oil of spike.

lavra see laura.

law courts, court-house; a building or part of a building where the rule of law is administered.

lawn in landscaping, a mowed and tended area of grass.

law of action and reaction Newton's law of mechanics which states that to every action there is an equal and opposite reaction.

law of inertia Newton's law of mechanics which states that a body remains inert, or moving at a constant velocity, unless acted on by an external force.

lawrencium a synthetic, radioactive, metallic chemical element, **Lr**.

Lawsonia inermis see henna.

Lawson's cypress, Port Orford cedar; [*Chamaecyparis lawsoniana*] a softwood from North America and the British Isles with pale yellow-brown timber, used in general construction work, for interiors and boat-building.

lay bar an intermediate horizontal glazing bar in a window. →111

lay-by, 1 draw-in, stopping place; an inset area or widening of a road to include a bus stop, or intended for vehicles to pull into and stop for loading and unloading etc.
2 see bus bay.
3 see rest area.

layer, level; an organizational device in computer-aided design and graphical software for subdividing information in a drawing file for ease of editing, accessibility and display.

laying-on trowel see plasterer's trowel. →43

laylight a horizontal window set into a suspended ceiling below a rooflight.

layout the schematic arrangement of parts of a building or other designs showing how component parts fit and function together.

layout drawing a design drawing showing the spatial relationships between buildings on a site or rooms in a building.

layout plan see site layout plan.

lazuline blue see lapis lazuli.

lazurite a blue sodium aluminium silicate crystalline mineral, the main constituent of the rock lapis lazuli.

L-beam 1 a beam which is L-shaped in cross-section, usually of concrete. →30
2 see boot lintel. →30

LCD liquid crystal display.

LD polythene low density polythene.

LDPE low density polythene.

lead 1 a soft, malleable, heavy metal, **Pb**, with a low melting point; used in traditional paints and coatings, and as sheetmetal for roof flashings.
2 the graphite-based content of a lead pencil.

lead 1 an insulated wire, fitted with a suitable connection at either end, which conveys electricity from a source to an appliance.
2 see electric lead.

lead acetate a poisonous white chemical compound, $\mathbf{Pb(C_2H_3O_2).3H_2O}$, used as a drier in paints and varnishes.

lead came a small lead glazing bar, H-shaped in cross-section, which holds panes together in leaded-light glazing.

lead carbonate a poisonous white chemical compound, $\mathbf{PbCO_3}$, used as a pigment in exterior paints.
see cerussite, white lead ore.

lead chromate a poisonous yellow chemical compound, $\mathbf{PbCrO_4}$, used as an industrial pigment in paints.
see crocoite, red lead ore.

lead drier a compound of lead used in solvent form in paints to speed up drying.

leaded brass an alloy of copper and zinc with additional lead to increase ductility and improve machinability.

leaded glass see leaded light.

leaded light, leaded glass, lead glazing; traditional glazing with small diamond-shaped or square panes of glass held in a mesh of lead glazing bars called cames.

leader header see rainwater head.

leader line see extension line.

lead-free paint any paint which does not contain lead compounds for health reasons, according to law.

lead glance see galena.

lead glass, crystal glass; a clear colourless glass containing lead oxide, used for optical devices and neon tubes.

lead glazing see leaded light.

lead grey a shade of grey which takes its name from the colour of the oxidized surface of the metal lead.

lead holder see clutch pencil. →130

leading hand see chargehand.

lead in oil a traditional paint of white lead ground into linseed oil.

lead molybdate $\mathbf{PbMoO_4}$, see wulfenite, yellow lead ore.

lead monoxide see lead oxide.

lead oxide, **1** lead monoxide; a chemical compound, **PbO**, used among other things in the manufacture of lead glass.
2 see red lead.
3 see massicot.

lead paint any paint which contains white lead or red lead.

lead pencil, **1** graphite pencil; a drawing and writing pencil with a rod of graphite encased in wood, available in a range of degrees of hardness from 6B (soft) to 9H (hard); the standard grade is HB. →130
2 see clutch pencil. →130
3 see carpenter's pencil. →130
4 see propelling pencil. →130

lead pigment **1** any pigment of lead salts such as lead chromate or lead carbonate, usually insoluble in water, poisonous and opaque.
2 see massicot (yellow).
3 see red lead.
4 see white lead.

lead plate thick rolled sheet manufactured from lead; used for soundproofing and radiation protection.
see *metal plate* illustration. →34

lead primer see red lead.

lead sheet **1** rolled sheet manufactured from lead; traditionally used for flashings, roof and wall claddings and damp proof courses.
2 see lead plate.

lead sulphate a chemical compound **$PbSO_4$**, found naturally as the mineral anglesite.

lead wool lead in fibrous form, used as sealing for pipes.

lead X-ray glass, X-ray resistant glass, radiation-shielding glass; glass which contains lead oxide and is relatively resistant to X-rays.

leaf, **1** wythe, withe (Am.); one single skin of brick, blockwork, concrete etc. in a cavity wall, or as facing for a steel or concrete frame.
2 see foil.
3 see door leaf. →50
4 see hinge leaf. →38

leaf and dart, heart and dart, waterleaf and dart; an ornamental motif consisting of a series of stylized leaves alternating with sharp dart-shaped forms. →82

leaf and rose scroll an ornamental motif consisting of a coiled leaf design with roses at the extremities of the coil. →82

leaf and tongue see leaf and dart.

leaf green **1** see chrome green.
2 see foliage green.

leaf moulding see foil moulding. →125

leaf ornament see foliated ornament. →82, →121

leaf scroll **1** a classical ornamental banded motif representing coiled foliage, especially acanthus, anthemion, lotus and palmette, and in medieval architecture, vines. →82
2 see leaf and rose scroll. →82

leafwork see foliated ornament. →82, →121

league a traditional British measure of linear distance equal to approximately 5 km or 3 miles.

leak **1** the unwanted escape of gas or liquid from a defective area of construction, a vessel, pipework or other technical installation.
2 the point at which this occurs.
3 the liquid or gas which thus escapes.

lean clay a soil type composed of 30–50% silty clays and clayey silts, generally of low to medium plasticity.

lean concrete concrete with a lower than usual percentage of cement.

lean lime low quality hydrated lime produced from impure limestone, which, when used as lime putty, cannot be spread evenly and has poor properties of plasticity and setting.

lean mix a mix of concrete or mortar which contains little binder.

lean-to roof, half span roof; a monopitch roof whose summit is carried on a wall which extends beyond the apex of the roof, often an overhang or canopy. →46

leasing **1** an agreement whereby buildings or land can be sold or transferred to a second party for a specified maximum length of time only, after which they return to the original owner.
2 a term used for long-term rental of vehicles, or sales with trade-back conditions.

leather **1** a sheet product made from the treated hides or skins of animals, used for upholstery, clothing etc.
2 see cocoa.

leather brown see cocoa.

leathercloth a plastic coated fabric having the appearance of leather, used in upholstery.

Leca see expanded aggregate.

lectern, lectorium (Lat.); a raised platform or desk with a sloping surface to hold an open book or notes from which a speaker, lecturer or priest may read.

lectorium see lectern.

lecture theatre a hall, often with banked seating, a podium and audiovisual equipment, in which lectures and demonstrations are presented.

ledge a horizontal structural rail in a ledged door, to which boards are fixed. →51

ledged and braced door a ledged door with diagonal bracing. →51

ledged door a simple door type whose leaf is constructed from vertical matchboarding nailed to a series of spaced horizontal members or ledges. →51

ledger **1** a scaffolding beam running parallel to the wall of the building under construction, which carries putlogs.
2 a large flat stone which covers a tomb or grave in a church.
3 see ligger. →48
4 tabloid; a North American standard paper size; 11" × 17", 279 mm × 432 mm. Table 6

leek green see chrome green.

left-handed, left-hung, LH; see handing.

left-hung see handing.

leg one of the two sides of a right-angled triangle, at right angles to one another.

legal a North American standard paper size; 8.5" × 14", 216 mm × 356 mm. Table 6

legget a steel-faced hammer used in thatched roofing for tapping and tightening the thatch and its fastenings.

legislation the action of making laws, the body of existing laws and their enactment.

legs anchor, hollow-wall plug; a range of nylon wall plugs for fastening to plasterboard hollow walls, with wings which spring out once pushed through a drilled hole and clamp to the reverse side. →37

Leipzig yellow see chrome yellow.

leisure centre, recreation centre; a commercial facility with halls, pools, courts, equipment etc. for sports, games and recreation; often synonymous with sports centre.

Leithner blue a form of the pigment cobalt blue.

lemon oil see oil of lemon.

lemon yellow, **1** citron yellow; a shade of yellow which takes its name from the colour of the peel of the ripe fruit of the lemon tree [*Citrus limon*]; equivalent to the colour of the pigment light chrome yellow.
2 barium yellow; also a general name for shades of pale yellow.

length **1** the basic measurement of linear distance, whose unit is the metre (m) (SI). →2
2 see overall length. →31

lengthening joint any joint used to join two long pieces or members together end on end to form one longer piece. →3
see scarf joint. →3

lengthening piece see extension.
lengthways referring to the orientation of an object with its longer dimension aligned with a particular direction or axis.
lens 1 a transparent solid optical object shaped to bend light passing through it in a controlled way.
2 glass lens; a translucent solid glazing unit made by a pressing process, embedded in cast concrete decks, floors and footways to provide natural lighting to spaces beneath.
Lentinus lepideus see scaly cap fungus.
Lenzites sepiaria see slash conk.
leper window, low side window, offertory window; a small church window set in the south wall of the chancel, to permit outsiders to see the altar and officiating priest; see also squint.
Lesbian cyma in classical ornamentation, a cyma reversa moulding enriched with leaf and dart ornament. →82
lesche, leskhe (Gk); an assembly room, or one for socializing, in ancient Greece. →92
lesene, pilaster strip; an exterior pilaster without a base or capital, found primarily in Romanesque churches providing lateral support for high walls. →13
leskhe Greek form of lesche. →92
let-in see housing. →5
letter a North American standard paper size; 8.5" × 11", 216 mm × 279 mm. Table 6
letter box, mail box, post box; an openable slotted container in which mail is placed awaiting collection before or after delivery.
letter-box plate see letter plate. →51
lettering 1 in technical drawing and graphics, the application of text, annotation, titles or other letters using a stencil, transfer lettering or by some other method.
2 annotation; in technical drawing and graphics, written explanatory words and titles.
lettering brush a finely pointed paintbrush used primarily for lettering on signs, plaques etc. →43
letter of attorney a legal document empowering one party to deal with matters on behalf of another.
letter of intent 1 a general communication from one party to another indicating a serious intention.
2 in contract administration, a formal letter from a client to the chosen tenderer stating that he proposes to enter into a contract with him.
letterpress a printmaking process for printing areas of typed text, produced by inking raised areas on a plate.
letter plate, letter-box plate, letter slot, mail slot; a slotted rectangular metal or plastics plate with covering hinged flap to allow for the conveyance of mail through a door leaf. →51
letter slot see letter plate. →51
letting, renting; the lending of property or a site for use or occupation by another party in return for regular payments.
lettuce green a shade of light green which takes its name from the colour of the leaves of the lettuce [*Lactuca sativa*].
leucite a whitish-grey silicate mineral which occurs in young volcanic rocks; it is used locally for potash fertilizer.
level 1 the height or datum of a point above sea level, as marked on drawings and maps.
2 see storey. →61
3 any instrument, apparatus or device for measuring true horizontal.
4 see levelling instrument.
5 see water level.
6 see spirit level.
7 see layer.
level crossing, grade crossing (Am.); an intersection of road and railway at the same level, often with hand-operated or automatic gates or a system of warning lights to alert traffic to the presence of an oncoming train.
level difference the vertical distance between two points or planes.
level invert taper in drainage and plumbing, a short piece of conical pipe or similar fitting for joining two pipes of different diameters so that their lower internal surfaces lie along the same line.
levelling compound, dressing compound, synthetic screed; in floor construction, a material such as cement or resin mortar applied in semi-liquid form in very thin layers, which sets to provide a level surface for flooring.
levelling instrument, level; in surveying, an optical instrument used in conjunction with a levelling staff for measuring levels.
levelling rod see levelling staff.
levelling staff, levelling rod; a long gradated rod used in surveying for ascertaining heights and levels from a known point.
lever handle a handle for a door or window casement, with a protruding lever, which operates a latch mechanism when turned downwards. →50, →51
lever-operated tap see lever tap.
lever tap, lever-operated tap; a water tap in which water flow is controlled by a lever.
Leyden blue a form of cobalt blue pigment.
LH see handing.
liability, debt; money owed by a company.
Liberty see Stile Liberty.
libitinensis see porta libitinensis. →90
libra a Roman unit of weight, equal to a pound, 12 unciae (Roman ounces) or 0.34 kg, later used in Italy, Portugal and Spain in various forms.
library a building, part of a building or room where books, papers and periodicals are stored and may be read or lent out.
lich gate see lych gate. →102
lierne a tertiary rib in a vault, which connects a point on a rib with a tierceron or another lierne; often for decorative rather than structural purposes. →101
life cycle the useful life of a building or product from its manufacture or construction from raw materials to its disposal or demolition.
lift, 1 elevator (Am.); a mechanical installation for lifting of passengers or goods from one level or storey in a building to another.
2 see lift car.
lift bank see lift battery.
lift battery, lift group, lift bank; a number of lifts in the same area whose controls are synchronized to work together.
lift bridge a bridge whose deck can be raised to allow vehicles, usually boats, to pass under. →64
lift car the lowered and raised compartment for carrying passengers and goods in a lift installation.
lift car door the inner door of a lift car, which moves up and down with it; a lift gate is usually a door of open lattice construction; see also landing door.
lift door see lift car door.
see landing door.
lift drive, lift machine; the machinery, motors or apparatus for moving and halting a lift.
lift gate see lift car door.
lift group see lift battery.
lift guide, lift runner; a rail attached to the wall of a lift shaft to guide the lift car.
lifting a defect in a paint finish consisting of the separation of a dry undercoat from a substrate on application of a successive coat of paint.
lifting equipment, hoisting plant; any equipment, cranes, hoists and elevators, used on a building site for lifting goods, machinery and people from one level to another.
lift landing an area of floor in front of a lift at which it stops.
lift machine see lift drive.
lift machine room, lift motor room, LMR; a space located adjacent to, above or below a lift shaft, with machinery to operate the movement of a lift car.

lift motor room see lift machine room.
lift-off butt hinge, lift-off hinge, loose butt hinge; a hinge whose central joining pin is welded to the upper part of one hinge leaf, permitting a door to be simply lifted on or off. →38
lift-off hinge see lift-off butt hinge. →38
lift pit, pit, run-by pit; a space at the base of a lift shaft to accommodate the underside of the lift car and counterweight.
lift pulley room a space located adjacent to a lift shaft, which contains pulleys which operate the lift, but no machinery.
lift runner see lift guide.
lift shaft see lift well.
lift shaft module a prefabricated unit of lift shaft which can be lifted into place.
lift sheave, sheave; a large pulley wheel around which lift cables, lift car and counterweight are hung in a lift installation.
lift slab construction a method of concrete construction in which concrete floor slabs are cast one above the other then raised into position for support by columns.
lift well, hoistway (Am.), lift shaft; the duct, tube or shaft in which a lift car moves.
lift well enclosure the structure that encloses a lift shaft.
lift well module see lift shaft module.
ligature see stirrup. →27
ligger a longitudinal timber used in thatched roofing to hold down thatch. →48
light 1 electromagnetic waves which can be seen by the human eye.
see artificial light.
see daylight.
see diffuse light.
see natural light.
2 any device for producing illumination; a lamp or luminaire.
droplight, see pendant luminaire.
see electric light.
see floodlight.
see spotlight.
3 an opening in a wall for a window; a small window or glazed unit.
see angel light.
see borrowed light.
see coupled light.
see domelight.
see fanlight.
see fixed light.
see lantern light.
see rooflight. →60
see side light. →52
see top light. →52
light alloy a mixture of light metals such as aluminium.
light blonde see beige.
light box an illuminated cabinet for viewing slides and transparencies on a flat horizontal opal glass bed with lamps behind.
lightbulb, lamp; a device which contains a gas or metal filament enclosed in a sealed glass vessel, excited by electricity to give off light.
light dispersivity in lighting design, the property of a surface to disperse light by interference or refraction.
light distribution curve, polar curve, candlepower distribution curve; a graphical representation of the light distribution characteristics of a particular luminaire or lamp, with luminous intensities for all directions from the source plotted on polar coordinates.
light expanded clay aggregate see expanded aggregate.
lightfast, light resistant; the property of a pigment, paint film or coloured coating to resist fading or deterioration of its colours on exposure to sunlight.
light filter see filter.
light fitting see luminaire. →60
see *light fitting* in office building illustration. →60
light fixture see luminaire. →60
lighthouse a tower with a powerful lamp on top for guiding ships and other seaborne vessels away from potential hazards and for aiding with navigation.
lighting, illumination; the provision of light for spaces in a building by the controlled placing of lights, windows etc.
lighting column see lighting post.
lighting controller see photoelectric lighting controller.
lighting fitting see luminaire. →60
lighting fixture see luminaire. →60
lighting mast, pylon; a tall freestanding structure for the high-level support of floodlighting, external area lighting etc.
lighting point 1 an outlet to which a light fitting can be connected to an electricity supply.
2 if located in a ceiling.
lighting post, lighting column; a freestanding column for supporting an exterior luminaire.
lighting track in artificial lighting, a surface-mounted conducting track to which movable spotlights can be attached.
light loss factor in lighting design, a measure of the aging of light sources, measured as a ratio of the illuminance after a specific period of time, to the illuminance of the source as new.
lightning-conductor, lightning-rod; a simple metal rod attached to the roof of a building or the top of a mast, connected to an earthed cable and used for conveying current from lightning strikes to earth.
lightning protection the physical protection of a building from random lightning strikes using rooftop installations to lead unwanted power surges safely to earth.
lightning protective installation any system of air terminations, down conductors and earth terminations to divert unwanted electric energy from lightning strikes away from a building.
lightning shakes see thunder shakes.
lightning-rod see lightning-conductor.
light output in lighting design, the quantity of luminous flux emitted by a source of light.
light-red silver ore see proustite.
light resistant see lightfast.
light sensitivity the property of a material or surface which has the tendency to react in some way to light which falls on it.
light shaft a narrow shaft either within a building or externally but surrounded by built form to introduce natural light to internal spaces, courtyards etc.
light table a large light box mounted on supporting legs for viewing slides, transparencies etc.
light transmittance in lighting design, the ratio of luminous flux transmitted through an area of material to that incident on it.
lightweight aggregate aggregate classified according to bulk density as less than 1200 kg/m^3 for fine aggregate, or 1000 kg/m^3 for coarse aggregate; types included as separate entries are listed below.
expanded aggregate. →49
expanded clay aggregate, expanded shale aggregate, see expanded aggregate. →49
light expanded clay aggregate, see expanded aggregate.
sintered aggregate.
wood particle aggregate.
lightweight aggregate concrete lightweight concrete which makes use of a lighter than usual coarse aggregate, often vermiculite, expanded clay, blast-furnace slag or in some cases a polymer or sawdust.
lightweight aggregate concrete block a concrete block manufactured using lightweight aggregate.

lightweight block see lightweight concrete block.

lightweight concrete concrete which has a bulk density range from 400 to 1760 kg/m^3 and is lighter than ordinary concrete, either by virtue of its lightweight aggregate (as in no-fines concrete, lightweight aggregate concrete), or entrained voids of air or gas (as in aerated concrete).

lightweight concrete block 1 a concrete block manufactured from lightweight concrete, or one with voids. →30
see *concrete block* illustration. →30
2 see lightweight aggregate concrete block.
3 see cellular block. →30

lightweight partition an interior non-loadbearing wall for dividing a space into rooms, often of plasterboard on a studwork frame.

lightweight plaster plaster which contains lightweight aggregate.

light well an external space surrounded by built form to provide light and ventilation to internal spaces, courtyards etc.
see *prehistoric structures* illustration. →65
see *Roman residential buildings* illustration. →88

lignin one of the organic polymeric substances which stiffens and bonds the cell structure in wood, extracted from paper pulp and used in the manufacture of plastics.

lignite, brown coal; a form of partially carbonized woody coal from the Cretaceous or Tertiary ages.

lignum vitae [*Guaiacum spp.*] a very heavy hardwood from the Caribbean and South America; its timber is greenish black, extremely hard and durable, and has a high oil content; used for machine rollers, mallet heads and 'woods' in the game of bowls.
Maracaibo lignum vitae, see verawood.

lilac a general shade of pale violet which takes its name from the colour of the flowers of the shrub *Syringa vulgaris*.

lilac grey a general name for shades of pale greyish violet.

Lilium see lily. →82, →121

lily 1 any of a number of species of flowering plant of the genera *Lilium*, *Nymphaea* etc. which have bulbous blossoms on long stems; a common motif in Egyptian (where it is also called a lotus), classical and heraldic ornament, symbolic of purity and the Virgin Mary in Christian ornament. →82, →121
2 see fleur-de-lis. →121
3 see lotus. →82, →121
4 blue lily, see blue lotus. →82, →121
5 see waterleaf. →82

lily capital an ancient Egyptian capital carved with decoration in imitation of stylized lily blossoms, also called a lotus capital. →73

lily moulding see fleury moulding. →125

lily white see chalky.

limba, afara; [*Terminalia superba*] a West African hardwood with straight-grained and coarse-textured yellowish timber, used for panelling, plywood and veneers.

lime, **1** basswood, European lime; [*Tilia spp.*] a number of species of hardwood tree from Europe and North America with pale, soft, light, fine textured timber; used for joinery, plywood and trim; see ***Tilia spp.*** for full list of species of lime included in this work.
2 chalk or limestone burnt in a kiln, used as a binder in cement and plaster; a generic name for quicklime, hydrated lime, lime putty, slaked lime, calcium oxide or calcium hydroxide. →Table 5

lime blue a form of Bremen blue pigment.

lime cement Portland cement to which lime has been added, used as a binder in masonry cement.

lime hydrate see hydrated lime.

lime mortar brickwork mortar consisting of slaked lime and sand in the ratio of 1:6 or other proportions depending on usage and exposure; may occasionally also include cement. →Table 5
cement lime mortar, see composition mortar.
see lime sand mortar.
see lime plaster.

lime plaster a form of crude plaster made from neat lime or a mixture of lime and sand. →Table 5

lime putty soft hydrated lime in solid but plastic form, used as a binder in plaster.

lime rock rock consisting largely of limestone or partially consolidated limestone, quarried from natural limestone deposits.

lime sand mortar, coarse stuff; mortar consisting of lime and coarse sand, often delivered to site ready mixed.

limestone a sedimentary rock composed of calcium carbonate, used extensively as building stone, and burnt to produce lime.

limewash see whitewash.

limewashing, whitewashing; the application of a solution of lime and water, or crushed chalk and water to a masonry surface as a clean, white finish.

lime white, **1** cream of lime, milk of lime; a watery or creamy emulsion of calcium hydrate or quicklime in water, traditionally used for whitewashing walls.
2 see bianco sangiovanni.

liming in landscaping and forestry, the addition of lime or any other calcareous material to the soil as fertilizer and to neutralize acid soils.

limited company, limited liability company (Am.), corporation, incorporated company (Inc.); abb. Ltd; a company whose owners are liable for potential debts only up to the value of their shares in that company.

limited liability company see limited company.

limited partner a member of a partnership whose liability for the debts of the company is restricted to the amount of his initial investment.

limited partnership a company formed by two or more people at least one of whom has limited liability for its potential debts up to the amount he or she has invested.

limiter see door chain. →51

Limnoria spp. see gribble.

limonite, brown iron ore; a brownish or yellowish earthy mineral, a natural oxide of iron, $Fe_2O_3.nH_2O$, used in various forms for pigments (yellow ochre); also an important iron ore.

linden see European lime.

linden green a shade of yellow green which takes its name from the colour of the seeds of the lime tree [*Tilia vulgaris*].

line 1 a measure of distance equal to one twelfth of an inch.
2 a longitudinal mark between two points made by a drawing instrument such as a pen.
3 the marking of a boundary or direction.
4 a series of events or products in industry or commerce.
5 see bricklayer's line.
6 see washing line.
7 see track.
8 see pipeline.
9 see power line.
10 see telephone line.

linear 1 in mathematics, referring to a function which can be calculated as responding to a straight line; generally, straight lined.
2 referring to a composition or form laid out lengthways or in such a way as to emphasize longitudinal effect.

linear city a city form which develops in a line along the sides of a main road, based on the principle that transport of people and goods is the ruling factor in urban design. →105

linear perspective the representation of three-dimensional objects in line on a two-dimensional surface by means of perspective projection.

linear strip see exposed runner.

lined paper any paper, usually writing paper, marked with a parallel series of evenly spaced horizontal lines.

line drawing any drawing composed entirely of lines rather than blocks of colour.

line engraving a method of making graphic prints by incising a pattern on a metal plate with a sharp instrument or burin; the tool makes a burred channel in the metal which serves to contain ink when printing.

line load see knife-edge load.

linenfold, drapery, linen scroll; carved decoration for wooden panelling, stone etc. representing hanging cloth with loose vertical folds. →123

linen scroll see linenfold. →123

line of draw ribbon-like variations in thickness of drawn glass caused by the manufacturing process, which give rise to visual distortion.

line of nosings, nose line, nosing line, pitch line; a theoretical line drawn between the front edge of the steps in a stair, parallel to the incline. →45

line printer a printer which prints one line of characters at one time in a sweep of its carriage; see also character printer, page printer.

liner a finely pointed paintbrush with bristles shaped to produce continuous lines, used for architectural rendering, decorative edges, lettering etc.; also called a lining brush. →43

line thickness, line weight, pen weight; in technical drawing, the continuous width of a drawn line, usually measured in decimal fractions of a millimetre.

line weight see line thickness.

linga, lingam; in Hindu architecture, a phallic symbolic statue or sacred representation of the god Siva. →68, →120

lingam see linga. →68, →120

lining 1 any dry covering of sheet, boarding etc. for cladding the interior surface of a wall or wall frame. →8
2 a surround for a door or window reveal, covering the joint and surface between frame and adjacent construction.
3 see breast lining.
4 see door lining.
5 drylining, see plasterboard drylining.
6 see formwork lining.
7 see flue lining. →56
8 see jamb lining.
9 see sock lining, resin lining.
10 see timber lining. →58
11 see wall lining.
12 see window lining.

lining brush see liner. →43

lining paper see wall lining.

linishing the smoothing of a surface, usually metal, using a continuously moving abrasive belt to produce a fine satin finish.

link 1 see stirrup. →27
2 see covered way.

link aerial see satellite link aerial.

linkage in traffic planning, the possibility to travel from one place to another by road, rail or public, private or other mode of transport.

link bridge an enclosed aerial walkway connecting two buildings above ground-floor level.

linked dwellings see link house.

link house, **1** linked dwellings; a form of low-rise residential building, similar to a terraced house, in which adjacent dwellings are connected by outhouses, car ports and pergolas. →61
2 see terraced house.

link mesh see chain link mesh. →34

link yoke in traditional timber frame construction, a piece joining the upper ends of principal rafters, supporting a ridge beam.

lino see linoleum. →44

linocut, linoleum cut; a method of making graphic prints by cutting a design out of a thick linoleum plate to which ink or paint is then applied with a roller.

linoleum a hardwearing, soft sheet flooring consisting of fibrous mineral material such as wood, chalk, cork and flax mixed with linseed oil and calendered; shortened form is 'lino'. →44

linoleum brown a shade of brown which takes its name from the colour of linoleum.

linoleum cut see linocut.

linseed oil 1 oil pressed from the ripe seeds of the flax plant [*Linum usitatissimum*], used as a vehicle and binder in paints.
2 see boiled linseed oil.

linseed oil putty see putty.

lintel, lintol; a beam above a window or door opening; types included as separate entries are listed below. →23, →22, →57
boot lintel. →30
corbelled lintel. →23
concrete lintel. →22
precast concrete lintel, see concrete lintel. →22
pressed steel lintel. →22
reinforced brick lintel. →22

lintel block, lintel unit; **1** a specially formed concrete or clay block with an indentation in its upper surface for grout and reinforcing bars; used in masonry beams as the tension flange or lower soffit.
2 see channel block. →30

lintel brick, beam brick, channel brick; a clay lintel block used over an opening in brickwork, having the same outward appearance, texture and size etc. as the other bricks. →16

lintel filler a preformed flashing, usually of sheetmetal, used over an opening.

lintel unit see lintel block.

lintol see lintel. →22, →57

Linum usitatissimum see flax.
see linseed oil.

lion depictions of the carnivorous feline *Panthera leo*, the 'king of the beasts'; symbolic in architectural ornament of courage, justice, power and heroism; attribute of the apostle Mark. →119
see chimera. →122
see lamassu. →75
see sea lion. →122
see Sekhmet. →74
see sphinx. →71
see Tefnut.

lion capital a capital carved with the images of two or four prostrate lions facing in opposite directions, typical of the edict columns of Indian architecture. →69

liparite see rhyolite.

liquefied gas a combustible hydrocarbon fuel such as propane gas stored in pressurized liquid form, used to produce energy for domestic and industrial use.

liquid 1 descriptive of one of the three states of matter, between a solid and a gas.
2 a substance which is able to flow but is virtually incompressible and thus stable in volume.

Liquidambar styraciflua see gum.

liquidated damages in contract administration, a predetermined amount taken from payments due to a contractor in the event of any delay on his part with regard to contractual obligation; a delay penalty.

liquidation in business management, a situation, usually occurring after bankruptcy, in which a company's assets are sold to meet debts.

liquid crystal display, LCD; a thin and light display, used especially for laptop computers and digital watches, in which crystals of certain compounds in liquid form can be charged so as to be temporarily visible to form numbers, letters and other characters.

liquid fuel any volatile liquid burned or otherwise used as an energy source.

liquid limit in soil mechanics, the maximum water content for a clay, which, when exceeded, promotes a change from the plastic to a liquid state.

Liriodendron tulipifera see tulipwood.

lispound a unit of weight formerly used in the Baltic shipping trade, which varied from 12 to 30 pounds or 5.5 to 13.5 kg.

listed building a building of recognized historical or cultural value which has official protected status against demolition, modification and disrepair.

list see listel. →14

listatum see opus listatum. →83

listel, list, tringle; a narrow flat fillet moulding. →14

lithium a soft, silver-white, chemical element, **Li**, the lightest of all metals.

lithography a graphic technique in which a drawing is made on a limestone block or zinc plate; during printing, ink adheres only to the drawn pattern.

lithopone, oleaum white; a fine white pigment consisting of zinc sulphide and barium sulphate which has good structural properties and is relatively cheap; used for exterior house paints and industrial coatings.

lithostratum opus see opus lithostratum.

litre abb. **l**; the SI unit of capacity equal to 100 mm × 100 mm × 100 mm.

litter unsightly waste in the form of paper, packaging and other small objects discarded into the environment by members of the public.

litter bin, waste bin; a container for the collection of litter, situated in a public place and emptied on a regular basis.

litter basket a small often non-fixed container for waste paper and similar rubbish.

live referring to a device, circuit or conductor which is connected directly to an electricity supply.

live knot see intergrown knot. →1

live load changing structural loads in a building imposed by the use of the building, its occupants, furnishings etc.

liver (brown) a shade of dark brown which takes its name from the colour of fresh liver.

Liverpool bond see English garden-wall bond. →19

live sawing see through and through sawing. →2

living area, lounge; a space or room in a residential building for leisure and communal activities.

living environment the various social and physical conditions for the occupants of a dwelling and its environment.

living room, lounge, sitting room; a central habitable room in a dwelling for recreation and relaxation; see also drawing room.
see *timber-framed building* illustration. →57
see *holiday home and sauna* illustration. →58
see *brick house* illustration. →59

living space space in a dwelling or residential establishment intended for leisure and communal activity.

living standard, standard of living; an empirical measure of the level of consumption and comfort of a community in terms of food, clothing, goods, materials, equipment, services etc. available to them.

Living Sculpture see Body Art.

LMR lift machine room.

load the forces imposed on a structure or structural member in use by building fabric and components, furnishings and services, internal forces and own weight, wind and snow etc.

loadbearing brickwork brickwork which has a structural function and transfers building loads to a foundation.

loadbearing capacity see bearing capacity.

loadbearing frame, structural frame; those parts of a building which carry structural loads to the foundations. →28

loadbearing structure see structure.

loadbearing wall, bearing wall; any wall which transfers structural loads from above and is part of the structure or structural frame of a building.
see *loadbearing external wall* in building frames illustration. →28

loadbearing wall construction, bearing wall system; a structural system in which the floors in a building are supported by loadbearing external walls and partitions. →28

loading 1 the imposition of a load on a structure or structural member.
2 the variation and types of load imposed on a structure.

loading bay a fixed raised platform for loading and unloading vehicles at a factory, commercial establishment or warehouse.

loading capacity see bearing capacity.

loan an agreement whereby money is lent on the understanding that it will be paid back over a specified period with interest.

lobate ornament see auricular ornament. →122

lobby 1 a circulation space adjacent to an external entrance or between stair flights which leads to other spaces.
2 see foyer.
3 see draught lobby. →59

lobster (red) a shade of red which takes its name from the colour of a cooked lobster [*Homarus vulgaris*] or crayfish [Astacidea spp.].

local air conditioning air conditioning for a specific room or targeted area within a room.

local centre see district centre.

local government, council, county council, municipal council; a democratically elected administrative body for a district.

local hue in painting, the true and inherent colour of an object or subject when viewed in diffuse light without alterations made by shadow or reflection.

localized lighting see local lighting.

local lighting, localized lighting; artificial lighting designed to provide a higher level of illumination in certain areas of a room or space.

local planning authority see planning authority.

local road a minor road conveying traffic to a local residential destination.

local ventilation mechanical ventilation for a specific room or targeted area within a room.

location, **1** site; the place where an object or area is placed or situated.
2 see position.

location block one of a number of small pieces placed under and around a glass pane or panel to prevent it moving in its frame during installation of glazing.

location drawing 1 a design drawing showing how or where a site, building or part of a building is situated with respect to its surroundings.
2 see general arrangement drawing.

location plan see block plan. →130

lock 1 a fastening mechanism for a door or gate, operated using an external mechanical or electronic device such as a key, push button or digital pad; types included as separate entries are listed below.
automatic lock, see coin operated lock.
bathroom lock. →39
cabinet lock. →39
check lock, see snib. →39
coin operated lock.
combination lock.
cylinder lock. →39
deadlock. →39
door lock. →51
electric lock.
electromagnetic lock.
furniture lock, see cabinet lock. →39
keyed lock.
magnetic lock, see electromagnetic lock.
mortise lock. →39
motor lock, see electromechanical lock.
padlock. →39
rim lock. →39
security lock.
solenoid lock.
thief-resistant lock, see security lock.
time lock.
toilet lock, WC lock, see bathroom lock. →39
Yale lock.

2 a chamber-like construction between two stretches of canal with different water levels consisting of two gates enclosing a body of water.
3 see air lock.
lock bolt see bolt. →39
lock case the protective casing or covering which houses the locking mechanism of a rim or mortise lock; in a cylinder lock this may be remote from the cylinder. →39
lock chisel a chisel with an L-shaped blade for cutting hidden mortises for locks.
lock control 1 the provision of security for a door or doors with the use of locks.
2 see electromechanical lock control.
3 see electric lock control.
4 see central locking.
lock cylinder see cylinder. →39
locked dovetailed notch see locked lap notch. →6
locked lap notch in log construction, a flush log joint in which the ends of corresponding logs are halved and cogged to form a tight interlocking joint; often called a locked dovetail notch if the cogs are splayed. →6
locker a cupboard with a lockable door for the storage of personal effects, often located in a changing room or at a railway station.
locker unit a furnishing unit containing a number of lockers.
lock faceplate see forend. →39
lock front see forend. →39
lock gate one of a pair of mechanical gates on a canal lock, opened to allow vessels to pass through.
locking 1 the securing of a lock with a key.
2 mechanisms and procedures associated with this.
locking bar a bar attached to a door leaf or pair of leaves to enable them to be fastened shut with a padlock.
locking snib 1 see thumb turn. →39
2 see snib. →39
lock nut 1 a nut with a nylon friction-ring cast into its threads to prevent it from working loose once attached. →37
2 see stop nut.
lock rail see middle rail.
lock ring 1 see circlip.
2 see lock washer.
lock saw see keyhole saw.
lock stile see shutting stile. →50, →51
lock suite see suite.
lock washer, **1** lock ring; any of a number of specially shaped, toothed or sprung washers for use under bolt heads to fasten a bolted joint. →37
2 especially one with a groove or projection to fit in a housing along a shaft and prevent it from rotating. →37
3 see spring lock washer.
loculus Lat.; pl. loculi; a niche or cell in a Roman chamber tomb. →89
lodge a temporary shelter or hut on a medieval building site where masons worked and stored their tools.
lodgepole pine, contorta pine, shore pine; [*Pinus contorta*] a planted softwood from the Rockies, Scotland and Scandinavia, used in the manufacture of chipboard.
lodging house an establishment providing short-term accommodation in return for rent; a hostel.
loess 1 in soil mechanics, fine material or silt which has been blown by the wind.
2 a porous, yellowish sedimentary rock formed from hardened wind-blown dust and containing the same minerals as clay.
loft 1 an accessible space within the roofspace of a building intended for habitation and frequently used for storage.
2 see garret.
loft ladder see disappearing stair.
log 1 the trunk of a felled tree, used for conversion into timber.
2 a piece of round unhewn timber used in log construction.
3 in computing, a file in which events, users and activities are registered chronologically in a file.
logarithm in mathematics, the power to which a specified number must be raised in order to produce a given number.
logarithmic spiral see Archimedean spiral.
log blue sap-stain in unseasoned logs.
log building 1 a building constructed of hewn or unhewn logs, principally horizontal timbers with interlocking corner joints.
2 see *log church* illustration. →102
log cabin a small hut or dwelling made of logs.
log cabin siding decorative timber cladding boards whose outer face is rounded so as to resemble log construction. →8
log church a traditional church with walls made of hewn logs. →102
log construction building frame construction using solid hewn or machined logs piled on top of one another horizontally, interlocking at the corners with joints known as notches; see also horizontal log construction. →6
see *log construction* illustration. →6
log corner joint see notch. →6
log crib see timber foundation grillage. →29
loge a private enclosure at an opera or theatre, a box.
logeion, logeum; Gk; in classical architecture, a raised speaking place, platform, stage or podium in a theatre or similar building. →89, →92
logeum Latin form of logeion. →89, →92
log extension, log overhang, flyway; in horizontal log construction, the length of log which extends outwards beyond a notched corner joint. →6
loggia in classical architecture, an arcaded or colonnaded porch or gallery of one or more stories attached to the ground storey of a building; also a separate colonnaded ornamental structure.
log grillage see timber foundation grillage. →29
logic 1 a branch of philosophy which deals with rational thought and reason.
2 a system of principles as applied to the physical working of an electronic or computing system.
logistics the discipline of arithmetical calculation applied to the movement of people, goods and vehicles.
log notch see notch. →6
logo the graphical symbol representing a commercial establishment, society or other institution.
log overhang see log extension. →6
log saw see tubular bow saw.
log wall a wall in a log building constructed from hewn horizontal logs placed one on top of another, caulked and held together with dowels and interlocked corner joints.
löllingite a silver-white or grey mineral, naturally occurring iron arsenide, $\mathbf{FeAs_2}$, used as an ore of arsenic.
Lombardic architecture the Romanesque architecture of Lombardy in northern Italy from c.600 to 1200 AD, characterized by areas of wall decorated with pilasters and blind arches.
Lombardy poplar [Populus nigra italica] a European hardwood, a variety of black poplar.
long and short work in stonework, a decorative quoin treatment for external masonry corners or jambs, using large stones interspersed vertically with flat stones. →12
long barrow see barrow.
long building see longhouse. →65
long-cornered chisel see skew chisel. →41
long cross see Latin cross. →117
long-grained plywood plywood in which the grain of the outer ply is approximately parallel to that of the longitudinal edge of the piece.
long groove in horizontal log construction, the groove hewn along the lower edge of a log to

suit the upper curved profile of the log course below, variously called a lateral, lateral groove, cope, Swedish cope or long notch. →6

longhorn beetle, longicorn beetle; [*Cerambycidae*] a family of insects whose larvae burrow under the bark of living softwoods.

longhouse an early Norse-influenced dwelling found in Scotland, Ireland and other parts of Northern Europe, a rectangular building often one room deep constructed within earth ramparts; similar models are also found in other primitive cultures. →65

long hundredweight see hundredweight.

longicorn beetle see longhorn beetle.

longitudinal beam a beam which lies parallel to the longer axis of a space or span.

longitudinal bevelled halved joint see bevelled scarf joint. →3

longitudinal church, nave-and-chancel church, axial church; a rectangular church type in which the main spaces are laid out in a linear fashion along a central nave, rather than centralized. →102

longitudinal reinforcement reinforcing bars which run parallel to the main axis of a reinforced concrete component, especially a beam or column. →27, →57

longitudinal rib a protrusion which runs along the length of a reinforcing bar.

longitudinal ridge rib, ridge rib; a horizontal rib which runs parallel to the main axis of a space at the ridge of a rib vault. →101

longitudinal section, long section; a sectional drawing of a building or object cut along its long axis.

longitudinal wave a waveform in which displacement is parallel to the direction of propagation.

long mesh fabric fabric reinforcement for concrete, with clearly elongated rather than square openings in its mesh.

long notch see long groove. →6

long radius bend a piece of curved drainage pipe with a large radius of curvature, designed for use at a gradual change in direction of the pipeline.

long section see longitudinal section.

long straw thatch see straw thatch.

long ton see ton.

lookout tower, observation tower, watch-tower; a tower with a clear view over the surrounding countryside or sea for defence or survey on a coastline, castle or other strategic place. →103

loop 1 a magnifying glass fitted into a cylindrical casing and used by watchmakers and graphic artists etc. for inspecting small or detailed objects.
2 an opening in a fortified wall through which weapons could be discharged; see arrow loop. →103
3 see arrow loop. →103
4 induction loop, see inductive loop.
5 see knuckle. →38

looped pile carpet a woven floor textile in which the weft or yarn formed in loops is left uncut at the surface.

loophole see arrow loop. →103

loop tracery a form of bar tracery found in Scotland in Gothic churches constructed from 1500 to 1545, dominated by large looped forms. →110

loose butt hinge see lift-off butt hinge. →38

loose-fill insulation insulation for roof spaces, wall cavities and floors consisting of lightweight granular or flaked material pumped into the void or laid in sacks; the most common forms are cellulose fibres, spun or expanded fibres or pellets of mineral material, glass etc.
see cellulose loose-fill insulation.

loose-joint butt hinge see loose-joint hinge.

loose-joint hinge, loose-joint butt hinge; a hinge which enables a door leaf to be lifted off without removing the hinge; a lift-off butt hinge.

loose knot a dead knot that is loose and may become detached from a piece of timber. →1

loose leaf the leaf of a hinge which swivels around the hinge pin. →38

loose piece mould in ornamental plastering, a mould consisting of a number of parts, used for taking or making casts from intricate or complex details.

loose pin butt hinge, loose pin hinge, pin hinge; a hinge with two rectangular metal leaves and a central joining pin which can be withdrawn for quick removal of a door leaf from its frame. →38

loose pin hinge see loose pin butt hinge. →38

loose rock fragmented rock types such as gravel and sand which do not occur naturally as solid masses.

loose rust, loose scale; flakes of rust loosely attached to the surface of steel delivered on site, which should be removed before priming and finishing.

loose scale see loose rust.

loose side, open face, open side, slack side; the side of a veneer sheet which has checks and markings from the cutting and is thus rougher than the face or tight side. →10

loose socket, collar; in plumbing and drainage pipework, a short fitting pushed over the adjacent ends of two aligned pipes to form a connection.

loose tongue see spline. →8

Lorraine cross, cross of Lorraine, double cross; a cross with two horizontal limbs which cross a vertical bar, one at the upper end, one at the lower; sometimes called a passion cross. →117

lorry, truck; a large motor vehicle, larger than a van, used for the transportation of goods.

Los Angeles coefficient, LA unit; a measure of the hardness and durability of aggregates, given as the percentage of detritus forming under standard grinding tests with ball-bearings in a rotating vessel.

loss 1 see attenuation.
2 in business management, a financial situation arising when costs exceed revenues.
3 see prestress loss.

lost formwork in concreting, any formwork left in place once the concrete has hardened.

lost-head nail, finishing nail, bullet-head nail; a round or oval nail with a small tapered head; used in situations where the nail should remain hidden. →35

loth a former unit of weight in the Netherlands, Germany, Austria, Switzerland and Scandinavia equal to half a local ounce.

Lotharingian cross a form of Lorraine cross in which the lower crossing bar is longer than the upper. →117

lotiform see lotus capital. →73

lotiform column see lotus column. →73

lotus 1 forms of flowering lily [*Nymphaea lotus* (white lotus), *Nymphaea caerulea* (blue lotus), *Nelumbo nucifera* etc.] sacred in ancient Egyptian, Buddhist and Hindu culture. →82, →121
2 an ornamental motif found in classical architecture based on the blue water lily [*Nymphaea caerulea*] or similar plants; heraldic plant of Upper Egypt (Nile Valley).
3 see lotus anthemion. →82
4 see waterleaf. →82

lotus anthemion painted ornamental banding from Mesopotamia, Egypt and Greece, depicting stylized lotus blooms alternating with other plant motifs such as pine cones, closed flower buds etc. →82

lotus and papyrus an ornamental motif consisting of stylized lotus and papyrus leaves. →82

lotus capital an ancient Egyptian capital carved in imitation of a stylized open or closed flower of the white lotus or water lily, Nymphaea lotus, or blue lotus, Nymphaea caerulea. →73
an Indian stone capital embellished with ovular lotus flower designs. →69

lotus column, lotiform column; an ancient Egyptian column type with a ribbed shaft carved in imitation of a tied bunch of lotus stems, or one surmounted by a lotus capital representing either open or closed lotus buds. →73

loudness in acoustics, the subjective phenomenon of sound measured in sones; one sone is equal to the perceived loudness of a 1000 Hz tone at a sound level of 40 dB.

loudness level in acoustics, the measure of loudness in phons; one phon is equal to the perceived sound level in decibels of a 1000 Hz tone above the audible sound threshold; it is thus a subjective version of the decibel, which is directly measurable.

loudspeaker, speaker; a device which turns electromagnetic signals into sound.

Louis XII, Louis Douze; pertaining to the French Renaissance style in architecture in France during the time of King Louis XII, 1498–1515.

Louis XIII, Louis Treize; pertaining to the style in architecture in France during the time of King Louis XIII, 1610–1643, French high Baroque.

Louis XIV style, Baroque classicism, Louis Quatorze style; late Baroque architecture in France during the reign of King Louis XIV (1643–1715) characterized by vast palaces and restrained ornament.

Louis XV style see rocaille.

Louis XVI, Louis Seize; pertaining to the style in architecture in France during the time of King Louis XVI, 1774–1792, French late Rococo.

Louis Douze see Louis XII.

Louis Quatorze style see Louis XIV style.

Louis Seize see Louis XVI.

Louis Treize see Louis XIII.

lounge, **1** living area; a space or room in a building for leisure, waiting and other communal activities.
2 see living room. →57, →59
3 a private hospitality room or suite of rooms in a commercial building, airport etc. for entertaining distinguished guests.
4 sun lounge, see conservatory. →57

loup see arrow loop. →103

loutron Gk; a bathtub in a Greek building, or a room housing one; also written loytron. →91

louver see louvre.

louvre, louver (Am.); **1** one of a series of horizontal slats in a grille, venetian blind etc.
2 a grille thus formed, used for shading devices, ventilation outlet covers.
3 see window louvre.

louvred blind see venetian blind.

louvred door a door with an open slatted construction to allow for the passage of air, used for the ventilation of plant rooms or for rooms in warm climates. →51

louvred shutters see persiennes.

louvred window a window with a series of pivoted horizontal glass louvres which may be rotated open to provide ventilation; also louvre window. →52

louvre window see louvred window. →52

love knot see Celtic love knot. →108

love seat, courting chair; an elaborately carved bench seating two, intended for couples to be married or in courtship.

Lovoa klaineana see African walnut.

Lovoa trichilioides see African walnut.

low carbon steel steel with a carbon content of 0.04–0.25%, used for wire and thin sheet.

low cost reasonably priced and costed.

low density fibreboard see softboard.

low density polythene, LD polythene, LDPE; a tough and resilient polythene which is soft and flexible.

low emissivity glass float glass with a transparent surface treatment to reflect longer, hotter wavelengths of solar radiation outwards.

lower chord, bottom chord; the lower longitudinal horizontal member in a truss. →33

Lower Egypt one of the two ancient Egyptian kingdoms, that which grew out of the Nile Delta; the other is Upper Egypt, the Nile valley; its Pharaoh wore the red crown, and its heraldic plant was the papyrus. →74

lower floor see downstairs.
see *lower floor* in brick house illustration. →59

lowest tender in tendering procedure, the lowest submission by a tendering contractor, to whom the contract is usually awarded.

low gloss see eggshell gloss.

low heat cement see low heat Portland cement.

low heat concrete concrete with a slow rate of heat release from the chemical reaction which takes place during setting.

low heat Portland blast-furnace cement a blended Portland blast-furnace cement in which the heat released in setting (heat of hydration) is significantly less than that for ordinary Portland cement.

low heat Portland cement, low heat cement; a Portland cement which generates less heat on setting than ordinary Portland cement.

low-level machine room a lift machine room located at or adjacent to the base of the lift shaft.

low pressure hot-water heating a hot-water heating system in which hot water produced for circulation and use is no more than 80°C.

low pressure sodium lamp a sodium lamp with a very efficient light source emitting strong yellow light, widely used for streetlighting.

low relief **1** see anaglyph.
2 see basso rilievo.

low-rise dwelling a class of residential buildings including detached houses, row and terraced houses, and multistorey residential buildings with few enough storeys to negate the need for a lift. →61

low-rise housing block a block of apartments usually up to three storeys in height. →61

low sheen see eggshell flat.

low side window see leper window.

low tide the occasion, usually occurring twice daily and caused by the action of the tide, at which the sea level is at its lowest, measured at a point on a coastline.

low velocity system, conventional system; an air-conditioning system using rectangular supply and return air ducting, in which air is conveyed at speeds of 3–8 m/s using conventional fans; cf. high velocity system.

low voltage a voltage in an electric circuit classified as less than 1000 V but greater than 50 V.

low water closet a self-contained toilet connected to a water supply, using small amounts of water for flushing waste.

loytron see loutron. →91

lozenge fret see diamond fret. →124

lozenge moulding see diamond fret. →124

L-profile **1** see edge strip. →2
2 see angle profile.

L-roof a hip and valley roof for a building which is L shaped in plan. →46

L-section see angle profile. →34

L-stair see quarter turn stair. →45

Ltd see limited company.

lug sill in masonry construction, a window or door sill which extends sideways beyond the edge of the opening, and is thus built into the wall at either side.

Luke see bull. →119

lumber (Am.) see timber.

lumen abb. **lm**; in lighting design, the SI unit of luminous flux.

luminaire, light fitting, light fixture (Am.), lighting fitting; an electric fitting to provide illumination, usually a lamp contained in a base with control equipment and a diffuser or shade; types included as separate entries are listed below.
see *light fitting* in office building illustration. →60
air-handling luminaire.

angle luminaire.
ceiling luminaire.
cove lighting.
downlight, downlighter.
droplight, see pendant luminaire.
exterior luminaire.
fixed luminaire.
floodlight.
fluorescent luminaire.
inground luminaire.
interior luminaire.
non-fixed luminaire.
pendant luminaire.
recessed luminaire.
spotlight.
surface-mounted luminaire.
uplighter.

luminance in lighting design, a measure of the brightness of a surface in a given direction, measured in candelas.

luminescence the emission of light by the excitation of a fluorescent or phosphorescent material etc. regardless of heat input.

luminescent concrete precast concrete to which luminescent material has been added, used in precast stair units to provide a low level of illumination in darkened stairways etc.

luminescent paint see luminescent pigment.

luminescent pigment, luminescent paint; various metal sulphides used in paint to provide luminescence or fluorescence, used especially in road signs and markings.

luminous ceiling, illuminated ceiling; a suspended ceiling whose ceiling panels are translucent glass or plastics sheets or baffles with luminaires behind, providing lighting for a space.

luminous efficacy see circuit efficacy.

luminous flux in lighting design, a measure of the flow of light energy from a light source or surface, measured in lumens.

luminous intensity in lighting design, the amount of energy in a cone of light, or solid angle from a light source, the ratio of luminous flux per solid angle, measured in candelas.

lump hammer see club hammer. →40

lump lime high quality quicklime in solid lump form.

lump sum contract, stipulated sum agreement; a form of building contract in which a single agreed sum is given as payment for work done.

lunette 1 an arched area, moulding or panel above a door, rectangular wall panel or window.
2 an arched or polygonal window in a roof or above a door.

lupine a shade of blue which takes its name from the colour of the blue flowers of the lupin [*Lupinus spp.*].

lutecium see lutetium.

lutetium, lutecium; a chemical element, **Lu**.

Lutheran cross a cross whose limbs have trefoil terminations, and with a circular void at the crossing. →118

lux abb. **lx**; in lighting design, the SI unit of illuminance, given as luminous flux per unit area or lumens per square metre (lm/m^2).

lych gate, lich gate; a roofed entrance gateway to a churchyard, usually of timber, originally for the purpose of resting coffins. →102

Lycopersicum esculentum see tomato red.

Lymexylidae see lymexylid beetle.

lymexylid beetle, ship timber beetle; [*Lymexylidae*] a family of insects which cause damage to standing trees and unseasoned hardwoods and softwoods by burrowing.

lyre a popular ancient Greek stringed plucking instrument with two projecting arms supporting a crossbar, from which seven strings are stretched down to the soundbox; a common decorative motif in antiquity. →123

lysis a plinth or extra step above the crepidoma of a classical temple, which surrounds the full extent of the stylobate.

M

Maat the ancient Egyptian goddess of harmony, justice, truth and order, portrayed as a female figure with a plume head-dress; also written as Mait. →74

macadam aggregate or crushed rock compacted for use in road construction.

Macassar ebony [*Diospyros celebica*] a hardwood from tropical Indonesia whose timber is very heavy and dark brown or black; used for decorative panelling.

macellum Lat.; in Roman architecture, an open colonnaded market square containing buildings with shops. →92

machicoulis a single opening in a machicolation; murder hole. →103

machicolation an exterior structure overhanging the walls of a fortification with openings in the floor from which missiles and boiling fluids could be dropped onto assailants; see murder hole. →103

machinability, workability; the ability of a material to be shaped with ease on a lathe or other cutting machine without flaking, blunting tools etc.

machine bend a bend in metal plumbing pipe produced with a bending machine; see pulled bend.

machine bit see cutter.

machine bolt a bolt whose shank has threads along its end portion only so a nut can be attached. →36

machine code see machine language.

machined log see milled log.

machine language, machine code; in computing, the specialized internal language in which programs and commands for computers are written.

machine mixing, mechanical mixing; the mixing of concrete or mortar with a spinning or oscillating device such as a drum or pan mixer.

machine room, 1 motor room; a plant room within a building containing equipment, motors, gear etc. for operating mechanical installations such as lifts, fans etc. →61

2 see lift machine room.

machine screw a screw with Whitworth or metric threads, a flat end, slotted head and a shank with an even diameter, fastened with a nut or into a predrilled hole. →36

machine trowel see power trowel.

machining, milling; a process of shaping materials such as metal, wood and plastics using a machine tool with a swiftly rotating bit, or by rotating the material to be worked.

machining tolerance in the machining of timber, a permissible variation in the dimensions of the machined piece.

machinist's hammer, peen; a metalwork hammer with a solid peen for shaping and bending. →40

macro a series of computer commands or a mini-program usually written by the operator to perform a specific subsidiary function, which can be recorded and used repeatedly.

macromolecule a very large molecule found in polymers, plastics, resins and rubbers, the smallest unit of the substance which cannot be divided without changing the basic property of the material.

madder [*Rubia tinctorum*]; see madder brown, madder lake, madder red, alizarin.

madder brown see alizarin brown.

madder lake, rose madder, natural madder; a red dyestuff made from the root of the madder plant (Rubia tinctorum), in use originally in Egypt, Greece and Rome, now mainly replaced by alizarin crimson.

madder red a red pigment traditionally produced from the root of the madder plant [*Rubia tinctorum*] and the various shades of red colour thus formed.

Madeira a shade of reddish brown which takes its name from the colour of the wine from Madeira.

madrasah, medresseh; a college building connected to a mosque in which teachings are given in Muslim theology.

maeniana plural form of maenianum. →90

maenianum 1 Lat.; a balcony in a Roman building.

2 a tier of seating in a Roman amphitheatre, theatre or circus which is bounded by two successive horizontal gangways (diazoma, praecintio); in an amphitheatre, each tier was reserved for a specific social class of spectator; plural maeniana. →90

maenianum medium, media cavea, maenianum secundum; 'middle tier' (Lat.); those tiers of marble seating in a Roman amphitheatre reserved for Roman citizens affluent enough to be able to wear a toga. →90

maenianum primum, ima cavea; 'first tier' (Lat.); the lowest tiers of marble seating in a Roman amphitheatre, directly above the emperor's podium, reserved for members of the equestrian order and aristocrats. →90

maenianum secundum 'second tier' (Lat.); see maenianum medium. →90

maenianum summum, summa cavea; 'highest tier' (Lat.); those tiers of limestone seating in a Roman amphitheatre reserved for poorer citizens (the pullati), slaves, freedmen, and foreigners residing in Rome, located between the maenianum medium and maenianum summum in lignis. →90

maenianum summum in lignis, summum maenianum in lignis; Lat.; a wooden gallery of seats at the upper tiers of a Roman amphitheatre reserved for the wives of senators and equestrians, protected from the sun and rain by a colonnaded canopy. →90

MAG welding, metallic active-gas welding; a method of arc welding of metals in which the arc is shielded with an active gas such as carbon dioxide or oxygen.

magazine a building or space for the storage of ammunition, especially explosives, in a castle or fortification.

Magen David, Mogen David, Star of David; 'shield of David' in Hebrew; a six-pointed star formed by the overlaying of two equilateral triangles, the symbol of the Jewish faith signifying God as the protective shield of David.

magenta 1 a deep purple pigment, one of the earliest dyes, named after the site of the Battle of Magenta in Italy in 1859.

2 a shade of purple which takes its name from the above.

magma rock in molten form from the interior of the earth.

magmatic rock see igneous rock.

magnesia white magnesium carbonate used as a white pigment.

magnesite, bitter spar; a mineral form of magnesium carbonate, used as a raw material in heat-resistant construction, as insulation and as a magnesium ore.

magnesite cement see oxychloride cement.

magnesium a pale, lightweight metal, **Mg**, which is ductile and easily machined.

magnesium carbonate a manufactured intense white chemical compound, $\mathbf{MgCO_3}$, used as a white pigment.

see magnesite, bitter spar.

magnesium oxychloride flooring see oxychloride cement.

magnet an object which has the property of attracting ferrous metals, which will align itself freely along an approximately north–south axis, and around which a magnetic field is formed.

magnetic catch a fastener used for furniture and other lightweight doors which holds by magnetic attraction.

magnetic disk a rotating magnetized circular computer board on which data, software, programs etc. are stored.

magnetic field a polarized field of force generated around a magnet or varying electric current.

magnetic flux a physical quantity whose SI unit is the weber (Wb), given as the amount of lines in a magnetic field which pass through an area.

magnetic flux density see magnetic induction.

magnetic induction, magnetic flux density; a measure of the strength of a magnetic field, given as the number of lines in the field per unit area, thus the amount of flux per unit area; its SI unit is the tesla (T).

magnetic iron ore see magnetite.

magnetic lock see electromagnetic lock.

magnetism a phenomenon whereby particular materials can be induced, or occur naturally, with a magnetic field, thereby attracting and repelling iron.

magnetite, black iron oxide, magnetic iron ore; a grey-black mineral oxide of iron, $\mathbf{Fe_3O_4}$, the most widespread and important iron ore also used as a pigment, polishing agent and in magnetic tapes.

magnifying glass a glass lens mounted on a base or with a handle used for magnifying images for the eye.

mahogany, 1 American mahogany, Cuban mahogany; [*Swietenia spp.*] a genus of tropical Central and South American hardwoods with heavy and extremely hard and durable red or golden brown timber; Swietenia is the true mahogany, although many other species are also sold as mahogany.
2 mahogany brown, mahogany red; a shade of reddish brown which takes its name from the general colour of the wood of the mahogany tree.

mahogany brown see mahogany.

mahogany red see mahogany.

maiden's blush a shade of pink which takes its name from the colour of the face when blushing.

maiden tree a tree which has been left undisturbed during landscaping, forestry felling etc.

mail box see letter box.

mail slot see letter plate. →51

main 1 a service pipe or cable which conveys electrical power, water or gas from a supplier to consumers.
2 see water main.
3 see gas main.

main bar one of the reinforcing bars in reinforced concrete which make up the main reinforcement.

main beam see principal beam.

main building the most important or conspicuous building of a building group or complex.

main contractor, general contractor, prime contractor; a contractor who is responsible for all work on site, though he may subcontract part of it.

main elevation the most important elevation of a building, usually one facing a street, axis or square.

main entrance, 1 front door; the principal door or means of entry into a building. →113
2 the most important or monumental entrance to a building, via which most of the building users will enter. →71, →91
3 see porta regia. →89

mainframe a powerful computer used for scientific and research projects.

main memory, primary memory; in computing, an integral high speed memory into which the computer loads programs and receives data for processing.

main reinforcement, principal reinforcement; reinforcement designed to resist principal loads in reinforced concrete. →27

main stair 1 the principal stair within or leading to a building.
2 a grand stair within or leading to the main entrance of a palace, castle, temple etc. for use of the most revered guests and dignitaries. →66

mains stopvalve, stopcock; the valve by which mains water supply to a building is controlled.

mains supply see mains voltage.

main switch a switch which shuts off electricity to all circuits in an electrical installation.

mains voltage, mains supply; the electrical potential supplied by mains electricity from generating plant, usually 220–240 V.

maintainability the property of how easily a component can be maintained and repaired.

maintenance, servicing; the care of a building, structure, system or technical installation in order to keep it functioning.

maintenance cost costs to an owner for keeping a building and its services in sound condition.

maintenance manual a document containing the basic requirements for maintaining and servicing the finishes, appliances and other components of a building or construction works.

maintenance painting see repainting.

maintenance period see defects liability period.

maisonette, duplex apartment; a dwelling of more than one storey within a larger residential block, with its own private internal vertical circulation.

Mait see Maat. →74

maize (yellow) a shade of yellow which takes its name from the colour of corn [*Zea mays*].

major road a large and important road, usually between urban centres, whose traffic has right of way over adjoining roads. →63

makore, African cherry, cherry mahogany; [*Tieghemella heckelii*, *Mimusops heckelii*] a hardwood from West Africa with pink to dark purple-red, stable and highly durable timber which has an abnormal blunting effect on tools; used for cabinets, flooring, boat-building and plywood.

malachite 1 an opaque yellowish green mineral, natural copper carbonate $\mathbf{Cu_2CO_3(OH)}$, polished as a gemstone, carved for ornamental work and ground as a pigment (see below).
2 Hungarian green, mineral green; the above used since ancient times as a bright green pigment.

malachite green see copper green.

mall 1 see maul.
2 see shopping centre.
3 see shopping arcade.

malleable cast iron cast iron which has been heat treated to improve its toughness and strength.

mallet a hammer with a wooden, rubber or plastic head, used for striking wooden or soft objects such as chisels, pegs etc. →40
see rubber mallet. →40
wooden mallet, see carpenter's mallet. →40

mallet-headed chisel a masonry chisel whose handle is shaped with an ovoid end, to take striking with a wooden mallet; cf. hammer-headed chisel. →41

mallow a shade of pink or pale red which takes its name from the colour of the flowers of the mallow plant [*Malva rotundifolia*].

Maltese cross a cross with four perpendicular wedge-shaped limbs which have indented ends; sometimes called a cross of promise. →118

maltha a mixture of wax, pitch, natural bitumen, olive pulp etc. used by the ancient Greeks as a sealant.

Malus sylvestris see apple.

mammisi, birth-house; a small Egyptian side temple, kiosk or tent shrine to celebrate the place where the god of the main temple was born, or where the goddess bore her children. →72

management 1 a body of people forming the administrative leadership of a company or business.
2 see administration.
3 see project management.

management audit a review of every aspect of the organization and running of a business at management level.

management contract a building contract in which a contractor provides consultation during the design stage and is responsible for planning and managing all post-contract activities and for the performance of the whole contract.

management contractor a person or organization, employed by the client, which is responsible for coordinating design and construction work in a building project.

manager 1 see construction manager.
2 see project manager.
3 property manager, see caretaker.

mandala 1 a magical figure representing the universe in Indian mythology, consisting of a circle and square with markings, used in the setting out and design of towns and buildings. →120
2 see yantra. →120
3 see cosmogram. →120

mandapa, 1 mantapam; a large open hall in a Hindu temple, used as a meeting place, and for theatre, instruction and dancing.
2 see ardhamandapa.

mandarin orange, orange peel, tangerine; a shade of orange which takes its name from the colour of the peel of the ripe fruit of the orange tree [*Citrus sinesis*], or mandarin orange tree [*Citrus reticulata*].

man-day, person-day; a measure of the amount of work done by a person over the period of one day, used in estimating potential labour costs for a project.

mandorla, mystical almond; in Early Christian art, an oval halo given to depictions of Christ, the Virgin Mary and others in images of the crucifixion. →119

manganese a metal, **Mn**, often used in steel alloys as a hardener.

manganese black a black pigment consisting of artificial manganese dioxide, used in cements and plasters.

manganese blue a brilliant blue pigment consisting of barium manganate.

manganese bronze, high tensile brass; an alloy of copper and zinc which contains small amounts of manganese and other metals to increase strength and improve resistance to corrosion.

manganese dioxide, MnO_2, see pyrolusite.

manganese green, baryta green, Cassel green, Rosenstiehl's green; a green variety of the pigment manganese blue.

manganese spar see rhodochrosite.

manganese steel an alloy of steel with manganese and carbon, which is extremely hard, brittle and resistant to abrasion.

manganese violet, mineral violet, permanent violet, Burgundy violet; a permanent inorganic violet pigment consisting of manganese chloride, phosphoric acid and ammonium carbonate; used in oil and tempera painting.

mangle an apparatus with rollers for squeezing the water out of laundry and flattening it.

manhole see inspection chamber.

manhole cover a removable cover for an inspection chamber, usually of concrete or cast iron.

man-hour, person-hour; a measure of the amount of work done by a person over the period of one hour, used in invoicing and estimating potential labour costs.

manière noire see mezzotint.

Manihot spp. see cassava.

Manila hemp fibre from a tropical plant [*Musa textilis*], used for making rope.

Manilla see Manila hemp.

manner a personal style of execution in art and architecture.

mannerism 1 any architectural style or detail which incorporates classical and other motifs in a frivolous, superficial and unconventional way.
2 Mannerism; a style in Italian Renaissance art and architecture which flourished from 1520, technically proficient and breaking away from classical harmony, with the emphasis on inner mysticism and external realism.
see *Mannerist portal* illustration. →113

mannerist referring to a work of art or architecture whose value is depreciated through its affected adherence to a certain style or aesthetic language; see also 2 above (of or pertaining to Mannerism).
see *Mannerist portal* illustration. →113

manometer see pressure gauge.

manor a landed estate, originally a division of land in feudal Britain worked by serfs, overseen and inhabited by the owner or lord.

manor house 1 the main residential building in a manor or estate in feudal medieval Britain.
2 a similar edifice for the Presbyterian Church in Scotland.

mansard an attic storey directly under a mansard or gambrel roof.

mansard roof 1 a hipped or gabled roof form in which each roof plane is doubly pitched. →46
2 see hipped mansard roof. →46

mansard roof truss a roof truss designed to maximize the use of interior roof space by having a large open central area topped by a king post truss and sided by rafters to produce a doubly pitched roof. →33

mansard tile a special roof tile manufactured for use at the joint of roof planes in a mansard roof.

manse the residence of a clergyman, especially of the Presbyterian Church in Scotland.

mansio Lat.; a Roman inn, especially for messengers and government officials.

mansion a large and prestigious residence.

mansion block see apartment house.

mansion-house the official residence of the Lord Mayors of London and Dublin.

mantapam see mandapa.

mantelpiece a decorative surround for an open fireplace, often forming a shelf above it; originally a beam across the face of a fireplace, supporting masonry above; also written as mantlepiece. →55

mantle 1 see gas mantle.
2 see mantling. →124

mantlepiece see mantelpiece. →55

mantling, mantle; stylized drapery hanging from the helm of a coat of arms; sometimes also called a lambrequin. →124

manual 1 see operating instructions.
2 see operation manual.
3 see maintenance manual.

manual metal-arc welding, MMA welding, shielded metal-arc welding (Am.), SMA welding (Am.), stick welding; a manual method of arc welding using electrodes covered with material that shields the arc.

Manueline a style of ornate late Gothic and early Renaissance architecture in Portugal during the reign of Manuel I (1495–1521).
see *Manueline style* in historical windows illustration. →111

manufactured aggregate aggregate produced as the result of an industrial process.

manufactured gas combustible gas manufactured from coal or oil and burnt to produce energy for domestic and industrial use; it has been largely superseded by natural gas.

manufacturer, producer; a person or organization which manufactures items such as building products, plant, and materials used in the building trade.

manufacturing see production.

manufacturing tolerance an acceptable range of dimensions or measurable quantities within which a manufactured item should be supplied to meet a specification.

manuring in landscaping and forestry, the addition of animal stool to soil in order to enhance plant growth.

man-year, person-year; a measure of the amount of work done by a person over the period of one year, used in estimating potential labour costs for a large project.

map an accurate scaled diagram of an area in plan, showing natural and man-made features, annotations etc.

maple [*Acer spp.*] a hardwood of North America and Europe with fine-textured, hard, strong, tough, flexible, cream-coloured timber; used for flooring, panelling, joinery, interiors and musical instruments; see ***Acer spp.*** for full list of species of maple and sycamore included in this work.

mapping, surveying; the making of a map or chart of an area of land on the basis of measurements and observations taken at various points.

maquette in sculpture, a small sketch model for a larger work, usually in wax or clay.

Maracaibo lignum vitae see verawood.

marble a metamorphic rock derived from limestone or dolomite, used extensively in building for floors and walls cladding, ground and polished as sheets or used as chippings in terrazzo and other composite materials.

marble dust small chips of ground marble used as aggregate in the plaster base of fresco and mural painting.

marble flour a fine form of marble dust used in fresco painting.

marble gypsum see alum gypsum.

marble stucco high quality polished stucco which resembles a marble surface, mixed from natural products including lime, marble dust, limestone and water. →83

marble white see alabaster.

marbling a decorative surface treatment applied by painting or other means in imitation of marble.

marcasite a yellow-green metallic mineral, naturally occurring iron disulphide, $\mathbf{FeS_2}$, an important raw material in the production of sulphur.

margin 1 the shaped exterior edge of a rectangular object such as a stone slab, tile, wooden table top etc. →14
2 see verge.
3 see dividing strip.

marginal draft see drafted margin.

marginal strip in road construction, a painted line or strip of material for marking out the edge of a carriageway. →62

margin knot a knot near a corner or arris of a piece of timber. →1

margin strip 1 in timber flooring, a board laid at the edge of a floor as a border.
2 see marginal strip. →62

margin trowel a narrow-bladed hand plasterer's trowel used for applying plaster to small, confined areas. →43

marigold window see rose window. →109

marina, yacht harbour; a harbour or row of jetties for the mooring of yachts and other small recreational vessels.

marine blue, Navy blue; a shade of blue which takes its name from the colour used to dye seamen's uniforms.

marine crustacean see gribble.

marine mollusc see shipworm.

marine plywood a grade of plywood manufactured from quality wood veneers bonded together with waterproof glues, used especially for applications in contact with seawater.

maritime transport see sea transport.

Mark see lion. →119

marker see marker pen.

marker pen, 1 marker; a pen containing permanent ink which has a felt or fibrous tip through which colour is transferred; see also felt pen, fibre-tipped pen.
2 see felt pen. →130

marker post one of a series of posts at the side of a road, often with reflectors, to mark out its edge.

market 1 in economics, trade in a specific item or service.
2 the section of population to which goods or services may be sold.
3 fair; a gathering of buyers and sellers and the place where their sales occur.

market cross, mercat cross; a stone cross erected in the market place or square of many market towns. →118

market hall see covered market.

market place, market square; an open area or widening of a street in the centre of a village, town or city in which goods are bought and sold.

market square 1 see market place.
2 see macellum. →92

market town a provincial town originally owing its existence to its market, which served the local rural area.

marking awl see scribe.

marking gauge, butt gauge; a device used in woodwork for marking out a cutting line on a piece of timber.

marking out see setting out.

marl a variety of clay containing a high proportion of calcium carbonate.

marlstone limestone with an abundance of clay material.

maroon a shade of violet brown which takes its name from the colour of the fruit of the sweet chestnut tree [*Castanea sativa*] ('marron' is French for chestnut).

marquetry inlaid work of different coloured veneers as surface decoration for panelling and furniture; see intarsia.

Mars black, black oxide of iron; a dense opaque black pigment consisting of black iron oxide, suitable for use in all types of paint.

Mars brown a form of synthetic brown iron oxide pigment.

Mars colour any of a range of coloured artificial iron oxides used as permanent pigments.

Mars orange see Mars yellow.

Mars yellow, iron yellow, Mars orange, yellow oxide of iron; a synthetic, organic, yellow iron oxide pigment which has good chemical and weather resistance.

marsh, marshland; an area of lowland covered with water, or having water near the surface.

marshland see marsh.

martensitic stainless steel a variety of stainless steel which contains 13% chromium.

martyrion, martyrium (Lat.); Gk; a burial place, place of martyrdom or a shrine with relics dedicated to a martyr.

martyrium Latin form of martyrion.

mascaron see mask. →122

mash hammer see club hammer. →40

mask, mascaron; carved ornamentation of a grotesque human or animal face or head, especially used for keystones and panels. →122

masking in painting and decorating, the temporary covering of boundary areas which are to remain free of paint with tape and paper.

masking tape pale brown adhesive paper tape used by painters and decorators for masking off boundaries of areas to be painted; also used as a general purpose tape, and often as draughting tape.

mason, stonemason; a skilled craftsman who works in stone, in building construction producing stone walling and embellishment.

masonry any construction in laid bricks, blocks or stone; types included as separate entries are listed below.
ashlar masonry, see ashlar. →12
blockwork.
brickwork. →20
cloisonné masonry.
coursed squared rubble masonry. →11
cyclopean masonry. →11
decorative masonry.
opus, Roman stonework. →83
Pelasgic masonry, see cyclopean masonry. →11
polygonal masonry. →11, →83
random squared rubble masonry, see uncoursed squared rubble masonry. →11
Roman stonework, see opus. →83
squared rubble masonry. →11
stone masonry. →11
stonework.
thin bed masonry.
uncoursed squared rubble masonry. →11

masonry arch a curved construction of wedge-shaped stones, blocks or bricks in compression, used to support loads between two points of support over an opening. →22, →23, →24
see *true arches* illustration. →24
see *flat, false and decorative arches* illustration. →23
see *arched and vaulted construction* illustration. →22

masonry axe a tempered steel, double-headed axe used for dressing and smoothing stonework; also variously called a stone, rock, stonemason's, masonry, trimming or chop axe. →40

masonry bit see masonry drill. →42

masonry block see block.

masonry capping, 1 coping block, coping stone; one of a series of bricks, blocks or stones placed along the top of a freestanding wall to protect it from the infiltration of rainwater.
2 see capping brick. →16
3 see coping brick. →16

masonry cement any cement used for bonding bricks, blocks or stones together in masonry walling, in particular Portland cement with finely ground lime, plasticizers or other additives.

masonry cement mortar a Portland cement-based mortar containing a fine mineral filler and air-entraining agent; it has good workability and is used in bricklaying.

masonry chisel any of a wide range of solid steel cold chisels used for shaping, carving and dressing stone; also called stonemason's, mason's, stone or stonecarving chisels; types included as separate entries are listed below. →41
see *masonry chisels* illustration. →41
batting tool. →41
boaster. →41
bolster. →41
broach. →41
claw chisel, claw tool. →41
clourer. →41
cold chisel. →41
driver. →41
fantail tool, see fishtail chisel. →41
fillet chisel. →41
fishtail chisel, fishtail tool. →41
hammer-headed chisel. →41
jumper. →41
mallet-headed chisel. →41
nicker, see splitter.
patent claw chisel. →41
pitching tool, pincher, pitcher. →41
point tool. →41
punch. →41
quirking tool. →41
sculptor's point. →41
spindle, see fillet chisel. →41
splitter.
tooth tool, see patent claw chisel.
tracer.
waster. →41

masonry drill, concrete drill, masonry bit; a drill bit for boring holes in masonry and concrete, usually tipped with a hard metal alloy such as tungsten carbide. →42

masonry finish see stonework finish. →12

masonry fireplace a fireplace laid in brick, block or stone as opposed to manufactured from steel or cast iron. →55

masonry joint any joint between adjacent stones, bricks etc. in masonry; the final shaped mortar in bed and vertical joints; see *types of masonry joint* illustration. →20

masonry mortar see bedding mortar.
see masonry cement mortar.

masonry nail a smooth round hardened steel nail used for fixing materials and components to masonry and concrete. →35

masonry paint, organic rendering, plastic paint, stone paint; a thick emulsion alkali-resistant paint used for masonry surfaces.

masonry primer a primer for use on a masonry surface.

masonry saw a machine tool with a diamond-tipped circular saw, often hand-held or bolted in place, for cutting openings in masonry walling, concrete etc.

masonry seal a masonry barrier constructed across the shafts of ancient Egyptian mastaba tombs and other burial structures to prevent the passage of grave robbers. →70

masonry screw see concrete screw. →36

masonry stove a solid-fuel heating stove constructed of laid stones or bricks in mortar. →56

Masonry style see Incrustation style.
see *Pompeian styles* illustration. →126

masonry trowel see bricklayer's trowel. →43

masonry unit any brick, block or stone used in the laying of a wall; a generic name for both bricks and blocks.

masonry vaulting see vaulting. →22, →23, →24

masonry wall a wall built of stones, bricks, blocks or other mineral products bonded together with mortar or cement.

mason's axe see masonry axe. →40

mason's chisel see masonry chisel. →41

mason's trowel see bricklayer's trowel. →43

mass 1 the quantity of matter a body contains, measured in kilograms.
2 a large solid volume in architectural composition.
3 a homogeneous body of malleable, plastic material.

mass centre see centre of gravity.

mass concrete, plain concrete; concrete containing no reinforcement, used in bulk solely for limited structural applications, fill etc.

mass density the mass per unit volume of a solid granular material, calculated to include the spaces between the granules; its units are kg/m^3.

massicot a yellow lead oxide pigment no longer in use, occurring naturally as soft, earthy deposits.

massing the location and size of the various built volumes and forms in an architectural composition.

massive rock see igneous rock.

massive wall see solid wall.

mass law in acoustics, an approximation according to which the acoustic insulation of a construction increases relative to its mass per unit area.

mass production a form of manufacturing using factory processes which turn out items in large quantities.

mass storage the area of a computer or peripheral device for storing large amounts of information not in continuous use, such as backup files.

mass transport see public transport.
mass transport vehicle a vehicle capable of carrying a large number of passengers, a bus, train, plane or ship.
mast a tall, relatively slender vertical structure or pole, often trussed or braced with guy ropes, used for supporting antennae, lighting, flags etc.
mastaba, **1** an Arabic stone bench or seat fixed to a dwelling.
2 mastaba tomb; a large ancient Egyptian stone tomb with sloping stone sides and a flat top, built over a burial ground or chamber. →70
mastaba tomb see mastaba. →70
mast church see stave church.
master key a key which fits all the locks in a suite of locks, each of which has a servant key.
mastic 1 natural resin gathered from a certain Mediterranean tree (Pistachia lentiscus), used with a solvent such as turpentine to form a varnish.
2 see sealant. →53
3 see sealing compound. →53
mastic asphalt a mixture of asphalt and chippings or sand laid hot but which is solid at normal temperatures; used for paving, flooring and roof waterproofing.
mastic asphalt surfacing in road construction, a surface layer or wearing course formed by successive layers of hot mastic asphalt.
masugumi, kumimono; an elaborate console or capital supporting a roof or canopy in Japanese wooden architecture. →68
masur birch an irregularity in birch wood which produces a speckled patterned surface; used in veneers and decorative surfaces.
mat see matting.
matchboard one of a number of tongued and grooved timber boards used in matchboard cladding or flooring.
matchboard door a simple ledge door faced with tongued and grooved boards.
matchboarding, tongue and groove boarding; timber boarding which has been milled with a tongue along one edge and a corresponding groove along the other; when laid, the tongue fits into the groove of the adjacent board. →8
matching 1 see tongue and groove jointing.
2 the alignment of adjacent sheets of patterned wallcovering so that the pattern is continuous.
3 the craft of arranging sheets of wood veneer into neat repeated or mirrored patterns for the surfaces of panels and tops or fronts of furnishings. →10
mate a labourer on a building site who helps a tradesman.
material, substance; a basic commodity used in the manufacture of products or constructions; the matter from which something is made.
maternity clinic part of a health centre which provides advice and health care for mothers and their young children.
math see mathematics.
mathematics, math (Am.), maths; the science of quantities and how they relate to one another.
maths see mathematics.
matrix 1 in mathematics, a system of numbers or values arranged in tabular form.
2 calcite or other material which binds the grains in stone, concrete etc. together; cementitious matrix.
3 see mould.
4 see dot matrix.
matrix printer, dot matrix printer; a printer in which colour is transferred to paper via a number of small pins pressing against an inked ribbon, forming a range of characters made up of small dots.
matroneum an upper gallery in a church reserved for womenfolk.
mat sinking see mat well.
matt see flat.
matte see flat.
Matthew see angel. →119
matting, mat; softish floor coverings such as rubber and synthetic matting, linoleum and various fibrous and fabric-based sheets, usually supplied in rolls; types included as separate entries are listed below.
carpet.
coir matting.
cork matting, see cork carpet. →44
doormat.
filter mat. →48
floor covering. →44
glassfibre mat.
linoleum. →44
rubber flooring.
sisal matting.
woven matting, see woven carpet.
maturity see concrete maturity.
mat well, mat sinking; a recess in floor construction in front of an external doorway, designed to house a doormat or grill so that it is flush with the floor surface.
mat well frame a frame for the perimeter of a mat well.
maul, 1 mall; a heavy hammer such as a sledgehammer or club hammer, used for crushing and driving. →40
2 see beetle.
3 see five pound maul. →40
4 see club hammer. →40
mausoleum a tomb or monument to an individual.
mauve, 1 Perkin's violet; a synthetic organic violet pigment manufactured from coal tar intermediaries, originally discovered by Sir William Perkin in England in 1856.
2 mauve Perkin; a shade of pale violet which takes its name from the above.
mauve Perkin see mauve.
maximum a highest point or value.
maximum load the largest structural load which a member or construction can safely withstand.
maximum temperature period in the steam curing of concrete, the period over which the temperature is maintained at a constant maximum level.
Maya architecture the architecture of the Mayan Indians in Central America and Mexico from c.400 to 900 characterized by ziggurats, planned gridiron towns, stone corbelled vaulting and the use of cement and concrete manufactured from burnt lime. see *Mayan teocalli* illustration. →67
Mayan pyramid see teocalli. →67
maze a labyrinth-like pattern which has dead-ends and false routes; a true labyrinth has only one route (unicursal) to the centre, one entrance and exit, no dead-ends and no intersecting paths; often mistakenly or loosely called a labyrinth. →123
see Classical maze, Cretan maze. →123
MDF medium density fibreboard.
mean in mathematics, the average value of a series of differing values.
meander, 1 labyrinth fret; a decorative pattern of intertwining perpendicular lines forming a band; a complex or intricate fret or key pattern, sometimes called an angular guilloche. →124
2 see potenty moulding. →125
mean deviation in statistics, the arithmetic mean of the deviations from the mean average value of a set of figures.
means of access a public or private roadway, driveway or path for use of vehicles or pedestrians to enter or approach a site.
means of egress, means of escape, escape route; a term appearing in fire regulations to mean the continuous and unobstructed way of exit travel during a fire or other emergency from any point in a building or facility to a public way.
means of escape see means of egress.
means of transport any system, machine or vehicle used to convey people or goods.

measure 1 the value or extent of a measured quantity.
2 a unit of measurement.
3 an implement used in measurement, such as a graded scale or graduated glass vessel.
4 see measuring tape, tape measure.
5 see dimension.
6 see circular measure.

measured drawing 1 a drawing to scale produced from a survey of an existing building or structure.
2 see record drawing.

measured work in contract management, site work paid on the basis of measurement of its scope and quantities after it has been undertaken.

measurement 1 the measuring of magnitude of an object, site, material, physical property or building work carried out.
2 the numerical quantity which results from measuring something.
3 see system of measurement.
4 see dimension.

measurement contract a form of building contract whose final sum is based on the total amount of work done, valued according to an itemized agreed schedule of rates.

measurement preambles in contract administration, clauses that explain or clarify methods of measurement for items in a bill of quantities.

measuring point in perspective, a vanishing point used to measure the lengths of lines parallel and perpendicular to the picture plane. →128

measuring tape 1 a long steel or fibrous rolled and gradated tape up to 30 m long for measuring long distances.
2 see flexible steel tape measure.

measuring telescope, scope; that part of an optical surveying instrument which contains a telescope whose sight is marked with a graduated scale and cross-hairs.

mechanical concerned with or operated by machines, machinery, tools or physical force.

mechanical adhesion the adhesion of two surfaces caused by bonding agents keying into porous or rough surfaces; cf. specific adhesion.

mechanical engineering see mechanical services engineering.

mechanical extract in ventilation, the removal of used air from a space, gases up a flue etc. with a fan or other mechanical plant.

mechanical input and extract ventilation, combined extract and input system; a mechanical ventilation system in which both supply and extract of air through terminal devices is controlled by a fan.

mechanical joint any joint fixed without the use of glue or other bonding medium. →3

mechanical mixing see machine mixing.

mechanical plastering see projection plastering.

mechanical services, heating and ventilation; heating, water supply and discharge, and ventilation services for a building.

mechanical services engineering 1 the building design and construction discipline encompassing heating, water supply, drainage and ventilation.
2 see HEVAC.

mechanical services installation the provision, apparatus and equipment to operate the heating, water supply, and ventilation requirements of a building.

mechanical smoke extraction system see fire venting installation.

mechanical trowel see power trowel.

mechanical ventilation, forced ventilation; the ventilation of a building which relies on mechanical plant to convey, introduce and remove air.

mechanics a branch of physics dealing with motion and equilibrium of bodies and the forces on them; includes statics and dynamics.

medallion a decorative round or oval framed wall panel either bare, ornamented or containing a portrait. →113

media cavea see maenianum medium.

median 1 in geometry, a line joining the apex of a triangle to the centre of the opposite side, thus bisecting the angle.
2 see central reserve. →63
3 see verge.
4 see dividing strip.

Medicago lupulina black medic, see shamrock. →121

Medieval architecture European architecture from the dissipation of the Roman Empire in 500 AD to the advent of the Renaissance in the 1500s, including Early Christian, Byzantine, Romanesque and Gothic architecture.
see *medieval castle* illustration. →103

medium 1 any substance or vehicle in which a body is, moves, or in which radiation extends.
2 see paint medium.

medium board a class of medium density fibreboards, including high density and low density medium board; density 350–800 kg/m^3.

medium carbon steel steel with a carbon content of 0.25–0.5%, used for forging.

medium density fibreboard, MDF; a dense and versatile fibreboard formed through a dry process in which the fibres are bonded together with urea formaldehyde resin; its density does not exceed 600 kg/m^3.

medium gravel in soil classification, a range of particles of mineral soil which vary in size from 6 mm to 20 mm.

medium grey, neutral grey; a general name for shades of grey towards the middle of the grey scale.

medium-hard rock according to a classification of hardness of rocks used by stone masons and construction technicians, rock which has a compressive strength between 800 kg/cm^2 and 1800 kg/cm^2.

medium sand in soil classification, a range of particles of mineral soil which vary in size from 0.2 mm to 0.6 mm.

medium silt in soil classification, a range of particles of mineral soil which vary in size from 0.006 mm to 0.02 mm.

medium strength in construction technology, a description of a member or structure which can withstand certain preclassified loading levels.

medresseh see madrasah.

medulla see pith.

medullary ray, pith ray; fine radial lines in wood extending outwards from the pith of a tree trunk.

Medusa a classical decorative motif based on the only mortal of three hideous sisters or Gorgons, from Greek mythology, with live snakes for hair and a gaze that turned its onlooker to stone. →121, →122

meeting, 1 conference; a formal occasion where parties with a common aim, project etc. gather to discuss matters and formulate decisions.
2 see site meeting.

meeting house a simple church or chapel devoid of ornament for Nonconformist, Baptist, Methodist, Quaker etc. worship based on readings from the bible.

meeting room, 1 conference room; a room within a building or place of work in which group meetings or discussions may be held. →60
2 see assembly room.
3 see ecclesiasterion. →92

meeting stile the vertical side member of the folding casement or double door leaf opposite that from which it is hung.

mega- abb. **M**; a prefix for units of measurement or quantity to denote a factor of 10^6 (one million). →Table 1

megabit a unit of computer memory capacity or data size of one million (or 1 048 576) bits.

megabyte a unit of computer memory capacity or data size of one million (or 1 048 576) bytes.

megalith a prehistoric structure such as a dolmen, chambered tomb or cist constructed from one or more large blocks of rough stone.

megalithic temple prehistoric temples such as those found at Tarxien, Malta, with walls constructed from shaped and placed upright blocks, or orthostats. →65

megalopolis 1 a large densely populated urban agglomeration or city chain such as those found along the east coast of the USA or in Japan.
2 according to Mumford's classification, the fourth stage of city growth, a consuming, bureaucratically and technocratically governed urban sprawl on the decline.

megaron Gk; **1** an early Greek or Mycenaean dwelling type. →65, →87
2 a long rectangular central hall in a Mycenaean dwelling or temple, with an entrance at one end; originally evolving from the Mycenaean dwelling type.
3 see megaron temple.

megaron temple a simple Greek temple type consisting of a columned pronaos leading to a single chamber containing a ritual hearth. →84

megilp a jelly-like mixture of linseed oil and the natural resin mastic, used as a medium in some artist's paints.

meh nesut see royal cubit. →106

melamine see melamine formaldehyde.

melamine faced chipboard chipboard manufactured with a surface coating of melamine impregnated paper or membrane, used for hardwearing table tops and kitchen surfaces.

melamine facing 1 the treatment of a surface by the thermal application of melamine impregnated sheet.
2 the finish formed by this.

melamine formaldehyde, MF, melamine; a clear, resistant thermosetting resin used for mouldings, hardwearing surface coatings and adhesives.

melamine formaldehyde glue a synthetic adhesive of melamine formaldehyde resin used for gluing veneers or laminated plastics.

melamine laminate any laminate whose main component is melamine formaldehyde resin, used for hardwearing surfaces of worktops and doors.

mélange yarn wound from fibres of a number of different colours.

melon dome see umbrella dome. →26

melting point the lowest temperature at which a solid will turn into a liquid.

memorial tablet, plaque; a stone or metal plate attached in proximity to a burial site or grave bearing the name of the deceased.

membrane a flexible tough sheet or thin covering layer incorporated in construction to prevent the passage of moisture; types included as separate entries are listed below.
air-gap membrane. →29, →57, →59
bitumen-polymer membrane.
bituminous membrane.
cavity drainage membrane, cavity membrane, see air-gap membrane. →29, →57, →59
damp proof membrane.
drainage membrane, see air-gap membrane. →29, →57, →59
geomembrane.
isolating membrane, see separating layer.
slip membrane.
tanking membrane, see air-gap membrane. →29
waterproofing membrane. →44

membrane absorber in acoustics, an absorbing construction consisting of a board or sheet material stretched between battens to absorb sound through sympathetic resonance.

membrane curing a method of curing concrete slabs by covering with a layer of impervious material such as polythene sheet or sprayed resin to prevent evaporation.

membrane roofing, membrane waterproofing; a general name for thin flexible sheet materials and products such as bitumen felt, plastic sheet or asphalt used to provide a waterproof upper layer in flat or pitched roof construction. →49

membrane theory a theory of shell structures which assumes that the considered construction behaves as a balloon and thus the only forces within it are tension or compression.

membrane waterproofing 1 a thin layer of waterproofing material or product, usually a membrane of bitumen or other polymeric resilient sheeting, laid as the final covering for flat roof construction. →49
2 see membrane roofing. →49

memo see memorandum.

memorandum, memo; a short, often informal written message circulated to a member or members of an organization.

memory that part of a computer in which data and instructions are stored.

mendelevium a chemical element, **Md**.

menhir a prehistoric monumental standing stone of Celtic origin, similar to an obelisk.

menorah a Jewish candelabrum with seven branches, a symbol of divine wisdom representative of the seven days of creation, the sun, moon and planets and the seven stars of Ursa Major; also a candelabrum with nine branches, called a chanukiah. →123

mensa 'table' (Lat.); see altar table. →116

menu 1 in computing, a display item consisting of a list of options to access files, run programs and perform other tasks.
2 Menu, see Min. →74

mercat cross see market cross.

mercury a silvery-white, highly poisonous liquid metal, **Hg**, found in the mineral cinnabar, and used in the production of thermometers and mirrors, and in alloys.

Mercury, staff of see caduceus. →120

mercury lamp see mercury vapour lamp.

mercury vapour lamp, mercury lamp; a discharge lamp whose light emphasizes yellow and blue colours, containing mercury vapour and argon in a sealed glass tube.

merging lane, acceleration lane; in highway design, a lane which provides an entry to a major road from a minor road or intersection, and on which traffic should increase speed to that of traffic on the major road.

merlon solid parts of a battlement parapet, alternating with openings or crenelles, which provide archers and artillery with shelter while defending a fortification. →103

Merulius lacrymans see dry rot.

Merovingian architecture the architecture of the German Franks from 480 to 750 AD in which Christian symbols are found alongside animal ornamentation, displaying influences from Byzantium and the Orient.

mesh 1 any product woven, welded or fused from sets of perpendicular strands to form an open sheet structure; if the openings are small it is called cloth; types included as separate entries are listed below.
see *wire mesh* illustration. →34
crimped wire mesh. →34
conveyor belt mesh. →34
chain link mesh. →34
fabric reinforcement.
insect mesh, see insect screen.
hexagonal mesh, see chicken wire. →34
steel mesh.
welded mesh. →34
see wire mesh.
woven wire mesh. →34
2 see mesh size.

mesh balustrade see wire-mesh balustrade. →54

mesh ceiling see open mesh ceiling.

mesh fence fencing constructed of wire mesh supported by regularly spaced posts.

mesh lathing 1 see wire lathing.
2 see expanded metal lathing.

mesh reinforcement see fabric reinforcement.
mesh size the measure of fineness of a wire mesh, the distance from centre to centre of adjacent parallel wires, sometimes given as the number of openings per unit measure (inch or cm); also simply called mesh; see opening size.
Meso-American architecture see Mixtec architecture.
mesolithic period, Middle Stone Age; a prehistoric period from c.8300 to 4000 BC, between the palaeolithic and neolithic, during which use of the axe became widespread and principal tools were struck from stone.
Mesopotamian architecture architecture from 3000 to 600 BC originating in the valleys of the rivers Tigris and Euphrates in what is now Iraq; characterized by lavish palaces, tombs and ziggurats in massive masonry and mud bricks.
see *Mesopotamian temple* illustration. →66
see *Mesopotamian stepped pyramid* illustration. →67
meta, plural metae; Lat.; a conical column for marking a turning place or boundary during chariot races in an ancient Roman circus; see meta prima, meta secunda. →89
metae plural form of meta. →89
metal 1 one of a class of elements which are malleable, ductile, lustrous and good conductors of heat and electricity; the principal metals used in the construction of buildings, or in alloys, are listed below.
aluminium, aluminum, **Al**.
brass.
bronze.
chromium, chrome, **Cr**.
cobalt, **Co**.
copper, **Cu**.
iron, **Fe**.
lead, **Pb**.
manganese, **Mn**.
nickel, **Ni**.
steel.
tin, **Sn**.
titanium, **Ti**.
vanadium, **V**.
zinc, **Zn**.
2 metal grey; a shade of grey which takes its name from the colour of a number of metals, also known as elephant skin.
metal bar any longitudinal solid length of metal manufactured with a uniform cross-section; used in construction.
see *metal bars* illustration. →34
metal cladding any metallic surface covering for a wall, building or structure, such as sheetmetal panelling products, plate, lathing, mesh, grilles etc.
metal component see prefabricated metal unit.
metal decking see profiled sheeting.
metal door 1 a door whose leaf and frame are made primarily from metal parts. →51
2 see glazed metal door. →51
metal drill a hardened steel spiral-cutting drill bit for cutting round holes in metal. →42
metal-electrode inert-gas welding see MIG welding.
metal-faced plywood plywood manufactured with a protective or decorative face layer of thin metal sheet.
metal-faced window a composite window unit with exterior metal sashes in a timber frame.
aluminium-faced timber window, see composite window. →53
metal flooring see expanded metal flooring.
see open bar metal flooring.
see open metal flooring.
metal foil see foil. →34
metal foil faced bitumen felt bitumen felt which has been treated on one side with a layer of metal foil and on the other with a surfacing of fine granular material.
metal foil wallcovering decorative wallcovering surface-treated with a layer of metal foil.
metal glazed door see glazed metal door. →51
metal grey see metal.
metal halide lamp, metallic-additive lamp; a high pressure mercury discharge lamp containing metal halide additives to alter the colour spectrum of its light output.
metal lathing a keying base for plaster of expanded metal sheet, mesh, metal slats or laths etc.; types included as separate entries are listed below.
expanded metal lathing.
mesh lathing, see wire lathing.
ribbed expanded metal lathing, rib lathing.
wire lathing, wire-mesh lathing.
metal lathing plaster plaster suitable for use with metal lathing.
metallic active-gas welding see MAG welding.
metallic-additive lamp see metal halide lamp.
metallic paint see metallic pigment.
metallic pigment, metallic paint; inorganic paint which contains tiny flakes of metal, producing a speckled metallic sheen when applied as a surface treatment.
metallic wood borer, buprestid beetle; [Buprestis spp.] a group of insects with hard shiny shells whose larvae burrow beneath the bark of living trees.
metallization see zinc spraying.
metallized wallcovering decorative wallcovering with a layer of metallized plastic film applied as a shiny surface finish.
metalloid, semi-metal; an element such as silicon or germanium which has the properties of both metals and non-metals.
metal multi-tile roofing a form of sheetmetal roofing, often organically coated, which has been rolled into embossed sheets in imitation of slate or tiled roofing. →49
metal pan see metal tray. →60
metal pipe pipes of copper, previously lead, mild steel and other metal used for conveying liquids and gases.
metal plate, flat plate; any metal product rolled in sheets over about 2–5 mm thick; actual thickness varies with national specification and type of metal; see also sheetmetal, foil; types included as separate entries are listed below.
see *metal plate* illustration. →34
aluminium plate.
chequerplate, checkerplate. →34
copper plate.
lead plate.
quarto plate.
steel plate.
metal primer a priming compound for use on a metal surface.
metal profile any length of metal preformed into a uniform cross-section of certain shape and dimensions, often synonymous with section, but usually more complex; used for patent glazing, door frames etc.
see *metal profiles* illustration. →34
metal products any components manufactured from metals and metal alloys used in the construction of buildings; structural work is usually in steel.
see *metal products* illustration. →34
metal roofing 1 see sheetmetal roofing. →49
2 see supported sheetmetal roofing. →49
3 see aluminium sheet roofing.
4 see corrugated sheetmetal.
5 see metal multi-tile roofing. →49
metal section any thin length of steel, aluminium, copper, brass etc. which has been preformed by a process of rolling, extrusion, bending etc. into a uniform cross-section of certain shape and dimensions.
see *metal sections* illustration. →34

metal sheet see sheetmetal.
see *metal sheet products* illustration. →34

metal spraying see zinc spraying.

metal structure any structure made of metal components.

metal tray, metal pan; a pressed metal ceiling panel in a suspended ceiling. →60

metal tube any long hollow structural member or vessel made of metal. →34
see *metal tubes* illustration. →34

metal window a window whose frame is made primarily from metal, most often steel or aluminium.

metalwork joint the various ways of joining metal components, by welding, bolting, riveting. →34

metamerism in lighting design, a phenomenon which occurs when two colours, which match under one set of lighting conditions, do not under another.

metamorphic rock rock which has been transformed in structure (and sometimes composition) from existing rock due to the action of high temperature or pressure; types included as separate entries are listed below.
amphibolite.
cipollino, cipolin.
contact metamorphic rock.
crystalline schist.
eclogite.
foliated gneiss, see gneissose mica schist.
gneiss.
gneissose mica schist, foliated gneiss.
granite-gneiss.
granulite.
hornfels.
marble.
mica schist.
phyllite.
quartzite.
schist.
serpentine, serpentinite.
slate.

metamorphism in geology, the transformation of igneous, sedimentary and older metamorphic rock types under the influence of high pressure and temperature, effecting chemical change and recrystallization.

meta prima Lat.; the turning marker situated at the curved end of a Roman circus. →89

meta secunda Lat.; the turning marker situated at the open end of a Roman circus. →89

meter 1 any measuring instrument which indicates quantities by means of a graduated scale or dial; see also gauge and below for list.
acoustic level meter, see sound level meter.
ammeter.
barometer.
consistometer.
cover meter.
electricity meter, electric meter.
gas meter.
hydrometer.
hygrometer.
manometer, see pressure gauge.
micrometer.
moisture meter.
oil meter.
parking meter.
psychrometer.
sound level meter.
tacheometer.
water meter.
2 American spelling of metre.

meter cupboard a small space which contains an electricity or gas meter.

meter cabinet a wall-mounted unit with a hinged door, often of sheetmetal, which contains an electricity meter.

methanal see formaldehyde.

method of diagonals a method of constructing perspective drawings using diagonal lines to determine the position of points measured away from the picture plane. →128

method of joints, joint method; in structural engineering, a method of calculating the forces acting on members in a truss by considering each portion of the triangulated construction as a static entity.

method of intersections a simplified method of constructing axonometric projections using a plan and an elevation, published by the Austrian mathematicians Theodor Schmid (in 1922) and L. Eckhart (in 1937). →127

method of sections, sections method; in structural engineering, a method of calculating the forces acting on members in a truss by considering each joint in turn as a static entity.

metope in classical architecture, one of a series of plain or carved rectangular panels lining a Doric frieze, separated by triglyphs. →78, →79

metre, meter (Am.); abb. **m**; the SI basic unit of length.

metres per second the SI basic unit of velocity, abb. m/s.

metric brick 1 see modular standard brick. →16
2 see metric standard brick. →16

metric carat see carat.

metric hundredweight see hundredweight.

metric modular brick see modular standard brick. →16

metric sabin, absorption unit; in acoustics, a unit of sound absorption equivalent to one square metre of perfect absorber.

metric standard brick a standard size of brick in use in Great Britain with regular dimensions of 215 mm × 102.5 mm × 65 mm. →16

metric system a system of weights and measures based on the metre and using the number ten as a basic division.

metric thread a standardized screw thread whose spacing is based on fractions of a metre; denser and at less of an angle than Whitworth thread.

metric ton see ton.

metro see underground railway.

metron anthropos Gk, see homo mensura.

metro station see underground railway station.

metropolis 1 a major urban centre, often a nation's capital or vibrant cultural and commercial city; in North America a city area which has a total population of 200 000 or more. →105
2 according to Mumford's classification, the third stage of city growth, an international city dependent on industry and foreign trade.

metropolitan railway, cross-link system; a rail network of commuter trains, underground trains and trams which serves an urban area.

metropolitan region see conurbation.

meurtrière see murder hole. →103

mews a row of town dwellings converted from stables, or any modern development of a similar character; originally dwellings converted from the Royal Stables in London.

mezzaluna see demilune. →104

mezzanine, entersole, entresol, intersole; an intermediate storey between two adjacent floors of a building, often a gallery, balcony or partial storey.

mezzo rilievo, demirelief, half relief; sculpture in which figures and elements project half their width from the background.

mezzotint, manière noire; a method of making graphic prints employing a scoured metal plate which will take ink evenly; a design, which remains white in the final print, is then worked into the surface with a burnisher or scraper.

mezzotinto see mezzotint.

MF melamine formaldehyde.

mica a shiny, soft potassium iron magnesium silicate found in mineral form as very thin flakes or small

plates in granite; used in the manufacture of plastics, in electrical and thermal insulation, and as an additive in paints for its structural qualities and sparkle.
see biotite.
see black mica.
see muscovite.

mica schist a grey, fine-grained metamorphic rock containing quartz, mica and muscovite; easily cleaved and used in building as paving and tiles.

micro see personal computer. →Table 1

micro- abb. **µ**; a prefix for units of measurement or quantity to denote a factor of 10^{-6} (one millionth).

microbiological corrosion the deterioration, chemical attack etc. of metals, concrete and other materials caused directly or by the acidic by-products of microbial activity in bacteria, algae, moulds or fungi.

microclimate a localized weather condition caused by the effects of natural features such as forest shelterbelts or hills, or by the massing, spacing and orientation of nearby buildings and landscaping.

microcline a form of the mineral orthoclase used as a raw material in the ceramic industry and for jewellery.

microcomputer see personal computer.

microdisk see diskette.

microfloppy see diskette.

micrometer, 1 micrometer gauge; an instrument with a G-frame and gradated screw for accurate measurement of fine thicknesses down to 0.001 mm.
2 see micron.

micrometer gauge see micrometer.

micrometre see micron.

micron, micrometre, micrometer (Am.); a unit of length equal to one millionth part of a metre, 1/1000 mm.

micropascal abb. **µPa**; in acoustics, a unit of measurement of sound pressure, one millionth of a pascal.

micropile see mini-pile.

microprocessor the centre of a microcomputer, one or a number of integrated circuits or chips comprising a processor unit.

microwave an electromagnetic wave with a wavelength of between 1 and 300 mm, used in radar transmissions, microwave ovens etc.

microwave oven an appliance which warms and cooks food by microwave action.

midden a prehistoric rubbish tip, often with archaeological relics such as shells, bones and artifacts.

Middle Kingdom the period of ancient Egyptian culture during the 11th and 12th dynasties from 2150 to 1785 BC, in architecture characterized by modest brick-filled pyramids, sun and mortuary temples, Hathor columns and the rock-tombs of private citizens. →72

middle oil see carbolic oil.

middle rail, lock rail; the intermediate horizontal framing member between the bottom and top rails in a framed door, where the lock is often fitted.

middle raker the middle slanting prop in a raking shore.

middle strip in concrete structures, that portion of a reinforced concrete slab spanning between columns, measured as the span of the slab with the width of the column strips subtracted.

Middle Stone Age see mesolithic period.

midnight (blue), night blue; a shade of dark blue which takes its name from the colour of a blackish blue material when illuminated by a weak light at night-time.

MIG welding, metal-electrode inert-gas welding; a method of arc welding light alloys and steels in which the arc is shielded with an inert gas.

migmatite a composite rock type consisting of metamorphic rock infused with bands of igneous rock when molten.

mignonette see reseda green.

migration the movement en masse of a people, population or animals from one location to another.

mihrab a praying niche or chamber in a mosque, facing the direction of Mecca.

mil a unit of measurement equal to one thousandth part of an inch or 0.02539 mm.

mild steel ductile steel with a carbon content of 0.15–0.25%, used for pipes, joists and bars.

mile, statute mile; abb. **mi**; an imperial unit of length equal to 1760 yards or 1.609 km.

mile castle small projecting fortlets constructed at intervals of one Roman mile (approximately 1500 m) along the length of fortified boundary walls (such as Hadrian's wall), each guarded by a small garrison of soldiers.

miles per hour abb. **mph**; an imperial unit of velocity equivalent to 0.447 m/s.

milieu see environment.

military base see garrison.

military encampment see castrum. →104

military fort see castrum. →104

military projection a form of oblique projection in which the X and Y axes are in true plan (laid at an angle) and the Y axis is drawn vertical, with scaling of lines on all axes equal; see cavalier, cabinet projections; sometimes called a planometric projection. →127

milk glass, opaline; ordinary glass to which ingredients are added at the molten stage to provide obscurance or translucency.

milk of lime see lime white.

milk white a shade of pale yellow which takes its name from the colour of unskimmed milk.

milky quartz an opaque white variety of crystalline quartz, used as a gemstone and carved for ornament.

milled log, machined log, engineered log; **1** an industrial timber product of uniform rectangular or round cross-section and cogged ends, machined from a single log and used in the construction of system-built and off-the-shelf log buildings.
2 see laminated log.

milled sheet lead lead sheet formed by a process of rolling.

miller's cross see cross fourchée. →117

Millettia laurentii see wenge.

milli- abb. **m**; a prefix for units of measurement or quantity to denote a factor of 10^{-3} (one thousandth). →Table 1

milliard see billion.

millimetre abb. **mm**; an SI unit of length equal to one thousandth part of a metre.

milling, 1 machining; the shaping of wood and other materials using a machine tool with a high speed rotary blade.
2 the shaping of metal pieces, circular in section, on a lathe.

millrind a heraldic figure representing the iron set into the centre of a millstone to hold it in place; also called a millrynd, fer de moline. →123

millrynd see millrind. →123

mill saw, donkey saw, frame saw, gang saw; an industrial saw for converting logs into timber sections with one or a series of oscillating blades held vertically in a frame.

mill scale iron oxide, Fe_3O_4, which forms on the surface of iron sections during hot rolling.

Milori blue see Prussian blue.

mimbar, minbar; a dais, pulpit or a set of steps in a mosque from which the sermon, or khutbah, is delivered.

mimosa (yellow) a shade of greenish yellow which takes its name from the colour of the flower of various species of the tropical plant, Mimosa spp.

Mimusops heckelii see makore.

Min the ancient Egyptian goddess of harvest and fertility, portrayed as a male in a mummy-dress with an erection and head-dress of feathers; written in Egyptian as 'Menu', 'Min' is Greek. →74

minaret a balconied tower in a mosque from which prayers and announcements are given, the faithful are called to prayer etc. →67

minbar see mimbar.

mineral any naturally occurring solid inorganic material with definite chemical composition and usually crystalline structure obtained by mining; usually rocky material such as quartz and feldspar; see below for list of minerals included in this work.

adularia.
agate.
alkali feldspar.
almandine.
amber, succinite.
amphibole.
andalusite.
andradite.
anglesite.
anhydrite.
anthracite.
antimonite, antimony glance, see stibnite.
antimony fahlerz, see tetrahedrite.
apatite.
aquamarine.
argentite.
arsenopyrite.
asbestos.
augite.
azurite.
barytes.
bauxite.
beryl.
biotite.
bismuthite.
bitter spar, see dolomite and magnesite.
black iron oxide, see magnetite.
black mica.
bloodstone.
blue john, see fluorite.
Bohemian garnet, see pyrope.
Bologna stone.
bornite.
boulangerite.
bournonite.
brown iron ore, see limonite.
brown millerite.
calcite.
Cape ruby, see pyrope.
carnelian, see cornelian.
carnonite.
cassiterite, tin-stone.
cerussite, white lead ore.
chalcocite, chalcosine, copper glance.
chalcopyrite, copper pyrites.
chlorite.
chromite.
chrysoberyl.
chrysolite, see olivine.
cinnamon stone, hessonite.
cobaltite, cobalt glance, cobaltine.
coccolite.
copper glance, see chalcocite.
cordierite, dichroite, iotite.
corundum.
cornelian.
covellite.
crocoite, red lead ore.
cuprite, red copper ore.
dark-red silver ore, see pyrargyrite.
dichroite, see cordierite.
diopside.
dioptase.
disthene, see kyanite.
dolomite, bitter spar.
emerald.
epidote, pistacite.
feldspar, felspar.
fluorite, fluorspar, blue john.
galena, lead glance.
garnet.
garnierite.
glauconite.
grossular, grossular garnet or grossularite.
gypsum.
haematite, hematite.
hematite, see haematite.
halite.
heavy spar.
heliodor.
heliotrope.
hessonite, cinnamon stone.
hornblende.
ilmenite.
iotite, see cordierite.
iron pyrites, pyrite, sulphur-ore.
iron spar, see siderite.
jade.
jadeite.
jasper.
kallaite, see turquoise.
kyanite, disthene.
labradorite, Labrador feldspar.
lazurite, lapis lazuli.
lead glance, see galena.
leucite.
light-red silver ore, see proustite.
limonite, brown iron ore.
löllingite.
magnesite, bitter spar.
magnetite, magnetic iron ore, black iron oxide.
malachite.
manganese spar, see rhodochrosite.
marcasite.
mica.
microcline.
molybdenite.
moonstone.
morganite.
muscovite.
nephrite.
niccolite, red nickel sulphide, nickeline.
nickeline, see niccolite.
olivine, peridot, chrysolite.
opal.
orpiment.
orthoclase, see potash feldspar.
peridot, see olivine.
phlogopite.
pistacite, see epidote.
pitchblende, uraninite.
plagioclase.
potash feldspar, orthoclase.
proustite, light-red silver ore, ruby silver.
psilomelane, hard manganese ore.
hard manganese ore, see psilomelane.
pyrargyrite, dark-red silver ore.
pyrite, see iron pyrites.
pyrites.
pyrolusite.
pyromorphite.
pyrope, Bohemian garnet, Cape ruby.
pyroxene.
pyrrhotite, pyrrhotine.
quartz.
red copper ore, see cuprite.
red lead ore, see crocoite.
red nickel sulphide, see niccolite.
rhodochrosite, manganese spar.
rhodonite.
ruby.
ruby silver, see proustite.
rutile.
sapphire.
sard.
selenite.
siderite, iron spar, sparry ironstone.
sillimanite.
skutterudite, smaltite.
smaltite, see skutterudite.

smithsonite, zinc spar.
sodalite.
sparry ironstone, see siderite.
spessartine.
sphene, titanite.
spodumene.
stannite, tin pyrites.
staurolite.
stibnite, antimonite, antimony glance.
sylvanite, graphic ore.
succinite, see amber.
sulphur-ore, see iron pyrites.
tetrahedrite, antimony fahlerz.
tin pyrites, see stannite.
titanite, see sphene.
topaz.
tourmaline.
turquoise, kallaite.
uraninite, see pitchblende.
uvarovite.
vanadinite.
white lead ore, see cerussite.
wolframite.
wulfenite, yellow lead ore.
yellow lead ore, see wulfenite.
zinc-blende, sphalerite.
zinc spar, see smithsonite.
zircon.
zoisite.

mineral acid any of a number of inorganic acids such as sulphuric, hydrochloric and nitric acid.

mineral blue see azurite.

mineral brown see burnt umber.

mineral fibre thin filaments of man-made mineral product, rock, glass etc. used in fireproofing and insulation.

mineral fibre reinforced referring to composites consisting of man-made mineral fibres in a cellulose binder; used for fire-resistant building boards and glazing channels.

mineral granule surfaced bitumen felt, coated felt, mineral-surfaced bitumen felt; bitumen felt which has been treated on one side with coloured mineral granules and on the other with a surfacing of fine granular material such as sand; used for roofing and general waterproofing.

mineral green see malachite.

mineral grey a certain shade of greenish grey.

mineral oil a general name for some crude petroleums after more volatile elements such as gasoline, mineral spirits and kerosene have been distilled off; viscous liquids used as lubricating oils and in some polishes and plastics.

mineralogy the science of minerals.

mineral pigment 1 a general name for natural or synthetic inorganic pigments such as umber, sienna, ochre (raw or burnt), and metal salts (chrome green, white lead); see earth colours for list of earth colours and mineral pigments.
2 see inorganic pigment.

mineral plaster rendering mortar containing coloured inorganic or mineral material, ground glass etc., which may be exposed in the surface by washing, scouring or sandblasting once the coating has hardened, producing a variegated coloured surface.

mineral render see mineral plaster.

mineral spirit see white spirit.

mineral-surfaced bitumen felt see mineral granule surfaced bitumen felt.

mineral violet see manganese violet.

mineral white gypsum used as an inert pigment.

mineral wool fibrous material produced by heating and spinning rock, glass or other mineral material, formed into soft slabs (known as bats) and used as thermal insulation for walls, floors and roofs. →44, →59
see glass wool.
see rock wool.

mineral yellow see Turner's yellow.

minette a form of the pigment yellow ochre.

Ming a period in Chinese culture during that of the autocratic Ming dynasty from 1368 to 1644, whose major cultural achievements were in painting and pottery.

minidisk see diskette.

mini-hacksaw a small hacksaw for cutting metal, plastics and wood.

mini-kitchen unit an appliance containing a hob, water connection, sink and fridge incorporated into one unit, used in dwellings where there is little space, holiday homes, boats, caravans etc.

minim a unit of liquid volume formerly used by apothecaries, one sixtieth part of a fluid drachm, equivalent in Britain to 0.059 cm^3, in North America to 0.063 cm^3.

minimal art see minimalism.

minimalism, minimal art; art or architecture which employs simple and often stark geometrical devices, colours, forms etc., unadorned surfaces and pared detail.

minimum a lowest point or value.

minimum gradient, self-cleansing gradient; the smallest possible slope of a drain etc. such that discharge will flow through and carry solid matter with it under the influence of gravity.

mining town a town whose inhabitants' main sources of income and work are from a local mining industry and which owes its existence to this.

mini-pile, micropile, pin pile; in foundation technology, a small pile whose diameter is less than 300 mm.

mini-roundabout a small urban roundabout designed to ease the flow of traffic at the meeting of two roads, often with a raised circular area of roadway at its centre. →62
see double mini-roundabout. →62

minium see red lead.

Minoan architecture the architecture of bronze-age Crete from 2800 to 1150 BC, characterized by massive masonry in stone, elaborate building plans and planned towns.
see *Asian and Mediterranean columns and capitals* illustration. →69

Minoan column, Cretan column, Mycenaean column, reverse taper column; a round column type with a smooth shaft tapering down to its base, surmounted by a wide cushion capital; found originally in the Minoan architecture of Crete, and later in Mycenae on mainland Greece. →69

minor road a local road with less traffic capacity than a major road, and one whose route is of lesser importance. →63

minor works contract a form of building contract designed for simple, low cost projects, interior design jobs, renovations etc., in which the freedom of the architect as client's representative is increased in the choice of subcontractors or suppliers.

minster a church which was once governed by a monastery. →97

minstrel gallery see singers' gallery. →98

minute 1 abb. ′; the angular measurement of a plane angle, equal to one sixtieth part of a degree.
2 abb. **min**; a basic unit of time equal to 60 seconds; not an SI unit.

mirador a lookout tower or pavilion in Spanish architecture.

mirror glass, or an object made from this, whose rear surface is coated with a material to provide accurate and intense reflections.

mirrored glass see mirror glass.

mirror gallery a long hallway, usually in a grand dwelling or palace, in which the side walls are covered with mirrors to enhance the impression of space.

mirror glass, 1 mirrored glass; any glass coated on one side with reflective material such as silver, from which a mirror is made.
2 see one-way glass.

3 see transparent mirror glass.
4 see Venetian mirror glass.

mirror screw a special screw for fixing mirrors and glass fronts, which comes supplied with a domed piece to cover the slotted head and provide a neat finish. →36

mirror test an inspection for possible obstructions in pipework using a mirror or periscope.

miserere see misericord.

misericord 1 an apartment or building in a monastery in which the usual strictness was relaxed for monks of special privileges.
2 miserere, subsellium (Lat.); a hinged and bracketed choir stall or priest's chair in a church which, when raised, gives support to a person standing.

mismatched see random match. →10

miss, holiday, skip; a defect in a paint finish consisting of areas which have not been painted.

mission tile see under-and-over tile. →47

mitre 1 a corner joint used in picture and glazing framing, fine joinery etc. in which two perpendicular pieces meet with joined ends splayed to 45°.
2 mitred edge; the end of one such piece cut with a 45° splay.
3 the tall, slender head-dress of a bishop, featured in religious art to symbolize position and power. →122

mitre block see mitre box.

mitre box, mitre block; a device for guiding a handsaw at a 45° or 90° angle when cutting a mitre in a piece of wood.

mitre brad see corrugated fastener. →35

mitre cramp see corner cramp.

mitred edge see mitre.

mitred joint see mitre joint.

mitre joint, mitred joint; any framing corner joint in which members are joined with mitred edges.

mitre square an implement for measuring and marking mitres consisting of a stock with a metal blade set at 45°.

mitre stop a piece of splayed board or sheeting placed in a mould to produce a mitred termination at the external corner of an ornamental plaster or concrete moulding.

Mittler's green a variety of viridian pigment.

mix 1 see mixture.
2 see concrete mix.
3 see plaster mix.

mixed concrete, site concrete; the dry constituents of concrete mixed with water ready for use on site.

mixed forest a classification of types of forest containing a number of different species of tree.

mixed garden bond a brickwork bond in which a course of alternating headers and stretchers alternates with between one and six courses of stretchers in no regular pattern.

mixed plywood plywood whose core veneers or inner plies are of a different species of timber from that of the outer plies. →9

mixer 1 see mixer tap.
2 see concrete mixer.
3 see cement mixer.

mixer tap, 1 mixer; a water tap in which hot and cold water are blended and released at a controlled temperature from a single nozzle.
2 see monobloc mixer.

mixing the mechanical stirring together, agitating etc. of component parts of a concrete or plaster mix to form a homogeneous mass before applying; the mixing of dry powders is often called blending or preblending.

mixing box, 1 mixing unit; in certain air-conditioning systems, a chamber in which air from two supply ducts containing air with differing temperatures and humidities are blended.
2 see dual duct terminal unit.

mixing unit see mixing box.

mixing valve in plumbing and drainage, a device containing a chamber in which hot and cold water supplies can be mixed into a single stream and to a regulated temperature.

mix proportions the proportions of each of the component parts in a concrete, mortar or plaster mix.

Mixtec architecture, Meso-American architecture; architecture of the Mexican and Central American Indians characterized by stone statues with astronomical and practical information, large centres of ceremony and fine palaces arranged around squares for the military elite.

mixtum see opus mixtum. →83

mixture, blend, mix; a combination of substances or ingredients which form a homogeneous whole while remaining chemically independent.

MMA welding see manual metal-arc welding.

moat a wide and deep excavation filled with water, or dry, surrounding the external wall of a medieval castle or other fortification as a line of defence; derived from motte, meaning the mound of excavated earth thereof. →103, →104

mobile any work of kinetic sculpture in which parts move, rotate or swing under the action of gravity or motors.

mobile home see caravan.

mobile home park, caravan park; an area where trailers are used as permanent dwellings, usually on designated sites provided with services such as water supply, drainage, and electricity; see also caravan site.

mobile scaffold scaffolding which can be moved from place to place without the need for dismantling; most often a framework on wheels furnished with a brake.

mobility in town planning, the calculation of inward and outward population migration for a particular area.

Mochica culture the ancient culture of the pre-Inca Mochica Indians living along the northern coast of Peru c.600–1000 AD.

modal split in traffic planning, a statistical model estimating the number of trips made per available mode of transport for a particular area or scenario.

model 1 a construction built as an example or pattern for a component or building.
2 see scale model.
3 computer model; a virtual three-dimensional computer representation of a design scheme, building, geographical area etc. used to test solutions, present proposals etc.
4 see fibrous plastering model.

modelling 1 the artistic shaping of wax, clay and other plastic materials.
2 the creation of a comprehensive three-dimensional virtual model of a building with computers as a design tool and for purposes of presentation.

modelling knife see craft knife.

modem in computing, a device used to transmit information between one computer to another using telephone communications.

mode of transport in transportation planning, the classification of type of vehicle, car, bus or train, used for a particular journey or by a specific user group.

modernism, 1 modern movement; an architectural and design movement originating in Europe in the 1920s and 1930s; it is based in the use of modern materials and methods, and disregards decoration and historical precedents.
2 architecture and art which is current and rejects traditional and classical ideologies and methods.

modern movement see modernism.

Modern Style the Art Nouveau style of decorative art and architecture in France.

modernum see opus modernum.

modification see variation.

modified binder a bituminous binder whose properties have been improved by the use of an additive.

modillion in classical architecture, one of a series of small ornate corbelled brackets which support a cornice of the Corinthian or Composite order.

modular brick 1 a mass-produced rectangular brick produced to metric standardized dimensions, coordinated in terms of height, length and width to a basic unit of 100 mm, varying in size from country to country and state to state. →16
2 see modular standard brick. →16
3 see US standard brick. →16
4 see cuboid brick. →16

modular component, module; any prefabricated building component which has been designed and dimensioned to be part of a modular building system.

modular coordination a design and construction system in which all components conform to an agreed set of sizes and are based on a single unit or module.

modular dimension see modular size.

modular floor see platform floor. →44

modular grid a grid of lines to which dimensions are coordinated, which marks out lines of modular coordination on a drawing.

modular size one of the basic starting dimensions used in a modular system.

modular standard brick, 1 modular brick, metric modular brick, metric brick, standard modular brick; a standard size of brick in use in Great Britain with regular dimensions of 190 mm × 90 mm × 65 mm. →16
2 see US standard brick. →16

module 1 a convenient unit of measurement used in design and construction as an aid in setting out, usually based on standard component sizes or a structural grid.
2 a prefabricated assembly of components brought to site for installation; often a whole working space such as a bathroom, staircase, serviced living accommodation etc.
3 see modular component.
4 see lift shaft module.

modulus of elasticity, elastic modulus, Young's modulus; the ratio of stress to strain within the elastic range of a material, whose SI units are MN/m or Gpa.

modulus of section see section modulus.

Mogen David see Magen David.

Moghul architecture see Mogul architecture.

Mogul architecture, Moghul, Mughal; Indian Islamic architecture of the great Mogul dynasty from c.1600, characterized by a mixture of Indian and Muslim styles in palaces and mausoleums, and the use of real arches and domes.

moist curing the curing of fresh concrete by covering it with a layer of damp material such as wet sand or sawdust, by ponding and by spraying with water.

moisture 1 water in the form of surface droplets or wetness contained within the fabric of a material or construction; see also humidity, dampness, condensation.
2 see building moisture.
3 see construction moisture.

moisture content the weight of contained or condensed water in a material expressed as a percentage of its dry weight.

moisture curing adhesive an adhesive which sets by polymerization and is cured by reaction with moisture from the air.

moisture meter 1 an instrument used for the rapid determination of moisture content in wood by electrical means.
2 see hygrometer.

moisture movement the change in dimensions of a material such as timber, concrete or mortar as a result of a change in water content.

moisture resistant 1 see damp proof.
2 see water resistant.
3 see waterproof.

moisture resistant adhesive, MR; a grade of adhesive which is relatively unresistant to hot water but which can withstand external exposure to weather and micro-organisms for a few years.

molding see moulding.

mole 1 in chemistry, the amount of a given substance which has a mass in grams numerically the same as its molecular weight.
2 taupe; a shade of grey which takes its name from the colour of the fur of a mole (Talpa europaea).

molecular weight see relative molecular mass.

molecule a number of atoms chemically bound together.

molet see mullet. →123

moline 1 referring to a cross whose limbs are split and curved back, resembling the form of a millrind; see cross moline. →117
2 fer de moline, see millrind. →123

molly 1 see hollow-wall plug. →37
2 see hollow-wall anchor. →37

molybdenite, molybdenum glance; a greasy, violet-tinged grey mineral, natural molybdenum sulphide, $\mathbf{MoS_2}$, the principal molybdenum ore.

molybdenum a pale, brittle metal, **Mo**, which, as an alloy, improves the corrosion resistance of stainless steel, especially in saline conditions.

molybdenum glance see molybdenite.

moment in mechanics, the turning effect of a force on a body around a given point, calculated by multiplying the imposed force by the perpendicular distance from its point of action.

moment of deflection see bending moment.

moment of gyration see moment of inertia.

moment of inertia, moment of gyration, second moment of area; the sum of the products of all the elementary areas of a section multiplied by their distances from the axis squared.

moment of resistance, resistance moment; in structural engineering, the highest bending moment which a beam can withstand.

momentum for a moving body, the product of its mass times its velocity: a measure of the quantity of its motion.

mon 1 a traditional Japanese family emblem, crest or trademark, often stylized images within a circle. →120
2 see tomoye. →120

monad see Great Monad. →120

monastery a religious community of monks with a church, accommodation, agricultural land and other buildings.
see *Carolingian monastery* illustration. →97

monastic cell a small room or apartment in a monastery for solitary habitation and prayer.

monastic church the main church of a monastery; an abbey or priory; types included as separate entries are listed below.
see *monastic church* in Carolingian monastery illustration. →97
abbey church.
Benedictine church.
convent church.
Franciscan church.
friary church.
priory church.

Monastral a proprietary name for certain blue and green phthalocyanine and red and violet quinacridone pigments.

Monastral blue see phthalocyanine blue.

Monastral green see phthalocyanine green.

money currency items with standardized values used in buying and selling, usually coins and banknotes.

Monge's projection in geometry and graphic representation, the description of three-dimensional objects or points in space as two-dimensional entities on a horizontal and vertical plane, in plan and elevation.

Mongol dynasty see Yuan dynasty.

monitor, 1 console; a long vertical strip window, part of a raised section of roof in factory buildings with sawtooth and similar roof forms.
2 screen; a television screen in a manufacturing plant, security system or control installation for surveillance of an area or process.
3 VDU, visual display unit; a television screen which displays information from a computer system.
monitor roof a pitched roof with a raised central area, also roofed, whose vertical walls often contain glazing. →46
monk bond, flying bond, Flemish double stretcher bond, Yorkshire bond; a brickwork bond in which each course consists of a repeated series of one header and two stretchers; alternate courses are laid symmetrically about the header. →18
monkey, ram; in piledriving, the weighted component in a drop hammer.
monks' choir that part of the chancel of a medieval church reserved for the use of monks. →97, →98
monobloc mixer, single-hole tap; a mixer tap to which the flow of hot and cold water are controlled separately but mixed in a single body and released through one nozzle.
mono-carriage, spine beam; in stair construction, a single string or beam which supports the treads from their midpoints so that they cantilever out from both sides. →45
Monochamus see sawyer beetle.
monochrome based on or containing one colour only.
monocular having one eye, lens etc. with which to see.
monogram a device, image or logo of intertwined letters, often initials; the stylized symbol of a person, event or word.
see Christ monogram. →119
see Jesus monogram. →119
see mon. →120
monolith any large block of rough stone, prehistoric standing stone or large freestanding pillar.
monolithic consisting of one large block of stone, or a solid unjointed mass of material such as cement, concrete or plastics.
monolithic concrete solid reinforced in-situ concrete construction for walls and slabs that has no joints other than construction joints.
monolithic temple see ratha.
monomer any chemical compound that can undergo polymerization and thus form long chain molecules.
monopitch roof, shed roof, single pitch roof; a roof with only one sloping plane. →46
monopteral, monopteros (Gk); a classical open temple type which is round in plan and whose roof is supported by a single outer ring of columns. →85, →94
monopteros Gk; a monopteral temple. →85, →94
monorail a metropolitan rail system in which specially constructed trains travel on a single elevated rail or track.
monostyle see henostyle. →77
monostyle temple a classical apteral temple type whose pediment is supported by a single column between protruding side walls; also described as monostyle in antis or henostyle in antis. →84
monotonous of architectural composition, dull and repetitive.
monotype a method of making one-off graphic prints by painting in inks or oils on glass, metal or polycarbonate.
monstrance in Roman Catholic churches, a glass and metal decorative receptacle containing sacred relics or the consecrated Host.
montage a work of art, decoration or pattern of different or differently coloured sheet material such as paper, cloth, photographs etc.
Monterey pine see radiata pine.
month 1 abb. **mo.**; a measure of time, one of the twelve named periods into which a year is divided, each ranging from 28 to 31 days in length.
2 see calendar month.
monthly salary a fixed wage paid to employees every month.
Montpelier yellow see Turner's yellow.
monument 1 an impressive building, structure or statue, especially one erected to commemorate an event, person or group of people.
2 see ancient monument, see historical monument.
see *Egyptian burial monuments* illustration. →70
monumental grand or impressive in architectural layout, size or style.
moon 1 a common decorative motif representing the celestial body which orbits the earth, often shown in its waning or waxing phase; depictive of the spouse of a major deity in many cultures, in Christian iconography representing the Virgin Mary. →120
2 see crescent. →120
3 see decrescent. →120
4 see increscent. →120
5 see star and crescent. →120
6 see demilune. →104
7 see Khonsu. →74
moonstone a transparent or translucent milky variety of the mineral adularia or similar stones, used in jewellery.
Moorish arch see horseshoe arch. →24
Moorish architecture the Islamic architecture of the Moors, peoples of Mauritania in North Africa who invaded Spain; characterized by polychromy, geometric forms, the horseshoe arch, and decoration based on mathematical constructions.
see Mudéjar architecture.
see *Moorish window* illustration. →111
see *medieval capitals* illustration. →115
moose fence see elk fence.
mopboard see skirting board. →2, →44
mopping in bituminous roofing and tanking, the application of hot bitumen or bonding compound with a brush or mop.
Moresque stylized Spanish Islamic and Moorish geometrical and foliated surface ornament and decorative art. →120
see *Moresque* in symbols and ornaments illustration. →120
see *Moresque capital* in medieval capitals illustration. →115
morganite a pale pink or violet variety of the mineral beryl, used as a gemstone.
morgue see mortuary.
mortality in town planning, the calculating of number of deaths or death rate for a particular area or period.
mortar coarse cement consisting of a binder, fine aggregate and water used for bedding and jointing of masonrywork and tiling, and as render; types included as separate entries are listed below.
bedding mortar.
cement mortar.
cement lime mortar, see composition mortar.
coarse stuff, see lime sand mortar.
coloured mortar.
composition mortar, compo.
fixing mortar. →11
jointing mortar. →11
lime mortar.
lime sand mortar.
masonry cement mortar.
pneumatical mortar, see sprayed concrete.
ready-mixed mortar.
refractory mortar.
tiling mortar. →59
mortar admixture a substance added to a mortar mix with the aim of changing its properties of drying, setting, workability etc.
mortar bedding the layer of mortar in which a brick, block or stone is laid to secure it in place in a wall.
mortar board see hawk.

mortar fillet, cement fillet, weather fillet; a triangular strip of mortar formed in roofing construction at the base of an upstand, to lessen the angle at an inside corner, raise a layer of tiles at a verge etc.

mortar fixing the fixing of tiles, stone facing etc. to a wall or floor surface by bedding them in mortar; also called cement fixing. →11

mortar mill, pug mill; a power-driven mixer for mixing mortar with blades or paddles for blending and breaking up lumps in stiff mixes.

mortgage a secured loan for the purchase of property, in which the property acts as the security.

mortice see mortise. →5

mortise, 1 mortice; a recess cut into a timber member to house a tenon, lock etc. →5
2 see hinge mortise. →38
3 see stopped mortise, blind mortise.
4 see slot mortise.

mortise and tenon joint, tenon joint; a strong timber framing joint in which the end of one member is cut with a tenon which fits into a housing or mortise in another. →5
see *timber mortise and tenon joints* illustration, and below for list of types included as separate entries. →5
abutting tenon joint. →5
barefaced tenon joint. →5
butt tenon joint, see abutting tenon joint. →5
cabinetmaker's tenon joint, see keyed tenon joint. →5
double tenon joint. →5
dovetail tenon joint. →5
edge-halved tenon joint. →5
fish tenon joint, see free tenon joint. →5
free tenon joint. →5
halved tenon joint. →5
haunched tenon joint. →5
joggle tenon joint, see stub tenon joint. →5
keyed tenon joint. →5
open tenon joint, see bridle joint. →5
pinned tenon joint, see keyed tenon joint. →5
shouldered tenon joint. →5
slip tenon joint, see free tenon joint. →5
splayed tenon joint. →5
stepped tenon joint, see shouldered tenon joint. →5
stopped tenon joint. →5
stub tenon joint, stub mortise and tenon joint. →5
stump tenon joint. →5
through tenon joint. →5
tusk tenon joint. →5
twin tenon joint, see double tenon joint. →5
undercut tenon joint. →5

mortise chisel, heading chisel, mortising chisel; a chisel with a narrow, thick blade for making holes and mortises in wood. →41

mortise gauge a device for marking out parallel lines for cutting mortises and tenons from a piece of wood, consisting of two spikes attached to a wooden body.

mortise latch a latch designed to be set into a mortise in the edge of a door leaf.

mortise lock a lock designed to be set into a mortise in the edge of a door leaf; see rim lock. →39

mortise lock chisel, swan-neck chisel; a narrow chisel with a hooked blade, used for cutting and cleaning out holes and mortises in wood. →41

mortiser see hollow-chisel mortiser.

mortising chisel see mortise chisel. →41

mortuary, morgue; a building or space where the dead are kept prior to burial.
see *mortuary in churchyard* illustration. →102

mortuary temple 1 in ancient Egyptian architecture, a place of worship of a deceased king or queen, especially one adjoining a pyramid or rock cut tomb, in which offerings of food and objects were made; also called a funerary temple. →70, →72
2 see pyramid temple. →70, →71

mosaic 1 one of a number of small tiles or pieces of glass, stone or ceramics used as a hardwearing and waterproof surface finish for walls and floors; see also sheet mosaic and below for list of types.
2 a decorative surface pattern for a wall or floor made up from the above.
Cosmati work. →123
Florentine mosaic.
glass mosaic.
intarsia.
marquetry.
opus alexandrinum.
opus musivum.
opus vermiculatum.
parquet mosaic, see parquet block. →44
sheet mosaic. →44
tessera.
wood mosaic, mosaic parquet. →44

mosaic flooring 1 flooring of small tiles of glass, ceramics or stone, used in Roman times for elaborately decorative flooring and nowadays for bathrooms and external surfaces. →44
2 see wood mosaic, mosaic parquet. →44

mosaic gold, aurum mussivum; metallic powder consisting mainly of bisulphide of tin, formerly used as a cheap substitute for powdered gold in ornament and painting.

mosaic parquet see wood mosaic. →44

mosaic tile small ceramic tiles used for bathroom walls and floors; often sheet mosaic. →44

mosaic tiling floor or wall facing in mosaic tiles. →44

Moslem architecture see Islamic architecture.
see *Abbasid spiral minaret* illustration. →67

mosque a building for the practice of Islamic worship.

moss green 1 a shade of dark green which takes its name from the colour of certain species of moss, such as *Hypnum triquetrum*.
2 see chrome green.

motel a building or complex consisting of a number of rentable rooms or cabins in which people, especially those travelling by motor vehicle, can stay overnight.

motherboard, backplane; in computing, the main component of a computer, a printed circuit board to which processors, memory chips and other electronic devices and drivers are attached.

mother-house in religious architecture, the founding establishment of a monastic order.

motif, 1 design, element; in architecture and ornament, a significant feature such as a component, sculpting or artwork, often repeated as part of a theme.
2 see ornamental motif. →14

motor car see automobile.

motor home a motor vehicle which contains habitable space and living facilities at the rear.

motorized damper in air-conditioning and mechanical ventilation systems, a thermostatically controlled damper which automatically regulates the flow of air in ductwork.

motor lock see electromechanical lock.

motor room see machine room. →61

motor vehicle a vehicle such as an automobile, motorcycle, bus or lorry which is driven by an internal combustion engine.

motorway, freeway (Am.); a major road with a number of continuous adjacent traffic lanes and a hard shoulder in each direction, designed for use by high speed vehicular traffic and connected to other roads via slipways and overhead or underpass junctions. →63
see *traffic interchange* illustration. →63
see *ideal city* illustration. →105

motte in English Norman architecture, an artificial mound on which a motte and bailey castle or keep was constructed.

motte and bailey a Norman fortification type consisting of an artificial mound or motte surmounted by a fortified structure, surrounded by a walled area, or bailey, which functioned as first line of defence and also for the keeping of livestock.

motto in heraldry, a phrase or sentence carried on the scroll below a shield, intended to state some guiding principle or idea of the bearer. →124

moucharaby an Arabic balcony screened off with a wooden lattice, found in North Africa.

mouchette a typical pointed tracery motif formed by intersecting glazing bars in the Gothic Curvilinear style; a curved dagger motif. →110

mould, 1 matrix; a hollow negative or female pattern into which material to be shaped by casting or pressing is placed; types included as separate entries are listed below.
battery mould.
bed mould. →78, →79
case mould.
fibrous plastering mould.
hood-mould. →110
horse mould, see running mould. →14
loose piece mould.
peg mould. →14
piece mould.
running mould, horse mould. →14
skin mould.
thumb mould.
waffle mould.
waste mould.
2 see formwork.
3 a fungal growth on the surface of wood or other damp surfaces, usually visible in the form of greenish black, blue or brown powdered residue.
4 see earth-coloured.

moulded boarding see bead boarding. →8

moulded brickwork brickwork whose bricks are moulded to special shapes before firing to form a decorative relief when laid.

moulded capital see bell capital. →115

moulding, molding (Am.); **1** a horizontal ornamental projecting band in a wall surface, often with running motifs and of carved stone, timber or plasterwork.
continuous mouldings. →14
repetitive mouldings. →124
classical mouldings. →80
2 profile, strip; a long, narrow piece of extruded metal, machined timber or preformed plastics formed into a specific uniform cross-sectional shape, used for various applications such as for covering construction joints, as glazing bars etc.
3 joinery moulding, see timber trim. →2
see *joinery mouldings* illustration. →2
4 strip; any long flat or profiled piece of timber or other material attached as decoration, or as an ornamental gutter, cornice or string course.
5 fillet; a long three-dimensional profiled strip in a wall surface.
6 band; a two-dimensional printed or rendered longitudinal decorative strip.
7 see bed mould. →78

moulding compound see flexible moulding compound.

moulding plane a woodworking plane with a base and blade specially shaped for working ornamental mouldings.

moulding wheel a power tool with a profile-formed rotating abrasive disc for grinding mouldings in stonework.

mould-made paper paper manufactured to resemble handmade paper.

mould mark see flash line.

mould oil, form oil; in concretework, lubricating oil applied to the inside face of formwork sheeting to permit easy and defect-free removal from the hardened concrete surface.

mound 1 in prehistoric architecture, earth either heaped over stone construction to form a series of subterranean spaces for tombs etc., or as an artificial hill for purposes of defence. →65
2 see burial mound.
3 see effigy mound.
4 see motte.

mountain ash see rowan.

mountain blue 1 see azurite.
2 see Bremen blue.

mountain green 1 see Bremen blue.
2 an outdated name for the mineral and pigment malachite.

mounted drawing see mounting.

mounting, 1 fitting; the fastening of a component, fixed furnishing, technical appliance, door leaf or services to a structural base such as a wall, floor or ceiling soffit.
2 see surface mounting.
3 mounted drawing; a drawing or a group of drawings which have been attached in some form to a stiff backing for use as presentation material.

mounting height the height at which a component is to be fixed in place, especially used in lighting design, where it is defined as the distance at which a luminaire is or should be mounted above the working plane or floor.

mouse in computing, a device for manual control of the cursor and for giving instructions to a computer without the use of a keyboard.

mouse grey, drab; a shade of brown grey which takes its name from the hair of a house mouse [*Mus musculus*].

mousetooth brickwork see dogtooth brickwork. →20

mousetooth moulding see dogtooth brickwork. →124

movable bridge a bridge which can be moved by raising, sliding or pivoting to allow larger vehicles or boats to pass by it. →64

movable partition a partition, often temporary, whose location within a space may be changed without alteration to the surrounding fabric.

movement joint a construction joint in a large rigid structure or monolithic concrete slab which allows for movement such as expansion or contraction to avoid the occurrence of cracks.

movie house see cinema.

movie theater see cinema.

moving load a structural live load imposed by a moving object; see rolling load.

moving staircase see escalator.

moving stairway see escalator.

moving walk see passenger conveyor.

Mozarabic art the art of Islamic Spain from c.800 to 1100 AD with Moorish and Romanesque elements and influences.

MR moisture resistant adhesive.

M-roof, double gable roof, trough roof, valley roof; a roof formed by the junction of two simple pitched roofs with a valley between them, resembling the letter M in section. →46

mud brick, sun-baked brick, sun-dried brick; an unfired clay brick which has been dried and hardened by heat from the sun, in use in various forms since ancient times.

Mudéjar architecture architecture in Spain from c.1200 to 1500 AD, characterized by the use of Moorish, Gothic and Renaissance features.

muffler, damper, silencer, sound attenuator; noise-reducing treatment or devices for air-handling ductwork within ceiling voids and other acoustically sensitive areas.

Mughal architecture see Mogul architecture.

mullet a heraldic star with five, six or eight points, also called a molet. →123
mullet of five points. →123
mullet of six points. →123
mullet of eight points. →123
see mullet pierced. →123

mullet pierced a five pointed star with a hole through the centre. →123

mullion, munnion, muntin (Am.); a vertical dividing or framing member in a window, proprietary glazing systems etc. →52, →110, →111

multifoil a decorative design consisting of a number of leaf motifs or lobes radiating outwards from a point. →108, →110

multifoil arch a decorative arch embellished with a number of lobes or foils, often more than five. →24

multifoliated arch 1 a decorative arch whose intrados is composed of a number of lobes or foils in a cloverleaf arrangement, and whose extrados is a round or pointed arch; especially found in Gothic architecture; see trifoliated, cinquefoliated. →23
2 see round multifoliated arch. →23
3 see pointed multifoliated arch. →23

multi-folding door a folding door with a number of side-hinged folding leaves.

multilayer chipboard chipboard manufactured in layers of chips of different sizes pressed together; the layers of finer chips on the exterior provide a denser and harder surface. →9

multilayer deposit a protective finish for a metal surface formed by successive deposition of a number of layers of different metals.

multilayer parquet parquet strip flooring of matched lengths of plywood, chipboard, blockboard etc. with a surface layer of hardwood veneer up to 5 mm thick; also called veneer or veneered parquet. →44, →59

multilevel car park see multistorey car park.

multilevel development modern urban planning in which various activities such as vehicular and pedestrian circulation, commerce, dwellings, utility services etc. are segregated and located on different vertical levels.

multilevel junction a road junction or interchange at which three or more major roads meet, and whose crossings are on more than two levels.

multilevel parking see multistorey parking.

multimedia in computing, communication and software systems which combine a number of media such as graphics, text and sound.

multiple span bridge a bridge with arches, beams or slabs spanning between a number of points of support; a masonry viaduct is an example of this. →32

multiple-view projection see multiview projection. →127

multiplication in mathematics, increasing a value a specified number of times to form a product.

multi-ply plywood consisting of more than three layers or plies. →9

multiprogramming see multitasking.

multipurpose plaster plaster which may be applied to a number of different backgrounds.

multipurpose workbench, Workmate bench; a proprietary portable workbench with a built-in vice and worktop.

multistorey building, block; any building with a number of storeys, usually more than three, divided into separate flats, offices etc. according to building usage.

multistorey car park, multilevel car park; a car park, usually situated in an urban environment, which provides parking for cars on many levels; often a ramp garage.

multistorey parking, multilevel parking; parking for vehicles usually situated in an urban environment where space is limited, with parking spaces on many levels.

multitasking, multiprogramming; the capacity of a computer to perform a number of functions, or run a number of programs concurrently.

multi-tile roofing see metal multi-tile roofing. →49

multiview projection a form of orthographic projection in which a number of plane views such as a plan and elevations of an object are shown in 'fold-out' format; see first and third angle projections; also called multiple-view projection. →127

mummy, Egyptian brown; a brown oil pigment in use until the 1920s, consisting of bone ash and asphaltum made by grinding up Egyptian mummies; also a synthetic equivalent.

Munich lake see carmine.

municipal building any building used for the administration of a municipality, town or city.

municipal centre see civic centre.

municipal council see local government.

municipality, county; a defined district within a country which has certain powers of self-government.

munnion see mullion. →51

muntin 1 a subsidiary vertical frame member between the stiles of a panelled or glazed door leaf. →51
2 see mullion.

muntin and plank construction a form of traditional timber wall construction in which heavy horizontal planks or boards are laid between a series of slotted posts at intervals. →7

mural, wall painting; a large-scale decorative painting or artwork for the wall of a building, especially that such as fresco applied directly to a wall surface.

mural wallcovering a wallcovering printed or manufactured with a non-repetitive pattern or image.

murder hole an opening in the floor of a castle or fortification over a gateway etc., through which implements, projectiles and boiling liquid could be dropped on attackers; see machicolation; also known as a meurtrière (French for 'murderer'), drop box, fall trap or spy hole. →103

Murex spp. see purple.
see Tyrian purple.

Murom culture the culture of the Finno-Ugric peoples living along the river Oka, a tributary of the Volga, in Russia from 900 to 1100 AD taking its name from the ancient town of Murom.

Murtrière see murder hole. →103

murus gallicus, Gallic wall, opus gallicum; Lat.; Roman stone and earth walling reinforced with rough timber beams and logs to withstand the impacts from the battering rams of attackers. →83

musaeum Lat.; an ancient Roman nymph temple or grotto of the Muses.

Musa sapientum see banana.

Musa textilis see Manila hemp.

muscovite a white variety of mica, a potassium aluminium silicate mineral.

Muse a typical subject of Renaissance painting, one of the mythological daughters of Zeus, inspiration of poetry and the arts.

museum a building or complex in which artifacts of cultural, historical and artistic value are stored and exhibited; a building for the display and storage of objects for research and study.

mushroom slab, flat slab; a beamless flat concrete slab used with concrete columns which have thickenings at their upper ends, so named because the columns resemble mushrooms. →27

music hall see concert hall.

musivum see opus musivum.

Muslim architecture see Islamic architecture.
see *Abbasid spiral minaret* illustration. →67

mustard brown a shade of brown which takes its name from the colour of dark mustard prepared from the seeds of the mustard plant [*Sinapis spp.*].

mustard yellow a shade of greenish yellow which takes its name from the colour of mustard; considerably lighter than mustard brown.

Mut the consort of the ancient Egyptian deity Amun, mother figure of the Theban triad, mistress of heaven, depicted wearing a vulture head-dress and Combined Crown of Egypt. →74

mutule in classical architecture, one of a number of projecting blocks on the underside of a corona, above a triglyph in a Doric pediment. →78

mutulus Latin form of mutule, plural is mutuli. →78

Mycenaean architecture the architecture of southern and central Greece in the late Bronze Age from 1700 to 1100 BC; see also Helladic period. →113

see *Mycenaean gateway* illustration. →23
see *Mycenaean tholos tomb* illustration. →65
see *Mycenaean portal* illustration. →113
see *Asian and Mediterranean columns and capitals* illustration. →69

Mycenaean column see Minoan column. →69

myrtle green **1** a shade of dark green which takes its name from the colour of the leaves of the evergreen myrtle tree [*Myrtus communis*].
2 see chrome green.

Myrtus communis see myrtle green.

mystery a typical subject of murals from classical and medieval times, portraying spiritual or religious symbolism.

mystical almond see mandorla. →119

N

nacarat carmine the finest grade of carmine pigment.

nail 1 a slender-shafted metal fastener driven in with a hammer to fix one component to another, relying on friction as a means of attachment. →35
see *types of nail* illustration; types included as separate entries are listed below. →35
annular nail. →35
bullet-head nail, see lost-head nail. →35
clout, clout nail. →35
concrete nail, see masonry nail. →35
convex head roofing nail.
copper nail.
corrugated fastener. →35
cut nail. →35
double headed nail. →35
dowel nail. →35
duplex nail, see double headed nail. →35
felt nail, see clout. →35
finishing nail, see lost-head nail. →35
forged nail. →35
form nail, formwork nail, see double headed nail. →35
French nail, see round wire nail.
gang nail, see nail plate. →35
improved nail, see annular nail. →35
jagged-shank nail, see annular nail. →35
lost-head nail. →35
masonry nail. →35
nipple head nail, see convex head roofing nail.
oval brad head nail, see brad. →35
oval wire nail.
pin. →35
plasterboard nail.
plug nail.
ring-shanked nail, see annular nail. →35
roofing nail.
round nail.
round wire nail.
scaffold nail, see double headed nail. →35
screw nail. →35
sleeved nail.
springhead roofing nail, see convex head roofing nail.
square twisted shank flat head nail, see screw nail. →35
staple, U-pin. →35
trenail. →3
upholstery nail, see upholstery tack. →35
wiggle nail, see corrugated fastener. →35
wire nail. →35
wrought nail, see forged nail. →35
2 see gutta. →78

nail claw, cat's paw, nail puller; a screwdriver-like hand tool whose blade is forked and bent; used for removing nails from wood.

nailed joint a timber joint in which the members are held together with nails. →3

nail float, devil float; a plastering hand float whose face has a series of projecting nails or spikes, used for scraping the plaster surface to make a key for the following coat. →43

nail gun a power tool which fires nails into surfaces to be fixed, operated by compressed air or electricity; see framing gun, bradder.

nail hammer a hammer used for driving nails, with a round flat face and claw. →40

nailhead 1 the flat or bulging shaped end of a nail, by which it is driven. →35
2 an ornamental motif consisting of a series of pyramid-shaped protrusions, resembling the heads of hand-forged nails. →124

nailhead moulding a moulding decorated with nailhead ornament.

nailing the fixing of timber and other members with nails. →3

nailing block see nog.

nail plate, gang nail, toothed plate fastener, truss plate; a toothed metal plate used for joining two timbers in the same plane, especially used in the manufacture of timber roof trusses. →35

nail puller see nail claw.

nail punch see nail set.

nail set, nail punch; a pointed metal rod used as a base for hammering nails beneath the surface.

naiskos Gk; a diminutive form of naos, a small ancient Greek shrine, often located within a naos. →85

naivism a movement in art originating in the late 1800s which draws from the expression of children and native cultures in an illustrative way, often by artists who have little professional training.

name-plate a rectangular plate or panel which bears the name, title etc. of the occupant of a room, dwelling or building. →51

Nankeen yellow a shade of yellow which takes its name from the colour of undyed cotton from Nanking; a pigment with this colour is known as Naples yellow.

nano- abb. **n**; a prefix for units of measurement or quantity to denote a factor of 10^{-9} (one thousand millionth). →Table 1

naos Gk; **1** the central space in a Greek temple containing a cult image; called a cella in a Roman temple. →85
2 a sanctuary in a Byzantine church.

naphtha any of a number of inflammable liquids refined from petroleum, coal tar, shale or coal, used as a source of energy and as a raw material.

naphthol carbamide a bluish red semi-transparent pigment, invented in 1921, suitable for use in printing.

naphthol red a bright red organic pigment used in watercolours, acrylics and oil paints.

Naples yellow, 1 antimony yellow, brilliant yellow, jaune brilliant, jaune d'antimoine; a highly poisonous heavy semi-opaque yellow pigment consisting of lead antimonite; an ancient pigment much used by painters.
2 see Nankeen yellow.

narrow grained see close grained.

narrow ringed see close grained.

narthex Lat.; a porch or vestibule situated at the west end of an Early Christian church, to which women and penitents were admitted.
see *Late Antique church* illustration. →95
see *Carolingian abbey church* illustration. →98
see *Romanesque church* illustration. →99

natality see fertility.

natatio Lat.; a swimming pool in an ancient Roman bath house. →91

natatorium Lat.; a room or building for an indoor swimming pool in an ancient Roman bath house.

National Insurance contributions see social security costs.

national park an area of countryside of cultural or environmental value owned by the state and conserved for recreational use by the public.

national planning a town planning strategy to improve and integrate living conditions, amenities, industry, transportation etc. on a nation-wide scale.

National Romanticism a style of architecture in Finland at the end of the 19th century characterized by naturalistic motifs, grotesque or rustic ornamentation in timber and granite and neo-medieval elements.

native green natural chrome oxide, formerly used as a pigment.

native plant see indigenous plant.

natural 1 pertaining to or originating from nature or natural processes.
2 see ivory.

natural aggregate aggregate found naturally or ground from natural minerals.

natural anhydrite the mineral anhydrite occurring in natural deposits in the earth.

natural brown iron oxide see burnt sienna.

natural convection see free convection.

natural draught burner, atmospheric burner; a gas heating appliance whose burner is provided with air at atmospheric pressure.

natural draught flue system a flue system in which draught is produced by heat from combustion.

natural exhaust in mechanical ventilation, the forced removal of stale air from a building through vents using internal pressure caused by the introduction of supply air.

natural fibre a general name for both animal and vegetable fibres.

natural gas naturally occurring gas consisting mainly of methane produced by the decay of living organisms, extracted from beneath the ground or sea bed; used for combustion, especially in gas heating.

natural gypsum, gypsum rock; the mineral gypsum which can be found in natural deposits in the earth's crust.

naturalism art, especially that of the late 1800s, which seeks to faithfully represent nature and reality.

natural light in lighting design, light which comes through windows, rooflights or openings directly or indirectly from the sun; cf. artificial lighting.

natural madder see madder lake.

natural pigment see earth colour.

natural resin a group of soft or hard oleoresins, hardened exudations from trees which have been refined by polymerization and other treatments.

natural rock asphalt a mixture of naturally occurring aggregate or crushed rock and bitumen, often found as sedimentary rock whose voids contain bitumen; see lake asphalt.

natural rubber rubber which has been produced from latex tapped from a rubber tree.

natural stone stone which has been quarried, cut, shaped and dressed for use in the construction industry; cf. artificial stone.

natural stone block any shaped, squared or dressed block of natural stone used in construction; nowadays usually as facing, walling etc. →12
see dimension stone. →12
see ashlar. →12

natural stone cladding external cladding in sheets or blocks of natural stone, hung from a wall frame or structure. →11
see *natural stone cladding* illustration. →11

natural stone facing external facing in natural stone, fixed to a wall frame or structure; often the same as natural stone cladding. →11

natural stone flooring see stone flooring.

natural stone paver, 1 flagstone; a flat rectangular paving stone made from cut or shaped natural stone. →15
2 see cobble. →15
3 see pebble. →15
4 see sett. →15
5 see cube. →15
6 see boulder. →15

natural stone paving see stone paving. →15
see stone block paving. →15

natural ventilation the ventilation of internal spaces of a building by natural convective movement of air via ducts, chimneys and openable windows without the use of mechanical plant.

naturalized plant any species of plant which does not naturally grow wild in a certain habitat, but is introduced and able to thrive and reproduce there.

nature the physical world including the earth, its water and atmosphere, fauna and flora.

nature reserve protected land designated by legislation and managed for the habitation and study of wildlife and natural features.

nautical mile a unit of distance used at sea, equivalent to 1852 m.

nave the main longitudinal space of a church, cathedral, basilica etc.; the body of a church between the west end and crossing.
see *Roman basilica* illustration. →93
see *Early Christian church* illustration. →95
see *Byzantine domical church* illustration. →96
see *Carolingian abbey church* illustration. →98
see *Romanesque church* illustration. →99
see *Gothic cathedral* illustration. →100
see *Scandinavian hall church* illustration. →102

nave-and-chancel church a church type emerging in the 800s, in which the nave extends up to the altar, beyond the transepts. →98

navel 1 see omphalos. →120
2 see Buddha's navel. →120

navel point see nombril. →124

navis media the central nave of a Roman basilica or early Christian church; 'nave' in Latin. →93
see *navis media* in Byzantine domical church illustration. →96

Navy blue see marine blue.

Naxian base a classical column base which is a simple stone block without mouldings, on which the fluted column rests. →81

NBR nitrile rubber.

neat cement grout see neat grout.

neat grout, cement grout, neat cement grout; a grout consisting of a mixture of a hydraulic binder such as cement and water, without fine aggregate or sand.

neat gypsum plaster plaster produced from the mineral gypsum, with no added aggregate or sand.

neat size see dressed size.

Nebthet see Nephthys.

nebule moulding, nebulé, nebuly; an ornamental Norman moulding consisting of a raised undulating line with a sunken lower edge. →124

nebulé moulding see nebule moulding. →124

nebuly moulding see nebule moulding. →124

necessarium see garderobe. →103

neck 1 the thin part of a chisel blade, which separates the handle from the cutting edge. →41
2 the thinning behind the bell or striking face of a hammerhead. →40
3 the part of the shank behind the flat head of a nail. →35
4 shank; the square protrusion in the underside of the head of a coach bolt or other similar fastener, which prevents it from turning. →36
5 in log jointing, the notched thinning at the extremity of a log to receive another log. →6
6 see necking. →81

necking 1 a narrow moulding at the top of the shaft of some classical columns, separating it from the capital. →81
2 see trachelion. →81

necropolis 1 a large cemetery, a city of the dead, especially in classical Roman or Egyptian culture, situated in or near a city, pyramid etc.
2 see *necropolis* in Egyptian pyramid complex illustration. →71
3 according to Mumford's classification, the final stage of city growth, in which the city has degenerated socially and economically, fallen into disrepair, and whose inhabitants have moved to rural areas or smaller settlements.

needle see Cleopatra's needle. →73

needle file a small, fine-toothed and thin-bladed hand tool used for the accurate filing, smoothing and grinding of metalwork.

needle-punch carpet a thin carpet made by mechanically punching an array of fibres into a supporting backing sheet.

negative ion see anion.

negative pressure ventilation see extract ventilation.

negotiated contract a form of building contract between a client and a single chosen contractor in which terms and financial matters are discussed and agreed beforehand, without recourse to a tendering procedure.

neighbourhood an area of a town or city that forms a relatively self-contained social unit.

neighbourhood centre see district centre.

neighbourhood unit an integrated and planned urban area consisting of residential districts, a school or schools, shopping facilities, religious buildings, open spaces, and small-scale service industry.

neighbours' approval see neighbours' consent.

neighbours' consent, neighbours' approval; the written approval from the occupants of an adjoining property to that for which planning permission has been applied, in the case that their living conditions, value of property etc. may be adversely affected by the forthcoming development.

Nekhbet the vulture goddess, protectress of ancient Upper Egypt.

Nelumbo nucifera see sacred lotus. →82, →121

neo-Babylonian period the last Babylonian period in Mesopotamian art, 625–539 BC, following the end of the Persian invasion.

Neo Brutalism see Brutalism.

neoclassicism an architectural style in Europe from the late 1700s and 1800s characterized by the use of monumental forms, strict adherence to the classical orders, and refinement of detail.
see *neoclassical church* illustration. →26
see *neoclassical window* illustration. →111
see *column styles in European architecture* illustration. →114
see Adam style.
see Empire style.
see *Empire style* facade in stone finishes illustration. →12
see Gustav III style.
see Louis Seize style, Louis XVI style.
see Palladianism.
see Regency style.

neodymium a metallic chemical element, **Nd**.

neodymium oxide lamp, daylight lamp, full-spectrum lamp; a standard lamp whose bulb is made of glass containing neodymium oxide, which causes the characteristic purplish hue in the glass and counteracts the adverse colour rendering of its otherwise yellow light.

neo-Gothic architecture any architecture which makes abundant use of Gothic motifs and elements, usually referring to architecture appearing in the late 1800s and 1900s.

Neo-Grec an architectural style in France from the 1840s; it is characterized by use of Greek motifs and forms in wrought ironwork.

neolithic period, New Stone Age; a prehistoric period in Europe from c.4000 to 2000 BC, after the mesolithic, during which the use of clay became widespread and the principal tools were finished by grinding.
see *prehistoric structures* illustration. →65

Neolithic Revolution the period in human development characterized by the change from hunting and gathering to farming and the domestication of animals, in Mesopotamia from c.7500 BC and in Europe from c.3000 BC.

neolithic village prehistoric settlements of rudimentary stone dwellings such as those at Skara Brae, Orkney Islands. →65

neon an inert gaseous chemical element, **Ne**, used in fluorescent lamps.

neon tube a high voltage fluorescent lamp which does not require a heated cathode, with a low light level meaning it is usually used for signs and advertising; usually contains neon, but in general, any cold cathode lamp.

neo-plasticism a style in abstract art founded in Holland around 1915 by Piet Mondrian (1872–1944) which emphasized the oneness of architecture, sculpture and painting, and is characterized by the use of primary colours and rectilinear patterns of lines.

neoprene a synthetic rubber with good resistance to oils and solvents, used for seals, roofing and gaskets; a trade name for chloroprene rubber.

neo-Renaissance eclectic Renaissance styles in architecture from the end of the 19th century.

neotechnic a term used by Patrick Geddes and Lewis Mumford to describe the later stage of the industrial age in which the main energy source is electricity and key inventions are radio, aircraft and the telephone, new materials steel, aluminium and light alloys.

nephrite a hard greenish mineral, often cut for decoration as jade.

Nephthys in ancient Egyptian mythology, the sister of Isis, Osiris and Seth, who assisted in the re-memberment of Osiris and his subsequent resurrection; also known as Nebthet.

Neptune's trident see trident. →120

neptunium a radioactive chemical element, **Np**, produced in nuclear reactors.

nest of saws a saw with several interchangeable saw blades which can be used at different times in the same handle.

net a description of the resulting basic value of price, income, weight etc. when all other factors have been deducted.

net floor area the floor area of a building excluding the thickness of the exterior walls.

net internal area 1 the total floor area of a building measured to the internal surface of the external walls, excluding all stairs, wells, internal walls, ducts etc.
2 the above when concerning particular premises such as an apartment within a larger building.

net usable area the useful floor area of a building, usually excluding circulation and service space such as corridors and stairs, plant rooms, foyers etc.

net price any price of goods or services from which all reductions and deductions have already been made.

net vault a vault whose ribs are arranged in an overlapping pattern, giving the impression of a net or mesh of rectangular or lozenge-shaped openings. →101

network 1 a number of computers which are linked by a telecommunications channel or central server for sharing of information, devices and storage capacity.
2 see gas distribution network.
3 see electricity supply grid.

neutral see colourless.

neutral axis a line, plane or surface within a structural member in bending, which is neither in tension nor compression, nor does it undergo deformation.

neutral grey see medium grey.

neutral pressure see pore-water pressure.

neutral stress see pore-water pressure.

neutron in chemistry, an uncharged subatomic particle found in the nucleus of an atom.

New Brutalism Brutalism in Britain from the 1950s and 1960s.

newbuild a generic term for the design and construction of new buildings as opposed to refurbishment or amendments to existing ones.

new building a project term describing a building designed and constructed from scratch rather than an alteration, remodelling or refurbishment.

newel, 1 newel post; a post used to support a stair balustrade at either end.
2 newel post; the central post onto which the steps in a circular stair are fixed. →45

newel post see newel. →45

New Kingdom the period of Egyptian culture during the time of the 18th to 20th dynasties, from 1580 to 1085 BC, characterized in architecture by the Amarna period and its temples, palaces, private dwellings and rock tombs.

newsagent see stationers.

New Stone Age see neolithic period.

new suburb originally denoting suburbs which were built after the Second World War, now referring to any newly planned area on a greenfield site.

newton abb. **N**; the SI basic unit of force, equal to that required to give a mass of one kilogram an acceleration of one metre per second per second; $1\,N = 1\,kg{\cdot}m/s^2$.

Newtonian laws the laws of statics and mechanics as formulated by Isaac Newton; the laws of inertia, acceleration, action and reaction.

newton-metre see joule.

new town one of a number of small and moderately sized towns constructed on rural greenfield sites after the Second World War, based on the nearness of services, places of work and recreational facilities near to residential areas.

nib, 1 cog; a projection at the upper end of a roof tile which, when laid, hooks over a roof batten to provide a secure fastening.
2 the shaped metal or plastic end of an ink pen, which makes contact with the paper on writing.

niccolite, red nickel sulphide, nickeline; a copper-red mineral, naturally occurring nickel arsenide, **NiAs**, an important ore of nickel.

niche 1 a recess within the thickness of a wall, usually for an ornament or artifact.
see *prehistoric structures* illustration. →65
see *pediment* illustration. →112
see *portal* illustration. →113
2 see aedicule. →112

nickel a whitish metal, **Ni**, used in alloys and for the protective coating of steel; it also improves the toughness of high chrome steel.

nickel azo yellow see green gold.

nickel brass see German silver.

nickel green a shade of dark green which takes its name from the colour of an arsenate of nickel.

nickeline see niccolite.

nickel plated referring to metals which have been treated with a thin protective coat of nickel.

nickel silver a hard and ductile alloy of copper and zinc with additional nickel to improve corrosion resistance.

nickel steel an alloy of steel containing nickel and carbon, with superior properties to those of carbon steel.

nicker see splitter.

Nicotiana tabacum see Havana (brown).

niello 1 a black mixture of sulphur, silver and lead or copper used to fill engravings in silver and other metals.
2 the decorative product thus formed.

night blue see midnight (blue).

Nile delta see Lower Egypt. →74

Nile (green) a shade of grey green which takes its name from the colour of the waters of the Nile.

Nile, key to see ankh. →117

Nile valley see Upper Egypt. →74

nimbus 1 Lat.; see aureole. →119
2 three-rayed nimbus, see triradiant halo. →119

nine inch wall see one-brick wall. →21

niobium a grey metallic chemical element, **Nb**, used in alloys and as a superconductor; occasionally known as columbium.

nipple see hexagonal nipple.

nipple head nail see convex head roofing nail.

Nissen hut, quonset (Am.); a temporary structure of corrugated sheet steel bent into a half cylindrical form, used for dwelling and storage.

nit abb. **nt**; the SI basic unit of luminance equal to one candela per square metre, cd/m^2.

nitch a bundle of combed wheat reed used as a basic roofing material in thatching; see also bunch.

nitrate a salt of nitric acid.

nitrate green a blue variety of chrome green pigment.

nitric acid a yellowish, corrosive, chemical compound, $\mathbf{HNO_3}$, used in the manufacture of explosives and fertilizers.

nitriding in metallurgy, the hardening of a steel surface by heating it in an atmosphere of ammonia and hydrogen to produce a very hard corrosion-resistant surface layer.

nitrile rubber, NBR; a resilient oilproof synthetic polymer manufactured from acrylonitrile and butadiene; used for seals, hoses, joints and storage vessels.

nitrocellulose lacquer a highly inflammable varnish used as a transparent finish for wood, made from treating cellulose with nitric acid.

nitrogen a colourless, odourless, gaseous chemical element, **N**, found in numerous compounds and the main constituent of air.

nitroglycerine an explosive oily liquid made from glycerine and sulphuric acid, used in blasting; see dynamite.

nobelium an unstable chemical element, **No**.

noble gas, inert gas, rare gas; the collective name for a group of chemically inert gaseous elements: argon, helium, krypton, xenon, neon and radon.

node see panel point. →33

nodular cast iron, spheroidal cast iron; a ductile form of cast iron produced by special heat treatment of normal cast iron.

no-fines concrete lightweight concrete consisting of coarse aggregate and cement, without sand or fine aggregate.

nog, 1 wooden brick, wooden block, fixing block, nailing block; a small piece of timber used like a brick, especially one built into brickwork as a nailing base in masonry.
2 see nogging.

nogging 1 in traditional timber frame construction, masonry infill for a timber stud frame.
see brick nogging.
see flint nogging.
see stone nogging.
2 in traditional timber frame construction, short horizontal timber struts inserted between adjacent uprights, posts, studs, rafters or joists to provide lateral support.
cross nogging, see herringbone strutting. →4

noise 1 sound in an environment which is made up of all frequencies with no regular pattern.
2 in acoustics, unwanted or disturbing sound.
3 interference; in an electronic or telecommunications system, interference caused by the obscuring action of an unwanted signal.

noise barrier in road engineering, a fence-like structure constructed alongside a busy roadway to reduce traffic noise in the surrounding environment.

noise bund in road engineering, an embankment, raised area of ground or other earthwork constructed alongside a busy roadway to reduce traffic noise in the surrounding environment.

noise control the careful planning of buildings and measures therein taken to reduce the amount of unwanted sound in spaces, achieved by the use of isolating construction and the addition of absorbing material to surfaces.

noise control glass see sound control glass.

noise level in acoustics, the measure of undesired or overloud sound level.

noise pollution sound from external sources, such as traffic, loud music etc., which causes a nuisance to those in nearby buildings or the immediate environment.

noise reduction in acoustics, reducing the sound pressure level or amount of unwanted noise between two adjoining spaces using careful planning, insulation and absorption.

noise reduction coefficient in acoustics, a measure of the sound absorption of a material or component, measured over a range of frequencies.

noise reduction glass see sound control glass.

nombril in heraldry, a point at the lower area of the shield, in the centre; also called a navel point. →124

nominal cover the specified thickness of concrete designed to cover reinforcing bars in reinforced concrete.

nominal dimension, nominal size; the size by which a component or material is specified; in reality it may be smaller or larger than this by an agreed tolerance.

nominal size see nominal dimension.

nominated subcontract a subcontract in which the client selects the contractor.

nominated subcontractor a subcontractor who has been appointed by the client, or his representative.

nomogram, graph; a diagram displaying the relationship between a number of variables, usually plotted against axes for use in calculation.

nomography the display of mathematical formulae in graphic form.

nonagon a planar regular or irregular nine-sided geometrical figure. →108

non-bearing wall see non-loadbearing wall. →28

non-combustible in fire testing, referring to a material which, under specified test conditions, can be considered not to burn.

non-conductive see insulating.

non-conforming use in town planning, a class of building or land use that does not conform to that stipulated in a development plan.

non-corridor block a multistorey residential building type in which all dwelling units on each floor are grouped around, and accessed from, a hallway within a central core; see point-access block. →61

non-destructive testing the physical and chemical testing of materials and components in such a way that they are in an unaltered state after testing.

non-drying oil a range of oils extracted from vegetable products, used in paints to add flexibility and reduce the speed of drying.

non-figurativism, non-objectivism; a general name for art which avoids the use of familiar objects or anything natural or recognizable as subjects.

non-fixed furnishing in interior design, furnishings such as tables, chairs, mats, curtains etc. which can be moved around or easily removed.

non-fixed luminaire a light fitting such as a table lamp or lamp stand not designed to be fixed to the building fabric.

non-loadbearing partition see lightweight partition.

non-loadbearing wall, non-bearing wall; any internal or external wall in a building which supports only its own weight, including fittings and wind loads, and which does not have a structural role.
see *non-loadbearing external wall* in building frames illustration. →28

non-metal a general name for all chemical elements which are not metals.

non-mortised butt hinge see non-mortised hinge. →38

non-mortised hinge, non-mortise butt hinge, surface-fixed hinge; a hinge with one flap shaped to fit in a cutout in the other, which, when closed, has the thickness of one flap only. →38

non-objectivism see non-figurativism.

non-plastic soil any granular soil type with a plasticity index of zero, or one for which a plasticity index cannot be determined.

non-return valve see check valve.

non-setting glazing compound a glazing compound which deforms plastically and remains in a semi-liquid state.

non-slip a treatment or fixing for floors and stairs in which the surface is roughened or profiled to provide friction on otherwise potentially slippery areas.

non-slip tile a ceramic tile manufactured with raised mouldings, grooves or a rough textured surface, designed for use at pool edges, stair nosings etc. →20

non-standard referring to any manufactured product or component which deviates from the usual standard form, usually requiring special manufacture.

non-vibration concrete see self-placing concrete.

non-volatile memory a computer memory in which data is retained when the power supply is switched off.

noraghe see nuraghe.

Norfolk reed see best reed.

norm, standard; an officially recognized exemplary standard of measurement, quality, regulative legislation or classification.

normal distribution, Gaussian distribution; a statistical distribution curve which follows the mathematical expression discovered by Gauss.

normalized steel a fine-grained, homogeneous, weldable steel which has been heat-treated by normalizing.

normalizing a heat treatment to refine grain size and increase the strength of steel by heating to a certain temperature and rapidly cooling in air.

Norman arch a round arch with a highly ornate archivolt, as found in Norman architecture.

Norman architecture, Anglo-Norman architecture; religious architecture in England after the Norman conquest in 1066, characterized by sparing use of detail, bulky forms and the round arch; known on the continent as Romanesque architecture.
see *Norman wheel-window* illustration. →109
see *medieval capitals* illustration. →115

Norman revival an architectural style in England from the 1800s characterized by an interest in forms and decoration from Norman and Romanesque architecture.

north one of the points of the compass, the direction opposite that at which the sun lies in the Northern hemisphere at midday.

north-east a direction halfway between that of north and east.

north-west a direction halfway between that of north and west.

northern red oak [*Quercus rubra*], see red oak.

northlight roof a sawtooth roof with north facing glazed lights used for industrial buildings in the northern hemisphere.

northlight shell roof a northlight roof in which the curved bands of roof between vertical lights are half barrel vaulted concrete shell structures; used for overhead illumination of industrial buildings.

Norway spruce [*Picea abies, Picea excelsa*] a common European softwood with soft, light, pale-coloured timber; used widely for framing, interior and exterior cladding and pulp.

Noryl a proprietary name for polyphenylene oxide plastic.

nose see nosing. →45

nose line see line of nosings. →45

nosing, nose; a horizontal protrusion of a stair tread beyond the riser. →45

nosing line see line of nosings. →45

nosing tile an L-shaped ceramic tile fitting designed for use at the front edge of a step. →20

no-slump concrete stiff concrete whose test sample exhibits very little slump.

nosocomion a Byzantine or Greek hospital or hospice.

notch 1 in timber frame construction and jointing, a small cutting made in the side of a framing member in order to fasten or stiffen a joint. →4

2 in log construction, the carefully hewn and crafted joint formed by cutting into overlaid crosswise logs so that they interlock with one another at the external corner of a log building; types included as separate entries are listed below. →6

boxed lap notch. →6

dovetailed notch. →6

lap notch, see boxed lap notch, locked lap notch. →6

locked dovetailed notch, see locked lap notch. →6

locked lap notch. →6

round notch, saddleback joint. →6

saddle notch. →6

3 see long groove. →6

notched and cogged joint a timber notched joint in which a cog is cut into the receiving member to further fasten the joint. →4

notched corner joint see notch (log construction). →6

notched housed joint in timber frame construction, a housed timber joint which has a notch cut in the end of one member for stiffening purposes.

notched joint 1 a timber joint in which a notch is made in one piece in order to fasten it in position; usually used for the fastening of joists on a wall plate or beam.

2 in timber frame construction, a crossing joint in which one or both members have a recess or notch cut to receive the other.

3 see single notched joint. →4

4 see double notched joint. →4

5 see notch (log construction). →6

notched lap joint a timber lap joint which has a notch in the lap and recess to strengthen the joint.

notched trowel a plasterer's trowel whose blade has a castellated edge to provide the plaster coat with a striated texture. →43

notch effect in structures, a local build-up of stress at the point in a member where it turns through a sharp angle, or is notched.

notching, cogging; in horizontal log construction, the shaping of the ends of logs to form a tight corner joint; the hewn cuts thus made.

notching saw see grooving saw.

notepad a loosely bound volume of usually cheap paper used for taking notes etc.

notice 1 a written announcement of intent by a client, contractor or local authority informing of an action which is being undertaken, or which should be carried out.

2 the announcement by one of the parties to a contract that it is to be terminated after a specific period of time.

noticeboard cork agglomerate cork available in sheet form and suitable for noticeboards.

notice to proceed in contract administration, a written announcement by a client to a contractor informing of the duration and starting dates of construction work.

not-pressed paper see cold-pressed paper.

nougat a shade of grey brown which takes its name from the colour of a French confection of the same name, made from nuts, almonds and caramel.

nowy cross 1 any cross with a boss, disc or lump at the crossing of the limbs; also called cross nowy. →117

2 nowy quadrant cross, see quadrant cross. →117

nozzle 1 the perforated outlet of a water- or gas-fed appliance such as a tap or shower which controls flow and direction.

2 see spout.

3 see jet inlet.

Nubian pyramid pyramid structures erected in groups by the Nubians as royal burial tombs over the period 300 BC–400 AD in Meroë, Sudan; steeper and more modest in scale than their Egyptian counterparts. →70

Nucella spp. see purple.

nuclear energy a form of energy generation from the decay of nuclear fuel; also called nuclear power, especially when used to drive a machine, vehicle etc.

nuclear fuel radioactive material such as enriched uranium which, by controlled reaction, is used as fuel in a nuclear power station.

nuclear power see nuclear energy.

nuclear power station, atomic power station; a power station in which electricity is produced by controlled atomic reaction.

nuclear radiation subatomic particles or rays emitted during nuclear decay of radioactive substances, used as a source of energy and relatively harmful in even small doses.

nuclear reactor that part of a nuclear power station in which energy is produced by controlled nuclear chain reaction.

nulled ornament see gadroon. →124

number, 1 amount, quantity; a value defining how many of an item there is.

2 the written form of such a value.

numerical based on numbers as opposed to symbols.

numerical value in mathematics, the result of calculation which can be expressed as a number.

Nun in ancient Egyptian mythology, the primeval watery chaos from which the world and sun-god Atum emerged.

nunnery, convent; a religious community or monastery inhabited solely by women.

nuragh see nuraghe.

nuraghe, noraghe, nuragh, pl. nuraghi; a prehistoric round fortified tower complex, built in cyclopean masonry and typical in Sardinia until the conquest of Rome in c.500 BC.

nursery, kindergarten, playschool, day-care centre; an establishment which provides daytime care for children under school age.

nursing home a communal residence for persons recuperating from illness or requiring constant nursing care.

nut 1 a hexagonal, octagonal or square fastener with a threaded hole to receive a bolt. →37

see *fixings and washers* illustration; types of nut included as separate entries are listed below. →37

acorn nut, see cap nut. →37

backnut.

butterfly nut, see wing nut. →37

cap nut. →37

castellated nut, castle nut. →37

dome nut, see cap nut. →37

hexagonal nut, hex nut. →37

lock nut. →37

seal nut. →37

square nut. →37

stop nut.

thumb nut.

wing nut. →37

2 the seeds of various fruit-bearing trees, used as a source of food and pressed for oils; these trees are often used for fine timberwork; see walnut, hazel, nut oil.

3 Nut; in ancient Egyptian mythology, the primeval deity of the sky, forming the cosmos together with Geb: earth, Shu: air, and Tefnut: moisture; depicted as a blue star-clad female on all fours, back arched to encompass the heavens. →74

nut oil various types of drying oils used as vehicles in paints, pressed from the dried kernels of nuts such as the walnut.
see hazelnut oil.
see walnut oil.

nutria a shade of dark brown which takes its name from the colour of the fur of the coypu (or nutria) [*Myocastor coypus*].

nylon any of a number of tough, whitish, durable polyamide thermoplastics used to produce fibres, hardware, coatings and garden furniture.

Nymphaea caerulea see blue lotus. →82, →121

Nymphaea lotus see white lotus. →82, →121

nymphaeum, pl. nymphaea; Lat.; in classical architecture, a temple, shrine or building dedicated to nymphs, mythological female water spirits; often built in proximity to a spring or water source; a fountain house. →91, →94

Nyssa spp. see tupelo.

O

oak [*Quercus spp.*] a group of tough, hard, heavy hardwoods of the temperate climates ranging in colour from light tan to pink or brown; used in construction and decoration, for interiors, flooring, boat-building and plywood; see ***Quercus spp.*** for full list of species of oak included in this work.

oak brown, oak wood; a shade of brown which takes its name from the colour of the wood of the oak tee [*Quercus spp.*].

oak wood 1 wood of the oak tree; often written as oakwood or oak-wood.
2 see oak brown.

oakum a stuffing for sealing and packing horizontal joints in log buildings and wooden ships made from hemp, old rope or other fibrous material.

oast house a cylindrical brick building with a conical roof and containing a kiln, used for the drying and storage of hops used in brewing.

obeche, samba, African whitewood, wawa, ayous; [*Triplochiton scleroxylon*] a West African hardwood whose light porous timber is pale brown to white; used for interior joinery and plywood.

obelisk 1 an Egyptian monolithic four-sided standing stone, tapering to a pyramidical cap, often inscribed with hieroglyphs and erected as a monument. →72, →73
2 see Cleopatra's needle. →73

oblique, skew; referring to a line, plane or building orientation at an angle to a major alignment or axis.

oblique butt joint a longitudinal timber butt joint in which the ends of one or both are splayed so that the members are at an angle to one another.

oblique cross see St Andrew's cross. →118

oblique joint see *types of timber oblique joint* illustration. →4

oblique perspective 1 see two-point perspective. →129
2 see three-point perspective. →130

oblique projection a parallel projection drawing in which the projectors are parallel but intersect the projection plane at an angle other than a right angle; one face of an object is thus drawn in true proportion, parallel to the picture plane, and the other axes are represented by extending oblique lines; see cavalier, cabinet, military projections. →127

oblique shake one of a series of cracks running across the grain of a timber board at an angle. →1

oblique tenon joint a mortise and tenon joint used when joining two timbers at an oblique angle to one another.

oblong a planar rectangular four-sided figure which is longer than it is wide and in which all internal angles are 90°.

obscurance see translucency.

obscured glass translucent glass of which one face has a diffuse surface produced by sandblasting, grinding, etching or acid embossing.
see reeded glass.

observation lift, scenic lift; a glazed lift for hotel foyers, shopping centres etc., designed to offer a view to the surrounding area.

observation tower see lookout tower. →103

observatory a building or structure designed to house telescopes and other astronomical instruments used for studying the heavens. →67

obsidian a form of dark, compact, naturally occurring volcanic glass, traditionally used for weapons and tools, now used for ornament.

obtuse angle a geometrical angle greater than 90° but less than 180°.

occupant one permanently resident in a dwelling, or renting space in a building.

occupant load in fire safety, a specified total number of occupants per floor area of building space.

occupation road a private road for use of the inhabitants of the dwellings which it serves.

ocean blue see sea blue.

ocean green see sea crest.

ocher see ochre.

ochre, ocher (Am.); a group of earth pigments, hydrated iron oxides with added clay, which range in colour from yellow to orange-red or brown; suitable for use in all types of paint; types included as separate entries are listed below.
brown ochre.
gold ochre.
red ochre, see red oxide paint.
Roman ochre, yellow ochre.
sil, yellow ochre.
yellow ochre.

Ochroma spp. see balsa wood.

octagon a planar regular or irregular eight-sided geometrical figure. →108

octagram a decorative star-shaped figure with eight points, constructed either with a single unbroken intersecting line or with two overlaid rectangles. →108

octahedron a solid shape whose surface is composed of eight planar faces.

octastyle in classical architecture, a portico supported by a row of eight columns. →77

octave in acoustics, the interval of eight notes on the diatonic scale between a doubling in frequency of sound.

octopartite vault a masonry vault sprung on eight points of support, octagonal or rectangular in plan and composed of eight curved roof surfaces. →26

octopus an eight-limbed marine invertebrate of the class of molluscs known as Cephalopoda, appearing in late Minoan and Mycenaean art and decoration with unknown significance, in other cultures symbolic of darkness and evil. →122

oculus, 1 pl. oculi; Lat.; a circular opening or rooflight in a roof or dome, especially that in a Roman building. →86
2 see roundel.

odd leg calliper see jenny leg calliper.

odeion Greek form of odeum. →89

odeon see odeum. →89

odeum, odeon, odeion (Gk); Lat.; a roofed theatre building in antiquity, especially one for the performance of vocal and instrumental music. →89

Odin's cross see wheel cross. →118

oecus Lat.; a main hall or dining room in a Roman dwelling, situated to one side of an open courtyard; called an andron in Greek architecture; cf. oikos. →88

oeillet an arrow loop; oeillet ('eyelet') often refers also to the rounded enlargements at either extremity of an arrow loop. →103

offer see bid.

offertory window see leper window.

office 1 space within a building used for business, clerical and administrative work.
2 see office space. →60
3 an administrative building or spaces from which a business operates.
4 see office building. →60

office block a multistorey building containing offices.

office building a building containing offices, used primarily for commercial, administration or clerical work.
see *office building* illustration. →60

office space any space within a building used or designated for clerical or administrative work etc. →60

offset handle see cranked pull handle. →51

offset match, half drop; a condition of patterned wallpaper which should be hung with adjacent lengths staggered vertically so that horizontal patterns match.

offset screwdriver a screwdriver whose bit and handle are not aligned, used for tightening screws in cramped positions, or for those requiring extra leverage. →41

offshore construction, platform; any maritime construction or platform such as an oil rig or lighthouse, which is floated out to sea and anchored to the sea bed.

off-white, broken white, faux blanc; a shade of white which has been slightly tinted with another colour, most often grey or yellow, to reduce its intensity or sterility.

ogee arch, 1 inflected arch; an arch whose intrados is composed of two mirrored ogees which meet at an apex. →24
2 see depressed ogee arch, two-centred ogee arch. →24
3 see bell arch, reverse ogee arch. →24

ogee brace in traditional timber-framed construction, a naturally S-shaped curved timber member used to brace the junction between a post and beam.

ogee moulding 1 a decorative moulding whose cross-section is that of an ogee or S-shaped profile, the concave part uppermost; called a cyma recta in classical architecture. →82
2 see reverse ogee moulding. →82
3 see cyma recta. →82
4 see cyma reversa. →82

ogee roof an ornamental roof form which is ogee shaped in cross-section. →26

ogee stop in ornamentation, the termination of a chamfered moulding or carving with a shallow S-shaped form.

ogival, lancet; a pointed arch; pertaining to Gothic architecture, as named by the French ('l'architecture ogival' or 'le style ogival').

ogive see diagonal rib. →101

ohm abb. Ω; the SI unit of electrical resistance, equal to that which will produce a current of 1 amp when a potential difference of 1 volt is passed across a resistor.

oikos Gk; a living room in a Greek dwelling.

oikos ekklesias Gk; a Greek Early Christian dwelling used as a church or place of worship; the Roman equivalent is domus ecclesius.

oil any greasy liquid, insoluble in water, obtained from animal, vegetable and mineral sources and used for lubrication, energy production etc.; types included as separate entries are listed below.
anthracene oil.
asphalt oil, see road oil.
blown linseed oil.
boiled linseed oil.
carbolic oil.
China wood oil, see tung oil.
clove oil, see oil of cloves.
cottonseed oil.
creosote oil, see creosote.
crude oil, see petroleum.
diesel oil.
drying oil.
essential oil, volatile oil.
fatty oil, fixed oil.
fixed oil, see fatty oil.
form oil, see mould oil.
fuel oil.
gas oil.
hempseed oil.
lemon oil, see oil of lemon.
lavender oil, oil of spike.
linseed oil.
middle oil, see carbolic oil.
mineral oil.
mould oil, form oil.
non-drying oil.
nut oil.
oil of cloves.
oil of lemon.
oil of spike, spike lavender.
oil of turpentine, see turpentine.
paraffin oil, see paraffin.
pine oil.
poppyseed oil, poppy oil.
road oil.
soya bean oil.
stand oil.
sun-bleached oil, sun-refined oil.
sunflower seed oil.
thyme oil.
tung oil, China wood oil.
volatile oil, see essential oil.
walnut oil.

oil based referring to a paint, sealant etc. whose medium is oil rather than water.

oil black a black pigment manufactured from the carbon deposits from burned oil.

oil burner a device in an oil heating system for converting fuel oil into a fine spray or vapour and igniting it.

oil crayon a hard oil pastel.

oiled charcoal a drawing crayon made by soaking charcoal in oil or wax.

oilet see oeillet. →103

oil fired referring to a heating system utilizing combustible fuel oil to produce heat.

oil-fired heating, oil heating; a heating system in which the fuel used is combustible oil.

oil fuel see fuel oil.

oil green a light yellow green variety of chrome green pigment.

oil heating see oil-fired heating.

oil interceptor a chamber in a drainage system where water-bound oil from drained surface water is deposited to prevent it from passing further along a drain.

oillet see oeillet. →103

oil meter a device for measuring and recording the flow and consumption of oil in an oil heating system.

oil of cloves, clove oil; an essential oil distilled from the dried buds (cloves) of the tropical myrtle plant *Eugenia caryophyllata* [*Syzygium aromaticum*], traditionally used as a slow drying solvent in paints and varnishes and as an odour-masking agent.

oil of lemon, lemon oil; oil extracted from the fresh peel of lemons, traditionally used in paints and varnishes to mask odours.

oil of spike, spike lavender; an essential oil distilled from the leaves of the broad-leaved variety of lavender, *Lavandula spica*, traditionally used as a solvent in paints and varnishes.

oil of turpentine see turpentine.

oil of vitriol see sulphuric acid.

oil paint any paint whose binder is an oil such as linseed oil, poppy oil etc., from which the solvent evaporates to leave a tough film; used for external joinery and furniture.

oil paste, colours in oil; a concentrated colour source consisting of pigment in an oil paste, used for tinting paints.

oil pastel, oil crayon; a soft stick of pigment in oils with a binder, used for drawing and painting.

oil ring main see cold oil ring main.

oil stain a translucent colouring agent for porous surfaces such as timber, consisting of a dye suspended in oil.

oilstone a fine-grained stone used with lubricating oil to sharpen the honed blades of tools.

oil storage tank a large vessel or similar construction for the storage of oil, especially for an oil heating system or other oil-fired installation.

oil terminal a harbour containing large oil storage vessels, in which oil is transferred to or from oil tankers.

oil varnish a glossy varnish containing oil and resin.

oil well a natural or bored hole in the ground or sea bed from which crude oil or natural gas is extracted from the earth's crust.

okoume see gaboon.

okribas see proscenium. →89

Old Kingdom, the age of pyramid builders; the period of the 3rd to 6th dynasties of ancient Egyptian culture from 2778 to 2423 BC, characterized by monumental stone edifices, mastabas, pyramids, sphinxes and the first sun temples with obelisks and lotus, papyrus and palm columns. →70, →71

old people's home a staffed communal residence equipped to take care of elderly persons; a nursing home.

old silver see silver.

Old Stone Age see palaeolithic period.

old testament cross see tau cross. →117

old woman's tooth see router plane.

Olea europaea see olive.

oleoresinous paint a traditional hard gloss paint containing oleoresin.

oleoresin, balsam; a thick viscous liquid exuded from certain conifers, used as a binder in some paints and as an additive to improve brushing and flexibility.

oleum white see lithopone.

olio d'abezzo see Strasbourg turpentine.

olive 1 [*Olea europaea*] a Mediterranean evergreen hardwood with hard and heavy greeny brown timber; used for joinery and turnery.
2 olive green; a shade of dark grey green which takes its name from the colour of fruit of the olive tree.

olive brown a general name for a shade of dark greyish brown.

olive green see olive.

olive grey a general name for a shade of dark greenish grey.

olive yellow a general name for a shade of yellow brown.

olivine, peridot, chrysolite; an olive green, crystalline magnesium iron silicate mineral.

Olmec architecture the architecture of the Indian peoples of the east coast of Mexico and Central America from c.1000 to 650 BC, typified by giant stone monoliths of human heads and jungle temples.

omega the final letter of the Greek alphabet, Ω, ω used to symbolize the unit of electrical resistance, the ohm; see alpha and omega. →119

omphalos 'navel' (Gk); a hemispherical marble stone at the temple of Delphi in Greece, traditionally believed to be the centre of the universe. →120

omu [*Entandrophragma candollei*] a tropical West African hardwood sold as mahogany; it has pale reddish brown timber and is used for plywood, veneered furniture and interiors.

one-and-a-half brick wall see brick-and-a-half wall. →21

one-brick wall, nine inch wall, whole-brick wall; a solid brick wall whose width is the length of one standard brick, 9″ or 215 mm. →21

one-coat plaster see single-coat plaster.

one-coat plasterwork see single-coat plasterwork.

one-component see one-pack.

one-family house a freestanding dwelling with living space for one family unit; see house. →61

one-pack, one-part, one-component; a description of products such as glues, sealants and paints which are supplied ready for use and do not require the addition of other components.

one-part see one-pack.

one-pipe system, single-pipe system; a central heating system in which each radiator is served by one pipe circuit, and the heating water is piped from one to the next.

one-point perspective a method of perspective drawing using only one vanishing point, producing a view in which verticals are seen as vertical and horizontals parallel to the picture plane are seen as horizontal; also known as central, Renaissance or parallel perspective.

one-room flat see bedsit.

one-turn stairs, full-turn stairs; a stair which turns through 360° on its ascent, formed from straight flights which meet at corner landings. →45

one-way glass, mirror glass; glass treated on one side with a transparent reflective finish or with a laminate so as to appear see-through from one side and as a mirror on the other.

one-way head screw, clutch head screw, butterfly head screw; a screw whose head has a slot so designed that it may be tightened but not undone by a cross-slot or traditional screwdriver. →36

one-way slab a reinforced concrete slab whose reinforcement is designed primarily to span parallel supports in one direction.

one-way stick adhesive, single spread adhesive; an adhesive applied to only one of the surfaces to be joined.

one-way street an urban road along which traffic is permitted to travel in one direction only to ease inner-city congestion.

one-way system an urban inner-city traffic network of one-way streets to alleviate congestion.

onion dome an ogee-shaped dome resembling an onion, pointed at the top, found in Russian, Byzantine and some Baroque architecture; a common motif in Indian and other Asian architecture; also called a bulbous dome. →26

on-street parking see street parking. →62

onyx a trade name for onyx marble.

onyx marble a pale brown or yellow banded calcareous rock used as decorative stonework in building.

oolite sedimentary rock, especially limestone, composed of spherical grains.

opacity, opaqueness, hiding power; a measure of the non-translucency of a paint, its ability to mask colours in coats beneath.

opaion Gk; in classical and Byzantine architecture, a roof lantern or oculus in a domed roof to admit light. →86

opal 1 a white or coloured mineral, an amorphous form of hydrated silica used for ornamentation, gemstones and jewellery.
2 opaline green; a shade of green which takes its name from the colour of the precious opal stone.
3 satin; in artificial lighting, the classification of the bulb of a lamp whose inner surface is treated with a white silica coating producing stronger obscurance of the filament and better diffusion than with a pearl finish.

opal glass, opalescent glass; opaque or translucent diffuse glass with a milky coloured or white appearance, produced by laminating clear glass with an obscuring plastic sheet or by introducing fine obscuring particles into the glass itself.

opalescent glass see opal glass.

opaline see milk glass.

opaline green see opal.

opaque referring to a material, surface or construction which inhibits the passage of light.

opaque glass 1 glass with a surface treatment or interlayer through which light does not penetrate, often used as cladding glass.

2 see coloured opaque glass.
3 see cladding glass.

opaqueness see opacity.

Op Art see optical art.

open-air museum an outdoor museum, usually containing traditional buildings or objects such as farm implements or vehicles in a natural or appropriate setting.

open-air swimming pool, outdoor swimming pool; an unroofed swimming pool or swimming bath which is open to the elements.

open-air theatre an outdoor arena for the presentation of theatrical works.

open balustrade a balustrade without infill between handrail and floor level; a railing. →54

open bar metal flooring metal flooring consisting of a grid of welded bars, used for maintenance platforms and walkways.

open-bed pediment see broken pediment. →112

open bidding see open tendering.

open boarding see spaced boarding. →8
see *timber cladding boards* illustration. →8
see *timber-framed building* illustration. →57
see *holiday home and sauna* illustration. →58

open caisson, cylinder caisson; a foundation caisson constructed in such a way so as to be open at both the top and bottom.

open capital see bell capital. →73

open ceiling 1 the underside of a timber roof or intermediated floor whose joists or beams are exposed from below.
2 a suspended ceiling of open baffles, mesh or grid, usually concealing luminaires and ventilation inlets.
3 see cell ceiling.
4 see open mesh ceiling.

open cell ceiling see cell ceiling.

open competition an architectural or planning competition in which all participants of a certain group (architects, citizens of a stated nation, or community etc.) are entitled to participate; see also invited competition.

open country, countryside, rural area; land outside an urban area with few or dispersed buildings, where the main source of livelihood is agriculture, forestry and recreation.

open cruck truss in traditional timber frame construction, a cruck truss which has no tie or collar-beam.

open eaves an eaves which has no soffit board and is open from below.

open-ended unit an apartment in a slab block which occupies a slice of its whole thickness, with windows on opposite walls, facing in opposite directions; also called a through apartment. →61

open excavation an excavation requiring no shoring, open to the elements and often with sloping sides.

open face see loose side. →10

open fire a fireplace, most often of masonry construction, in which the combustion chamber has no doors or hatches and is open to a room. →55

open fireplace see open fire. →55

open front seat, cut-away-front seat; a WC seat in the shape of a horseshoe with its opening at the front.

open grained see coarse textured.

open-hearth process, Siemens-Martin process; a steelmaking process developed in the 1860s for producing steel on a large scale from scrap and pig iron; it utilizes hot gases to heat up the metal while removing unwanted carbon, manganese, silicon, phosphorus and sulphur.

opening a hole in a wall, floor etc. for the fitting of a door, window, hatch, or simply left open; if in a floor it is called a void. →4
damper opening, see throat. →55
door opening, see doorway. →28, →51
see window opening. →28

opening size the side of a door leaf or window casement which opens away from the frame. →50, →51

opening light a hinged or sliding part of a window unit or glazed screen which can be opened. →52

opening size a measure of fineness of a wire mesh, the open space between adjacent parallel wires; see mesh size.

open joint a construction joint left open between two adjacent components, without jointing compound, seals or covering.

open mesh ceiling a suspended ceiling system formed from rectangular mesh panels to allow for the passage of air and light from services located in the ceiling void.

open metal flooring metal flooring of perforated panels in or on a frame.

open mortise see slot mortise.

open mortise joint a mortise and tenon corner joint in which the mortise cut into the end of one piece is open on three sides to receive a tenon in the other; often called a bridle joint. →5

open pediment, 1 broken-apex pediment, open-topped pediment; a Baroque or Neoclassical pediment with an opening where the apex should be. →112
2 see open segmental pediment. →112

open piling the open stacking of timber or other wood products in layers separated to allow for air circulation during seasoning and drying.

open plan offices large open office space without permanent dividing walls.

open rise the open space between treads in a stair with no risers.

open rise stair see open riser stair. →45

open riser stair, ladder stair, open rise stair, skeleton stair; a stair with no infill construction between its treads. →45

open roof, open timbered roof; pitched roof construction in which the roof structure or rafters are not concealed with a lining or ceiling and are visible from the space below.

open section a cold formed or cold pressed metal section which is not a hollow section, one bent or formed into an open shape. →34

open segmental pediment a segmental pediment whose upper curve has a central opening. →112

open side see loose side. →10

open space areas between buildings or groups of buildings for recreational use; any public open urban land such as parks, gardens or squares on which no buildings have been constructed.

open spandrel bridge an arch bridge with voids between the extrados of the supporting arch and the deck structure; often one of concrete with a series of columns supporting the deck from the main arch. →32

open stile balustrade a balustrade with a series of vertical parallel stiles between handrail and floor level to provide an intermediate barrier. →54

open tendering, open bidding (Am.); a competitive tendering procedure in which any suitable firm or person can submit a tender for a building contract, usually as a result of a public announcement for calls to tender.

open tenon joint see bridle joint. →5

open timbered roof see open roof.

open time in painting and decorating, the time elapsed before a freshly painted surface has dried sufficiently for an adjacent coat to be painted next to it.

open-topped pediment see open pediment. →112

open tongue and groove boarding tongue and groove boards with rebated external edges to form longitudinal indents between adjacent laid boards. →8

opera Lat.; plural form of opus.

opera coronata see crownwork. →104

opera house a building with stage, auditorium and other facilities required for the public production and performance of operatic and other musical works.

operating cost the cost of running a building, organization, piece of machinery etc.

operating instructions, manual; written instructions setting down the principles of usage for a system or installation.

operating loss an actual net financial loss made by a business over a period of time.

operating profit an actual net financial gain made by a business over a period of time.

operating system in computing, a program which makes the running of specific programs on a particular computer possible.

operation manual a written document with specifications and a description of a particular appliance or piece of equipment, and instructions and advice for its use.

operative a skilled or semi-skilled person who carries out work on a site involving operating a machine.

Ophiostoma minus see blue stain fungus.

opisthodomos, epinaos, posticum; in classical architecture, an enclosed room or open space at the rear of a Greek, especially amphiprostyle, temple, often used as a treasury; it is a called posticum in Roman architecture. →84

oppidum 1 Lat.; a Gallic walled and fortified town or stronghold, as named by the Romans.
2 a line of buildings, gates and towers which delineated the end of a Roman circus, so called because of its resemblance to the above.

opportunity model in traffic planning, a synthetic trip distribution model which studies all the possible modes of transport and routes between two specified points without taking into account expense, distance or time.

optical art, Op Art, retinal art; a movement in abstract art originating in the 1960s, concerned with the optical effects of line, form and repetition on the eye.

optical fibre a very fine, high quality glass tube in which light is used as a medium in telecommunications systems.

optical mixing in colour theory, the merging of small dots of colour to form different colours when viewed at a distance.

optical smoke detector, visible smoke detector; a fire detector which, using a photocell or other sensor, reacts to the disturbing effects on a light or laser beam as it passes through smoke from fire.

opus, pl. opera, work (Lat.); an artistic composition or pattern, especially as used in relation to Roman stonework.
see *Roman walling* illustration. →83

opus africanum 'African work' (Lat.); classical Roman concrete masonry of massive horizontal and vertical dressed stone blocks, interspersed with panels of smaller masonry blocks, mud brick, or faced concrete, particularly common in North Africa. →83

opus albarium, albarium opus; Lat.; in Roman and Renaissance architecture, a coating of stucco for masonry surfaces, especially interior walls and ceilings. →83

opus alexandrinum Lat.; classical Roman paving in mosaic and large pieces of marble or stone.

opus antiquum Lat.; see opus incertum. →83

opus caementicium, opus concretum, opus structile, structura caementicia; Lat.; concrete or rubble work in Roman architecture. →83

opus concretum Lat.; see opus caementicium. →83

opus craticium Lat.; the Roman name for traditional Roman and ancient European timber-framed structures with infill panels, primarily of wattle and daub. →83

opus francigenum Lat.; see opus modernum.

opus gallicum Lat.; see murus gallicus. →83

opus incertum, opus antiquum; Lat.; classical Roman masonry of rough stones set in mortar. →83

opus interrasile Lat.; classical Roman ornament carved in relief.

opus isodomum Lat.; classical Roman and Greek masonry with blocks of identical size laid with the vertical joints of a course centred over the blocks in the course below. →83

opus italicum Lat.; a medieval term for masonry building.

opus latericium, opus lateritium; Lat.; classical Roman masonry which makes use of bricks and tiles, often bedded in concrete. →83

opus lateritium Lat.; see opus latericium. →83

opus listatum Lat.; classical Roman masonry with alternating courses of brick and rubblestone. →83

opus lithostratum, lithostratum opus; Lat.; any classical Roman and Greek ornamental pavement.

opus mixtum 1 Lat.; Roman walling of bands of coursed regular stone alternating with courses of brick, or masonry simply using both stone and brick. →83
2 see opus reticulatum mixtum. →83
3 see opus vittatum mixtum. →83

opus mixtum vittatum Lat.; see opus vittatum mixtum. →83

opus modernum, opus francigenum; Lat.; the modern or French style, a name by which Gothic architecture was known as it spread across Europe c.1150–1200.

opus musivum Lat.; classical Roman mosaic which makes use of coloured glass or enamelled pieces.

opus pseudoisodomum Lat.; classical Roman masonry with courses of uneven height. →83

opus quadratum Lat.; classical Roman masonry of squared stones in regular courses. →83, →126

opus quasi-reticulatum Lat.; Roman concrete walling faced with rough squared blocks forming a random surface pattern. →83

opus reticulatum Lat.; classical Roman masonry of small pyramid-shaped tufa blocks with square bases, laid with their pointed ends embedded in concrete to form a diagonal grid pattern on the surface; similar patterns in tile and rectangular blocks. →83

opus reticulatum mixtum Lat.; classical Roman concrete-core masonry of small squared tufa blocks laid diagonally with alternating bands or surrounding fields of horizontal brick courses. →83

opus scoticum Lat.; a medieval term for timber construction.

opus sectile, sectile opus; Lat.; classical Roman marble paving using varying sized and shaped pieces.

opus signinum Lat.; classical Roman render of broken tiles or tesserae and concrete used especially as a coating for aqueducts, barrack buildings etc. →83

opus siliceum Lat.; Roman polygonal masonry. →83

opus spicatum, spicatum opus; Lat.; classical Roman masonry and paving in herringbone pattern. →83

opus structile Lat.; see opus caementicium. →83

opus tectorium Lat.; in Roman architecture, a coating of stucco formed from three or four coats of gypsum, chalk, sand and additives, often polished. →83

opus tesselatum Lat.; classical Roman paving of large evenly sized tesserae.

opus testaceum Lat.; classical Roman facing of broken tile or triangular brick embedded into the surfaces of concrete walling structures. →83

opus vermiculatum Lat.; classical Roman mosaic laid in a pattern of intricate wavy lines.

opus vittatum mixtum, opus mixtum vittatum; Lat.; Roman concrete-core walling faced with courses of brick alternating with large rectangular blocks. →83

orange a colour of the visible spectrum which represents a range of wavelengths from 585 m to 640 m.

orange grey see alabaster.
orange peel see mandarin orange.
orangepeel, orange peeling; a defect in which a dry paint or lacquer finish has a dimpled surface resembling orange peel, caused by lack of solvent in the paint or poor workmanship.
orange peeling see orange peel.
orangery a building, construction, or part of a building often set in parkland or on an estate, with large areas of glass to provide a controlled environment for the growing of exotic plants.
orange vermilion a variety of cinnabar.
orans figure see orant figure. →95
orant figure, orans figure; a standing figure with both arms raised in prayer, as found in Greek and Early Christian art and architectural ornamentation. →95
oratorium Latin form of oratory.
oratory a small building or part of a church intended for private prayer; Latin form is oratorium.
orb a decorative motif of a golden globe surmounted by a cross, symbolic of regal power and the monarchy. →122
orbital sander a portable power tool with a rectangular sanding surface driven with a rapid oscillating action.
orchard a plantation of apple or pear trees, grown for their fruit. →97
orchestra, orkhestra (Gk); **1** a semicircular platform between the stage and auditorium of an ancient Greek theatre, from where the choir or chorus is performed. →89
2 seats reserved for the senate and dignitaries in a Roman theatre.
orchestra pit a sunken layer of floor area in which the orchestra in a theatre, opera house or the ballet is situated.
orchid lilac a shade of pale violet which takes its name from the colour of the flowers of certain orchid plants (Orchidacae).
orchid purple a shade of purple which takes its name from the colour of the flowers of certain orchid plants (Orchidacae).
order 1 one of the predominating styles in classical architecture, a classical order.
see *orders* in Roman amphitheatre illustration. →90
2 one of a series of projecting bands above the intrados of an arch making up an archivolt.
order book in manufacturing, the volume of future orders for goods that a supplier has agreed to produce.
ordinary cement see ordinary Portland cement.
ordinary Portland cement, ordinary cement; a Portland cement, used in general construction, formed by mixing Portland cement clinker and calcium sulphate.
ordinate the distance of a point from the X or horizontal axis measured along the Y or vertical axis in a geometrical system of Cartesian coordinates. →127
Ordnance Survey of Britain the independent governmental cartographic department in Britain, which produces accurate maps of the British Isles.
ore mineral material extracted from the ground containing metals or other materials which are of commercial and industrial value.
Oregon pine see Douglas fir.
organic 1 referring to a substance, a chemical compound of carbon, which is found in or derived from living organisms.
2 biogenic; of soil, some foodstuffs and other products, based on or manufactured using living organisms.
organic architecture architecture which seeks to physically, ecologically and environmentally unify buildings with their surrounding environment through careful planning, use of materials, form and technology.
organic coating 1 see plastics coating.
2 see stove enamelling.
3 see powder coating.
organic planning town planning characterized by organized growth and balanced central development, using to advantage the existing environmental and climatic conditions and local topography while taking into account future change.
organic rendering see masonry paint.
organic roof any roof whose roofing is of organic materials such as wood, bark, turf, planting etc. →48
organic soil in ground engineering, soil containing decayed remnants of plants and animals, rich in organic material and with a poor bearing capacity.
organic solvent see solvent.
organic waste, biodegradable waste; waste material from industrial processes, residential establishments etc. which is organic and can be broken down with microbes.
organ loft a gallery or upper level in a church where an organ is situated.
see *organ loft* in Scandinavian hall church illustration. →102
organosol a dispersion of particles of a plastisol, resin or synthetic polymer in an organic solvent, which can be converted to a solid on heating; used for PVC coatings for roofing and other sheetmetal components.
organ screen an ornamental screen in a church over which an organ is situated.
oriel see oriel window.
oriel window, oriel; an upper storey window which protrudes from the elevational plane of a building; see bay window.
Oriental blue a shade of blue, greener than Delft blue, which takes its name from the colour of traditional colours used in dyeing and pottery in the Orient.
Orientalism any architectural style which borrows motifs from the Arab world, India and the Far East.
orientation, 1 direction; the angle that an object, main axis of a building or street makes with respect to due north.
2 the location of a building on its site and the arrangement of spaces therein so as to take into account the direction of sun and prevailing winds, views and disturbing factors according to the points of the compass.
3 see single orientation. →61
oriented strand board, oriented structural board, OSB; a building board manufactured of layers of flakeboard glued together with the flakes or strands at right angles to those in adjacent layers. →9
oriented structural board see oriented strand board. →9
Orient red see blood red.
Orient yellow a variety of deep cadmium yellow pigment.
origin the point at which the axes in a system of Cartesian coordinates meet, usually 0,0,0. →127
original a version of an architectural drawing or document, to which possible amendments are made and from which copies are taken for distribution.
originality the quality of a design or scheme of being unique, unusual or having little or no precedent.
orkhestra Gk; see orchestra. →89
Orlon a proprietary name for polyacrylonitrile plastics, used for fibres and textiles.
ornament 1 two- or three-dimensional decoration, sculpture, carving etc. for the surfaces or spaces of a building or other object.
see *continuous mouldings* illustration. →14
see *floriated and foliated ornament* illustration. →82
see *repeated mouldings* illustration. →124
see *fret and heraldic mouldings* illustration. →125

see *geometrical figures* illustration. →108
see *symbols and ornamental motifs* illustrations. →119, →120, →121, →122, →123
see *cross* illustrations. →117, →118
2 see running ornament. →124

ornamental bed an area of landscaped ground prepared and planted with plants and flowers as decoration.

ornamental brickwork 1 see decorative masonry.
2 see patterned brickwork.
3 see polychrome brickwork.

ornamental motif, decorative motif; a design, pattern, sculpture, symbol etc. used as surface decoration for the surface of a building or other object; often with specific meaning, message or symbolic value. →14

ornamental plaster moulding see fibrous plaster moulding.

ornamental plasterwork see fibrous plasterwork.

Ornamental style, Third Pompeian style, Closed style; a style of Roman mural painting from Roman Pompeii depicting mythical themes on a flat background of coloured panels (see Architectural, Incrustation style).
see *Pompeian styles* illustration. →126

ornamental tile 1 any roof, wall or floor tile with decorative profiled edges, embossing, patterns etc.
2 especially a clay roof tile used for decorative eaves, verge or ridge embellishment.

ornamentation see enrichment.

orphanage an establishment which provides care for children who have lost their parents.

Orphism a movement in cubist art from the beginning of the 1900s characterized by the use of colour harmonies in abstract compositions.

orpiment a greasy, lemon yellow mineral, natural arsenic trisulphide, As_2S_3, used as the pigment king's yellow, for removing hair from animal skins and as a source of arsenic.

orthoclase see potash feldspar, alkali feldspar.
see adularia.
see microcline.
see moonstone.

orthodox cross see Russian cross. →117

orthogonal 1 relating to objects, axes, grids or lines which lie at right angles to one another.
2 a line at right angles to an axis, line or plane.

orthogonal projection 1 any projection drawing in which projectors meet the picture plane at right angles, producing a plan, elevation, side view etc.
2 see orthographic projection. →127

orthographic axonometric projection see axonometric projection. →127

orthographic dimetric projection see dimetric projection. →127

orthographic isometric projection see isometric projection. →127

orthographic projection a drawing which shows a surface or section drawn at scale as if from infinity, at right angles to the cutting plane or elevation; in architectural drawing the result is a plan, elevation or sectional drawing, though sometimes extended to include true axonometric projections; also called an orthogonal projection. →127
orthographic axonometric projection, see axonometric projection. →127
orthographic dimetric projection, see dimetric projection. →127
orthographic isometric projection, see isometric projection. →127
orthographic trimetric projection, see dimetric projection. →127

orthographic trimetric projection see dimetric projection. →127

orthography the art of drawing parallel projections.

orthostat a large stone slab laid vertically in a structure or set in the ground, such as a prehistoric standing stone, a large stone in the lower part of a Greek temple or a decorated Mesopotamian monolith in the foundations or interior of a building.
see *Pompeian styles* illustration. →126

orthotropic slab a reinforced concrete floor slab, such as a one-way slab, in which reinforcement in the direction of span is greater than that perpendicular to it.

OSB oriented strand board. →9

oscillation repeated or swinging movement back and forth across an axis.

osier see withe.

Osirian column see Osiris column. →73, →76

Osirid column see Osiris column. →73, →76

Osiride column see Osiris column. →73, →76

Osiris in ancient Egyptian mythology, originally the corn-god of the Nile Delta, later principal deity of the Old Kingdom, who ruled the world with his brother Seth, by whose hand he died; king and judge of the underworld, depicted in mummy-dress wearing a crown of plant stems; brother of Isis, father of Horus; 'Asar' in Egyptian, 'Osiris' in Greek. →74

Osiris column, Osiris pillar; an ancient Egyptian column carved in an image of Osiris, god of the underworld, with arms crossed; also known as an Osiris, Osirid, Osiride or Osirian pillar or column. →72, →73, →76

osmium the heaviest metal yet discovered, **Os**, very durable and often found in conjunction with platinum.

ossuarium Latin form of ossuary.

ossuary, ossuarium (Lat.); a construction, often at a cemetery or the crypt or undercroft of a church, intended for the storage of bones of the dead; a charnel house.

ostium Lat.; the doorway or space between vestibule and atrium in a Roman building.

ostrum see Tyrian purple.

Ostrya carpinifolia see European hop-hornbeam.

Othman architecture see Ottoman architecture.

Ottoman architecture, Othman architecture; the architecture of the Ottoman dynasty in Turkey from 1300 to 1923, especially Islamic architecture from 1400 to 1600 in which the mosques displayed Byzantine influence, spreading building masses, large saucer-domed spaces, minarets and simple exteriors.

Ottonian architecture the architecture of the East Frankish dynasty of the Holy Roman Empire in Germany (962–1030) during the rule of Otto I, characterized by Byzantine and Italian influences.

oubliette a windowless basement cell in a medieval castle or fortification with a sole opening in its roof, into which prisoners were thrown and left to rot. →103

Oulu school a movement in timber and brick architecture in northern Finland from the 1980s which has overt postmodernist influences.

ounce 1 abb. **oz**; a unit of weight equal to one sixteenth of a pound avoirdupois, equivalent to 28.35 grams.
2 see troy ounce.

oundy moulding, swelled chamfer, undy moulding, wave moulding; an ornamental motif consisting of a series of lines representing the breaking of waves. →125

outbuilding, ancillary building; a subsidiary building such as a bin store, barn, garage, bicycle shelter, workshops, shed etc. situated in a yard, garden or estate of a residential or main building, or connected to it.

outcrop, exposed rock; an area of uncovered rock exposed at the surface of the earth.

outdoor furniture see garden furniture.

outdoor swimming pool see open-air swimming pool.

outdoor temperature the temperature as measured in an external environment.

outer court, an area of walled open ground directly in front of the main walls of a castle, palace or temple; a forecourt.

outer glazing see external glazing. →52

outer leaf 1 the outer skin of masonry in a brick cavity wall or other sandwich construction.
see *concrete outer leaf* in concrete frame illustration. →28
see *outer leaf brickwork* in brick house illustration. →59
2 see external leaf.

outer ply in plywood, the surface layer or veneer.

outer sash the sash of a coupled window facing the exterior of a building. →52

outer suburbs see outskirts.

outer surface, external surface, exterior; the surface of a component or construction which faces outwards, or towards the open air.

outerwork see outwork. →104

outflow heater a device for preheating oil from a storage tank to reduce its viscosity prior to use as fuel in an oil heating installation.

outhouse, 1 privy, latrine; an outside toilet, often a rudimentary structure containing a closet without flushing or piped drainage.
2 a shed or storehouse built in the grounds of a dwelling.

outlet 1 a component through which water drains off a level roof or paved etc. surface into a drain, a gully.
see balcony outlet. →54
floor outlet, see floor drain. →58
see gully.
see rainwater outlet.
see rainwater spout.
roof outlet, see rainwater outlet.
2 a component through which fresh air is introduced to a space, or stale air, smoke etc. extracted from it. →60
see air outlet, see supply air terminal unit. →60
see exhaust outlet. →58
see fire vent.
see smoke outlet.
3 drain, waste; the point at which an appliance or sanitary fixing is connected to a drainage system; a drainage outlet.
4 the point at which a connection can be made to a service or public utility provided to a building.
see socket outlet.
see spray outlet.
see telecommunications outlet.
see water outlet.

outlet grating 1 see outlet strainer, wire balloon.
2 see domical grating.

outlet strainer a wire balloon, grating or other device placed over a roof gulley or rainwater outlet to prevent the passage of leaves and other detritus into the drainage system.

outline 1 the bounding line of a two-dimensional image, object or shape.
2 a preliminary or initial version of a design, plan or document.
3 see plan.

outline drawing see sketch drawing.

outline planning permission planning permission for a development granted in principle, without official status and subject to approval of further details of siting, planning or external appearance.

outline programme, tender programme; a proposed programme of work and programme chart sometimes submitted by contractors who are tendering for a project.

output 1 any information produced by a computer, process or specialist field.
2 in manufacturing, the quantity of products made by a company or a unit in that company.
3 see light output.

outside air, external air; the air surrounding a building.

outside calliper an instrument for measuring the outside diameter of pipes and other round objects, consisting of a pair of curved hinged legs.

outside corner the meeting of two perpendicular walls, vertical surfaces etc. which form an angle greater than 180°; also called an external corner or external angle. →14

outside corner trowel see external angle trowel. →43

outside face the face of a piece of sawn timber which is furthest from the heart when cut from a log. →2

outside glazing glass or other glazing products which have been added to the outer surface of external glazing.

outskirts, urban fringe, outer suburbs; the outlying areas of a town or city, outside the central area.

outward opening referring to a window casement or door which opens outwards with respect to the exterior of a building.

outwork an outlying fortifying element of a castle or fortification, often of earth and separated from the main body of fortifications; also called an outerwork. →104
see *fortification* illustration; types of outwork included as separate entries are listed below. →104
advanced work. →104
barbican.
counterguard. →104
demilune. →104
ditch. →104
earthwork.
forework, see advanced work. →104
half moon, see demilune. →104
moat. →103, →104
rampart, see earthwork.
redan. →104
redoubt. →104
ravelin. →104
tenaille. →104

oval a planar geometrical figure, a squashed circle similar to an ellipse, but not necessarily constructed in the same way. →108

oval brad head nail see brad. →35

oval countersunk screw see oval head screw. →36

oval head screw, raised countersunk screw, oval countersunk screw; a countersunk screw with a convex head which protrudes above the surface into which it is fixed. →36

oval house a prehistoric Minoan dwelling type from Crete, with a roughly oval plan characterized by a series of rooms surrounding a small open courtyard containing a well or cistern. →65

oval knot a knot in seasoned timber which has been cut at an angle to the branch and is thus oval in shape.

oval wire nail a slender nail with an oval shank 13 mm–150 mm in length and a small bulging head.

oven the heated chamber in a fireplace or cooker or kiln, in which food is cooked or ceramic products fired; often taken to mean the whole appliance or construction.

overall cost see total cost.

overall dimension, 1 overall size; the largest measurement of an object in any direction.
2 see external dimension.
3 see overall length. →31

overall length the total dimension of the long side of an object. →31

overall programme a diagrammatic scheme produced by a main contractor indicating the various jobs of work on site pertaining to a building project, their scope, sequencing of construction, and proposed duration.

overall size see overall dimension.

overbridge in traffic planning, any bridge which spans a carriageway; variously known as an overpass or flyover. →64

overcloak the upper overlapping part of a folded sheetmetal roofing seam or welt, which covers an undercloak. →49

overconsolidated a description of soils, especially clays, which are in a state of compression caused by previous loading from overlying ground, buildings etc. which are subsequently removed.

overcrowding in town planning, a phenomenon which occurs in urban districts with an excess of people or dwellings in too small an area, leading to a lack of individual space for its inhabitants.

overcurrent a current in an electric circuit exceeding the rated value.

overflow 1 the escape of liquid from a vessel which is too full.
2 an opening in the side of a basin or other vessel, usually with a suitable fitting, through which water can escape into a drain if the water level rises too high.
3 see weir overflow.

overflow pipe a drainage pipe connected to a basin or other vessel to lead water into a drain to avoid water flooding over the rim of the vessel.

overgrainer a paintbrush with groups of soft fibres tied in a row of bundles, used in decorative graining to imitate the shaped grain of hardwoods. →43

overhand struck joint see struck joint. →16

overhang 1 see projection.
2 see log extension. →6

overhead, indirect cost; in business management, a cost incurred by such items as rent, insurance premiums and maintenance.

overhead cable electrical power supply and telecommunications cables supported between poles or pylons.

overhead clearance see headroom.

overhead door 1 a door which runs on vertical tracks and, when open, is stored in position above the door opening; see also up-and-over door. →50
2 see up-and-over door. →50
3 see sectional overhead door. →50
4 see roller shutter. →50

overhead door closer a door closer designed to be mounted to the door head and the upper edge of the door leaf.

overhead heating downward radiant heating provided by heating panels hung high in a space.

overhead projector an image projector with a horizontal light bed and series of lenses to project images from transparencies, used primarily for presentations.

overhead shutter a lightweight shutter designed to provide night security at open shop fronts, often of lattice construction and contained in a recess or overhead or side space when not in use.

overlaid plywood plywood whose face plies have been coated with an overlay such as paper, plastics, resins, metal etc.

overlap 1 a defect in veneering and plywood caused by the overlapping of two adjacent veneers.
2 see lap. →3

overlap and double cut in wallpapering, a method of ensuring even vertical butt joints by overlapping adjacent sheets then cutting through with a knife.

overlay drafting, pin-registration drafting, registration drafting; the use in computer-aided design and drafting of base or background drawings to provide reference information, positioning of elements, datum heights etc. common to both.

overlay flooring 1 prefabricated pre-finished panels or proprietary interlocking wood strips designed to be laid directly onto a structural floor slab. →59
2 see parquet strip.

overload a structural load greater than that for which a structural system or member is designed.

overload current an electric current which exceeds the rated value without damaging an electric circuit.

overload trip, trip switch; a switch in a circuit which turns off electric current in the event of dangerously high levels or surges which may damage equipment and appliances.

overpainting see repainting.

overpass 1 see flyover. →63, →64
2 see footbridge.

overrun a space at the top of a lift shaft to allow for inaccuracies of control and to accommodate necessary apparatus.

overspill in town planning, an excess of population from a particular overcrowded area due to redevelopment, an increase in space for the inhabitants etc.

overtaking lane in road design, a lane intended for overtaking of other vehicles moving in the same direction.

overtime 1 work done over and above an agreed amount.
2 money paid for this.

ovolo moulding 1 a decorative convex moulding, semi-elliptical in cross-section. →14
2 a quadrant moulding found at the internal junction of perpendicular planar surfaces. →14

ovum mundi a mystical decorative symbol, an omphalos. →120

ownership the state of legally owning an item, property etc.

ox see bull. →119

Oxalis acetosella wood sorrel, see shamrock. →121

oxblood red a shade of reddish brown used by porcelain manufacturers, which takes its name from the colour of the blood of a bull [*Bos taurus*].

oxidation the reaction of chemical elements with oxygen.

oxidation tank see aeration tank.

oxidative drying a process of drying of paints and coatings in which the evaporation of contained solvents is followed by chemical reaction between the binder and oxygen in the surrounding air.

oxide a chemical compound formed when an element reacts with oxygen; oxides included as separate entries are listed below.
aluminium oxide, see alumina.
black iron oxide, see iron oxide.
brown iron oxide, see burnt sienna.
calcium oxide.
carbon monoxide.
cobalt oxide, see black oxide of cobalt.
chromium oxide green.
dioxide.
emerald chromium oxide, see viridian.
ferric oxide, see iron oxide.
ferrous ferric oxide, see iron oxide.
ferrous oxide, see iron oxide.
hydrogen peroxide.
hydroxide.
natural brown iron oxide, see burnt sienna.
polyphenylene oxide.
red iron oxide, see iron oxide.
trioxide.
zinc oxide.
zirconium oxide.

oxide of chromium see chromium oxide green.

oxide red, Indian red, Persian red, Venetian red; a range of red pigments manufactured by the oxidation of ferrous salts.

oxidization a process whereby a compound, metal etc. is brought in contact with oxygen, activating an oxidation reaction.

oxidized bitumen see blown bitumen.

oxychloride cement, magnesite cement, sorel cement; a hard, strong cement of calcined magnesite and magnesium oxychloride with an aggregate filler, used for hardwearing in-situ floor surfacing.

oxygen a colourless, odourless, gaseous chemical element, **O**, essential for combustion and forming about 20% of the earth's atmosphere.

oxygen trim a method of controlling the air/fuel ratio fed into a gas or oil burner according to the proportion of oxygen measured in flue gases.

oylett see oeillet. →103

oyster grey, oyster white; a shade of pale grey which takes its name from the colour of the inside surface of the shell of an oyster [*Ostrea edulis*].

oyster white see oyster grey.

P

PA polyamide.
PA-system public address system.
Pacific red cedar [*Thuja plicata*] see western red cedar.
package deal see design and construct contract.
packing, compression; the computerized consolidation of the contents of a computer-aided drawing or other computer file into one location to free up memory space.
packing piece see glazing block. →53
packway see bridleway.
pad 1 any material, block, component etc. used as a buffer, abutment, rest, bearing or support.
bridge pad, see bridge cap. →31
gilder's pad, see gilder's cushion.
see paint pad. →43
see push pad.
2 block; a bound series of sheets of paper fixed along one side, used as a notepad for writing and or sketchpad for drawing.
see notepad.
see sketchpad.
padauk [*Pterocarpus spp.*] a group of hardwoods from Africa and Asia with red or purple-brown streaked timber; used in cabinetmaking and veneers.
padding, cushioning; soft or resilient material used as a base in furnishings, as protection in packing or to dissipate vibrations from heavy plant.
paddle mixer see rotating pan mixer.
paddling pool in landscape design, a shallow pool for children to play in.
paddock a fenced area of ground in proximity to farm buildings for the containment of livestock.
pad foundation, column footing, isolated footing; a precast or in-situ rectangular block foundation of reinforced concrete which transmits vertical point loads such as those from columns to the underlying ground. →29
padlock a small detachable lock with a fastening ring, openable with a key. →39
padlock eye one of a pair of perforated metal plates attached to the edge of a hinged door and its frame, enabling it to be secured with a padlock. →39
pad saw 1 a small saw with a thin tapering blade used for cutting curves or holes.
2 see keyhole saw.
pad seat see inset seat.
pagoda a multistorey Buddhist temple with projecting roofs at storey level, often replicated in Europe in the 1800s as an ornamental pavilion in gardens and parks. →68
pailou a Chinese ornamental temple gateway consisting of a series of beams, the uppermost of which curves upwards, supported on columns; in Japan it is called a torii.
pain threshold see threshold of pain.
paint a liquid substance used for providing a protective or decorative surface coating, consisting of a pigment and a binder which sets or is treated to form a resistant film.
paint binder the component of paint which forms film and produces a bond to the surface being painted.
paintbrush a hand-held implement used for applying paint, consisting of fibres, bristles or hairs bound to a wooden or plastic handle, available in a range of widths, shapes and sizes. →43
see types of *paintbrush* illustration; types included as separate entries are listed below. →43
distemper brush. →43
dragger, see flogger. →43
dusting brush. →43
flat brush. →43
flat varnish brush. →43
flat wall brush, see flat brush. →43
flogger. →43
lettering brush. →43
liner, lining brush. →43
overgrainer. →43
paint pad. →43
paint roller, see roller. →43
radiator brush. →43
rigger brush, rigger. →43
round brush. →43
script brush. →43
scrubbing brush. →43
varnish brush, see flat varnish brush. →43
wall brush, see flat brush. →43
painter a tradesman or skilled labourer who does painting work in buildings.
painterly in fine art, referring to the good use of light, shade and colour rather than line and outline to represent form in a painting.
painter's and decorator's a commercial service which specializes in the painting and decorating of buildings and parts of buildings.
painter's putty in painting and decorating, linseed oil putty used as a filler by a painter.
paint finish a surface coating of paint, the material and process therein.
paint finish see finishing.
painting 1 the trade of applying paint to surfaces.
2 art which represents form in terms of applied colour and pattern.
paint medium the liquid component of paint, in which pigments and fillers are suspended.
paint pad a paint applicator for delicate areas, edges etc. consisting of a rectangular piece of soft material with a sponge back, a short nap and a handle. →43
paint removal, paint stripping; in painting and decorating, the removal of old paintwork before a new surface is applied.
paint remover, paint stripper; in painting, a liquid applied to soften hardened paint thus enabling it to be easily removed with a scraper, spatula or abrasive substance.
paint roller see roller. →43
paint scraper see scraper. →41
paint shop the part of a factory, works, establishment, or separate space where components are painted, usually by spraying.
paint spray gun a device with a nozzle connected to a supply of paint and powered by compressed air, used for projecting paint in a fine spray; see spray painting.
paint stripper see paint remover.
paint stripping see paint removal.
paint system a number of layers of paint applied in the correct order to provide a durable and attractive finish.
paint tray see roller tray. →43
paintwork 1 the painted surfaces in a building.
2 the job or contract for carrying out the above.
pair of compasses see compass.
pair of pliers see pliers.
pair of scales see scales.
pair of scissors see scissors.
pair of tweezers see tweezers.
PAL permanent artificial lighting.

palace a luxurious residence, especially the stately residence of a sovereign, ruler, aristocrat or other ruling figure such as a bishop.
see palace in Mesopotamian temple illustration. →66

palace chapel a building or room in a palace for prayer and religious services. →66

palace courtyard an open space at the heart of a palace, surrounded on four sides by rooms. →66

palaeolithic period, Old Stone Age, paleolithic; a prehistoric period from c.600 000 to 8000 BC, predating the mesolithic period and characterized by the rise to dominance of the human species, Homo sapiens, during which the first implements were struck from stone.

palaestra Lat.; in classical architecture, a place used for the instruction and practice of wrestling and athletics. →91

palazzo an Italian stately residence, often in an urban setting.

pale 1 a timber post driven into the ground which may be part of a wall, fence or palisade.
2 see timber pile. →29
3 a vertical timber board or strip in a palisade fence, nailed at its upper and lower edges to rails.
4 a vertical band, strip or line down the middle of a heraldic shield, often dividing areas of different colours. →125

paled fortification a fortification wall constructed of timber stakes driven side by side into the ground; a palisade or stockade.

paleolithic see palaeolithic period.

paleotechnic a term used by Patrick Geddes and Lewis Mumford to describe the early stage of the industrial age, in which the main source of power was provided by steam and key inventions were the railway, the Bessemer process and automated spinning and weaving devices.

Palestine cross see Jerusalem cross. →118

palette 1 the thin wooden board on which an artist mixes his paints.
2 the range or choice of colours used by an artist or other colour-renderer.

palette floor see platform floor. →44

palette knife a tool with a handle and flat blade used by an artist for mixing paint on the palette or applying it to the canvas.

pale turquoise see horizon blue.

paling 1 a series of pales driven into the ground to form a fence or timber wall.
2 a series of pales, timber boards or strips, in a fence.

palisade 1 a fence or wall made from timber posts driven into the ground.
2 see stockade.

palisander a name for various tropical timbers from South America, especially rosewoods [*Dalbergia spp.*], used for high quality work.

Palladianism an architectural style originating in Italy from the theories and practice of Andrea Palladio (1508–1580); it is characterized by close adherence to Roman orders, symmetry and proportion.

Palladian motif, Serlian motif, Venetian motif; a Renaissance motif such as a door, window or other opening in a wall which is divided into three, and whose central portion is arched. →24

Palladian window see Venetian window. →24

palladium a light, durable, greyish-white metal, **Pd**, often alloyed with gold and other metals; a member of the platinum group.

pallet in heraldry, a narrow pale. →125

palm 'shep, shesep'; an ancient Egyptian unit of measurement equal to one seventh part of a royal cubit, approximately 75 mm; also called a palm-width. →106

palm capital, palmiform; an ancient Egyptian capital carved in imitation of bunches of stylized palm fronds tied round the head of a pole, sometimes called a plume capital by virtue of its resemblance to a series of feathers bound at their base. →73

palm column an ancient Egyptian column surmounted by a palm capital. →73

palmette 1 a decorative motif found in the architecture of antiquity, consisting of a stylized fan-shaped palm leaf. →82, →121
2 see palmette heart. →121

palmette capital see illustration. →73

palmette heart, heart-palmette; palmette ornament in a heart-shaped border. →121

palmiform see palm capital. →73

palm leaf a decorative motif used in antiquity, often to represent peace and victory, based on the stylized fan-shaped or rounded leaves of one of a large number of species of subtropical and tropical plants.

palm-width see palm. →106

pamment a thin square paving brick or tile between 9" and 12" long.

pan 1 in computer-aided design, viewing parts of an image which is too large to fit on screen by virtually moving the cursor or crosshair from side to side or up and down.
2 see water closet pan.
3 see metal tray.
4 see ash pan. →56
5 see condensates pan.
6 a satyr with goat's legs and horns; plural is panes. →122

PAN polyacrylonitrile.

pan and roll tiles see Italian tiles. →47

pane 1 a piece of glass or glazed unit fitted in a window frame or as glazing. →52, →111
2 see peen. →40

panes plural form of pan, the satyr. →122

pane size, glazing size, glass size; in glazing, the actual size of a pane of glass cut or manufactured for use in a frame.

panel 1 a prefabricated cladding unit fixed to a structural frame, a cladding panel.
2 a distinct area of material or ornament on the surface of a wall, ceiling or vault.
3 a framed decorative tablet on a wall, door or ceiling surface, or a painting or decorative motif therein.
4 in structures, the open space delineated by members or lines of force in a truss.
5 the main area of a panelled door, joinery panelling etc., housed by framing members.
6 see door panel. →51
7 see ceiling panel.
8 see formwork panel.
9 see solar panel.

panel clamp a mechanism for holding formwork together during the casting of a concrete panel.

panel construction a form of construction used for panelled doors and partitions, in which main framing members have infill panels of a non-loadbearing material.

panel door see panelled door. →51

paneled door see panelled door. →51

panel form a small standard-sized plywood unit used in series to form a larger formwork component such as one for casting a wall or floor.

paneling see panelling.

panelled door, framed door, panel door; any door whose main members (rails and stiles) are tenon jointed, forming a rigid frame for infill boarding, glazing or panelling; also written as paneled door. →51

panelling, paneling (Am.), panelwork; **1** internal joinery cladding for ceilings and walls.
2 the construction of the above.
3 see wall panelling.

panel of judges see board of assessors.

panel pin a slender small-headed nail whose shank is 13 mm–50 mm, used in joinery, glazing etc. where it can be nailed beneath the surface. →35

panel planer see thicknessing machine.

panel point, node; the meeting point of two members in a triangulated structure such as a truss. →33

panel product see wood-based panel product. →9

panel radiator, pressed-steel radiator; a radiator manufactured from pressed sheetmetal with cavities in which hot water for space heating circulates.

panel saw a small handsaw with a long blade 250 mm–600 mm long, used for cutting across the grain of softwood boards and sheet materials.

panel tracery see rectilinear tracery. →110

panel wall a wall or partition, usually of brickwork or blockwork used as a non-structural infill within a structural frame.

panelwork see panelling.

pan form see waffle mould.

panic bar proprietary hardware for an escape door consisting of a horizontally pivoted rod which, when pushed, opens a latch; see panic latch.

panic bolt, fire-exit bolt; a fastener fitted on the inside of a double escape door, consisting of a horizontal bar at waist height which, when pushed, will open the door.

panic hardware any mechanisms for opening escape doors from the inside with a simple pushing action without a key during a building fire or other emergency.

panic latch a latch for a single escape door operated during an emergency by pushing against a panic bar or lever, or by some other simple action.

pan mixer a concrete mixer with a horizontally rotating pan in which the constituent materials are mixed.

Pannetier's green see viridian.

panorama in landscape design, a wide view, often of countryside, which opens out from an elevated place.

pantheon Gk; a circular domed building, similar to its predecessor in Rome which was used for the worship of all deities; Latin form is pantheum.

Panthera leo see lion. →119

pantile, 1 S-tile; a clay roof tile which is S shaped in section to overlap with adjacent tiles in the same course. →47

2 see double pantile. →47

3 Roman pantile, see Roman tile. →47

pantograph in technical drawing, a mechanical device consisting of a number of concertina-joined arms, used for copying an image or pattern at an enlarged or reduced scale.

pantry a small domestic room adjacent to a kitchen in which provisions, stores and equipment are kept.

papal cross a cross with three horizontal transoms at its upper end, decreasing in length towards the top; symbol of the papacy; also sometimes called a pontifical cross, Roman cross, or western triple cross. →117

Papaver rhoeas the common or corn poppy, see coqueliquot.

paper thin sheet material produced primarily from wood fibres matted together with varying amounts of china clays, increasingly made from recycled material; used for drawing, writing, packing, facing and many other purposes.
see 'paper size' for list of standard international and regional paper sizes. →(Table 6)

paper backed referring to a sheet product such as gypsum board, wire mesh or tiling which has been backed with paper as reinforcement.

paper birch [*Betula papyrifera*] a North American hardwood with brown timber; used as sawn boards, in plywood, furniture and interiors.

paperboard see cardboard.

paper clip a bent wire clip of copper used for the temporary fastening together of sheets of paper.

paper cutter a device with a hinged or sliding blade for cutting and cropping sheets or stacks of paper.

paper faced referring to a sheet product such as plywood or gypsum board which has been faced with paper.

paperhanging see wallpapering.

paper shop see stationers.

paper size paper manufactured to internationally and regionally agreed sizes; see list below and table. →(Table 6)
A0, 841 mm × 1189 mm (33" × 46¾"). →130, →(Table 6)
B0, 1000 mm × 1414 mm (39" × 55"). →(Table 6)
C0, 917 mm × 1297 mm (36" × 51"). →(Table 6)
antiquarian; 31" × 51", 787 mm × 1346 mm. →(Table 6)
cartridge; 12" × 26", 305 mm × 660 mm. →(Table 6)
crown; 15" × 20", 318 mm × 508 mm. →(Table 6)
double crown; 20" × 30", 508 mm × 762 mm. →(Table 6)
double elephant; 27" × 40", 686 mm × 1016 mm. →(Table 6)
double foolscap; 17" × 27", 432 mm × 686 mm. →(Table 6)
executive; 7.5" × 10", 190 mm × 254 mm. →(Table 6)
foolscap; 13½" × 17", 343 mm × 432 mm. →(Table 6)
ledger, tabloid; 11" × 17", 279 mm × 432 mm. →(Table 6)
legal; 8.5" × 14", 216 mm × 356 mm. →(Table 6)
letter; 8.5" × 11", 216 mm × 279 mm. →(Table 6)
post; 15¼" × 19", 387 mm × 483 mm. →(Table 6)
quad crown; 30" × 40", 762 mm × 1016 mm. →(Table 6)
see quad double crown; 40" × 60", 1016 mm × 1524 mm. →(Table 6)
royal; 20" × 25", 508 mm × 635 mm. →(Table 6)
tabloid, see ledger. →(Table 6)

papilio Lat., pl. papiliones; a Roman military tent measuring ten Roman feet square for housing eight legionaries.

paprika (red) see capsicum red.

papyriform 1 see papyrus capital. →73
2 see papyrus column. →73

papyrus 1 a type of paper made originally by the Egyptians from the leaves of the rusk-like plant *Cyperus papyrus*, of the genus *Cypereae*, an aquatic sedge found in tropical and subtropical regions.
2 an ornamental motif found in classical and Egyptian architecture consisting of a series of stylized leaves from the papyrus; heraldic plant of Lower Egypt (Nile Delta). →82, →121

papyrus-bundle column see papyrus column. →73

papyrus capital, papyriform; an Egyptian capital carved in imitation of a tied bundle of papyrus leaves, either open, as in a bell capital, or closed, as a bud capital. →73

papyrus column, papyrus-bundle column; an Egyptian column type whose shaft is carved to resemble a bunch of tied papyrus stems, surmounted by a papyrus capital. →73

parabola a geometrical curve formed by slicing through a cone parallel to its main axis.

parabolic having the form of a parabola or paraboloid.

parabolic arch an arch whose form traces out a parabola. →24

paraboloid a three-dimensional geometric form constructed by rotating a parabola around its axis of symmetry.

parachute dome see umbrella dome. →26

paradise 1 an open space in front of a church or monastery; see parvis, atrium paradisus. →95, →96, →98
2 the open space in the cloister or garden of a church or monastery.

paraffin, 1 kerosine, kerosene, paraffin oil; a product of the fractional distillation of crude oil, a volatile pleasant-smelling oil used as fuel for some vehicles, lamps and flueless heating appliances.
2 see paraffin wax.

paraffin oil see paraffin.

paraffin wax a soft, waxy, white, solid residue from the distillation of petroleum, used as a fuel in candles and in some polishes and surface treatments.

paragone a variety of black Italian marble.

paraline drawing a drawing such as an isometric or axonometric projection, constructed of a series of parallel lines; an alternative name for a parallel projection drawing.

parallax the apparent change in the position or direction of an object as viewed from two different points.

parallel referring to two lines or planes which have the same direction and whose perpendicular distance from one another is constant.

parallel connection the arrangement of appliances in an electric circuit so that each receives the same voltage.

parallelepiped, parallelipiped, parallelopiped; a solid shape whose surface is composed of six planar parallelograms.

parallel-grain plies plywood plies laid with their grain running in the same direction. →9

parallel-grain plywood plywood in which the grain of each ply runs in the same direction; used for beams and other applications where loading is one-sided.

parallel-grain plywood beam. →7

parallelipiped see parallelepiped.

parallelogram a planar four-sided regular figure in which opposite sides are parallel. →108

parallelopiped see parallelepiped.

parallel perspective 1 an outdated name for parallel projection. →127

2 see one-point perspective.

parallel projection a method of drawing projections in which all the projectors for a given axis or direction are parallel to one another, as if the viewpoint is an infinite distance from the viewed object; often referred to as axonometry; cf. perspective projection. →127

see *parallel projection* illustration; types included as separate entries are listed below. →127

axonometric projection. →127

axonometry. →127

oblique projection. →127

orthographic projection. →127

parallel ruler a draughting device for drawing a series of parallel lines, consisting of a table-top ruler guided by a system of wires. →130

parallel tread see flier. →45

parament any ecclesiastical vestment, hanging or other textile used in religious services. →116

parameter, variable; in mathematical functions, a value which is constant in certain cases but may change under other circumstances.

Parana pine [*Araucaria angustifolia*] a South American softwood with pale cream-coloured and straight grained timber; used for interior joinery, staircases and furniture.

parapet 1 a low wall, barrier or balustrade at the edge of a roof, balcony, terrace or bridge.

2 the junction at which an external wall and a flat roof meet.

see *parapet detail* illustration. →49

3 see bridge parapet.

parapetasma a curtain covering the doors and side constructions of a Greek theatre building; called a siparium in Roman equivalents. →89

parapet capping a pressed metal capping to protect the upper surface of a parapet against the elements. →49

parapet gutter in roof construction, a gutter at the junction of a roof plane and a parapet.

parapet walk see alure. →103

parascaenium Lat.; see parascene.

parascene, parascaenium, parascenium, paraskenion (Gk); 'beside the skene'; architectural projections one or two storeys high on either side of the stage building (skene, scaena) in a classical theatre; called versurae in a Roman theatre; Latin form is parascaenium, Greek form paraskenion. →89

parascenium see parascene.

paraskenion Gk; see parascene.

parchment traditional paper made from the skin of calves, goats or sheep and treated with lime and pumice; used for manuscripts, calligraphy etc.; see also vellum.

parclo see partial cloverleaf junction. →63

parclose, perclose; a screen in a church to seclude a chapel from the main space. →100

parecclesion, parekklesion; a chapel flanking the sanctuary or narthex of a Byzantine church. →96

parekklesion see parecclesion. →96

parentheses, 1 round brackets; in mathematics or written text, symbols (and) for isolating a function, statement or clause.

2 see square brackets.

parge a traditional render of cow dung, hair and lime sand mortar used as a smooth interior lining for brick chimneys; modern equivalents; also called parging, pargeting. →55

pargeting, parging; **1** a decorative, patterned or scored coat of render.

2 see parge. →55

parging see pargeting. →55

paring chisel, joiner's chisel; a light, long-bladed chisel used without a mallet in joinery and cabinetwork. →41

Paris black an inferior grade of ivory black pigment.

Paris blue see Prussian blue.

Paris green see emerald green.

parish centre, parochial centre; a religious building or building group in the immediate vicinity of a church, used for receptions, gatherings, administration and ecclesiastic affairs other than services.

Paris white high grade whiting.

Paris yellow see chrome yellow.

parish hall see church hall.

park a landscaped area of planted land in an urban setting for public recreation.

Parker's cement see Roman cement.

parking the temporary storage or keeping of a vehicle or vehicles when not in use.

parking bay see parking space. →62

parking for the disabled, disabled parking; parking places reserved for the disabled, in which parking is allowed by special permit only. →62

parking garage, car park; a building or part of a building designed for the parking of motor vehicles. →62

parking hall see parking garage. →62

parking lot an area of land with marked spaces, designated for the parking of motor vehicles.

parking meter a mechanism located adjacent to parking spaces for measuring the duration of specific parking periods and collecting payments.

parking requirement the number of parking spaces for a particular facility as required by a brief or regulatory norms.

parking space, parking bay; a marked space designated for the parking of a single vehicle. →62

parking standard the number of parking spaces for a development as required by statutory norms or a town plan.

parkland an area of rural land, often landscaped with trees and grass, set aside or designated for public recreation.

parkway an urban expressway or motorway situated within park-like or landscaped surroundings and for which heavy traffic is usually excluded.

parlatorium Lat.; see parlatory.

parlatory, parlatorium (Lat.); a room in a monastery for socializing and conversation.

parliament hinge, H-hinge, shutter hinge; a surface-mounted hinge with T-shaped leaves which open out from a central knuckle into the shape of the letter H; its pin is not in the same plane as the leaves allowing a door or shutter to swing back against an adjacent wall. →38

parliament house the main building of a nation's parliament.

Parma violet a shade of dark greyish violet which takes its name from the colour of the flowers of a type of violet [*Viola parmensis*] associated with Parma, Northern Italy.

parochial centre see parish centre.

parodos Gk; a gangway or entrance leading to the orchestra of a classical theatre, between the side wall of the auditorium wall and the skene or scaenia. →89

parpen see parpend.

parpend, perpend stone, perpent, perpin, through stone, parpen; in masonry construction, a bonding stone or brick which is visible on either face of a wall.

parquet, 1 parquetry; hardwearing flooring of solid or laminated strips, blocks or staves of timber laid in rows or various rectangular arrangements; types included as separate entries are listed below.
floor square, see parquet floor square. →44
herringbone parquet. →44
mosaic parquet. →44
multilayer parquet. →44, →59
parquet batten, see parquet block. →44
parquet block. →44
parquet composite, see parquet strip. →59
parquet floor square. →44
parquet flooring. →44
parquet mosaic, see parquet block. →44
parquet strip. →44
parquet tile, see parquet floor square. →44
parquet work, see parquetry.
solid parquet. →44
strip parquet, see parquet strip. →44
veneer parquet, veneered parquet, see multilayer parquet. →44
wood mosaic, mosaic parquet. →44
2 see stalls.

parquet batten see parquet block. →44

parquet block one of the small pieces of wood that make up a mosaic parquet floor; also sometimes called a stave, batten or mosaic. →44

parquet composite see parquet strip. →59

parquet flooring floor surfacing consisting of wood blocks or thin strips, often on plywood or softwood backing, laid in a patterned or parallel arrangement; see below and **parquet** entry. →44
multilayer parquet, veneer parquet. →44
solid parquet. →44
wood mosaic, mosaic parquet. →44

parquet floor square a square or rectangle of parquet flooring, often with battens laid in a pattern which is repeated once the squares are laid in series; a parquet tile. →44

parquet mosaic see parquet block. →44

parquet stave see parquet block. →44

parquet strip, 1 parquet composite, overlay flooring; thin tongued and grooved boards of solid hardwood or hardwood-surfaced composite used as a hardwearing wooden flooring surface. →44, →59
2 see solid parquet. →44
3 see multilayer parquet, veneer parquet. →44

parquet tile see parquet floor square. →44

parquetry 1 see parquet.
2 parquet work; the laying of parquet flooring; the result of this.

parquet work see parquetry.

parrot green a shade of green which takes its name from the colour of the plumage of certain parrots [*Psittacus spp.*].

parsley green a shade of dark green which takes its name from the colour of the leaves of the parsley plant [*Petroselinum crispum*].

parsonage the residence of a clergyman, especially a priest of the Protestant church.

parterre the ground floor of a theatre auditorium immediately in front of the orchestra.

Parthian art ancient Persian art of the Parthians in Mesopotamia from 247 BC to 226 AD, in architecture characterized by the use of vaulted halls opening out into courtyards.

partial cloverleaf junction a cloverleaf junction based on the cloverleaf model, but with fewer ramps, in general only two loops and two slip roads; also called a parclo or half cloverleaf junction. →63

partial handover, partial possession; in contract administration, the process of the contractor delivering up part of the site and building works thereon to the client prior to full completion.

partial possession see partial handover.

partial release, strain relief; in the pretensioning of concrete, the stressing of the setting concrete with part of the stresses held by the prestressing tendons.

partially crushed gravel a coarse aggregate containing gravel, some of which has been crushed.

participation taking part or being involved in common or public action such as local meetings, summaries of proposals and idea competitions.

particle in mathematics, a theoretical point having mass but no magnitude.

particle analyser a device for measuring the size, quantity and consistency of particles in a gas, usually air.

particleboard a range of non-structural building boards manufactured from chips or fibres of wood bonded together with resin then pressed into sheets; although the term particleboard includes products such as chipboard, flakeboard, flaxboard, and OSB, most often it is synonymous with chipboard. →9
see *particleboard* illustration; types included as separate entries are listed below. →9
chipboard. →9
fibreboard. →9
flakeboard. →9
flaxboard. →9
oriented strand board. →9
softboard.
waferboard. →9

parting chisel 1 see parting tool.
2 see bruzz chisel. →41

parting compound see release agent.

parting tool, parting chisel; a turning chisel with a flat blade pointed at its end, used for removing a piece of work from a lathe once it has been shaped. →41

partition 1 a lightweight, non-loadbearing wall dividing interior space in a building. →28
2 see interior wall.
3 see lightweight partition.
4 see screen.

partition block an unperforated concrete block used for constructing internal walls, providing good sound insulation between adjacent rooms. →30

partner one of a group of people in charge of a partnership, company or firm, and liable for its debts.

partnership 1 a company or business formed by two or more people.
2 see general partnership.
3 see limited partnership.

part perspective a perspective of part of a building, object or scene.

part plan a drawing which represents a certain area of a building shown on plan, usually at an enlarged scale to allow for greater detail.

party floor 1 see separating floor.
2 see fire floor.
party wall see separating wall.
parvis, parvise; a colonnaded entrance court in front of a church or cathedral. →95, →96, →99
parvise see parvis. →95, →96, →99
pascal abb. **Pa**; the SI unit of pressure, equal to one newton per square metre (1 N/m^2).
pass door see wicket door.
passage 1 a narrow exterior or subterranean circulation space intended for pedestrians, bounded on both sides and sometimes covered; also called a passageway.
2 see path.
3 see thoroughfare.
4 see access.
5 see dromos. →91
see *prehistoric structures* illustration. →65
see *rock-cut tomb* illustration. →74
passage grave, passage tomb; a stone-age chambered tomb from western Europe, with a long passage leading to a burial chamber or chambers. →65
passage tomb see passage grave. →65
passageway 1 see passage.
2 see entranceway.
3 see *passageway* in prehistoric structures illustration. →65
passenger car see automobile.
passenger conveyor, moving walk (Am.); a moving horizontal or sloping belt of rubber or metal slats functioning as a means of circulation for pedestrian users of a large building such as an airport.
passenger lift a lift designed to carry people.
passenger traffic in transportation planning, traffic such as trains, buses etc. consisting of vehicles conveying passengers.
passe-partout a frame for a photograph, graphic image or other displayed item consisting of a piece of card with a rectangular opening cut into it.
passing bay see passing place.
passing place, passing bay; a widening in a narrow road to allow two vehicles to pass one another.
Passion cross 1 see Calvary cross. →117
2 see Latin cross. →117
3 see Lorraine cross. →117
passivation the treatment of freshly machined metal surfaces with acids or pastes to remove contaminants and leave a very thin protective layer to improve corrosion resistance.
passive earth pressure the pressure of earth acting against the lower side of a retaining wall and which prevents it from moving.
passive fire protection the design and planning of a building with fire safety in mind, with compartments, designated escape routes, fire-resistant materials and structure etc.
passive solar energy solar heating based on the planning, orientation, construction techniques and mass of a building rather than solar panels and collectors.
pastas Gk; a long hall running along the centre of certain types of Greek dwelling, affording access to rooms; most often serving as a veranda open to a court on one side. →87
pastas house a dwelling type from the classical period of northern Greece, 423–348 BC, with a courtyard in the centre of the south side and deep columned veranda or pastas affording access to rooms; cf. prostas house. →87
paste, gum; a simple thick adhesive mixed from an organic material such as flour, or a polymer which swells in water, used for gluing paper and wallpaper.
paste blue see Prussian blue.
pasteboard see cardboard.
pastel a soft dry stick of coloured pigment mixed with an oil, gum, wax or kaolin binder, used for drawing.
pastel blue a general name for shades of pale blue.
pastel colour, tint; in painting and colour science, any pale hue which contains a large amount of white colour.
pastel drawing drawing, rendering or painting with pastels.
pastel green a general name for shades of pale green.
pastel grey a general name for shades of pale grey.
pastel pink a general name for shades of pale pink.
pastel red a general name for shades of pale red.
pastel violet a general name for shades of pale violet.
pastel yellow a general name for shades of pale yellow.
pasticcio see pastiche.
pastiche, pasticcio; a work of art or architecture which imitates motifs and styles from a previous age, often without meaning or purpose.
pastophorion Gk; see pastophorium. →95
pastophorium, pastophorion, pastophory; Lat.; the temple apartment of a priest at the side of the bema or sanctuary of an early church, translated in later Byzantine architecture as a chamber to the side of the apse; a prothesis or diaconicon.
see *Late Antique church* illustration. →95
see *Byzantine domical church* illustration. →96
pastophory see pastophorium. →95
pastose referring to art rendered in thick paint; see impasto.
patch 1 a piece of material used to repair a damaged or defective surface construction.
2 a piece of veneer used in the repair of plywood.
3 insert, plug; a small piece of wood glued into a wooden surface in order to cover a defect, loose knot etc.
patching 1 the repair of holes, pitting and other defects in concretework, veneerwork, plasterwork and other finishings and coatings.
2 the filling of voids, cracks etc. and repairing of defects in a plaster or cast concrete surface with mortar.
3 see concrete patching.
4 see remedial plastering.
patée see cross patée.
patent axe a metal mason's tool with raised teeth or blades, used for dressing hard stone and granite. →40
patent claw chisel, tooth tool; a masonry claw chisel with a replaceable blade. →41
patent glazing, system glazing; a dry glazing system of proprietary metal structural framing members with glazing infill, used for large glazed areas and curtain walls; also other proprietary systems with a predesigned set of accessories, gaskets and fixings, structural glass, frameless glazing etc. →53
patent stone see cast stone.
patent yellow see Turner's yellow.
patera, phiala; Lat.; a decorative ornament resembling a round dish, flat vase or flower in low relief. →121
paternoster 1 a continuous, slow moving lift with a number of twinned cars arranged in a rotating formation so that one side moves upwards and the other downwards.
2 see beaded moulding. →124
path, 1 pathway, passage, pedestrian way; a route, track or lane for pedestrian use only. →62
2 see track.
3 see footway.
4 a written string of characters defining the location of a file or program in the storage system of a computer.
pathogenic the property of certain substances to cause disease through contact or inhalation.
pathway see path.

patina, patination; a coloured protective layer of oxide forming naturally on the surface of some metals such as copper and bronze (green) and lead (dark grey) on exposure to the elements.

patina green a shade of grey green which takes its name from the colour of patina on the trunks of trees and rocks; similar to bronze green.

patination 1 the act of artificially inducing a patina on a copper or bronze surface as a hardwearing finish.
2 see patina.

patio a paved external area directly outside a dwelling at ground floor, furnished with seats for recreation, taking outdoor meals etc. →57

patio house see atrium house.

patonce see cross patonce. →118

patriarchal cross a cross with two horizontal transoms, a shorter one above; symbol of the Roman Catholic church. →117

pattée see cross patée. →118

pattern 1 an abstract design of lines, dots or forms for decorating a surface.
2 a diagram showing how something, a model or part of a design, is made.
3 see template.
4 see distribution pattern.
5 see key pattern. →124
6 sawing pattern, see blade set.
7 see paving pattern. →15

patterned brickwork 1 decorative brickwork in different coloured and textured bricks.
2 see polychrome brickwork.

patterned glass rolled glass treated with a patterned relief to obscure one or both surfaces.

patterned plasterwork see textured plasterwork.

pattern flooring raised pattern flooring, see studded rubber flooring. →44

pattern paver any specially shaped concrete paving unit which is laid to create a regular pattern; see interlocking, key, hexagonal and interweave pavers. →15

pattern spar see cross spar. →48

paty see cross patée. →118

pavement 1 the main structural and surface construction of a road, laid in courses of concrete, stone or asphalt above a subgrade.
2 see footway. →62
3 see concrete paving.
4 see pavimentum.

pavement concrete concrete used as surfacing for external areas such as roads, pavements etc.

pavement light a square or circular glass lens incorporated into a concrete slab to allow natural lighting to a space below.

paver any brick, concrete or natural stone product etc. used for paving external surfaces; also called a paving stone, pavior or paviour. →15
see paving brick.
see concrete paver.
see concrete block paver. →15
see concrete paving slab. →15

pavilion a small ornamental structure or shelter set in parkland as a summer-house, bandstand or to provide changing facilities and stores at a sports ground.
see *pavilion* in Asian temples illustration. →68

pavilion roof a hipped roof with a square or polygonal plan, composed of a number of triangular roof planes. →46

pavimentum, pavement; Roman paving of broken stone or tile set into a bed of ash or cement.

paving 1 blocks, precast units or thin slabs of stone, brick, concrete or ceramic material laid horizontally as a hardwearing external surface; see stone paving, brick paving, concrete paving, tiled paving. →15
see *paving* illustration. →15
2 the trade of laying floor slabs and paviors with butting joints as covering for external areas.
see stone paving. →15
see brick paving. →15
see cellular paving, grass paving. →15
see tiled paving.
see concrete block paving.

paving block see concrete block paver. →15

paving brick, paviour brick, paver; a brick of special dimension and durability used for paving. →15

paving pattern the various patterns in which stone and concrete pavers, slabs etc. can be laid as paving. →15
see *paving pattern* illustration. →15

paving slab see concrete paving slab. →15

paving stone, stone paver; any natural stone product used for paving. →15

paving unit see concrete paving slab. →15

pavior 1 see paver. →15
2 see slab.

paviour see paver. →15

paviour brick see paving brick. →15

Pavo cristatus see peacock blue.

Paxillus panuoides see roll-rim.

pay see wages.

pay as you earn see tax deduction.

payback period 1 the agreed amount of time over which a loan should be paid back.
2 in business, the time taken for money invested to return a profit.

pay-day in business management, the day on which wages are paid.

PAYE acronym for pay-as-you-earn; see tax deduction.

payment 1 a sum of money to be paid in regular instalments for a job of work, loan etc.
2 see fee.
3 see interim payment.

payment date see due date.

pay phone, pay station (Am.); a public telephone operated by coins or a debit card.

pay station see pay phone.

PC 1 see polycarbonate.
2 acronym for personal computer.

PCB printed circuit board.

PE polyethylene.

peach a shade of pale orange which takes its name from the colour of the ripe fruit of the peach tree [*Prunus persica, Amygdalus persica*].

peacock blue a shade of dark turquoise which takes its name from the colour of the blue feathers of the peacock (Pavo cristatus).

peacock green a shade of green which takes its name from the colour of the green feathers of the peacock; see peacock blue.

peacock tail pattern see fantail pattern. →15

peak hour clearway a through road on which vehicles are not permitted to stop at certain times of congestion, usually rush hour.

peanut gallery (Am.); the highest gallery in a theatre or grandstand.

pear [*Pyrus communis*] a European hardwood with rosy pink, fine-grained wood used in veneers, furniture, turned bowls and parts of musical instruments for the decorative value of its grain.

pearl, frosted; in artificial lighting, the classification of a bulb of a lamp which has a diffuse inner or outer surface produced by etching or sandblasting to obscure the filament; cf. opal lamp.

pearl moulding see beaded moulding. →124

pearl stone see perlite.

peasant blue a certain shade of dark blue; supposedly a popular colour among European peasantry in the past.

peat a dark and fibrous soil type formed from the decomposition of organic matter.

pebble, duckstone, cobble; naturally weathered rounded stones, larger than shingle, used in a cement or concrete base as wall facing, surface paving for driveways etc., or laid loose around borders. →15

pebbledash, dry dash; a weatherproof finish for masonry and concrete with a coating with pebbles or gravel embedded into wet mortar.

pecked finish 1 see picked finish.
2 see sparrowpecked finish.

pedestal 1 a columnar support for an object.
2 a rectangular masonry block on which a classical column, statue, caryatid etc. is supported, consisting of a plinth and dado, often surmounted with a cornice. →76
see *classical orders* illustrations. →78, →79, →80
see *spiral column* illustration. →114

pedestal bidet a bidet supported by the floor on a short column.

pedestal pile see under-reamed pile. →29

pedestal washbasin a washbasin supported by the floor on a column rather than being attached to the wall.

pedestal WC pan a WC supported by the floor on a short column.

pedestrian one who travels on foot.

pedestrian bridge see footbridge. →64

pedestrian crossing, crosswalk (Am., Aus.); in traffic planning, a marked area of carriageway designated as a safe crossing point for pedestrians.

pedestrianization in town planning, the converting of vehicular roads and urban streets or zones for the sole use of pedestrians and cyclists.

pedestrian precinct an urban street where vehicular traffic is restricted, reserved for the use of pedestrians and light traffic only.

pedestrian subway see subway. →63, →64

pedestrian way 1 see footway. →62
2 see path.

pedestrian zone an urban area for the sole use of pedestrians.

pediment 1 the triangular gabled portion of a classical portico or building; forerunners of this.
2 fronton; in Renaissance, Baroque and Neoclassical architecture, a triangular or segmental ornamental device, panel or canopy above doorways, windows and panels. →112
see *classical pediments* illustration. →112
see triangular pediment. →112
see segmental pediment. →112
see fastigium. →86

pedunculate oak, common oak; [Quercus robur]; a European hardwood with heavy, hard and strong pale brown timber marketed as European or English oak.

PEEK polyetheretherketone.

peel tower see pele tower.

peelable wallcovering wallcovering which can be removed once dry so that its backing or webbing remains attached to the wall.

peeled veneer see rotary cut veneer. →10

peeler block a timber from which veneer is peeled.

peeling 1 a defect in a paint or plaster finish caused by separation from its underlying coat or surface.
2 see veneer peeling. →10

peeling chisel see barking chisel.

peeling iron see barking chisel.

peen, 1 pein, pane; the end of the head of a hammer opposite its striking face, shaped with a point, ridge, ball, claw etc. for a variety of uses. →40
2 see machinist's hammer.

peen hammer a hammer with a peen opposite its striking face. →40
see cross peen hammer, Warrington hammer. →40
see ball peen hammer. →40
see straight peen hammer. →40

peen sledge see engineer's sledge. →40

peephole see door scope. →51

peg 1 in traditional timber frame construction, a small piece of wood or dowel used for fastening or tightening joints; a timber nail. →3
2 see dowel. →5
3 see trenail. →3
4 see wood key. →6

peg board, perforated hardboard; hardboard manufactured with a regular grid of holes; uses include decorative and acoustic linings. →9

pegged joint a timber joint fastened by pegs or wooden nails.

pegging the fastening of joints in timber construction with timber pegs hammered into predrilled holes.

pegmatite a very coarse-grained crystalline igneous rock often containing rare minerals.

peg mould in ornamental plasterwork, a template drawn across a plaster surface between two pegs set apart, forming a curving moulding; a curved running mould; see run moulding. →14

pein see peen. →40

Pelasgic masonry see cyclopean masonry. →11

pele tower, peel tower; a small fortified medieval dwelling found especially in Scotland and northern England, often a simple masonry tower.

pelican the large pouch-billed bird of the genus *Pelicanus*, symbolic in ornament of Christ's sacrifice on the cross, resulting from the belief that it fed its young on its blood by piercing its breast with its beak. →119

pelican crossing in traffic planning, a pedestrian crossing controlled by traffic lights or signals.

pellet moulding a narrow Romanesque or Gothic ornamental moulding decorated with a series of small hemispheres or raised flat discs. →124

pelmet a board or trim above a window opening to cover a curtain rail or blind.

pelta pelte (Lat., Gk); a stylized half-moon motif based on a Greek shield, used as decoration for wall surfaces and metalwork.

pen a drawing instrument utilizing ink or another liquid as its drawing medium; an ink pen is usually a pen which is refillable with ink; types included as separate entries are listed below.
ball pen, ball point pen.
dip pen.
drafting pen, see draughting pen. →130
draughting fountain pen, see Graphos.
draughting pen. →130
drawing pen, see draughting pen. →130
felt pen, felt-tipped pen. →130
fibre-tipped pen, see fibre tip.
fountain pen.
ink pen, see pen.
marker pen.
reed pen.
reservoir pen.
stylo pen, see draughting pen. →130
technical pen, see draughting pen. →130

penalty, fine; compensation to be paid by one who breaks an agreement or contract, or financial punishment of one who breaks the law.

penalty clause in contracts administration, a condition stating the details of the terms and amount to be paid if the contract is broken.

pencil 1 a drawing instrument with a stick of graphite or other mineral product in solid form as its drawing medium; see also lead pencil, coloured pencil, clutch pencil; types included as separate entries are listed below.
all-surface pencil.
builder's pencil, see carpenter's pencil. →130
carpenter's pencil. →130
Chinagraph pencil.
clutch pencil.
coloured pencil.
drawing pencil.
eraser pencil. →130
graphite pencil, see lead pencil.
lead pencil.
propelling pencil. →130

2 a fine brush with hairs tapered to a point, used in artwork and for applying painted decoration.

pencil arris see pencil round. →14

pencil drawing any drawing in lead pencil.

pencil holder a device used for holding short or partly used pencils which makes drawing easier.

pencil round the blunting of the sharp edges of rectangular stone, woodwork, glass etc. objects by slight sanding or grinding, usually with less than 3 mm chamfer, also referred to as a pencil or eased arris, or an arrised or eased edge. →14

pencil sharpener a device for sharpening the lead in a pencil, usually by rotary action. →130

pendant an elongated decorated round piece or boss hanging down at the join of ribs or other members in a vault or ornamental ceiling. →101

pendant luminaire, droplight; a fixed light fitting designed to be hung from a roof, structure or ceiling, and which sheds most of its light downwards.

pendentive a curved segmental surface or construction for joining the round base of a masonry dome or opening to a square structure beneath.

pendentive dome any dome constructed on pendentives; often a sail dome. →26

penetration 1 the place at which a component such as a pipe or chimney passes through a floor, wall or roof, usually requiring special measures to ensure weatherproofing and fireproofing. →56

2 see roof penetration. →56

penetration testing in soil investigation, the testing of the stiffness of non-cohesive soils and gravel by sinking a special implement into the ground and measuring the force required to do so.
see cone penetration testing.
deep penetration testing, see cone penetration testing.
see dynamic penetration testing.
see static penetration testing.
see vane testing.

peninsula a body of land projecting into and surrounded by water.

penknife, pocket knife, clasp knife, jack knife; a knife which has one or more hinged blades which can be turned back into its hollow handle when not in use.

penning see pitching.

penny washer see flat washer. →37

pension fund money set aside by a private company or other institution from which pensions are paid to employees, often used in the interim for investment.

pent roof see penthouse roof. →46

pentagon a planar regular or irregular five-sided geometrical figure. →108

pentagram a five-pointed star, a mystical decorative motif constructed with one unbroken line. →108

pentahedron a solid shape whose surface is composed of five planar faces.

Pentarthrum huttonii see wood weevil.

pentastyle in classical architecture, a portico which has five supporting columns in a row. →77

penthouse an apartment or suite of rooms at the top of a high-rise building. →61

penthouse roof, pent roof, shed roof; a monopitch roof which covers the top of a higher wall on which its upper end is supported; see also lean-to roof. →46

pentimento the showing through of previous painting in a work of art that has been overpainted.

pentise roof a monopitch roof built against a wall as a canopy.

pentlandite, iron nickel sulphide; a yellow or brown mineral, naturally occurring iron nickel sulphide, $\mathbf{(Fe,Ni)_9S_8}$, the most important ore of nickel.

pen weight see line thickness.

peperino volcanic tuff found in the areas south-east of Rome, used as a building stone by the Romans; also called lapis albanus.

pepper red see capsicum red.

per cent %; one hundredth part.

perch, 1 pole, rod; a traditional unit of length equal to 5½ yards or 50292 m.

2 a measure for the volume of stone equivalent to 0.7008 m^3.

perclose see parclose. →100

percussive bored pile in foundation technology, a bored pile in which excavation is carried out using repeated blows or vibration of the pile casing.

percussive welding, resistance percussive welding; a method of resistance welding in which a local electric current is passed concurrently with the sudden application of a high pressure.

perennial any species of flowering plant that lives for many years, usually dying down at winter and regrowing from shoots the following spring.

perfect frame see statically determinate frame.

perfect gas see ideal gas.

perfect market an economic situation in which enough buyers and sellers affect or define the price of goods or services to keep them static.

perforated brick, 1 cored brick; a clay brick which has a pattern of vertical holes through it for weight reduction, but also to save on material and improve the insulation properties of the brickwork; the maximum permitted amount of perforation is usually governed by a national standard, less than 25% in Great Britain. →16

2 see ventilating brick, air brick. →16

3 see hollow clay block. →16

4 see hollow brick. →16

perforated hardboard see pegboard. →9

perforated masonry unit 1 any brick, block or stone perforated with holes, indentations or cavities.

2 see perforated brick, cored brick. →16

3 see air brick, ventilating brick. →16

perforated panel absorber in acoustics, an absorbing construction consisting of a perforated board with an air gap or mineral wool behind.

perforated pipe a clay or plastics pipe with slotted perforations along its length; see drain pipe. →59

perforated sheetmetal a sheetmetal product manufactured with a series of regular circular or rectangular openings. →34

perforated underlay bitumen felt, vented underlay, venting layer; bitumen felt manufactured with perforations and treated with granular material on its reverse side, used in a warm flat roof as an underlay to allow for the movement of air within roof construction.

perforation 1 the drilling, punching or forming of holes through components, sheet materials etc.

2 the holes or pattern of openings thus made.

performance the specified, expected or actual behaviour of a building material, component or building while in use.

performance specification a technical specification that outlines, lists and documents the behaviour or use of a product, process, installation or service.

pergelisol see permafrost.

pergola in landscape and garden design, a passage, walkway, gateway etc. with a canopy of trelliswork on which climbing plants are trained to grow.

periaktos Gk; movable scenery from an ancient Greek theatre.

peribolos Gk; see peribolus. →85

peribolus, peribolos (Gk); a surrounding wall or area for a classical temple or Early Christian basilica. →85

Pericopsis elata see afrormosia.

peridot see olivine.

peridotite a dark, coarse-grained igneous rock type used as building stone.

peridrome peridromos (Gk); the passage formed between the rows of columns and outer wall of the cella in a Greek or Roman temple; this area is also known as the pteroma. →85

peridromos Gk; see peridrome. →85

perimeter the enclosing external boundary of an area.
perimeter fencing see boundary fencing.
perimeter surveillance the use of cameras and alarms on boundary fencing and gates to prevent the entry of intruders.
perimeter trim a profile fixed to a wall at the edges of a suspended ceiling to provide support to ceiling panels. →60
perimeter wall **1** a masonry wall constructed around an area such as a churchyard. →102
2 see enceinte.
perinone orange a strong, clean reddish orange organic pigment used in acrylic paints, discovered in 1924.
periodic table a table displaying all the chemical elements in order of atomic weight and grouped according to chemical property. →Table 4
period of final inspection in contract administration, the time during which measurement of the completed works takes place and the final account is agreed.
peripheral, device; in computing, any of the hardware such as printers, modems, scanners, remote drives etc. used in conjunction with a computer.
peripteral in classical architecture, referring to a temple type, known as a peripteros, whose cella is surrounded on four sides by a single row of columns. →85
see *peripteral* in peristyle temple illustration. →85
see dipteral. →85
see pseudoperipteral. →85
see pseudodipteral. →85
peripteral temple see peripteros. →85
peripteros (Gk); a peripteral temple, one surrounded by a single row of columns. →85
peristasis 'circumstance' (Gk); the outer row of columns surrounding the cella of a Greek or Roman temple. →85
peristylar temple see peristyle temple.
peristyle, 1 peristylium (Lat.), peristylion (Gk); in classical architecture, a row of columns surrounding a building or open courtyard.
2 the open courtyard or temple thus surrounded.
see *Greek residential building* illustration. →87
see *Roman residential building* illustration. →88
peristyle house a Greek dwelling type whose open courtyard is surrounded by a colonnade on all sides, often more luxurious than a prostas or pastas house. →87
peristyle temple, peristylar temple, peristylos (Gk); a classical temple type which is surrounded by a colonnade on all sides; types included as separate entries are listed below.
see *peristyle temple* illustration. →85
see *classical temple* illustration. →86
peripteral. →85
dipteral. →85
pseudoperipteral. →85
pseudodipteral. →85
peristylion Gk; a peristyle in a Greek building. →87
peristylium Lat.; a peristyle in a Roman building. →88
peristylos see peristyle temple.
Perkin's violet see mauve.
perlite, pearl stone; dark, natural volcanic glass composed of small nodules, used as a lightweight building material for filtering, filling, fireproofing and for insulation.
perlite plaster, gypsum-perlite plaster, fire-retardant plaster; plaster containing perlite aggregate in place of sand as thermal and fire resistance.
Perlon a proprietary name for a polyamide plastic, a variety of nylon produced by the polymerization of caprolactam.
permafrost, pergelisol; a condition of permanently frozen ground in arctic and subarctic regions.
permanence the property of a pigment or paint to retain the strength of its colour under prolonged exposure to light.
permanent artificial lighting, PAL; the continuous lighting with luminaires of deep office or windowless spaces in which the amount of natural light is insufficient.
permanent formwork in concreting, formwork of plywood, plastics or steel sheet, which remains in place once the concrete has hardened.
permanent load see dead load.
permanent supplementary artificial lighting of interiors, PSALI; continuous artificial lighting provided to supplement daylighting in interiors where the illumination level would otherwise be insufficient.
permanent violet see manganese violet.
permanent white see blanc fixe.
permanent yellow a loose name for barium yellow pigment.
permeability **1** the property of a porous solid to permit the passage of liquids through due to differential pressure.
2 see water permeability.
permeability-reducing admixture see pore filler.
permissible stress, working stress; in structural design, the maximum stress which can be applied to a structure or structural member; usually set by a standard equivalent to a specified fraction of the tested failure stress of the structure.
permit an official document issuing permission to carry out a certain task or function such as construction, demolition and various types of hazardous work; examples included as separate entries are listed below.
building permission, see planning permission.
building permit.
conditional planning permission.
demolition permit.
neighbours' consent, neighbours' approval.
outline planning permission.
planning permission, planning approval, planning consent.
work permit.
permitted development building work and other development that does not require planning permission.
permittivity in electronics, the ratio of electric displacement to the electric field intensity producing it.
permutation in mathematics and statistics, the change in arrangement of a series of values or objects and the arrangements that follow.
peroxide see hydrogen peroxide.
perpend, perpend joint, cross joint, head joint, header joint; **1** in masonry construction, a vertical joint between adjacent bricks or stones in the same course. →20
2 see parpend.
perpendicular **1** a line at right angles to another line or axis.
2 the relationship of lines arranged as such.
Perpendicular style, Rectilinear style; the last and longest of three phases of English Gothic architecture from 1350 to 1550 characterized by a vertical emphasis in decoration and tracery, large glazed areas and elaborate fan vaulting.
perpendicular tracery tracery of the Perpendicular style; see rectilinear tracery. →110
perpend joint see perpend. →20
perpend stone see parpend.
perpent see parpend.
perpin see parpend.
perron **1** one or a number of staircases leading to a raised platform in front of a grand building.
2 a raised platform in front of a stately building.
Persian in Greek architecture, a telamon rendered in Persian dress. →76

Persian art the Mesopotamian art of the Persians from 539 to 331 BC up to the conquest of Babylonia by Alexander the Great; in a wider context, also the art of the Parthians and the Sassanids.
see *Asian and Mediterranean columns and capitals* illustration. →69

Persian blue a shade of blue which takes its name from the colour of Persian porcelain and certain fabric dyes.

Persian orange a shade of deep yellow which takes its name from the colour of the pigment Persian yellow, a compound of sulphur and arsenic.

Persian red see oxide red.

Persian walnut see European walnut.

persiennes, louvred shutters; a pair of hinged external window shutters to provide shading by means of louvres held in a light frame.

personal computer, microcomputer, micro, PC; a small table-top computer which functions as an independent unit, with a monitor, keyboard and associated auxiliaries.

person-day see man-day.

person-hour see man-hour.

personification the depiction of an idea, emotion, phenomenon or object as a human figure.

personnel management the supervision of the needs, careers, training, salaries etc. for employees of an organization.

person-year see man-year.

perspective 1 the optic phenomenon in which objects in the distance are perceived as smaller than objects in the foreground.
2 a technique for rendering three-dimensional objects in a realistic way on a flat surface using converging projectors; sometimes called linear perspective to distinguish it from other forms of perspective rendering.
3 the art or science of perspective drawing.
see *perspective* illustrations; types included as separate entries are listed below. →127, →128, →129
aerial perspective.
angular perspective, see two-point perspective. →129
atmospheric projection, see aerial perspective.
axonometric perspective. →127
bird's-eye perspective.
central perspective, see one-point perspective.
colour perspective.
divergent perspective.
exterior perspective.
interior perspective.
linear perspective.
oblique perspective, see two-point perspective, see three-point perspective. →129
one-point perspective.
parallel perspective. →127
part perspective.
Renaissance perspective, see one-point perspective.
sectional perspective.
size perspective.
three-point perspective. →129
two-point perspective. →129
worm's-eye perspective.

perspective drawing a drawing which has been constructed according to the rules of perspective; see previous entry for list of types.

perspective grid a network of converging predrawn lines to aid in the construction of a perspective drawing; an orthogonal grid superimposed onto a three-dimensional visualization to represent the ground or datum plane.

perspective projection a three-dimensional representational drawing in which lines converge as if viewed normally. →128
see *perspective projection* illustrations. →127, →128, →129

perspective section see sectional perspective.

perspective sketch a perspective drawing which has been created freehand without precise construction.

Perspex 1 a proprietary name for thin sheets of acrylic used as glazing, translucent roofing and for cladding.
2 see polymethyl methacrylate.

pervious macadam a low splash, porous and self-draining road surfacing consisting of bitumen, aggregate and a filler.

perylene, perylene red; a transparent red pigment used in watercolours and oil paints.

perylene red see perylene.

PET polyethylene terephthalate.

peta- abb. **P**; a prefix for units of measurement or quantity to denote a factor of 10^{15} (a thousand million million). →Table 1

pet-cock see air release valve.

Peter's cross St Peter's cross, see inverted cross. →117

petrifaction see fossil.

petrography see petrology.

Petroselinum crispum see parsley green.

petrol, gasoline, gasolene (Am.); a strong-smelling volatile liquid obtained by the distillation of petroleum, used as a solvent and as vehicular fuel.

petroleum, crude oil; an inflammable oily liquid found naturally in deposits in the earth's crust, from which petrol is refined.

petroleum gallon see gallon.

petroleum spirit see mineral spirit.

petrol intercepting trap an outlet construction for separating petrol and oil from waste water to inhibit its passage into the drainage system; found in garages, petrol stations and repair shops.

petrol interceptor a chamber in a drainage system in which petrol and other volatile liquids are evaporated off from the surface of waste water.

petrology, petrography; the science and study of rocks.

petrol station, filling station; an establishment where motor vehicles can be taken to be filled up with fuel.

pew 1 one of a number of long benches or stalls in a church arranged in rows to seat the congregation.
see *pew* in Scandinavian hall church illustration. →102
2 see box pew. →102

pewter grey see pewter.

pewter a grey alloy of tin, antimony and copper or tin and lead used primarily for kitchen utensils and ornament.
pewter grey; a shade of bluish grey which takes its name from the colour of the above.

PEX cross-linked polyethylene.

PF phenol formaldehyde.

pH see pH-value.

phantom in drawing, part of an object or building that has been shown transparent or in outline only so that what is behind may be shown.

phantom line a dotted or broken line in drawing which represents part of an object or building shown as transparent so that what is behind may be revealed; it also may represent a displaced part or property line.

pharmacy see chemist.

phase 1 one of a number of sections of work in a large building development, often with its own contractual agreements for design, management and construction that arises from splitting up the project to make it more manageable.
see stage.
2 a particular point or stage in the cycle of a wave, process etc.
see single-phase.
see three-phase.

Phellinus ignarius see false tinder fungus.

Phellinus pini see red ring rot.

phenocrystal see porphyritic.

phenol, carbolic acid; any one of a group of acidic compounds used in the manufacture of epoxy resins.

phenol formaldehyde, PF, bakelite; a tough, brittle, dark-coloured thermosetting resin used for moulded products and in paints and adhesives.

phenol formaldehyde glue 1 a thermosetting, moisture-resistant, synthetic adhesive used for gluing plywood plies, veneer etc.
2 see film glue.

phenolic resin resin formed from phenol and formaldehyde; see also phenol formaldehyde.

phenomenology the philosophy and study of phenomena with regard to human experience and without preconceptions.

phiala see patera. →121

Philip's cross see St Philip's cross. →118

Phillips head screw a screw with a patented cross-shaped indentation in its head for turning with a special screwdriver or bit. →36

phloem, inner bark; the layer of living cells directly beneath the bark of a tree, which conduct synthesized food down from the leaves. →1

phlogopite a greyish yellow or green-brown scaly metallic mineral, used for electrical insulation.

Phoenicopterus roseus see flamingo.

phoenix a decorative motif depicting a mythological bird rising from the ashes, symbolic of rebirth. →119

phon in acoustics, a unit of perceived loudness equivalent to 1 decibel at a frequency of 1000 Hz.

phone see telephone.

phosphate a salt of phosphoric acid.

phosphating the pretreatment of a metal surface with hot phosphoric acid to form a corrosion-resistant layer of iron, zinc or manganese phosphate to enhance bonding of subsequent coatings.

phospho gypsum the mineral gypsum produced as a by-product of the manufacture of phosphoric acid.

phosphoric acid a colourless, water-soluble chemical compound, H_3PO_4, used for the pretreatment of metal surfaces to be painted.

phosphorus a chemical element, **P**, compounds of which are used in matches and fertilizers.

photo brown a shade of dark brown which takes its name from the colour of early photographs.

Photo Realism see Super Realism.

photocell see photoelectric cell.

photocopier an electromechanical device for producing copies of images from one piece of paper to another.

photocopy, copy; a paper print taken from an original using a photocopier.

photocopying the process of taking copies with a photocopier.

photoelectric cell, 1 photocell; a device designed to convert light into electricity.
2 see solar cell.

photoelectric lighting controller, automatic lighting controller; electronic control equipment for switching on electric lights and lighting systems automatically when darkness falls, operated by a signal from a photocell reacting to the level of illuminance.

photogrammetrical reconstruction the technique of producing perspective drawings by tracing through from underlayed photographic images.

photogrammetry the technique of using photographs for measurement and to make maps and drawings.

photography the production of images using a camera followed by an image-developing process or image-storage process.

photomontage an image produced using parts of a number of photographs joined; a drawn image superimposed onto a photograph.

Phragmites australis common reed, see best reed, Norfolk reed.

phthalocyanine blue, intense blue, Monastral blue, thalo blue; a deep greenish blue opaque organic pigment, invented in 1935, consisting of copper phthalocyanine, similar in properties to Prussian blue.

phthalocyanine green, Monastral green, thalo green; a bright bluish green poisonous pigment, developed in 1938, consisting of organic polychloro copper phthalocyanine and suitable for use in all kinds of paints.

phthalocyanine pigment a group of brilliant, transparent, blue and green synthetic organic pigments developed in the 1930s.

pH-value in chemistry, a measure of the acidity of a solution from 0 to 14; pH7 is neutral, under 7 is acidic and over 7 is alkaline.

phyllite a dark grey fine-grained metamorphic rock, the surface of which, when cleaved, is shiny with minute grains of mica.

physical conservation, remedial conservation; active building conservation in which direct measures are taken to prevent further deterioration of structures and properties in a state of disrepair.

physical drying the drying of paints or other coatings by simple evaporation of contained solvents.

physical planning in town planning, the preparation of proposals for land use within an area or district and the control of development therein.

physical record a batch of computer information recorded in the storage system of a computer.

physical threshold in threshold analysis, a natural feature or existing land use which presents a barrier to further urban expansion.

PIR polyisocyanurate.

piano hinge, continuous hinge; a long, slender butt hinge continuously formed into standard lengths which may be cut to suit the size of door or hinged surfaces; originally used for piano lids, now mainly in use for furnishings. →38

piano nobile the main living spaces of an Italian palazzo or townhouse, located over subsidiary rooms, above the basement or ground floor level.

piazza 1 a square or open space in an Italian town or city.
2 a veranda or covered walkway in front of a building or square.

piazzetta a small piazza.

Picea spp. see spruce.
Picea abies, see Norway spruce.
Picea engelmannii, see Engelmann spruce.
Picea excelsa, see Norway spruce.
Picea glauca, see white spruce (Canada spruce).
Picea mariana, see black spruce (Canada spruce).
Picea obovata, see Siberian spruce.
Picea sitchensis, see Sitka spruce.

pick 1 an axe whose head is sharply pointed at both ends, used for hacking stone and masonry, in demolition and excavation work etc.; also called a pickaxe. →40
2 see rock pick. →40
3 see pick hammer. →40

pickaxe see pick. →40

picked finish, pecked finish; a rough stonework finish produced by dressing with a pick or point.

pick hammer a small hammer with a sharp peen, used in plastering, for removing scale, raking out mortar joints etc. →40

pickling the removal of oxides, scale, rust and other compounds from steel surfaces by dipping in sulphuric acid before priming or other surface treatments.

pico- abb. **p**; a prefix for units of measurement or quantity to denote a factor of 10^{-12} (one million millionth). →Table 1

Pictish stone a rough prehistoric standing stone with Pictish or ancient Scottish carvings.

pictorial space the illusion of three-dimensional space produced on a two-dimensional surface, as in perspective drawing.

picture a depiction of a scene, object, people etc. made by painting, drawing, photography or some other method.
picture element see pixel.
picturesque 1 referring to attractive townscape or the countryside which has the visual quality of a painting or illustration.
2 a style in English country houses and mansions from the 1700s and early 1800s in which asymmetrical building masses and groups are set in romantic parkland.
picture frame cramp see corner cramp.
picture house see cinema.
picture plane the imaginary plane on which a projection drawing is produced; sometimes called the image plane or plane of delineation. →128
picture varnish a general name for any final protective coating for oil or tempera paintings.
picture window a large window which frames a particular exterior view.
piecemeal development small-scale and fragmentary urban development undertaken bit by bit without adhering to a town plan or taking into account its surroundings.
piece mould in various casting processes, a mould composed of a number of pieces which are assembled for casting and disassembled to remove the cast.
piece of furniture, non-fixed furnishing; an interior utility object such as a table, chair, bed, cupboard etc. which is not fixed to the fabric of a building.
piend see hip.
pier 1 a masonry column or small section of masonry walling between two adjacent openings. →21
see attached pier.
see bridge pier.
engaged pier, see engaged column. →13
2 a heavy stone column or pillar, especially a compound column in a medieval religious building.
see bundle pier. →13, →101
see compound pier, clustered pier. →13, →101
filleted pier, see filleted column.
3 a vertical protruding rib built at right angles to a wall surface to stabilize it; a buttress or counterfort. →21
4 see brick pier. →21
5 see counterfort.
6 a buttress. →102
7 a structure built on stilts or supported by other means, projecting over a body of water such as the sea or lake, and used as a landing stage for boats and for recreational activities; a seaside pier.
pierced cross 1 a cross which has a hole or perforation in the centre. →118
2 see restoration cross. →118
pierced mullet see mullet pierced. →123
Pietà a religious work of art depicting the Virgin Mary with the dead body of Christ in her lap.
pietre dure see Florentine mosaic.
pigeon blue a shade of pale bluish grey which takes its name from the typical colour of the feathers of a feral pigeon [*Columba livia*].
pigeon house see dovecote.
pigeonhole one of a number of open compartments in a furnishing unit in which papers, letters and memos etc. may be stored for easy access and distribution.
pig iron crude iron produced by smelting iron ore in a blast-furnace, cast in rough pieces.
pigment fine coloured powder which may be mixed with (but not dissolved into) a liquid medium such as oil or water to form paint.
pigment figure grain figure in wood with colour variation from absorbed material.
pignon, pynnion; a gable in traditional timber frame construction.
pilaster a vertical rectangular protrusion in a wall, often carved or decorated to resemble a column and usually for ornamental rather than structural purposes. →13
pilaster block see column block. →30
pilaster strip see lesene. →13
pile in foundation technology, any vertical structural member of concrete, steel or timber used in series as a foundation on types of soil with poor or uneven bearing capacity; it transmits building loads deep into the ground or to bedrock, or functions as an earth retaining structure; vertically loaded piles are generally called bearing or foundation piles.
see **types of pile** in foundation drawing; types included as separate entries are listed below. →29
anchor pile, see piled anchorage, see tension pile. →29
augered pile. →29
batter pile, see raking pile. →29
bearing pile. →29
belled pile, see under-reamed pile. →29
bored pile. →29
box pile. →29
cast-in-place pile, cast-in-situ pile. →29
cohesion pile. →29
composite pile.
concrete pile. →29
driven pile. →29
end-bearing pile. →29
enlarged base pile. →29
foundation pile, see bearing pile. →29
Franki pile.
friction pile. →29
H-pile. →29
in-situ pile, see cast-in place pile. →29
inclined pile, see raking pile. →29
jacked pile.
large diameter pile.
micropile, see mini-pile.
mini-pile.
pedestal pile, see under-reamed pile. →29
percussive bored pile.
pin pile, see mini-pile.
pipe pile. →29
point-bearing pile, see end-bearing pile. →29
precast pile, prefabricated pile. →29
preliminary pile.
raking pile. →29
screw pile.
segmental pile.
sheet pile, see steel sheet pile. →29
steel pile. →29
steel sheet pile. →29
tension pile.
test pile.
timber pile. →29
trial pile.
tubular pile, see pipe pile. →29
under-reamed pile. →29
wooden pile, see timber pile. →29
working pile.
pile building see pile dwelling.
pile cap 1 a steel plate at the upper end of a pile to provide protection during driving.
2 a footing or concrete beam which transmits loading from a structure to a series of piles.
3 in foundation engineering, a concrete plate to which the upper ends of groups of piles are attached, through which loading from the building is transmitted.
pile casing a length of steel tubing sunk into the ground as permanent or temporary formwork for a concrete pile. →29
piled anchorage, anchor pile; a buried pile or stake attached with ties to the rear of a retaining wall to provide a restraining anchorage. →29
piled foundation any foundation system which makes use of piles to transmit building loads to the underlying bedrock or ground. →29

pile driver, piling frame; site plant for hammering piles into the ground with a repeated percussive action, usually a winch, frame and heavy weight or drop hammer.
piledriving, piling; the placing of concrete or timber piles into the ground by repeated downward blows from a hammer, pile driver or similar plant.
pile dwelling, lake dwelling; a prehistoric dwelling type often situated over a lake, water or swampy ground, constructed on piles driven into the ground; traditional and modern equivalents of this.
pile-placing see piling.
pile yarn in the making of carpets, rugs and mats, yarn which forms the final wearing surface of the mat as opposed to the structure.
pilgrimage church a medieval Romanesque church along a pilgrimage route to Santiago di Compostela in Spain, containing sacred relics for worshippers.
piling, 1 pile-placing; the process of casting, installation or driving of foundation piles on site.
2 see piledriving.
piling frame see pile driver.
pillar a heavy masonry column or pier, freestanding or supporting a structure, often other than round in plan. →13
see block pillar. →102
brick pillar, see brick column. →21
see cross pillar. →118
see edict pillar. →69
see Egyptian heraldic pillar. →73
pillar box a freestanding cylindrical or rectangular slotted hollow steel vessel for collecting mail; a freestanding letter box.
pillow in traditional timber frame construction, a small horizontal timber piece added to the top of a post to spread the load of a beam; a timber capital. →4
pilot project see experimental project.
pin 1 a small nail with a slender shank; examples included as separate entries are listed below. →35
drawing pin.
escutcheon pin. →35
gimp pin.
hardboard pin. →35
panel pin. →35
U-pin, see staple. →35
2 in timber frame construction, a wooden peg with round cross-section driven into the sides of a joint as a fixing. →3
dowel. →5
hook pin.
trenail. →3
wood key. →6
3 see hinge pin. →38
4 see cotter pin.
pinacotheca, pinakotheke (Gk); a picture gallery in ancient Greece or Rome; originally a wing of the Propylaea of the Acropolis in Athens containing art works, later a domestic gallery containing objects of art.
pinakotheke see pinacotheca.
pincers a metal scissor-like hand tool with hinged jaws used for removing nails, gripping and cutting.
pinched finish see pitched finish. →12
pincher see pitching tool. →41
pine [*Pinus spp.*] a group of common softwoods found in the Northern hemisphere with pale reddish brown timber; used for general constructional, cladding and joinery; see ***Pinus spp.*** for full list of species of pine included in this work; see also Oregon pine, Parana pine.
pineapple a decorative ovoid finial carved with a web of diagonal lines or bands, resembling a pineapple; similar to pine cone. →121
pine cone depictions of the cone-shaped fruit of a conifer, as found in ancient banded ornament and mouldings, or sculptured as a terminating element for newel posts, pendants, balustrades, finials etc.; similar to pineapple. →82, →121
pine needle see fir (green).
pine oil oil extracted from the needles, wood and resin of pine trees, with characteristic odour, used as an additive in insecticides, detergents and some paints.
pine soot black a variety of Chinese lampblack pigment.
pin hammer see tack hammer. →40
pin hinge 1 see loose pin butt hinge. →38
2 see fast-pin hinge. →38
pinhole 1 a small round hole in wood caused by the infestation of insects.
2 see pinholing.
pinholing, pinhole; a defect in a paint finish consisting of tiny holes produced by bursting bubbles of air or gas introduced into the paint during mixing or application.
pin joint, hinge joint; any joint which is free to rotate about a pivot, or can be regarded as such for purposes of structural calculation. →33
see pinned joint. →35
see dowel joint. →5
pin knot, cat's eye; a small knot in seasoned timber, less than 6 mm or ¼" in diameter. →1
pin leaf the leaf of a hinge to which the hinge pin is fixed. →38
pinnacle a small pointed or pyramidical turret in Gothic architecture, often adorning buttresses, doorways and roofs and ornamented with crockets and finials. →100, →109
pinned joint a timber joint in which wooden or metal round pins are laterally driven in to fasten and tighten members together. →35
see dowel joint. →5
pinned tenon joint see keyed tenon joint. →5
pin pile see mini-pile.
pin-registration drafting see overlay drafting.
pint a unit of liquid capacity equal to one eighth of a gallon; in Britain, an imperial pint is equal to 20 fluid ounces or 34.66 cu.in., equivalent to 0.57 l; in North America a US pint is equal to 28.87 cu.in. or 0.47 l for liquid capacity, and 33.60 cu.in. or 0.551 l for dry capacity.
pintle a hinge pin in a lift-off hinge. →38
pin tumbler one of a number of moving pins in a lock mechanism which holds the bolt fast until lifted with a suitable key.
Pinus spp. see pine.
Pinus cembra, see Siberian yellow pine.
Pinus contorta, see lodgepole pine.
Pinus monticola, see western white pine.
Pinus nigra, see Corsican pine.
Pinus radiata, see radiata pine.
Pinus strobus, see yellow pine.
Pinus sylvestris, see Scots pine.
pipe 1 a rigid, hollow tubular product of plastics, ceramics, concrete or metal, usually used to convey liquids or gases.
2 see pipeline.
3 see gas pipe.
4 steel pipe, see circular hollow section. →34
pipe bracket a support for fixing a pipe to the building fabric.
pipe circuit a system of pipes in which liquid or gas flows for a particular function such as heating, cold water supply etc.
pipeclay an impure variety of kaolin.
pipe clip see saddle clip.
pipe closer see fire stop sleeve.
pipe duct, 1 conduit; a length of usually plastic pipe built into construction to provide an unobstructed route for installation cabling and pipework.
2 see cable duct.
3 see pipework duct.
pipe fitting, connector, coupler, coupling; a length of special pipe attached to a pipeline to alter the direction or action of the flow or to

connect two pipes together; types included as separate entries are listed below.
bend.
branch fitting.
breech fitting.
bush.
compression fitting.
connector.
coupling.
cross.
elbow.
fire stop sleeve.
gully.
hexagonal nipple.
knuckle bend.
reducing fitting, reducer.
screwed pipe.
slotted waste.
taper.
tee.
union.
waste coupling, waste.
Y branch.

pipe fixing a bracket, hanger or other means for securing a pipe to supporting construction.

pipe flashing in roof construction, a strip of impervious sheet material used to waterproof the junction where a pipe or other component penetrates roofing, decking etc.; also called a cover soaker, roof soaker or vent soaker.

pipe hanger a component for hanging a pipe from a soffit or overlying structure.

pipe-in-pipe in a district heating system, a composite tube consisting of a pipe wrapped with insulation in a hard casing, in which heated water is conveyed.

pipe interrupter a device containing apertures for the introduction of air to inhibit the backflow of water into sanitary pipework; a form of backflow valve.

pipelaying the installation of lengths of pipeline for drainage, water supply or district heating, into trenches in the ground, along the sea bed etc.

pipeline, line; a length of pipe as part of an installation for gas, water, sewage etc.

pipe pile, tubular pile; in foundation engineering, a pile formed from a steel pipe. →29
see box pile. →29

pipe saddle, saddle fitting, service clamp; a pipe component with a suitably shaped curved flange and socket to make a connection from a new drain to an existing sewer.

pipe shoe, rainwater shoe; a kinked fitting at the lower end of a rainwater pipe to throw water away from the surface of a building.

pipe sleeve a length of pipe built into floor or wall construction to provide an opening through which pipes or cables can later be passed.

pipe system test a test for blocks, interruptions and leaks in a system of pipework; types included as separate entries are listed below.
air test.
gas soundness test.
hydraulic test, see water test.
mirror test.
pipe system test.
pneumatic test, see air test.
smoke test.
soundness test, see gas soundness test.
water test.

pipe tongs see footprints.

pipework 1 the job of installing and mounting pipes for a water, drainage, heating or gas system.
2 the pipes themselves.
3 see pipe circuit.
4 see plumbing.
5 see gas installation pipework.

pipework duct, pipe duct; a service duct for carrying pipework.

pipework test see pipe system test.

pipe wrench, Stillson wrench; an adjustable metal hand tool with jaws for gripping pipes and other round objects.

PIR see polyisocyanurate.

pisces Lat.; plural form of piscis, fish. →119, →123

piscina, 1 sacrarium; Lat.; a stone basin in a church for washing the communion vessels and draining the water used in the Mass, usually set in a recess.
see *Byzantine domical church* illustration. →96
2 an ornamental pool, reservoir, basin or fishpond in Roman architecture. →88
see *Roman residential buildings* illustration. →88

piscina limaria Lat.; a reservoir constructed at the termination of a Roman aqueduct to collect water and allow solid material to settle out before it is distributed for use; a Roman water-purification plant or settling tank.

piscis Lat.; see fish. →119, →123

pisé, rammed earth construction, pisé de terre; a traditional walling construction of clay laid and compacted in boarded formwork, allowed to dry in the sun and often faced with stucco.

pisé de terre see pisé.

pistache (green) a shade of pale greyish green which takes its name from the colour of the green seed of the pistachio tree (Pistacia vera).

pistacite see epidote.

pit 1 a defect in a concrete or other finish caused by a small recess in the surface.
2 see excavation.
3 the part of the ground floor of a theatre auditorium behind the stalls.
4 orchestra pit.
5 see lift pit.

pitch 1 the angle of a sloping plane measured as a fraction or percentage.
2 see slope.
3 see rise. →22
4 see roof pitch.
5 slope; the angle of a stair from the horizontal, measured along the line of nosings.
6 the sloping of the face of a saw tooth relative to the vertical.
7 the distance between adjacent ridges in a screw thread, a measure of its fineness. →36
8 in acoustics, the subjective frequency of a sound as perceived by the human ear.
9 a dark resinous residue formed from the distillation of coal, crude turpentine and tar, used for caulking and waterproofing timber constructions; also any similar bituminous products.
10 see resin.

pitch black a shade of dark black which takes its name from the colour of pitch.

pitchblende, uraninite; a black mineral, naturally occurring uranium oxide, UO_2, the most important ore of uranium.

pitch line see line of nosings. →45

pitch pine [Pinus spp.] a collective name for a number of pines from the Americas with resinous timber; used for heavy construction work and in the manufacture of turpentine.

pitch pocket, resin pocket; a flattened round or oval separation containing resin in the grain of certain grades of softwood. →1

pitch streak, resin streak; a local accumulation or streak of resin in the grain of certain grades of highly resinous softwood. →1

pitched beam a concrete or steel beam whose longer upper edge is V shaped, with a ridge in the middle. →30

pitched finish, pinched finish; a stonework finish which resembles natural rock, produced by dressing with a pitching tool; the same result as a quarry finish. →12

pitched roof 1 a roof form of two sloping roof planes meeting at a ridge, terminating at either end with either hips or gables. →46
2 any sloping roof, usually one with a pitch of more than 20°. →46

pitcher see pitching tool. →41

pitch-faced see pitched finish, quarry finish. →12

pitching, armour, penning, rubble revetment, soling; stones of 180–450 mm used as revetment for embankments.

pitching hammer a mason's hammer used for striking a pitching tool or punch. →40

pitching tool, pincher, pitcher; a chisel-like masonry tool with a blunt end, used for the initial rough dressing of stone surfaces. →41

pitchstone a form of dark, naturally occurring glass which has a resinous lustre; used as aggregate.

pit corrosion one of the most destructive forms of corrosion of metals, localized attack resulting in surface holes.

pit dwelling a prehistoric dwelling whose floor is excavated to below ground level and material dug out used for walling, with a roofing of turf.

pith, medulla; the small core of soft spongy tissue at the centre of a tree trunk.

pith flecks in timber, longitudinal discolorations of wound tissue caused by fly larvae of the genus Agromyza.

pith ray see medullary ray.

pit lime good quality slaked lime which has been produced and aged for a period of years in pits excavated in the ground, stored as a wet paste and used as a binder in fresco paints and a raw material in lime mortar.

pivot bridge see swing bridge. →64

pivot damper see swivel damper. →55

pivot window 1 a window with an opening light hung centrally on pins attached to the frame, either vertically or horizontally, about which it opens. →52
2 see vertical pivot window. →52
3 see horizontal pivot window, tip-up window. →52

pixel abb. of picture element; one of the multitude of basic square units or grains of uniform colour or illumination of which a television screen image or graphic print is composed, which defines its resolution.

pixel graphics graphic images composed of a great number of pixels.

place 1 any open space, location or defined area; a particular volume of three-dimensional space or two-dimensional area.
2 see square.
3 see parking place.
4 a seat in a theatre or arena.

placement see concrete placing.

placing see concrete placing.

plafond, 1 ceiling painting; a decorative painting applied to a roof or ceiling surface.
2 a richly decorated or ornate ceiling.

plagiary the reproduction or adaption of a creative work without acknowledgement of the original author.

plagioclase one of a group of sodium-calcium mineral feldspars.
see labradorite, Labrador feldspar.

plain bar a reinforcing bar whose surface is smooth with no ridges or ribs. →27

plain carbon steel any steel which contains carbon but does not contain substantial proportions of alloying element.

plain concrete, unreinforced concrete; concrete without steel reinforcement.

plain cut joint see flush joint. →16

plain cut veneer see flat cut veneer. →10

plain reinforcing bar see plain bar. →27

plain sawing see through and through sawing. →2

plain sawn, flat grain, flat sawn, slash grain, slash sawn, tangentially cut; a description of sawn timber which has been cut approximately tangentially from the log.

plain tile a standard flat rectangular roof tile, usually of clay and with holes or nibs for fixing. →47

plain washer see flat washer. →37

plain weatherboard a horizontal timber cladding board, wedge shaped in cross-section.

plan 1 a horizontal section of a building or area drawn to scale, showing the relationships between spaces therein; a floor plan. →130
2 one of the principal design drawings of a building.
3 outline; a series of decisions based on an idea, the structural formulation for realization of an idea or aim.
4 see programme, schedule.

planar a description of a surface or system with all points lying on a single plane; two dimensional.

planar glazing see structural glazing. →53

plane 1 a two-dimensional flat surface; examples included as separate entries are listed below.
bedding plane.
bond plane.
cleavage plane.
coordinate plane. →127
cutting plane.
datum plane, see datum level.
drawing plane.
front plane, see vertical plane. →127, →128
ground plane. →127, →128
horizon plane. →128
horizontal plane. →127, →128
image plane, see picture plane. →128
picture plane. →128
profile plane. →127, →128
projection plane. →128
side plane, see profile plane. →127, →128
vertical plane. →127, →128
working plane.
2 see roof plane.
3 [*Platanus spp.*] a hardwood from Europe, western Asia and North America; see *Platanus spp.* for list of species.
4 a powered or hand tool with a cutting edge for shaping and smoothing primarily wood, but sometimes metal and plastics.
angle plane, see corner scraper. →41
bench plane.
block plane.
circular plane, see compass plane.
combination plane.
compass plane.
convex plane, see round plane.
cow plane, see roughing plane.
dado plane.
French plane, see corner scraper. →41
granny's tooth, see router plane.
gutter plane, see round plane.
hag's tooth, see router plane.
hollow plane.
jack plane.
jointer plane.
moulding plane.
old woman's tooth, see router plane.
rebate plane, rabbet plane.
roughing plane.
round plane.
roundsil, see compass plane.
router plane.
scrub plane, see roughing plane.
scud plane, see roughing plane.
scurfing plane, see roughing plane.
shoulder plane.
side rabbet plane.
smoothing plane.
spout plane, see round plane.
trying plane, see jointer plane.
universal plane, see combination plane.
5 see planer.

plane angle an angle marking out a two-dimensional plane as opposed to a three-dimensional cone, measured in degrees or radians; see solid angle.

planed see dressed. →2

planed all round, por, surfaced four sides (Am.); a description of sawn timber which has been smoothed with a plane on all four sides. →2

planed square edged board, PSE; a timber board which is rectangular in cross-section and has been smoothed by a plane on all sides. →2, →8

planed timber see dressed timber. →2

planed tongued and grooved board a timber board which has been planed and milled with a tongue and groove. →2

plane frame a two-dimensional framework of structural members.

plane geometry geometry in two dimensions.

plane iron the sharpened metal cutting part of a plane.

plane of delineation see picture plane. →128

planer, 1 plane, planing machine; a machine with a wide rotating cutter mounted into a bench for smoothing or milling timber and other materials in a variety of ways; see surface planer or thicknesser.
2 rotary planer; a hand-held power tool with a narrow rotating cutting blade for planing wood.

plane truss a truss in which all members lie in the same plane.

plane wave in acoustics, a theoretical wave pattern describing a wave front in terms of a flat plane, used in modelling and calculations.

planing see dressing.

planing machine see planer.

planing mill an establishment where timber is sawn and planed.

plank a long piece of sawn softwood with cross-sectional dimensions of 38–100 mm thick and over 175 mm wide, used for flooring and walling; any wooden section of similar section, a timber board. →2
see concrete plank.
double T plank, see double tee beam.
glass plank, see channel glass. →53
gravel plank, see gravel board.
see gypsum plank.
see hardwood plank.
plasterboard plank, see gypsum plank.
precast concrete plank, see concrete plank.
ridge plank, see ridge board. →33
see softwood plank.

plank construction a form of traditional timber construction in which timbers are laid vertically, side by side, to form a wall. →7
see muntin and plank construction. →7

plank flooring see wide plank flooring. →44

planner see town planner.

planning, 1 spatial planning; in architectural design, the creation of functional layouts or sequences of the rooms or spaces as required by the brief.
2 see city planning.

planning appeal in town planning, an official complaint to a planning authority in order to reverse or reconsider a planning decision, either by submission of documents or by holding a public inquiry.

planning application a formal written request to a local planning authority for permission to carry out development or building work on a designated site, in the form of drawings and explanatory documentation.

planning approval see planning permission.

planning area an area of land for which a town plan is prepared.

planning authority a local authority department which prepares plans and oversees the control of building development for a particular region through processes of planning permits and building control.

planning blight a loss in the value of existing land and property through planning proposals or future development.

planning competition, town planning competition; an ideas or design competition whose purpose is to devise outline or detail solutions for the design and use for an area of land, for use as the basis of a town plan.

planning condition a restriction or provision imposed by a local authority as a condition of granting planning permission for a building or development.

planning consent planning permission for demolition, extension or alteration works, especially regarding listed or protected buildings, monuments etc.

planning control, development control; in town planning, the various processes of planning applications and enforcement of planning legislation by which a planning authority controls building development; see also building control.

planning decision an official statement by a local planning authority to a planning application stating whether planning permission is refused, approved or granted conditionally.

planning gain an obligation by a developer to provide associated facilities, utilities, infrastructure or amenities additional to those in a planning application, imposed by a planning authority as a condition for planning permission.

planning department see town planning department.

planning federation see International Federation for Housing and Planning.

planning inquiry a town planning tribunal in which an appointed inspector is employed to hear evidence and arbitrate a dispute between a local authority and a private party.

planning office see town planning department.

planning permission, 1 planning approval, building permission, planning consent; compulsory official approval of proposed building designs or development by a local planning authority or building control department after inspection to ensure that they conform with a town plan and local bye-laws; a legally binding requirement obtained prior to commencement of building work, valid for only a limited period.
2 see outline planning permission.
3 see conditional planning permission.

plan of work a document that outlines the principal stages in the design, construction and maintenance of a project and that identifies main tasks and persons; also called a work plan or programme.

planometric projection any geometrical projection drawing in which faces drawn parallel to the horizontal plane are true and the scales of the axes are the same.
see military projection. →127

plan projection method see common method. →129

plant 1 any heavy machinery or other mechanical devices used on a construction site; site equipment or site plant.
2 machinery which operates heating, air conditioning and other installations in a building or construction.
3 see equipment.
4 a living vegetable organism.
5 see establishment.

plantation castle a castle or fortification used by a garrison of invading troops as a base to protect further expansion and domination in Ireland in the 1500s and 1600s, built as a result of the Plantations, the colonizing of Ulster by the English.

planter a vessel or container of concrete, clayware, timber or plastics for decorative planting, placed on or built into hard landscaping, balconies, pedestrian areas etc.

planting in landscape design, an area which has been planted with selected plants, groundcover, trees or shrubs. →15

plant ornament see *plant and leaf decoration* illustration. →82, →121

plant room, machine room, service space; a room or space within a building containing machinery and equipment which operate technical services, air conditioning, heating, electrical and lift installations. →61

plan view in projection drawing, the orthographic planar projection made of an object or building on the horizontal or ground plane, as if viewed from above; also called a top view. →127

plaque see memorial tablet.
see name-plate. →51

plasma cutting a method of cutting metals with an intense flame of ionized gas.

plasma welding arc welding in which hot plasma, an ionized gas containing electrons and free positive ions, is used as the heat source.

plaster, 1 plaster mix, plastering mix; a mixture of a hydraulic binder such as lime, gypsum or Portland cement with water and sand, used as a surface treatment for walls; the term plaster is usually used nowadays in reference to interior work, when used outside it is called render; types included as separate entries are listed below.
2 see render.
3 see stucco.
4 gypsum plaster; a mixture of calcined gypsum (sulphate of lime) and water used for finishing interior walls and ceilings and moulding into ornaments.
acoustic plaster.
base coat. →83
board finish plaster, board plaster.
bonding plaster.
browning plaster.
casting plaster.
cement plaster, see cement render; see Portland cement plaster.
coarse plaster, see coarse stuff.
damp resisting plaster.
dry mix plaster, see preblended plaster.
exposed aggregate plaster.
fibrous plaster, fibre-reinforced plaster, fibred plaster.
finish plaster.
fire-retardant plaster, fireproof plaster.
gauged lime plaster, see gauged stuff.
gypsum-perlite plaster, see perlite plaster.
gypsum-vermiculite plaster, see vermiculite plaster.
gypsum plaster.
hemihydrate gypsum plaster, see hemihydrate plaster.
interior plaster, internal plaster.
lightweight plaster.
lime plaster.
metal lathing plaster.
mineral plaster.
multi-purpose plaster.
neat gypsum plaster.
one-coat plaster, see single-coat plaster.
perlite plaster.
plaster of Paris, see hemihydrate plaster.
polymer plaster, see polymer render.
Portland cement plaster.
preblended plaster.
premixed plaster.
projection plaster.
Rabitz plaster.
ready-mixed plaster.
reinforced plaster.
renovation plaster.
sanded plaster.
sawdust plaster, see wood-fibred plaster.
scratch plaster.
single-coat plaster.
spray plaster, see projection plaster.
thin coat plaster.
thin wall plaster.
undercoat plaster.
vermiculite plaster, vermiculite-gypsum plaster.
waterproof plaster, see damp resisting plaster.
wood-fibred plaster.
X-ray resisting plaster.

plaster batch in plasterwork, an amount of plaster mixed for use at any one time.

plasterboard, gypsum plasterboard; a very inert building board made from a thin layer of gypsum plaster cast between two sheets of paper, easily cut and screw-fixed to a frame and used as a drylining, internal wall cladding etc.
see *plasterboard lining* in timber-framed house illustration. →57
see *plasterboard ceiling* in brick house illustration. →59

plasterboard composite see gypsum plasterboard composite.

plasterboard drylining, plasterboard drywall; a lining for lightweight partitions etc. made from gypsum wallboard, requiring no wet trades.
see *plasterboard lining* in timber-framed house illustration. →57

plasterboard drywall see plasterboard drylining.

plasterboard joint the joint or seam formed by the butting of the edges of adjacent sheets of plasterboard, often strengthened with tape and skimmed.

plasterboard nail a galvanized nail with a large flat head and annulated shaft for greater holding power, used for fixing plasterboard to timber studs.

plasterboard plank see gypsum plank.

plasterboard screw see drywall screw. →36

plasterboard seamless drylining a drylining made from gypsum wallboard with seamless joints.

plasterboard seamless joint a smooth plasterboard butt joint which has been covered with tape and jointing compound.

plaster cast see fibrous plaster cast.

plaster coat a single layer of plaster laid at any one time; types included as separate entries are listed below.
backing coat, see plaster undercoat.
brown coat, see base coat.
browning coat.
face coat, see final plaster coat. →83
final plaster coat.
finish coat, see final coat.
finishing coat, see final plaster coat. →83
first plaster undercoat, first coat.
floated coat, see float-finished rendering.
floating coat, see first plaster undercoat.
key coat.
plaster undercoat.
pricking-up coat, see first plaster undercoat.
primary coat, see key coat.
render coat.
scratch coat, see first plaster undercoat.
second plaster undercoat, second coat. →83
setting coat, see final plaster coat.
skimming coat, see final plaster coat.
straightening coat, see first plaster undercoat; see second plaster undercoat.

plaster dabs see plaster dots.

plaster dots, plaster dabs; in plastering, a number of blobs of wet plaster thrown onto a wall at intervals and flattened as a guide to define the thickness of the plaster coat and provide a key.

plaster draught see fibrous plaster draught.

plasterer a tradesman or skilled labourer who does building work on site in plaster, render and plasterboard.

plasterer's float see plastering float. →43

plasterer's trowel, 1 laying-on trowel; a steel-bladed hand tool for applying and smoothing plaster. →43
2 see finishing trowel. →43

plastering the process of applying a coat of plaster to a wall surface; see below for examples.
fibrous plastering.
hand-plastering.
in-situ plastering.
mechanical plastering, see projection plastering.
projection plastering.
remedial plastering.
rendering.
solid plastering, see in-situ plastering.
spray plastering, see projection plastering.
trowelled plastering, see hand-plastering.

plastering background, backings; in plasterwork, any surface or structure to which plaster or plaster casts are applied.

plastering dabs see plaster dots.

plastering dots see plaster dots.

plastering float a flat bladed hand tool used in plastering for the application and smoothing of plaster. →43

plastering mix see plaster.

plastering model see fibrous plastering model.

plastering mortar mortar designed especially for use in plastering, with good adherence and resistance to cracking; also called plastering mix.

plastering mould see fibrous plastering mould.

plastering screed 1 a narrow band of plaster initially laid on a wall surface as a guide to thickness and aligning of a subsequent coat of plaster.
2 see screed rail.
3 see collar screed.

plaster lathing see lathing and below for list.
bruised lath.
expanded metal lathing.
mesh lathing, see wire lathing.
see metal lathing.
ribbed expanded metal lathing, rib lathing.
timber lath.
timber lathing.
wire lathing, wire-mesh lathing.

plaster mix see plaster.

plaster mixer pump in plastering and rendering, a device for mixing plaster and pumping it to a spray gun, ready for application.

plaster mould see fibrous plastering mould.

plaster moulding see fibrous plaster moulding.

plaster of Paris see hemihydrate plaster.

plaster ornament see plasterwork enrichment.

plaster pump in plastering and rendering, a device for pumping plaster to a spray gun, ready for application.

plaster spray gun a device for spraying plaster onto a surface, operated by compressed air.

plaster undercoat, backing coat; in plastering, a layer of plaster applied to a surface, which provides a base and key for the final coat.

plasterwork 1 construction work in gypsum plaster for coating walls, rendering, ornamental mouldings etc.; types included as separate entries are listed below.
2 the finished work thus resulting.
acoustic plasterwork.
combed plasterwork, see comb-finish rendering.
dragged plasterwork, see comb-finish rendering.
fibrous plasterwork.
in-situ plasterwork.
one-coat plasterwork, see single-coat plasterwork.
ornamental plasterwork, see fibrous plasterwork.
patterned plasterwork, see textured plasterwork.
rendering.
run-moulded plasterwork. →14
single-coat plasterwork.
solid plasterwork, see in-situ plasterwork.
stucco.
textured plasterwork.
three coat plasterwork.
two coat plasterwork.

plasterwork cove see gypsum cove.

plasterwork enrichment, plaster ornament, stucco ornament; any ornament in plaster, especially decorative plasterwork casts which are difficult to cast in situ and are added to wet plaster mouldings and surfaces.

plastic 1 relating to a material which, when deformed with a force, will not return to its original shape once the force is released.
2 a description of concrete which is easy to work.
3 sculptural; relating to the form of a building or object, free and often expressive as if moulded from clay.
4 pertaining to any product made of organic polymers; often used in the form plastics when used as an adjective; see **plastics** for full list of organic polymers and resins.

plastic art any art in three-dimensional solid form such as sculpture, pottery etc.

plastic cracking cracks caused by plastic shrinkage during the setting of fresh concrete.

plastic deformation, plastic flow, plastic yield; the change in dimension of a member under load which is permanent and will not be reversed once the load is released.

plastic eraser a rubber used by artists and designers for rubbing out pencil and ink on artwork and drawings; made from white or coloured vinyl.

plastic-faced window a composite window in which plastic framed sashes are fixed into timber or metal frames.

plastic flow see plastic deformation.

plasticity 1 the property of a material or substance which enables it to be worked or deformed into a permanent reshapen state using mechanical force.
2 the property of how well a soil will remain whole and homogeneous under mechanical force.
3 workability, fatness; the property of how well a mortar and cement can be mixed, laid and applied.
4 an aesthetic property of architecture or sculpture, as if moulded or sculpted from clay.

plasticity index, index of plasticity; in soil analysis, a measure of the range of water contents for clay at which it remains plastic.

plasticized concrete concrete containing an admixture to increase workability when fresh.

plasticizer 1 see plasticizing admixture.
2 see water reducing admixture.

plasticizing admixture, densifier, plasticizer; in concreting, either a water reducing admixture or a superplasticizing admixture, included in the mix to increase workability.

plastic limit in soil analysis, the lowest water content for which a clay remains in the plastic state.

plastic paint 1 see masonry paint.
2 see emulsion paint.

plastics any of a vast range of polymeric organic materials derived from petroleum or coal which can be shaped by heat or pressure at some stage in production; types included as separate entries are listed below.
acrylonitrile butadiene styrene, ABS.
acetal, see polyoximethylene.
acetate.
acrylic.
alkyd resin.
amino-plastic.
bakelite, see phenol formaldehyde.
cellophane.
celluloid.
cellulose acetate, CA.
cellulose acetate butyrate, CAB.
cellulose nitrate, CN.
cross-linked polyethylene, PEX, XLPE.
Dacron, see polyethylene terephthalate.
Delrin, see polyoximethylene.
Dralon, see polyacrylonitryl.
epoxide resin, epoxy resin, EP.
expanded polystyrene, EPS.
extruded polystyrene, XPS.

fibre-reinforced plastic, FRP.
foamed plastics.
foamed polystyrene, see expanded polystyrene.
foamed polyurethane.
furan.
furfuraldehyde, furfural.
gutta-percha.
high density polythene, HDPE.
isocyanurate, see polyisocyanurate.
laminate.
low density polythene, LDPE.
melamine formaldehyde, melamine, MF.
Noryl, polyphenylene oxide.
nylon, polyamide.
Orlon, polyacrylonitrile.
Perlon, polyamide.
Perspex, polymethyl methacrylate.
phenol formaldehyde, phenolic resin, PF.
polyacetal, polyacetate, see polyoximethylene.
polyacrylonitrile, PAN.
polyamide, PA.
polycarbonate, PC.
polyester.
polyester resin, UP.
polyetheretherketone, PEEK.
polyethylene, PE.
polyethylene terephthalate, PET.
polyformaldehyde, see polyoximethylene.
polyisocyanurate, PIR.
polymethyl methacrylate, PMMA.
polyolefin.
polyoximethylene, POM.
polyphenylene oxide, PPO.
polypropylene, PP.
polystyrene, PS.
polysulphone, PSU, polysulfone (Am.).
polytetrafluoroethylene, PTFE.
polyurethane, PU.
polyvinyl acetate, PVAC.
polyvinyl alcohol, PVA.
polyvinyl chloride, PVC.
polyvinyl fluoride, PVF.
polyvinylidene chloride, PVDC.
polyvinylidene fluoride, PVDF.
reinforced plastic, see fibre-reinforced plastic.
Rilsan, polyamide.
silicone, SI.
styrene-acrylonitrile, SAN.
Teflon, polytetrafluoroethylene.
thermoplastics.
thermosetting plastics.
unsaturated polyester, see polyester resin.
urea formaldehyde, UF.
vinylidene chloride, see polyvinylidene chloride.

plastics coated fabric woven textile which has been coated with flexible plastic as waterproofing or decoration.

plastics coated paper paper to which a coating of flexible plastics has been applied.

plastics coating, organic coating; the electrostatic application of a protective surface layer of polyester or other plastics to metal surfaces for resistance to corrosion.

plastics door a door whose leaf is made primarily from plastic.

plastic settlement see secondary consolidation.

plastic sealant flexible sealant with plastic properties, which undergoes permanent change of form as a response to movement between jointed components or materials.

plastics granulate see granulate.

plastic sheet curing see membrane curing.

plastic shrinkage the shrinkage and cracking of fresh concrete as it loses moisture due to the effects of temperature, lack of humidity and wind after placement, but before any strength development has occurred, a problem especially in hot countries.

plastics laminate see laminate.

plastic soil the classification of very cohesive soils which can be rolled into thin threads without crumbling.

plastics pipe stiff pipe formed from a polymer such as polythene and unplasticized polyvinyl chloride, used for a number of applications including drainage pipework.

plastics wallcovering hardwearing and water-resistant decorative wallcovering made of plastics, supplied in rolls and used for wet areas etc.

plastics window see PVC-U window.

plastic yield see plastic deformation.

plastisol a thin coating, often polyvinyl chloride dissolved in a plasticizer, baked to provide a hardwearing and corrosion-resistant surface for steel components.

plastomer a molecule or combination of molecules that form the basis of a plastic, usually a resin or other thermosetting polymer.

Platanus spp. see plane.
Platanus acerifolia, see European plane.
Platanus hybrida, see European plane.
Platanus occidentalis, see American plane.

plat band a flat decorative horizontal band or course slightly projecting from the surface of a masonry wall.

plate 1 any thin, rigid sheet or piece of material, structural layer etc.
see metal plate, flat plate. →34
see *metal plate* illustration. →34
see quarto plate.
see chequerplate, checkerplate. →34
see kicking plate. →51
see name-plate. →51
see push plate. →51
key plate, see escutcheon.
2 any horizontal member fixed to walling and used as a bearing for joists and other members.
see wall plate. →4, →33
see sole plate. →58

plate floor a solid concrete floor slab of even thickness in which bottom reinforcement compensates for the lack of supporting beams.

plate girder, welded plate girder; an I-beam welded from steel plate, used for long spans; the thickness and size of the flange and web may be varied according to loading requirements. →34

plate glass, 1 polished plate glass; thick cast glass which has been ground and polished; largely replaced with float glass.
2 see clear plate glass.

platen-pressed chipboard, pressed chipboard; chipboard manufactured by pressing between flat steel plates. →9

plate rack see draining rack.

plateresque a rich decorative style in Spain in the 1500s with influences from early Italian Renaissance, late Gothic and Moorish architecture.

plate tracery early Gothic tracery consisting of a simply divided arched opening with solid plate of masonry or spandrel above, into which a foil or other shape has been cut. →110

platform 1 any artificially raised area higher than its surroundings, usually on stilts, piers or a structural base.
2 any level area at the top of a building or construction. →67, →70
3 a level construction for the siting of cannon, a battery or emplacement in a castle or fortification; see terreplein; a gun platform. →103
4 a long raised area used for passengers embarking or disembarking vehicles such as trains, trams and buses.
5 see offshore construction.
6 see sauna bench. →58
7 see plinth.

platform floor, modular floor, palette floor, raised access floor; floor construction supported on a series of props above the main floor structure to allow for the passage of cables and ducts. →44

platform frame, platform framing, western framing; a form of multistorey timber frame construction in which single-storey stud walls bear on the floor or platform constructed at the level below. →57

platform framing see platform frame. →57

platform roof see flat roof.

platinum a heavy, ductile, silver-coloured metal, **Pt**, which is corrosion resistant and has a high melting point.

platinum blonde see ivory.

Platonic body see Platonic solid.

Platonic solid, Platonic body, regular polyhedron; one of five geometrical solids whose faces are regular polygons: tetrahedron, cube, octahedron, dodecahedron, icosahedron.

play area an external area reserved for children's recreation, often in the vicinity of residential buildings.

playground, play park, children's playground; an external area with recreational apparatus and sandpits designed for children's play.

playhouse 1 a small structure in which children can play, often a scaled model of a larger building.
2 a theatre.

playing field, athletic field, sports field; an area of level ground, often of grass, marked out and equipped for the pursuit of sports.

play park see playground.

playschool see nursery.

plaza 1 a Spanish urban square.
2 any large open urban space, often linked to a prestigious building.

pleasure-ground see amusement park.

pleat a localized defect in veneering and plywood caused by lifting and folding of plies.

Plebejus argus the silver-studded blue butterfly, see butterfly blue.

pledge in finance, an item of value given up as security for a loan or debt.

plenum barrier the upper extension of a partition into a ceiling void providing an acoustic barrier to inhibit the transmission of sound to adjacent spaces.

Plessey's green a variety of chromium oxide green pigment.

Plexiglas a proprietary name for thin sheets of acrylic used as glazing, translucent roofing and for cladding.

pliability the property of a solid material which is easily bent or folded.

pliable tube metal or plastics pipe which can be bent into shape with pipe benders etc. without fracturing.

pliers, pair of pliers; a metal scissor-like tool used for gripping objects.

plinth 1 a thickening or base at the base of a wall, column or building, on which it stands.
2 the round or square construction on which a classical column is supported; the lowest part of a classical base or pedestal. →76, →80
3 see plinth brick. →16

plinth brick, plinth; a special brick with one upper edge splayed along its length, used in a brick coping, above a projection etc. →16
see header plinth. →16
see stretcher plinth. →16

plinth header see header plinth. →16

plinth stretcher see stretcher plinth. →16

plot ratio an indication of the density of building for a particular area, the ratio of built floor area to area of site on which a building stands.

plotter originally a mechanical device with moving pens for producing drawings from computer files; nowadays any large printer which prints CAD files is called a plotter.

ploughing see snowploughing.

plucking a defect in concretework caused by the separation of surface material from the concrete on striking of the formwork.

plug 1 a rubber, metal or plastics accessory for a sink or basin to temporary close the outlet to a discharge pipe.
2 see stopper.
3 see electric plug.
4 see patch.
5 see wall plug. →37
6 see hollow-wall plug. →37

plug adaptor an electrical fitting to join a plug with a plug socket in which it would not otherwise be suitable.

plug and feathers an implement for cleaving stone in a quarry, consisting of two semicircular metal plates inserted into a shallow hole; a wedge, known as a plug, is then driven between, causing the stone to cleave.

plug cock see cock.

plug cutter a drill bit for cutting circular wooden inserts to conceal the heads of submerged screws. →42

plug gauge, hole gauge; a cylindrical metal bar with stepped or cone-shaped machined ends used for the accurate measurement or checking of round holes.

plugmold see skirting trunking.

plug nail a fastener consisting of a serrated nail in a plastics wall plug, used for fixing components to concrete or masonry.

plug socket see socket outlet.

plug tap see cock.

plug valve see cock.

plum 1 [*Prunus domestica*] a hardwood with dense, fine-grained timber used mainly for the decorative value of its grain in veneers and quality furniture.
2 displacer, plum stone; in concretework, a large stone or piece of hardened concrete placed in the pour as a space filler.

plumb in surveying, setting out and construction work, measured as or installed exactly vertical.

plumb line a device used to indicate true vertical by means of a length of fine cord with a weight hung on the end. →43

plumbago see graphite.

plumber a tradesman who installs and repairs water pipes, drains, sanitary fittings and other water systems.

plumbing 1 the job of installing the pipework and other assemblies for a functioning water supply or drainage system.
2 pipework; the various systems of pipes and fittings thus installed.
3 the measuring or setting up of a construction to true vertical.

plumbing unit a prefabricated assembly of water fittings or sanitary appliances with supporting framework, which can be installed and connected as a unit.

plume capital see palm capital. →73

plum purple a shade of dark violet which takes its name from the colour of the ripe fruit (dark variety) of the plum tree [*Prunus spp.*].

plum stone see plum.

plunge bath a large bathtub for use of a number of people at one time.

plutonic rock, plutonite, intrusive rock, deep seated rock; types of coarse-grained igneous rock which form from slowly solidified magma in the lower part of the earth's crust; these include granite, diorite, gabbro and peridotite.

plutonite see plutonic rock.

plutonium a radioactive metallic chemical element, **Pu**.

ply 1 a layer of sheet material in laminated construction.
2 a layer of veneer in plywood.
3 see plywood. →9

ply-web beam see plywood web beam. →7
see corrugated ply-web beam. →7

plywood, ply; a timber building board manufactured by gluing an odd number of thin timber veneers or plies face to face under pressure; each alternate veneer is arranged with its grain at 90° to the adjacent veneer to increase strength; also called veneer plywood; types included as separate entries are listed below. →9
bent plywood. →9
birch plywood.
cellular plywood, cellular board.
coated plywood.
core plywood. →9
cross-grained plywood.
exterior plywood.
film-faced plywood.
finger-jointed plywood.
foil-faced plywood.
formply.
hardwood plywood. →9
homogeneous plywood.
inserted plywood.
interior plywood.
long-grained plywood.
marine plywood.
metal-faced plywood.
mixed plywood. →9
multi-ply. →9
overlaid plywood.
parallel-grain plywood.
prefinished plywood.
preformed plywood. →9
raw plywood.
repaired plywood.
sanded plywood.
scarf-jointed plywood.
scraped plywood.
softwood plywood. →9
special plywood.
treated plywood.
unsanded plywood.
wood-based core plywood.

plywood beam see below. →7
see corrugated ply-web beam. →7
see laminated web beam.
plywood box beam, see box beam. →7
see plywood web beam, ply-web beam. →7

plywood flooring flooring consisting of plywood boards, often with matched edges. →44

plywood web beam, ply-web beam; a composite beam made with an upper and lower chord of a timber section with a plywood web in between. →7
see corrugated ply-web beam. →7

PMMA polymethyl methacrylate.

pneumatically applied concrete see sprayed concrete.

pneumatical mortar see sprayed concrete.

pneumatic caisson see compressed air caisson.

pneumatic concrete placer a machine for pumping concrete into formwork, operated by compressed air.

pneumatic concreting see concrete spraying.

pneumatic document conveyor see tube conveyor.

pneumatic structure see air-supported structure.

pneumatic test see air test.

Poaceae see grass.

pocket see box out.

pocket calculator see calculator.

pocket chisel see butt chisel. →41

pocket knife see penknife.

pocket rot localized fungal decay in timber, surrounded by sound wood.

pod urinal see bowl urinal.

podium, 1 dais, stand; a platform, stage or raised area of floor in a hall or auditorium for a speaker, committee, dignitaries or for a presentation etc.
2 a raised platform from which speeches and other performances are given.
3 see bema. →92
4 Lat.; in classical architecture, a wall and raised platform surrounding the arena in an amphitheatre or theatre, reserved for the seating of high ranked officials.
see *podium* in amphitheatre illustration. →90
see *podium* in classical theatre illustration. →89
5 see logeion. →89, →92
6 in classical Roman architecture, the high base on which a temple, column or statue stands; see crepidoma. →86

podzol a light, grey soil type common to cold and damp climates, in which most of the soluble minerals have been leached to underlying soils by rainwater.

point, 1 point tool, clourer; a pointed masonry chisel, used for the initial rough shaping of stone surfaces, or to produce a pitted finish to smooth stonework. →41
2 see electric point.
3 see lighting point.
4 see typographical point.

point-access block 1 any multistorey building, usually a residential block, whose means of vertical circulation is a central core with a stair, lifts and hallway, from which flats or spaces are accessed; also called a single stair building or central core building. →61
2 point-access slab block, see slab block. →61

point-bearing pile see end-bearing pile. →29

pointed arch any arch with a pointed apex; sometimes called a Gothic arch; types included as separate entries are listed below. →24
equilateral arch. →24
Italian pointed arch. →23
lancet arch. →24
pointed cinquefoil arch. →24
pointed cinquefoliated arch. →23
pointed horseshoe arch. →24
pointed multifoliated arch. →23
pointed Saracenic arch.
pointed segmental arch. →24
pointed trefoil arch. →24
pointed trifoliated arch. →23
Saracenic pointed arch, see pointed Saracenic arch.
stilted pointed arch, see pointed Saracenic arch.
Venetian arch, see Italian pointed arch. →23

pointed architecture see Gothic architecture.

pointed barrel vault, Gothic vault; a curved masonry roof vault which is pointed in uniform cross-section, found especially in Gothic churches. →25

pointed cinquefoil a decorative design consisting of five intersecting pointed arches radiating outwards from a point. →108

pointed cinquefoil arch an arch composed of five pointed lobes or foils in a cloverleaf arrangement. →24

pointed cinquefoliated arch a decorative arch whose intrados is composed of five pointed lobes or foils, and whose extrados is a pointed arch. →23

pointed cross 1 see fitched cross. →117
2 see cross urdy. →117

pointed equilateral arch see equilateral arch. →24

pointed horseshoe arch an arch composed of two segments of a circle which meet at an apex and bow outwards. →24

pointed multifoliated arch a decorative arch whose intrados is composed of a number of pointed lobes or foils, and whose extrados is a pointed arch; see trifoliated, cinquefoliated. →23

pointed quatrefoil a decorative motif of four intersecting pointed arches radiating outwards from a point. →108

pointed Saracenic arch, stilted pointed arch; a pointed arch whose arched form begins above the line of imposts.

pointed segmental arch any type of pointed arch composed of two segments of a circle leaning in on one another. →24

pointed trefoil a decorative motif of three intersecting pointed arches radiating outwards from a point. →108

pointed trefoil arch an arch composed of three pointed lobes or foils in a cloverleaf arrangement. →24

pointed trifoliated arch a decorative arch whose intrados is composed of three pointed lobes or foils in a cloverleaf arrangement, and whose extrados is a pointed arch. →23

pointed vault see pointed barrel vault. →25

pointer in computing, the exact position or address of a record or other data grouping stored in a file.

pointillism, pointillisme, Divisionism, stippling; a method of painting devised by some Impressionist artists, in which colour is applied in small dots with a brush, producing the illusion of a far greater range of colours.

pointillisme see pointillism.

pointing the filling of masonry joints with better quality mortar after the bedding mortar has hardened in order to provide a smooth, compressed and attractive surface. →16

pointing compound a flexible joint filler used in glazing.

pointing mortar mortar designed especially for use in pointing brickwork and masonrywork. →11

point load, concentrated load; a structural load imposed over a small area, in theory a point, as opposed to being spread evenly over a larger area.

point of inflection see inflection point.

point of sight see station point. →128

points per inch see PPI.

point tool see point. →41

point tool finish a finish for concrete produced by dressing with a point tool.

poison any substance which may cause damage or death to a living organism, even in small amounts.

poison green a shade of clear harsh green which takes its name from the colour of certain poisonous pigments from which it was originally reproduced; now synonymous with signal green.

poisonous referring to a substance which has a toxic effect on human health.

poker vibration see immersion vibration.

poker vibrator see immersion vibrator.

poker-work 1 the burning of a design or decoration onto a wooden surface with a heated metal instrument.
2 the product of this process.

polar coordinates a system of coordinates in which a point on a plane is defined by its distance from an origin and angle from a straight line drawn through it.

polar curve see light distribution curve.

pole see perch.

pole plate in traditional timber roof construction, a horizontal timber supported by the lower end of principal rafters, which carries the lower end of common rafters.

police station, precinct house (Am.); a building for the administration of police services.

policies, grounds; an area of land, gardens or an estate belonging to a building in Scotland.

poling board in excavation work, one of a series of vertical timber boards which support the sides of a trench or excavation.

polis Gk; an ancient Greek city state.

polish, polishing agent; a minutely abrasive substance rubbed into a smooth surface to provide a glossy sheen as a finish.

polished a description of an easily scratched glossy finish in stonework caused by the natural reflection density of the stone's crystals, created by treating with a very high diamond abrasive such as 8000 grit, polishing bricks or powders; similar glossy finishes for other materials. →12

polished plate glass see plate glass.

polishing 1 the finish treatment of a smooth surface by rubbing with very fine abrasives, leather or cotton fabric until a glossy sheen is produced; see also burnishing.
2 see French polishing.

polishing agent see polish.

pollution 1 substances or phenomena, hazardous to health, which contaminate the environment.
2 see noise pollution.
3 see air pollution.

polonium a radioactive chemical element, **Po**.

polyacetal see polyoximethylene.

polyacetate see polyoximethylene.

polyacrylate rubber, ACM, acrylic rubber; a synthetic rubber with good oil and heat resistance, used for seals, gaskets and hoses.

polyacrylonitrile, PAN; any of a range of acrylic plastics based on acrylonitrile, resilient and UV-resistant plastics sold as Dralon and Orlon and used as fibres.

polyaddition see addition polymerization.

polyamide, PA; any of a range of synthetic resins whose chemical units are linked together with amide molecules; proprietary names are Nylon, Perlon and Rilsan.

polybutadiene see butadiene rubber.

polycarbonate, PC; a dense, hard, tough, transparent thermoplastic used as a glazing material.

polycarbonate cellular glazing see polycarbonate cellular sheet.

polycarbonate cellular sheet, cellular polycarbonate; lightweight cellular sheet glazing or cladding manufactured from two sheets of transparent polycarbonate separated by an insulating cellular polycarbonate structure.

polychloroprene see chloroprene rubber.

polychrome brickwork brickwork which makes use of bricks of differing colours for decorative effect.

polychromy the use of a range of different colours in architecture and painting for decorative effect.

polycondensate a polymer produced by the process of polycondensation.

polycondensation polymerization in which a simple molecule such as water is condensed out.

polyester a group of plastics which are polymerized from ester; used for making fibres for fabrics and textiles.

polyester base felt roofing roofing felt whose fibrous mat is primarily of polyester fibres.

polyester resin, UP, unsaturated polyester; a thermosetting resin which hardens without heat or pressure, used in glass-reinforced plastics and paints, varnishes and floor coverings.

polyetheretherketone, PEEK; a high strength radiation-resistant engineering plastic used in electrical installations and appliances for the chemical industry.

polyethylene, polythene, PE; a chemically resistant thermoplastic, a polymer of ethylene used for drainage and water pipes, membranes and concrete curing sheets.

polyethylene terephthalate, Dacron, PET; a strong, tough, heat-resistant polymer used to make textile fibres.

polyformaldehyde see polyoximethylene.

polygon 1 a planar many-sided figure, either a regular polygon with all sides of equal length, or irregular, with sides of unequal length. →108
2 see regular polygon. →108
3 see funicular polygon.

polygonal fortification a fortification laid out in the form of a polygon, with a number of bastions connected by curtain walls, a bastion trace; sometimes called the German system. →104

polygonal masonry, 1 cyclopean masonry; uncoursed masonry walling laid of large irregular

stones in rough polygonal shapes to fit in with adjacent stones, often without mortar. →11, →83
2 Roman polygonal masonry, see opus siliceum. →83

polygonal shell see folded plate. →27

polygonal truss a roof truss whose upper chord is made up of more than two angled segments of a polygon. →33

polygonal wall see polygonal masonry. →11, →83

polyhedron a solid shape whose surface is composed of many polygonal planar faces.

polyisocyanurate, isocyanurate, PIR; a non-flammable urethane foam used as thermal insulation in composite structures.

polyisoprene a polymer of isoprene, one form of which is natural rubber.

polyline in geometry, a line made up of a number of joined segments of line at different angles.

polymer any chemical compound consisting of long chains of similar repeated molecules; most plastics are polymers; see **plastics** for full list of organic polymers and resins.

polymer adhesive see polymerizing adhesive.

polymer binder, polymeric binder; a synthetic resin binder for paints and glues that sets by polymerization.

polymer concrete, polymer Portland cement concrete, resin concrete; chemically resistant concrete whose binder is an organic polymer.

polymer fibre one of a number of thin filaments of polypropylene or other plastics used for concrete reinforcement.

polymer fibre-reinforced concrete concrete reinforced with polypropylene fibres, used for in-situ concrete and piles.

polymer glue see polymerizing adhesive.

polymeric binder see polymer binder.

polymeric roofing see calendered polymeric roofing.

polymer impregnated concrete concrete which, when hard, has been impregnated with a polymer.

polymer modified concrete concrete which contains an emulsion of PVC to increase strength and resistance to oil and abrasion.

polymer plaster see polymer render.

polymer Portland cement concrete see polymer concrete.

polymer render types of render or plaster designed for difficult external wall surfaces, consisting of mineral aggregate in a polymer binder; also called polymer plaster.

polymerization the chemical action of forming polymers or long chain molecules from simple repeated molecules; most plastics are formed by this process.

polymerizing adhesive any adhesive which sets by polymerization.

polymethyl methacrylate, PMMA, polymethyl methylacrylic; a clear acrylic resin used in sheets for glazing and roofing, and formed into light fittings, basins, urinals and signs; sold variously as Perspex and Plexiglas.

polymethyl methylacrylic see polymethyl methacrylate.

polymorphism the use of a repeated element, form, volume or space in a number of different ways in architectural composition etc.

polyolefin any plastic manufactured by the additional polymerization of ethylene and propylene; used for synthetic fibres.

Polyommatus amandus the Amanda's blue butterfly, see butterfly blue.

polyoxymethylene, polyacetal, polyacetate, polyformaldehyde, POM, acetal, Delrin; a tough, strong polymer manufactured from formaldehyde and used for wearing parts of bearings, cogs, taps, pumps, zips and valves.

polyphase current a number of electric currents supplied with identical frequency but differing phases.

polyphenylene oxide, PPO, Noryl; a high strength, temperature and moisture-resisting plastic used for computer equipment, appliances and pipes.

polypore see conk.

polypropylene, PP; a thermoplastic used for drainage pipes and fittings, road gullies, WC seats and cavity trays.

polyptych an altarpiece consisting of more than three hinged panels.

polystyrene, PS; a brittle, flammable, low cost thermoplastic, clear in unmodified form, used for light fittings, formwork, paints and as expanded and extruded polystyrene.
bead polystyrene, see expanded polystyrene.
see expanded polystyrene.
see extruded polystyrene.
foamed polystyrene, see expanded polystyrene.

polystyrene foam board see extruded polystyrene.

polysulphide a synthetic rubber used in mastics and sealants.

polysulfone see polysulphone.

polysulphone, PSU, polysulfone (Am.); a tough, strong, stiff, heat- and chemical-resistant synthetic resin used for plumbing fixtures, automotive parts and cable insulation.

polytechnic, institute of technology; an educational and research facility, building or group of buildings in which specialist education is given in science and technology.

polytetrafluoroethylene, PTFE, Teflon; a resistant, expensive thermoplastic used for non-stick surfaces, dirt-repellant coatings and sliding expansion joints in large structures.

polythene the more common abbreviated name for polyethylene.
see high density polythene.
see low density polythene.

polythene sheet curing see membrane curing.

polyurethane, PU; a hardwearing, resilient, stable thermosetting plastic used for paints, varnishes, sealants, sheeting and foams.

polyurethane foam, PU foam; an expanded plastic made from polyurethane and freon gas, used for rigid thermal insulation in cavities and composite products.

polyurethane powder coating a pigmented polymeric powder coating whose binder is polyurethane.

polyurethane varnish, urethane varnish; a clear, waterproof, durable gloss varnish which contains polyurethane as a binder.

polyvinyl acetate, PVAC; a thermoplastic used in wood glues, emulsion paints, plaster, screed bonding agents and in-situ floor coverings.

polyvinyl acetate glue, PVA glue; an emulsion glue with a binder of polyvinyl acetate, used for gluing paper and card.

polyvinyl alcohol, PVA; a resin formed by treating polyvinyl acetate with acids or alkalis, used in paints and adhesives, for films, and as a raw material in textile fibres.

polyvinyl chloride, PVC; a versatile, low cost thermoplastic used for coatings, pipes and trim.

polyvinyl fluoride, PVF; a thermoplastic used as a decorative and protective surface film for metals and plywood.

polyvinylidene chloride, PVDC, vinylidene chloride; a plastic manufactured into extruded films for the packaging industry.

polyvinylidene fluoride, PVDF; a plastic used for injection-moulded products and extruded films.

polyvium Lat.; an urban place or square, originally a Roman forum, at which more than three main radial roads meet; see also trivium.

POM polyoximethylene.

pomée see cross pommelé. →117

pomegranate the reddish fruit of the tree *Punica granatum* with many seeds and a hard rind; in classical ornament, symbolic of fertility, love, and of life and death; in the medieval Catholic church, symbolic of the blood of the Virgin Mary. →121

pomerium see pomoerium.

pommy see cross pommelé. →117

pomoerium, pomerium; Lat.; an area of land on either side of a Roman city or castrum wall marking a sacred city boundary or extent, on which the construction of buildings was forbidden, and, for cities, within which weapons were banned.

pompae see porta pompae. →90

Pompeian blue see Egyptian blue.

Pompeian red a shade of brownish red which takes its name from the colour of a pigment used in Roman Pompeii.

Pompeian style forms of wall-painting and interior decoration typical of dwelling houses in Roman Pompeii from 200 BC to 100 AD; see also Incrustation, Architectural, Ornamental and Fantastic styles; also written as Pompeiian.

Pompeian yellow a shade of yellow ochre which takes its name from the colour of a pigment used in Roman Pompeii.

Pompeiian alternative form of Pompeian.

pomy see cross pommelé. →117

ponceau see coqueliquot.

pond, 1 abb. **p**; a unit of measurement of force defined as the gravitational force acting on one gram of mass.
2 a very small lake or body of water, often man-made.

ponding, 1 water seasoning; a process in which logs are stored under water to protect them from insect and fungal attack.
2 the curing of fresh concrete by pouring a shallow layer of water on top of it.

pontifical cross see papal cross. →117

pontoon, float; a floating support such as an air-filled barrel used to support a bridge, jetty or temporary structure on water. →64

pontoon bridge see floating bridge.

pood a Russian measure of weight equivalent to 16.38 kg.

pool an open area of water or small artificial lake for ornament or recreation.
see swimming pool.
see paddling pool.
see cesspool.
see piscina. →88

pop art art originating in the 1950s based on themes of modern consumer culture: television, advertising, music, fashion and the media.

pop classicism, postmodern classicism; light-hearted modern architecture with both classical and current motifs in new materials, plastics, steel and glass etc., and bright primary colours.

poplar [*Populus spp.*] a group of hardwoods from Europe and North America with soft, pale timber which does not splinter; used for furniture, packaging, panelling and plywood; see ***Populus spp.*** for full list of related species included in this work.

poppy (red) see coqueliquot.

poppy oil, poppyseed oil; a clear, slow-drying oil pressed from the seeds of the poppy plant, used as a vehicle in paints.

poppyseed oil see poppy oil.

pop rivet a light, hollow aluminium rivet used to form quick and clean joints in sheetmetalwork using special pliers.

population the inhabitants of a particular area or region.

population study in town planning, the estimating of the current population and forecasting of future population changes and patterns.

Populus spp. see poplar.
Populus alba, see white poplar.
Populus balsamifera, see balsam poplar.
Populus canescens, see grey poplar.
Populus nigra, see black poplar.
Populus nigra italica, see Lombardy poplar.
Populus tacamahaca, see balsam poplar.
Populus tremula, see aspen.
Populus tremuloides, see aspen, quaking aspen.
Populus trichocarpa, see black cottonwood.

pop-up waste a pipe fitting for joining a sink or basin to a discharge pipe at a plug-hole, which incorporates a raisable plug operated by a lever.

por see planed all round.

porcelain, 1 a ceramic material similar to vitreous china but made from higher quality products under more controlled conditions; used for high class crockery and electrical insulators.
2 porcelain blue; a shade of blue which takes its name from the colour of certain cobalt-based pigments used in porcelain and ceramic glazes.

porcelain blue see porcelain.

porch 1 a space immediately in front of the external door of a building, usually unheated and sometimes glazed.
see *timber-framed house* illustration. →57
2 the main entrance door and surrounding wall fabric of a temple, church or other religious building, often highly ornate.
see *Gothic cathedral* illustration. →100
3 an enclosed and roofed entrance room or space in a church.
see *Carolingian abbey church* illustration. →98
see *Romanesque church* illustration. →99
see *Scandinavian church* illustration. →102
4 see portico.
5 see chalcidicum. →93
6 see prodomos. →87
7 see antecella. →84

pore a cross-cut vessel in the structure of hardwood, or small void in soils, mortar and concrete etc.

pore filler, permeability-reducing admixture; a mineral admixture included in a concrete mix to reduce the size of voids or pores by filling them.

pore water in soil mechanics, water contained in voids or pores in the soil.

pore-water pressure, neutral pressure, neutral stress; in soil mechanics, the pressure of water contained in voids or pores in saturated soil.

porosity a measure of the ratio of voids to total volume in a granular or porous solid.

porous concrete see aerated concrete.

porous wood wood with longitudinal cells which transport water in a living tree; these same cells in converted timber form the basic structure of hardwood.

porphyritic, phenocrystal; a description of types of rock which contain distinct crystals in a homogeneous mineral matrix.

porphyry an igneous rock with large red or white feldspar crystals set in a fine-grained mass.

port 1 a town or city containing a port or harbour, on which its economic livelihood is partly dependent.
2 a waterside area of a town or city containing docks and berths for loading and unloading ships.
3 a harbour, especially that used for the mooring of ships bringing goods and passengers.
4 in computing, a terminal into which a device may be plugged.

porta Lat.; a Roman gateway or doorway; plural form is portae. →89, →104
see porta decumana. →104
see portae hospitales. →89
see porta libitinensis. →90
see porta pompae. →90
see porta praetoria. →104
see porta principalis. →104
see porta quintana.

see porta regia. →89
see porta sanavivaria. →90
see porta triumphalis. →90

portability the ability of a component, furnishing or construction to be easily carried or moved without excess difficulty, heavy transport or machinery.

portable computer see laptop computer.

porta Caesarea 'Caesar's gate'; see Imperial gate. →96

porta decumana Lat.; the rear gate at the short end of a Roman military camp, at the end of the via decumana, directly opposite the porta praetoria. →104

portae Lat.; plural form of porta, a Roman gate or doorway. →90, →104

portae hospitales 'guest doors' (Lat.); the two doors on either side of the central main door (porta regia), leading to the stage from backstage in a Roman theatre building. →89

portal a grand, often ornamental gateway, porch or main entrance for a castle, religious or large public building. →113
see *historical styles of portal* illustration. →113

portal bridge see portal frame bridge. →32

portal dolmen a prehistoric rectangular burial chamber found mainly in Ireland and Wales, lower and narrower towards the rear and fronted by two portal stones.

portal frame, rigid frame; a simple beam and column framework with rigid joints, often of welded steel girders or lattice construction. →33

portal frame bridge a bridge whose concrete or steel deck and supports form a portal frame, with rigid joints; also called a portal bridge or rigid frame bridge. →32

porta libitinensis 'funerary gate' (Lat.); one of the gates leading from the arena of a Roman amphitheatre or circus, named after Libitina, the goddess of funerals, through which the dead and injured were carried or dragged out; see porta triumphalis. →90

portal tomb see dolmen.

porta pompae 'ceremonial gate' (Lat.); one of the gates leading to the arena of a Roman amphitheatre, through which contestants and players made their ceremonial entrance. →90

porta praetoria 'praetorian gate' (Lat.); the main gate at the short end of a Roman military camp, at the end of the via praetoria, facing the direction of potential threats or aggressors, from which the troops departed and returned for battle. →104

porta principalis 'principal gate' (Lat.); one of two gates at either side of a Roman military camp, connected by the via principalis; the one on the right side is called the porta principalis dextra, the one on the left side, the porta principalis sinistra. →104

porta quintana Lat.; one of a pair of gates on opposite long sides of a Roman military camp, connecting the ends of the via quintana; often omitted and replaced with watchtowers.

porta regia 'Royal door' (Lat.); the central main door to the stage from backstage in a Roman theatre building; sometimes written as porta reggia. →89

porta sanavivaria 'gate of life' (Lat.); one of the gates leading from the arena of a Roman amphitheatre, through which those gladiators departed who had been defeated but spared. →90

portatile a portable altar used in medieval churches which did not have a reliquary shrine; more fully known as altare portatile, altare mobile. →116

porta triumphalis 'triumphal gate' (Lat.); the exit gateway of a Roman arena, amphitheatre or circus through which victorious horsemen, gladiators etc. passed (see also porta libitinensis); also a grand urban archway or gateway through which a victorious general entered the city. →89, →90
see *Roman amphitheatre* illustration. →90
see *Roman hippodrome and circus* illustrations. →89

portcullis a main castle gate of iron and timber of open-grid construction, lowered vertically with a system of chains or ropes to prevent entry.

porte cochère a doorway or porch designed to allow for the passage of a vehicle, originally one to allow the passage of carriages into a courtyard.

portfolio a leather, board or plastic case for containing drawings or artwork in transit.

portico 1 a formal ornamental gateway, porch or main covered entranceway for a classical temple, religious or public building etc. consisting of rows of columns which support a roof, often pedimented.
see *classical temple* illustration. →86
see *Roman basilica* illustration. →93
see *Carolingian abbey church* illustration. →98
2 see chalcidicum. →93

porticus 1 Lat.; any open Roman building, canopy or structure whose roof is supported on one side by a row of columns; a portico.
see *Roman basilica* illustration. →93
2 the roofed veranda around the edges of a peristyle in a Roman dwelling. →88
see *Roman residential buildings* illustration. →88
3 shallow side spaces off the nave of a Saxon church.

porticus villa Lat.; a Roman villa consisting of a long row of rooms opening out onto a road, court or seafront, with a colonnade or porticus in front; often a villa maritima.

Portland blast-furnace cement a blended cement formed by a ground mixture of blast-furnace slag, Portland cement and calcium sulphate.

Portland cement an active hydraulic binder (so named because it resembles Portland stone) formed by grinding the clinker which is produced by burning clay and lime in a kiln; nowadays all cement used in concrete is Portland cement.

Portland cement clinker, Portland clinker; clinker composed mainly of calcium silicates made by burning clay and lime in a kiln, used in Portland cement.

Portland cement concrete concrete whose binder is Portland cement.

Portland cement plaster plaster produced with Portland cement as a binder.

Portland clinker see Portland cement clinker.

Portland pozzolana cement a blended cement formed from a ground mixture of Portland cement and pozzolan.

Portland pulverized fuel-ash cement, fuel-ash cement; a blended cement formed from a ground mixture of Portland cement and pulverized fuel-ash.

Port Orford cedar see Lawson's cypress.

portrait a form of art which developed in the 1400s, the drawing or painting of a human figure or bust.

Portuguese cross a cross whose limbs terminate with concaved enlargements. →117

portus post scaenium a portico or passage behind the scaenium in a Roman theatre building. →89

port wine a shade of dark red which takes its name from the colour of wine produced in the Douro valley around the Portuguese city of Porto.

Poseidon's trident see trident. →120

position, location, situation; a defined site or place in which a building, object or event is situated.

positive ion see cation.

possession 1 see possession of site.
2 see handover.

possession of site, site possession; the contractor's legal right to occupy a site after the signing of a building contract in order to carry out construction work.

post 1 any slender column, often round in plan; either freestanding as a fixing for lighting etc. or supporting a fence or overlying structure.
2 a structural timber laid vertically to act as a column or strut. →4, →8

3 see lighting post.

4 a British standard paper size, 15¼" × 19", 387 mm × 483 mm. →Table 6

post and beam construction a structural framing system for a building in which floor and wall loads are transferred via framing beams to a grid of supporting columns down to foundations; also called post and lintel construction, column and beam construction (especially in concrete or steel construction), trabeated construction. →27, →28

post and lintel construction see post and beam construction. →27, →28

post and rail balustrade a balustrade constructed of horizontal rails supported by regularly spaced uprights, with or without an infill material of glass, mesh, boarding etc.

post box see letter box.

post-contract stage in contract management, the range of sitework, construction and administration events commencing from the point at which a contract is signed.

poster a printed sheet of paper, cloth etc. designed to be hung up for decoration, or as an announcement or advertisement.

poster paint an opaque water-based paint with a gum binder.

postern 1 a secondary, side or rear doorway in a fortified wall.

2 a secondary gateway in the wall of an enclosure such as a churchyard. →102

posticum Lat.; an opisthodomos in Roman architecture. →84

postmodern classicism see pop classicism.

Post-Modernism an architectural style in Europe and America from the 1970s and 1980s; it is characterized by frivolous and colourful use of historical motifs.

see *Post-Modern portal* illustration. →113

post office an establishment for handling, sorting and delivering mail.

Post Office red see cherry (red).

postscaenium 1 'behind the scenes' (Lat.); the main rear wall or area of a Roman theatre, where staging equipment was kept, and where the players changed costume.

2 see portus post scaenium. →89

post-tensioned concrete a form of prestressed concrete, usually manufactured on site, in which the tendons are stressed once the concrete has hardened; see pretensioned concrete.

post-tensioning a method of prestressing concrete in which tendons are placed in tension once the concrete has hardened.

postulate see axiom.

potable water, drinking water, supply water; water deemed fit for human consumption.

pot life, working life; the period of time after mixing during which an adhesive or varnish remains in a usable state.

pot sink, utensil sink; a metal sink designed for the washing of cooking and working utensils in hot water.

potash a crude form of potassium carbonate.

potash alum see alum.

potash feldspar, orthoclase; a potassium silicate mineral used as a raw material in the ceramic and glass industries.

see adularia.

potash water glass a thick alkaline liquid, potassium silicate, which dries to form a weak type of glass used as a glaze or medium in some painting.

potassic a description of a mineral substance which contains a higher than average amount of potassium.

potassium a soft, pale-coloured, metallic chemical element, **K**, which appears naturally along with sodium salts.

potassium carbonate, potash; an alkaline compound used in the production of washing powders and some types of glass; potash is a crude form.

potent 1 a stylized handle, crutch or T-shaped motif in ornament and heraldry. →125

2 see cross potent. →117

3 see potenty moulding. →125

potential the electrical force at any point in a circuit caused by the presence of an electric charge.

potential difference see voltage.

potenty moulding classical fret ornament made up of a series of crutch-like forms joined end on end. →125

potstone see soapstone.

Potter's flint any silica or quartz-based material ground to a powder as a basic material in ceramics.

pottle a traditional measure of capacity for liquids and loose foodstuffs, half a gallon or 2.3 l.

poultice corrosion see deposit corrosion.

pound 1 abb. **lb**; an avoirdupois unit of weight equal to 16 ounces or exactly 0.454 kg.

2 a unit of weight equal to 12 troy ounces or 373.2 g.

3 a prehistoric enclosure of drystone masonry to protect livestock from predators and poachers.

pounds per square inch abb. **psi**; an imperial unit of pressure equivalent to 0.07 kp/cm^2.

powder coating 1 a hardwearing protective or decorative coating formed by the application of a finely divided powder pigmented organic polymer fused into a continuous film by the application of heat during a baking process.

2 see acrylic powder coating.

power 1 a measure of rate of exchange of energy in a system, a physical quantity whose SI unit is the watt (W).

2 a number or symbol, written as a superscript, which signifies by how many times a mathematical function is multiplied by itself.

power bender see bar bending machine.

power drill, electric drill; a hand-held machine tool for boring holes.

power factor the ratio of active power to apparent power in an electric circuit; the lower the power factor, the less efficient the circuit.

power float, 1 rotary float; a machine tool for the finishing of concrete slabs after the initial set with rotating steel smoothing blades, a horizontal disc or some other smoothing mechanism.

2 especially one with a horizontal rotating disc.

3 see power trowel.

power floated finish, power trowelled finish; a smooth concrete floor finish formed with a power float.

power generating board see electricity board.

power line 1 any main cable used for distribution of electricity.

2 electric transmission line; a cable, usually supported on steel pylons, to transmit electricity over long distances.

power plant 1 an establishment or part of a building in which electricity is generated for a special use, group of dwellings etc.

2 see central energy station.

power point see electric point.

power saw any saw or sawing device powered by electricity.

power station an industrial complex designed for the production of electricity on a large scale.

power supply network see electricity supply grid.

power trowel, helicopter, mechanical trowel, machine trowel, rotary trowel; a power-driven machine having a number of rotating blades in its base, used for producing a smooth finish on freshly cast concrete floors; cf. power float.

power trowelled finish see power floated finish.

Pozidriv head screw a screw whose head has a patented cross-shaped indentation similar to the

Phillips, but with small oblique notches for added grip when turning. →36

pozzolan, pozzolana, pozzuolana; a siliceous volcanic duct occurring naturally in Pozzuoli, Italy and used by the Romans in their concretework; nowadays a finely ground manufactured product, it sets in the presence of calcium hydroxide and water to form a hardwearing cement binder.

pozzolana see pozzolan.

pozzolanic cement a blended cement formed from a ground mixture of Portland cement and a pozzolan (which has to have passed a pozzolanicity test).

pozzuolana see pozzolan.

Pozzuoli blue see Egyptian blue.

PP polypropylene.

PPI points per inch; a measure of the fineness of a saw blade, the number of points of sawteeth per inch.

PPO polyphenylene oxide.

practical spreading rate the rate at which a coating can be applied to a surface under normal conditions.

pradakshina a symbolic pathway around the base of a Buddhist stupa. →68

praeceptoria Lat.; see preceptory.

praecinctio Lat.; a horizontal gangway between alternative banks of seats in a Roman theatre or amphitheatre; called a diazoma in a Greek theatre. →89, →90

praefurnium Lat.; the furnace room of a Roman bath house, providing heat to the warm baths and heated spaces. →91

praetentura Lat.; the front area of a Roman military camp situated nearest the enemy, where the elite troops were billeted; see retentura. →104

praetoria 1 Lat.; see porta praetoria. →104
2 see via praetoria. →104

praetorium, pretorium; 'praetor's residence' (Lat.); the official residence of the governor of a Roman province, or the tent or house of the commander of a military camp and the place where it was pitched. →104

Prairie style a modern style in American bungalow architecture initiated by Frank Lloyd Wright at the beginning of the 1900s.

pram a wheeled carriage for conveying a baby.

pram shelter a roofed area, room or canopy in or under which prams can be stored.

pram store a room or space within a building for the temporary storage of prams.

praseodymium a metallic chemical element, **Pr**.

Pratt truss a form of lattice beam or triangular truss patented by the Americans Thomas and Caleb Pratt in 1844, in which, by virtue of the layout of the members, all diagonals are in tension and all verticals in compression, the opposite of those in a Howe truss; in the triangular truss diagonals form an A-pattern and in flat trusses a V-pattern, see Howe truss, Vierendeel truss, Warren truss. →33

preblended mortar the component parts of a mortar mix, mixed together as dry powder before supply, and mixed with clean water on site prior to use; also known as premixed mortar or dry mix mortar.

preblended plaster the component parts of a plaster mix, mixed together as dry powder before supply, and mixed with clean water on site prior to use; also known as premixed plaster or dry mix plaster.

preblending the mechanical stirring together of dry or powdered component parts of a concrete, plaster, paint etc. mix to form a homogeneous mass; packed and supplied in bags as dry mix.

pre-Christian cross see tau cross. →117

pre-Columbian pertaining to the art, architecture and cultures in existence in the American continent before the arrival of Columbus in 1492.

pre-contract stage in contract administration, the stage of design work, tendering, administration etc. prior to the point at which a contract for construction work on site is placed.

precast beam, 1 beam unit; a concrete beam manufactured in a plant, brought to site ready made with reinforcement and fixings for erection. →28
2 see concrete plank.
3 see hollow-core beam. →28

precast column, column unit; a concrete column manufactured in a plant, brought to site ready made with reinforcement and fixings for erection. →28

precast concrete 1 constructional concrete in the form of prefabricated units and manufactured products that are cast and cured under controlled conditions in a factory or plant and transported to a building site for installation or erection.
2 see hollow-core beam. →28
3 see precast column. →28
see *precast concrete frame* illustration. →28

precast concrete beam see precast beam. →28

precast concrete column see precast column. →28

precast concrete construction any construction methods using precast concrete units, especially for structural wall units and cladding panels.

precast concrete culvert see precast concrete ring.

precast concrete flag see concrete paving slab.

precast concrete frame a concrete building frame whose beams, columns, slabs etc. have been cast elsewhere, and brought to site for assembly. →28

precast concrete lintel see concrete lintel. →22

precast concrete panel a precast concrete unit for wall structure or cladding; types included as separate entries are listed below.
edge panel.
external wall panel.
precast concrete panel.
precast concrete unit.
sandwich panel. →28
wall panel. →28
window panel.

precast concrete paver see concrete block paver. →15

precast concrete plank see concrete plank.

precast concrete ring a large-bore precast concrete pipe used for manholes, wells, soakaways etc.

precast concrete slab unit see precast slab unit. →28

precast concrete stair unit see precast stair unit.

precast concrete unit a concrete component, usually for floor or wall construction, that is cast in a factory under controlled conditions, then assembled on site as a unit when hardened and cured; see all entries under precast concrete.

precast concretework the casting, finishing and installing of precast concrete panels and units.

precast culvert see precast concrete ring.

precast flag see concrete paving slab. →15

precast frame see precast concrete frame. →28

precast foundation, 1 footing unit, foundation block; any rectangular foundation products prefabricated from cast concrete and installed on site.
2 see footing block.

precast lintel see concrete lintel. →22

precast panel 1 see precast concrete panel.
2 see precast concrete unit.

precast paver see concrete block paver. →15

precast pile in foundation technology, a pile consisting of a prefabricated prestressed or reinforced concrete unit. →29

precast plank see concrete plank.

precast ring see precast concrete ring.

precast slab unit, slab unit; any of a number of prefabricated concrete units used as floor structure in multistorey buildings. →28

precast stair unit a prefabricated stair flight of concrete or other cast material.

precast unit 1 see precast concrete unit.
2 see precast slab unit.

3 see precast stair unit.
4 see prefabricated unit.
5 see concrete block paver. →15
6 see precast concrete panel.

preceptory a medieval building or lands belonging to the Knights Templar.

pre-chased brick a special brick manufactured with a rebate in its side to provide a vertical slot for subsurface electrical wiring when laid in walling. →16

precinct 1 see pedestrian precinct.
2 see ward.
3 see shopping arcade.
4 see temple precinct. →68
5 (Am.) a particular area patrolled by police.

precinct house see police station.

precinctio see praecinctio. →89, →90

precinct planning in town planning, the exclusion of vehicular traffic from designated inner-city shopping streets to provide safe areas for pedestrians and ease congestion.

precious stone, gemstone; a general term for minerals which are of some value, used as ornament or in jewellery.

precipitate see sediment.

precipitation 1 the separation of a solid from a liquid as the result of a chemical process.
2 water falling from the atmosphere as rain, snow or hail.

precision engineering the accurate design, manufacture and maintenance of machines, devices and appliances which have small components.

precision tube relatively thin-walled manufactured steel tubing used for applications such as bicycle frames, furnishings and trim.

precompression see prestressing.

preconsolidation the process of compacting the ground upon which foundations of a building are to be laid by using a preload or other techniques prior to construction in order to limit the amount of final settlement.

predecorated, prefinished; pertaining to wallboard and other sheet or strip products which have been given a factory finish.

predella the long horizontal structure at the base of an altarpiece. →116

pre-emption in property law, the right of one party to purchase something before it is offered for sale to others.

prefabricated, factory-made; referring to a product or component which is manufactured or assembled in a factory as opposed to on site; precast is the term used for prefabricated concrete products.

prefabricated building any building for which the majority of elements and components are prefabricated elsewhere for assembly on site; called a kit building if consisting of a set of standard prefabricated parts. →28

prefabricated component see prefabricated unit.

prefabricated concrete frame see precast concrete frame. →28

prefabricated construction see prefabrication.

prefabricated gypsum wallboard panel a prefabricated partition panel consisting of gypsum wallboard fixed to either side of a frame or core.

prefabricated metal unit, metal component; any prefabricated partition, flooring, roofing or stair unit whose structure is of steel or aluminium.

prefabricated partition see prefabricated gypsum wallboard panel.

prefabricated pile see precast pile. →29

prefabricated stair, stair unit; a stair of timber, concrete or steel assembled or installed on site, having been manufactured elsewhere. →45

prefabricated stair unit part of a stair, a flight or series of steps which has been produced in a factory and fixed in place on site.

prefabricated timber unit a building element such as part of a timber-framed wall or floor which is factory-made with openings, fittings and cladding and brought to site for erection.

prefabricated tread, tread unit; a prefabricated or precast plank product fixed to stringers or a newel to form a step in a stair.

prefabricated unit, 1 prefabricated component, unit; any building component or set of components which have been manufactured and assembled prior to arrival on site.
2 see precast concrete unit.
3 see prefabricated timber unit.

prefabrication, prefabricated construction; a quick and clean method of construction in which components or groups of components are made under workshop conditions and transported to site for installation.

prefinished see predecorated.

prefinished plywood plywood whose face plies have been surface treated at the manufacturing stage.

preform, blank; the basic shape of a key or other moulded product before it has been cut for use.

preformed plywood plywood which has been bent or moulded during the gluing stage of production, using clamps, heat treatment etc. →9

preformed rope, trulay rope; metal or plastics rope whose strands or wires have been bent into their final helical shape before laying to remove internal stresses and prevent fraying when cut.

preformed wire rope preformed rope manufactured from metal wires, used for tension and bracing cables.

prefurnium see praefurnium. →91

preheater see bulk heater.

prehistoric referring to an age which predates written historical records.

prehistoric fortress see ancient stronghold.

prehistoric site, area of archaeological interest; an area of land of cultural and historical value by virtue of a prehistoric structure or habitation thereon, or as the site of archaeological findings, often protected by legislation.

prehistoric structure dwellings, rudimentary temples, standing stones, burial grounds etc. constructed by stone-age peoples. →65
see *prehistoric structures* illustration. →65

preliminaries in contract administration, that part of a bill of quantities or specification that describes not the work itself, but associated matters such as site use, facilities, security etc.

preliminary, draft; a rough or initial version of a drawing or document, often used as a basis for further design development.

preliminary drawing see sketch drawing.

preliminary pile 1 in foundation technology, a pile sunk prior to foundation construction to test design criteria, structural suitability and dimensions of the piling system.
2 see test pile.
3 see trial pile.

preload embankment, preload fill; a pile of earth placed over the location of future foundations of a building for a period of time prior to commencement of construction to compress the ground beneath and limit the amount of settlement of the building once constructed; see preconsolidation.

preload fill see preload embankment.

premature stiffening see false set.

premises a building or part of a building with land on which it stands, rented or owned as a package, usually for business purposes.

premium 1 of highest quality, without defects or blemishes.
2 see insurance premium.

premixed mortar mortar delivered on site as a dry powder in a ready mixed condition.

premixed plaster plaster delivered on site as a dry powder in a ready mixed condition.

pre-packed concrete see grouted concrete.
prepaint process see coil coating.
prepayment see advance.
preplaced concrete see grouted concrete.
prepolymer in plastics technology, an intermediate product of polymerization processes used as a raw material and fully polymerized at a later stage in manufacture.
pre-Romanesque architecture post-Roman styles of European architecture leading up to the emergence of the Romanesque style in the 11th century; e.g. Merovingian, Carolingian, Ottonian and Lombardian architecture. →115
see Carolingian.
see Lombardic architecture.
see Merovingian architecture.
see Ottonian architecture.
see *medieval capitals* illustration. →115
presbyterium Lat.; see presbytery. →98
presbytery, presbyterium (Lat.); the area east of the choir in a church or cathedral, in which the high altar is situated.
see *Carolingian abbey church* illustration. →98
see *Romanesque church* illustration. →99
presentation model a scale model of the final design for a project or proposal, constructed for the purposes of presenting or selling the scheme to clients.
preservation 1 the treatment of timber with a preservative to protect it from fungal decay and insect attack.
2 see landscape preservation.
3 see building preservation.
preservative, 1 wood preservative; any substance used to protect timber from fungal decay or insect attack.
2 see fungicide.
pressed brick a brick made by moulding under high pressure.
pressed chipboard see platen-pressed chipboard. →9
pressed metal capping 1 preformed sheetmetal construction of galvanized steel, zinc or aluminium used as a weatherproof covering for an exposed abutment, parapet, upstand or upper surface of a freestanding wall.
2 see parapet flashing. →49
3 see pressed metal coping.
pressed metal coping a sheetmetal capping for the exposed top of a freestanding wall or parapet.
pressed metal facing unit see sheetmetal cladding panel. →60
pressed metal flashing 1 a pressed sheetmetal component included above openings and at junctions etc. in construction to direct water to the outside of a building.
2 see eaves flashing. →49
pressed metal sill a sill of pressed sheetmetal beneath a window to protect the join between window frame and wall from infiltration by rainwater.
pressed steel lintel a proprietary or standard steel beam for supporting walling loads over a window or door opening. →22
pressed-steel radiator see panel radiator.
pressing 1 one of a number of products such as sheetmetal flashings or some solid plastic components which are formed in batches by compressing raw material in moulds or by the application of localized pressure.
2 the mechanical processes of producing such products, natural oils etc.
pressure the physical quantity of force per unit area, whose SI unit is the newton-metre, N/m.
pressure gauge, manometer; an instrument for measuring the pressure of fluids or gases.
see barometer.
pressure grouting a strengthening process in which voids and air pockets in hardened concrete and soil are filled with grout, cement or mortar injected under pressure.
pressure gun see caulking gun.
pressure impregnated timber timber which has been saturated with preservative, usually a toxic liquid compound of copper with chromium or arsenic, in a sealed vacuum or under pressure, to ensure deep penetration.
pressure impregnation, pressure treatment; the preservation of timber by the forcing, in a vacuum, of preservative into the wood, see above.
pressure reducing valve, reducing valve; a valve which maintains a constant pressure in pipework regardless of the changes in pressure of gas entering it.
pressure surge see water hammer.
pressure tank 1 any vessel for storage of gases and liquids under pressure.
2 a water tank to which pressurized gas is applied, providing the force for circulation in a high pressure hot-water heating system.
pressure treatment see pressure impregnation.
pressure ventilation see input ventilation.
pressure vessel any pipe, chamber or boiler in a heating system whose pressure is greater than that of the surrounding air.
pressure water heater a water heater in which water is heated to over boiling point under pressure.
pressure welding, solid-phase welding; a method of welding in which heated parts to be joined are held together under pressure, either by machine or by hammering.
pressurized space any space in which air pressure is maintained at a higher level than in surrounding spaces, often for purposes of industry, ventilation or research.
prestress see prestressing force.
prestressed the condition of a structural concrete component of being internally compressed by steel tendons in tension prior to use to compensate for tensile stresses when the component is under load.
prestressed concrete reinforced concrete placed in a state of permanent compression by stretched high tensile steel wires, strands or tendons within its fabric; these enable the component to withstand higher tensile loading than normal; see also post-tensioned, pretensioned concrete.
prestressed concrete beam a concrete beam which contains tensioned cables or tendons which enable it to withstand greater loads than a simply reinforced concrete beam.
prestressed concrete pavement a structural base and surfacing of large prestressed concrete decking slabs for roads, factory floors and airstrips.
prestressing, precompression; the application of an internal force to a concrete component, usually with tensioned steel tendons, to put it in a state of compression when in a normal non-loadbearing condition, thus improving its strength under tensile loading.
prestressing force, prestress; in prestressed concrete, the tensile loading applied to prestressing tendons, which, on their release, exerts an internal compressive force on the concrete.
prestressing strand in prestressed concrete, a prestressing cable formed from a number, usually 6, 19 or 37, of cold drawn wires wound together round a central core wire.
prestressing system the proprietary assembly, fixings, anchors and tendons that are used in the prestressing of concrete members.
prestressing tendon see tendon.
prestress loss in prestressed concrete, the difference in theoretical prestressing force and that occurring after transfer, due to shrinkage of the concrete and creep of the steel tendons.
pretensioned concrete prestressed concrete, usually precast units, in which the tendons are

placed in tension before the concrete is cast around them; the hardened concrete is placed in compression when the force on the tendons is released.

pretensioning a prestressing method of placing a concrete unit in continual compression to enable it to resist tensional loading, using embedded steel tendons which are placed in tension while the concrete is wet.

pretensioning tendon a steel prestressing rod, cable or strand in pretensioned concrete.

pretorium see praetorium. →104

pretreatment any treatment for a product or surface, often factory produced, which cleans or primes it to receive a finish; a similar stage in other production processes.

price the sum of money to be paid for goods or services when they are bought.

price adjustment see formula price adjustment.

price competition trading competition in goods and services, based on price alone as opposed to quality.

priced bill of quantities a bill of quantities in which a contractor has entered rates and costs against items to produce a total tender sum.

price index see retail price index.

price level the general cost of services and goods in any particular economy.

price list see tariff.

price variation formula in contract administration, a standardized method of amending contract prices to reflect variation in economic conditions, cost and price fluctuations etc.

pricing the specification of the sale price of goods or services.

pricking-up coat see first plaster undercoat.

primary beam see principal beam.

primary coat see key coat.

primary colour any of the three main colours from which all other colours can be mixed: red, green and blue for light, and red, yellow and blue for pigments.

primary compression see primary consolidation.

primary consolidation, primary compression; the reduction in volume of soil beneath the foundations of a new building due to the gradual squeezing out of water from it.

primary memory see main memory.

primary red see signal red.

primary route a main through road or route other than a motorway.

prime coat see priming coat.

prime contractor see main contractor.

primed referring to a component or surface to which a treatment has been applied prior to a subsequent or final coating.

primed and filled chipboard smooth chipboard supplied with its surface treated with a filler to even out irregularities and a primer to reduce porosity and receive a finish.

prime number any number which is only divisible by itself or one to produce a whole number.

primer, priming paint; a paint or liquid compound applied to a surface to ensure that subsequent coats will adhere, to seal a porous base etc.
see masonry primer.
see metal primer.
see sealant primer.
see wood primer.

primer-sealer paint applied to a surface to reduce its absorbency and ensure that subsequent coats will adhere.

priming the treating of a surface with a primer.

priming coat, prime coat; an initial coat applied to seal a wall surface, steel component etc. as a base onto which successive coats or a final coat may be applied; a coat of primer.

priming paint see primer.

primitive in computer-aided design and geometry, a simple geometric entity such as a line, arc, point etc.

primitivism a form of art which imitates that of children or native cultures, or seeks to free itself from the strictures of academia.

primrose yellow 1 a loose name for the pigments cadmium yellow, cobalt yellow and zinc yellow, after the flower of the primrose [*Primula vulgaris*].
2 a general name for shades of pale yellow.

princess blue a shade of blue, slightly greener than royal blue.

princess post in traditional timber roof construction where a queen post is used for long spans, an intermediate post between the queen post and eaves.

principal 1 see principal beam.
2 see principal rafter. →4, →33

principal arch one of a series of major arches lining the sides of the nave of a vaulted building such as a Romanesque basilica church, supported on columns; any similar or large arch in a modern structure. →25

principal beam, principal, main beam, primary beam; a beam which bears major structural loading or which supports other beams. →4

principal designer the coordinating professional or firm in a construction project responsible for the overall design of the building, usually a qualified architect.

principal entrance see main entrance. →71, →91

principalis 1 see porta principalis. →104
2 see via principalis. →104

principal point see centre of vision. →128

principal post, teagle post; in traditional timber frame construction, a main post at a corner or meeting of walls responsible for the support of the building.

principal rafter, 1 principal; in timber roof construction, a main rafter supporting purlins, which in turn support rafters. →4, →33
2 see cantherius. →47

principal reinforcement see main reinforcement. →27

principal roof truss in framed roof construction, a roof truss which provides intermediate support for purlins, which in turn carry rafters. →33

principal shaft a large or main shaft in a bundle or clustered column, essentially found in Gothic architecture. →13

principia Lat.; the headquarters of a Roman military camp, in which speeches were given, meetings held, the legionary eagle kept etc.; situated at the meeting of the via principalis and via praetoria. →104

print 1 the product of a printing process.
2 paper or cloth printed with a design, pattern or with words.
3 see copy.

printed circuit board, 1 PCB; electronic circuitry with microchips, serving a specific function and manufactured by printing on an insulating board.
2 see expansion board.

printer an electronic device for producing printouts from computer files and other media.

printer's see print shop.

printing 1 a method of making graphic designs and patterns by transferring ink from a treated block or plate onto paper, cloth, or other medium.
2 the process of reproducing the content of a computer file on paper using a printer.

printout any printed matter produced by a computer or printer.

print shop, copy shop, printer's; an establishment where copies or prints are taken from drawings, documents.

priority see right of way.

priority road a road on which traffic has right of way over traffic on other roads meeting it at junctions and crossroads.

priory 1 a monastery governed by a prior or prioress, next in rank below an abbot.
2 a priory church.
priory church the church of a priory.
prism 1 a solid geometrical figure in which the two ends are identical parallel polygons and each side is a parallelogram.
2 a transparent object with two adjacent faces set at an angle to one another, used in optics to bend light.
prison, gaol, jail, jailhouse; a building or institution containing accommodation and facilities for the enforced confinement of persons as punishment, or for those awaiting trial.
prison cell see cell.
privacy, seclusion; the provision of occupants of a space with visual isolation, physical separation, screening from noise or protection from other disturbance.
private apartment a suite of rooms in a public building, castle, palace etc. for the private use of a dignitary or ruler and his or her family. →66
private company see private firm.
private enterprise commercial activity, industry and business owned by an individual or private company as opposed to the government.
private firm, private company; a business owned by an individual or group of individuals as opposed to shareholders or the government.
private house a residential building owned by an individual or private company rather than by the state or local council.
private road a road in private ownership and use, not maintained by a local authority, to which the public does not have right of way.
private sewer a sewer owned and maintained under private jurisdiction, which conveys foul water to a public sewer.
private space any space in which the occupants can enjoy privacy.
private suite see private apartment. →66
privy 1 see garderobe. →103
2 see outhouse.
prize see award.
probability a branch of mathematics that deals with the likelihood of occurrence of events.
probe, sensor; a metal extension to a measuring instrument by which temperature, moisture level etc. can be measured.
problem 1 any dilemma which requires a solution.
2 a mathematical proposition or task to which a solution can be found by algebraic etc. means.
problem waste see hazardous waste.
procedure, routine; in computing, a secondary part of a program for carrying out a certain task within a main program.
Process Art a movement in art originating in the 1960s in which the creative process involved is more important than the product, and itself becomes the work of art.
processional way a predetermined or traditional route in temples, towns etc. along which ceremonial processions and parades are held.
processor the main calculating unit in a computer, a series of microchips.
prodigy house an ornate Elizabethan mansion.
prodomos Gk; a porch-like space in front of a Mycenaean megaron dwelling. →87
producer see manufacturer.
product 1 an object, material or component produced as a result of a manufacturing process.
see building product.
see by-product.
panel product, see wood-based panel product. →9
see metal products. →34
2 in mathematics, the result of multiplication.
production, 1 manufacturing; the industrial making or preparing of materials and products.
2 see batch production.
production card see job card.
production drawing, working drawing; an annotated and scaled design drawing intended for use by a contractor as a guide to the manufacture of components and construction of parts of a building.
productivity in manufacturing, the amount of products made, or rate of production achieved by a company or a unit in that company.
profession a skilled occupation, usually one requiring specific education, training, knowledge or experience.
professional engineer see chartered engineer.
professional practice the practising of an occupation according to accepted professional procedures, ethics and guidelines.
profile 1 the outline shape of an object or form as if viewed in projection; a silhouette or sectional cut.
see en profil.
see moulding.
ground profile, see topography.
2 any length of material preformed into a uniform cross-section of certain shape and dimensions; often synonymous with section, but in metals usually more complex, thin walled or hollow, used for patent glazing, door frames etc.; types included as separate entries are listed below.
see *joinery profiles* illustration. →2
see *metal profiles* illustration. →34
aluminium profile.
angle profile. →34
C-profile, see C-section, channel.
L-profile, see edge strip. →2
metal profile. →34
joinery profile, see timber trim. →2
steel profile.
thermal-break profile. →53
U-profile, see channel.
3 see template.
profiled sheet roofing roofing of proprietary sheets of metal, plastics or fibre cement formed into a wavy or undulating profile to increase stiffness along their length; see troughed sheet, corrugated sheet. →49
profiled sheeting, 1 metal decking, tray decking; structural roofing or decking formed of sheetmetal or plate ribbed with deep corrugations to provide a loadbearing base for further construction. →49
2 troughed sheeting; roofing formed of sheeting (usually treated steel, plastic or aluminium) ribbed with a continuous series of shallow corrugations to give it added stiffness in one direction. →49, →58
3 ribbed-sheet roofing; the same as the previous entry, but with only occasional or spaced ribs. →49, →58
4 see corrugated sheeting. →49
see *profiled sheet roofing* in holiday home and sauna illustration. →58
see *profiled sheet steel roofing* in office building illustration. →60
profile glass see channel glass. →53
profile plane in parallel and perspective projection, the vertical coordinate plane which is perpendicular to the vertical or front plane and the horizontal or ground plane, on which points are defined by y and z coordinates; also known as the side plane. →127, →128
profile view see side view. →127
profit money gained in business through selling products or services at a higher price than manufacturing, processing or buying costs.
profit and loss account, gain and loss account; in business management, a document which lists total profits and losses of a company over the period of a year.
profit-sharing in business management, the distribution of the company's profits to the workforce.

program see computer program.
program language in computing, the synthetic language in which a computer program is written.
programme, 1 schedule; a written or graphical statement of the sequence and timing of operations of work on a construction project.
2 see brief.
3 see site preparation programme.
4 see design programme.
programme chart a graphic representation of a programme of work or overall programme, showing various stages and their timing etc.
progressive tax a system of taxation in which the rate of tax increases with increase in value of the taxable item.
prohedria Gk; a row of marble armchairs situated around the edge of the orchestra in a classical theatre building, reserved for distinguished guests. →89
project 1 an undertaking, plan, commission or process intended to put into action and bring to completion a conceived idea or design; a design project is one on which an architect will work.
2 see development.
3 see public housing.
projecting headers headers in brickwork bonds laid projecting from a wall surface for decorative effect.
projecting window 1 a window which projects from the exterior wall plane of a building. →60
2 see oriel window.
3 see bay window.
projection 1 the technical drawing of three-dimensional objects on a two-dimensional plane by extending imaginary lines, called projectors from a point or from infinity through the object to be visualized onto the plane; types included as separate entries are listed below.
2 the drawing resulting from this method, a projection drawing.
atmospheric projection, see aerial perspective.
axonometric projection. →127
azimuthal projection.
cabinet projection. →127
cavalier projection. →127
central axis of vision. →128
dimetric projection. →127
first angle projection, first quadrant projection. →127
gnomonic projection.
isometric projection. →127
military projection. →127
Monge's projection.
multiview projection, multiple-view projection. →127
oblique projection. →127
orthogonal projection.
orthographic projection. →127
paraline drawing.
parallel projection. →127
perspective projection. →128
planometric projection.
stereographic projection.
third angle projection, third quadrant projection. →127
trimetric projection. →127
view.
zenithal projection, see azimuthal projection.
3 overhang; part of a building such as a balcony, oriel window, moulding, upper storey etc. which projects outwards from an external wall.
projection drawing a two-dimensional line drawing of a three-dimensional object constructed using perspective or parallel projection methods.
projection line see projector. →127
projection method a method of representing a three-dimensional object in two dimensions using geometrical techniques.
projection plane the imaginary plane on which a three-dimensional object is projected in a projection drawing; in perspective projection called the picture plane. →128
projection plaster, spray plaster; plaster suitable for use in projection plastering.
projection plastering, mechanical plastering, spray plastering; plasterwork applied by spraying and finished with tools or left as a textured surface.
projection welding, resistance projection welding; industrial resistance welding utilizing an electric current passed through a number of points of contact provided by small surface projections; similar to spot welding.
project management, management; the profession of running construction projects on behalf of a third party.
project manager, client's representative; a professional person or body whose task is to run construction projects for a client.
projector, 1 projection line, sight line; an imaginary construction line in a projection drawing from the object to be represented to the picture plane. →127
2 see overhead projector.
project representative see clerk of works.
project signboard a large sign or plaque erected at the edge of a building site containing information pertaining to the building under construction, listing who commissioned and paid for it, its designers, engineers, consultants and contractors, and its completion date.
project specification a specification of works written for a particular construction project, rather than a standard document.
prolongation an extension to a building contract period that requires the payment of costs by the client to the contractor or vice versa.
promenade a wide paved path or elegant urban street along the sea front for recreational walks etc.
promethium a metallic chemical element, **Pm**.
promontory fort see cliff castle.
promoter see catalyst.
pronaos Gk; in classical architecture, an open portico or vestibule in a Greek temple, lined with walls and fronted by a row of columns; it is called an antecella in Roman architecture. →84
see *pronaos* in apteral and peristyle temple illustrations. →84, →85
prop a short timber member used in construction for temporary vertical support and shoring of groundwork, scaffolding, unfinished construction etc.
propagation see sound propagation.
propane see commercial propane.
propellant the compressed inert gas in an aerosol can or similar device which provides the pressure to expel its contents.
propelling pencil a pencil whose lead is held in a jaw mechanism so that it may be retracted or exposed by a push-button in a similar way to a ball-point pen. →130
property, 1 real estate; land and buildings.
2 real estate; land and buildings, or a specific building, which are owned, up for sale, being developed etc.
property inspection see property survey.
property management, estates management; the job of upkeep, maintenance and servicing of a building or property.
property manager see caretaker.
property survey, property inspection; a detailed inspection by an official, qualified professional or specialist to assess the condition of a building.
property valuation the calculation or estimation of the price of an existing building for purposes of sale or insurance.
propigneum Lat.; the central heating room in a Roman bath house, producing hot air for use in the hypocausts; see praefurnium. →91
proportion 1 an aesthetic quality relating to the massing and relative sizes of forms, lines etc.

see *studies of proportion* illustration. →106, →107

2 the empirical or numerical comparison of one dimension or quantity with another.

3 see mix proportions.

proportioning, batching; in concreting, the measuring out of the constituent parts of concrete into their correct amounts prior to mixing.

proportioning by weight see weight batching.

proportioning by volume see volume batching.

proposal 1 a design, idea etc. presented for assessment, approval or discussion.

2 see competition entry.

proprietary referring to a product made and manufactured under patent or licence.

proprietor the legal holder of a piece of property.

propugnaculum Lat.; a space between successive gateways to a Roman city, from which attackers who had broken through the exterior gate could be hindered from the flanks.

propylaea Lat.; plural form of propylaeum, used for the gateway to the Acropolis, Athens. →92

propylaeum, propylon (Gk); Lat.; in classical and Egyptian architecture, a monumental gateway to a sacred enclosure, fortification, town or square; often used in the plural form propylaea.

see *propylaeum* in Greek buildings illustration. →92

propylon Gk; see propylaeum. →92

proscaenium Lat.; see proscenium. →89

proscenion see proscenium. →89

proscenium, 1 proskenion (Gk), proscenion, proscaenium (Lat.); 'in front of the skene'; the stage area between the skene (scaena) or background and the orchestra in a classical theatre; the front wall of the stage building; also called an okribas. →89

2 in modern times, part of the stage between the curtain and the auditorium or orchestra pit.

proskenion Gk; see proscenium. →89

prostas a vestibule or open anteroom in certain types of Greek dwelling, often a large niche with columns in antis, affording access to suites of rooms on all sides, open to a colonnaded court. →87

prostas house a Greek dwelling type entered from the street via a passage to an open courtyard, around which all spaces are arranged; the principal rooms are accessed via a niche-like anteroom or prostas; cf. pastas house. →87

prostyle 1 in classical architecture, referring to a temple or building which has a row of columns carrying a portico in front of the main entrance, but not along the sides. →84

2 see amphiprostyle. →84

prostyle temple see above. →84

protactinium a radioactive metallic chemical element, **Pa**.

protected corridor, protected lobby; part of a fireproofed escape route within the storey height of a building, which leads to an exit.

protected lobby see protected corridor.

protected membrane roof see upside down roof.

protected space space to which entry by undesired persons or objects is restricted.

protective coating see protective finish.

protective finish, protective coating; a layer of material such as paint, anodization, zinc coating etc. applied to the external surface of a component as protection against wear, weathering and corrosion.

protein glue glue made from vegetable or animal proteins.

prothesis Gk; in Byzantine and Early Christian churches, a small table or niche to the left side of the altar, reserved for objects used in worship; also the side chapel in which this was situated.

see *Late Antique church* illustration. →95

see *Byzantine domical church* illustration. →96

prothyron a space or recess in front of the entrance door of an ancient Greek urban dwelling or subsequent building. →87, →96

protium the lightest and most common isotope of the element hydrogen.

proto-Doric column an Egyptian column of the Old Kingdom, polygonal or fluted in section and with a simple capital, often thought to be the forerunner of the Greek Doric column. →73

proto-geometric style a decorative style from Archaic Greece (1100–900 BC) preceding the Geometric period, during which line patterns and concentric circles were typical, especially for vase painting.

protoma see protome. →115

protome, protoma; a classical decorative or sculptural motif depicting the forepart and head of an animal. →115

protome capital a decorative capital carved with the stylized head and upper body of an animal or animals, found especially in medieval architecture, sometimes written as 'protoma'. →115

proton in chemistry, a positively charged subatomic particle found in the nucleus of an atom.

proto-Renaissance architecture regarded as being the direct forebear of Renaissance, such as the severe Tuscan Romanesque architecture with classical influences c.1100–1200 or that from the lower reaches of the Rhone.

protractor an instrument for measuring and marking angles, consisting of a semicircular transparent disc with a degree scale marked around its circumference.

proustite, light-red silver ore, ruby silver; a red-coloured mineral, silver arsenic sulphide, an important ore of silver.

provincialism a generally derogatory term for architecture which has local or vernacular themes, or which was borne outside the main cultural centres of a nation.

pruning in landscaping and forestry, the upkeep of trees by removing unhealthy, old or unwanted branches.

Prunus spp. see cherry.

Prunus amygdalus, the almond tree; see almond green.

Prunus armeniaca, see apricot.

Prunus avium, see sweet cherry.

Prunus cerasus, see sour cherry.

Prunus domestica, see plum.

Prunus dulcis, the almond tree; see almond green.

Prunus padus, see bird cherry.

Prunus serotina, see American cherry.

Prussian blue a deep intense opaque greenish-blue pigment consisting of ferric-ferrocyanide; it was simultaneously discovered by Diesbach in Berlin and Milori in Paris in the early 1700s and is used in oil and watercolour paints; variously known as Berlin blue, iron blue, Milori blue, Paris blue, paste blue, steel blue.

Prussian brown, iron brown; a permanent opaque brown pigment, natural red iron oxide, formed by burning Prussian blue pigment.

prytaneion Gk; see prytaneum. →92

prytaneum, pl. prytanea; Lat.; a public town hall for the citizens of ancient Greece, containing state banquet halls, hospitality suites etc. and the eternal sacred flame; also prytaneion. →92

PS polystyrene.

PSALI acronym for permanent supplementary artificial lighting of interiors.

PSE planed square edged board.

pseudo cruciform church a church type whose plan is cross shaped, but whose transepts are taken up with secondary spaces such as a vestry or almonry. →102

pseudo four-centred arch a triangular arch whose extremities are curved.

pseudodipteral in classical architecture, referring to a temple which has a double row of columns at the front and rear, and a single row of columns at the sides; usually a temple which was originally planned to have been dipteral. →85

pseudodipteros Gk; a pseudodipteral temple. →85

pseudoisodomum see opus pseudoisodomum. →83

pseudoperipteral in classical architecture, referring to a temple which has a single row of columns in front, and rows of attached columns or pilasters at the rear and sides, in imitation of a peripteral temple. →85

pseudoperipteros Gk; a pseudoperipteral temple. →85

pseudoprostyle in classical architecture, referring to a prostyle temple or building which has a row of pilasters in place of its columns. →84

pseudo three-centred arch an arch with a flat intrados whose sides are curved downward. →23

Pseudotsuga douglasii see Douglas fir.
Pseudotsuga menziesii, see Douglas fir.
Pseudotsuga taxifolia, see Douglas fir.

psilomelane, hard manganese ore; a fine-grained, black, metallic mineral, a mixture of natural oxides of manganese; an important ore of manganese.

PSU polysulphone.

psychrometer a hygrometer for measuring atmospheric humidity with dry bulb and wet bulb thermometers.

Ptah in pre-Dynastic ancient Egyptian mythology, the Great Craftsman or Divine Artificer, inventor of metallurgy and engineering; in Memphis regarded as the Great Creator, depicted as a white mummy; his temple in Memphis, Hekuptah, was later corrupted by foreigners into the word 'Egypt'. →74

Pteridium aquilinum the common bracken fern, see bracken green.

Pterocarpus spp. see padauk.

pteroma Gk; the space or passage formed between the pteron (outer colonnade) and the side walls of the cella in a Greek or Roman peristyle temple; this space is also called a peridrome. →85

pteron 'wing' (Gk); a colonnade running along the long side of a Greek peristyle temple. →85

PTFE polytetrafluoroethylene.

Ptolemaic period the Grecian period in ancient Egyptian culture from 323 to 30 BC; in architecture characterized by a wider range of column and capital types integrated with temple types familiar during the New Kingdom.

P trap a drainage trap in the shape of the letter P lying on its back, with a vertical inlet and a horizontal outlet.

PU polyurethane.

pub see public house.

public address system, PA-system; a system of loudspeakers installed at key points in a building or complex for relating audial messages to occupants.

public baths 1 see baths.
2 see thermae. →91, →94
3 see balneum. →88

public building an administrative or recreational building maintained by local or national government with taxpayers' money.

public convenience a toilet for public use.

public domain software, shareware; computer software which is distributed or can be downloaded free of charge.

public footpath a path designated as a public route across privately owned land or rural areas.

public house, bar, pub, inn; an establishment in which the principal business is sale of alcoholic liquors to be consumed on the premises.

public housing, council housing, housing project (Am.), project (Am.), social housing; affordable rented housing provided by a town council, municipality or the state for its citizens.

public participation, 1 citizen participation; in town planning, procedures by which members of the public are able to take part in the planning processes which shape their local area.
2 see community forum.

public relations the communication and advertising of the policies, intentions and operations of a particular group to influence another group or public opinion in a positive way.

public sector that part of an economic, commercial, industrial or administrative process which is run by a state-owned authority.

public sewer a system of sewers laid, run and maintained by a municipality or public water treatment company, which conveys foul water to a water treatment plant.

public space space to which the public has right of access.

public-service vehicle a vehicle employed as public transport, a public bus, train or tram.

public telephone a telephone located in a public place for use by members of the public, most often a pay phone.

public transport, mass transport; buses, trains, boats and planes which run to schedules on advertised routes for use by the general public.

puddingstone see conglomerate.

puddling furnace a small furnace in which pig iron and millscale are heated to produce wrought iron.

pueblo an Indian settlement in south-western United States or Latin America, often with buildings of adobe or stone terraced into the hillside and entered by ladder via the roof.

pueblo Baroque the Baroque architecture of South and Central America, especially Mexico.

PU foam see polyurethane foam.

pugging boards, sound boarding; boards attached between or to the underside of floor or ceiling joists, traditionally used to carry sand or other material as thermal and acoustic insulation (pugging). →6, →8

pug mill see mortar mill.

pulled bend in plumbing and drainage, a bend in metal pipework formed by mechanical bending with special tools.

pulley room see lift pulley room.

pull handle 1 a handle fixed to a door, window or hatch, containing a grip by which it can be pulled open. →51
2 see bow handle.
3 see cranked pull handle, offset handle. →51
4 see wire pull handle, wire handle. →51

pulpit a raised structure in a church from which a sermon is delivered.
see *Romanesque church* illustration. →99
see *Scandinavian hall church* illustration. →102
see *altar* illustration. →116

pulpitum Lat.; the raised stage area of an ancient Roman theatre. →89

pulverized fuel-ash, fly-ash; a fine material extracted from the combustion gases of bituminous coal, used as a binder in some cements.

pulvin 1 'cushion'; see dosseret. →115
2 see pulvinus. →90

pulvinar Lat.; the private box or enclosure of the Emperor, consuls or other dignitaries at a Roman amphitheatre, theatre or circus; also called a pulvinarium; plural is pulvinaria. →90

pulvinus 1 'cushion' (Lat.); the baluster-shaped piece at the sides of an Ionic capital, which joins the paired volutes on either face. →90
2 see dosseret. →115

pumice a light, porous lava stone or volcanic glass with a high silica content, used as an abrasive and a polishing compound.

pump 1 a mechanical device for providing the force to move mass materials in liquid, granular or gaseous form, or to compress gases.
2 see concrete pump.
3 see site pump.

pumpable concrete concrete of a consistency that enables it to be placed with a pump when fresh.

pumped circulation the circulation of water supply, gas or other liquid in a mechanical service installation, induced by pressure from a pump.

pumped drainage, pumped sewerage; an installation in which sewage and foul water are conveyed from a building to a sewer at a higher level, requiring mechanical pumps or compressed air.

pumped sewerage see pumped drainage.

pumping the action of using a pump to move gases, liquids and granular solids, or of altering the pressure of gases.

pumping aid an admixture included in a concrete mix to reduce friction while pumping it into formwork.

pumping station 1 a structure or building designed to house machinery for pumping water, sewerage etc.
2 see sewage pumping station.

pumpkin dome see umbrella dome. →26

pump room a room or small building, often part of a waterworks, in which a pump is situated.

pump screwdriver see spiral ratchet screwdriver.

punch 1 a hard metal tool consisting of a shaft with a patterned end, used with a hammer or press for embossing designs and lettering into a metal surface.
2 a pointed steel masonry chisel used for the rough dressing of stone. →41
3 see centre punch.
4 see nail set.

puncheon in traditional timber frame construction, a vertical framing member or stud in a wall.

puncheon flooring timber flooring of halved logs with their flat faces upwards.

puncheon roof traditional timber roofing of split logs or puncheons laid longitudinally from ridge to eaves; the join between adjacent puncheons with flat side upwards is covered with a puncheon with flat side downwards. →48

pund a traditional Scandinavian unit of weight equivalent to 425.1 g, nowadays interpreted as a metric unit equal to 500 g.

Punica granatum see pomegranate. →121

punning see tamping.

purchase 1 the exchange of money for goods.
2 a proposal in an architectural competition which is adjudged to be of certain merit, and for which a lesser sum of money is awarded.

purchaser a person or organization which buys goods and services.

purchasing officer a contractor's employee responsible for buying materials and components and scheduling their delivery to site.

pure aluminium aluminium which contains less than 1% of impurities or alloys.

puree Indian yellow pigment in crude form.

purging the displacement of unwanted air etc. by another gas in a gas pipeline.

purification plant an establishment in which contaminated material such as waste or soil water is purified.

Purism a style in art from 1918 based on cubism, in which forms and subjects are rendered geometrically and the use of colour follows a strict system.

purity see colour purity.

purlin 1 in roof construction, a horizontal beam running parallel to the ridge to give added intermediate support for roof joists or rafters. →4, →33
2 see trussed purlin. →33
3 see steel purlin. →60
4 see templum. →47

purlin brace see wind brace.

purline outdated spelling for purlin. →33

purlin roof, 1 double roof; roof construction in which secondary support is given to rafters by purlins. →33
2 see trussed purlin roof. →33

purple a shade of colour between crimson and violet, formed when red and blue are blended, originally obtained as a pigment from the shellfish Murex purpurea, Murex brandaris, or other molluscs of the genera Nucella, Thais; it is the complementary colour for green and does not appear in the visible spectrum; see below for list of purple and violet pigments.
alizarin violet.
Burgundy violet, see manganese violet.
Byzantine purple, Byzantium purple.
cobalt violet.
dioxazine purple.
Grecian purple, see Tyrian purple.
magenta.
manganese violet.
mineral violet, see manganese violet.
ostrum, see Tyrian purple.
permanent violet, see manganese violet.
purple of the ancients, see Tyrian purple.
purpurin.
quinacridone violet.
Tyrian purple.
violet madder lake, see alizarin violet.

purple of the ancients see Tyrian purple.

purpose made brick a non-standard clay brick specially shaped, or of unusual colour or consistency for a particular purpose; see also special brick. →16

purpurin a red-coloured substance obtained from the root of the madder plant [*Rubia tinctorum*], used as a colourant in dyeing processes.

push button a disc or button-like mechanism which operates an electrical or mechanical device when pressed with the thumb or forefinger.

push-button timer see timer.

pushchair, stroller (Am.); a lightweight wheeled chair, often foldable, for conveying young children.

push pad a protective plate attached to a door leaf but slightly apart from it, by which it can be pushed open.

push plate, finger plate; a protective metal or plastics plate attached to a door leaf, by which it can be pushed open at approximately waist height. →51

push-pull fastener a catch which holds a door closed but releases it on application of pressure to the door leaf.

putlog in scaffolding, horizontal members supporting a walkway.

putlog hole in medieval masonry, one of a number of recesses left in the wall during construction for the insertion of putlogs or scaffolding bearers.

putlog scaffolding scaffolding supported on one side by props or standards and on the other by the building itself.

putti plural form of putto. →123

putto, pl. putti; in Renaissance and Baroque art, the representation of a naked male child, with or without wings, often used as a motif in frescos. →123

putty, 1 glazier's putty, glazing putty; a mixture of chalk and linseed oil traditionally used for the fixing of glazing into a window frame, for stopping or spackling etc.
2 see glazing compound.
3 a shade of yellowish grey which takes its name from the colour of linseed oil putty.

putty fronting, face putty, front putty; in glazing, a triangular fillet of putty applied to the external edges of a window pane to hold it in place.

putty knife, spackling knife, stopping knife; a knife with a metal blade used by a decorator and glazier for applying filler, stopping, putty etc. →43

putty rubber, kneaded rubber; a soft, pliable eraser used by artists and illustrators for rubbing out pencil and crayon marks.

PVA polyvinyl alcohol.

PVAC polyvinyl acetate.
PVA glue polyvinyl acetate glue.
PVC polyvinyl chloride.
PVC-U window plastics window; a window whose frame is made primarily from PVC-U plastics.
PVDC polyvinylidene chloride.
PVDF polyvinylidene fluoride.
PVF polyvinyl fluoride.
pwree see Indian yellow.
pycnostyle 'close columned'; in classical architecture, the spacing of rowed columns (intercolumniation) at a distance of one and a half column diameters between adjacent columns. →77
pylon **1** in Egyptian architecture, one of a pair of gigantic tapered stone towers surrounding a monumental temple gateway. →72
2 a large freestanding open-lattice steel structure for carrying overhead power lines.
3 a tall steel or concrete tower from which suspension or cable-stay bridge cables are strung; a bridge pylon. →32
4 see lighting mast.
pylon temple an Egyptian temple type with monumental gateways formed by twinned pylons. →72
pynnion see pignon.
pyramid **1** a solid shape in which one surface is a polygon and the others are triangles which meet at a single point.
2 a huge monumental Egyptian stone tomb, the burial place of a Pharaoh, usually consisting of four sloping triangular sides culminating at an apex; an Egyptian pyramid. →70, →71
3 see step pyramid. →70
4 see bent pyramid, blunt pyramid. →70
5 see Nubian pyramid. →70
6 see ziggurat. →67
7 see teocalli, Mayan pyramid. →67
pyramid builders, the Age of see Old Kingdom. →70
pyramid causeway in ancient Egyptian architecture, a covered ceremonial route or corridor leading from a valley temple to a mortuary temple at the foot of a pyramid, notably at sites of the Nile valley pyramids. →71
pyramid complex the ceremonial area of buildings and structures surrounding an ancient Egyptian pyramid. →70, →71
pyramidion a small pyramid such as the pyramid-shaped termination of an Egyptian obelisk. →73
pyramid roof a hipped roof on a square plan whose four identical triangular roof planes meet at a central point.
pyramid stop see broach stop.
pyramid temple a mortuary temple connected specifically to a pyramid, or part of an Egyptian pyramid complex. →70, →71
pyrargyrite, dark-red silver ore; a dark red mineral ore of silver, similar to proustite.
Pyrex a trade name for borosilicate glass.
pyrite see iron pyrites.
pyrites hard, pale-coloured crumbly mineral sulphides of metal in mineral form, especially iron disulphide; see iron pyrites.
pyroclastic rock any rock which has been ejected by volcanic action.
pyrogenic rock see igneous rock.
pyrolusite a grey metallic mineral, natural manganese dioxide, $\mathbf{MnO_2}$, used for colouring glass and an important ore of manganese.
pyrolysis the decomposition or chemical alteration of a substance by the action of heat.
pyromorphite a green, brown, orange or white, greasy mineral, chloritic lead phosphate, a locally important ore of lead.
pyrope, Bohemian garnet, Cape ruby; a reddish variety of the mineral garnet.
pyroxenite a dark-coloured igneous rock composed almost entirely of the mineral pyroxene.
pyroxene a dark green, black or brown mineral composed of calcium and magnesium silicates; a common component of igneous rocks.
see augite.
see coccolite.
pyrrhotine see pyrrhotite.
pyrrhotite, pyrrhotine; a brownish-yellow metallic mineral, naturally occurring iron sulphide, **FeS**; in nickel rich form, used as an important ore of nickel.
Pyrus communis see pear.
pyx in religious architecture, a vessel in which the consecrated bread of the Eucharist is kept.

Q

qibla see kiblah.
qiblah see kiblah.
Qing see Ching.
quad see quadrangle.
quad crown a British standard paper size; 30" × 40", 762 mm × 1016 mm. →Table 6
quad double crown a British standard paper size; 40" × 60", 1016 mm × 1524 mm. →Table 6
quadrangle 1 any planar four-sided figure with four internal angles.
2 quad; an open square or rectangular space wholly surrounded by buildings, often with a central lawn and within a college or monastery.
quadrant 1 a sector of a circle bounded by two radii at right angles to one another and the enclosed length of circumference; one quarter of a circle.
2 a decorative strip or moulding which is a quarter circle in cross-section. →14
3 a piece of joinery trim which is a quarter circle in cross-section. →2
quadrant cross, quadrate cross, nowy quadrant cross; a cross with a square transcribed across the crossing of the arms. →118
quadrate cross see quadrant cross. →118
quadratic cross see Greek cross. →118
quadratum see opus quadratum.
quadrifrons Lat., see quadrifrontal arch. →93
quadrifrontal arch (Lat. quadrifrons) a Roman urban monument situated at the meeting of two crossing streets, with four arches, one on each side, to allow passage through in all directions. →93
quadriga Lat.; in classical architecture, a triumphal statue or rendering of a chariot pulled by four horses. →89
quadrilateral 1 a planar four-sided figure.
2 a description of a shape or area with four defined boundaries.
quadripartite vault a masonry vault sprung on four points of support, square or rectangular in plan and composed of four curved roof surfaces or compartments divided by ribs. →26
quadriportico an area closed off on four sides by building form or masonry, with an entrance portico on each side.
quadro riportato decorative ceiling painting which depicts scenes in normal perspective.
quaestorium Lat.; the administrative and financial building of a Roman military camp, the paymaster's office. →104
quaking aspen [*Populus tremuloides*]; a species of aspen found in North America; see aspen for further information.
quality, grade; the classifiable characteristics of a material or product as demanded by use or suitability.
quality competition trading competition based on quality alone rather than price of goods and services supplied.
quality control a system whereby products or services are checked for a specified quality at each stage in processing.
quality grading the classification of sawn timber according to visual defects.
quantity 1 the amount in weight, running length or number of a product, material or component required for a constructional project.
2 those physical properties of things which can be measured.
quantity survey a central contract document itemizing materials, products and components used in a building, their amounts and costs, undertaken by a qualified quantity surveyor, and presented as a bill of quantities prior to construction.
quantity surveyor a qualified professional responsible for drawing up bills of quantities and advising the client on contractual and financial matters.
quarry 1 a place where building stone and other minerals are excavated from the ground.
2 see quarry tile. →44
quarry finish an uneven, rough-textured stone surface treatment, produced by dressing with hand or machine tools to resemble stone in its natural state; also variously called rubble or scabbled finish, or pitch or rock faced, and hammer dressed or pitched when produced by hand tooling. →12
quarrying the extraction of rock from the ground for use in construction etc.
quarry tile, floor quarry; a thick unglazed clay floor tile formed by extrusion. →44
quart a unit of liquid volume equal to one quarter of a gallon; in Britain equivalent to 1.14 l, in North America equal to 0.95 l for liquids and 1.10 l for dry capacity.
quarter 1 a unit of weight equal to one fourth part of a hundredweight; in Britain equal to 28 lb or 12.7 kg, in North America equal to 25 lb or 11.3 kg.
2 a unit of length equal to one fourth part of a yard, equal to 9" or 22.86 cm.
3 a unit of length in North America equal to one fourth part of a mile.
4 a unit of nautical distance equal to one fourth part of a fathom.
5 see quarter bat.
6 an urban district with its own cultural or functional identity.
7 any of four equal divisions of a shield in heraldry. →125
quarter bat, quarter; a brick which has been cut to one quarter of its length for use in brickwork bonding. →21
quarter brick wall a thin brick wall laid with bricks on edge, whose thickness is the same as the height of a brick. →21
quarter cut see quarter sliced veneer. →10
quartering way see cleavage plane.
quarterpace stairs, quarter-space stair; an L-shaped stair which turns through 90° at a landing. →45
quarter round 1 a decorative moulding which is a quarter of a circle in cross-section; a quadrant. →14
2 see cock beak moulding, thumbnail bead moulding. →14
quartersawing, 1 radial cutting, rift sawing; a method of converting timber by sawing a log radially into quarters and then converting the segments to provide fine quality timber boards with relatively even perpendicular end grain. →2
2 see sawing round the log. →2
quartersawn, 1 edge grained, radially cut, rift sawn, vertical grained; a description of timber sawn approximately radially from a log.
2 see quarter sliced veneer. →10
3 see quartersawing. →2
4 see sawing round the log. →2
quarter sliced veneer a decorative veneer formed by the radial slicing of a quarter log or flitch; also called quarter cut or quartersawn. →10
quarter-space stairs see quarterpace stairs. →45
quarter turn stair, 1 angle stair, L-stair; an L-shaped stair which turns through a right angle on its ascent, either with a landing, as with a quarterpace stair, or with a series of wedge-shaped steps. →45
2 see quarterpace stairs. →45

quarto plate, heavy plate; relatively thick, uncoiled and heavy steel plate rolled to individual specification regarding composition and size, manufactured on a special quarto plate mill.

quartz a very hard, transparent, whitish mineral form of silica, often found naturally in the form of hexagonal crystals; a violet form is known as amethyst; all types included as separate entries are listed below.
amethyst.
chalcedony.
citrine.
milky quartz.
quartzite.
rose quartz.
smoky quartz.

quartz diorite an igneous rock, similar to granite and diorite, containing a high proportion of quartz; its uses in building are similar to that of granite.

quartz glass see fused silica glass.

quartzite a white, grey or reddish metamorphic or sedimentary rock which consists almost wholly of quartz; it is durable and resistant to chemical and frost action, and is used for flooring tiles.

quartz porphyry see rhyolite.

quasi-reticulatum see opus-quasi reticulatum. →83

quasi-satellite in town planning, a town located near to a large urban centre, which in character resembles a suburb of that city rather than an independent town.

quatrefoil **1** a decorative motif consisting of four stylized leaf designs radiating out from a point. →108, →109, →110
2 see pointed quatrefoil. →108

quatrefoil arch an arch composed of four lobes or foils.

quatrefoil church see tetraconch church.

quattrocento Italian early Renaissance in art and architecture in the 1400s.

quay a solid stone or masonry structure, part of a harbour to which boats can be moored, loaded and unloaded etc.

qubbah the domed shrine of an Islamic nobleman or saint.

Queen Anne arch a pointed arch over a tripartite window, with a horizontal intrados and a protruding arched portion in the centre.

Queen Anne revival a revival style in town house architecture in England from the 1800s, characterized by the use of red brick, white framed windows, bay and oriel windows and dramatic roof forms.

Queen Anne style an architectural and interior decoration style in England during the reign of Queen Anne (1702–1714), evident principally in urban buildings and residences and characterized by the use of red brickwork in a mix of Renaissance and Baroque motifs from Holland and England.

queen closer **1** a cut brick which shows a half-header width in a brick wall; a brick halved lengthways to fit in with a bonding pattern. →21
2 a quarter bat.
3 a three quarter brick which has been cut in half lengthways. →21

queen post in traditional timber roof construction, one of a pair of posts carrying purlins in a queen post truss. →33

queen post bridge a bridge whose main support is a framework in the shape of a queen post truss. →32

queen post collar rafter roof in traditional timber roof construction, a collar roof with purlins supported on queen posts. →33

queen post rafter roof in traditional timber frame construction, a rafter roof with purlins supported on queen posts. →33

queen post roof see queen post rafter roof. →33

queen post truss in timber roof construction, a timber truss consisting of a tie beam, a pair of vertical queen posts, a collar or straining beam and principal rafters. →33

queen strut in timber roof construction, a queen post that does not carry a purlin directly. →33

queen strut roof truss in timber roof construction, a timber truss in which rafters are supported by purlins carried on queen struts. →33

quenching in the tempering of metals, rapid cooling of the heated metal by plunging it in water or some other liquid.

Quercus spp. see oak.
Quercus alba, see white oak, American white oak.
Quercus mongolica, see Japanese oak.
Quercus petraea, see durmast (oak).
Quercus robur, see pedunculate oak.
Quercus rubra, see red oak, northern red oak.
Quercus suber, see cork oak.

query language a synthetic computing language in which non-expert users can access a database.

quicklime, anhydrous lime, burnt lime, caustic lime; lime which has been produced by the burning of limestone or calcium carbonate, **$CaCO_3$**, to form calcium oxide; mixed with water to form slaked lime. →Table 5

quick-setting Portland cement a Portland cement which sets more rapidly than ordinary Portland cement.

quicksilver a traditional name for the metal mercury.

quick strip formwork formwork used for casting and supporting the underside of a concrete slab, which can be removed without necessitating the removal of its supports.

quill an ink pen made from a feather whose end is cut, shaped and split; a simple dip pen used for drawing and writing.

quilted figure a decorative figure in veneers cut from irregular grained timber, especially bigleaf maple, as if the surface is quilted.

quinacridone red a synthetic lightfast organic red pigment used in many types of paint.

quinacridone violet a synthetic organic violet-red pigment used since the 1960s in oil, watercolour and acrylic paints.

quincunx Lat.; an arrangement of five objects in a square formation with one at each corner and one in the centre; found as a derivative form in Roman town planning and the basic layout of some Byzantine churches.

quincunx church see cross-domed church. →95

quintana **1** see porta quintana.
2 see via quintana. →104

quire **1** a measure of paper, 25 (formerly 24) sheets.
2 archaic spelling of choir.

quirk a narrow decorative cutting in a moulding or ornate surface to separate main elements such as beads, rolls etc.

quirk bead moulding, **1** bead and quirk moulding, quirked bead moulding; a decorative moulding whose cross-section is that of a bead or ovoid formed with a quirk or notch on one or both sides. →14
2 see flush bead moulding. →14

quirked bead moulding see quirk bead moulding. →14

quirking tool a small masonry chisel for cutting narrow grooves or quirks in decorative stonework. →41

quoin one of a series of staggered corner stones or brick at an external masonry corner, often of a different material or colour to the rest of the wall as decoration; also spelled coign or coin. →12

quoining masonry blocks or bricks added to the external corner of a building's wall as quoins. →12

quoit see dolmen.

quonset see Nissen hut.

quotient in mathematics, the result of division of one value by another.

R

Ra the ancient Egyptian sun god, carried on his solar barque across the sky each day; depicted with the head of a falcon (Ra-Horakhti); also written as Re. →74
rabbet see rebate. →5
rabbet plane see rebate plane.
Rabitz plaster special gypsum lime plaster reinforced with a mesh and animal hair, invented by Karl Rabitz in 1878, used primarily for domes and other vaulted structures.
raceway see trunking.
rack and pinion see rack railway.
rack railway, rack and pinion; a railway system for mountainous regions, which uses a system of powered cogs to achieve uphill locomotion.
racking see raking. →21
racking back see raking. →21
rad and dab see wattle and daub.
radial see radial brick.
radial arm saw a circular saw suspended from and moving along a cantilevered arm, used for various cross cuts in wood.
radial block a concrete block manufactured with curving vertical faces, designed for use in curved wall construction. →30
radial brick, arch brick; any special brick shaped for use in a curved or vaulted brick surface such as a well or barrel vault; see also radial stretcher, radial header, culvert stretcher, culvert header. →16
see culvert header. →16
see culvert stretcher. →16
see radial header. →16
see radial stretcher. →16
tapered header, see culvert stretcher. →16
tapered stretcher, see culvert header. →16
radial circuit an electric circuit with a number of appliances attached to a single power supply.
radial configuration the arrangement of cables in a cable-stayed bridge so that they all fan out from a single point near the top of supporting pylons; see harp configuration, fan configuration. →32
radial cutting see quartersawing. →2
radial header a special brick which is wedged shaped in plan, used as a header in a curving brick wall, circular well or chimney stack etc. →16
radial joint one of the joints between voussoirs in a masonry arch.
radially cut see quartersawn.
radial plan a town plan in which urban development occurs primarily along main roads radiating outwards from a city centre.
radial road an urban road providing a link between the central city area and outerlying districts.
radial stretcher a special brick which is bow shaped in one of its long faces and wedge shaped in plan, used as a stretcher in a curving brick wall. →16
radial surface see edge. →2
radian abb. **rad**; the SI unit of angular or circular measurement, equal to the length of one radius along the circumference of the same circle.
radiant heater, radiant panel, radiator; any heating device which imparts thermal energy primarily by radiation.
radiant heating heating in which thermal comfort is provided by radiant heat, as opposed to warm air, convection etc.
radiant moulding see rayonny moulding. →124
radiant panel see radiant heater.
radiata pine, Monterey pine; [Pinus radiata] a softwood from temperate regions with pale pink timber; a very widely planted conifer, used for exterior cladding, flooring and joinery.
radiating chapels a series of projecting chapels radiating from the apse or ambulatory of a Romanesque or Gothic church or cathedral. →100
radiation 1 the transmission of energy in the form of electromagnetic waves.
2 see nuclear radiation.
3 see thermal radiation.
4 see cold radiation.
radiation detector see flame detector.
radiation resistance the ability of a material or construction to resist penetration by nuclear radiation.
radiation-shielding glass 1 any protective glass designed with interlayers and added compounds to reflect or absorb radiation and restrict its transmission.
2 see lead X-ray glass.
3 see electronic shielding glass.
radiation-shielding mortar see X-ray resisting plaster.
radiator 1 a space heating appliance, which may be part of a central heating system or an individual heater, in which hot liquid (water or oil) circulates in a metal chamber.
2 see radiant heater.
radiator brush a long-handled painter's and decorator's brush with either a kinked or a perpendicular wire handle, used for painting difficult or constrained areas such as behind radiators and crevices. →43
radiator heating a hot-water central heating system in which heating water is circulated to radiators.
radical in mathematics, pertaining to or forming the root of an expression.
radioactivity 1 the property of certain chemical elements to decay and release X-rays and gamma-rays.
2 the emissions thus released.
radio studio a building or part of a building from which radio programmes are broadcast.
radium a radioactive, metallic chemical element, **Ra**.
radius 1 in geometry, a line or length from a point around which a curve is described.
2 the length of this line.
3 see bending radius.
radius of curvature in mathematics, the constant dimension from a centre point to the surface of a curve.
radius of gyration in mechanics, the effective distance of the centre of mass of an object from its centre of rotation or oscillation.
radon an inert, radioactive, gaseous, chemical element, **Rn**.
rafter 1 one of a series of timber beams carrying roofing in a sloping roof; the upper member of a roof truss or a sloping roof joist; types included as separate entries are listed below. →33, →48
2 see roof beam. →59
angle rafter.
common rafter.
hip rafter.
horizontal rafter, see common purlin.
jack rafter.
principal rafter.
trimmed rafter.
trimming rafter.
valley rafter.
rafter bracket a roofing accessory for fixing an eaves gutter to the end of a rafter.
rafter roof in timber roof construction, a roof in which rafters are the basic frame supporting the roof covering. →33

raft foundation a foundation consisting of a continuous reinforced concrete slab (usually the lowest floor slab of a building) which transmits overlying loads over its whole area. →29

rag paper high quality durable paper used for banknotes, certificates and for drawing, manufactured from cotton and linen fibres.

ragbolt see anchor bolt. →36

raguly see cross raguly. →118

raguly moulding a crenellated moulding whose castellations are slanting, resembling the stumps left when branches are sawn from a tree trunk. →125

ragwork 1 masonry walling of rough thin stones laid horizontally. →11
2 see slate walling. →11
3 crazy paving, random stone paving; stone paving of irregularly shaped and randomly sized stones. →15

Ra-Horakhti see Ra. →74

rail 1 a horizontal frame member in a door leaf, sash, casement or other framework. →5, →51
see bottom rail. →51, →52, →111
see middle rail, lock rail. →51
see intermediate rail. →51
see top rail. →51, →52, →111
2 a horizontal profile, moulding or section in a balustrade or similar framework. →5, →51
see intermediate rail. →54
3 a lightweight balustrade, open waist-height barrier, handrail etc., see railing. →54
see altar rail, communion rail. →116
see guard rail.
see handrail. →54
see safety rail. →54
see stair rail. →45
see timber handrail.
4 a shaped metal supporting bar for a moving system such as a track, sliding screen or electrical installation.
see chair rail.
see cladding rail. →11
see curtain rail.
dado rail, see chair rail.
see towel rail, drying rail.
5 a steel product, one of a pair of formed bars of specified cross-sectional profile laid side by side to form a railway track.
see monorail.
6 see screed rail.

rail balustrade see railed balustrade. →54

rail bolt see joint bolt.

rail bridge see railway bridge. →64

railed balustrade a balustrade with a number of horizontal parallel rails between handrail and floor level to provide an intermediate barrier; also called a rail balustrade. →54

railing a fence, balustrade or low barrier of metal bars fixed to a frame structure, supported by posts at regular intervals; often used in the plural. →54

railroad see railway.

rail transport any mode of transport in which vehicles travel on a system of preconstructed rails: a generic term for railway, underground and tram systems.

railway, railroad (Am.); a line of parallel rails, a track on which a train can travel.
see *railway* in ideal city illustration. →105

railway bridge a bridge which carries a railway over an obstacle such as a road or river. →64

railway sleeper see sleeper.

railway station an establishment with platforms and associated buildings for a train to pick up and put down passengers.
see *railway station* in ideal city illustration. →105

rain water precipitated from clouds as falling droplets.

rainbow roof a roof in the cross-sectional form of a pointed arch.

rain cap, flue cap; a lightweight protective construction fitted over the upper outlet of a flue to prevent the passage of rainwater and snow. →56, →58

rainproof referring to a component or construction which is impervious to rain or resistant to the penetration of rainwater.

rainwater water precipitated as rain.

rainwater fittings see rainwater goods.

rainwater goods, rainwater fittings; gutters, downpipes and other metal, plastic or ceramic fittings, often part of a manufacturer's system of parts, used to convey rainwater from roofs and other surfaces into drains.

rainwater gully, surface water gully; an inlet to lead surface water and rainwater from paved external areas and downpipes to a drainage system.

rainwater gutter, roof gutter; a slightly sloping channel at an eaves, abutment etc., to collect rainwater from a roof surface and convey it to a downpipe. →46

rainwater head, conductor header (Am.), hopper head, leader header (Am.), rainwater header, rainwater hopper; in roof construction, a funnel-shaped vessel designed to collect rainwater from a gutter and convey it to a downpipe. →46

rainwater header see rainwater head. →46

rainwater hopper see rainwater head. →46

rainwater outlet, roof outlet, roof gully; a component, fitting or construction through which rainwater collecting on a flat roof surface is led out to a drain, downpipe etc.

rainwater pipe 1 a drainpipe conveying rainwater away from a roof or paved surface. →46
2 see downpipe. →46

rainwater shoe see pipe shoe.

rainwater spout, gargoyle, outlet, water spout; in roof construction, a piped fitting to cast rainwater from a gutter or roof surface away from the roof and wall surfaces of a building. →100

rainwater system a system of gutters, channels, outlets and pipes which collects water from roofs and other areas and conveys it to a drainage system.

raised access floor see platform floor. →44

raised countersunk head screw see oval head screw. →36

raised fillet a plain, thin decorative moulding, protruding from a flat surface. →14

raised floor 1 any floor which has been raised as a dais, platform, stage or access floor.
2 see access floor. →44

raised grain in woodworking, the natural raising of wood fibres after the wet application of a finish, sanded down on drying before a final coat.

raised hearth fireplace a fireplace whose hearth is constructed at a distance above floor level. →55

raised moulding see bolection moulding.

raised pattern flooring see studded rubber flooring. →44

raised pattern plate see chequerplate. →34

rake see batter.

rake angle see cutting angle.

raked joint, keyed joint, raked-out joint, recessed joint; a brickwork mortar joint which has been recessed to a certain depth either as a key for plaster or pointing, or for decorative effect. →16

raked-out joint see raked joint. →16

raker 1 in bricklaying, a simple metal tool used for removing excess or old mortar from a joint.
2 one of the slanting support props in a raking shore.
see bottom raker.
see middle raker.
see top raker.

raking 1 referring to vertical joints in adjacent courses of bonded masonry which form a regular diagonal sawtoothed pattern in a wall surface; bricks are laid with one quarter brick overlap. →18
2 racking back, raking back; the laying of bricks or stones in stepped layers at the end of a brick wall

under construction to support a builder's line and ease the laying of the rest of the wall. →21
3 using a rake to even out a granular surface, or remove excess material from a lawn or other landscaped surface.
raking arch see rampant arch. →24
raking back see raking. →21
raking bond any brickwork pattern whose vertical joints form a regular diagonal sawtoothed pattern in the wall surface.
see raking Flemish bond. →18
raking Flemish double stretcher bond, see Flemish double stretcher bond. →19
see raking stretcher bond. →17
raking flashing in roofing, a flashing at the junction of the side of a sloping roof and a parapet or wall; the upper surface of its upstand is sloping at the same pitch as the roof plane.
raking Flemish bond brickwork laid in Flemish bond with a quarter brick overlap between courses so that the vertical joints form a regular diagonal sawtoothed pattern in the wall surface. →18
raking pile, batter pile; in foundation technology, any pile placed at a slant to the vertical; often a tension pile. →29
raking shore excavation shoring in the form of a series of slanting props to support a wall.
raking stretcher bond 1 a brickwork bond consisting entirely of courses of stretchers, in which alternate courses are laid with a quarter brick overlap. →17
2 the same with modular bricks in which alternating courses are laid with a one third brick overlap.
ram 1 see monkey.
2 see Khnum. →74
RAM random access memory.
ramin [*Gonystylus spp.*] a group of hardwoods from South-East Asia with pale, featureless, timber; it smells unpleasant when freshly cut and is used for joinery and furniture.
rammed earth construction see pisé.
ramming see tamping.
ramp 1 a sloping planar surface providing access from one level to another.
see *ramp* in Egyptian mortuary temple illustration. →72
2 see apron.
3 see slip road. →63
4 see vehicular ramp.
ramp garage a multistorey car park in which traffic ascends and descends via a series of ramps between floors.
ramp stair a gradually ascending stair with deep treads and short risers, resembling a ramp. →45
rampant arch, raking arch; an arch whose imposts are at different levels. →24
rampant vault a masonry vault which is a rampant or asymmetrical arch in uniform cross-section, used over stairs and changes in level. →25
rampart 1 the fortified wall or earthwork surrounding a castle, encampment or town, used as a defensive barrier, see enceinte; originally the embankment of earth excavated from a surrounding ditch. →103
2 see agger. →104
3 see alure. →103
4 see earthwork.
5 see vallum. →104
ramped floor a sloping deck in a multistorey car park, part of the circulation system on which vehicles are also parked.
ranch a large cattle farm, usually in America, complete with fields and farmhouse.
ranch house 1 the dwelling house on a ranch.
2 a single storey American dwelling type built in a rustic style to imitate a house on a ranch.
random-access memory, RAM; a temporary storage area in a computer, from which data is lost when the computer is switched off.
random ashlar 1 see uncoursed ashlar. →11
2 see coursed squared rubble. →11
random bond 1 see irregular bond. →17
2 see random paving. →15
random match, mismatched; veneering using veneers which are variable in grain pattern and are glued in no strict pattern. →10
random paving 1 paving in rectangular pavers of differing sizes in no particular recognizable pattern. →15
2 see ragwork. →15
random rubble masonry construction of roughly shaped stones not laid in courses; also called uncoursed rubble. →11
random squared rubble masonry see uncoursed squared rubble masonry. →11
random stone paving see ragwork. →15
range a traditional coal or wood-fired masonry or cast-iron stove with hot plates on top, kept continually warm and used for cooking food.
ranger see waling.
range work 1 stonework of coursed ashlar in small laid stones.
2 stonework which is composed of coursed ashlar with small stones; same as bats.
rank see taxi rank.
Ranunculus spp. see buttercup yellow.
rapakivi, rapakivi granite; a reddish or brown porphyritic hornblende granite originating in Finland, characterized by roundish deposits of feldspar, prone to decay and used as building stone for cladding.
rapakivi granite see rapakivi.
rapid-hardening Portland cement, high early-strength cement; a Portland cement that produces concrete which hardens more rapidly in early stages than ordinary concrete.
rapid-transit a form of urban public transport which runs on a system of rails or preconstructed tracks.
rare gas see noble gas.
rasp a toothed metal tool or coarse file for rough shaping and smoothing of wood and plastics.
raspberry (red) a shade of red which takes its name from the colour of the ripe fruit of the raspberry plant [*Rubus idaeus*].
ratan see rattan.
ratch see ratchet.
ratchet, ratch; a gear wheel with slanting teeth and a stopper or pawl which allows for turning in one direction only; used in some winches, hand drills and screwdrivers.
ratchet screwdriver a screwdriver with a ratchet mechanism to operate in one selected direction at a time.
rate a regulated scale of prices and fees for goods and services.
rate of combustion see combustion rate.
rate of growth see growth rate.
rate of placement see rate of placing.
rate of placing, rate of placement; the speed at which concrete is placed in formwork, regulated to prevent drying, cracking or the formation of voids.
rath see ringfort.
ratha, monolithic temple; an Indian temple carved out of rock.
ratification in town planning, final approval of a town plan at the highest level, after which it becomes a legal document.
ratio the proportion of one quantity in relation to another, expressed as a fraction.
rational endowed with or based on reason.
rational number in mathematics, a number expressible as an integer or a ratio of integers.
rationalism a movement in architecture which sought to rationalize the process of design and construction.
rationalization the act of reordering a system, structure, business or plan in a logical way.

rattan, ratan; the dried stems of a range of tropical climbing palms used for making cane furniture and fittings.

rat-trap bond, Chinese bond, rowlock bond, silverlock bond; a brickwork bond in which all bricks are laid on edge with each course consisting of alternating headers and stretchers in a similar way to Flemish bond, used for hybrid cavity wall construction. →17

ravelin a detached angular or V-shaped outwork in front of a rampart to provide protection for a castle wall or fortification; see also demilune. →104

raven a shade of deep black which takes its name from the colour of the raven [*Corvus corax*].

raw cork untreated cork which has been cut from a cork oak.

raw plywood plywood whose face plies have undergone no treatment during manufacture other than sanding or scraping.

raw sewage, crude sewage, untreated sewage; sewage which has yet to undergo any treatment at a water treatment plant.

raw sienna see sienna.

raw umber, Sicilian brown, terra ombre; dark brown iron oxide containing manganese hydroxide, used as a pigment in a similar way to ochre.

raw water water obtained by a water board for distribution to a water supply, to which further purifying aids are sometimes added.

ray the perceived straight line along which any given radiation travels.

ray acoustics see geometrical acoustics.

ray figure, ray fleck, splash figure, storied rays, ripple marks; a decorative figure produced by the radial slicing of certain hardwoods for veneers, caused by the rays in the wood appearing as ripples in the surface.

ray figured veneer decorative veneer with ray figure.

ray fleck see ray figure.

Rayonnant style the middle phase of French Gothic architecture from the 1200s and 1300s, characterized by radiating lines in tracery.

rayonny moulding banded ornament consisting of a series of flame-like motifs; primarily found in heraldic motifs; also called radiant, rayonnant, rayoné moulding. →124

rays tissues in the structure of wood radiating in bands from the pith towards the bark of a tree.

r.c., r-c, rc reinforced concrete.

r-c column 1 reinforced concrete column, see concrete column.
2 see precast column.

Re see Ra. →74

reaction 1 a physical force exerted to counteract an imposed force in a state of equilibrium.
2 see chemical reaction.

reaction wood wood with unevenly spaced growth rings, which is weak and prone to warping, resulting from abnormal growth of a tree. →1

reactor see nuclear reactor.

reading a value which can be read from a gauge or meter.

reading room a room intended for study and reading, often part of a library or educational facility.

read-only memory, ROM; a data storage device or disk which retains computer information permanently in an unalterable state.

readymix concrete see ready-mix concrete.

ready-mixed concrete concrete which has been mixed either in a suitable vehicle or off-site mixing plant, and is delivered for immediate use on site; also written as readymix.

ready-mixed mortar mortar delivered to site mixed and with water added; also written as readymix.

ready-mixed plaster plaster delivered to site mixed and with water added; also written as readymix.

real estate 1 see landed property.
2 see property.

realism a movement in art from the 1800s which sought to represent reality such as it is perceived; any art which sets out with similar objectives.

realization see completion.

real number a number in mathematics which has no part which contains the square root of a negative number.

real property a traditional English term for immovable property, see landed property.

real value the commercial value of an item without respect to fluctuation in the value of currency; the amount of goods which can be purchased with a sum of money.

ream a measure, 500 sheets of paper.

reamer a hand tool or drill bit with a straight or tapered serrated blade, used for enlarging or cleaning out drilled holes. →42

reaming the enlargement or finishing of a drilled hole in metal, rock and other materials.

rear elevation an elevation of a building which faces towards a courtyard or garden; a minor elevation at the back of a building.

rebar see reinforcing bar. →27

rebate, 1 rabbet; a step-shaped reduction along the edge of or in the face of a piece of timber or other component, usually to receive another piece. →5
2 a housing in a window or door frame in which a door leaf, casement or pane of glass is fitted.
3 see glazing rebate.
4 a hinge rebate, see hinge mortise. →38
5 a sum of money paid back or deducted as a result of commercial dealings.
6 discount; a reduction in the basic price of goods and services.

rebated block channel a drainage channel which is rectangular in cross-section, shaped with a semi-circular recess and rebates to house a grating along its upper face.

rebated corner joint a lapped corner joint used in cabinetmaking for joining boards and sheets at right angles, in which the end of one piece is grooved near its edge to receive the rebated edge of the other piece. →5

rebated door a door whose leaf has edges rebated to form a small overlap with surrounding framing members. →51

rebated featheredged board timber cladding board, wedge shaped and rebated in cross-section. →8

rebate joint a timber joint in which one piece has been rebated to receive another.
see lapped corner joint. →5
see rebated corner joint. →5

rebate plane, rabbet plane; a plane for cutting a groove or rebate in a piece of wood.

rebound material from spray concreting and painting processes which does not adhere to the intended surfaces and bounces off or is otherwise lost as waste.

recaulking the refilling of horizontal timber joints in log construction with caulk after the initial settlement of the building frame.

receipt, bill of sale, voucher; a written or printed document which serves as proof that an item has been sold, or that the ownership of an item has changed hands.

reception, reception area; an area, desk or foyer in a hotel, hospital or other public building in which visitors may check in and receive information.

reception area 1 a space in a building for receiving visitors, making appointments and dealing with reservations.
2 see reception.

reception room see reception area, a closed space, room or hall with the same function.
see apadana.
see durbar.
see salon.
see tablinum. →88

recercelée see cross moline. →117

recess 1 any setting back or a depression of a wall in plan, often to allow for servicing installations, a door or window, or ornament.
2 see niche.
3 see fireplace recess. →55
4 dining recess, see dinette.

recessed bead moulding see flush bead moulding. →14

recessed column a column incorporated within a small recess in an adjacent wall. →13

recessed fixing see flush mounting.

recessed joint see raked joint. →16

recessed luminaire a light fitting designed to be flush mounted into a ceiling, or set into a suitable niche or recess.

recessed portal a main doorway in a Romanesque or Gothic church, stepped inwards with columns bearing sculpted figures. →113

recessed screw cup, countersunk washer, inset screw cup; a pressed metal recessed ring for a countersunk screw to protect the base into which it is being fixed. →36

reciprocal, inverse; in mathematics, the quotient resulting from the division of one (1) by a given number or function.

recirculated air in air conditioning, return air which is reused once it has been pumped back to the plant rooms.

recirculation duct in air conditioning, a duct conveying return air back to a plant room for reuse.

reconditioning the steam treatment of improperly seasoned timber to reduce distortion and warping.

reconstituted marble see reconstituted stone.

reconstituted stone, reconstituted marble; a stone product consisting of fragments of marble or other soft rock embedded in a matrix of resin, cement or marble dust, cast, cut and shaped as building stone.

reconstructed stone see cast stone.

reconstruction 1 restoring or rebuilding a dilapidated, ruined or non-existent building, often using archive material.
2 the product of this process.
3 see reorganization.

record 1 in computer-aided design, a set of one or more consecutive fields of data on a related subject treated as a unit.
2 see physical record.

record drawing, survey drawing; a drawing produced from data and measurements taken during a land or building survey; a measured drawing.

recording studio see sound recording studio.

recoverable tie a formwork tie removed for reuse once formwork is struck.

recoverable waste, recyclable waste; refuse such as organic matter, glass, metals, plastics and paper, sorted and reused in the manufacturing industry.

recreation activities which people do for amusement, entertainment and relaxation in their free time and of their own free will.

recreation area an area such as a park, playground, public open space or sports field intended for recreational use by the public.

recreation centre see leisure centre.

recreation ground an area of land, often grassed, designated for recreation and sports.

recreation room see activity space.

rectangle a planar four-sided figure in which opposite sides are parallel and all internal angles are 90°; see also square, oblong.

rectangular column a column whose shaft is rectangular in cross-section.

rectangular grid floor see waffle floor.

rectangular gutter see box gutter.

rectangular hollow section, RHS; a rectangular hollow steel section formed by rolling and welding steel plate, used for structural purposes such as framing, columns, posts etc. →34

rectangular tile any tile whose face is rectangular in shape. →20

rectangular tube a metal profile of hollow rectangular cross-section; when in steel and used for structural purposes, it is called a rectangular hollow section, RHS. →34
see *metal tubes* illustration. →34
see rectangular hollow section. →34

rectification 1 in map-making, the correction of perspective effects in aerial photographs to produce exact plan views of an area.
2 the purifying of alcohols by repeated distilling.
3 the conversion of alternating current into direct current.

Rectilinear style see Perpendicular style.

rectilinear tracery, panel tracery, perpendicular tracery; Gothic tracery found in churches of the Perpendicular style, characterized by the use of a lacework of vertical glazing bars. →110

recyclable waste see recoverable waste.

recycling the process whereby waste materials are collected, sorted, treated in some way and reused for new materials or products.

red a general name for a range of wavelengths of coloured light from the visible spectrum between 640 and 780 m.
see list of red pigments under **red pigments**.

red alder [*Alnus rubra*] a North American hardwood with rich reddish timber, stronger than common alder, used for furniture and as a substitute for mahogany.

redan a small angular outwork to provide protection for a castle wall or fortification; a small ravelin, also written as reden. →104

red brick a very common clay brick containing iron oxide which gives it a reddish brown colour.

red cedar [*Thuja plicata*] see western red cedar.

red copper ore see cuprite.

red crown the symbolic head-dress of ancient Lower Egypt, a low red garment with a staff at the rear; often later subsumed into the Combined crown of the New Kingdom. →74

red deal the timber from a Scots pine tree.

reddle see red oxide paint.

reden see redan. →104

redevelopment 1 the rebuilding, reshaping or improvement of a building, block or urban area.
2 see urban renewal.
3 see comprehensive redevelopment.

redevelopment area an area of land on which redevelopment has been planned or realised.

redoubt a small polygonal fortified structure or earthwork outlying a castle or fortification, one serving as a refuge; also written as redout, reduit. →104

redout see redoubt. →104

red gold a metal alloy consisting of 95% gold and 5% copper.

red iron oxide see iron oxide.

red knot an intergrown knot in softwood. →1

red lead, 1 lead oxide, lead primer, minium; a heavy poisonous lead oxide ($\mathbf{Pb_3O_4}$) pigment used in paints, metal primers, glass, glazes, putties and batteries.
2 see coqueliquot.
3 saturnine red, minium; a poisonous opaque red pigment consisting of lead monoxide and lead peroxide; used for its physical and chemical properties for exterior use and the priming of steel.

red lead ore see crocoite.

red maple [*Acer rubrum*] a North American hardwood; a soft maple used for furniture and panelling.

red nickel sulphide see niccolite.

red oak [*Quercus spp.*] a group of hardwoods, especially the northern red oak, Quercus rubra, from eastern North America with light reddish brown timber which is relatively hard, heavy, strong, coarse grained and used for external cladding and interiors.

red ochre see red oxide paint.

red oxide iron oxide when used as a red pigment.

red oxide paint traditional paint used for external timber surfaces, a mixture of earth rich in iron oxide and oil; the earth, used in differing mediums as paint is variously known as red ochre, reddle, ruddle and terra rossa.

red pigments
alizarin.
aniline colour.
anthraquinoid red.
antimony vermilion.
cadmium red.
carmine.
carthame, see safflower.
Chinese red, see chrome red.
Chinese vermilion.
chrome red.
cinnabar.
cochineal.
Derby red, see chrome red.
English vermilion.
ferric oxide, see iron oxide.
garance.
haematite, see iron oxide.
iron oxide.
kermes.
madder lake.
mauve.
minium, see red lead.
Munich lake, see carmine.
nacarat carmine.
naphthol carbamide.
natural madder, see madder lake.
orange vermilion.
perinone orange.
Perkin's violet, see mauve.
perylene.
purpurin.
quinacridone red.
red iron oxide, see iron oxide.
red lead.
red ochre, see red oxide paint.
rose madder, see madder lake.
safflower.
saturnine red, see red lead.
scarlet vermilion, see vermilion.
selenium red, see cadmium red.
toluidine red.
vermilion.
Vienna lake, see carmine.
zinnober, see cinnabar.

red ring rot, canker rot, honeycomb rot, red rot, ring scale fungus, white pocket rot, white pitted rot, white speck; [*Phellinus pini*, *Fomes pini*, *Trametes pini*] a fungal decay in living conifers in Europe and North America which, in its early stages, forms a red stain in the heartwood, spreading as pockets of white filaments which weaken the timber.

red rot see red ring rot.

reducer 1 see thinner.
2 see reducing fitting.

reducing 1 making the size or quantity of something smaller.
2 in design and graphics, the changing in scale of an object so that it appears smaller.

reducing bend a piece of curved pipe for changing the direction of flow and reducing the diameter of a pipeline.

reducing bush see socket reducer.

reducing cross a pipe fitting to connect two smaller bore subsidiary pipes at right angles to a main pipe.

reducing elbow a piece of bent pipe for providing a sharp change of direction of flow and for reducing the bore of a pipeline.

reducing fitting, reducer; a pipe fitting for joining two pipes of different diameters.
see straight reducer.

reducing socket a short length of connecting pipe which is internally threaded and shaped for joining pipes of different diameters.

reducing tee a pipe fitting for connecting a smaller bore subsidiary pipe at right angles to a larger-bore main pipeline.

reducing valve see pressure reducing valve.

reduction, smelting; the process of heating metal ore in order to extract useful metal.

reduit see redoubt. →104

redundant frame see statically indeterminate frame.

redundant building a building no longer needed for its original purpose, which has fallen into disuse as a result of this.

redwood, sequoia; [*Sequoia sempervirens*] a softwood from North America with dark red-brown heartwood and white sapwood, resistant to fungal attack; used for vats, tanks, joinery, plywood and construction work.

reed 1 a grassy plant found growing near water and on marshland, with long, hollow stems used for thatching roofs, matting, reed pens etc.
2 [*Arundo phragmites*, *Phragmites australis*]; common reed, see best reed, Norfolk reed.
3 a thin decorative band; see reeded, reeding.

reed and tie moulding a decorative moulding representing a parallel set of reeds bound intermittently with diagonal crossed ribbons.

reeded referring to a surface that has been cut or formed with a series of parallel convex ridges; see fluted.

reeded boarding see bead boarding. →8

reeded glass glass which has been obscured with a reeded pattern of parallel grooves impressed into one side.

reeded moulding any horizontal flat or torus moulding scored with a series of parallel indentations, convex carvings or protrusions. →14

reeded torus moulding a semicircular decorative moulding carved with reeds or parallel convex projections. →14

reeding an ornamental motif or surface treatment for masonry, glass, sheet products etc. with a series of parallel convex carvings or protrusions.

reed pen an ink pen made from a piece of hollow reed whose end is cut, shaped and split; a simple dip pen used for drawing and calligraphy.

reed thatch thatching material of dried unbroken reed stems. →48

reel see fire-hose reel.

reel and bead see bead and reel. →124

refectorium Lat.; see refectory.

refectory 1 a dining hall in a monastery; a frater.
see *refectory* in Carolingian monastery illustration. →97
2 any room, hall, facility etc. in which a group of people, especially students or monks, take communal meals.

reference drawing see base sheet.

reference line, construction line; in technical drawing and lettering, a fine line drawn to aid the construction or setting out of an item to be drawn.

reflectance 1 in lighting design, a measure of the reflectivity of a surface given as a fraction of the luminous flux that is reflected from it; albedo refers to the reflectance of a planet or moon.
2 see value.

reflected glare in lighting design, glare caused by light from an indirect or reflected source.

reflected sound in acoustics, sound which reaches the listener after bouncing off a wall, floor or ceiling surface.

reflecting road stud, cat's eye; a component sunk in series into a road surface for marking out the edge of a lane, which, at night, reflects the headlights of oncoming cars by means of embedded glass balls or reflectors.

reflecting surface in acoustics, a non-absorbent surface from which sound in a space is reflected.

reflection 1 the bouncing or turning back of wave motion as it strikes a smooth surface.
2 see sound reverberation.
3 see specular reflection.

reflective float glass see surface coated float glass.

reflective glass 1 solar control glass surface treated or coated with a layer to reflect solar radiation.
2 see surface coated float glass.

reflector that part of a lamp, luminaire, sign or treated surface designed to direct reflected light in a certain direction.

reflector lamp, spot lamp; a lamp with an internally silvered lining to reflect light outwards with a directional narrow beam.

reflex angle in geometry, an angle of greater than 180°, but less than 360°.

reflux valve see check valve.

reformatory see community home.

reform school see community home.

refraction the change in direction of a wave such as a beam of light as it enters a medium of different density at an angle.

refractive index, index of refraction; the ratio of the speed of an electromagnetic wave in a certain material to that in a vacuum.

refractory brick see firebrick. →56

refractory concrete concrete designed to withstand high temperatures for use in flues, fireboxes etc., prepared with calcium aluminate cement and refractory aggregate.

refractory lining see fireproof lining. →56

refractory mortar finely crushed mortar, often made from fireclay, silica sand and firebrick, able to withstand high temperatures and used for masonry flues and ovens.

refrigerant a liquid medium through which energy in air-conditioning refrigeration plant and other cooling installations is transferred.

refrigerated store a cold room maintained at a temperature higher than the freezing point of its contents.

refrigeration, chilling; the cooling of something to a low temperature, often to below zero Celsius.

refrigeration unit, chiller; an air-conditioning appliance for producing a cold stream of liquid used in cooling conditioned input air.

refrigerator, fridge; a cupboard-like storage appliance for keeping food cool.

refuge, traffic island; in traffic design, a raised central area of the carriageway between lanes or at a junction to provide a safe area for pedestrians and to direct or divert traffic. →63

refund money returned for defective, unsatisfactory or unused goods and services.

refurbishment, renovation; the action of bringing buildings, structures and their technical installations up to modern requirements, or restoring them to meet current functional standards.

refusal, first refusal; the right or privilege of one party to accept something before it is offered to others.

refuse solid waste products from consumption, manufacture, industrial processes etc.

refuse bin, ashcan (Am.), bin, dustbin, trash can (Am.), rubbish bin; in waste management, a container for the storage of household and commercial solid waste.

refuse chute see waste chute.

refuse collection, waste collection; the organized collection of waste material from buildings, and its transportation to a refuse dump.

refuse collection and disposal the organized collection of household and industrial waste and its transport to a place of disposal.

refuse dump see rubbish dump.

refuse sack a large plastic or paper bag in which household and other waste is collected and transported to a place of disposal.

refuse sack holder see sack holder.

refuse store see bin store.

refuse tip see rubbish dump.

refuse vehicle see waste collection vehicle.

Régence style see Regency style.

Regency style 1 an architectural style in England from the early 1800s between the Georgian and Victorian periods when George, Prince of Wales, was regent; it is characterized by use of classical proportion and eclectic motifs.
2 a style of Rococo and early Baroque architecture in France from the early 1700s during the period when Philip, Duke of Orleans, was regent.

reggia see porta regia. →89

regia see porta regia. →89

region see district.

regional planning in town planning, physical planning for a wider area of country, encompassing towns and countryside.

regional policy in town planning, the policy of local government which determines the economic and social structure of a district or area.

registered chisel a sturdy chisel used for heavy work, with has a ferrule at either end of the handle to prevent it from splitting when struck with a mallet.

register ton a unit of freight capacity in shipping equal to 100 cubic feet or 2.83 m^3.

registration drafting see overlay drafting.

regula, guttae band; Lat.; in classical architecture, one of a series of plain fillets situated below the tenia, which line a Doric architrave and correspond with triglyphs, underlaid with guttae. →78

regular hexagon see hexagon. →108

regularized timber timber which has been resawn or planed on four sides to an accurate dimension.

regularizing the planing of seasoned softwood sections on four sides to produce an accurately measured cross-section.

regular polygon a planar many-sided figure in which all sides are of equal length. →108

regular polyhedron see Platonic solid.

regular prism a prism whose ends are regular polygons.

regular tetrahedron a tetrahedron whose faces are equilateral triangles.

regulating valve see control valve.

regulation 1 a rule provided by an authority indicating the way in which a matter should be undertaken.
2 see building regulation.

regulator see control device.

rehabilitation an action of bringing buildings, structures and their servicing back to a state of functional repair.

rehabilitation centre a hospital or other establishment which cares for people who have suffered drug, alcohol or other intoxicant abuse.

reheating in certain air-conditioning systems, the final heating up of conditioned air, governed by a thermostat within the space, prior to release as supply air.

Re-Horakhti see Ra. →74

rehousing in town planning, the relocation of residents from a particular building or area into new or alternative dwellings.

reindeer fence a barrier by the side of roads in Lapland to prevent reindeer from wandering into the path of traffic.

reinforced blockwork blockwork with reinforcing bars laid in bed joints to withstand structural loading.

reinforced brick lintel, brick beam; a laid-in-situ or prefabricated beam of bricks and reinforcing bars in bed joints, used over openings in walls. →22

reinforced brickwork brickwork with reinforcing bars laid in bed joints to withstand structural loading.

reinforced concrete, ferroconcrete, steel concrete; structural concrete containing inlaid steel reinforcing bars or a mesh to increase strength in tension.

reinforced concrete column 1 see concrete column. **2** see precast column.

reinforced concrete lintel see concrete lintel. →22

reinforced concrete pavement see continuously reinforced concrete pavement.

reinforced concrete structure any structure designed to make use of concrete and its contained steel reinforcement acting together to withstand loading.

reinforced earth earth with inlaid layers of binding reinforcement such as geotextile, used for stabilizing embankments and earthworks.

reinforced felt, sarking felt; bitumen felt reinforced with a hessian web, used beneath tiled or slate roofing.

reinforced joint a horizontal joint in which reinforcing bars have been set; used in structural brickwork over openings etc. →22

reinforced plaster any plaster or render which has been strengthened with or supported by a steel mesh.
see fibrous plaster, fibre-reinforced plaster, fibred plaster.
see metal lathing plaster.
see Rabitz plaster.

reinforced plastic see fibre-reinforced plastic.

reinforced render see reinforced plaster.

reinforcement 1 any rods, fibres, mesh or fabric added to a mass product (concrete, plaster or plastics) to withstand the loading against which the material itself is weak.
2 see concrete reinforcement.
see *concrete reinforcement* illustration; types included as separate entries are listed below. →27
beam reinforcement. →27
binder, see stirrup. →27
bottom reinforcement. →27
cage.
column reinforcement. →27
compression reinforcement.
concrete mesh reinforcement, see fabric.
concrete reinforcement.
fabric reinforcement.
foundation reinforcement. →27
helical reinforcement.
lateral reinforcement. →27
ligature, see stirrup. →27
link, see stirrup. →27
longitudinal reinforcement. →27, →57
main reinforcement. →27
mesh reinforcement, see fabric reinforcement.
principal reinforcement, see main reinforcement. →27
secondary reinforcement.
shear reinforcement.
slab reinforcement. →27
steel reinforcement, see concrete reinforcement.
stirrup. →27
tension reinforcement, tensile reinforcement.
top reinforcement. →27
transverse reinforcement, see lateral reinforcement. →27
two-way reinforcement.
wall reinforcement. →27
web reinforcement, see shear reinforcement.
wire-mesh reinforcement, see fabric reinforcement.
3 see reinforcing bar. →27
4 see steel fixing.
5 see soil reinforcement.
6 see fibre reinforcement.

reinforcement schedule see bar schedule.

reinforcement spacer see spacer.

reinforcing bar one of a number or configuration of deformed steel bars used in reinforced concrete to provide resistance to tensile stresses; also called a rebar or reinforcement. →27
see *reinforcing bars* illustration. →27

reinforcing cage see cage. →30

reinforcing fabric an area of plaster-soaked textile used in plaster casting as structural reinforcement.

reinforcing strip see taping strip.

reinspection a subsequent building inspection held after defects in building work have been made following an initial inspection, or where work has not been ready or the approved plans and specifications are not on site during an initial inspection.

reinstatement the restoring of public areas, infrastructure, landscaping and surroundings which have been affected by construction work to their pre-existing state after the completion of building work.

reject a material or product which is not acceptable for use in construction work due to its poor quality, imperfections or faults, or because it does not meet a specification.

relational database in computing, a system arranged so that data can be used in a number of different applications.

relative atomic mass, atomic weight; the ratio of the average mass of an atom of a certain chemical element to that of one twelfth part of a carbon-12 atom.

relative humidity the ratio of the humidity of air to the saturation point of air at the same temperature and pressure.

relative molecular mass, molecular weight; in chemistry, the sum of the atomic weights of the atoms in a molecule.

relaxation in structural engineering, the loss of stress in a loaded tensile member due to creep.

relay an electromagnetic switch in an electric circuit.

release agent, parting compound; in concreting, a material or compound applied to formwork to facilitate its removal from the concrete.

reliability the ability of a component or construction to perform a required function under certain conditions for a specified time.

relic 1 a religious artifact, garment or the belongings of a revered saint or martyr, kept as objects of worship.
2 see ancient relic.

relief, 1 relievo; a two-dimensional design, pattern or sculpture which is raised partly or entirely above a flat surface to appear as if in three dimensions.
2 decorative ornament carved, embossed or otherwise pressed into a surface.
see sunk relief, cavo-relievo, intaglio rilevato.
see anaglyph.
low relief, bas-relief, see basso relievo.
half relief, see mezzo rilievo.
high relief, see alto rilievo.

relief block printing see relief printing.

relief printing, relief block printing; a general name for woodcut, wood engraving and linocut methods of making graphic prints; also other materials and textures stuck onto a board, from which prints can be taken.

relief road a road designed to direct traffic around an urban centre, roadworks or other source of congestion.

relief wallcovering wallcovering with a face surface rendered or embossed with a raised pattern.

relieving arch, discharging arch; a blind arch built into masonry above a window or door opening to spread loading to side wall abutments. →23

relieving vault a simple vaulting system found above chambers in the Egyptian pyramids and other massive stone monuments, whose purpose is to redirect loads bearing directly onto the chamber roof to side abutments. →71

relievo see relief.
see basso relievo.
cavo relievo, see sunk relief.

religious building, sacral building; a building such as a church, mosque or temple which has religious significance or in which sacred rituals are performed.

reliquary a casket in a catholic church, containing the relics of a saint. →116

reliquary altar an altar with a reliquary. →116

relocatable partition see demountable partition.

remainder in mathematics, the result of one value subtracted from another.

remedial conservation see physical conservation.

remedial plastering the repairing of pits and cracks in an existing plaster surface using small areas of fresh plaster, having first removed loose material and wetted the treatable areas; also known as patching.

remedial work see renovation.

remoulded sample, disturbed sample; a soil sample which has been manipulated on removal from the ground and has had its structure altered.

removability the ability of a component or construction to be easily taken away or dismantled.

Renaissance the rebirth of classicism, a cultural movement originating in Florence, Italy in the 1400s; in architecture it is characterized by the use of classical elements for primarily secular buildings; styles of Renaissance included as separate entries are listed below.
cinquecento, Italian high Renaissance.
early Renaissance.
high Renaissance.
late Renaissance.
Mannerism.
neo-Renaissance.
proto-Renaissance.
quattrocento, Italian early Renaissance.
see *Renaissance portal* illustration. →113
see *column styles in European architecture* illustration. →114
see *Renaissance systems of proportion* illustration. →106

Renaissance perspective see one-point perspective.

render, 1 rendering; an exterior finish for concrete, masonry and rough stonework consisting of a mixture of cement, sand and water, applied wet; commonly also known as plaster, though this usually applies to traditional methods and materials, or interior work; types included as separate entries are listed below.
cement render.
cement lime render, see composition render.
composition render, compo render.
fibre-reinforced render.
insulated render.
mineral render, see mineral plaster.
polymer render.
reinforced render, see reinforced plaster.
scratch render, see scratch plaster.
thin coat render, thin section render.
waterproof render, see damp resisting plaster.
2 see rendering mortar.

render and set see two coat plasterwork.

render coat 1 a single layer of render laid as surfacing for a wall at any one time.
2 see first plaster undercoat.

rendered brickwork brick masonry waterproofed with a render finish. →12

render, float and set see three coat plasterwork.

rendering 1 the process of applying a coat of render to a wall surface.
2 the render thus applied; see plaster, plasterwork, render, stucco.
see coloured rendering.
see comb-finished rendering.
see float-finished rendering.
organic rendering, see masonry paint.
see trowel-finished rendering.
3 see daubing.
4 see torching.
5 in computer graphics and CAD, the application of surface colour or texture to an image or model.
see colour rendering.

rendering mortar mortar designed especially for use in rendering and plastering, with good adherence and resistance to cracking; also called render.

renewal see urban renewal.

renovation, 1 remedial work, repair work; the action of repairing or remodelling a building or a space within a building to meet current requirements.
2 see refurbishment.

renovation plaster plaster used for repairs in old buildings where the background may be damp.

rental agreement see tenancy agreement.

renting 1 the making of regular payments to an owner in return for use of a property or site.
2 see letting.

reorganization, reconstruction; the rearranging of the contents or methods of operation of an existing building, organization or business to improve its performance or effectiveness.

repainting, 1 maintenance painting; in painting and decorating, the addition of a fresh coat of paint to an existing painted surface, including filling cracks, removing hardened paint which is loose etc.
2 overpainting; the adding of subsequent coats of paint to a freshly painted surface.

repair 1 the action of restoring an item, part of a building or component which is broken or in poor condition to its original functional state.
2 the result of this action.

repairability the ease with which a system, device or component can be mended if it falls into a state of disrepair.

repaired plywood plywood in which defects in the face plies have been patched or filled.

repair shop 1 an establishment or workshop for mending mechanical devices and components.
2 see garage.

repair work see renovation.

repeated see running.

repetition in architectural composition and planning, the recurrence of a motif or element in plan or elevation.

repetitive moulding any decorative moulding carved or rendered with an ornamental motif repeated in series along its length; see also running ornament. →124

replacement cost the cost at current price level of replacing goods and property which are outdated, dysfunctional, or have been lost or destroyed.

replica 1 an exact copy of a work of art.
2 see duplicate.

representative 1 one chosen to stand for a group; see project manager, clerk of works.
2 see sales representative.

reprocessing the industrial recycling of waste material into new materials or products.

reproduction copying or imitating; a copy made of a work of art, photograph or graphic image by a printing process.

request for bids the stage in a contract tendering procedure during which sets of tender documents are sent to a number of potential contractors, to which they will supply a tender price or bid; also called request for tender.

request for tender see request for bids.

required life a specified service life for a product or installation.

requirement in design and construction, a local authority, client or contractual condition, obligation, standard or imposition which should be fulfilled.

reredorter a latrine block in a monastery. →97

reredos, altar screen; a decorated screen hung behind the altar in a church. →95

resawing the longitudinal sawing of converted and seasoned timber into smaller sections. →2

resawn a description of converted timber sawn into smaller pieces after seasoning.

research park see science park.

Reseda spp. **1** *Reseda luteola* (dyer's rocket plant), see weld.
2 see reseda green.

reseda green a shade of dark green which takes its name from the colour of the leaves of the mignonette plant, Reseda odorata.

reservation 1 a tract of land protected as a living habitat and breeding grounds for certain species of animal, birds and native cultures.
2 see verge.
3 see central reserve. →63

reserve 1 in business and building management, a sum of money left aside from profits or during a budgeting process, part of the assets of a company.
2 see central reserve. →63

reserved matter in town planning and building control, a matter that requires subsequent approval by a local planning authority following the granting of outline planning permission.

reserve water tank a tank of water from which extinguishant water is pumped in the event of a building fire.

reservoir 1 a natural or man-made lake for the storage of a large volume of water.
2 any vessel which temporarily stores liquid used in a process, installation etc.

reservoir pen an ink pen containing a built-in ink reservoir.

residence 1 the official dwelling of a monarch or notable official or minister.
2 the usual abode of a person, his or her home.

resident one who permanently lives in a dwelling.

residential area, 1 housing area; an urban district consisting principally of dwellings. →105
2 an area on a town plan designated for dwellings.

residential block see apartment block. →61

residential building, dwelling house; a building which contains one or a number of dwellings, or one whose sole purpose is to serve as such. →61
see *types of residential building* illustration. →61
see *residential building* in ideal city illustration. →105
see *Greek residential buildings* illustration. →87
see *Roman residential buildings* illustration. →88

residential development, 1 housing project; a new area of dwellings under design or construction.
2 see housing estate.
3 see housing development.

residential home a communal residence staffed and equipped to take care of the elderly or infirm.

residential scheme, housing scheme; a distinct unit of new housing, usually arranged around a yard and with certain communal facilities.

residential street a quiet street lined with dwellings in a residential area, mainly used by the inhabitants.

residential suburb an area of a town containing principally residential buildings, whose inhabitants commute to work in other areas. →105

resident parking an area of parking designed for the use of residents of adjacent dwellings.

residual stress internal stresses in a structural member or component caused by manufacturing processes etc. rather than applied loading.

residue waste or unusable material deposited from a chemical or sedimentation process.

resilient channel a metal acoustic channel fixing to prevent any vibration of fittings and wall surfaces being transmitted to the building fabric.

resilient clip a metal fixing clip used in acoustic construction to prevent any vibration of fittings etc. being transmitted to the building fabric.

resilient mounting any flexible support or fixing designed to prevent vibration from fittings, mechanical plant etc. being transmitted to the building fabric.

resin 1 a natural or synthetic organic polymer used in the manufacture of varnishes, adhesives, paints and plastics; types included as separate entries are listed below.
2 pitch; the viscous secretion from the resin canals of some pines, distilled to form tar, oil of turpentine and other products; see also natural resin.
alkyd resin.
amber, succinite.
bakelite, see phenol formaldehyde.
coumarone resin, see coumarone indene.
damar resin, see damar.
epoxide resin, epoxy resin, EP.
fossil resin.
gutta-percha.
melamine formaldehyde, melamine, MF.
natural resin.
oleoresin, balsam.
phenol formaldehyde, phenolic resin, PF.
polyester resin, UP.
polysulphone, PSU, polysulfone (Am.).
polyvinyl alcohol, PVA.
unsaturated polyester, see polyester resin.
urea formaldehyde, UF.

resin adhesive see synthetic resin adhesives.

resin concrete see polymer concrete.

resin glue see synthetic resin adhesives.

resin lining see sock lining.

resin pocket see pitch pocket. →1

resin streak see pitch streak. →1

resistance 1 the force of a body opposing motion or a liquid resisting flow.
2 see electrical resistance.
3 see thermal resistance.
4 see sound resistance.

resistance butt welding see butt welding.

resistance flash welding see flash welding.

resistance moment see moment of resistance.

resistance percussive welding see percussive welding.

resistance projection welding see projection welding.

resistance seam welding see seam welding.

resistance spot welding see spot welding.

resistance welding a range of welding processes in which metal objects to be welded are pressed together and heat for fusion is provided by electrical resistance; examples of this are spot, seam, projection and butt welding.

resistant 1 see heat resistant.
2 see damp proof.
3 see fireproof.
4 see lightfast.

resistor see electrical resistor.

resolution the amount of graphic detail which can be distinguished by the human eye, given as the density or clarity of visual information in a print or photograph.

resonance a physical phenomenon, the lively sympathetic vibration of an object or component at certain frequencies of induced vibration.

resonant frequency in physics and acoustics, a frequency at which resonance occurs.

resonator in acoustics, a construction designed to absorb sound of a narrow band of frequencies by sympathetic resonance; a type of absorber.

resorcinol formaldehyde glue a synthetic resin adhesive which is water soluble for several hours, then insoluble and chemically resistant.

resources raw materials, money, labour, infrastructure and assets available for use in a project, production process or business.

rest area, lay-by; a paved area alongside a motorway or busy road into which vehicles may pull in for brief stops.

restaurant a commercial facility whose principal business is the provision and serving of food to be consumed on the premises.

restoration 1 the action of bringing a building, piece of furniture or work of art back to its original state by repair work, cleaning etc.
2 see land restoration.

restoration cross a Greek cross with a circular hole in the centre, as used in heraldry during the reign of Henry VIII of England; a pierced cross. →118

restrictor see throat restrictor. →56

resultant see resultant force.

resultant force, resultant; in mechanics, the overall force vector resulting from all the different forces acting on a body or at a joint.

retable a low decorated framework, ledge or shelf behind a church altar, to which ornaments or images are fixed. →116

retail park a suburban area of large stores, supermarkets and retail outlets landscaped with adequate parking.

retail price index a statistic which lists the prices of basic goods and services and their variation over a period of time.

retainage see retention sum.

retainer 1 see retention sum.
2 insulation retainer, see insulation clip. →22

retaining ring see circlip.

retaining wall a structural wall designed to withstand lateral forces from the abutting ground or a body of water on one side of it; types included as separate entries are listed below. →29
see types of *retaining wall* illustration. →29
analemma. →89
anchored retaining wall. →29
buttress wall, see counterfort wall. →29
cantilever wall, cantilever retaining wall. →29
counterfort wall. →29
cribbing, cribwork. →29
gabion wall. →29
gravity retaining wall, gravity wall. →29
iskhegaon, see analemma. →89
sheet piling, trench sheeting. →29
wing wall. →31

retarded concrete concrete which contains an admixture to increase its setting time.

retarder, retarding agent; an additive for cement, plaster and glues to slow down the rate of setting.

retarding agent see retarder.

retempering, knocking up; the addition of water to concrete or mortar in order to increase its workability, which also reduces its final strength.

retention sum, retainage; in contract administration, a sum retained for a certain period by the client to offset costs that may arise from the contractor's failure to comply fully with the contract.

retentura the rear area of a Roman military camp, where the cavalry, workshops and craftsmen were situated. →104

reticulated finish an irregularly lined or grooved finish in stonework produced by dressing with a point tool.

reticulated tracery Gothic tracery of vertical members which are interlaced in the upper arch of a window with undulating ogee forms. →110

reticulatum see opus reticulatum. →83

reticulatum mixtum see opus reticulatum mixtum. →83

retinal art see optical art.

retouching the process of repairing or improving a painting, graphic image or photograph by the further addition of colour, removing blemishes or by sharpening detail etc.

retouch varnish a general name for varnishes used for bringing out the colour of old oil paints on canvas prior to resuming painting.

retractable bridge, traversing bridge; a type of bridge whose deck can be temporarily retracted to one side, usually on rollers, to allow vehicles or vessels to pass by. →64

retrenchment an inner line of defence for a castle or fortification consisting of a ditch or trench and parapet.

retrochoir a chapel or space in a large church or cathedral extended eastward beyond the high altar. →116

retrofit the installation of components and plant after the usual completion of a building or surrounding construction.

retrospective an art exhibition in which a sample of the life's work of a particular artist or designer is on display.

return 1 a short perpendicular change in direction at the end of a wall, moulding etc.
2 yield; in finance, money paid back on an investment.
3 see return pipe.

return air, extract air; in air conditioning and mechanical ventilation, stale air extracted from a space.

return-air duct, extract duct, exhaust duct; a mechanical ventilation or air-conditioning duct carrying stale air away from a space.

return-air terminal unit, air intake, extract unit; in air conditioning and mechanical ventilation, a grille or other device through which stale air is sucked out of a space.

return end, return wall; a short perpendicular change in direction at the end of a wall.

return latch, catch bolt, latch bolt, spring latch, tongue; the bevelled metal springloaded tongue in a latch, which engages in a plate fixed to a door jamb and retracts when a door handle is turned. →39

return main in a district heating system, a pipeline which conveys water from its place of use back to heating plant.

return pipe, return; a pipeline which conveys fluid from a place of use such as a radiator back to a storage or plant facility.

return stair see dogleg stair. →45
see double return stair. →45

return wall see return end.

return water water in a hot-water heating circuit which is returned from radiators etc. for reheating.

reuleaux triangle, curved triangle; a three-sided geometrical figure in which each equilateral side is constructed by scribing an arc around the opposite apex, and whose height measured through its centre is, like a circle, a constant; often found as a decorative motif in Byzantine, Syrian and Gothic architecture, symbolic of the manifestation of divine will. →108

reusable formwork in concreting, specialized or proprietary formwork which is not destroyed on striking, and can be used over again.

reuse the use of waste materials in the manufacture of new products; the use of redundant buildings and plots for new and different purposes; see also recycling.

reveal, jamb; the vertical side surfaces of an opening in a wall, usually at right angles or splayed with respect to the main wall surface.

revel spur revel, see spur rowel. →108

revelation temple an ancient Babylonian temple type with a cult room to the rear of a rectangular courtyard, functioning both as a sacred area and a hub of commerce and production. →66

reverberation 1 see sound reflection.
2 see sound reverberation.
3 see water hammer.

reverberation time in acoustics, the time taken for the sound pressure level to drop below 60 dB after the initial sound has stopped.

reverberatory a description of a room with spatial conditions and reflective surfaces which produce long reverberation times.

reverse, back; the rear side of a component or product, not usually visible after fitting.
reverse alternate lengths a method of hanging wallpaper in which every other vertical length is laid upside down.
reverse box match a veneering pattern in which four triangular pieces of straight-grained veneer are laid in a rectangular arrangement with diagonal joints in such a way that the direction of grain is from the centre point outwards. →10
reversed cross see inverted cross. →117
reverse diamond match a veneering pattern in which four rectangular pieces of straight-grained veneer are laid in a group so that the grain of each is at an angle and radiating away from the centre point. →10
reverse ogee arch, 1 bell arch; a decorative round or pointed arch formed of two back-to-back ogees with their concave parts meeting at the apex. →24
2 see keel arch. →24
reverse ogee moulding a decorative moulding whose cross-section is that of an ogee, the convex part uppermost; called a cyma reversa in classical architecture. →82
reverse taper column see Minoan column. →69
reverse toothing recesses left in the face of a brick wall under construction into which lapping courses in a perpendicular cross wall can be bonded; also called indents. →21
reversionary development development which returns land or buildings to their original use or state, after a period specified in planning permission.
revestry see vestiary. →95, →102
revetment 1 a layer of binding material, concrete, stone etc. laid over a natural embankment or sloping earthwork as stabilization. →31
2 a retaining wall for an earthwork or embankment.
revibration the recompaction of concrete a few hours after placing using a vibrator to reduce settlement cracks, release trapped water and increase bonding with reinforcement.
revised drawing see revision.
revision, 1 amendment; an annotated change to documentation due to alterations in a design.
2 revised drawing; a documentation or design drawing which has been altered because of the above.
revision arrow see arrowhead. →130
revision cloud a rough ring added to draw attention to recent alterations in a drawing, also called an amendment cloud. →130
revision panel tabulated information in a drawing, listing the revisions made, dates etc., also called an amendment block. →130
revival style a general name for styles in architecture such as the Greek revival and Gothic revival which derive forms and motifs from historical precedents and bygone eras.
revolving door a door with a number of leaves which revolve around a central axis. →50
RH see right-handed.
rhenium a metallic chemical element, **Re**, used in thermocouples.
rheology a science which deals with the flow and deformation of matter.
rhodium a light, durable, greyish-white metal, **Rh**, from the platinum group.
rhodochrosite, manganese spar; a red, brown or pinkish mineral, natural manganese carbonate, $\mathbf{MnCO_3}$, used as a local manganese ore and polished for jewellery and ornamental stone.
rhodonite a black-veined, pink or red mineral, a silicate of manganese used in the art trade and occasionally as an ore of manganese.
rhomb see rhombus. →108
rhombi plural of rhombus.
rhomboid a parallelogram whose adjacent sides are of unequal length.
rhomboid pyramid see bent pyramid. →70
rhombus, rhomb; a parallelogram in which all sides are equal but whose adjacent internal angles are unequal. →108
rhone see half round gutter.
RHS 1 see rectangular hollow section. →34
2 see rolled hollow section.
rhyolite, liparite, quartz porphyry; a silica-rich, fine-grained volcanic rock used as aggregates and chippings, for paving and as ornamental stone.
RIAI, Royal Institute of the Architects of Ireland, the; a professional body to further the interests and rights of its architect members in Ireland.
RIAS, Royal Institute of the Architects of Scotland, the; a professional body to further the interests and rights of its architect members in Scotland.
rib 1 in reinforced concrete construction, one of a number of projections on a deformed reinforcing bar to provide a better bond with the concrete matrix; see longitudinal rib, transverse rib.
2 the main structural member in a rib vault, or a line of stone which marks it; types included as separate entries are listed below. →101
arc doubleau, see transverse rib. →101
diagonal rib. →101
groin rib, see diagonal rib. →101
ogive, see diagonal rib. →101
lierne. →101
longitudinal ridge rib. →101
ridge rib, see longitudinal ridge rib, transverse ridge rib. →101
secondary rib, see tierceron. →101
tertiary rib, see lierne. →101
tierceron. →101
transverse rib. →101
transverse ridge rib. →101
RIBA, Royal Institute of British Architects, the; a professional body to further the interests and rights of its architect members in Great Britain.
ribbed bar see deformed bar. →27
ribbed board hardboard with one face moulded with a ribbed texture.
ribbed expanded metal lathing, rib lathing; lathing, a base for plaster, made from expanded metal which has been ribbed to give a better key.
ribbed vault see rib vault. →26, →101
ribbed-sheet roofing see profiled sheeting. →58
ribbon a narrow flat woven band often used as a decorative motif in carved stonework, woodwork and plasterwork.
ribbon development in town planning, concentrated development along main roads leading to a city centre or built-up area.
ribbon figure, ribbon grain, stripe figure; a decorative striped figure in sawn timber and veneers produced by the radial cutting of the wood from the log.
ribbon grain see ribbon figure.
ribbon window see window band.
Riber rubrum the redcurrant bush, see currant red.
rib lathing see ribbed expanded metal lathing.
rib vault, ribbed vault; a vault constructed of structural arched stone members or ribs with an infill of masonry; often with tiercerons or secondary ribs, and liernes or tertiary ribs. →26, →101
see *Gothic rib vault* illustrations. →26, →101
rice paper thin, fragile, absorbent paper made from the pith of the ricepaper plant *Tetrapanax papyriferus* [*Aralia papyrifera*], used in traditional watercolour painting by the Chinese and Japanese.
rich concrete, fat concrete; a concrete mix whose proportion of cement is greater than usual.
rich lime see fat lime.
rich mix, fat mix; a mix of concrete or mortar with a high content of binder.

ridge the longitudinal apex where two sloping planes in a pitched roof meet; the straight line running along the highest point of a sloping roof. →46

ridge beam, 1 ridge purlin, rooftree; in timber roof construction, a horizontal timber which supports the ends of coupled rafters at the ridge. →33
2 see columen. →47

ridge board, ridge plank, ridge piece; in timber roof construction, a horizontal board at ridge level onto which rafters bear. →33

ridge capping, ridgecap, ridge covering; a longitudinal construction or component for covering the ridge of a roof, often a channel, board, row of U-shaped tiles etc.

ridge capping board timber boards used as a ridge capping in traditional timber roof construction.

ridge capping tile see ridge tile.

ridge covering see ridge capping.

ridge end 1 in roofing, a special tile or other construction at the end of a ridge.
2 see block end ridge tile.

ridge gusset in timber roof construction, a fish plate for connecting a pair of rafters at the ridge.

ridge piece see ridge board. →33

ridge plank see ridge board. →33

ridge plate in timber pitched roof construction, a piece placed at ridge level onto which the ridge capping may be fixed.

ridge pole a ridge beam in traditional and log construction.

ridge purlin see ridge beam. →33

ridge rib see longitudinal ridge rib. →101
see transverse ridge rib. →101

ridge tile, 1 ridge capping tile; a special roof tile formed to cover the ridge of a roof.
2 see ventilating ridge tile.
3 see dry ridge tile.
4 see angular ridge tile.
5 see block end ridge tile, ridge end.

ridgecap see ridge capping.

riding shore a slanting prop or raker sprung from another raker in a raking shore.

rift crack see heartshake. →1

rift sawing see quartersawing. →2

rift sawn see quartersawn.

rift sliced veneer a decorative veneer formed by the oblique slicing of a quarter log or flitch.

rigger see rigger brush. →43

rigger brush a slender paintbrush with very long fibres culminating in a point, used by artists and decorators for precision work; also simply called a rigger. →43

right angle in geometry, an angle of 90° formed by two intersecting lines which are perpendicular to one another.

right-angled triangle, right triangle; a triangle in which one internal angle is 90°.

right-handed, right-hung, RH; see handing.

right hexahedron a three-dimensional solid with six flat, rectangular faces.

right-hung see right-handed.

right-of-occupancy, right-of-tenancy; a tenancy agreement in which the occupier pays a specified percentage of the price of the dwelling, and thereon a reduced rent in return for rights as if he or she were the owner.

right-of-tenancy see right-of-occupancy.

right of way, 1 priority; in traffic planning, the right of vehicles travelling on one road over those on another road to proceed first at a junction or interchange between the two.
2 a path or lane across private land which the public has the legal right to use.

right triangle see right-angled triangle.

rigid 1 the property of a structure which will resist deformation under load due to adequate bracing and stiff joints.
2 see stiff.

rigid body a body or structure which resists change in shape under the action of forces.

rigid composite pavement road construction of a structural concrete slab surfaced with layers of bituminous material.

rigid frame see portal frame. →33

rigid frame bridge see portal frame bridge. →32

rigidity, stiffness; the property of a material or structure to resist bending, stretching and deformation.

rigid joint any joint between two members which is fixed in place and implies no rotation about a pivot for purposes of structural calculation. →33

rigid pavement road construction consisting of a concrete slab providing both structure and surfacing.

rigid pipe pipes of ceramics, metal, concrete etc. which are brittle and cannot be deformed without fracturing.

rilevato 1 see relief.
2 intaglio rilevato, see sunk relief.

rilievo see relief.

Rilsan proprietary name for a tough, polyamide thermoplastic used as fibres.

rim latch a latch attached to the surface of a door rather than incorporated into its thickness.

rim lock a lock attached to the surface of a door rather than incorporated into its thickness; see also mortise lock. →39

rinceau Gothic and Romanesque decorative ornament in low relief with representations of foliage, acanthus, vines and berries.

rind gall the growth of new tissue over a surface wound in a growing tree.

ring 1 see annual ring. →1
2 see annulet. →81

ring circuit a ring-shaped electric circuit connected to a power supply.

ring cross 1 see Celtic cross. →117
2 see cross annuletty. →118

ringed column 1 see annulated column. →114
2 see rusticated column. →13, →114

ring failure see cup shake. →1

ringfort, rath; a fortified settlement or farmstead from Iron Age Britain and Ireland, consisting of a circular mound of earth, with or without a timber palisade, surrounding buildings.

ring main 1 a pressurized pipe circuit for the continuous supply of hot water to a building.
2 see cold oil ring main.

ring porous wood hardwood with relatively large pores concentrated in early wood and small pores in latewood.

ring pull a handle consisting of a hinged ring by which a door, drawer, hatch etc. is pulled open.

ring road, 1 beltway (Am.); an urban road or route which diverts traffic around a city centre or other built-up area.
2 see circular road.

ring scale fungus see red ring rot.

ring seat a WC seat in the shape of a ring hinged at the rear to the pan.

ring shake see cup shake. →1

ring-shanked nail see annular nail. →35

ringwork a fortification for a village, garrison or encampment, consisting of a circular surrounding earthwork and external ditch, punctured with an entrance or entrances.

rink see ice rink.

Rinman's green see cobalt green.

rinsing sink, scalding sink, sterilizing sink; a metal sink used in hospitals and laboratories for washing and sterilizing utensils and sample vessels in water.

rip saw a saw with teeth adapted for cutting along the grain of wood; see cross-cut saw.

rip-sawing see flat cutting.

ripper a tool consisting of a steel bar for removing old surface construction such as plasterwork, boarding etc.

ripping see flat cutting.
ripping chisel a large chisel used for heavy and rough work. →41
ripple marks see ray figure.
rip-rap 1 rubble and loose stone used to form a foundation, ramp, bridge abutment, bank or breakwater; a construction thus built. →31
2 loose stones 7–70 kg used as a covering for a revetment.
rise, 1 pitch; the vertical distance measured from the impost to the crown of an arch. →22
2 the vertical height of a step, or the vertical distance between adjacent treads in a stair. →45
riser 1 the vertical surface forming the front face of a step. →45
2 see rising main.
3 ventilation riser, see ventilation stack. →56
rising-butt hinge see rising hinge. →38
rising hinge, gravity door hinge, rising-butt hinge; a hinge with two metal flaps and a central joining pin, whose housing is cut with a helix so that the door rises slightly when opened, and swings shut under its own weight. →38
rising main, riser; a vertical service main to provide a water, electricity, gas, telecommunications supply or service to upper floors of a multistorey building.
rising sun see Khepri. →75
riveling see wrinkle.
riven finish, cloven finish; a stonework finish produced by cleaving or splitting; the finished surface is the same as the cleavage plane.
river a naturally moving stream of water from precipitation collected on hills and uplands flowing towards a sea.
rivet a short flat-headed metal pin used for fixing metal sheet or plate by inserting it into holes in the sheets to be fastened and hammering to flatten the other end.
riveted joint a metalwork joint fastened with rivets.
see *metal products* illustration. →34
see *sheetmetal roofing* illustration. →49
riveting 1 the process of fixing metal plates together with rivets.
2 the result of this action.
riveting hammer a hammer with a small face and cross peen used in riveting work.
road a route or way which has been designed and surfaced for use by vehicular traffic.
roadbase see base course. →62
road bridge a bridge which carries a road over an obstacle such as a railway or river. →64
road construction the building of roads, including all subterranean, surfacing and technical works.
road hump, speed control hump, sleeping policeman; a short area of raised carriageway, a bump, hump or obstruction designed to reduce the speed of vehicles in residential and built-up areas.
road junction the meeting of two or more roads such that traffic may flow from one road to another; see crossroads. →62
see *at grade junctions* illustration. →62
see *grade-separated junctions* illustration; types included as separate entries are listed below. →63
at-grade junction. →62
cloverleaf junction. →63
diamond junction. →63
directional T junction. →63
dumbbell junction. →63
fork junction, forked junction. →62
grade-separated junction. →63
grade-separated fork junction. →63
interchange. →63
roundabout. →62
mini-roundabout. →62
roundabout junction. →63
scissor junction. →62
staggered junction. →62
T junction, tee junction. →62
trumpet junction. →63
Y junction. →62
road map a map whose primary purpose is to show roads and their networks.
road marking any marking on a road to indicate priority, zones or restrictions to the road user.
road of Jerusalem a circular labyrinth pattern on the floor of some medieval churches (notably at Chartres), a symbol of the pilgrimage trail; the original name in French, 'chemin de Jerusalem', is sometimes also translated as 'road to Jerusalem'. →123
road oil, asphalt oil; a viscous oily substance distilled from crude oil, used as a surface treatment or binder in road construction.
road safety measures taken to reduce the amount of road accidents and danger to pedestrians, road users etc. caused by traffic.
road sign, traffic sign; any fixed sign providing vehicular or pedestrian traffic with information, instructions or warnings.
road surfacing see surfacing. →63
road tar a blend of coal tar and tar oil used in road construction.
road to Jerusalem see road of Jerusalem. →123
road transport a mode of transport in which vehicles travel on roads as opposed to by rail, air or water.
roadway see carriageway. →63
robbers' cross 1 see tau cross. →117
2 see furca, forked cross. →117
robinia, false acacia, black locust (Am.); [*Robinia pseudoacacia*] a hardwood of Europe and the USA with golden brown, hard and heavy timber; used for furniture, fences and posts.
Robinia pseudoacacia see robinia.
rocaille, French Rococo, Louis XV style; an exuberantly decorative style of Rococo architecture in France during the reign of Louis XV (1715–1774).
rock 1 a naturally occurring agglomeration of minerals forming a distinct and definable geological body.
2 stone in its natural habitat within the earth's crust.
3 an expanse of stone exposed at the surface of the earth as an outcrop.
4 see boulder.
see **igneous rock** for ancient igneous rock types (granite, basalt etc.).
see **metamorphic rock** for metamorphic rock types (marble, schist, slate etc.).
see **sedimentary rock** for types of sedimentary rock (limestone, sandstone etc.).
rock anchor, rock anchorage; a system of steel rods, guys or braces to fix a structure firmly to the bedrock. →29
rock anchorage see rock anchor. →29
rock axe see masonry axe. →40
rock burst, rock bursting; the breaking away of a larger area of rock face than intended during blasting excavation.
rock bursting see rock burst.
rock bolt a fixing which receives the forces from a rock anchorage and transmits them to the bedrock in which it is embedded.
rock-cut temple, cave temple, rock temple; a temple cut into a sheer rock face, a building type found in the Indian architecture of the early middle ages. →68, →72
rock cutting an open passage for a railway line or road cut into rock below ground level.
rock-cut tomb a subterranean tomb, often found in Mediterranean regions, which has been hewn out of solid rock and is generally intended for collective burial; also called a rock tomb; see sepulchre. →74
rocket dyer's rocket plant (*Reseda luteola*); see weld.
rock-faced see quarry finish. →12
rock flour rock which has been crushed into a powder with grains which are well under 1 mm in size.

rock joint in geology, a crack or fissure in rock with the layers or bedding planes still aligned; when displacement occurs it is known as a fault.

rock maple see sugar maple.

rock pick a small hammer with a bladed peen, used for careful removal of stone from surfaces, geological specimens, archaeological finds etc. →40

rock plant any species of landscaping plant which usually grows and thrives in rocky or dry areas.

rock pocket see honeycombing.

rock salt see halite.

rock shoe see rock socket.

rock socket, rock shoe; the lower end of a foundation pile, by which it is bored into and connected to bedrock.

rock temple see rock-cut temple. →68, →72

rock tomb see rock-cut tomb. →74

rock wool mineral wool produced from volcanic rock or other rock types, used for thermal insulation.

Rococo an architectural and decorative style originating from France c.1725–1775, characterized by abundant lightweight ornament.
see *Rococo window* illustration. →111
see *Rococo portal* illustration. →113

rod 1 any thin long solid length of material, usually metal.
2 see perch.

rodded joint see keyed joint. →16

rodding see tamping.

rodding eye see cleaning eye.

rod of Hermes see caduceus. →120

rod of Mercury see caduceus. →120

roll billet see round billet. →124

rolled asphalt asphalt laid hot and compacted by rolling plant, used for wearing courses, basecourses or roadbases in road construction.

rolled concrete, roller-compacted concrete; stiff concrete compacted using a vibrating roller, used for roads and pavements.

rolled glass glass manufactured by passing molten glass between steel rollers, often shaped to provide patterned surfaces.
see patterned glass.

rolled hollow section, RHS; a structural steel section formed by processes of rolling, whose uniform cross-section is mostly a hollow rectangle (also RHS), but may also be a square or circle. →34
see circular hollow section. →34
see rectangular hollow section. →34
see square hollow section. →34

rolled steel joist see I-section. →34

rolled steel section a structural steel profile with a uniform cross-section produced by rolling.

roller, paint roller; a hand-held implement consisting of a roll of absorbent material on an axle, used for the rapid application of paint to a surface. →43

roller bearing a structural bearing consisting of one or more cylindrical pieces which transfers loading between parallel plates.

roller blind an internal fabric window blind with a spring mechanism to enable it to be retracted by rolling up around a central rod above the window opening.

roller catch a fastening device fixed into the edge of a door leaf to hold it in a closed position by means of a sprung cylinder in a casing; see also ball catch. →39

roller compaction see rolling.

roller door see roller shutter. →50

roller marks see feed-roller marks. →1

roller painting the application of paint on wall surfaces with a paint roller.

roller shutter 1 any door, gate, shutter or screen which is rolled up around an overhead horizontal axle when in an open position.
2 an overhead door or shutter made up from hinged slats, cloth etc. which roll up around a drum above the opening; usually a high speed motorized door. →50

roller tray a shallow plastic vessel in which paint is held while being transferred to a paint roller; also called a paint tray. →43

roller-compacted concrete see rolled concrete.

rolling, 1 roller compaction; in road construction, the compaction and evening of a freshly laid surface or substrate with heavy rolling plant.
2 in landscaping, the evening and flattening of lawns etc. with a manual roller.
3 the production of metal bars, plate etc. with a uniform cross-section in a rolling mill using industrial methods.
cold rolling, see cold forming.
see hot rolling.

rolling ball writer a ball pen with a small nylon sphere at its point, which, through rolled contact with the paper or base, regulates the flow of spirit-based ink.

rolling load a structural live load imposed by a moving vehicle; see also moving load.

roll joint, 1 batten roll joint, conical roll joint, wood roll joint; in sheet roofing, a joint formed by dressing roofing material around a timber fillet with welded joints, or nailing the sheet material to the fillet and fixing a capping on top. →49
2 see hollow roll joint. →49

roll-jointed roof a sheetmetal roof whose adjacent strips of roofing are connected with roll joints. →49

roll-jointed roofing felt or sheetmetal roofing in which adjacent seams running from ridge to eaves are formed using roll joints. →49

roll moulding, 1 round moulding; a decorative moulding which is half round (or a greater part of a circle) in cross-section. →14, →80
2 see scroll moulding.
3 roll billet, see round billet. →124

roll-rim [*Paxillus panuoides*] a brown rot fungus which attacks timber in damp conditions, forming brown lobed shelf-like growths.

roll tile a pantile or Roman tile. →47

ROM read only memory.

Roman arch a masonry arch whose intrados describes half a circle; a semicircular arch. →22, →24

Roman architecture the post-Etruscan classical architecture of the Romans from 750 BC to 476 AD, characterized by Greek-influenced temples, theatres, baths and tenements, and by engineering ingenuity for structures such as roads, bridges and conduits. →79, →81, →111
see *Roman residential buildings* illustration. →88
see *apteral temple* illustration. →84
see *peristyle temple* illustration. →85
see *classical temples* illustration. →86
see *classical public and commercial buildings* illustration. →92
see *classical stages and spectator structures* illustration. →89
see *Roman baths* illustration. →91
see *Roman amphitheatre* illustration. →90
see *classical Roman orders* illustration. →79
see *classical capital and bases* illustrations. →81

Roman basilica see illustration. →93

Roman brick 1 a thin brick used by the Romans and often reused for later buildings on the same sites.
2 a Roman clay brick, see later. →83
3 other Roman baked ceramic products, see testa. →83

Roman cement 1 a pozzolanic cement used in Roman times, made from natural pozzolan mixed with lime.
2 Parker's cement, brown cement; a proprietary form of cement produced from burnt clay and used as render in England in the 1800s.

Roman column 1 see classical column. →79
2 see columna caelata.
3 see columna rostrata. →69
4 see Composite column. →79
5 see Tuscan column. →79
see *classical Roman columns* illustration. →79

Roman concrete Roman walling construction made from two skins of rubble with an infill of cement and small stones poured at intervals during construction. →83
see opus and *Roman walling* illustration. →83

Roman Corinthian order a variation of the Greek Corinthian order, especially favoured during the Renaissance, in which bare columns are crowned with tall Corinthian capitals, and the entablature has richer embellishment. →79

Roman cross see papal cross. →117

Roman Doric capital a capital at the top of a column of the classical Roman Doric order, consisting of a decorated echinus above an annulet, surmounted by an abacus edged with a cyma moulding. →81

Roman Doric order, Doric Roman order; a Roman and Renaissance version of the Doric order comprising columns with fluted shafts, simple capitals and bases, and an entablature with triglyphs and metopes. →79, →81

Romanesque religious architecture in Western Europe in the early 11th century, characterized by bulky massing, sparing use of detail and the round arch; known in England as Norman architecture.
see *Romanesque church* illustration. →99
see *Romanesque columns* illustration. →114
see *Romanesque capitals* illustration. →115
see *Romanesque window* illustration. →111
see *Romanesque recessed portal* illustration. →113
see Carolingian. →98
see Lombardic architecture.
see Norman architecture. →98, →109

Romanesque arch a round arch with a heavy intrados, found in Romanesque architecture.

Romanesque church **1** see Romanesque; see *Romanesque church* illustration. →99
2 see triconch church, three-apsed church. →99
3 see basilica church. →99

Romanesque Revival an architectural style from the late 1800s, characterized by an interest in forms and decoration from Romanesque architecture.

Romanesque vault heavy semicircular masonry vaults used in Romanesque and Norman churches for roofing the nave and aisles. →25

Roman fort see castrum. →104

Roman holy cross a form of complex gammadion or swastika emblem, in Christian symbolism representing the return of Christ. →117

Roman Ionic order a Roman variation of the Greek Ionic order whose volutes have greater sculpturing than the original. →80
see *Roman Ionic order* illustration. →80

Roman Iron Age a period in central and northern European history from c.0–400 AD during which the peoples living beyond the boundaries of the Roman Empire came into contact with Roman culture.

Roman military fort see castrum. →104

Roman ochre a variety of yellow ochre pigment, either one used in ancient Rome or found naturally in Italy.

Roman orders Roman and Etruscan versions of the Greek classical orders, often with columns used as decorative rather than structural devices; see Roman Corinthian, Roman Doric, Roman Ionic, Tuscan. →79

Roman pantile see Roman tile. →47

Roman residential buildings the residential masonry building types of ancient Roman towns; see villa, insula, atrium house; see *also Roman residential building* illustration. →88

Roman roof tile see Roman tile. →47

Roman stonework see opus. →83

Roman temple see *apteral and peristyle temple* illustrations. →84, →85

Romanticism a movement in the arts from the late 1700s and early 1800s concerned with subjective emotions, legends, fables and a return to medieval themes rather than the strictures of classicism; in architecture it is represented by the neo-Gothic.

romantic planning town planning practice based on the idealization of rural and medieval unmechanized life rather than industrial and bureaucratic development, manifested by urban landscaped parks and garden cities.

Roman tile a single-lap roof tile moulded into a profile with one or two convex projections abutting a flat channel or waterway; sometimes called a Roman pantile. →47
see double Roman tile. →47
see imbrex. →47
see kalypter. →47
see single Roman tile. →47
see stegaster. →47
see tegula. →47

Roman tiled roof see illustration. →47
see Corinthian roofing. →47
see Laconian roof tiling. →47
see Sicilian roofing. →47

Roman vault round barrel masonry vaults found in Roman construction, one of the basic defining elements in Roman architecture and engineering. →25

Roman walling see 'opus' and *Roman walling* illustration. →83

Romayne pertaining to decorative carving, furniture and panelling in England in the early 1500s, typically characterized by foliage and medallions and with Italian Renaissance influences.

rood a large crucifix in a church. →117

rood altar an altar against a rood screen, facing the nave of a church. →116

rood arch the main arch in a rood screen.

rood beam a beam spanning across the chancel of a church to support a rood screen.

rood loft a gallery running along the top of a rood screen intended to carry candles, effigies or a crucifix.

rood screen a screen in a church which separates the nave and chancel and is intended to carry a crucifix or rood. →95, →99, →100

rood spire a spire over the crossing of a church.

rood tower a tower above the crossing of a church.

roof **1** those parts of the top of a building which provide shelter against the elements. →46
2 the uppermost weatherproof level in a building.
3 see roofing, roof covering.
roof types according to structure, method of construction and materials are listed below; roof types according to shape are listed under **roof form**.
angel roof.
bark-thatched roof. →48
barrel vaulted roof.
boarded roof. →48
clapboard roof. →48
clasped purlin collar rafter roof.
close couple roof, close couple rafter roof. →33
cold roof.
collar roof, collar rafter roof. →33
common purlin roof, horizontal rafter roof.
couple roof, coupled rafter roof. →33
crown post rafter roof, crown post and collar purlin roof. →33
crown post rafter roof, crown post roof. →33
double roof, see purlin roof. →33
glazed roof, glass roof. →60
grass roof, see turf roof, green roof. →48
green roof. →48
hammer-beam roof. →33
horizontal rafter roof, see common purlin roof.
inverted roof, see upside down roof.
king post roof. →33
northlight shell roof.
open roof, open timbered roof.
organic roof. →48
protected membrane roof, see upside down roof.
puncheon roof. →48
purlin roof, double roof. →33
queen post collar rafter roof, queen post roof. →33
queen post rafter roof. →33

rafter roof. →33
roll-jointed roof. →49
Roman tiled roof illustration. →47
scissor roof, scissor rafter roof. →33
shake roof. →48
sheetmetal roof.
shell roof.
shingle roof. →48
single roof. →33
slate roof.
span roof, see close couple roof. →33
thatched roof. →48
tie beam roof.
tiled roof, tile roof.
timber roof. →33
trussed purlin roof. →33
trussed rafter roof. →33
trussed roof, triple roof. →33
turf roof. →48
unventilated roof.
upside down roof.
ventilated roof.
warm roof.

roof access ladder see access ladder.

roof batten one of a number of timber strips laid to provide a nailing base and a ventilation gap for roofing material.
see *roof batten* in holiday home and sauna illustration. →58

roof beam one of a series of horizontal or slanting structural members for supporting roof construction; see also rafter. →48, →59

roof boarding, sarking; in roof construction, timber boards laid onto rafters as a base for roofing material such as felt, sheetmetal, turf etc. →48

roof box in prehistoric architecture, a rectangular opening above the entrance to a passage grave to allow the sun's light in to illuminate the inner chambers on the dawn of the winter solstice, notably at Newgrange, Ireland. →65

roof channel see box gutter. →60

roof comb in Pre-Columbian architecture, a large stone crested throne-like structure which surmounts a Mayan pyramid or teocalli. →67

roof conductor the metal components attached to a roof in a lightning protection system, which direct current from strikes to a down conductor.

roof construction the component parts or layers of the uppermost level in a building, including structure, insulation and roofing material.
see *roof construction* in brick house illustration. →59

roof covering see roofing.

roof decking, roof sheathing; in roof construction, any stiff sheet material such as plywood, boarding etc. laid above rafters or trusses as a base for roofing material. →57, →59

roof extractor in air conditioning and ventilation, a protected fan unit situated on a roof or at the top of flues, ducts etc. to extract waste gases.

roof form the shape of the roof of a building; roof types according to shape are listed below; roof types according to structure, method of construction and materials are listed under **roof**. →46
see *roof form* illustration. →46
butterfly roof, Y-form roof. →46
catslide roof. →46
clerestory roof, see split-level roof. →46
clipped gable roof, see half-hipped roof. →46
conical roof.
crossform roof. →46
curb roof, double pitched roof, knee roof.
domed roof, domical roof.
double gable roof, see M-roof. →46
double hipped roof.
double lean-to roof. →46
double pitched roof, see curb roof.
duopitch roof, see saddleback roof. →46
flat roof, platform roof.
gable roof, gabled roof. →46
gabled mansard roof, gambrel roof. →46
gambrel roof, gablet roof.
half span roof, see lean-to roof. →46
half-hipped roof. →46
helm roof.
hip and valley roof. →46
hip roof, hipped roof. →46
hipped gable roof, see half-hipped roof. →46
hipped mansard roof. →46
hyperbolic paraboloid roof.
jerkinhead roof, see half-hipped roof. →46
knee roof, see curb roof.
lean-to roof, half span roof. →46
L-roof. →46
M-roof. →46
mansard roof. →46
monitor roof. →46
monopitch roof. →46
northlight roof.
ogee roof. →26
pavilion roof. →46
penthouse roof, pent roof. →46
pentise roof.
pitched roof. →46
platform roof, see flat roof.
pyramid roof.
rainbow roof.
saddleback roof, saddle roof. →46
sawtooth roof. →46
shed roof, see monopitch roof, see penthouse roof. →46
shread head roof, see half-hipped roof. →46
single pitch roof, see monopitch roof. →46
skirt roof. →46
southlight roof.
spire roof.
split-level roof, clerestory roof. →46
station roof, umbrella roof.
suspended roof, suspension roof.
trough roof, see M-roof. →46
valley roof, see M-roof. →46
Y-form roof, see butterfly roof. →46

roof glazing see glazed roof, rooflight. →60

roof gully see rainwater outlet.

roof gutter see rainwater gutter. →46

roof hatch a small openable hinged panel in roof construction to afford access to the roof surface.

roofing, 1 roof covering, weatherproofing; in roof construction, the impermeable outer surface and finish material which provides waterproof and weatherproof protection for a roof; various types of roofing are listed below.
2 the laying of weatherproof roofing material, or the construction of a roof.
aluminium sheet roofing, aluminium roofing.
asphalt roofing.
bitumen felt roofing, built-up roofing. →49
bituminous roofing.
board on board roofing.
built-up roofing, built-up felt roofing. →49
calendered polymeric roofing.
clapboard roofing. →48
Corinthian roofing. →47
corrugated sheet roofing. →49
felt roofing, see bituminous felt roofing. →49
flexible metal roofing, see supported sheetmetal roofing. →57
lap-jointed roofing. →49
membrane roofing. →49
metal multi-tile roofing. →49
metal roofing, see sheetmetal roofing. →49
polyester base felt roofing.
polymeric roofing, see calendered polymeric roofing.
profiled sheet roofing. →49
ribbed-sheet roofing, see profiled sheeting. →58
roll-jointed roofing. →49

seam-welded roofing. →49, →57
sheet roofing. →49
sheetmetal roofing. →49
Sicilian roofing. →47
strip slate roofing.
supported sheetmetal roofing. →49, →57
tiled roofing, see roof tiling. →47, →59
troughed sheet roofing.

roofing bolt a metal bolt with an integrated sealing washer, used for attaching profiled or other sheet roofing onto a frame. →36

roofing cleat see cleat.

roofing felt **1** sheet roofing material composed of a thin fibrous mat soaked in a waterproofing compound such as bitumen, supplied in rolls. →57
2 see bitumen felt.

roofing nail a galvanized or stainless steel nail used for fixing down tiles, slates, roofing battens or roof sheeting; often provided with a soft washer or shaped head to seal the nail hole.
see convex head roofing nail.

roofing screw **1** a pointed metal screw with an integrated sealing washer, used for fastening profiled sheet roofing to a base. →36
2 see sheetmetal screw. →36

roofing sheet see roof sheeting.

roofing slate, roof slate, slate; a piece of thin stone, usually slate, nailed to battens in overlapping rows as roofing.

roofing system proprietary roofing supplied with all relevant fixings, seals and sealant, flashings, trim and special components included.

roofing tile see roof tile. →47

roofing underlay a layer of roofing felt used as a waterproof underlay for profiled sheet, tiled or slate roofing; also called sheathing. →49, →57

roofing upstand the turning up of the edges of roofing felt or sheetmetal roofing against a vertical verge, parapet or abutment. →57

roof insulation those layers of roof construction which provide thermal insulation. →49

roof joist **1** a beam which supports a roof; see rafter.
2 see *roof joist* in holiday home and sauna illustration. →58

roof ladder a ladder attached externally to the sloping plane of a roof, from eaves to ridge, to provide maintenance access for chimneys, rooflights, roofing etc.

rooflight, 1 roof window, skylight; a window or glazed panel in a roof to provide natural lighting for the interior; may be horizontal or at an angle.
see *rooflight* in office building illustration. →60
2 see lantern light.

rooflight sheet translucent sheet material such as glass or plastics laid alongside similarly formed opaque roof sheeting to allow light into spaces below.

roofline see skyline.

roof outlet see rainwater outlet.

roof parking an area of parking for motor vehicles on a suitably prepared flat roof of a building.

roof penetration the place at which a chimney, flue or other component passes through a roof, requiring particular measures to ensure weatherproofing and waterproofing. →56

roof pitch the slope of a roof plane, given as a percentage or ratio.

roof plan an architectural drawing showing the roof of a building in plan, including any equipment, gradients, critical dimensions etc. thereon. →130

roof plane one of the flat surfaces which make up the outer surface of a roof.

roof plate in timber roof construction, a horizontal member running parallel to the ridge, which spreads the load of roof trusses onto a wall or beam.

roofscape the view over the tops of roofs in an urban environment.

roof screen a fire barrier within or above a roof space.

roof sheathing see roof decking. →57, →59

roof sheeting, 1 roofing sheet; rigid sheet material such as sheetmetal, fibre cement sheet, profiled plastics sheeting used as impervious roofing material.
2 see sheet roofing. →49
3 see sheetmetal roofing. →49

roof slab a concrete slab cast or laid as roof structure. →49

roof slate see roofing slate.

roof soaker see pipe flashing.

roof space, roof void; the uppermost level beneath the pitched roof of a building; often a loft or attic.

roof structure 1 the structural elements which form a roof and support the layers of decking and waterproofing.
see *concrete roof structure* in concrete frame illustration. →28
see *timber roof structure* in holiday home and sauna illustration. →58
2 see roof slab. →49
3 see roof truss.

roof surfacing a layer of chippings or other material used as a protective covering for bituminous roofing against the elements.

roof terrace an outdoor space at roof level of a building for the recreation of the occupants.
see *residential building* illustration. →61
see *brick house* illustration. →59

roof tile, roofing tile; a flat slab of burnt clay, concrete, or other rigid material fastened, overlapping or interlocking in series as a roof covering; types included as separate entries are listed below.
see *roof tile* illustration. →47
angular hip tile.
block end ridge tile.
bonnet hip tile.
clay roof tile.
cloaked verge tile.
concrete roof tile.
double Roman tile. →47
dry ridge tile.
eaves tile.
half tile.
hip tile.
interlocking tile. →47
kalypter. →47
mansard tile.
ornamental tile.
pantile. →47
plain tile. →47
ridge tile.
Roman tile. →47
shingle tile. →47
single Roman tile. →47
roofing slate.
stegaster. →47
strip slates. →49
top course tile.
under-and-over tile. →47
valley tile.
ventilating tile.
verge tile.

roof tiling, tiled roofing; a roof surface or roofing of interlocking or overlapping tiles.
see *roof tiling* illustration. →47
see *roof tiling* in brick house illustration. →59

rooftop parking see roof parking.

rooftree see ridge beam. →33

roof truss in roof construction, a triangulated timber frame which supports secondary construction and roofing material.
see *types of roof truss* illustration. →33
see **truss** for list of different types of roof trusses. →33

roof valley see valley. →46

roof vent a component for ventilating a closed roofspace or roof construction. →49

roof ventilation the natural circulation of outside air through roof construction and voids to remove unwanted moisture. →49

roof void 1 a space in between the uppermost habitable room and the roofing in a building too small to stand up in.
2 see roof space.
roofway see catwalk. →46
roof window see rooflight. →60
room 1 any enclosed space within a building excluding circulation space.
2 see habitable room.
see *rooms* in brick house illustration. →59
room acoustics the characteristics of a space with respect to sound quality and audibility.
room air-conditioner see unit air-conditioner.
room heater, domestic solid-fuel appliance, heating stove; a wood or coal fired heater, range or other closed flued appliance used in the home to provide occasional heating. →56
room formwork see apartment formwork.
room height see ceiling height.
room index in lighting design, a design formula relating to the geometry of a space, given as follows: $(l \times w)/h(l + w)$, where h is the working height.
room temperature the normal internal temperature of the habitable spaces of a building, usually between 15°C and 21°C.
root in mathematics, the value which, when multiplied by itself a specific number of times, will produce a given quantity.
root barrier that layer of resilient sheeting laid beneath landscaped planting, green roofs etc. to prevent roots from growing plants damaging waterproofing membranes and other underlying construction. →48
root rot see annosus root rot.
root store, underground store, vegetable store; a rudimentary structure for storing root vegetables and other commodities on a farm or homestead, hollowed out from the ground or an embankment to maintain a cool temperature during hot summers and cold winters.
rope a thick wound twine of fibrous material, plastics or metal consisting of a core around which at least three strands are spirally wound.
rope bridge a rudimentary suspension bridge with ropes or cables strung between two points, supporting a lightweight deck of boards or similar material.
rope moulding see cable moulding. →125
ropeway see aerial ropeway.
rose 1 a metal plate or fitting for covering the hole in a door through which the spindle of a door handle passes. →39
2 see shower head.
3 see centrepiece.
4 see rosette. →123
5 see Tudor rose. →121
6 see whorl. →123
rose cross a Greek cross which has a rose motif at the crossing of its limb; used as an emblem by the Rosicrucian brotherhood in the 16th century. →118
rose dawn see aurora.
rose madder see madder lake.
Rosenstiehl's green see manganese green.
rose quartz a cloudy, pink variety of quartz used for ornament and as a gemstone.
rosette, 1 rose; a decorative circular ornament which represents a stylized rose or any other similar flower. →82, →123
2 see whorl. →123
rose window, marigold window; in medieval religious architecture, a large round ornamental window with tracery. →109
see types of *rose window* illustration. →109
rosewood 1 [*Dalbergia spp.*] hardwoods from South America and India with purplish brown timber and decorative grain, used for decorative panelling, furniture and cabinets; other similar species are often sold as rosewood; often also called palisander; see ***Dalbergia spp.*** for full list of related species included in this work.
2 bois de rose; a shade of reddish brown which takes its name from the colour of the above.
Rosicrucian cross see rose cross. →118
rosin, colophony, Greek pitch; a hard transparent brittle resinous residue formed during the production of turpentine, used with a solvent as a weak adhesive and in some paints.
rostra Lat.; a Roman speakers' rostrum, especially that of the Forum Romanum, so called because it was decorated with the prows of ships captured at Antium in 338 BC.
rostral column see columna rostrata. →69
rostrum a platform for public speaking, a podium.
rosy cross see rose cross. →118
rot, decay, fungal decay; the decomposition of wood by the attack of fungi and other micro-organisms; see list of wood-attacking fungi under **fungi**.
rotary cut veneer, peeled veneer; veneer cut from a rotating log or flitch to produce a continuous sheet; sometimes called unrolled veneer. →10
rotary float see power float.
rotary planer see planer.
rotary trimmer a device for trimming and cropping sheets of paper, light card etc. by means of a blade-carrying mechanism which slides along a straight bar across the surface of the sheet.
rotary trowel see power trowel.
rotating damper a rotating metal flap incorporated within a flue or chimney to regulate the amount of draught for combustion, or to shut off the flueway completely. →56
rotating pan mixer, paddle mixer; in the production of concrete, a pan mixer which has rotating mixing baffles.
rotation the turning of an object around an axis.
rotten knot see unsound knot. →1
rotunda a classical circular domed building used for ceremonial or public functions. →86
rough board finish a finish for concrete in which the grain and sawing pattern of the boards used as formwork are evident in the surface.
rough arch see rough brick arch. →22, →23
rough brick arch, rough arch; a structural arch laid with rectangular bricks in wedge-shaped joints. →22, →23
roughcast, 1 trullisatio; the first undercoat or key layer of rough plaster added to a masonry surface onto which a fresco is to be painted; see intonaco, arriccio.
2 see wet dash.
roughcast glass 1 glass with an obscuring surface on one side, traditionally produced by casting molten glass on a bed of sand.
2 see cast glass.
rough grounds see grounds.
roughing plane, cow plane, scrub plane, scud plane, scurfing plane; a woodworking hand tool with an uneven blade for shaping and roughing timber surfaces prior to gluing.
roughness a description of a material or surface with an uneven, irregular or angular texture.
rough paper very coarse-grained paper used for watercolour painting.
rough planed a classification of a timber surface which has undergone preliminary smoothing with a plane.
rough t and g board a timber cladding board which has been sawn, as opposed to milled, with a tongue and groove. →8, →44
round 1 see circular.
2 a milled joinery profile which is round in cross-section; also called a dowel. →2
3 see round bar. →34
roundabout 1 a road junction designed to ease the flow of traffic, with a small one-way distributing ring road to which all roads meeting at that point are connected. →62
2 see mini-roundabout. →62

roundabout interchange see roundabout junction. →63

roundabout junction a variation on the diamond junction, with a flyover roundabout located at the meeting of all ramps to ease traffic flow; also called a roundabout interchange or grade-separated roundabout junction. →63

round arch any arch whose intrados is the arc of a circle; types included as separate entries are listed below. →24
circular arch. →24
Florentine arch. →23
horseshoe arch. →24
Italian round arch, see Florentine arch. →23
Norman arch.
Roman arch. →22, →24
Romanesque arch.
round cinquefoliated arch. →23
round horseshoe arch, see horseshoe arch. →24
round multifoliated arch. →23
round trefoil arch. →24
round trifoliated arch. →23, →110
segmental arch, segmented arch. →22, →24
semicircular arch. →22, →24

round-arris boarding see round-edged boarding. →8

round bar a metal bar with a circular cross-section; uses in construction include framing, brackets, tie rods, concrete reinforcement, stakes and ornamental work. →27, →34

round billet, roll billet; an ornamental billet moulding consisting of a chequerwork of elongated convex forms or cylinders. →124

round brackets see parentheses.

round brush any paintbrush with a round head and round handle; used primarily in decorative work and stencilling. →43

round church a medieval church type with a round central area or nave.

round cinquefoliated arch a decorative arch whose intrados is composed of five circular lobes or foils, and whose extrados is a semicircle. →23

round column see circular column. →13

rounded aggregate coarse aggregate whose particles are rounded in shape.

rounded arris see pencil round. →14

rounded edge see bullnose. →14

round-edged boarding, round-arris boarding; timber cladding boards with rectangular cross-section whose outer edges have been rounded, used for decking, outdoor furniture etc. →8

roundel, 1 oculus, round window; a window which is round in shape; see also bullseye, rose window. →23
2 a decorative circular panel, tablet, relief or window. →24, →110
3 see tondo. →123
4 see medallion. →113
5 a round or semicircular turret in a castle or fortification.
6 any straight decorative moulding which is half a circle or more in cross-section; an astragal, roll moulding, bead moulding etc. →14

round head screw see dome head screw. →36

round hollow section see circular hollow section. →34

round horseshoe arch see horseshoe arch. →24

round house 1 stone dwelling types of prehistoric and native cultures which have circular plans; in Britain, particularly those of early Celtic origin. →65
2 see wheelhouse. →65
3 see broch. →65
4 see rotunda. →86

round knot a knot in a sawn timber surface, roughly circular in shape. →1

round log a log from which the branches and bark have been removed, used in horizontal log construction.

round moulding 1 see roll moulding. →14
2 see half round moulding. →14
3 see three-quarter round. →14
4 see torus. →14, →80
5 see bowtell. →14

round multifoliated arch a decorative arch whose intrados is composed of a number of circular lobes or foils, and whose extrados is a semicircle; see trifoliated, cinquefoliated. →23

round nail any nail whose shank is round in cross-section.
see round wire nail.

round nose pliers a pair of pliers whose jaws are smooth but rounded conical rods, used for gripping and bending wire.

round notch in log construction, the simplest of log corner joints, in which the underside of each log has a hewn transverse concave notch to fit with the curvature of the log below; also often known as a saddleback joint, and sometimes erroneously called a saddle notch. →6

round plane, convex plane, gutter plane, spout plane; a woodworking plane with a convex base and blade for cutting concave rebates; usually sold in a pair with a hollow plane.

round section 1 see circular hollow section. →34
2 see round bar. →34

roundsil see compass plane.

round temple, 1 circular temple; any temple type whose plan is based on a circle. →66, →85
2 see monopteral. →85
3 see tholos. →85
4 see thymele. →85

round tower a slender, round stone construction with a conical pointed roof, found in Early Christian Ireland and used for defence or as a look-out; any such structure similar to this. →103

round trefoil arch a decorative arch with three circular lobes or foils in a cloverleaf arrangement. →24

round trifoliated arch a decorative arch whose intrados is composed of three circular lobes or foils in a cloverleaf arrangement, and whose extrados is a semicircle. →23, →110

round tube a metal profile of hollow round cross-section; when in steel and used for structural purposes, it is called a circular hollow section. →34
see *metal tubes* illustration. →34
see circular hollow section. →34

round window 1 see roundel. →23
2 see Catherine wheel window. →109
3 see rose window, marigold window. →109
see *styles of round window* illustration. →109

round wire nail, French nail; a nail with a round shank and flat chequered head, 13–150 mm in length.

route in traffic planning, the particular series of directions and distances, usually along defined roads or paths, determining the way from one place to another.

router a motor-driven hand-held cutter for making a variety of cuts in wood, including grooves, rebates, housings or mouldings.

router plane, granny's tooth, hag's tooth, old woman's tooth; a two-handled woodworking plane with a narrow protruding blade for cleaning out and smoothing the base of grooves.

routine see procedure.

roving in glassfibre construction, a number of parallel glass strands wound through one full turn to form a loose bundle, used as a basis for woven glassfibre fabric.

rowan, mountain ash; [*Sorbus aucuparia*] a European hardwood with hard yellow-brown timber; used for small items, tool handles and spinning wheels.

row house any small dwelling constructed in a row, with common party walls or subsidiary buildings joining one to another, see terraced house, linked dwellings. →61

rowel see spur rowel. →108

rowlock, bull header; a brick on edge with its end showing in a masonry wall. →20

rowlock bond see rat-trap bond. →17

rowlock course, bull header course; a brickwork course made up entirely of rowlocks. →20

royal a British standard paper size; 20" × 25", 508 mm × 635 mm. →Table 6

Royal Air Force blue see cadet blue.

royal cubit 'meh nesut'; an ancient Egyptian Old Kingdom unit of measurement equivalent to approximately 52 cm in length, used to measure building dimensions, land, quantities of grain etc. →106

Royal door see porta regia. →89

Royal green see chrome green.

Royal Institute of British Architects, the see RIBA.

Royal Institute of the Architects of Scotland, the see RIAS.

Royal Institute of the Architects of Ireland, the see RIAI.

royal purple a shade of purple, originally crimson, which takes its name from the colour of dyes used by the Phoenicians for colouring the royal wardrobe.

Royal yellow see king's yellow.

RSI-value, internal surface resistance value; a theoretical measure of the thermal insulation properties of the internal surface of a given construction or component parts of a given construction, used in the calculation of U-values; units are m^2 C/W.

rsj rolled steel joist, see I-section. →34

RSO-value, external surface resistance value; a theoretical measure of the thermal insulation properties of the external surface of a given construction or component parts of a given construction, used in the calculation of U-values; units are m^2 C/W.

rubbed brickwork see gauged brickwork.

rubbed finish a smooth finish in stonework, brickwork and concreting produced by manual rubbing with abrasives.

rubbed joint a brickwork mortar joint flush to the brickwork surface, formed by clearing off excess mortar with a rag when wet. →16

rubber 1 a synthetic organic polymer or natural product obtained as sap from certain species of plants and trees with good properties of elasticity and waterproofing; used in the construction industry for seals and waterproofing, as latex in paints, in paints etc.; types included as separate entries are listed below.
acrylic rubber, see polyacrylate rubber.
bromine butyl rubber, BIIR.
butadiene rubber.
butyl rubber.
cellular rubber.
chloroprene rubber, CR.
ethylene propylene diene rubber, EPDM.
expanded rubber.
foam rubber.
isoprene rubber, IR.
natural rubber, NR.
nitrile rubber.
polyacrylate rubber, ACM.
polyisoprene.
silicone rubber.
sponge rubber, see foam rubber.
styrene-butadiene rubber, SBR.
synthetic rubber.
2 a small piece of rubber, vinyl or other abrasive material used for rubbing out marks in drawings and designs, also known as an eraser. →130
clutch rubber.
indiarubber, see caoutchouc.
kneaded rubber, see putty rubber.
ink rubber, see ink eraser.
putty rubber.

rubber adhesive 1 see elastomeric adhesive.
2 see rubber solution.

rubber flooring 1 durable flooring in sheet or tile form, manufactured in rolls from natural or synthetic rubber.
2 see studded rubber flooring. →44
3 see cement rubber latex flooring.

rubber glue 1 see elastomeric adhesive.
2 see rubber solution.

rubber latex cement flooring see cement rubber latex flooring.

rubber mallet a mallet whose head is made of rubber, used for jobs where a steel head may cause damage. →40

rubber set an outdated name for false set.

rubber solution, rubber glue; glue manufactured from natural or synthetic rubber and used for gluing rubber products.

rubber spreader see spreader. →43

rubbing 1 see flatting down.
2 see frottage.

rubbish solid waste, especially that collected from habitation, consumption etc.; household waste, called garbage in North America.

rubbish bin see refuse bin.

rubbish dump, refuse tip, rubbish tip; a designated area of public land, often fenced and maintained by a local authority, to which waste material from a particular area is brought.

rubbish tip see rubbish dump.

rubble 1 any broken pieces of brick, stone, concrete etc. resulting from demolition work and building waste; used as fill and hardcore.
2 see hardcore.
3 roughly cut or irregular stones used in masonry walling; types included as separate entries are listed below. →11
coursed rubble. →11
coursed squared rubble masonry. →11
emplecton, opus antiquum. →83
opus concretum, opus caementicium. →83
random rubble. →11
squared rubble masonry. →11
random squared rubble masonry, see uncoursed squared rubble masonry. →11
uncoursed rubble, see random rubble. →11
uncoursed squared rubble masonry. →11

rubble basket see gabion. →29

rubble chute see drop chute.

rubble concrete concrete containing large pieces of broken stone, masonry, concrete and building rubble as a filler.

rubble finish see quarry finish. →12

rubble facing stone facing of a rough or rustic nature for masonry walling, used to provide a fine finish at a lower cost than rubble masonry.

rubble revetment see pitching.

rubblestone walling masonry of rough coursed stones with varying height.

rubble wall 1 a masonry wall constructed from roughly cut or irregular stones; sometimes also called ragstone wall; types included as separate entries are listed below. →11
coursed rubble. →11
random rubble. →11
squared rubble masonry. →11
uncoursed rubble, see random rubble. →11
2 see gabion wall. →29
3 see dry-stone wall.

Rubens brown a form of Vandyke brown earth pigment.

Rubens madder a brownish shade of alizarin crimson pigment.

Rubia tinctorum common madder plant; see alizarin.

rubicund see ruddy.

rubidium a silver-white, metallic chemical element, **Rb**, used in the manufacture of photoelectric cells.
rubstone an abrasive stone used for sharpening chisels or for producing a fine surface on stonework. →41
Rubus idaeus see raspberry (red).
ruby 1 a red variety of the mineral corundum, used as a gemstone, often produced artificially.
2 ruby red; a general name for shades of strong, dark bluish reds named after the above.
ruby red see ruby.
ruby silver see proustite.
ruddle see red oxide paint.
ruddy, rubicund; a shade of red which takes its name from the colour of the effects of wind and weather on the facial complexion.
ruin the dilapidated and uninhabited remains of a building, usually of historical importance.
rule 1 see ruler.
2 see scale rule.
3 see screed board.
ruled joint see scored joint. →16
rule joint hinge, table hinge; a backflap hinge with one leaf wider than the other, used for hinged table tops. →38
ruler, 1 rule; a long scaled rod, bar or strip of metal, wood or plastic used for measuring and drawing straight lines.
2 see parallel ruler. →130
rumble strip, serrated strip; in traffic design, a series of raised lines, bumps etc. for marking the edge of a carriageway and to reduce the speed of traffic at junctions by producing a warning vibration in the vehicle when driven over.
run 1 a defect in a paint finish caused by drips from thickly painted areas running down the surface once setting has begun.
2 see going. →45
3 see total going. →45
4 drain run, see discharge pipe. →58
run-by pit see lift pit.
run cast in decorative plasterwork, a preformed plaster cast formed of fibrous plaster by running a template known as a run mould across it when wet. →14
Rundbogenstil an architectural style in Germany from the mid-1800s characterized by the eclectic use of Romanesque and Renaissance elements.
rung a horizontal bar which functions as a step in a ladder. →54
run-moulded plasterwork plasterwork shaped into a profiled moulding by dragging a template or running mould across it. →14
run moulding, horsed moulding; an ornamental plasterwork moulding shaped by dragging a template in the profile of the final moulding across wet plaster.
runner 1 in excavation work, one of a series of timber boards driven into the earth at the side of a proposed trench, after which soil is removed from the trench side. →30
2 in thatched roofing, a flexible stick of hazel or willow used to tie thatch to rafters; see withe. →48
3 in timber frame construction, a horizontal timber member to which other members including joists are fixed. →57
4 see ceiling runner. →60
5 see lift guide.
running, 1 repeated; a description of ornament, decoration and brick bonds etc. which are composed of the same interlinked recurring motif; see running bond, running ornament.
2 in ornamental plasterwork, the making of run mouldings such as cornices by drawing a shaped profile across the face of wet plaster.
3 the operation of software by a computer.
running bond 1 see stretcher bond. →17
2 a paving pattern in which alternate rows of rectangular pavers are laid with a half-stone overlap with respect to neighbouring rows; similar patterns in parquetry and tiling. →15
running dimensions dimensioning for a drawing, usually a survey, in which all measurements in any one line are taken from a single reference point.
running dog classical ornament made up of a series of S-shaped curves joined end on end, synonymous with Vitruvian scroll; sometimes rendered as a fret with squared lines or fillets. →125
running mould, horse mould; a metal or wooden template drawn across a plaster surface to form an ornamental moulding with a uniform cross-section; see run moulding. →14
running ornament any banded ornamental motif made up of a pattern of wavy lines which intermingle to form a continuous design, rather than having simple distinct repeated motifs. →124
running rule in making a plaster moulding, a long strip of timber used as a guide for a running mould.
running sand a soil type, sand saturated with water, which behaves in a similar fashion to a liquid.
runway a flat paved strip designed to accommodate the taking off and landing of aircraft.
Rupicapra rupicapra the chamois antelope, see chamois leather.
rupture a break in a material or component which can lead to failure.
rural architecture see rustic architecture.
rural area see open country.
rural depopulation the result of migration of people from rural to urban areas in search of work.
rural planning, country planning; the same processes of physical planning that occur in town planning applied to areas of countryside.
rush hour in town planning, a daily period in an urban area during which vehicular congestion may occur due to an excess of traffic as people travel to or from their workplaces.
Ruskinian an architectural movement in England from the 1800s linked to the Arts and Crafts, which championed the Venetian Gothic style advocated by the writer John Ruskin and sought solutions to industrial living from medieval precedent.
Russian constructivism see constructivism.
Russian cross, eastern cross, orthodox cross; a three-barred cross indicative of the crucifixion cross, whose upper limb represents a plaque and lower skewed limb a footrest; the Symbol of the Greek and Russian Orthodox churches. →117
rust 1 the reddish-brown product of oxidation which forms on the surface of untreated iron and steel when in prolonged contact with water or air.
2 see hazel.
rust brown see hazel.
rustic architecture, rural architecture, vernacular architecture; traditional architecture based on the culture of the countryside, built with local materials, methods and craftsmanship.
rustic ashlar see rusticated ashlar. →12
rusticated ashlar, rustic ashlar; coursed and dressed stonework with edges and joints emphasized by rustication. →12
rusticated brick, rustic brick; any brick whose face has been treated or pressed with a pattern or texture.
rusticated column a column with a series of square blocks arranged vertically up its round shaft, often decorated with surface texture; found primarily in classical architecture from the late Renaissance onwards; may also be called a banded or ringed column. →13, →114
rustication 1 in masonrywork, decorative rebates or sinkings around the edges of individual stones to emphasize joints and give articulation to the surface; especially prevalent in Renaissance architecture. →12
2 see textured finish.

rustication strip strip material attached to the inside of formwork to provide grooves and indentations in cast concrete surfaces.

rustic brick see rusticated brick.

rustic finish see textured finish.

rust inhibiting see corrosion inhibiting.

ruthenium a light, spongy, white, durable metal, **Ru**, from the platinum group.

rutile a metallic mineral, natural titanium dioxide, $\mathbf{TiO_2}$, an important ore of titanium.

R-value, coefficient of thermal resistance; a theoretical measure of the thermal insulation properties of a given construction or component parts of a given construction, the reciprocal of C-value, whose units are m^2 C/W.

S

S trap a drainage trap shaped in the letter 'S' lying on its side, with both the inlet and outlet vertical and a water seal contained in the lower bed.

sabin see metric sabin.

sabre saw see jigsaw.

sacellum 1 Lat.; a small Roman unroofed chapel containing a sacrificial altar.
2 a sepulchral chapel in a church.

sackcloth see hessian.

sack holder a metal frame attached to the inside of a waste bin to support disposable plastic or paper refuse sacks.

sacral building see religious building.

sacrarium 1 Lat.; a sacred space, shrine or room in a Roman dwelling for the keeping of objects of worship.
2 see piscina.
3 see sanctuary.

sacred fig tree see tree of Buddha. →121

sacred ibis see Thoth. →74

sacred lotus the blue lotus, [*Nelumbium nucifera*], as used in eastern ornament; see lotus. →121

sacred scarab see scarab, Khepri. →75

sacrificial altar an altar, stone table etc. on which live offerings were ritually sacrificed in the name of a deity.
see *sacrificial altar* illustration. →116
see *Mesopotamian temple* illustration. →66
see *Egyptian pyramid* illustration. →70

sacrificial chapel a sacred space within a temple or shrine, in which sacrificial offerings were made.
see *sacrificial chapel* in mastaba illustration. →70

sacrificial stone 1 a pagan stone altar, slab etc. at which ritual sacrifices were performed. →116
2 see cupstone. →116

sacristy a chamber in a church or cathedral near the sanctuary, where the robes and various utensils of the clergy are kept, and in which they were prepared for service; often the same room as a vestiary or vestry.
see *Early Christian church* illustration. →95
see *Scandinavian church* illustration. →102
see *Romanesque church* illustration. →99

saddle 1 see bolster. →4
2 in thatched roofing, long straw laid over a ridge and secured with hazel or willow branches; see also brotch, ligger. →48
3 see chimney saddle.
4 see saddle junction.
5 see pipe saddle.
6 see saddle scarf. →6

saddleback see saddleback coping. →16

saddleback capping brick a saddleback coping brick whose length matches the width of the wall on which it is laid, without overhangs on either side. →16

saddleback coping, saddleback, saddle coping; a coping stone, brick or other construction with a central linear ridge and two downwardly sloping upper faces, forming a weatherproof capping for the top of a masonry wall or parapet. →16

saddleback coping brick a special brick with a ridged upper surface and throated overhangs to provide a saddleback coping on top of freestanding walls. →16

saddleback joint see round notch. →6

saddleback roof, duopitch roof, saddle roof; a pitched roof of two sloping planes which meet at an upper ridge with a gable at either end. →46

saddle clip, pipe clip; a U-shaped metal fixing with protruding lugs, designed to attach a pipe to the building fabric with screws.

saddle coping see saddleback coping. →16

saddle fitting see pipe saddle.

saddle junction, saddle; in plumbing and drainage, a branch connection made by boring a hole in a main pipeline and joining a subsidiary pipe with a special fitting.

saddle notch in log construction, a simple log corner joint in which the underside of each log is cut with a transverse V-shaped notch to fit with the corresponding shape of the upper surface of the log below. →6
see round notch. →6

saddle roof see saddleback roof. →46

saddler's hammer a tack hammer with a small claw attached perpendicular to its peen, used for pulling out tacks. →40

saddle scarf in horizontal log construction, the cutting of a V-shaped long groove in the lower edge of a log to prevent large gaps opening up during drying and settling; also called a saddle. →6

saddle stone, apex stone; the uppermost stone in a gable, pediment or other triangular or conical stone construction.

sadzhen, sagene; a traditional Russian unit of distance equal to 3 arshins, equivalent to 7 English feet or 2.134 m.

SAFA acronym for Suomen Arkkitehtiliitto Finlands Arkitektförbund, the Finnish Association of Architects.

Safavid architecture the Islamic architecture of Persia from 1500 to 1600, characterized by the use of coloured wall tiling, ornamental scripts and woven carpets.

safe anchorage a fixing or cleat anchored to a roof surface for tying safety ropes and cables during maintenance.

safety the range of legislation and codes of practice for building construction pertaining to structural stability, constructional integrity, measures taken to prevent and protect against fire damage etc.

safety barrier see vehicle safety barrier.

safety curtain see fire curtain.

safety deposit box a lockable receptacle for the storage of valuable items, stored in a vault.

safety factor see factor of safety.

safety glass 1 glass which resists breakage, or breaks in such a way as to reduce the risk of injury to a minimum; includes toughened glass, laminated glass and wired glass. →53
2 see laminated safety glass.

safety glazing glazing designed to withstand a specified level of physical impact without breaking; see safety glass.

safety level a measure of the level of risk from hazards such as fire and explosion.

safety lighting, 1 emergency lighting; auxiliary lighting used in emergencies to provide illumination for escape during fire, power failure etc.
2 see standby lighting.

safety officer a local authority inspector who ensures that designs, constructions and site procedures comply with safety standards and regulations.

safety rail a light open balustrade or railing at the side of access stairs, gantries, platforms etc. to afford protection during maintenance. →54

safety sign 1 see fire safety sign.
2 see fire exit sign.

safety valve a valve operated automatically or manually to release excess pressure in any system of pipework and vessels containing a gas or liquid.

safflower, carthame; a red dye made from the dried petals of the flowers of the safflower plant [*Carthamus tinctorius*].

saffron 1 a yellow pigment, used in Roman times, obtained from crushing the dried petals of the flower *Crocus sativa*.
2 see flame yellow.

sag, curtain, curtaining, sagging; a defect in a paint finish caused by an area of thickly applied paint which begins to run down the surface producing a horizontal ridge.

sagene see sadzhen.

sagging see sag.

sag pipe, inverted siphon; drainage, a kink in a horizontal inground drainpipe or sewer to convey its contents under an obstacle, relying on siphonage to function.

sagularis see via sagularis. →104

Sahara a shade of brown which takes its name from the colour of the sands of the Sahara desert.

sahn in Islamic architecture, the colonnaded inner courtyard of a mosque.

sail dome, sail vault; a round or hemispherical dome constructed on pendentives, so named because it resembles the form of a billowing sail with arched openings between its corners; see also pendentive dome. →26

sailor a brick on end with its bed showing in the face of a masonry wall, used in a row for string courses, fill and decorative effects. →20

sailor course a brick course made up entirely of sailors. →20

sail vault see sail dome. →26

saint see list of saints used in architectural ornament listed under 'St'. →118

Sakhmet see Sekhmet. →74

sal ammoniac see ammonium chloride.

salamander a portable heater used during cold weather for curing freshly poured concrete with a naked flame.

salary 1 money or wages paid on a regular basis to an employee for work or services, usually of a professional or non-manual nature.
2 see monthly salary.

sale the exchange of goods for money.

sales 1 in commerce, the selling of products.
2 the amount of goods or products sold.

sales representative a person or organization involved in the marketing of products, not necessarily employed by the manufacturer.

saliant variation of salient. →104

salient (angle) in military architecture, the obtuse external angle between two faces of a bastion; the salient is the point thus formed, projecting towards the enemy. →104

Salix spp. see willow.
Salix alba, see white willow.

sallent variation of salient. →104

sallied half lap joint a timber lengthening joint in which the halved ends of both pieces are splayed with a V-shaped or sallied end termination to fit into corresponding cuttings. →3

sallow, wan; a shade of greyish yellow which takes its name from the colour of a sickly facial complexion.

sally see birdsmouth.

sally port a small gate or subterranean passageway used to link the outer walls of a castle or fortified settlement with a keep or central fortified building; used by defenders to make surprise attacks or sorties.

salmon a shade of pink which takes its name from the colour of the fresh flesh of the Atlantic salmon [*Salmo salar*].

salomonica see spiral column. →114

salon 1 a reception room in a grand dwelling or palace.
2 a commercial fashion establishment such as a hairdresser, beautician or fashion boutique.

salt see halite.

salt glazing the glazing of ceramics by covering with a layer of common salt which fuses on firing to provide a protective surface.

saltire see St Andrew's cross. →118

salt stone see halite.

salutatorium 1 Lat.; the reception hall of a Roman Caesar or Roman Catholic bishop.
2 salutatory; a porch or chamber in a medieval church where the clergy and commoners could meet.

salutatory see salutatorium.

salvage, scrap; solid metal waste which can be recycled.

Samanid architecture the Islamic architecture of what is now Turkmenistan and Uzbekistan, ruled by a Muslim dynasty from 873 to 999 AD.

samarium a hard silvery metallic chemical element, **Sm**.

samba see obeche.

Samian base a classical Ionic column base in which the lower end of the column rests on a spira, a cushion-like protrusion with horizontal fluting. →81

sample 1 a section of a building or construction, interior space, component, product, material or colour which has been assembled or presented to give an indication of how it will function or appear once finished.
2 a part removed from a whole for testing; a soil sample, concrete test sample or component from a batch.
3 an example for demonstration, as with a product sample or colour sample.

samson post in traditional timber frame construction, a freestanding post for carrying a beam, supported directly from a floor. →4

SAN styrene-acrylonitrile.

sanatorium, sanitarium (Am.); a building or complex for the residence of those recuperating from long illness, or with a terminal illness.

sanavivaria see porta sanavivaria. →90

sanction a punitive measure taken to force a person, company or nation to obey the law.

sanctuary 1 the most sacred area of a temple or church containing the divinity; a shrine.
see *Egyptian temple* illustration. →72
2 a bounded or raised area in a church or cathedral surrounding the high altar; also called sacrarium. →116
see *Romanesque church* illustration. →99
see *Scandinavian hall church* illustration. →102
3 see adytum. →85
4 see cella. →66
5 see fanum.
6 see holy of holies.
7 see naos.
8 see templum. →84
9 see barque sanctuary. →72
10 see bird sanctuary.

sand 1 mineral soil composed of particles between 0.06 mm and 2 mm in size; classified variously as fine sand, medium sand, coarse sand.
2 see ivory.

sandalwood [*Santalum spp.*] a tropical evergreen hardwood from Asia and Australia whose timber is used in decorative work.

sandarac natural resin gathered from the gum juniper tree [*Tetraclinis articulata, Callitris quadrivalvis*] from North Africa, used with a solvent such as turpentine in artist's oil paints; also known as gum sandarac.

sand bedding a layer of sand spread over a structural base, in which paving stones are laid. →15

sand blasting a smoothing, finishing or cleaning treatment for concrete, glass or masonry surfaces in which sand or other particles are mechanically projected at high velocity by compressed air; also written as sandblasting.

sand curing a method of curing concrete by placing a layer of wet sand on top.

sand drain, vertical sand drain; in soil mechanics, a bored excavation filled with sand to drain and consolidate clay and silty soils.

sanded a description of an even, smooth and matt surface or finish produced by rubbing or blasting with abrasives.

sanded chipboard chipboard whose surface has been sanded smooth during manufacture.

sanded finish a relatively even masonry finish produced by rubbing or blasting with abrasives.

sanded plaster a plaster mix containing a high proportion of sand.

sanded plywood plywood whose face plies have been sanded smooth during manufacture.

sander a machine tool used for smoothing timber surfaces; see belt sander, orbital sander.

sand-faced brick a brick one end and one side of which have been given a coating of sand before firing.

sanding 1 the producing of an even, unpitted, smooth surface finish in timber, stone etc. using an abrasive. **2** see joint sanding.

sanding block a small block of wood, rubber or cork around which sandpaper is wrapped during manual sanding. →41

sand joint a joint between adjacent laid paving stones, filled with brushed sand. →15

sand jointing see joint sanding. →15

sand-lime brick see calcium silicate brick.

sandpaper, emery paper; paper coated with an abrasive such as powdered glass, mineral, emery or hard metal for sanding by hand or machine. →41

sandpaper block see glasspaper block.

sand piling see deep compaction.

sandpit a play area for children consisting of a framed area of sand.

sandstone a brown, beige or reddish sedimentary rock formed of particles of quartz cemented together by other minerals, relatively easy to shape and used extensively as a building stone.

sandwich panel a prefabricated composite concrete wall panel consisting of an inner structural and outer cladding leaf bonded on either side of a layer of fluted insulation. →28

sandy see arenaceous.

sanguine a red or flesh-coloured drawing crayon whose colour is derived from iron oxide.

sanitarium see sanatorium.

sanitary appliance any device in a building supplied with water and connected to a drain, used for drinking, cleaning or disposal of foul water.

sanitary module a prefabricated assembly of sanitary fittings with surrounding fabric and finishes, used on large projects with a high degree of prefabrication, brought to site and connected to structure and service outlets.

sanitary pipework, sanitary plumbing; the system of drain pipes which convey foul water from a building to an inground drain or sewer.

sanitary plumbing see sanitary pipework.

sanitary space a general term for washrooms and toilets.

sanitary ware sanitary fittings such as basins, WCs and urinals, moulded from vitreous china and glazed.

sanitation installation an installation of plumbing and appliances in a building for providing water and disposal of waste.

sanmon the main gateway of a Japanese temple. →68

Santalum spp. see sandalwood.

Santiago cross see cross of St James. →117

sap the water and dissolved sugars and nutrients in a living tree.

sapele [*Entandrophragma cylindricum*] a West African hardwood with red to golden brown, strong and durable timber; used as a substitute for mahogany in furniture, panelling, flooring and veneers.

sap green a shade of yellowish green which takes its name from the colour of blooming buds in spring.

sapling a young tree with a thin stem, planted as such in new areas of landscaping.

saponification a defect in paints caused by the breakdown of the oil medium to form a soft soapy mass in the presence of alkalis and moisture, especially occurring when applied to mineral-based surfaces such as masonry, new concrete, plaster and render.

sapphire a coloured variety of the mineral corundum, usually blue, occurring naturally or produced artificially; used as a gemstone.

sapphire blue a shade of dark blue which takes its name from the colour of the precious stone of the same name.

sap-stain a fungus which leaves a dark tinge, usually bluish, on the surface of timber.

sapwood, alburnum; living wood found in the outer area of a tree trunk; timber converted from this. →1

sapwood rot fungal decay in the sapwood of timber.

Saracen a name for peoples or objects of Muslim and Arab origin, in use in the Middle Ages.

Saracenic architecture see Islamic architecture.

Saracenic pointed arch see pointed Saracenic arch.

sarcelly see cross moline. →117

sarcophagal altar a typical altar type from the Baroque period, reminiscent of a sarcophagus. →116

sarcophagus a stone coffin, often decorated with inscriptions and carvings.
see *mastaba* illustration. →70
see *Egyptian rock-cut tomb* illustration. →74
see *altar* illustration. →116

sard a reddish-brown microcrystalline variety of the mineral chalcedony, used as a gemstone and for decoration; a form of cornelian.

sarking see roof boarding. →48

sarking and sheathing grade insulating board a grade of insulating board suitable for cladding roofs and walls.

sarking felt see reinforced felt.

Sarouk see Saruk.

sarsen a rough unhewn boulder of sandstone which occurs naturally on the surface of the land, often previously used as building stone.

Saruk, Sarouk; a shade of brownish beige which takes its name from the colour of certain Persian rugs from the Iranian village of Saruq.

Sasanian see Sassanian.

sash, window sash; an openable framed part of a window opened either by sliding or on hinges; a casement is a hinged sash.

sash chisel see butt chisel. →41

sash cramp see joiner's cramp.

sash handle a device or fitting used for opening a window sash.

sash window, 1 double-hung sash window, hanging sash window, vertical sliding window; a window with an openable sash or sashes which slide vertically in a frame. →52
2 sliding sash window, see sliding window. →52

Sassanian, Sasanian, Sassanid; pertaining to the architecture of the peoples of Persia from 226 to 651 AD after the Parthians, characterized by domed palaces whose walls are decorated with blind arcades.

Sassanid see Sassanian.

satellite a sophisticated telecommunications device, orbiting the earth in space, which receives and transmits electromagnetic signals to and from points around the globe.

satellite antenna see satellite link aerial.

satellite aerial see satellite link aerial.

satellite dish 1 a dish aerial for picking up signals transmitted by a satellite.
2 see satellite link aerial.

satellite link aerial, satellite antenna; a telecommunications receiver for relaying electromagnetic signals via a satellite; a round satellite aerial is called a dish.

satellite town, industrial suburb; a self-contained town separated by distance and open countryside from a larger metropolis, but linked economically via transport systems.

satin 1 see opal.
2 see eggshell gloss.

satin white a shade of white which takes its name from the colour of uncoloured satin or silk.
satinwood [*Chloroxylon swietenia*] see Ceylon satinwood.
saturated colour in colour theory, a colour whose outward appearance cannot be intensified by the addition of more of the same coloured pigment.
saturated soil soil whose voids are filled with water.
saturation 1 the relative amount of water filling voids in soil or other porous or absorbent substance; especially its maximum possible water content.
2 see colour saturation.
saturation point 1 see fibre saturation point.
2 see dewpoint.
saturnine red see red lead.
satyr a decorative motif depicting woodland or mountain spirits which appeared as men with the ears and tail of an ass, representing the fertility of the wilderness; a goat-legged satyr was known to the Romans as faun (pl. fauni) or pan (pl. panes) and the elder one as a silenos (pl. sileni). →122
saucer dome a dome whose height is small in relation to its diameter, a shallow dome. →26
sauna a building, room or series of spaces with wooden benches and a stove for bathing in steam.
see *sauna* illustration. →58
see *brick house* illustration. →59
sauna bench one of a number of raised timber platforms for sitting on in a sauna or steam room, usually of soft, porous timbers such as obeche, aspen or spruce. →58
sauna heater, sauna stove, stone heater; a heating appliance for a sauna consisting of a nest of stones above a heating element or firebox, on which water is thrown to produce steam. →58
see electric sauna heater.
sauna stove see sauna heater. →58
saving 1 the setting aside of money as an investment for future use.
2 a reduction in cost, energy, fuel or water.
saw one of a wide range of hand or machine tools with toothed blades, used for cutting materials; types included as separate entries are listed below.
backsaw.
bandsaw.
bayonet saw, see jigsaw.
bead saw.
bench saw.
bow saw.
bracket saw, see fretsaw.
cabinet saw.
carborundum saw.
chainsaw.
circular saw.
compass saw.
concrete saw.
coping saw.
cross-cut saw.
crown saw, see hole saw. →42
diamond saw.
donkey saw, see mill saw.
dovetail saw.
drunken saw.
felling saw.
fillet saw.
flexible saw, see saw chain.
floor saw.
flooring saw.
forester's saw, see tubular bow saw.
frame saw, see gang saw, mill saw.
fretsaw.
grooving saw.
hacksaw.
handsaw.
hole saw. →42
inside start saw, see flooring saw.
jigsaw.
joiner saw, see bench saw.
keyhole saw.
lock saw, see keyhole saw.
log saw, see tubular bow saw.
masonry saw.
mill saw.
mini-hacksaw.
notching saw, see grooving saw.
pad saw.
panel saw.
power saw.
radial arm saw.
rip saw.
sabre saw, see jigsaw.
scribing saw, see coping saw.
scroll saw, see fretsaw.
stairbuilder's saw, see grooving saw.
steel bow saw, see bow saw.
Swedish saw, see tubular bow saw.
tenon saw.
trenching saw, see grooving saw.
tubular bow saw.
tubular saw, see hole saw. →42
turning saw.
two-man cross cut saw, see felling saw.
veneer saw.
web saw, see turning saw.
wire saw.
wobble saw, see drunken saw.
saw buck see saw horse.
saw chain, flexible saw; a saw consisting of a barbed chain pulled back and forth across wood; a manual chainsaw.
sawdust the fine powdered wood resulting from sawing, sanding and milling timber.
see **sawdust** fill in floor construction of log building. →6
sawdust concrete see wood-cement concrete.
sawdust plaster see wood-fibred plaster.
sawed see sawn.
saw horse, saw buck, trestle; a timber A-frame structure on which wood may be sawn.
sawing the cutting of timber, stone etc. with a saw; types included as separate entries are listed below.
band sawing.
flatsawing, plain sawing, through and through sawing. →2
flitch sawing. →2
live sawing. →2
sawing round the log. →2
resawing. →2
rift sawing, quartersawing. →2
rip-sawing, see flat cutting.
see *wood and sawn timber* illustration. →1
see *conversion of timber* illustration. →2
sawing defect defects and blemishes in sawn timber caused by blunt or poorly adjusted machining tools. →1
sawing pattern see blade set.
sawing round the log a method of quartersawing timber by removing four thick sectors and resawing them into relatively even-grained boards, thus leaving a square central section; often used for logs with heart rot. →2
saw jointer a filing tool used in the first stage of sharpening a saw, which joints the teeth to an equal length.
sawmill an industrial plant for converting timber from logs into sawn boards.
sawn, sawed; **1** a description of a surface or object, often timber, board, stone or concrete, that has been cut or worked with a saw.
2 one of the industrial surface finishes available for building stone, obtained by sawing blocks into slabs or cutting stones to required sizes, with cutting marks from diamond disc or gangsaw blades clearly visible on the surface. →12
see *wood and sawn timber* illustration. →1
see *conversion of timber* illustration. →2

sawn finish **1** a rough but even surface on timber boards, stone etc. produced by conversion with a band saw or circular saw; see also previous entry.
2 an even finish produced by sawing stone; see sawn. →12
sawn softwood the generic term for sawn commercial softwood timber.
see *wood and sawn timber* illustration. →1
see *conversion of timber* illustration. →2
sawn timber timber converted into sections by sawing. →2
see *wood and sawn timber* illustration. →1
see *conversion of timber* illustration. →2
sawn veneer high quality decorative veneer cut with a fine saw.
saw set a slotted tool for setting the teeth of a saw.
saw tooth each of the small cutting serrations along a saw blade.
sawtooth moulding see indented moulding. →124
sawtooth roof an industrial roof type having a number of parallel roof surfaces of triangular section with a profile similar to the teeth in a saw; the steeper side, usually vertical, is often glazed; see also northlight roof, southlight roof. →46
sawyer beetle a longhorned beetle of the genus [Monochamus], whose larvae cause damage to conifers by boring.
Saxon architecture see Anglo-Saxon architecture.
Saxon blue see smalt.
SBR styrene-butadiene rubber.
scabbled finish see quarry finish. →12
scabbler see scabbling hammer. →40
scabbling in concretework, the removal of a surface layer of hardened concrete to expose the aggregate; see tooling.
scabbling hammer a mason's hammer whose head has a sharp point at one end, used for the rough dressing of granite and other hard stone. →40
scaena, scena; Lat.; a backdrop structure or stage building, a skene, in a Roman theatre, sometimes richly decorated and with spaces inside for the players; often used in the plural scaenae. →89
scaena ductilis Lat.; a movable decorative backdrop screen in a Roman theatre.
scaena frons Lat.; the decorated front surface of a scaena in a Roman theatre. →89
scaffold, scaffolding; a temporary structure erected alongside the external wall of a building under construction or repair to support workmen and materials.
scaffold boards see scaffolding boards.
scaffold nail see double headed nail. →35
scaffolding see scaffold.
scaffolding boards, scaffold boards; boards used to form a walkway or working platform in a scaffold.
scagliola a decorative masonry finish imitating marble used in classical Rome, composed of an applied mixture of alabaster gypsum, lime, marble and cement which is heated and polished to a very high sheen; sometimes referred to as stucco lustro, though generally regarded as its precursor.
scalar a mathematical quantity which expresses only magnitude, not direction; see vector.
scalding sink see rinsing sink.
scale **1** the proportion relative to full size at which a design drawing, model or map is produced.
2 see extent.
3 see scale rule. →130
4 see scales.
5 furring; in plumbing and hot-water installations, an undesirable hard chalky deposit from hard water building up on the inside surface of water pipes and heating vessels.
6 see fee scale.
7 see grey scale.
8 see human scale.
9 loose scale, see loose rust.
10 see mill scale.
11 vernier scale, see vernier callipers.
scale model, model; a three-dimensional realization of a design, usually to a smaller scale and to a lesser degree of complexity, for the purposes of presentation and as a design aid.
scale rule, scale; in scaled technical drawing, a plastic, wooden or metal scaled slat, often triangular in cross-section, with markings in a range of different scales. →130
scales, pair of scales; an instrument or apparatus used for measuring weight.
scaling the manual removal of loose rock and stones from a freshly blasted rock surface.
scaling hammer a hand-held hammer whose head has one chisel edge and a sharpened edge opposite, used for removing deposits, rust and scale from metal and stonework. →40
scallop **1** ornamental carving or decoration with a stylized fan-shaped shell motif. →123
2 see scallop moulding. →124
scallop capital, scalloped cushion capital; a capital found in Norman architecture, consisting of a squared block with its lower edges cut with radiating reed ornamentation resembling a scallop shell. →115
see double scallop capital. →115
scalloped cushion capital see scallop capital. →115
scallop moulding, invected moulding; a Romanesque decorative moulding consisting of a series of stylized scallop shells, a series of arcs joined end on end. →124
scalpel, surgical scalpel; a knife with a very sharp disposable steel blade held in a metal handle, used by surgeons, designers and modelmakers. →130
scaly cap fungus, scaly lentinus; [*Lentinus lepideus*] a brown rot fungus with a scaly cap and white flesh which attacks timber in contact with damp ground.
scaly lentinus see scaly cap fungus.
scamillus Lat.; diminutive form of scamnum; a small unadorned plinth beneath the bases of Ionic and Corinthian columns.
scamna plural of scamnum.
scamnum, pl. scamna; 'bench', Lat.; a residential block in a Roman city or military settlement which has its end walls facing the main street; see striga.
Scandinavian hall church see Scandinavian church illustration. →102
scandula Lat.; pl. scandulae; a timber roofing shingle in Roman architecture.
scanner an electronic device for converting an image into digital information so that it can be viewed, transmitted and manipulated by electronic media, computers etc.
scanning the converting of an image into digital form using a scanner or similar device.
scantling a piece of sawn timber with cross-sectional dimensions of 38 mm–75 mm thick and 75 mm–175 mm wide. →2
scarab **1** ancient Egyptian ornament depicting a scarab or dung-beetle, revered symbol of the sun deity, creation and resurrection. →75
2 see Khepri. →75
scarf joint, 1 scarfed joint; a timber lengthening joint for connecting two timbers end to end by cutting and overlapping to provide a gluing or fixing edge. →3
see *types of timber scarf joint* illustration. →3
2 see splayed scarf joint. →3
scarf-jointed plywood, scarfed plywood; plywood extended or lengthened using scarf joints.
scarfed joint see scarf joint. →3
scarfed plywood see scarf-jointed plywood.
scarlet vermilion see vermilion.
scarp a steep defensive slope surrounding the base of a fortification, usually a bank of earth forming the inner side of a ditch; also known as an escarp, escarpe or escarpment; see counterscarp. →104

scattering the spreading out or diffusing of radiation when passing through matter; in lighting design, the diffusing of sunlight when passing through the earth's atmosphere.

scena see scaena (Lat.). →89

scenario a conceived outline or plan for an ensuing series of events.

scene see skene (Gk), scaena (Lat.). →89

scenery the view of a surrounding environment, external landscape etc.

scenic lift see observation lift.

scenography 1 the art of antique theatre set design or perspective drawing.
2 the representation of an object, building or scene in perspective.

schedule 1 written design documentation for doors, windows, ironmongery etc. in the form of tables or detailed lists specifying type, finish, quantity, location and other information not found on drawings.
2 see drawings schedule.
3 see window schedule.
4 see schedule of defects.
5 see programme.

scheduled fabric in reinforced concrete, fabric reinforcement defined by specifying the size and spacing of the wires or bars.

schedule of defects, defects schedule; a list of defects, omissions and errors, poor workmanship etc. in building work drawn up during the final inspection of a building nearing completion, obliging the contractor to make reparations accordingly.

schedule of drawings see drawings schedule.

schedule of fixtures and finishes a contract document specifying surface finishes, interior materials and fixed fittings for each space in a building.

schedule of rates a schedule in which the prices applicable to various items of work are listed.

schedule of works in contract administration, an itemized list of work to be undertaken for a construction project, often written prior to the contract stage, or forming the basis of a contract without a bill of quantities.

scheme, 1 design; designs of a building project or development presented as drawings, models or computer generations; the building produced from these designs.
2 see building group.

schist a group of medium-grained metamorphic rocks in which the minerals are arranged in parallel layers similar to that of sedimentary rocks.
see crystalline schist.
see gneissose micaschist, foliated gneiss.
see mica schist.

schistose rock rock containing schist or with a texture similar to schist.

Schmid and Eckhart method see method of intersections. →127

Schnitzer's green see chromium oxide green.

schola, 1 schola labri; a recess in a Roman bathhouse containing a bathtub or pool.
2 an alcove in a classical palaestra for recreation and relaxation. →91
3 see schola cantorum. →95

schola cantorum that part of an Early Christian church reserved for the choir, or liturgical singers; often a raised platform surrounded by a low balustrade. →95

schola labri see schola.

school a building or complex designed for education.

School of Amsterdam see Amsterdam, School of.

Schweinfurt green see emerald green.

science park, technology park, research park; an industrial building community, often constructed in parkland, which specializes in technological and industrial research.

scissor brace in traditional timber frame construction, the cross bracing of pairs of common rafters.

scissor gate see collapsible gate.

scissor junction a road junction of two roads crossing obliquely and at the same vertical level. →62

scissor lift a steel platform raised and lowered by the hydraulic action of a hinged scissor-like structure beneath, used in loading bays etc. for raising goods through short distances.

scissor rafter roof see scissor roof. →33

scissor roof, scissor rafter roof; a timber roof which has diagonal cross braces, called scissor braces, as a means of supporting and stiffening the rafters. →33

scissors, pair of scissors; an implement for cutting sheet material such as paper or cloth with two hinged blades which have loops for finger and thumb at the non-cutting end.

scissors truss a pitched truss whose lower chords cross to form an inverted V shape. →33

scoinson see scuntion.

sconce 1 a bracket fixed to a wall to hold a candle; a candleholder. →116
2 a secondary fortification to protect a castle entrance.

sconcheon see scuntion.

scontion see scuntion.

scoop see scorp.

scope 1 see extent.
2 see measuring telescope.
3 see endoscope.
4 see fibrescope.
5 see videoscope.
6 see door scope. →51
7 see episcope.
8 hagioscope, see squint.

scope of contract the range of tasks which a particular contractor or subcontractor has contractually agreed to undertake within a building project; the boundary thus formed between work undertaken by similarly obligated contractors; also referred to as extent of contract.

scored joint, ruled joint; a horizontal brickwork joint with lines scribed in the mortar to sharpen the appearance. →16

scorp, scoop; a drawing knife used for scooping out hollows in wood.

Scotch glue a variety of animal glue.

scotia, 1 gorge, trochilus; a horizontal moulding found especially in the bases and capitals of classical columns, consisting of a deep concave asymmetrical cutting in cross-section. →14, →80
2 a strip of wood, metal or plastics with a uniform cross-section shaped with a concave recess, used as trim for covering the internal join between two perpendicular surfaces. →2

scoticum see opus scoticum.

Scots pine, European redwood; [*Pinus sylvestris*] a northern European softwood with pale reddish timber sold as red or yellow deal, used in all timber industries.

Scottish baronial style baronial architecture in Scotland, influenced by the writings of Sir Walter Scott.

***Scotylidae* 1** see bark beetle.
2 see ambrosia beetle.

scour, erosion; the gradual wearing away of a surface layer (a coastline, river-bed, pipelines) due to the effects of a flowing liquid.

scourge see flail. →74

scouring in plastering, compacting and smoothing of the surface of a fresh coat using a float worked in a circular motion; also called float-finishing.

scrap see salvage.

scraped plywood plywood whose face plies have been smoothed with a mechanical scraper during manufacture.

scraper, 1 devil, dumb scraper; a small piece of sharpened steel plate used for smoothing and scraping the surface of wood and other materials as a finish. →41

2 see Japan scraper. →41
3 paint scraper, scraping iron; a hand tool with a lateral metal blade fixed to a handle, used for the removal of old paint, dirt and coatings from surfaces prior to refinishing. →41
4 see scraping tool. →41

scraperboard, scratchboard (Am.); a method of drawing in which a board is coated first with chalk or gesso and then with ink; this is then worked at with a pointed tool when dry to produce patterns of lines.

scraping iron see scraper. →41

scraping tool, scraper; a turning chisel used for the accurate shaping of wood, available with a number of different shaped blades. →41

scratch the undesirable linear marking or scoring of a surface, coating or component, a defect occurring during manufacture or handling.

scratchboard see scraperboard.

scratch coat see first plaster undercoat.

scratcher, comb, drag; a hand tool used to provide a key for subsequent coats of plaster, or to spread tiling mortar etc., consisting of a set of steel points or a serrated blade set in a handle.

scratch plaster patterned plaster which has been scored with a nail float after application, producing a rough striated surface; also called scratch render.

scratch render see scratch plaster.

scratch resistance the ability of a surface such as a paint film or other coating to resist scratching or abrasion, measured by standardized tests.

screed 1 a layer of concrete, mortar or cement up to 75 mm thick applied to a horizontal concrete slab as a level and smooth base for a floor finish. →44
2 see screed board.
3 see screed rail.
4 see vibrating screed board.
5 see plastering screed.
6 see collar screed.

screed batten in concretework, one of a pair of wooden strips fixed to a base to define the thickness of a screed cast in between, along which a screed board is guided.

screed board, screeding board, screed, straightedge, rule, tamper; a board dragged across the surface of fresh concrete between two screed rails, used for the production of an even and level surface, or screed.

screeding 1 the dragging of a board across wet plaster between guides to form a level surface and strike off unwanted material.
2 the laying of an even surface layer of concrete up to 75 mm thick on a floor slab using a screed board and rails.

screeding board see screed board.

screed rail, 1 plastering screed; in plastering a strip of wood or cast plaster used to regulate the thickness of a plaster surface.
2 a batten or rail for regulating the thickness of a horizontal concrete screed.

screen, 1 sieve; a graded wire mesh in a frame used for the sorting by size of granular material such as aggregate.
2 partition; a lightweight interior wall, often freestanding or with upper glazing, used for dividing up a larger space.
3 any vertical wall-like barrier, often with perforations, to provide visual separation, privacy, protection from the wind and sun etc.
4 the large vertical surface onto which films displayed in a cinema are projected.
5 see monitor.

screen façade, false front; the non-structural grand front of a building, especially in Italian Renaissance architecture, which disguises the true interior form or size of the building.

screening 1 a method of grading aggregate by passing it through screens of a certain mesh size to separate out particles of that size.
2 in the treatment of waste water, the process of straining out some of the larger solids, paper etc. from the incoming sewage using a coarse screen of bars.
3 a subsequent process using fine mesh screens to remove grit etc.

screen printing see silkscreen printing.

screen wall a regularly perforated wall of mesh, slats, louvres etc. used for internal separation, visual separation and to give privacy to an area.

screw a pointed fastener with a helical threaded shank and head which has a shaped indentation, allowing it to be fixed by turning with a screwdriver or similar tool. →36
see *screws and bolts* illustration; types included as separate entries are listed below. →36
adjustment screw.
allen head screw. →36
bugle head screw. →36
butterfly head screw, see one-way head screw. →36
clutch head screw, see one-way head screw. →36
coach screw. →36
concrete screw. →36
countersunk screw, countersunk head screw. →36
cross-slot screw. →36
dome head screw. →36
dowel screw. →36
drive screw, see screw nail. →35
drywall screw. →36
fillister head screw. →36
flat head screw. →36
general purpose screw. →36
hook screw, see screw hook. →36
lag screw, see coach screw. →36
machine screw. →36
masonry screw, see concrete screw. →36
mirror screw. →36
one-way head screw. →36
oval countersunk screw, see oval head screw. →36
Phillips head screw. →36
plasterboard screw, see drywall screw. →36
Pozidriv head screw. →36
raised countersunk head screw, see oval head screw. →36
roofing screw. →36
round head screw, see dome head screw. →36
self-tapping screw.
set screw. →36
sheetmetal screw. →36
tapping screw, see self-tapping screw.
thumb screw. →36
Torx head screw. →36
wood screw. →36

screw anchor see concrete screw anchor. →36

screwback see skewback. →22

screw cap, Edison screw cap; the metal part of an electric lightbulb to which an electric supply is connected, provided with a screw thread as a means of connecting it to a holder.

screw cup, finish washer; **1** a pressed metal raised ring for a countersunk screw to protect the base material into which it is being fixed. →36, →37
2 see recessed screw cup.

screwdriver a hand tool with a steel blade for fixing screws with a turning action; types included as separate entries are listed below. →41
impact screwdriver.
offset screwdriver. →41
ratchet screwdriver.
spiral ratchet screwdriver.

screwdriver bit an interchangeable steel attachment for an electric drill or power screwdriver whose end is suitable for tightening screws. →42

screwed boss a threaded spout protruding from an appliance or pipeline to which a pipe can be fitted.

screwed pipe any cast-iron or steel pipe or pipe fitting joined via threaded ends and connectors.

screwed union a short pipe fitting threaded at both ends, used for connecting a threaded pipe to the outlet of an appliance.

screw eye a wire fixing whose end is shaped into a closed loop, with a threaded end for screwing into a wall surface. →36

screw head the enlarged slotted part of a screw, by which it is driven in with a screwdriver. →36

screw hinge see screw hook and eye hinge. →38

screw-hole a hole into which a screw is fixed, either pre-bored or made by the screw as it is tightened. →36

screw hook, hook screw; a wire fixing in the shape of a hook with a threaded end for screwing into a wall surface. →36

screw hook and eye hinge a rudimentary hinge used for hanging gates, consisting of two threaded and pivoting shanks one of which is screwed into the gate and the other to its gatepost. →38

screw nail, drive screw, square twisted shank flat head nail; a nail with a square spiralled shank to increase its fixing strength when driven in. →35

screw pile in foundation technology, a pile for soft silts and sands whose base is helically tipped to enable it to be screwed into the ground, and to provide a greater bearing area.

screw thread see thread. →36

scribe, marking awl, scriber; a sharp-pointed metal instrument for marking out lines on metal, timber and stone surfaces.

scribed edge in horizontal log construction, the edge of the long groove, in contact with the upper surface of the log below, which provides a closure against the elements. →6

scriber see scribe.

scribing saw see coping saw.

scrim coarse fabric or a mesh product used in plastering as reinforcement for wallboard joints and fibrous plasterwork.

script brush a finely pointed paintbrush with bristles shaped to produce fine lines, used for intricate decoration, especially flowing writing. →43

scriptorium Lat.; a room in a monastery for writing, copying and illuminating manuscripts. →97

scroll an ornamental motif resembling a coiled band or line, or a scroll of paper; types included as separate entries are listed below. →123
linen scroll, see linenfold. →123
double C-scroll. →108
leaf and rose scroll. →82
leaf scroll. →82
Vitruvian scroll. →125
volute. →80

scroll bow-saw see bow saw.

scrolled pediment a segmental broken pediment whose upper extremities are terminated with scrolls. →112

scroll moulding, roll moulding; a decorative moulding which is scrolled in cross-section.

scroll ornament any ornament, medallion etc. with spirals, coiled lines or bands. →123

scroll saw see fretsaw.

scrubbable describing a finish which may be washed with water, a soft brush and soap without causing damage to it.

scrubbing brush a simple unhandled brush with short stiff bristles, used for heavy surface scouring and cleaning. →43

scrubboard see skirting board. →2, →44

scrub plane see roughing plane.

scrub-up trough a specialist sink used by medical employees in a hospital after performing surgery.

scruple an old apothecaries weight of $^1/_{24}$ part of an ounce.

scud plane see roughing plane.

scullery a room adjoining a kitchen used for washing dishes, cleaning pots and pans etc.

sculptor's point a pointed mason's chisel used for carving detail on stonework. →41

sculptural see plastic.

sculpture a three-dimensional work of art. →112

sculptured portal a main doorway in a medieval church, with sculptured jamb and trumeau figures of saints, prophets, nobility etc. →113

scum channel a drainage channel in a swimming pool surround through which water is circulated for cleansing.

scuncheon see scuntion.

scuntion, esconson, scoinson, scontion, sconchion, scuncheon; a reveal at an opening in a wall.

scuola any of various buildings in Venice used as a meeting place of the medieval guilds; a guildhall.

scupper in roof construction, an opening in a parapet from which rainwater from a gutter or roof surface may drain.

scurfing plane see roughing plane.

scutch see scutch hammer. →40

scutch hammer, scutch; in bricklaying, a small pick-like tool with a blade on either end of the head, used for shaping and cutting bricks and blocks. →40

scutcheon 1 see escutcheon. →39, →51
2 see shield. →122

sea blue, ocean blue; a shade of dark turquoise similar in colour to aquamarine.

sea chart see chart.

sea crest, ocean green; a shade of green which takes its name from the colour of the ocean.

seal 1 a component or product used to form a weathertight, watertight or airtight joint.
2 see draught excluder, weatherstrip, weatherseal.
3 see gasket.
4 see glazing gasket.

sea lane, shipping route; a marked route at sea to direct large vessels in congested waters and near coastlines. →64

sealant 1 any resilient material used to seal a joint.
2 building sealant, joint sealant, mastic, sealing compound; a soft, flexible compound applied to construction joints between components or material as weatherproofing. →53
3 see glazing compound.

sealant primer a priming treatment for construction joints in porous materials prior to the application of a sealant.

sealant strip see jointing strip. →53

sealed expansion vessel see expansion tank.

sealed glazed unit, hermetically sealed multiple glazed unit, insulating glass unit, insulated glazing unit; an insulating glazing component with two or more panes of glass sealed around an edging strip and the gap between each pane filled with an inert gas. →53

sealed glazing unit see sealed glazed unit. →53

sealer any material applied in liquid form to porous surfaces as waterproofing, sealing, or to reduce their absorptivity prior to painting and finishing.

sea level the theoretical height of the surface of the sea, taken as a datum from which all heights on land are measured.

sealing compound, 1 mastic; solid or semi-solid plastic material used as a sealant for joints between components or parts of construction. →53
2 lap cement; in built-up roofing, cold liquid bitumen used for sealing the lapped joints between layers of bitumen felt.
3 see sealant.

sealing strip a flexible strip applied to construction joints between components or material as weatherproofing.

sea lion a decorative and heraldic motif of a mythical sea monster composed of the forepart of a lion with webbed paws and the dorsal fin and tail of a fish or dragon. →122

seal nut a nut with an incorporated rubber bung, which seals any opening over which it is tightened. →37

seam 1 the joint between adjacent sheets of sheetmetal, linoleum, matting and cloth.
2 see standing seam. →49

seaming the forming of folded and rolled seams between adjacent strips in supported sheetmetal roofing using a special tool or machine.

seam-welded roofing supported sheetmetal roofing whose joints are seam welded on site by machine. →49, →57

seam welding, resistance seam welding; a method of resistance welding to produce continuous joints in overlapping metal sheets by means of an electric current passed via a pair of rollers which press the components together.

search the process of finding information from computer files or databases using special software and applications which carry out systematic examinations.

search time see access time.

seaside pier see pier.

seasonal variation a variation in events, phenomena, cost etc. depending on the time of year.

seasoning, drying; the process of drying timber using natural or artificial methods to produce a product with minimal warpage and cracking; an equivalent process for stone. →1

seasoning defect defects and warpage in sawn timber sections which occur as a result of improper seasoning. →1
see *seasoning defects* illustration. →1

seasoning shake a split in the surface of a timber piece which appears as a result of uneven shrinkage during incorrect seasoning; also called a check. →1

seat a piece of furniture or other base for sitting on.
balanced seat, see self-raising seat.
see bank seat.
bearing seat, see bridge cap. →31
bridge seat, see bridge cap. →31
cut-away-front seat, see open front seat.
see inset seat.
see love seat.
see open front seat.
pad seat, see inset seat.
see ring seat.
see self-raising seat.
see WC seat.
see window seat.

seat cushion in interior design, fixed or removable padded upholstery for the seat of a chair or bench.

sea-town a coastal town in which the sea plays an important part in local livelihood.

sea traffic see sea transport.

sea transport, maritime transport, sea traffic; sea-going vessels used to transport goods and people.

secco see fresco secco.

Secessionist, Sezessionstil; a naturalistic movement in architecture in Vienna during the late 1800s, Austrian Art Nouveau.

seclusion, see privacy.

second 1 abb. **s**; the SI basic unit of time, one sixtieth part of a minute.
2 a unit of angular dimension equal to one sixtieth part of a minute, 1/3600 degree.

secondary beam one of a number of regularly spaced beams, joists etc. which are supported by heavier principal crossbeams.

secondary colour in colour theory, a hue formed by mixing two of the three primary colours together in equal parts.

secondary consolidation, plastic settlement; the permanent reduction in volume of soil beneath the foundations of a new building due to compression caused by the weight of the building.

secondary glazing, 1 applied sash glazing, secondary sash glazing; a lightweight glazed sash added at a later stage to the inner face of single glazing to form a kind of double glazing.
2 see subsidiary glazing.

secondary production those areas of human production using raw materials which have already undergone a process of production or refining, such as manufacturing of goods, building and road construction etc.

secondary reinforcement concrete reinforcement designed to distribute loads resisted by main reinforcement, and resist shear and thermal expansion.

secondary rib see tierceron. →101

secondary roof truss in traditional timber roof construction, a smaller roof truss supported by purlins between the principal roof trusses. →33

secondary shaft a small or minor shaft in a bundle or clustered column, essentially found in Gothic architecture. →13

secondary sash glazing see secondary glazing.

second coat see second plaster undercoat. →83

second family gas a commercial gas which has a Wobbe number of 48.2–53.2 Mj/m^3, used as fuel in gas heating.

second growth timber grown on land from which forest has recently been harvested or destroyed.

second moment of area see moment of inertia.

second plaster undercoat, floating coat, straightening coat; the second coat of plaster in three coat plastering, applied above the first coat to provide a smooth base for the final coat.
see *second plaster coat* in Roman walling illustration. →83

Second Pompeian style see Architectural style.
see *Pompeian styles* illustration. →126

secret dovetail joint a cabinetmaking dovetailed joint in which the various cuts are concealed within the assembled joint. →5

secret fixing, concealed fixing; the fastening of timber boarding and other components so that the fixings are not visible in a finished surface.

secret gutter a roof gutter concealed from view, often included in the thickness of roof construction or behind a parapet.

secret hinge see invisible hinge.

secret joint a timber joint in which cuttings such as dovetails, notches, tables are concealed within the assembled joint.

secret nailing, blind nailing, concealed nailing; the nailing of timber boarding so that the nails remain hidden. →3

secret wedge see fox wedge.

sectile opus see opus sectile.

sectio aurea Lat.; see golden section. →107

section 1 any thin length of material which has been preformed by a process of rolling, extrusion, sawing etc. into a uniform cross-section of certain shape and dimensions; see also bar, profile.
see metal section entry for list of sections and *metal sections* illustration; types included as separate entries are listed below. →34
aluminium section.
bar.
channel, channel section. →34
circular hollow section. →34
cold formed section. →34
C-profile, see C-section, channel. →34
C-section.
customized section.
H-section. →34
hollow section. →34
hot-rolled steel section. →34
I-section. →34
L-profile, see angle profile.
open section. →34
profile.
rectangular hollow section, RHS. →34
rolled hollow section, RHS. →34

rolled steel section.
round hollow section, round section, see circular hollow section. →34
square hollow section. →34
steel section.
structural hollow section. →34
T-section, T-bar, tee section. →34
tubular section, see hollow section. →34
UB section, see I-section. →34
UC section, see H-section. →34
U-section. →34
Z-section. →34
2 cross-section, cut, sectional drawing; a design drawing or view representing a theoretical cut through a site, building or object, showing objects in view from the cutting plane and the construction of the structure which is cut. →130
3 see sectional perspective.

sectional drawing see section. →130

sectional overhead door an overhead door whose leaf is made up of horizontal hinged segments, opened by pulling it upwards between vertical tracks on either side; the door leaf is horizontal and above the door opening once open. →50

sectional perspective a sectional drawing in which the area visible behind the cutting plane is represented in perspective; also called a perspective section.

section foreman a contractor's representative responsible for supervising part of the work on site.

section modulus, modulus of section; in structural engineering, the moment of inertia of a beam section divided by the distance from the extreme fibre to the neutral axis.

sections method see method of sections.

sector 1 in geometry, a planar figure or area defined by two radii of a curve, usually a circle, and the arc between the ends of these radii.
2 an area of political, industrial or economical activity.

secular building any lay building not used for religious practices or ceremonies.

secured loan a sum of money lent with the guarantee of repayment with goods or property if the loan is not repaid.

security 1 protective measures taken in a building to prevent unauthorized intrusion and burglary.
2 guarantee, collateral; a sum of money, assets or property agreed as a guarantee for a loan; if the loan is not repaid, this is taken instead.
3 see bond.

security bolt see hinge bolt. →38

security door chain see door chain. →51

security glass laminated glass specially designed to resist vandalism, burglary or penetration during physical attack. →53
see anti-bandit laminated glass.
see anti-vandal glass.
see blast-resistant laminated glass.
see bullet-resistant laminated glass, armour-plated glass.

security glazing glazing with security glass and specially approved secure glazing beads designed to withstand intrusion.

security level a measure of the level of protection with alarms, resilient construction, surveillance equipment etc. against entry by unauthorized persons into a building.

security lock, thief-resistant lock; a lock designed to prevent the inward entry of intruders but to allow outward passage in the event of an emergency.

sedge a species of grass, [*Cladium mariscus*], whose cut and dried stems are particularly used for ridges in thatched roofing.

sedile Lat.; singular of sedilia.

sedilia Lat.; seating in a church for the clergy, usually three seats recessed in the south chancel wall.

sediment, precipitate; solid insoluble particles or other granular material which gradually sink to the bottom of the liquid in which it is suspended.

sedimentary rock forms of rock formed by the layered deposition of granular material; types included as separate entries are listed below.
arenaceous rock, arenite.
bauxite.
calcareous rock.
chert, hornstone.
clastic sedimentary rock.
clayslate, killas.
limestone.
loess.
natural rock asphalt.
oolite.
quartzite.
sandstone.
selenite.
shale.
siliceous rock.
tufa.

sedimentation, settling; **1** the gradual sinking of granular solid particles dispersed in a liquid.
2 the mechanical process of water purification by allowing solid matter to sink to the bottom of a sedimentation tank.

sedimentation tank, settling tank, clarifier; in sewage treatment, a tank through which raw sewage passes slowly so that the solid components sink to the bottom and the liquid effluent passes on for further treatment.

sediment trap a device for inhibiting the passage of suspended granular solids suspended in surface water into a drain.

SE duct a ducted flue system in which air is drawn in at the base and released as combustion gases at the top.

seedling in landscaping, a young plant grown from seed.

see-through fireplace, through fireplace; an ornamental fireplace open or glazed on two or more faces, so that the fire can be viewed from opposite sides. →55

segment in mathematics, an area bounded by a curve and a line drawn between two points on that curve, or a three-dimensional solid bounded by the intersection of a plane and a curved surface.

segmental arch, segmented arch; an arch composed of an arc of a circle which is less than a semicircle. →22, →24

segmental barrel vault, segmental vault, surbased vault, cambered vault; a shallow masonry barrel vault whose curvature is less than a semicircle. →25

segmental coping 1 a coping stone or masonry unit whose upper surface is convex in cross-section. →16
2 see half round coping. →16

segmental pediment in classical, especially Neoclassical, architecture, a pediment in which the upper chord is a segment of a circle. →112
see broken segmental pediment. →112
see open segmental pediment. →112

segmental pile in foundation technology, a pile formed from short lengths of concrete placed on top of one another.

segmental vault see segmental barrel vault. →25

segmented arch see segmental arch. →22, →24

segregation 1 see concrete segregation.
2 see vehicular segregation.

seicento the 1600s in Italian art and architecture.

Seker see Sokar.

Sekhmet an ancient Egyptian deity, 'the Powerful', daughter of the sun god Re and consort for Ptah; symbolic of the sun's destructive force and prowess in battle; depicted as a female figure with the head of a lioness; also written as Sakhmet. →74

sekos Gk; an enclosed sacred inner courtyard in an ancient Egyptian or Greek temple. →85

selective tendering competitive tendering in which a limited number of persons or firms are invited to submit a tender.

selenite gypsum in crystalline form or a sedimentary rock based on this mineral, used in building as decorative stone.

selenium a poisonous, non-metallic chemical element, **Se**, used in the manufacture of solar cells.

selenium red see cadmium red.

self-build, do-it-yourself, DIY; building processes, usually small scale and domestic in nature, in which the owner or client is responsible for organizing labour, acquiring materials, and is often involved in the actual construction work.

self-cleansing gradient see minimum gradient.

self-compactable concrete see self-placing concrete.

self-consolidating concrete see self-placing concrete.

self-contained air-conditioner see unit air-conditioner.

self-contained toilet a toilet not attached to a drainage system, in which waste is stored in a collecting bin and often treated before periodical emptying.

self convection see free convection.

self-employed person a person employed in an independent capacity in private enterprise, regarded as such for the purposes of fees, tax, contributions and benefits.

self-levelling concrete self-placing concrete used for screeds and flooring, which, due to its low viscosity, will flow into a naturally horizontal surface without the need for vibration or floating.

self-placing concrete types of very workable and easily placeable concrete used for densely reinforced structures, difficult voids, intricate formwork etc., which will settle or flow into its final position without the need for compaction or vibration; also known as self-compactable concrete, self-consolidating concrete, flowable concrete or non-vibration concrete.

self-raising seat, balanced seat; a WC seat which raises automatically when not in use.

self-siphonage the sucking out of a water seal from a trap by siphonage induced by the introduction of water from a sanitary appliance or a fluctuation in pressure.

self-supporting referring to a component or member capable of supporting its own weight without the need for a structure or frame.

self-tapping screw, tapping screw; a screw which makes its own hole and cuts its own threads as it is screwed in, used for fixing metals, wood etc.

Seljuk architecture the Islamic architecture of what is now the land between Syria and Pakistan ruled by a Turkish dynasty from 1055 to 1307 AD.

semantic error a logical programming error in a computer command which may produce an unexpected result or failure to perform a required function.

semeiology see semiology.

semi see semi-detached house.

semi-aquatic plant any species of landscaping plant which usually thrives in shallow water.

semi-arch an arch with only half a curve, terminating at its crown, as with a flying buttress.

semicircle half a circle.
see half round. →2

semicircular arch an arch whose intrados describes half a circle. →22, →24

semicircular capping see half round capping. →16

semicircular channel see half round channel.

semicircular coping see half round coping. →16

semicircular gutter see half round gutter.

semicircular moulding see half round. →14

semicircular stair, semi-spiral stair; a stair which is a half circle in plan, with wedge-shaped steps arranged radially around a single newel post or opening. →45

semi-detached house, duplex house, semi, two-family house; a residential building of two dwellings structurally joined but separated by a common dividing wall or intermediate floor. →61

semi-direct lighting artificial lighting in which luminaires distribute 60–90% of the emitted light downwards or to the area to be illuminated.

semi-dome see half dome. →26

semi-dry pressing see dry pressing.

semi-gloss the fourth of five grades of glossiness in a dry paint surface, slightly less glossy than full gloss.

semi-indirect lighting artificial lighting in which luminaires distribute 10–40% of the emitted light downwards or to the area to be illuminated.

semi-metal see metalloid.

semiology, semeiology, semiotics; the modern science based around the meanings of signs and signals appearing and employed in all social activities.

semiotics see semiology.

semi-precious stone a general term describing stones used in jewellery which are less valuable than precious stones.

semi-skilled worker a construction worker with a level of skill between a tradesman and labourer.

semi-spiral stair see semicircular stair. →45

sense of place, genius loci, spirit of place; a characteristic feature, identifying emotion etc. of a particular natural or built environment.

sensitive clay clay which loses compressive strength when moulded.

sensitivity 1 in soil mechanics, a proportional measure of how much a sample of clay will change its strength characteristics once it has been remoulded.
2 see light sensitivity.

sensitivity ratio in soil mechanics, a measure of the sensitivity of clay defined as its compressive strength in the undisturbed state to that of a sample which has been reworked.

sensor 1 see probe.
2 see detection device.

separate drainage see separate system.

separate sewerage see separate system.

separate system, separate drainage; a drainage or sewerage system in which surface water and sewage are conveyed in separate pipes.

separating floor, party floor; a floor slab or structure which divides adjacent premises or dwellings within the same block, often with different ownership, and usually has to meet certain requirements of fire resistance and sound insulation.

separating layer in floor and roof construction, a layer of impervious sheet material used to isolate layers in construction to prevent bonding; also called an isolating membrane or bond breaker.

separating wall, common wall (Am.), party wall; a wall which divides adjacent premises or dwellings within the same block, often with different ownership, and usually has to meet certain requirements of fire resistance and sound insulation.
see fire wall.

sepia a dark greenish brown pigment extracted from the ink sacs of the cuttlefish [*Sepia officinalis*]; nowadays produced synthetically for watercolour paints.

septic tank, settlement tank; in the treatment of waste water, a small-scale treatment plant for one building or complex, in which the solid matter in sewage settles, and the remaining effluent is purified and released.

sepulchre 1 a burial tomb, especially one cut in rock or constructed in stone.
2 Easter sepulchre; a recess in a church wall, symbolic of Christ's burial tomb, where the sacrament is received at Easter. →116

sequencing of operations see construction sequence.
sequoia Sequoia sempervirens, see redwood.
seraglio, serai; a Turkish palace, especially that of the Sultan in Istanbul.
serai 1 see caravansary.
2 see seraglio.
serdab 1 a passage or walled-up chamber in an ancient Egyptian tomb, containing a statue.
2 a subterranean chamber in a Mesopotamian dwelling, used as a living room during the summer months.
serial contract a contract let for work of a similar nature to previous work, or following directly on from it.
serial number a number identifying or coding objects in a series such as manufactured products, objects in a computer file etc.
serial printer in computing, a printer which receives information bit by bit and prints as it receives, as opposed to printing once all the information has been received.
series connection the arrangement of appliances in an electric circuit so that each receives the same current.
serigraphy see silkscreen printing.
Serinus canarius the canary bird, see canary yellow.
Serlian motif see Palladian motif. →24
serpent see Wadjet. →74
see uraeus. →74
serpent column, Aesculapian column, Asclepian column; an ornamental freestanding Greek column constructed as part of a monument commemorating victory in battle, with three spirally intertwined snakes carrying a golden cauldron on their heads; also named after Aesculapius, the Greek god of healing and medicine. →69
serpentine, 1 serpentinite; a soft, dark green, metamorphic rock composed of hydrated magnesium silicate, often richly patterned, easily polishable and used as decorative stone in building, for jewellery etc.
2 a greenish or yellow mineral found in veins in metamorphic rock, especially the above.
serpentinite see serpentine.
serpent staff see staff of Asclepius. →120
Serpula lacrymans see dry rot.
serrated strip see rumble strip.
servant key a key which operates only one or a limited number of locks in a suite of locks for which there is a master key.
server in computer networks, a central computer which manages shared resources for a number of workstations.
servery a room or space between a kitchen and dining area from which meals are served and cutlery and crockery are kept.
service, 1 technical installation, utility; any system, installation etc. in a building providing water, air, gas, communications and electricity or disposing of waste; see also services.
2 community services, see community facilities.
serviceability the property of a component to be suitable for a particular function, compatible, in working order and able to be replaced or maintained if need be.
service area an area at the edge of a highway with services such as toilets, food, fuel etc. for the drivers and passengers of vehicles.
service clamp see pipe saddle.
serviced housing see sheltered housing.
service duct a duct for cables, pipes or equipment that also allows space for working.
service illuminance 1 in lighting design, a measure of the illuminance of a surface or space averaged over the maintenance cycle of the luminaires and the space in which they are situated.
2 see standard service illuminance.
service industry any industry concerned with the provision of a service as opposed to production of goods.
service life the period of time for a component or installation during which no excessive costs are expended in relation to operation, maintenance or repair.
service lift a lift designed to carry goods for providing a service to a building, too small to carry people.
service pipe a pipeline which conveys water or gas from a supply main to a building.
service reservoir, distribution reservoir, clear-water reservoir; an area storage tank for a water supply system.
service road a road leading to a building, used by service or maintenance traffic and emergency services.
services 1 the provision of water, gas, electricity, phone lines and other basic infrastructure for a building.
2 the provision by a local authority of schools, hospitals, transport, information, maintenance etc. for a community.
3 community services, see community facilities.
service space 1 a space within a building involved in its maintenance or servicing.
2 see plant room.
3 a secondary space whose function is to serve a major space.
4 see utility room.
service stair see access stair.
service station a commercial establishment located on or near a motorway or major road to provide refuelling and other services for vehicles and passengers.
service traffic vehicular and other maintenance traffic arriving at a building along clearly designed routes to provide a service such as delivery, refuse collection etc.
servicing see maintenance.
servicing valve a plumbing valve attached to an appliance or pipeline for switching off a water supply during maintenance.
sesquipedalis Lat.; a Roman triangular or square brick of which two adjacent sides are one and a half Roman feet long (444 mm), or sometimes half of that (222 mm). →83
sessile oak see durmast oak.
set 1 see setting.
2 the slight bending to either side of alternate teeth in a saw blade to allow for easier movement of the saw through wood.
3 see feint.
4 see set of copies.
5 see accelerated set.
Set, see Seth. →74
set accelerating admixture, accelerator; an admixture included in a concrete mix to increase its setting rate.
setback the recessing of the facade of a building, usually at ground floor or upper storey level.
Setekh see Seth. →74
Seth in ancient Egyptian mythology, brother of Osiris, whom he murdered to usurp the more fertile lands by the Nile; god of storms, the desert and chaos, also written as Set, Setekh or Sutekh. →74
set of copies a number of copies produced from the same drawing.
set retarding admixture an admixture included in a concrete mix to reduce its setting rate.
set screw a threaded fastener without a head, used to secure a sleeve, collar or gear on a shaft by compression, preventing relative movement. →36
set square a technical drawing implement for drawing perpendicular or angled lines, a right-angled triangular piece of thin transparent plastic, wood etc. with either two 45° angles or 30° and 60°. →130
see adjustable set square. →130

sett, cobble; a small hewn rectangular block of natural stone such as granite or sandstone used in series as paving for roads and hard areas; ranging in size from 50 mm × 50 mm × 50 mm to 300 mm × 200 mm × 100 mm; sometimes called a cobble; a small sett is known as a cube. →15

settecento the 1700s in Italian art and architecture.

settee see sofa.

set theory a branch of mathematics dealing with sets regardless of what their composition is.

setting 1 in general construction, the hardening to its usable form of any material applied or cast as a liquid or paste.
2 set; the hardening of the cement in concrete from a liquid to a soft crumbly solid, occurring before the hardening or strength-gaining stage.
3 in the sharpening of a saw, the action of bending over teeth alternatively to one side and then the other so that the saw cut is greater than the thickness of the saw blade.

setting block see glazing block. →53

setting coat see final plaster coat.

setting out, 1 marking out, staking out; the marking of boundaries and levels on a construction site for a prospective building before construction begins.
2 the laying out of the parts of a technical or design drawing, various projections, title block, borders etc. on the paper or drawing plane.

setting stuff plaster used for finishes, produced from lime putty and fine sand.

setting time 1 the period of time after application over which a liquid such as glue turns into a solid.
2 the time taken for the cement in a concrete mix to harden to the required degree, measured by a standard test.

setting up see upsetting.

settlement 1 the collection of particles suspended in a liquid at the bottom due to the action of gravity.
2 the movement of a building downwards soon after construction as ground material underneath is compressed.
3 see immediate settlement.
4 see creep settlement.
5 a small village or community, usually in a rural area.
6 the act of occupation of an area of land by a population for purposes of dwelling and livelihood.

settlement damage problems of cracking, structural damage and doors and windows that don't open, caused by the differential settlement of a building after construction.

settlement tank see septic tank.

settling see sedimentation.

settling tank see sedimentation tank.

sett paving a paved surface made up of setts.

setup the preparation of initial settings for the working of a computer's operating system and programs.

severity see fire severity.

severy see cell. →25, →101

sewage soil water and solid human waste, not surface water, conveyed in a sewer away from buildings for treatment.

sewage disposal, sewage treatment; the screening, sedimentation, filtration etc. of waste water and solids from a sewer, and the disposal of settled sludge in digestion tanks or on drying beds.

sewage pumping station pumping plant for raising sewage from a drainage system to a sewer located at a higher level.

sewage tank see cesspool.

sewage treatment see sewage disposal.

sewage treatment plant the apparatus, vessels and pumps, filters, pipework etc. for treating raw sewage.

sewer a large diameter pipe which conveys waste liquids and solids in suspension away from a building's soil and foul water drainage systems to a treatment plant; any pipeline or channel which conveys foul waste.

sewerage, sewerage system; a public drainage installation consisting of branch and main sewer pipes, inspection chambers, pumps, valves etc. which convey foul water to a sewage treatment plant.

sewerage system 1 the network of sewers which convey discharge from buildings in a district to a sewage treatment plant.
2 see sewerage.

sewer pipe a length of proprietary pipe with suitably formed interconnecting ends, joined in series to form a sewer.

sexfoil a decorative motif found in Gothic tracery consisting of six lobes or pointed arched protrusions radiating outwards from a central point. →110

sexpartite vault, hexapartite vault; a vault sprung on six points of support, hexagonal or rectangular in plan, composed of six ribbed bays and with curved roof surfaces. →26

sextant a hand-held optical instrument used for measuring angles, originally up to one sixth part of a whole circle, with the use of mirrors; used particularly in nautical navigation and astronomy.

Sezessionstil see Secessionist.

sfairisterion see sphaeristerium. →91

sfumato in painting, the softening of outlines and gradual fading of colours from light to dark.

sgraffito, graffito; in coloured plasterwork and pottery, a pattern scratched in surface material which allows for a backing material or colour to shine through.

shack a rudimentary hut or cabin of timber, tin etc.

shackle, bail; any looped metal bar or construction such as the fastener for a padlock, used in fixing, securing gates and scaffolding, attaching chains etc. →37, →39

shade 1 in lighting design, an area over which direct light, especially sunlight, does not fall.
2 a device placed externally over a window or around a light fitting to prevent glare or diffuse direct light.
3 see awning.
4 see sunshade.
5 see lampshade.
6 see tint.

shading in drawing, the adding of dark edge areas to produce a three-dimensional effect.

shadow graphical hatching and other darkened areas added around a plan or projection drawing of a building to show apparent shade, cast shadow or depth.

shadow bead a strip of planed timber or other material with a rebated or recessed edge, used as trim to form a recessed joint between adjacent components. →2

shaft 1 the straight vertical part of a column, by which loads are transmitted to a base or foundation; a column shaft. →76
see *column shaft* in classical orders illustrations. →78, →79, →80, →81
see *Asian and Mediterranean columns and capitals* illustration. →69
2 one of the distinctly carved merged piers in a Gothic compound column, which continues in vaulting as a rib. →13
see principal shaft. →13
see secondary shaft. →13
3 the longitudinal body of a component such as an axe, hammer, drill bit or other device, usually connecting one part to another. →40, →41, →42
4 see shank. →35, →36
5 an enclosed vertical opening, hole etc. in a building or the ground; see well, chute.
see *shaft* in mastaba illustration. →70
see chimney shaft.
lift shaft, see lift well.
see light shaft.

see stairwell. →45
see ventilation shaft. →56

shaft grave an Early Bronze Age grave or tomb type, especially those richly furnished examples found at Mycenae, whose roofed burial chamber was reached by a vertical shaft, which was subsequently filled in.

shaft module see lift shaft module.

shaft ring see annulet. →81

shake 1 a crack which occurs in timber due to natural causes.
see cup shake. →1
see heartshake. →1
see oblique shake. →1
see seasoning shake, check. →1
see straight shake. →1
see wind shake. →1
2 dry, shakes; a fine crack or vent which occurs across the cleavage plane of rock or stone due to a natural imperfection.
3 split shingle; a thin timber cladding or roofing tile made by splitting a short log of timber along the grain. →48

shake roof a roof with timber shakes as the roofing material. →48

shakes see shake.

shale a layered, crumbly argillaceous sedimentary rock formed by the deposition of clay and silt.

shallow foundation any foundation, such as a footing, pad or raft foundation, which does not require a deep excavation. →29

shamrock a decorative motif derived from the three-lobed leaf of various plants, principally that of the wood sorrel, *Oxalis acetosella*, but also white clover, *Trifolium repens* and black medic, *Medicago lupulina*; the symbol of St Patrick of Ireland; cf. cloverleaf. →121

Shang the first historical dynasty in Chinese history from 1450 to 1050 BC.

shank, 1 shaft; the straight slender body of a nail, screw, bolt etc., between its head and tip. →35, →36
2 see neck. →36

shanty a rough hut or cabin, often hastily constructed and with whatever materials come to hand.

shanty town an unorganized settlement established illegally on the outer fringes of a metropolis by immigrants, the destitute etc. with an array of makeshift homes with little infrastructure.

shape, form; the two- or three-dimensional profile of an object.

shape code in reinforced concrete, the standard notation for the shape of a reinforcing bar.

shaping 1 see forming.
2 in the sharpening of a saw, the filing of teeth to a uniform shape after they have been topped.

shareware see public domain software.

sharpener 1 see pencil sharpener. →130
2 see dowel sharpener. →42
3 see grindstone. →41

sharpening 1 the producing of a sharp edge to metal cutting tools using abrasives.
2 the final action of sharpening each tooth of a saw with a file after topping, shaping and setting.

shave hook a scraping tool consisting of a thin blade attached perpendicular to a handle, used by a painter for removing unwanted paint splashes from glazing and other surfaces. →41

shaving a strip or flake of refuse wood left over from milling and planing, often reused in the manufacture of particleboard and other products.
see **shavings** fill in floor construction of log building. →6

shaving knife see drawing knife.

shear, shear force; an internal splitting force caused by two forces acting in opposite directions at a distance to one another on the cross-section of a structural member.

shear crack one of a number of diagonal cracks which may appear in the web of a beam or bracing wall due to shear stresses exceeding shear strength.

shear force see shear.

shearing stress load on a structural member due to shear forces exceeding shear strength.

shear plate connector in timber frame construction, a round flanged metal plate housed between two bolted timber members to strengthen the joint. →35

shear reinforcement, web reinforcement; in reinforced concretework, reinforcement designed to resist shear forces.

shears see tin snips.

shear strength the stress at which a material, component or construction will structurally fail in shear.

shear stress the force per unit area in kN/m^2 acting on the cross-section of a structural member due to external forces acting on it in opposite directions but not along the same line.

shear wall a wall designed to resist horizontal forces along its length, used to provide bracing for concrete frames.

sheath in post-tensioned concrete, a pipe cast into the concrete into which the prestressing cables are placed so that they will not adhere to the concrete while it is hardening.

sheathing 1 see sheeting. →30
2 a layer of roofing felt used as underlay for profiled sheet roofing. →57
3 see boarding.
4 roof sheathing, see roof decking. →59
5 the outer insulating and protective covering for electric wires in a cable.

sheathing board plywood, coated fibreboard or similar products used to clad the timber frame of a building on the exterior side of the thermal insulation layer to reduce the effects of wind and reduce the movement of moisture. →8

sheathing grade insulating board see sarking and sheathing grade insulating board.

sheath knife a short, thick-bladed general purpose knife which usually has a plastic or leather pouch to protect the blade when not in use.

sheave see lift sheave.

shed, outhouse; an often crude ancillary building or shelter used for storage.

shed roof 1 see monopitch roof. →46
2 see penthouse roof. →46

sheen a grade of paintwork finish which appears glossy at an angle but appears matt when viewed straight on.

sheer legs a simple hoisting device consisting of a crude tripod over which a rope is slung.

sheet 1 any material or product manufactured into planar sizes of preset length with a thickness of between 0.15 mm and 10 mm.
see *metal sheet products* illustration. →34
2 see sheetmetal. →34
3 see glass sheet.

sheet curing see membrane curing.

sheet flooring flooring of sheet material, boarding etc. with butt or housed joints.

sheet glass, drawn sheet glass, drawn glass; glass manufactured by vertical drawing of molten glass from a furnace in a continuous sheet, rarely used nowadays because of its uneven surfaces.
see *glazing* illustration. →53

sheeting 1 any material or surface construction formed into continuous rigid or flexible sheets with a thickness of between 0.15 mm and 10 mm.
2 sheathing, shuttering; sheet material or rough boarding used in formwork to support and form the shape of cast concrete while it is hardening. →30

sheet laminate a durable facing product of layers of paper, wood, glass fibre or fabrics impregnated with synthetic resins and pressed into sheets.

sheetmetal, metal sheet; metal produced in sheets less than about 2 mm–5 mm thick according to type of metal; see also metal plate, foil.
see *sheetmetal* illustration; types included as separate entries are listed below. →34
aluminium sheet.
copper sheet.
corrugated sheetmetal.
expanded metal. →34
lead sheet.
perforated sheetmetal. →34
sheet steel.

sheetmetal capping see pressed metal capping.

sheetmetal coping see pressed metal coping.

sheetmetal cladding panel, pressed metal facing unit; a prefabricated exterior cladding unit made of pressed sheetmetal with turned-in edges and proprietary fixings. →60

sheetmetal cleat, roofing cleat, latchet, ear; a small L-shaped metal fixing for attaching sheetmetal roofing to decking below, and included in standing seams and roll joints; also called clip, tie and shingle.

sheetmetal duct a ventilation or air-conditioning duct made from galvanized sheetmetal, often rectangular in cross-section.

sheetmetal flashing, 1 pressed metal flashing; a strip of sheetmetal laid over a joint to inhibit or divert the passage of water.
2 see eaves flashing.

sheetmetal joint 1 see *sheetmetal joint* illustration. →49
2 see welt. →49
3 see standing seam. →49

sheetmetal roof a roof clad with thin metal sheet, either supported or profiled and usually of aluminium, lead, copper or galvanized or coated steel.
see *sheetmetal roof* in office building illustration. →60

sheetmetal roofing, roof sheeting; roofing of profiled or seamed sheets of steel, stainless steel, lead, zinc or aluminium. →49
see supported sheetmetal roofing. →49, →57
see aluminium sheet roofing.
see corrugated sheetmetal.
see metal multi-tile roofing. →49

sheetmetal screw 1 a self-tapping screw with a flat head, used for fixing sheetmetal to a frame or base. →36
2 see roofing screw. →36

sheetmetal sill see pressed metal sill.

sheetmetal work any work on a construction site using sheetmetal, usually by folding and spot welding or pop-riveting.

sheet mill that part of a steel rolling mill which rolls ingots into steel sheet and plate.

sheet mosaic mosaic tiles or tesserae fixed to a paper- or mesh-backed web to enable them to be easily laid on floors and wall surfaces. →44

sheet pile see steel sheet pile. →29

sheet piling, trench sheeting; vertical members of interlocking profiled steel plate driven into the ground to support the sides of a major excavation. →29

sheet products see *metal sheet products* illustration. →34

sheet roofing any roofing material manufactured and laid in sheets: bitumen felt, sheetmetal, ribbed polymer sheeting etc.; types included as separate entries are listed below. →49
aluminium sheet roofing.
bituminous roofing.
corrugated sheet roofing. →49
felt roofing, bituminous felt roofing. →49
membrane roofing. →49
profiled sheet roofing. →49
profiled sheeting, ribbed-sheet roofing. →49, →58
sheetmetal roofing. →49

sheet steel, steel sheet; steel rolled into sheets not more than 3 mm thick.
see *sheetmetal* illustration. →34

shelf 1 a horizontal surface or level on which goods and effects are stored, fixed to a wall or part of a furnishing unit; often used in the plural, shelves.
2 see smoke shelf. →55

shelf fungus see conk.

shelf life, storage life; the length of time an adhesive, paint or other building material can be kept in storage without deterioration.

shelf unit, shelves; a piece of furniture consisting of a shelf or shelves.

shell 1 a thin, hard, structural or protective outer facing for a building, construction or component.
2 see shell construction, shell structure. →27
3 see scallop. →123
4 see conch. →123

shellac a natural resin gathered from the twigs of certain Indian fig trees, mixed with a solvent such as alcohol and used as a varnish.

shell construction a thin curved loadbearing concrete, steel or plastics slab used for loadbearing roof forms; also called a shell structure; types included as separate entries are listed below.
barrel shell. →27
concrete shell. →27
polygonal shell, see folded plate. →27
prismatic shell. →27
see *folded plate and shell structures* illustration. →27

shell keep in military architecture, a keep which is roughly round in plan and has accommodation on its inner face, arranged around a courtyard. →103

shell pink a shade of pink which takes its name from the colour of the inside of certain sea shells.

shell roof a thin self-supporting roof construction of reinforced or prestressed concrete or other plastic material, often designed in three-dimensionally curving forms.

shell shake see cup shake. →1

shell structure see shell construction. →27

shelter 1 a simple roofed construction designed to provide protection from the elements, open on one or all sides.
2 see cabin.
3 see civil defence shelter, air-raid shelter. →61
4 a rudimentary building, movable or fixed, providing protection from the elements.
5 see bothie.

shelterbelt a row or rows of landscaped trees or shrubs forming a shelter against wind, sun, noise etc.

sheltered housing, serviced housing; housing or a residential block for the handicapped or elderly with communal facilities and staff on call in case of emergency.

shelves 1 plural of shelf.
2 see shelf unit.

shep see palm. →106

shepherd's cross a cross whose apex is hooked like the upper end of a shepherd's crook, symbolic of religious guidance and the saving of lost souls. →117

sherardizing a rust-proofing treatment for a steel or iron surface consisting of a coating of zinc dust applied at a temperature slightly below its melting point.

shesep see palm. →106

shewbread table, showbread table; an ancient Babylonian or Jewish table structure on which food offerings were presented to God. →116

shield, escutcheon, scutcheon; a warrior's hand-held protective device, the symbolic base of heraldic designs and coats of arms, much used as a decorative motif in architectural ornament. →122, →124

shielded metal-arc welding see manual metal-arc welding.

shielding angle a measure of glare in artificial lighting design, the angle to horizontal above which a lamp in a ceiling luminaire can be seen through a diffuser.

shielding glass 1 see radiation-shielding glass.

2 see electronic shielding glass.
3 see lead X-ray glass.

shield of David see Magen David.

shift work jobs which are continuous or involve such long hours that a group of workers will work back-to-back, handing over to another group after an agreed period of time.

shikhara, sikhara; a tower in a Hindu temple over its most sacred point.

shim a thin strip of veneer used in the repair of veneerwork or plywood.

shiner, bull stretcher; a brick on edge laid with its bed showing in a masonry wall. →20

shiner course, bull stretcher course; a brickwork course made up entirely of shiners. →20

shingle 1 naturally rounded stones of variable size used as coarse aggregate and for surfacing flat roofs and driveways.
2 see gravel.
3 a sawn timber tile used for cladding roofs and walls. →48
4 felt shingles, see strip slates. →49

shingle dash, dry dash; a weatherproof rendered finish for masonry and concrete with a coating of shingle embedded into wet mortar.

shingle roof a pitched roof clad in timber shingles. →48

shingle tile a clay or concrete roof tile manufactured in imitation of a wooden shingle, often with a rustic surface and a curved or decorative tail. →47

Shingle style a style in American vernacular domestic architecture from the 1870s characterized by the use of ornate timber shingles for roof and wall cladding.

shingling the trade of laying shingles as roofing and external wall cladding.

ship canal a canal large enough to be used by ships.

shiplap boarding rebated and recessed timber cladding boards laid horizontally so that adjacent boards overlap one another. →8

shiplap joint a timber joint used in overlapping boarding, with the edges of each board rebated to receive an adjacent board. →8

shipping route see sea lane. →64

shipping terminal a building or group of buildings where passengers and goods embark or disembark from ships.

shippound a unit of weight used in the Baltic shipping trade, equal to 20 lispounds and varying from 300 lb to 400 lb.

ship timber beetle see lymexylid beetle.

shipworm, marine mollusc; [*Teredo spp.*] a marine organism which causes damage to wood submerged in seawater by boring.

shipyard, dockyard; a facility in which boats and ships are constructed, maintained or repaired.

shoddy fibrous material made from old cloth, used as caulking in horizontal log construction.

shoe see driving shoe.

shoe rack a low domestic shelf unit on which shoes are stored.

shoji a sliding door in a traditional Japanese building consisting of a timber frame surfaced with paper.

shop 1 a building or space within a building for the sale of merchandise or the provision of services.
2 see paint shop.
3 see workshop.
4 see print shop.
5 see taberna. →88, →91

shop picture see bottega.

shopping arcade, mall, precinct; a covered and sometimes arched passage, often constructed through existing urban fabric, with shops on one or both sides.

shopping centre, mall, shopping mall (Am.); a building or complex containing a number of shops and associated facilities.

shopping mall see shopping centre.

shopping street a street in an urban environment lined with shops or one well known for its shops.

shop window see display window.

shore 1 a temporary support or prop for an excavation or work under construction; types included as separate entries are listed below.
dead shore.
flying shore.
horizontal shore, see flying shore.
jack shore.
raking shore.
riding shore.
single flying shore.
sloping shore.
vertical shore, see dead shore.
2 the meeting of a body of water such as a sea or lake and land; the area of land around this.

shore pine see lodgepole pine.

shoring 1 the erection of one or a configuration of slanting timber props or shores as temporary support for a structure under construction or under repair.
2 the construction thus formed.
3 see excavation shoring.

short circuit the situation occurring in an electric circuit when two points with different voltages come into direct contact with little resistance, causing a surge which may damage equipment and appliances.

shortest-route procedure in traffic planning, a trip assignment method based on computer modelling of available routes and modes of transport which seeks to minimize time, cost and distance of journey.

short grained see brashy.

short hundredweight see hundredweight.

short message service, SMS; in wireless telephone communications, a cheap way of communicating using written messages in the form of digitized text strings.

short ton see ton.

shotcrete sprayed concrete containing aggregate over 10 mm in particle size, placed by spraying it against a surface using pneumatic pressure.

shotcreting 1 see concrete spraying.
2 see spray concreting.

shot firing see blasting.

shothole a 2 mm–3 mm diameter hole in the surface of wood, caused by burrowing insects.

shoulder 1 in timber tenon jointing, the timber surface at the base of a tenon which abuts the face of the mortised member. →5
2 the widening of the blade of a chisel between the neck and cutting area. →41
3 see hard shoulder. →63

shoulder angle in military architecture, the obtuse external angle between the face and flank of a bastion. →104

shouldered scarf joint see housed scarf joint. →3

shouldered tenon joint, stepped tenon joint; a framing mortise and tenon joint for the ends of joists and window and door headers, in which the mortised member is cut to incorporate the side of the tenoned piece; often the same as an undercut tenon joint. →5

shoulder fitting see barrel nipple.

shoulder plane a narrow plane with a chamfered blade used for cleaning up the inside corners of shoulders, grooves and rebates in wood.

shove see bunch.

shovel a spade used for transferring loose material from one place to another.

showbread table see shewbread table. →116

shower a sanitary installation with a controllable spray or jet of water for washing and cleaning.

shower cubicle see shower unit.

shower curtain a screen of textiles or plastic sheeting drawn in front of a shower to contain splashing and provide privacy.

shower head, shower rose; the perforated part of a shower assembly through which water is ejected, usually a spray outlet.

shower mixer see shower tap.
shower room a room in which a shower can be taken, with shower units, drains etc.
shower rose see shower head.
shower screen a lightweight partition, usually of plastics or glass, used to separate a shower cubicle from an adjacent space or other shower cubicle.
shower tap, shower mixer, shower unit; the mechanism by which the supply of hot and cold water to a shower head is controlled.
shower tray a shallow bath connected to a drain to collect waste water beneath a shower.
shower unit, 1 shower cubicle; a light, often transparent construction consisting of a shower tray with glass or plastic side screens and a door to contain splashing.
2 see shower tap.
shread head roof see half-hipped roof. →46
shrine 1 see temple.
see *shrine* in Egyptian temples plan illustration. →72
2 a chapel within a church, or a separate chapel, containing an effigy of a saint.
shrinkability the ability of a material to decrease in size without compression.
shrinkage 1 the reduction in volume of a material due to compression, evaporation of water, or change in state or temperature.
2 the reduction in dimensions of timber as it dries.
3 see plastic shrinkage.
4 see autogenous shrinkage.
5 see chemical shrinkage.
6 see dry shrinkage.
shrinkage crack a crack occurring during the setting of concretework as a result of the evaporation of water.
shrinkage joint see contraction joint.
shrinkage preventer an admixture included in a concrete mix to inhibit shrinkage.
shroud see crypt. →99
shrub layer, understorey; in landscaping and forestry, the layer of plant growth composed mostly of woody, perennial shrubs and young, small trees less than 3 m in height.
SHS see square hollow section. →34
Shu in ancient Egyptian mythology, one of the primeval twin deities (along with Tefnut), air, spat forth by the sun-god Atum; see Tefnut.
shutter, 1 window shutter; an opaque or louvred panel, usually hinged or sliding, used to cover or shade a window.
2 gate; an often light or lattice construction used to close off an opening such as a shop front or doorway.
3 see persiennes.
4 see fire shutter.
5 see fire damper.
shutter hinge 1 a hinge used to hang a shutter.
2 see parliament hinge. →38
shuttering 1 see formwork.
2 see sheeting. →30
shutting jamb, closing jamb; the vertical framing member against which a window casement or door leaf shuts and into which a lock, latch or catch engages. →50, →51
shutting stile, closing stile, lock stile; the vertical side framing member of a window casement or door leaf opposite that from which it is hung, often containing a lock or fastening device. →50, →51
SI 1 silicone.
2 International System of Units, see SI-system.
Siberian fir [*Abies sibirica*] a Siberian softwood used for pulp and fibres, and planted in parks as an ornamental tree.
Siberian larch [*Larix russica, Larix sibirica*] a softwood from eastern Siberia with typical properties of larch; one of the most common sources of larchwood in Europe.
Siberian spruce [*Picea obovata*] a Russian softwood from the Siberian taiga with pale timber, logged as construction timber.
Siberian yellow pine, cembra pine; [*Pinus cembra*] a Siberian pine with long needles, used for cabinetwork.
siccative see drier.
Sicilian brown see raw umber.
Sicilian roofing the antique term for classical clay roof tiling laid with flat, lipped tiles capped with rows of concave tiles; nowadays also known as Italian tiling. →47
side 1 one of the external flat surfaces of an object, building etc.
2 one of the long rectangular surfaces of a brick; when exposed in a masonry wall, it is called a face. →21
side aisle see aisle.
side altar, by-altar; a secondary altar in a church or cathedral.
see *Early Christian and Late Antique church* illustration. →95
see *Byzantine domical church* illustration. →96
see *Carolingian church* illustration. →98
see *Romanesque church* illustration. →99
side board in the conversion of timber, a rectangular sawn board cut tangentially from the edge of a log, with end grain forming a series of concentric arcs. →2
sideboard, buffet; a piece of furniture, usually in a dining room or dining area, used for the storage of crockery, and from which food can be served.
side chapel a small chapel for private worship situated to the side of the choir or in the aisle of a church.
see *Early Christian basilica* illustration. →95
see *Romanesque church* illustration. →99
see parecclesion. →96
side elevation see end elevation.
side form see edge form.
side hung referring to a window, casement or hatch whose opening leaf is hinged at the side, see following entries.
side-hung casement window a window type whose opening casement is hinged at the side. →52
side-hung door a term which distinguishes doors which have hinges along one vertical edge, rather than sliding, tilting or other mechanisms; the most common category of door. →50, →51
sidelap the overlap of adjacent parts of roofing material such as tiles or roof sheeting on either side.
side light 1 a glazed panel at the side of a doorway.
2 a narrow glazed casement at the side of a window unit, hinged on one vertical edge. →52
side-opening door a double sliding door in which both leaves slide to one side of the door opening; lift doors are typical examples. →50
side plane see profile plane. →127, →128
side purlin in timber roof construction, a purlin situated between ridge and eaves level for supporting common rafters. →33
side rabbet plane a small woodworking plane with a narrow blade for widening and shaping rebates; it may sometimes have two blades for cutting in either direction.
side rezor, side wevor, side wyver; in traditional timber frame construction, a side purlin.
siderite, iron spar, sparry ironstone; a yellowish, black or brown mineral, natural iron carbonate, **$FeCO_3$**, an important iron ore.
side street, cross-street; a minor or subsidiary road in a town which meets a main road at right angles, or which runs parallel to it.
side view in projection drawing, the orthographic planar projection made of an object or building on the side or profile plane, as if viewed at right angles to it; often a secondary or shorter elevation of a building, called a profile view, or end view if of the shorter side. →127
sidewalk see footway. →62
side wevor see side rezor.
side wyver see side rezor.

siding see weatherboarding (also for list of different types of weatherboarding). →8
see *timber cladding boards* illustration. →8
see *holiday home and sauna* illustration. →58

Siemens-Martin process see open-hearth process.

Siena see sienna.

sienna, 1 Terra Sienna, raw sienna; a form of yellowish brown native pigment, named after earth found near the Italian city of Sienna, consisting of hydrated mineral iron oxide, used in watercolour and oil paints.
2 see burnt sienna.

sieve 1 see screen.
2 see strainer.

sieving, grading; a method of sorting aggregate by passing it through successive sieves of certain mesh size to separate out grains of the required size.

sight in surveying, a device connected to an optical instrument or level to guide the eye or to visually ascertain an alignment.

sight distance, visibility distance; in road design, the distance at which an object becomes clearly visible to the driver of a vehicle moving along a road, taking account of curves and topography.

sight line see projector. →127

sight point see station point. →128

sight size, daylight size; the size of the opening in glazing or a window frame, measured from inner edge to opposite inner edge; smaller than the tight size. →52

sign 1 the graphic representation of a message, instruction or advertisement.
2 the device or board on which it is presented.
3 see street sign.

signal green a shade of harsh bright green which loosely takes its name from the colour of green traffic lights; nowadays the same shade as poison green.

signal red, high red, primary red, vivid red; a basic shade of bright red which has a high saturation of colour but a high degree of lightness.

signal yellow a shade of bright yellow, the colour of light chrome yellow pigment, which takes its name from the colour of traffic lights.

signature 1 the handwritten name or insignia of a party as used as proof on documents, contracts etc.
2 the signed name or mark of the artist on a work of art.

signinum see opus signinum. →83

sikhara see shikhara.

sil Lat.; the Roman name for yellow ochre pigment.

Silesian bond see Flemish garden-wall bond. →18

silencer see muffler.

sileni plural form of silenos. →122

silenos in classical mythological ornament, an elderly drunken satyr, a companion of Dionysus; plural is sileni. →122

siles see crucks. →7

silhouette 1 the outline of an object seen as a dark shape against a contrasting light background.
2 see skyline.

silica, silicon dioxide; a mineral chemical compound, SiO_2, used in the manufacture of glass, porcelain and abrasives and in metallurgy; found naturally in sandstones, quartz, flint and agate.
see opal.
see quartz.

silica gel a gelatinous form of silica used as a desiccant.

silica glass see fused silica glass.

silicate a salt derived of silicic acids; also any of the largest group of minerals which includes clay, quartz, mica and feldspar.

silicate mortar types of mortar containing silicates of potassium etc., used for their resistance to high temperatures and acidic conditions.

siliceous rock types of sedimentary rock which have a silica content of over 50%; includes chert and flint.

siliceum see opus siliceum. →83

silicon a common chemical element, **Si**, found in the earth's crust in minerals and rocks; used in the production of glass, bricks and alloys, and in steelmaking; not to be confused with silicone.

silicon brass see silicon bronze.

silicon bronze, silicon brass; a durable copper alloy with zinc, silicon and small quantities of other metals such as manganese and beryllium; used for corrosion-resistant fixings.

silicon carbide, carbon silicide; an extremely hard crystalline chemical compound, **SiC**, used as an abrasive, for fireproof products and for electrical resistors in high temperature applications.

silicon dioxide see silica.

silicone, SI; a clear, flexible, waterproof thermosetting resin used as a sealant and in paints; not to be confused with silicon.

silicone paint a durable heat-resistant paint consisting of silicone solutions mixed with polymers.

silicone rubber an elastomer made from silicone, used for seals and electrical insulation.

silicone sealant a silicone-based flexible sealant with a characteristic acidic odour, applied with a caulking gun for sealing internal corners in tiling and other wet applications.

silk see eggshell flat.

silk cotton see kapok.

silkscreen printing, screen printing, serigraphy; a method of making graphic prints in paint or ink which is pushed through a fine mesh, originally of silk, masked off with a patterned stencil.

silk-screened glass, silkscreen glass; decorative, reduced-glare or obscured glass whose surface is silk-screen printed with a pattern of baked enamel, paint or frit during tempering.

silkscreen glass see silk-screened glass.

sill, 1 cill; the lowest horizontal member in a door, window or other vertical framework; see window sill, door sill.
2 see window sill. →52
3 see ground plate. →6

sill block a concrete block with a sloping upper surface, designed for use as a sill below a window opening. →30

sill board see window board. →53

sill plate, cill plate; a horizontal timber base member fixed to a footing or foundation, onto which a timber frame is constructed. →57
see ground plate. →6

sillimanite a hard, greenish or brownish aluminium silicate mineral; used for gemstones and in ornament.

silo a tall hollow structure for the storage of granular material such as grain or sand, often a series of connected masonry or metal cylinders; also a subterranean missile store.

silt a soil type composed of particles between 0.002 mm and 0.06 mm in size; see also fine, medium, coarse silt.

silvanite see sylvanite.

silver 1 a heavy, pale, soft and malleable metal, **Ag**; a good conductor of electricity used as a decorative coating on other metals and in some photographic compounds.
2 silver grey, old silver; a shade of slightly brownish grey which takes its name from the colour of tarnished silver.

silver arsenic sulphide arsenic sulphide, see proustite.

silver birch see European birch, [*Betula pendula*].

silvered-bowl lamp see crown silvered lamp.

silver fir [*Abies alba*] the largest European softwood with light brown timber; used in all kinds of construction work and joinery.

silver glance see argentite.

silver grey see silver.

silvering, silver plating; the coating of an object with a thin layer of silver.

silver leaf sheets of silver beaten or rolled as thin as 0.001 mm, used as surface decoration, usually treated with varnishes to prevent the blackening effects of oxidation.

silverlock bond see rat-trap bond. →17

silver maple [*Acer saccharinum*] a North American hardwood with light brown timber, marketed as soft maple; used for furniture, panelling and packaging.

silver plating see silvering.

silver point a method of drawing with a silver rod on a chalk-coated ground with or without added coloured pigment; a forerunner of the lead pencil.

silver poplar see white poplar.

silver stylus a metal drawing instrument with a sharp silver point used for making delicate brown line drawings, often miniatures, on a ground of gesso or other material.

silver sulphide a chemical compound, **AgS**, found naturally as the mineral argentite, an important ore of silver.

silver white a shade of pale grey which takes its name from the colour of shiny silver.

silviculture the planting and cultivation of trees in a natural environment as woodland or forest.

sima see cymatium. →78, →79

simple span bridge see single span bridge. →32

simply supported stair a stair in which each step is supported at both ends. →45

sine a trigonometric function for an angle, defined by the length of the side of a right-angled triangle opposite to the angle, divided by the length of the hypotenuse.

singers' gallery a balcony or gallery overlooking the main body of a church or medieval hall etc. intended for the performances of singers and musicians; also called a minstrel gallery or cantoria. →98

single-coat plaster, one-coat plaster; plaster designed to be both an undercoat and a final coat, laid over a base as a single layer.

single-coat plasterwork, one-coat plasterwork; plasterwork laid as one thin layer of final plaster.

single digging in excavation and landscaping, manual digging to the depth of a spade's blade.

single door a door with only one side-hinged door leaf; see also double door. →50

single drainage system an outdated drainage system in which foul water and surface water from domestic premises are combined in a single drain.

single-family house see one-family house. →61

single Flemish bond a brickwork bond giving the appearance of a Flemish bond on the outer face of a brick wall more than 9" thick.

single flying shore a flying shore in which the supporting element is a single member.

single glazing glazing with a single uninsulated layer of glass separating the inside and outside of a building.

single-hole tap see monobloc mixer.

single layer chipboard, standard grade chipboard; chipboard manufactured from chips of an even size, or of chips of varying size evenly distributed throughout the thickness of the board; see also graded density chipboard, multilayer chipboard. →9

single lever tap a lever tap in which hot and cold water supplies are mixed and their temperature and pressure controlled, operated by one lever fitted on a ball joint.

single-loaded corridor block a multistorey residential building type in which apartments are arranged with their entrance doors on one side of a corridor or access gallery on each floor. →61

single-lock cross-welt see single-lock welt. →49

single-lock welt, single-lock cross-welt; a sheetmetal roofing joint in which the edges of two adjacent sheets are bent over each other then hammered down. →49

single notched joint, trenched joint; a timber crossing joint in which the face of one member is cut with a notch or groove to receive a second member. →4

single orientation referring to an apartment or dwelling unit with windows on one external wall only, opening out in the same direction. →61

single-phase a description of alternating current at 240 volts with one phase or with phases at an angle of 180°; used for normal applications such as residential and office buildings.

single-phase current see previous entry.

single-pipe system see one-pipe system.

single pitch roof see monopitch roof. →46

single-purpose planning town planning in which priority is given to one area such as transport policy, and other issues left with insufficient consideration.

single Roman tile a wide single-lap roof tile with one flat waterway or channels between convex projections. →47

single roof a roof construction in which rafters are unsupported by purlins or primary beams. →33

single sized aggregate aggregate consisting of particles of relatively even size.

single span bridge a bridge whose main spanning member is a single arch, beam or slab between two supports; also called a simple span bridge. →32

single spread adhesive see one-way stick adhesive.

single stair building see point-access block. →61

single-storey referring to a building with only one habitable floor; a bungalow is a single-storey dwelling.

single track road a narrow road wide enough for the travel of only one vehicle at a time, often with passing places.

single welt see welted edge.

sinister in heraldry, the part of a shield to the left of the wearer or bearer; to the right as viewed by the spectator. →124

sink a sanitary vessel of vitreous china or stainless steel for washing utensils, hands etc., connected to a drainage system, fixed to a wall or furnishing at waist height and usually fitted with a plug-hole and taps.

sinking a recess or groove cut into a surface, especially stone or timber.

sink top a kitchen worktop with an integrated sink or sinks, often a pressed stainless steel unit containing a drainer and taps.

sinter a range of yellow-brown minerals and rocks formed as a build-up of deposits from mineral-rich spring water; includes calcareous tuff and travertine.

sintered aggregate lightweight aggregate produced from particles which have fused together on heating.

sintering the process of heating particles of mineral matter to such a temperature that they fuse together to form a porous solid without becoming liquid.

sinuous flow see turbulent flow.

sinuous grain see wavy grain.

siparium Lat.; a side or secondary curtain in a Roman theatre. →89

siphon a tubular apparatus for transferring liquid over an obstacle from one level to a lower level, which operates by the pressure difference acting on columns of water within the tube.

siphonage, 1 siphonic action; the conveyance of a liquid using a siphon, or by such principles.
2 see induced siphonage.

siphonic action see siphonage.

siphonic WC pan a WC in which soil falls into a water-filled bowl and is removed by the siphonic action of flushing water.

sipo see utile.

Siricidae see wood wasp.

sisal the dried leaf-fibre from one of a number of Central American plants, especially *Agave sisalana*, used for making ropes and matting.

sisal matting a natural floor covering woven from sisal fibres.

sistrum an ancient Egyptian musical instrument composed of a metal handled loop and crossbar with perforated discs threaded onto it; making a gentle rattling sound and used in sacred rituals of the cow-goddess Hathor, it features in many ornamental motifs and column capitals. →73

SI-system International System of Units.

site 1 the place at which construction work is undertaken; a building site.
2 an area of land designated by a planning application for a specific development, or one for which a proposed building is to be designed.
3 see location.

site access, site road; either a road which permits access from a public right of way to a private plot, a point of access for vehicles entering a building site, or a temporary road on the building site itself.

site accommodation, site hut; a temporary portable shelter with electricity and water supply used by the contractor and other site employees for on-site administration, storage and as sanitary facilities during a construction project.

site agent a contractor's representative responsible for managing and supervising work on a small site.

site assembly pertaining to components and parts of construction which are built or assembled on site rather than by a process of prefabrication.

site boundary the official boundary of ownership or right of use for a particular plot of land, often a building plot.

site clearing see clearing.

site concrete see mixed concrete.

site engineer a contractor's representative responsible for overviewing external and structural work, setting out and foundations etc.

site equipment, site plant; plant, heavy tools and other machinery used in on-site building construction, rather than that installed in the building itself.

site hut see site accommodation.

site information in contract administration, details of location, access, ground conditions etc. provided to tenderers.

site inspection the initial overviewing of a building plot or site prior to site investigation, surveys and the commencement of construction.
an inspection of building works under construction, carried out on site.

site investigation an investigation of the subterranean site conditions of a building site prior to foundation design to ascertain soil types, bearing capacity and evidence of toxic substances.

site layout plan a drawing produced by a contractor to show means of access to a building site, location of stores, materials, signs, any demolition work, huts and other site arrangements during construction.

site manager a contractor's representative responsible for managing and supervising work on a large site.

site meeting a meeting held at or near a construction site in which the designers, contractors, client representatives and other associated parties meet to discuss progress and problems regarding the project, make decisions etc.

site mixed concrete concrete mixed on site rather than delivered pre-mixed or ready-mixed.

site office a temporary office on a building site where site administration is carried out, and in which site meetings are held.

site plan a drawing showing in plan the layout of a site and buildings, roads and landscape thereon.

site plant see site equipment.

site possession see possession of site.

site preparation programme a series of documents and drawings produced by a contractor to indicate means of access to a site, location of stores, materials, signs, any demolition work, huts and other site arrangements during construction.

site pump mobile mechanical plant for pumping rainwater and groundwater from surface areas and excavations, and for lowering the water table on a building site.

site road see site access.

site utilization factor in town planning, a value stipulated for a particular site by a planning authority limiting the amount of development on that site.

Sitka spruce [*Picea sitchensis*] a Canadian spruce with high quality, relatively knot-free pale pink timber; used for building construction, cladding and joinery.

sitting room 1 see living room. →57, →59
2 a room in a residential building or establishment for the leisure activities of its occupants.

situation see position.

sitz bath see hip bath.

six-pointed star 1 a decorative motif of a star with six pointed limbs radiating out from a central point at equal intervals; in French heraldry it is called a mullet. →123
2 see Star of David, hexagram. →108

size 1 the magnitude of an object; examples of sizes used in dimensioning and construction are listed below.
actual size.
daylight size, see sight size. →52
dressed size, dressed dimension.
external dimension.
finished size.
full size, see tight size. →52
glass size, glazing size, see pane size.
grain size.
measurement.
mesh size.
modular size, modular dimension.
neat size, see dressed size.
see nominal dimension, nominal size.
opening size.
overall dimension, overall size.
paper size. Table 6
span dimension.
pane size.
sight size. →52
tight size. →52
2 sizing; a clear water-based glue or varnish used for sealing porous surfaces such as painting canvas or plaster before the application of paint, wallcovering etc.; see below.
bole.
glue size.
gold size.
gilding size, see gold size.
varnish size.

size perspective a way of indicating depth in drawing by rendering objects, people etc. in the foreground larger than those in the distance.

size water a water-based solution of gelatine used for slowing down the setting rate of casting plaster.

sizing 1 the sealing of a painter's canvas, plaster wall or other absorbent surface with size before painting.
2 see size.

skating rink see ice rink.

skeleton see frame.

skeleton stair see open riser stair. →45

skene, scene, scena, scaena (Lat.); Gk; in classical Greek architecture, a back stage building for the players, facing the audience in a theatre. →89

skenotheke Gk; in classical Greek theatre architecture, a back stage storage building within the skene. →89

sketch 1 an initial outline design or drawing.
2 see croquis.

sketchbook see block.

sketch drawing, preliminary drawing, outline drawing; a drawing made at an early stage in the design of a building to show the designer's concept and initial layout of spaces and massing etc.

sketchpad a loosely bound volume of usually cheap paper used for drawing, sketching etc.

sketch paper very fine, white, translucent paper used by architects and designers for lead pencil sketches, designs and drawings.

skete (Gk sketos, asketes); the dwelling of a monk in an Orthodox monastery.

skew see oblique.

skew arch a form of arch whose abutments or supporting structural elements are on different lines in plan to the face of the arch.

skewback, screwback; the wedge-shaped masonry abutment or splayed stone at the springing of an arch to transmit its thrust downward. →22

skew bridge a bridge which crosses a road, waterway or obstacle at an oblique angle. →64

skew chisel, long-cornered chisel; a straight-bladed turning chisel whose cutting edge is set at an angle, used for smoothing and accurate shaping of wood on a lathe. →41

skew filler piece a proprietary component fitted beneath profiled roof sheeting at a slanting eaves or hip to block up the corrugations.

skew nailing the hammering of nails into a surface at an angle when attaching a timber on end or to provide a stronger fixing; also called toe nailing or dovetail nailing. →3

ski jump a tall ramped structure and the landing strip below it to provide a run for ski-jumpers.

ski lift an outdoor lift to convey skiers to the top of a ski-slope.

skilled labourer, craft operative, skilled operative; a construction worker whose skill is equivalent to that of a tradesman, often one skilled in a modern trade.

skilled operative see skilled labourer.

skimming coat see final plaster coat.

skimming float a thin-bladed hand float used for the application of finish plaster.

skin a lightweight and non-structural outer facing, cladding or layer for a wall or component.

skin mould in ornamental plastering, a membrane-like flexible mould in which decorative castings are made.

skip 1 see miss.
2 any large open steel container for collecting building rubbish, conveying material etc.
3 see crane skip.
4 see waste skip.
5 see concrete skip.

ski rack a rack at a ski resort against which skis can be temporarily stored.

skirting 1 an area of roofing which has been turned upwards against an abutment to provide protection at the upper edge of a roof.
2 a strip of material, not necessarily of wood, for covering the join between floor and wall in a room. →2
3 see skirting board. →2

skirting board, baseboard, mopboard, scrubboard, washboard; a board, trim or strip which covers the construction joint between floor and wall surfaces; a component produced for this purpose. →2, →44

skirting tile 1 a ceramic tile designed for use at the lowest edge of a tiled wall, where it meets the floor. →20
2 see coved skirting tile. →20

skirting trunking, plugmold, wireway (Am.); an openable conduit for cables and wiring in an electric installation, which also functions as skirting.

skirt roof a false overhanging roof or canopy fixed to a wall at storey level. →46

skutterudite, smaltite; a metallic white or grey mineral, naturally occurring cobalt arsenide, $CoAs_3$, an important ore of cobalt.

sky blue 1 a pale form of ultramarine blue pigment.
2 bleu-ciel; a shade of blue which takes its name from the colour of a clear summer noonday sky.

sky component see sky factor.

sky factor, sky component; in daylight calculations for a room, the portion of daylight which is diffuse radiation from the sky as opposed to direct sunlight.

sky grey a shade of blue grey which takes its name from the colour of an overcast sky on a rainy day.

skylight, 1 indirect solar radiation; in lighting design, that part of solar illuminance that reaches the ground as diffuse light from the sun.
2 see rooflight. →60

skyline, roofline, silhouette; in urban design, townscape etc. the meeting point of built form and the sky, the forms of roofs, towers and structures perceived on the near horizon.

skyscraper a tall modern building, usually offices or dwellings, situated in an urban environment.

slab 1 any thin horizontal plate-like structure, usually of solid in-situ concrete or precast concrete units, which functions as a floor or roof structure.
see types of structural concrete slab listed under 'concrete slab'.
see balcony slab. →54
see floor slab.
see roof slab. →49
2 flag, pavior; a hard, thick, fairly large cladding tile for floors or external areas, usually of stone, clay or a mineral-based material such as concrete.
see concrete paving slab. →15
3 in the conversion of timber, curved-edged or waney boards cut from the edge of a log, often with attached bark. →1, →2

slab block an elongated multistorey residential block, most often rectangular in plan, whose dwelling units are arranged around and accessed by a series of vertical circulation cores with stairs and lifts. →61

slab bridge a bridge constructed from a single monolithic slab of material such as concrete or stone. →32
see single span bridge. →32
see continuous slab bridge. →32

slab-on-grade see ground supported floor. →59

slab reinforcement steel reinforcement for a reinforced concrete slab. →27

slab unit see precast slab unit.

slab urinal a urinal consisting of a sheet fitted to a wall, down which collected discharge flows into a floor channel.

slack side see loose side. →10

slag see blast-furnace slag.

slag concrete, blast-furnace concrete; lightweight concrete using granulated blast-furnace slag as a coarse aggregate.

slag wool a brittle fibrous material formed by the heating and spinning of blast-furnace slag; manufactured into slabs and used as thermal and acoustic insulation.

slaked lime hydrated lime or calcium hydroxide in liquid form, produced on site by the addition of an excess of water to quicklime; used as a binder in plaster and as an opaque white pigment in whitewash. →Table 5

slaking 1 the mixing of water with quicklime (calcium oxide) to form slaked lime (carbon hydroxide). →Table 5
2 see wet slaking.
3 see dry hydrate.

slap dash see wet dash.

slash conk [*Gloephyllum sepiarium*, *Lenzites sepiaria*] a form of brown rot which attacks timber whose moisture content alternates between being damp and dry.

slash grain see plain sawn.

slash sawing see through and through sawing. →2

slash sawn see plain sawn.

slat a thin piece of wood or other material used in a shading device or grille.

slate 1 a dark grey aluminium silicate metamorphic rock formed in thin layers; it can be easily cleft into sheets and is used for roof tiles and paving slabs.
2 see roofing slate.
3 see strip slates. →49

slate black a greyish black pigment of powdered slate or shale used in some water-based paints.

slate fillet one of a series of pieces of slate laid in mortar as an upstand in traditional roofing construction.

slate grey a shade of either dark greyish brown or dark bluish grey which takes its name from the colour of slate.

slate hanging the hanging of slates on battening as cladding for external walls.

slate roof a sloping roof whose weatherproofing is provided by rows of overlapping roofing slates nailed to horizontal battens.

slate walling masonry walling of pieces of slate laid horizontally and bedded in mortar. →11

slating the trade of laying slates as roofing; the work thus done.

slatting in timber-clad construction, battening laid with spaces between the ends of the battens to allow for the passage of ventilating air within construction.

slaughterhouse see abattoir.

sledge see sledgehammer. →40

sledgehammer, sledge; a heavy two-handed hammer with a long shaft and heavy iron or steel head, used for crushing, breaking and driving; types included as separate entries are listed below. →40
beetle.
blacksmith's hammer. →40
club hammer. →40
double face hammer. →40
drilling hammer. →40
engineer's hammer. →40
engineer's sledge. →40
lump hammer, mash hammer, see club hammer. →40
maul, mall. →40
peen sledge, see engineer's sledge. →40
smith's hammer, see blacksmith's hammer. →40
striking hammer. →40

sleeper 1 railway sleeper; a timber or precast concrete member laid at intervals for supporting railway tracks.
2 see ground plate. →6

sleeper wall a low masonry wall which carries timber floor joists at intervals between side walls, usually in honeycomb bond to allow for underfloor ventilation.

sleeping policeman see road hump.

sleeve 1 see pipe sleeve.
2 see ferrule.

sleeve anchor see wedge anchor. →37

sleeved nail a round-shanked nail with an outer sleeve which expands as the nail is driven home.

sliced veneer, knife cut veneer; veneer produced by moving a log or flitch vertically against a fixed veneer knife.

slicing see veneer slicing. →10

slide bolt, 1 snib bolt; a secondary bolt incorporated in a rim latch, operable from the inside only.
2 thumb slide; a small barrel bolt. →39

slide damper in air conditioning and mechanical ventilation installations, a damper which functions by sliding across a duct to control the flow of air.

slide rule a traditional calculating device based on sliding graded scales.

sliding bearing a structural bearing consisting of two surfaces which can move horizontally with respect to one another.

sliding bevel a bevel square which has a slot through the blade so that it may be extended for added versatility.

sliding damper a sliding metal flap incorporated within a flue or chimney to regulate the amount of draught for combustion. →56

sliding door a door opened by sliding its leaf along an upper or lower track, with manual or motorized action. →50
see double sliding door. →50
see sliding folding door. →50
see centre-opening door, bi-parting door. →50

sliding door gear mechanisms for opening and closing an automatic sliding door, operated by a signal from a detector device, remote controls etc.

sliding door handle a device or fitting by which a sliding door may be pulled open.

sliding folding door, concertina door; a sliding door whose leaf is also hinged so that it slides along a track and folds with a concertina action. →50

sliding folding window a sliding window whose sash is hinged so that it also folds, thus increasing the area of openable window. →52

sliding hatch a hatch for sales, serveries, information desks etc., which opens and shuts by sliding horizontally in tracks.

sliding sash a framed light in a window, opened by sliding.

sliding sash window see sliding window. →52

sliding window, 1 horizontal sliding window, sliding sash window; a window with a sash or sashes that slide open horizontally within a frame. →52
2 see sliding folding window. →52
3 vertical sliding window, see sash window. →52

sling see crane sling.

slip 1 see engobe.
2 see brick slip.

slipform, continuously moving form; proprietary formwork used for large-scale and seamless concretework, consisting of a rig which moves continuously along a plane while casting is taking place.

slipform casting the in-situ casting of concrete in continuously moving formwork; see slipform.

slip layer a coating applied to the shaft of a foundation pile to minimize friction between it and the surrounding ground during piledriving.

slip match a veneering pattern in which similar pieces of veneer are glued side by side to form a repeated pattern. →10

slip membrane one or two layers of sheet material, often polyurethane sheet, used to provide a horizontal movement joint between successive layers of floor construction.

slip road, ramp; a length of single-directional roadway providing access to or from major roads meeting at different levels. →63

slip sill in masonry construction, a window or door sill which does not extend beyond the edge of the opening into which it fits, and is not built into the wall at either side.

slip tenon joint see free tenon joint. →5

slit coil a steel product from a rolling mill; coil which has been cut lengthways into strips.

slope 1 the angle that a stair, roof etc. makes with the horizontal.
2 an area of terrain or land at an angle to the horizontal.
3 see pitch, gradient.

sloping see inclined.

sloping bridge a bridge whose deck is at an angle to the horizontal along its length. →32

sloping grain, diagonal grain; grain in a piece of sawn timber which is not parallel to one of its straight edges. →1

sloping roof see pitched roof.

sloping shore a flying shore assembled at an angle for increased stability etc.

slop moulding see soft-mud process.

slot 1 any long, narrow recess or gap formed into a surface.

2 the sinking in the head of a screw or other fastener, by which it is rotated with a tool. →36
3 see straight slot. →36

slot mortise, open mortise; a mortise for a timber joint that is cut through the end of a piece, having three open sides.

slot overflow a rectangular opening near the rim of a basin or sink through which water can flow into a drain if the water level rises too high.

slotted panel absorber an acoustical absorbing construction consisting of a perforated board with an air gap or mineral wool behind.

slotted waste a pipe fitting at a slot overflow, which joins a sink or basin to a discharge pipe.

slow grown see close grained.

sludge waste solid particle matter in thick liquid suspension resulting from a straining or deposition process.

slum a residential area within a large city which is overcrowded, densely built, unhygienic and dilapidated.

slum clearance the organized demolition of substandard housing to make way for new residential redevelopment and provide better housing conditions in dilapidated urban areas.

slump test an on-site test to determine the consistency of fresh concrete by filling a metal cone-shaped mould and measuring how much it subsides when the mould is removed.

slurry 1 a mixture of fine solid particles suspended in a liquid and having the general flow properties of a thick liquid.
2 see cement slurry.

slurrying in stonework under construction or repair, the application of a temporary coating of lime and stone dust to provide protection during further construction, washed off on completion of works.

slurry seal a liquid material used for patching and filling cracks in worn road surfaces, consisting of a binder such as cement or bitumen, fine aggregate and water.

slype a covered passageway in a monastery or monastic church between the transept and a chapter house. →97

smallholding an agricultural establishment of only a few hectares, smaller than a normal farm, for growing crops, horticulture, raising livestock etc.

smalt, Saxon blue; a form of ground potassium blue glass with traces of cobalt used as a pigment in paints, glass, ceramics and enamels.

smaltite see skutterudite.

smaragd green see viridian.

smart key a range of electronic products used as a key for access control and automated access systems, in which the personal information of the carrier, and his or her accessibility credentials, are encoded within; see following entry.

smart card a personalized card with a microchip or magnetized strip containing information which can be updated, used for phonecards, credit and swipe cards etc.

SMA welding acronym for shielded metal-arc welding, see manual metal-arc welding.

smelting see reduction.

smith's hammer a blacksmith's hammer. →40

smithsonite, zinc spar; a whitish mineral, naturally occurring zinc carbonate, $\mathbf{ZnCO_3}$, an important ore of zinc.

smith welding see forge welding.

smithy, forge; a traditional workshop in which a blacksmith plies his craft.

smog a form of pollution occurring in densely populated urban areas consisting of smoke mixed with fog.

smoke gases given off during combustion which contain fine particles of burnt material.

smoke alarm an alarm triggered by the presence of smoke.

smoke blue a shade of blue which takes its name from the colour of smoke viewed against a dark background.

smoke brown a shade of greyish brown which takes its name from the colour of coal smoke viewed against a dark background.

smoke chamber the space in a fireplace formed by a throat, gather and smoke shelf. →55, →56

smoke control measures taken in design and practice to control the flow of smoke outwards from a hazardous building fire.

smoke control door see smoke door.

smoke damper 1 a hinged or sliding metal flap in a fireplace flue for regulating the amount of draught for combustion; sometimes called a throat restrictor. →55, →56
2 see sliding damper. →56
3 see rotating damper. →56

smoke detector a fire safety sensor or fire detector which reacts to the presence of smoke and triggers fire safety measures and warnings.

smoke developed rating a standardized classification of the amount of smoke given off by the combustion of an interior finish; sometimes also known as smoke development rating.

smoke development rating see smoke developed rating.

smoke dispersal see dispersal, fire venting.

smoked glass glass manufactured with a grey or brown body tint, achieved by the addition of nickel, iron, copper or cobalt oxide.

smoke door, smoke control door, smoke stop door; an approved door type with seals around its edges to prevent the passage of cold smoke.

smoke extract fan a fan which removes smoke from hazardous building fires by blowing it along designed routes, corridors or ducts to the outside.

smoke grey a shade of grey which takes its name from the colour of smoke viewed against a light background.

smoke outlet 1 an opening in the upper part of an external wall, shaft etc. through which smoke from a building fire may be vented to the outside.
2 see fire vent.

smoke pipe see flue. →55, →56

smoke sauna a traditional wood-fired sauna building with no flue, ventilated before use to evacuate the smoke from combustion.

smoke shelf an upwardly curving ledge in a fireplace to direct smoke up the flue. →55

smoke shutter an automatic door, hatch or shutter designed to close and prevent smoke spreading from one space into another during a building fire.

smoke stop door see smoke door.

smoke test a test for unwanted openings and flow in a system of plumbing pipes or ventilation ducts by introducing smoke or other coloured non-toxic gas.

smoke vent see fire vent.

smoke venting see fire venting.

smoke venting rooflight a rooflight which also functions as a fire vent.

smoky quartz a brownish or smoke-coloured variety of quartz used for ornament and for gemstones.

smooth, flush; a description of a surface which is relatively even, has no projections and is not pitted.

smoothing 1 see sanding.
2 see dressing, surfacing.
3 see float-finishing.

smoothing compound a material applied in semi-liquid form to interior floor construction, which sets to provide a smooth flooring.

smoothing plane a small bench plane used for the final smoothing or cleaning off of work.

smoothing trowel see finishing trowel. →43

smoothness evenness of surface texture.

smooth planed a description of sawn timber which has been smoothed with a plane to produce a finished surface.
smouldering in the development of a fire in buildings, burning without flame.
SMS short message service.
snake see Wadjet. →74
see uraeus. →74
snaked finish a smooth, lightly polished matt finish in stonework produced by rubbing with a fine abrasive or whetstone.
snap header, half bat; a half brick used in walling to appear in a wall surface as a header. →21
snap line see chalk line.
snapping line see chalk line.
sneck a small stone used in rough masonry joints as a gap filler and to stabilize walling.
snib, check lock, locking snib, thumb slide; a mechanism in a lock or latch to hold its bolt in a closed or open position, usually operated by a sliding button in the forend. →39
snib bolt see slide bolt.
snib latch see indicating bolt. →39
snow white hexagonal crystals of frozen moisture from the atmosphere.
snow barrier a rudimentary fence constructed at the side of roads in rural areas to prevent snow drifting onto the carriageway.
snowboard, snow cradling; a board laid at eaves level on a pitched roof to act as a snowguard.
snow clearance the removal of snow from areas and building surfaces; see also snowploughing.
snow cradling see snowboard.
snow density a measure of the water content of snow expressed as the ratios of depths before and after total melting.
snow disposal site a designated site in regions with cold climates where snow which has been removed from roads, streets and public areas is dumped.
snow fence a screen by the side of a carriageway designed to prevent snow from drifting into the path of traffic.
snowguard a horizontal bar or rail fixed at eaves level on a pitched roof to prevent the slippage of snow onto the ground below. →46
snowhook a bent metal component or loop fixed at eaves level to support a snowguard or snowboard.
snow load a structural live load imposed by the weight of snow on a roof.
snow melt water conveyed into drains which arises from melted snow and ice during a period of thaw.
snowploughing, snow clearance; the clearing of streets, roads and railways of snow using a snowplough.
snow white 1 see zinc white.
2 see chalky.
snuff (brown) see Havana (brown).
soakaway a rudimentary drain consisting of an excavated pit filled with sand, gravel or stones, into which waste water is discharged and from which it leaks away into the surrounding soil. →58
soaker 1 in roof construction, a small piece of metal sheet laid beneath roof tiles at a hip, valley or abutment.
2 roof soaker, see pipe flashing.
3 a strip of waterproofing material laid between courses of roof shingles in exposed areas.
soap a special brick with a square profile, usually 50 mm × 50 mm × 215 mm. →16
soapstone, 1 steatite, potstone; a soft, grey rock whose surface has a soapy feel; it contains a high proportion of talc and is used for baths, sinks, fireplaces and in industry.
2 see French chalk.
Sobek the ancient Egyptian crocodile deity, focus of worship in the Middle Kingdom, bodyguard of the kings; depicted as a man with the head of a crocodile. →74
social engineering the improvement of societies according to social theories and precepts.
social group a collection of people linked by common social ties providing a sense of belonging and social relationships through awareness of shared interests or experiences.
social housing see council housing.
social security costs, National Insurance contributions; a levy from wages that employers and employees are obliged to pay towards maintaining social services.
social structure the whole complex of relationships which forms the social framework of people's lives.
social welfare study in town planning, a study of social conditions based on surveys of health, education, standard of living, crime and delinquency, family structure etc. in a particular area.
sociology the science of developing and systemizing an understanding of how human collectives function, flourish, and perish.
sociomorphic fallacy the town planning concept that humans instinctively know what other people should want, irrespective of local tradition and circumstance, information to the contrary etc.
socket, 1 bell (Am.); the enlarged end of a drainage pipe to fit over the end of another pipe and form a join.
2 a short length of connecting pipe which is internally threaded.
3 see socket outlet.
4 see telecommunications outlet.
socket outlet, plug socket; electric installation casing and switches to receive an electric plug at a power point.
socket reducer, reducing bush; a small pipe fitting attached to the socketed end of one pipe to reduce its bore for the attachment of a smaller bore pipe.
sock lining a method of repairing a leak or hole in underground pipes by inserting a resin-soaked felt 'stocking' into the pipe and then expanding it against the pipe wall with compressed air or water; this provides a seal when the resin sets; also called resin lining.
soda-lime glass the most common type of glass, manufactured from sand, soda ash and limestone, used for flat glass, bottles and light bulbs.
sodalite a blue or yellowish white aluminium silicate mineral, a major constituent of lapis lazuli, used for jewellery and fashioned into ornamental objects.
sodium a soft, silver-white metallic chemical element, **Na**, found in common salt and discharge lamps.
sodium bicarbonate, sodium hydrogen carbonate; a white, water-soluble chemical compound, $NaHCO_3$, used in fire extinguishers and baking.
sodium borate see sodium tetraborate.
see borax.
sodium chlorate a colourless, water-soluble chemical compound, $NaClO_3$, used in explosives, matches and as a bleaching agent.
sodium chloride common salt, **NaCl**, see also halite.
sodium cyanide a white, poisonous chemical compound, **NaCN**, used in the surface treatment of metals and for carburizing steel alloys.
sodium hydrogen carbonate see sodium bicarbonate.
sodium hydroxide, caustic soda; a corrosive alkaline chemical compound, **NaOH**, used in the manufacture of pigments, soap, cellulose and paper.
sodium hypochlorite a pale green, crystalline chemical compound, **NaOCl**, used as a bleaching agent in the textile and paper industries, in water purification, and for domestic use.
sodium lamp, sodium-vapour lamp; a discharge lamp used primarily for street and external lighting, producing yellow light from sodium vapour.

see high pressure sodium lamp.
see low pressure sodium lamp.

sodium nitrate a crystalline, water-soluble chemical compound, $NaNO_3$, used in explosives, fertilizers, the manufacture of glass, and as a colour stabilizer in processed meat.

sodium silicate, water glass; one of a number of chemical compounds used in the production of soaps, detergents, in the textile industry, as wood preservative, and in the manufacture of paper products and cement.

sodium sulphate a white, crystalline, water-soluble chemical compound, Na_2SO_4, used in the manufacture of dyes, soaps, glass and ceramic glazes.

sodium tetraborate, sodium borate; a chemical compound, $Na_2B_4O_7$ ($10H_2O$), used for dissolving metal oxides, cleaning soldered surfaces and in glazing and enamelling; found naturally as borax.

sodium-vapour lamp see sodium lamp.

sofa, settee; an elongated upholstered easy chair with a back and armrests which seats two or more people.

soffit, 1 undersurface; the lower face of any building component or structure such as a ceiling, arch or slab.
2 see intrados. →22
3 see soffit board. →46
4 head; the upper undersurface of a window or door opening.
5 see window soffit.
6 see door head.

soffit bearer in timber roof construction, a small horizontal timber at eaves level to which a soffit board is nailed.

soffit board, soffit; a horizontal board or boarding fixed to the underside of the ends of joists or rafters in a projecting eaves. →46

soffit formwork, decking; formwork for casting and supporting the underside of a concrete slab.

softboard, insulation board; a lightweight timber-based sheet product with porous construction, a low density fibreboard whose density is less than 350 kg/m^3, used for sound and thermal insulation.

soft face hammer a hammer with a plastic, leather or rubber head for hammering easily breakable surfaces. →40

soft maple [*Acer saccharinum, Acer rubrum*] a collective name for the timber of the North American silver and red maples.

soft-mud process, slop moulding; a process of forming bricks or other ceramic products from wet clay which contains 20–30% water.

soft pine see western white pine.

soft rock, soft stone; according to a hardness classification of rocks used by stone masons and construction technicians, rock which has a compressive strength below 800 kg/cm^2; includes sandstones and limestones.

soft soap a concentrated semi-liquid soap made with potassium hydroxide (potash), used in the textile industry and as a household cleaning fluid.

soft solder an alloy of tin with a low melting point, used in soft soldering.

soft soldering the normal method of soldering used for joining copper and brass pipes and electronic components using soft solder, an alloy of tin with a low melting point.

soft stone see soft rock.

software the collective names for computer programs and programmed applications; see hardware.

softwood the collective name for timber from any coniferous tree, in general light-coloured with pronounced growth rings, which, despite its name, may sometimes be harder than some hardwoods; see below for list of species of conifers (softwood tree) included in this book.
cedars, see *Cedrus spp.*; for other trees called by the name cedar: see *Calocedrus decurrens, Chamaecyparis lawsoniana, Juniperus communis, Thuja.*
cypresses, *Cupressus spp.*; Lawson's cypress, see *Chamaecyparis lawsoniana*; southern cypress, see *Taxodium distichum.*
firs, see *Abies spp.*; Douglas fir, see *Pseudotsuga douglasii.*
hemlocks, *Tsuga spp.*
juniper, eastern red cedar, see *Juniperus communis*
larches, see *Larix spp.*
pines, see *Pinus spp.*; Oregon pine, see *Pseudotsuga douglasii*; Parana pine, see *Araucaria angustifolia.*
spruces, see *Picea spp.*
yew, *Taxus baccata.*

softwood board a piece of sawn softwood with cross-sectional dimensions of less than 47 mm thick and greater than 100 mm wide. →2

softwood plank a piece of sawn softwood with cross-sectional dimensions of 47 mm–100 mm thick and greater than 275 mm wide. →2

softwood plywood plywood whose veneers are made from softwood. →9

softwood scantling a piece of sawn softwood with cross-sectional dimensions of 47 mm–100 mm thick and 50 mm–125 mm wide. →2

softwood strip a piece of sawn softwood with cross-sectional dimensions of less than 50 mm thick and less than 125 mm wide.

soil 1 granular mineral material within the earth's crust, crushed rock and humus, classified according to composition and grain size.
2 fragmented or loose mineral or organic material, including humus, consisting of weathered and crushed rock; earth above the bedrock.
3 natural granular material with appropriate nutrients, laid as a growing medium for planting; see below. →15
coarse soil, see granular soil.
cohesive soil.
fine-grained soil.
granular soil.
growing medium. →48
non-plastic soil.
organic soil.
plastic soil.
saturated soil.
subsoil.
topsoil.
vegetable soil. →15
4 see soil water.

soil amelioration in landscaping, the improvement of the quality and drainage of soil by the addition of granular material.

soil anchorage a system of steel rods, guys or braces to fix a structure firmly to the underlying ground.

soil appliance, soil fitment; any appliance for the disposal of human waste, a toilet or urinal, connected to a soil drain.

soil binder plants and bushes planted on embankments whose roots provide reinforcement for the soil.

soil cement cement with soil as its aggregate, used in road construction and soil stabilization.

soil classification, classification of soils; the classification of soil types according to properties, granular range and content.

soil conditioning in landscaping, the improvement of the quality and drainage of soil by the addition of chemical material.

soil drain see soil water drain.

soil fitment see soil appliance.

soil mechanics the science surrounding the investigation of soils by the collection and testing of samples in order to provide information used for foundation design.

soil reinforcement, ground improvement; the strengthening of soil to be used for loadbearing earthworks, soil structures, embankments and under foundations using geotextiles and other reinforcing measures.

soil sample a sample of loose subterranean material or earth taken from a site to ascertain bearing conditions, contamination etc.

soil stabilization the strengthening, reinforcing, supporting or compacting of weak and porous soils to prevent erosion and provide a structural base for roads and other earthworks.

soil stack a vertical drainage pipe into which soil water is discharged into a soil drain.

soil water, soil; discharge containing human solid waste from WCs.

soil water drain, soil drain; a horizontal pipe buried beneath the ground for leading soil water from a building to a private or public sewer.

Sokar the pre-Dynastic Egyptian god of darkness and death, protector of tombs, depicted with the head of a falcon; also written as Seker.

Solanum melongena see aubergine.

solar altitude in lighting design, the height of the sun in the sky, measured in degrees above the horizon.

solar azimuth in lighting design, the direction of the sun, measured in degrees from due north.

solar building a building heated wholly or partly by energy from the sun.

solar cell one of the photoelectric cells in a solar panel which converts light into electricity.

solar collector that part of a solar heating system designed to absorb solar energy and heat up water or other liquids.

solar constant the average amount of the sun's energy received by the earth, measured as that received over unit time by a unit area of the earth's surface at a theoretical mean perpendicular distance from the sun, taken as approximately 1.94 cal/min/cm^2.

solar control glass, anti-sun glass; glass which has been treated with a body tint or reflective coating to improve solar absorption and reflection; types included as separate entries are listed below.
absorbing glass, see tinted solar control glass.
anti-fading glass.
heat-absorbing glass, see tinted solar control glass.
laminated solar control glass.
low emissivity glass.
reflective glass.
surface coated float glass.
surface-modified tinted float glass.
tinted solar control glass.

solar cross see wheel cross. →118

solar declination in lighting design, the angular distance of the sun measured north or south of a plane traced out by the equator.

solar disc see winged sun disc. →75
see Aten. →74

solar energy energy received as radiation direct from the sun, or electricity produced from this.

solar god see Aten. →74
see Atum. →74
see Khepri. →75
see Ra. →74

solar heating any system which makes use of the radiant energy of the sun to provide heat; see passive solar energy.

solarium 1 a device for providing ultraviolet radiation for health or therapy.
2 a room at a beauty parlour, hospital or health club with such a device.
3 any glazed or open porch or terrace exposed to the sun.
4 see Imperial chapel. →98, →99

solar panel in a solar heating system, a device containing solar cells for converting radiant energy from the sun into electricity.

solar power electricity produced by a solar cell or panel.

solar power station a large-scale plant containing a battery of solar panels to generate electrical energy from sunlight.

solar radiation electromagnetic radiation from the sun, including visible light, ultraviolet light and infrared radiation.

solder 1 a metal alloy used in joining metals together by soldering; usually an alloy of lead and tin for soft soldering or copper and zinc for brazing.
2 see soft solder.
3 see hard solder.

soldered joint a joint in plumbing or other metalwork formed and sealed by soldering.
see *soldered joint* in sheetmetal roofing illustration. →49

soldering the joining of metals together by melting a soft metal alloy or solder at a join and allowing it to harden, widely used for fastening electronic components and metal plumbing connections; see also soft soldering, brazing.

soldering iron a tool with a thin copper blade heated electrically or by gas, used for melting solder and applying it to metal connections.

soldering torch a device consisting of a vessel containing a combustible liquid or gas attached to a nozzle, which, when ignited, produces a flame used to provide melting heat for soldering.

soldier in brickwork, a brick on end with its face showing in a masonry wall, used in a row for copings, string courses and in flat arches. →20

soldier course a course of bricks made up entirely of soldiers, usually for decorative bands, above openings etc. →20

solea in Early Christian and Byzantine architecture, a raised part of the floor in front of a doorway or chapel, for use of the clergy. →95

sole member see sole plate. →8, →57, →58

solenoid a coil of metal wire, usually copper, that becomes magnetized when a current is passed through it.

solenoid lock an electric lock whose latch is restrained or freed for use by means of a solenoid.

sole piece 1 in traditional timber frame construction, a short horizontal lateral timber which provides the bearing for a common rafter onto a wall.
2 see sole plate. →8, →57, →58

sole plate, base plate, sole member, sole piece; in timber frame construction, the lower horizontal member in a stud wall, onto which vertical framing members are fixed. →8, →57, →58

solid one of the three states of matter in which a material is able to maintain its form under certain conditions of temperature and humidity, and is stable in mass and volume.

solid angle in three-dimensional geometry, an angle marked out in three dimensions as a cone-shaped part of a sphere.

solid background any solid masonry or concrete surface, as distinct from lathing or battening, to which plasterwork or plasterboard is applied.

solid balustrade a balustrade whose infill is of solid or sheet material with no perforations or openings. →54

solid brick a brick without indentations or perforations in its bed. →16

solid concrete slab a monolithic reinforced concrete floor or roof slab of even thickness. →44, →60

solid floor a floor slab of solid concrete without voids. →44

solid floor slab see solid floor. →44

solid fuel any solid material such as coal, wood etc. used as fuel to provide energy when burned.

solid-fuel appliance see solid-fuel stove. →56

solid-fuel heater see solid-fuel stove. →56

solid-fuel heating, wood-fired heating; heating of a building or space by the combustion of solid fuels such as wood, peat or coal.

solid-fuel stove, cast-iron stove; a freestanding heater which burns coal and wood as fuel; usually a patented product of metal plate or cast-iron construction connected to a flue. →56
solid geometry, stereometry, three-dimensional geometry; geometry in three dimensions.
solidification point the temperature at which a liquid turns into a solid on cooling.
solid map see bedrock map.
solid model the definition of a three-dimensional object in computer-aided design, rather than vectors defining its points of extremity.
solid parquet parquet strip flooring of solid matched lengths of hardwood laid in parallel arrangement. →44
solid-phase welding see pressure welding.
solid plastering see in-situ plastering.
solid plasterwork see in-situ plasterwork.
solid rock rock which consists of a consolidated and unfragmented mass of mineral material.
solid spandrel bridge an arch bridge with solid unvoided masses of masonry filling the triangular areas between the arched extrados and the bridge deck; also called a closed spandrel bridge, cf. open spandrel bridge. →32
solid timber beam 1 a beam produced from a single piece of sawn or hewn timber. →7
2 a timber beam of solid wood, either as described above or one of glue-laminated rather than composite or built-up construction.
solid timber flooring flooring material of planed timber sections rather than parquetry or wood products. →60
see *floors and flooring* illustration. →44
see *office building* illustration. →60
solid wall, massive wall; a wall with no cavities or one not of composite laminated construction; usually a concrete, brick or block wall.
solid waste relatively unusable solid material left over from an industrial process, habitation etc.; often referred to as refuse, rubbish or garbage.
solid wood timber products or sections which are unprocessed wood throughout their thickness rather than veneered board, framed panels, facing etc.; often includes glue-laminated timber beams and planks.
soling see pitching.
Solomonic column see spiral column. →114
Solomon's shield see Star of David. →108
Solomon's seal see Star of David. →108
solubility the ability of a material to be dissolved in a liquid.
soluble blue a form of water-soluble Prussian blue pigment.
solute a material that is dissolved in another.
solution 1 a chemical mixture consisting of a material dissolved in a liquid.
2 an answer, series of decisions or outcome to a particular problem or dilemma.
solvency the financial position of a company whose assets are of greater value than its debts.
solvent, 1 dissolvent; a liquid in which another substance will dissolve.
2 organic solvent; any highly volatile organic liquid used as a vehicle in paints and adhesives, and for paint and grease removal.
solvent adhesive a polymer-based adhesive for plastics which dissolves surfaces to be joined, forming a bond as its solvent evaporates.
solvent-based adhesive see solvent borne adhesive.
solvent borne adhesive, solvent-based adhesive; any adhesive whose binder is dissolved in an organic solvent which sets by evaporation.
Somalis a shade of brown which takes its name from the colour of the native people of Somalia, East Africa.
sone in acoustics, a unit of subjective loudness equivalent to a tone of frequency 1000 Hz at a sound pressure level of 40 dB.
Song period, Sung; a period in Chinese history from 960 to 1279 AD.
soot fine-grained carbon, especially that deposited on the inside of flues; the product of imperfect combustion.
soot brown a shade of dark brown which takes its name from the colour of soot.
soot door a hatch at the base of a chimney or fireplace through which a flue can be swept. →56
sopraporta, supraporta; a framed painting or decoration above a door, window or portal.
Sorbus aucuparia see rowan.
sorel cement see oxychloride cement.
sorrel wood sorrel, see shamrock. →121
sort the process of arranging the records or parts of a computer file in sequence according to specific predefined requirements.
sound 1 a sensation produced in the ear by rapid waves of pressure in a body of material, often air or water.
2 a description of a construction, structure, material etc. which is unbroken, stable, in good working order or without defects.
sound absorber see absorber, muffler.
sound absorption the ability of a material or construction to absorb sound by inhibiting or preventing reflections from its surface; also called acoustic absorption.
see *sound absorption* in floors and flooring illustration. →44
sound absorption coefficient in acoustics, the proportion of sound energy incident on a surface which is absorbed by that surface.
sound attenuation in acoustics, the prevention of echoes, reverberation and reflections of sound in a space due to scattering and absorbing of sound waves by surface treatments and careful design; also called acoustic attenuation.
sound attenuator see muffler.
sound boarding see pugging boards. →8
sound control glass window glass whose properties of sound insulation are improved with extra thickness, added compounds or special interlayers; also variously called acoustical glass, acoustic control glass, noise control glass, noise reduction glass, sound insulation glass and sound reduction glass.
see laminated sound control glass.
sounder that part of a fire alarm, doorbell or other device designed to produce a noise by mechanical or electronic means.
sounding 1 in soil investigation, the driving of a steel rod into the ground to discern the level of underlying bedrock.
2 depth sounding; a process of determining the depth of a body of water by various methods including dropping weighted lines or echo-sounding.
sounding board see tester. →102
sound insulation, 1 soundproofing, sound isolation; dense material used to prevent the travel of sound from one space in a building to another; also called acoustic insulation.
see *soundproofing* in floors and flooring illustration. →44
2 the prevention of travel of sound from one space to another; also called acoustic isolation.
3 see impact sound isolation. →59
sound insulation glass see sound control glass.
sound intensity in acoustics, the rate at which sound energy progresses through a given medium; measured in units of W/m^2; also called acoustic intensity.
sound intensity level the measure of relative sound intensity, in decibels.
sound isolation 1 see sound insulation.
2 see impact sound isolation. →59
sound knot a knot in seasoned timber which is free from decay and as hard as the surrounding wood. →1
sound level in acoustics, the make-up and intensity of a sound source, measured by a microphone linked to a calibrated electronic sound level meter.

sound level meter an electronic instrument used in acoustics for measuring sound pressure levels.

soundness, integrity; the property of a material, structure or product which is free of defects, whole and unbroken.

soundness test see gas soundness test.

sound power in acoustics, the sound energy per time emitted by a sound source.

sound power level in acoustics, a measure of sound pressure.

sound pressure in acoustics, a measure of the pressure at any point in a sound wave.

sound pressure level in acoustics, the logarithm of the ratio of a given sound pressure to a reference sound pressure.

soundproof in acoustics, referring to a material or component which inhibits the transmission of sound through its mass, structure or envelope.

soundproofed a description of a space, duct, chamber etc. constructed with sound insulating material and resilient joints to prevent sound from passing in or out of it.

soundproofing see sound insulation.
see *soundproofing* in floors and flooring illustration. →44

sound propagation in acoustics, the travel of sound via wave movement.

sound recording studio, recording studio; a specially equipped building, part of a building or complex where sound, especially music, is recorded.

sound reduction in acoustics, the ability of a material or construction to inhibit the transmission of airborne and impact sound through it.

sound reduction glass see sound control glass.

sound reduction index in acoustics, a measure of the sound transmission through an object or material.

sound reflection, reverberation; in acoustics, the various ways in which sound is reflected within a space, dependent on its shape, surface materials and treatment.

sound resistance the ability of a given material or construction to inhibit the transmission of sound.

sound reverberation in acoustics, a number of late secondary reflections in a space which unite to form a continuous aftersound.

sound source in acoustics, the source from which sound is emitted.

sound spectrum see audio spectrum.

sound timber timber which is free from fungal decay or insect attack.

sound wave a longitudinal pressure wave in air or other media which produces the sensation of sound in the ear.

sour cherry [*Prunus cerasus*] a European hardwood whose timber is used for musical instruments and for the decorative value of its grain.

souterrain see fogou.

south one of the points of the compass, the direction in which the sun in the Northern hemisphere lies at midday.

south-east a direction halfway between that of south and east.

southern cypress, swamp cypress (Am.); [*Taxodium distichum*] a deciduous softwood from the swamps of east and south USA; its timber is yellow brown and used for interior and exterior cladding and furniture.

southlight roof a sawtooth roof with south-facing glazed lights used for industrial buildings in the Southern hemisphere.

south-west a direction halfway between that of south and west.

soya bean oil a drying oil used as a vehicle in paints, pressed from soya beans; used widely as an industrial substitute for linseed oil.

soya glue glue made from soya bean meal after the extraction of its oil.

spa see health resort.

space 1 an area or volume bounded actually or theoretically; a continuous extension in three dimensions; a bounded area within a building.
2 see parking space.
3 the measured length from one point of a sawtooth to the next, a measure of the fineness of the cut of a saw.

space coordinates see three-dimensional coordinates.

spaced boarding, open boarding; sawn timber boards laid on a building frame with noticeable gaps between each, often as a base for cladding, roofing or flooring. →8
see *timber cladding boards* illustration. →8
see *timber-framed building* illustration. →57
see *holiday home and sauna* illustration. →58

space frame, space structure; any three-dimensional framework, especially a deck structure for long spans consisting of a three-dimensional lattice of triangulated members, usually steel tubes connected at their ends. →33

space heating see heating.

space lattice a space frame assembled from a number of parallel lattice girders connected with lateral members. →33

spacer, 1 cover block, reinforcement spacer; in reinforced concrete, a small piece of concrete, plastic or steel fixed over reinforcing bars to provide the appropriate amount of concrete cover between the bar and the formwork surface.
2 glazing unit spacer; a hollow metal tube sealed around the edges of adjacent panes in a sealed glazing unit to keep them apart and provide an insulating gap. →53

space structure see space frame. →33

spacial see spatial.

spacing see centres.

spacing plate a large perforated plate placed underneath a bolt-head or nut in a bolt fixing, which acts as a spacer and transfers the pressure of the fixing over a wider area.

spacious referring to an internal or external area, room etc. which has, or appears to have, an abundance of space; one which is open, high-ceilinged etc.

spackling 1 a very fine paste which sets to form a hard, smooth surface; applied in thin layers by a painter to fill small cracks, holes, joints and other blemishes in a surface prior to painting or wallcovering; also called spackling compound, stopping or filler.
2 the job of applying the above; also called stopping or filling.

spackling compound see spackling.

spackling knife see putty knife. →43

spade a hand tool for digging and shifting granular solids by means of a metal blade fixed to a handle.

spaded concrete see tamped concrete.

spading see tamping.

spall in masonry construction, flakes of stone removed during dressing with a tool, or which become detached due to frost or chemical action.

spall hammer, spalling hammer; a mason's hammer for the rough dressing of hard stone by spalling off small pieces. →40

spalling a defect in a stone, masonry or plaster finish caused by the separation of pieces from the surface.

spalling hammer see spall hammer. →40

spalt an early form of white rot in timber causing white areas surrounded by dark lines.

span 1 the area or axis over which the unsupported part of a beam or arch lies, between adjacent or main supports.
2 the horizontal distance between adjacent columns or supports which carry a beam or arch, measured from centre to centre.
see *span* in bridge structure illustration. →31

3 the distance between supports of an arch. →22
4 see clear span.

span bridge 1 see single span bridge. →32
2 see multiple span bridge. →32

span dimension the measured distance between two points of support of a beam, arch etc.

spandrel 1 an almost triangular area of wall bounded by an arch and a rectangle which surrounds it, often embellished.
2 the area of wall between two adjacent arches in an arcade.
3 a triangular area of wall beneath a stair.

spandrel braced arch bridge a bridge supported by a truss whose lower chord is arched to form a central opening beneath, and whose upper chord is horizontal, at deck level. →32

spandrel glass see cladding glass.

spandrel step one of a number of solid steps, triangular in cross-section, which form a stair with a smooth sloping soffit.

Spanish bond a paving pattern of a series of square pavers bordered with smaller stones, resembling basketweave pattern, but with arrangements of stones forming rectangular areas; similar patterns in parquetry and tiling. →15

Spanish brown see burnt umber.

Spanish chestnut see sweet chestnut.

Spanish green see green of Greece.

Spanish tile see under-and-over tile. →47

Spanish white high grade whiting in lump form.

spanner, wrench (Am.); a simple steel tool with jaws fixed at a certain width for undoing or tightening nuts.

span roof see close couple roof. →33

spar 1 a structural timber or mast, circular in cross-section.
2 see brotch.
3 see cross spar.

spar dash, dry dash; a rendered finish for masonry and concrete in which white spar pebbles are applied to a surface coating of mortar.

spare part one of a range of replacement parts for a particular device, installation or appliance, kept in storage and installed during repairwork.

sparrowpecked finish, stugged finish; a relatively even stonework finish produced by dressing with a small pick.

sparry ironstone see siderite.

sparsely populated area a rural area with low density of human settlement.

spatial, spacial; relating to the quality and characteristics of an interior or exterior space.

spatial coordinates see three-dimensional coordinates. →127

spatial planning see planning.

spatterdash 1 a mix of cement and sand thrown roughly onto a masonry wall surface as a key for further rendering or plasterwork.
2 a wet mix of plaster flicked onto a masonry wall by hand or machine to provide a mottled external finish.

spatula a bladed hand tool used in painting and decorating, plastering and masonry for applying and smoothing fillers, plasterwork and mortar. →43

speaker see loudspeaker.

speaking-tube a rudimentary communicating device, an open tube through which one can speak to the occupants of an adjoining space.

special 1 referring to any product or component which is available in non-standard form, one which has unusual properties, or one which has been produced for a specific purpose.
2 see special brick. →16

special brick, 1 special, special shape brick (Am.); any brick in a manufacturer's mass-produced range which is of non-standard shape or size; sometimes also called a standard special brick; types included as separate entries are listed below. →16
angle brick. →16
arch brick, see radial brick. →16
birdsmouth brick. →16
bullhead brick, see cownose brick. →16
bullnose brick. →16
cant brick. →16
capping brick. →16
coping brick. →16
cove brick. →16
cownose brick. →16
culvert header. →16
culvert stretcher. →16
featheredged coping. →16
header plinth. →16
plinth brick. →16
plinth header, see header plinth. →16
plinth stretcher, see stretcher plinth. →16
pre-chased brick. →16
radial brick. →16
radial header. →16
radial stretcher. →16
saddleback coping brick. →16
soap. →16
stretcher plinth. →16
tapered header, see culvert stretcher. →16
tapered stretcher, see culvert header. →16
2 see purpose made brick. →16

special colour any colour which is not standard for ranges of supplied proprietary items, or is unusual because of its composition.

special glass any glass such as tempered, toughened, coated, body-tinted or laminated glass which has been given special properties of strength, durability or colour.

specialist one who has certain specific knowledge or experience of a particular field, often employed in professional capacity because of this.

speciality contractor see specialized contractor.

specialized contractor, speciality contractor, trade subcontractor; a building contractor employed to carry out work on site requiring specialized skills or expert knowledge.

specialized work work on a building site requiring contractors or tradesmen with skills in unusual or demanding areas of construction, modern technologies etc.

special plywood plywood manufactured or processed for a particular or demanding use.

special road a road authorized for use by certain classes of traffic, or one of unusual construction.

special roof tile any roof tile in a manufacturer's mass-produced range which is of non-standard shape or size, for use at particular junctions or penetrations; types included as separate entries are listed below.
angular hip tile.
block end ridge tile.
bonnet hip tile.
cloaked verge tile.
dry ridge tile.
eaves tile.
half tile.
hip tile.
mansard tile.
ornamental tile.
ridge tile.
top course tile.
valley tile.
ventilating tile.
verge tile.

special shape brick see special brick. →16

species a group of plants or animals whose members share the same certain common characteristics and are able to interbreed; pl. species.

specific heat the heat required to raise the temperature of one unit of a particular material by 1°C, measured in MJ/kg°C.

specification 1 see specification of works.
2 see descriptive specification.

3 see performance specification.
4 see project specification.
5 see technical specification.

specification of works, specification; a written contract document that describes in detail all parts of work for a construction project to be carried out by a contractor, including standards of workmanship, testing and other procedures.

specified see as specified.

spelling checker computer software designed to detect and sometimes automatically correct misspellings in text.

specimen sample components or material removed as an example for testing and examination.

spectacula Lat.; the original name for a Roman amphitheatre, as used by Roman citizens. →90

spectral colour see chromatic colour.

Spectrolite the trade name for the rock anorthosite containing a high proportion of labradorite; a dark rock, iridescent with blue reflective plates when polished; used for decorative effect and exported from Finland.

spectrum 1 the range of wavelengths of any type of wave.
2 see visible spectrum.
3 see audio spectrum, sound spectrum, acoustic spectrum.

specular reflection the reflectance of visible light without distortion or dispersion, as if by a perfect mirror.

speculation investment, often of a risky nature, for short-term profit.

speculative builder a person or construction company who constructs buildings without having a buyer or occupant for them in advance, and thus bears the inherent financial risk.

speculative development the practice by a builder, developer, financier etc. of having buildings designed and constructed with a view to selling them to previously unknown buyers, often before the completion of the buildings themselves.

specus Lat.; a cave or channel in a Roman aqueduct along which water flows.

speed control hump see road hump.

speer see spere.

sper see spere.

spere, speer, spier, spur; a screen or construction placed near a door in medieval buildings to prevent draughts.

spessartine an orange-brown variety of the mineral garnet.

sphaeristerium Lat.; a room or space in a Roman bath house for ball games; called a sfairisterion in a Greek gymnasium. →91

sphalerite see zinc-blende.

sphene, titanite; a yellow, green or brown mineral, a calcium titanium silicate used as gemstones and occasionally mined as a source of titanium.

sphere a solid geometrical figure whose surface is formed by the rotation of a circle through 180° around its diameter; a ball.

spherical wave in acoustics, the spreading out of sound in all directions from a point source.

spheroidal cast iron see nodular cast iron.

sphinx an ancient Egyptian sculpted figure which has the prostrate body of a lion and the head of a human (androsphinx) or other animal such as a ram (criosphinx). →75
see *types of sphinx* illustration. →75
see *Egyptian pyramid complex* illustration. →71
see *Egyptian temple plan* illustration. →72
see androsphinx. →75
see criosphinx. →75
see hieracosphinx. →75

spicae testaceae Lat.; rectangular paving bricks or blocks used in Roman herringbone paving, opus spicatum.

spicatum opus see opus spicatum. →83

spick see brotch.

spier see spere.

spigot the plain or threaded end of a drainage pipe shaped to fit into the socket of another pipe and form a join in a pipeline.

spigot-and-socket joint, bell-and-spigot joint (Am.), spigot joint; a joint formed between two pipes by means of a socket enlargement at the end of one pipe which fits over the end of another and is sealed.

spigot joint see spigot-and-socket joint.

spike a large cut iron nail traditionally used in framing. →35

spike knot a knot in seasoned timber formed from a branch that has been cut lengthways. →1

spike lavender see oil of spike.

spike plate a small serrated metal washer clamped between two timbers in a bolted joint to provide stiffness. →37

spill-over level the level of liquid in a basin, bath, sink or other vessel at which it will spill over the rim.

spina 'spine' (Lat.); a longitudinal central dividing wall between the metae in the arena of a Roman circus. →89

spinach green a shade of dark green which takes its name from the colour of the leaves of the spinach plant [*Spinacia oleracea*].

Spinacia oleracea see spinach green.

spindle 1 a square metal rod that fits into a handle on one or both sides of a door leaf and turns a latch mechanism. →39
2 see fillet chisel. →41

spindle moulder a woodworking machine tool with a rapidly rotating cutter for machining housings and mouldings; a router mounted upside down on a bench.

spin drier an appliance with a rapidly rotating drum for drying washed laundry by centrifugal action.

spine beam see mono-carriage. →45

spine wall a principal loadbearing wall parallel to the main axis or structural layout of a building. →60

spira Lat.; a cylindrical torus moulding in an Ionic or Corinthian column base. →81

spiral, 1 volute; a curve which may be constructed mathematically, consisting of a line or lines rotating around a fixed point with a steadily decreasing distance; often used as a decorative device.
2 see continuous coil spiral. →125

spiral column 1 a column type with a shaft carved into a helical form, appearing in Late Gothic and Baroque architecture, and found in the legendary temple of King Solomon; variously called a barley-sugar column, salomonica, Solomonic column, torso, twisted column, wreathed column. →114
2 see serpent column. →69

spiral cutter a woodworking tool for machining decorative spirals or threads onto dowel.

spiral grain, torse grain; contorted grain in a piece of sawn timber which makes it difficult to work, formed by steep spiral arrangements of fibres in the tree trunk from which it was cut. →1

spiral ramp see helical ramp. →67

spiral ratchet screwdriver, double spiral screwdriver, in-and-out screwdriver, pump screwdriver, spiral screwdriver, Yankee screwdriver; a screwdriver with a spiral mechanism to enable screws to be tightened or loosened simply by pressing down on its handle.

spiral screwdriver see spiral ratchet screwdriver.

spiral stair, corkscrew stair, helical stair, spiral staircase; a stair which is usually circular in plan, with steps arranged radially around a single newel post or opening. →45

spiral staircase see spiral stair. →45

spire the tall pointed roof of a church tower, which may be round, polygonal or square in plan and resembles a very steep pavilion or conical roof.
see *church tower* illustration. →26
see *Scandinavian hall church* illustration. →102

spire roof a very sharply pointed hipped or conical roof.

spirit level a device for indicating true horizontal, by means of an air bubble sealed in a marked, liquid-filled glass tube mounted in a frame; the tube is horizontal when the bubble is between two marks.

spirit of place see sense of place.

spirit stain a translucent colouring agent consisting of a dye suspended in spirits, used for porous surfaces such as timber.

spirits of turpentine see turpentine.

spit 1 in manual excavation work and landscaping, a depth of soil equal to the length of the blade of a spade.
2 a small peninsula or headland which projects into the sea or a lake.

splash figure see ray figure.

splashback an area of sheetmetal or other sheet material such as plastics or coated plywood attached behind a sink as waterproof protection for an adjacent wall.

splashboard, waterboard; a strip of timber or other material attached to the base of a door or cladding to throw rainwater away from the surface or threshold.

splay 1 the surface formed when a corner is removed from a rectangle; a chamfer or bevel.
2 a splayed moulding, see bevel moulding. →14

splayed and tabled scarf joint, hooked scarf joint; a timber lengthening joint formed by making a slanting Z-shaped cut in the end of both timbers to fit each other. →3

splayed corner joint see bevelled corner joint. →4

splayed halved joint see bevelled halved joint. →4

splayed moulding see chamfered moulding. →14

splayed scarf joint a timber lengthening joint formed by splaying the ends of both timbers; often simply called a scarf joint. →3

splayed tenon joint a timber joint in which two tenons inserted in a common mortise from opposite sides are splayed to abut one another. →5

splay knot in timber grading, an elongated oval knot formed from a branch that has been cut lengthways, which crosses an arris on a sawn board. →1

spliced joint, fish joint, fish plate joint; a longitudinal timber joint in which fish plates are fixed on either side to strengthen the joint. →3

spliced scarf joint a timber lengthening joint with a splicing piece added as strengthening. →3

splice plate see fish plate. →3

splicing piece a piece fixed to or incorporated in a timber lengthening joint to strengthen or stiffen it. →3

spline, loose tongue, feather; a thin piece of material inserted into a longitudinal grooved joint as a strengthening piece. →5, →8

spline joint, feather joint; a timber joint in which timbers are joined lengthways by cutting a groove in the edges of each and inserting a tongue or spline.

spline-jointed boarding, feather-jointed boarding; timber cladding boarding with grooved edges into which a loose connecting spline is concealed to provide rigidity. →8

split face brick a facing brick whose rough texture is achieved by splitting off the surface layer.

split-level house a house type for a sloping site, in which floor levels on the high side of the site are half a storey higher than those on the low side, with entrances at either side on different levels. →61

split-level ramp a sloping accessway which joins floors at half-level intervals in a multistorey car park.

split-level roof, clerestory roof; a pitched roof with two roof planes separated vertically by an area of walling, used for buildings with a varying number of stories or on sloping sites; either with roof planes parallel or in mirror image. →46

split ring connector in timber-framed construction, a split metal ring housed between two bolted timbers to strengthen a joint between timbers. →35

split-ring washer see spring lock washer. →37

split shingle see shake.

splitter, nicker; a wide-bladed masonry chisel whose cutting edge is approximately 2 mm thick.

split tile a tile manufactured by splitting an extruded tile, once fired, through its thickness into two.

splitting hammer a mason's hammer with a sharp axe-like blade, used for splitting stone; often held by one person against the stone surface while another strikes with a sledgehammer. →40

spodumene a pale grey or green translucent mineral, natural lithium aluminosilicate, used for gemstones and as a source of lithium.

spokeshave a small winged woodworking plane for planing curved surfaces.

spokeshave scraper see cabinet scraper.

sponge a soft, porous cleaning implement used for soaking up water, wiping, texturing plaster and concrete etc. →43

sponge float in concretework and plastering, a hand float whose blade is coated with a synthetic sponge, used on a wet surface to produce a specific finish. →43

sponge rubber see foam rubber.

spongeable describing a surface such as a wallcovering or other finish which may be wiped clean with a moist cloth without damaging it.

spongeable wallcovering wallcovering that can be cleaned by wiping with a damp sponge or rag.

spoon gouge, front bent gouge; a gouge with a hooked, spoon-shaped blade, used for carving deep recesses in wood. →41

sports centre 1 a building providing facilities and equipment for a range of different sports.
2 see leisure centre.

sports field see playing field.

sports hall a building or hall in which facilities are provided for one or more indoor sports.

sports pavilion a building adjoining an outdoor sports field, providing facilities for changing and storage of sports equipment.

sports stadium see stadium.

spot 1 see spotlight.
2 see reflector lamp.

spot board see hawk.

spot gluing the adhesion of one material to another using small areas of glue as opposed to a uniform glue film.

spot lamp see reflector lamp.

spotlight, spot; a luminaire which emits a narrow beam of light, used for highlighting features, task lighting, exhibitions etc.

spotlighting directional lighting for highlighting features of an elevation or interior, ornament, displays etc.

spot welding, resistance spot welding; a method of resistance welding for sheetmetal, using electric current passed through small diameter electrodes which press the components together and cause a localized fusing at that point.

spout 1 see rainwater spout.
2 nozzle; the outlet pipe or assembly of a tap, from which water is discharged.

spout plane see round plane.

sprawl see urban sprawl.

spray adhesive, aerosol glue; an adhesive stored in a pressurized can and applied by spraying.

spray concreting, shotcreting; the application of concrete to a surface by firing it at high velocity through a nozzle, propelled by compressed air; used for stabilizing and sealing rock faces, tunnel walls and embankments.

sprayed concrete, pneumatically applied concrete, pneumatic mortar; concrete placed by spraying through a nozzle against a surface using pneumatic pressure, used for stabilizing rock walls and repairing reinforced concrete; see shotcrete, gunite.

sprayed mineral insulation see firespraying.

spray gun 1 see paint spray gun.
2 see plaster spray gun.

spraying 1 the application of liquid paints, glues and other surface treatments under pressure as a spray of fine droplets.
2 see concrete spraying.
3 a method of curing concrete with a continuous spray of water to keep it moist and inhibit evaporation.
4 see zinc spraying.

spray nozzle see spray outlet.

spray outlet, spray nozzle; a perforated outlet for a tap or valve designed to produce a spray or shower of droplets rather than a stream of liquid.

spray paint any paint with a consistency suitable for spray painting, including aerosol paints.

spray painting an efficient form of painting using a spray gun, aerosol etc. to apply a smooth, even film of paint.

spray plaster see projection plaster.

spray plastering see projection plastering.

spreader 1 a rubber or plastic hand-held implement with a bevelled edge, used by a painter and decorator for applying and spreading glue and filler, smoothing and shaping etc. →43
2 see glue spreader. →43
3 see squeegee. →43
4 see box spreader.
5 sparge pipe; a device for flushing a urinal.

spread foundation any foundation, as distinct from pile and special foundation systems, which transmits loading to the ground beneath by means of a widened plate or raft beneath a wall, column etc. →29

spreading rate the unit area covered by unit quantity of paint or glue.

spreadsheet computer software which organizes data in the form of tables for correlating and handling batches of information.

sprig see glazing sprig.

spring 1 an elastic device of coiled metal etc., which can be wound or tensioned to store mechanical energy.
2 see crook. →1
3 a natural source of water from the ground.

spring clamp in joinery and cabinetmaking, a clamp whose pressing force is provided and released with a spring.

spring clip any small metal fixing for securing components in place with a push-pull action; especially used for holding infilling, glazing etc. in frames before the application of fronting or capping.

spring green a shade of green which takes its name from the colour of foliage in spring.

springer, springing stone; one of the two lowest wedge-shaped pieces or voussoirs on either side of a true masonry arch. →22

springhead roofing nail see convex head roofing nail.

spring hinge 1 a hinge containing a spring mechanism to return it to its folded position, used for closing a door or flap automatically.
2 see double-acting spring hinge.

springing line see spring line. →22

springing stone see springer.

spring latch see return latch. →39

spring line, springing line; a theoretical horizontal line from which the curvature of an arch begins. →22

spring lock washer, split-ring washer, compressive washer; a slightly helical washer inserted beneath a screw or bolt head, which, when tightened, compresses to form a firm joint. →37

spring tide an especially high tide which occurs directly after a new moon.

spring toggle, butterfly toggle; a toggle bolt whose locking part is made up of paired wings which open under a spring action and clamp against the rear of a construction. →37

spring washer see spring lock washer. →37

springwood see earlywood.

sprinkler 1 see sprinkler system.
2 see sprinkler head.

sprinklered referring to a space protected against the spread of fire with a sprinkler system.

sprinkler head the specially shaped outlet nozzle of a sprinkler, through which water is released and dispersed in the event of a building fire.

sprinkler system a fire safety system of ceiling-mounted water sprinklers, connected to a main, which shower water into a space in the event of a building fire.

sprinkling in landscaping, the watering of dried areas of planting, lawns etc. using spray outlets.

sprocket, cocking piece; in timber roof construction, a piece of timber attached to a rafter at eaves level forming a sprocketed eaves.

sprocketed eaves in timber roof construction, an eaves which has a smaller fall than the common rafters.

spruce, 1 Canadian spruce, Norway spruce, Sitka spruce; [*Picea spp.*] a common softwood found in the Northern hemisphere with pale timber similar in properties to pinewood, used in general construction and for cladding and joinery; see ***Picea spp.*** for full list of species of spruce included in this work.
2 a shade of green which takes its name from the needles of the above.

spruce beetle 1 a small group of longhorn beetles [*Tetropium fuscum, Tetropium castaneum*] whose larvae kill living trees by tunnelling beneath the bark and disrupting the transfer of nutrients; mainly found on spruce trees in Europe but also known to attack other conifers and occasionally hardwoods.
2 [*Tetropium fuscum*], brown spruce longhorn.
3 [*Tetropium castaneum*], black spruce beetle.

spruce green see fir.

spur 1 in Byzantine, Romanesque or early Gothic architecture, one of a number of decorative devices set at the corners of a square or polygonal base supporting a round column, often of leaf or grotesque ornament; also called a griffe. →115
2 see spere.

spur revel see spur rowel. →108

spur rowel, spur revel; a symbol representing the star-shaped wheel attached to the spurs of horsemen; representative in heraldry of equestrianism and the cavalry. →108

spy hole see murder hole. →103

square 1 a planar figure with four sides of equal length, with each internal angle a right angle; a pattern or figure derived from this. →108
see crossed square. →118
floor square, see parquet floor square. →44
2 a piece of sawn timber, square in cross-section, 25 mm–100 mm in size.
3 a triangular or L-shaped implement for measuring and marking angles; see below.
bevel square.
carpenter's square, see framing square.
combination square, see try and mitre square.
framing square.
mitre square.
set square. →130
T-square. →130
try and mitre square.
try square.
4 place; an urban public open space, often planted or paved, surrounded on all sides by, in front of or between buildings.
market square, see market-place.
agora. →94
forum. →104

square bar a manufactured steel bar, square in cross-section, used in welded steel construction, detail work etc. →34

square billet an ornamental billet motif consisting of a chequerwork of squares. →124

square brackets a mathematical symbol '[' or ']', used to enclose and unite functions.

square column a column whose shaft is square in cross-section. →13

square cup hook a square screw hook with a collar above the threaded shank to restrict its screw-in depth and cover the edges of the hole. →36

squared see edged.

squared log a log which has been hewn or sawn to square off the rounded edges; may have wane.

squared paper any paper marked out with an orthogonal grid of lines, used in detail drawing, measuring, marking and scaling etc.

squared rubble masonry roughly squared pieces of stone laid as a masonry wall; may be constructed in courses (coursed) or laid with no definable courses (random, uncoursed). →11

square-edged boarding, butt-edged boarding; timber boards with rectangular cross-section laid horizontally as cladding for a wall frame. →8
see planed square edged board. →2, →8

square external angle trowel a hand tool for smoothing external corners in plasterwork with a handled blade of bent steel sheet. →43

square fillet a thin straight decorative moulding, square in profile. →14

square foot abb. **sq.ft**; an imperial unit of area equivalent to 0.093 m^2.

square halo in Christian art and symbolism, a square-shaped halo around the head of a figure, identifying a living person presumed to be a saint.

square hollow section, square tube; a hollow steel section, square in cross-section, formed by rolling and welding steel plate, used for structural purposes such as framing, columns, posts, balustrades etc. →34

square hook a screw hook which is L shaped. →36

square inch abb. **sq.in.**; an imperial unit of area equivalent to 6.45 cm^2.

square internal angle trowel a hand tool for smoothing internal corners in plasterwork with a handled blade of bent steel sheet. →43

square kilometre abb. **km^2**; an SI unit of surface area equal to the area enclosed by a square whose sides are one kilometre in length.

square metre abb. **m^2**; an SI basic unit of surface area equal to the area enclosed by a square whose sides are one metre in length.

square mile abb. **sq.mi.**; imperial unit of area equivalent to 2.59 km^2.

square millimetre abb. **mm^2**; an SI unit of surface area equal to the area enclosed by a square whose sides are one millimetre in length.

square nut a nut which is square in form. →37

square pattern a paving pattern in which rows of square pavers or paving slabs are laid to form a simple grid pattern; when alternate stones are of different colours it may be called a checkered, chequered or checkerboard pattern; similar patterns in parquetry, tiling and veneering. →15

square root in mathematics, the second root; see root.

square temple any temple which is roughly square in plan. →66

square tile any ceramic tile whose exposed face is square in shape. →20

square tube a metal profile of hollow square cross-section; when in steel and used for structural purposes, it is called a square hollow section or SHS. →34
see *metal tubes* illustration. →34
see square hollow section. →34

square twisted shank flat head nail see screw nail. →35

square yard abb. **sq.yd**; an imperial unit of area equivalent to 0.836 m^2.

squatting plate WC footplates in a stand-up toilet, on which the squatter must place himself.

squatting WC pan a WC designed to be used in a squatting position, with footplates in place of a seat.

squeegee a hand-held implement with a wide flexible rubber blade attached to a handle, used for wiping and spreading liquids. →43

squinch, squinch arch; a series of adjacent masonry arches, each successive arch larger than the last, used as corner vaulting to support a polygonal structure or dome on a square base. →26

squinch arch see squinch. →26

squint, 1 hagioscope; a small oblique opening in the wall of a church to allow people in the side aisles and transepts to see the altar.
2 see squint brick. →16

squint brick a special angle brick with a shaped chamfered end, designed for use at an external obtuse corner in a brick wall; manufactured for standard corners of 30°, 45° or 60°. →16

St Andrew's cross, crux decussata (Lat.), oblique cross, saltire; a cross composed of two diagonally crossing limbs. →118

St Andrew's cross bond see English cross bond. →19

St Anthony's cross see tau cross. →117

St Bride's cross see St Bridget's cross. →117

St Bridget's cross 1 a variation of the cross patée with a roundel incorporated within each limb, and one at the crossing, emblem of the Swedish St Bridget, also known as Brigit or Birgitta. →118
2 a cross of straw or rushes reputedly woven by St Bridget of Ireland at the deathbed of a dying pagan; symbols associated with this; also known as St Bride, Brigit, Brigid. →118

St Catherine see Catherine wheel. →122
see Catherine wheel window. →109

St Han's cross see Bowen knot. →123

St James' cross see cross of St James. →117

St John see eagle. →119

St John's white see bianco sangiovanni.

St Luke see bull. →119

St Mark see lion. →119

St Matthew see angel. →119

St Peter's cross see inverted cross. →117

St Philip's cross a Latin cross on its side. →118

stability the ability of a structure to resist buckling, bending and collapse.

stabilization see soil stabilization.

stable 1 the state whereby a body will attempt to return to its original position under the action of a force.
2 a building or part of a building in which horses are kept. →102

stable door a door type whose leaf is composed of two parts hinged separately, one above the other. →50

stack 1 see discharge stack.
2 see soil stack.
3 see chimney stack.
4 see ventilation stack. →56

stack bond, 1 stacked bond; a brickwork bond with courses of bricks on end and continuous vertical joints; not a true bond. →17
2 a paving pattern in which rows of rectangular pavers are laid with joints running in orthogonal lines, forming a chequered pattern; similar patterns in parquetry and tiling. →15

stacked apartments a cross between a detached or row house and an apartment block, with dwelling units stacked in two or three storeys, but with each having direct access from the outside. →61

stacked bond see stack bond. →17

stacked joint see straight joint.

stack effect a thermal phenomenon governed by the tendency of heated gases to rise causing suction beneath, an effect on which the functioning of chimneys, fire venting and natural ventilation rely.

stack vent, stench pipe, vent pipe; a length of ventilating pipe attached to the upper end of a discharge stack or pipe, to relieve pressure and through which foul air from a drain can pass into the open air.

stadion an ancient Greek elongated sports venue with rounded ends, surrounded on all sides by banked spectator stands; a stadium. →89, →91, →94

stadium, 1 sports stadium; a sports field surrounded by terraces and stands, often roofed, for spectators.
2 see stadion. →89, →91, →94

staff see crook. →74

staff facility an area within a workplace containing rest and recreation spaces, lockers, washing and showering facilities etc.

staff of Aesculapius see staff of Asclepius. →120

staff of Asclepius, (Lat. Aesculapius), serpent staff; ornament depicting a rod with a serpent twined around it; architectural ornament and symbol of medicine, named after Asclepius, an ancient Greek physician deified as the god of medicine. →120

staff of Bacchus see thyrsus. →120

staff of Dionysus thyrsos, see thyrsus. →120

staff of Hermes see caduceus. →120

staff of Jupiter see thunderbolt. →120

staff of Mercury see caduceus. →120

staff of Neptune see trident. →120

staff of Poseidon see trident. →120

staff of Zeus see thunderbolt. →120

Staffordshire blue brick, blue brick; a hard, dense dark blue brick made from the shales of Staffordshire, England, and used for engineering and industrial purposes.

staff room a communal room used by employees for relaxation; a private room for teachers in a school.

stage 1 a raised platform in a theatre or auditorium for performance.
2 that area of a theatre in front of the seats from which a performance is carried out.
see *stage* in classical theatre illustration. →89
3 one of a series of sections of work in a construction project; also called phase.
see design stage.
see phase.
see post-contract stage.
see pre-contract stage.
4 see landing stage. →64

staggered 1 referring to a pattern of lines, construction joints or a layout in which adjacent elements are slightly overlapping and every other element is aligned, as with crenellations or brickwork.
2 referring to vertical masonry joints in adjacent courses of brickwork or stonework which form a regular toothed pattern, achieved by laying bricks with a quarter brick overlap; cf. raking. →18, →19

staggered bond any brickwork pattern whose joints form a regular vertical toothed pattern in the wall surface.
staggered Flemish bond, see Dutch bond. →18
staggered Flemish double stretcher bond. →19

staggered Flemish bond see Dutch bond. →18

staggered jointing in built-up roofing, the laying of successive layers of bitumen felt such that the joints between them are covered by the sheet above; the similar overlapping in other repeated construction such as brickwork and roof tiling.

staggered junction a road junction in which two roads approach a major road from opposite directions but do not meet at the same point. →62

staggered siding see board on board cladding. →8, →57

staggered stud partition an acoustical stud wall construction in which alternate studs are placed off-centre in the thickness of the wall to prevent direct transmission of sound through them.

stain 1 a defect in a surface occurring due to the presence of unwanted colour.
2 a translucent colourant for porous surfaces consisting of a dye suspended in a clear liquid; when used on timber the liquid penetrates the surface and allows the underlying pattern or grain to show through.
3 see oil stain.
4 see spirit stain.

stained glass coloured and patterned surface-tinted decorative glass held in lead cames, often depicting biblical scenes in ecclesiastical buildings.

stainer, colouring pigment, tinter; a translucent colouring agent for paints consisting of a pigment suspended in an oil paste.

staining 1 the colouring of a timber surface with coloured stain.
2 an unsightly defect in a finish or surface caused by uneven discoloration.

staining power see tinting strength.

stainless steel a range of types of silver-coloured alloy steel with good corrosion resistance, usually containing a high proportion of chromium (up to 18%) and nickel (up to 8%); used for structural members, cladding, furniture and fittings, hardware, tubes, windows and fixings.

stair, stairs, staircase, stairway; a means of vertical circulation consisting of a number of steps from one level to another; although usually called 'stairs' in the colloquial, 'stair' may be used in preference, to denote a single unit of vertical circulation; types included as separate entries are listed below. →45
see *stairs* illustration. →45
access stair.
alternating tread stair. →45
angle stair, see quarter turn stair. →45
cantilevered stair. →45
ceremonial stair. →66
circular stair. →45
closed riser stair. →45
concrete stair. →45
corkscrew stair, see spiral stair. →45
curving stair. →45
disappearing stair.
dogleg stair, dog-legged stair. →45
double cantilevered spiral stair.
double cantilevered stair. →45
double return stair. →45
emergency stair, see escape stair.
escape stair.
external stair.
fire stair, see escape stair.
geometrical stair. →45
grand stair. →67
halfpace stair. →45
half turn circular stair. →45
half turn stair. →45
helical stair, see spiral stair. →45
ladder stair, see open riser stair. →45
L-stair, see quarter turn stair. →45
main stair.
open rise stair, see open riser stair. →45
prefabricated stair. →45
quarter turn stair. →45
ramp stair. →45
return stair, see dogleg stair. →45
semicircular stair, semi-spiral stair. →45
service stair, see access stair.
simply supported stair. →45
skeleton stair, see open riser stair. →45
spiral stair. →45
straight flight stair. →45
three-quarter turn stair. →45
turning stair. →45
wall-stair. →103

winding stair, see turning stair. →45

stair balustrade a balustrade for the sides of a stair; see also banister. →45

stairbuilder's saw see grooving saw.

staircase 1 originally the space occupied by a stair and its structure, nowadays the stair itself. →45
2 a grand, main or public stair.
3 see stairway. →45
see *staircase* illustration. →45
see *residential buildings* illustration. →61

stair clearance see stair headroom. →45

stair clear width the minimum unobstructed width of a stair on plan, measured at right angles to the direction of travel. →45

stair enclosure that part of the building fabric in which a stair is enclosed. →45

stair flight see flight. →45, →61

stair headroom, clearance; in stair and ramp design, the minimum vertical height from a stairline, slope or landing to the lowest overhead obstruction. →45

stair landing 1 see intermediate landing. →45, →61
2 see storey landing. →45, →61

stairlift a domestic lift designed for the disabled or elderly to operate along the line of a stair.

stair nosing see nosing. →45

stair rail 1 a light balustrade for the side or sides of a stair.
2 the handrail of a stair, often fixed to the wall of a stair enclosure, or atop a stair balustrade. →45

stair riser see riser. →45

stairs see stair.
see *stairs* illustration. →45

stair shaft see stairwell. →45

stair spandrel in stair construction, a triangular-shaped infill construction or panelling beneath a string and the floor.

stair tower a tower articulated on the outside of a medieval or later historical building containing a spiral or winding staircase; a similar element in a modern multistorey building.
see *stair tower* in Carolingian abbey church illustration. →98

stair tread see tread. →45

stair type a stair as classified by material, form or function etc.; see *stair type* illustration. →45

stair unit 1 see precast stair unit.
2 see prefabricated stair.

stairway, 1 staircase; an enclosed space containing a stair. →45
2 see stair. →45
see *staircase* illustration. →45
see *stairway* in residential buildings illustration. →61

stairwell 1 the space within a stair enclosure in which stair flights and landings are located; also called a stair shaft. →45
2 the open void between adjacent flights of a stair, or a full height shaft-like opening at the side of a stair. →45

stair width in stair design, the clear width of a stair flight, often including handrail and stringers. →45

stake, 1 stave; a timber post driven into the ground as part of a foundation structure, for marking out etc.; a timber pile.
2 see pale.
3 see timber pile. →29

staking out see setting out.

stalactite capital a Moorish capital carved with embellishment resembling stalactite work. →115

stalactite work in Islamic decoration, clustered small pendant-like secondary vaults which hang down in geometrically arranged tiers from main vaulting, resembling geological formations called stalactites; also known as honeycomb work. →115

stalk the downward vertical flange of a precast concrete tee beam.

stall 1 see booth.
2 see choir stalls. →99

stalls, 1 parquet (Am.); any of the seats in a concert hall or theatre immediately in front of the pit; seats on the ground floor of a cinema.
2 a row of seats, each set in its own compartment, defined by a partition or arm rest.
3 see choir stalls.

stall urinal a urinal with a curved console fitted to a wall, down which urine flows into a drainage channel.

stamp duty tax paid on the transfer of land, shares and property to a new ownership, and for obtaining official documents.

stanchion a column of metal, usually steel; types included as separate entries are listed below.
battened stanchion.
braced stanchion, lattice stanchion.
composite stanchion.
laced stanchion.
steel stanchion.

stand 1 a stepped structure for seating spectators in tiers; see also grandstand.
2 see booth.
3 see taxi rank.

standard 1 any product, method, process or procedure which has been established as an exemplar, is a stock or basic item or otherwise represents the norm.
2 see norm.
3 a vertical scaffolding post.
4 upright; one of a series of spaced vertical framing members in a balustrade, to which infill, rails, a handrail etc. are fixed. →54

standard brick any mass-produced rectangular brick produced to standardized dimensions, often coordinated in terms of height, length and width, varying in size from country to country and state to state. →16
1 see metric standard brick. →16
2 see imperial standard brick. →16
3 see US standard brick. →16
4 see modular standard brick. →16

standard colour one of a number of set colours in which proprietary items of a particular range of prefinished products are usually supplied.

standard concrete cube see test cube.

standard concrete cylinder see test cylinder.

standard grade chipboard see single layer chipboard. →9

standard hardboard hardboard that has defined minimum properties of strength and dimensional stability.

standard lamp see floor lamp.

standard modular brick 1 see metric brick. →16
2 see US standard brick. →16

standard of living see living standard.

standard service illuminance the recommended level of illuminance for a specific space, setting or task.

standard special brick see special brick.

standby lighting building lighting with an independent power source, used in an emergency during the failure of normal lighting.

standby pump in sewage pumping and other pumped installations, a reserve pump which cuts in automatically if the main pump fails.

standing seam a sheetmetal roofing joint in which two adjacent sheets are bent over each other and left standing perpendicular to the roof plane. →49

standing stone a prehistoric monumental stone, often one of a group placed in an arrangement for some ritual or symbolic purpose.

standing wave, stationary wave; an acoustical phenomenon in corridors or narrow rooms with smooth parallel walls, in which sounds of certain frequencies are intensified, caused by waves whose positions of maximum and minimum oscillation remain stationary.

stand oil a heavy, viscous refined linseed oil which has been polymerized by heating to over 500°C for a number of hours, used as a vehicle in paints.

standpipe a vertical water pipe, usually from a water main to domestic premises, with a tap fitted to its upper end.
Stanley knife see trimming knife.
stannite, tin pyrites; a dark greenish grey metallic mineral, used as a local ore of tin and copper.
stanza a room, apartment or chamber in an Italian building, especially a hall in the Vatican.
staple, 1 U-pin; a U-shaped nail, used to fix boards, cable etc. →35
2 a small U-shaped wire fastener, projected from a hand-held device to fix sheet material together, or to another component.
3 see brotch.
4 see box staple.
5 an authorized town which formerly bore the sole rights to export and import particular commodities.
staple gun, stapler, stapling machine; a power tool used for fixing light board to a frame with wire staples, driven by compressed air or electricity.
stapler 1 a small, hand-held device for fixing paper, fabric and other thin sheet material together or to a base with staples.
2 see staple gun.
stapling machine see staple gun.
star a figure or design with pointed protrusions radiating out from a central area; see below. →108
three-pointed star. →108
four-pointed star. →118
five-pointed star, see pentagram. →108
six-pointed star, hexagram, see Star of David. →108
eight-pointed star, see octagram. →108, →123
star of Ishtar. →120
Star of David. →108
estoile. →123
star and crescent ornament depicting a crescent with a star within, an ancient symbol associated in early Sumerian civilization with the sun God and moon Goddess; common symbol of the Islamic faith. →120
starch adhesive an adhesive for internal use made from vegetable starch mixed with water.
star cross see four-pointed star. →123
star formation the arrangement of adjacent plies in plywood with their grains at a noticeable angle to one another, not necessarily a right angle as with crossbanding. →9
starling, cutwater; in bridge construction, a pier which is pointed in profile at its lower edge, so as to be streamlined against the flow of a river. →31
Star of David, hexagram; a six-pointed star formed by the superimposition of two equilateral triangles; the symbol of Judaism and the state of Israel; also called Magen David, Mogen David (in Hebrew) or the Shield of David, Solomon's seal. →108
Star of Ishtar a symbol of the Mesopotamian goddess Ishtar (or Anath, Astarte, Inanna), with eight points representing the movements of the planet Venus associated with her. →120
star-ribbed vault see stellar vault. →101
star shake see heartshake. →1
star sun see four-pointed star. →123
starter 1 see lamp starter.
2 see starter bar.
starter bar, starter, stub bar; a reinforcing bar which protrudes from cast areas of reinforced concrete, to which reinforcement in the next batch or stage can be attached.
starting device see lamp starter.
starting gate see carceres. →89
star vault see stellar vault. →101
starved joint a poorly bonded glue joint caused by lack of applied adhesive.
stately home a palatial country house.
statement 1 in computing, an expression or command in a program.
2 financial statement; a periodic record of the state of a financial account showing all transactions.
state of equilibrium see equilibrium.
static not moving, in equilibrium.
statically determinate frame, isostatic frame, perfect frame; a structural frame with no redundant members, in which all the forces, loads and bending moments can be determined by the laws of statics.
statically indeterminate frame, hyperstatic frame, redundant frame; a structural frame in which all the forces, loads and bending moments cannot be determined by the laws of statics, due to the presence of redundant members.
static load a structural load which is non-moving and unchanging in terms of magnitude and direction.
static moment, first moment of area; in structural statics, the sum of products obtained by multiplying the area of a structural section by its distance from an axis.
static penetration testing in soil investigation, penetration testing using a testing implement which is pushed with a steady force into the soil.
statics, theory of structures; a branch of mechanics which studies the forces on bodies at rest.
station a building or establishment with personnel and facilities for a particular purpose such as vehicular control, sales, firefighting and policing; see below.
cattle station.
police station.
bus station.
coach station.
petrol station.
railway station.
service station.
fire station.
stationary wave see standing wave.
station building a building at a station, especially the main building of a railway station.
stationers, newsagent, paper shop; a shop which sells books, papers and writing and drawing accessories.
station point in perspective drawing, the apparent point of the observer, from which the projection is constructed; also known as the viewpoint, eye point, centre of projection, sight point or point of sight. →128
station roof, umbrella roof; a roof used for open shelters, canopies etc., carried on a single row of stanchions or columns, cantilevered on one or both sides.
statistics a branch of mathematics which deals with the collection and collation of information and its use for presentation of data, calculation of probabilities and forecasting.
statue 1 a sculpture of a human or animal figure. →112
2 a sculptural monument situated in a public place.
statute a law, rule or enactment as made by a head of state, guild, corporation or local government.
statute mile see mile.
staurolite a hard iron aluminium silicate mineral.
stave 1 see stake.
2 see pale.
3 see timber pile. →29
4 see parquet block. →44
stave church, mast church; a timber church typical in medieval Scandinavia with wall construction of vertical palisaded planks and steeply pitched roofs of shingles, often highly ornamented.
stave building a primitive building type whose walls are of upright logs driven directly into the ground.
stave construction a traditional form of timber construction based on a series of staves or pales driven into the ground side by side as side walls.
stay 1 a structural member such as a prop, pier, buttress or cable, which gives support to a construction.
2 see support.

3 see guy.
4 a simple device for holding a window or door open or in a certain fixed position.
5 see casement stay.
6 door stay, see door stop. →51

stayed bridge see cable-stayed bridge. →32

steady flow see streamline flow.

steam water either in the form of hot water vapour or as a gas.

Steamboat Gothic an architectural style in North America from the 1800s, particularly Ohio and Mississippi, influenced by the use of carved and cast decoration from the riverboats.

steam curing the curing of concrete by placing it in a chamber with steam to speed up its gain of strength and reduce dry shrinkage; see autoclaving, low pressure steam curing.

steam heating an industrial space-heating system in which the heating medium is steam, circulated from a main heating plant.

steam room the central chamber of a sauna or steam bath facility, containing a stove and benches, in which bathers are immersed in steam. →58

steatite 1 see soapstone.
2 see French chalk.

steel 1 a versatile, strong, finely crystalline alloy of iron with a carbon content of up to 2%, one of the most common building and structural materials.
2 steel grey; a shade of grey which takes its name from the colour of steel.

steel angle, angle bar, angle iron; a structural steel section whose uniform cross-section resembles the letter L, formed by a process of rolling.
see *angle profile* illustration. →34

steel bar any longitudinal solid length of steel rolled into a uniform cross-section; used in construction.
see *metal bars* illustration. →34

steel beam 1 any beam rolled, welded or manufactured from steel.
see *steel beam* in office building illustration. →60
2 see pressed steel lintel. →22

steel blue see Prussian blue.

steel bow saw see bow saw.

steel cable 1 see cable.
2 see high tension steel cable.

steel column 1 a column manufactured from steel; often a standard steel section.
2 see stanchion.
3 universal column, see H-section.

steel concrete see reinforced concrete.

steel construction building work using structural steel; the product of this; see steelwork.

steel deck floor see composite floor slab.

steel door a door whose leaf is made primarily from steel; a steel-framed door.

steel fibre thin crimped filaments of steel, approximately 50 mm long and 0.5 mm thick, used in bulk as concrete reinforcement.

steel-fibre reinforced concrete sprayed or cast concrete reinforced with less than 2% steel fibres with dimensions under 1 mm thick and 100 mm in length, used for road and floor surfaces, pipes and thin structural sections.

steel fixing, reinforcement; in reinforced concretework, the cutting, bending, binding and placing of steel reinforcement prior to pouring the concrete.

steel flat a flat bar manufactured from steel.
see *flat bar* illustration. →34

steel frame any frame structure composed of steel beams, columns, bracing etc. joined at their ends, onto which cladding components, flooring, roofing etc. are fixed.

steel-framed door see steel door.

steel-framed window see steel window. →53

steel grey see steel.

steel ingot a basic unit of steel cast in a blast furnace prior to further manufacture or forming by rolling, extrusion or forging.

steel joist rolled steel joist, see I-section. →34

steel lintel see pressed steel lintel. →22

steel mesh 1 any mesh product manufactured primarily of steel; see **wire mesh** for list of mesh types.
see *wire mesh* illustrations. →34
2 see welded mesh.
3 see fabric reinforcement.

steel mesh reinforcement see fabric reinforcement.

steel nail a round nail made from tempered steel, used for nailing to concrete and masonry surfaces.

steel pile any foundation pile fabricated from steel. →29
see box pile. →29
see H-pile. →29
see pipe pile. →29
tubular pile, see pipe pile. →29

steel pipe see circular hollow section. →34

steel plate flat plate manufactured from steel.
see *metal plate* illustration. →34
see quarto plate.
see chequerplate, checkerplate. →34

steel products any components such as sections, sheet, coil plate etc., manufactured from steel and steel alloys, used in the construction of buildings; structural work is usually in steel.
see *steel products* illustration. →34

steel profile any length of steel preformed into a uniform cross-section of certain shape and dimensions, often synonymous with section, but usually more complex; used for patent glazing, door frames etc.
see *metal profiles* illustration. →34

steel purlin a lightweight secondary steel beam laid in series for supporting floor or roof construction; usually a Z-, C- or I-profile. →60

steel reinforcement 1 see concrete reinforcement.
2 see reinforcing bar. →27
see *concrete reinforcement* illustration. →27

steel rule a straight parallel-sided strip of steel, often gradated, used for scribing and measuring.

steel section any thin length of steel which has been preformed by a process of rolling, extrusion, bending etc. into a uniform cross-section of certain shape and dimensions; see steel bar, steel profile.
see *metal sections* illustration. →34
see hollow section, structural hollow section. →34

steel sheet see sheet steel.
see *steel sheet products* illustration.

steel sheet pile, sheet pile; in excavation work, one of a series of interlocking steel profiles driven into the ground prior to excavation to retain the sides of the subsequent excavation. →29

steel sheet piling a number of interlocking steel sheet piles forming a retaining wall for an excavation.

steel stanchion a column built up from one or a number of structural steel sections.

steel tape measure see flexible steel tape measure.

steel window a window whose frame is made primarily from coated steel; a steel-framed window. →53

steelwork, steel construction; **1** framing construction work in welded or bolted steel sections, usually structural steelwork.
2 the construction and structure resulting from this.

steeple the combined tower and spire of a church. →102

stegaster Gk; an ancient Greek flat clay roof tile, equivalent to a Roman tegula, whose side joints, when laid, are capped by rows of concave tiles; cf. kalypter. →47

stela, stele (Gk); Lat.; a slab or upright stone in antiquity with inscriptions and carvings; often a gravestone or commemorative pillar. →77

stele see stela. →77

stellar cross see four-pointed star. →123

stellar vault, star-ribbed vault, star vault; a masonry vault used for medieval church roofs, whose ribs, tiercerons and liernes form a star-shaped pattern in the interior ceiling. →101

stellated cross see four-pointed star. →123

stellite a cobalt-chromium-tungsten metal alloy, used for hard facings for cutting tools, bearings, valves and other components prone to wear.

stench pipe see stack vent.

stencil, template; a template used for lettering in printing and draughting.

stencilling, stencil painting; a form of applied decoration produced by painting over sheet material with patterned perforations to leave a negative design on a surface.

stencil painting see stencilling.

step 1 a shallow platform or construction designed to negotiate a pedestrian change in level by means of a short horizontal surface connected to a vertical riser, either on its own or as part of a stair; types included as separate entries are listed below. →45
balanced step, see dancing step. →45
corbie steps, see crow steps.
dancing step, French flier. →45
doorstep. →28
flier. →45
kite step, kite winder. →45
parallel tread, see flier. →45
spandrel step.
tapered step. →45
tread. →45
wheel step, wheeling step, see winder. →45
2 see rung. →54

step iron one of a number of iron fastenings in series providing vertical stepped access to a shaft, manhole or up the side of a chimney stack.

stepladder a ladder whose rungs are flat steps and which has a triangulated propped construction to make it freestanding.

step-off part of the horizontal end of an escalator made up of two stair units, from which a passenger steps to leave the escalator.

step-on part of the horizontal beginning of an escalator made up of two stair units, onto which a passenger initially steps.

stepped block a row house or slab block constructed on a sloping site, whose upper parapet is stepped back allowing for a series of roof terraces over the upper storey spaces of neighbouring units; if a low-rise building, all flats will have access at ground level; also called a terraced block. →61

stepped flashing in roof construction, an upstand flashing at the junction of the verge of a sloping roof and a masonry parapet or wall, whose upper surface is stepped and housed in horizontal joints in the masonry.

stepped gable see crow steps.

stepped pyramid see step pyramid. →67, →70

stepped tenon joint see shouldered tenon joint. →5

step pyramid, 1 stepped pyramid; a pyramid type whose sides are stepped with tiers rather than smooth, in Egypt predating the true pyramids; the primary existing Egyptian example is that of King Zoser at Saqqara, south of Cairo. →70
2 see ziggurat. →67
3 see teocalli. →67
see *ziggurats and stepped pyramids* illustration. →67

steps an external solid stair in a garden, park, yard or urban environment.

steradian abb. **sr**; the SI unit of solid angle equal to an area marked out by the angle on the surface of a sphere divided by the radius of the sphere squared.

stereobate in classical architecture, a masonry base or visible foundation for a column or wall; the base or foundation on which a building is constructed; see also stylobate. →86

stereographic projection a geometrical projection of the surface of a sphere onto a flat plane touching its surface, with projectors radiating out from a point on the surface of the sphere diametrically opposite to that which is in contact with the plane.

stereometry see solid geometry.

Stereum sanguinolentum see bleeding Stereum.

sterile 1 the property of a material or space which is free from bacteria and living microbes.
2 a description of an environment perceived as lifeless and uninspiring.

sterile room see clean room.

sterilizing sink see rinsing sink.

stibium a traditional name for the chemical element antimony.

stibnite, antimonite, antimony glance; a dull grey mineral, antimony trisulphide, $\mathbf{Sb_2S_3}$, the most important ore of antimony.

stick, sticker; a strip of wood for separating layers of piled timber being seasoned or stored to aid air circulation.

stick charcoal drawing charcoal made from charred sticks of willow or vine.

sticker see stick.

stick welding see manual metal-arc welding.

stiff referring to a material with the property of resisting bending or stretching; see rigid.

stiffened concrete laid or cast concrete that has hardened to a degree that it is no longer workable.

stiffening see frame bracing.

stiffening beam a main longitudinal beam or girder beneath the deck of a suspension bridge, which provides structural bending strength; similar beams in other structures. →32

stiff-leaf carved decoration of stylized foliage motifs found in Norman architecture.

stiff-leaf capital a Norman capital consisting of a block carved with formalized leaf ornament; possibly inspired by the classical Corinthian equivalent. →115

stiffness see rigidity.

stilb abb. **sb**; a unit of luminance equal to one candela per square centimetre; cd/cm^2.

S-tile see pantile. →47

stile 1 a vertical side framing member of a door leaf or window casement. →5, →52, →111
see door stile.
2 a low external construction of steps to provide passage over a wall or fence in rural areas for people but not animals.

Stile Liberty, Liberty Style; the Art Nouveau style of decorative art and architecture in Italy.

stillicidium Lat.; a board or similar construction fixed at the eaves of a Roman building as a drip or to throw off water.

Stillson wrench see pipe wrench.

stilted arch 1 an arch whose curvature begins above the impost, as if on stilts.
2 stilted pointed arch, see pointed Saracenic arch.
3 see stilted semicircular arch.

stilted pointed arch see pointed Saracenic arch.

stilted semicircular arch a semicircular arch whose curvature begins above its impost.

stipes a stem-like support, especially for an altar table. →116

stipple see stippler.

stippler, stippling brush, stipple; a stiff brush, sponge, or similar hand-held implement for applying a stippled finish to paint and plaster.

stippling 1 the producing of a decorative mottled surface for paint or plaster by regular dabbing with a brush or similar implement.
2 a branch of fine art in which colour is applied in dabs or dots.
3 see pointillism.

stippling brush see stippler.

stipulated sum agreement see lump sum contract.

stirrup 1 in timber frame construction, a metal strip or belt fixing for two perpendicular pieces, fastened to both sides of one piece and wrapped around the other.

2 one of a number of bent secondary reinforcing bars which bind the main reinforcement and resist shear forces in a reinforced concrete beam or pile; also called a link, binder or ligature. →27

stoa Gk; a colonnaded court in Greek classical architecture, usually surrounding an agora or with shops and offices. →92, →94

stock 1 see building stock.
2 see housing stock.

stock exchange an establishment in which stocks, bonds and currencies are traded.

stockade, palisade; a fortified enclosure constructed of timber stakes driven into the ground side by side to form a wall.

stockroom see store.

stomion Gk; in Mycenaean architecture, the entranceway to a tholos tomb, opening from the passage or dromos into the vaulted space. →65

stone 1 a unit of weight for people and animals, equal to 14 lb or 6.35 kg.
2 a generic name for the rigid mineral material forming the earth's crust, used in building construction as masonry, paving, cladding, concrete aggregates, decoration etc.; see **rock** for references to lists of building stones, rocks and minerals.
3 see natural stone.
4 see cast stone.
5 an imperfection in manufactured glass caused by a small solid lump or fleck of opaque mineral material.
6 see stone grey.

Stone Age a prehistoric period from about 600 000 BC to 1200 BC during which the most important utensils were made from stone, usually divided into the Old, Middle and New Stone age.

stone axe see masonry axe. →40

stone block see natural stone block. →12
see dimension stone. →12
see ashlar. →12

stone block paving a paved surface made up of evenly sized stone units or slabs. →15

stone carving the carving of patterns, sculpture, ornament and lettering into stone with tempered steel tools.

stonecarving chisel see masonry chisel. →41

stone chisel see masonry chisel. →41

stone circle a prehistoric arrangement of standing stones set in a circle whose function, though uncertain, was probably linked to astronomy and ritual gatherings.

stone cladding see stone facing, natural stone cladding.
see *stone cladding* illustration. →11

stone-coal see anthracite.

stone column see vibroreplacement.

stone facing any cladding in sheets or fragments of natural stone cemented or hung on a base of brick, concrete etc.; see natural stone facing, ashlar facing, rubble facing; if in thin precut sheets it is called stone veneer. →11
see *stone facing* illustration. →11
see *Egyptian tombs* illustration. →70

stone flooring hardwearing or decorative flooring of natural or cast stone slabs.

stone grey a shade of grey which takes its name loosely from the colour of light grey stone, similar to the colour of cement.

stone heater see sauna heater.

stone labyrinth ancient patterns of rough stones laid down in labyrinth formations in Scandinavia and other parts of coastal Europe by fisher cultures; thought to represent a symbolic wind trap to bring good weather for sea journeys. →122

stonemason see mason.

stone masonry masonry in roughly hewn, cut or sawn stones laid as structural walling, arches, vaults, cladding etc. →11

stonemason's axe see masonry axe. →40

stonemason's chisel see masonry chisel. →41

stone nogging stone infill for the timber stud frame of a traditional half-timbered building.

stone paint see masonry paint.

stone paver 1 see natural stone paver.
2 see paving stone. →15

stone paving, 1 natural stone paving; shaped flat slabs of natural stone laid horizontally as a hardwearing external surface. →15
2 see pebble. →15
3 see sett. →15
4 crazy paving, random stone paving; see ragwork. →15

stone slab 1 a large solid flattish slab of natural stone, worked into shape, used for many purposes in construction.
see *stone walling* illustration. →11
see *Egyptian mastaba* illustration. →70
2 see standing stone.
3 see paving stone. →15

stone veneer see stone facing. →11

stone wall a low freestanding wall of laid stones built as a boundary wall for a plot of land, often in dry-stone construction.

stone walling masonry in laid blocks or pieces of stone.

stoneware a hard ceramic material containing a relatively high proportion of glass, fired at high temperatures of 1200–1300°C and used for unglazed drainage products, pipes, channels etc.

stonework any part of a building, structure, cladding or paving, which incorporates natural stone as a primary material; construction and detailing in stone.
see *stonework* illustrations; some types included as separate entries are listed below. →11, →12
diamond work. →19
long and short work. →12
ragwork. →11
range work.

stonework finish the various factory or tooled treatments applied to the stone surfaces of a building, or natural stone slabs. →12
see *stonework finishes* illustration. →12

stonework joint any joint between adjacent stones etc. in stone masonry; the final shaped mortar in bed and vertical joints; see *types of masonry joint* illustration. →20

stool a simple seat with three or four legs and no backrest.

stool bottomgrate a cast-iron grated podium in an open hearth fire, on which solid fuel rests during combustion so that air may be drawn up through it. →55

stop 1 a rebate in a door or window frame, against which the door leaf or window casement rests when closed.
2 see door stop. →50, →51
3 in stonework and carving, a decorative terminating element for horizontal mouldings.
4 a termination or closing construction for a long component or construction such as a gutter.

stopcock 1 see stopvalve.
2 see mains stopvalve.

stop end, 1 gutter end; the closed end of an eaves gutter, or a terminating component which achieves this. →46
2 see stopped end. →21
3 see stop end form.
4 see stop-end outlet.

stop end form, day joint, form stop; formwork sheeting placed at a joint, at the edge of a component or to contain the edge of concrete being cast.

stop-end outlet a terminating drainage channel or guttering section blocked at one end, with an opening in its base to release drainage water.

stop notice a notice served by a planning authority requiring building work, demolition or other activity on site that is in contravention of planning control to be immediately stopped.

stop nut, back nut, lock nut; a nut screwed tightly against the back of another nut to prevent it from working loose.

stopped a description of a timber joint in which a mortise or recess is cut only part way into the timber receiving a tenon, rather than right through.

stopped dovetail joint see lapped dovetail joint. →5

stopped end 1 the end of a laid masonry wall which terminates in a straight vertical line through use of bonding stones. →21
2 see return end.

stopped mortise, blind mortise; in timber mortise and tenon jointing, a mortise that does not fully penetrate the piece into which it is cut.

stopped tenon joint a timber mortise and tenon joint whose tenon does not fully penetrate the piece into which it is fitted. →5
see stub tenon joint. →5

stopper, 1 plug; a simple conical, wedge-shaped or threaded component for closing an opening or orifice in a tube, pipework, duct etc.
2 see tap-hole stopper.

stopping 1 the filling of cracks, holes, joints and other blemishes in a surface with filler prior to painting.
2 the product used for this, usually a very smooth paste which sets to form a smooth finish; spackling or filler.
3 see caulking.
4 see putty.

stopping in in plasterwork, the filling and smoothing of joints in plasterboard construction and ornamental plasterwork.

stopping knife see putty knife. →43

stopping place see lay-by.

stopping sight distance in road design, the minimum specified sight distance over which a vehicle travelling within the speed limit is able to stop.

stopvalve, stopcock; a valve in a system of water or gas pipework to shut off flow.

storage building see store.

storage cylinder a closed cylindrical pressure vessel for storing hot water for domestic use.

storage heater, 1 thermal storage heater; a unit heater consisting of electrodes embedded in a mass of material with a high thermal capacity surrounded by insulation; the electrodes heat up the mass with off-peak electricity during the night and the resultant heat is given off slowly during the day.
2 hot water storage heater, storage water heater; in hot-water systems, a hot-water storage vessel in which water is also heated.

storage heating space heating with a series of storage heaters utilizing off-peak electricity, or with massive masonry fireplaces providing slow release of heat.

storage life see shelf life.

storage space 1 a room or space in a building in which objects, implements, goods etc. are stored when not in use.
2 see store.

storage tank 1 see oil storage tank.
2 see cistern.

storage unit a piece of domestic or office furniture or in-built fitting containing a number of cupboards for storage.

storage water heater see storage heater.

store 1 a building or room within a building devoted to storage or distribution of supplies. →59
2 storage space; a space or part of a space within a building for the storage of equipment, supplies or goods.
see *prehistoric structures* illustration. →65
see *Carolingian monastery* illustration. →97
see *brick house* illustration. →59
see *office building* illustration. →60
3 stockroom; the storeroom of a retail outlet.
4 storage building, storehouse; a building which is used for storage of goods and supplies.
5 storeroom; a room in a building for the storage of goods.
6 warehouse; a building or structure for the storage of retail goods.
7 a building or space within a building for the sale of merchandise.

storehouse 1 see store.
2 a traditional agricultural building for storing goods and implements.

storeroom see store.

storey, floor, story (Am.), level; **1** one of the horizontal floor levels in a building with one or more of these. →61
2 the area between vertically adjacent floors of a building.
3 see basement storey. →61
4 see ground floor. →61

storey height see floor height.

storey landing a stair landing at the same level as adjacent floor construction. →45

storey rod see gauge rod.

storied rays see ray figure.

stories, number of see height in stories.

storm drain, storm sewer, stormwater sewer; a municipal or private drain for conveying water directly to a river in the event of heavy rainfall.

storm sewage see stormwater.

storm sewer see storm drain.

stormwater, storm sewage; rainwater from heavy rainfall which has been collected as runoff from external surfaces of a building and conveyed to storm drains, often mixed with foul water to prevent overflow.

stormwater sewer see storm drain.

story see storey. →61

stoup a basin in a church for holy water, often set into a recess or onto a pedestal near the entrance.

stove a closed appliance for heating a space, often freestanding and connected to a flue if solid fuel, gas or oil fired, ventilated if operated by electricity; types included as separate entries are listed below.
cast-iron stove. →56
cooker.
masonry stove. →56
room heater.
sauna heater.
solid-fuel stove.

stoved see stove enamelled.

stoved acrylic see acrylic powder coating.

stoved enamel see baked enamel.

stoved finish see baked enamel.

stove enamel see baked enamel.

stove enamelled, stove finished, baked, stoved; the description of a component coated with a stove or baked enamel.

stove enamelling, baking, stoving; the process of drying or fusing an applied polymeric coating by the application of artificial heat.

stove finished see stove enamelled.

stoving see stove enamelling.

stoving enamel 1 see acrylic stoving enamel.
2 see alkyd stoving enamel.

stoving lacquer lacquer dried by a sustained period of baking or application of heat.

straight angle see flat angle.

straight arch see flat arch. →23

straight bands those internal plies in the thickness of plywood whose grain is in the same direction as the face plies.

straight bevelled halved joint see bevelled scarf joint. →3

straight bridge any bridge which crosses a road, waterway or obstacle at a right angle. →64

straight cut veneer see flat cut veneer. →10

straightedge 1 a long straight rod used for measuring and setting out.
2 see screed board.

straightening coat 1 see first plaster undercoat.
2 see second plaster undercoat. →83

straight flight stair a stair which consists of a single linear flight with no intermediate landing; see also straight stairs. →45

straight grained a description of a piece of sawn timber whose grain is approximately parallel to an edge.

straight-grained float a flat-bladed wooden float used for smoothing plastering, whose timber grain is parallel to its length.

straight joint, stacked joint; a vertical brickwork joint which rises through more than one course and provides a weak bond.

straight line in geometry, the shortest distance between two points.

straight match a condition of decorative or patterned wallpaper which should be hung with horizontal patterns aligned on adjacent sheets.

straight peen hammer a hammer whose peen is aligned with its shaft. →40

straight reducer a pipe fitting for joining two pipes of different diameters in a straight line.

straight-run stairs see straight stairs. →45

straight shake a crack running along the grain of a timber board. →1

straight slot the elongated indentation in the head of a normal screw which allows tightening with a screwdriver. →36

straight stairs, 1 straight-run stairs; a stair which ascends in a straight line, with or without intermediate landings. →45
2 see straight flight stair. →45

strain in structural mechanics, unit deformation of a member resulting from applied stress.

strain energy the energy stored in an elastic body under stress.

strainer 1 a coarse filtering device or sieve for preventing solid matter in liquid suspension from passing a certain point in a flow system such as sewage treatment.
2 see outlet strainer.

strainer arch a supplementary masonry arch constructed part way down a high opening to prevent buckling of its sides. →23

straining arch a structural arch which functions as a brace, as in a flying buttress.

straining beam in traditional timber roof construction, the upper beam between the tops of queen posts in a queen post truss. →33

straining sill in traditional timber roof construction, timbers attached to the top of a tie beam to prevent the base of a queen post from moving.

strain relief see partial release.

strand 1 one of the wound fibres, filaments or threads in a rope, cable or cord.
2 a bundle of many glass fibres, often hundreds, used as reinforcement in fibreglass.
3 see prestressing strand.

stranded caisson see box caisson.

strap 1 a metal strip or belt fastened across a joint to secure a fixing in timber frame construction.
2 ceiling strap, see ceiling hanger. →60
3 see anchor strap. →22

strap hinge, 1 flap hinge; a surface-mounted hinge with long, tapered or straight flaps. →38
2 see tee hinge. →38

strapwork surface decorative of interwoven bands rendered as if cut from a sheet material such as leather, originating in the Netherlands in the 1500s. →122

Strasbourg turpentine, olio d'abezzo; a variety of turpentine exuded from the silver fir [*Abies pectinata*], used as a medium in paints, varnishes and adhesives.

stratification a defect in cast concrete resulting from overvibration, causing lighter constituent materials such as water and cement to rise to the surface.

stratum see bed.

straw stems of dried grasses such as wheat, oats or barley used as roof thatching material, reinforcement in clay construction etc.

strawberry see cardinal (red).

strawboard, compressed straw slab; an insulating building board manufactured by compressing straw under heat between sheets of card.

straw thatch, long straw thatch; roofing thatch of unbroken, dried wheat, barley, rye or sedge stalks.

straw yellow a shade of greyish yellow which takes its name from the colour of straw or dried hay.

streak in geology, the coloured residue left by a piece of stone drawn across a piece of porcelain; a useful device for identifying rock types.

streamline flow, laminar flow, steady flow, viscous flow; in hydraulics, the flow of a fluid which is continuous and undisturbed rather than turbulent.

street a road in a town or city which has buildings along one or both sides and is serviced with lighting, a system of drains, road marking etc.

streetcar see tram.

street corner a place formed by the meeting of two crossing streets.

street frontage see frontage.

street furniture any fixed objects in the urban environment such as signage, lighting, pillar boxes, benches and litter bins.

streetlamp see streetlight.

streetlight, streetlamp; a light, often with supporting structure, used for illuminating exterior areas, especially roadways.

streetlighting a series or system of streetlights.

street parking, on-street parking, kerb parking, curb parking (Am.); the provision of parking places in marked spaces lining the edge of a street carriageway. →62

streetscape, urban milieu; the perceived environment caused by the visual pattern and variety of buildings in an urban area.

street sign a printed or embossed plate fixed to a wall or pole indicating the name of a street.

strength the property of a material or component to withstand forces without fracture or failure.

strength accelerating admixture, accelerator; an admixture included in a concrete mix to increase its hardening rate.

strength of materials a branch of engineering, the study of stresses, deflection and failure in materials.

strength test see compressive strength test.

stress 1 the effect of an external force or forces on a structure or structural member.
2 the force per unit area resulting from external loads on a structure, or internal forces such as drying, in units of N/m.

stress corrosion corrosion leading to potentially disastrous cracking and failure taking place in steel structural members under tensile stress.

stressed skin component a prefabricated structural timber walling or flooring component consisting of boarding fixed on either side of a timber frame.

stressed skin construction a method of construction of walls, floors and panels in which boards or membranes are fixed to either side of a frame or series of structural members as bracing.

stressed skin panel a rigid structural element consisting of a frame onto which boards or sheets are fixed as bracing.

stress grading the classification of sawn timber according to structural defects.

stressing the application of stress or load to a structure or structural member.

stretcher a bonded brick or stone laid with its long side or face exposed in the surface of a masonry wall. →20

stretcher bond, 1 running bond; a brickwork bond consisting entirely of courses of stretchers, with alternate courses laid with a half brick overlap. →17
2 any brickwork bond consisting of single courses of Flemish etc. interspersed with an odd number of courses of stretchers.
see Flemish stretcher bond. →18
Flemish double stretcher bond, see monk bond. →18
see raking stretcher bond. →17

stretcher course, stretching course; a course of bonded brickwork which consists entirely of stretchers. →20

stretcher face the visible side of a brick when laid in masonry as a stretcher. →20

stretcher plinth, plinth stretcher; a special brick whose upper arris has been chamfered along one of its long sides, used as a stretcher in a brick coping or above a projection. →16

stretching course see stretcher course. →20

striated finish see batted finish. →12

striga, plural strigae; Lat.; a residential block in a Roman city or military settlement whose longer walls face the main street; see scamnum; the rectangular divisions of a Roman military camp for the erection of tents and, later, buildings.

strigae plural form of striga.

strigil ornament in Roman architecture, a decorative motif of shallow recurring S-shaped carvings for vertical surfaces; it takes its name from the curved implement used by wrestlers to scrape the oil, sweat and dust from their bodies after bouts. →125

strike see striking plate.

strike plate see striking plate.

striking, stripping; the removal of formwork from hardened concrete.

striking face see face. →40

striking hammer 1 a heavy hammer or maul used for striking cold chisels and other cutting and shaping tools in stone and metalwork. →40
2 see drilling hammer. →40
3 see mallet. →40

striking piece in concreting, a piece of formwork sheeting which can easily be removed to aid dismantling of the rest of the formwork.

striking plate, keeper, strike, strike plate; a metal plate with a rectangular perforation, attached to a door jamb to receive a latch or bolt when the door is closed.

striking time, stripping time; the time from placing of cast concrete after it has reached an accepted degree of hardness so that formwork can be safely removed.

string 1 see cord.
2 stringer; an inclined beam which carries the treads in a stair. →45

string course see band course.

stringer see string. →45

stringline see bricklayer's line.

strip 1 see moulding.
2 backing strip, see back-up material.
3 cant strip, see angle fillet. →49
4 see carpet strip. →2
5 see ceiling strip.
6 see column strip.
7 see cover strip.
8 see draught strip, weatherstrip. →52
9 door strip, see door seal.
10 see edge strip. →2
11 see floor strip.
12 see gum strip.
13 pilaster strip, see lesene. →13
14 see rumble strip.
15 see window strip. →53

stripe figure see ribbon grain.

strip flooring 1 see wood strip flooring. →44
2 see wide plank flooring. →44
3 see solid parquet. →44
4 see parquet strip.

strip footing see strip foundation. →29

strip foundation, 1 strip footing; a wall foundation consisting of a continuous horizontal strip of concrete. →29
see *strip foundation* in brick house illustration. →59
2 see widestrip foundation. →29

strippable wallcovering wallcovering which can be removed in one piece once dry.

strip parquet see parquet strip.

strippers see wire strippers.

stripping 1 see striking.
2 see paint removal.
3 see hot-air stripping.

stripping knife a flat-bladed spatula used for removing old paintwork and wallcoverings.

stripping time see striking time.

strip slates a roofing product of small pieces of shaped bitumen felt laid in the same manner as roof tiles; if sold in attached groups they are called strip slates or tiles, if sold as single nailable items, they are variously known as asphalt, bitumen, composition or felt shingles. →49

strip slate roofing roofing of small pieces of shaped bitumen felt laid in the same manner as roof tiles; see previous entry.

strip soaker a strip of waterproofing material laid between courses of roof shingles in exposed areas.

strip tie see strip wall tie. →22

strip tiles see strip slates. →49

strip wall tie any wall tie formed from metal strip rather than wire; see vertical twist tie, fishtail tie. →22

strip window see window band.

stroller see pushchair.

strongroom, vault; a storeroom for valuables built within bedrock or of reinforced concrete to provide a high degree of security against fire and burglary.

strongback a structural member used as a spreader beam, soldier or as waling in formwork. →30

stronghold 1 any strongly fortified place used for defence or as a place of refuge during conflict.
2 the fortified centre of a castle complex, its last position of defence. →103
3 see ancient stronghold.
4 see citadel.
5 see acropolis. →94
6 see keep.

strongroom door see vault door.

strontium a metallic chemical element, **Sr**, used in fireworks, flares and some armaments.

strontium sulphate see strontium white.

strontium white strontium sulphate ($SrSO_4$) used as a pigment in the same way as blanc fixe and barytes.

strontium yellow a pale bright yellow pigment manufactured from strontium chromate, now almost obsolete.

struck joint, 1 overhand struck joint; a horizontal brickwork mortar joint used for interior and sheltered work, which is slanting in cross-section and made by pressing the mortar in at the bottom of the joint. →16
2 see weathered joint. →16

structile opus structile, see opus caementicium.

structura caementicia Lat.; see opus caementicum. →83

structural 1 pertaining to loadbearing systems, forces or elements.
2 referring to a material, member etc. whose function is loadbearing.

structural adhesive a strong and durable adhesive for joining structural components.

structural arch see arched structure.

structural board any building board used for its loadbearing properties as decking, bracing etc.

structural brickwork brickwork which is designed to be loadbearing.

structural concrete concrete designed to carry loads or be part of the structure of a building.

structural concretework any work on site involving reinforced concrete frames, including formwork erection, casting, installation of precast panels etc.

structural defect an imperfection affecting the strength of the structure of a building, component, or material such as timber.

structural design the design, theoretical testing and calculation of structural loads, stresses and sizing of structural members undertaken by a structural engineer.

structural drawing a design drawing produced by a structural engineer to show the layout, materials and sizing of structural units of a building.

structural engineer a qualified professional responsible for designing structures and supervising their construction and maintenance.

structural engineering the engineering discipline which deals with the design, calculation and testing of structures.

structural floor those loadbearing layers of floor construction designed to support dead and imposed loading, over which flooring is laid. →44

structural frame see loadbearing frame. →28

structural glazing, frameless glazing, planar glazing; a system of glazing in which the glass itself has a structural role, usually unframed sheets of toughened glass hung on patch or spot fittings with sealed butt joints. →53

structural grid 1 the orthogonal layout of columns and main structural elements in a building.
2 see grid.

structural hollow section a structural steel section formed by rolling or welding, whose cross-section is a hollow rectangular, circular or other shaped tube. →34

structural log see laminated log.

structural member one of the component parts of a structural system designed to carry load.

structural skeleton, frame; the primary framework for a building or structure.

structural steel a general name for rolled steel sections, beams and columns used in construction for framing and other loadbearing functions; structural steel sections are listed below.
see *metal sections* illustration. →34
bar.
channel, channel section. →34
circular hollow section. →34
C-section.
H-section. →34
hollow section. →34
hot-rolled steel section. →34
I-section. →34
L-profile, see angle profile.
rectangular hollow section, RHS. →34
rolled hollow section, RHS. →34
rolled steel section.
round hollow section, round section, see circular hollow section. →34
square hollow section. →34
structural hollow section. →34
T-section, T-bar, tee section. →34
tubular section, see hollow section. →34
UB section, see I-section. →34
UC section, see H-section. →34
U-section. →34
Z-section. →34

structural steelwork any structural work or loadbearing frames consisting of steel sections fixed together.

structural threshold in threshold analysis, existing built form or urban grain which presents a barrier to further urban expansion.

structural timber timber and timber products used in construction for their structural and loadbearing properties in framing, beams, trusses etc. →2
see *conversion of timber* illustration. →2
see *timber frame* illustration. →57, →58

structure, 1 loadbearing structure; a combination of parts joined together to form a loadbearing or rigid whole; types included as separate entries are listed below.
2 composition; the construction or make-up of an object, compound, material such as stone or timber, organism or component and the relationship of parts therein.
air-supported structure.
amusement structure.
arched structure.
bridge structure.
cable-stayed structure.
cable-supported structure.
concrete roof structure. →28
floor structure.
frame structure.
lattice structure, see truss.
metal structure.
pneumatic structure, see air-supported structure.
prehistoric structure. →65
reinforced-concrete structure.
roof structure.
shell structure, see shell construction. →27
social structure.
space structure, see space frame. →33
substructure.
superstructure.
suspended structure.
timber structure. →57
urban structure.

structure borne sound in acoustics, sound transmitted by the fabric or other components of a building.

structure borne sound transmission in acoustics, sound transmission through the building fabric.

structure of wood see *wood and sawn timber* illustration. →1

structure plan in town planning, a policy-based plan for a county or greater urban area, which presents general proposals concerning land use patterns, population distributions and their analysis and transportation systems etc.

strut 1 any structural member which resists forces in compression along its length.
2 a vertical member which resists compressive forces, a column.
3 in timber roof construction, a secondary member carrying the thrust from purlins or otherwise adding support to a rafter. →33
4 see capreolus. →47
5 see diagonal. →33

strut beam see collar beam. →33

strutting see herringbone strutting. →4

Stuart architecture an architectural style in England during the reigns of Charles II and James II (1660–1688); it is evident principally in secular palaces and country houses, and is characterized by use of Baroque elements.

stub bar see starter bar.

stub mortise and tenon joint see stub tenon joint. →5

stub stack a vertical pipe, closed at its upper end, into which a number of sanitary appliances at one level may discharge.

Stub's wire gauge see Birmingham wire gauge.

stub tenon joint, joggle tenon joint, stopped tenon joint, stub mortise and tenon joint; any mortise and tenon joint in which the mortise does not penetrate right through to the other side of a receiving member. →5

stucco 1 any plaster used for facing the outside of buildings, for decorative castings etc.; stucco usually refers to textured renderwork in lime mortar, cement mortar or lime cement mortar, especially fine plasterwork for classical or Baroque decorative work, columns, rustication etc. in imitation of stone.

2 see hemihydrate gypsum plaster.
3 see marble stucco. →83

stucco architecture ornate architectural styles in which stonework is imitated in decorative plasterwork, much in vogue in the eclecticism of the 1800s.

stucco lustro a technique of marble-imitation plasterwork invented in the 17th century, in which coloured pigments, marble dust etc. are sprinkled or painted over the plaster when wet, then the surface is polished to a sheen with a hot iron; sometimes called marmorino or, for high quality interior finishes, Venetian stucco.
see scagliola.

stucco ornament see plasterwork enrichment.

stud 1 in timber frame construction, spaced vertical timber members in a wall frame, to which external cladding and internal lining are attached. →8, →57, →58
2 a spaced vertical timber or pressed metal framing member in a lightweight partition.
3 a metal fixing consisting of a short steel rod threaded at one or both ends to take a bolt.
4 a bolt or nail attached by firing with a special pistol.

studded rubber flooring proprietary sheet or tile flooring of natural or synthetic rubber whose surface has been textured with low projections to provide friction; also known as raised-pattern, coin-pattern or coin flooring. →44

studding 1 see studwork.
2 see threaded rod. →36

student hostel, hall of residence; a building containing student living accommodation.

stud gun a robust nail gun for firing nails or fixings into masonry and concrete.

studies of proportion see *studies of proportion illustrations*. →106, →107

studio, 1 atelier; the workshop or working space of an artist.
2 a large spacious room for drawing at a school of art or design.
3 a specialized room in which film, radio and television is produced and presented.

studio apartment see bedsit.

stud partition a lightweight internal dividing wall constructed with a frame of spaced verticals lined with a building board.

stud wall in frame construction, any wall framed with spaced vertical timbers or studs.

stud welding a method of resistance welding threaded studs onto steel frames using special guns, as a fixing for claddings and other components.

studwork 1 timber or pressed metal sections laid vertically as a framework for lightweight partitions.
2 studding; the verticals in a timber frame wall.

study a room for studying, reading and similar activities. →57

study bedroom 1 one of a number of rooms in a student dormitory which have shared kitchen, sanitary and recreational facilities.
2 a room in a student residence in which the student both sleeps and studies, a bedroom which is also a study.

stugged finish see sparrowpecked finish.

stump 1 in landscaping and forestry, the lower part of a tree's trunk and rootage which remains when a tree has been felled.
2 a rod of rolled paper, sharpened at both ends, used in pencil and charcoal drawing for smoothing tones and various shading effects.

stump chipping in site clearance, landscaping and forestry, the disintegration of unwanted tree stumps in situ.

stump grubbing see grubbing.

stump tenon joint in timber frame construction, a joint in which the end of a post is received into a housing in a horizontal sill or head member. →5

stupa a dome-shaped sacred Buddhist building, often surrounded by a freestanding wall or railing and containing holy relics. →68

style 1 the categorization of art and architecture according to aesthetic persuasion, era, artist, nationality, ideology, materials etc.
2 see order.

Style Moderne see Art Deco.

style ogival, le see ogival.

stylization the abstracted representation of recognizable forms in art and ornamentation.

stylobate 1 in classical architecture, the upper stepped course of a crepidoma, on which a temple stands. →86
2 a plinth or base for a colonnade.

stylo pen see draughting pen. →130

stylus see silver stylus.

styrene a clear volatile liquid produced from benzene and used in the manufacture of plastics.

styrene-acrylonitrile, SAN; a thermoplastic formed by copolymerization of styrene with acrylonitrile, used in the automotive industry, for kitchenware, appliances and furniture.

styrene-butadiene rubber, SBR; a resilient synthetic rubber used for car tyres, carpet-backing and wire insulation.

styrofoam see extruded polystyrene.

sub-base 1 in foundation, paving and road construction, a layer of material such as hardcore, cement etc. laid beneath the substructure to spread loading evenly to underlying soil, to restrict frost heave and as drainage. →15, →62
2 see flooring sub-base. →44, →59

sub-basement a storey under the main basement of a building.

sub-contract a contract to carry out part of a larger contract, paid for and managed by the main contractor.

sub-contracting a procedure that enables a contractor to contract part of the work, often of a specialist nature, to another contractor.

subcentralization in town planning, the outward movement of industries, businesses etc. from urban centres to outlying areas.

subcontractor a building contractor which carries out specific parts of building work or trades according to a contract or agreement with a contractor.

subdirectory a lower hierarchy of a computer's directory system, in which files or folders are stored.

subfloor 1 those layers of floor construction above a structural floor, which provide a base for the flooring material. →44, →57, →59
2 see flooring sub-base. →59

subframe wall framing at the edges of a door or window opening, to which a door or window frame is directly fixed. →28, →53

subgrade 1 in paving and road construction, that part of the ground or an earthwork which bears loads from the overlying road structure. →15
2 see foundation.

sublimation the change from a solid directly into a gas on heating without turning into a liquid first; on cooling, the gas will turn directly back into a solid.

submerged-arc welding a method of arc welding steel plates in which an electric arc is applied across an intermediate electrode, carried out under a mass of molten flux.

submersible pump a small pump for drawing relatively clean water from wells, excavations etc. by immersion in the water.

subsellium 1 see misericord.
2 Lat.; a seat in a Roman amphitheatre.

subsidiary glazing, secondary glazing; proprietary glazing units, usually in metal frames, attached to the front side of old or leaky windows to improve performance.

subsidy government or private financial aid given for such purposes as starting a business, reducing the price of manufactured goods, sponsoring the arts etc.

subsill 1 the lower member of a window opening, formed into a sill onto which a window frame rests and is fixed. →53
2 see timber subsill.

subsoil 1 a layer of soil immediately above solid ground, but below topsoil.
2 see foundation.

subsoil drain 1 a perforated pipe laid beneath the ground in sand or gravel to dry out damp soil and lead seepage water away from the substructure of a building or road to a public drain.
see *foundation* illustration. →29
see *brick house construction* illustration. →59
2 irrigation drain; in the treatment of waste water, a perforated drain which discharges effluent from a septic tank into the surrounding soil.

subsoil drainage see land drainage.

substance see material.

substation an electric power installation and its sheltering structure containing a transformer for distribution of electricity to a local area.

substrate any surface to which a finish, coating or adhesive may be applied; also called a base or ground. →20

substructure 1 that part of the structure of a building which transmits loading to the ground below.
2 particularly those constructed below ground.
3 see bridge substructure. →32

subsurface drain see subsoil drain. →59

subtenant a person or concern which rents or leases property from a tenant, not directly from the owner.

subtopia a loose town planning term describing suburbs which are untidy, poorly designed and sprawling.

subtraction in mathematics, the process of taking one number away from another to determine the difference in their values.

subtractive mixture in colour science, darker colours formed when colours are combined, each absorbing a part of the light incident on it.

suburb a predominantly residential area on the outskirts of a city or town, usually with its own commercial and municipal services.

suburban area, suburbia, suburbs; an outlying residential zone of a town or city.

suburban expansion, suburbanization; in town planning, the migration of people from inner-city residential areas to the outlying suburbs in the hope of more space and relatively inexpensive property.

suburban growth in town planning, typical urban growth in outlying areas due to suburban expansion.

suburbanization see suburban expansion.

suburban traffic vehicular traffic which travels along routes between a residential suburb and a town centre, or traffic within a suburban area.

suburbia see suburban area.

suburbs see suburban area.

subway, 1 pedestrian subway; an underpass designed for the use of pedestrians and cyclists beneath a busy road or railway. →64
2 see underground railway.

succinite see amber.

suction the ability of a material or installation to absorb or draw water from a damp substance or surface with which it is in contact.

sudatorium Lat.; a steam or hot air room in a Roman bath house. →91

sugar maple, rock maple; [*Acer saccharum*] a hardwood from North America with hard, heavy, cream-pinkish timber and elegant grain; a hard maple used for furniture, flooring, plywood, tools and musical instruments.

sui generis use 'of its own kind, unique' (Lat.); in planning control, a class of development which does not fit into any of the main defined classes.

suite, 1 lock suite, suite of locks; a group of locks within a building which can be opened by a single master key, and each has its own individual key which fits only that lock.
2 three-piece suite; a set of furniture comprising a sofa and two armchairs of the same or similar style.
3 see WC suite.

suiteing the planning and formulation of a suite of locks within a building or complex to suit the needs of user groups, but in such a way that all are openable by a master key.

suite of locks see suite.

sulfate see sulphate.

sulfur see sulphur.

sulphate, sulfate (Am.); any of a number of water-soluble compounds formed by the reaction of minerals or metals with sulphur, used in traditional paints as fixatives and as to prevent attack of timber by insects and fungi.

sulphate attack a fault in hardened concrete caused by the attack of dissolved sulphate salts.

sulphate-resistant cement see sulphate-resisting Portland cement.

sulphate-resisting Portland cement, sulphate-resistant cement; a Portland cement, low in tricalcium aluminate, which has a better resistance to attack by sulphates dissolved in water than ordinary Portland cement.

sulphur, sulfur (Am.); a yellow chemical element, **S**, used in matches, explosives and the vulcanization of rubber.

sulphur blue a shade of pale blue which takes its name from the colour of a flame produced by sulphur when it burns.

sulphur dioxide a poisonous, gaseous, chemical compound, $\mathbf{SO_2}$, used in bleaching; a major source of air pollution.

sulphuric acid, oil of vitriol; a dense, oily, corrosive chemical compound, $\mathbf{H_2SO_4}$, used in the chemical industry, pickling of steel surfaces and in dye manufacture.

sulphur-ore see iron pyrites.

sulphur yellow a shade of pale yellow which takes its name from the colour of refined sulphur.

sum the result of adding arithmetic functions.

Sumerian art the art of the Babylonian civilization from 2900 to 2000 BC, coinciding with the beginnings of monumental architecture in Mesopotamia.

summa cavea see maenianum summum. →90

summer, summer beam, summer tree; in traditional timber-framed building, a heavy main beam which carries a wall or other continuous load.

summer beam see summer.

summer-house 1 a recreational building, structure or shelter in a garden or parkland to provide shade and shelter.
2 see summer residence. →58

summer residence, holiday home, country cottage, summer-house; a cottage, villa or chalet in a rural setting, used as holiday accommodation. →58
see *holiday home and sauna* illustration. →58

summer tree see summer.

summer triclinium see triclinium aestivum. →88

summerwood see latewood.

summum maenianum in lignis see maenianum summum in lignis. →90

sun ornament depicting a burning or flamed globe, often symbolizing a principal deity; in Christian art symbolic of immortality and resurrection. →120

sun-baked brick see mud brick.

sun-bleached oil see sun-refined oil.

sunburn a shade of reddish brown which loosely takes its name from the colour of skin tanned by the sun.

sunburst matching a veneering pattern for round or polygonal tabletops in which segmental slices of burl or crotch veneer are glued side by side to form a repeated star-like pattern.

sun cross see wheel cross. →118

sundial a device or construction for displaying the hour of day by casting a shadow of sunlight on a marked scale.

sun disc 1 see winged sun disc. →75
2 see Aten. →74

sun-dried brick see mud brick.

sunflower see buttercup yellow.

sunflower oil see sunflower seed oil.

sunflower seed oil, sunflower oil; a drying oil pressed from the seeds of the sunflower plant [*Helianthus annuus*], used as a vehicle in paints.

sun god see Aten. →74
see Atum. →74
see Khepri. →75
see Ra. →74

Sung period see Song period.

sunk bead a thin hollow moulding, semicircular in profile. →14

sunken half round a hollow moulding, semicircular in profile. →14

sunk fillet a thin hollow moulding, rectangular in profile. →14

sunk relief, cavo-relievo, cavo-rilievo, intaglio rilevato; carved ornament or decoration which does not project from the surface into which it is carved.

sunlight, direct solar radiation; in lighting design, that part of illumination reaching the ground as direct, unobscured and unreflected light from the sun.

sun lounge see conservatory. →57

sun-refined oil, sun-bleached oil; traditional linseed oil refined by leaving it in the sun in glass vessels for a number of weeks; used as a vehicle in paints.

sunshade, shade; any grill, set of baffles or blind fixed externally above a window or glazing to provide shade from the sun.

sunshine yellow see sun yellow.

sun temple a shrine to the sun deity, a building type typical to the ancient cultures of South America, Egypt etc. →72

sun wheel a prehistoric symbol of the sun, a spoked cross inscribed in a circle; a wheel cross. →118

sun yellow, sunshine yellow; a shade of light yellow which takes its name from the colour of sunlight which has passed through the atmosphere.

super abacus see dosseret. →115

supercalendered paper paper manufactured by rolling through metal calenders to produce a smooth surface.

supercapital see dosseret. →115

super computer a vague term to describe any computer capable of carrying out very complex calculations.

superelevation, banking, cant; the cross-sectional inclination built into bends on some main roads.

super glue see cyanoacrylate adhesive.

superimposed orders the stacking of classical orders as elevational devices in successive storeys of a classical building, by convention (from the bottom) Tuscan, Doric, Ionic, Corinthian and Composite. →90, →114

supermarket a retail outlet selling food and other consumer items and run on a self-service principle.

superplasticized concrete liquid concrete with a superplasticizer added to increase workability, used for patching structural defects in reinforced concrete.

superplasticizer see superplasticizing admixture.

superplasticizing admixture, high range water-reducing admixture, superplasticizer; in concretework, a powerful admixture included in the mix to maintain workability with a reduced water content.

superposition principle a structural theory for calculating forces in redundant frames by dividing them up into a number of superimposed perfect frames.

Super Realism, Hyper Realism, Photo Realism; a movement in art from North America in the 1970s concerned with painting subjects with a photographic and exaggerated attention to detail.

superstructure 1 that part of the structure of a building or bridge above its substructure or foundations.
2 parts of a building which remain above ground level.
3 see bridge superstructure. →32

supersulphated cement blended cement composed of blast-furnace cement mixed with calcium sulphates and lime or cement clinker.

superterranean see surface.

suppedaneum, altar platform; a raised platform or plinth beneath or in front of a church altar, originally the ledge on the cross supporting the feet of Christ during crucifixion.
see *Scandinavian hall church* illustration. →102
see *altar* illustration. →116
see *cross* illustration. →117

supplementary angle in geometry, one of two angles whose sum is 180°.

supplier a commercial organization which stocks, produces or delivers materials, components or products for a building project.

supply 1 goods or services which are provided or available.
2 the conveyance of electricity, gas, water or other service to a building via a main.
3 in mechanical ventilation and air conditioning, the introduction of ducted fresh air into a space using fans.
4 see electricity supply.
5 see gas supply.
6 see water supply.

supply air, 1 input air; treated air introduced into a space by an air-conditioning system.
2 fresh air; air pumped into a space by mechanical ventilation plant to replace stale air.

supply air terminal unit, outlet, input device; in air conditioning and ventilation, any device, grille, diffuser etc. through which air is supplied to a space.
see *supply air terminal unit* in office building illustration. →60

supply grid see electricity supply grid.

supply network 1 see gas distribution network.
2 see electricity supply grid.

supply pipe that part of the service pipe of a water or gas supply installation which connects the supply of a building to the communication pipe, lies inside a site boundary and is not maintained by the supplier.

support, 1 stay; any construction or component which keeps something in place or bears a load such as a prop, beam, bracket, cleat or column.
2 system support; a phone-based supplier's or manufacturer's service giving information, advice, maintenance and dealing with computing queries.

supported sheetmetal roofing, flexible metal roofing; roofing of thin, flat sheets of metal laid in bands with longitudinal joints, standing seams etc.; seams over boarding or decking; unlike profiled sheeting, it is not self-supporting. →49, →57
see seam-welded roofing. →49, →57

supporter in heraldry, stylized figures, beasts or birds on either side of a shield, apparently supporting it. →124

supraporta see sopraporta.

Suprematism a movement in modern art originating in Petrograd in 1915, which attempted to break free from representation through the use of pure geometric form in boundless space.

surbased vault see segmental barrel vault. →25

surcharge the overflowing of a drain or sewer caused by an excess of pressure or capacity.

surface 1 the outermost bounding layer of an object, especially when coated or treated.
2 superterranean, above ground; referring to any construction work undertaken above ground level.

surface-acting agent, surfactant; **1** an additive which reduces the surface tension in a liquid, used in detergents and to make paint more brushable.
2 an additive for concrete which lowers the surface tension in mixing water to aid penetration of the concrete into formwork voids, and dispersion and foaming of other additives.

surface area, area; a measure of the two-dimensional space taken up by a surface, abb. **a**.

surface box, valve box; a receptacle with a hinged lid, submerged into hard external surfaces, floors, footpaths etc., to offer protection to a valve or pipe fitting, and from which it can be operated and serviced.

surface checks surface splitting in the face of an improperly seasoned timber board. →1

surface coated float glass, reflective float glass; float glass treated with a transparent but reflective surface layer of metal oxide or other material to reduce transmission of solar radiation.

surface coefficient in thermal calculations for thermal conductivity of a construction, the heat loss per °C of temperature difference between a surface and the surrounding air; units are W/m_2 °C; see also U-value, C-value.

surface condensation undesirable water vapour or steam which condenses on cool internal surfaces such as ceilings, window frames or walls as droplets of water.

surfaced see dressed. →2

surfaced bitumen felt see mineral granule surfaced bitumen felt.

surfaced four sides (Am.) see planed all round. →2

surfaced paper see coated paper.

surfaced sawn, surfaced two sides (Am.); a description of sawn timber which has been planed on three sides only, leaving one face unplaned.

surfaced timber see dressed timber. →2

surfaced two sides see surfaced sawn.

surface filler see filler.

surface-fixed hinge see non-mortised hinge. →38

surface hardening, hardening; a process of hardening the surface of steel for use in tools by various heat-treatment processes.

surface hinge a hinge designed to be mounted to the face of a door, gate or hatch rather than its edge.

surface-modified tinted float glass float glass treated with a layer of tinting metal ions during manufacture to reduce transmission of solar radiation.

surface-mounted door closer a door closer designed to be fixed to the face of a door leaf.

surface-mounted luminaire a luminaire designed to be fixed to and protrude from a surface, rather than being sunken into it.

surface mounting the fixing of electric cables and other services to the surfaces of ceilings, floors and walls as opposed to installing them in ducts, housings or trunking.

surface planer, surfacer; a machine with a wide rotating cutter mounted into a bench for planing a flat even surface on a wooden board; see thicknessing machine.

surfacer see surface planer.

surface retarder a material applied to concrete formwork to slow down the setting of surface concrete, providing an exposed aggregate finish once the formwork is struck.

surface temperature temperature measured at the external surface of a body.

surface tension a property of the surface of a liquid to behave as if covered with a supporting film.

surface treatment, finish; the protective or decorative treatment of a surface by mechanical or chemical means, or by the application of a coating to produce a finish.
see stonework finish. →12

surface vibration the compacting of fresh concrete by applying vibration to its outer surface rather than immersing a vibrator into it; see also poker vibrator.

surface vibrator in the compaction of fresh concrete, a concrete vibrator which vibrates the exterior surface of fresh concrete; see also immersion vibrator.

surface water rainwater which falls on the ground, roofs of buildings, roads and paved areas and is collected in a drain.

surface-water drainage the conveyance of rainwater from the slightly sloping surface of paving, roads etc. into a system of drains.

surface-water erosion the erosion caused by surface water running over loose and granular soils, causing damage and subsidence and contributing sedimentation to streams and drainage systems.

surface water gully see rainwater gully.

surfacing 1 see dressing.
2 in road construction and landscaping, a layer or layers of material such as tarmac, paving or concrete which form a hardwearing surface; in road construction this is made up of the base course and wearing course. →62
3 see roof surfacing.

surfactant see surface-acting agent.

surform tool a hand tool with a multi-toothed blade for rough shaping and smoothing of wood and plastics.

surgical scalpel see scalpel. →130

surplus the amount by which supply exceeds demand in manufacturing, the amount by which revenues exceed expenditure in accounting.

surround 1 see fireplace surround. →55
2 see Gibbs surround.

surroundings the external environment in immediate proximity to a building or buildings.

surrounding wall see perimeter wall.
see *surrounding wall* in Egyptian burial monuments illustration. →70

surround lighting see general surround lighting.

surveillance see camera surveillance.
see perimeter surveillance.

surveillance camera, closed circuit television camera; one of a network of cameras installed at key points in or around a building to provide security monitoring of the movement of people.

survey the gathering of information from samples, research, measurement, photographs etc. for a particular purpose; types included as separate entries are listed below.
aerial survey.
building survey.
geotechnical survey.
investigation.
land survey.
quantity survey.
property survey.

survey drawing see record drawing.

surveying 1 see land surveying.
2 see mapping.

surveyor 1 see building surveyor.
2 see land surveyor.
3 see quantity surveyor.

suspended base floor the lowest structural floor in a building which transmits loading via foundations, but is not constructed directly onto the ground or bedrock below.

suspended ceiling a ceiling system of hangers, runners and panels hung from the soffit of floor construction above, in which light fittings, ducting and outlets are incorporated; sometimes called a hung ceiling.
see *suspended ceiling* in office building illustration. →60

suspended floor a floor construction which spans between points of support rather than being fully supported over its whole area by the underlying ground.

suspended roof, suspension roof; a roof supported by cables.

suspended scaffold a scaffold with a working stage which is hung from a counterweighted cantilever from the ridge or eaves of a building.

suspended slab any floor or roof slab supported at intervals by columns or cross walls, which does not bear directly onto the ground. →29

suspended structure a structure such as a suspension bridge, which relies solely on the force of tension to support loads.

suspender see bridge suspender. →32

suspension a liquid containing minute particles of a solid or liquid suspended in it.

suspension agent see thickening admixture.

suspension bridge a bridge hung from a system of primary and secondary cables strung between tall towers known as pylons.
see *suspension bridge* illustration. →32
see chain bridge.

suspension bridge anchorage see anchorage. →32

suspension bridge cable one of the two principal supporting cables in a suspension bridge, from which the bridge deck is supported by vertical hangers; also called a catenary cable. →32

suspension cable see suspension bridge cable. →32

suspension roof see suspended roof.

suspension track a proprietary profile of metal or plastics with rollers or guides for overhead mounting of blinds, signage and lighting.

Sussex bond see Flemish garden-wall bond. →18

Sutekh see Seth. →74

swag see festoon. →121

swallowtailed cross, bifurcated cross; a cross whose limbs are terminated with a V-shaped notch. →117

swamp cypress see southern cypress.

swan-neck chisel see mortise lock chisel. →41

sward in landscaping, an area of tended lawn.

swastika, fylfot, tetraskelion; an ancient cross or symbol in which the extremity of each arm has a perpendicular extension, scribing out a square; a gammadion, later the emblem of the Third Reich. →118

sway in thatched roofing, a long rod of hazel, elm or willow for fastening down a course of thatch. →48

sway brace see wind brace.

Swedish cope see long groove. →6

Swedish green see cobalt green.

Swedish saw see tubular bow saw.

sweeping see chimney-sweeping.

sweet cherry, wild cherry; [*Prunus avium*] a European hardwood with deep red-brown timber; used for the decorative value of its grain in interiors and in musical instruments.

sweet chestnut, Spanish chestnut; [*Castanea sativa*] a European hardwood with golden-brown, rough-textured, durable timber, whose uses are similar to that of oak.

sweetgum see gum.

swelled chamfer see oundy moulding. →125

swelling the increase in volume of a body due to absorption of a liquid.

Swietenia spp. see mahogany.
Swietenia macrophylla, see Honduras mahogany.

swill solid or partially liquid food waste from domestic and residential establishments, hospitals etc., used as animal feed.

swimming baths, 1 swimming pool; a facility with one or a number of swimming pools, changing rooms etc.
2 see bath house.

swimming pool 1 an indoor or outdoor pool for recreational swimming, water sports etc.
2 see natatio. →91
3 see swimming baths.

swing 1 a recreational swinging seat suspended on wires, ropes or by some other construction, situated in a children's playground or garden.
2 see door swing. →50

swing bridge, pivot bridge, turn bridge; a bridge designed to move horizontally to one side on pivots to allow vehicles, usually boats, to pass by.

swing door a door whose leaf is hinged so that it may open in both directions. →50

swing door hinge 1 see double-acting hinge.
2 see double-acting spring hinge.

swing door operator a motorized lever or hinge mechanism for opening and closing an automatic swing door, operated by a signal from a detector device, remote control etc.

swirl the irregular grain pattern that surrounds knots or crotches in a piece of sawn timber.

Swiss chalet a timber dwelling or holiday home characterized by steeply pitched roofs and rustic ornament, originating in the mountainous areas of Alpine Europe.

Swiss trowel a hand tool used for smoothing plaster in projection plastering by means of a rectangular flat blade attached to a handle.

switch a manual or automatic device for closing or opening an electric circuit.

swivel bridge see swing bridge. →64

swivel damper a smoke or flue damper which opens and closes by means of a pivot, about which it rotates; also called a pivot damper. →55

sycamore, 1 harewood; [*Acer pseudoplatanus*] a hardwood with tough, light, fairly strong perishable yellowish timber, used for flooring and veneer.
2 see American plane.

syenite a coarse-grained, grey, bluish or reddish crystalline igneous rock containing feldspar and hornblende.

sylvanite, graphic ore; a dark grey mineral, an important ore of gold and silver; also written as silvanite.

symbol a sign, mark or image whose purpose is to signify, represent or have associations with some ideal, message, institution etc.

Symbolism a movement in art and literature originating in France in the 1880s and making use of mystical and allegorical figures, signs etc. to express subjective feeling.

symmetrical 1 well proportioned, harmonious, in balance.
2 in geometry, pertaining to a figure which, when bisected by an axis, is divided into two areas which are mirror images of one another.

symmetrical composition see axial composition.

symmetry the quality of an object which is symmetrical.

sympathetic resonance see resonance.

sympathetic vibration see resonance.

synagogue a building for the practice of Jewish worship. →94

syndicate see group.

synergy improved efficiency, results, achievements etc. gained by the combined action or cooperation of a number of bodies or processes.

synoecism a term coined by Aristotle to describe the administrative coming together of several proximate villages to form a town.

synthesis the chemical formation of a compound by combining its constituent parts.

synthetic man-made, as opposed to occurring naturally.

synthetic anhydrite the mineral gypsum produced as a by-product of another process, or calcium sulphate manufactured under controlled conditions.

synthetic fibre see artificial fibre.

synthetic grass, astroturf, synthetic turf; a hardwearing surface covering for sports fields, a mat of raised tough plastic strands manufactured in imitation of grass.

synthetic model, analogous model; in traffic planning, a trip-distribution model which takes account of future radical changes in patterns of land-use and modes of transport.

synthetic resin adhesive a group of adhesives whose main constituent is a synthetic phenolic or aminoplastic resin.
see melamine formaldehyde glue.
see phenol formaldehyde glue.
see resorcinol formaldehyde glue.
see urea formaldehyde glue.

synthetic rubber rubber produced from synthetically manufactured latex.

synthetic rubber glue see elastomeric adhesive.

synthetic screed see levelling compound.

synthetic turf see synthetic grass.

synthronon a small amphitheatre-like podium at the far end of the altar in an Early Christian, Greek orthodox or Byzantine church, with banked rows of seating surmounted by the tribune of a high priest; sometimes benches placed on either side of the cathedra; also called a synthronos. →95, →116

synthronos see synthronon. →95

Syrian arch, arcuated lintel; a major masonry arch supported on columns, often a large decorative arch in an arcade or colonnade with walling above, especially one marking an entranceway or other portal. →24

Syringa vulgaris see lilac.

system a functional organized construction, process or set of laws or guidelines.

systematic art a form of abstract painting expressing the idea of a logical system through repetition or regeneration of simple motifs.

system building a modern method of construction in which all or a certain major part of the building components for a construction project are prefabricated to save time and labour on site; see also prefabrication.

Système Internationale d'Unites see International System of Units.

system glazing see patent glazing. →53

system of coordinates see coordinate system. →127

system of measurement an agreed system of unified units of measurement, such as the metric system or SI-system, by which size, quantity, mass and other physical phenomena can be quantified.

system of proportion a set of rules, principles or numbers governing the layout and relative arrangement of aesthetic forms.
see *Egyptian and Renaissance systems of proportion* illustration. →106
see *Vitruvian systems of proportion* illustration. →107

system scaffolding proprietary scaffolding of specially made tubes, fixings, housings and shackles for quick and easy assembly, dismantling and storage, and automatic compliance with regulations.

system support see support.

systyle 'narrow columned'; in classical architecture, the ordered spacing of rowed columns at a distance of two column diameters between the centres of adjacent columns. →77

Syzygium aromaticum see oil of cloves.

T

t&g see tongue and groove.
taberna Lat.; pl. tabernae; a shop, workshop, dwelling or inn, open to the street in the lower floor of an urban Roman residential block, insula, thermae etc. →88, →91, →92
tabernacle 1 in Jewish worship, a sacred canopy shrine.
2 in Christian worship, a recess or niche in a wall with an ornate canopy for housing a statue.
tabernacle-work carved decorative work in a church especially for a tabernacle and its canopy, but found on other furnishings such as pulpits, screens or stalls.
tabernae plural form of taberna.
table 1 a diagram for presenting information in a regular and clear way in columns and rows.
2 a piece of furniture with a flat horizontal working or activity surface supported on legs or a base of some sort.
3 the horizontal upper flat slab of a precast concrete tee beam.
tabled scarf joint, hooked scarf joint; a timber lengthening joint whose halved surfaces are set back or tabled along their length for added strength. →3
table formwork large-scale proprietary formwork used for casting and supporting the underside of concrete slabs in multistorey buildings, which has its own supports so that it can be easily moved and reused in subsequent locations.
table hinge see rule joint hinge. →38
table sharpener a pencil sharpener designed to be mounted onto a work surface and which contains a large chamber for collecting shavings or sharpenings.
tablet a magnetized and calibrated plate with a preloaded menu, used in conjunction with a mouse in computer-aided design.
tablet flower an ornamental motif consisting of a series of embossed square flowers. →121
tablinum Lat.; a reception room situated off the atrium opposite the main entrance in a Roman dwelling, the study and private living room of the master of the house, containing family archives and hereditary statues; in larger villas it may be a transition space between two courtyards. →88
tabloid see ledger. →Table 6
tabula the flat top of an altar table. →116
tabularium Lat.; see tabulary.
tabulary, tabularium (Lat.); a Roman archive building for the storage of public documents; the name is sometimes given to a modern building with equivalent use.
tacheometer an instrument used in surveying for measuring distances, direction and level differences.
tack 1 a flat-headed nail or pin for attaching building paper, fabric and carpets. →35
2 see upholstery tack. →35
tack free a stage in the drying of paint at which the painted surface is not sticky, but not fully hard.
tack hammer, brad hammer, pin hammer; a small hammer with a lightweight steel head for driving small nails, pins, brads or tacks. →40
tacking see tack welding.
tack welding, tacking; the fixing of metal pieces together or in position with temporary welds before final welding.
taenia Lat.; see tenia. →78
tai-chi see yin-yang. →120
tail the lower edge of a roofing slate or tile. →47
tai-qi see yin-yang. →120
takspån see shingle.
talc, soapstone, steatite; natural magnesium silicate, ground and used as a filler in paints.
tallow-wood [*Eucalyptus microcorys*] an Australian hardwood with heavy, yellow-brown timber, used for all kinds of construction work.
talus see batter. →103
tamarack, eastern larch; [*Larix laricina*] a North American softwood with resistant red-brown timber, used for posts and packing.
tambour, drum; a wall which supports a dome or cupola, cylindrical, square or polygonal in plan and often punctuated with openings. →26
tamped concrete, spaded concrete; concrete compacted by repeated tamping with a hand tool.
tamper see screed board.
tamping, punning, ramming, rodding, spading; the compaction of fresh concrete by the repeated manual thrusting of a sharp metal tool into it to release air voids; spading uses a spade-like tool, rodding uses a long steel rod.
tan see cocoa.
t and g see tongue and groove.
tang 1 the pointed spike at one end of a chisel blade, drill bit or file, designed to be housed into its handle or chuck. →41, →42
2 see Tang period.
tangent in geometry, a line touching a curve, at right angles to its radius at that point.
tangerine see mandarin orange.
tangentially cut see plain sawn.
tangential surface the surface of a piece of sawn timber which has been cut tangentially from the log.
Tang period a period in Chinese history from 619 to 906.
tank any open or closed vessel for the storage of liquids or gases; types included as separate entries are listed below.
aeration tank.
cistern.
expansion tank.
gas tank.
oil storage tank.
oxidation tank, see aeration tank.
pressure tank.
reserve water tank.
sedimentation tank.
septic tank.
settlement tank, see septic tank.
settling tank, see sedimentation tank.
sewage tank, see cesspool.
storage tank.
water tank.
tanking 1 an impervious layer of asphalt, bitumen or bituminous felt for waterproofing the outer surface of subterranean concrete or masonry structures.
2 see air-gap membrane. →29
tanking membrane see air-gap membrane. →29
tantalum a rare metal, **Ta**, used for special applications such as surgical instruments.
tap 1 any fitting by which piped water, gas etc. can be drawn off for use.
see water tap.
2 a hard metal hand tool consisting of a threaded rod, used for cutting female or internal threads into prebored round metal holes.
tap aerator a device attached to or incorporated into the nozzle of a water tap for introducing air into the stream of water.

tape 1 any thin strip of flexible material.
2 see adhesive tape.
tape measure 1 see measuring tape.
2 see flexible steel tape measure.
taper a conical pipe fitting for joining two pipes of different diameters.
tapered brick tapered header, see culvert stretcher. →16
tapered stretcher, see culvert header. →16
tapered edge gypsum wallboard gypsum wallboard whose edges are tapered on the face side to enable butt joints to be made more easily.
tapered header see culvert stretcher. →16
tapered step, tapered tread; a wedge-shaped step whose front and back edges are not parallel, such as one in a spiral stair. →45
tapered stretcher see culvert header. →16
tapered tread see tapered step. →45
tapered tube a metal tubular product whose circumference decreases with length, used for flagpoles, masts and floodlighting poles.
tapestry, wall hanging; a textile hung on a wall as decoration, woven or embroidered with depictions, designs or patterns.
tap-hole stopper a plug accessory designed to cover a tap-hole in a sink, in the case that no tap is to be installed.
taping strip, reinforcing strip; in built-up roofing, strips of material laid over joints in the underlying structure before the laying of bitumen felt.
tapping the cutting of internal screw threads in a bored hole.
tapping screw see self-tapping screw.
tar a black viscous liquid with a smoky odour, manufactured from the destructive distillation of wood or coal, traditionally used as a wood preservative.
tarantula any of a group of large spiders, a typical stylized motif in Mediterranean and Asian decoration. →120
tar black a shade of black which takes its name from the colour of the particles of charcoal formed in tar during its distillation from wood.
tare the weight of packaging material for a product, reduced from the total to give a net weight.
tar epoxy paint tar-based epoxy resin paint used for waterproofing concrete or steelwork.
target cost contract a form of cost-reimbursement contract in which a nominal cost is estimated beforehand; on completion of the work, the difference in value between this target cost and the actual cost is divided between the client and contractor according to pre-agreed terms.
tariff, price list; a list of prices or rates for goods and services.
tarmac see tarmacadam.
tarmacadam, coated macadam, tarmac; a hardwearing road surfacing made from graded aggregate coated with bitumen or road tar to bind the particles together.
tar paper building paper saturated with tar, used as a moisture barrier in wall construction.
tarpaulin a thin sheet of waterproof material, originally waterproofed fabric, used for the temporary protective covering of constructions and materials on site.
tar paving tarmacadam, tar slurry or other bituminous cements containing road tar as a binder, used for surfacing pedestrian areas and those designed for light traffic.
tarsia see intarsia.
task lighting artificial lighting designed to provide a higher level of illumination for certain localized activities such as reading, writing, drawing etc.
tau cross, St Anthony's cross, crux commissa; a cross in the shape of the letter T or tau, the nineteenth letter of the Greek alphabet; sometimes also called an advent cross, anticipatory cross, T-cross, Egyptian cross, robbers' cross, pre-Christian cross or old testament cross. →117
taupe a shade of grey which takes its name from the colour of the fur of the mole [*Talpa europaea*]; taupe is 'mole' in French.
tax a percentage of monies from earnings, profits or goods sold, business, inheritance etc. collected by the state to provide revenues for the upkeep of government services such as political administration, education, health services, roads and public utilities.
tax brick a brick of larger than normal size which originated in England to avoid a brick tax levied from 1784 to 1850.
tax deduction 1 certain items of expenditure, sales etc. which for various reasons lie outside the taxable realm or can be used in a compensatory manner, according to the tax authority.
2 PAYE, pay as you earn; money deducted by an employer on behalf of an employee as income tax.
taxi lane a lane in a vehicular road reserved for the use of taxi traffic.
taxi rank, taxi stand; a designated location from which a taxi may be hailed, either on the spot or by phone.
taxi stand see taxi rank.
Taxodium distichum see southern cypress.
Taxus baccata see yew.
tax year a twelve month period for which taxes are calculated and collected.
T-bar see T-section. →34
T-beam, tee beam; a flanged beam, T-shaped in cross-section to withstand greater compressive stresses. →30
tchetvert an old Russian measurement of capacity equivalent to 8.6 kg of grain.
T-cross see tau cross. →117
teagle post see principal post.
teak, Indian oak; [Tectona grandis] a hardwood from Burma, India and Thailand with durable, oily, dark yellow or brown timber; used for interior construction, plywood, boat-building and decorative panelling.
teak (brown) a shade of dark brown which takes its name from the colour of the wood from the teak tree [*Tectona grandis*].
tear see lachryma. →78
tear fungus see dry rot.
tearoom see cafe.
teazle tenon in traditional timber-framed construction, a tenon made in the top of a post, housed in a mortise in a horizontal member above.
technetium a chemical element, **Tc**.
technical concerning machines, technology or applied science.
technical installation see service.
technical pen see draughting pen. →130
technical specification a document outlining a technical description of a product, process or service, and the requirements to be fulfilled by it.
technocratic planning a rationalist planning philosophy which views the city as a machine and is characterized by technological invention in transport planning and construction methods, vast building complexes and the systematic zoning of activity.
technological threshold in threshold analysis, the rehabilitation of existing coordination of old and new technical infrastructure systems etc. which present a barrier to further urban expansion.
technology 1 the practical use of science to perform a useful function.
2 engineering sciences and their application in industry.
technology park see science park.
Tectona grandis see teak.
tectonics 1 the art of building.
2 a pictorial composition which takes into account the structural qualities of line and surface.

tectorium see opus tectorium.
tee a pipe fitting to connect one pipe to another at right angles.
tee beam see T-beam. →30
tee half lap joint a timber halved joint of one member meeting another at right angles, forming a tee shape.
tee hinge, strap hinge, T-hinge; a surface-mounted hinge which has one long tapered flap and one small flap, which forms a tee-shape when opened out. →38
tee junction see T junction. →62
tee section see T-section. →34
teeth per inch see TPI.
Teflon trade name for polytetrafluoroethylene.
Tefnut in ancient Egyptian mythology, one of the primeval twin deities (along with Shu), representing rain, dew, moisture, spat forth by the sun-god Atum; sometimes depicted as a lion; see Shu.
tegula, plural tegulae; 'tile' in Latin; a flat tray-shaped roofing tile used in conjunction with an imbrex or covering tile in Italian and Roman tiling. →47
tegula mammata Lat.; a special Roman tile used in hypocaust construction, cast with short protrusions at each corner to permit the flow of hot air behind. →83
telamon see atlas. →76
telamones plural of telamon. →76
tele a prefix denoting an action or activity which happens at a distance from its source, especially in relation to electronic communication.
telecommunications the transmission of signals and messages over long distances usually by electronic means, using cables or satellites.
telecommunications exchange, exchange, telephone exchange; a telecommunications station where messages are connected and transmitted.
telecommunications network a telecommunications system comprising all outlets, exchanges, transmitters, relays, cables, satellites, antennae etc., via which signals are transmitted.
telecommunications outlet, telecommunications socket; a plug-hole by which a telecommunications transmission device can be connected to a network or transmission system.
telecommunications socket see telecommunications outlet.
telecommuting see telework.
telecopier see telefacsimile.
telefacsimile see telefax.
telefax, 1 telecopier (Am.); abbreviated form of telefacsimile; an electronic device for digitizing graphic images and simultaneously sending them along phone lines to be printed by a receiving device.
2 a message received or sent on a such a device.
telegraph pole, telephone pole; one of a series of poles laid vertically to support telephone cabling above ground.
telematics long distance communication using computers.
telemetry the practice of taking measurements with instruments which transmit data automatically in digital form to distant receivers.
telephone 1 an electronic communications system which enables sound, most often human speech, to be transmitted by cable over great distances.
2 see telephone set.
telephone box, phone booth, telephone kiosk, call box; a small shelter or construction, often with a door, which contains a public telephone.
telephone charge a cost of running a telephone, made up of installation, connection, rental and calls.
telephone company a commercial establishment which operates a telephone network and provides associated services.
telephone connection a telephone line activated or connected by agreement with a telephone company, so that calls can be made from a telephone handset.
telephone entry system, door phone; security telecommunications between an external door or gate and a restricted area, usually a send-and-receive unit connected to a monitoring centre, occupant's residence etc.; often the same as an entry-phone.
telephone exchange 1 see telecommunications exchange.
2 see telephone office.
telephone hood a small canopy fitted over a public telephone to provide acoustic privacy, shelter from rain etc.
telephone kiosk see telephone box.
telephone line a cable along which telephone signals are transmitted.
telephone network a system of telephones, including handsets, cables, exchanges and other links.
telephone office, telephone exchange; the central administration and installation establishment which maintains a telephone network.
telephone pole see telegraph pole.
telephone set, phone, telephone; a device containing a transmission and receiving set, linked to a telephone network.
telephone socket see telecommunications outlet.
telephone system a digital, wireless, analogue, local, international, manual or automatic communications network using telephones.
telephone traffic the entirety of phone signals running through a telephone system at any one time.
teleprinter a telecommunications device for receiving and typing out telex messages.
telescopic crane, telescopic jib crane; a crane whose boom or jib is telescopic and can be easily hydraulically extended or retracted, often mounted on a vehicle.
telescopic prop a proprietary steel strut whose length can be adjusted, used for temporary propping of slabs and horizontal formwork; also called an adjustable prop. →30
telescopic jib crane see telescopic crane.
telesterion Gk; an ancient Greek temple of the Mysteries, with a shrine or anactoron in the centre, surrounded by banked seating. →92
television 1 the sending and receiving of moving pictures and sound.
2 television set; a device for receiving these signals.
3 see closed circuit television.
television centre a building from which television programmes are produced and broadcast.
television set see television.
television survey see closed circuit television survey.
telework, telecommuting; work undertaken at home or away from the workplace proper using computers, faxes and telecommunications and networks as a means of communication.
telex 1 a telecommunications system in use previously for international communication, whereby printed messages are sent to typewriter-like receiving machines (teleprinters) along telephone lines.
2 a message received on this system.
tell an earthen mound in Middle Eastern countries, based on the accumulations of previous settlements, often the sites of significant archaeological finds; many place names bear this prefix.
tellurium a silvery, crystalline chemical element, **Te**, used in alloys and as a colourant in glass and ceramics.
temenos Gk; the sacred area or enclosure surrounding a classical Greek temple. →94
tempera paint consisting of oils in an emulsion, used with water as a medium, which dries to form a hard, durable surface.
temperature a measurable level or degree of heat, coolness etc. of a physical body or environment,

whose basic unit is the degree Celsius or degree Kelvin (°C, °K).

temperature difference the difference in level of heat between two taken measurements, in degrees Celsius, °C .

tempered glass see toughened glass. →53

tempered hardboard dense fibreboard impregnated with oil or resin for added strength, water resistance and abrasion resistance.

tempering heat treatment to increase the ductility of hardened steel by reheating it to a temperature below that of hardening, and allowing it to cool.

templa plural form of templum.

Templar cross see cross capital. →117

template 1 any flat sheet of stiff material which has been profiled, shaped or had patterned holes cut out of it, used in marking out, draughting, lettering, and as a pattern in milling and turning on a lathe; variously called a stencil, templet, pattern or profile.
2 see circle template. →130
3 see dovetailing template.

temple, **shrine** a building or consecrated space for the worship of a deity or effigy; types included as separate entries are listed below.
see *Mesopotamian temple* illustrations. →66
see *classical apteral and peristyle temple* illustrations. →84, →85
see *Asian temples* illustration. →68
see *ziggurats and stepped pyramids* illustration. →67
amphiprostyle temple. →84
antis temple. →84
apteral temple, apteros. →84
Asian temple. →68
Buddhist temple, see *temple precinct* illustration. →68
cave temple, see rock-cut temple. →68
circular temple, see round temple. →85
classical temple. →86
cult temple. →66
double antis temple. →84
double temple. →85
Etruscan temple. →84
fort temple. →66
funerary temple, see mortuary temple. →70, →72
Greek temple, see apteral and peristyle temple illustrations. →84, →85
hearth temple, see hearth shrine. →66
megalithic temple. →65
megaron temple. →84
monolithic temple, see ratha.
monopteros. →85, →94
monostyle temple. →84
mortuary temple. →70, →72
peripteral temple, see peripteros. →85
peristyle temple.
prostyle temple. →84
pylon temple. →72
pyramid temple. →70, →71
revelation temple. →66
rock-cut temple. →68, →72
Roman temple, see apteral and peristyle temple illustrations. →84, →85
round temple. →66, →85
square temple. →66
sun temple. →72
templum. →84
terraced temple. →72
valley temple. →71

temple court see temple courtyard. →66, →72, →85

temple courtyard 1 an open space at the heart of a temple or temple precinct, surrounded on four sides by built form. →66, →72, →85
2 see sekos. →85

temple precinct 1 the sacred area or walled enclosure surrounding a temple or shrine, including buildings therein. →68
see *Buddhist temple* illustration. →68
2 see pyramid complex. →71

templet see template.

templum, pl. templa **1** Lat.; a Roman sacred place or sanctuary. →84
2 a purlin in Roman timber roof construction. →47

templum in antis 1 Lat.; see antis temple. →84
2 see double antis temple. →84

temporary works work on site which is demolished or dismantled after use and is not part of the completed construction, usually work carried out to stabilize or protect an existing building or as an aid to construction such as formwork, scaffolding etc.

tenaglia see tenaille. →104

tenaille 'pincers' Fr.; a low work in a castle or fortification, consisting of two walls at an angle to each other, situated in a ditch between bastions or behind a ravelin, designed to protect the main fortification; also known as a tenaglia (Italian) or tenaillon. →104

tenaillon see tenaille. →104

tenancy agreement, rental agreement; a contract made when a property is rented out.

tenant one who rents a piece of property and has the legal right to occupy it.

tender 1 a written offer to carry out work or supply goods or services in given conditions at a stated price; a bid.
2 see competitive tendering.

tender document any document which is part of a package sent out to tender; a contract document.

tendering 1 see competitive tendering.
2 see tendering procedure.
3 see two-stage tendering.

tendering procedure the procedure for the invitation, selection and acceptance of tenders.

tender programme see outline programme.

tender sum in construction planning, the sum which a potential contractor offers as a fee for work to be undertaken, stated in his tender.

tendon, prestressing tendon; in prestressed concrete, a steel bar, wire, strand or cable stretched within the concrete to place it in compression.

tenement a multistorey block of rental apartments accessed from a single stairway and often without a lift, especially found in Scottish and American cities. see insula. →88

tenement block see tenement.

tenia, taenia (Lat.); in classical architecture, a thin moulding which runs along the top of a Doric architrave, below the frieze. →78

tennis court an area of level, surfaced ground or lawn with a net and standard marked boundaries for playing tennis.

tenon a rectangular protrusion cut into the end of a timber member, which fits into a recess or mortise to create a mortise and tenon joint. →5

tenoned purlin see butt purlin.

tenoned scarf joint a timber lengthening joint in which the end of one or both pieces is fashioned with a tenon to increase the strength of the joint once assembled. →3

tenon joint see mortise and tenon joint for list of joints in this category. →5
see *timber mortise and tenon joints* illustration. →5

tenon purlin see butt purlin.

tenon saw a medium-sized saw with a reinforced back, 250 mm–350 mm in length, used for general accurate benchwork.

tensile failure the failure of a structural member due to excess tensile force.

tensile force, tension; a pulling or stretching force in a structural member.

tensile reinforcement see tension reinforcement.

tensile strength in structural design, the greatest tensile stress that a member can withstand on a permanent basis.

tensile stress pulling or stretching force per unit area.

tension 1 the state of being stretched or pulled apart by such a force.
2 see tensile force.

tension brace 1 in traditional timber frame construction, a curved convex brace running from post to sole plate for stiffening the frame, often exposed on the exterior of a half-timbered building.
2 see tie rod. →54

tensioning the application of tensile stress or load to a structure, structural member, prestressing strands etc.

tension pile, anchor pile; in foundation technology, a pile designed to resist a downwards or lateral tensile force, often a raking pile.

tension reinforcement, tensile reinforcement; reinforcing bars whose primary task is to resist forces in tension rather than shear in reinforced concrete.

tension rod see tie rod. →54

tension wood reaction wood from the upper surfaces of branches and leaning trunks of a hardwood tree.

tented arch see draped arch. →24

tent-pole capital an ancient Egyptian stone capital carved in imitation of the billowing fabric structure of a tent. →73

tent-pole column an ancient Egyptian stone column with a tent-pole capital. →73

tent shrine an ancient Egyptian temple type reminiscent of the portable cloth shrines of the predynastic age, in which slender stone columns or arches support a canopy. →72

teocalli 'house of God'; an ancient Mexican or Central American temple on a truncated pyramid-shaped mound of earth and stone or brick. →67

teopan an Aztec teocalli, a stepped pyramid temple. →67

tephra see tuff.

tepidarium Lat.; pl. tepidaria; a warm room in a Roman bath house, one with moist heat. →91

tera- abb. **T**; a prefix for units of measurement or quantity to denote a factor of 10^{12} (one million million). →Table 1

terbium a silvery metallic chemical element, **Tb**.

Teredo spp. see shipworm.

term contract a form of building contract that enables the client to order work over a prescribed period at agreed rates.

terminal 1 a central station for loading and unloading passengers and cargo for road, rail and air transport.
2 a group of access devices for a computer; a keyboard, monitor and mouse, connected to a central computer or network.

Terminalia ivorensis see idigbo.
Terminalia superba, see limba.

terminal unit 1 see air terminal unit. →60
2 see supply air terminal unit. →60

termination 1 the end or uppermost element or component in a building or structure.
2 the point in a technical installation at which there is an interface, such as an air-conditioning outlet.

termite, white ant; [*Isoptera spp.*] a group of insect species of tropical and sub-tropical origin which cause serious damage to timber.

terms of agreement see conditions of contract.

terms of contract see conditions of contract.

terpene an oily hydrocarbon obtained from coniferous and citrus trees, used in the manufacture of solvents and germicides.

terra see earth colour.

terra alba a white powdery form of the mineral gypsum.

terrace 1 a raised external level or platform in a garden, park, protruding from a building etc. for promenading or leisure.
see *terrace in Egyptian mortuary temple* illustration. →72
2 an external raised area in front of a grand building or mansion, often with ornate staircase and balustrade.
3 see roof terrace. →59
4 an urban street lined with similar buildings joined together; the row of buildings in such a street.

terrace house see terraced house.

terraced block see stepped block. →61

terraced house, terrace house; one of a row of dwellings joined together by dividing walls, each having its own entrance at ground level and often a small garden; called a row house in the USA. →61

terraced temple a temple type of the ancient Egyptian Middle and New Kingdom, in which a rock-cut tomb is reached via a number of terraced levels linked by ramps. →72

terracotta 1 a fine-grained red clay from which hollow clay blocks and tiles are manufactured.
2 see brick red.

terra di Siena see sienna.

terrain an area of land as regards topography and natural physical conditions, aspect, rock formations etc.

terramare a late neolithic pile village in northern Italy surrounded by man-made earth ramparts, ditches or water, with dwellings arranged in aligned blocks; also a single dwelling in such a village and the earthy deposit found therein.

Terramare culture, singular is Terramara; a culture which arose in Emiliae in northern Italy south of the Po river, whose habitations consisted of piled dwellings surrounded by a vallum as protection from floods.

terra merita yellow pigment made from saffron or turmeric root.

terra ombre see raw umber.

terra rossa see red oxide paint.

Terra Sienna see sienna.

terra verde see green earth.

terrazzo, terrazzo concrete; a smooth concrete surface finish or thin finish facing of cement and marble or other attractive aggregate chips laid in a screed then ground and polished. →44

terrazzo concrete see terrazzo. →44

terrazzo tile a concrete floor or wall tile with a surface of prefabricated terrazzo.

terreplein a level earthwork behind a parapet in a castle or fortification, on which cannon are mounted; a battery or emplacement. →103

tertiary rib see lierne. →101

tesla abb. **T**, SI unit of magnetic induction or magnetic flux density, $1\ T = 1\ weber/m^2$.

tessera Lat.; a small, thin rectangular or polygonal unit of glass, stone or ceramic material used as cladding for walls and floors; its plural is tesserae; see mosaic.

tesserae plural form of tessera.

test see testing.

testa Lat.; pl. testae; any Roman baked ceramic product, concrete aggregates, bricks, earthenware etc. →83

testaceum see opus testaceum. →83

testae plural of testa. →83

test core a concrete test specimen, often cylindrical, removed from an existing structure by drilling.

test cube, standard concrete cube; a specially cast and hardened sample concrete cube used to compression test a particular batch of concrete.

test cylinder, standard concrete cylinder; a specially cast and hardened sample concrete cylinder used to compression test a particular batch of concrete.

tester, sounding board; a board hung above a podium or pulpit to project the voice of a speaker forwards into the auditorium.
see *tester* in Scandinavian hall church illustration. →102

testing a process of defining the properties of a material or component with regard to strength, fire resistance, durability etc. through a series of standardized controlled tests; types included as separate entries are listed below.
air test.

compressive strength test.
concrete flow test.
concrete slump test.
cone penetration testing, deep penetration testing.
core test.
cube test.
cylinder test.
destructive testing.
dynamic penetration testing.
fire test.
flow test, see concrete flow test.
gas soundness test.
hydraulic test, see water test.
mirror test.
non-destructive testing.
penetration testing.
pipe system test.
pneumatic test, see air test.
slump test.
smoke test.
soundness test, see gas soundness test.
static penetration testing.
strength test, see compressive strength test.
vane testing.
VB-consistometer test.
Vebe test, see VB-consistometer test.
water test.
works cube test.

test piece, test specimen; a specially made concrete cube, cylinder or prism used in the compression testing of hardened concrete.

test pile **1** a foundation pile sunk prior to construction to determine loading conditions, settlement characteristics etc. in a particular location.
2 see trial pile.
3 see preliminary pile.

test pit see trial pit.

test specimen see test piece.

testudinate a description of a Roman atrium which has a ridged roof with no compluvium; also called atrium testudinatum.

testudo Lat.; a Roman arched masonry ceiling or vault.

Tetraclinis articulata the gum juniper tree, see sandarac.

tetraconch church, quatrefoil church; a Byzantine church type whose plan is composed of four half-domed semicircular apses around a central space.

tetrahedrite, antimony fahlerz; an olive grey mineral, naturally occurring copper antimony sulphide, used occasionally as an ore of copper.

tetrahedron a solid shape whose surface is composed of four triangular planar faces.

tetrakionia Gk; a four-columned monument situated at the meeting of two major streets in a classical town or city. →93

Tetrapanax papyriferus see rice paper.

tetrapylon Gk; a Roman urban monument placed at the meeting of two streets, with four columned arches permitting passage through in all directions. →93

tetraskele see tetraskelion. →118

tetraskelion Gk; a four-legged symbol now more commonly known as a swastika. →118

tetrastyle **1** in classical architecture, a portico with four supporting columns in a row. →77
2 referring to a Roman atrium with a column at each of the four corners of the impluvium; called an atrium tetrastylum.

Tetropium castaneum black spruce beetle, see spruce beetle.

Tetropium fuscum brown spruce longhorn, see spruce beetle.

teutonic cross see cross capital. →117

tex a unit of measurement of yarn given as the weight in grams of a length of 1000 m.

text **1** any written words used to annotate a drawing or as part of a larger written work.
2 in computing, that part of a message, in character form, which contains information to be conveyed.

text editing see word processing.

text file in computer-aided design, a file made up of data in character form, often contained on a separate word processing application.

text processing see word processing.

textile any sheet product woven or bonded from fibres.

textile wallcovering wallcovering whose outer surface is of fabric.

texture **1** a property relating to the smoothness, softness, coarseness etc. of a surface.
2 the structural character of a solid object or granular material.

textured finish, rustic finish, rustication; a rough face treatment for bricks achieved by scoring, blasting or other means.

textured plasterwork, patterned plasterwork; plasterwork whose surface has been rendered or tooled with a scratched, embossed or stamped pattern or texture after application, but prior to setting.

textured wallcovering a wallcovering treated with a surface layer of straw, cork or other granular material to provide a texture.

tezontle a light, porous, workable volcanic rock found locally in South America and used by the Aztecs and their forebears as building stone.

Thais spp. see purple.

thalami plural form of thalamus.

thalamos **1** ancient Greek version of thalamus.
2 the innermost chamber of a Mycenaean megaron dwelling. →87

thalamus, pl. thalami Lat.; in classical architecture, an inner chamber or apartment for women; see also thalamos (Gk).

thallium a soft, bluish, metallic chemical element, **Tl**, used in alloys and as a pesticide.

thalo blue see phthalocyanine blue.

thalo green see phthalocyanine green.

thatch a traditional roofing material of bunches of straw, reed or other dried plant matter. →48

thatch coat a layer of roofing thatch laid over a whole roof plane.

thatched roof **1** a roof whose weatherproofing and insulating material is bundles of straw or reed (or in some cases heather or bark) held down with timber rods, wire etc. →48
2 see bark-thatched roof.

theater see theatre.

theatre, 1 theater (Am.); a building or arena with a stage and auditorium for the production and performance of theatrical works; an indoor theatre is sometimes called a playhouse.
2 see theatrum. →89
see *classical theatre* illustration. →89
see *theatre* in Hippodamian town plan illustration. →94

theatron Gk; the auditorium of a classical theatre, where the public were seated. →89

theatrum Lat.; a Roman theatre building or structure. →89

theatrum tectum, (Lat.) odeum; a roofed classical theatre. →89

Theban Triad the ancient Egyptian trio of deities, Amun, Mut and their son Khonsu, subject of cult worship in New Kingdom Karnak. →74

Thénard's blue see cobalt blue.

Theobroma cacao see cocoa.

theodolite, transit (Am.); an optical measuring instrument used in surveying for measuring angles in both planes by means of a sighted telescope which can be turned through both horizontal and vertical axes.

theorem in mathematics, an expression which can be proved by logic to be true or correct.

theory of structures see statics.

therm singular form of thermae.

thermae Lat.; ancient classical public baths with associated recreational facilities. →91, →94

thermal break an insulated break in construction between interior and exterior to prevent the passage of heat and cold bridging.

thermal-break profile, thermally broken profile; a proprietary metal window or door framing profile which is manufactured with an integrated plastics bridging piece to minimize loss of heat across its construction. →53

thermal bridge see cold bridge.

thermal capacity, heat capacity, thermal inertia; a measure of the ability of a material or construction to store thermal energy and of how rapidly it warms up, given as the quantity of heat required to raise the temperature of a given construction by unit temperature.

thermal column the rising column of hot air, smoke, ash and other debris over a fire; also called a convection column.

thermal comfort the sensation of physical well-being caused by the effects of temperature, draught and humidity in a space, an empirical measure used in heating and ventilation design for an internal environment.

thermal conductance the rate of flow of thermal energy through a material or construction of given thickness, whose unit of measurement is the C-value.

thermal conduction the transfer of heat through a solid or stagnant liquid or gas by the excitation of adjacent particles within it.

thermal conductivity the rate of flow of thermal energy through a homogeneous material or construction, whose unit of measurement is the K-value.

thermal convection the transfer of heat in a liquid or gas by internal thermal currents.

thermal expansion the increase in size of a material caused by an increase in temperature.

thermal finish see flamed finish. →12

thermal image see thermogram.

thermal imaging see thermographic imaging.

thermal inertia see thermal capacity.

thermal insulation, heat insulation; a layer of lightweight material added to building construction to restrict the flow of heat to the outside; insulation for boilers and pipes is called lagging; types included as separate entries are listed below.
see *timber cladding* illustration. →8
see *concrete frame* illustration. →28
see *brick house* illustration. →59
cellulose loose-fill insulation.
expanded polystyrene.
extruded polystyrene.
frost insulation. →59
glass wool.
loose-fill insulation.
mineral wool. →44, →59
rock wool.
roof insulation. →49

thermally broken profile see thermal-break profile. →53

thermal printer a printer which prints characters and designs by applying heat to thermally sensitive paper, often used in conjunction with a computer, calculator or telefax machine.

thermal radiation the transfer of heat in the form of electromagnetic infrared waves.

thermal resistance 1 a physical quantity whose basic unit is m °C/W, the inverse of thermal conductance.
2 see R-value.

thermal storage heater see storage heater.

thermal transmittance the empirical measure of a given construction to conduct heat; its basic unit of measurement is the U-value.

thermal wheel see heat recovery unit.

thermit welding, alumino-thermic welding, thermite welding; a method of fusion welding steel rails in which aluminium powder and iron oxide form a reaction which melts the steel in close proximity.

thermite welding, thermit welding; the process of igniting a mix of high energy materials that produce a metallic slag that is poured between the working pieces of metal to form a joint.

thermo-differential detector, heat differential detector; a fire detector which measures the rate of temperature rise and issues an alarm at a prespecified value.

thermodynamic equilibrium see heat balance.

thermo-forming a method of forming thermoplastic mouldings by pressing sheet material against a one-sided mould and heating.

thermogram, thermal image; an image of a surface or area taken by a special camera which reacts to infrared radiation to show heat variations in a body or system.

thermographic imaging, thermal imaging; a method of creating pictures based on heat or infrared energy emitted by a viewed scene, used for checking or surveying buildings for missing or damaged insulation, air infiltration or interstitial moisture.

thermoplastic adhesive, hot-melt adhesive, hot-melt glue; glue made from a plastic which softens on heating and becomes rigid again on cooling, applied as a strip with a special electric glue gun.

thermoplastic elastomer, TPE; types of rubbery thermoplastics which remain elastic at moderate temperatures but can be easily remoulded to new forms at high temperatures.

thermoplastic glue see thermoplastic adhesive.

thermoplastics a group of plastics which always soften when heated and regain their hardness on cooling; cf. thermosetting plastics.

thermosetting adhesive, hot setting glue; a synthetic resin adhesive which sets into its final shape under the application of temperatures above 50°C, and cannot be reshaped by reheating once cool.

thermosetting plastics a group of plastics which undergo an irreversible chemical change on heating and become hard; cf. thermoplastics.

thermostat a simple control device which maintains the temperature of a system at a constant level.

thermostatic mixer, thermostatic mixing tap, thermostatic valve; a tap for sinks and showers in which hot and cold water supplies are mixed and their temperature and pressure controlled.

thermostatic mixing tap see thermostatic mixer.

thermostatic valve see thermostatic mixer.

thesauros Gk; a treasury, storehouse or chest in ancient Greece for keeping valuables and riches; a casket for offerings at a sacrificial altar or a shrine reputedly intended for safekeeping valuables. →84
see *prehistoric structures* illustration. →65
see *apteral temple* illustration. →84

thick bed designating a layer of mortar over 10 mm in thickness, enabling tiling and paving to be laid onto uneven surfaces.

thickening admixture, suspension agent, thickening agent; an admixture included in a concrete mix to improve viscosity and prevent segregation and bleeding of the concrete.

thickening agent see thickening admixture.

thickness the dimension of a body, sheet product, construction or layer as measured perpendicular to its main planar surface; the diameter of a longitudinal profile. →2

thicknesser see thicknessing machine.

thicknessing machine, panel planer, thicknesser; a milling machine for planing the rear side of a flat board or piece to the required thickness so that both faces are parallel; see surface planer.

thief-resistant lock see security lock.
thief's cross see furca, forked cross. →117
thimble see wire rope thimble. →37
thin bed the fixing of tiling and paving in a layer of mortar less than 3 mm thick.
thin bed masonry a modern masonry practice of laying accurately sized and shaped bricks, blocks, tiles etc. in a bed of specially developed glue mortar, with joints between blocks of less than 2 mm.
thin coat plaster plaster designed to be applied in very thin layers.
thin coat render render designed to be applied in very thin layers so that the texture in the substrate (brickwork etc.) will be evident in the finish, also called thin section render.
T-hinge see tee hinge. →38
thinner, diluent, reducer (Am.); a volatile liquid which lowers the viscosity of paint and makes it flow more easily.
thin section render see thin coat render.
thin wall plaster final coat plaster which includes a binder that hardens by drying.
third angle projection a standard draughtsman's method of arranging the six planar orthographic projection drawings of main views of a building or object in relation to one another, as if unfolding the hinged sides of an imaginary cube onto which the projections have been made; also called a third quadrant projection, it is widely favoured in North America; see also first angle. →127
third family gas a commercial gas used for combustion and heating which has a Wobbe number of 72.6–87.8 Mj/m^3.
Third Pompeian style see Ornamental style.
see *Pompeian styles* illustration. →126
third quadrant projection see third angle projection. →127
thixotropic referring to a viscous liquid or gel which becomes fluid when agitated.
thixotropy the property of a gel or viscous liquid to become fluid when shaken or brushed, useful for non-drip paints.
tholobate a cylindrical base which supports a dome. →86
tholos, 1 tholus, beehive tomb; 'vault' (Gk); a dome-shaped corbel-vaulted masonry tomb from the Mycenaean period of ancient Greece. →65
2 any classical Greek building type with a circular plan, especially a round peripteral temple. →85, →92
tholos tomb a tomb complex whose main chamber is a corbel-vaulted chamber or tholos. →65
tholus see tholos. →65
thorium a grey, radioactive, metallic chemical element, **Th**, used in alloys and for filaments in some lamps.
thorny crown see crown-of-thorns. →119
thoroughfare, throughfare, passage; permitted or possible access or travel along a way, through an opening etc.
Thoth in ancient Egyptian mythology, the divine scribe and reckoner of time, later attribute of the moon and knowledge; depicted as a male figure with the head of a sacred ibis, or as a large white baboon; known also as Djehuty. →74
thread 1 a thin cord of natural, synthetic or metal strands which have been wound together.
2 screw thread; the helical moulded windings along the shaft of a screw or bolt, or internally in a nut or cap, which provide a mechanical fixing. →36
threaded bar see threaded rod. →36
threaded boss see screwed boss.
threaded pipe see screwed pipe.
threaded rod, studding, threaded bar; a length of threaded stainless or galvanized steel rod on which bolts are screwed to form joints and connections. →36
thread gauge a simple device with a number of calibrated saw-toothed blades for defining the gauge of a screw thread.
threading the cutting of external screw threads on a screw.
three-aisled church a church type which has a central nave with aisles on either side, separated by rows of columns. →102
three-apsed church see triconch church. →99
three-centred arch, 1 anse de panier, basket arch; an arch whose intrados is composed of curves of differing radii constructed from three centres of curvature. →24
2 see pseudo three-centred arch. →23
three coat plasterwork, render, float and set; plasterwork for rough surfaces laid in three separate layers; the first filling coat, the second coat which smooths off the surface and provides a key, and the final coat which provides a finish.
threefoil cross see cross botonée. →117
three-dimensional referring to an object or geometrical system which has length, breadth and depth.
three-dimensional coordinates a system of defining three-dimensional space on a flat plane, or as a series of numbers, using three mutually perpendicular coordinate planes, by convention referred to as horizontal or 'XY' plane, vertical or 'XZ' plane and side, profile or 'YZ' plane; also called spatial or space coordinates. →127
three-dimensional geometry see solid geometry.
three-faced fireplace a fireplace open or glazed on three sides. →55
three-hinged arch, three-pinned arch; an arch which has pin joints at both its abutments and at its crown.
three-phase referring to electricity supply, usually used for providing power at 415 volts, in which there are three live conductors plus a neutral wire.
three-piece suite see suite.
three-pinned arch see three-hinged arch.
three-pointed arch see equilateral arch. →24
three-pointed star a decorative motif of a star with three pointed limbs radiating out from a central point at equal intervals. →123
three-point perspective a perspective drawing constructed from three vanishing points, producing a view of converging lines parallel to all three major axes; sometimes also known as oblique perspective in North America. →129
see *three-point perspective* illustration. →129
three quarter see three quarter bat. →21
three quarter bat, three quarter; a brick cut to three quarters of its length for use in brickwork bonding. →21
three quarter brick see king closer. →21
three-quarter round 1 an ornamental moulding which is semicircular in cross-section. →14
2 see bowtell. →14
three-quarter turn stair a stair which turns through 270° on its ascent. →45
three-rayed nimbus see triradiant halo. →119
threshold 1 the place in a doorway at floor level between two adjacent spaces. →51
2 the lowest member in a door frame, a door sill. →50, →51
threshold analysis a town planning method of identifying the physical, technological, or natural limitations to urban development and analysing the affect of expenditure needed to overcome these barriers.
threshold of hearing in acoustics, the lowest sound pressure which gives rise to a sensation of sound in the human ear.
threshold of pain, pain threshold; in acoustics, the lowest sound intensity which gives rise to a sensation of pain in the human ear.
throat 1 see drip.
2 damper opening; a narrow opening between the outlet of a fireplace and a flue, over which a flue

damper is often situated, to improve draught and reduce pressure in the smoke chamber. →55

throat restrictor an adjustable device to regulate the size of a throat in a flue system or chimney; a smoke damper. →55, →56

throating see drip.

throne the ceremonial seat of a king or other leader. see cathedra. →95

throne room a grand hall in a castle or palace with a throne or thrones for the seating of the governing officials, used primarily for ceremonial functions.

through a through stone, see parpend.

through and through sawing, 1 flatsawing, plain sawing, slash sawing; the conversion of logs by sawing into planks or boards longitudinally along the grain. →2

2 live sawing; the conversion of logs as above, but by first edging the log to provide a flat even surface on one or both sides; the flitch thus produced is sawn into sections of even dimension.

through apartment see open-ended unit. →61

through bridge a bridge constructed from a deck hung from side beams, girders or trusses, often tied at their upper ends, between which the bridge is crossed.

throughfare see thoroughfare.

through fireplace see see-through fireplace. →55

through mortise and tenon joint see through tenon joint. →5

through purlin, trenched purlin, laid on purlin; in timber roof construction, a purlin resting on the backs of principal rafters or notched into their upper surface.

through stone see parpend.

through tenon joint a timber mortise and tenon joint whose tenon fully penetrates the piece into which it is fitted. →5

through traffic in traffic planning, traffic which passes through a certain area en route to some other destination.

throw, blow; in air conditioning and mechanical ventilation, the distance that a jet of air extends out from a supply air inlet to that point at which its air speed is a specified value.

thuja, arborvitae, thuya; [*Thuja spp.*] a genus of East Asian and North American softwoods with weak, soft but durable timber; used for telephone poles, railway sleepers and exterior cladding.

Thuja occidentalis, see white cedar.

Thuja plicata, see western red cedar.

thulium a metallic chemical element, **Tm**.

thumb 1 an old Scandinavian unit of length which takes its name from the width of a thumb, equal to one tenth of a Scandinavian foot, equivalent to 29.69 mm.

2 an old Scandinavian unit of length 24.74 mm; a Scandinavian inch.

thumb mould a small running mould used to make ornamental plasterwork mouldings.

thumb moulding 1 a decorative moulding whose cross-section is that of a round edged fillet, oblique to the vertical. →14

2 see gadroon. →124

thumbnail bead moulding a decorative moulding whose cross-section is that of a quadrant of a circle, its upper face convex or concave, often found at the lower join of two perpendicular planes. →14

thumb nut 1 any nut which can be tightened by hand.

2 see wing nut. →37

thumb screw a threaded fastener with a large round textured head, designed to be tightened by hand for applications such as removable access panels, computer casings etc. →36

thumb slide 1 see slide bolt. →39

2 see snib. →39

thumb turn a small sprung handle turned to operate a latch or lock by grasping between thumb and forefinger; often used to operate a door from the inside; called a locking snib if used for locking a bathroom lock. →39

thumbtack see drawing pin.

thunder blue a shade of bluish grey which takes its name from the colour of sky during a thunderstorm.

thunderbolt an ancient symbol depicting a rod or staff with lightning at both ends; in classical mythology the staff or arrow of Zeus (Greek) and Jupiter (Roman). →120

arrow of Jupiter. →120

arrow of Zeus. →120

thunder shakes, cross shakes, lightning shakes; a timber defect caused by cross grain faults in a living tree, resulting in abrupt failure and general weakness.

thuya see thuja.

thyme oil an aromatic essential oil produced from the herb thyme [*Thymus vulgaris*], whose active component is thymol, used in painting to increase the durability of watercolours and as a fungicide and disinfectant.

thymele 1 Gk; in classical architecture, a sacrificial altar within the orchestra of a theatre, especially to Dionysus. →89, →116

see *thymele* in classical theatre illustration. →89

2 a round temple building which contains a sacrificial altar. →85

thyroma, pl. thyromata (Gk); a main door in the skene of an ancient Greek theatre, usually one of three used by actors on entering the stage. →89

thyron see thyrorion. →87

thyroreion Greek form of thyrorion. →87

thyroreum Latin form of thyrorion. →87

thyrorion, thyron, thyroreum (Lat.); a passage leading from the entrance of an ancient Greek (or Roman) dwelling to a colonnaded courtyard; also spelled thyroreion. →87

thyrsos see thyrsus. →120

thyrsus Lat.; architectural ornament depicting a staff tipped with a pine cone ornament and twined with ivy, as carried by the Roman god of wine, Bacchus (Dionysus in Greece), revellers and satyrs; thyrsos in Greek. →120

staff of Bacchus. →120

staff of Dionysus. →120

tiara, triregnum; a beehive-shaped layered ornamental crown of Persian kings and later the Pope, ornamented with gemstones and pearls, symbolic in decoration and ornament of the papacy and its power. →122

ticket hall a space or room in a station or theatre building for the sale and checking of tickets.

tide the alternating movement of the seas due to the gravitational attraction of the moon and sun, see also ebb tide, flood.

tie 1 any structural bracing or stabilizing member which resists forces in tension; types included as separate entries are listed below.

2 a stirrup in a vertical reinforced concrete component.

3 see clip.

4 see tie rod. →54

angle tie.

cavity tie, see wall tie.

diagonal tie, see angle tie.

dragon tie, see angle tie.

formwork tie, form tie.

king tie.

recoverable tie.

wall tie. →22

tie beam 1 a beam for tying the ends of supporting posts, walls, rafters or columns together. →33

2 especially one in traditional timber framing and roof construction. →33

3 see transtrum. →47

4 a timber tie beam for connecting the upper ends of parallel side walls to prevent them from splaying outwards.

5 see ground beam.

tie beam roof in timber roof construction, a rafter roof with tie beams to prevent rafters and underlying walls and posts etc. from splaying outwards.

tie beam truss 1 a simple roof truss with rafters tied at their lower edges by a horizontal member or tie beam. →33
2 a roof truss with a large tie beam as the main supporting member for the rafters, struts and other subsidiary members.

tied arch a structural arched beam, usually of steel or concrete, which is braced at its lower extremities by a horizontal tie beam, to prevent them from splaying outwards; a simple bowstring truss used in bridges etc., often with vertical hangers between upper and lower chords. →32

tie plate a steel or wrought-iron plate bolted to either end of a tie rod to bear the outward thrust of a loaded masonry wall.

tie rod, 1 tension rod, tension brace, hanger; a steel rod by means of which any component such as a balcony or canopy is hung from overlying structure. →54
2 a steel or wrought-iron rod threaded at either end and often added to construction as a remedial measure, used in conjunction with tie plates to prevent parallel masonry walls and vaulting from buckling outwards under loading.

Tieghemella heckelii see makore.

tierceron in masonry vaulting, a subsidiary rib which connects a point on the ridge rib or central boss with one of the main springers or supports. →101

tiering see torching.

tiger grain see wavy grain.

tightening the act of securely fastening a component or assembly with a fixing, locking screw, wedge or other device.

tight knot, adhering knot; a live or dead knot in timber held firmly in place by the surrounding wood.

tight side, closed face, closed side; the outer side of a veneer sheet as peeled from a flitch, which has fewer checks and markings from the cutting or slicing than the loose side. →10

tight size, full size; in glazing, the size of the opening in the frame, measured from inner edge of rebate, in which the pane fits; larger than the sight size. →52

tight-pin hinge see fast-pin hinge. →38

tignum Lat.; a timber beam or joist in a Roman building.

TIG welding, gas tungsten arc welding (Am.), GTA welding (Am.), tungsten inert-gas arc welding; a method of welding in which an arc is formed using a tungsten electrode shielded by an inert gas such as argon.

tile any thin, rectangular or polygonal product of mineral, plastics or organic material used in series to form a protective or weatherproof finish; types included as separate entries are listed below.
brick tile.
ceramic tile. →20
floor tile. →20
ornamental tile.
parquet tile, see parquet floor square. →44
roof tile. →47
strip tiles, see strip slates. →49
wall tile.

tile accessory any component such as clips, spacers, special tiles etc. designed for use in the laying or fixing of tiles.

tile cladding 1 a weatherproof facing of tiles for an exterior wall or other surface.
2 see tiling.

tile clip a small metal fixing for mechanically attaching a roofing or other tile in position.

tile cutter 1 any tool used for cutting and cropping tiles.
2 a scissor-like tool for cutting or snapping ceramic tiles along prescribed cutting lines of weakness.

tiled finish see tiling.

tiled flooring see tile flooring. →44, →59

tiled paving ceramic tiles laid horizontally as a hardwearing external surface.

tiled roof, tile roof; a roof whose weatherproofing is provided by roofing tiles.
see *Roman tiled roof* illustration. →47
see *tiled roofing* illustration. →47

tiled roofing see roof tiling. →47, →59
see *tiled roofing* illustration. →47
see *brick house* illustration. →59

tiled upstand see tile fillet.

tiled valley in tiled roofing, a valley formed entirely of specially formed tiles.

tile facing see tiling.

tile fillet, tile listing, tiled upstand; roofing tiles set in mortar below a parapet or abutment to act as a flashing; a tiled upstand.

tile fitting any specially shaped roofing tile.

tile flooring floor surfacing of laid tiles. →44, →59

tile grout a cementitious compound applied to fill the joints between adjacent laid ceramic tiles.

tile hanging, vertical tiling, weather tiling; tiles hung vertically in overlapping courses as an external cladding for walls.

tile layer see tiler.

tile listing see tile fillet.

tiler, tile layer; a tradesman or skilled labourer who lays tiles.

tile red see brick red.

tile roof see tiled roof.

Tilia spp. see lime.
Tilia americana, see basswood.
Tilia europaea, see European lime.
Tilia vulgaris, see European lime.

tiling 1 the trade of laying tiles with butting joints as flooring, wall covering etc.
2 the resulting surface or construction.
see *paving and tiling* illustration. →15
3 tiled finish, tile cladding, tile facing; a wall, floor or ceiling surface laid with a facing of tiles.
see roof tiling. →59
see floor tiling. →59
see wall tiling.

tiling base the wall or floor surface below tiling, onto which tiles are fixed; see substrate. →20

tiling batten one of a series of timber strips fixed across rafters or decking as a base for tiling. →59

tiling mortar, bedding mortar, fixing mortar; mortar used for fixing ceramic tiles to a wall. →59

tiling pattern the various patterns in which ceramic and other tiles can be laid. →15
see *tiling and paving pattern* illustration. →15

tiling substrate see tiling base. →20

till 1 see boulder clay.
2 see basal till.

tilting drum mixer a concrete mixer with a rotating hinged drum in which the constituent materials are mixed, which can be tilted to enable emptying.

tilting fillet see doubling piece.

tilt-up formwork special formwork in which concrete is cast horizontally, then rotated to enable lifting to another location, used for casting prefabricated units.

timber, 1 lumber (Am.); wood used for constructional purposes. →1
see *wood and sawn timber* illustration. →1
2 wood converted from sawlogs.
see *conversion of timber* illustration. →2
see list of species of tree from which softwood is obtained under **softwood**.
see list of species of tree from which hardwood is obtained under **hardwood**.

timber-based board see wood-based panel product. →9
see *timber-based building board* illustration. →9
see coreboards. →9
see particleboards and chipboards. →9
see plywoods. →9

timber beam any composite, solid or built-up beam made principally of wood or wood products.
see *timber beam* illustration; types included as separate entries are listed below. →7
anchor beam.
binder.
built-up beam. →7
corrugated ply-web beam. →7
dragon beam, dragging beam.
glued and laminated beam, glulam beam, see laminated timber beam. →7
hammer beam. →33
joggle beam. →7
laminated timber beam. →7
laminated web beam.
plywood box beam, see box beam. →7
plywood web beam, ply-web beam. →7
ridge beam. →33
rood beam.
solid timber beam. →7
straining beam. →33
strut beam, see collar beam. →33
summer beam, see summer.
trabs, trabes. →47

timber board 1 a planed section of timber of similar dimensions used in finished flooring, external cladding, linings etc.
see *timber cladding boards* illustration. →8
see *timber-based building board* illustration. →9
2 timberboard, see bargeboard.

timber building 1 any building whose structure, cladding etc. are principally of timber. →8
2 see timber frame building. →57, →58
3 see log building. →6

timber church see wooden church. →102

timber cladding cladding of sawn timber boards or joinery panels for the frames of walls, floors and roofing; also called timber facing, or, if external, weatherboarding. →8
see *timber cladding boards* illustration. →8
see weatherboarding (also for list of different types of weatherboarding). →8, →58

timber cladding board see *timber cladding boards* illustration. →8

timber connector any fixing for attaching timber sections together.
see toothed plate connector. →35
see split ring connector. →35
see shear plate connector. →35
truss plate, gang nail; see nail plate. →35

timber construction 1 building activity in which the principal framing material is wood or wood products for wall, floor or roof construction, log walls, panel products etc.
2 any building or structure produced in this way, primarily of wooden parts.
see *traditional timber structures* illustration. →7

timber conversion see conversion. →2

timber decking see decking. →58

timber defect an imperfection which lowers the quality of a piece of sawn or dressed timber.
see growth defect. →1
see seasoning defect. →1
see conversion defect. →1
see sawing defect. →1

timber door 1 a door whose leaf and frame are made primarily from timber. →51
2 see glazed timber door. →51

timber facing see timber cladding. →8

timber floor any floor whose structure and/or finish is of wood. →44

timber flooring any flooring material whose finish is treated wood, veneer or wood product; also generally called wood and wooden flooring.
see *timber flooring* illustration; MSP 38 types included as separate entries are listed below. →44
see *timber cladding boards* illustration. →8
block flooring, see end-grain wood block flooring. →44
board flooring.
chipboard flooring.
end-grain wood block flooring. →44
floorboards. →58
see *floorboards* in timber frame illustration. →58
overlay flooring. →59
parquet flooring. →44
plank flooring, see wide plank flooring. →44
plywood flooring. →44
puncheon flooring.
solid timber flooring. →60
see *solid timber flooring* in office building illustration. →60
strip flooring, see wood strip flooring. →44
timber flooring.
wide plank flooring. →44
wide strip flooring, see wide plank flooring. →44
wood block flooring, see end-grain wood block flooring. →44
wood board flooring. →44
wood flooring.
wood strip flooring. →8, →44

timber floor joist a floor joist which is a solid or laminated timber section. →8

timber foundation grillage, log grillage, log crib; a grillage of timber logs or members placed in the ground in perpendicular layers to form a base for a foundation under heavy loads. →29

timber frame 1 a structural frame for a building, partition etc. made of timber sections fixed at their ends.
see *timber frame* illustration. →57, →58
see *conversion of timber* illustration. →2
see *cladding boards* illustration. →8
2 see A-frame.
3 see balloon frame. →57
4 see platform frame. →57
see *traditional timber structures* illustration. →7

timber frame building see timber-framed building. →57, →58

timber-framed building, 1 timber frame building; any building whose structural frame is of timber members clad and lined with sheet material. →57, →58
see *timber-framed building* illustration. →57, →58
2 especially a building with a frame of vertical spaced timber studs clad with sawn boards.
3 see half-timbered building.
4 see timber building.

timber-framed window see timber window. →53

timber frame wall wall construction of a frame of timber sections.

timber framing joint see framing joint. →4
see *types of timber framing joint* illustration. →4

timber glazed door see glazed timber door. →51

timber grillage see timber foundation grillage.

timber handrail a handrail made of sawn, turned, machined or carved wood.

timber joint a mechanical, glued or nailed joint formed between two or more timber members.
see *types of timber scarf joint* illustration. →3
see *types of timber framing joint* illustration. →4
see *timber mortise and tenon joints* illustration. →5
bridle joint. →5
double tenon joint. →5
cabinetmaker's joint, see mortise and tenon joint. →5
carpenter's joint, see framing joint. →4
corner joint.
crosslap joint, see cross half lap joint. →4
dado joint, see housed joint. →5
dovetail joint.
halved joint, halving joint, halflap joint. →4
housed joint, housing joint. →5
joinery joints, see mortise and tenon joint. →5
lengthening joint. →3
mortise and tenon joint. →5
oblique joint, see *types of timber oblique joint* illustration. →4
scarf joint. →3
tenon joint, see mortise and tenon joint. →5

timber joist a roof, floor or ceiling joist made of timber, usually a sawn timber section.

timber lath a split timber batten fixed to a base in rows over a frame as a base for plasterwork; see lathing.

timber lathing a base for plaster made from thin strips of timber fixed to a base or structural members. see bruised lath.

timber lining any covering of boards, plywood and other wood products for the inner surface of a wall frame or structure. →58

timber pile a foundation pile hewn or fabricated from timber. →29

timber roof a roof whose structure or skeleton is of timber members. →33

timber scaffolding scaffolding whose structural members are timber sections.

timber seasoning see seasoning. →1

timber stud see stud. →57, →58

timber structure the loadbearing elements of a building when made of wood; see *timber frame* illustration. →57
see *traditional timber structures* illustration. →7

timber subsill the lower framing member of a window opening, a timber plate incorporated into wall construction onto which a window frame can be attached. →53

timber trim, joinery profile, joinery moulding; a narrow strip of machined wood used in construction as decorative edging, for covering unsightly joints, glazing beads etc. →2
see *timber trim* illustration. →2

timber truss a truss whose members are wooden.

timber unit see prefabricated timber unit.

timber upper floor the floor construction of a building above ground floor and below the roof, which has timber joists as its structure.

timber veneer see veneer. →10

timber window 1 a window whose frame is made primarily from treated timber; a timber-framed window. →52, →53
2 aluminium-faced timber window, see composite window. →53

timberwork the construction work of a building on site involving timber, carried out by a carpenter; see also joinery, carpentry.

timberwork see **joint** timber joint.

timber yard a place for the seasoning, storage and sale of sawn timber.

time a measurable extent of physical existence or duration whose SI unit is the second, abb. **s**.

time control the automatic switching on and off of lighting and other technical systems for preset periods using control gear containing a timer device.

time for completion see contract time.

time lock a lock controlled by a timer device which permits opening only at specified times.

timer, 1 timer switch; a switch operated by a mechanism which turns an electric current on or off after a specific duration.
2 push-button timer; a switch used for corridor lighting etc. which, when pressed, will open a circuit for a specified duration before closing it automatically.

timer switch see timer.

Timonox a trade name for antimony white pigment.

tin a chemically durable, soft, pale metal, **Sn**, with a low melting point, often used for the protective coating of other metals such as iron and copper.

tin bronze an alloy of copper with tin; true bronze.

tin dioxide SnO_2, see cassiterite.

tingle see clip.

tinner's hammer a hammer with a square flat face for beating and dressing sheetmetal panels. →40

tinning, tin plating; the coating of a metal such as copper or iron with a thin protective layer of tin; also the result of this process.

tin plate steel sheet manufactured with a protective coating of tin, used especially to make tin cans, pots etc.

tin plating see tinning.

tin pyrites see stannite.

tin shears see tin snips.

tin snips, hand shears, tin shears; a tough, scissor-like hand tool with high leverage handles for cutting sheetmetals.

tin-stone see cassiterite.

tint, 1 shade; a colour formed when a number of pigments are mixed together.
2 see pastel colour.

tinted glass 1 transparent glass coloured either with a body-tint or with a coloured interlayer.
2 see body-tinted glass.

tinted solar control glass, heat-absorbing glass, absorbing glass; glass manufactured with a body tint to absorb heat from the sun, reduce glare etc.

tinter see stainer.

tinting strength, staining power; the ability of a coloured pigment to modify the colour of white paint.

tip-up window see horizontal pivot window. →52

tissue paper a very fine, light, unsized paper used in various crafts, and for wrapping or protecting objects etc.

titanite 1 see rutile.
2 see sphene.

titanium a grey, hard, light metal, **Ti**, which is corrosion resistant and used for the toughening of steel.

titanium dioxide a white, non-poisonous, chemical compound, TiO_2, used as an opaque pigment in paints (titanium white) and in plastics.
see rutile.

titanium oxide see titanium dioxide.

titanium pigment see titanium white.

titanium white, blanc titane, titanium pigment; a permanent and opaque white pigment whose chief component is titanium dioxide, suitable for use in oils and glues.

titano gypsum the mineral gypsum occurring as a by-product of the manufacture of titanium oxide.

Titanox a trade name for titanium white pigment.

tithe barn a barn traditionally used for storage of the tithe, one tenth of the yearly harvest given over to a landowner as a rent for the land.

Titian red a shade of brownish red which takes its name from the colour used by the Italian Renaissance painter Titian (Tiziano Vecelli).

title heading information such as name, author and publisher on printed matter, drawings and documentation.

title block an area or table of text located at the bottom right-hand corner of a design drawing, containing information about its content, scale, designer and date; also called a title panel. →130

title church see titular church. →95

title page see title sheet.

title panel see title block. →130

title sheet, title page; an initial sheet of a document or set of drawings which contains a title and other general explanatory information.

titular church, title church, titulus; any of the original legal parish churches in Rome, often initially private houses, headed by a cardinal. →95

titulus 1 Lat.; pl. tituli; a name plate attached to the wall of a dwelling in ancient Rome, subsequently any engraved plaque.
2 see titular church. →95

T junction 1 a road junction in which one road meets another at right angles; also written 'tee junction'. →62
2 see directional T junction. →63

tobacco (brown) see Havana (brown).

toe nailing see skew nailing. →3

toggle 1 see toggle bolt. →37
2 see hollow-wall plug. →37
3 see hollow-wall anchor. →37

toggle bolt 1 a metal threaded fastener for fixing to drywall or hollow wall surfaces by means of a pivoted or sprung 'job' which is clamped against the reverse side of construction once the bolt has been pushed through a bored hole. →37
2 see spring toggle. →37
3 see gravity toggle. →37

toilet 1 a room or building furnished with one or a number of water closet suites, urinals and wash basins; variously called a lavatory, convenience, cloakroom, closet or WC. →57
2 see WC. →60
3 a receptacle for collecting human waste, a WC or water closet suite.

toilet lock see bathroom lock. →39

toilet roll holder a wall fitting to hold or contain toilet rolls.

tolbooth, tollbooth; an old Scottish term for a town hall, often containing a jail.

tolerance an acceptable range of variation in size or magnitude of a manufactured, supplied or constructed object to that specified; a permissible range of inaccuracy in measuring.

tollbooth 1 see tolbooth.
2 see tollhouse.

tollhouse a hut or series of booths constructed at the side of a road or turnpike for the collection of dues for vehicular use of a toll road, bridge, tunnel etc.

toll road, turnpike (Am.); a stretch of road for which a payment is collected for vehicular use.

Toltec architecture architecture from the Nahuatl peoples from the Gulf of Mexico and the Yucatán peninsula in c.750–1450 AD, characterized by severe geometrical human statues, reticular relief ornament and the first planned gridiron walled towns on the continent.

toluidine red an organic solvent-based vivid red pigment.

tomato red a shade of red which takes its name from the colour of the ripe fruit of the tomato plant [*Lycopersicum esculentum*].

tomb a monument or elaborate grave for the dead; types included as separate entries are listed below.
see *tomb* in Egyptian pyramid illustration. →70
altar tomb. →116
beehive tomb, see tholos. →65
chambered tomb. →65
house tomb.
mastaba tomb, see mastaba. →70
passage tomb, see passage grave. →65
portal tomb, see dolmen.
pyramid. →71
rock-cut tomb.
sepulchre.
tholos tomb. →65
tower tomb. →93
tumulus tomb.
wedge-tomb.

tomb sculpture a sculpture which ornaments a tomb.

tombstone see gravestone.
see *tombstone* in Egyptian burial monuments illustration. →70

tomb tower see tower tomb. →93

tomoye a tripart circular symbol from Japanese Samurai heraldry and ancient Shinto religion, similar to a Greek triskelion, depicting the revolution of the universe. →120

ton, 1 metric ton, tonne; an SI unit of weight equal to 1000 kg.
2 long ton; a unit of weight used in Great Britain, equal to 20 hundredweight, 2240 pounds, equivalent to 1016 kg.
3 short ton; a unit of weight used in North America, equal to 20 hundredweight, 2000 pounds, equivalent to 907 kg.
4 see register ton.

tondo 1 a round painting, or a carving set in round space. →122, →123
2 see medallion. →113

tone see colour saturation.

tongue 1 the projection along one edge of a tongue and groove board. →2
2 see return latch. →39

tongue and groove, tongued and grooved, t and g, t&g; referring to joints, boards and other sheet products whose edges are matched with tongue and groove joints.

tongue and groove joint, 1 tongued and grooved, t and g, t&g; a joint for flush timber boarding, chipboard etc. in which each board is milled with a flange or tongue along one long edge and a channel or groove along the other, designed to fit into one another when the boards are laid edge-on as flooring and cladding.
2 see barefaced tongued and grooved joint

tongue and groove boarding 1 see matchboarding. →8
2 see open tongue and groove boarding. →8
3 see rough t and g board. →8

tongue and groove jointing, matching; the milling of the edges of building boards with a tongue and groove.

tongued and grooved see tongue and groove.

tongued and grooved board any building board machined with tongued and grooved edges.

tongued and grooved chipboard chipboard whose edges have been milled with a tongue and groove, used for matched flooring and sheathing.

tonne see ton.

tool 1 a simple implement used to make a job easier, often hand-held.
2 see utility.

tool box a container for tools, often with a closable lid and carrying handles.

tooled finish any stonework finish in which the marks of the tools are evident.

tooling, hacking, scabbling; the working of the surface of exposed concrete or stone with a chisel, point tool or mechanical device to produce a patterned or textured finish or to roughen the surface as a key for a finish.

tool shed an outhouse of light construction for storing agricultural, household and garden implements.

tooth 1 see saw tooth.
2 tooth ornament, see dogtooth. →122
3 granny's, hag's or old woman's tooth, see router plane.

toothed plate connector, bulldog plate; in timber frame construction, a toothed metal plate placed between two timbers bolted together to strengthen the joint. →35

toothed plate fastener see nail plate. →35

toothed washer see tooth washer. →37

toothing 1 the toothed end of a partially laid brickwork wall formed by overlapping alternate courses, used for bonding subsequent work. →21
2 see reverse toothing. →21

tooth ornament see dogtooth. →122

tooth tool see patent claw chisel.

tooth washer, toothed washer; a circular metal washer whose inner or outer edge is stamped with crimped serrations to provide a tight bolted joint by compression. →37
see internal tooth washer. →37
see external tooth washer. →37

topaz 1 a colourless or coloured vitreous aluminium orthosilicate mineral used as gemstones.
2 a shade of yellow brown which takes its name from the colour of the above.

top chord see upper chord. →33

top course tile a special roof tile which is shorter than other tiles, used for the uppermost course in roofing.

top dressing the addition of any mineral, organic or chemical material to the surface of planted and landscaped areas to improve the quality of the soil.

top edge the upper part of a sloping roof plane at a ridge or abutment.

top floor the uppermost storey in a building containing usable habitable space.

top form formwork used for casting and supporting the upper side of concrete slabs, walls etc.; top formwork, in full.

top hung referring to a window, casement or hatch whose opening leaf is hinged at its upper edge.

top-hung casement window, awning window; a window type whose opening casement is hinged at its upper edge. →52

top light 1 a narrow glazed casement at the top of a window unit, hinged at the top. →52
2 any glazing above a main window, partition or door. →60, →111
3 see fanlight.

topographical map a map showing the natural features and contours of a certain area of land.

topography 1 the measuring, surveying and representation in map form of natural and artificial features in the landscape.
2 ground profile, contour; the shape of an area of land according to the changes in vertical level of its surface.

topology 1 a branch of mathematics which deals with the properties of geometrical forms which remain constant under deformation or transformation.
2 the geographical study of historical topography.

topping 1 see concrete topping. →49
2 see wearing course. →62
3 the first stage of the sharpening of a saw by levelling of the tips of its teeth with a file.

topping out the stage in a project when the structure of a building under construction has reached its full height or is completed, often marked by a small on-site ceremony.

top rail the upper framing member of a window casement or door leaf. →52, →111

top raker the uppermost slanting prop in a raking shore.

top reinforcement main reinforcement for a reinforced concrete beam or slab placed near the upper surface to resist tensile forces near beams, fixed ends and cantilevers. →27

topsoil 1 soil occurring at the earth's surface, rich in root, fibrous and organic material.
2 see growing medium. →48

top view see plan view. →127

toran see torana. →68

torana, toran; the ornamental gateway to a Buddhist stupa. →68

torch 1 see soldering torch.
2 a blowtorch, see blowlamp.

torching, rendering, tiering; a traditional practice in tiled and slate roofing whereby lime mortar is laid under the heads of roof tiles and slates as a secondary fastening and to prevent the passage of drifting snow.

tori plural of torus.

torii 1 a Japanese ornamental gateway to a Shinto shrine consisting of a series of beams, the uppermost of which curves upwards, supported on columns; in China it is called a pailou. →120
2 plural form of torus.

torn grain a sawing defect resulting in wood fibres frayed loose at the surface after cutting and converting timber, caused by a blunt saw or wet timber. →1

toroid any three-dimensional geometrical form whose basis is a torus, a doughnut or ring-like tubular formation.

torque the magnitude of an axial twisting or rotating action produced by a force, equal to the actual force multiplied by the perpendicular distance from the centre of the axis about which it acts.

torque wrench a manual wrench with a gauge or meter to indicate the amount of torque transferred to the nut or bolt, and so control its final tightness.

torse see wreath. →124

torse grain see spiral grain. →1

torsion in mechanics, a twisting action on an object caused by two forces working in opposite directions perpendicular to its main axis.

torso 1 a statue of a man or beast lacking limbs and a head.
2 a spiral column in the architecture of the middle ages. →114

tortil see wreath. →124

tortillion a rod or small round stump of rolled paper sharpened at one end, used in pencil and charcoal drawing for smoothing tones and various shading effects.

tortuous flow see turbulent flow.

torus 1 a three-dimensional shape formed by the rotation of a circle or conic section through 360° around a point; plural is tori.
2 a decorative convex moulding, larger than an astragal, found in classical bases. →14, →80, →115
3 see spira. →81

Torx head screw a screw whose head has a patented star-shaped or serrated indentation, tightened with a special screw bit, usually used on finishing and precision work. →36

total cost, overall cost; **1** a cost which has all factors included.
2 the cost of all works, labour, construction materials and design in a construction project.

total going, run (Am.), going; the horizontal dimension of a stair flight as measured on plan. →45

touch dry, dry to touch; in painting, a stage in drying at which finger marks will not be left on the painted surface.

touching up in painting and decorating, the covering of small missed or damaged areas with paint after the main body of painting work has been carried out.

toughened glass, 1 tempered glass; glass that has been heated and then cooled rapidly during manufacture to produce controlled internal stresses as strengthening and to make it less dangerous on shattering; cf. annealed glass. →53
2 see chemically strengthened glass.
3 see heat-soaked glass.

toughness the property of a material to withstand repeated deformations without breaking, through ductility and tensile strength.

Toulouse cross see cross of Toulouse. →118

tourelle see turret. →104

touret see turret. →104

tourmaline a colourful boron aluminium silicate mineral used for its unusual thermoelectrical properties and as a gemstone.

tow rough fibrous material made from hemp and flax used for caulking horizontal log buildings.

towel rail 1 a rail fixed near a basin, bath or shower, on which a towel is hung for use and to dry.
2 drying rail; a series of pipes connected to a hot water supply to provide warming in a bathroom, on which towels and other household fabrics are hung to dry.

tower any tall, slender structure, building or part of a building; types included as separate entries are listed below.
church tower. →26
belltower, belfry. →102
clocktower.
control tower.
cooling tower.
drum tower, round tower. →103
gate tower.
high-rise building, high-rise block. →61
lookout tower, observation tower, watch-tower. →103
pele tower, peel tower.
pylon. →32
rood tower.

stair tower. →98
tomb tower, see tower tomb. →93
water tower.
watch-tower, see lookout tower. →103

tower block a tall apartment block containing a number of flats on many floors. →61

tower bolt a large barrel bolt.

tower crane a high site crane with hoisting equipment, a control booth and a counterweighted boom or jib fixed atop a tall trussed stanchion, either static or running on rails.

tower house a fortified medieval dwelling in the form of a simple masonry tower containing stores on the ground floor and living quarters above, found especially in Scotland and Ireland.

tower tomb, tomb tower; a family tomb in the form of a masonry tower, built above ground, often with a number of stories with separate burial chambers. →93

towing path see towpath. →31

town an organized and regularly built urban settlement with housing, services and employment for its inhabitants, and some form of elected independent administrative body.

town centre the focal area of a town, usually its centre of business, culture, administration, entertainment and shopping.

town church the principal church of a town.

town council see council.

town gas combustible gas manufactured from the distillation of coal or oil and burnt to produce energy for domestic and industrial use; it has been largely superseded by natural gas.

town hall 1 a building or group of buildings in a town, used for local government administration, the seat of the town council.
2 see prytaneum. →92

town house a tall narrow residential building which is part of a row, often more than two storeys in height and situated in the residential area of a town or city. →61

town plan 1 the layout of streets and activities in a town; a statutory document which stipulates types of use, land use restrictions, layout of areas for residential and other forms of use etc.
see Hippodamian system. →94
2 see grid plan. →94
3 see ideal city. →105
4 see linear city. →105
5 see garden city. →105

town planner, planner; a person or organization responsible for designing and developing town, area and general plans.

town planning see city planning.

town planning competition see planning competition.

town planning department, planning department, planning office; the administrative department of a local authority which prepares town plans for the regional area.

town planning federation see International Federation for Housing and Planning.

townscape the visual and spatial quality of streets, buildings, parks, squares and other elements in a built-up area.

Town truss a type of lattice beam patented by Ithiel Town in 1820, consisting of a series of fairly densely spaced crossing diagonals tied between an upper and lower chord. →33

towpath, towing path; a road or path which runs along the banks of a canal or river, originally used for the towing of barges by humans or horses. →31

toxicity the measure of the poisonousness of a material or substance with regard to living organisms.

toxic waste waste material or products left over from a process or use which may pose a contamination hazard to the environment and should be disposed of using special measures.

TPE thermoplastic elastomer.

TPI the fineness of the cutting blade of a saw, measured in teeth per inch.

trabeated describing a structural system based on the use of columns and beams; see post and beam construction.

trabeated construction see post and beam construction. →27, →28

trabes Lat.; see trabs. →47

trabs, trabes; Lat.; a large principal beam, often a main rafter or architrave in classical architecture, or one supporting a crucifix in a church. →47

tracer a large masonry chisel used for splitting rock.

tracery Gothic ornamental stone and woodwork decoration carved into an intricate vertical and interwoven framework of ribs for the upper parts of openings such as windows or perforated screens, or for the surface of vaults and walls. →110
see *types of Gothic tracery* illustration; types included as separate entries are listed below. →110
bar tracery.
blind tracery, blank tracery.
branch tracery, astwerk.
decorated tracery.
fan tracery, fanwork.
flamboyant tracery.
flowing, curvilinear, undulating tracery.
geometrical tracery, geometric tracery.
intersecting tracery.
Kentish tracery.
loop tracery.
rectilinear, panel, perpendicular tracery.
plate tracery.
reticulated tracery.
Y-tracery.

trachelion, necking, trachelium; the upper part of the shaft of a classical Doric column, below the shaft ring and above the hypotrachelion; sometimes also called a collarino. →81

trachelium see trachelion. →81

trachytic tuff see trass.

tracing the transferring of an image onto translucent sheet by drawing through or copying information from a base drawing placed under.

tracing paper paper with a degree of transparency or translucency, used for sketching and tracing out designs.

track 1 a preformed steel or plastics section for guiding and supporting rollers in the operating mechanism of a sliding door, curtain etc.
2 see lighting track.
3 see suspension track.
4 path; a small unpaved road or route.
5 line; an assembly of rails, sleepers and fixings for a rail-transport system.

TRADA roof truss a standardized timber roof truss, developed in Britain to make use of truss plates, used as a primary truss on which purlins may rest.

trade 1 one of the various skilled or semi-skilled technical on-site occupations, often demanding training, required in the construction of a building.
2 see commerce.

trade contractor see specialized contractor.

trade discount a reduction in prices offered by a supplier to trade customers from which the client may be entitled to benefit under terms of a building contract.

trade effluent 1 contaminated water discharged as waste from commercial premises.
2 see commercial waste.

trade mark, brand; a symbol or figure, often patented or under copyright, used by a company for their products.

trade name the name by which a product or material is sold.

trade secret a matter, formula, material, construction or strategy kept secret from the competitors of a commercial enterprise.

trades foreman a contractor's representative responsible for supervising construction work on site carried out by specific tradesmen.

tradesman a person skilled in a particular job of work, employed on a construction site.

trades union, trade union; an organized body which looks after the interests and rights of the labour force of a particular trade or profession.

trade union see trades union.

trade waste see commercial waste.

trading company, trading house; a company which buys and sells goods.

trading house see trading company.

trading standards department see fair-trading, department of.

traditional building 1 see vernacular architecture.
2 see rustic architecture.
see *traditional timber structures* illustration. →7
see *prehistoric structures* illustration. →65

traffic 1 systems and processes relating to the mass movement, circulation and conveyance of people, motor vehicles and goods.
2 see telephone traffic.

traffic assignment see trip assignment.

traffic barrier see vehicular barrier.

traffic control see traffic management.

traffic engineering the design and construction of roads and associated systems for vehicular traffic.

traffic island 1 in traffic design, a raised area of carriageway designed to direct or divert traffic at a road junction. →63
2 see refuge. →63

traffic lane in road design, a marked area of carriageway reserved for a single line of vehicles moving in the same direction; types included as separate entries are listed below. →63
acceleration lane, see merging lane.
bicycle lane, see cycle lane.
bus lane.
climbing lane.
crawler lane, see climbing lane.
cycle lane.
deceleration lane, see diverging lane.
diverging lane.
merging lane.
overtaking lane.
taxi lane.

traffic light see traffic signal. →64

traffic management the organization of traffic movement within a given street system by arranging for efficient traffic flow, controlling intersections and regulating the times and location of parking; also known as traffic control.

traffic noise noise pollution from vehicular traffic.

traffic plan, 1 transportation plan (Am.); outline urban design proposals for various transportation systems for a particular area based on study of living and working patterns, population densities, behavioural models and land use.
2 traffic scheme; designs, drawings and other documents outlining the functioning of a traffic system for a particular district.

traffic planning, transportation planning (Am.); planning for traffic, including action to improve accessibility within urban areas by reducing traffic congestion and upgrading and extending the road system.

traffic scheme 1 see traffic plan.
2 see traffic system.

traffic sign see road sign.

traffic signal, traffic light; in traffic management, a series of coloured lights arranged vertically, indicating whether traffic may move or is obliged to stop; other similar lights for directing traffic. →64

traffic study, transportation study (Am.); in town planning, a survey of traffic routes, destinations, the influence of land use on traffic systems and the evaluation of existing traffic capacity.

traffic system the system of roads, markings, traffic lights, signs and other control devices in a particular district.

traffic volume in design for road and traffic systems, the number of vehicles or pedestrians passing a given point on a lane or carriageway over a given time span.

trailer see caravan.

trailer mixer a mobile concrete mixer designed to be towed by a vehicle.

trailer park see caravan site.

train a mode of public rail transport consisting of a number of passenger wagons pulled by a locomotive.

training centre a building or complex for the instruction of professions, occupations, specialist tasks, crafts etc.

tram, tramcar, streetcar; a passenger vehicle in a tramway system.

tramcar see tram.

Trametes pini see red ring rot.

tramline see tramway.

trammel 1 a compass-like device used as a guide for making an elliptical plastering moulding. →14
2 see beam compass.

trammel rod a timber strip used in conjunction with a trammel for making an elliptical plastering moulding. →14

tramway, tramline; an urban rail-transport passenger system in which special vehicles run on tracks laid down in the streets, usually powered by overhead electricity.

transaction in computing, an input record used to update an existing file.

transaction file a computer file of transaction records to be processed against a master file.

transenna a perforated screen in an early Christian church; originally referring to early forms of window with small panes made from thin sheets of translucent marble or alabaster. →96, →111

transept the transverse space to either side of the crossing in a cruciform church or cathedral, the 'arms' of the cross which meet the nave and chancel.
see *Carolingian abbey church* illustration. →98
see *Romanesque church* illustration. →99
see *Gothic cathedral* illustration. →100

transfer 1 in prestressed concrete, the transfer of loading from the concrete to the prestressing tendons.
2 see detensioning.
3 see data transfer.
4 see bank transfer.
5 patterns, lettering, symbols or figures, vehicles and plants printed onto thin adhesive transparent plastic sheet and added as embellishment to drawings.

transfer file a computer file format for transferring data from one device or program to another.

transfer lettering in drawing and graphic design, lettering of varying styles and sizes applied to a drawing by rubbing against the backing sheet on which it is printed.

transfer moulding a method of forming thermoplastics and thermosetting plastics products by heating material in a mould then applying pressure to force it through channels into its final shape; used for delicate castings.

transformer an electrical device for transmuting electrical energy to a different voltage and current level with minimal power loss.

transit see theodolite.

transit mixer see truck mixer.

transitional igneous rock see hypabyssal rock.

transitional style a style in architecture which occurs during the change from one style to another, such as from Romanesque to Gothic or from Gothic to Renaissance.

translucency, obscurance; the property of a material to allow the passage of light without being fully transparent.
translucent referring to a material which allows the passage of light but provides visual obscurance.
translucent glass see diffuse reflection glass.
transmission the passing of radiation, pressure waves and similar migrations through a medium.
transmittance 1 see light transmittance.
2 see thermal transmittance.
transom, transome; a horizontal framing member in a window or door frame, between two openable panels such as a door and fanlight above, or between two sashes in the same frame; also the horizontal bar in a cross. →110, →111
transome see transom. →111
transom light see fanlight.
transom window see fanlight.
transparency 1 the property of a material which permits the undiffused passage of light through it.
2 a sheet of clear acrylic or other plastic with an image or text printed on one side; used in conjunction with an overhead projector or other projecting device.
3 a print applied to transparent or translucent material such as plastics or paper.
transparent, clear; a description of materials such as clear glass or plastics which permit the undiffused passage of light.
transparent gold ochre see Turner's yellow.
transparent mirror glass glass treated with a thin metallic foil to reflect most of the light which falls on it, rendering it transparent under certain lighting conditions and a mirror under others.
transparent oxide of chromium see viridian.
transport 1 vehicular conveyance, associated infrastructure etc., classified by vehicular mode such as air transport, rail transport.
2 see mode of transport.
3 see vehicle.
transportability the ability of components, constructions or plant to be easily transported.
transportation the action of conveying people, animals or goods in vehicles.
transportation charge see delivery charge.
transportation plan see traffic plan.
transportation planning see traffic planning.
transportation study see traffic study.
transportation system the system of roads, public and private transport, terminals, bus stops etc. for a particular area; the means by which people and goods are conveyed, the organization of this.
transport planning physical planning for transport systems.
transtrum a wooden transverse, cross or tie beam in Roman roof construction. →47
transverse arch 1 one of a series of arches crossing the main body of a vaulted building such as a Romanesque basilica church, supported on columns on ether side of the nave; any similar or crosswise arch in a modern structure. →25
2 an arch in a groin, rib or fan vaulted roof which separates one vaulted bay from another. →101
transverse beam see cross beam.
transverse joint see cross joint. →20
transverse reinforcement see lateral reinforcement. →27
transverse rib 1 a lateral protrusion in a reinforcing bar.
2 arc doubleau; a rib which runs across the space at the edge of a rib vault. →101
transverse ridge rib a horizontal rib which runs across the space at the ridge of a rib vault. →101
transverse section, cross-section; a drawing representing a cut through the shorter dimension of a site, building or object.
transverse warping see cup. →1
transverse wave a waveform in which displacement is perpendicular to the direction of propagation.
trap a device or construction at a drain, gully or drainage outlet, filled with water to prevent the passage of foul air from a sewer back into the building or area.
trapdoor 1 a horizontal hinged hatch in a floor.
2 see access door.
trapdoor handle a device or fitting for pulling opening a trapdoor.
trapezium a planar four-sided figure in which only two sides are parallel.
trapezoid a planar four-sided figure in which no sides are parallel.
trapless gully a drainage gully with no trap, through which gases from the drain can freely escape.
trapped gully a gully containing a trap to prevent gases and odours escaping from the drain to which it is connected.
trapped purlin see clasped purlin.
traprock see diabase.
trashcan see refuse bin.
trass, trachytic tuff; a variety of volcanic tuff which, by virtue of its hydraulic properties, is often used as an admixture in cement in underwater construction.
trave see bay. →25, →101
travelled way the part of a road used by continuous vehicular traffic, excluding stopping places, bus lanes and the like. →63
traverse in military architecture, a wall or building which divides a line of defence into two independent units.
traversing bridge see retractable bridge. →64
travertine a variety of porous, pale-coloured limestone, tufa, deposited by springwater, often containing fossils; used in building for decorative stonework and ornament.
tray see metal tray.
tray decking see profiled sheeting. →49
trayle see vignette. →82
tread the horizontal upper surface of a step, or the shallow platform which forms a step. →45
parallel tread, see flier. →45
see prefabricated tread.
tapered tread, see tapered step. →45
wheel tread, see winder. →45
treadmill a large wooden wheel traditionally used to provide the power for hoisting, lifting etc., operated by the action of men walking inside it.
tread plate see chequerplate. →34
tread unit see prefabricated tread.
tread width in stair design, the horizontal distance from the nosing to the rear edge of a tread, often greater than the going.
treasury see thesauros. →84
see *prehistoric structures* illustration. →65
see *apteral temple* illustration. →84
treated plywood plywood whose veneers or adhesive have been treated with preservatives or resins.
treatment 1 the application of a process or material to a surface, object or component in order to improve its properties.
2 see acoustic treatment.
3 see surface treatment.
4 see air treatment.
treatment bath a hospital bath designed for hydrotherapy.
trecento the 1300s in Italian art and architecture.
tree one of a vast range of large plants with a woody stem and foliage, usually growing to a height of over 5 m, planted as landscaping and used as a source of wood and other products. →1
see *parts of a tree* illustration. →1
see list of species of tree from which softwood is obtained under **softwood**.
see list of species of tree from which hardwood is obtained under **hardwood**.

tree of Buddha, bodhi tree; the sacred fig tree [*Ficus religiosa*] under which Buddha gained enlightenment, stylizations of which are typical motifs in eastern art and decoration. →121

Tree of Jesse a religious ornamental motif representing the family tree of Christ growing from Jesse, father of David, who is lying prostrate.

tree of life 1 a symbolic figure appearing in many different forms in ornament and art, often a Y-shaped motif with an extra vertical limb or an abstracted depiction of a real tree. →117, →121
2 the carnauba palm, see carnauba wax.

tree store a traditional Lappish timber food store constructed on top of a post or severed trunk of a tree to discourage unwanted visitors.

trefoil 1 a decorative design consisting of three leaf motifs or lobes radiating outwards from a point. →108, →109
2 see pointed trefoil. →108

trefoil arch an arch composed of three lobes or foils in a cloverleaf arrangement. →24

trefoil cross see cross botonée. →117

trefoil moulding a decorative moulding with a series of trefoil motifs joined end on end; primarily found in heraldic designs; also called cloverleaf moulding. →125

trellis a loose screen with a grid or rows of jointed timber strips for supporting climbing plants.

tremie concrete underwater concrete pumped into place using a tremie, a long flexible pipe with a funnel-shaped upper end into which concrete is poured, whose other end is located in the fresh concrete which has already been placed.

tremie concreting the process of underwater concreting using a tremie; see above.

trenail a large hardwood pin, peg or nail used for fastening traditional timber joints. →3

trench a long, narrow excavation.

trenched joint see single notched joint. →4

trenched purlin see through purlin.

trench-fill foundation a rough foundation constructed by excavating a longitudinal excavation, laying reinforcing bars, and filling it with concrete, without the need for formwork. →29

trenching saw see grooving saw.

trench sheeting see sheet piling. →29

trestle see saw horse.

trial hole see trial pit.

trial period any period over which an employee, product or building is tested for suitability before any firmer action is taken.

trial pile 1 in foundation technology, a pile sunk prior to foundation construction to determine the suitability of its functioning and design.
2 see test pile.
3 see preliminary pile.

trial pit, trial hole, test pit (Am.); in site investigation, an excavation made on site prior to commencement of construction to ascertain the soil type, existing services, depth of bedrock etc.

triangle a planar regular or irregular three-sided figure; a regular triangle is known as equilateral; see below. →108
equilateral triangle. →108
isosceles triangle. →108
reuleaux triangle. →108
right-angled triangle.

triangular arch an arch composed of two flat leaning slabs which meet at an apex to form a triangular opening; not a true arch. →23

triangular fillet see angle fillet. →49

triangular pediment a Renaissance, Baroque or Neoclassical pediment with a central apex, cf. segmental pediment. →112
a broken-apex pediment, see open pediment. →112
see broken segmental pediment. →112

triangulation 1 a method of surveying and mapping which employs trigonometry to divide an area into a grid of triangles between known fixed points.
2 in structures, the use of diagonal struts in pin-jointed frames to provide stiffening.
3 in drawing composition, the use of diagonals to define key points and assess proportions.

tribelon a triple-arched opening at the esonarthex of a medieval church. →96, →99

tribunal 1 a platform or stage from which Roman magistrates or military leaders made speeches; a tribune.
2 Latin form of 'tribune'.

tribunal arch an upper arch between the choir and apse of a church or basilica. →99

tribune 1 an apse in a basilica. →93
2 a gallery in a church above a side aisle and opening out onto a nave.
3 an important room in an Italian villa, a balcony or gallery therein.
4 a raised platform for a speaker; see tribunal.
5 see cathedra. →95

triceps 'three-headed' (Lat.); an ancient geometrical symbol with three lozenge shapes radiating out from a point, arranged in a triangular formation; in Nordic and Anglo-Saxon cultures symbolic of divine power, now the logo of the Mitsubishi company. →108

trickle ventilator a venting device incorporated into a high performance window unit to permit ventilation without draught caused by an opening. →52

triclinium 1 Lat.; a Roman dining room or other space in which couches surround a table on three sides. →88
2 see triclinium aestivum.

triclinium aestivum, summer triclinium; Lat.; an open outdoor dining space in a Roman atrium dwelling. →88

triconch church, three-apsed church; a form of long church whose choir terminates in three apses, arranged in a trefoil arrangement around the crossing. →99

trident in ornament and decoration, a three-pronged spear as brandished by the Roman sea-god Neptune (Poseidon in Greek mythology) and Britannia. →120

trifoliated arch 1 a decorative arch whose intrados is composed of three lobes or foils in a cloverleaf arrangement, and whose extrados is a round or pointed arch; especially found in Gothic architecture. →23, →110
2 see round trifoliated arch. →23
3 see pointed trifoliated arch. →23

Trifolium repens white clover, see cloverleaf, shamrock. →121

triforium in Romanesque or Early Gothic religious architecture, an inwardly facing open wall passage, often arcaded, running above the nave arcade below clerestory level in a cathedral. →100

triglyph 1 in classical architecture, one of a series of grooved blocks or panels which line a Doric frieze and are separated by metopes. →78
see *triglyph* in classical orders illustration. →78, →79
2 see glyph. →78

triglyphs, controversy of see corner contraction. →77

trigonometric based on or dealing with trigonometry.

trigonometry a branch of mathematics which deals with the relationship between the sides and angles in a triangle.

trilith see trilithon.

trilithon, trilith; a prehistoric structure constructed from two large blocks of rough stone, monoliths, with a large lintel placed between them.

trillion 1 one million billion, 10^{18} in UK and Germany.
2 see billion.

trim 1 a narrow strip of wood or other material used in construction as surface decoration or for covering a joint or seam.
see *timber trim* illustration. →2

2 a generic term for all thin sections of timber or other material attached as mouldings, beads, rails, and cover strips.
3 a strip of material used to cover a gap between frame and adjacent construction in a window or door opening, an architrave.
4 see door trim.
5 see window trim. →53
6 see moulding.
7 see perimeter trim. →60
8 see timber trim. →2

trimetric projection 1 'three measurements'; in general, any axonometric or oblique projection drawing in which lines parallel to all three main axes are drawn at different scales; scales and angles are chosen to produce the most realistic depictions. →127
2 in particular, any of a number of standardized axonometric projections in which the X and Y axes are drawn at different angles above the horizontal and the Z axis is vertical; all three axes have different scales. →127

trimmed beam, trimmed joist; in timber frame construction, a beam shortened to accommodate an opening or otherwise cropped, carried by a trimmer joist or beam at the edge of the opening. →4

trimmed joist see trimmed beam. →4

trimmed rafter in timber roof construction, a rafter shortened to accommodate an opening in the frame, carried by a trimmer at the edge of the opening.

trimmed veneer a sheet of veneer of which at least one edge has been cut straight before gluing.

trimmer, trimmer beam; in timber-framed construction, a lateral member which frames the edge of an opening in a floor or roof, and bears the ends of trimmed joists. →4

trimmer beam see trimmer. →4

trimmer joist in timber frame construction, a lateral floor joist which frames the edge of an opening and from which trimmed rafters are supported, thus acting as a trimmer. →4

trimmer's hammer a lightweight hammer used by a flooring carpenter. →40

trimming 1 the removal of the ends of batches of converted timber sections to produce pieces of the same lengths for shipping and sale.
2 in timber frame construction, the cutting and framing of timbers around an opening. →4

trimming axe see masonry axe. →40

trimming joist in framed floor and wall construction, a joist bounding an opening, from which trimmers are supported. →4

trimming knife, general purpose knife, Stanley knife, utility knife; a knife used by workmen, designers and modelmakers for cutting sheet material such as card and linoleum, with an interchangeable blade held in a stocky metal or plastic handle.

trimming rafter in timber roof construction, a rafter, from which trimmers are supported, which bounds an opening in the roof.

trinacria an ancient triangular symbol with three radiating limbs, as found in Celtic and other traditional art; the Greek name for Sicily.

tringle see listel. →14

Trinidad bitumen a form of lake asphalt which used to be imported from Trinidad.

trinity see Holy Trinity. →119

trinitas Lat.; see Holy Trinity. →119

trioxide an oxide with three atoms of oxygen in its chemical formula.
see arsenic trioxide.

tripartite vault a masonry vault sprung on three points of support, triangular in plan and composed of three curved roof surfaces. →26

trip assignment, traffic assignment; in traffic planning, the prediction or estimation of routes taken for trips using a series of models.

trip distribution in traffic planning, the prediction or estimation of the arrivals and departures of trips between specified zones using a series of models.

trip-end estimation see trip generation.

trip-end model in traffic planning, a modal split model applied to determine which destinations are achievable with each mode of transport.

trip generation, trip-end estimation; in traffic planning, a set of models used to estimate the total number of arrivals and departures for each zone of a specific area.

tri-phosphor lamp a fluorescent lamp with good colour rendering and circuit efficacy whose colour spectrum is made up of three distinct peaks.

trip-interchange model in traffic planning, a modal split model applied to determine which mode of transport is used for a specified trip.

triple cross 1 a cross whose stem is crossed by three horizontal bars. →117
2 western triple cross, see papal cross. →117

triple-glazed unit a sealed glazed unit made of three parallel sheets of glass sealed around air gaps.

triple-glazed window a window thermally insulated with three successive panes of glass, either forming a sealed unit, glazed individually or a combination of the two.

triple glazing glazing in which three parallel layers of glass separate the inside and outside of a building to provide thermal and acoustic insulation.

triple roof see trussed roof. →33

Triplochiton scleroxylon see obeche.

tripod a portable three-legged support used as an adjustable but steady mounting for an optical instrument.

trip switch 1 see overload trip.
2 see circuit breaker.

triptych an altarpiece or other work of art consisting of three panels, usually hinged together; see diptych, polyptych. →116

triquetra a three-pointed decorative motif formed by the intersection of three arcs; in Christian art it is the symbol of the Holy Trinity, when inscribed in a circle it symbolizes eternity. →108

triradiant halo, three-rayed nimbus; a crossed halo surrounding the head of a depicted sacred figure. →119

triregnum see tiara. →122

triskele see triskelion. →119

triskelion, triskele; a decorative motif consisting of three bent legs radiating outwards from a common centre point, in use since ancient times; in the Middle Ages used as a symbol of the Holy Trinity. →119

tristram see Bowen knot. →123

tristyle in classical architecture, a portico which has three supporting columns. →77

Triticum vulgare wheat, see golden wheat.

tritium a radioactive isotope of hydrogen.

triumphal arch (Lat. arcus triumphalis); a large arched monument constructed in a public urban place to commemorate a great event, usually a victory in war. →93

triumphal gate see porta triumphalis.

triumphalis see porta triumphalis.

trivium Lat.; an urban place or square, originally a Roman forum, at which three main radial roads meet.

trochilus 1 a deeply recessed moulding, ovoid in cross-section; also called gorge. →14
2 see scotia. →14, →80

trompe l'oeil see illusionism.

trophy sculpted decoration depicting helmets, garlands, flags or weapons, signifying the celebration of victory in battle. →122

trough cistern see flushing trough.

troughed sheet roofing metal and plastics profiled sheet roofing formed with a series of stiffening toothed protrusions in profile; steel troughed sheeting has structural strength and is often used for decking.

troughed sheeting see profiled sheeting.

trough mould a formwork mould for producing an elongated recess or channel in a concrete slab.

trough roof see M-roof. →46

trough urinal a urinal consisting of a wall-hung channel fixed at a suitable height to collect discharge.

trough vault a barrel vault whose ends are closed with vaults. →25

trowel a hand tool for the application, jointing, smoothing and shaping of plaster, filler, mortar etc. by means of a flat metal blade fixed to a short handle; types included as separate entries are listed below. →43
see *trowels* illustration. →43
angle trowel. →43
bricklayer's trowel, brick trowel. →43
corner trowel, see angle trowel. →43
external angle trowel. →43
finishing trowel. →43
gauging trowel. →43
helicopter, see power trowel.
internal angle trowel, inside corner trowel. →43
jointing trowel. →43
laying-on trowel, see plasterer's trowel. →43
machine trowel, see power trowel.
margin trowel. →43
mason's trowel, masonry trowel, see bricklayer's trowel. →43
mechanical trowel, see power trowel.
notched trowel. →43
outside corner trowel, see external angle trowel. →43
plasterer's trowel. →43
power trowel.
rotary trowel, see power trowel.
smoothing trowel, see finishing trowel. →43
spatula. →43
square external angle trowel. →43
square internal angle trowel. →43
Swiss trowel.
twitcher trowel, twitcher. →43

trowel-finished rendering rendering whose wet surface has been worked with a hand-held trowel to produce a smooth, even finish.

trowelled finish a finish for concrete produced by smoothing with a power or hand trowel.

trowelled plastering see hand-plastering.

troy ounce a traditional unit of weight used by dealers in precious metals, equivalent to 31.315 g.

Troytown see Cretan maze. →123

truck see lorry.

truck mixer, 1 transit mixer; a concrete mixer attached to a vehicle, which can mix the concrete in transit to site.
2 see agitating vehicle.

true arch a masonry arch constructed from wedge-shaped stones supporting overlying loads by internal compressive forces. →24

true fresco see buon fresco.

true-lover's knot see Bowen knot. →123

true view a projection drawing showing only those features which lie on a plane parallel to the projection plane.

trulay rope a proprietary name for preformed rope.

trulli plural form of trullo.

trullisatio see roughcast.

trullo, pl. trulli; a traditional rendered stone dwelling in Apulia, southern Italy, in which square chambers are roofed with conical vaulted roofs.

trumeau a masonry column, pillar or pier between two openings, often in religious buildings supporting the centre of the tympanum in an arched doorway or window. →113

trumeau figure a carved statuesque figure decorating a trumeau, depicting a religious person or saint. →113

trumpet capital a Gothic capital whose diameter increases in size towards the top; also called a bell capital. →115

trumpet interchange see trumpet junction. →63

trumpet junction 1 a flyover road junction in which one major road meets another obliquely or at right angles, with a loop ramp and slip roads permitting free flow of traffic in all directions; also called a trumpet interchange. →63
2 see directional T junction. →63
3 see double trumpet junction. →63

trunk the main stem of a tree. →1

trunking, raceway (Am.); openable casing for cables and wiring in an electric installation.

trunnel see gutta. →78

truss, 1 lattice structure; a structural element consisting of a number of members pin-jointed at their ends to form a beam which resists loads by means of triangulation; types included as separate entries are listed below. →33
2 in particular one of steel or timber used for supporting floors and roofs. →33
see *types of truss* illustration. →33
arch braced roof truss.
arched truss, arch truss, see trussed arch. →33
attic truss. →33
base cruck truss.
Belfast truss. →33
Belgian truss, see fink truss. →33
bowstring truss. →33
closed cruck truss.
collar and tie beam truss. →33
composite truss.
couple truss, see coupled rafters. →33
cruck truss.
double hammer beam truss.
fan truss. →33
Fink truss. →33
fish-bellied truss. →33
flat top truss, flat truss. →33
French truss, see fink truss. →33
full cruck truss, see closed cruck truss.
half truss.
hammer-beam roof truss. →33
Howe truss. →33
joggle truss.
king post roof truss. →33
mansard roof truss. →33
open cruck truss.
plane truss.
polygonal truss. →33
Pratt truss. →33
principal roof truss. →33
queen post truss. →33
queen strut roof truss. →33
roof truss.
scissors truss. →33
secondary roof truss.
tie beam truss. →33
timber truss.
Town truss. →33
TRADA roof truss.
Vierendeel truss. →33
Warren truss. →33
W truss, see fink truss. →33

trussed arch a roof truss in which both upper and lower chords are arches, with diagonal web members between; also known as an arch truss. →33

trussed arch bridge 1 a steel arch bridge whose main arch is a lattice or trussed structure, carrying a series of members supporting the deck. →32
2 see spandrel braced arch bridge. →32

trussed beam, framed beam, lattice beam; a compound beam of upper and lower chords which take compression and tension stresses respectively, and intermediate triangulated struts which hold them apart. →33
see *traditional trussed beam* illustration. →7
see *types of truss* illustration and list of types of roof truss under **truss**. →33

trussed bridge a bridge whose main structural support is a trussed beam; types included as separate entries are listed below.
bowstring bridge. →32
spandrel braced arch bridge. →32
trussed arch bridge. →32
trussed construction any triangulated frame construction braced to form a rigid loadbearing structure.
trussed purlin a trussed beam which functions as a purlin. →33
trussed purlin roof a roof with purlins which are trussed beams. →33
trussed rafter roof a pitched roof with all opposite pairs of common rafters triangularly braced. →33
trussed rafters in pitched roof construction, coupled rafters with or without subsidiary supporting or bracing members. →33
trussed roof, triple roof; a roof structure of roof trusses held together by purlins. →33
truss-out scaffolding scaffolding supported by and projecting from the building for which it has been erected, used where the ground cannot provide support.
truss plate see nail plate. →35
truss plate construction timber frame construction in which timber members are held together by truss plates.
try and mitre square, combination square; an adjustable carpenter's tool used as a try square, mitre square, level, marking gauge plumb, and straight edge.
trying plane see jointer plane.
try square a measuring instrument for marking lines perpendicular to a surface or checking perpendicularity, consisting of a wooden stock and straight metal blade fixed at right angles to one another.
T-section, T-bar, tee section; a structural steel section formed by rolling, whose uniform cross-section resembles a letter T with equal width of flanges. →34
Tsing see Ching.
T-square a T-shaped drawing instrument for ruling straight parallel lines, with a wooden or plastic ruler and perpendicular piece guided by hooking it over the edge of a drawing board or table. →130
Tsuga spp. see hemlock.
Tsuga canadensis, see eastern hemlock.
Tsuga heterophylla, see western hemlock.
tube 1 any rigid hollow product of plastics, ceramic or metal, used for structure, framing, electrical protection, for conveying liquids or gases etc.
2 see fluorescent lamp.
3 see neon tube.
4 the underground railway in London.
tube conveyor, pneumatic document conveyor; an in-house system for conveying light goods such as documents or money in sealed units along pipelines from one room or floor to another, driven by compressed air.
tube station see underground railway station.
tubular bow saw, forester's saw, log saw, Swedish saw; a metal-framed bow saw used for cutting up logs and other rough work.
tubular pile see pipe pile. →29
tubular saw see hole saw. →42
tubular scaffolding scaffolding of steel or aluminium tubes, often with proprietary jointing and shackles, supporting scaffolding boards or grilles.
tubular section see hollow section. →34
tubulus (Lat.); a Roman clay pipe of relatively even diameter, especially one for distributing hot air in a hypocaust.
tuck-in in bituminous roofing, the edge of a sheet of bitumen felt skirting tucked into a chase in an abutment.
tuck pointing in brickwork jointing, light-coloured mortar pushed into darker coloured pointing to create the illusion of thin joints between bricks.
Tudor arch, 1 four-centred pointed arch; a pointed arch composed of four arc segments struck from different points, sometimes with straight upper edges. →24
2 see pseudo four-centred arch.
Tudor architecture architecture in England during the reign of the Tudors (Henry VII–Elizabeth I, 1485–1603), evident principally in secular palaces and country houses, and characterized by the gradual transition from Gothic to Renaissance elements.
Tudor flower an English Gothic decorative motif depicting a stylized ivy leaf. →82, →121
Tudor rose a decorative design of a red and white rose combined in a single motif, the symbol of a united England after 1485. →121
tufa a porous sedimentary rock, usually limestone, formed from the deposits of mineral enriched springs or pools; see calcareous tufa.
tuff, 1 volcanic tuff, tephra; volcanic rock formed by the consolidation of ash and other ejected products of volcanic action, used as building stone.
2 trachytic tuff, see trass.
3 welded tuff, see ignimbrite.
tuffite rock consisting of volcanic tuff mixed with sedimentary rock.
tufted carpet a type of carpet with pile tufts mechanically inserted into a prewoven backing by needles.
tulipwood, American whitewood, canary wood, yellow poplar; [*Liriodendron tulipifera*] a hardwood from North America and Europe with soft greenish brown timber, used for plywood and interior furniture.
Tum see Atum. →74
tumble drier a domestic appliance which dries washed laundry with warm air in a slowly rotating drum.
tumbler one of a number of pivoted pins or discs which holds the bolt in a lock mechanism fast until lifted with a suitable key.
tumulus see barrow.
tumulus tomb an Etruscan tomb-type consisting of a burial mound surrounded by a stone base.
tung oil, China wood oil; a high quality drying oil pressed from the nuts of the Chinese trees *Aleurites fordii* and *Aleurites montana*, used as a vehicle in industrial varnishes to produce tough, strong coatings.
tungsten, wolfram; a heavy, grey metal, **W**, which has a high melting point, used for the filaments of electric lamps and as an alloy in steel.
tungsten carbide a very hard alloy of the metal tungsten used for tipping the edges of cutting tools.
tungsten-halogen lamp see halogen lamp.
tungsten inert-gas arc welding see TIG welding.
tungsten steel steel alloyed with tungsten and small quantities of carbon.
tunnel a subterranean passage excavated to provide a pedestrian or vehicular route beneath an obstacle.
tunnel formwork see apartment formwork.
tunnel shower a communal showering space with a row of shower nozzles, used at sports and recreational facilities, schools etc.
tunnel vault see barrel vault. →25
tunnland a traditional Scandinavian unit of land area equal to 32 kapplands or 4936.4 m^2.
tupelo, black gum (Am.); [*Nyssa spp.*] a lightweight hardwood from North America with grey sapwood and creamy yellow heartwood; used for railway sleepers, flooring, furniture and plywood.
turbulent flow, eddy flow, sinuous flow, tortuous flow; in hydraulics, the unsteady and swirling flow of a liquid when moving at high velocity.
turette see turret. →104
turf roof, 1 grass roof; a roof whose weatherproofing is provided by growing turf laid over a waterproof membrane. →48
2 see green roof. →48

Turkey blue see Delft blue.
Turkey red see blood red.
Turkish blue see Delft blue.
Turkish red see blood red.
turn see thumb turn. →39
turn bridge see swing bridge. →64
turnbuckle a mechanism for tensioning bracing wires, cables or rods joined end on end by means of two threaded connections housed in a sleeve, which is turned to produce a tightening force. →37, →54
Turnbull's blue a form of potassium ferrous ferricyanide used as a pale blue pigment.
turn button see button.
Turner's yellow, Kassler yellow, mineral yellow, Montpelier yellow, patent yellow, transparent gold ochre; an obsolete yellow lead oxychloride pigment used extensively in the past in watercolour, oil and chalk paints.
turning the shaping of wooden pieces on a lathe to create items which are predominantly circular in section.
turning catch see turning latch.
turning chisel a woodworking chisel used for shaping wood on a lathe. →41
see *turning chisels* illustration. →41
turning circle in traffic design, the minimum distance needed for the turning of a particular class of vehicle, measured variously as the outer radius or diameter of the circle it inscribes when turning through 180°.
turning gouge a turning chisel with a concave blade for removing wood, rough shaping and smoothing. →41
turning latch, turning catch; a simple latch which holds a door leaf or casement in a closed position by means of a rotating piece of stiff material attached to the frame.
turning piece, camber slip, camber piece; a piece of timber with a slightly curved upper edge, used as temporary support for a flat or shallow cambered masonry arch during construction. →22
turning saw, web saw; a workshop saw with a wooden frame constraining a blade tightened into place, which can be turned along its axis for greater flexibility in cutting curves etc.
turning stair, winding stair; a stair whose direction of travel changes as it ascends; types included as separate entries are listed below. →45
curving stair. →45
half turn stair. →45
one-turn stairs. →45
quarter turn stair. →45
turnkey contract see design and construct contract.
turnover the total sales or business in monetary terms carried out by a company over a specified period of time.
turnpike see toll road.
turnsole see folium.
turn-up in bituminous roofing, the edge of a sheet of bitumen felt which acts as a skirting at an abutment.
turpentine, 1 oil of turpentine, spirits of turpentine; volatile distillations of the resinous liquid exuded from certain pines and other coniferous trees, used in the preparation of oil paints and as a thinner.
2 originally the resinous secretion itself, distilled into oil of turpentine and rosin.
turquoise, kallaite; a semi-translucent blue or blue-green mineral polished or carved as decoration and ornament.
turquoise white a general name for a shade of white tinged with turquoise.
turret a smaller defensive or decorative corner or boundary tower in a castle, fortification or palace, often with a platform and battlements; also sometimes called a tourelle, touret or turette. →104
Tuscan column a column of the Roman Tuscan order, distinguished by a gap between the shaft ring and capital. →79
Tuscan capital a simple capital at the top of a column of the classical Roman Tuscan order, consisting of an echinus above an annulet, surmounted by an abacus edged with a cyma moulding. →81
Tuscan order, Etruscan order; a simple classical Roman order, influenced by the old brick and timber temples of the Etruscans, and the Greek Doric, with smooth-shafted columns, a simple capital, base and entablature. →79, →81
see *classical Roman orders* illustration. →79
see *Tuscan order* in superimposed orders illustration. →114
tuscanicum, Etruscan hall; Lat.; an atrium in a Roman dwelling which has surrounding hipped roofs; more fully called an atrium tuscanicum.
tusk tenon joint in timber frame construction, a specially hewn tenon joint for housing the ends of joists, pinned to increase its bearing capacity. →5
TV see television.
TV survey see closed circuit television survey.
tweezers, pair of tweezers; a pair of fine pincers used for gripping and plucking small objects.
twilight area in town planning, an urban area surrounding the centre of a town in which housing, the physical environment and infrastructure are in an outdated, substandard condition and in need of redevelopment.
twining stem a decorative moulding representing the coiled stem of a climbing plant. →125
twinned see coupled.
twinned columns see coupled columns. →13, →114
twin tenon joint see double tenon joint. →5
twin triangle tie double triangle wall tie. →22
twist an end-to-end rotational warping of an improperly seasoned timber board on drying, making it propeller shaped. →1
twist drill a hardened steel drill bit with spiral cutting edges, used for boring holes in metal or wood. →42
twisted bar see cold twisted bar. →27
twisted column see spiral column. →114
twist gimlet see gimlet. →42
twisting fibres see interlocking grain.
twist tie see vertical twist tie. →22
twitcher see twitcher trowel. →43
twitcher trowel, angle trowel, twitcher; a hand tool for smoothing internal corners in plasterwork with a handled blade of bent steel sheet. →43
two-brick wall a solid bonded brick wall whose width is the sum of two brick lengths plus one intermediate joint. →21
two by four the traditional term for sawn timber whose cross-section is 50 mm × 100 mm; refers to dimensions in inches.
two-centred ogee arch, depressed ogee arch; an ogee arch with lower haunches constructed around two centres of curvature, lower or fatter than a normal ogee arch. →24
two coat plasterwork, render and set; plasterwork consisting of two separate layers; the first coat which smooths off the surface and provides a key, and the final coat which provides a finish.
two component adhesive see two part adhesive.
two component sealant, two-part sealant; a sealant such as polyurethane products, supplied as two separate components, which must be mixed before application.
two-dimensional referring to a body or system which has length and breadth but little or no depth.
two-faced fireplace a fireplace open or glazed on two sides. →55
two-family house see semi-detached house. →61
two-man cross cut saw see felling saw.
two pack adhesive see two part adhesive.
two part adhesive, two pack adhesive, two component adhesive; adhesive mixed from two separate parts before use.

two-part sealant see two component sealant.

two-pipe system a central heating system in which each radiator is served by two pipe circuits, one for input hot water, and the other for return water to the heating plant.

two-point perspective a perspective drawing constructed from two vanishing points, producing a view in which verticals are seen as vertical and lines on other axes are seen as converging; also called angular perspective and, in Great Britain, sometimes called oblique perspective. →129
see *two-point perspective* illustration. →129

two-roomed flat a dwelling which contains two habitable rooms and a kitchen or kitchenette.

two-stage competition an architectural or planning competition in which certain proposals are chosen for further development after initial assessment, usually involving a greater depth of detailed design; from these, a winner is chosen.

two-stage tendering in contract administration, a tendering procedure in which a contractor is selected on the basis of an approximate bill of quantities, and the price negotiated on the basis of contractor's advice at the design stage.

two-way reinforcement concrete slab reinforcement consisting of sets or a mesh of parallel reinforcing bars laid in two perpendicular directions to provide resistance to tensile forces along two major axes.

two-way slab a reinforced concrete slab whose reinforcement is designed to span in two perpendicular directions.

two way stick adhesive any adhesive applied to both surfaces to be joined.

tying wire see binding wire.

tympan see tympanum.

tympanum, 1 tympan; Lat.; an area of wall, panel or space enclosed within an arch and its horizontal line of springing.
2 the triangular panel or surface on the front face of a classical pediment or decorative gable. →86, →113
see *tympanum* in classical temple illustration. →86
see *Gothic tympanum* illustration. →113
3 see aetos. →86
4 see dado. →76, →80

type a characteristic of a group of objects by which the group can be classified, or which distinguishes it.

typical decay see advanced decay.

typographical point a unit of measurement of typefaces, equivalent to 0.376 mm.

tyrannopolis a later stage of urban development according to Mumford, characterized by an ecologically degenerate environment, totalitarian government rule and the prevalence of violence and crime.

Tyrian purple, Grecian purple, ostrum, purple of the ancients; a purple pigment used by the Romans for imperial dress, originally obtained from the shellfish Murex trunculis and Murex brandaris and later manufactured synthetically; now superseded by other pigments.

Tyrolean finish a surface coating of mortar for masonry and concrete, textured after application; textured or patterned render or plasterwork.

U

Uadjet see Wadjet. →74
Udjet see Wadjet. →74
UB section see I-section. →34
UC section see H-section. →34
UF urea formaldehyde.
UIA Unione Internationale des Architectes.
Ulmus spp. see elm.
Ulmus americana, see American elm.
Ulmus glabra, see wych elm.
Ulmus procera, see English elm.

ultimate compressive strength the stress at which a material or structural component fails in compression or is crushed.

ultimate load the greatest load a structure or structural member can withstand before it fails.

ultimate strength, breaking strength; in the study of materials, the stress at which a material or component fails under increasing load.

ultrabasic rock a form of igneous rock whose silica content is less than 45%.

ultramarine, ultramarine blue; a greenish blue pigment originally made from the mineral lapis lazuli until an artificial method of production was discovered in 1828; also the name given to the shade of colour of this; types included as separate entries are listed below.
artificial ultramarine.
cobalt ultramarine.
French blue, French ultramarine, see artificial ultramarine.
Gmellin's blue, see artificial ultramarine.
green ultramarine, see ultramarine, ultramarine green.

ultramarine blue see ultramarine.

ultramarine green a greenish form of ultramarine pigment.

ultramarine yellow an old name for barium yellow pigment.

ultrasonic pertaining to ultrasound.

ultrasonic welding a method of welding stainless steels and other alloys by the application of ultrasonic vibration and light pressure.

ultrasound sound with a frequency greater than that which can be heard by the human ear (greater than 15–20 kHz).

ultraviolet control glass see laminated ultraviolet light control glass.
see anti-fading glass.

ultraviolet lamp an electric lamp which produces light from the ultraviolet end of the spectrum.

ultraviolet light resistance the ability of a material or surface to inhibit the transmission of ultraviolet light, or to be unaffected in its presence.

ultraviolet radiation, UV; that part of the electromagnetic spectrum beyond the cool violet end, with wavelengths between 400 nm and 40 nm, shorter than radiation of the visible spectrum; often known as ultraviolet light when produced by lamps.

Umayyad architecture early Islamic architecture of a ruling Muslim dynasty from Damascus in 661–750, with Hellenistic and Coptic influences.

umber, umbre; a general name for brown native pigments rich in oxides of iron and manganese; its colour may range from yellowish to greenish and reddish and is usually darker than sienna and ochre; see below for list of umber pigments.
burnt umber.
chestnut brown, raw umber.
jacaranda brown, see burnt umber.
mineral brown, see burnt umber.
raw umber.
Sicilian brown, see raw umber.
Spanish brown, see burnt umber.
terra ombre, see raw umber.

umbre see umber.

umbrella dome, melon dome, parachute dome, pumpkin dome; a domical vault which, in plan, is a polygon whose sides are arcs of a circle. →26

unbroken a description of a wall surface, line etc. which has no breaks or openings.

uncoursed ashlar, random ashlar; ashlar masonry with stones of different sizes laid in a rough bond with no or few horizontal running joints. →11

uncoursed rubble see random rubble. →11

uncoursed squared rubble masonry roughly squared pieces of stone laid as masonry with no definable coursed pattern; also called random squared rubble masonry. →11

uncrushed gravel coarse aggregate processed from naturally occurring gravel which has not undergone further processing of mechanical crushing.

unctuarium Lat.; see alipterion. →91

under-and-over tile, Spanish tile, mission tile (Am.); a U-shaped clay roof tile laid alternately convexly and concavely in courses to overlap one another. →47

underbridge in traffic planning, a bridge which supports a carriageway over another road or obstacle. →64

undercloak the lower overlapping part of a folded sheetmetal roofing seam or welt, covered by an overcloak. →49

undercoat 1 a coat of paint or treatment applied to prepare, seal or colour a surface prior to a final or finish coat.
2 see plaster undercoat.

undercoat plaster plaster laid directly onto a wall or ceiling as a base onto which further coats are applied.

undercroft 1 the vaulted cellar of a building, used for storage.
2 the vaulted cellar of a church, a crypt.
see *Early Christian basilica* illustration. →95
see *Romanesque church* illustration. →99

undercrossing a structure which allows a road to pass under an obstruction such as a railway, park, buildings or another road. →64

undercut tenon joint a timber tenon joint in which a sloping cut is made into the receiving piece to provide a greater gluing area for the tenoned end, or a ledge on which it rests. →5

under-deposit corrosion see deposit corrosion.

underfelt 1 see underlay.
2 see felt underlay.

underfloor heating, floor heating; electric wires or hot-water pipes laid under a floor or within floor construction as space heating and to provide a pleasantly warm floor surface in bathrooms etc.

underground see underground railway.

underground parking an area of parking located below ground, either in specially excavated structures or in the basements of buildings. →62

underground railway, metro, subway, tube, underground; an urban railway system in which trains travel for the most part in tunnels constructed under the city.

underground railway line an urban rail-transit route located partially or wholly in subterranean tunnels.

underground railway station, metro station, tube station; a stop on an underground line for dropping off and picking up passengers.

underground store see root store.
underground streetcar a form of underground railway in which the vehicles are trams.
underground watering in landscaping and forestry, the provision of water directly to the roots of plants by burying perforated pipes in the soil.
undergrowth, understorey; the lowest layer of plants and shrubs that grow on a woodland floor or landscaped area.
underinsuring insurance of goods and property which does not cover the real value of the items insured.
underlay, 1 underfelt; a base layer of sheet material such as expanded polystyrene or cork sheeting laid beneath a floor covering as a vibration or noise attenuator and to provide an even base; flooring underlay.
2 in roof construction, a layer of impervious material such as polythene sheet or roofing felt laid beneath roofing such as slates, tiles, profiles sheeting etc. as secondary protection against the penetration of water. →57
3 see base sheet.
4 see felt underlay. →57
5 see roofing underlay. →49, →57
6 see sheathing.
7 vented underlay, see perforated underlay bitumen felt.
underlining, underscoring; a continuous line under text or headings as emphasis, highlighting etc.
underpass a road, passage or carriageway which passes beneath another road or obstruction in a short tunnel or shaft. →63, →64
underpinning 1 the addition of support beneath the foundations of an existing structure to account for an increase in loading or altered ground conditions.
2 the same operation beneath a column or pillar.
underpitched vault a cross vault in which the arches at the edges of the bay are smaller than those across the bay. →101
under-reamed pile in foundation technology, a bored pile whose base is enlarged; also called a belled pile or pedestal pile. →29
underscoring see underlining.
underside the lower side of an object or building component.
understorey 1 see shrub layer.
2 see undergrowth.
undersurface see soffit.
underwater concrete concrete which is placed, and hardens, under water.
undisturbed sample a soil sample which has been removed from the ground as a core sample and largely represents the properties in analysis of the soil from which it was taken.
undulating moulding see wave moulding. →124
undulating tracery see flowing tracery. →110
undy moulding see oundy moulding. →125
unearned increment in town planning, the increase of rents and property values in expanding urban areas due to local land use, allocation of activity and population density as stipulated in the plan, rather than the enterprise of landowners.
unedged a description of converted timber which contains wane, or has been sawn on two opposite sides but not at the edges.
unemployment the condition of being without paid employment.
unequal angle a steel angle in which the limbs are of differing lengths when viewed in cross-section. →34
uneven grain a pronounced visual difference between earlywood and latewood in a piece of sawn timber.
unexcavated referring to an area of a construction site which has not been dug or excavated during construction work.
unframed door 1 a rudimentary door whose leaf is made from vertical matchboarding held together with horizontal members or ledges nailed to one side, often with diagonal braces for additional stiffness.
2 see all glass door.
unglazed door a door whose leaf has no glazed lights. →51
unheated space space in a building which contains no heating appliance and is kept at about the same temperature as external air.
unicorn a decorative motif depicting a mythological horselike creature with a single horn, symbolic of power and purity. →122
Uniform Building Code laws in Australia and the USA which control the layout, safety, health, materials and fire regulations in buildings; see Building Regulations.
uninhabitable describing a building deemed to be unfit for occupation because of its state of disrepair, contamination, fire damage etc.
uninhabited referring to an area or building in which nobody lives.
unique character, uniqueness; the properties of a particular natural area, old building, urban environment etc. which distinguish it from all others and make it worthy of preservation.
uniqueness see unique character.
union 1 a pipe fitting with a loose coupling nut at its end, used for connecting a threaded pipe to an appliance.
2 see screwed union.
3 see trades union.
union clip an accessory for joining two sections of rainwater guttering or similar component end to end.
Unione Internationale des Architectes, UIA; a professional body to further the interests and rights of its international architect members.
unit, 1 unit of measurement; a value or size used by convention as a measure of a quantity (metre, second).
2 a component or group of components viewed as a whole; a module.
3 see prefabricated unit.
4 see precast concrete unit.
5 see cladding unit.
6 see concrete paving slab. →15
7 see dwelling unit. →61
unit air-conditioner, cooler unit, room air-conditioner, self-contained air-conditioner; an independent air-treatment unit situated within the space it serves.
unit cost 1 the price per unit (square metre, kilogram) of a commodity.
2 see cost per square metre.
unit of measurement see unit.
unit paver see concrete block paver. →15
unit paving see concrete block paving. →15
unit price contract a standard prime contract in which a contractor agrees to carry out construction work according to a predetermined, fixed sum for each specified unit of work performed; the final price is determined by multiplying the unit price for each unit by the measured quantity of work carried out.
universal beam see I-section. →34
universal column see H-section. →34
universal plane see combination plane.
university, institute of higher education; an educational and research facility, building or group of buildings in which specialist education is given in the sciences and humanities.
university town a town whose university plays an integral part in its livelihood and environment.
unreinforced a description of structural concrete which does not contain steel reinforcement.
unreinforced concrete see plain concrete.
unrolled veneer see rotary cut veneer. →10

unsanded plywood plywood which has not been finished by sanding.
unsaturated in colour science, referring to pale shades of colour which are not as intense as the same hue without white.
unsaturated polyester see polyester resin.
unskilled labourer a construction worker with little formal training, who usually works as a builder's hand.
unsound knot, decayed knot, rotten knot; a knot in timber, softer than the surrounding wood as a result of fungal attack. →1
unstable see labile.
untreated sewage see raw sewage.
unventilated roof roof construction which contains a vapour control layer to restrict movement of vapour above the insulation layer, and has no need for a ventilation gap within the construction.
UP polyester resin.
up-and-over door an overhead door whose single door leaf is opened by lifting it into a horizontal position on a system of pivots, levers and springs above the door opening. →50
upholsterer's hammer a small hammer used for hammering tacks in upholstery work; it often contains a magnet in its head for holding nails. →40
upholstery fabric covering for furniture and fittings.
upholstery nail see upholstery tack. →35
upholstery tack, upholstery nail; a small nail with a dome-shaped head, used for fastening upholstery to furniture. →35
upholstery textile in interior design, cloth used for cladding or covering furnishings and other interior components.
U-pin see staple. →35
uplighter a luminaire which indirectly illuminates a space or area by directing light upwards onto a ceiling or wall plane.
uplighting lighting designed to provide indirect light to a space by illumination of ceiling and upper wall surfaces.
upper chord, top chord; the upper member in a truss. →33
Upper Egypt one of the two ancient Egyptian kingdoms, which grew along the banks of the river Nile; the other is Lower Egypt, the Nile Delta; its Pharaoh wore the white crown, and its heraldic plant was the lotus, a species of water lily. →74
upper floor 1 one of the stories above ground level in a building with two or more stories.
see *upper floor in brick house* illustration. →59
2 see intermediate floor. →28
upper floor construction see intermediate floor construction. →59
see *upper floor construction* in brick house illustration. →59
upper glazing see top light. →60, →111
upper king post see king tie.
upright see standard. →54
upright freezer a freezer with a side-hung door, similar in form to a fridge.
U-profile see channel.
upsetting, setting up; the making thicker of the end of a metal bar by hammering it on end while hot, as with the fixing of rivets.
upside down roof, inverted roof, protected membrane roof; a roof whose insulation is laid above the waterproofing membrane and is held in position by ballast such as shingle or concrete slabs; the insulation thus protects the waterproofing from the effects of weathering and thermal variation.
upstairs the upper floor of a building above the ground floor.
see *upstairs in brick house* illustration. →59
upstand an area of waterproof membrane or sheeting turned up against a wall abutment or parapet to provide a secure edge joint. →56, →57
see roofing upstand. →57
see slate fillet.
tiled upstand, see tile fillet.
see water check.
upstand beam a beam which protrudes from the upper face of a concrete slab, which it supports.
upstand flashing in roofing, a flashing which forms an upstand at an abutment but is not dressed into the abutting wall; it is covered by a cover flashing. →56, →57
uraeus in ancient Egyptian mythology and decoration, a fire-spitting snake motif worn at the front of a royal head-dress, protectress of the kings, closely linked to Wadjet. →74
uraninite see pitchblende.
uranium a white, radioactive, metallic chemical element, **U**, used in the nuclear industry and armaments.
uranium yellow a permanent, expensive pigment made from uranium oxide; used in ceramics.
urban pertaining to the nature of a town or city.
urban development the construction of whole areas of a town or city, controlled by planning processes to enhance or improve conditions therein.
urban fabric see urban structure.
urban form see urban structure.
urban freeway (Am.), urban motorway; a local motorway which runs through a city, or which connects one part of a city to another.
urban fringe see outskirts.
urban milieu see streetscape.
urban motorway (Am.) see urban freeway.
urban park, city park; a public park in urban surroundings, for the recreation of inhabitants etc.
urban planning 1 town planning concerned with the nature, structure, and functioning of human collectives in physical space.
2 see city planning.
urban redevelopment 1 see urban renewal.
2 see comprehensive redevelopment.
urban renewal, urban redevelopment; the reconstruction and rehabilitation of blighted or decaying urban areas and communities.
urban sociology a social science which describes and documents the impact of urban concentrations on social behaviour.
urban sprawl a typical development in modern city growth related to the unconstrained and messy extension of suburban areas around shopping centres and outlying commercial districts.
urban structure, urban fabric, urban form; the overall shape and pattern of an urban area based on its visual and material impact, density, traffic patterns and topography.
urbanization the change of a rural or suburban area to one with urban character.
urdy cross see cross urdy. →117
urdy moulding a crenellated moulding whose upper and lower castellations have sharpened extremities; sometimes called a vair moulding in heraldry. →125
urea formaldehyde, UF; a clear thermosetting resin used for mouldings, WC seats, paints and stove enamels.
urea formaldehyde glue a synthetic resin glue made by chemically condensing urea with formalin.
urethane varnish see polyurethane varnish.
urinal 1 a soil appliance for receiving urine and flushing it away into a drain.
2 see bowl urinal.
urn 1 a decorative motif depicting a Greek urn.
2 see cinerary urn.
use see use class.
use class in planning control, an official classification of proposed and existing building development according to types of use, whether residential, commercial, recreational, industrial etc.
use classes order in planning control, an official document specifying classes of use for building development, so that a change of use within the same class is not taken to involve development requiring planning consent.
U-section a metal section whose cross-section resembles the letter C or U; see channel. →34

user a person, animal or object for whom a building is designed and constructed.

user interface hardware devices such as keyboard, mouse, display etc. and programs which allow the user to communicate with a computer.

US gallon see gallon.

US gill see gill.

US pint see pint.

US standard brick a standard size of brick in use in North America with regular dimensions of 8" × 4" × 2⅔" (203.2 mm × 101.6 mm × 67.7 mm), also confusingly called a modular brick. →16

ustrinum Lat.; in Roman architecture, a place for incineration of the dead.

utensil sink see pot sink.

utile, sipo; [*Entandrophragma utile*] a hardwood from West Africa with strong, heavy, rich tawny timber used for furniture, panelling and construction work.

utilitarian planning, commercial-utilitarian planning; a town planning practice based on laissez-faire policies and economic forces, characterized by the provision of dense built form and buildings geared to private financial gain rather than recreational areas and public buildings for the common good.

utility, 1 tool; auxiliary computing software for performing a simple routine task such as sorting, searching or inspecting.
2 see service.

utility knife see trimming knife.

utility room 1 a room adjoining a kitchen for providing additional facilities for washing, storage and other domestic activities. →59
2 service space; a subsidiary space or room used in conjunction with the functioning or servicing of a building or adjacent major space, largely for storage, preparation etc.

utilization factor in lighting design, the ratio of the luminous flux received by a surface to the total luminous flux produced by individual lamps.

utopian planning theoretical town planning which seeks to provide for a society of the future, often based on an idealistic model or a forecasted future living environment.

UV see ultraviolet radiation.

U-value, air-to-air heat transmission coefficient, coefficient of thermal transmittance, coefficient of heat transfer; a basic quantity used for heat loss calculations for external wall, roof and floor constructions, whose units are $W/m^2\ °C$; a measure of how well the given construction will conduct heat and available from standard empirical tables of data, based on experimentation by measuring the rate of heat flow per square metre of surface for every degree of temperature difference on either side of the construction, with a surface coefficient added to allow for exposure to wind and rain.

uvarovite an emerald green variety of the mineral garnet.

V

V-joint a brickwork mortar joint in which the mortar is shaped with a pointed tool to form a V-shaped depression. →16

vacuum breaker see anti-vacuum valve.

vacuum concrete, vacuum dewatered concrete; concrete to which a vacuum is applied after placing in order to extract the excess water not needed for hydration.

vacuum concreting working with vacuum concrete.

vacuum dewatered concrete see vacuum concrete.

vacuum dewatering, vacuum processing; the compaction of fresh concrete by the application of a controlled vacuum to suck out excess water.

vacuum forming a method of forming thermoplastic moulded products by sucking sheet material against a perforated one-sided mould using a vacuum.

vacuum pressure impregnated timber see pressure impregnated timber.

vacuum processing see vacuum dewatering.

vacuum sewerage a sewerage system for flat or low lying areas in which sewage is sucked along plastic pipelines with vacuum pressure induced by a pumping station.

vacuum WC a sealed WC for use on trains, ships and aircraft in which soil is discharged into a collecting tank by means of a partial vacuum induced by a pump.

vair moulding same as urdy moulding. →125

valence, valency; in chemistry, the relative power of atoms in joining other atoms in the formation of compounds.

valency see valence.

valetudinarium the soldiers' hospital in a Roman military camp. →104

valley 1 the inside join formed by the junction of two pitched roofs meeting at an angle; a roof valley. →46

2 see tiled valley.

3 Nile valley, see Upper Egypt. →74

valley board in timber frame construction, a wide board which runs the length of a valley as a base for the valley gutter.

valley gutter in sheetmetal and other pitched roofing, a pressed sheetmetal component or other construction included in a valley for the runoff of water to a gutter or outlet.

valley rafter in timber roof construction, a diagonal rafter supporting the meeting of two sloping roofs at an inside corner or valley.

valley roof see M-roof. →46

valley temple a temple pavilion in an ancient Egyptian pyramid complex, connected via a covered causeway to a mortuary temple at the foot of a pyramid; used for preparing the Pharaoh for his final journey. →71

valley tile a special roof tile manufactured for use in a roof valley.

valli plural form of vallum. →104

vallum Lat.; pl. valli; the upper rampart, palisade etc. built on top of the embankment or agger surrounding a Roman military encampment; a single stake in a palisade thus formed. →104

value, reflectance; in colour science and painting, the relative darkness or lightness of a colour, the amount of light reflected from it; see below for list of other types of value.

aggregate impact value.
book value.
C-value.
calorific value.
exchange value.
external surface resistance value, see RSO-value.
face value.
heat transmission value, see k-value.
heating value, see calorific value.
internal surface resistance value, see RSI-value.
iodine value.
k-value.
land value.
numerical value.
pH-value.
real value.
RSI-value.
RSO-value.
R-value.
U-value.

value added the increase in the value of a product as a result of a stage in the production process.

value added tax, VAT; a tax added to the sale price of goods and services.

valve a control device for closing off and regulating flow of liquids and gases in pipework.

valve box see surface box.

vanadinite a yellow, brown or orange-red mineral used as a local source of lead and vanadium.

vanadium a metallic chemical element, **V**, used as an alloy to toughen steel.

vandalproof see vandal resistant.

vandal resistant, vandalproof; a description or property of a component, construction or finish which is designed to resist deliberate damage from vandalism by virtue of robust construction, Teflon coatings etc.

Vandyke brown, 1 Rubens brown; a native earth pigment composed of clay and iron oxide with included organic matter.

2 a shade of dark brown used by the Flemish painter Antonius van Dyck in the 1600s; the colour of the pigment burnt umber.

vane see weather-vane. →102

vane testing in soil investigation, the on-site testing of the stiffness of soft and silty clays by sinking a winged implement inside a tube into the soil and measuring the force required to turn it.

vanishing point 1 in perspective drawing, one of the points at which lines converge, constructed as if at infinity. →128

2 see diagonal vanishing point. →128

see accidental point.

vanishing trace in perspective, a line along which all sets of parallel lines will appear to converge.

vanity basin, counter top basin; a domestic wash basin housed in a hole cut in a worktop, usually as part of a bathroom cabinet.

vaporarium Lat.; a steam room in a Roman bath house, one in which bathers sweated. →91

vaporizing oil burner a burner in an oil heating system whose oil is vaporized and mixed with air prior to combustion.

vapour the result of the boiling of a liquid; a liquid in droplet form at or near its boiling point; see steam, water vapour.

vapour barrier, vapour check; an impervious membrane incorporated into wall construction to inhibit the passage of moisture. →8, →59

vapour blasting see wet blasting.

vapour check see vapour barrier. →8, →59

vapour control layer a layer of impervious material or membrane included in wall, roof, floor etc. construction to inhibit the passage of water vapour.

variable 1 in mathematics, a quantity which does not remain constant in a function.
2 see parameter.

variable air volume system, variable volume system, VAV system; an air-conditioning system in which temperature of input air is a constant, but actual room temperature is governed by the amount of air provided to each space with the use of localized fan units.

variable cost in business management, a cost which varies dependent on production and staffing levels, material costs etc.

variable volume system see variable air volume system.

variation, change (Am.), modification (Am.); a change in the nature or the extent, conditions or programming of construction work from that stipulated in a building contract, agreed and billed by a contractor extra to the contract.

variation formula see price variation formula.

variation of price contract 1 a form of building contract in which prices may be amended to reflect changes in economic conditions.
2 see formula variation of price contract.

variation order in contract administration, an instruction from the client or client's representative that implements a change in the nature or extent of constructed work.

varnish a liquid coating applied to a surface, usually timberwork, joinery or furniture which forms a hardwearing transparent film.

varnish brush see flat varnish brush. →43

varnish size size made from varnish diluted with a solvent or thinner.

VAT value added tax.

vault 1 a three-dimensional arched ceiling construction to support a floor or roof, often of masonry; types included as separate entries are listed below. →25
see *arched and vaulted construction* illustration. →22
see *Roman and Romanesque vaulting* illustration. →25
see *Gothic rib vault* illustrations. →26, →101
annular vault.
barrel vault. →25
cambered vault, see segmental barrel vault. →25
cloister vault. →25, →26
conical vault.
corbelled vault. →65
coved vault. →25
cradle vault, see barrel vault. →25
cross vault, see groin vault. →25
cylindrical vault, see barrel vault. →25
dome. →26
domical vault, see cloister vault. →25, →26
dormer vault. →25
expanding vault, see conical vault. →25
fan vault. →101
Gothic vault. →101
groin vault, groined vault. →25
hexapartite vault, see sexpartite vault. →26
intersecting barrel vault, see groin vault. →25
net vault. →101
octopartite vault. →26
pointed barrel vault, pointed vault. →25
quadripartite vault. →26
rampant vault. →25
relieving vault. →71
rib vault, ribbed vault. →26, →101
Roman vault. →25
Romanesque vault. →25
sail vault, see sail dome. →26
segmental barrel vault, segmental vault. →25
sexpartite vault. →26
stellar vault, star vault, star-ribbed vault. →101
surbased vault, see segmental barrel vault. →25
tripartite vault. →26
trough vault. →25
tunnel vault, see barrel vault. →25
underpitched vault. →101
wagon vault, wagonhead vault, see barrel vault. →25
2 see cellar.
3 see strongroom.

vault door, strongroom door; an approved door type reinforced with steel and concrete and with special locks to meet certain standards of security and fire resistance, used for vaults and secure storage areas.

vaulted construction see *arched and vaulted construction* illustration. →22

vaulting 1 the curved surfaces of a vault.
2 the making of masonry vaults. →25
see *arched and vaulted construction* illustration. →22
3 a series of vaults.

VAV system see variable air volume system.

VB-consistometer test, VB-test, Vebe test; a test for the workability of fresh concrete, in which the time of collapse of a concrete cone on a vibrating table is measured.

VB-test see VB-consistometer test.

VDU 1 acronym for visual display unit; see display unit.
2 see monitor.

Vebe test see VB-consistometer test.

vector a mathematical quantity which has both magnitude and direction; see scalar.

vector graphics computer-aided design drawing using lines defined by their end points in space.

vedika a stone balustrade surrounding a Buddhist stupa. →68

vedro a Russian measure of liquid capacity equivalent to 12.3 l.

veduta a landscape or townscape painting based on accurate observation rather than fictitious or romantic premises.

vegetable fibre thin fibres of plant material such as wood, hessian, sisal or jute used as reinforcement in composite materials or woven to form matting.

vegetable fibre reinforced referring to composites consisting of vegetable fibres in a binder such as clay, mud, cement or plaster; traditionally used for cast and in-situ work.

vegetable glue glue made from plant matter, especially starch glue (cassava), protein glue (soya glue), or glue from oils pressed from nuts and rape seed.

vegetable preparation sink a commercial or domestic sink with special facilities for cleaning and washing vegetables.

vegetable soil a thin layer of dark crumbly soil, usually topsoil, containing a large proportion of decayed vegetable matter or humus. →15

vegetable store see root store.

vehicle 1 the main liquid body of a paint, including a thinner.
2 a wheeled mechanical device, a mode of transport for conveying people and goods; a car, bus, lorry, train, bicycle etc.

vehicle access route, fire service access; a prescribed means of access to a building which the fire service may use when arriving to fight a fire.

vehicle heating point, car heating point; an electrical point installed in unheated car parks and outdoor parking areas to which engine and in-car heating devices can be connected in cold weather.

vehicle safety barrier, crash barrier, vehicle safety fence; a low metal or concrete barrier at the edge of a carriageway, ramp etc. to prevent vehicles from veering off, and to protect the surroundings.

vehicle safety fence see vehicle safety barrier.

vehicular access 1 a road, canal, railway etc. which makes travel to a place by vehicle possible.
2 a road or track which provides site access for motor vehicles.

vehicular barrier, traffic barrier, access barrier; any fixed or temporary barrier, a boom, balustrade or bollard for inhibiting the passage of vehicular traffic.

vehicular ramp an inclined carriageway in a car park, roadway etc. for vehicles to move from one level to another.

vehicular segregation the separation of pedestrian and vehicular traffic in a traffic planning system for reasons of road safety, pollution etc.

vein a linear marking or band of a different colour or material to the base matrix in rock and ornamental stone, especially marble and limestone.

velarium see velum; pl. velaria.

vellum a fine, smooth paper, less coarse than parchment, made from the skin of a calf, lamb or kid.

velocity the speed of a moving body in a given direction, measured in m/s.

velodrome a modern sports arena with a banked track for cycling competitions.

velum, velarium; Lat.; pl. vela; in a Roman amphitheatre, forum or theatre, an awning stretched above the audience or public as protection from the sun and elements.

velvet carpet a type of cut-pile carpet of a basic Wilton type.

veneer 1 sheets of wood less than 6 mm in thickness cut from a log by slicing, peeling or sawing; glued together as plywood or to cheaper boards as a decorative finish; often called wood veneer to distinguish it from brick and other veneers. →10
see *veneering* illustration, and veneering pattern entry for list of matches; types included as separate entries are listed below. →10
back cut veneer.
burl veneer.
flat cut veneer.
half round veneer.
quarter sliced veneer.
rotary cut veneer, peeled veneer.
2 brick veneer, see brick facing.
3 stone veneer, see stone facing. →11

veneer bolt, veneer flitch; a piece of wood or log from which veneer is peeled or sliced. →10

veneer cutting decorative veneer produced either by slicing or peeling. →10

veneered chipboard chipboard surfaced with a wood veneer, used for high quality interior linings and furnishings.

veneered parquet see multilayer parquet. →44, →59

veneered wall an external wall whose cladding or facing is non-structural.

veneer flitch see veneer bolt. →10

veneer hammer, veneering hammer; a hammer with a long thin flat face used in veneerwork for pressing down veneers during gluing. →40

veneering, veneerwork; **1** the process of cutting and gluing decorative glued veneers. →10
see *veneering* illustration, and veneering pattern entry for list of matches. →10
2 a decorative facing of veneer on board, plywood or lower quality timber.

veneering hammer see veneer hammer. →40

veneering pattern the various patterns in which veneers are glued to a base; types included as separate entries are listed below. →10
see *veneering pattern* illustration.
bookmatching, book match. →10
box match. →10
butt match. →10
centre match. →10
chevron match, see V-match. →10
diamond match. →10
herringbone pattern, herringbone match. →10
random match. →10
reverse box match. →10
reverse diamond match. →10
slip match. →10
sunburst matching.
vertical butt and horizontal bookmatching. →10
V-match. →10

veneer parquet see multilayer parquet. →44

veneer peeling decorative veneer produced by cutting the surface layer from a rotating log or flitch. →10

veneer pin a small round pin, 10 mm–38 mm in length, used for temporarily fastening veneers in position until the glue has set.

veneer plywood see plywood. →9

veneer slicing decorative veneer produced by straight cutting of a half log or flitch. →10

veneer saw a small fine-toothed saw for cutting veneers.

veneerwork see veneering. →10

Venetian arch 1 a decorative arch form whose intrados is formed of two adjacent semicircular arches, and whose extrados is of one, double width semicircle; the spandrel left between often contains a circular opening or panel. →23
2 a decorative pointed arch form whose intrados and extrados are further apart at the crown than at the springing; an arch whose intrados is an elliptical arch and extrados is an ogee is also sometimes called a Venetian arch. →23

venetian blind, louvred blind; a raisable window-blind consisting of a number of horizontal slats of wood, metal or plastics hung by string or tape one above the other, whose angle is adjustable to allow more or less light through.

Venetian dentil moulding a dentil moulding cut with a splayed base or background. →124

Venetian Gothic an architectural style in Victorian England characterized by use of Venetian medieval elements and polychromatic brickwork.

Venetian mirror glass mirror glass coated with wide strips of mirrored surface interspersed with narrower clear strips, used for providing one-way vision from surveillance and control rooms, offices etc. to larger spaces.

Venetian motif see Palladian motif. →24

Venetian red see oxide red.

Venetian window, Palladian window; an ornamental window with three openings, the central portion arched. →24

Venice turpentine a variety of turpentine exuded from the Austrian larch (Larix decidua), used as a medium in paints, varnishes and adhesives.

vent, ventilator; **1** a grille or other device to allow the passage of fresh air to a space from the outside, or for release of stale air. →56
2 an openable hatch or window to provide ventilating air.
see fresh-air vent. →58
see exhaust vent. →58
see *roof vent* in parapet illustration. →49
see ventilation pipe.

vented underlay see perforated underlay bitumen felt.

ventilated roof roof construction with a planar gap within its thickness above the insulating layer, for the circulation of air, removal of moisture etc.

ventilating brick see air brick. →16

ventilating column a vertical ventilating pipe for an underground sewer.

ventilating pipe a pipe in a drainage system for the ventilation and pressure release of a discharge pipe.

ventilating ridge tile a special ridge tile with perforations to allow for the passage of ventilating air.

ventilating tile a special roof tile with perforations to permit ventilation.

ventilation 1 the maintenance of the air quality of spaces in a building by continual provision of fresh air from the outside, either by natural or mechanical means.
see *ventilation* in sauna illustration. →58

2 the natural passage of air into rooms to provide fresh air, and through gaps or cavities within roof, wall and floor construction to convey excess moisture out thus inhibiting mould and fungal attack; types included as separate entries are listed below.
see natural ventilation.
see mechanical ventilation.
see roof ventilation. →49

ventilation duct 1 an air duct used in a mechanical ventilation installation.
see *ventilation duct* in office building illustration. →60
2 a closed flue or other channel through which stale air from a space can pass to the outside.
see *ventilation duct* in chimney illustration. →56

ventilation gap a space between layers in a roof or wall construction allowing for the passage of circulating air to remove unwanted moisture.
see *ventilation gap* in brick house illustration. →59

ventilation installation see ventilation plant.

ventilation pipe, vent, vent pipe; a pipe connected to a drainage system which conveys foul air upwards out of the building, easing the flow of water in drains.

ventilation plant, ventilation installation; the pumps, fans, ductwork and other equipment that make up the mechanical ventilation system of a building.

ventilation plant room, air-handling plant room; a service space in a building containing intakes, mixing chambers, fans and main delivery ducts for a ventilation system.

ventilation riser see ventilation stack. →56

ventilation shaft a large vertical ventilation duct. →56

ventilation stack a closed flue or other vertical channel through which stale air is released to the outside, usually via natural convection; also called a vent stack or ventilation riser; if large, may be called a ventilation shaft. →56

ventilation rate see air-change rate.

ventilator 1 see vent.
2 see trickle ventilator. →52
3 see eaves ventilator.

venting see fire venting.

venting layer see perforated underlay bitumen felt.

venting panel see blast venting panel.

vent pipe 1 see stack vent.
2 see ventilation pipe.

vent stack see ventilation stack. →56

vent soaker see pipe flashing.

veranda, 1 verandah; a roofed open space, terrace or porch providing shelter and shade along the sides or front of a building.
see *timber-framed house* illustration. →57
see *sauna building* illustration. →58
2 see pastas. →87
3 see porticus. →88

verandah see veranda. →58

verawood, Maracaibo lignum vitae; [*Bulnesia arborea*] an extremely heavy Venezuelan tropical hardwood.

verchok a traditional Russian unit of distance equal to a sixteenth part of an arshin or 44.45 mm.

verdigris see green of Greece.

verge 1 the join of roof and wall at a gable or sloping end of a pitched roof. →46, →57
2 margin, median, reservation; a strip or area adjoining a carriageway for emergency stopping etc. →63
3 see dividing strip. →63
4 see hard shoulder. →63

verge tile a special roof tile for use at a verge.

vergeboard see bargeboard.

verism a naturalistic style in art in which subjects are depicted using accurate observation rather than aesthetic embellishment.

vermiculation the dressing of a stonework or plaster surface with random worm-like decorative recesses or wavy lines, especially used for quoins or finer stones. →12

vermiculatum see opus vermiculatum.

vermiculite any of a group of hydrous silicates of aluminium, magnesium or iron, used loose as thermal insulation and fire-retardant coatings.

vermiculite-gypsum plaster see vermiculite plaster.

vermiculite plaster, gypsum-vermiculite plaster, vermiculite-gypsum plaster, fire-retardant plaster; plaster containing fine exfoliated vermiculite aggregate, used as a fire-retardant coating for steelwork.

vermilion, scarlet vermilion; a bright red inorganic pigment, originally manufactured from the mercury sulphide ore, cinnabar, which since 1789 has been synthetically produced.

vernacular architecture 1 any architecture, often in rural areas, which makes use of local forms, methods and materials.
2 see rustic architecture.

vernier 1 two adjacent sliding calibrated scales which, when read in conjunction with one another, provide a more accurate reading for measurements of linear size.
2 see vernier callipers.

vernier callipers, calliper gauge, vernier gauge, vernier scale; a metal or plastic instrument with sliding jaws, used for taking small-scale but accurate measurements by reading from a vernier scale.

vernier gauge see vernier callipers.

vernier scale see vernier callipers.

verst a Russian and Scandinavian measure of distance equivalent to 1.07 km.

versurae see parascene. →89

vert emeraude see viridian.

vertical 1 a description of a body placed or lying perpendicular to a flat horizontal plane; see also plumb.
2 an upright member in a structural system such as a truss. →33

vertical boarding timber cladding boards laid with their long faces vertical. →8

vertical butt and horizontal bookmatching a veneering pattern in which bookmatched veneer sheets are also matched with an array of mirrored sheets end on end, used in cases where veneers being used are not long enough to cover the whole panel heights; often simply called butt match. →10

vertical circulation the means of changing from one level to another within a building using stairs, lifts and ramps.

vertical folding door 1 an overhead door with sections hinged horizontally, which fold up into an overhead space on opening. →50
2 see bi-part folding door. →50

vertical glazing bar an intermediate vertical glazing bar in a window; often called a mullion. →111

vertical grained see quartersawn.

vertical pivot window a window with an opening light hung centrally on pins at top and bottom of the frame, about which it opens. →52

vertical plane in parallel and perspective projection, the coordinate plane which is perpendicular to the horizontal or ground plane and the side or profile plane, on which points are defined by x and z coordinates; also known as the front plane, and often the picture plane. →127, →128

vertical sand drain see sand drain.

vertical section a scaled drawing representing a vertical cut through a site, building or object.

vertical shore see dead shore.

vertical sliding window see sash window. →52

vertical tiling see tile hanging.

vertical twist tie any wall tie formed out of metal strip with a twist along its length to provide a suitable drip for gathered water; a strip tie. →22

vesica piscis, fish bladder; Lat.; a decorative motif composed of two circular arcs joined facing each other to form a vertical pointed oval; a geometrically stylized variation of an ancient fish symbol used in ecclesiastical ornament as a halo, and to denote the receptacle of Christ, innocence and purity. →108

vessel a longitudinal cell in hardwood in which water is conveyed within the original tree.

vestiarium Lat.; a vestiary in a monastery. →95, →102

vestiary, revestry; a vestry or sacristy. →95, →102

vestibule 1 a space or room directly beyond the external door of a dwelling, public building or church; also called an entrance hall, lobby or porch. →57
2 see chalcidicum. →93
3 see vestibulum. →88, →91

vestibulum Lat.; an entrance hall or passage in a Roman building; a vestibule. →88, →91

Vestorian blue a variety of Egyptian blue pigment.

vestry the room in a church or monastery where ceremonial garments, vestments etc. were kept; often the same room as a sacristy. →95, →102

via Lat.; a Roman road or way; plural form is viae; see below. →104
via decumana. →104
via principalis. →104
via praetoria. →104
via quintana. →104
via sagularis. →104

viable see feasible.

via decumana 'way of the tenth' (Lat.); the road in a Roman military camp leading to the porta decumana at the rear, running along the main long axis of the camp, the decumanus. →104

viaduct a high-level masonry bridge with many arched spans, designed to carry a railway or road between two elevated points over a valley, waterway or low lying ground. →32

viae plural form of via. →104

via praetoria 'praetorian way' (Lat.); the road in a Roman military camp leading along the main long axis of the camp, the decumanus, from the porta praetoria at the front, to the headquarters building, the principia, where it meets the via principalis. →104

via principalis 'principal road' (Lat.); one of the main roads in a Roman military camp, running along the short axis of the camp (cardo) in front of the headquarters building (principia), connecting the two principal gates (portae principali). →104

via quintana 'way of the fifth' (Lat.); the road in a Roman military camp running parallel to the via principalis, at which the via decumana terminates. →104

via sagularis 'cloaked way' (Lat.); the road running around the perimeter of a Roman military camp, inside the main ramparts; also known as the intervallum road. →104

vibrated concrete concrete compacted by vibration.

vibrating screed board, screed; mechanical plant for levelling and compaction of a concrete floor slab, a screed board with the capacity for motorized vibration.

vibrating table a machine for compacting precast concrete by means of a vibrating platform onto which the fresh concrete and formwork are placed.

vibration 1 the rapid oscillation of mechanical plant etc. causing unwanted pressure waves to be transmitted through the air as sound, and surrounding building fabric as mechanical energy.
2 the compaction of fresh concrete by the application of mechanical vibration to release air pockets using an immersion or surface vibrator.

vibration insulation the placing of flexible material in strategic joints to attenuate vibration from mechanical plant and other sources of vibration.

vibration insulator, damper, vibration isolator (Am.), isolation mount; a layer of resilient material onto which mechanical equipment is placed to reduce the transmission of sound and vibration into the surrounding fabric.

vibration isolator see vibration insulator.

vibration limit in the setting of concrete, the time after which concrete will no longer respond to vibration.

vibrator see concrete vibrator.

vibrocompaction, vibroflotation; a method of stabilization for soft ground in which a large vibrating poker is sunk into the soil using water jets from the base of the vibrator; the ground is compacted by the vibrations to form wide earth columns of compacted soil.

vibroflotation see vibrocompaction.

vibroreplacement, stone column; a method of stabilization for soft ground similar to vibrocompaction, in which gravel is introduced into the ground during compaction to form a wide stone pile.

vicarage the residence of a priest of the Christian church.

vice, vise (Am.); a cast metal or wooden screwed device for holding and gripping objects in place while they are being worked, fixed to a workbench.

Victorian architecture architecture in England during the reign of Victoria (1837–1901), characterized by lavish ornament and eclectic styling of all types of buildings.

victory flag see labarum. →119

videoscope an endoscope with a flexible tube and a camera at the end, whose image is transmitted to a remote video monitor.

video surveillance 1 the monitoring of internal and external space in a building using a system of fixed video cameras linked to centralized monitors.
2 see camera surveillance.

videotex a system for accessing a database on a television screen or display, used for digital information boards and teletext.

Vienna blue a form of the pigment cobalt blue used in glass and enamels.

Vienna lake see carmine.

Vierendeel truss a flat trussed beam with vertical web members only connected to upper and lower chords with rigid joints; named after the Belgian engineer Arthur Vierendeel, its inventor in 1896. →33

view 1 a drawing or rendering depicting how an object, building, site or interior would look once complete; see below.
2 a constructed drawing showing the projected face of an object or elevation of a building in true scale; a projection.
3 the visual impact of a landscape or townscape as gained from a particular point, or from a certain direction.
aerial view.
bird's-eye view.
cross-section, see section.
cut, see section.
elevation.
front view. →127
interior view.
panorama.
plan view. →127
section.
side view. →127
top view, see plan view. →127
true view.
worm's-eye view.

viewer door viewer, see door scope. →51

viewpoint see station point. →128

viewport, window; in computing, a mode of showing different views of a drawn object on the same screen.

vignette, trayle, vinette; an ornamental motif consisting of stylized vine leaves and grapes. →82

vihara a Buddhist monastery building.

villa 1 Lat.; a large classical Roman country house with an estate; originally divided into two parts, the pars urbana, or living area, and pars rustica, or working area; see below. →88
2 in more modern times, any well-to-do detached house, country house on an estate, holiday home or a so-named suburban dwelling.
villa maritima Lat.; a luxury seaside mansion constructed by wealthy urban Romans for recreational use, usually palatial and with panoramic coastal views.
villa rustica Lat.; any Roman country dwelling from rudimentary cottages to palatial complexes; in general a walled country estate with stores and farm buildings, owned by wealthy Romans as a source of income.
village an urban settlement smaller than a town but larger than a hamlet, which has no council or financial powers of self-government.
villa suburbana Lat.; a walled suburban mansion with colonnades and gardens, constructed by wealthy urban Romans outside the city walls as a response to population pressure within the city.
vimana a small Hindu temple capped with a tower. →68
vine an ornamental motif consisting of stylized leaves and stems of the vine plant, *Vitis vinifera*. →82, →115
see vignette. →82
see *vine* in foliated ornaments illustration. →120
see *vine leaf capital* in medieval capitals illustration. →115
vine black, grape black; a bluish black pigment consisting of carbon with impurities obtained from burnt and ground wood and other vegetable products, traditionally made from charred twigs of the vine (*Vitis vinifera*); also known as blue black, coke black, cork black, drop black, German black, kernel black or yeast black, depending on country of origin or raw material used.
vine leaf capital a medieval capital embellished with vine leaf designs. →82, →115
vinette see vignette. →82
see vine. →82, →115
vinyl chloride a poisonous colourless gas used in the production of PVC and other polymers.
vinylidene chloride see polyvinylidene chloride.
vinyl paint an acid-, alkali- and weather-resistant emulsion paint based on a dispersion of vinyl or PVC in water, used on exterior masonry and plaster surfaces.
vinyl wallcovering wallcovering of a paper or fabric base with a PVC coating, available in rolls.
violaceous a shade of violet which takes its name from the colour of the flowers of the violet (Viola odorata).
Viola odorata the violet flower, see violaceous.
Viola parmensis see Parma violet.
violation of agreement see breach of contract.
violet a general name for bluish purple colours in the visible spectrum with wavelengths between 380 and 430 m; named after the flower of the violet plant, *Viola spp.*; see purple for list of purple and violet pigments.
see Viola spp.
violet madder lake see alizarin violet.
viridian a bright, transparent, permanent green pigment consisting of hydrated chromium oxide, suitable for use in oil, watercolour and acrylic paints; variously known as Casali's green, emerald chromium oxide, emeraulde green, Guinet's green, Mittler's green, Pannetier's green, smaragd green, transparent oxide of chromium, vert emeraude.
viridine green a shade of light green, often associated with the colours of the pigments Schweinfurt green and hydrated chrome oxide.
virus in computing, programming introduced to a system with the intention of subversion, disruption and destruction.
viscose a cellulose sodium salt solution used in the manufacture of artificial silk and other plastics.
viscosity, internal friction; in hydraulics, the resistance of a liquid to flow.
viscous flow see streamline flow.
vise see vice.
visibility distance see sight distance.
visible smoke detector see optical smoke detector.
visible spectrum the range of wavelengths of the electromagnetic spectrum comprising the colours in light which can be seen by the human eye.
visitor parking an area of parking or parking places reserved for the use of visitors to a building or complex.
visorium (Lat.); the spectator seating areas of a Roman amphitheatre; the cavea. →90
vista 1 in landscape design, a view along a main or grand axis, in the urban milieu lined by built form, in rural areas marked out by landmarks or bounded by natural features.
2 a longitudinal view framed by built form.
visual art any art such as painting, sculpture, photography, video or film in which the sense of sight is primarily used.
visual cone see cone of vision.
visual display unit 1 see display unit.
2 see monitor.
visualization the explanation or presentation of a proposal, design or idea in terms of a drawing, diagram, chart or model.
visual ray see central axis of vision. →128
visual ray method a method of constructing a perspective projection of an object using two stations or viewpoints, projectors, a picture plane and two planar views, but no vanishing points; also known as the direct plan projection method. →128
Vitis vinifera the vine plant, see vine. →82, →115
see wine yellow.
see vine black.
vitreous china a ceramic material with a relatively high glass content, used for sanitary fittings such as WC bowls and sinks.
vitreous enamel see enamel.
vitrification the conversion of mineral compounds into glass by fusion in high temperatures.
vitrine see display case.
vitriol a traditional name given to any of a number of hydrated sulphates of metals such as iron, copper, zinc, cobalt and aluminium, or for sulphuric acid.
Vitruvian man a popular theme in theories of art and architecture from Renaissance times, depicting a man of ideal proportions with arms outstretched within a circle and square, thus proposing the proportions of the human body as a basis for aesthetic design in accordance with the canons of proportion suggested by Vitruvius. →107
Vitruvian scroll, running dog, Vitruvian wave, wave scroll; an ornamental motif consisting of a series of interconnected leaning S-shaped figures. →125
Vitruvian wave see Vitruvian scroll. →125
vittatum see opus vittatum mixtum. →83
vivid blue a general name for shades of strong primary blue colour.
vivid green a general name for shades of strong primary green colour.
vivid red see signal red.
vivid violet a general name for shades of strong basic violet.
vivid yellow a general name for shades of strong primary yellow colour such as cadmium or flame yellow and chrome yellow.
V-match, chevron match; a veneering pattern in which veneers with slanting grain are glued side by side in mirror image along a centre line, forming a series of V shapes. →10

vocabulary see architectural language.

void 1 an opening in a floor or wall construction, such as one in a floor slab to afford light and a visual link with the storey below.
see *timber framing* illustration. →4
see *office building* illustration. →60
2 a space within a building or component, usually for technical installations, weight reduction etc. which is enclosed and to which access is provided usually for maintenance only; see below.
ceiling void. →60
roof void.
3 air- or water-filled spaces or channels within a porous solid such as concrete or wood.
see air void.
see water void.

void box see void form.

voided cross a cross drawn or made in outline only, or with a hollow centre. →118

void form, void box; a formwork mould for creating a void or opening in a cast concrete component.

voids ratio in concretework, the ratio of the volume of air to the total volume.

volatile referring to a liquid which will readily evaporate at room temperature.

volatile memory in computing, a memory in which data is not retained once the power supply has been switched off.

volatile oil see essential oil.

volcanic glass uncrystalline vitreous rock formed when molten lava cools down very quickly.

volcanic rock, vulcanite, effusive rock, extrusive rock; types of igneous rock originally formed from rapidly solidified magma pushed to the surface of the earth's crust; these include basalt, dacite and tuff.

volcanic tuff see tuff.
see peperino.

volt abb. **V**; the SI unit of electromotive force or potential difference; one volt produces a current of one amp in a resistor with a resistance of one ohm.

voltage, potential difference; electromotive force in an electric circuit measured in volts.

voltage drop the loss in electrical pressure or voltage caused by resistance of cables, power lines and other transmission devices.

voltage tester a screwdriver-like device with an insulated handle containing a small lamp which lights up when a current flows through the blade.

voltaic couple see galvanic couple.

volume 1 the physical measurement of three-dimensional space (length × width × height) whose SI unit is the cubic metre (m^3).
2 see gross building volume.
3 see traffic volume.

volume batching, proportioning by volume; the measuring out of the component parts of concrete into the desired ratio by volume as opposed to weight.

volume yield see concrete yield.

volute, 1 helix; in classical architecture, a spiral scroll found typically as a motif in classical Ionic, Corinthian and Composite capitals; any similar ornament. →80, →113
2 see spiral.

volute capital any capital which contains paired volutes; an Ionic, Aeolic or other capital from Asia or the Mediterranean. →69
see Aeolic capital. →69
see *Carolingian volute capital* illustration. →115
see Ionic capital. →80, →81

vomitorium Lat.; pl. vomitoria; the stepped entrance to a Roman auditorium or theatre. →90

vortex a violent spirally swirling mass of liquid or gas, as with a whirlpool or cyclone.

vortices plural of vortex.

voucher see receipt.

voussoir a wedge-shaped stone or brick used in the construction of a true masonry arch. →22

vulcanite 1 see volcanic rock.
2 see ebonite.

vulcanization the process of treating rubber with sulphur at a high temperature to increase strength and elasticity.

Vulpes vulpes see fox.

vulture see Nekhbet.

W

Wadjet the cobra goddess, protectress of ancient Lower Egypt; other spellings are Wedjet, Uadjet, Udjet. →74
Wadjet eye see eye of Horus. →75
waferboard flakeboard with specially shaped flakes. →9
waffle floor, honeycomb floor, rectangular grid floor; a concrete floor slab constructed of a grid of downstand beams with a pattern of hollows or coffers in the soffit, both for economy of concrete and for aesthetic effect.
waffle form see waffle mould.
waffle mould, pan form, waffle form; plastic, plywood or steel reusable moulds or formwork used to cast rectangular recesses in the underside of a concrete slab to form waffle slabs and coffered ceilings.
waffle slab, coffered slab, honeycomb slab; a ribbed reinforced concrete floor or roof slab whose underside is indented with a regular arrangement of hollows; see waffle floor. →27
wage, pay, wages; money paid to employees and others in return for work or services rendered, usually on a regular basis; see also salary.
wagonhead vault see barrel vault. →25
wagon vault see barrel vault. →25
wainscot, wainscoting; timber or joinery panelling, originally of oak, fixed to an interior wall below waist height.
wainscoting see wainscot.
waist 1 a thinning out in the middle of a component or element.
2 in concrete stair design, the minimum thickness of a flight, measured between the soffit and meeting of tread and riser.
waiting room a room for people awaiting transport, medical attention etc.
wale, 1 waler, whaler; in timber construction and formwork, a horizontal timber member which binds together vertical boards or sheet material.
2 see waling.
waler 1 see waling.
2 see wale.
waler plate a long plate which transfers loading evenly from a form tie to formwork. →30
waling, 1 wale, waler, ranger; a horizontal beam or other structural member which holds formwork sheeting in place around cast concrete, or at the edge of an excavation. →30
2 in excavation work, a horizontal intermediate support for poling boards, held apart by horizontal struts across the trench.
walk a lane, track or street intended for pedestrians.
walking line a theoretical line joining the nosings in a stair, given as the average position in plan of a person using the stair and taken by convention as 457 mm from the handrail. →45
walk-up apartments an apartment building less than three storeys in height, with access to all flats via external stairs or a stair core. →61
walkway, 1 access bridge; a suspended platform or gangway on a construction site, theatre or roofspace etc. for material conveyance, access to services and circulation, often with safety balustrades.
2 see catwalk. →46
3 see gantry.
4 see access balcony.
5 see footbridge. →64
6 see footway. →64
wall a vertical construction delineating and enclosing space inside a building, forming the external envelope, freestanding etc.; it may be loadbearing or non-loadbearing.
wall anchor 1 see toggle bolt. →37
2 see hollow-wall anchor. →37
wall base, base wall, foundation wall; that part of an external wall below a damp proof course or that part of a foundation wall above ground, on which an external wall is constructed.
see *Roman walling* illustration. →83
see *concrete frame* illustration. →28
see *timber-framed building* illustration. →57
see *blockwork wall base* in brick house illustration. →59
wallboard any board product such as gypsum board, fibre board, plywood or laminates used in construction as cladding for a wall frame, as a base for a finish, or as a lining.
wallboard panel see prefabricated gypsum wallboard panel.
wall brush see flat brush. →43
wall cap see coping.
wall cladding weatherproofing components, sheet material etc. for cladding the exterior wall frame and construction of a building.
see *wall cladding* in office building illustration. →60
wallcovering any material in thin sheet form, wallpaper, textiles, vinyl sheeting etc., supplied in rolls and applied to interior walls as a finish or a base which can be painted.
wallcovering support the surface onto which a wallcovering is fixed; a wall or ceiling.
walled town a medieval town surrounded by a fortified wall as defence and to preserve the health and financial status of its inhabitants.
wall end 1 see stopped end. →21
2 see return end.
wallette a model wall built for test purposes.
wall foundation see wall base.
wall hanging see tapestry.
wall hung bidet a bidet appliance supported by a bracket from a wall, so that there is a gap between it and the floor.
wall hung WC pan a WC supported by a bracket from a wall, so that there is a gap between it and the floor, its drain penetrating the rear wall.
walling the process and product of constructing walls in masonry.
see *Roman walling* illustration. →83
see *brickwork* illustrations. →20, →21
wall joint in masonry construction, an internal joint which remains hidden in the thickness of a wall. →20
wall lining, lining paper; paper wallcovering hung as a base for a subsequent wallcovering.
wall painting see mural.
wall panel a prefabricated cladding or infill panel for walling. →28
wall panelling boards or joinery fixed as a timber lining for a wall, often framed.
wallpaper wallcovering of decorated or embossed sheets of sized paper, supplied in rolls.
wallpapering, paperhanging; the trade of fixing wallpaper to an internal wall surface.
wallpaper paste adhesive for fixing wallpaper, consisting of a powder such as flour or methyl cellulose mixed with water.
wall plate a longitudinal member incorporated into or placed on a wall, onto which another construction is fixed. →4, →33

see *timber framing joints* illustration. →4
see *rafter and purlin roof* illustration. →33
see *timber floor* illustration. →44
see *timber-framed building* illustration. →57
see *holiday home and sauna* illustration. →58
see *brick house* illustration. →59

wall plug 1 a plastic fixing sleeve inserted into prebored holes, enabling metal screws to be anchored to masonry and other difficult surfaces. →37
2 see legs anchor. →37
3 see hollow-wall plug. →37

wall reinforcement steel reinforcement for a reinforced concrete wall. →27

wall-stair a stair constructed within a hollow in the thickness of a masonry wall, often in a castle or fortification. →103

wall thickness 1 the perpendicular measurement of any wall from inner to outer surface.
2 the thickness of a brick wall, measured in fractions of the length of a brick, one brick, one-and-a-half brick etc.

wall tie a galvanized steel or twisted wire fixing laid at regular intervals into a masonry wall to provide stability by connecting masonrywork to a structural base, or by linking inner and outer leaves of brickwork; called a cavity tie when used in cavity walls. →22
see *types of wall tie* illustration; types included as separate entries are listed below. →22
see *wall tie* in brick house illustration. →59
butterfly wall tie. →22
double triangle wall tie. →22
fishtail wall. →22
strip wall tie. →22
twin triangle tie, double triangle wall tie. →22
vertical twist tie. →22

wall tile any tile used for facing an internal or external wall surface. →20, →44

wall tiling 1 the laying of wall tiles.
2 the product of this process.

wall-to-wall carpet see fitted carpet. →44

wall unit see wall panel. →28

wall-walk see alure. →103

walnut [*Juglans spp.*] a group of hardwoods from Europe, Asia and America valued for their decorative grain figure; used for furniture and veneers; see American walnut, European walnut; see ***Juglans spp.*** for full list of species of walnut included in this work.
see African walnut, *Lovoa trichilioides*, *Lovoa klaineana*.

walnut oil a drying oil used as a vehicle in paints, pressed from the dried kernels of the common or English walnut.

wan see sallow.

wane the curved edge of a timber board cut from the edge of a log, with or without bark. →1

waney a description of a sawn timber with wane on one or both edges. →1

waning moon see decrescent.

ward, 1 precinct (Am.); a political or administrative division of a town, borough or city.
2 a communal room in a hospital, equipped with beds for overnight patients.
3 see bailey. →103
4 see inner ward. →103

wardrobe 1 a piece of furniture or built-in cupboard with shelves and a rail for the storage of clothes.
2 see airing cupboard.
3 a room or space in a theatre in which costumes are kept.

warehouse a large building for storing goods and products prior to distribution; a storehouse.
see *warehouse* in Hippodamian town plan illustration. →94

warm-air heater, fan heater; a space-heating appliance which blows out a stream of warmed air.

warm-air heating, fan heating; a heating system in which warm air is blown into spaces to maintain a certain temperature level.

warm-air unit a device which discharges a flow of warm air to provide heating and ventilation.

warm boot restarting a computer after a software fault has occurred or after installing hardware etc.

warm colour in colour theory, any colour dominated by red, orange or yellow, and which produces a subjective feeling of warmth.

warm roof roof construction in which insulation is laid below the waterproofing, and a vapour barrier below the insulation.

warp 1 the distortion in shape of a piece of improperly seasoned timber due to uneven drying.
see *seasoning defects of timber* illustration. →1
2 see warp yarn.

warp yarn in weaving, carpetmaking and tapestry, a suspended lengthwise structural thread onto which the weft or crosswise threads are woven.

warranty see guarantee.

Warren truss a trussed beam patented by the British engineers James Warren and Willoughby Monzoni in 1848, whose web members form a series of equilateral or isosceles triangles joined by upper and lower chords; sometimes its end struts are vertical; see also Howe truss, Pratt truss, Vierendeel truss. →33

Warrington hammer see cross peen hammer. →40

wash 1 a watery solution of material applied as a treatment or finish.
2 see acid wash.
3 see whitewash.
4 see cleaning.
5 in watercolour painting, a layer or area of thin, transparent, watered-down colour often used as a base.

washability in paintwork, the ability of a coat to withstand washing.

washable describing a finish which may be washed with water and soap without causing damage.

washbasin see handrinse basin.

washboard see skirting board. →2, →44

washdown WC pan the most common type of WC in which waste is removed by flushing water.

washer a perforated plate beneath a bolt-head or nut which acts as a spacer in a bolt fixing and transfers the pressure of the fixing over a wider area; types included as separate entries are listed below. →36
see *fixings and washers* illustration. →37
flat washer. →37
lock washer.
spring lock washer.
tooth washer. →37

wash fountain, ablution fountain; a large circular or polygonal communal washbasin which accommodates a number of people washing at any given time.

wash-house, laundry; a space or separate building for the use of the inhabitants of a residential facility to wash clothes and other fabrics.

washing line, clothes line; a length of tensioned cord strung between two points, on which washed clothes and fabrics are hung up to dry.

washing machine a domestic appliance for washing clothes and fabrics, connected to a drainage system and water supply.

washing machine valve a water fitting for turning on or off a cold water supply to a washing machine.

washing trough, ablution trough; a large, long, rectangular communal washbasin which accommodates a number of people washing at any given time.

washout WC pan a WC in which soil falls into a water filled bowl and is removed by the downthrust of flushing water.

washroom, 1 lavatory; a room with running water for personal cleaning, nowadays with washbasins, WCs etc.
2 see lavatrina. →88

waste 1 material left over from an industrial, commercial or consumer process which is relatively unusable; waste may refer to both solids and liquids, refuse is usually solid; types included as separate entries are listed below.
biodegradable waste, see organic waste.
commercial waste.
construction waste.
domestic refuse.
flush grated waste.
garbage, see rubbish.
hazardous waste.
household waste, see domestic refuse.
industrial waste.
organic waste.
problem waste, see hazardous waste.
recoverable waste.
recyclable waste, see recoverable waste.
rubbish.
sewage.
soil water.
solid waste.
toxic waste.
trade waste, see commercial waste.
waste water.
2 the metal ring-shaped component fixed at the base of a sink, handbasin or sanitary appliance, through which waste water passes via a trap into a drain; often supplied with a fitted plug; see waste coupling.
outlet.
pop-up waste.
slotted waste.

waste bin see litter bin.

waste chute, refuse chute; a chute within a building into which waste material can be tipped, often with a collecting vessel or rubbish room at its base.

waste collection see refuse collection.

waste collection vehicle, dustcart (Am.), dustbin lorry, refuse vehicle; in waste management, a lorry equipped with a container and waste compressor for the organized collection of waste.

waste compactor a hydraulic or pneumatic device to compress collected waste into a reduced volume.

waste coupling, waste; a pipe fitting at a plug-hole or other appliance outlet for joining it to a discharge pipe.

waste disposal unit a powered device for shredding organic household waste prior to its discharge into a drain.

waste management the storage, collection, disposal and treatment of household refuse and industrial and commercial waste.

waste mould in ornamental plastering, a mould which has to be destroyed in order to release the casting.

waster a masonry chisel with a flat, toothed or profiled blade for producing a rough stone finish. →41

waste skip in waste management, a large transportable metal container for the collection of commercial and building waste.

waste sorting in waste management, the sorting of collected waste into categories of material for recycling.

waste storage chamber a space or building for the storage of refuse bins.

waste storage container a vessel for the temporary storage of solid or liquid waste prior to transport to a place of disposal.

waste water water which results from household processes, cleaning and food preparation but not from WCs or industrial processes.

waste water appliance any sanitary appliance, basin etc. for washing, fitted with a water supply and outlet connected to a waste water drain.

watch-tower see lookout tower. →103

water a very common chemical compound, **H_2O**, a colourless and odourless substance in its liquid state between the temperatures of 0° and 100°; essential for life on earth and a basic constituent of concrete, plasters and many other building materials.

water bar, water stop; a strip of metal or plastic embedded into a sill or threshold to inhibit the passage of water.

water-based, aqueous; referring to paints, varnishes and other similar liquids which consist of a solid or liquid dissolved, suspended or dispersed in water.

water-based adhesive see water borne adhesive.

water-based paint any paint in which the pigment is suspended or dissolved in water; often emulsion paint.

water blue a shade of blue which takes its name from the colour of water at a depth; the colour of the pigment Bremen blue.

waterboard see splashboard.

water borne adhesive, aqueous adhesive, water-based adhesive; any adhesive whose binder is dissolved or dispersed in water.

water burnt lime slaked lime which has been incompletely mixed with water giving a coarse texture.

water/cement ratio in concretework, the ratio of water to cement in the mix, regulated to affect its compressive strength.

water check an upstand or raised fillet in a flat roof plane to convey water away from vulnerable areas.

water closet see WC.

water closet pan see WC pan.

water closet suite see WC suite.

watercolour paints and painting techniques using opaque or transparent water-soluble pigments; see gouache, aquarelle.

watercolour paper, aquarelle paper; absorbent textured paper, used for watercolour painting, often made by hand.

water content the mass of water per unit volume of mix, especially in concreting, plastering and painting.

water distribution system a system of pipes, vessels and associated devices through which water is conveyed to a building or area.

water engineering in civil and ground engineering, the design and control of the flow, treatment and disposal of ground and surface water.

waterfall water flowing over a vertical precipice in a river or stream; often included in landscaped gardens as a feature.

water fitting in hot and cold water installations, a tap, valve or other fitting connected to a water supply to control its flow or draw water off for use.

water gain see concrete bleeding.

watergate a gate or entrance which leads from a building directly onto a waterway; in fortifications it may be the defended gateway through which supplies are delivered. →103

water glass see sodium silicate.

water green a shade of grey green which takes its name from a loose association with the colour of sea water.

water hammer, reverberation, pressure surge; the sudden change of velocity of water in pipework inducing pressure waves which cause a hammering noise.

water heater a device or installation for heating water in a hot water supply system.
see electric water heater.
see pressure water heater.

water-heating plant see boiler plant.

watering the addition of water to construction processes, planting etc. by pouring, spraying or sprinkling.

water installation see water system.

waterleaf 1 any decorative motif based on the stylized leafs of the water lily (called lotus in antique times); found especially in Roman and Greek architecture, and in different form in the capitals of medieval Byzantine and Romanesque architecture. →82
see classical *waterleaf and dart* in floriated and foliated ornament illustration. →82
2 carved decoration of stylized unribbed broad leaf motifs found adorning capitals in Norman architecture.
see *water leaf capital* in medieval capitals illustration. →115

waterleaf and dart see waterleaf and tongue, leaf and dart. →82

waterleaf and tongue an ornamental motif consisting of a series of stylized leaves alternating with ovoid forms; same as or similar to leaf and dart. →82

waterleaf capital any capital embellished with water leaf designs, especially a Norman capital with a squared block whose lower corners are carved with a leaf motif. →115

water level, 1 hydrostatic level; a simple site instrument for measuring level differences between two points on a building site, consisting of a flexible tube filled with water.
2 the level at which the upper surface of water usually rests, whether in a gauge, waterway or the water table.
3 see water-line.

water lily 1 see lily. →82, →121
2 see lotus. →82, →121
3 see waterleaf. →82

water-line a horizontal mark indicating water level when a cistern, storage vessel etc., is full.

water main a main water distribution pipe from a water authority, to which individual users or buildings can be connected.

watermark in paper production, a distinctive manufacturer's emblem incorporated into the paper, which shows when held up against the light.

water meter a device for measuring the quantity of water for consumption supplied to a building.

water of hydration in concreting and plasterwork, the water that combines chemically with a hydraulic binder.

water outlet one of the points in a building where hot or cold water supply can be drawn off for use, usually fitted with a tap or valve.

water permeability the property of a porous solid such as stone or concrete to permit the passage of water through due to differential pressure.

water pipe a pipe, usually of copper, through which water is conveyed to and within a building; part of any technical installation in which water is conveyed.

water pressure the force exerted by a mass of water either to propel itself, or exerting a load on a surrounding structure.

waterproof the ability of a material or construction to resist the penetration of water.

waterproof adhesive see water-resistant adhesive.

waterproof glue see water-resistant adhesive.

waterproofing admixture see water-resisting admixture.

waterproofing membrane a layer of impervious sheet material, usually bitumen based, incorporated into flat roof construction to prevent the passage of water downwards. →44

waterproof ink ink that is not soluble in water once dry.

waterproof plaster see damp resisting plaster.

waterproof render see damp resisting plaster.

water reducer see water reducing admixture.

water reducing admixture, plasticizer, water reducer; in concretework, a plasticizing admixture included in the mix to increase workability with a lower water content.

water reed [*Arundo phragmites*, *Phragmites australis*]; see best reed, Norfolk reed.

water-repellent cement see hydrophobic cement.

water resistant, 1 moisture resistant; a description or specification of a material or construction which resists penetration by, and chemical reaction with, water and is otherwise physically unaffected by contact with water.
2 see waterproof.

water-resistant adhesive, waterproof glue; any adhesive which maintains its bond strength when in contact with water.

water-resisting admixture, waterproofing admixture; in concretework, an admixture included in the mix to inhibit the absorption or passage of water.

water seal water in the vessel of a drainage trap to prevent the passage of foul air from a drainage system.

water seasoning see ponding.

watershed a ridge or area of raised land between two waterways or drainage areas, from which water flows in different directions.

waterside plant any species of landscaping plant which usually grows near water, but not necessarily in it.

watersplash see ford.

water spout see rainwater spout. →100

water stain a translucent colouring agent for porous surfaces such as timber consisting of a dye suspended in water.

water stop see water bar.

water storage tank see water tank.

water supply 1 the supply of water for a building from a main.
2 see water system.

water supply system see water system.

water system, water installation, water supply; the piped supply of water, pipe fittings, appliances etc., for a building.
see hot water supply system.

water table, groundwater table, groundwater level; the upper level of water in the ground, varying according to locality, rainfall, excavation and mining etc.

water tank a closed pressure vessel for storing water for use in a water supply system; see cistern.
see reserve water tank.
see cistern. →91

water tap, faucet (Am.), tap; a water fitting, usually attached to a basin, sink or bath, from which hot or cold water can be drawn off for use.

water test, hydraulic test; a test for leaks, unwanted openings and water flow in pipework by introducing water into a closed or restricted circuit at high pressure.

watertight referring to the ability of a material or product to keep out water.

water tower a tall structure containing stored water at high level to provide pressure for water distribution to mains supply.

water transport a mode of transport using boats, ships or other vessels over water.

water vapour small droplets of airborne water, usually condensation from boiled or evaporated water.

water void in concretework, small spaces or voids in hardened concrete containing excess water not bound by the hydration reaction, which may render the concrete susceptible to frost damage; see capillary space.

waterway 1 an area of sea, lake, river or canal, especially when used as a route by water traffic.
2 in plumbing and drainage, any pipe, channel or vessel for conveying water.

waterway bridge a bridge carrying traffic over a body of water such as a river, estuary, lake etc. →64

watt abb. **W**; SI basic unit of power, 1 W = 1 J/s.

wattle see flaking.

wattle and dab see wattle and daub.

wattle and daub, 1 rad and dab, wattle and dab; a traditional form of infill walling construction for timber frames etc. consisting of woven horizontal twigs, often willow, covered with clay or mud.
2 see opus craticium, Roman wattle and daub construction. →83

wave 1 a series of oscillations which transfers energy through a medium without the transference of the matter itself.
2 see sound wave.
3 see wave moulding. →124
4 wave scroll, see Vitruvian scroll. →124

waveform a graphic representation of the shape of a wave.

wave front in wave motion, the extent of a wave perpendicular to the direction of propagation.

wavelength the measure of a length of a physical waveform, measured as the distance between two adjacent crests.

wave motion a physical form of motion which propagates through a medium with an oscillating action, as with the surface of water.

wave moulding, 1 undulating moulding; an ornamental motif consisting of a pattern of undulating lines. →124
2 see oundy moulding. →125
3 Vitruvian wave, see Vitruvian scroll. →125

wave pattern a paving pattern of small stones or cobbles laid in a series of undulating and interweaving curves, resembling guilloche ornament. →15

wave scroll see Vitruvian scroll. →125

wavy grain, curl, sinuous grain, tiger grain; an undulating grain formation found in certain hardwoods with an irregular cell structure, used in decorative veneers.

wavy paver a specially shaped concrete paving unit with a wavy profile, laid to create a regular pattern. →15

wawa see obeche.

wax 1 a solid greasy extract from vegetable, animal and mineral sources, used in the production of paints and varnishes, as a protective finish for wooden surfaces and as a binder in wax and pastel crayons.
2 see beeswax.

wax crayon a drawing stick consisting of pigment in a wax binder, used for drawing and colouring.

waxing the application of a coating of wax to a surface as a finish.

waxing moon see increscent.

wax white a shade of pale yellowish grey which takes its name from the colour of bleached beeswax.

wax yellow a shade of pale yellow which takes its name from the colour of beeswax.

WC, 1 water closet; a room containing a water closet suite connected to a drain and water supply; see toilet. →57
2 see WC suite.
see *WC* in office building illustration. →60

WC cover a hinged lid for a WC seat.

WC lock see bathroom lock. →39

WC pan, 1 water closet pan; the ceramic bowl in a water closet suite where human waste is deposited.
2 see close coupled WC pan.

WC seat the hinged part of a WC suite which provides a place to sit; types included as separate entries are listed below.
balanced seat, see self-raising seat.
cut-away-front seat, see open front seat.
inset seat.
open front seat.
pad seat, see inset seat.
ring seat.
self-raising seat.

WC suite, water closet suite; a device with a pan, seat and flushing cistern for collection and disposal of human waste; commonly called a WC or toilet.

wear the mechanical degeneration of a surface, construction or appliance due to continual use, exposure to the elements etc.

wearing course, topping, carpet; in road construction, the uppermost layer of hardwearing material in contact with traffic, usually asphalt or concrete. →62

wearing surface in road construction, the uppermost surface of the wearing course in direct contact with traffic.

weatherboarding, siding; exterior cladding of horizontal or vertical sawn timber boards for a building frame, laid side by side or overlapping. →8
see *types of weatherboarding* illustration; types included as separate entries are listed below. →8
see *weatherboarding* in holiday home and sauna illustration. →58
bead boarding. →8
bead edged boarding. →8
board and batten cladding. →8
board on board cladding. →8, →57
butt-edged boarding, see square-edged boarding. →8
ceiling boarding. →57, →59
clapboarding. →8
close boarding. →57
colonial siding, see clapboarding. →8
diagonal boarding. →8
exterior boarding, external boarding, see weatherboarding. →8
feather-jointed boarding, see spline-jointed boarding. →8
featheredged boarding, featherboarding. →8
floorboards, floorboarding.
gapped boarding, see spaced boarding. →8, →57, →58
horizontal boarding. →8
log cabin siding. →8
matchboarding. →8
moulded boarding, see bead boarding. →8
open boarding, see spaced boarding. →8
open tongue and groove boarding. →8
reeded boarding, see bead boarding. →8
roof boarding. →48
round-edged boarding, round-arris boarding. →8
shiplap boarding. →8
sound boarding, see pugging boards. →8
spaced boarding. →8
spline-jointed boarding. →8
square-edged boarding. →8
staggered siding, see board on board cladding. →8, →57
tongue and groove boarding, see matchboarding. →8
vertical boarding. →8

weathercock a weather-vane in the shape of a cockerel.
see *weathercock* in Scandinavian hall church illustration. →102

weathered 1 referring to materials that have been in external conditions for some time with consequent surface deterioration such as discoloration, corrosion, exfoliation etc.
2 referring to a sill or coping laid at a slope to allow for the runoff of rainwater.

weathered joint, weather joint, weather-struck joint, struck joint; a horizontal brickwork joint whose mortar is pressed in at the top, slanting in cross-section. →16

weathered pointing in brickwork, the making of weathered joints.

weather fillet see mortar fillet.

weathering 1 the effect of rain, moisture, sun, wind and external pollutants on materials that have been in external conditions for some time.

2 the discoloration, greying, and disintegration of untreated external wood surfaces due to the effects of the weather.
3 see brickwork weathering.

weathering steel steel with a high copper content, whose surface corrodes to form an oxide coating with good resistance to corrosion; see Cor-Ten.

weather joint see weathered joint. →16

weatherproof see weather resistant.

weatherproofing see roofing.

weather resistant, weatherproof; referring to a material, product or construction which is resistant to the attack of the elements.

weather seal see weatherstrip. →53

weather shingling timber shingles laid vertically as cladding for a wall.

weatherstrip, draught strip, draught excluder, weather seal; a strip of impervious material applied to joints between a door leaf or window casement and its frame to prevent the passage of water and air draughts, and as soundproofing.
see *weatherstrip* in window illustration. →53

weather-struck joint see weathered joint. →16

weather tiling see tile hanging.

weather-vane, vane, weathercock; a flat piece of metal which is free to rotate around a central pivot, fixed to a roof or high point to indicate the current wind direction.
see *weather-vane* in Scandinavian hall church illustration. →102

web 1 part of a beam between the upper and lower chords or surfaces, which resists shear forces within the beam; the material, flange etc. forming this. →33
2 the surface of a vault, see cell. →25, →101

weber abb. **Wb**; SI unit of magnetic flux, equal to the amount of flux that produces an electromotive force of one volt as it is reduced to zero in one second; 1 Wb = 1 volt per second.

web reinforcement see shear reinforcement.

web saw see turning saw.

wedge 1 in timber jointing, a tapered piece, used for tightening joints and fixings. →3
2 see folding wedges. →3
3 see fox wedge.

wedge anchor, sleeve anchor, expansion bolt; a heavy duty metal threaded fastener for fixing to concrete or masonry, inserted in a bored hole then twisted to retract its wedged termination into a split sleeve, which expands to lock tight against the edge of the hole. →37

wedge bead a small wedge-shaped machined timber profile used primarily as a glazing bead. →2

wedged scarf joint see keyed scarf joint. →3

wedged joint 1 any timber tenon joint using wedges driven in as tightening. →5
2 see fox-wedged joint. →5
3 see keyed tenon joint. →5

wedge-tomb a type of chambered tomb, found in Ireland, with a wedge-shaped burial chamber.

Wedjet see Wadjet. →74

week abb. **wk**; a measure of time equal to 7 days; not an SI unit.

weem see fogou.

weep-hole a gap for ventilation and to allow water to run out of the lower edges of cavity brickwork above a damp proof course, usually made by leaving the mortar out of vertical joints.

weevil 1 [*Curculionidae*] a family of insects, some species of which cause great destruction to timber by boring.
2 see eremotes weevil.
3 wood weevil.

weft yarn in weaving, carpetmaking and tapestry, a crosswise thread woven onto the warp or structural threads, forming the main surface of the fabric.

weight a measure of the heaviness of an object, whose SI unit is the kilogram.

weight batching, proportioning by weight; the measuring out of the component parts of concrete into the desired ratio by weight as opposed to volume.

weir a damming waterfall in a waterway to control the level of water upstream, often sloping downstream.

weir overflow a weir in a vessel down which water can flow into a drain if the water level rises too high.

weld 1 the act or result of welding.
2 see welded joint. →34
3 a yellow vegetable pigment produced from the dyer's rocket plant [*Reseda luteola*].

weldability the ability of a metal, plastic or other material to be welded.

welded fabric 1 welded mesh, especially when used as concrete reinforcement. →34
2 see fabric reinforcement.

welded joint, weld; a joint between metal components which has been formed by welding. →34
see butt weld. →34
see fillet weld. →34
see lap weld. →34

welded mesh, 1 welded wire mesh, welded fabric; a product manufactured from two sets of parallel steel strands or wires spot welded at right angles to one another to form a mesh, used for fences, partitions, lathing and as concrete reinforcement. →34
2 see fabric reinforcement.
3 see welded mesh fencing.

welded mesh fencing, welded mesh fabric; a steel mesh product of slender steel bars welded together, used for fences and screens.

welded plate girder see plate girder. →34

welded tuff see ignimbrite.

welded wire mesh see welded mesh. →34

welding 1 the joining together of metal (and plastics) components by melting or pressure or a combination of both; see fusion welding, resistance welding.
2 see heat welding.

weld line the visible line along a joint, formed when two materials are welded together.

weld-on hinge a heavy-duty hinge for use with steel-framed doors and windows, of which one swivelling part is welded to the frame and one to the leaf or casement. →38

welfare study see social welfare study.

well 1 a traditional source of drinking and household water, a hole bored in the ground into which fresh groundwater naturally gathers. →92
artesian well.
oil well.
2 shaft; a vertical void through a building to provide light and ventilation, or for a lift installation or staircase; see below for examples.
lift well.
stairwell.
light well.
mat well.

well enclosure see lift well enclosure.

well-house a small building or structure which shelters a well, often containing a holy shrine or healthy waters.

well module see lift shaft module.

well-proportioned, harmonic; of a building or composition, visually harmonized with regard to relative proportions and scale.

welt, welted seam; a fastened seam or joint between two adjacent sheets of supported sheetmetal roofing. →49
see welted edge.
see cross-welt. →49
see single-lock welt. →49
see double welt. →49

welted edge, single welt; the bent over edge of a sheetmetal component, roofing etc. to provide rigidity.

welted seam see welt.

wenge [*Millettia laurentii*] a hardwood from Central and East African rainforests with dark brown-black, extremely tough timber; used for furniture, exterior and interior joinery.

west one of the points of the compass, the direction at which the sun sets and lies at six o'clock in the evening in the Northern hemisphere.

west chancel a choir at the west end of a medieval double-chancel church. →97

west end the end of a church traditionally opposite the east-facing principal altar, in Gothic architecture a highly ornate facade with towers and a main entrance. →100

western framing see platform frame. →57

western hemlock [*Tsuga heterophylla*] a western North American softwood with white to yellowish brown timber, one of the lightest softwoods in use; used for general construction and plywood.

western larch [*Larix occidentalis*] a North American softwood with coarse-textured reddish brown wood; used in building construction and flooring.

western red cedar, British Columbian cedar, giant cedar, Pacific red cedar, red cedar, giant arborvitae; [*Thuja plicata*] a North American softwood with weak but durable reddish brown timber; used for shingles and exterior boarding.

western triple cross see papal cross. →117

western white pine, soft pine; [*Pinus monticola*] a softwood from the USA with pale yellow-red-brown heartwood; used for interiors and plywood.

westwork a high narthex at the west end of some Romanesque and Carolingian basilica churches, often bounded by towers and encompassing both nave and aisles in a number of storeys; the forebear of ornate facades at the west end of later Gothic churches.
see *Carolingian abbey church* illustration. →98
see *Romanesque church* illustration. →99

wet analysis in soil classification, the analysis of fine particular soils by allowing a sample to slowly settle in water and measuring the densities of the sediment at regular intervals.

wet and dry paper a fine abrasive paper used for sanding and smoothing, wetted with water as lubrication and to prevent the abrasive surface from clogging up.

wet area a bath, shower or other space in a building in which water can be expected to flow freely, requiring water-resistant finishes and specially located electrical fittings.
see *wet area flooring* illustration. →44

wet blasting, vapour blasting; the sandblasting of masonry with an abrasive and water, included to inhibit the spread of dust.

wet dash, dashed finish, harl, roughcast, slap dash; a rendered finish for external masonry in which mortar or plaster is thrown on a wall rough, either by hand using a trowel, or by machine using an applicator.

wet-mix process a sprayed concrete process in which premixed concrete, including water, is projected through a nozzle at high velocity by a pump; see dry-mix process.

wetness the state of being coated or soaked in water.

wet-pipe system a sprinkler system whose pipes are always full of water, connected to a permanent supply; see dry-pipe system.

wet removable wallcovering a wallcovering which can only be removed by scraping, having been treated by soaking in water or a stripper, or by steaming.

wet rubbing the smoothing of a surface with a fine abrasive such as sandpaper in the presence of water to clean and remove dust.

wet sieving the segregation of coarse concrete aggregate from finer particles by placing in water and sieving the mixture through a 0.075 mm mesh prior to use in concrete.

wet slaking the slaking of lime using an excess of water than is needed for hydration.

wettability the ability of a liquid to become immersed in solid and make it wet.

wetting the application of water to a surface or solid mass, as in curing of concrete, raising of timber grain prior to final smoothing etc.

Weymouth pine see yellow pine.

whaler see wale.

wharf a mooring structure of masonry or timber for the loading and unloading of ships and other water-borne vessels; a landing stage. →64

wheat see golden wheat.

wheel a circular component which revolves around an axis, used in many machines and devices for propulsion and transfer of power; in ornament symbolic of movement and cyclic events; types included as separate entries are listed below. →120
Catherine wheel. →122
colour wheel.
cross wheel, see wheel cross. →118
dharma wheel, see dharma chakra. →120
emery wheel.
Ferris wheel.
grinding wheel.
moulding wheel.
sun wheel, see wheel cross. →118
thermal wheel, see heat recovery unit.
the wheel of law, see dharma chakra. →120

wheelbarrow, barrow; a general-purpose one-wheeled cart with two handles, used on a building site for carrying soil, construction materials, building waste etc.

wheel cross, sun cross, solar cross; a circular emblem enclosing a cross motif, one of the oldest religious symbols; also known as the sun or cross wheel, and Odin's or Woden's cross in Viking Scandinavia. →118
sun wheel. →118
Odin's cross. →118

wheelhouse a round prehistoric dwelling with a circular open central court and radiating walls defining interior space, occurring predominantly in Scotland. →65

wheeling step see winder. →45

wheel of law see dharma chakra. →120

wheel ore see bournonite.

wheel step see winder. →45

wheel tread see winder. →45

wheel window see Catherine wheel window. →109
see types of *wheel window* illustration. →109

whetstone see hone.

whip 1 in landscaping, a young slender stemmed tree under two years old.
2 see flail. →74

whirlpool bath a bath with in-built water jets for massage and other purposes; see also jacuzzi.

whispering gallery an acoustic space under a dome in which even a quiet noise such as a whisper may be heard all around its circumference.

white a general name for achromatic shades of colour; the lightest colour of the grey scale; white pigments include white lead, zinc white, titanium white and chalk; see below for list of white pigments.
antimony white.
barium sulphate, see blanc fixe.
baryta white, see blanc fixe.
biacca.
bianco sangiovanni.
bismuth white.
blanc fixe.
blanc titane, see titanium white.
Bougival white.
ceruse.
Chinese white.
constant white, see blanc fixe.
Cremnitz white.

Dutch white.
enamel white, see blanc fixe.
English white, see whiting.
Flemish white, see flake white.
French white, see flake white.
Krems white, see Cremnitz white.
lime white.
lithopone.
magnesia white.
magnesium carbonate.
mineral white.
oleum white, see lithopone.
Paris white.
permanent white, see blanc fixe.
snow white, see zinc white.
Spanish white.
St John's white, see bianco sangiovanni.
strontium white.
terra alba.
Timonox.
titanium white.
white lead.
whiting.
zinc white.

white alder (Am.) see grey alder.

white ant see termite.

white ash see American ash; [*Fraxinus americana*].

white cast iron rapidly cooled cast iron, harder and more brittle than grey cast iron; used as a base for steel and malleable cast iron.

white cedar [*Thuja occidentalis*] a North American softwood with light brown timber; used in boat-building and construction work.

white cement see white Portland cement.

white concrete a light-coloured finish concrete made with white Portland cement and a pale-coloured aggregate.

white crown the symbolic head-dress of ancient Upper Egypt, a tall white hood with a bulb at its top; often later subsumed into the combined crown of the New Kingdom. →74

white fir [*Abies concolor*] a North American softwood used for sawn boards.

white land in town planning, undeveloped land with no particular zoning use associated with it or allocated to it in a town plan.

white lead a poisonous opaque white pigment used since ancient times in paints; composed of lead carbonates and lead sulphates.

white lead ore see cerussite.

white lily the white lotus, *Nymphaea lotus*; see lotus. →82, →121

white lotus *Nymphaea lotus*; see lotus. →82, →121

white noise, white sound; in acoustics, unobtrusive noise of a wide range of frequencies introduced into a space to mask out unwanted background noise.

white oak [*Quercus spp.*] a group of hardwoods from North America, especially the American white oak, Quercus alba, with heavy durable timber which is grey to reddish brown; used for flooring, panelling and trim.

white pigments see white.

white pine see yellow pine.

white pitted rot see red ring rot.

white pocket rot see red ring rot.

white poplar, silver poplar, abele; [*Populus alba*] a hardwood from Europe and Central Asia; see poplar.

white Portland cement, white cement; a Portland cement, made with iron-free raw materials, used to provide white cements and concretes.

white rot a general term for fungal decay which attacks cellulose and lignin in timber and leaves a whitish stringy residue.

white rot fungus a large group of fungi which attack both the cellulose and lignin of dead wood to leave a white residue behind, causing serious decay and weakening of timber construction.

white spongy rot [*Antrodia serialis*] a brown rot fungus which causes decay in wooden posts and timberwork in poorly ventilated, damp underfloor spaces.

white sound see white noise.

white speck 1 a form of white pocket rot which causes rice-sized cavities or specks in living timber.
2 see red ring rot.

white spirit, mineral spirit, petroleum spirit; a volatile liquid manufactured from the distillation of petroleum; used as a thinner and as a substitute for turpentine.

white spruce [*Picea glauca*] a softwood marketed as Canadian spruce.

white walnut see butternut.

whitewash, limewash, whiting; a solution of lime or crushed chalk and water used to whiten masonry and plastered wall surfaces.

whitewashing see limewashing.

white willow, common willow; [*Salix alba*] a deciduous tree commonly planted in parks and gardens as ornament.

whiting 1 natural calcium carbonate which is ground, washed and refined; used as an inert pigment in paints, a white pigment in water-based media, and mixed with oil to form putty.
2 see Paris white.
3 see whitewash.

Whitworth thread, BSW thread; a standardized range of screw threads whose dimensions are based on number of threads per inch.

whole brick see full brick. →21

whole-brick wall see one-brick wall. →21

whorl decoration based on a spiral or swirling flower motif. →123

wicket door, 1 pass door; a small integral hinged door within a larger overhead or sliding door in factories or loading bays for the use of staff.
2 a gate to an area such as a churchyard or field.

wide plank flooring timber flooring consisting of wooden boards over 100 mm wide, or rough planks, laid parallel to one another. →44

wide strip flooring see wide plank flooring. →44

widestrip foundation a foundation type consisting of a wide rectangular concrete casting beneath a wall, requiring transverse reinforcement; used to spread the bearing of heavy loads over a larger area than with a normal strip foundation. →29

width, breadth; the shorter or transverse dimension of an object. →2

wiggle nail see corrugated fastener. →35

wild cherry see sweet cherry.

willow [*Salix spp.*] a genus of hardwood bushes, shrubs and trees often planted as decoration and with light, resilient, pinkish white timber; its timber is used for furniture, joinery, panelling, cricket bats and artificial limbs etc., its branches for holding down thatch and for basketwork; see ***Salix spp.*** for full list of species of willow included in this work.

Wilton carpet a thick and durable woven carpet which has its woven loops cut open.

wimble see gimlet. →42

winch, hoist; a lifting or pulling device in which a wire or cable supporting a load is wound around a drum or similar construction. →64

Winchester bushel see bushel.

wind a natural flow of external air in a certain direction, usually parallel to the ground, caused by pressure differences in the atmosphere.

wind beam see collar beam. →33

wind brace 1 any structural member designed to maintain the rigidity of a structure against the forces of wind.
2 sway brace, purlin brace; in traditional timber frame construction, a brace at the angle of a rafter and a purlin to stiffen the roof against wind and other lateral loads.

wind bracing bracing in the structural frame of a building designed to resist forces generated by wind loads.
windbreak in landscaping, a natural barrier or fabricated screen constructed to provide shelter from the wind.
wind deposit see aeolian deposit.
winder, wheeling step, wheel tread; a tapered step in a spiral stair, whose front and back edges radiate from a single point, often attached to a newel post. →45
winder flight a series of winders or tapered steps which turn a corner in a turning stair.
winding stair see turning stair. →45
windlass a traditional implement for raising loads on site, a hand-cranked wooden cylinder or barrel around which a load-supporting rope is wound.
windmill a structure with large sails or aerofoil blades which rotate in the wind to provide mechanical or electrical power, traditionally for grinding corn.
wind load the structural load on the external surfaces of a building imposed by the action of wind.
window 1 an opening in an external wall of a building for allowing light into a space; may be a simple opening or an assembly of parts.
see *window types* illustration. →52
see *glazing* illustration. →53
see *windows of different styles* illustration. →111
2 see window assembly.
3 see window unit.
types of window listed below.
access window, see access door.
aluminium-faced timber window, see composite window. →53
aluminium window, aluminium-framed window. →53
angel light.
arch window, arched window. →111
awning window, see top-hung casement window. →52
barred window.
bay window.
blank window.
blind window, see false window.
borrowed light.
bottom-hung casement window. →52
bow window.
casement window. →52
Catherine wheel window. →109
clerestory window, clearstory window.
composite window, compound window. →53
coupled light.
coupled window.
display window.
domelight.
dormer window.
double glazed window.
double-hung sash window, see sash window. →52
double sash window.
double window.
factory glazed window.
false window.
fanlight.
fire window.
fixed light.
flanking window.
folding window, see sliding folding window. →52
French window, see casement door.
hanging sash window, see sash window. →52
horizontal pivot window. →52
horizontal sliding window, see sliding window. →52
Jesse window.
lancet window.
lantern light.
leper window.
light.
louvred window, louvre window. →52
low side window, see leper window.
marigold window, see rose window. →109
metal-faced window.
metal window.
offertory window, see leper window.
oriel window.
Palladian window, see Venetian window. →24
picture window.
pivot window. →52
plastic-faced window.
plastics window, see PVC-U window.
projecting window. →60
PVC-U window.
ribbon window, see window band.
rooflight, roof window. →60
rose window. →109
round window, roundel. →23
sash window. →52
shop window, see display window.
side-hung casement window. →52
side light. →52
sliding folding window. →52
sliding window, sliding sash window. →52
steel window, steel-framed window. →53
strip window, see window band.
timber window, timber-framed window. →53
tip-up window, see horizontal pivot window. →52
top-hung casement window. →52
top light. →52
transom window, see fanlight.
triple glazed window.
Venetian window. →24
vertical pivot window. →52
vertical sliding window, see sash window. →52
wheel window, see Catherine wheel window. →109
4 in computing, an area on the display screen selected by the operator for closer inspection.
window acceptor see acceptor.
window apron 1 that part of external wall construction beneath a window; see window back.
2 a decorative panel or cladding beneath a window, either externally or internally.
window assembly all the parts of a window: the outer frame, sashes and glazing.
window back the internal lining between the bottom of a window and the floor; a window apron.
window band, ribbon window, strip window; a long narrow horizontal window, or windows grouped together in the same opening.
window bar see glazing bar. →111
window board, elbow board, sill board, window stool; a horizontal board fitted internally at the base of a window opening to form a shelf or window sill. →53
window box a container for decorative planting hung externally beneath a window, situated on a balcony etc.
window buck see buck. →6
window casing in traditional timber window construction, the external covering surround for a window frame.
window component any part of a window, including ironmongery, frame, gasket or glazing unit.
window construction the materials, frames, glass and seals from which a window is made. →53
window former a formwork mould to create an opening for a window in a concrete wall.
window frame 1 the surrounding construction for a window unit, which holds the glazing in place and in which openable parts are hung. →52, →53
2 see casement frame. →53
window glass glass manufactured for use in glazing; either float glass or sheet glass. →53
window grille a series of iron or steel bars fixed to the exterior of a window as protection, security or as decoration.
window head 1 the uppermost horizontal member of a window or window frame. →52, →111
2 see window soffit.
window hinge a hinge for a window casement; a casement hinge. →52, →53

window jamb 1 a vertical side member in a window frame or window opening. →52, →111
2 see window reveal.
window lining facing for a window reveal which covers the join between frame and wall.
window louvre, grille; a construction or grille of slatted bars, profiles etc. located externally in front of glazing to provide shade or as an external feature.
window opening an opening in the walling fabric of a building, into which a window is fixed. →28
window pane a piece of glass fitted in a window frame. →52, →111
window panel in prefabricated construction, a prefabricated wall unit which contains a fitted window.
window post in timber-framed construction, a vertical member to which the window frame is fixed at the edge of a window opening.
window reveal, window jamb; the vertical portion of wall between a window frame and the main wall surface of a building, the side wall of a window opening.
window sash see sash.
window schedule a written document listing and specifying the windows and associated accessories for a construction project.
window seat an interior window sill low and wide enough to be used as a seat, often situated in a bay window.
window shutter see shutter.
window sill 1 an external horizontal protruding construction at the base of a window for throwing off water. →53
2 the lowest horizontal member in a window frame. →52, →111
window soffit the upper horizontal undersurface of a window opening.
window stay see casement stay.
window stile a vertical side framing member of a window casement. →111
window stool see window board. →53
window strip a draught excluder for a window. →53
window trim a strip of material around a window for covering joints between a window frame and surrounding wall construction. →53
window type a window as classified by material, function, opening mechanism or manner etc.; see *window types* illustration. →52
window unit a prefabricated glazing component of glass in a frame, often containing openable casements, fittings etc.
window wall, 1 glazed wall; a wall, part of a wall, screen or partition made up partly or entirely of glazing.
2 a wall which contains a window or windows.
wind shake a crack in timber, the segregating of the growth rings caused by wind strain during growth. →1
wind stop see draught excluder.
wine red, Bordeaux (red), claret; a shade of red which takes its name from the colour of red wines produced in the Bordeaux region of France.
wine yellow a shade of dull yellow which takes its name from the colour of white wine made from the grapes of the vine [*Vitis vinifera*].
wing a longitudinal extension of a building, often containing additional or subsidiary spaces.
see aile.
see pteron. →85
see bat's wing. →123
wing compass, wing dividers; in technical drawing, a compass with a lockable thumbscrew which can be tightened onto a protruding steel band to lock the arms to a set dimension.
wing dividers see wing compass.
winged altar an altar whose altarpiece is of two or more decorated panelled wings joined or hinged to a central section, situated on a podium. →116
winged bull see bull. →119
winged disc see winged sun disc. →75
winged knot see branched knot. →1
winged ox see bull. →119
winged sun disc 1 an ancient Egyptian apotrope, a winged disc often carved above doorways and gates, symbolic of the god Horus. →75
2 see feroher. →75
wing light see flanking window.
wing nut, butterfly nut, thumb nut; a threaded fixing for a bolt with wing-like protrusions for tightening by hand. →37
wing wall in bridge construction, an oversailing retaining wall at right angles to the line of the bridge, containing piled earth at a bridge abutment. →31
winter bricklaying, cold-weather bricklaying; bricklaying in conditions where the temperature is around or below freezing point, requiring special measures to ensure good results.
winter concreting, cold-weather concreting; concreting which takes place when the average temperature is below 5°; special measures and mixes have to be used to prevent water in the fresh concrete from freezing.
winter garden see conservatory.
winter hardy plant any species of landscaping plant which can survive outdoors during the winter months.
wire 1 a thin strand of metal.
2 see electric cable.
wire balloon a small wire basket attached to the outlets of external drainage and vent pipes, gullies etc. to prevent blockage by fallen leaves, nesting birds etc.; an outlet strainer.
wire balustrade 1 see cable balustrade. →54
2 see wire-mesh balustrade. →54
wire basket a domestic storage container made from plastic-coated welded metal mesh, often mounted in a storage unit as a sliding drawer.
wire brush a brush with bristles of steel wire used for roughing, scratching, cleaning up surfaces and removing scale from steel; other softer metals such as copper are sometimes used for the bristles. →41
wirecut brick a mass-produced brick manufactured by extruding clay through a suitably shaped die and cutting it into suitably sized pieces with a slanting wire.
wired cast glass see wired glass.
wired glass, wired cast glass; glass which has been rolled with a reinforcing wire mesh in the middle.
wire drawing see cold drawing.
wire-frame model in computer-aided design, objects described as points and lines in three dimensions.
wire gauge a simple device for defining the gauge or diameter of wire, consisting of a plate with a number of calibrated holes or notches.
wire handle see wire pull handle. →51
wire lathing galvanized wire mesh base tied at intervals to wall surfaces to provide a key for plasterwork and renderwork; wire-mesh lathing.
wireless communication network, cellular phone system; a telecommunications network in which mobile telephones and local boosting antennae form the basis of the communications system.
wire mesh any mesh product manufactured from two series of parallel metal wires woven, welded or crimped perpendicular to one another.
see *wire mesh* illustrations; types included as separate entries are listed below. →34
chain link mesh. →34
conveyor belt mesh. →34
crimped wire mesh. →34
fabric reinforcement.

hexagonal mesh, see chicken wire. →34
insect mesh, see insect screen.
steel mesh.
welded wire mesh, see welded mesh. →34
woven wire mesh. →34

wire-mesh balustrade a balustrade with an infill of wire mesh in a steel or aluminium frame. →54

wire-mesh lathing see wire lathing.

wire-mesh reinforcement see fabric reinforcement.

wire nail a nail manufactured by mechanically stamping lengths of wire, obtainable in a range of lengths from 12 mm to 200 mm. →35
French nail, see round wire nail.
see oval wire nail.
see round wire nail.

wire pull handle a slender pull handle made from a single U-shaped metal rod. →51

wire rope see cable.

wire-rope balustrade see cable balustrade. →54

wire-rope clamp, wire-rope clip, cable clamp; a bolted metal ring fastening for clamping two lengths of wire rope together side by side. →37

wire-rope clip see wire rope clamp. →37

wire-rope thimble, cable thimble; a metal harness for strengthening a loop at the end of a wire rope or tensioning cable. →37

wire saw a saw whose blade is a piece of wire coated with a hard abrasive material such as carborundum grit, used for cutting ceramics, metal and plastics.

wire strippers a scissor-like tool with notched jaws used for stripping the plastic insulation from electric cable.

wire tie wire wall tie. →22

wire wall tie any wall tie bent or twisted into shape from galvanized steel wire. →22

wireway see skirting trunking.

wiring 1 the laying of cables and wires in an electric installation to form circuits.
2 the circuits thus formed.
3 in reinforced concreting, the job of binding reinforcing bars together with wire.

wismuth a traditional name for the chemical element bismuth.

withe, osier; in thatched roofing, short flexible branches of willow, hazel etc. twisted together to form a runner, with which thatch can be bound to rafters; also written as wythe; see brotch.
see leaf.

withe braiding see flaking.

with the grain in the milling of timber, the direction of cutting in which the grain of the piece is sloping downwards and into the milling edge.

woad a traditional blue dye made from the leaves of the woad plant Isatis tinctoria.

Wobbe number an index relating to the heat released when a specific commercial heating gas is burned, equal to its calorific value per square root of density.

wobble saw see drunken saw.

Woden's cross see wheel cross. →118

wolfram see tungsten.

wolframite a black metallic mineral, natural iron manganese tungstate, **(Fe,Ma)WO$_4$**, the principal ore of tungsten.

womb chamber see garbha-griha. →68

wood 1 an organic material made up of lignin and cellulose, obtained from the trunks of trees, called timber when used in construction. →1
see *structure of wood* illustration. →1
see list of species of tree from which softwood is obtained under **softwood**.
see list of species of tree from which hardwood is obtained under **hardwood**.
2 see woodland.

wood adhesive, wood glue; any adhesive suitable for gluing wood.

wood axe see felling axe.

wood-based core plywood core plywood with a core of wood.

wood-based panel product, timber-based board; a building or insulating board produced from wood products (particles, veneers, strips) pressed together with a binder or adhesive. →9
see *wood-based panel product* illustration. →9

wood block flooring 1 see end-grain wood block flooring. →44
2 see parquet.

wood board flooring, board flooring; traditional flooring of large solid timber planks laid side by side on joists. →44

woodcarving the working of wood with hand tools to create decorative mouldings, carvings and artifacts.

woodcarving chisel, carving chisel; a chisel used by a woodcarver for shaping, sculpting and decorative work, available in a variety of shaped blades for different uses. →41

wood cement chipboard, cement bonded chipboard, wood cement particleboard; chipboard whose particles are bonded together with Portland cement as opposed to resin.

wood-cement concrete, sawdust concrete; a lightweight concrete made with wood chips, wood fibres or sawdust as an aggregate.

wood cement particleboard see wood cement chipboard.

wood chipboard see chipboard. →9

woodchip wallpaper, ingrain wallcovering; cheap wallpaper with small chips of wood embedded in it to provide a textured finish.

woodchips see chips.

wood cramp a wooden clamping device used by a joiner, tightened with a screw or folding wedges.

woodcut 1 a form of printing in which a pattern is carved into the side grain of a piece of wood, which is then given a coating of ink and prints taken from it; see wood engraving.
2 a print from this process.

wood drill a hardened steel spiral-cutting drill bit, often with a positioning spur at its end, for cutting accurate holes in wood. →42

wooden block see nog.

wooden brick see nog.

wooden church a church whose principal structural and constructional material is wood. →102

wooden door see timber door. →51

wooden fencing fencing of vertical or horizontal timber boards supported on a frame or by spaced posts.

wooden flooring same as wood or timber flooring.
see *wooden flooring* illustration. →44

wood engraving, xylography; a form of woodcut developed by Thomas Bewick in the late 1800s, in which cuttings are made in the end grain of a polished hardwood block, used as a printing plate.

wooden mallet see carpenter's mallet. →40

wooden pile see timber pile. →29

wood-fibred plaster plaster containing an aggregate of wood fibres for increased strength.

wood-fired heating see solid-fuel heating.

wood float a wooden board with a handle, used for smoothing and levelling concrete and plaster surfaces. →43
see cross-grained float.
see straight-grained float.

woodfloat finish a concrete surface which has been smoothed with a wood float.

wood flooring flooring such as wood-block, floorboards or parquet which form a hardwearing wooden surface; also called timber flooring.
see *wood flooring* illustration. →44

wood glue see wood adhesive.

wood-inhabiting fungus any fungus which causes deterioration of wood.

wood joint a mechanical, glued or nailed joint between two or more wooden members; see timber joint for list of types of joints and illustrations.

wood key long round or square pegs driven into vertical pre-bored holes in horizontal log construction to tie adjacent courses together and provide lateral stability; a large dowel, peg or pin. →6

woodland, wood; a natural tract of land covered with trees.

woodland plant in landscaping, any species of plant which usually grows in a shaded environment such as woodland or forest.

wood mastic a compound consisting of sawdust and a binder used for filling cracks and joints in timber boarding and boardwork.

wood mosaic, mosaic parquet; decorative timber flooring in wooden strips, usually less than 10 mm thick, laid in a repeated square patterned arrangement. →44

wood particle aggregate lightweight concrete aggregate manufactured from treated wood chips.

wood plastic composite, WPC; a wood product which has been impregnated with a plastic to restrict its moisture movement.

wood preservative see preservative.

wood primer a primer for sealing, preserving or pretreating a timber surface prior to painting.

wood roll joint see roll joint. →49

wood screw a screw for joining or attaching to pieces of timber, often self-tapping and with threads which are wider and steeper than those used for other purposes. →36

wood sorrel see shamrock. →121

woodstain 1 stain used on timber surfaces.
2 see exterior woodstain.

wood strip flooring 1 timber flooring consisting of matched wooden boards up to 100 mm wide laid parallel to one another; wood strip flooring most often refers to hardwood flooring placed on battens over a solid structural base; cf. floorboards. →8, →44
2 see solid parquet. →44

wood turpentine turpentine manufactured by the distillation of wood.

wood wasp, horntail; [*Siricidae*] a family of insects whose larvae bore into softwood, causing weakening of the timber and loosening of the bark.

wood weevil, wood boring weevil; [*Pentarthrum huttonii*] an insect which causes damage to damp infected timber by burrowing.

wood veneer see veneer. →10

woodwool slab a thick board manufactured by compressing a mixture of wood shavings and cement; used as thermal and sound insulation and cladding.

woodwork the panelling and decorative construction work of a building on site involving timber, carried out by a joiner; framing is usually referred to as timberwork; see also joinery, carpentry.

woodworking chisel a hand tool with a metal blade sharpened at one end for cutting and shaping wood. →41
see *woodworking chisels* illustration; types included as separate entries are listed below. →41
barking chisel.
bench chisel. →41
bevelled-edge chisel, bevel edge chisel. →41
bruzz chisel. →41
butt chisel. →41
cant chisel, see framing chisel.
carving chisel, see woodcarving chisel. →41
caulking chisel, caulking iron.
corner chisel, see bruzz chisel. →41
dogleg chisel, see bruzz chisel. →41
drawer lock chisel.
firmer chisel. →41
floor chisel.
framing chisel.
gouge. →41
heading chisel, see mortise chisel. →41
hinge chisel.
joiner's chisel, see paring chisel. →41
lock chisel.
long-cornered chisel, see skew chisel. →41
mortise lock chisel. →41
mortising chisel, mortise chisel. →41
paring chisel. →41
parting chisel, parting tool.
peeling chisel, peeling iron, see barking chisel.
pocket chisel, see butt chisel. →41
registered chisel.
ripping chisel. →41
sash chisel, see butt chisel. →41
scraping tool, scraper. →41
skew chisel. →41
swan-neck chisel, see mortise lock chisel. →41
turning chisel. →41
turning gouge. →41
woodcarving chisel. →41

woodwork joint see wood joint, timber joint.

woodworm see furniture beetle.

wool any loose material made up of a tangle of slender fibres, see below; especially that shorn from sheep and used in the cloth and yarn industries.
glass wool.
lead wool.
mineral wool. →59
rock wool.
slag wool.
woodwool slab.

woolly grain see fuzzy grain. →1

word processing, text processing, text editing; in computing, software for handling, editing, printing and storing text documents.

word processor a computer programed to handle written tasks, or one in which word processing software is installed.

work 1 in mechanics, the distance through which a force operates, measured in Nm or joules; one joule is the work required to move one newton through one metre; see energy.
2 a military structure built as a fortification, a bastion, rampart or outwork. →104
see *fortification* illustration; types of works included as separate entries are listed below. →104
advanced work. →104
crownwork. →104
forework, see advanced work. →104
hornwork. →104
outwork, outerwork. →104
ringwork.
3 see opus (Roman masonrywork).
4 see list of types of sitework under **construction work**.
5 see list of types of ornamentation under **decorative work**.

workability 1 the ability of a material, especially wood or stone, to be easily shaped with cutting and abrasive tools.
2 see machinability.
3 the ability of a plastic material to be shaped with ease.
4 the property of concrete that is able to be placed, pumped and vibrated with ease.
5 see plasticity.

workability retention aid in concreting, an admixture included in the mix to increase the time during which the concrete is workable.

work-based trip in traffic planning, a trip by any mode of transport, travelling to or from a place of work.

workbench a robust wooden bench containing in-built vices, used by a joiner in the workshop.

worker's housing housing built near a large industrial complex, often by its owner or managing body, as dwellings for the workers.

work face see face side.

workforce, labour, labour force; human resources available for or employed in a particular job of work; those employed by a company or for a particular project.

working drawing, production drawing; a design drawing for the construction industry providing information about structure, components and materials in a project or development, from which it can be realized.

working environment a place of work, its location and conditions for the workforce, when considered as a whole.

working life see pot life.

working model a rough scale model made of a proposal at design stage to test ideas of space and massing.

working pile in foundation technology, any pile used as part of the foundation system of a building. see **types of pile** in foundation drawing. →29

working plane in lighting design, a hypothetical horizontal, vertical or tilted plane for which lighting conditions are calculated; usually assumed to be 0.7 m above floor level for offices, 0.85 m for industrial applications.

working space, work space; space required for an installation, servicing or operation of an appliance, or for carrying out work.

working stress see permissible stress.

workmanship a required, specified or accepted standard of work on a building site, or by a craftsman.

Workmate bench see multipurpose workbench.

work of art the product of creative aesthetic action.

work permit an official certificate or document permitting a non-national or company to work in a given area or state.

work plan see plan of work.

work programme see plan of work.

workroom a room, study, studio or workshop for an activity such as studying, research, clerical work etc.

works 1 the body of building or construction work involved in a project; construction works.
see external works.
see temporary works, falsework.
see groundwork.
2 military fortifications, see work. →104
see *fortification* illustration. →104
3 a manufacturing or production plant.
see brickworks.
see gasworks.

works contract 1 see electrical works contract.
2 see minor works contract.

works cube test a test for concrete used for a particular development, carried out on site during the progression of work by destructive crushing of a sample cube.

workshop, 1 shop; a building or part of a building in which a particular activity such as metalwork, woodwork etc., or a stage in a manufacturing process is carried out. →97
2 see taberna. →88, →91

work space see working space.

workstation in computing, a set-up including a computer, keyboard, monitor and associated devices, at which one person can work.

work surface see worktop.

worktable a table on or at which work is done; it may be a workbench, desk or drawing board.

worktop, work surface; the flat horizontal upper surface or component of a kitchen unit, desk, table etc.

worm's-eye perspective a worm's-eye view constructed as a true perspective.

worm's-eye view a view, scene or pictorial projection of an object from below.

wormhole, borehole; a small round hole in wood caused by burrowing insects, evident as a defect in the surface.

worse face see back.

worsted yarn, combed yarn; a strong yarn spun from long fibres of wool combed prior to spinning.

woven carpet carpet manufactured by weaving crosswise threads known as weft onto suspended lengthwise structural threads, warp.

woven matting see woven carpet.

woven mesh see woven wire mesh. →34

woven roving see glassfibre cloth.

woven wire fencing, 1 anti-intruder chain link fencing; security fencing material made of woven wire.
2 see chain link mesh. →34

woven wire mesh 1 a metal mesh product manufactured from two sets of wire strands woven together in an orthogonal arrangement, with square or polygonal openings between. →34
2 see chain link mesh. →34
3 see conveyor belt mesh. →34
4 see chicken wire, hexagonal mesh. →34

wove paper paper manufactured on a fine wire roll, which has no marks on its surface.

WPC wood plastic composite.

wpm waterproofing membrane. →44

wrack poor quality timber, unsuitable for use in construction.

wreath 1 ornament depicting a twisted ring of foliage, flowers etc. →121
2 see laurel wreath.
3 tortil, torse; a heraldic embellishment of woven leaves set between the crown and helmet in a coat of arms. →124

wreathed column see spiral column. →114

wrecking strip a piece of formwork sheeting which can easily be removed to aid striking, and is destroyed in the process.

wrench see spanner.

wright see carpenter.

wrinkle, riveling; a defect in a paint finish consisting of one or a number of small creases in the surface.

write protect referring to a computer file or disk whose content cannot be erased or modified.

writing chalk see chalk.

wrot see dressed.

wrought iron a form of ductile iron, fibrous in structure, which has little or no carbon added, easily forged and welded and used for water pipes and rivets.

wrought nail see forged nail. →35

W truss see fink truss. →33

wulfenite, yellow lead ore; a yellow-orange mineral, natural lead molybdate, $\mathbf{PbMoO_4}$, a locally important ore of molybdenum.

wych elm [*Ulmus glabra*] a European hardwood, see elm for further information.

wythe 1 see withe.
2 see leaf.

xenodochium Lat.; in classical and monastic architecture, a room, building or apartment for the reception of guests or strangers; alternative Greek spelling is xenodokheion; a hostel suite. →92

xenon a heavy, inert, gaseous chemical element, **Xe**, used in television and fluorescent tubes.

Xestobium rufovillosum see death watch beetle.

XLPE cross-linked polyethylene.

xomsa see hand of Fatima. →120

XPS see extruded polystyrene.

X-ray resistant glass see lead X-ray glass.

X-ray resisting plaster, radiation-shielding mortar; plaster containing barytes, which is relatively resistant to the penetration of X-rays.

X-rays penetrating short wave, high energy electromagnetic emission from naturally radioactive elements; their uses in construction include non-destructive inspection of welds and other opaque constructions.

xylography see wood engraving.

xyst see xystus.

xystus 1 Lat.; an open passage, courtyard or park in a Roman building, used for sport and recreation. →91

2 the inner colonnaded portico or hall in an ancient Greek dwelling, used for exercise and recreation. →91

3 xyst; pl. xysti; a cloister in a medieval monastery.

Y

yacht harbour see marina.
Yale lock a proprietary cylinder lock.
Yankee screwdriver see spiral ratchet screwdriver.
yantra a Tibetan mandala pattern of intersecting triangles, squares and circles. →120
yard 1 abb. **yd**; imperial unit of length equal to 3 feet or 0.9144 m.
2 an area of land surrounded by, linked to or belonging to a building or buildings.
yard blue, deal yard blue; blue stain found in timber in storage.
yarn a product manufactured of strands or fibres wound together and used in the fabrication of textiles.
yasti a mast or spire for supporting the royal parasol or chattra on the top of an Indian stupa. →68
Y branch a Y-shaped pipe fitting for merging pipelines in a drainage system.
Y-cross see forked cross. →117
year abb. **yr**; a period of time equivalent to that taken by the earth to orbit the sun once, roughly equal to 52 weeks or 365–366 days.
yeast black a variety of vine black pigment.
yeba see finger. →106
yellow a colour of light from the visible spectrum which represents a range of wavelengths from 560 m to 585 m; see list of yellow pigments below.
alizarin yellow.
antimony yellow, see Naples yellow.
arsenic yellow, see king's yellow.
arylide yellow.
aureolin, see cobalt yellow.
auripigmentum, see king's yellow.
aurora yellow, see cadmium yellow.
barium yellow.
brilliant yellow, see Naples yellow.
buttercup yellow, see zinc yellow.
cadmium yellow.
Chinese yellow.
chrome yellow.
citron yellow, zinc yellow.
cobalt yellow.
gamboge.
Hansa yellow, see arylide yellow.
Indian yellow.
indanthrene.
jaune d'antimoine, jaune brilliant, see Naples yellow.
Kassler yellow, see Turner's yellow.
king's yellow.
Leipzig yellow, see chrome yellow.
massicot.
Montpelier yellow, see Turner's yellow.
Naples yellow.
Orient yellow, cadmium yellow.
Paris yellow, see chrome yellow.
patent yellow, see Turner's yellow.
permanent yellow.
puree, pwree, Indian yellow.
Royal yellow, see king's yellow.
strontium yellow.
terra merita.
transparent gold ochre, see Turner's yellow.
Turner's yellow.
ultramarine yellow.
uranium yellow.
yellow lake.
see yellow ochre.
yellow oxide of iron, see Mars yellow.
yellow ultramarine, see barium yellow.
zinc yellow.
yellow birch [*Betula alleghaniensis*] a North American hardwood with light brown to deep russet hardwearing timber; used for plywood and turning.
yellow cedar [*Chamaecyparis nootkatensis*, *Cupressus nootkatensis*] a softwood from Alaska and the west coast of North America; used in interiors, furniture and boat-building.
yellow deal commercial timber from the Scots pine tree.
yellowing the weathering of a colour, treated surface or material from white or clear to shades of yellow due to reaction with light, lack of light, heat or airborne pollution.
yellow lake a general name for a number of transparent yellow pigments.
yellow lead ore see wulfenite.
yellow ochre a dull yellow pigment in use since prehistoric times, yellow or yellowish brown hydrated iron oxide produced from yellow clays.
yellow oxide of iron see Mars yellow.
yellow pigments see list of yellow pigments under **yellow**.
yellow pine, Weymouth pine, white pine; [*Pinus strobus*] a softwood from eastern USA with pale yellow-brown, soft timber; used for non-structural interior work, crates and boxes.
yellow poplar see tulipwood.
yellow ultramarine see barium yellow.
yett an iron defensive door in a Scottish castle.
yew [*Taxus baccata*] the heaviest softwood in Europe with strong, resilient, reddish or purple brown timber; used for decorative inlays and veneers and the English longbow in the Middle Ages.
Y-form roof see butterfly roof. →46
yield 1 in mechanics, the permanent deformation which happens to a material, especially a metal, under stress beyond its elastic limit.
2 see concrete yield.
3 see return.
yield point, yield stress; in mechanics, the stress at which a body under stress suddenly deforms rapidly, shortly before failure.
yield stress see yield point.
yin-yang an ancient oriental circular symbol divided into scrolled black and white areas; symbolic of the universe, feminine (yin, dark) and masculine (jang, white) duality; also called tai-chi or tai-qi. →120
Y junction a road junction in which one road meets another road obliquely in plan. →62
yocto- abb. **y**; a prefix for units of measurement or quantity to denote a factor of 10^{-24}. →Table 1
yoke in traditional timber roof construction, a member joining and bracing the upper ends of rafters.
yolk yellow a shade of bright yellow which takes its name from the colour of egg yolk.
yoni in Hindu art and architecture, a symbolic statue or sacred representation of the female genitalia. →68, →120
Yorkshire bond see monk bond. →18
yotta- abb. **Y**; a prefix for units of measurement or quantity to denote a factor of 10^{24}. →Table 1
Young's modulus see modulus of elasticity.
youth centre see youth club.
youth club, youth centre; an establishment which provides social, leisure and recreational facilities for young people.
youth hostel a reasonably priced and rudimentary hostel, especially for travellers and young tourists.
ypsilon cross see forked cross. →117

Y-tracery bar tracery found in Gothic churches of the 1300s, in which each mullion branches into a Y shape at its upper end. →110

ytterbium a rare metallic chemical element, **Yb**.

Yuan dynasty, Mongol dynasty; a Chinese cultural dynasty from 1279 to 1368 established by Mongol nomads under Ghengis Khan, and spread by his grandson Kublai Khan, which made Peking China's capital.

Z

zaffer, zaffre; an impure form of cobalt oxide used as a blue colourant for ceramics and glass.
zaffre see zaffer.
Zapotec architecture the architecture of the Indian peoples of Mexico and Central America from 0 to 400 AD, succeeding the Olmecs and predating the Mayans and Aztecs.
Z-bar see Z-section. →34
zebra crossing in traffic planning, a pedestrian crossing marked with a series of alternating light and dark stripes.
zenana the private living quarters of women of high caste in an Indian dwelling; a harem.
zenithal projection see azimuthal projection.
Zentner see hundredweight.
zepto- abb. **z**; a prefix for units of measurement or quantity to denote a factor of 10^{-21}. →Table 1
zero the starting point in any scale of numbers, graphs or tables; a value equal to nothing.
zetta- abb. **Z**; a prefix for units of measurement or quantity to denote a factor of 10^{21}. →Table 1
Zeus, arrow of see thunderbolt. →120
Zhou, Chou; a period in Chinese history from 1050 to 256 BC during the Zhou dynasty.
ziggurat an ancient Babylonian, Mesopotamian or Assyrian tiered structure of sun-baked bricks, similar to a stepped pyramid on a rectangular or ovoid plan, with straight or spiral ramped access to a summit temple, approached by a processional way; also similar structures in early Central and South American cultures.
see *ziggurat* in Mesopotamian temple illustration. →66
see types of ziggurat illustration. →67
zigzag 1 see chevron. →124
2 see indented moulding. →124
zinc a bluish-white, fragile metal, **Zn**, with good resistance to corrosion; used as a protective coating for other metals, especially steel.
zinc-blende, sphalerite; a black or brownish mineral, natural zinc sulphide, **ZnO**, a principal ore of zinc.
zinc carbonate $ZnCO_3$, see smithsonite, zinc spar.
zinc chromate a chemical compound, **$ZnCrO_4.7H_2O$**, used as a corrosion inhibitor and a yellow pigment in paints and metal primers; see also zinc yellow.
zinc chrome see zinc yellow.
zinc coated steel see galvanized steel.
zinc coating 1 the corrosion protection of ferrous metals by application of a thin layer of zinc.
2 the protective coating thus formed.
zinc green see cobalt green.
zincite a naturally occurring oxide of zinc, **ZnO**, blood-red in colour.
zinc oxide 1 a chemical compound, **ZnO**, used in the manufacture of cements and glass, and as a white pigment.
2 see zinc white.
zinc phosphate a paint used as a corrosive coating for priming steel.
zinc-rich paint a protective surface treatment for steel sheeting consisting of paint which contains 90–95% fine zinc powder, the application of this is often known as cold galvanization.
zinc silicate paint a two component paint used for priming steel.
zinc spar see smithsonite.
zinc spraying, metallization, metal spraying; the application of a protective coating of atomized zinc to the surface of metals by spraying; aluminium is often also used.
zinc sulphide ZnO, see zinc-blende, sphalerite.
zinc white, Chinese white; a harsh white pigment, often pure zinc oxide, used in paints for its properties of durability, colour retention and hardness.
zinc yellow, buttercup yellow, citron yellow, zinc chrome; a pale poisonous semi-opaque yellow pigment consisting of zinc chromate, no longer in use.
zinnober an alternative spelling of cinnabar.
zinnober green see chrome green.
zircon a colourless or coloured mineral, zirconium silicate, **$ZrSiO_4$**, the most important ore of zirconium, used also as a gemstone.
zirconium a corrosion-resistant grey metal, **Zr**, with properties similar to those of titanium; used principally in the nuclear industry, but also in some alloys and for valve and pump components.
zirconium oxide a chemical compound, **ZrO_2**, used in the manufacture of ovens.
zircon white zirconium oxide used as a white pigment in ceramics.
zoisite a grey, green, pinkish or blue vitreous mineral used as a gemstone and for ornamental stone.
zoning in town planning, the division of a larger area of urban land into zones or districts, and the establishment of regulations within each zone to govern the scope of development with regard to land-use, height and volume of buildings etc. to form the basis of a local plan.
zoning legislation a legal framework of regulations for designating use for specific areas of land, ensuring that town planning is carried out in a controlled fashion.
zoning ordinance in town planning, the system which regulates development through the process of zoning, and stipulates regulations for land use, heights, bulk and shape within each of these zones.
zoning regulations in town planning, a written document outlining detailed stipulations such as particular land use, parking standards, heights and sizes of buildings, materials used etc. for a zone.
zoo see zoological gardens.
zoological gardens, zoo; a recreational establishment or area of specialist parkland containing captive wild animals in paddocks and enclosures for display and research; often in an urban setting.
zoom in computer-aided design, an enlargement of objects proportionally on the screen for closer inspection.
zoomorph a symbolic representation of natural animal forms in art and architecture, especially a standing stone in Central and South America sculpted with men and beasts intertwined.
zoophoros Gk; see zophorus. →78, →80
zophorus, zoophoros (Gk); Lat.; a classical frieze with animal or human ornamentation. →78, →80
Z-section a structural steel section, formed by rolling, forming or bending, whose uniform cross-section resembles the letter Z; sometimes called a Z-bar when of hot-rolled steel. →34

Part II

Illustrations

1 WOOD AND SAWN TIMBER

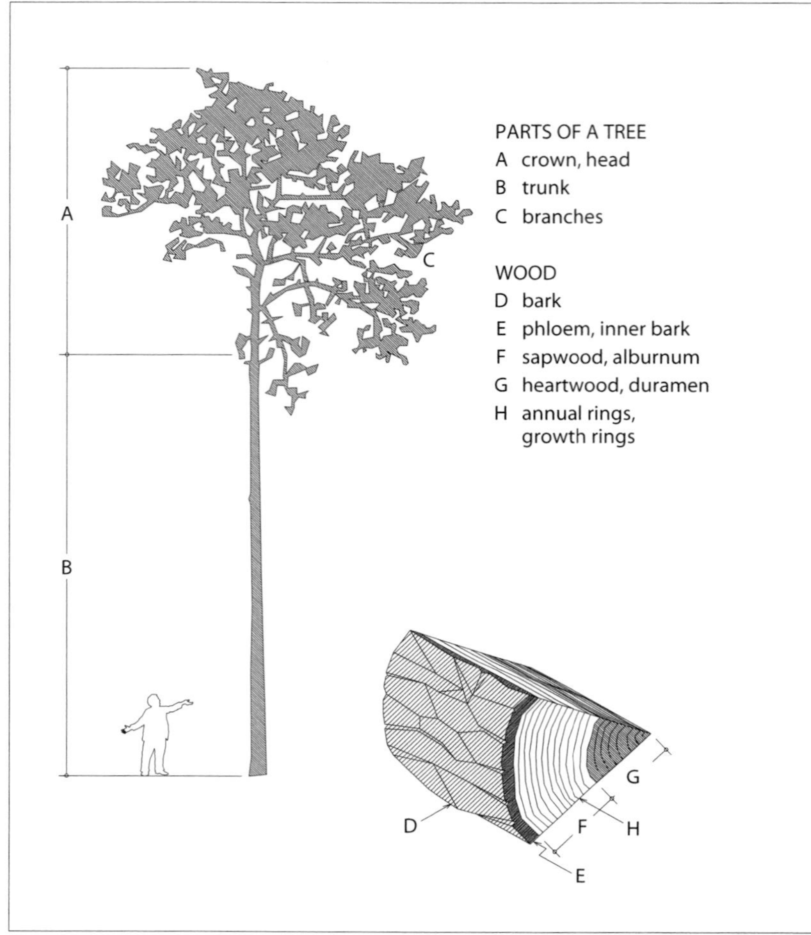

tree
one of a vast range of large plants with a woody stem and foliage, usually growing to a height of over 5 m, planted as landscaping and used as a source of wood and other products

wood
an organic material made up of lignin and cellulose, obtained from the trunks of trees, called timber when used in construction

timber, lumber (Am)
1 wood used for constructional purposes
2 wood converted from sawlogs

knot
a hard, ovoid or swirling growth evident in the surface of sawn timber, a branch stem in the original tree cut through its width

KNOTS AND GROWTH DEFECTS
1 slab
2 surface check, seasoning shake
3 cup shake, wind shake, ring shake, shell shake
4 heartshake, heart check, rift crack, star shake
5 wane, waney timber
6 pitch streak, resin streak, pitch pocket, resin pocket
7 spiral grain, torse grain, sloping grain, diagonal grain
8 compression wood
9 tension wood, reaction wood
10 intergrown knot, live knot, sound knot, red knot
11 round knot
12 dead knot
13 loose knot
14 knot hole
15 encased knot, bark-ringed knot
16 unsound knot, decayed knot, rotten knot
17 splay knot
18 arris knot
19 spike knot, margin knot
20 branched knot, winged knot
21 knot cluster
22 pin knot, cat's eye

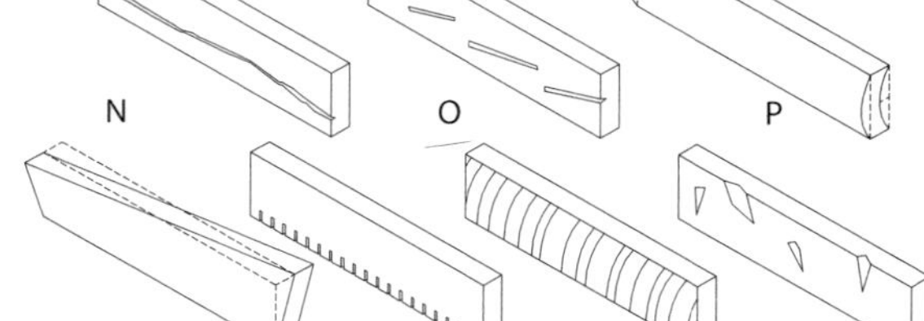

SEASONING AND CONVERSION DEFECTS IN TIMBER
J kink
K crook, spring
L bow, camber
M diamonding
N straight shake
O oblique shake
P cup, transverse warping
Q twist
R feed-roller marks
S sawing defect
T chipped grain, torn grain
U fuzzy grain, woolly grain

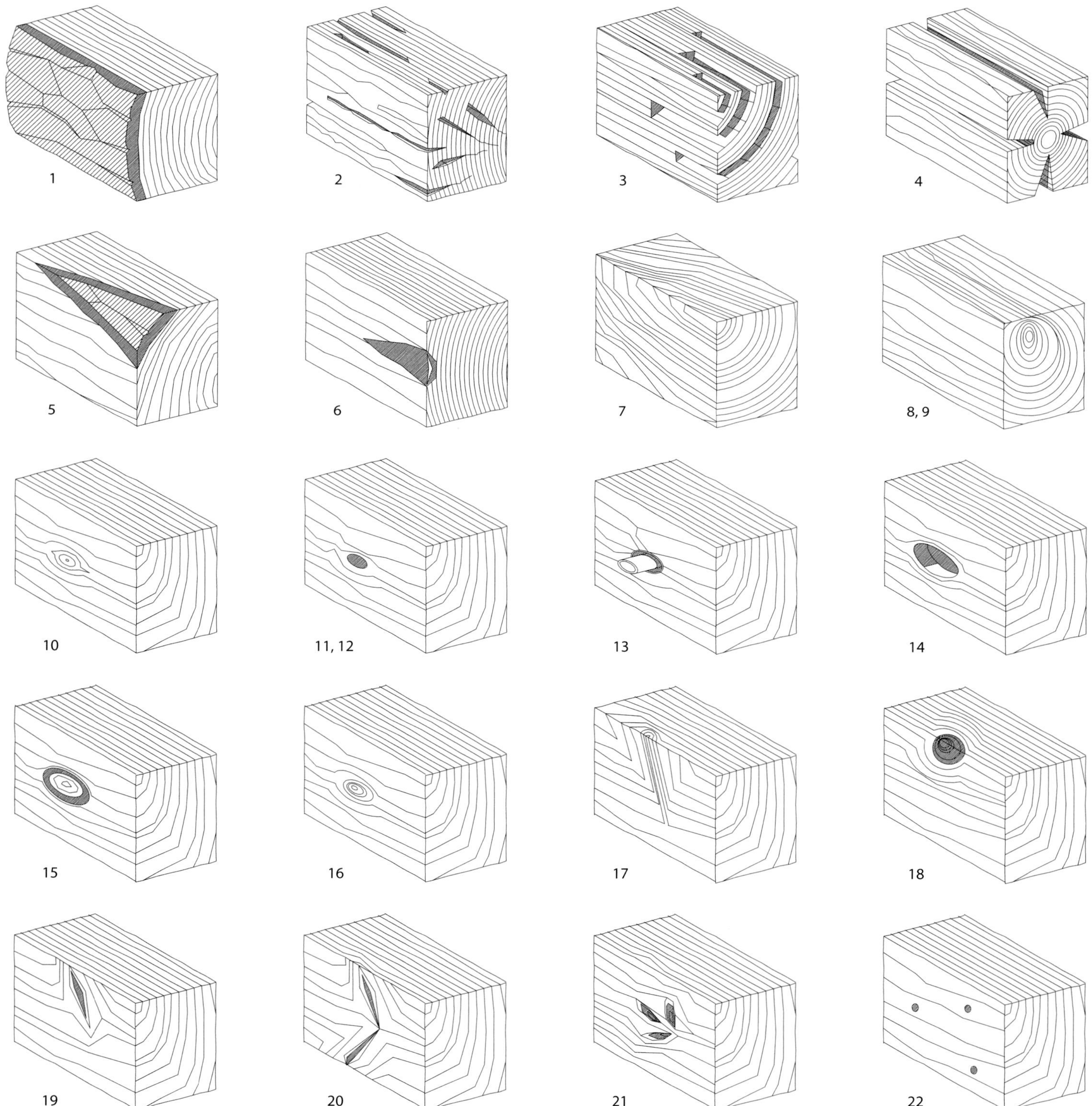
1
2
3
4
5
6
7
8, 9
10
11, 12
13
14
15
16
17
18
19
20
21
22

2 CONVERSION OF TIMBER

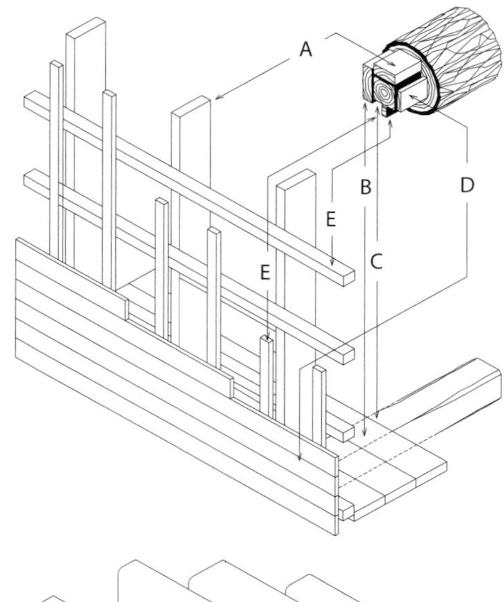

STRUCTURAL TIMBER

A scantling
B deal, plank
C baulk, bauk, balk
D board
E batten

conversion
the sawing of logs into large timber sections, profiles and mouldings for use in building

sawmill
an industrial plant for converting timber from logs into sawn boards and other sections

grade, class
the classification of converted timber according to quality

dressing
1 planing, surfacing; the smoothing or finishing of a timber surface with a plane or planer
2 the surface-smoothing of rough timbers with an adze

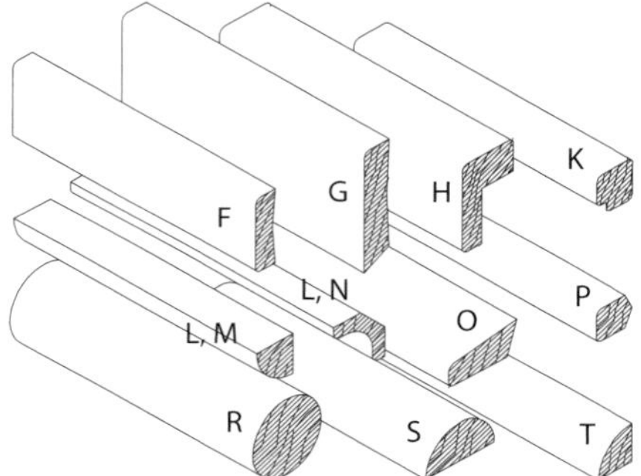

TIMBER TRIM, JOINERY PROFILES, JOINERY MOULDINGS

F cover fillet, capping strip
G skirting, skirting board, baseboard, mopboard, scrubboard, washboard
H edge strip, edging, edge bead, angle bead, corner bead, L-profile, hockey stick
K shadow bead
L angle bead, corner bead
M quadrant
N scotia
O wedge bead
P glazing bead
R dowel, round
S half round
T carpet strip, flooring bead

DRESSED, SURFACED OR PLANED TIMBER

U planed square edged board, planed all round timber
V planed tongued and grooved board, planed t&g board

CONVERSION METHODS

1 live sawing, through and through sawing, edging
2 flitch sawing, resawing
3 through and through sawing, flatsawing, plain sawing, slash sawing; (Am.) bastard sawing
4 edging, resawing
5 quartersawing, radial cutting, rift sawing
6 sawing round the log
7 flitch, cant

BOARDS

8 slab
9 side board
10 centre board
11 outside face
12 end grain
13 inside face
14 edge, radial surface
15 arris
16 tongue
17 groove
18 thickness
19 width, breadth
20 length

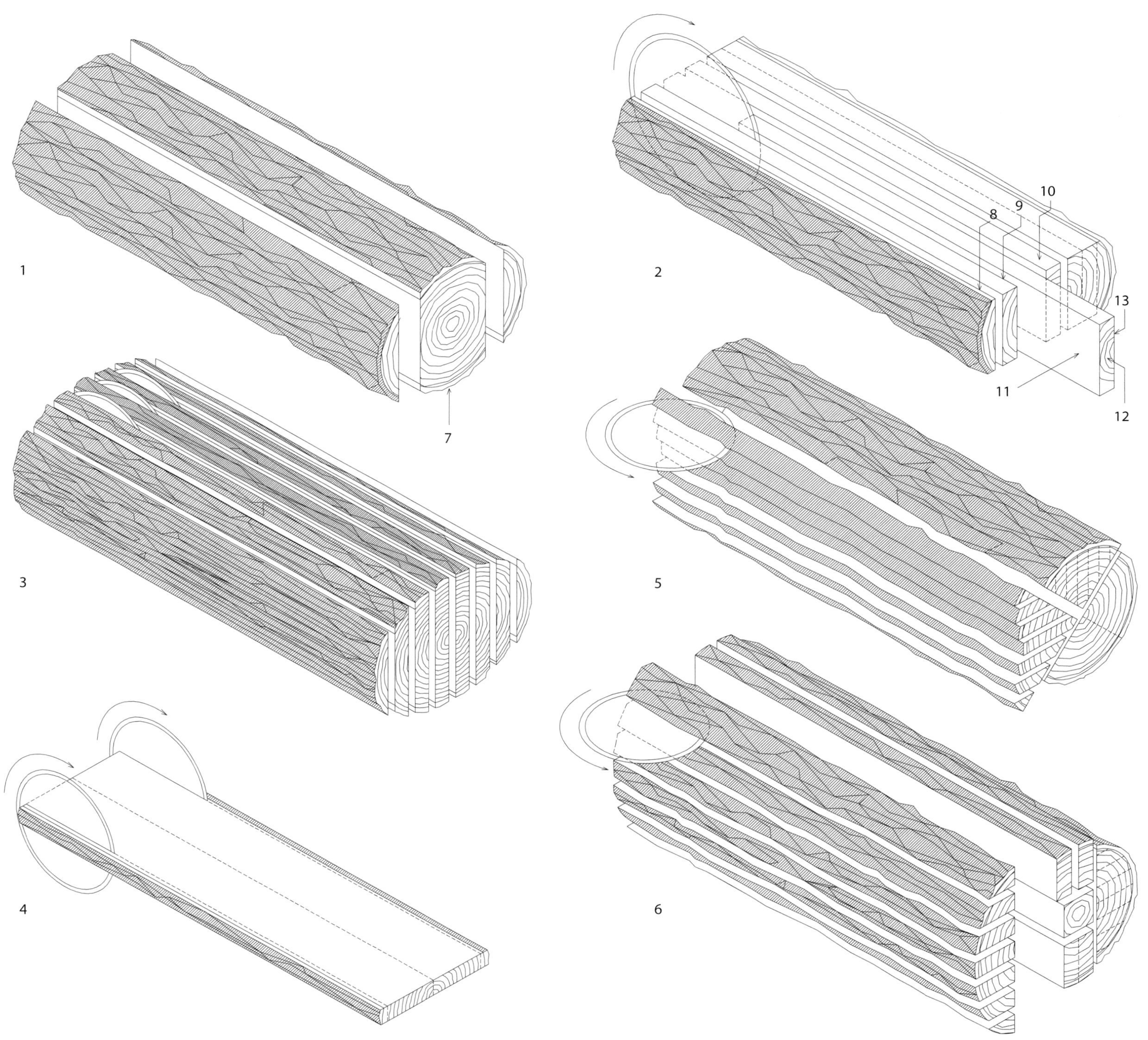
1
7
2
8
9
10
13
11
12
3
5
4
6

3 SCARF JOINTS

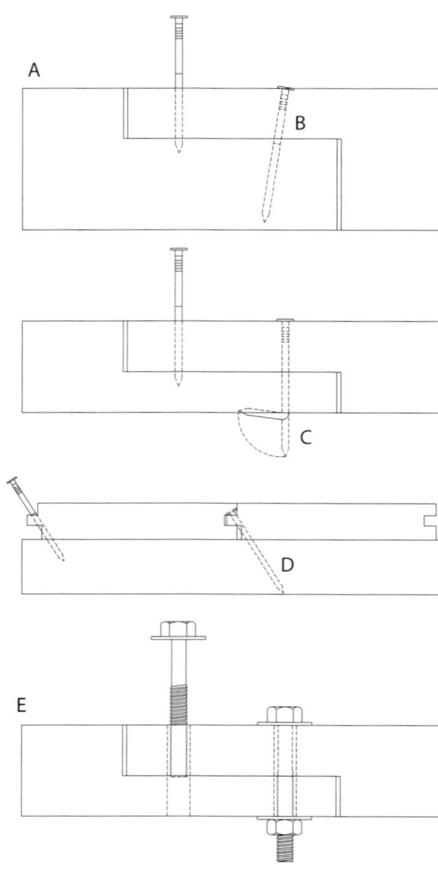

MECHANICAL JOINTS

A nailing, nailed joint
B skew nailing, toe nailing
C clinching, clenching
D secret nailing, blind nailing, concealed nailing
E bolted joint

lengthening joint
any joint used to join two long pieces or members together end on end to form one longer piece

scarf joint, scarfed joint
a timber lengthening joint for connecting two timbers end to end by cutting and overlapping to provide a gluing or fixing edge

mechanical joint
any joint fixed without the use of glue or other bonding medium

splicing piece
a piece fixed to or incorporated in a timber lengthening joint to strengthen or stiffen it

LENGTHENING JOINTS, BUTT JOINTS, END JOINTS

1 butt joint, end joint
2 splayed scarf joint, oblique scarf joint
3 joggle-spliced scarf joint
4 joggled scarf joint
5 spliced joint, fish plate joint, fish joint
6 double lap joint
7 bridled scarf joint

HALVED SCARF JOINTS, LAP JOINTS, LAPPED JOINTS

8 halved scarf joint
9 tabled scarf joint, hooked scarf joint
10 bevelled scarf joint
11 sallied half lap joint
12 splayed and tabled scarf joint, hooked scarf joint
13 keyed, splayed and tabled scarf joint, keyed or wedged scarf joint

TENONED SCARF JOINTS

14 halved and tenoned scarf joint
15 housed or shouldered scarf joint
16 dovetail scarf joint
17 finger joint

SPLICING PIECES

21 dog, dog iron, cramp, crampon
22 abutment, butt
23 joggle piece, joggle
24 hooked joggle, hook joggle
25 fish plate, fish piece, splice plate, splicing piece
26 trenail, peg, pin
27 lap, lapping, overlap
28 lap joint, lapped joint
29 wedge
30 folding wedges

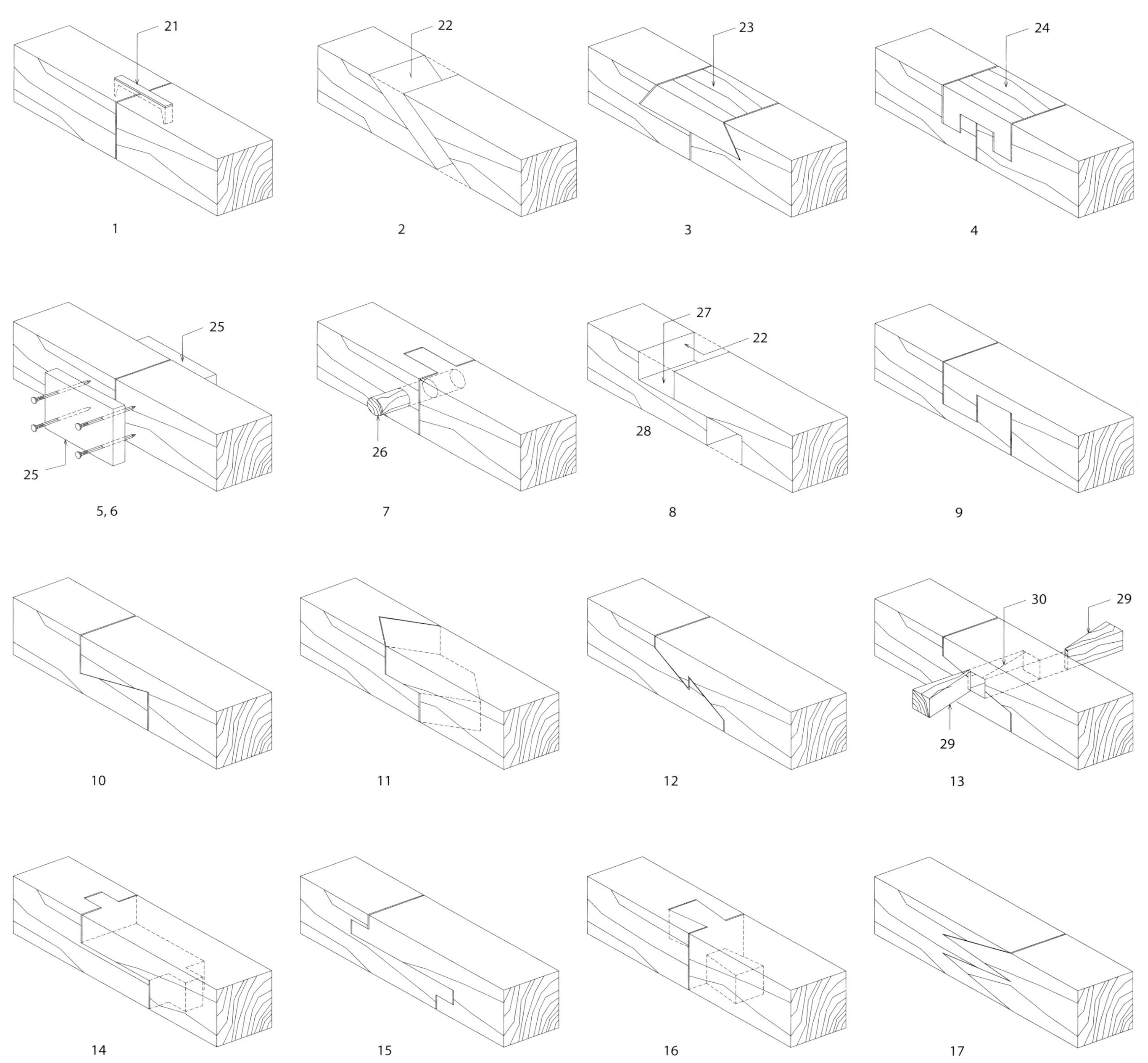
21
1
22
2
23
3
24
4
25
25
5, 6
26
7
27
22
28
8
9
10
11
12
30
29
29
13
14
15
16
17

4 FRAMING JOINTS

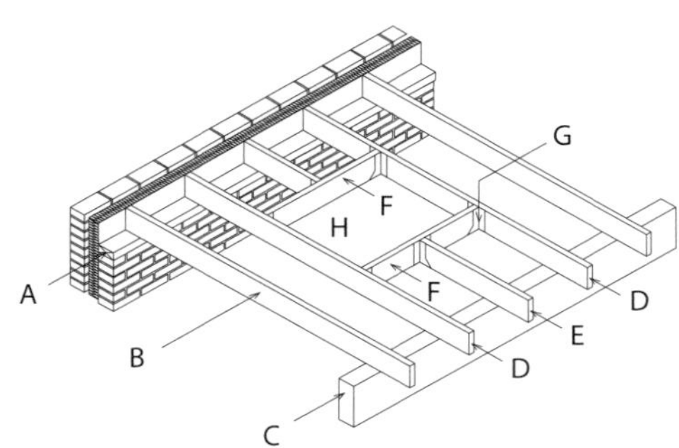

TRIMMING

- A wall plate
- B ceiling joist, floor joist
- C purlin, dormant
- D trimming joist
- E trimmed joist
- F trimmer beam, trimmer joist, trimmer
- G joist hanger
- H void, opening

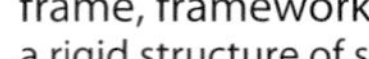

frame, framework
a rigid structure of slender loadbearing members joined together, for attaching and supporting cladding, infill and other components

skeleton
the loadbearing elements of a building, erected first, onto which cladding and other components are fixed

carpentry
construction work in timber; in North America this also includes joinery

carpenter
a craftsman or tradesman who works on site in structural and framing timber; in North America this also includes one who works in joinery

trimming
the cutting and framing of timbers around an opening in construction

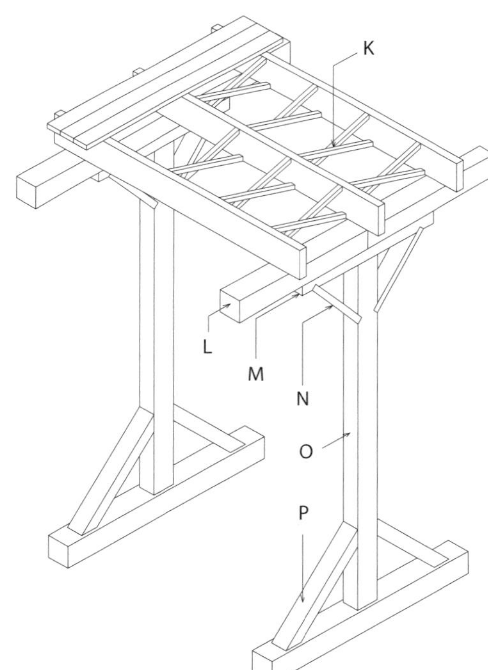

SAMSON POST

- K herringbone strutting
- L binder, principal beam
- M saddle, pillow, bolster
- N brace, knee brace, angle strut
- O post
- P foot brace – prop, stay

CROSS JOINTS, CROSSING JOINTS, CROSSLAP JOINTS

1 single notched joint
2 double notched joint
3 double cogged joint

HALVED JOINTS, HALVING JOINTS

4 cross half lap joint, crosslap joint, halved crossing joint
5 notched and cogged joint, cogged halved joint
6 halved joint, cross half lap joint, crosslap joint, halved crossing joint
7 dovetail halved joint, dovetail lap joint
8 dovetail halved joint, dovetail lap joint, dovetailed housing
9 cogged corner joint
10 bevelled halved joint, splayed halved joint
11 bevelled halved joint, splayed halved joint
12 bevelled corner joint, splayed corner joint
13 bevelled notched housing

OBLIQUE JOINTS

14 dovetailed housing
15 birdsmouth, sally
16 housing
17 birdsmouth housing
18 notched housing, sallied housing
19 mortised housing
20 sallied mortised housing
21 notched mortised housing
22 bridled housing
23 cog
24 notch

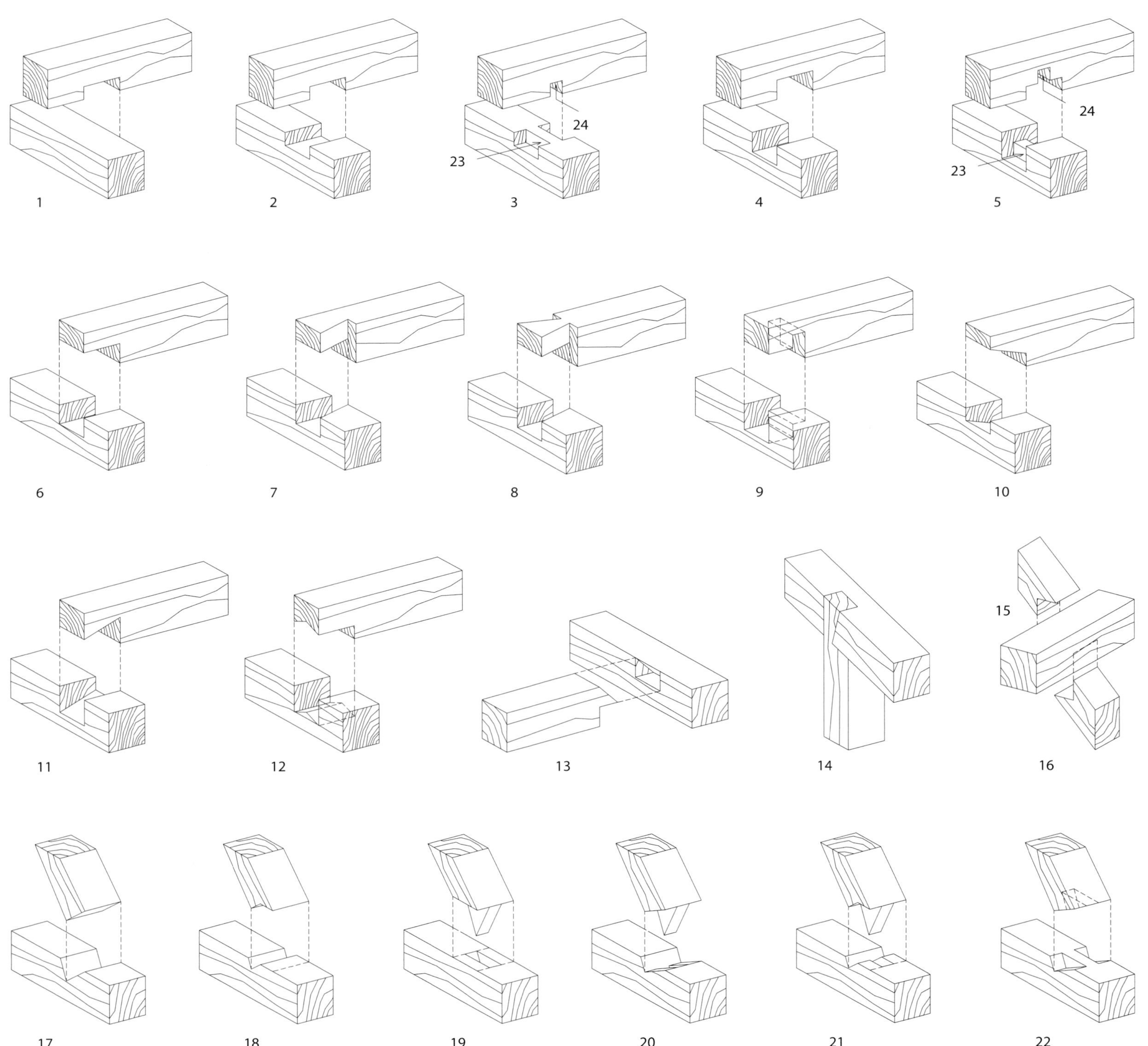
1
2
24
23
3
4
24
23
5
6
7
8
9
10
11
12
13
14
15
16
17
18
19
20
21
22

5 MORTISE AND TENON JOINTS – JOINERY JOINTS, CABINETMAKER'S JOINTS

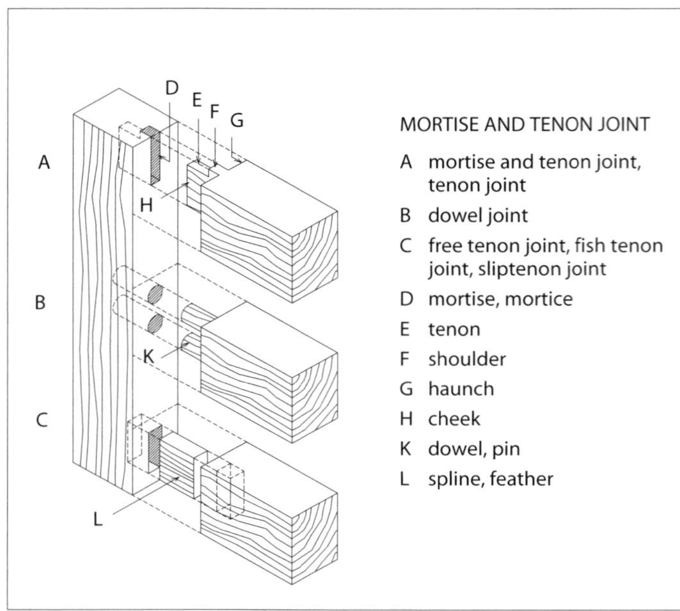

MORTISE AND TENON JOINT

- A mortise and tenon joint, tenon joint
- B dowel joint
- C free tenon joint, fish tenon joint, sliptenon joint
- D mortise, mortice
- E tenon
- F shoulder
- G haunch
- H cheek
- K dowel, pin
- L spline, feather

joinery, finish carpentry (Am)
fine woodwork such as doors, window frames, trim and panelling in a building

cabinetwork
the trade of making fine furnishings, joinery and veneerwork; the furnishings thus produced

joiner
a tradesman responsible for the non-structural timberwork such as furniture, interiors and panelling in a building

mortise and tenon joint, tenon joint
a strong timber framing joint in which the end of one member is cut with a rectangular protrusion (a tenon) which fits into a housing (a mortise or mortice) in another

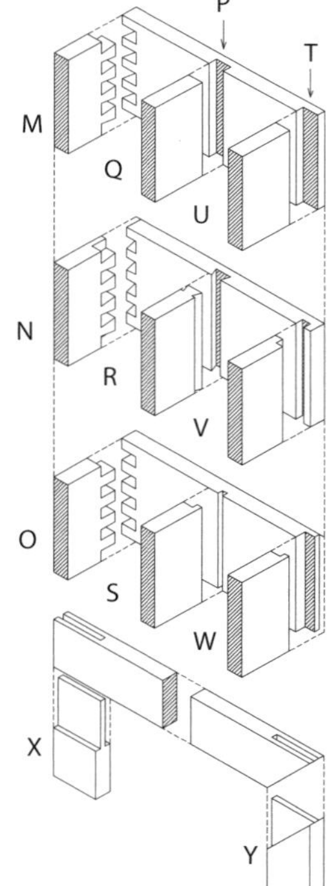

BOX CORNER JOINTS

- M box dovetail, dovetailed corner
- N lapped dovetailed corner, stopped or concealed dovetailed corner
- O finger joint, combed joint, comb joint

HOUSED JOINTS, DADO JOINTS

- P housing, chase, dado
- Q dado joint, straight housing
- R dovetailed housing
- S rebated housing

REBATE, RABBET or LAP JOINTS

- T rebate
- U lapped corner
- V rebated corner
- W lapped and rebated corner

BRIDLE JOINTS

- X bridle joint, open tenon joint
- Y mitred bridle joint, splayed bridle joint

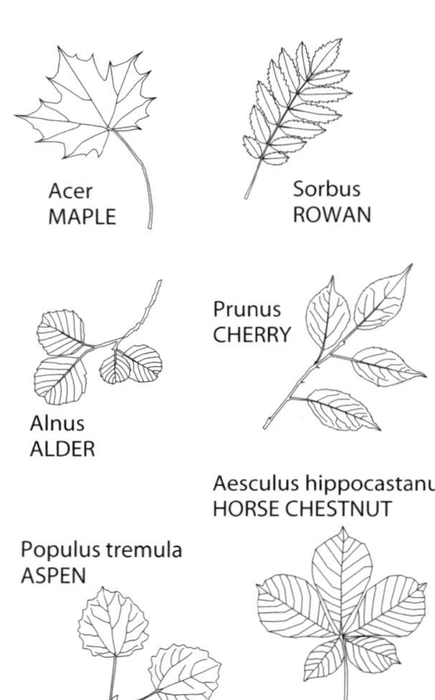

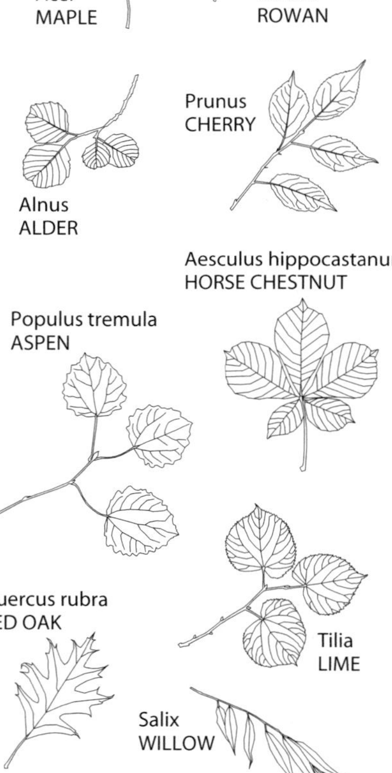

MORTISE AND TENON JOINTS

1. through tenon joint
2. edge-halved tenon joint, stopped tenon joint
3. haunched tenon joint
4. barefaced tenon joint
5. bridle joint
6. double tenon joint
7. twin tenon joint
8. tusk tenon joint
9. dovetail tenon joint
10. wedged joint
11. fox-wedged joint
12. keyed tenon joint, pinned tenon joint, cabinetmaker's tenon joint
13. open mortise and tenon joint
14. shouldered tenon joint, stepped tenon joint, undercut tenon joint
15. free tenon joint, fish tenon joint, slip tenon joint
16. open slot mortise joint
17. abutting tenon joint, butt tenon joint
18. halved tenon joint
19. splayed tenon joint
20. crossed tenon joint
21. teazle tenon joint
22. stub tenon joint, joggle tenon joint, stopped tenon joint
23. notched crossing bridle joint
24. stump tenon joint

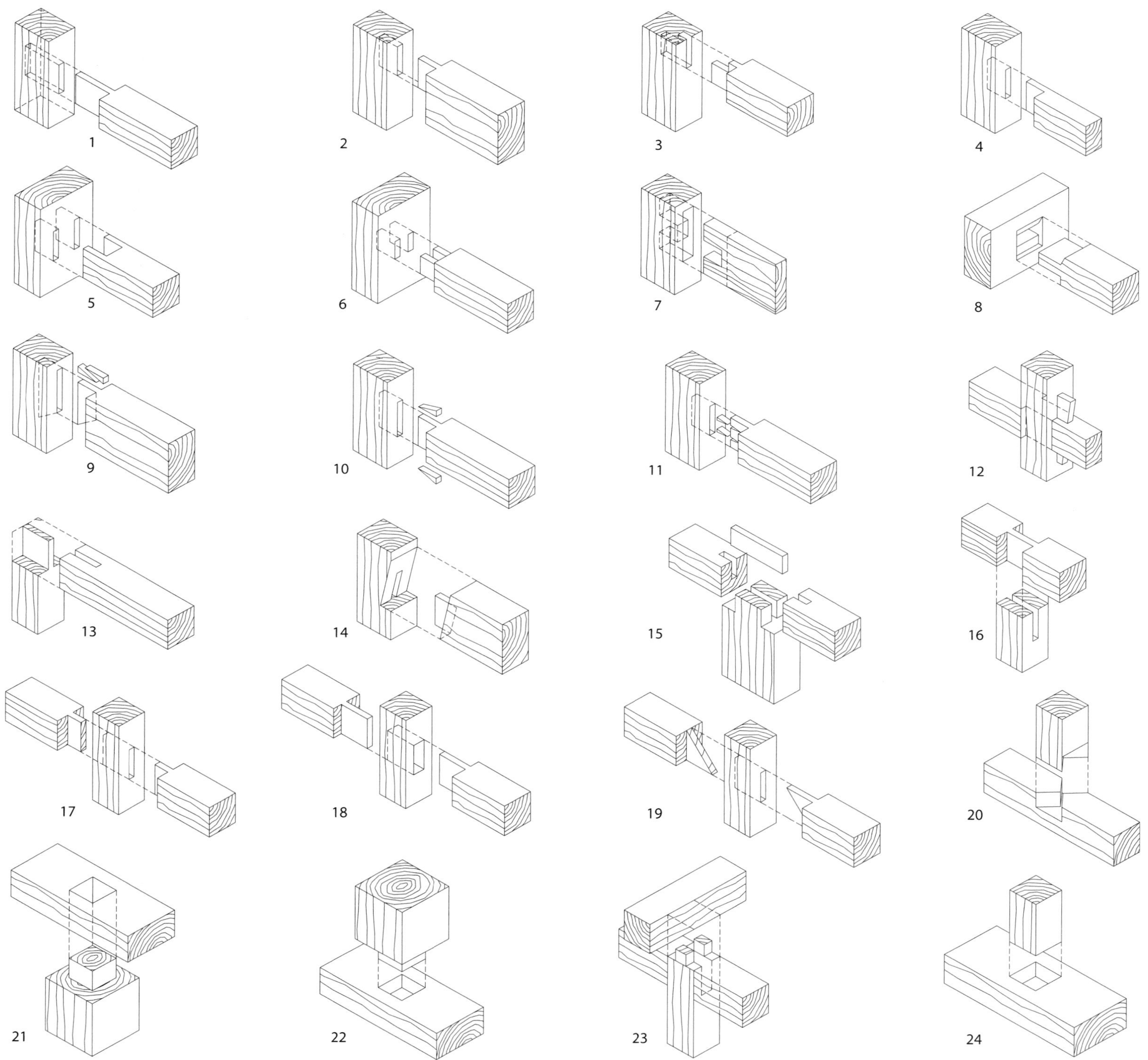

1
2
3
4
5
6
7
8
9
10
11
12
13
14
15
16
17
18
19
20
21
22
23
24

6 LOG CONSTRUCTION, BLOCKWORK

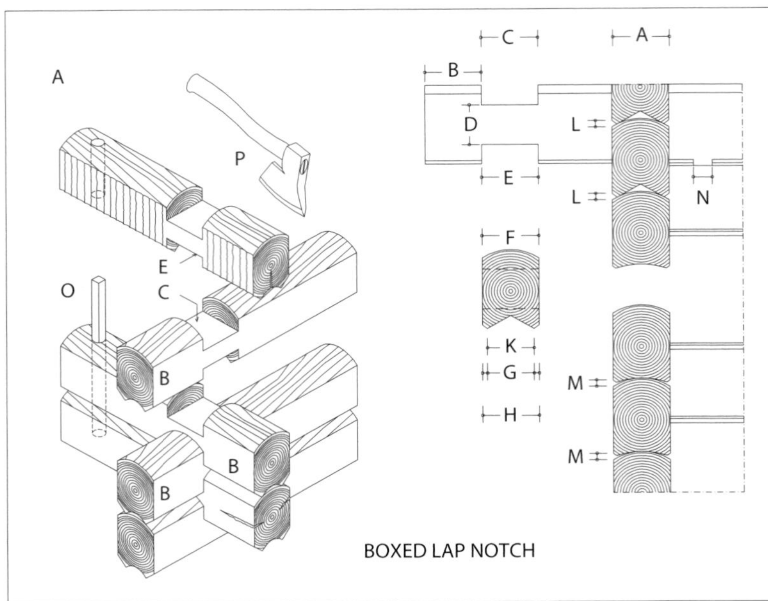

BOXED LAP NOTCH

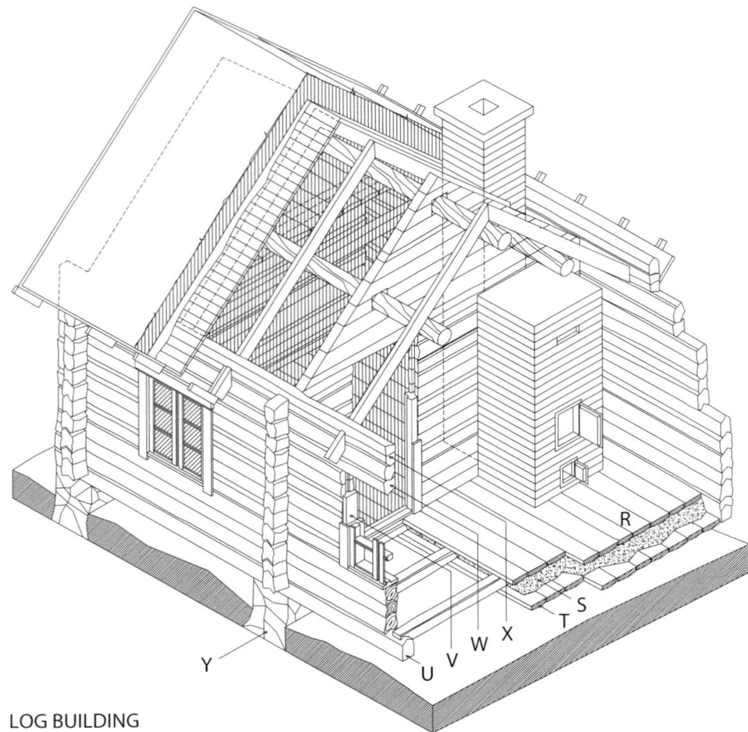

LOG BUILDING

A notched corner joint, log jointing, cobwork
B log extension, flyway, log overhang
C notch, upper notch
D neck
E notch, lower notch
F width of log
G long groove, lateral groove, long notch, Swedish cope
H scribed edge
K chink gap, saddle scarf
L closed fit
M open fit
N cog
O wood key, pin, peg, dowel
P hewing axe
R suspended and ventilated timber ground floor
S sawdust – shavings
T pugging boards
U sill log, ground sill, sleeper
V rough buck, settling piece, key piece
W header log, lintel
X plate log, header
Y bedstone

OVERHANG CORNERS, EXTENDED CORNERS

1 round notch, saddleback joint
2 rough hewn notch
3 boxed lap notch (round log)
4 square notch, double-scribed notch, sheep-head notch
5 boxed lap notch (variation)
6 mitred lap notch, diamond notch
7 lapped notch
8 boxed lap notch (splayed variation)
9 saddle notch (round log)
10 saddle notch (squared log)
11 blind notch

FLUSH CORNERS

12 dovetailed notch (variation)
13 dovetailed notch
14 locked lap joint
15 cogged joint, locked lap notch
16 dovetail joint (keyed)

log
1 the trunk of a felled tree, used for conversion into timber
2 a piece of round unhewn timber used in log construction

log construction, blockwork
building frame construction using solid hewn or machined logs laid on top of one another horizontally, interlocking at the comers with joints known as notches

milled log, machined log, engineered log
an industrial timber product of uniform rectangular or round cross section and cogged ends, machined from a single log and used in the construction of system-built and off-the-shelf log buildings

laminated log, glue-laminated log, lam-log, structural log
an industrial timber product of uniform rectangular or round cross section and cogged ends, glue-laminated and machined from strips of wood and used in the construction of system-built and off-the-shelf log buildings

notch
in log construction, the carefully hewn and crafted joint formed by cutting into overlaid crosswise logs so that they interlock with one another at the external comer of a log building

1
2
3
4
5
6
7
8
9
10
11
12
13
14
15
16

7 TRADITIONAL TIMBER FRAME STRUCTURES AND BEAMS

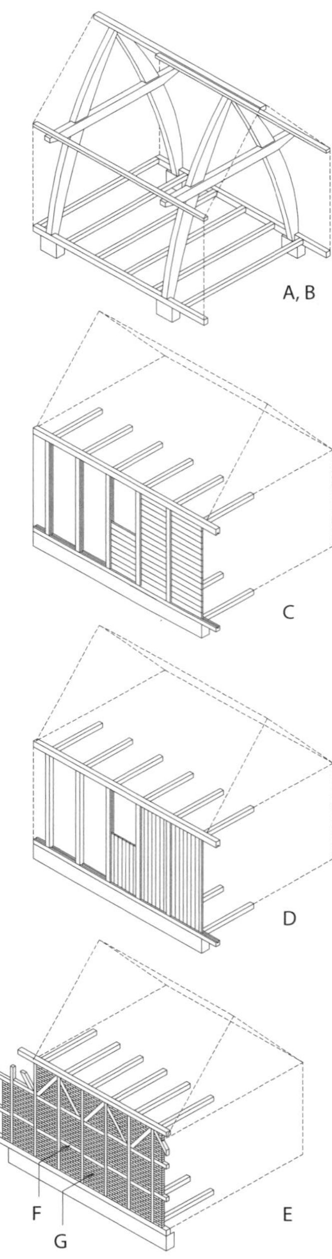

FRAME TYPES

A cruck construction
B A-frame
C muntin and plank construction
D plank construction
E half-timbered construction, black and white work
F nogging, nogging piece
G nogging, brick nogging

BEAM TYPES

H simple beam, simply supported beam
K cantilever beam
L bowstring beam
M simply supported wall, pier and panel wall
N cantilever wall

MULTIPLE-SPAN GIRDERS

O continuous beam
P sleeved beam, cantilever span beam
Q suspended span beam

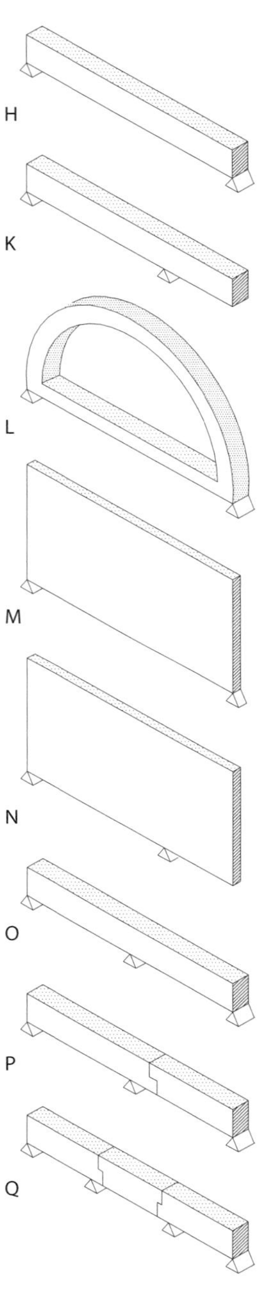

TIMBER BEAMS

1 solid timber beam
2 laminated timber beam
3 parallel grain plywood beam
4 plywood box beam
5 ply-web beam
6 corrugated ply-web beam
7 braced timber beam, traditional braced beam
8 joggle beam
9 traditional trussed beam
10 traditional trussed beam
11 braced timber beam
12 composite trussed beam
13 composite trussed beam
14 composite built-up beam (bound)
15 cambered composite built-up beam (bolted)
16 composite built-up beam (bolted)

carcass, carcase
the frame of a building excluding wall and roof cladding, services, fittings and finishes; the term usually refers to timber framed construction

beam
a horizontal structural member which supports loads over an opening, transferring loading from above to its bearing points on either side

built-up beam
a beam made from more than one timber fixed together by bolts or splices to provide greater bearing capacity

span
the area or axis over which the unsupported part of a beam or arch lies, between adjacent or main supports

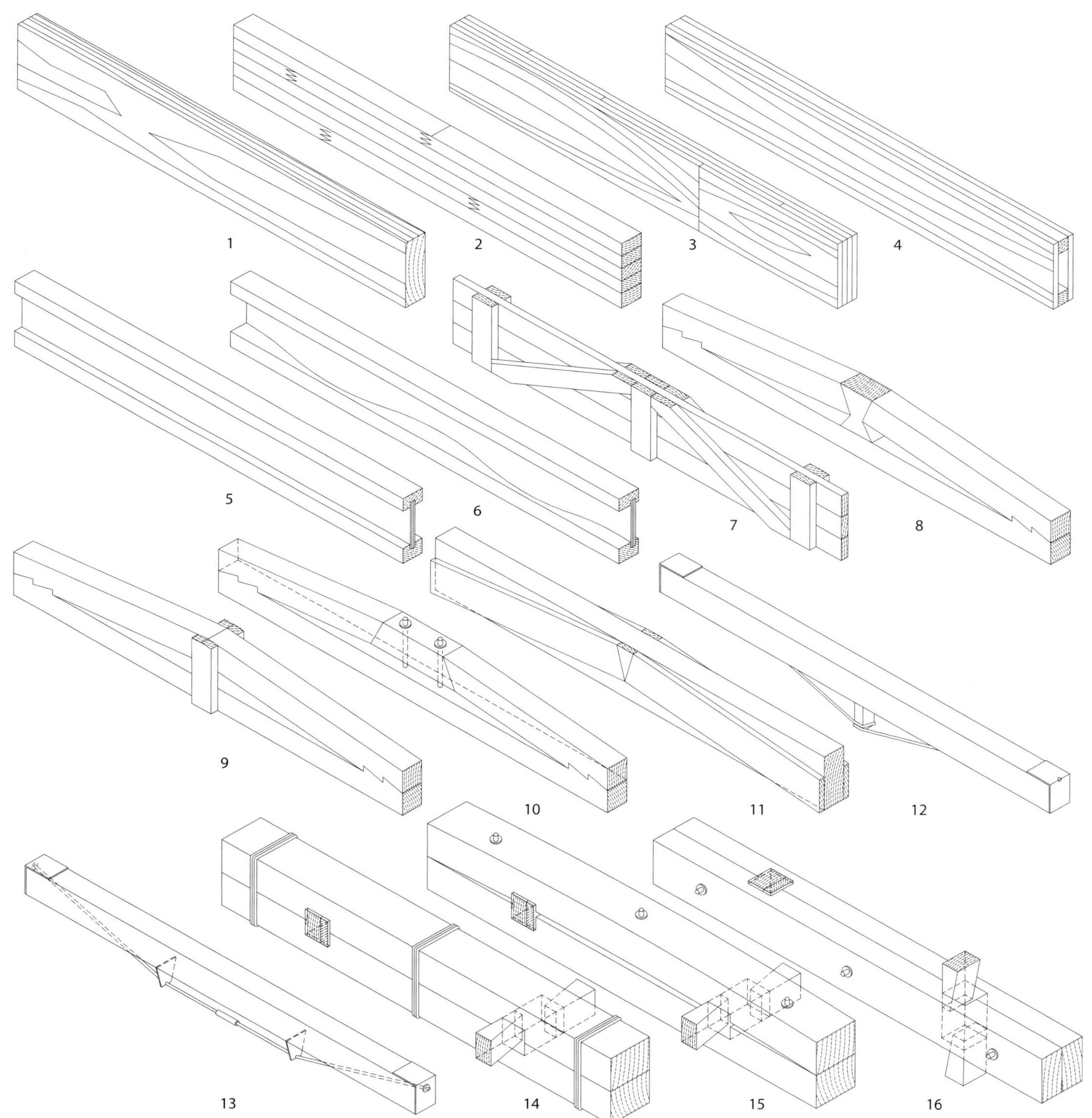

1
2
3
4
5
6
7
8
9
10
11
12
13
14
15
16

8 WEATHER BOARDS, TIMBER CLADDING BOARDS

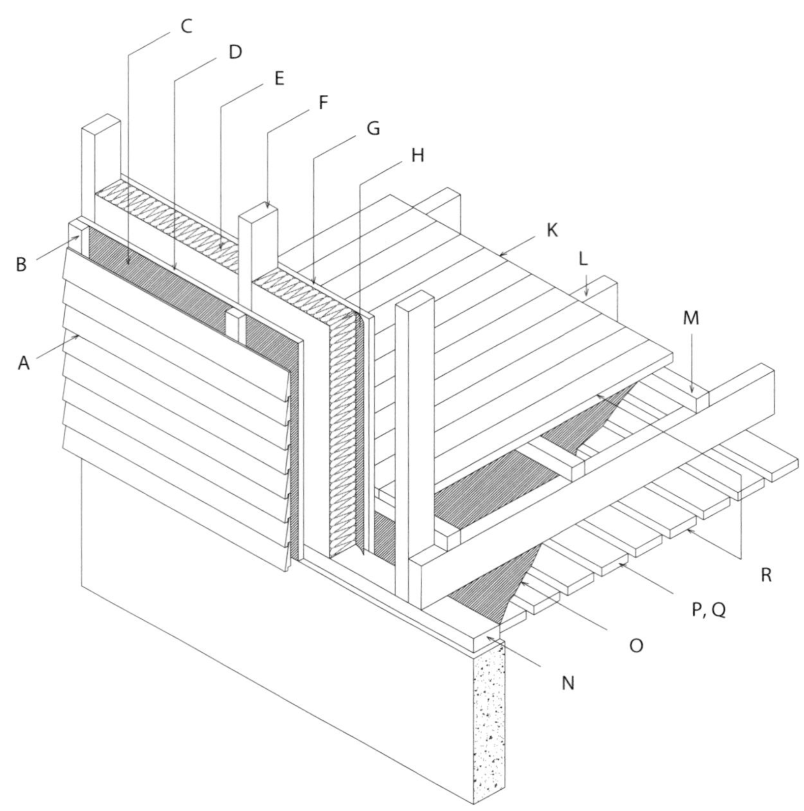

HORIZONTAL BOARDING

1 square-edged boarding, butt-edged boarding
2 round-edged boarding, round-arris boarding
3 clapboarding, colonial siding
4 featheredged boarding, featherboarding
5 rebated featheredged boarding
6 shiplap boarding
7 matchboarding, tongue and groove boarding
8 open tongue and groove boarding
9 bead-edged boarding
10 log cabin siding
11 bead board, moulded board-bead-board cladding
12 spline-jointed boarding, feather-jointed boarding

VERTICAL BOARDING

13 square-edged boarding
14 board-on-board cladding, staggered siding
15 board and batten cladding
16 spaced boarding, open boarding
17 diagonal boarding, diagonal sheathing
18 spline, loose tongue, feather

TIMBER CLADDING

A siding, external cladding boards
B battening
C air gap, gap, cavity
D sheathing board
E thermal insulation
F stud, post
G lining
H vapour barrier, vapour check
K floorboarding, timber flooring, wood strip flooring
L floor joist
M firring, furring
N baseplate, sole plate, sole piece
O building paper, kraft paper
P spaced boarding, open boarding
Q pugging boards
R suspended timber floor with pugging

cladding, facing
any non-loadbearing system of boards, prefabricated components, stone, brick, sheeting etc. attached to a building frame as weatherproofing or as an exterior or interior finish

weatherboarding, siding
exterior cladding of horizontal or vertical sawn timber boards for a building frame, laid side by side or overlapping

tongue and groove joint, tongued and grooved, t and g, t&g
a joint for flush timber boarding, chipboard etc. in which each board is milled with a flange or tongue along one long edge and a channel or groove along the other, designed to fit into one another when the boards are laid edge-on as flooring and cladding

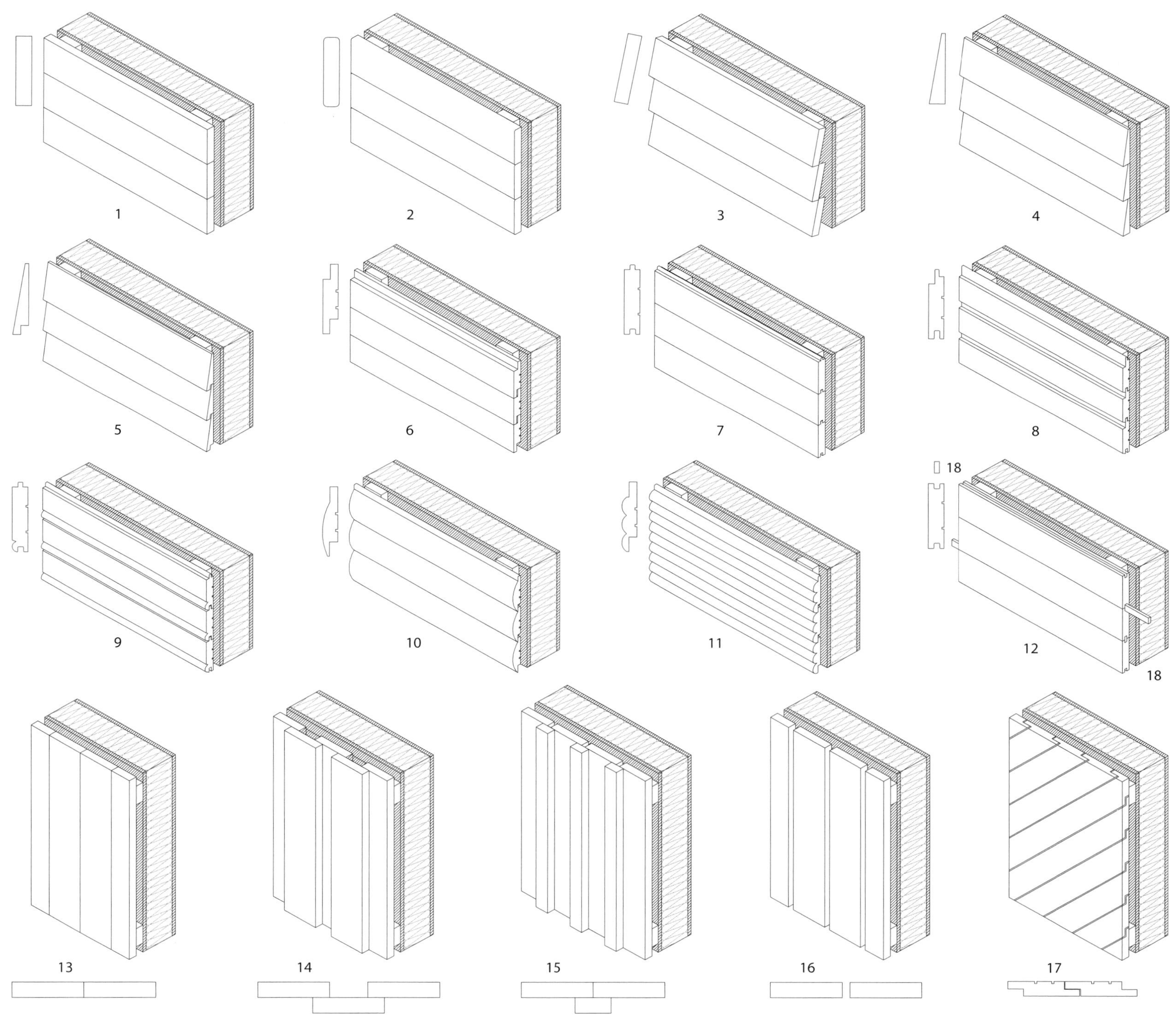
1
2
3
4
5
6
7
8
9
10
11
12
18
18
13
14
15
16
17

9 TIMBER-BASED BUILDING BOARDS

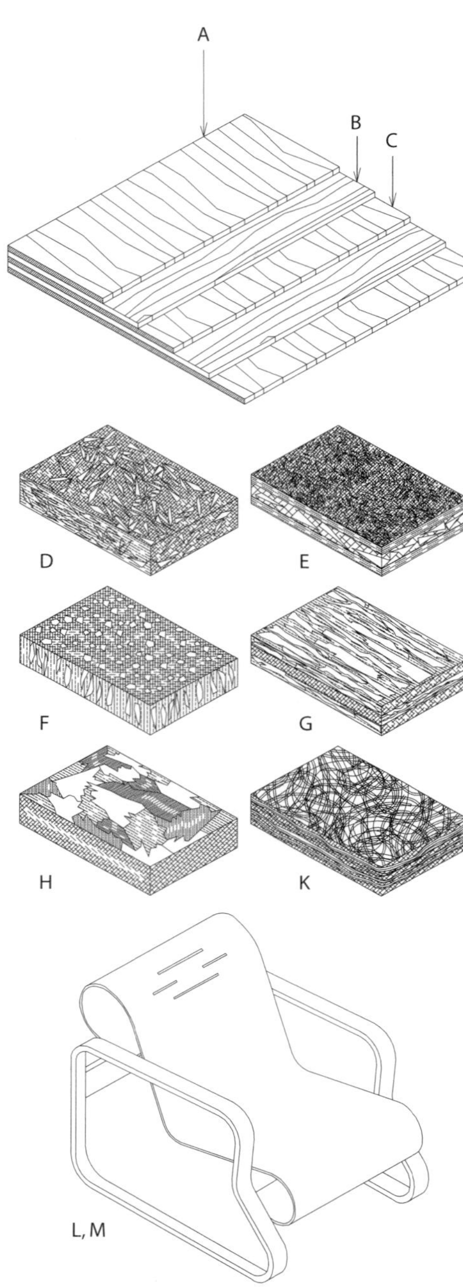

Alvar Aalto 1933: Paimio chair

CROSSBANDING,
balanced construction

A face veneer, face ply
B inner ply
C central ply, core ply

TYPES OF PARTICLEBOARD

D platen-pressed chipboard, pressed chipboard
E graded density chipboard
F extruded particleboard, extruded chipboard
G oriented strand board, OSB
H flakeboard, waferboard
K flaxboard
L bent plywood
M preformed plywood

COREBOARDS, CORE PLYWOODS

1 laminboard
2 core
3 blockboard
4 battenboard
5 cellular board, cellular plywood
6 composite board

PLYWOOD

7 hardwood plywood
8 mixed plywood
9 softwood plywood
10 multi-ply
11 crossbanding
12 star formation
13 parallel-grain plies

CHIPBOARD

14 single layer chipboard, standard grade chipboard
15 multilayer chipboard

FIBREBOARD, FIBRE BUILDING BOARDS

16 peg board, perforated hardboard
17 hardboard

building board
any rigid sheet material of timber, mineral fibre, plastics, gypsum etc. used in construction for cladding and lining frames, as a surface for a finish, as insulation or as bracing

balanced construction
the pairing of matched layers in plywood or composite boards around either side of the central layer to form a symmetrical construction and prevent warping

crossbanding
the laying of alternate plies in the thickness of plywood perpendicular to one another for increased strength

particleboard
a range of non-structural building boards manufactured from chips or fibres of wood bonded together with resin then pressed into sheets; although the term particleboard includes products such as chipboard, fibreboard, flakeboard, flaxboard, and OSB, most often it is synonymous with chipboard

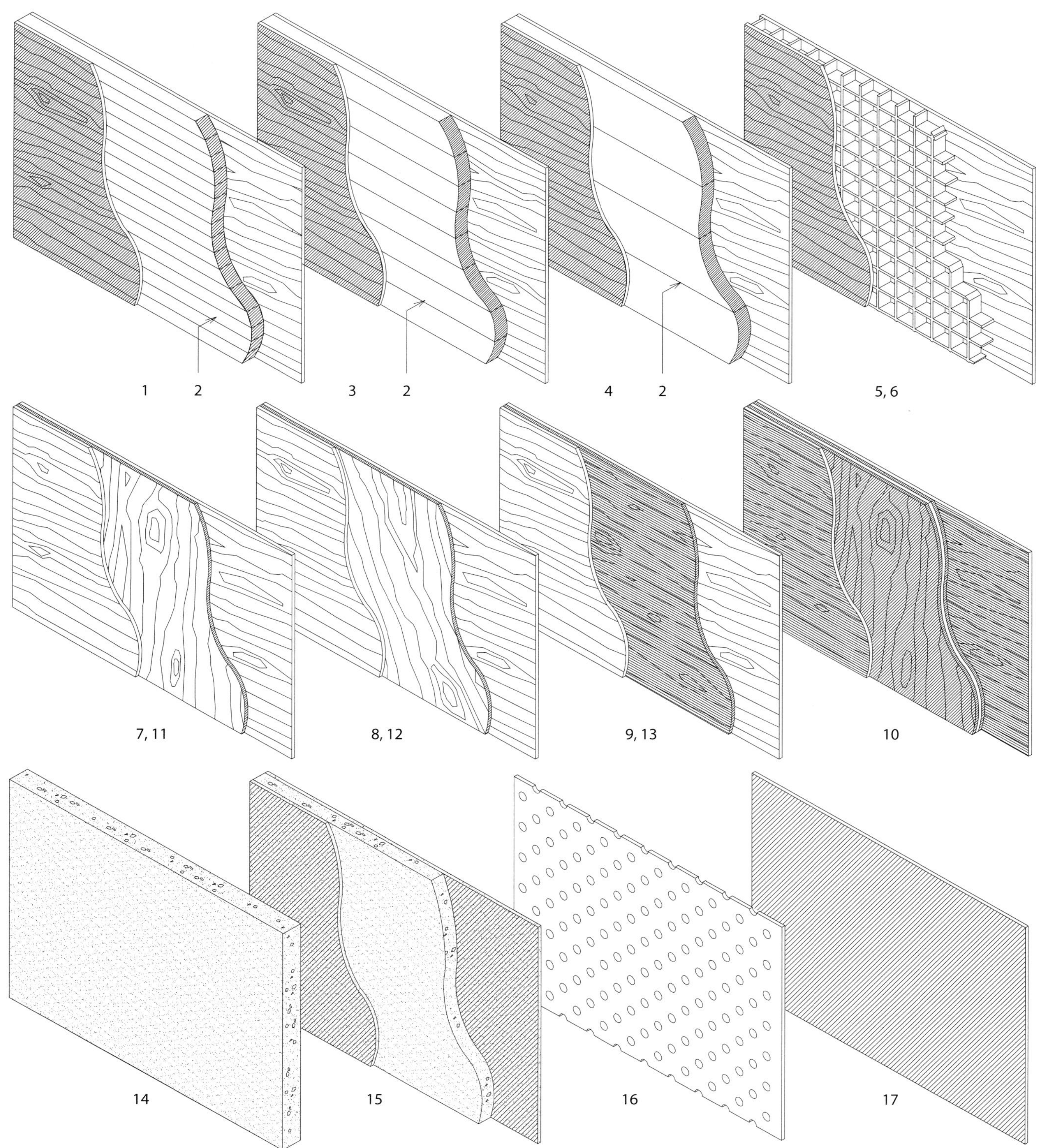
1
2
3
2
4
2
5, 6
7, 11
8, 12
9, 13
10
14
15
16
17

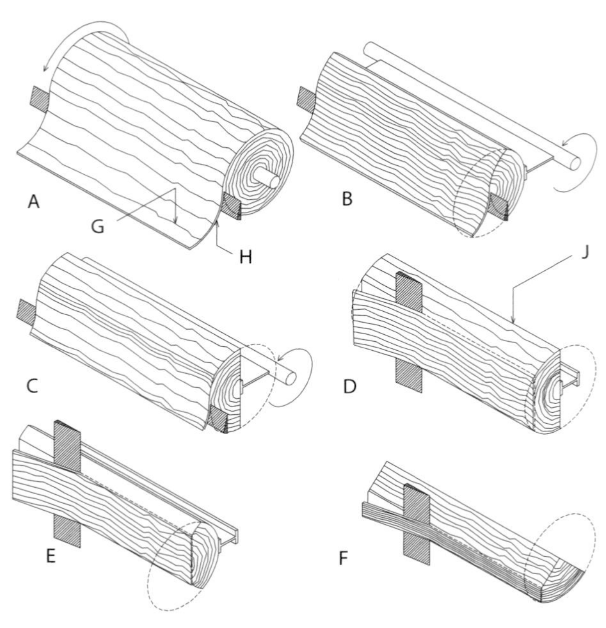

CUTTING OF VENEER

A peeled veneer, rotary cut veneer, unrolled veneer
B back cut veneer
C half round veneer
D flat, plain or straight cut veneer
E back sliced veneer
F quarter sliced, quarter cut or quartersawn veneer
G tight side, closed face, closed side
H loose side, slack side, open face, open side
J veneer bolt, veneer flitch

VENEERING PATTERNS

1 random match, mismatched
2 slip match
3 book match, bookmatching
4 centre match
5 vertical butt and horizontal book match, butt match
6 basketweave, chequerboard
7 herringbone match or pattern
8 chevron match, V-match
9 diamond match
10 box match
11 reverse diamond match
12 reverse box match

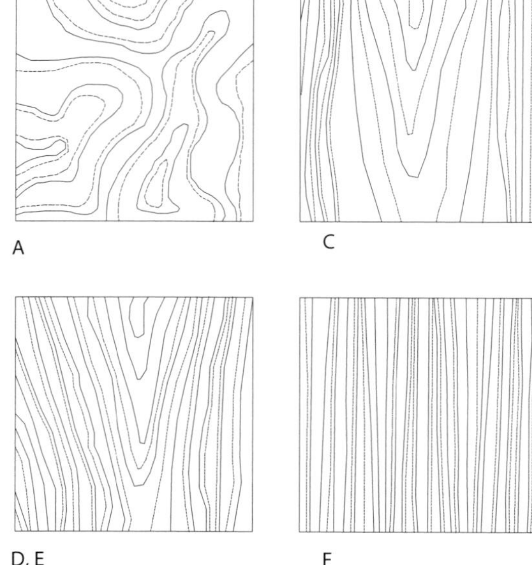

veneer
sheets of wood less than 6 mm in thickness cut from a log by slicing, peeling or sawing; glued together as plywood or to cheaper boards as a decorative finish; often called wood veneer to distinguish it from brick and other veneers

veneering, veneerwork
the process of cutting and gluing decorative veneers

grain
the arrangement and direction of the fibres in wood

figure
the pattern caused by grain on a wooden surface

matching
the craft of arranging sheets of wood veneer into neat repeated or mirrored patterns for the surfaces of panels and tops or fronts of furnishings

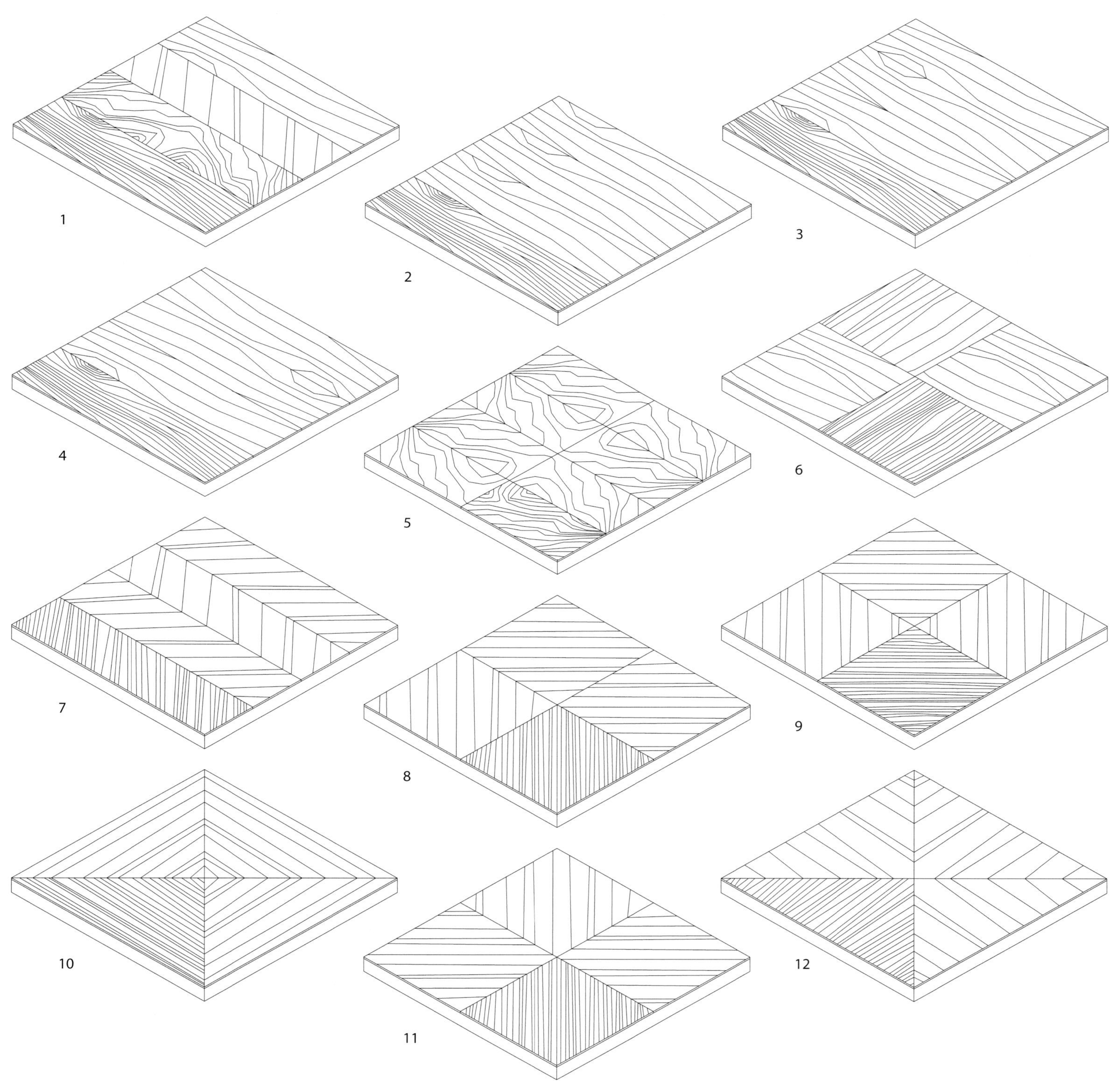
1
2
3
4
5
6
7
8
9
10
11
12

11 STONE WALLING

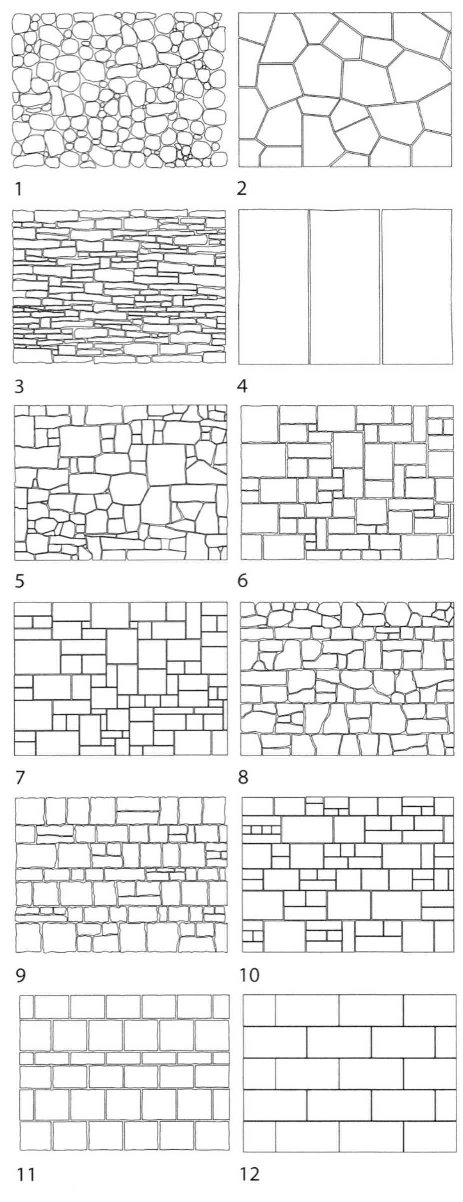

VARIETIES OF STONE WALLING

UNCOURSED MASONRY

1 cobblestone wall, cobble wall, uncoursed field stone, rough rubble wall, common rubble wall

2 polygonal wall, cyclopean masonry, Pelasgic masonry

3 ragwork, slate walling

4 wall of stone slabs

5 random rubble wall, uncoursed rubble wall

6 uncoursed squared rubble wall

7 uncoursed ashlar wall

COURSED MASONRY

8 irregular coursed rubble wall

9 coursed squared rubble wall

10 coursed ashlar wall

11 regular coursed rubble wall

12 regular ashlar wall

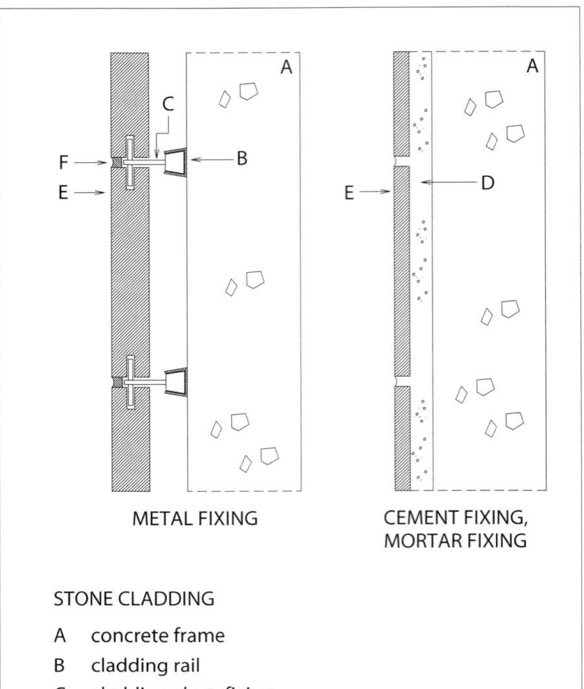

METAL FIXING

CEMENT FIXING, MORTAR FIXING

STONE CLADDING

A concrete frame

B cladding rail

C cladding cleat, fixing, holdfast

D fixing mortar

E stone cladding, stone veneer, stone facing

F joint sealant or jointing mortar

masonry
any construction in laid bricks, blocks or stone

mason, stonemason
a skilled craftsman who works in stone, in building construction producing stonework, stone walling and embellishment

walling
the process and product of constructing walls in masonry

ashlar, ashlar masonry
masonry blocks or facing stone which has been dimensioned, squarely dressed and laid in bonded courses with narrow joints

1
2
3
4
5
6
7
8
9
10
11
12

12 STONE FINISHES AND RUSTICATION

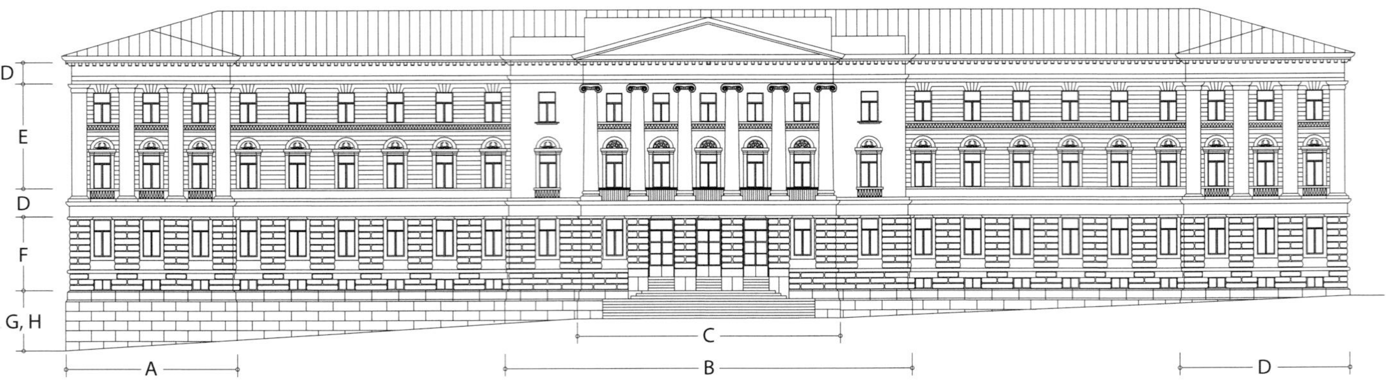

EMPIRE FACADE (NEO-CLASSICISM) University of Helsinki, Helsinki, 1828–33, C.L.Engel 1/500

A corner bay, flanking bay
B central bay
C frontispiece
D rendered brickwork
E banded rustication, channel jointed rustication
F rusticated wall
G regular ashlar wall
H ashlar footing, stone footing

stonework
any part of a building, structure, cladding or paving, which incorporates natural stone as a primary material; construction and detailing in stone

rustication
in masonrywork, decorative rebates or sinkings around the edges of individual stones to emphasize joints and give articulation to the surface; especially prevalent in Renaissance architecture

natural stone
stone which has been quarried, cut, shaped and dressed for use in the construction industry

stonework finish
the various factory or tooled treatments applied to the stone surfaces of a building, or natural stone slabs

RUSTICATION

1 bossage, rusticated ashlar, rustic ashlar
2 banded rustication, channel jointed rustication
3 quoining, long and short work
4 alternating rustication

ASHLAR MASONRY

5 quoin
6 pitched quarry stone (hammer-dressed, pinched)
7 ashlar, natural stone block, cut stone, dimension stone
8 anathyrosis
9 rusticated block
10 draft, drafted margin
11 smooth-faced rustication
12 bevel margin, facet
13 diamond-pointed block, prismatic block
14 drafted diamond-pointed block
15 sunk margin
16 double-sunk margin
17 rounded sunk margin
18 beaded margin, rounded margin
19 coved margin
20 coved and sunk margin

INDUSTRIAL FINISHES FOR NATURAL STONE

21 quarry finish, rubble finish, pitch-faced, rock-faced
22 sawn finish, cut finish
23 flame finish, thermal finish
24 milled finish, planed finish
25 honed finish
26 sand-blasted finish
27 polished finish

HAMMER-DRESSED AND TOOLED FINISHES

28 bush-hammered (all stones)
29 pointed, pecked (hard stones)
30 tooth chiselled, drove finish, boasted finish (soft stones)
31 batted or striated finish
32 vermiculation

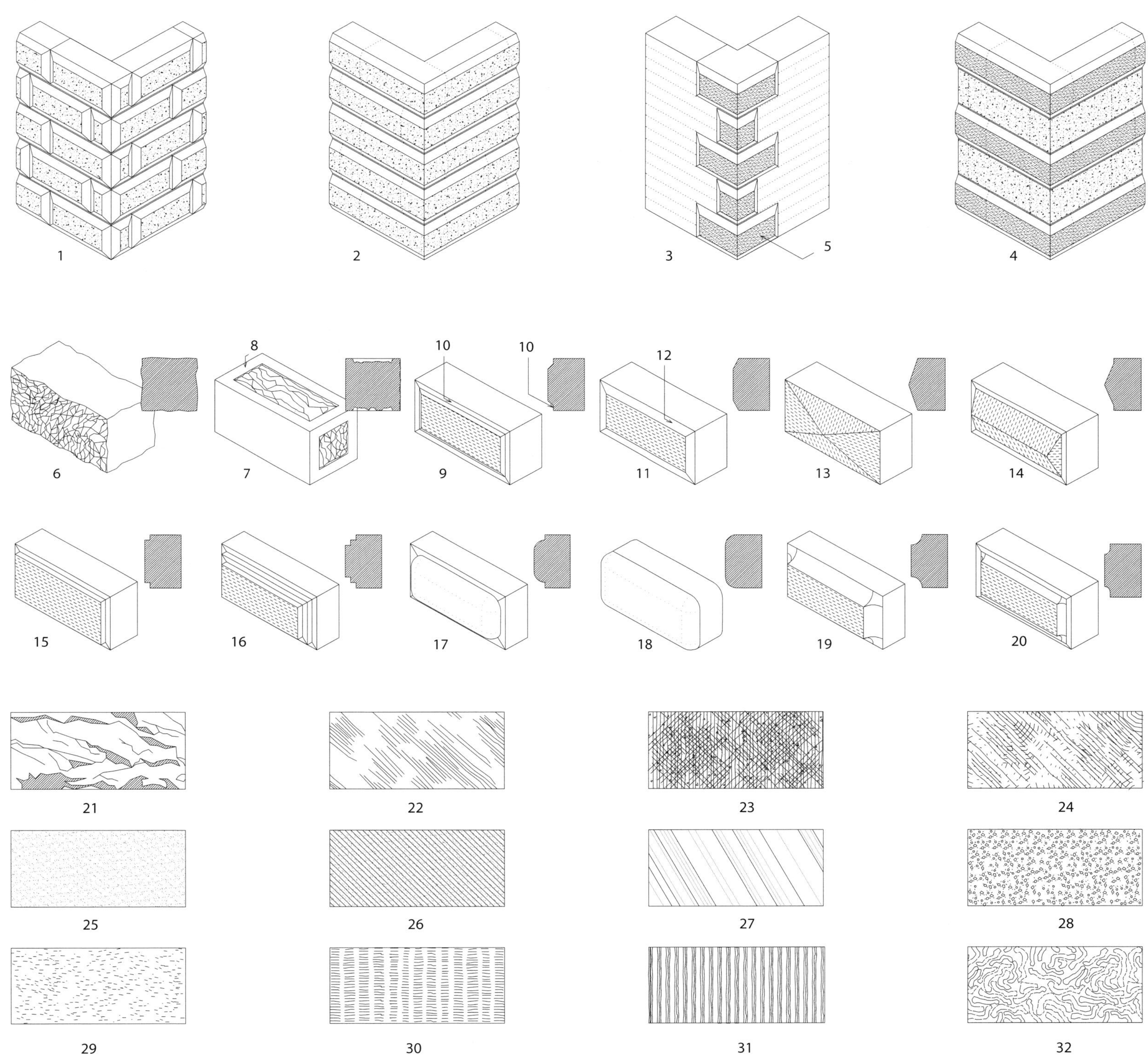

1
2
3
5
4
6
8
7
10
9
10
12
11
13
14
15
16
17
18
19
20
21
22
23
24
25
26
27
28
29
30
31
32

13 TRADITIONAL COLUMN AND PILLAR TYPES

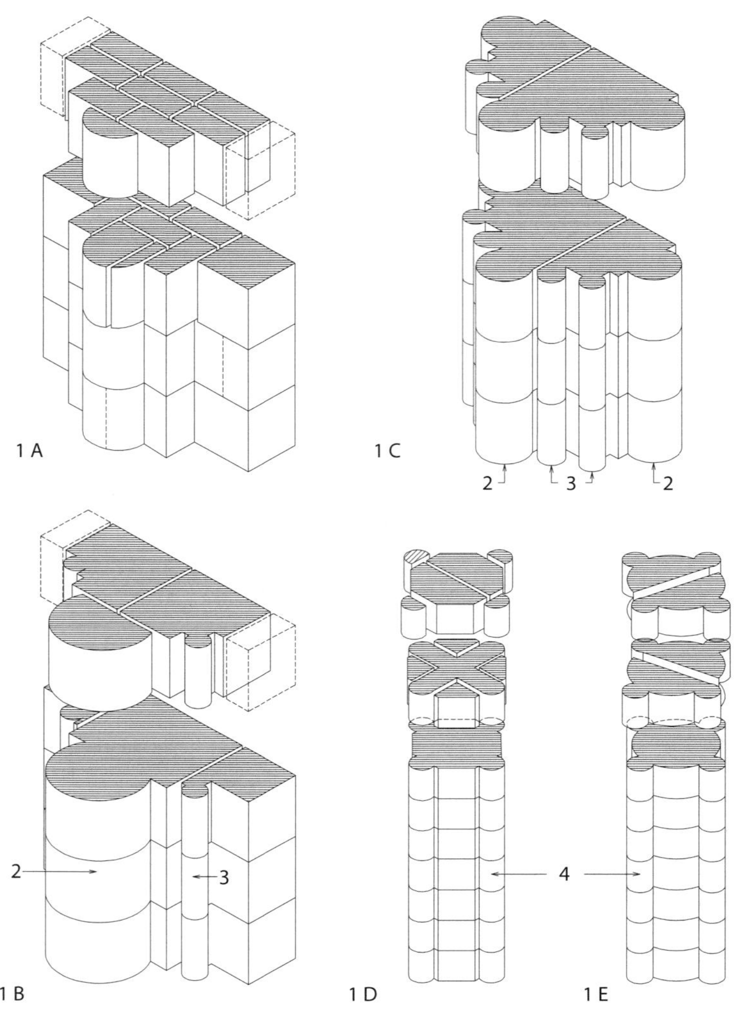

COMPOUND PIERS, COMPOUND COLUMNS

1 compound pier, bundle pier, clustered pier
2 principal shaft
3 secondary shaft
4 shaft, merged shaft, semi-merged shaft

COMMON COLUMNS

5 round column, circular column
6 coupled columns, twinned columns
7 bundle column, compound column
8 rusticated column
9 square column, pillar, 'Attic column'
10 edge rolled column
11 detached column

ENGAGED COLUMNS

12 engaged column or pier, applied column, attached column, inserted column
13 demi-column, half-column
14 recessed column
15 pilaster
16 lesene, pilaster strip

column
a structural shaft of concrete, masonry, metal or timber which transfers applied vertical loads through its length to its base

pillar
a heavy masonry column or pier, freestanding or supporting a structure, often other than round in plan

detached column
a column adjacent to a wall, but not physically attached to it, often a decorative column on a pedestal or plinth

engaged column, attached column, engaged pier, applied column, inserted column
a column built into, adjacent or physically attached to a wall, either for structural stability or for decorative effect

Compound piers from French cathedrals: A) Jumièges, 1037–67; B) Amiens, 1220–69; C) St. Denis, 1135–1144; D) Chartres, 1134–1220; E) Reims, 1211–1255

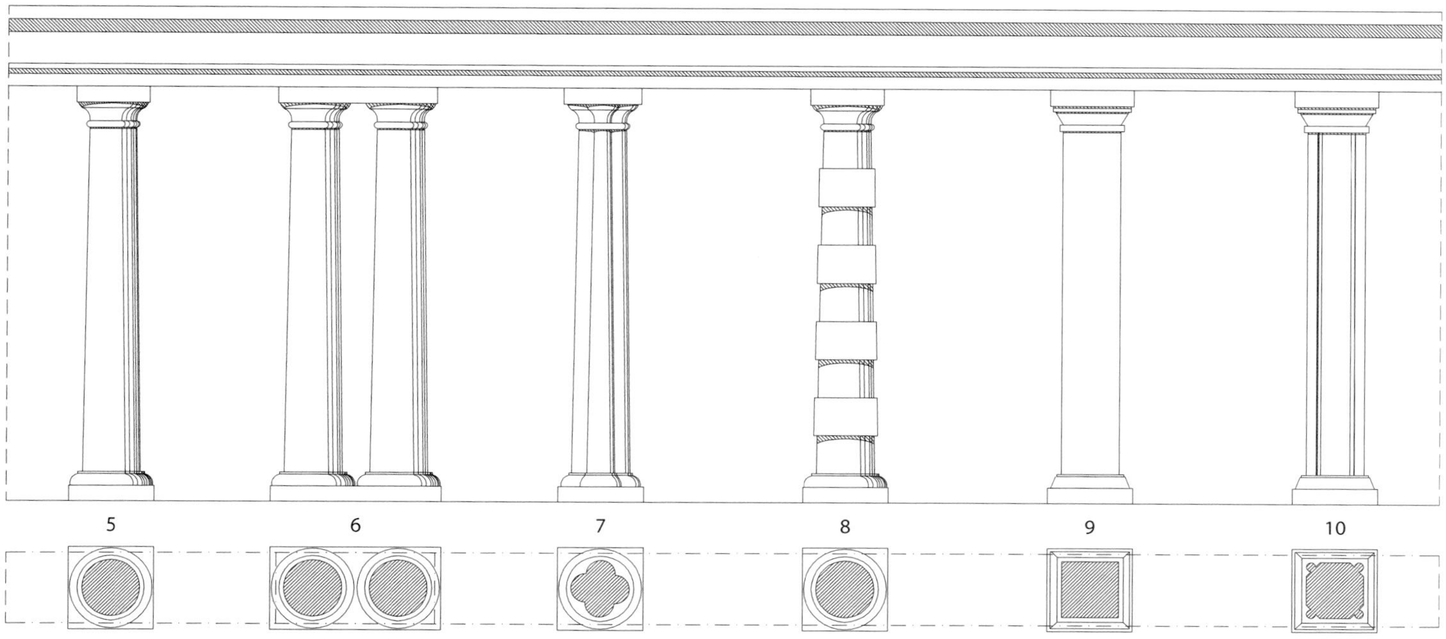

5 6 7 8 9 10

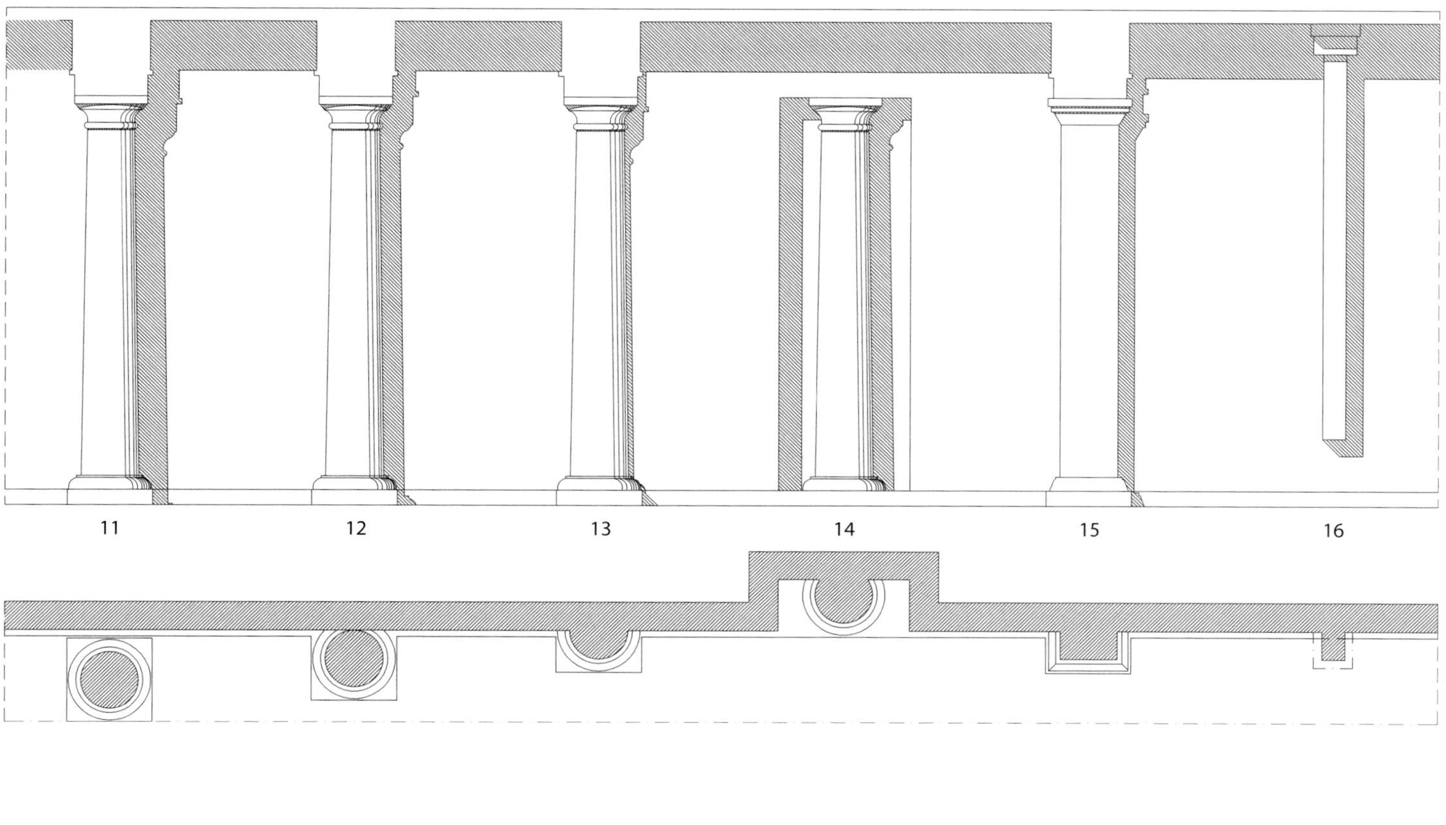

11 12 13 14 15 16

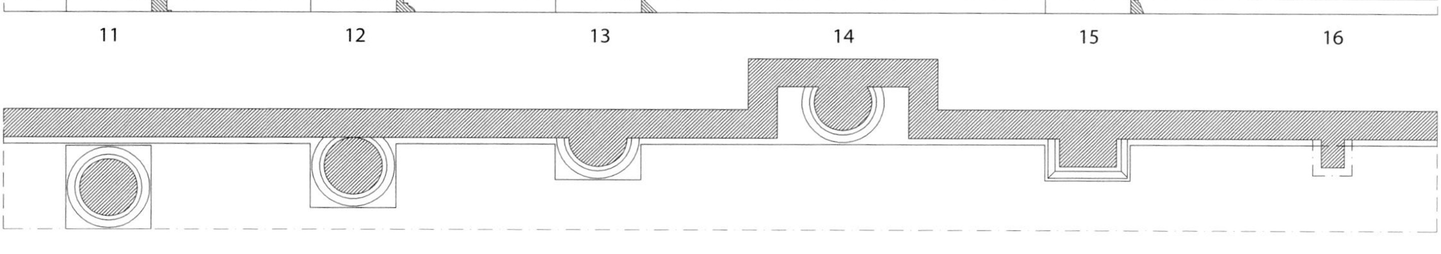

14 CONTINUOUS MOULDINGS, RUN-MOULDED PLASTERWORK

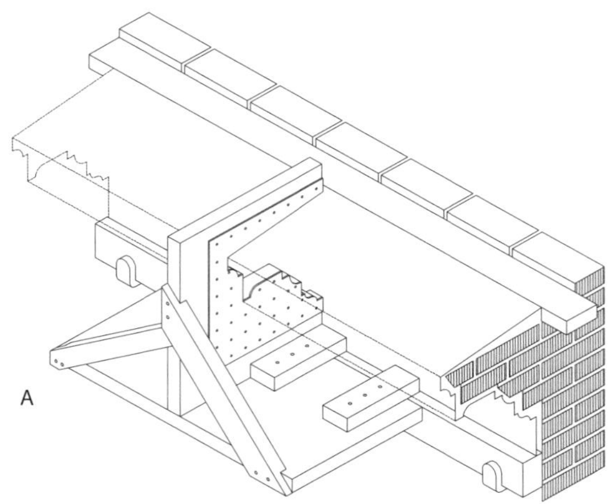

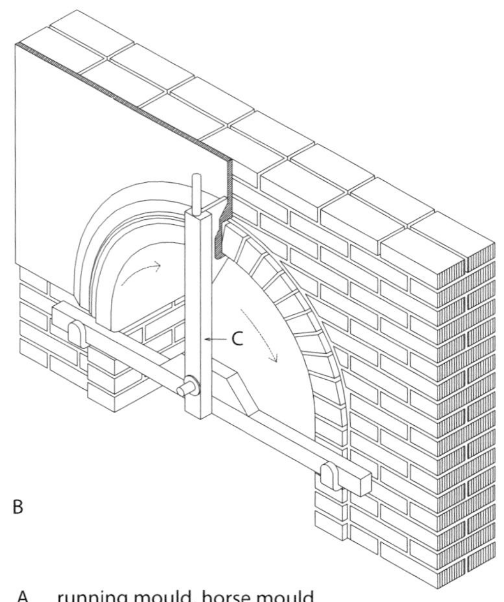

A running mould, horse mould
B peg mould
C trammel rod

MOULDINGS

1 fillet, fascia, listel, list, tringle
2 raised fillet, square fillet
3 corona moulding
4 roundel, roll moulding, bowtell, round moulding, three-quarter round
5 half-round, roll moulding, torus, astragal, round bead, bead moulding
6 quirk bead moulding, quirked bead moulding, bead and quirk moulding, flush bead moulding, double-quirked bead moulding, recessed bead moulding
7 ovolo
8 beak moulding, thumbnail bead, quarter round, quadrant
9 beak moulding, bird's beak moulding, cock beak moulding
10 keel moulding
11 brace moulding, bracket moulding, double ogee moulding
12 thumb moulding
13 cavetto, cove, congé
14 hollow moulding, trochilus, gorge
15 scotia, gorge, trochilus
16 sunk fillet
17 sunken half round, sunk bead
18 eased sunken half round
19 reeded moulding, reeding
20 fluted moulding, fluting
21 reeded torus moulding

INSIDE CORNERS, INTERNAL CORNERS

22 splayed moulding
23 cove, coving
24 angle bead, corner bead, ovolo moulding, quadrant
25 bowtell, boltel, boutel, bowtell, edge roll

OUTSIDE CORNERS, EXTERNAL CORNERS, MARGINS

26 bevel, chamfer, splay
27 bevel, facet
28 bullnose, rounded edge
29 pencil round, pencil arris, eased arris, eased edge, arrissed edge
30 sunk margin
31 edge strip, edging, edge bead
32 edge roll, bowtell

moulding, molding (Am)

1 a horizontal ornamental projecting band in a wall surface, often with running motifs and of carved stone, timber or plasterwork
2 profile, strip; a long, narrow piece of extruded metal, machined timber or preformed plastics formed into a specific uniform cross sectional shape, used for various applications such as for covering construction joints, as glazing bars etc.
3 strip; any long flat or profiled piece of timber or other material attached as decoration, or as an ornamental gutter, cornice or string course
4 fillet; a long three-dimensional profiled strip in a wall surface

run moulding, horsed moulding

an ornamental plasterwork moulding shaped by dragging a template in the profile of the final moulding across wet plaster

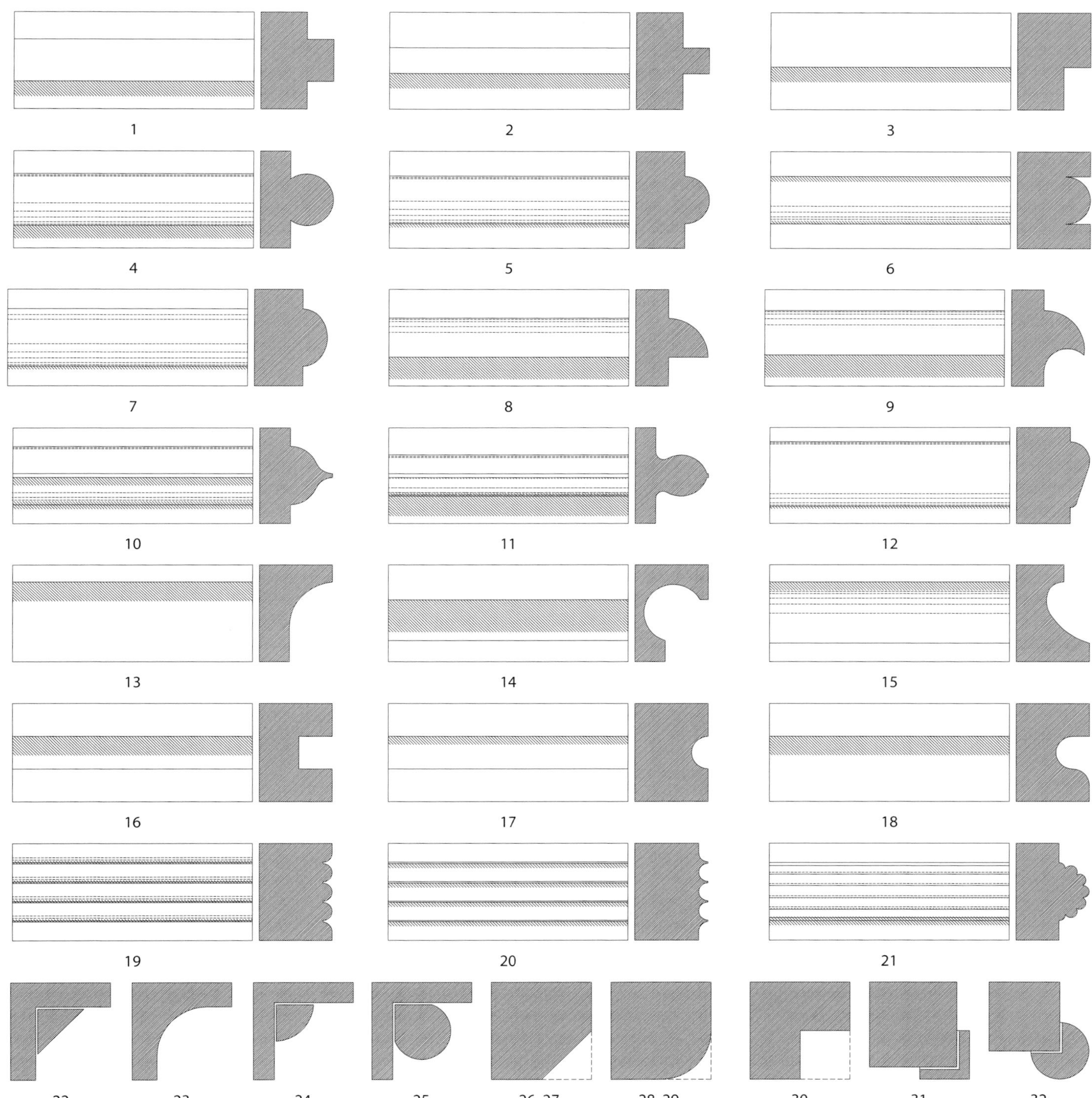

1
2
3
4
5
6
7
8
9
10
11
12
13
14
15
16
17
18
19
20
21
22
23
24
25
26, 27
28, 29
30
31
32

15 PAVING AND TILING

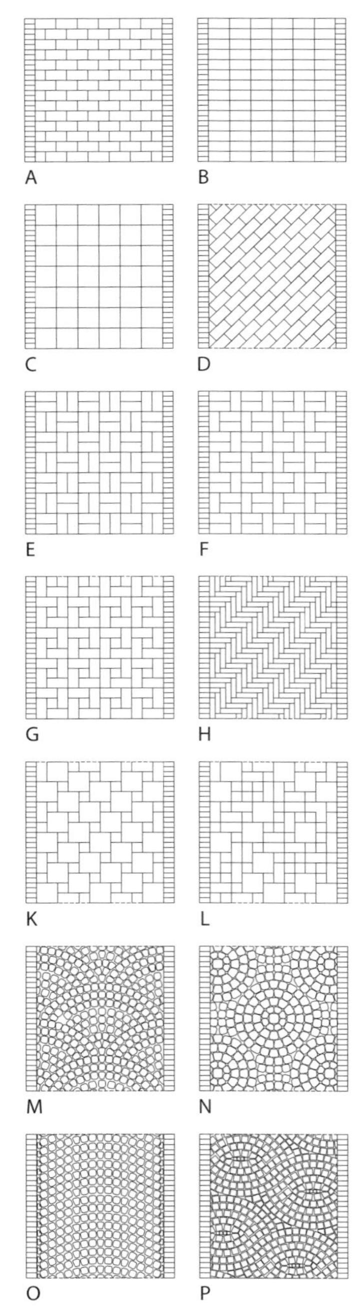

PAVING PATTERNS

A running bond
B stack bond
C square pattern, chequered pattern
D diagonal pattern
E basketweave paving
F half-basketweave paving
G Spanish bond
H herringbone paving (brick-on-edge)
K herringbone paving (Dutch paving)
L random paving
M fan pattern, fantail pattern, peacock tail pattern
N circular pattern, concentric pattern
O arc pattern
P wave pattern

SECTION THROUGH PAVEMENT

a paver
b sand bedding
c sub-base
d subgrade, formation level
e sand joint
f kerb, curb, edging
g vegetable soil
h planting

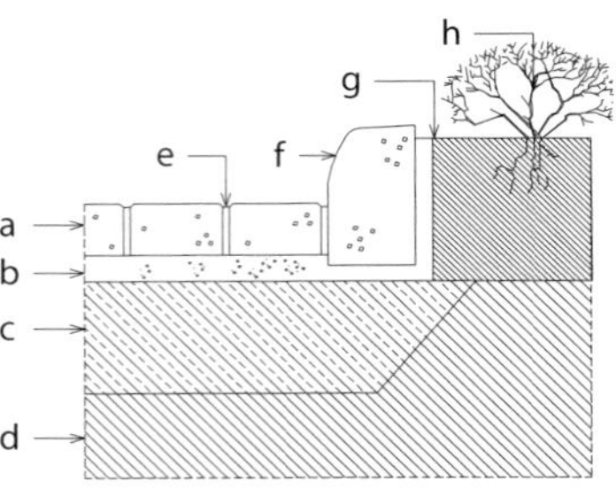

paving
blocks, precast units or thin slabs of stone, brick, concrete or ceramic material laid horizontally as a hardwearing external surface

paver
any brick, concrete or natural stone product etc. used for paving external surfaces; also called a paving stone, pavior or paviour

tiling
the trade of laying tiles with butting joints as flooring, wall covering etc.; the resulting surface or construction

tile
any thin, rectangular or polygonal product of mineral, plastics or organic material used in series to form a protective or weatherproof finish

NATURAL STONE PAVING

1 sett, cobble
2 cube, cobble
3 pebble, cobble
4 large pebble, boulder, cobble
5 crazy paving, random paving

BRICK PAVING

6 brick-on-flat paving
7 brick-on-edge paving
8 brick-on-end paving

CONCRETE BLOCK PAVING

9 hexagonal paver
10 key paver, interlocking paver, interpaver
11 interweave paver
12 pattern paver
13 wavy paver
14 crib paver, cellular paver, grass paver
15 crib paver, cellular paver, grass paver
16 flag, paving slab

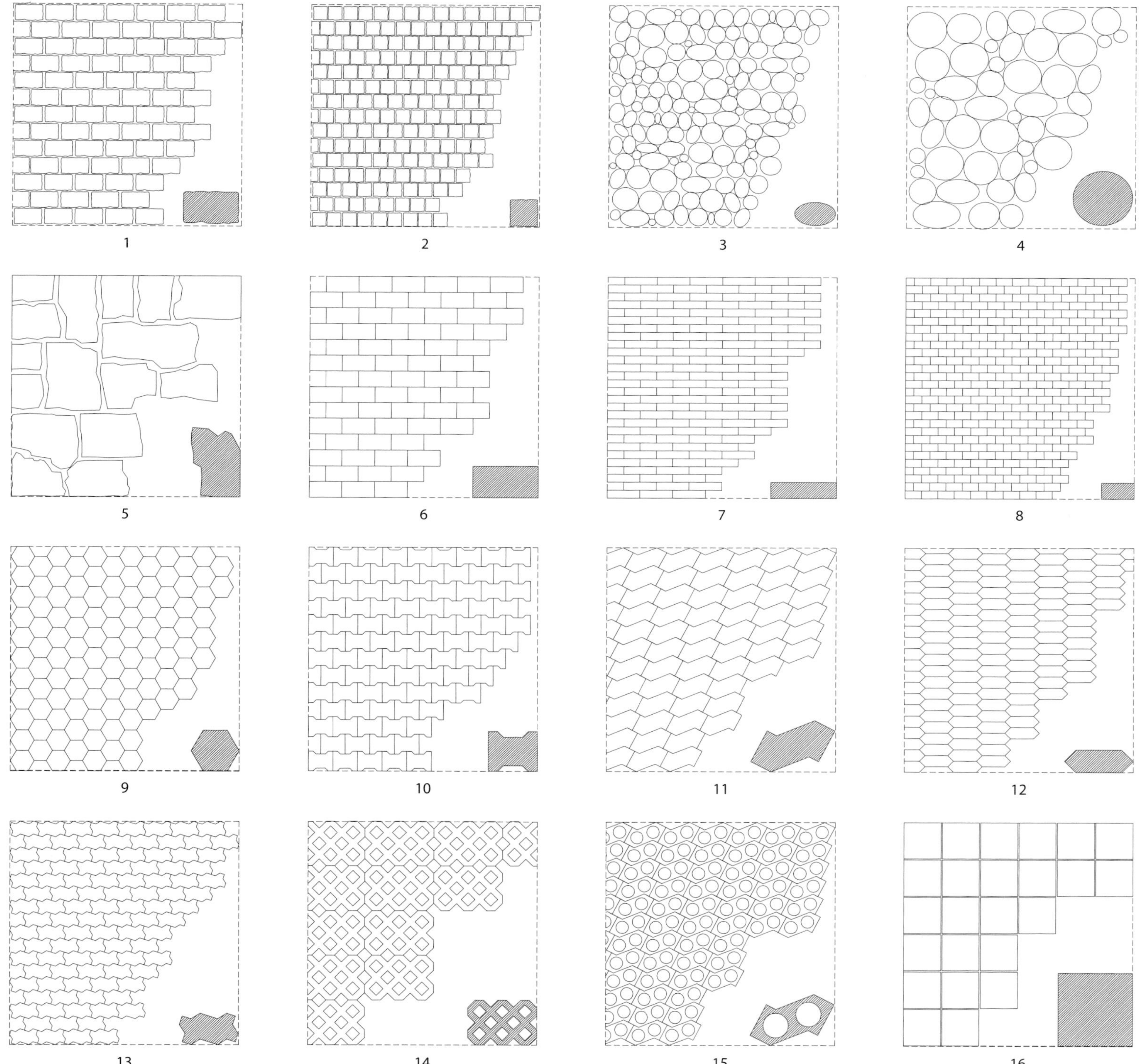
1
2
3
4
5
6
7
8
9
10
11
12
13
14
15
16

16 FIRED CLAY BRICKS

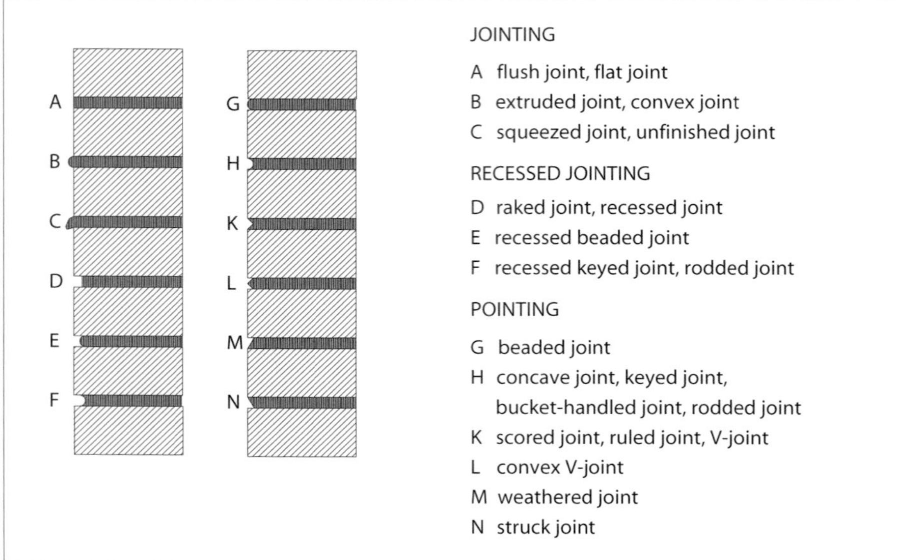

brick, building brick
a rectangular block made of fired clay, burnt mud, concrete or other mineral material, used for building walls, paving and other constructions; its size is usually no larger than 338 x 225 x 113 mm, so it can be held in one hand for ease of laying

jointing
1 bedding; the binding of bricks together using mortar
2 the tidying up and smoothing of excess wet mortar from a brickwork joint, and shaping it into the desired form

pointing
the filling of masonry joints with better quality mortar after the bedding mortar has hardened in order to provide a smooth, compressed and attractive surface

special brick
1 special, special shape brick (Am); any brick in a manufacturer's mass-produced range which is of non-standard shape or size; sometimes also called a standard special brick
2 purpose made brick; a non-standard clay brick specially shaped, or of unusual colour or consistency for a particular purpose

common brick, common
a standard general-purpose rectangular mass-produced brick with untreated faces; not generally used for special applications or visual quality

COMMON BRICKS/SOLID BRICKS

1 standard brick, metric (European)
2 standard brick, coordinating (European)
3 flue brick, flue block, chimney block
4 modular brick, metric brick (European)
5 cuboid brick, soap
6 standard brick, imperial (British)
7 standard brick, metric (British)
8 modular brick, metric brick (British)

PERFORATED BRICKS

9 perforated brick, cored brick
10 perforated brick, cellular brick
11 hollow clay block
12 air brick, ventilating brick

SPECIAL BRICKS, SPECIAL SHAPE BRICKS, PURPOSE-MADE BRICKS

13 hollow brick, cavity brick
14 pre-chased brick
15 lintel brick, beam brick, channel brick
16 frogged brick
17 cove brick
18 stretcher plinth, plinth stretcher
19 header plinth, plinth header
20 cant brick, angle brick
21 squint, squint brick
22 birdsmouth brick
23 angle brick
24 bullnose brick
25 cownose brick, bullhead brick

RADIAL BRICKS, ARCH BRICKS

26 radial stretcher
27 radial header
28 culvert header, tapered stretcher
29 culvert stretcher, tapered header

COPING AND CAPPING BRICKS

30 featheredged capping, featheredged coping
31 saddleback capping
32 saddle coping, saddleback coping
33 half round capping, segmental capping
34 half round coping, segmental coping

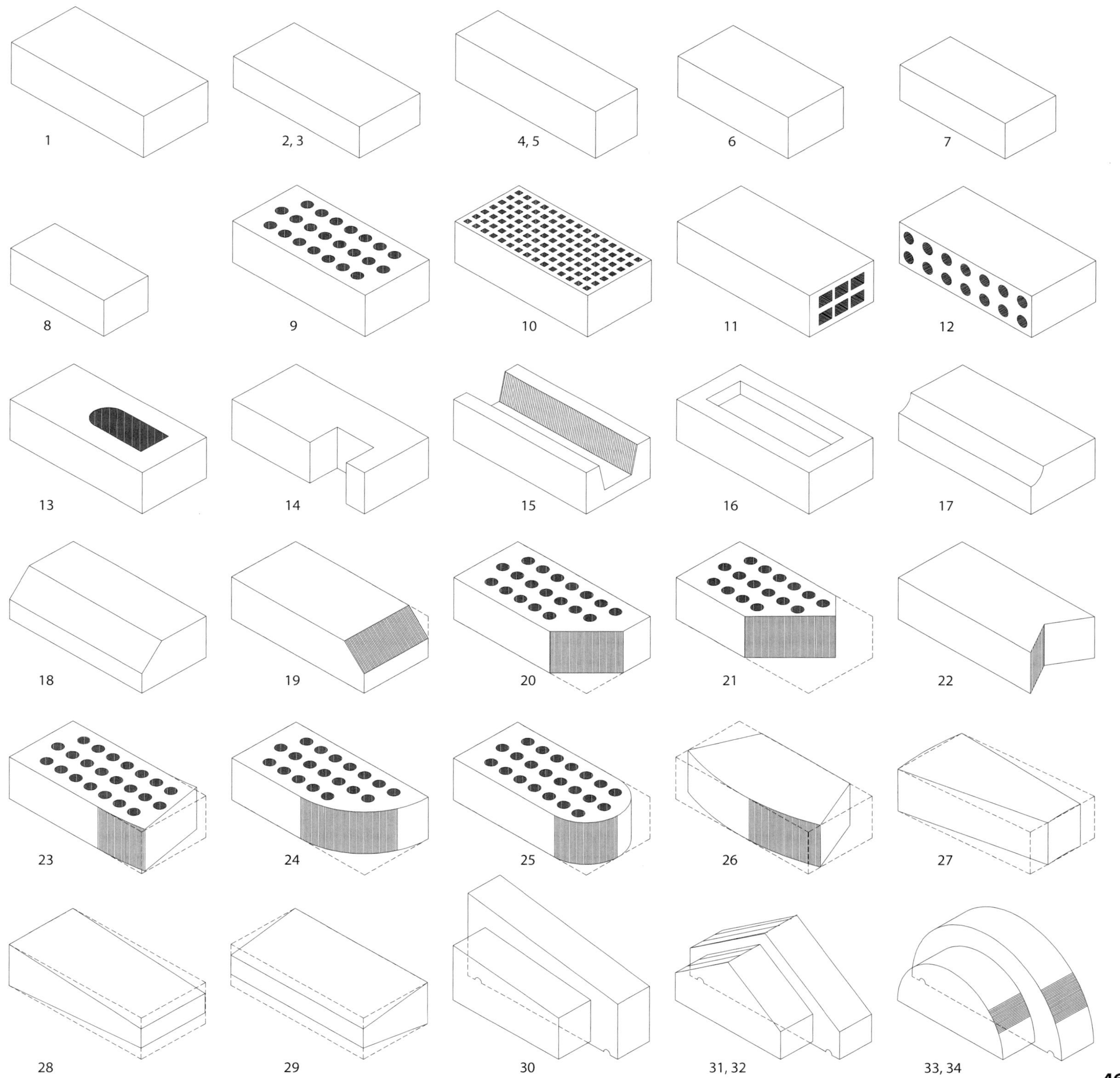
1
2, 3
4, 5
6
7
8
9
10
11
12
13
14
15
16
17
18
19
20
21
22
23
24
25
26
27
28
29
30
31, 32
33, 34

17 BRICKWORK BONDS

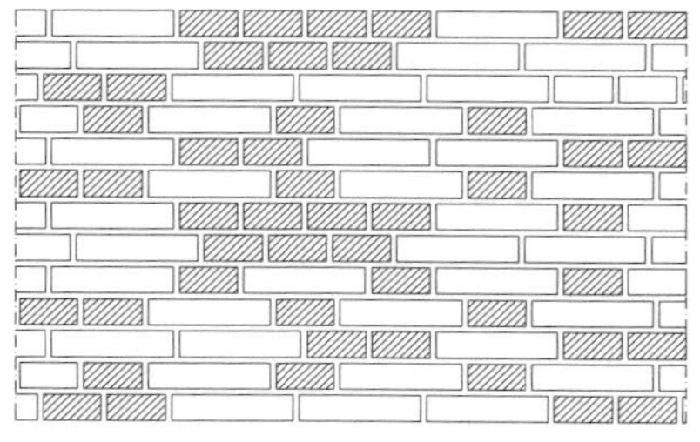
1

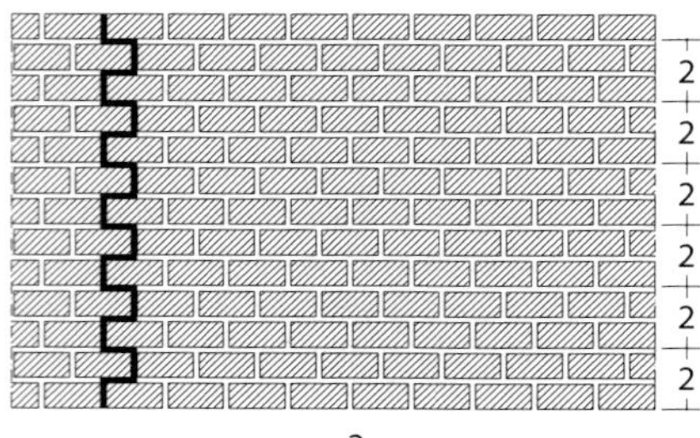

2

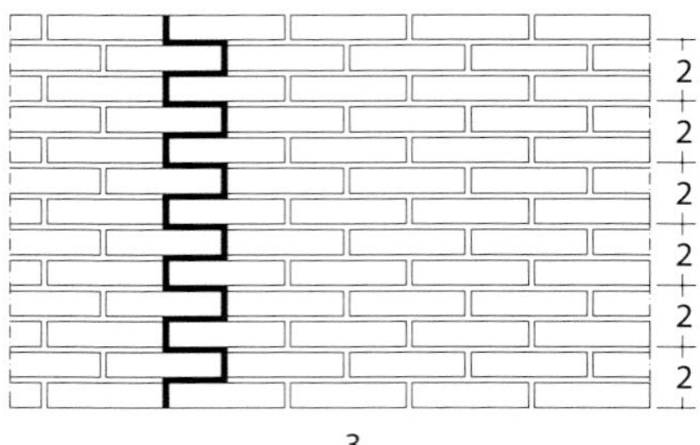

3

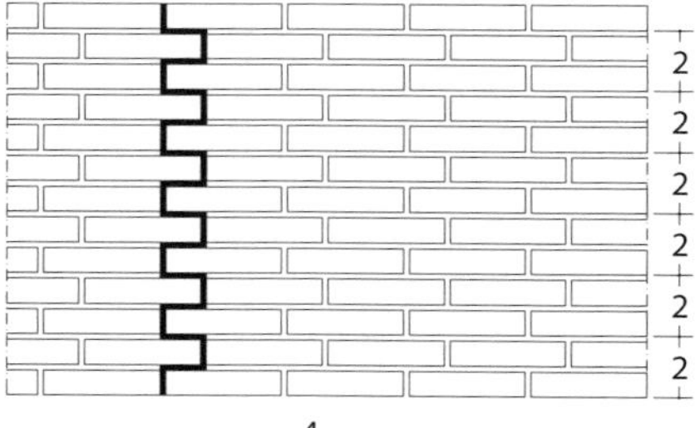

4

5

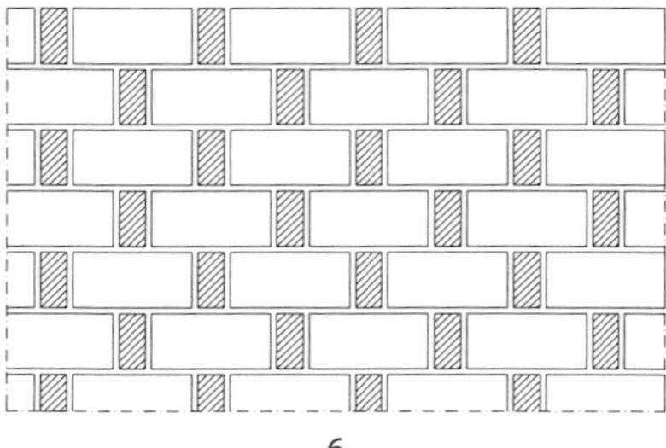
6

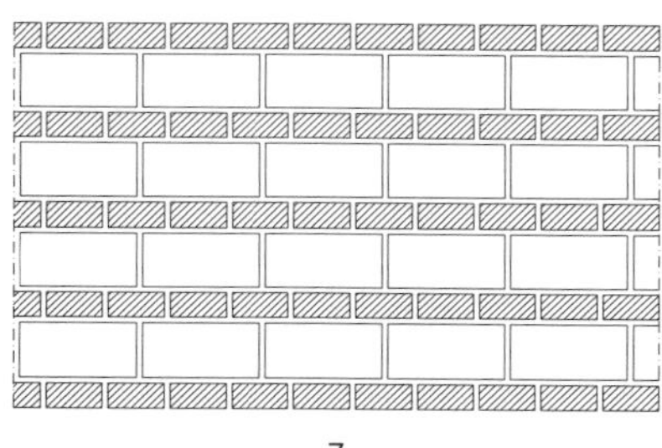
7

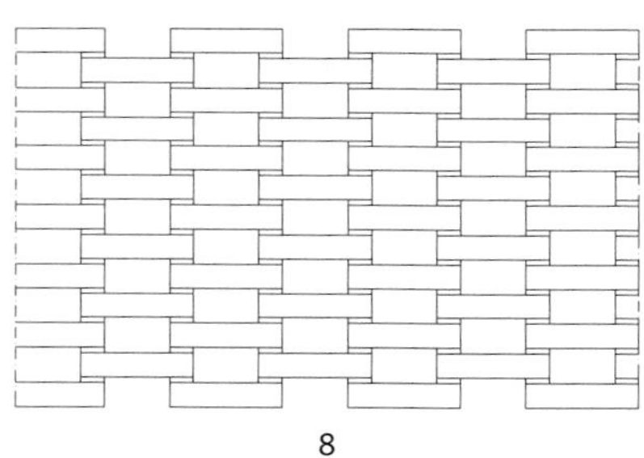
8

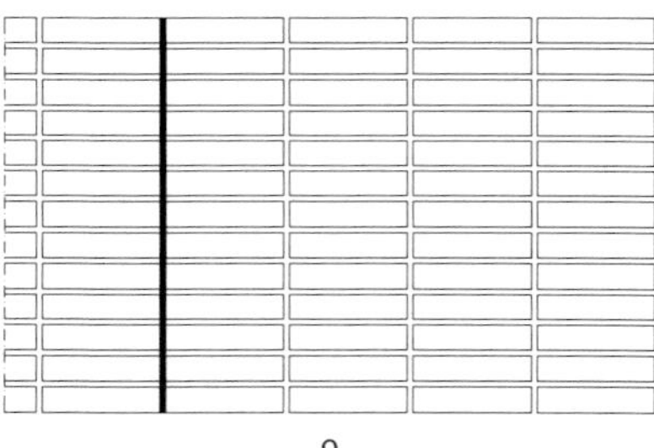
9

1 irregular bond, random bond

2 header bond, heading bond

3 stretcher bond, running bond (½ brick overlap)

4 raking stretcher bond (1/3 brick overlap)

5 herringbone bond, herringbone brickwork

6 rat-trap bond, Chinese bond, rowlock bond, silverlock bond, cavity bond

7 Dearne's bond, hollow wall bond, cavity bond

8 honeycomb brickwork

9 stack bond, stacked bond (false bond)

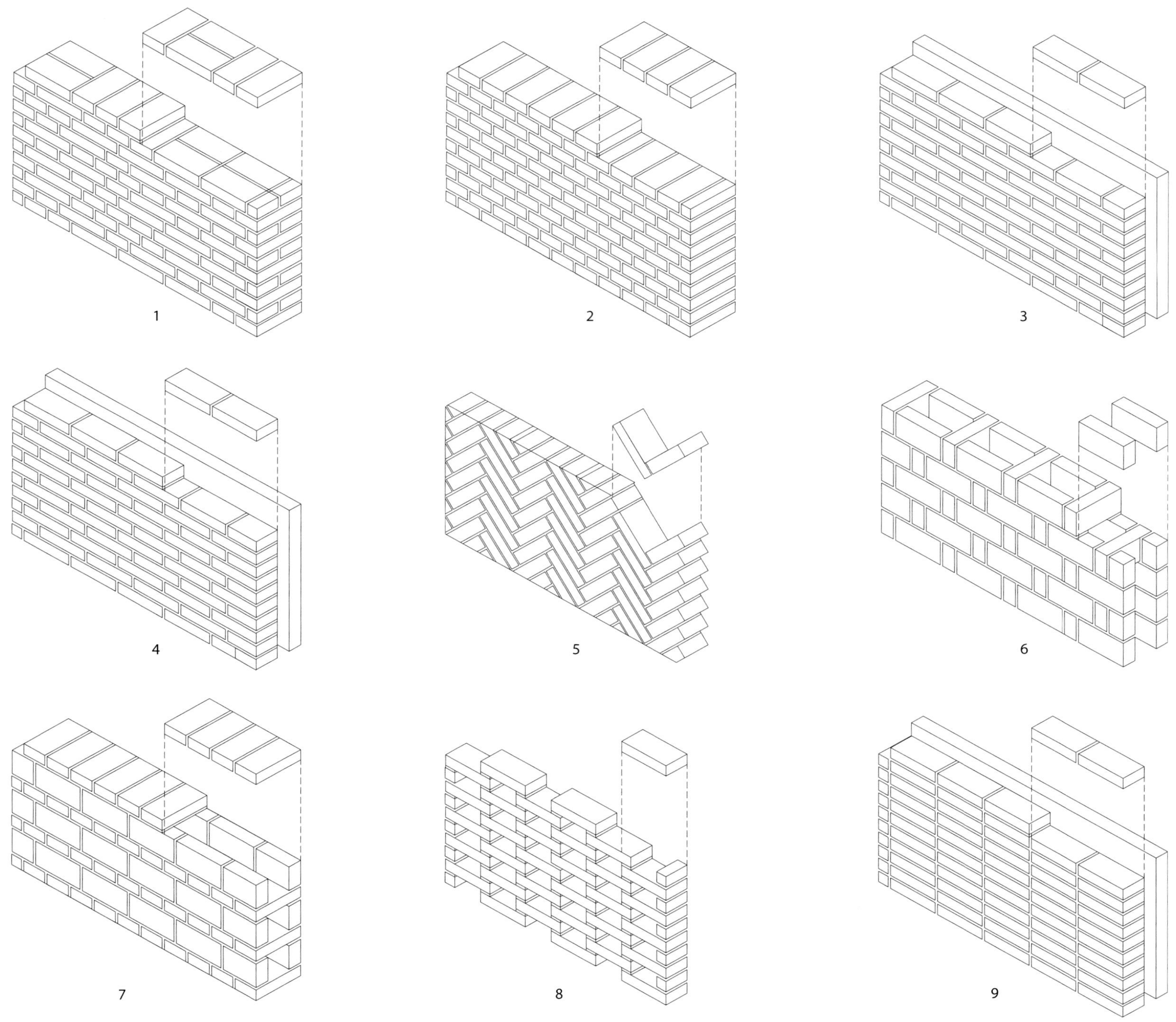
1
2
3
4
5
6
7
8
9

18 FLEMISH BONDS

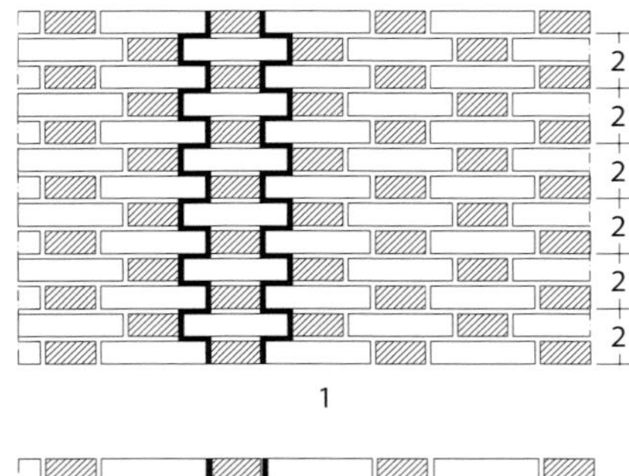

1

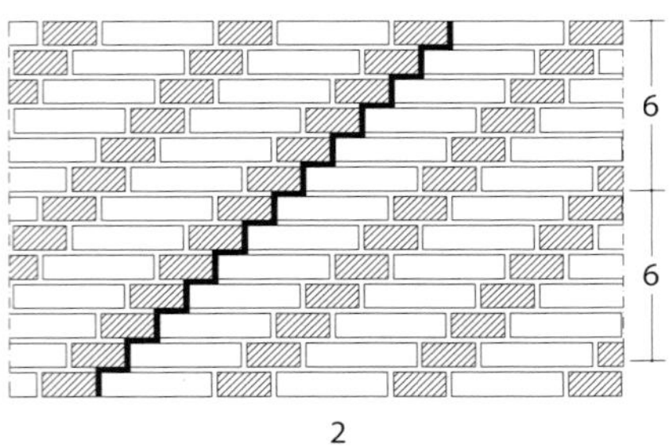

2

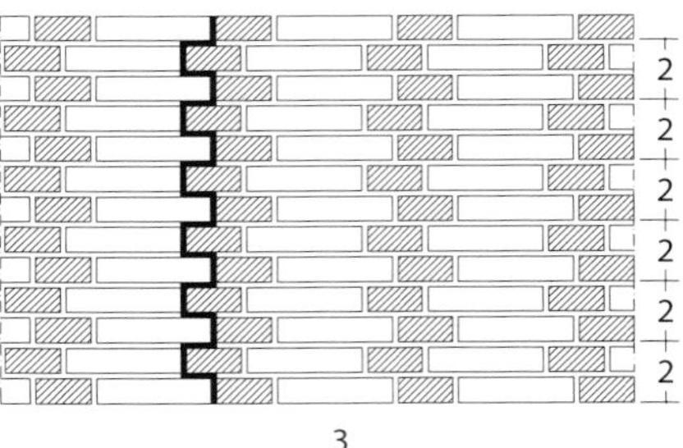

3

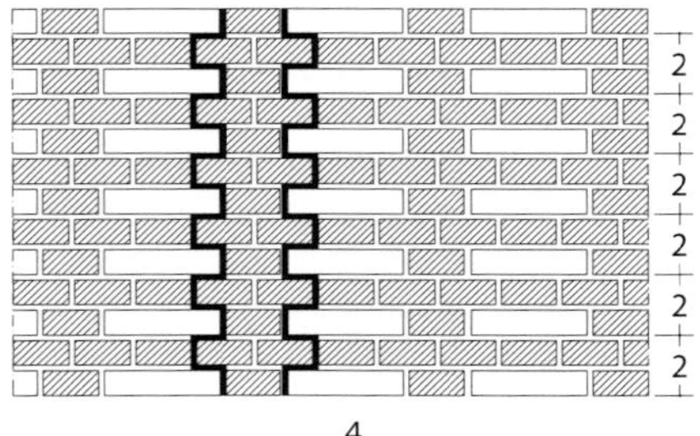

4

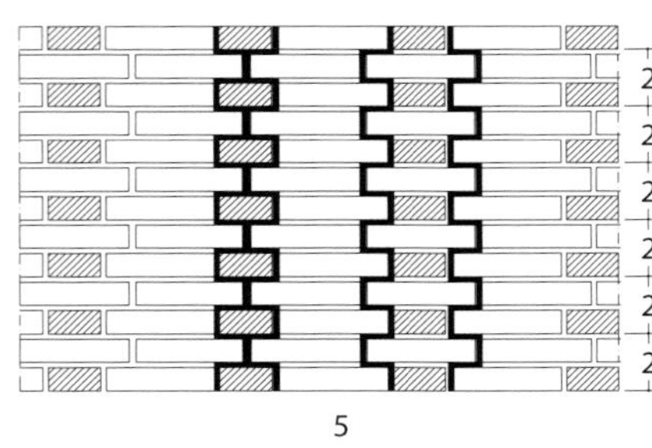

5

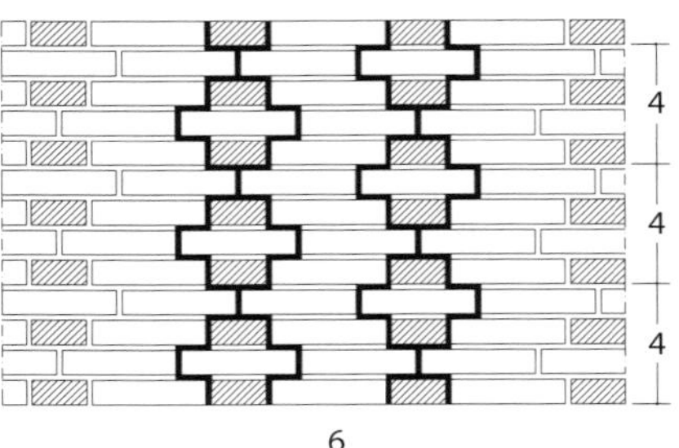

6

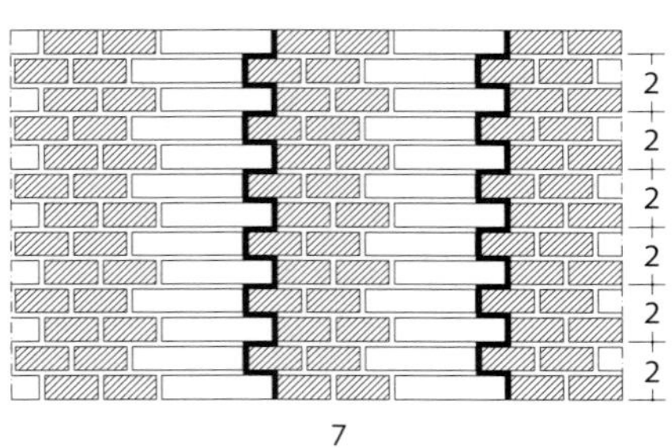

7

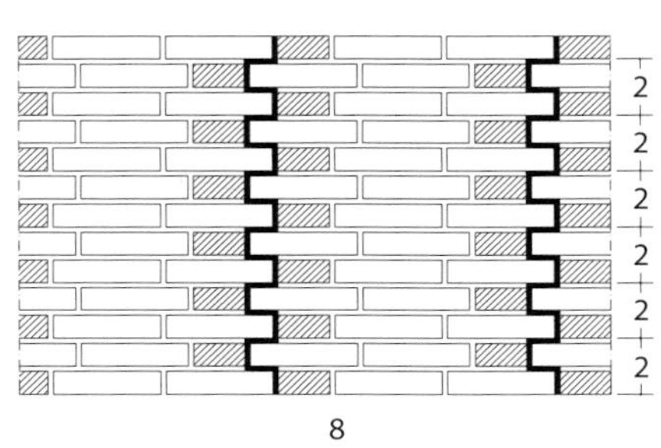

8

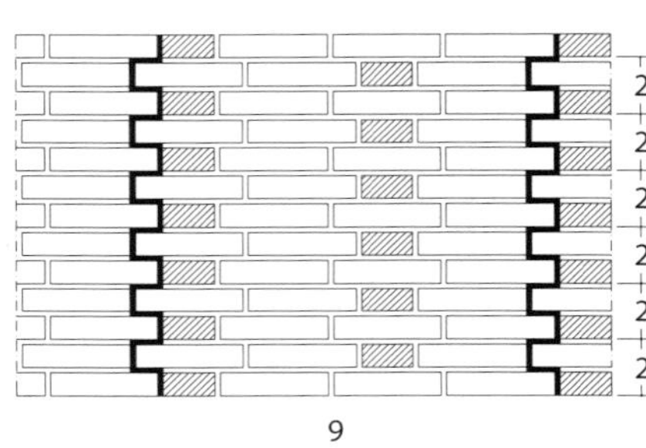

9

1 Flemish bond

2 raking Flemish bond

3 Dutch bond, staggered Flemish bond

4 Flemish header bond

5 Flemish stretcher bond, American with Flemish bond, common bond

6 Flemish cross bond

7 Flemish double header bond

8 monk bond, flying bond, Yorkshire bond, Flemish double stretcher bond

9 Flemish garden-wall bond, Sussex bond, Silesian bond

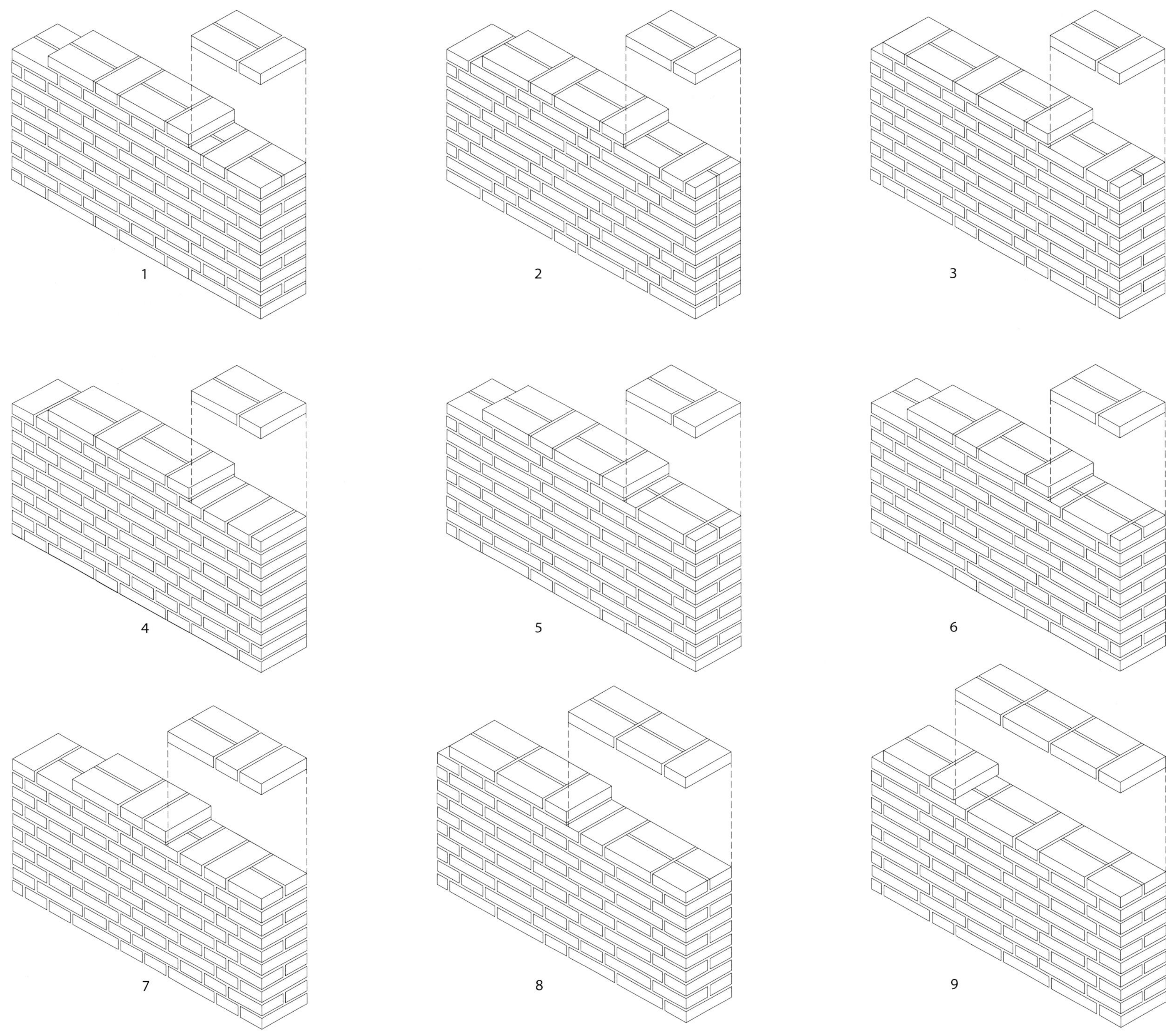
1
2
3
4
5
6
7
8
9

19 FLEMISH DOUBLE-STRETCHER AND ENGLISH BONDS

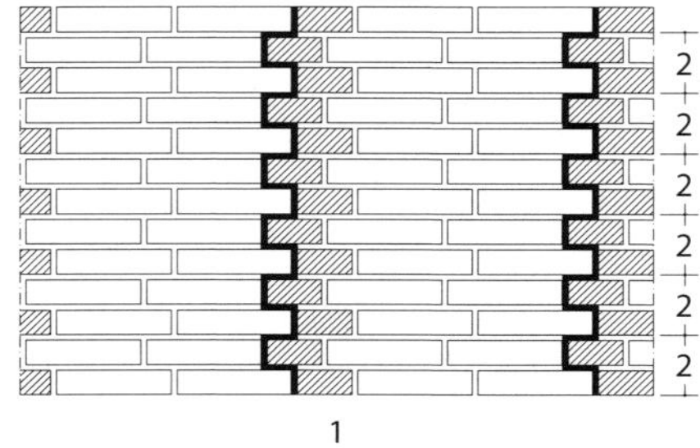

1

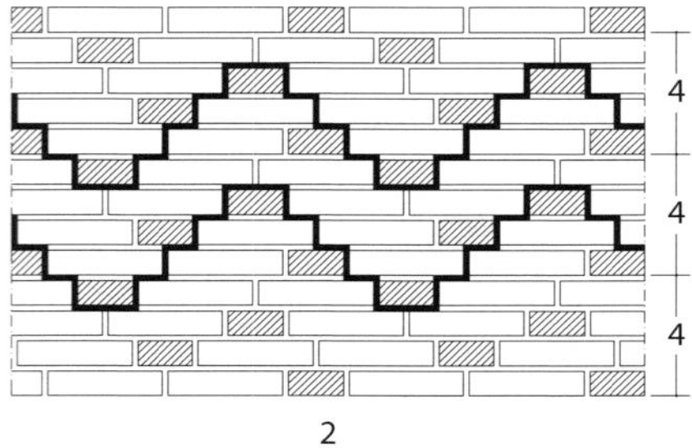

2

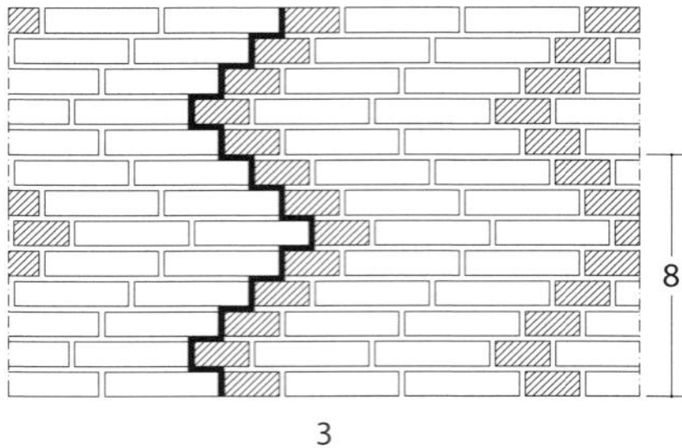

3

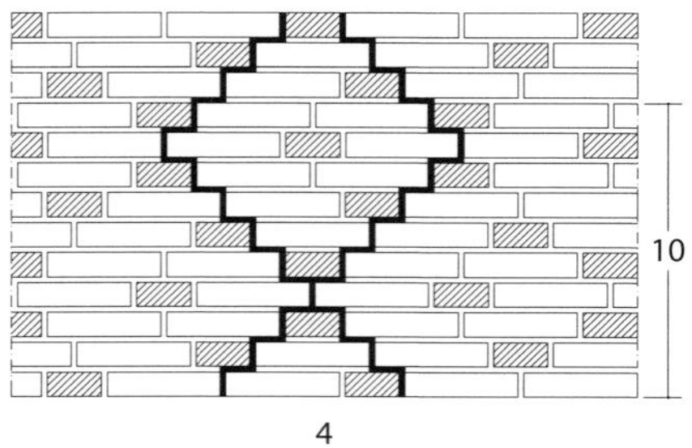

4

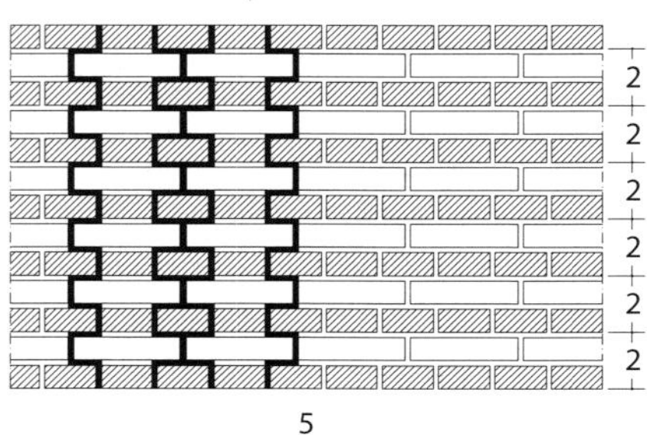

5

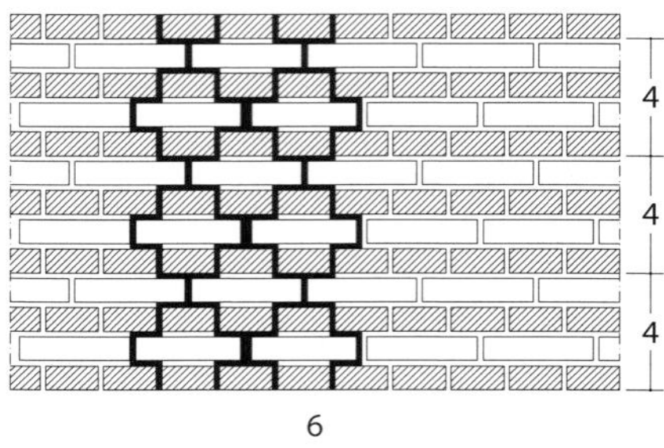

6

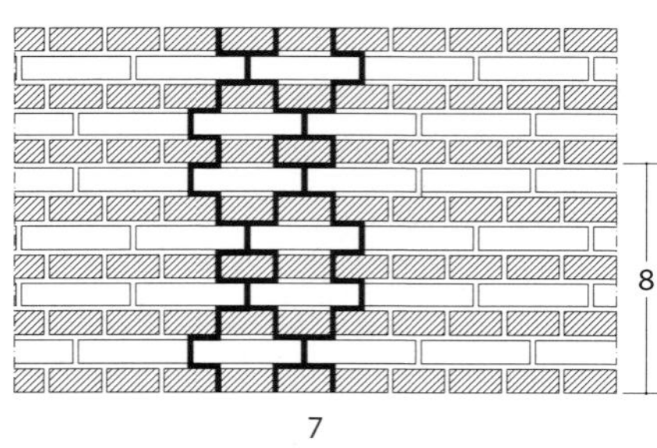

7

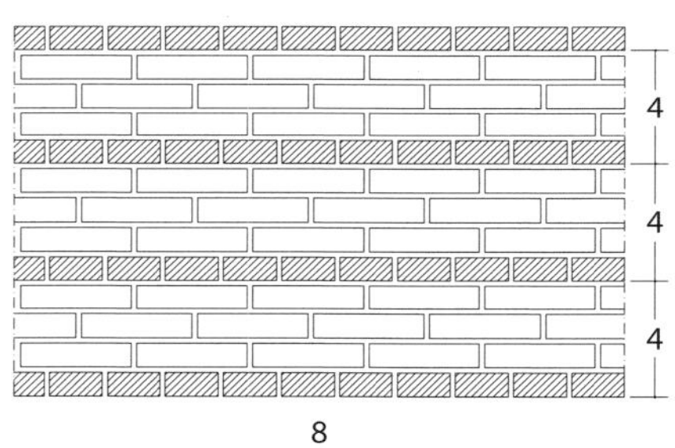

8

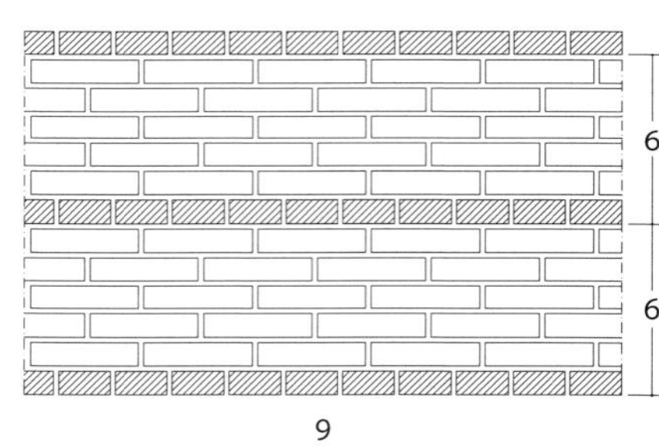

9

1 Flemish double stretcher bond, staggered

2 Flemish double stretcher bond, raking variation

3 Flemish double stretcher bond, diagonal variation

4 Flemish double stretcher bond, Flemish diagonal bond, diaper, diamond work

5 English bond

6 English or St Andrew's cross bond

7 English bond (variation), Danish bond, Koch's bond

8 English garden-wall bond, American bond, common bond, Liverpool bond

9 English garden-wall bond, American bond, common bond, Liverpool bond

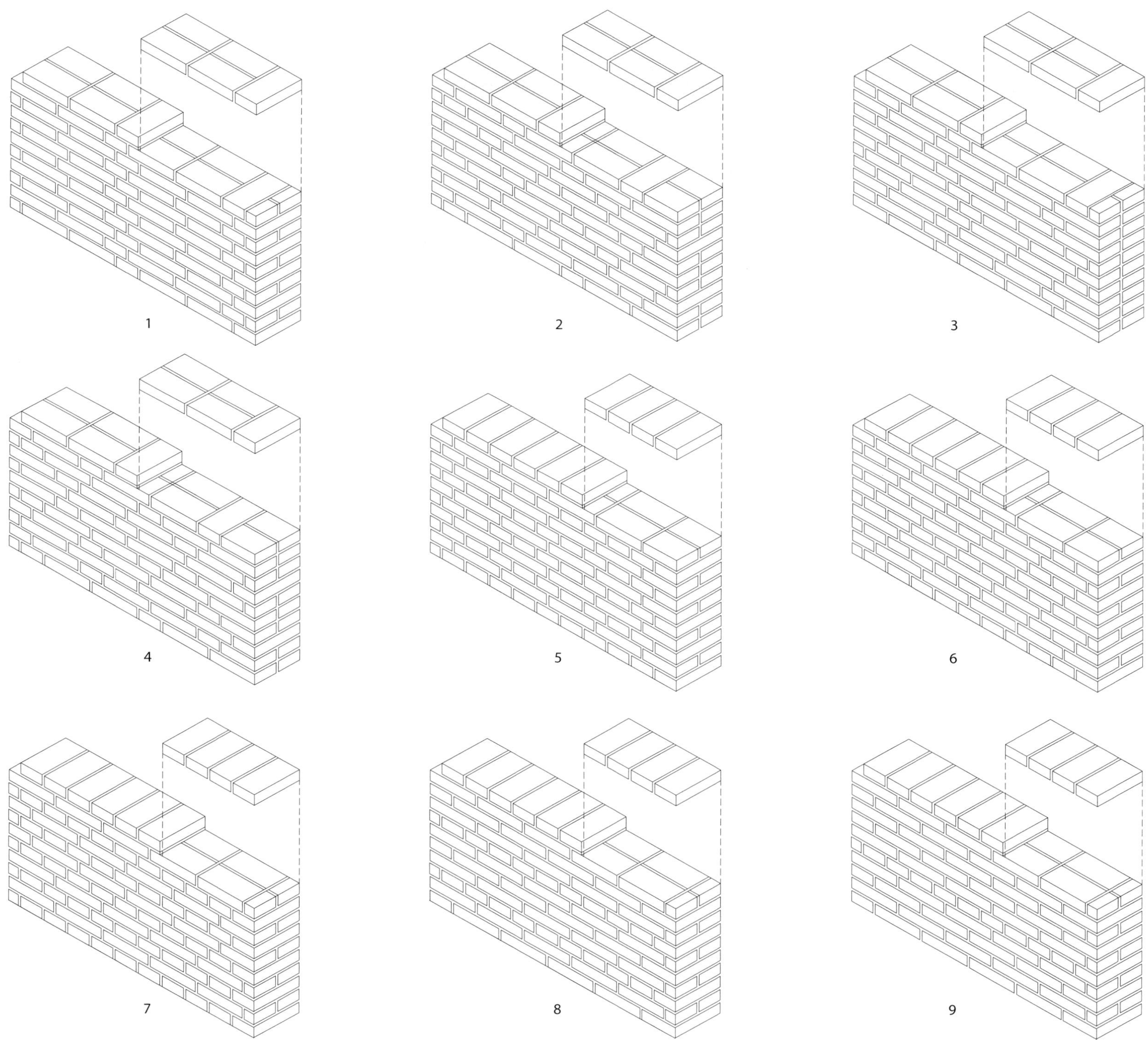

1
2
3
4
5
6
7
8
9

20 BRICK COURSES AND JOINTS

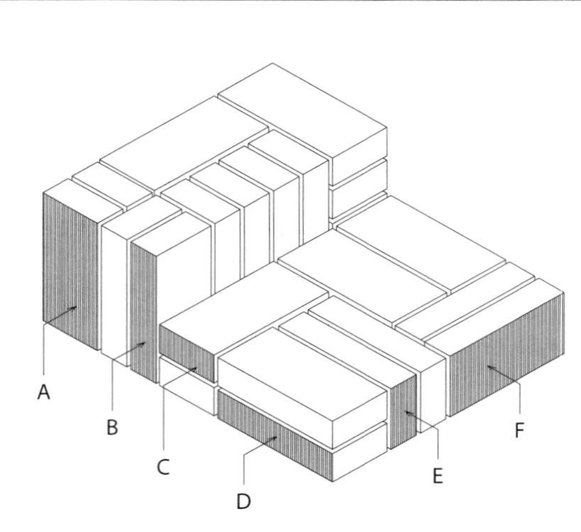

BONDING OF COORDINATED BRICKWORK

- A brick on end (sailor)
- B brick on end (soldier)
- C brick on flat (header)
- D brick on flat (stretcher)
- E brick on edge (rowlock, bull header)
- F brick on edge (shiner, bull stretcher)

brickwork bond
the overlapping and interlocking of bricks laid in mortar in successive courses to provide strength and for decorative effects

course
a row of bricks, stones or blocks which form a horizontal band in masonry walling construction, either one brick or stone high, or of uniform height

header
a brick or stone laid with its short side or end exposed in a masonry surface

perpend, perpend joint, cross joint, head joint, header joint
in masonry construction, a vertical joint between adjacent bricks or stones in the same course

stretcher
a bonded brick or stone laid with its long side or face exposed in the surface of a masonry wall

bedding
1 the laying of a brick, block or stone into mortar or another cementitious material, and tapping it into the correct position
2 bed; the layer of material, often mortar, in which a brick, block or stone is laid

BRICK MASONRY

1 stretcher course, stretching course
2 stretcher
3 header course, heading course
4 header, inbond (Scot.)
5 shiner course, bull stretcher course
6 shiner, bull stretcher
7 rowlock course, bull header course
8 rowlock, bull header
9 soldier course
10 soldier
11 sailor course
12 sailor
13 dogtoothed brickwork, bricks on flat
14 dogtoothed brickwork, bricks on edge
15 dogtoothed brickwork, bricks on end
16 stretcher course
17 stretcher face
18 binding course, header course
19 header face
20 perpend, header joint, perpend joint
21 bed joint, horizontal joint
22 cross joint
23 wall joint

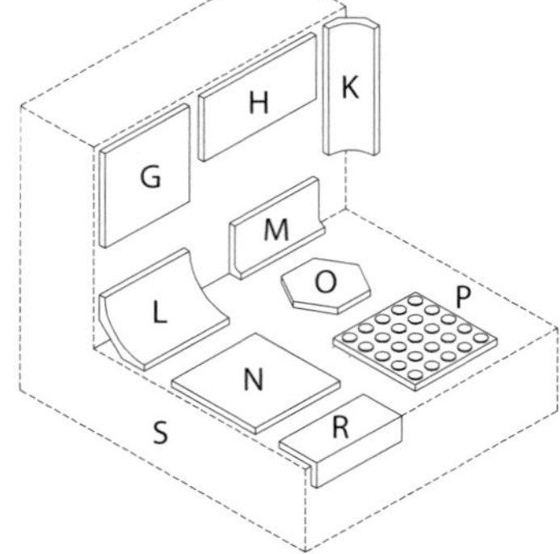
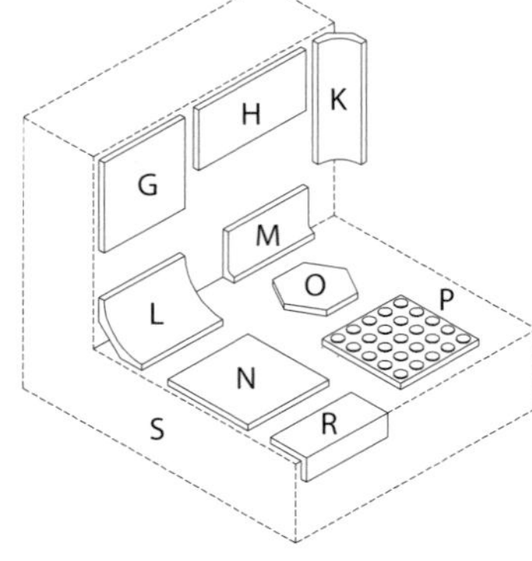

CERAMIC TILES

WALL TILES

PORCELAIN TILES; DRY-PRESSED AND GLAZED TILES

- G square tile
- H rectangular tile

CAST TILES

- K inside corner tile
- L cove tile
- M skirting tile

VITREOUS TILES – UNGLAZED TILES

- N floor tile, flooring tile
- O geometric tile – hexagonal tile
- P non-slip tile
- R nosing tile
- S tiling base, ground, substrate

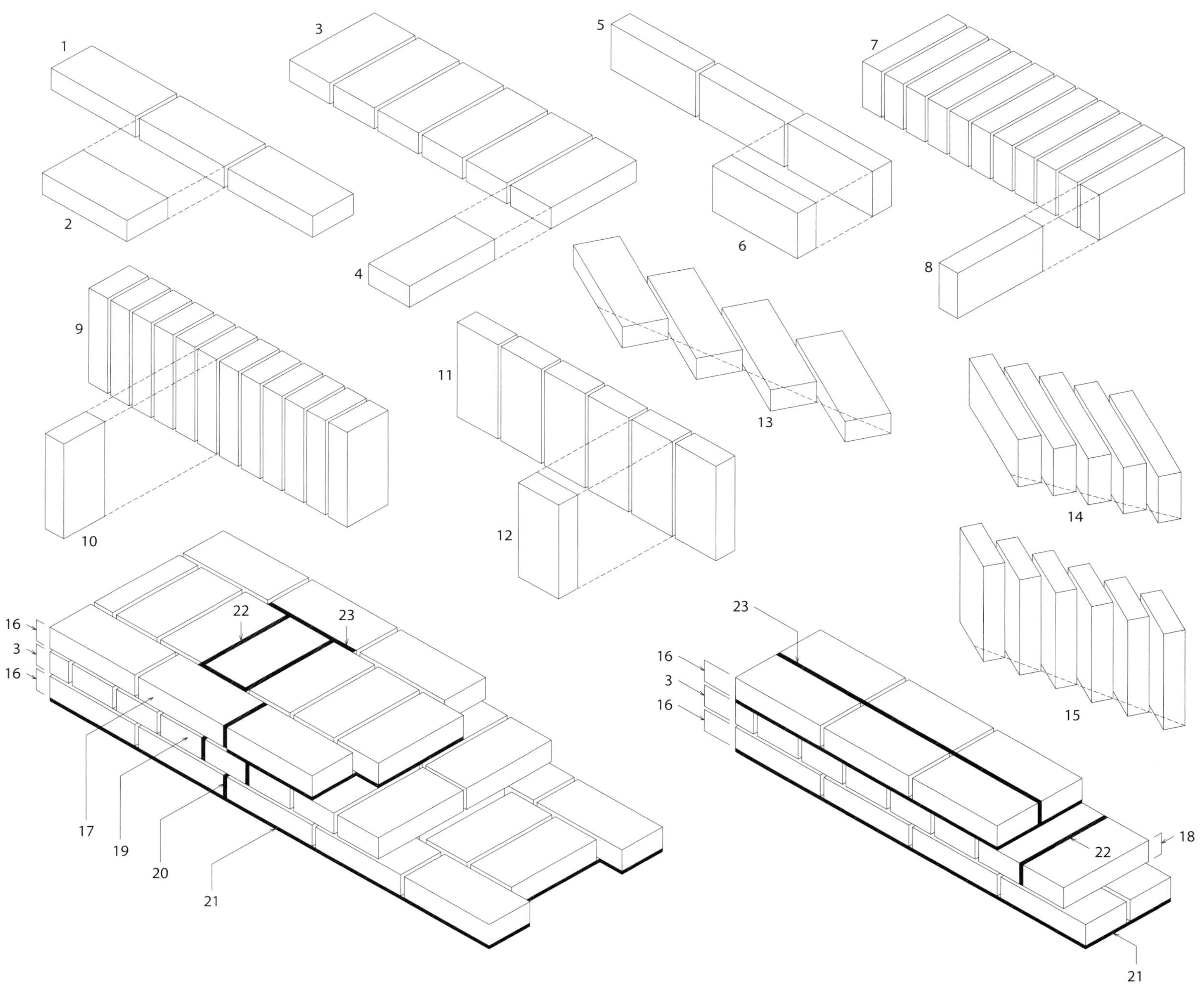
1
2
3
4
5
6
7
8
9
10
11
12
13
14
15
16
3
16
22
23
17
19
20
21
23
16
3
16
18
22
21

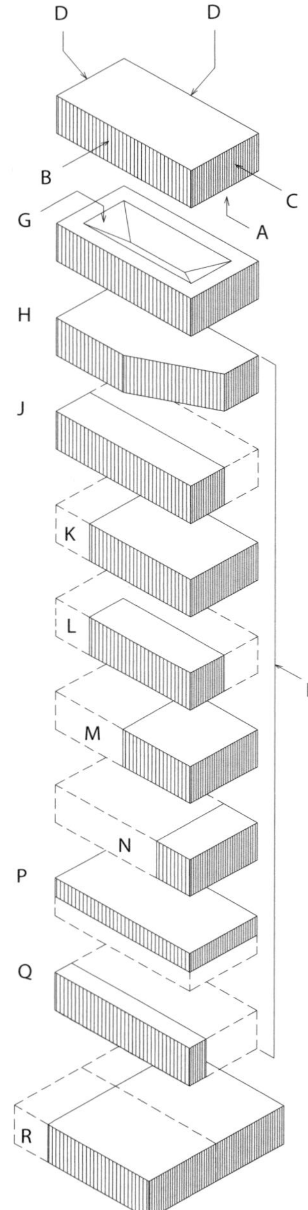

brickwork
any construction in bricks laid with a binder such as mortar

cut brick
any brick shaped by cutting, sawing or breaking on site, most often used for making up space in brickwork bonds

bat, brickbat
a full brick cut down to size in order to act as a space filler in bonded brickwork; often larger than a quarter brick

closer
1 the last brick in a brick course at a stopped end or corner, often manufactured to a non-standard large or small size to make up space in a brickwork bond
2 a brick which exposes a half-header or header in brickwork, usually used to make up space in the brick bond

FULL BRICK

A bed
B side, face
C end, header face
D arris, edge

CUT BRICKS, BONDING BRICKS

F cut brick, bonding brick
bat, brickbat
G frog
H king closer, three quarter brick
J queen closer
K three quarter bat
L halved three quarter bat,
queen closer
M half bat, snap header
N quarter bat, quarter
P brick tile, brick slip
Q brick tile, brick slip
R closer

WALL THICKNESSES

1 quarter brick wall (stretcher bond)
2 half-brick wall (stretcher bond)
3 one-brick wall, nine inch wall,
whole brick wall (header bond)
4 brick-and-a-half wall, one-and-half
brick wall (English bond)
5 two-brick wall (English cross bond)
6 edge bedding
7 closer
8 cavity wall, hollow wall
9 pier, pilaster, buttress

BONDING OF JUNCTIONS

10 indents, reverse toothing
11 toothing
12 raking, racking back
13 brick pier
14 dentilation
15 stopped end
16 brick column, brick pier
17 chimney bond, column bond

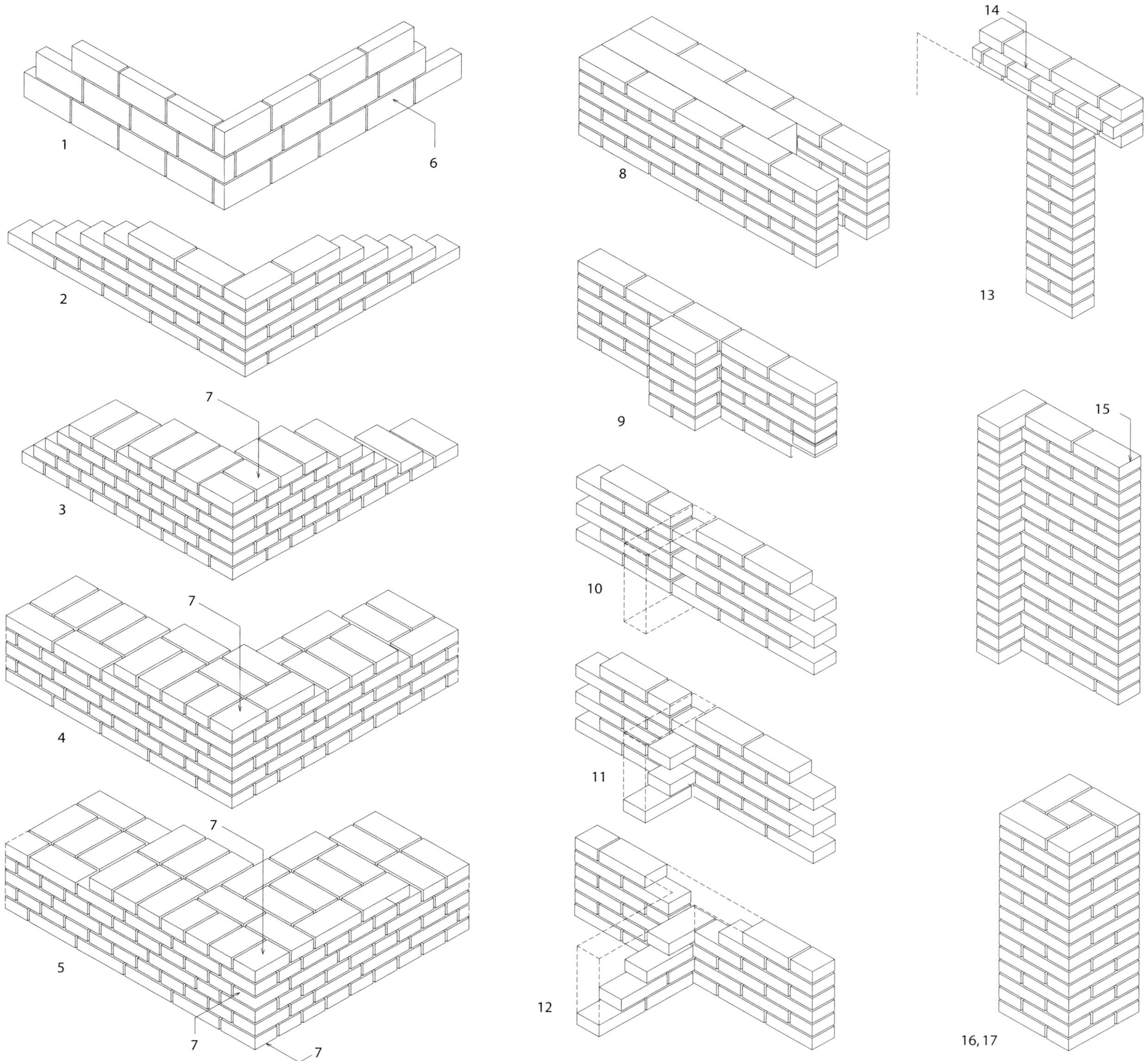
1
6
2
7
3
7
4
7
5
7
7
8
9
10
11
12
14
13
15
16, 17

22 ARCHED AND VAULTED CONSTRUCTION, MASONRY ARCHES

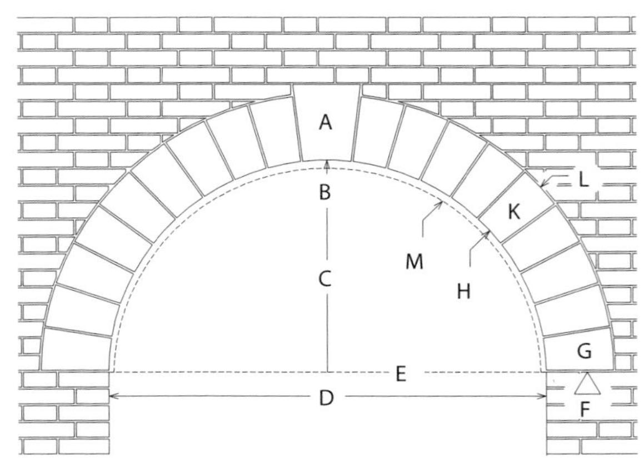

GAUGED ARCH

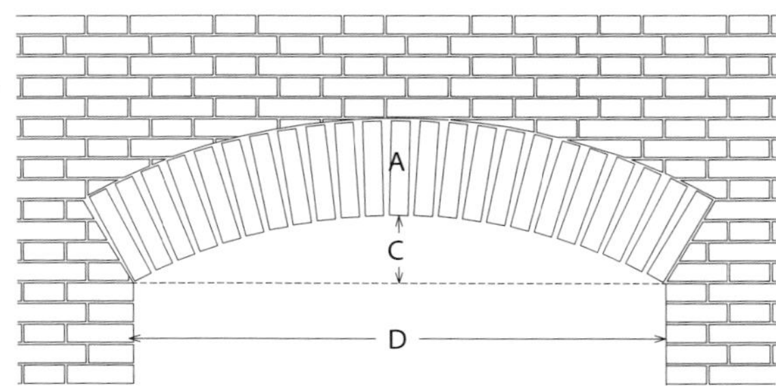

ROUGH ARCH, ROUGH BRICK ARCH

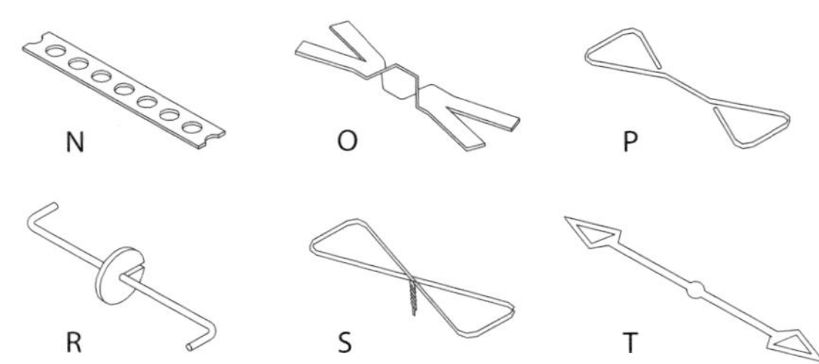

WALL TIES AND ANCHOR STRAPS

ANATOMY OF AN ARCH

A keystone, key block
B crown
C rise, pitch
D span
E springing line
F abutment, impost
G springer, springing stone, skewback
H intrados, soffit
K voussoir
L extrados
M haunch

WALL TIES AND ANCHOR STRAPS

N anchor strap
O fishtail tie
P double or twin triangle tie
R wire tie with insulation clip/retainer
S butterfly tie
T proprietary wall tie

CONSTRUCTING AN ARCH

1 centering for semicircular arch construction
2 centre, centering
3 shuttering, sheathing
4 strongback, spreader beam, yoke
5 strut, prop
6 centering for segmental and camber arch construction
7 turning piece

LINTELS

8 pressed steel lintel
9 proprietary reinforcing strap
10 precast concrete lintel with brick slip facing
11 reinforced bed joint
12 reinforced brick lintel, brick beam

arch
a two-dimensionally curved beam construction for supporting loads between two points of support over an opening; traditional masonry arches were constructed from wedge-shaped stones locked together by loading from above

lintel, lintol
a beam above a window or door opening

centering, centres
a temporary curved frame of wood or other material for supporting a masonry arch while it is being constructed

wall tie
a galvanized steel or twisted wire fixing laid at regular intervals into a masonry wall to provide stability by connecting masonrywork to a structural base, or linking inner and outer leaves of brickwork; called a cavity tie when used in cavity walls

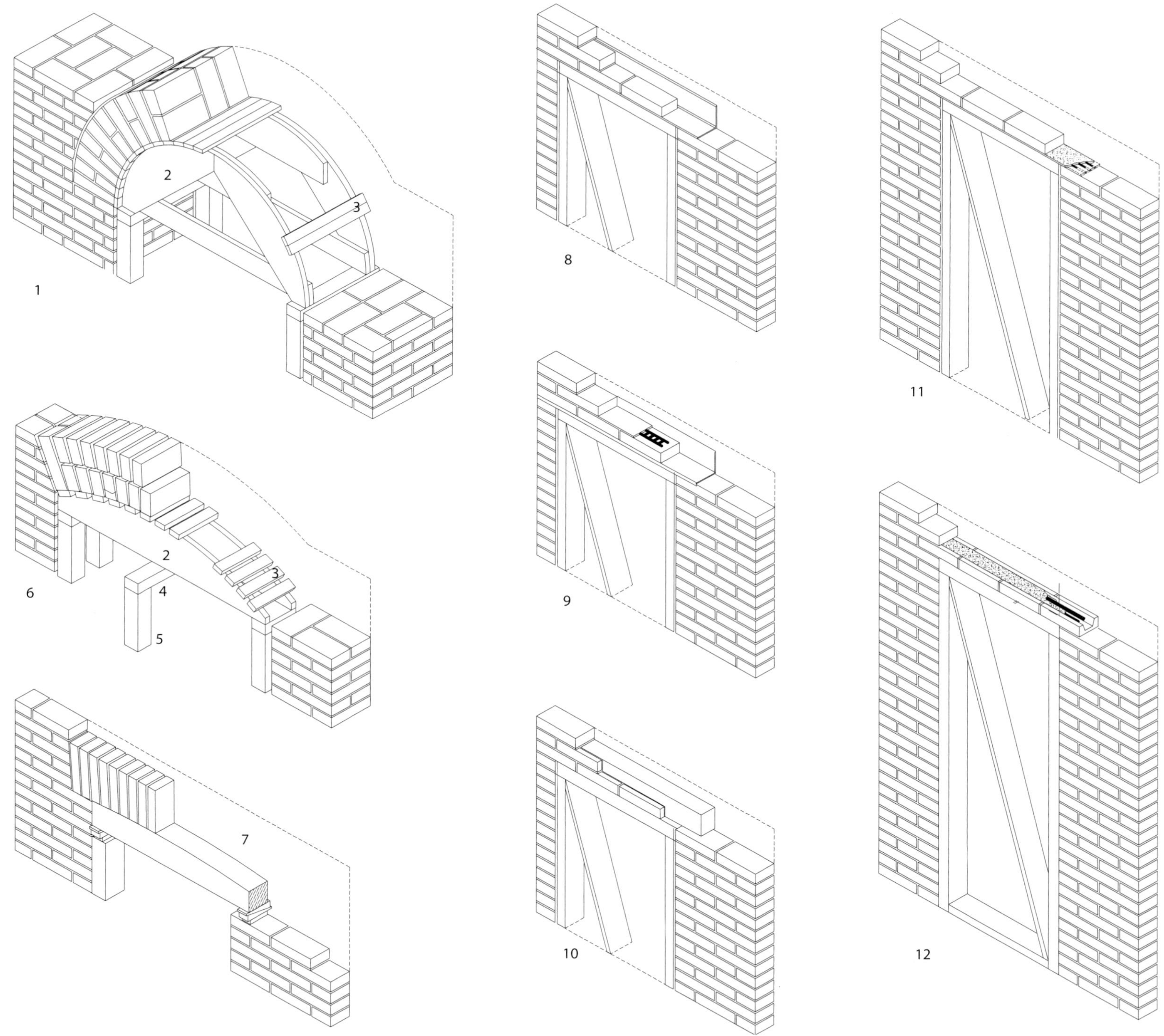
2
3
1
8
11
2
3
6
4
5
9
7
10
12

23 FLAT, FALSE AND DECORATIVE ARCHES

CORBELLED ARCH WITH LINTEL
Lion Gate, Mycenae, c.1250 BC, Greece

VARIATIONS OF THE VENETIAN ARCH

FALSE ARCHES

1 triangular arch
2 corbel arch, corbelled arch
3 corbelled lintel

FLAT ARCHES, JACK ARCHES, STRAIGHT ARCHES

4 rough brick arch
5 gauged arch
6 Dutch arch, Welsh arch
7 joggled arch, crossette
8 pseudo three-centered arch
9 pseudo four-centered arch

ITALIAN ARCHES

10 Venetian arch
11 Florentine arch
12 bell arch
13 relieving arch
14 strainer arches
15 roundel

DECORATIVE ARCHES

16 pointed trifoliated arch
17 pointed cinquefoliated arch
18 pointed multifoliated arch
19 round trifoliated arch
20 round cinquefoliated arch
21 round multifoliated arch
22 corbel, impost block

false arch
types of arch such as triangular or corbelled arches which do not utilize masonry voussoirs to provide support over an opening

corbel
a masonry bracket projecting from the face of a building surface to provide support for an overhanging object or member

foliated
having been carved or rendered with decorative leaf motifs, or foils

foil
a decorative design consisting of one of a number of stylized leaf motifs or lobes radiating outwards from a point, found especially in medieval architecture

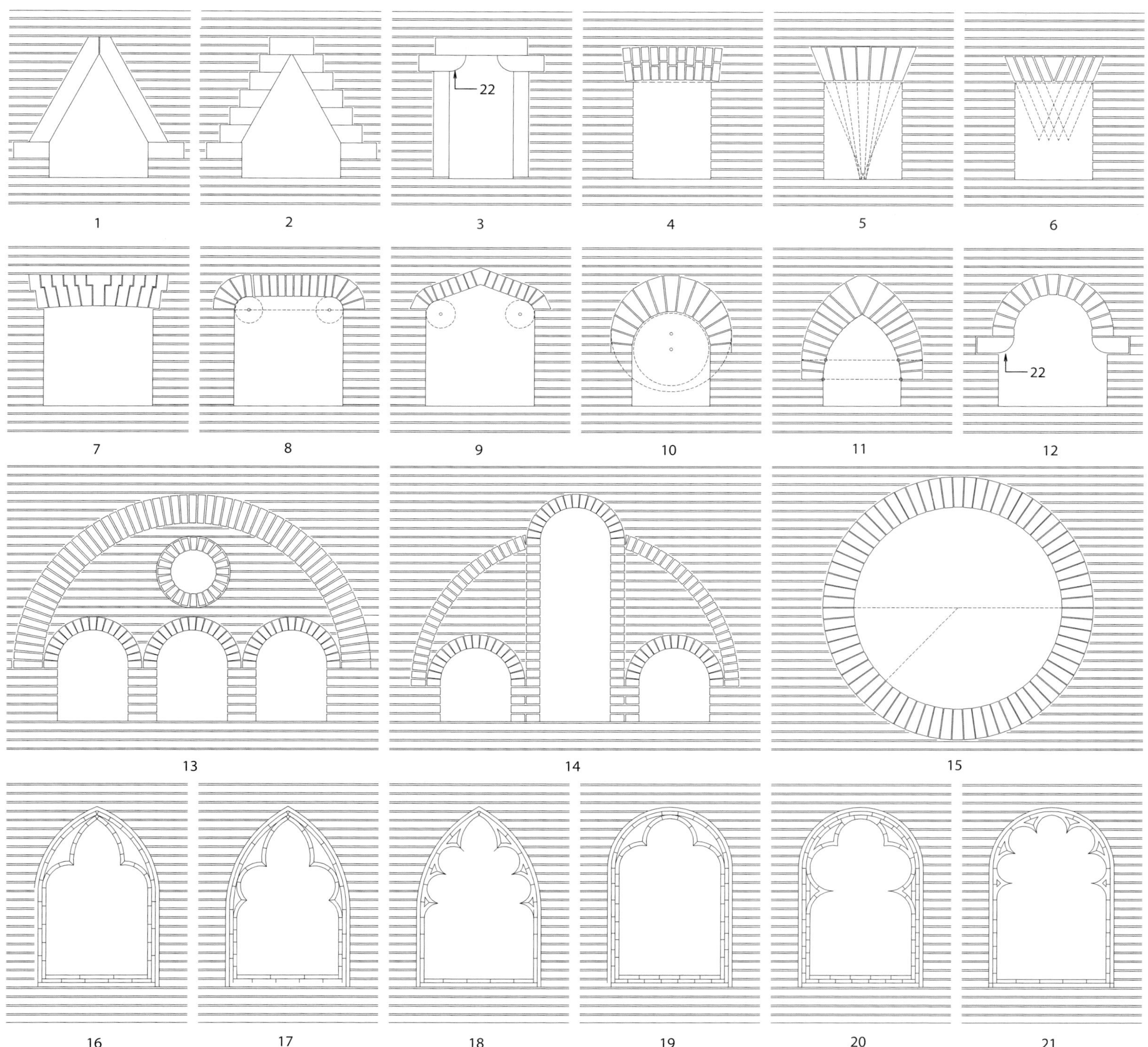
22
1
2
3
4
5
6
22
7
8
9
10
11
12
13
14
15
16
17
18
19
20
21

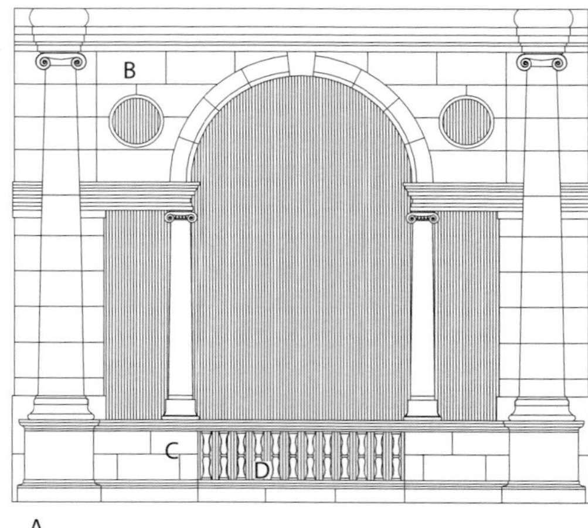

A

arch
a two-dimensionally curved beam construction for supporting loads between two points of support over an opening; traditional masonry arches were constructed from wedge-shaped stones locked together by loading from above

archivolt
arcus volutus (Lat.); a decorated band above or on the soffit of the intrados in an arch

intrados
the lower line, underside, soffit or face of an arch

extrados
the upper line of the voussoirs in an arch

voussoir
a wedge-shaped stone or brick used in the construction of a true masonry arch

E

E) Temple of Hadrian, 117–138, Ephesus, Turkey

- A Palladian motif, Serlian motif, Venetian motif (Queen Anne arch, Venetian window)
- B roundel
- C balustrade
- D baluster
- E Syrian arch, arcuated lintel

TYPES OF ARCH

1 semicircular arch, circular arch, round arch, Roman arch
2 round horseshoe arch, Arabic arch, Moorish arch
3 segmental arch, segmented arch
4 three-centred arch, basket arch, anse de panier
5 five-centred arch, elliptical arch
6 rampant arch, raking arch
7 parabolic arch
8 equilateral arch, three-pointed arch
9 lancet arch, acute arch
10 drop arch, depressed arch
11 four-centred arch, pointed segmental arch, Tudor arch
12 ogee arch, inflected arch
13 two-centred ogee arch, depressed ogee arch
14 tented arch, draped arch
15 tented arch, draped arch
16 trefoil arch
17 pointed trefoil arch
18 cinquefoil arch
19 pointed cinquefoil arch
20 multifoil arch
21 reverse ogee arch, bell arch
22 keel arch
23 inverted arch
24 pointed horseshoe arch
25 flat arch, jack arch, straight arch

1
2
3
4
5
6
7
8
9
10
11
12
13
14
15
16
17
18
19
20
21
22
23
24
25

25 ROMAN AND ROMANESQUE VAULTING

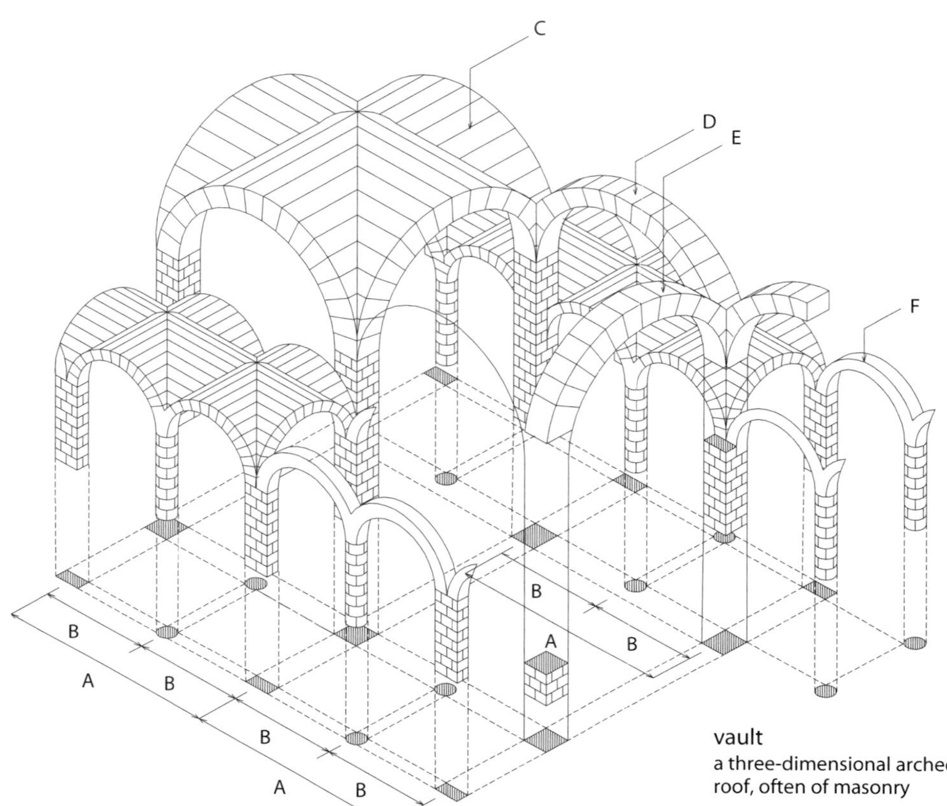

DOUBLE-BAY SYSTEM, ENGAGED SYSTEM

ABBA alternation of support, alternating system of support

A, B bay
C web, cell, severy
D principal arch
E transverse arch
F wall arch

TYPES OF VAULT

1 barrel vault, tunnel vault, wagon vault, cradle vault
2 pointed barrel vault, pointed vault, Gothic vault
3 rampant vault
4 conical vault, expanding vault
5 cloister vault, domical vault
6 pointed cloister vault, domical vault
7 groin vault, cross vault, intersecting barrel vault
8 pointed groin vault, pointed cross vault
9 dormer vault
10 trough vault
11 coved vault
12 segmental vault, segmental barrel vault

vault
a three-dimensional arched ceiling construction to support a floor or roof, often of masonry

vaulting
1 the curved surfaces of a vault, or a series of vaults
2 the making of masonry vaults

Romanesque
religious architecture in Western Europe in the early 11th century, characterized by bulky massing, sparing use of detail and the round arch; known in England as Norman architecture

alternation of support, alternating system of support
a system of columnar supports for a Romanesque arcade or vaulting, in which alternating columns or piers have variations in column-type, cross-section of shaft, embellishment etc.

double-bay system, engaged system
a pattern of columns to support vaulting in Romanesque basilicas where the side aisles are half the width of the nave, requiring columns for aisle vaulting at half-bay widths along the sides of the nave

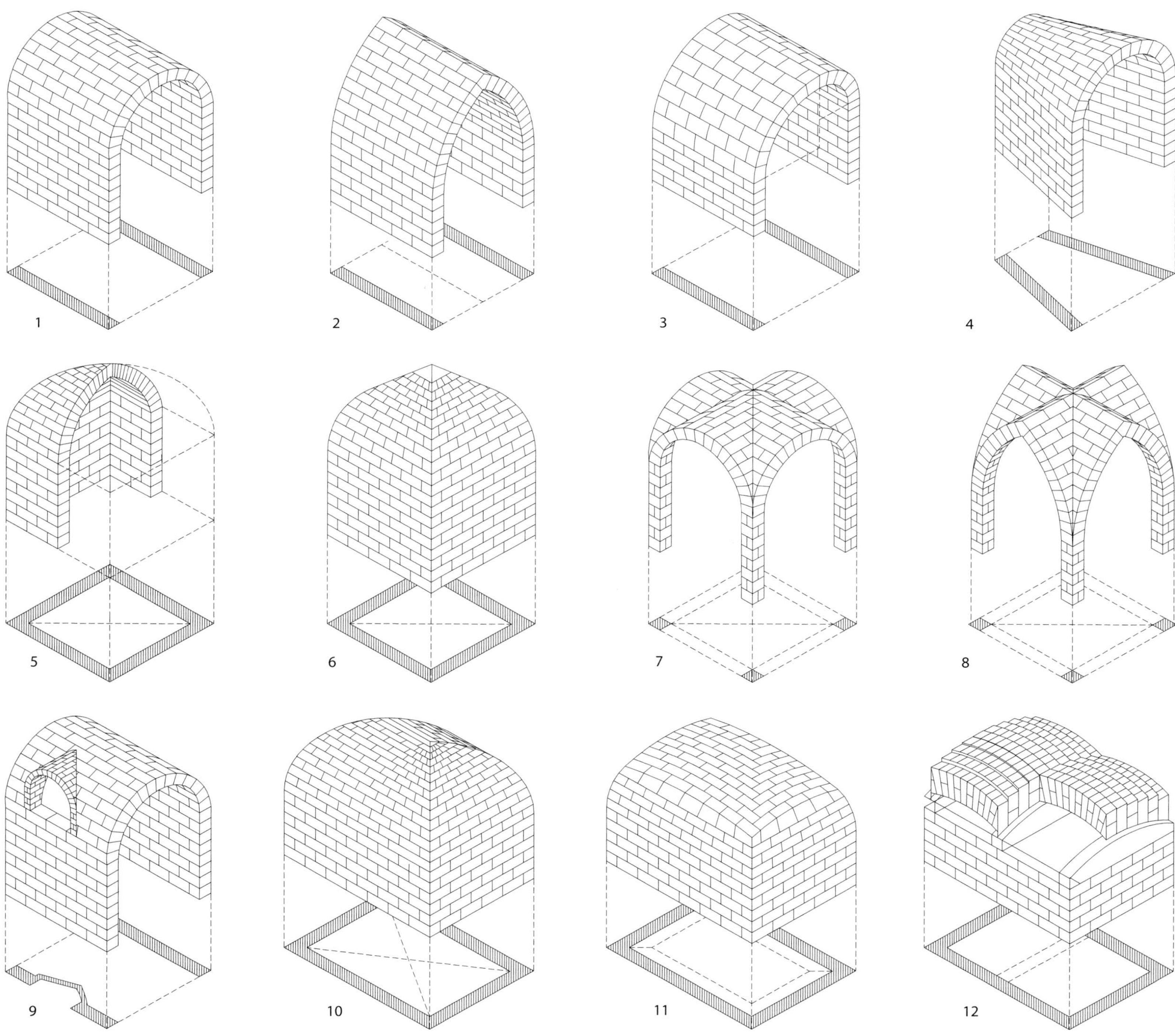
1
2
3
4
5
6
7
8
9
10
11
12

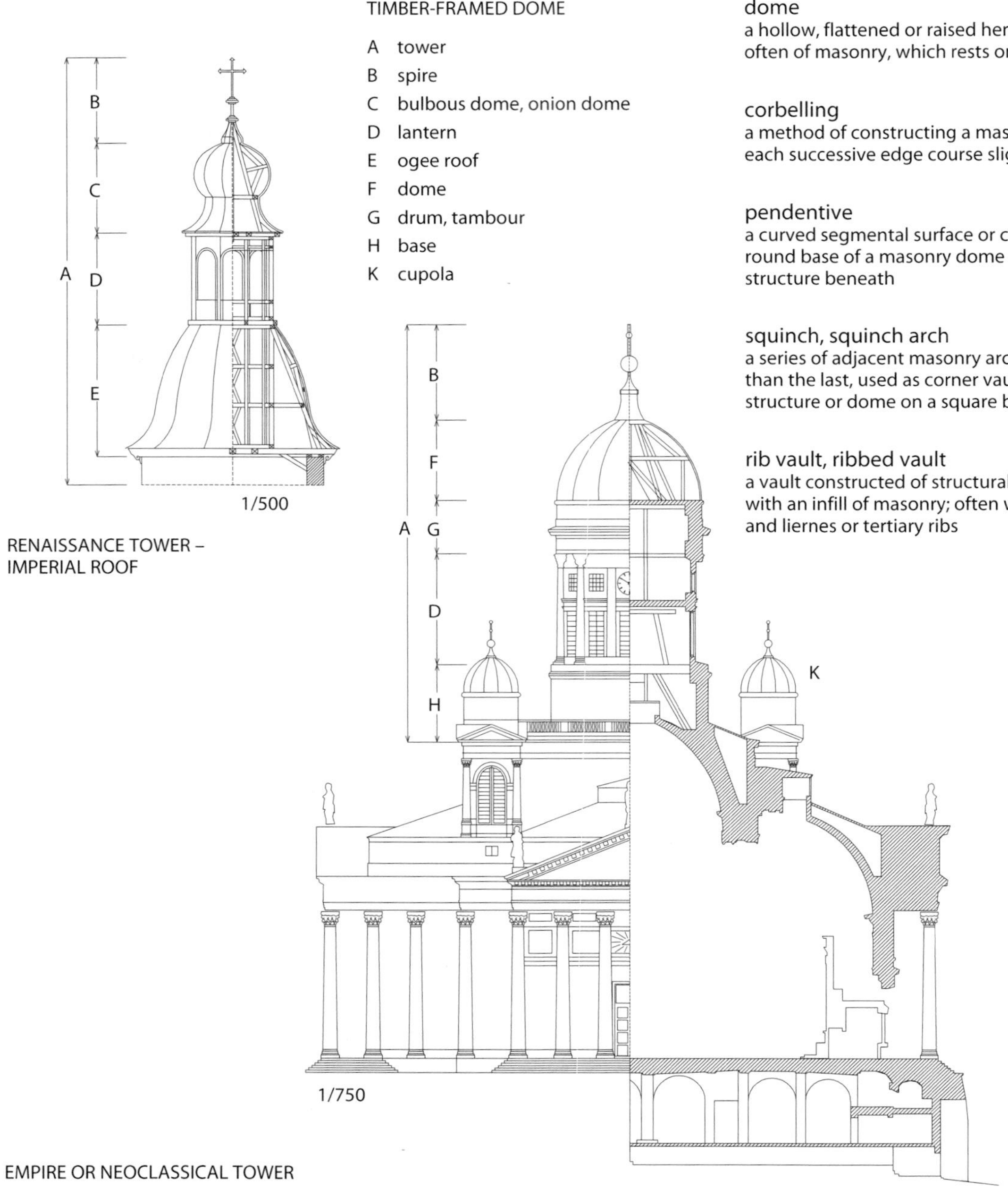

TIMBER-FRAMED DOME

A tower
B spire
C bulbous dome, onion dome
D lantern
E ogee roof
F dome
G drum, tambour
H base
K cupola

RENAISSANCE TOWER – IMPERIAL ROOF

EMPIRE OR NEOCLASSICAL TOWER

F–K) Cathedral of St Nicholas, Helsinki, Finland, 1830–52, C.L. Engel

dome
a hollow, flattened or raised hemispherical roof structure, often of masonry, which rests on a circular, square or polygonal base

corbelling
a method of constructing a masonry overhang by projecting each successive edge course slightly outward

pendentive
a curved segmental surface or construction for joining the round base of a masonry dome or opening to a square structure beneath

squinch, squinch arch
a series of adjacent masonry arches, each successive larger than the last, used as corner vaulting to support a polygonal structure or dome on a square base

rib vault, ribbed vault
a vault constructed of structural arched stone members or ribs with an infill of masonry; often with tiercerons or secondary ribs, and liernes or tertiary ribs

MASONRY DOMES

1 umbrella dome, melon dome pumpkin dome, parachute dome
2 cloister vault, domical vault
3 sail vault, sail dome
4 dome on corbelling
5 dome on squinches
6 pendentive dome
7 half dome, semi-dome, conch
8 calotte, saucer dome
9 corbelling
10 squinch
11 pendentive

RIBBED VAULTS

12 tripartite vault
13 quadripartite vault
14 sexpartite vault, hexapartite vault
15 octopartite vault

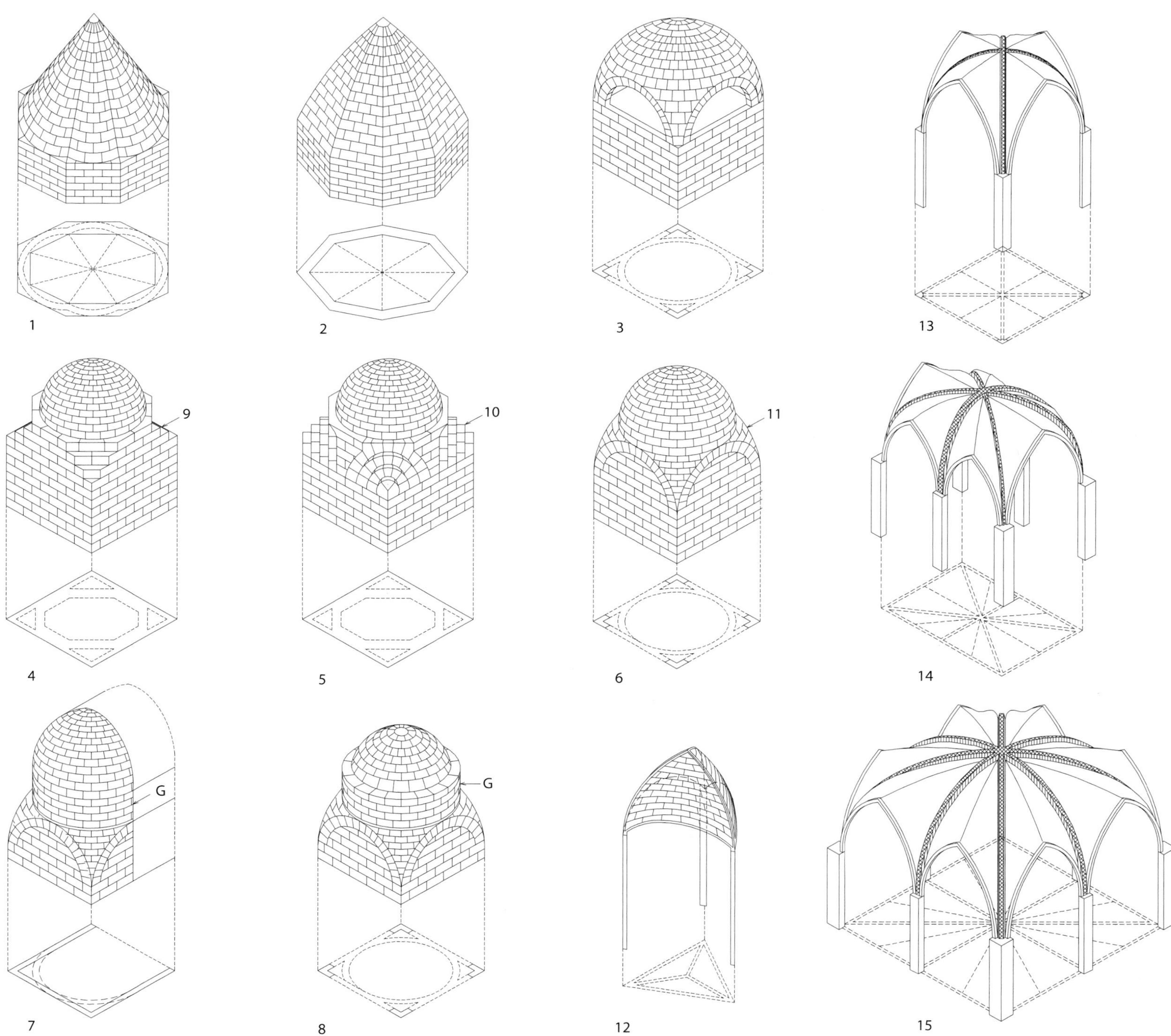
1
2
3
13
4
9
5
10
6
11
14
7
G
8
G
12
15

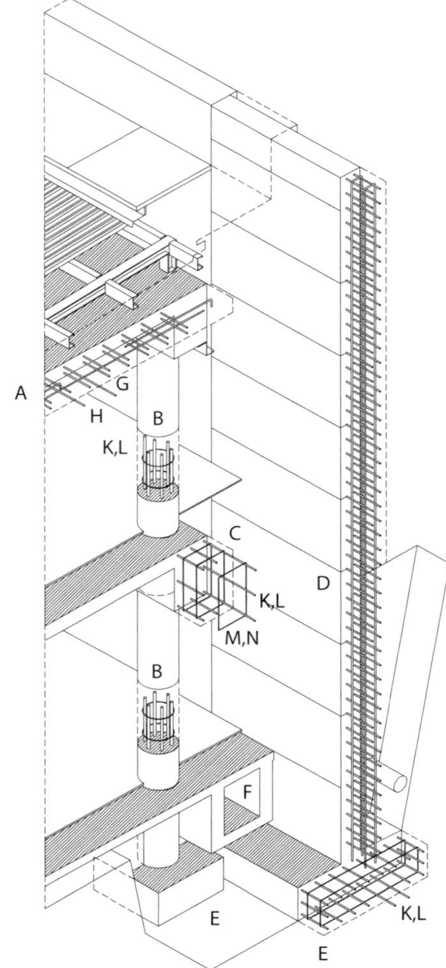

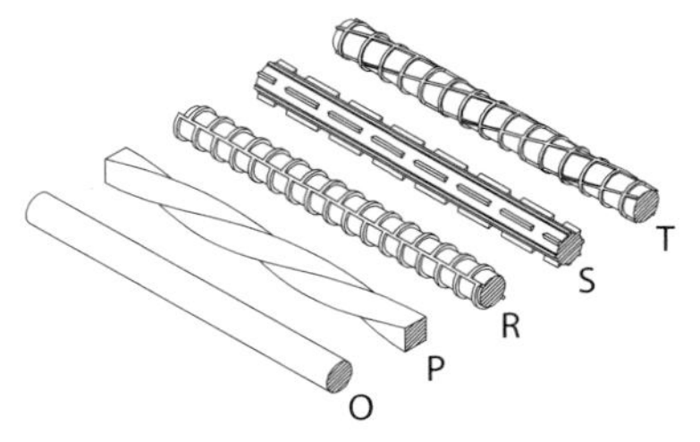

IN-SITU CONCRETE ELEMENTS AND REINFORCEMENT

A in-situ concrete slab, slab reinforcement

B in-situ concrete column, column reinforcement

C in-situ concrete beam, beam reinforcement

D in-situ concrete wall, wall reinforcement

E in-situ concrete footing, foundation reinforcement

F in-situ concrete duct

G top reinforcement

H bottom reinforcement

K main reinforcement, principal reinforcement

L longitudinal reinforcement

M lateral reinforcement, transverse reinforcement

N stirrup, binder, link, ligature

REINFORCING BARS, REBARS

O round bar, plain bar

P twisted bar

R deformed bar, ribbed bar

S deformed bar, ribbed bar

T ribbed and twisted bar

FOLDED SLAB STRUCTURES

1 right prismatic folded slab, prismatic barrel vault with solid diaphragm

2 prismoidal folded slab, hipped folded slab

3 folded slab with rigid frame

COMBINED FOLDED SLABS

4 folded slab with counterfolds

5 folded frame (portal frame)

6 folded frame with counterfolds

7 folded slab with triangular panels

CURVED SHELL STRUCTURES

8 barrel vault

9 inclined barrel vault, cant barrel vault

10 conoidal vault

DOUBLY CURVED SHELLS

11 hyberboloid parabolic shell

12 umbrella shell

COLUMN AND SLAB SYSTEMS

13 column and slab construction (column strips)

14 mushroom slab

15 column slab

16 column, beam and slab construction

17 composite construction

18 hollow core slab

19 double tee slab

20 waffle slab

21 end frame, diaphragm

concrete
a mixture of sand, aggregate, cement and water, often including admixtures, which sets to form a hard, versatile building material, mainly used for its structural properties

in situ, cast-in-place (Am), cast-in-situ
referring to concrete and other similar materials which have been cast fresh on site as opposed to being prefabricated; written in-situ when used as an adjective

reinforced concrete, ferroconcrete, steel concrete
structural concrete containing inlaid steel reinforcing bars or a mesh to increase strength in tension

aggregate
inert granular material such as sand, gravel, crushed rock and clinker used as a main solid constituent in concrete, plaster, tarmacadam and asphalt

cement
a powdered mineral substance, usually containing lime or gypsum, mixed with water to form a paste which will set to form a hard, brittle material; used as a binder in concrete, mortars, plasters etc.

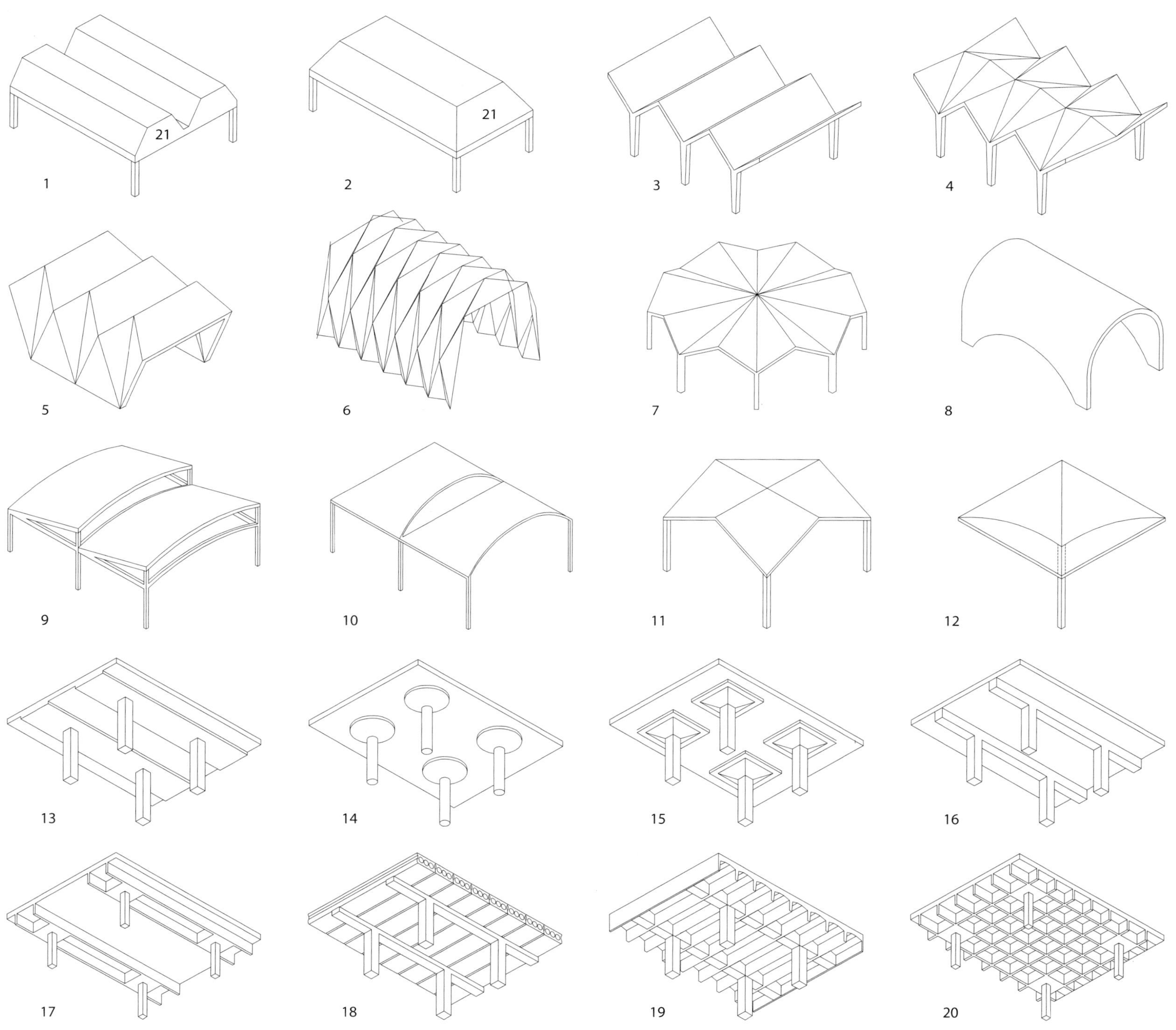
21
1
21
2
3
4
5
6
7
8
9
10
11
12
13
14
15
16
17
18
19
20

28 LARGE PANEL CONSTRUCTION AND BUILDING FRAMES

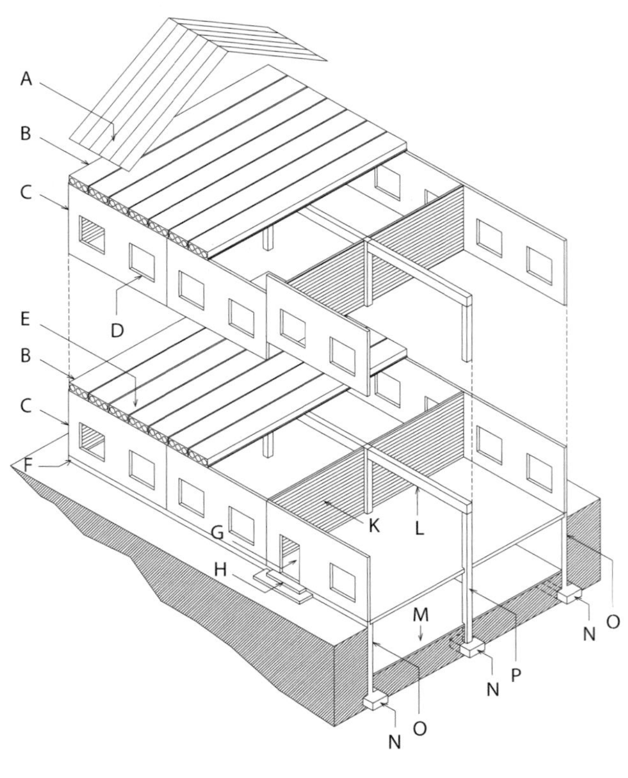

FULLY PRECAST BUILDING

BUILDING ELEMENTS

A roof, roofing

B roof slab – precast slab, slab unit – hollow-core slab, hollow-core beam

C external wall – load bearing wall unit, load bearing wall panel

D window opening

E intermediate floor

F base wall, wall base

G doorway, door opening

H doorstep

K internal wall, partition

L precast beam, beam unit

M base floor, bottom floor

N footing, foundation

O foundation wall

P precast column, column unit

R infill concreting, infill casting

S outer leaf: precast panel

T thermal insulation

U inner leaf: structural wall

V subframe, closure piece

LOADBEARING FRAME, STRUCTURAL FRAME

1 loadbearing wall construction, bearing wall system

2 crosswall construction (monolithic in-situ)

3 crosswall construction (precast)

4 column and slab construction

5 post and beam construction, post and lintel construction, column and beam construction (monolithic in-situ)

6 post and beam construction, post and lintel construction, column and beam construction (precast)

7 bearing wall and trabeated construction

8 cellular structure

9 module construction

10 spatial unit, module

SANDWICH PANEL

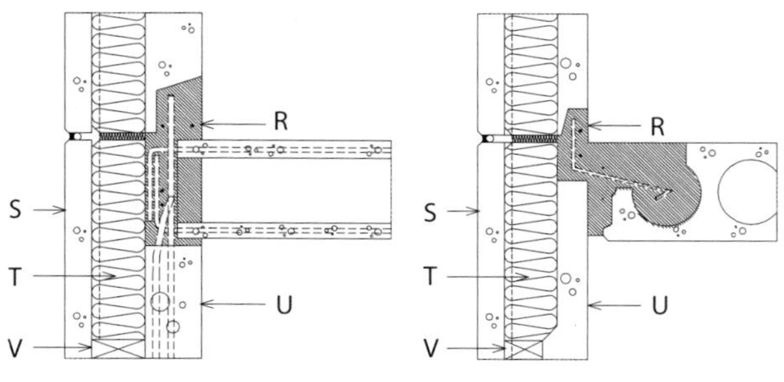

loadbearing external wall   non-loadbearing external wall

prefabrication, prefabricated construction
a quick and efficient method of construction in which components or groups of components are made under workshop conditions and transported to site for installation

large-panel construction
industrialized building using precast concrete panels for structural frame and cladding of buildings, involving careful design to ensure that components fit together on site, but saving time and expense at construction stage

precast concrete
constructional concrete in the form of prefabricated units and manufactured products that are cast and cured under controlled conditions in a factory or plant and transported to a building site for installation or erection

sandwich panel
a prefabricated composite concrete wall panel consisting of an inner structural and outer cladding leaf bonded on either side of a layer of fluted insulation

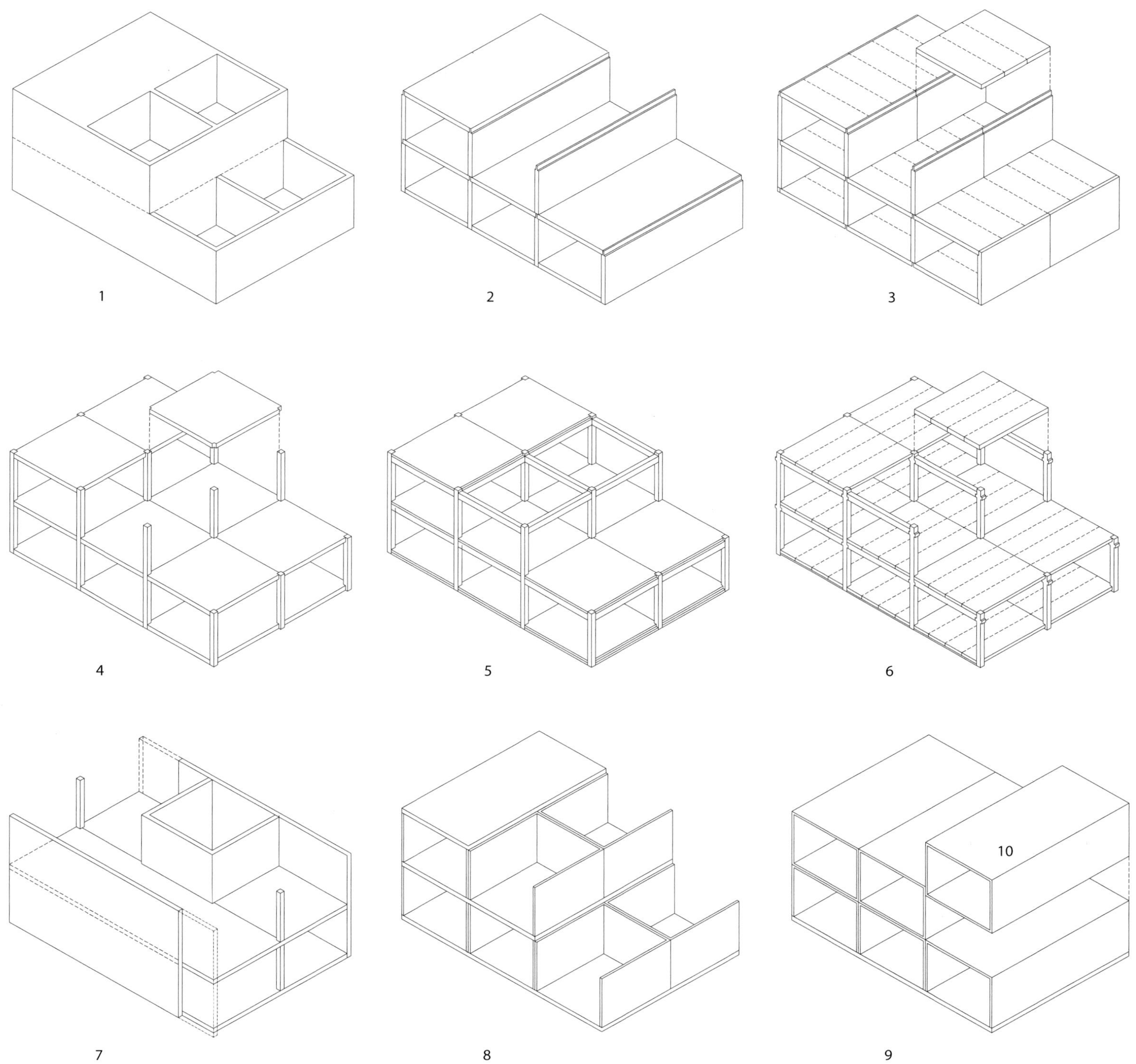
1
2
3
4
5
6
7
8
9
10

29 FOUNDATION TYPES

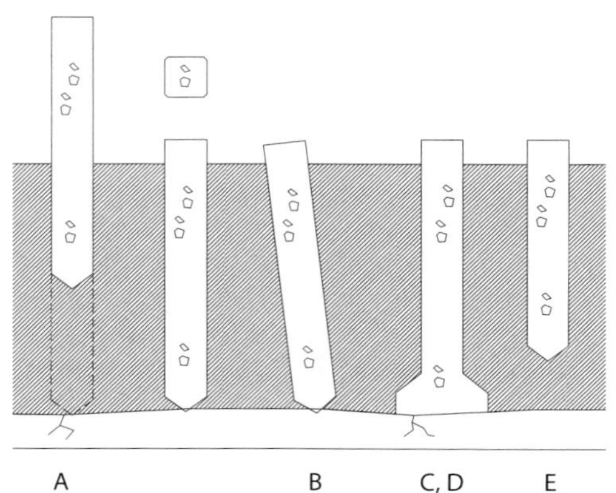

foundation
1 a subterranean structure designed to transmit the structural loading of a building to the underlying ground
2 formation, subgrade, subsoil, ground; the bearing layer of soil or rock below the substructure of a building or other construction

pile
in foundation technology, any vertical structural member of concrete, steel or timber used in series as a foundation on types of soil with poor or uneven bearing capacity; they transmit building loads deep into the ground or to bedrock, or function as earth retaining structures; vertically loaded piles are generally called bearing or foundation piles

retaining wall
a structural wall designed to withstand lateral forces from the abutting ground or a body of water on one side of it

SPREAD FOUNDATIONS

1 shallow foundation
2 deep foundation
3 strip foundation
4 widestrip foundation
5 trench-fill foundation
6 pad foundation, column or isolated footing
7 pad foundation, column or isolated footing
8 foundation column, pier or pillar
9 ground beam
Am: grade beam
10 raft foundation
11 bedrock foundation
12 log grillage, log crib
13 log grillage, log crib

RETAINING WALLS

14 gravity wall
15 cantilever wall
16 counterfort wall
17 counterfort
18 cribbing, cribwork
19 crib
20 gabion wall
21 gabion, rubble basket
22 anchored retaining wall; ground anchor, rock anchor
23 anchored retaining wall; deadman
24 anchored retaining wall; piled anchorage, anchor pile
25 sheet piling, trench sheeting
26 steel sheet pile

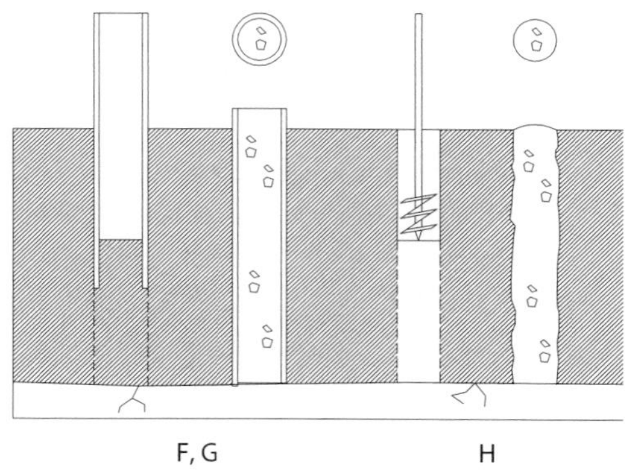

PILED FOUNDATIONS

CONCRETE PILES

A driven pile, precast pile
B batter pile, raking pile, inclined pile
C underreamed pile, belled pile, pedestal pile, enlarged base pile
D end-bearing pile, point-bearing pile
E friction pile, cohesion pile
F cast-in-place pile, in-situ pile, bored pile
G pile casing
H augered pile, bored pile

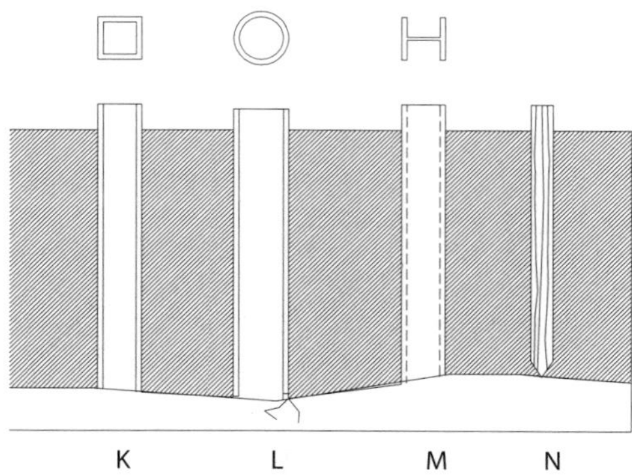

STEEL AND TIMBER PILES

K box pile
L pipe pile, tubular pile – augered steel pile
M H-pile
N timber pile, wooden pile

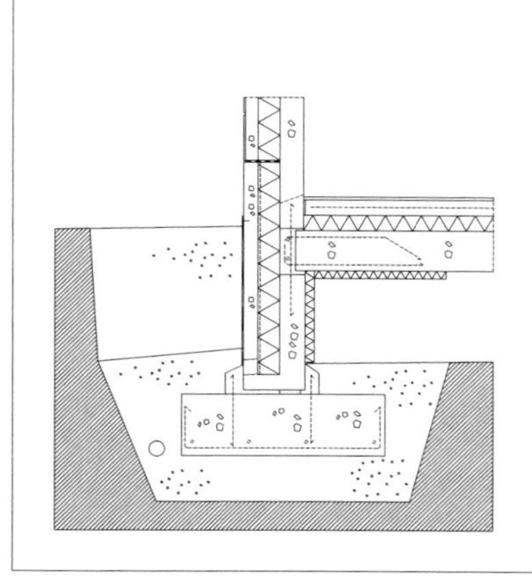

27 FOUNDATION
28 base wall, wall base
29 granular or gravel backfill
30 tanking, drainage membrane
31 foundation wall
32 footing, foundation
33 subsoil drain
34 suspended slab
35 gravel, hardcore
36 foundation, formation

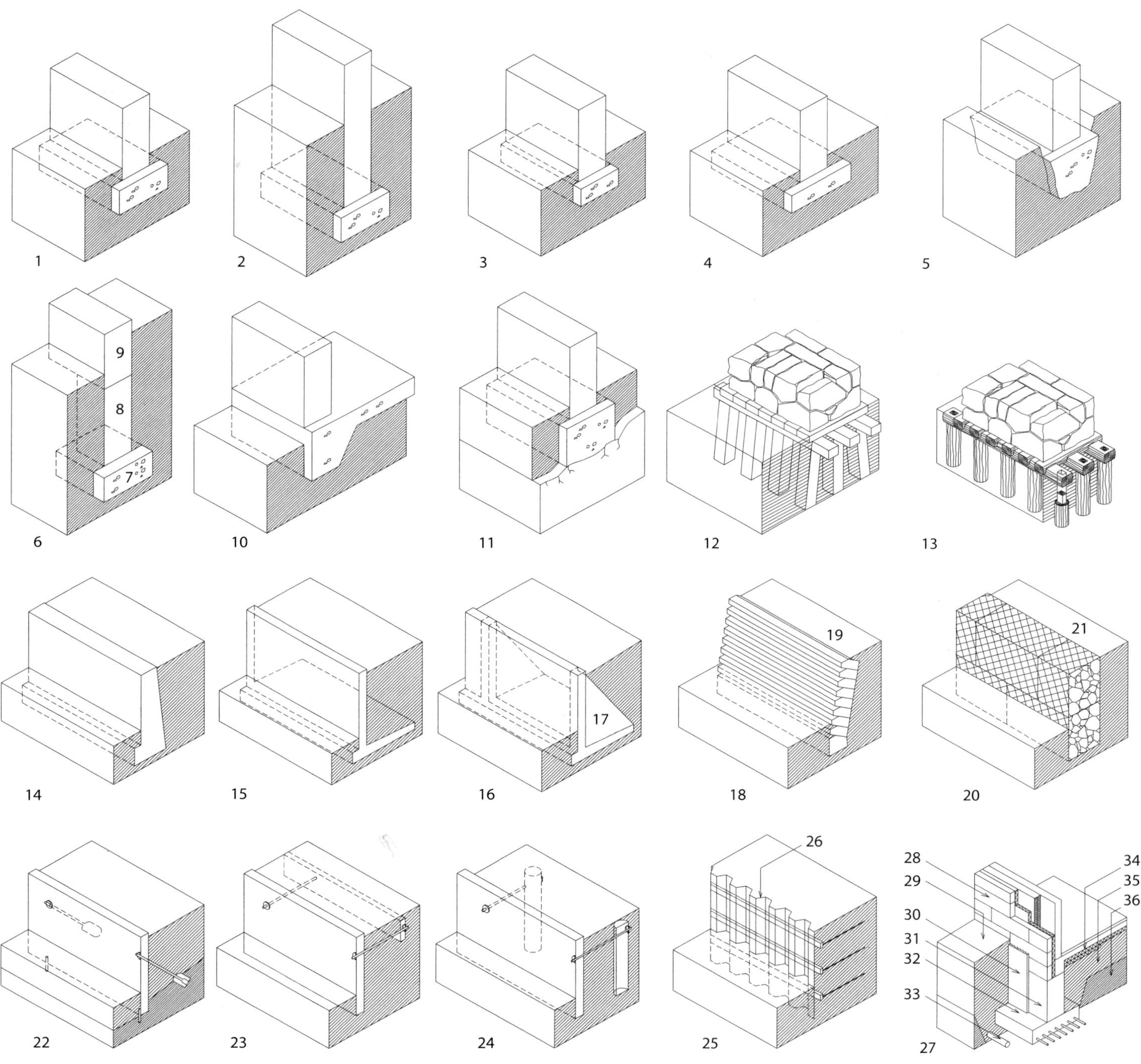
1
2
3
4
5
9
8
7
6
10
11
12
13
14
15
17
16
19
18
21
20
22
23
24
26
25
28
29
30
31
32
33
34
35
36
27

30 CONCRETE BEAMS, LIGHTWEIGHT CONCRETE AND GLASS BLOCKS

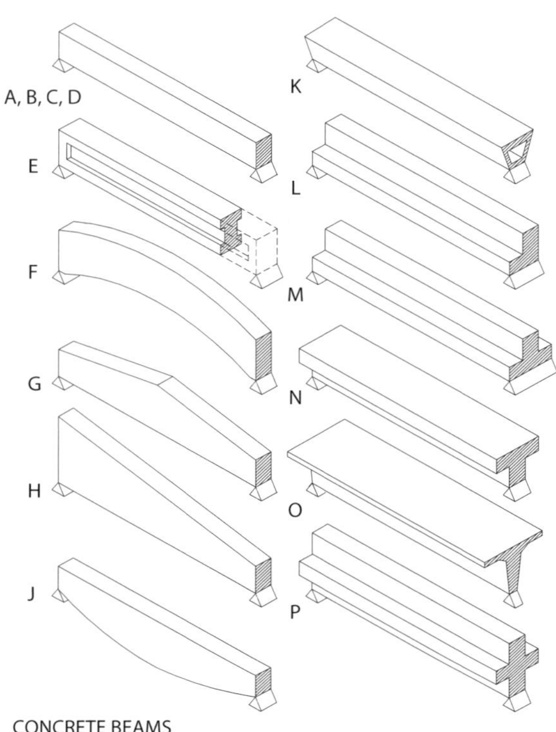

CONCRETE BEAMS

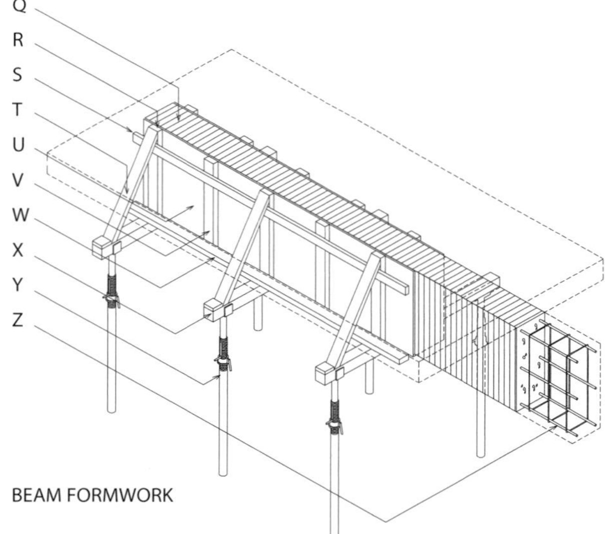

BEAM FORMWORK

A plain beam, straight beam
B flat beam
C rectangular beam
D solid beam, rectangular beam
E I-beam
F cambered beam, arched beam
G pitched beam, saddle beam
H monopitch beam, tapered beam, wedge beam, sawtooth beam
J fishbellied beam
K box beam, hollow beam
L L-beam, boot lintel
M flanged beam
N T-beam, tee beam
O downstand beam, ribbed beam
P cruciform beam
Q cast concrete
R formwork support
S wale, waler, waler plate
T strut
U formwork, sheathing, shuttering
V runner
W wale, waler, waler plate
X strongback, spreader beam, yoke
Y strut, prop: adjustable prop, telescopic prop
Z reinforcing cage

LIGHTWEIGHT CONCRETE BLOCKS

1 concrete brick
2 partition block, breeze block
3 breeze block
4 cellular block
5 insulated block
6 channel block
7 column block, pilaster block
8 radial block
9 coping block, capping block
10 footing block, foundation block

GLASS BLOCKS

11 plain glass block
12 wired glass block
13 wavy glass block
14 reeded glass block
15 double reeded glass block
16 chequered glass block
17 prismatic glass block

formwork, casing, mould, shuttering
concreting moulds of boarding, sheet material or specialized construction to give temporary support for in-situ concrete while it hardens

prestressed concrete
reinforced concrete placed in a state of permanent compression by stretched high-tensile steel wires, strands or tendons within its fabric; these enable the component to withstand higher tensile loading than normal

lightweight concrete
concrete which has a bulk density range from 400–1760 kg/m^3 and is lighter than ordinary concrete, either by virtue of its lightweight aggregate (as in no-fines concrete, lightweight aggregate concrete), or entrained voids of air or gas (as in aerated concrete)

concrete block
a masonry block manufactured from precast concrete, usually of cellular or aggregate construction

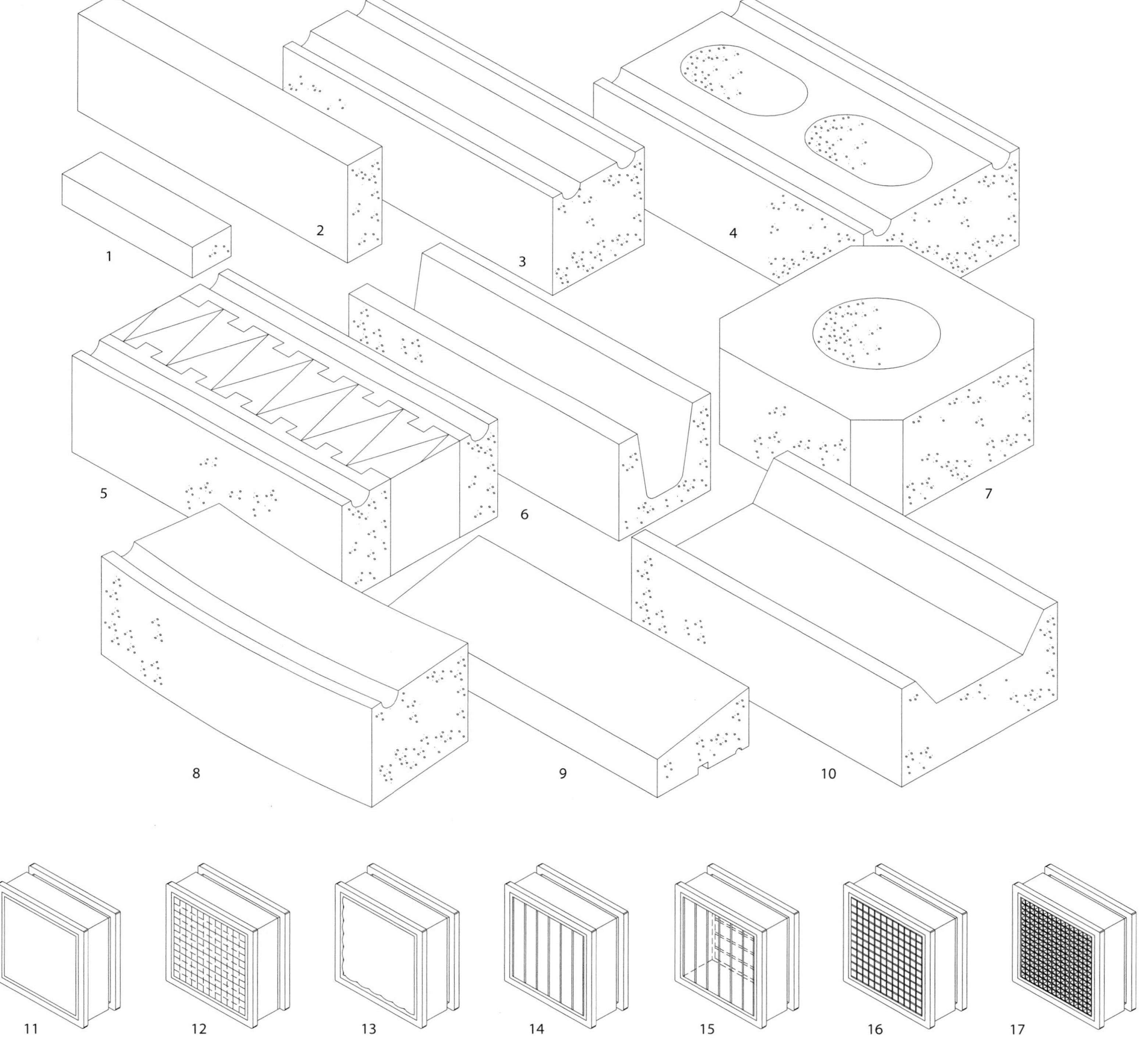

1
2
3
4
5
6
7
8
9
10
11
12
13
14
15
16
17

31 BRIDGE STRUCTURE

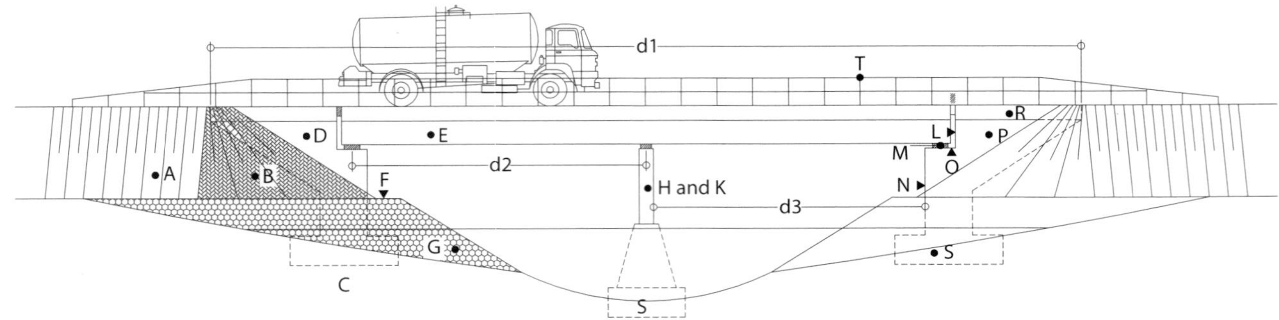

d1 total length, overall dimension
d2 span
d3 clear span

ANATOMY OF A BRIDGE

A embankment
B slope
C bank seat
D bridge abutment (substructure)
E deck (superstructure)
F towpath
G rip-rap, revetment
H bridge pier
K starling, cutwater
L abutment
M bearings
N abutment face
O bridge seat, bearing pad
P wing wall
R spandrel beam
S footing
T balustrade, parapet

bridge
a construction built between two points of support over an obstacle or ravine to enable passage of a road, railway or pathway

bridge deck
the structural slab-like base or flooring superstructure of a bridge, which supports traffic and transfers loads to the substructure

substructure
that part of the structure of a bridge below the bridge deck, which supports it

bridge superstructure
the structural parts of a bridge supported by its piers and buttresses

BRIDGE DECKS

1 solid slab bridge
2 solid slab bridge
3 prefabricated slab
4 central beam bridge
5 central beam bridge
6 hollow core slab
7 trough bridge
8 ribbed slab bridge
9 prefabricated beam bridge
10 box girder bridge
11 box girder bridge
12 box girder bridge
13 orthotropic steel deck bridge
14 composite girder bridge
15 composite girder bridge

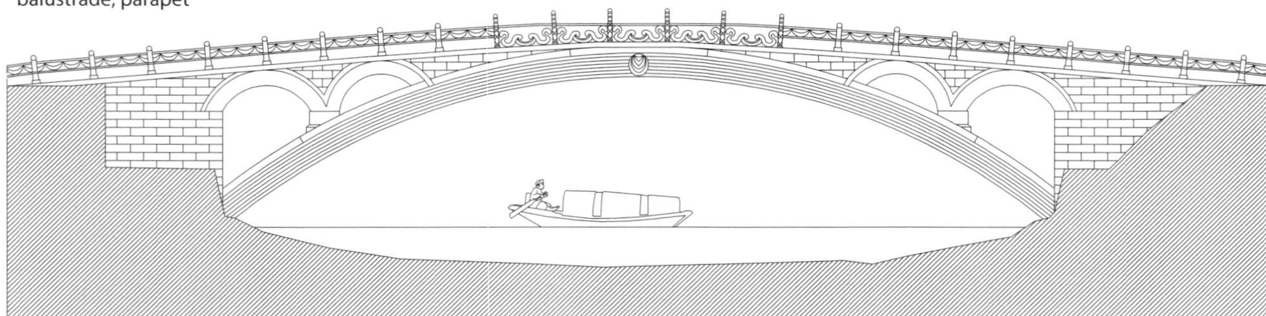

An Ji bridge at Zhao Xian, Hebel province, China, 605 AD, span 37 m (121 ft)

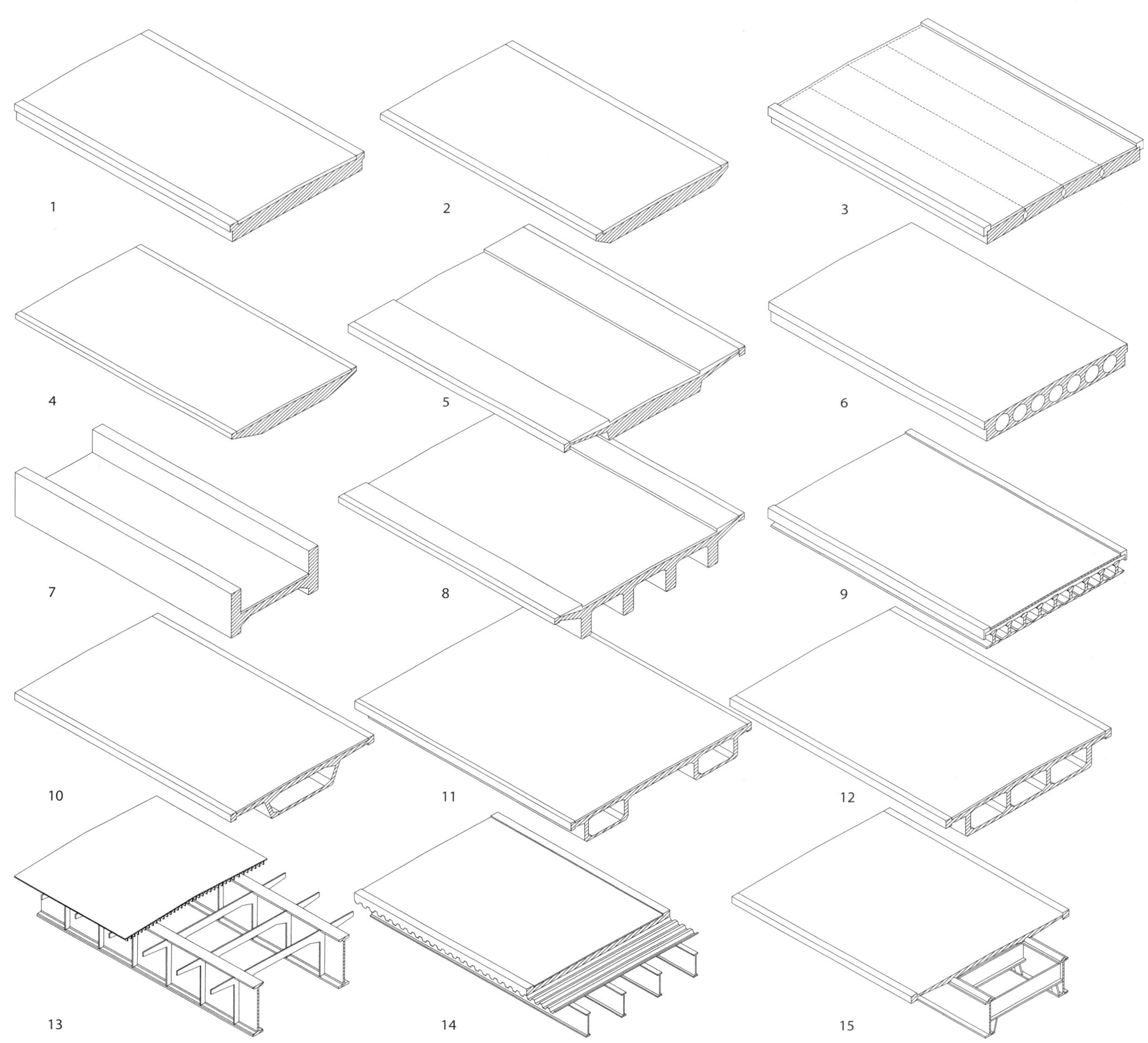
1
2
3
4
5
6
7
8
9
10
11
12
13
14
15

32 BRIDGE TYPES

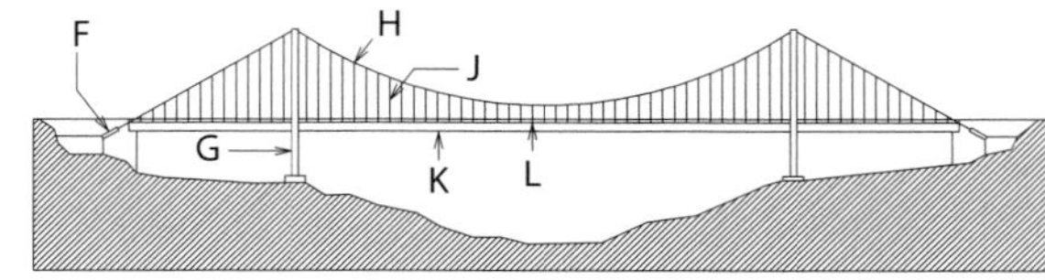

A

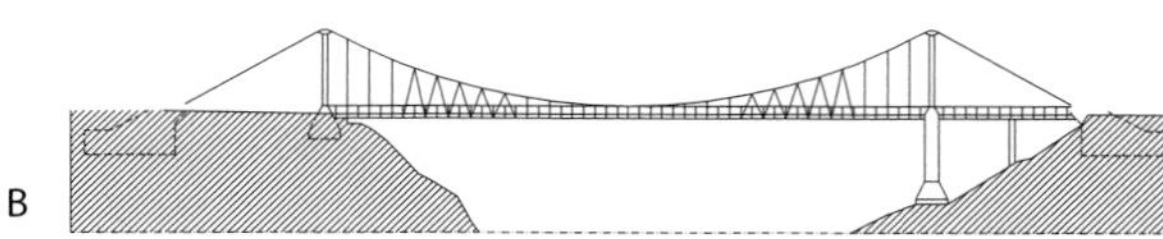

B

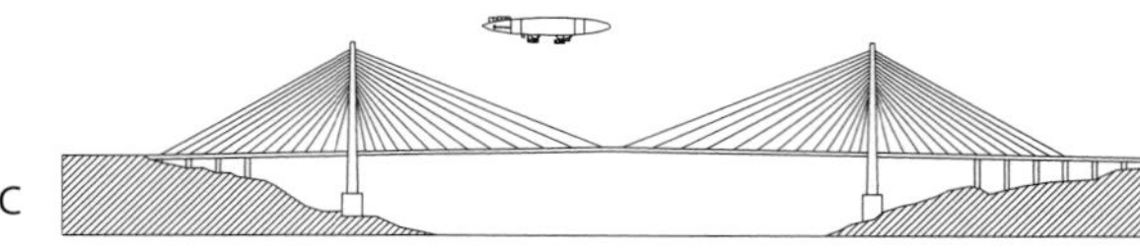

C

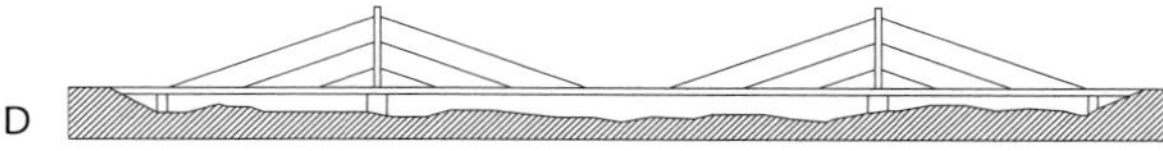

D

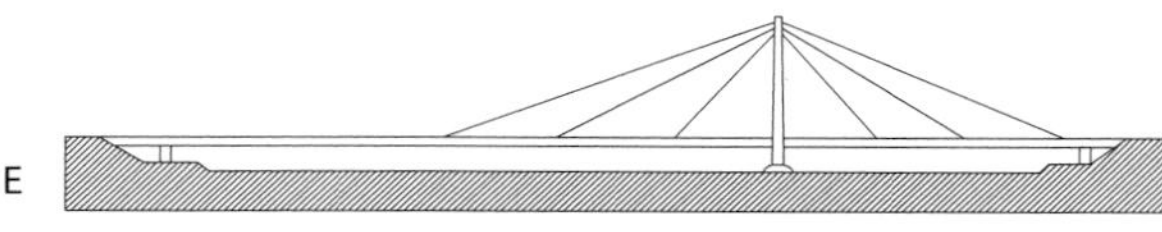

E

SUSPENSION BRIDGES

A suspension bridge with hangers

B suspension bridge with hangers and braces

CABLE-STAYED BRIDGES

C fan configuration

D harp configuration

E radial configuration

PARTS OF A SUSPENSION BRIDGE

F anchorage

G pylon

H suspension cable, catenary cable

J hanger, suspender

K stiffening beam (substructure)

L bridge deck (superstructure)

BRIDGE TYPES

1 horizontal bridge

2 sloping bridge

3 cambered bridge, bowed bridge, hump-back bridge

4 concave bridge

TRUSSED FRAME BRIDGES, RIGID FRAME BRIDGES

5 king post bridge

6 queen post bridge

7 portal truss bridge, rigid frame truss bridge

8 portal truss bridge, rigid frame truss bridge

9 portal bridge, rigid frame bridge

GIRDER BRIDGES

10 slab bridge, single span bridge, simple span bridge

11 continuous span bridge

12 cantilever span bridge

ARCH BRIDGES

13 solid spandrel bridge, earth-fill

14 viaduct, multiple span bridge

15 open spandrel bridge, solid ribbed arch bridge, deck arch bridge

16 open spandrel bridge

17 tied arch bridge, bowstring bridge

18 tied arch bridge, bowstring bridge

STEEL TRUSS BRIDGES

19 trussed arch bridge

20 spandrel braced arch bridge

21 polygonal truss bridge

suspension bridge
a bridge hung from a system of primary and secondary cables strung between tall towers known as pylons

cable-stayed bridge, stayed bridge
a bridge whose deck is supported by a series of inclined cables or rods strung from one or a number of pylons or towers

span
the horizontal distance along the unsupported superstructure of a bridge, between adjacent piers or main supports

C) Skarnsundet, Trondheimsfjord, Norway (530 m, 1991)
D) Severin, Cologne, Germany (301 m, 1960)
E) Nord Elbe, Hamburg, Germany (172 m, 1962)

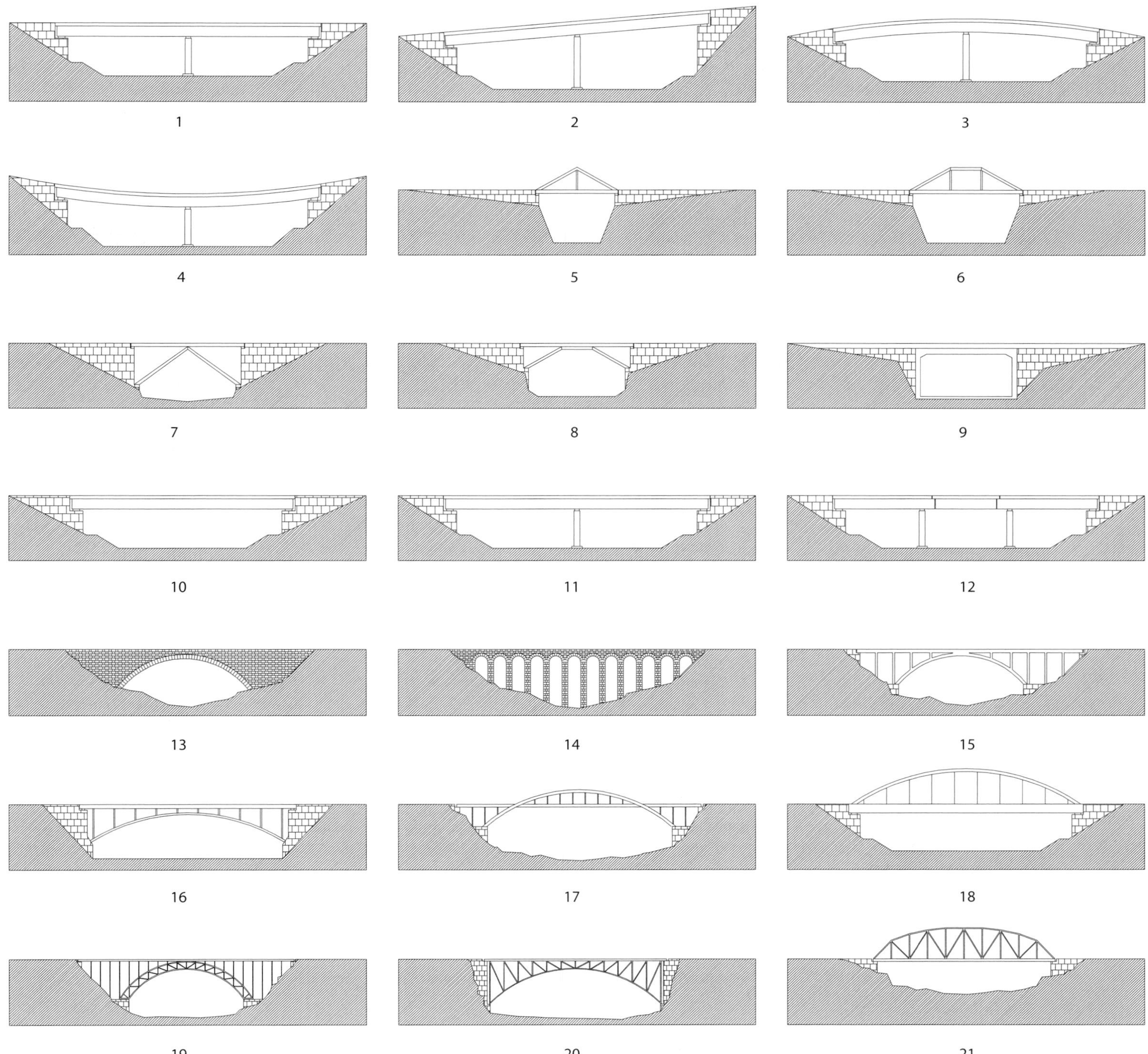
1
2
3
4
5
6
7
8
9
10
11
12
13
14
15
16
17
18
19
20
21

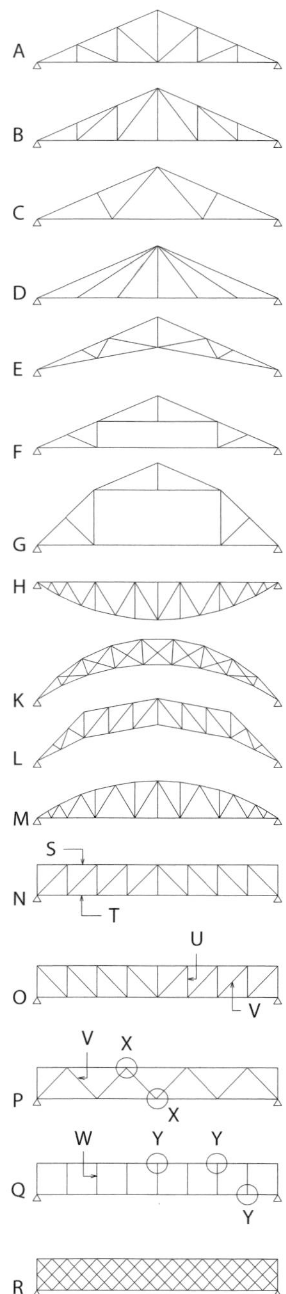

ROOF TRUSSES

A Howe gable truss
B Pratt gable truss
C Fink truss, French truss, Belgian truss
D fan truss
E scissors truss
F attic truss
G mansard truss

TRUSSED BEAMS, LATTICE BEAMS

H fishbellied truss
K trussed arch, arch truss
L polygonal truss
M Belfast truss, bowstring truss

FLAT TRUSSES

N Howe truss
O Pratt truss
P Warren truss
Q Vierendeel truss
R Town truss, lattice truss
S upper chord
T lower chord, bottom chord
U web member, brace
V brace, diagonal brace
W strut, vertical
X pin joint, node
Y rigid joint
Z bearing point

ANATOMY OF A TRUSSED RAFTER

a rafter, common rafter
b ridge board
c collar, collar beam
d tie beam
e collar purlin
f ashlar post, strut
g sole piece
h roof plate, binder
k ceiling joist
m ridge beam
n purlin, side purlin
o wall plate
p crown post
q king post
r principal rafter
s queen strut
t queen post
u straining beam
v principal roof truss
w secondary roof truss
x hammer beam
y hammer post
z strut

TRADITIONAL TRUSSED ROOFS, SINGLE ROOFS

1 collar and tie beam truss
2 couple roof, coupled rafter roof
3 collar roof, collar rafter roof
4 tie beam truss, close couple roof, span roof
5,6 'Swedish truss'
7 scissor roof, scissor rafter roof

DOUBLE ROOFS

8 purlin roof
9 purlin roof
10 trussed purlin roof
11 crown post roof
12 queen post collar rafter roof

TRUSSED ROOFS, TRIPLE ROOFS

13 king post roof
14 king post roof
15 queen strut roof
16 queen post roof
17 portal frame, rigid frame
18 hammer-beam roof
19 flat trusses
20 space frame, space deck

truss, lattice structure
a structural element consisting of a number of members pin-jointed at their ends to form a beam which resists loads by means of triangulation, in particular one of steel or timber used for supporting floors and roofs

strut
any structural member which resists forces in compression along its length

tie
any structural bracing or stabilizing member which resists forces in tension

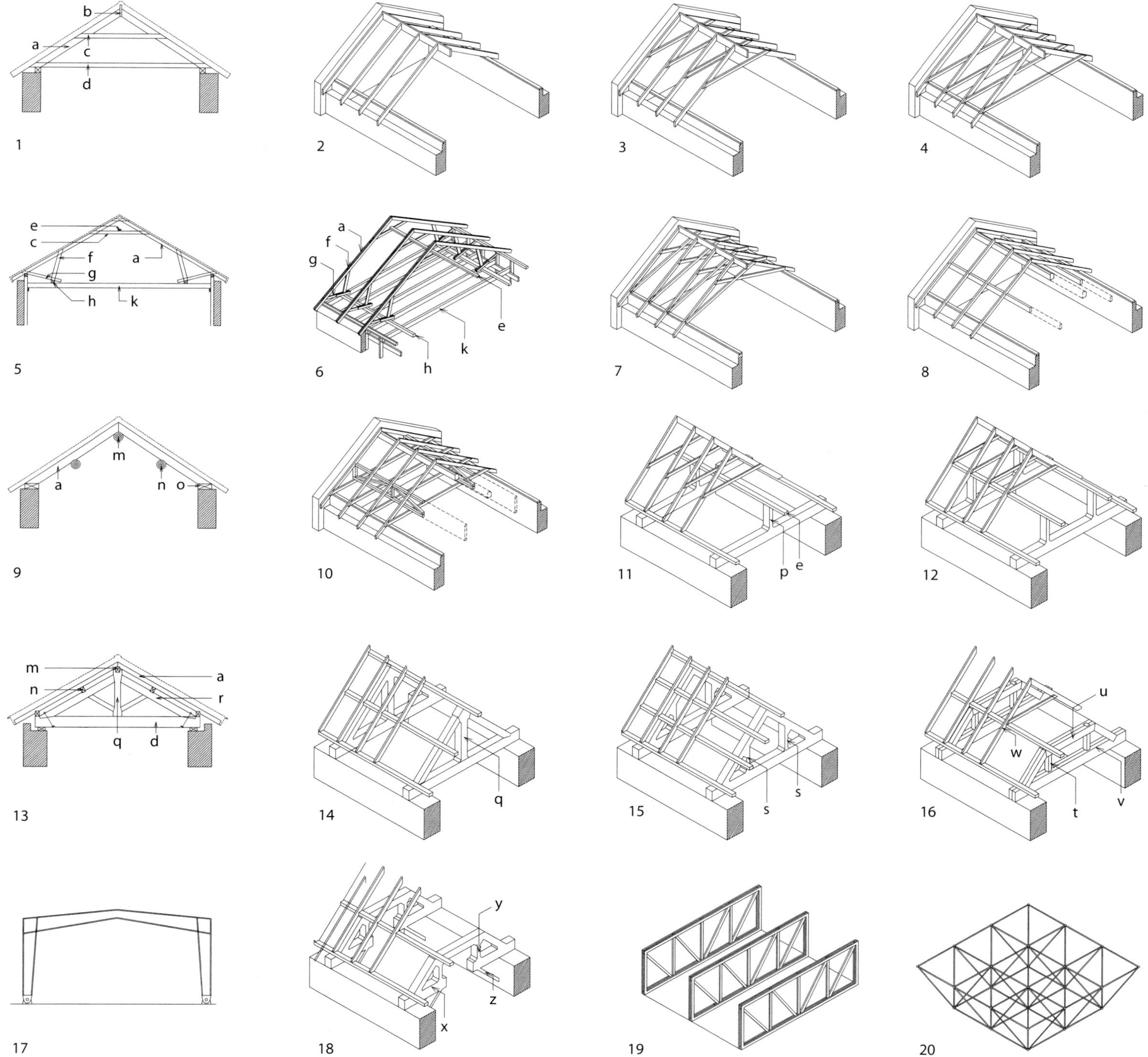

b
a
c
d
1
2
3
4
e
c
f
a
g
h
k
5
a
f
g
e
k
h
6
7
8
m
a
n
o
9
10
p
e
11
12
m
a
n
r
q
d
13
q
14
s
s
15
u
w
t
v
16
17
y
z
x
18
19
20

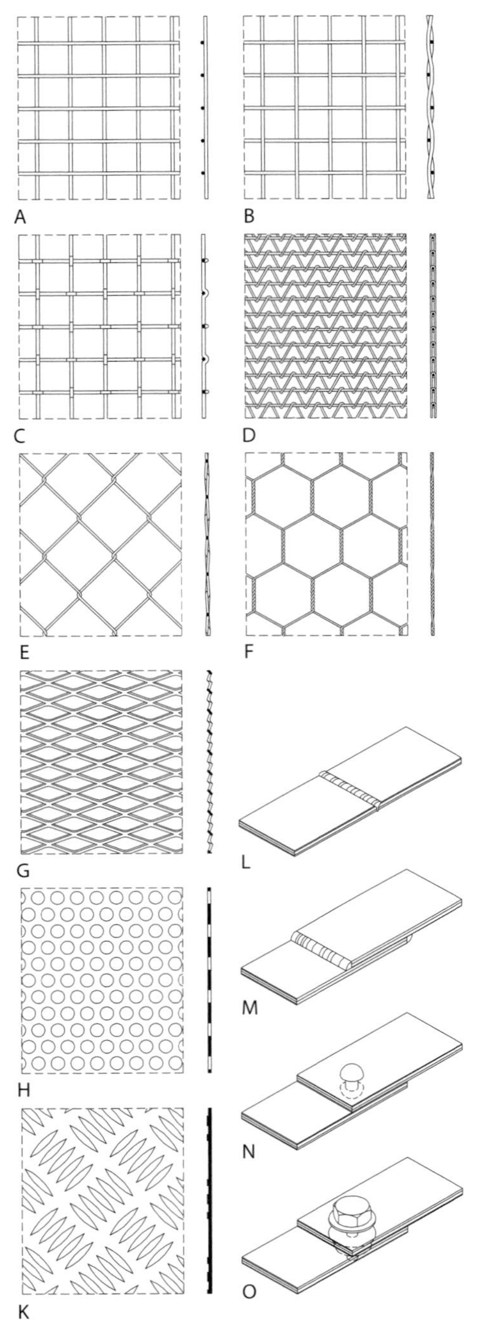

WIRE MESHES AND PATTERNED PLATES

A welded wire mesh
B woven wire mesh
C crimped wire mesh
D conveyor mesh, belt mesh
E chain link mesh
F chicken wire, hexagonal mesh
G expanded metal
H perforated sheetmetal
K chequerplate, checkerplate tread plate

WELDED JOINTS, WELDS

L butt weld, fillet weld
M lap weld
N riveted joint
O bolted joint

METAL PROFILES BARS

1 flat bar, flat
2 round bar
3 square bar
4 hexagonal bar

HOLLOW SECTIONS AND TUBES

5 round hollow section, round tube
6 square hollow section, SHS, square tube
7 rectangular hollow section, RHS, rectangular tube

ANGLES AND OPEN SECTIONS

8 equal angle
9 equal angle (structural)
10 unequal angle
11 unequal angle (structural)
12 T-bar, structural tee
13 Z-bar
14 channel, U-section, C-section
15 I-section, universal beam, UB section
16 H-section, universal column, UC section
17 cold formed or cold rolled steel beam
18 hot rolled steel beam
19 plate girder, welded plate girder

SHEET PRODUCTS

20 metal foil, foil
21 metal sheet, sheetmetal
22 metal plate

steelwork
framing construction work in welded or bolted steel sections, usually of a structural nature

welding
the joining together of metal components by melting or pressure or a combination of both

zinc coating, galvanization
the corrosion protection of ferrous metals by application of a thin layer of zinc

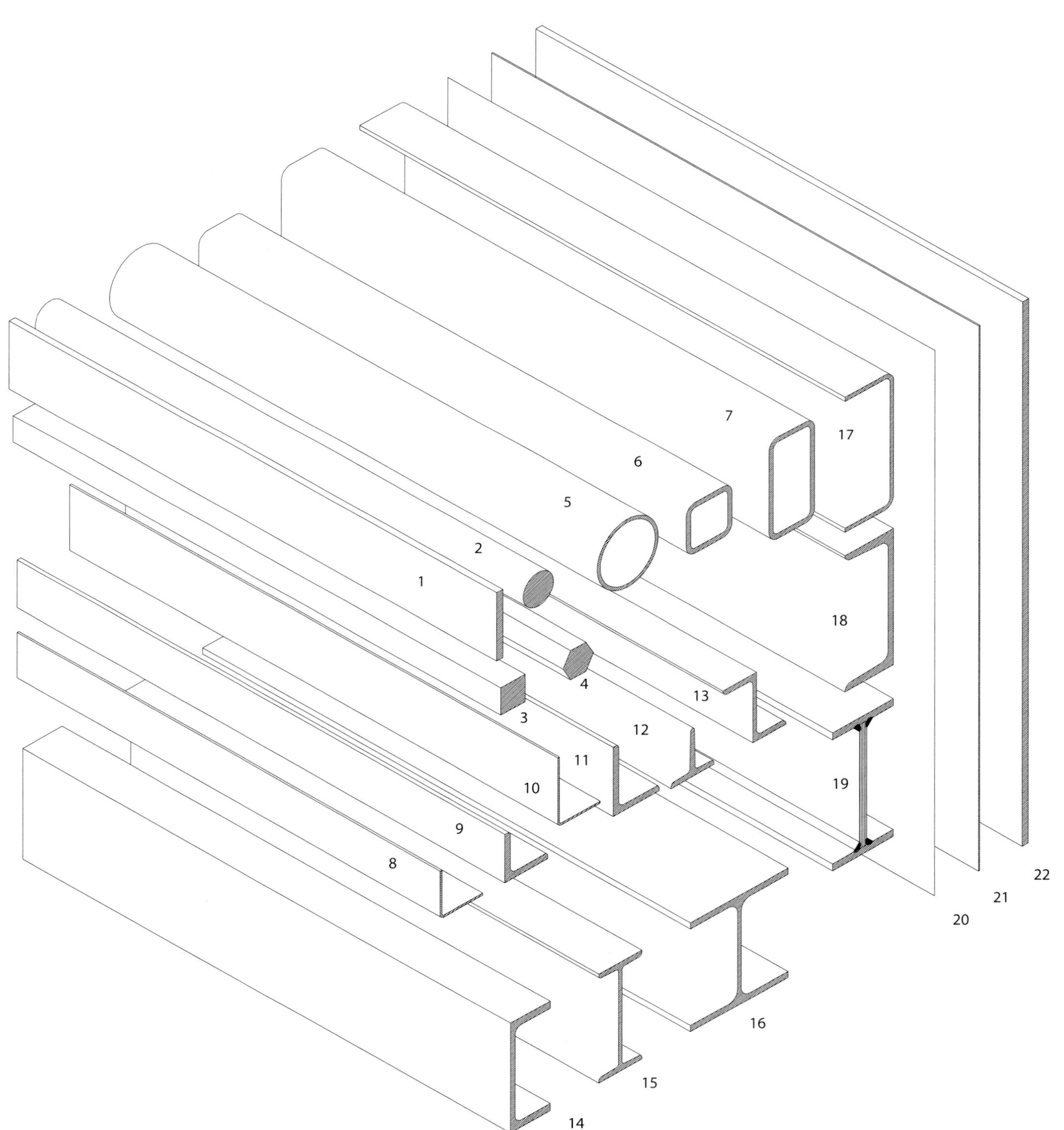

7
17
6
5
2
1
18
4
13
3
12
11
19
10
9
8
22
21
20
16
15
14

35 NAILS

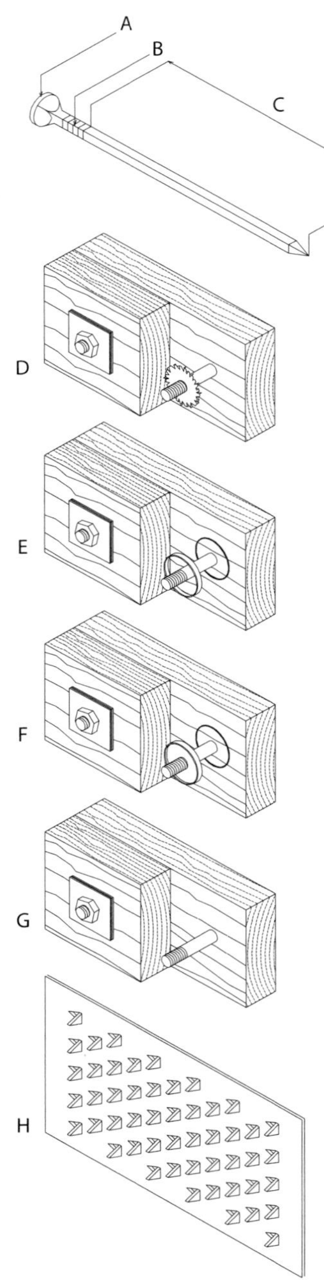

PARTS OF A NAIL

A nailhead, head
B neck
C shaft, shank

TIMBER CONNECTORS

D toothed plate connector, bulldog plate
E split ring connector
F shear plate connector
G pinned joint
H nail plate, gang nail, truss plate, toothed plate fastener

TYPES OF NAIL

1 wire nail
2 lost-head nail, finishing nail, bullet-head nail
3 concrete nail, masonry nail
4 cut nail, spike
5 forged nail, wrought nail
6 annular nail, improved nail, ring-shanked nail, jagged-shank nail
7 anchor nail
8 roofing nail, nipple-head nail
9 convex-head roofing nail, nipple-head nail
10 double headed nail, duplex nail, scaffold nail, form nail
11 screw nail, drive screw, twisted shank nail
12 pin, concrete nail
13 dowel nail
14 hardboard pin
15 panel pin
16 tile clip, holding down clip
17 clout, clout nail, felt nail
18 pin, panel pin, beading nail, headless nail, headless pin, sprig
19 cut nail
20 cut nail
21 cut nail, T-nail
22 U-pin, staple
23 brad, hook nail
24 escutcheon pin
25 upholstery tack, upholstery nail
26 shoe nail, sprig
27 tack
28 corrugated fastener, mitre brad, wiggle nail

connector
any accessory for fixing two components or members together

nail
a slender-shafted metal fastener driven in with a hammer to fix one component to another, relying on friction as a means of attachment

nail gun
a power tool which fires nails into surfaces to be fixed, operated by compressed air or electricity

pin
a small nail with a slender shank

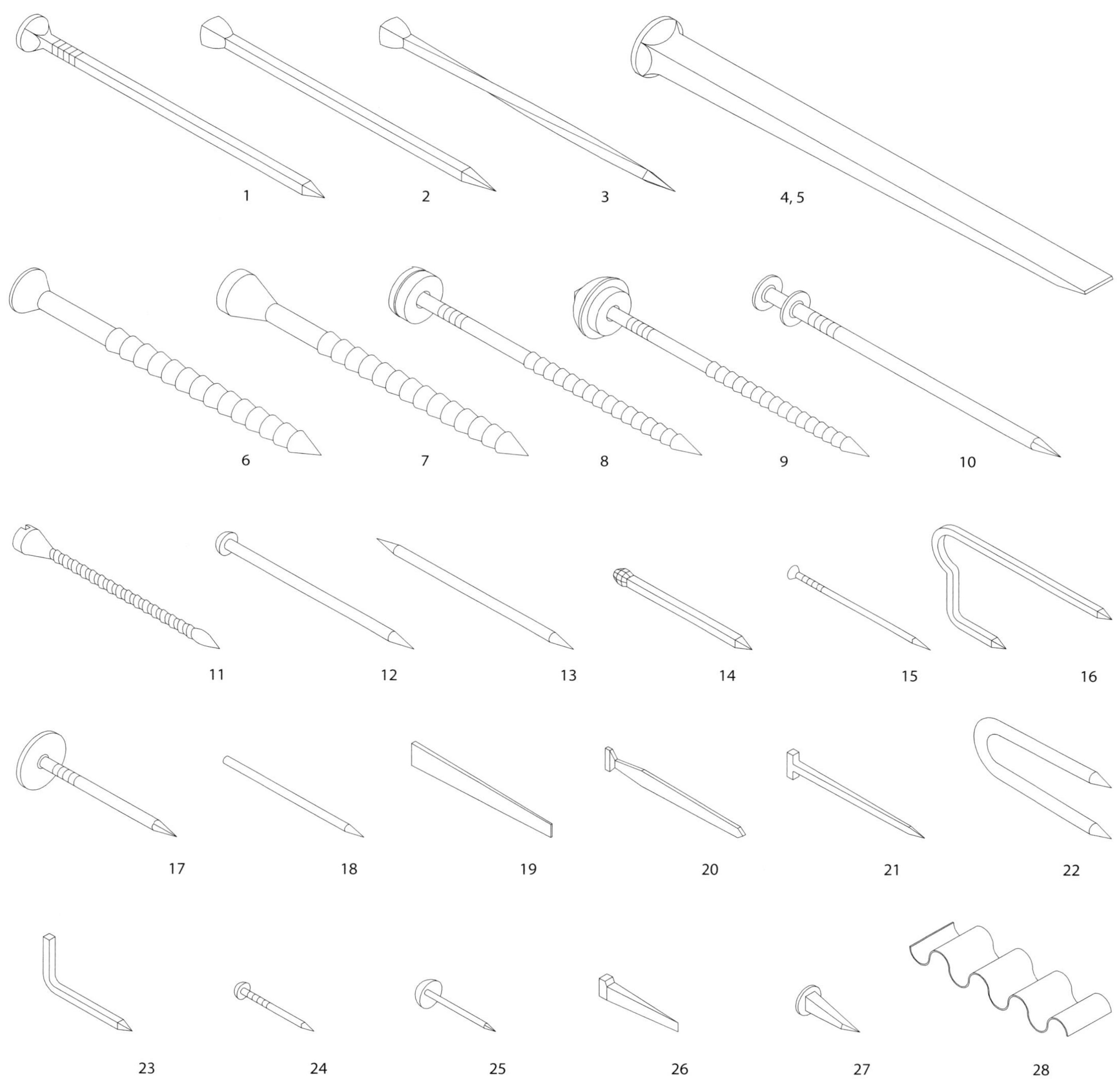
1
2
3
4, 5
6
7
8
9
10
11
12
13
14
15
16
17
18
19
20
21
22
23
24
25
26
27
28

36 SCREWS AND BOLTS

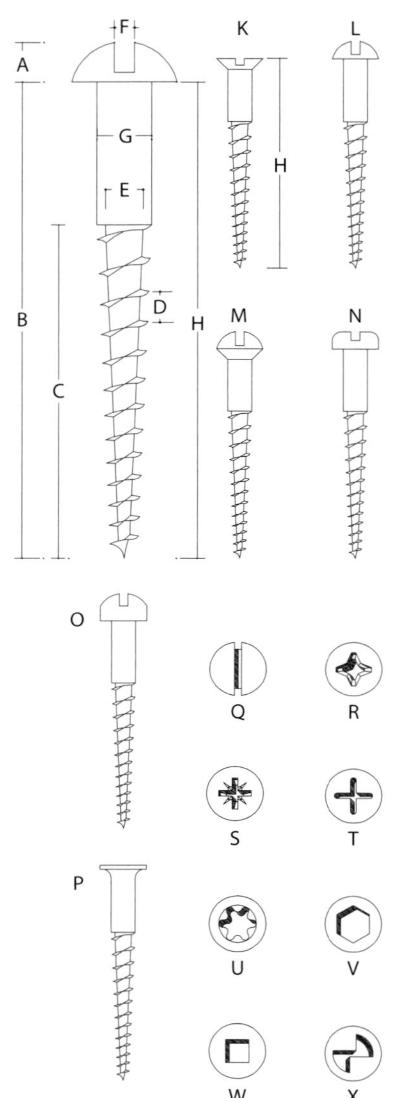

PARTS OF A SCREW

- A screw head
- B shaft, shank
- C screw thread
- D pitch
- E stem
- F slot
- G width of screw
- H length of screw

SCREW HEADS

- K flat head, countersunk head
- L round head, dome head
- M oval head, raised countersunk head
- N panhead screw, cheesehead screw
- O fillister head screw
- P bugle head screw

SLOTS

- Q straight slot
- R cross slot, Phillips head
- S Pozidriv head
- T Supadriv slot
- U Torx head
- V Allen head
- W square slot, Robertson slot
- X one-way head, clutch head, butterfly head

screw
a pointed fastener with a helical threaded shank and head which has a shaped indentation allowing it to be fixed by turning with a screwdriver or similar tool

bolt
a flat-ended fastener with a helically threaded shank whose head has a hexagonal, octagonal or square projection allowing it to be tightened to a nut using a spanner

thread, screw thread
the helical moulded windings along the shaft of a screw or bolt, or internally in a nut or cap, which provide a mechanical fixing

metric thread
a standardized screw thread whose spacing is based on fractions of a metre; denser and at less of an angle than whitworth thread

Whitworth thread, BSW thread
a standardized range of screw threads whose dimensions are based on number of threads per inch

TYPES OF SCREW AND BOLT

1. countersunk head screw, countersunk screw
2. dome head screw, round head screw
3. oval head screw, raised countersunk head screw, oval countersunk screw
4. dowel screw
5. general purpose screw
6. roofing screw
7. roofing bolt
8. dowel screw/stud bolt
9. coach screw, lag bolt, lag screw
10. sheetmetal screw
11. drywall screw, plasterboard screw
12. concrete screw anchor, concrete screw, masonry screw
13. mirror screw
14. screw hook, hook screw
15. cup hook
16. screw eye with ring
17. square hook
18. square cup hook
19. screw eye, eye
20. hook and eye
21. machine screw
22. hexagonal bolt, hex-head bolt
23. countersunk head bolt
24. threaded rod, studding, threaded bar, set screw
25. thumb screw
26. neck, shank
27. coach bolt, carriage bolt
28. machine bolt
29. anchor bolt, foundation bolt, ragbolt

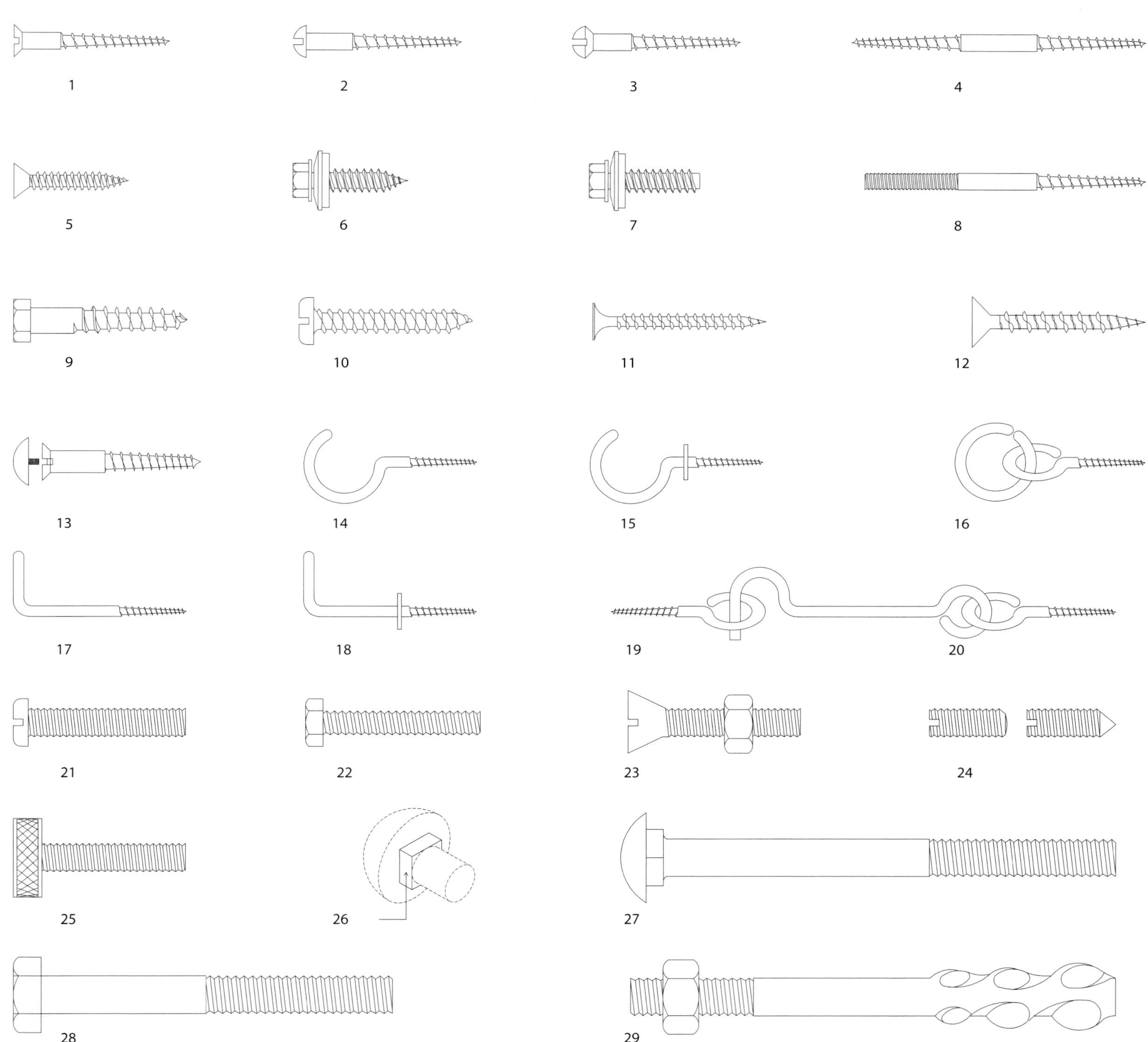
1
2
3
4
5
6
7
8
9
10
11
12
13
14
15
16
17
18
19
20
21
22
23
24
25
26
27
28
29

37 FIXINGS AND WASHERS

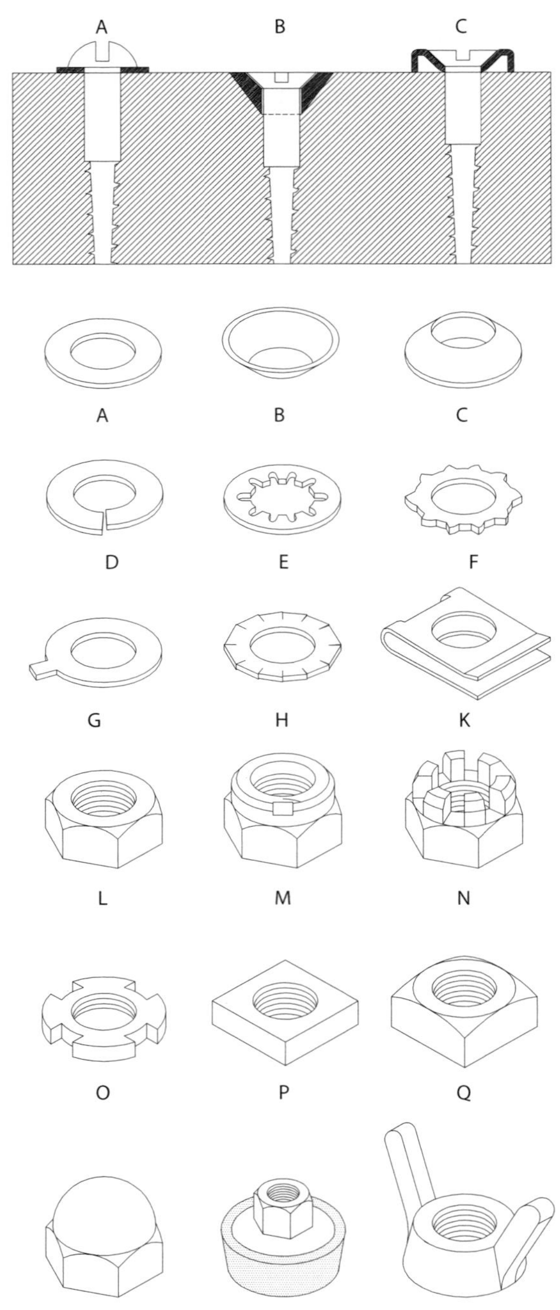

WASHERS

- A plain washer, flat washer, penny washer
- B recessed screw cup, countersunk washer, inset screw cup
- C screw cup, finish washer
- D spring lock washer, split-ring washer, compressive washer
- E internal tooth washer, toothed washer
- F external tooth washer, toothed washer
- G lock washer, lock ring
- H spike plate

NUTS

- K plate nut
- L hexagonal nut, hex nut
- M lock nut
- N castellated nut, castle nut
- O round nut, disc nut
- P flat square nut
- Q square nut
- R cap nut, acorn nut, dome nut
- S seal nut
- T wing nut, thumb nut, butterfly nut

FIXINGS

1. wall plug
2. wedge anchor, sleeve bolt, expansion bolt
3. legs anchor, hollow-wall plug
4. toggle bolt, gravity toggle
5. hollow-wall plug, molly, toggle
6. toggle bolt, spring toggle, butterfly toggle
7. hollow-wall anchor, molly, toggle
8. turnbuckle
9. shackle, clevis
10. wire rope clamp, cable clamp, wire rope clip
11. cable thimble, wire rope thimble

fixing, fastener
any hardware such as nails, screws, bolts etc. used to attach components in place or connect them together

nut
a hexagonal, octagonal or square fastener with a threaded hole to receive a bolt

toggle bolt
a metal threaded fastener for fixing to drywall or hollow wall surfaces by means of a pivoted or sprung 'job' which is clamped against the reverse side of construction once the bolt has been pushed through a bored hole

washer
a perforated plate beneath a bolt-head or nut which acts as a spacer in a bolt fixing and transfers the pressure of the fixing over a wider area

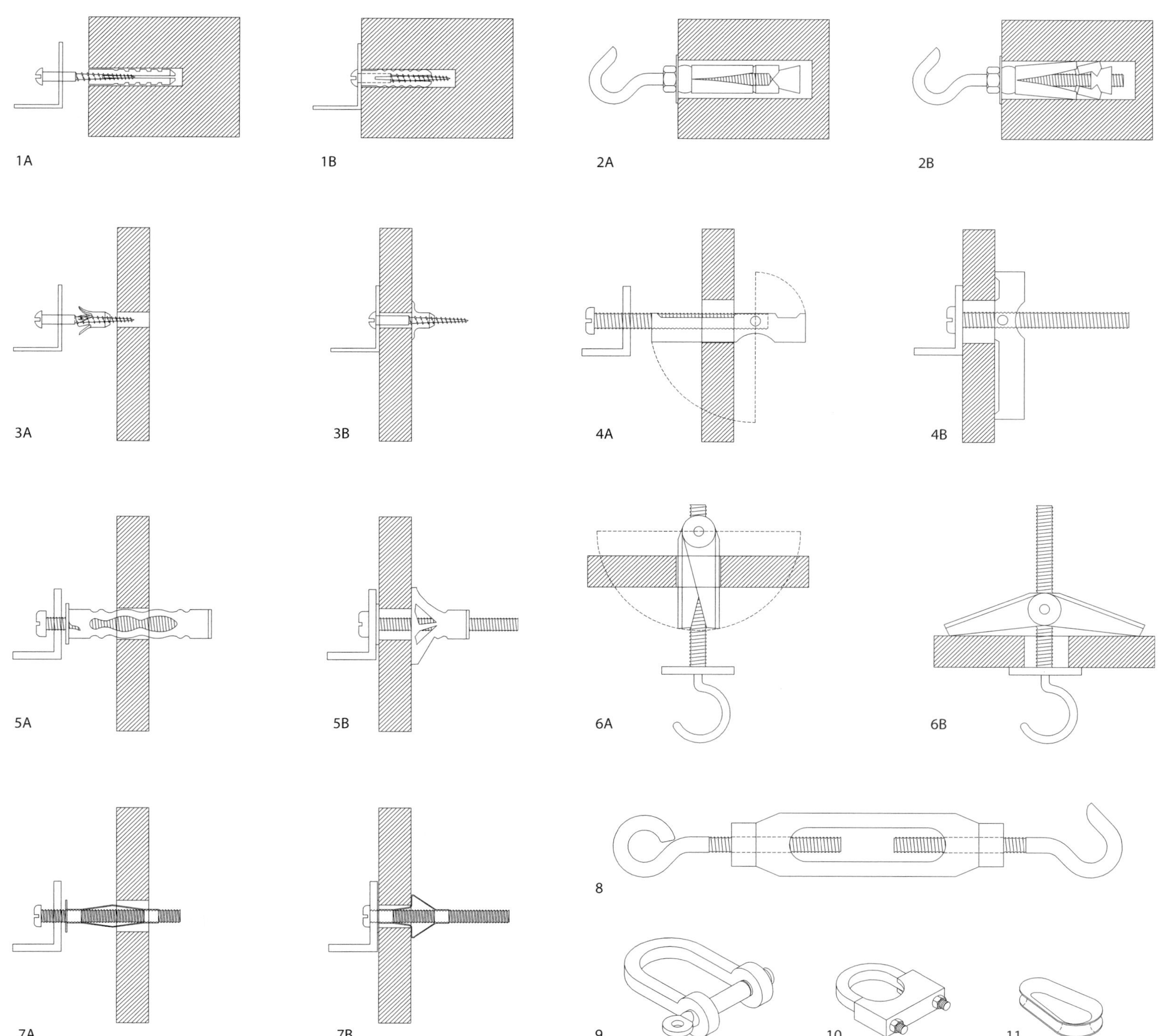
1A
1B
2A
2B
3A
3B
4A
4B
5A
5B
6A
6B
7A
7B
8
9
10
11

38 HINGES

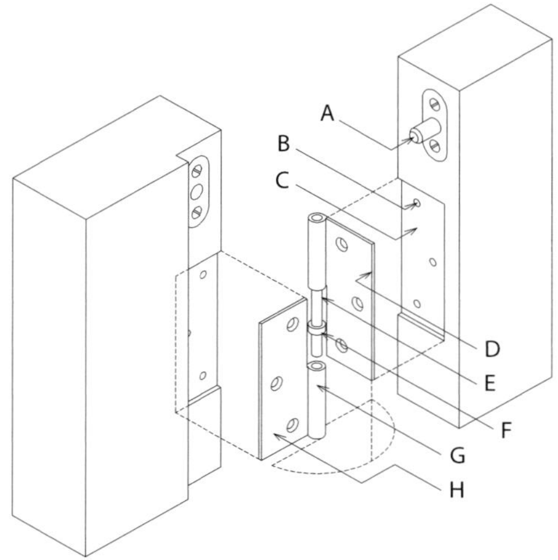

PARTS OF A HINGE

A hinge bolt, security bolt, dog bolt
B screw-hole
C hinge mortise, hinge rebate
D hinge leaf, pin leaf
E pin, hinge pin, pintle
F ball-bearing
G knuckle
H hinge leaf, loose leaf

1 butt hinge, fast-pin hinge, tight-pin hinge
2 lift-off hinge, loose-butt hinge
3 ball-bearing butt hinge
4 ball-bearing butt hinge, ball-bearing hinge
5 pin hinge, loose-pin hinge
6 non-mortise hinge, surface-fixed hinge
7 falling-butt hinge
8 rising hinge, gravity-door hinge
9 cranked hinge, easy-clean hinge, cleaning hinge
10 cylinder hinge, barrel hinge
11 cabinet hinge, furnishing hinge
12 table hinge, rule-joint hinge
13 butterfly hinge
14 parliament hinge, H-hinge, shutter hinge
15 strap hinge, flap hinge
16 A-hinge
17 screw hook-and-eye hinge
18 band and hook hinge, hook and band hinge
19 T-hinge, tee hinge, surface-fixed hinge
20 weld-on hinge
21 piano hinge, continuous hinge
22 loose pin

hinge
a pivoting mechanism to provide a fixing and rotating action to framed door leaves, window casements etc.

butt hinge
a hinge with two rectangular metal leaves and a central joining pin, usually inset into the edge of a door leaf and its frame

handing
a term describing which direction a hinged door or window opens and the side on which it is hinged, affecting its hardware specification, denoted as right-handed or left-handed; there is no universal rule about which is which, and definition of handing varies from country to country; according to the Scandinavian classification, a left-hand door which opens outwards has its hinges on the left, and so on; in Britain and North America this is most often called a right-hand door, but not always

1
2
3
4
5
22
6
7
8
9
10
11
12
13
14
15
16
17
18
19
20
21

 39 LOCKS

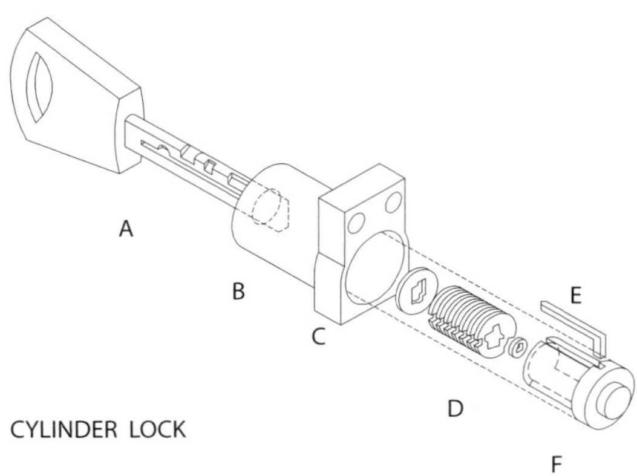

CYLINDER LOCK

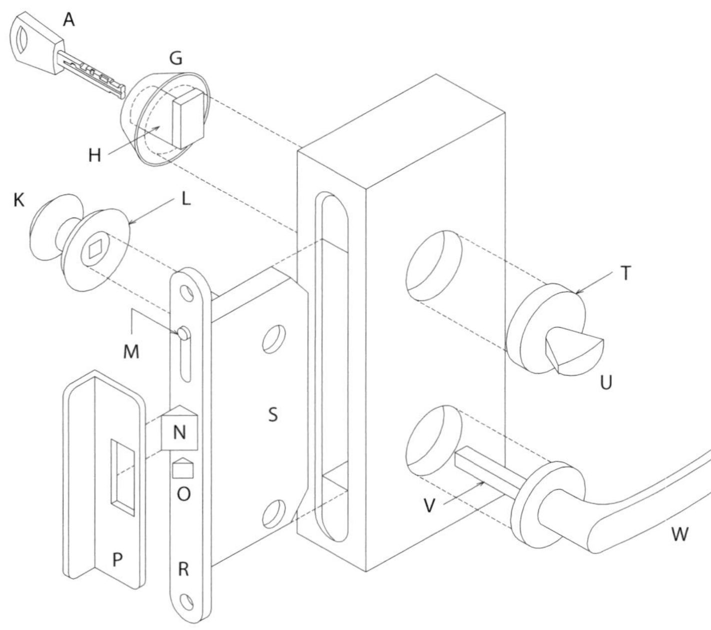

LATCH, LATCHSET

PARTS OF A LOCK

A key
B cylinder body
C cam
D tumblers
E lever tumbler
F cylinder plug

LOCK CYLINDER

G cylinder guard
H cylinder
K door knob
L rose
M locking snib, thumb slide
N lock bolt, draw bolt
O guardbolt, trigger bolt
P striking plate, keeper, striker
R forend, faceplate, lock front
S lock case
T escutcheon, scutcheon
U thumb turn
V spindle
W door handle, lever handle

TYPES OF LOCK

1a deadlock
1b surface lock, recessed lock
2 rim lock
3 mortise lock
4 padlock
5 padlock eye
6 padlock
7 shackle, bail
8 box strike
9 rim lock
10 cabinet lock, furniture lock
11 key plate, escutcheon
12 bathroom lock, indicator lock
13 cabinet lock, furniture lock
14 catch
15 barrel, foot or slide bolt
16 return latch, spring latch, latch bolt, catch bolt, tongue
17 dead bolt
18 hook bolt
19 claw bolt
20 anti-friction latchbolt
21 roller catch
22 ball catch, bullet catch
23 guardbolt, trigger bolt

lock
a fastening mechanism for a door or gate, operated using an external mechanical or electronic device such as a key, push button or digital pad

latch
any lock-like fastening mechanism for a door or gate, in which a handle rather than a key is pushed or turned to disengage a bolt

latchset
a set of door fittings comprising a latch, two door handles, two roses, two cover plates and a spindle

key
a small portable implement by which a lock can be operated

bolt, draw bolt, lock bolt
that part of a latch or lock which engages with a striking plate in the frame to hold the door in a closed position

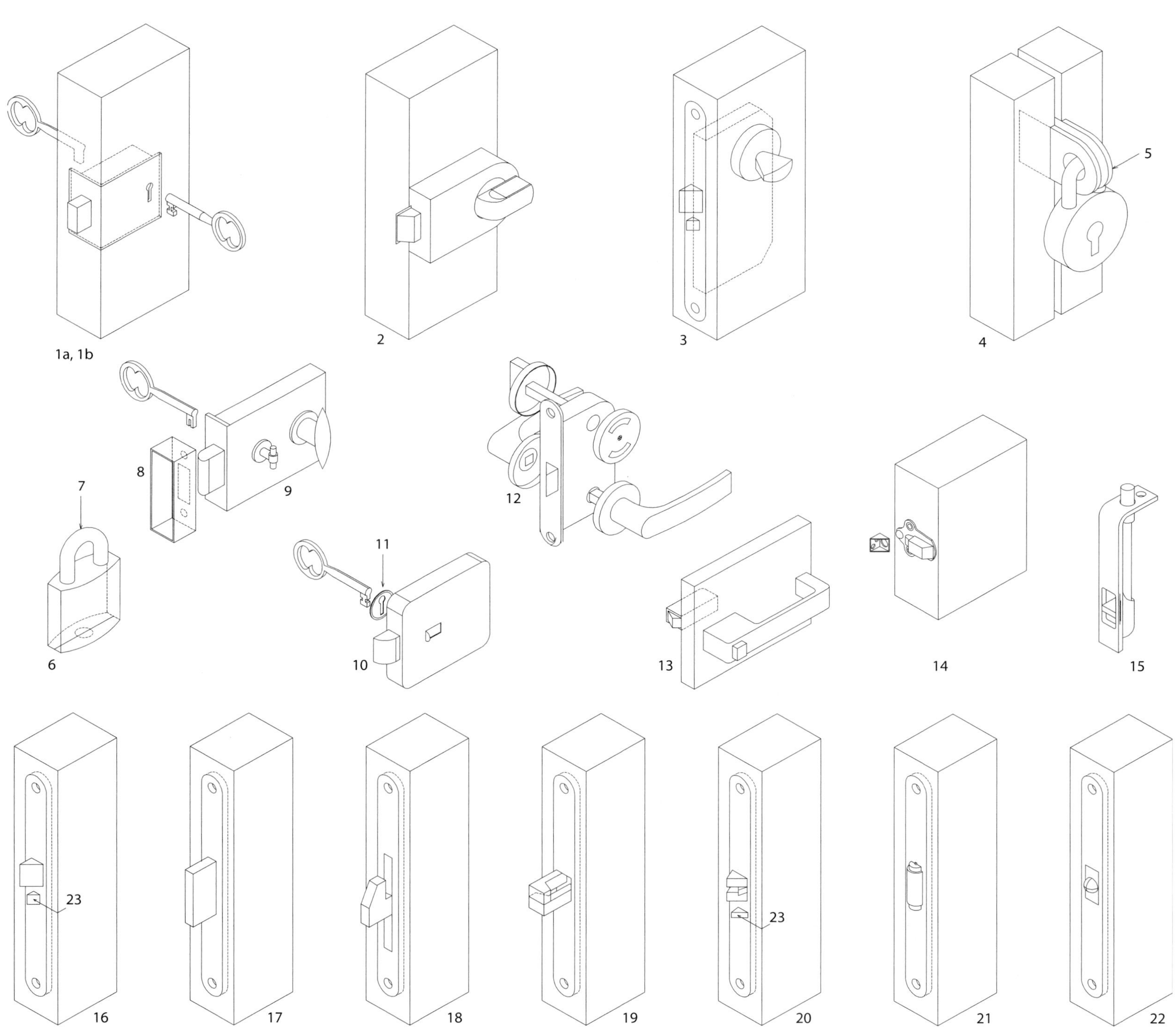
1a, 1b
2
3
4
5
6
7
8
9
10
11
12
13
14
15
16
17
18
19
20
21
22
23
23

40 HAMMERS AND MALLETS

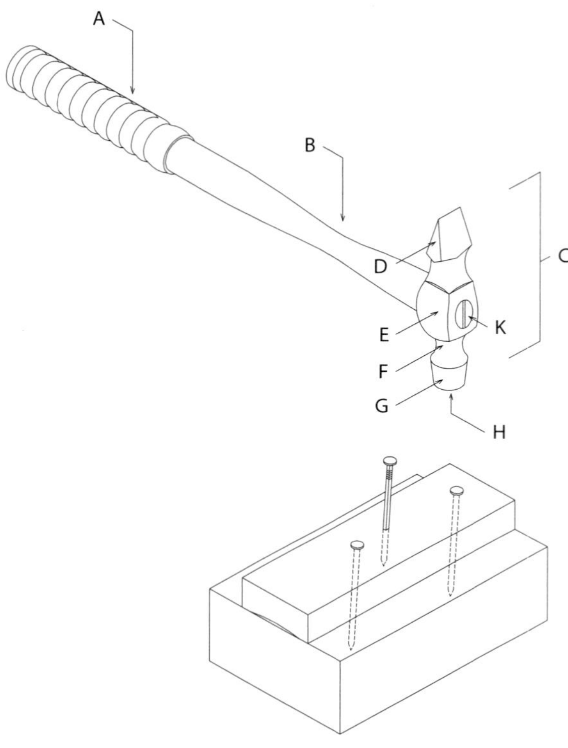

PARTS OF A HAMMER

- A grip, handle
- B handle, shaft
- C hammerhead, head
- D peen, pein, pane
- E cheek
- F neck
- G bell
- H striking face, face
- K eye

hammer
a hand tool with a shaft and heavy metal head for striking, breaking or driving nails

axe
a hand tool with a handle and sharpened steel head for felling trees, shaping and chopping wood and stone etc.

mallet
a hammer with a wooden, rubber or plastic head, used for striking wooden or soft objects such as chisels, pegs etc.

maul, mall
a heavy hammer such as a sledgehammer or club hammer, used for crushing and driving

pick
an axe whose head is sharply pointed at both ends, used for hacking stone and masonry, in demolition and excavation work

sledgehammer, sledge
a heavy two-handed hammer with a long shaft and heavy iron or steel head, used for crushing, breaking and driving

BELL FACE HAMMERS

1 claw hammer, nail hammer
2 framing hammer
3 ball peen hammer
4 peen hammer, cross peen hammer, Warringon hammer
5 straight peen hammer
6 joiner's hammer
7 bricklayer's hammer, brick axe, brick hammer, scutch hammer
8 upholsterer's hammer, tack hammer
9 saddler's hammer
10 glazier's hammer
11 veneer hammer, veneering hammer
12 double-clawed hammer
13 soft face hammer, replaceable tip hammer, replaceable face hammer
14 rubber mallet
15 dummy
16 carpenter's mallet, wooden mallet

BUSHING TOOLS

17 patent hammer, patent axe, toothed axe
18 bush hammer
19 bush hammer, bouchard, boucharde
20 mason's axe, stoneaxe, stonemason's axe, masonry axe
21 scabbling hammer, napping hammer

MAULS AND SLEDGES

22 drilling hammer, hand hammer, maul
23 pitching hammer, striking hammer
24 machinist's, blacksmith's, forge or engineer's hammer
25 peen sledge, engineer's sledge
26 splitting hammer, spalling hammer
27 scabbling hammer, trimming hammer, mason's hammer
28 scaling hammer, rock pick
29 pick hammer, scutch
30 club hammer, mash hammer, lump hammer, maul
31 double-faced sledgehammer
32 pick, pickaxe

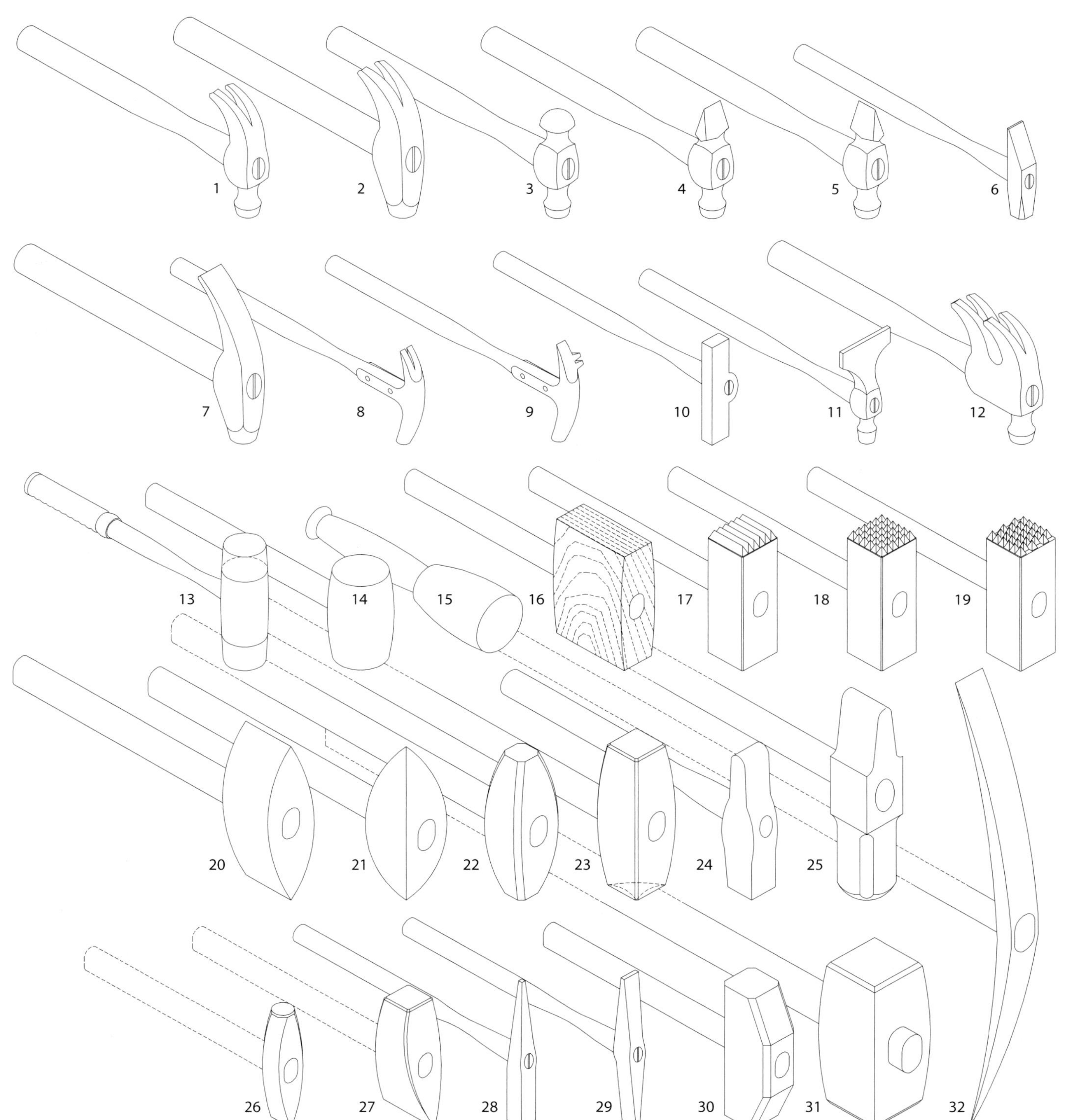
1
2
3
4
5
6
7
8
9
10
11
12
13
14
15
16
17
18
19
20
21
22
23
24
25
26
27
28
29
30
31
32

41 CHISELS AND SCRAPERS

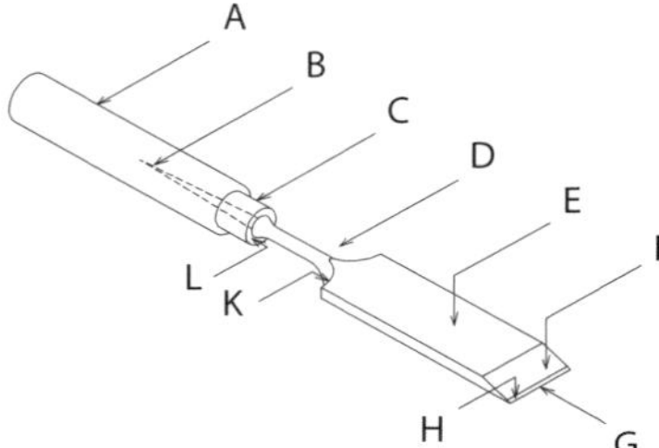

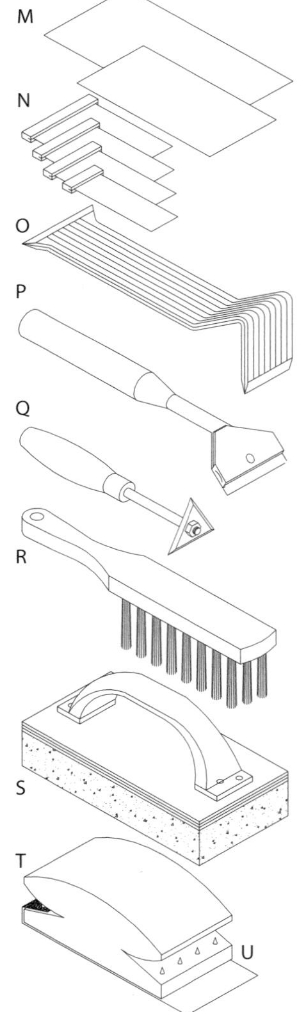

PARTS OF A CHISEL

- A handle
- B tang
- C ferrule
- D neck
- E blade
- F grinding bevel, ground bevel, cannel
- G cutting edge
- H honing bevel
- K shoulder
- L bolster

SCRAPERS

- M scraper, devil, dumb scraper
- N Japan scraper
- O scraper, paint scraper, scraping iron
- P window scraper, edge paint scraper, replaceable blade scraper
- Q corner scraper, angle plane, French plane, shave hook

HONING IMPLEMENTS

- R wire brush
- S grindstone, rubstone
- T sanding block
- U sandpaper, emery paper, glasspaper

chisel
a hand tool whose metal blade is sharpened at one end, used for cutting and shaping timber and stone

scraper
a piece of sharpened steel plate or bladed hand tool, used for smoothing and scraping the surface of wood and other materials as a finish or to remove old paint, dirt and coatings from surfaces prior to refinishing

sanding
the producing of an even, unpitted, smooth surface finish in timber, stone etc. using an abrasive

honing
the sharpening of the tip of a metal blade of a hand tool or the production of a matt surface on stonework using a fine grindstone or hone

WOODWORKING CHISELS

1 firmer chisel, bench chisel
2 butt chisel, sash chisel, pocket chisel
3 bevelled-edge chisel, bevel edge chisel
4 paring chisel
5 mortise chisel, heading chisel, mortising chisel

WOODCARVING CHISELS

6 gouge
7 bruzz chisel, corner chisel, dogleg chisel, parting chisel
8 swan-neck chisel, mortise-lock chisel
9 spoon gouge, front bent gouge

TURNING CHISELS

10 turning gouge
11 scraping tool, scraper
12 skew chisel, long-cornered chisel
13 parting tool, parting chisel
14 screwdriver
15 offset screwdriver

STONE CHISELS, COLD CHISELS, HAMMER-HEADED CHISELS

16 fillet chisel, spindle, quirking tool
17 waster, driver
18 fishtail chisel, fantail tool
19 point, punch, jumper
20 punch
21 pitcher, pitching tool

MALLET-HEADED CHISELS

22 bolster
23 boaster, batting tool, broad tool
24 claw tool, tooth tool, waster

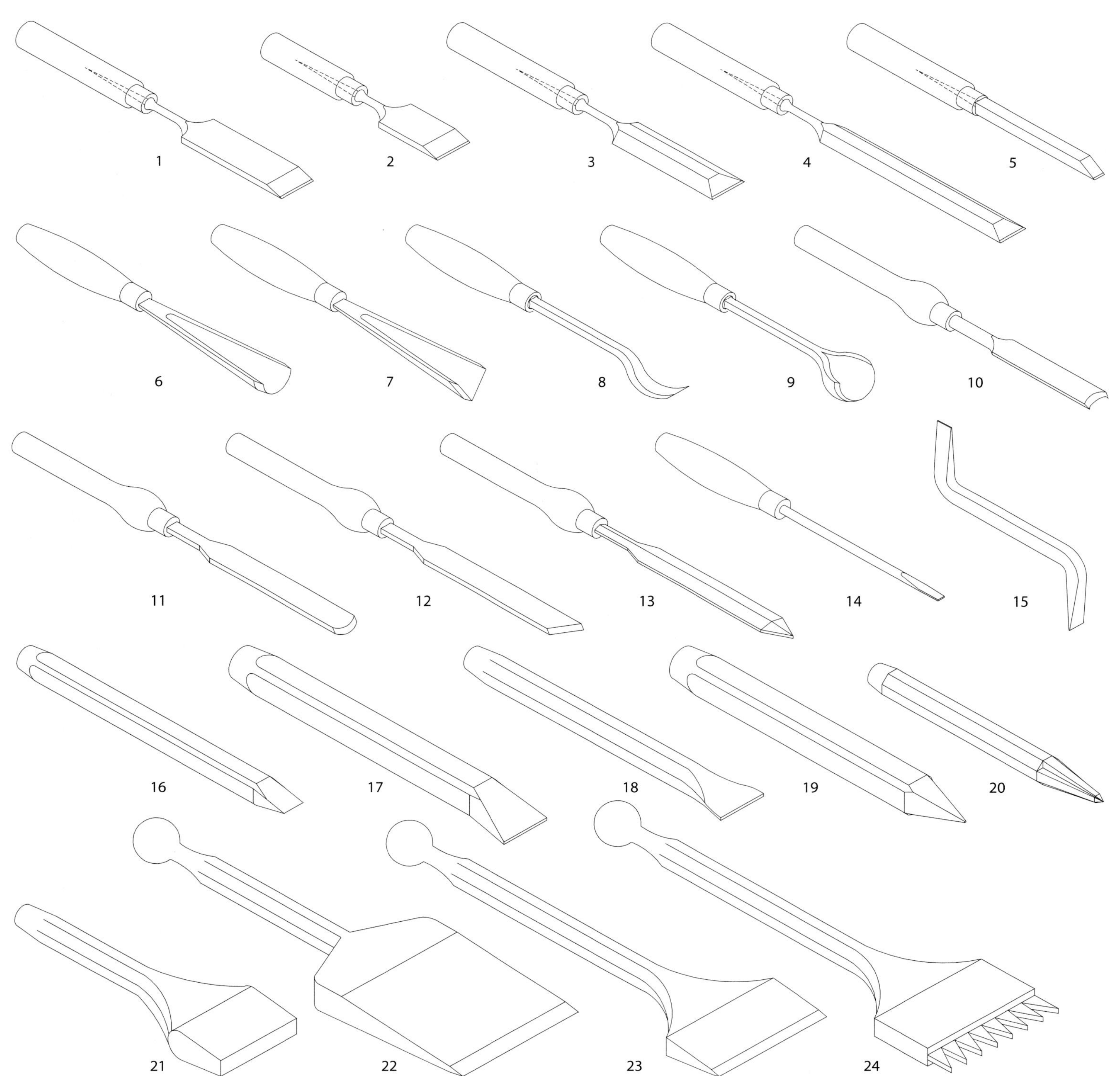
1
2
3
4
5
6
7
8
9
10
11
12
13
14
15
16
17
18
19
20
21
22
23
24

42 DRILL BITS AND GRINDING WHEELS

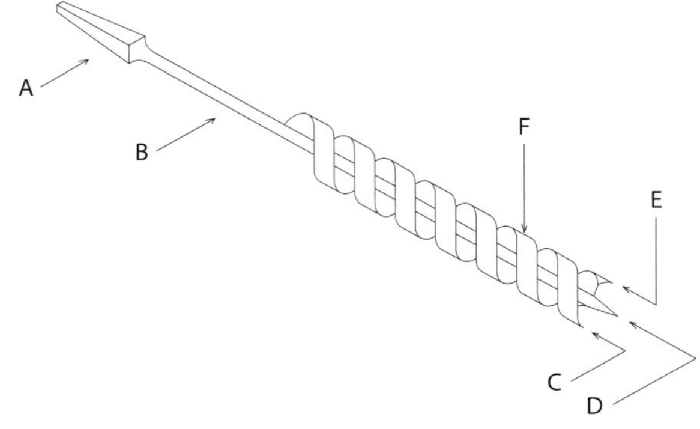

ANATOMY OF A DRILL BIT – AUGER BIT

A tang
B shaft
C spur, spur cutter
D point, screw point, feed screw
E router
F twist

drill
1 a tool or machine for drilling or boring a hole
2 a drill bit

brace
a hand tool with a crank and handle for boring holes; a large manual drill with a kinked shaft

breast drill
a drill with an attachment which is pressed against the chest to provide additional force in drilling

drill bit
a sharpened metal blade for boring holes, often helically shaped, attached to and rotated by the chuck of a brace or drill

hammer drill
a drill for boring a hole in masonry and concrete with a drill bit which oscillates back and forth with a chattering action

power drill, electric drill
a hand-held machine tool for boring holes, with a drill bit held in an adjustable jaw mechanism called a chuck

WOOD DRILLS

1 centre bit
2 auger bit, Jennings pattern bit
3 brad point drill, dowel bit, wood drill
4 flat spade drill
5 combination drill bit
6 expansive bit, expansion bit
7 Forstner bit
8 countersink
9 dowel sharpener, dowel pointer
10 hole saw, annular bit, crown saw, hole cutter, tubular saw
11 plug cutter

OTHER DRILL BITS

12 twist drill, metal drill
13 masonry drill, masonry bit, concrete drill
14 glass drill, glass bit
15 screwdriver bit
16 gimlet, twist gimlet, wimble
17 centre punch
18 bradawl, awl – sharp and flat

REAMERS

19 straight reamer
20 tapered reamer
21 grinding burrs

WHEELS, DISCS

22 cut-off wheel
23 depressed wheel
24 straight (grinding) wheel
25 tapered grinding wheel
26 straight grinding cup
27 flaring grinding cup

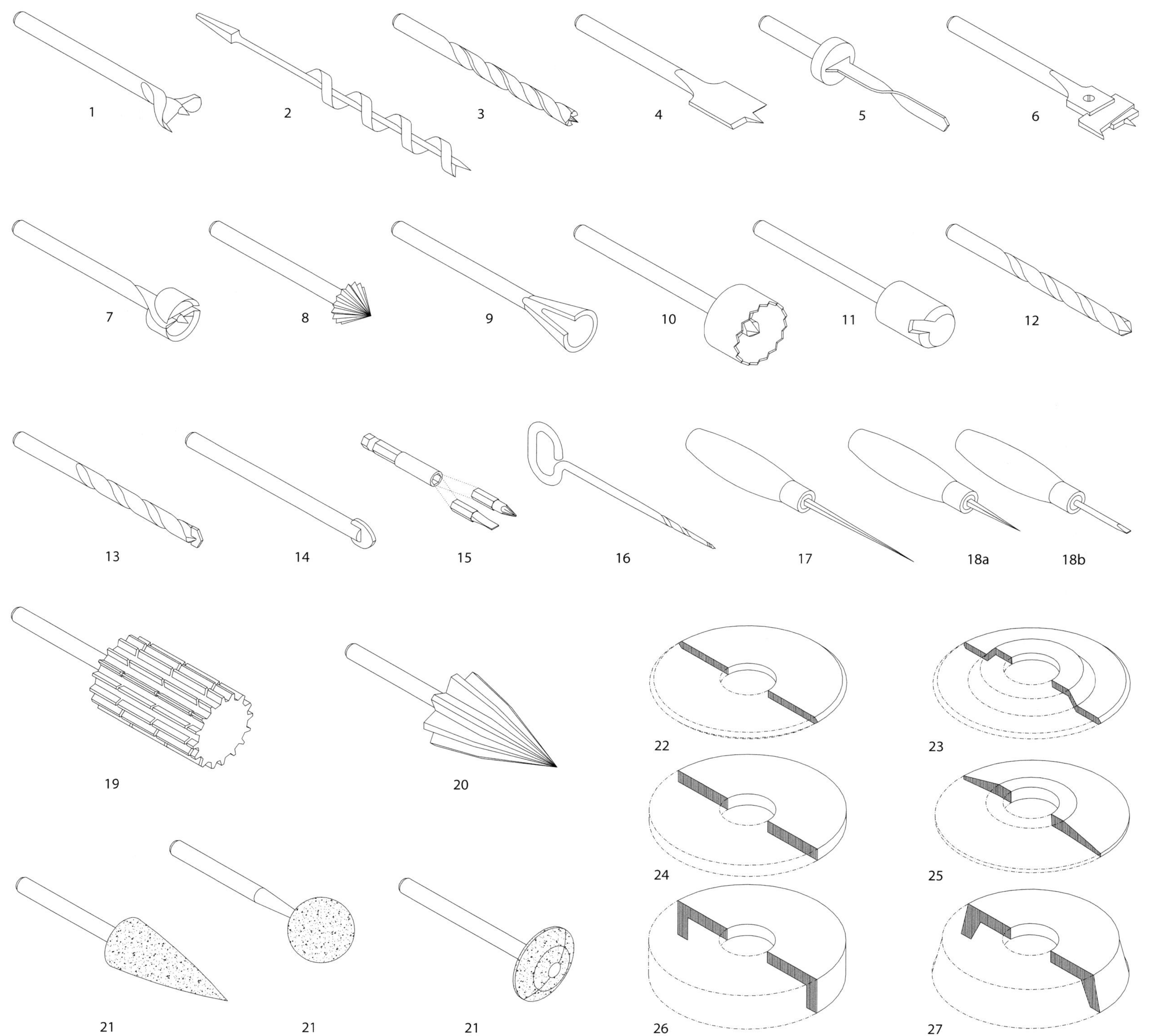
1
2
3
4
5
6
7
8
9
10
11
12
13
14
15
16
17
18a
18b
19
20
21
21
21
22
23
24
25
26
27

43 PAINTING AND PLASTERING IMPLEMENTS

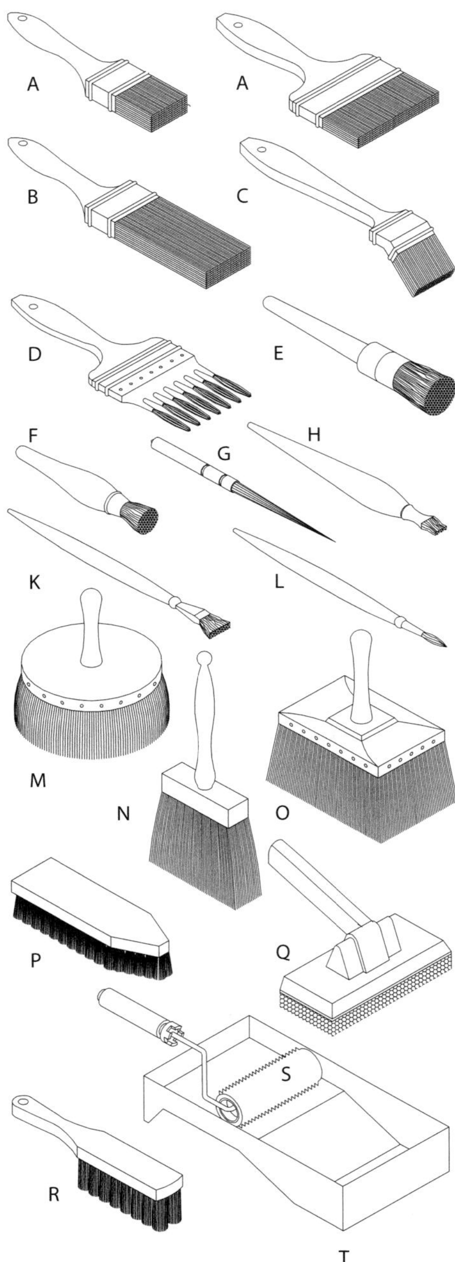

PAINTBRUSHES

A flat brush, flat varnish brush
B flogger, dragger
C radiator brush
D overgrainer, grainer
E round brush
F dabber, stencil brush
G rigger brush
H lining tool, liner
K lettering brush, fitch
L script brush
M liming or whitewashing brush
N softener, blender
O distemper brush
P scrubbing brush
Q paint pad
R dusting brush
S paint roller
T roller tray, paint tray

MASONRY AND PLASTERING IMPLEMENTS

1 plasterer's trowel, laying-on trowel
2 bricklayer's trowel, brick trowel, mason's trowel, masonry trowel
3 finishing trowel, smoothing trowel
4 notched trowel
5 margin trowel
6 gauging trowel
7 jointer, jointing trowel, jointing tool
8 internal angle trowel, inside corner trowel, twitcher trowel, angle trowel
9 external angle trowel, outside corner trowel
10 spatula, putty knife, spackling knife, stopping knife
11 drag, comb, spreader
12 wood float, floater, plasterer's float, plastering float
13 nail float, devil float
14 rubber spreader
15 sponge float
16 plumb line
17 squeegee
18 hawk, mortar board
19 sponge
20 darby, derby, Darby float

paint

a liquid substance used for providing a protective or decorative surface coating, consisting of a pigment and a binder which sets or is treated to form a resistant film

paintbrush

a hand-held implement used for applying paint, consisting of fibres, bristles or hairs bound to a wooden or plastic handle, available in a range of widths, shapes and sizes

plaster

1 a mixture of a hydraulic binder such as lime, gypsum or Portland cement with water and sand, used as a surface treatment for walls; the term plaster is usually used nowadays in reference to interior work, when used outside it is called render
2 gypsum plaster: a mixture of calcined gypsum (sulphate of lime) and water used for finishing interior walls and ceilings and moulding into ornaments

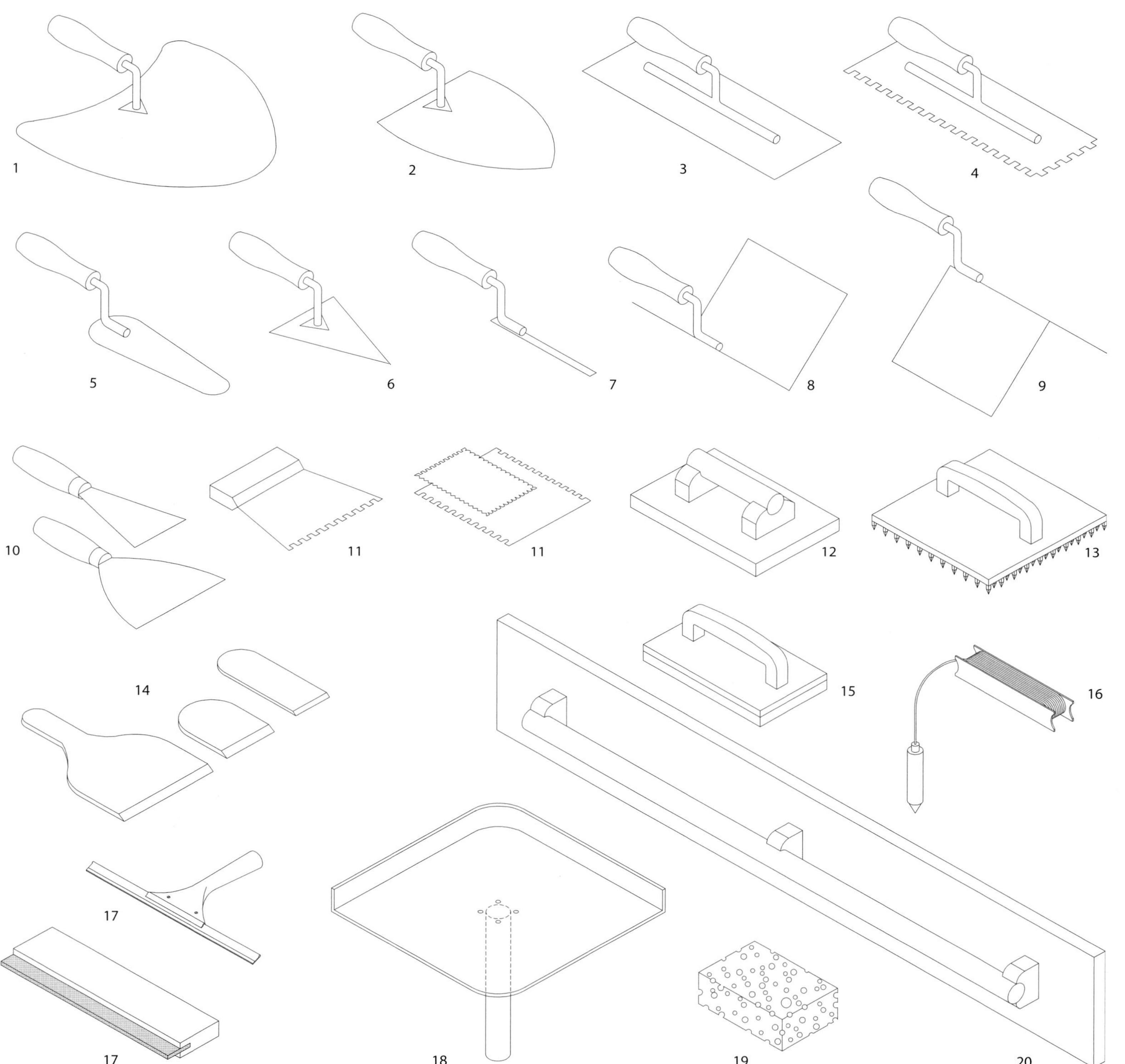
1
2
3
4
5
6
7
8
9
10
11
11
12
13
14
15
16
17
17
18
19
20

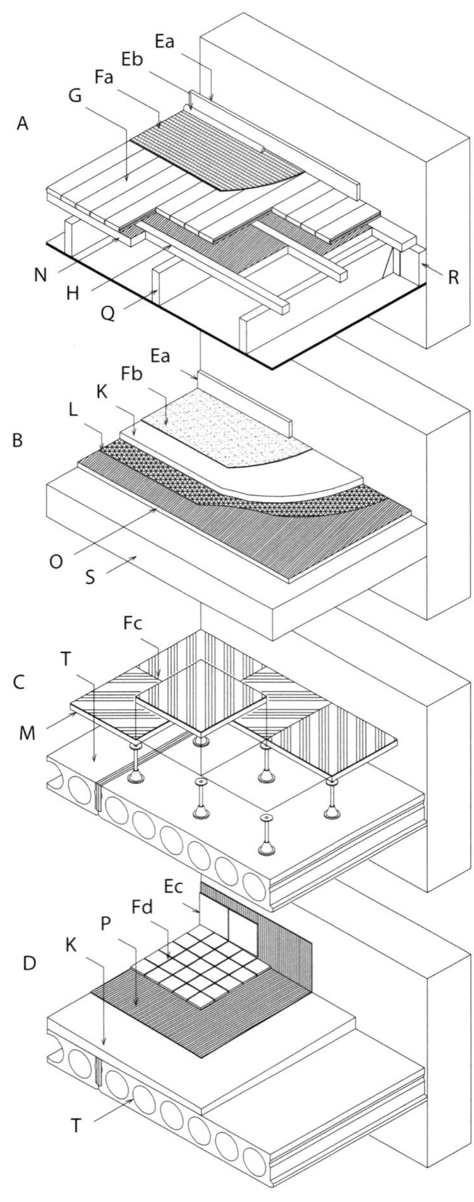

DRY AREA

A timber floor

B solid floor slab – floating floor, floating screed

C access floor, cavity floor, raised floor, platform floor, palette floor

WET AREA

D waterproofed hollow core slab

FLOOR STRIPS, SKIRTINGS

Ea skirting board, baseboard, mopboard, scrubboard, washboard

Eb flooring bead, carpet strip

Ec wall tile

FLOOR COVERINGS

Fa cork carpet, cork matting, linoleum flooring, lino

Fb wall-to-wall carpet, fitted carpet – felt carpet, felt matting

Fc plastics tile, quartz vinyl tile

Fd floor tiling – ceramic tile

FLOORING SUB-BASE, SUBFLOOR

G timber subfloor – rough t&g boarding

H battening

K cement screed, screeding

L placing filter – filter fabric

M building board

INSULATING MATERIALS

N mineral wool – soundproofing

O expanded polystyrene, EPS – sound absorption

P waterproofing membrane, wpm

STRUCTURAL FLOOR, FLOOR BASE

Q floor joists

R wall plate

S solid concrete slab, in-situ floor

T hollow-core slab

SOLID TIMBER FLOORING

1 plank flooring

2 t&g strip flooring

3 end-grain woodblock flooring

4 block flooring, wood strip, solid parquet – chequered pattern

5 parquet block flooring – basketweave pattern

6 mosaic parquet, wood mosaic – herringbone pattern

7 wood tile flooring, parquet tile, floor square

VENEERED PARQUETS, MULTILAYER PARQUETS

8 veneered strip parquet

9 parquet tile composite flooring, laminated floor square

TILED FLOORING

10 stone tile or cement tile

11 clinker tile, vitreous tile

12 mosaic tile

13 terrazzo screed

POLYMER FLOORING

14 vinyl sheet flooring, vinyl sheet

15 studded rubber flooring, raised or coin-pattern flooring

floor
the horizontal lower surface of a room or interior space and its supporting construction; see also flooring, floor covering, floor construction

flooring
any material used for surfacing a floor or providing a floor finish

floor covering
thin sheet material such as linoleum, carpet or plastics matting used for providing a finish to a floor

subfloor
those layers of floor construction above a structural floor, which provide a base for the flooring material

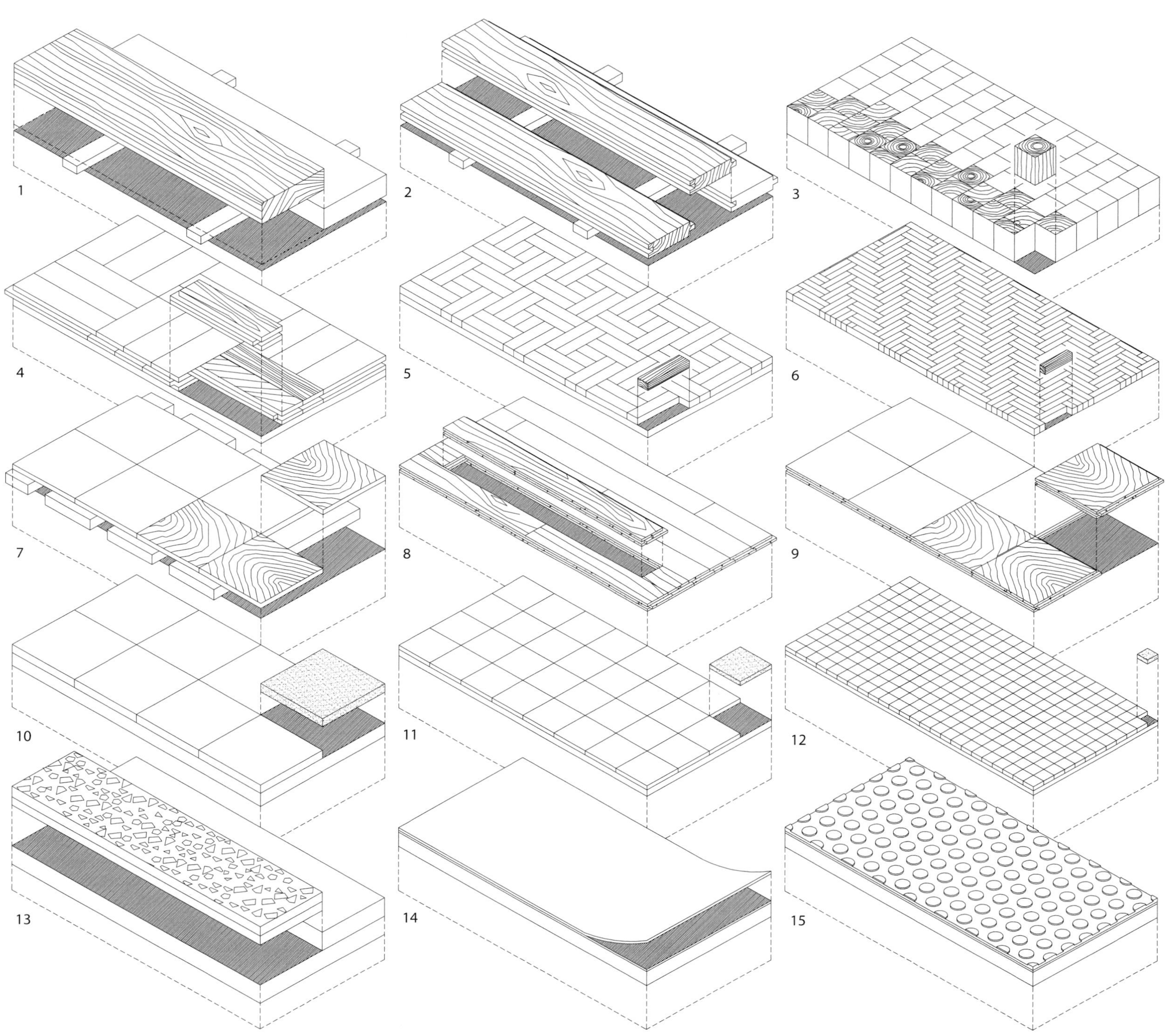
1
2
3
4
5
6
7
8
9
10
11
12
13
14
15

45 STAIR

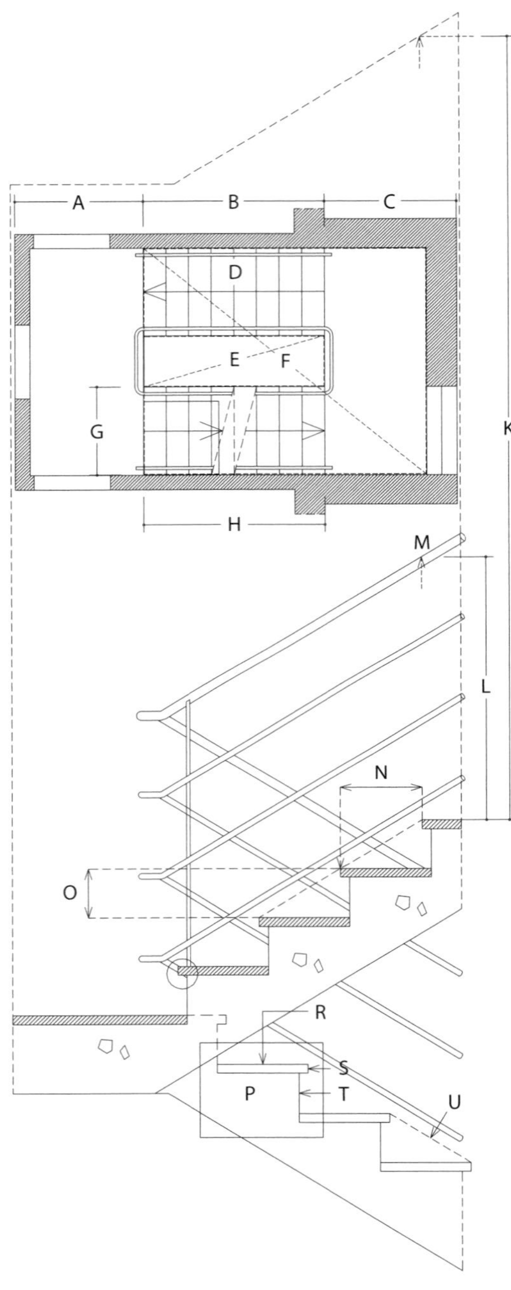

STAIR ENCLOSURE, STAIRWAY, STAIRCASE

A storey landing
B stair flight
C intermediate landing, stair landing, half-landing
D walking line
E stairwell
F stair shaft
G stair width, stair clear width
H run, total going
K stair clearance, stair headroom
L balustrade height
M stair balustrade, stair rail
N going, run
O rise
P step
R stair tread
S nosing
T stair riser
U line of nosings, nose line, pitch line

stair, stairs, staircase, stairway
a means of vertical circulation consisting of a number of steps from one level to another; although usually called 'stairs' in the colloquial, 'stair' may be used in preference, to denote a single unit of vertical circulation

escape stair, fire escape, fire stair, emergency stair
a protected or outdoor stair which is part of an escape route for use in the event of a fire or other emergency in a building

step
a shallow platform or construction designed to negotiate a pedestrian change in level by means of a short horizontal surface connected to a vertical riser, either on its own or as part of a stair

tread
the horizontal upper surface of a step, or the shallow platform which forms a step

1 straight stair
2 straight-run stair
3 solid concrete stair
4 closed riser stair
5 open riser stair, ladder stair, skeleton stair
6 cantilevered stair, flying stair
7 double cantilevered stair
8 simply-supported stair
9 prefabricated stair
10 straight-run stair

TURNING STAIRS, WINDING STAIRS

11 quarter turn stair, L-stair, angle stair, quarterpace stair, quarter space stair
12 halfpace stair, half-space stair, dogleg stair, dog-legged stair, return stair
13 double return stair
14 half turn stair, three-flight stair
15 three-quarter turn stair, four-flight stair
16 one-turn stair, full-turn stair

CIRCULAR STAIRS

17 curving stair
18 semicircular stair, semi-spiral stair
19 full-turn spiral stair, helical stair, corkscrew stair
20 alternating tread stair
21 ramp stair
22 mono-carriage, spine beam
23 string, stringer
24 newel
25 dancing step, balanced step, French flier
26 tapered step, tapered tread
27 winder, wheel step, wheeling step, wheel tread
28 parallel tread, flier, flyer

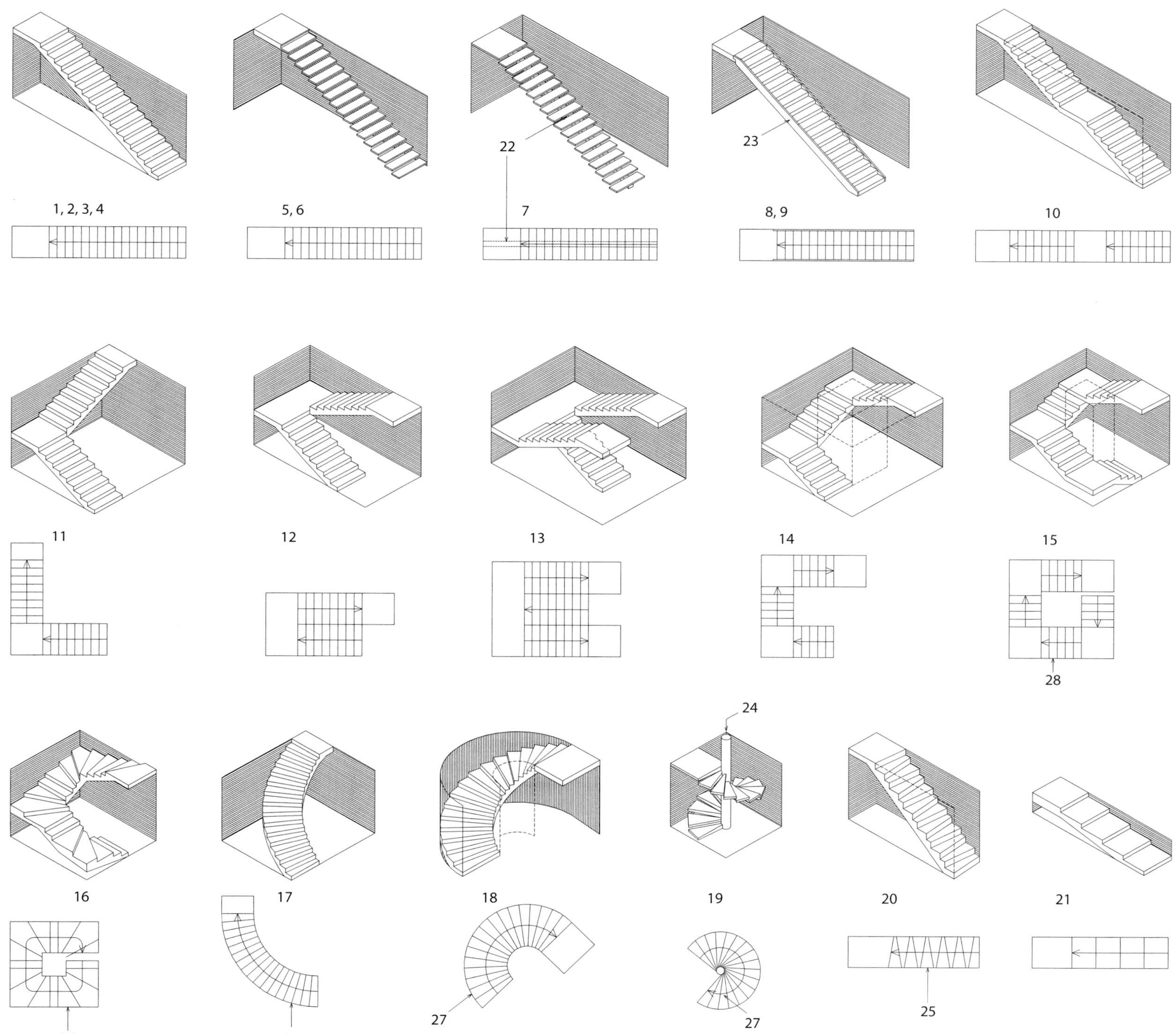
22
23
1, 2, 3, 4
5, 6
7
8, 9
10
11
12
13
14
15
28
24
16
17
18
19
20
21
25
26
27
27
25

46 PITCHED ROOFS

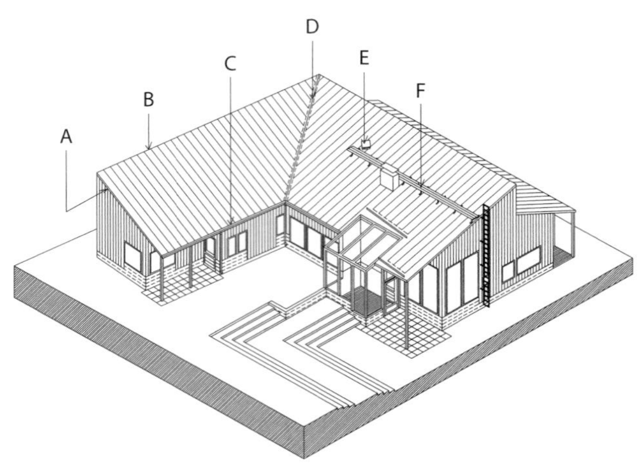

A verge
B ridge
C eaves
D valley, valley gutter, centre gutter
E roof hatch, access hatch
F walkway, catwalk, roofway
G snowguard
H eaves gutter, roof gutter, rainwater gutter
K gutter stop, gutter end, stop end
L gutter bearer, gutter bracket
M rainwater header, leader header, (Am.) hopper head
N downpipe, rainwater pipe
O soffit board, eaves soffit, soffit boarding
P soffit bearer
Q hip
R hip, hip end, hipped end
S gable

1 monopitch roof, penthouse roof, pent roof, shed roof
2 duopitch roof, pitched roof, saddleback roof, saddle roof
3 pavilion roof
4 hip roof, hipped roof
5 gable roof, gabled roof
6 gabled mansard roof; Am.: gambrel roof
7 jerkinhead roof; (Am.): hipped gable roof, half-hipped roof, clipped gable roof, shreadhead roof
8 hipped mansard roof
9 gambrel roof
10 knee roof
11 hipped knee roof
12 half hip and gable roof
13 L-roof, hip and valley roof
14 heel gable roof
15 crossform roof
16 monitor roof
17 split-level roof, clerestory roof (duopitch)
18 split-level roof, clerestory roof (monopitch)
19 catslide roof
20 skirt roof
21 catslide roof
22 butterfly roof, double lean-to roof, Y-form roof
23 M-roof, double gabled roof
24 sawtooth roof
25 lean-to roof, half span roof, pentise roof

roof
those parts of the top of a building which provide shelter against the elements

pitched roof
any sloping roof, usually one with a slope of more than 20°, or a roof form of two sloping roof planes meeting at a ridge, terminating at either end with either hips or gables

eaves
the junction of the roof and wall of a building

gable
the triangular upper portion of wall at the end of a double pitched roof

hip
1 hip end, hipped end; the sloping triangle of a roof plane at one or both ends of a hipped roof
2 piend; the sloping ridge formed by two pitched roofs which meet at an outside corner

ridge
the longitudinal apex where two sloping planes in a pitched roof meet; the straight line running along the highest point of a sloping roof

G
H
K
L
M
N
O
P

SECTION THROUGH EAVES

A–E) Risku House, Pello, Finland 1986, Erkki Jokiniemi

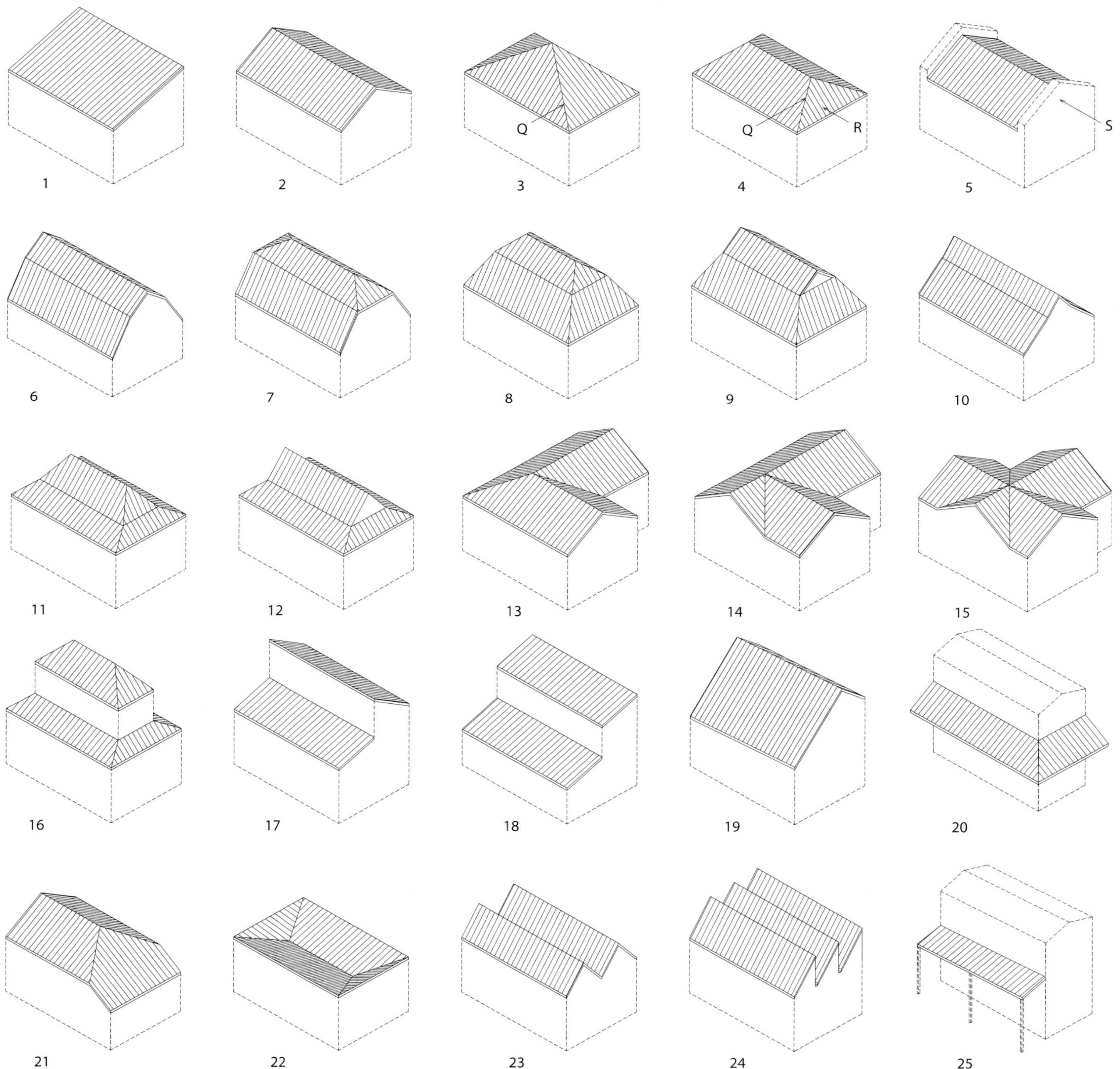

1
2
Q
3
Q
R
4
S
5
6
7
8
9
10
11
12
13
14
15
16
17
18
19
20
21
22
23
24
25

47 TILED ROOFING

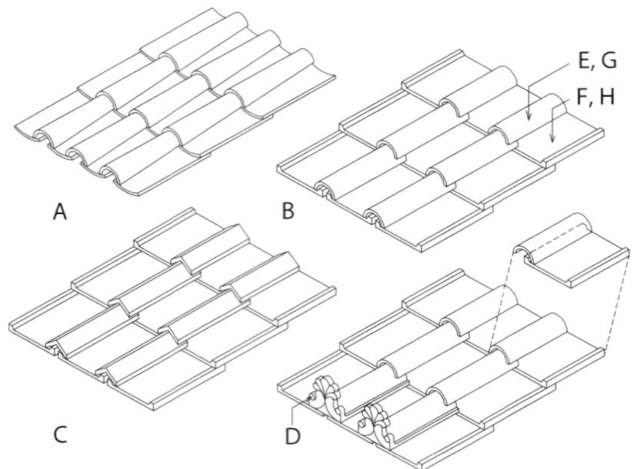

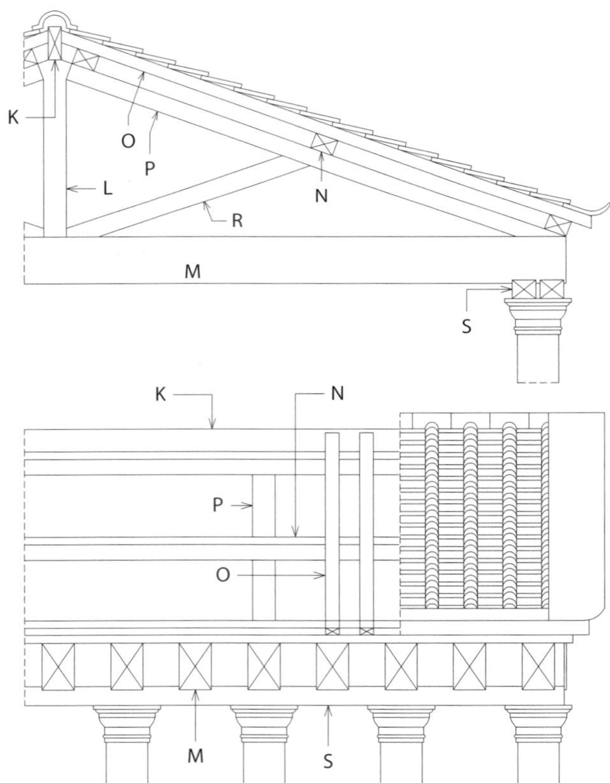

ROMAN TILED ROOFING AND ROOF TRUSS

ROMAN TILED ROOF

A Laconian roofing
B Sicilian roofing
C Corinthian roofing
D antefix: eaves piece
E kalypter (Gr.): cover tile
F stegaster (Gr.): roof tile
G imbrex: cover tile
H tegula: roof tile
K columen: ridge beam
L columna: king post
M transtrum: tie beam
N templa: purlins
O asseres: common rafters
P cantherii: rafters
R capreolus: strut
S trabs, trabes: architrave, main beam

TYPES OF ROOF TILE

1 Spanish tiles, mission tiles
2 Italian tiles, pan-and-roll roofing tiles
3 shingle tile roofing
4 single Roman tile roofing, roll tile
5 double Roman tile roofing, bold roll tile
6 plain tile roofing
7 pantile, S-tile, roll tile
8 double pantile, double-S tile, bold roll tile
9 interlocking tile
10 tail
11 head

tiled roofing, roof tiling
a roof surface or roofing of interlocking or overlapping tiles

roof tile, roofing tile
a flat slab of burnt clay, concrete, or other rigid material fastened overlapping or interlocking in series as a roof covering

tile hanging, vertical tiling, weather tiling
tiles hung vertically in overlapping courses as an external cladding for walls

clay roof tile
any roof tile manufactured from fired clay

concrete roof tile
any roof tile manufactured from concrete

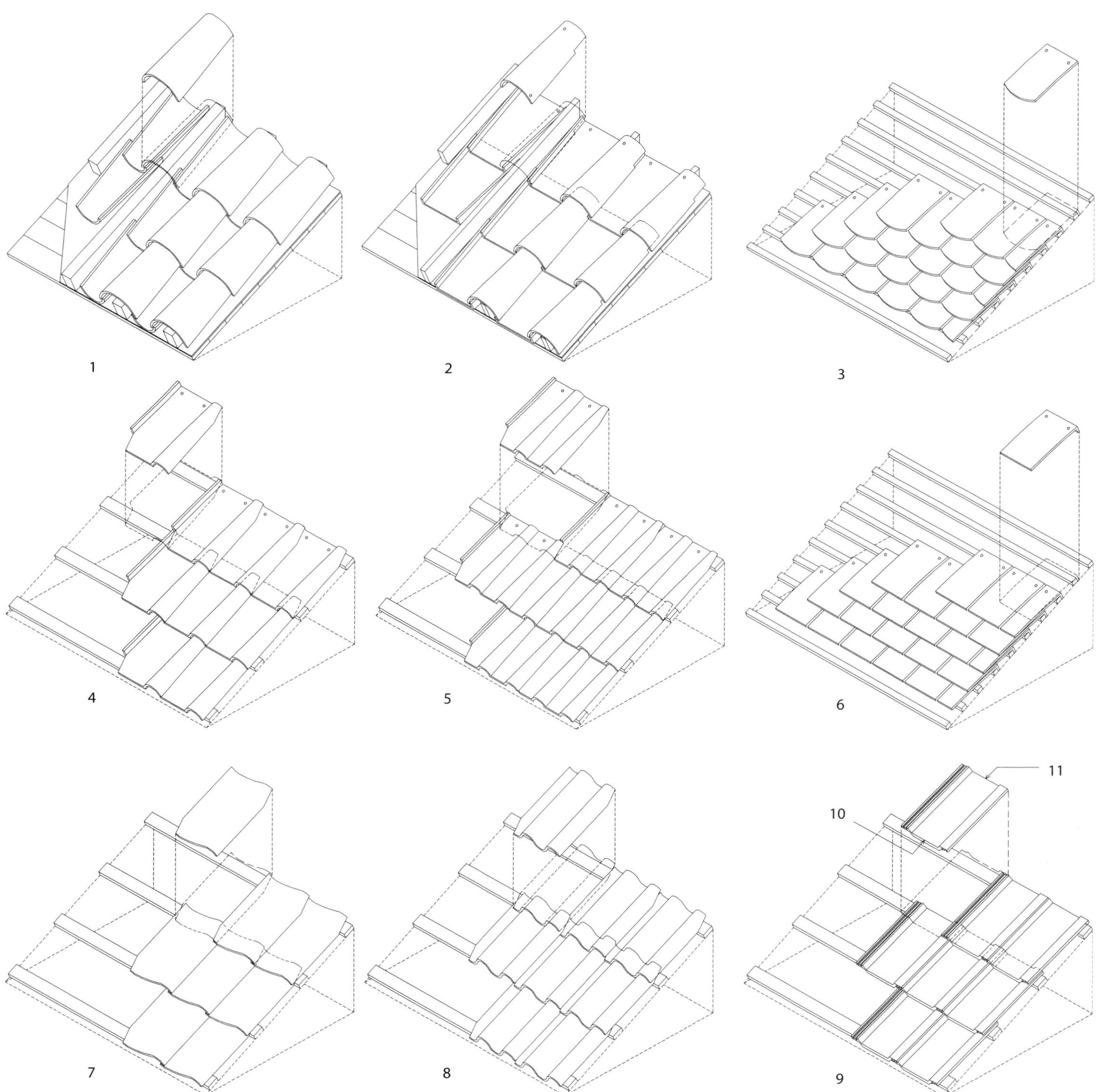
1
2
3
4
5
6
7
8
9
10
11

48 ORGANIC ROOFING

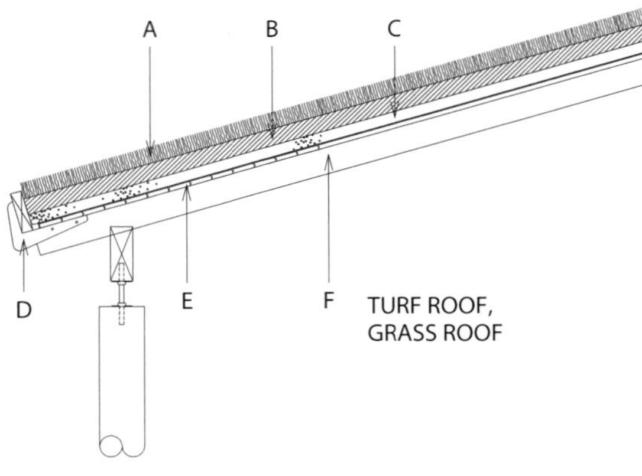

TURF ROOF, GRASS ROOF

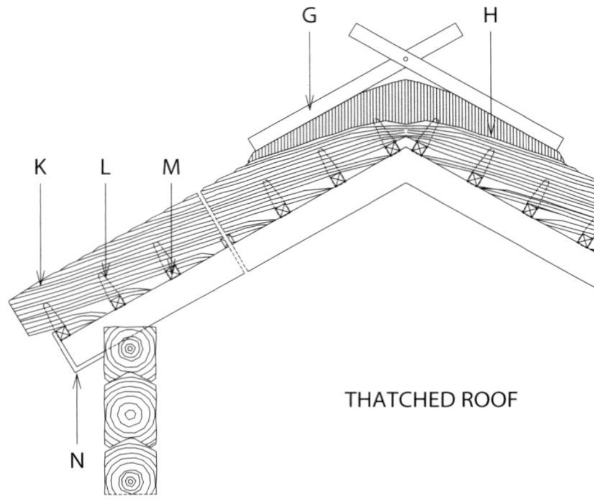

THATCHED ROOF

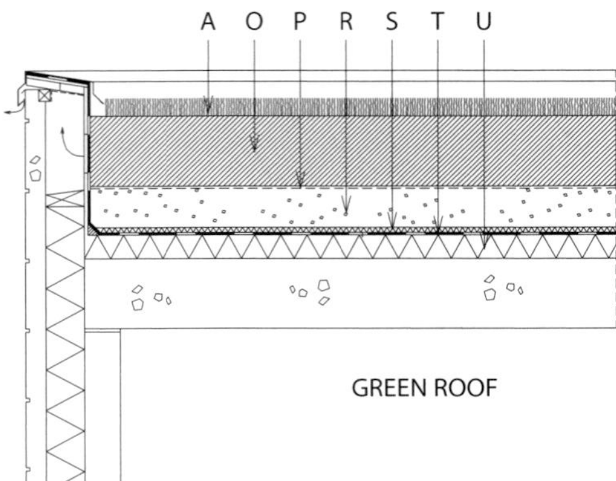

GREEN ROOF

TURF ROOF

A vegetation layer: turf
B rooting layer: humus
C drainage layer: gravel
D wooden retaining hook
E roof boarding, sarking
F roof beam, rafter

THATCHED ROOF

G cross spar, pattern spar
H ridge saddle
K reed thatch
L brotch, spike, staple
M ligger, runner, sway
N fascia board

GREEN ROOF

O growing medium
P filter mat
R drainage layer: leca
S root barrier
T waterproofing: bitumen membrane
U thermal insulation: polystyrene

TRADITIONAL WOODEN ROOFING

1 bark roof with weighting spars
2 birch–bark roofing
3 spruce–bark thatched roofing
4 'lath roof, slat roof': bark roof with slat covering

BOARDED ROOFING

5 puncheon roof
6 'channel roof': hewn puncheon roof
7 board and batten roof
8 groove-boarded roof
9 clapboard roof

WOODEN TILE ROOFING

10 shake roof
11 shingle roof

organic roof
any roof whose roofing is of organic materials such as wood, bark, turf, planting etc.

turf roof, grass roof
a roof whose weatherproofing is provided by growing turf laid over a waterproof membrane

thatched roof
a roof whose weatherproofing and insulating material is bundles of straw or reed (or in some cases heather or bark) held down with timber rods, wire etc.

green roof
roof construction comprising growing plant material laid in soil over a drainage layer and waterproofing membrane; the soil layer provides insulation and protection from the elements

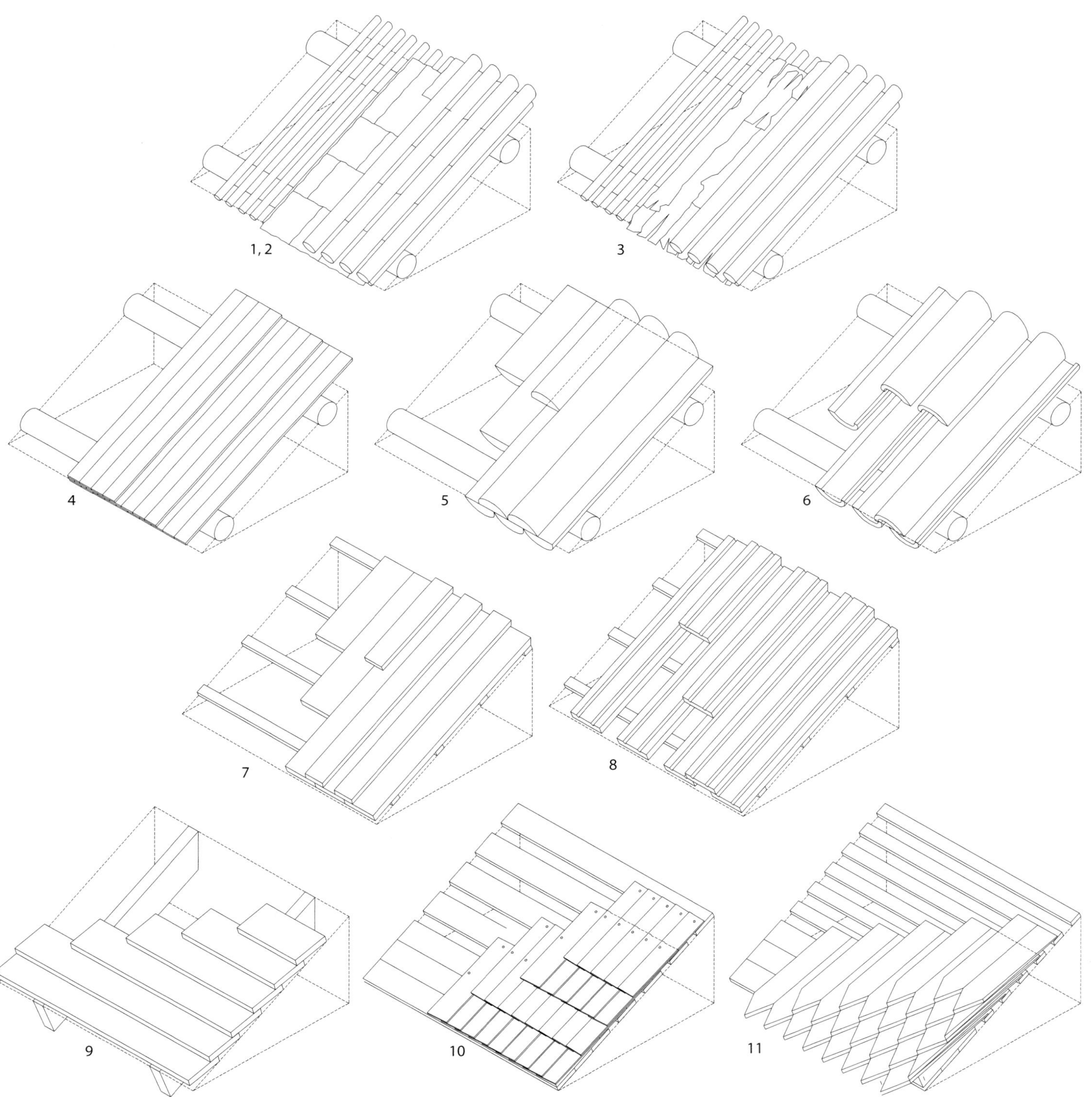
1, 2
3
4
5
6
7
8
9
10
11

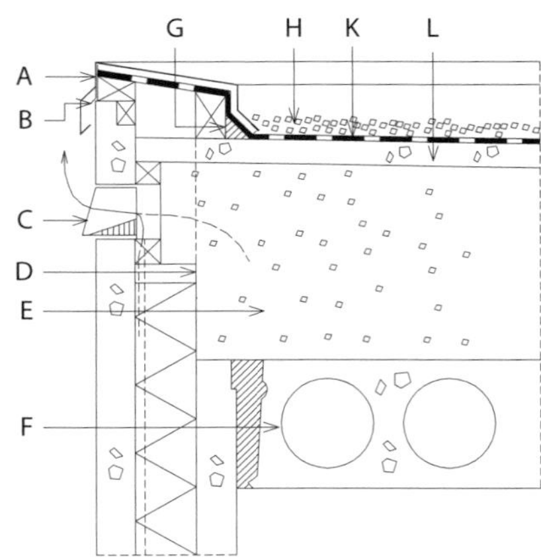

PARAPET OF FLAT ROOF

A parapet capping
B eaves flashing
C vent, ventilation of roof structure
D dense-weave mesh
E expanded clay aggregate
F concrete roof slab
G angle fillet, arris fillet, cant fillet
H chippings, gravel surfacing, granular surfacing – shingle
K membrane waterproofing
L concrete topping

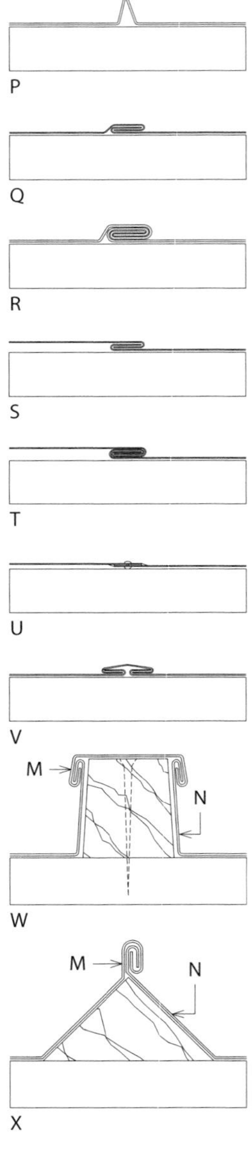

WELTS, WELTED SEAMS

M overcloak
N undercloak
O standing seam, single
P standing seam, double
Q lock welt, single lock welt
R double welt, double-lock welt, clink
S cross welt, single
T cross welt, double
U lap joint, riveted and soldered joint
V hollow roll joint
W roll joint, batten roll joint, wood roll joint
X conical roll joint

PROFILED SHEET ROOFING

1 trough sheeting, tray decking
2 ribbed-sheet roofing
3 corrugated sheet roofing, corrugated sheeting

SHEETMETAL ROOFING

4 metal multi-tile roofing
5 supported sheet metal roofing, flexible metal roofing
6 roll-jointed flexible metal roofing
7 seam welded roofing

MEMBRANE AND FELT ROOFING, BITUMINOUS ROOFING

8 roll-jointed bitumen roofing
9 lap-jointed bitumen felt roofing
10 built-up roofing
11 strip slate or tile roofing, bitumen shingles, asphalt shingles
12 roofing underlay

sheet roofing
any roofing material manufactured and laid in sheets: bitumen felt, sheetmetal, ribbed polymer sheeting etc.

membrane roofing, membrane waterproofing
a general name for thin flexible sheet materials and products such as bitumen felt, plastic sheet or asphalt used to provide a waterproof upper layer in flat or pitched roof construction

flat roof, platform roof (Scot.)
a roof which has a slope of less than 10°

parapet
a low wall, balustrade at the edge of a roof, or the junction at which an external wall and a flat roof meet

welt, welted seam
a fastened seam or joint between two adjacent sheets of supported sheetmetal roofing

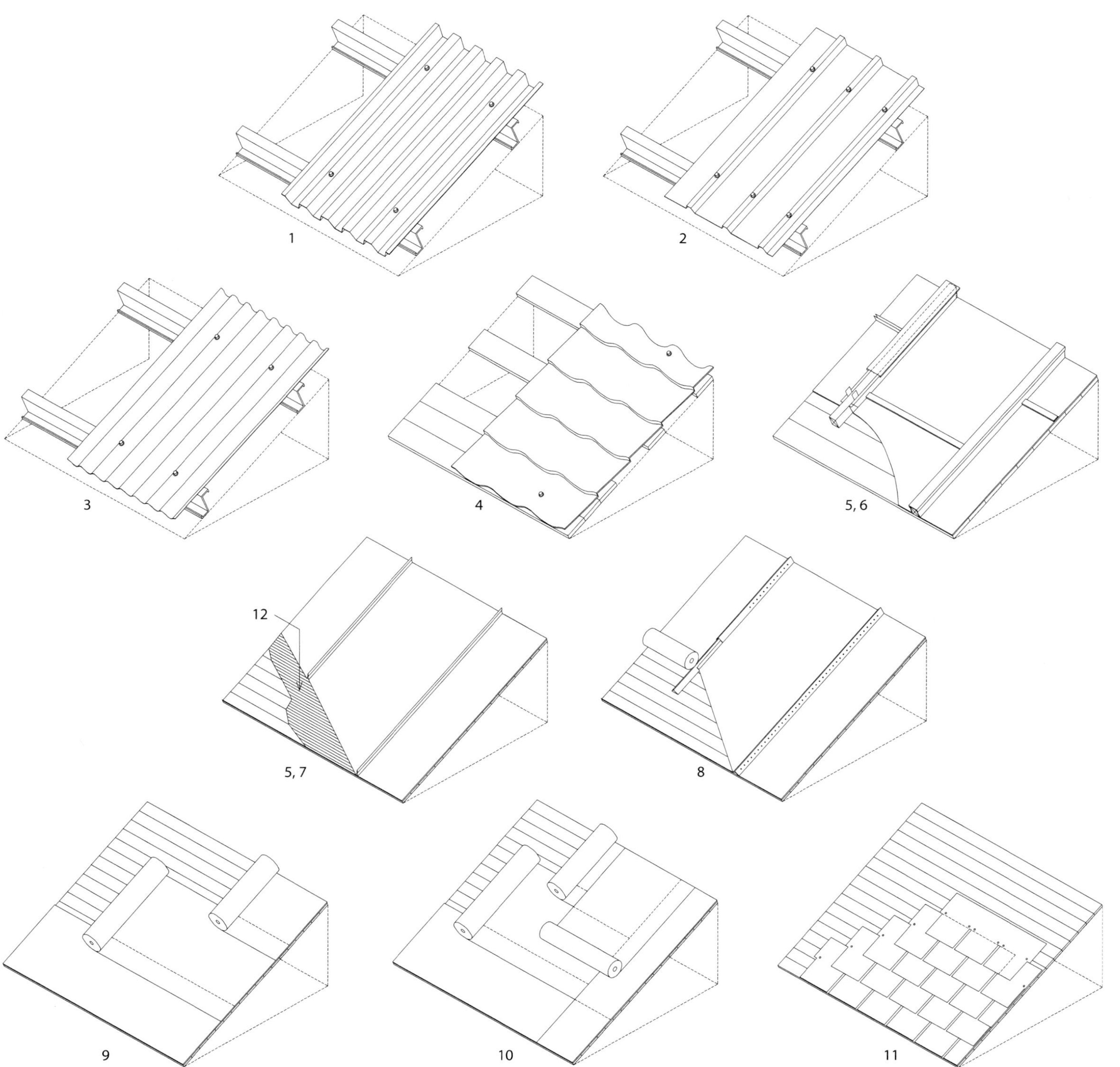
1
2
3
4
5, 6
12
5, 7
8
9
10
11

50 DOOR TYPES BY ACTION

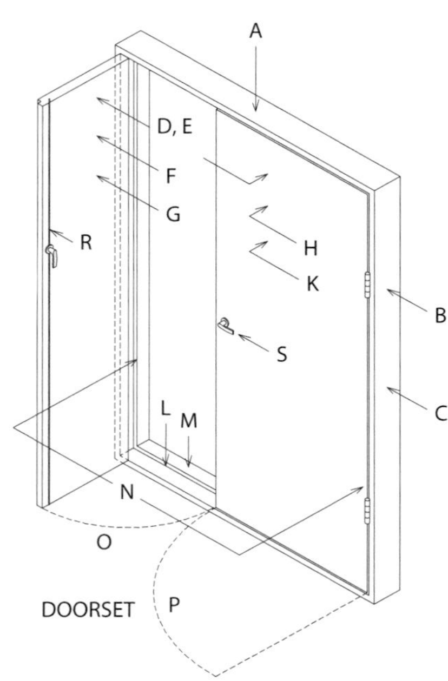

JAMB OF GLAZED DOOR

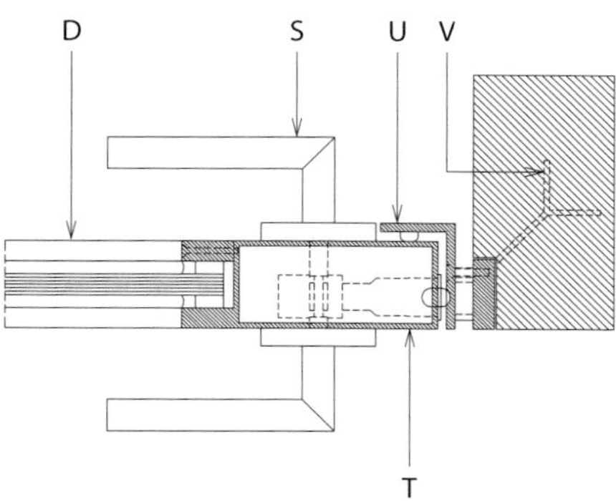

ANATOMY OF A DOOR

A door head
B door jamb
C hanging jamb
D door leaf
E door face
F inactive leaf
G shutting face, closing face
H active leaf
K opening face
L threshold
M door stop, rebate
N doorway

DIRECTION OF SWING – HANDING

O left-handed door, left hung door
P right-handed door, right hung door
R panic bolt, fire-exit bolt; cremone bolt
S lever handle; door handle
T door stile – shutting stile, closing stile, lock stile
U shutting jamb, closing jamb
V door-frame anchor

SIDE HUNG DOORS

1 single door, hinged
2 double door
3 double door
4 swing door
5 stable door
6 coupled door

REVOLVING DOORS

7 balanced door
8 revolving door

FOLDING DOORS

9 concertina door, multi-folding door
10 accordion door, pleated door
11 sliding folding door, bi-fold door

SLIDING DOORS

12 sliding door (single-leaf)
13 centre-opening door
14 telescopic door, side-opening door
15 overhead door
16 bi-part folding door, vertical folding door
17 up-and-over door
18 sectional overhead door
19 roller shutter

door
1 an opening in a wall with a hinged or sliding partition to allow access from one space to another, also called a doorway or door opening
2 the partition itself, called a door leaf
3 the partition and its associated frame, with or without door fittings, also called a doorset or door assembly

door swing
the curve traced by the edge of a door leaf as it opens, as marked on plan drawings

door jamb
1 one of the vertical members of a door frame
2 a door reveal

door reveal
the vertical flat side of a doorway, perpendicular or skew to the main wall surface; also called a door jamb

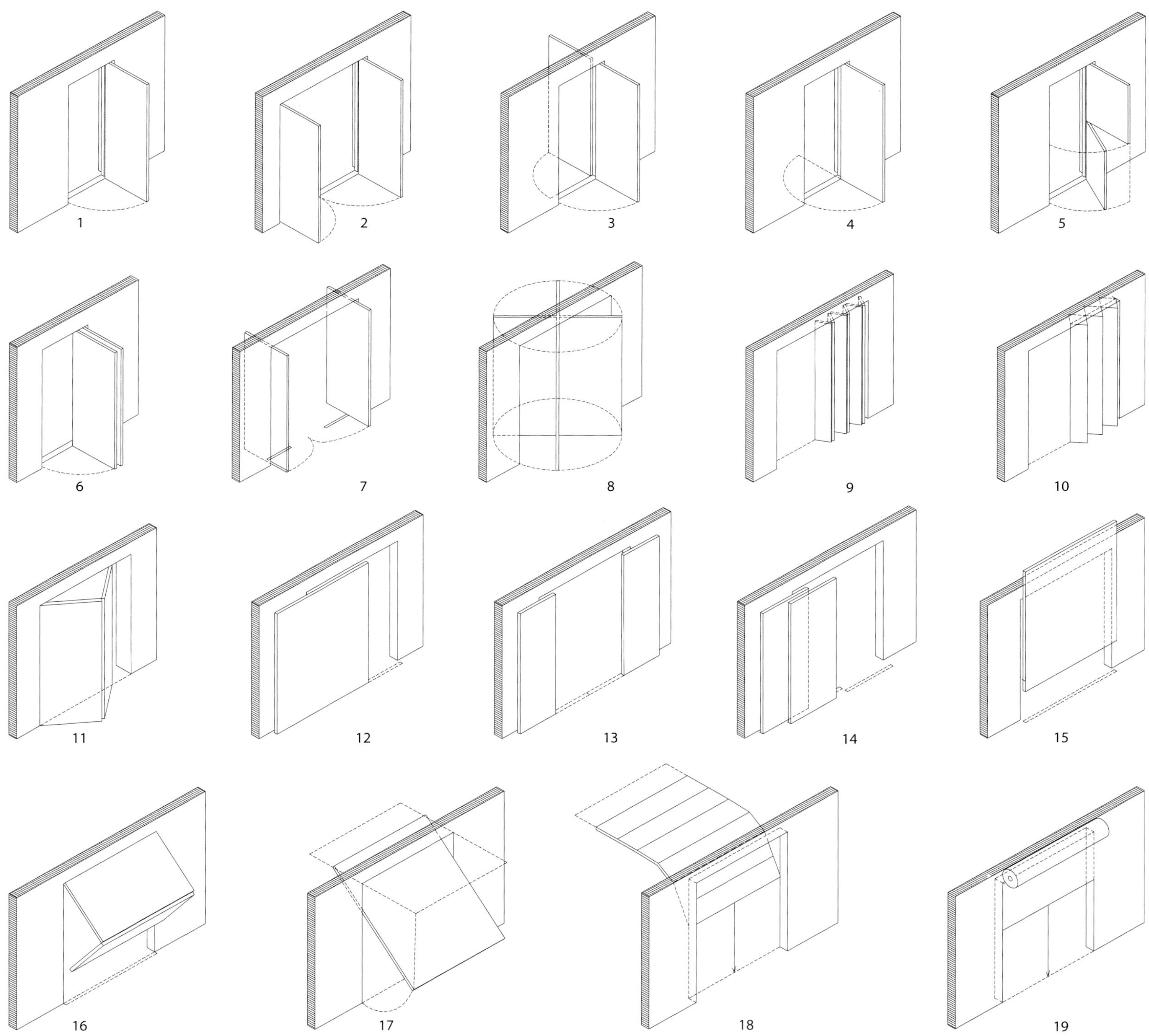
1
2
3
4
5
6
7
8
9
10
11
12
13
14
15
16
17
18
19

51 SIDE HUNG DOORS

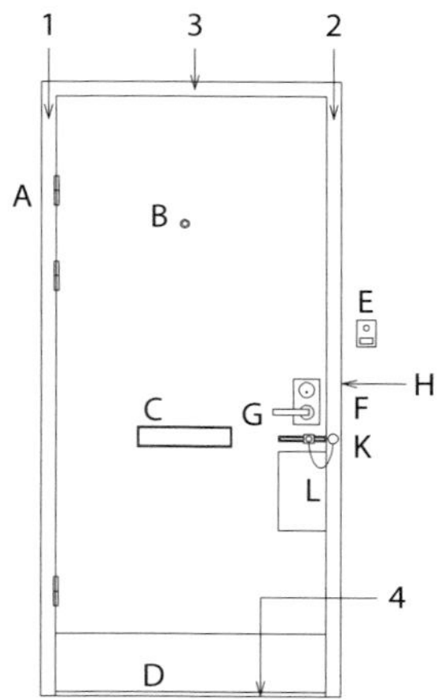

DOMESTIC ENTRANCE DOOR

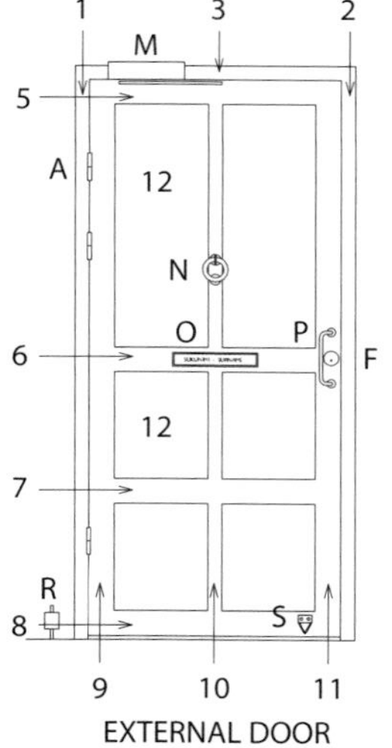

EXTERNAL DOOR

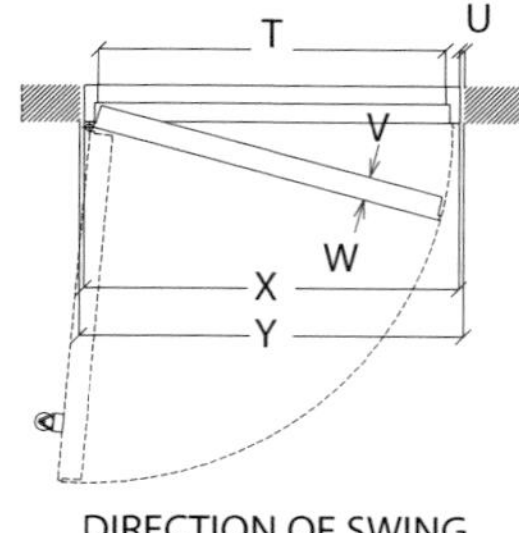

DIRECTION OF SWING

DOOR FURNITURE

- A door hinge
- B door scope, door viewer, peephole
- C letter plate, mail slot
- D kicking plate, kick plate, door plate
- E doorbell
- F key plate, escutcheon plate, scutcheon
- G lever handle
- H door lock
- K door chain, door limiter, security chain
- L push plate, finger plate
- M door closer
- N door knocker
- O name plate
- P door handle – wire pull handle – cranked pull handle, offset pull handle
- R door stop, door stay, door buffer
- S door holder
- T door clearance
- U installation allowance, door clearance
- V shutting face
- W opening face
- X door width
- Y doorway

FRAME

1 jamb – hanging jamb
2 jamb – shutting jamb
3 door frame – head
4 threshold

STILES, FRAMING

5 rail – top rail
6 intermediate rail – upper intermediate rail
7 intermediate rail – bottom intermediate rail
8 bottom rail
9 stile – hanging stile
10 muntin; (Am.) munnion
11 stile – closing stile, shutting stile, lock stile
12 panel – door panel

SOLID DOORS, UNGLAZED DOORS

13 ledged door
14 ledged and braced door
15 framed door
16 panel door
17 flush door
18 non-rebated door
19 solid core door
20 door without threshold
21 rebated door
22 hollow-core door
23 metal door

GLAZED DOORS

24 timber glazed door
25 metal glazed door
26 all-glass door
27 louvred door
28 ledge

door furniture, door ironmongery, door hardware
any fittings such as hinges, door handles and closers for the operation and functioning of a door

rail
a horizontal frame member in a door leaf, sash, casement or other framework

stile
a vertical side framing member of a door leaf or window casement

door schedule
a contract document listing types of door, their ironmongery, fire-rating and other specifications for a project

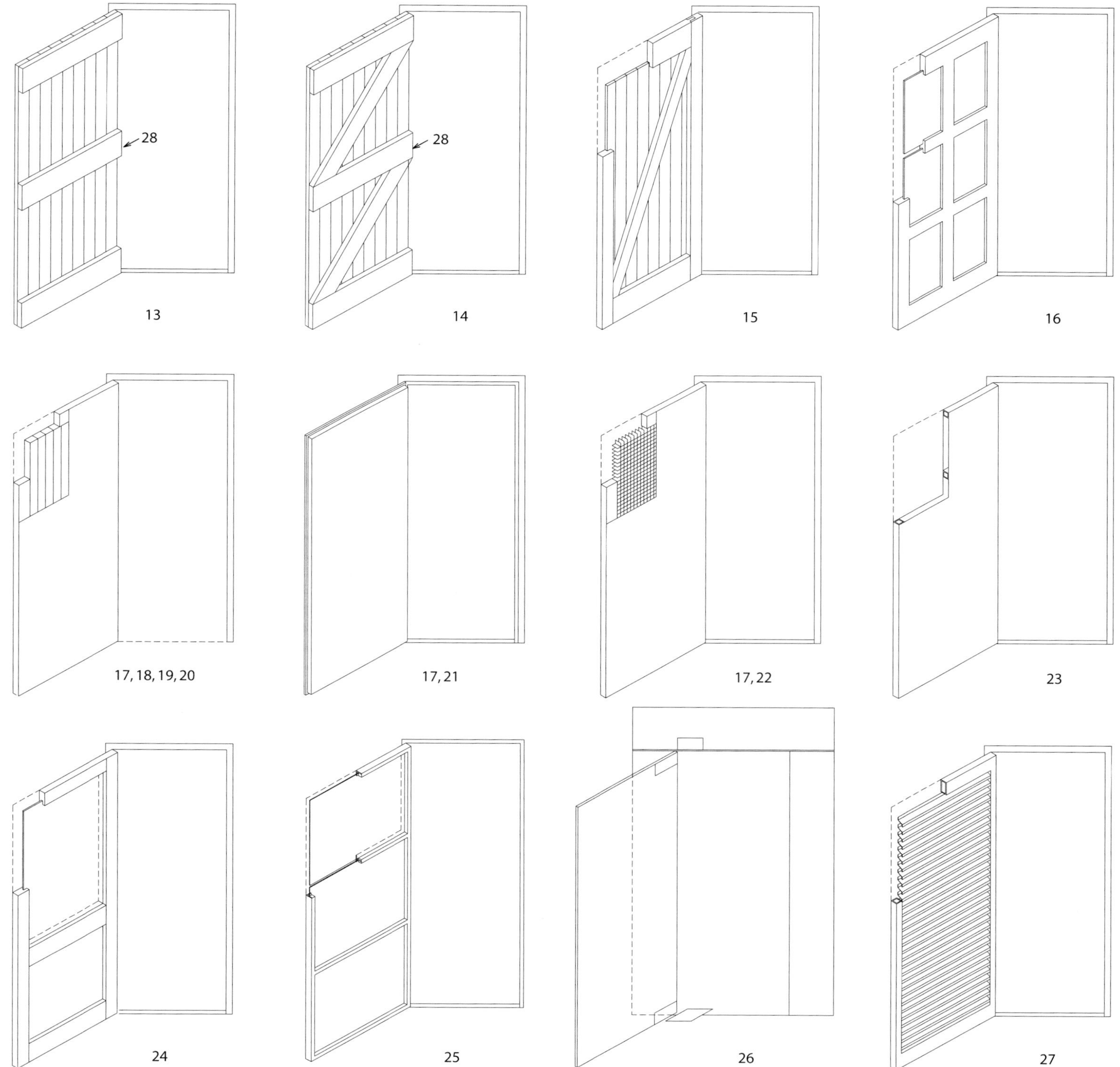
28
28
13
14
15
16
17, 18, 19, 20
17, 21
17, 22
23
24
25
26
27

52 WINDOW TYPES

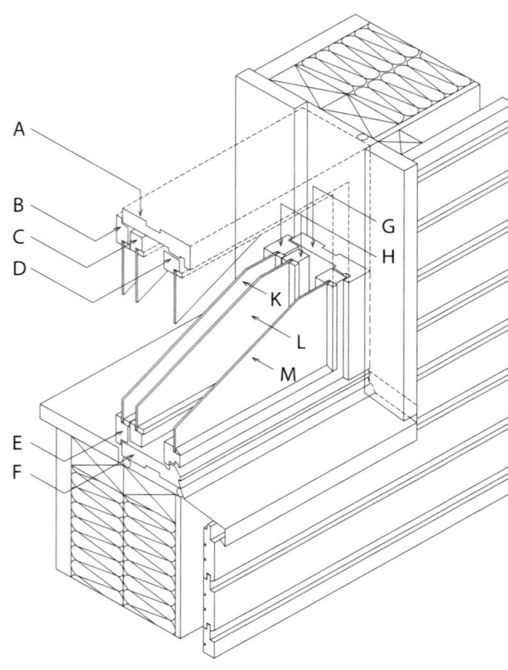

TIMBER WINDOW, TIMBER-FRAMED WINDOW

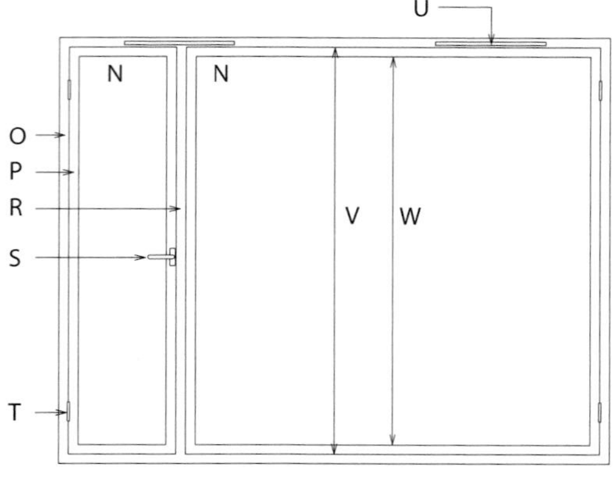

SIDE-HUNG CASEMENT WINDOW

TRIPLE-GLAZED INWARD-OPENING WINDOW

A head, window head
B top rail – inner sash
C top rail – intermediate sash
D top rail – outer sash
E bottom rails
F sill, window sill
G jamb
H stiles
K internal glazing
L intermediate glazing
M external glazing
N window pane
O window frame
P window casement
R mullion
S casement handle
T window hinge
U trickle ventilator
V light size, full size
W sight size, daylight size

WINDOW TYPES

1 side-hung casement window
2 side light
3 top light
4 sliding folding window
5 top-hung casement window, awning window
6 bottom-hung casement window, hopper window
7 horizontal pivot window
8 vertical pivot window
9 top-hung sliding window
10 vertical sliding sash window
11 horizontal sliding window
12 louvred window
13 centre hinge, centre pivot hinge

window
an opening in an external wall of a building for allowing light into a space; may be a simple opening or an assembly of parts

window assembly
all the parts of a window: the outer frame, sashes and glazing

window unit
a prefabricated glazing component of glass in a frame, often containing openable casements, fittings etc.

sash
an openable framed part of a window opened either by sliding or on hinges; a casement is a hinged sash

casement
an openable, framed, glazed and hinged light in a window unit

1
2
3
4
5
6
13
7
13
8
9
10
11
12

53 GLAZING AND WINDOW SYSTEMS

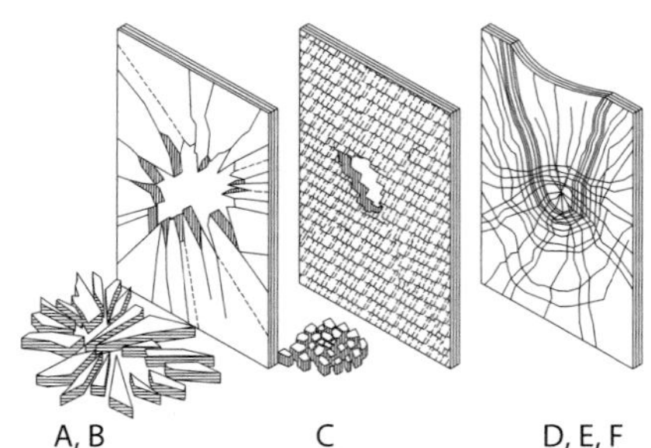

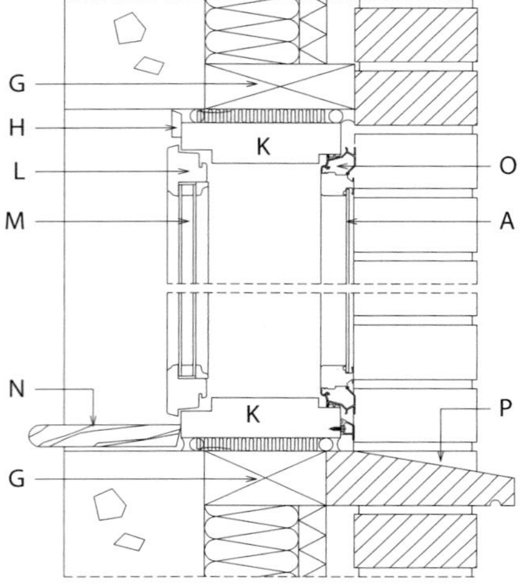

COMPOUND WINDOW

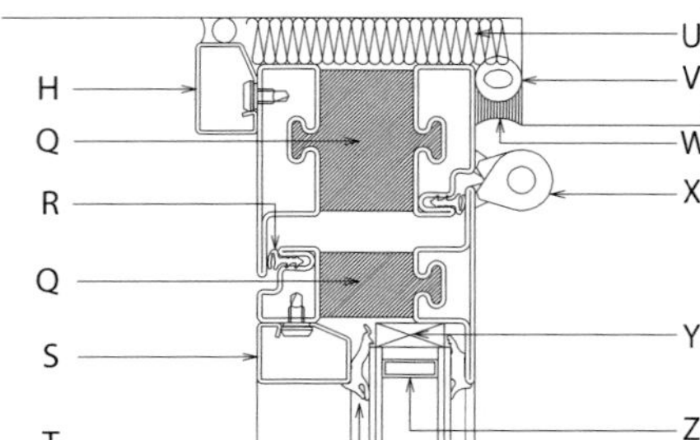

THERMAL-BREAK PROFILES, DRY GLAZING

SHATTERING OF GLASS

NORMAL WINDOW GLASS

A float glass
B sheet glass, drawn glass

SAFETY GLASS

C toughened glass
D laminated glass
E anti-bandit glass, anti-vandal glass
F bullet-resistant laminated glass

WINDOW CONSTRUCTION

G timber subsill, subframe
H window trim
K timber window frame
L inner sash (timber)
M sealed glazed unit
N window board, window sill
O outer sash (aluminium)
P window sill, subsill
Q thermal-break profile, thermally broken profile
R draught strip, weatherstrip, window strip
S glazing bead
T glazing gasket
U polyurethane joint filler
V jointing strip, backing strip
W sealing compound, joint sealant
X window hinge, casement hinge
Y glazing block, setting block, packing piece
Z spacer

WINDOWS BY CONSTRUCTION

1 steel-framed window
2 aluminium-framed window
3 timber-framed window
4 aluminium-faced timber window (composite window, compound window)

SYSTEM GLAZING, GLAZING SYSTEM

5 patent glazing system, dry glazing
6 prefabricated glazing system
7 planar glazing system, structural glass
8 channel glass system, profile glass system
9 glass block walling

glass
a hard, impermeable, transparent material formed from sand, soda ash, limestone and dolomite; used for many applications especially window glazing

glazing
1 the installation of glass, glass panels or products into frames or other supporting systems
2 the resulting glass panels and windows thus installed

safety glass
glass which resists breakage, or breaks in such a way as to reduce the risk of injury to a minimum; includes toughened glass, laminated glass and wired glass

solar control glass, anti-sun glass
glass which has been treated with a body tint or reflective coating to improve solar absorption and reflection

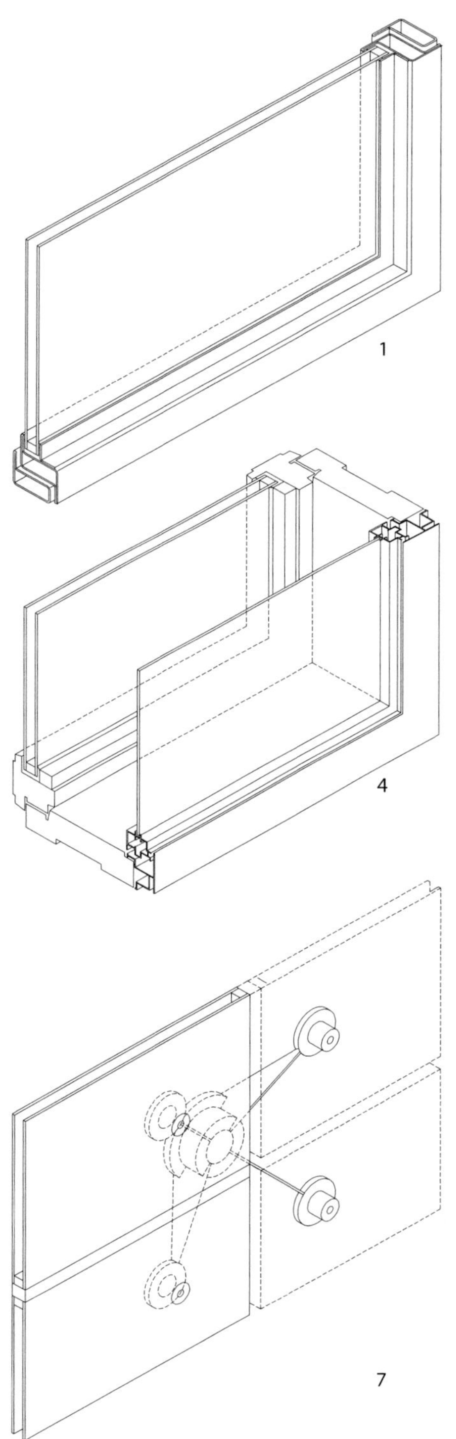

1
4
7

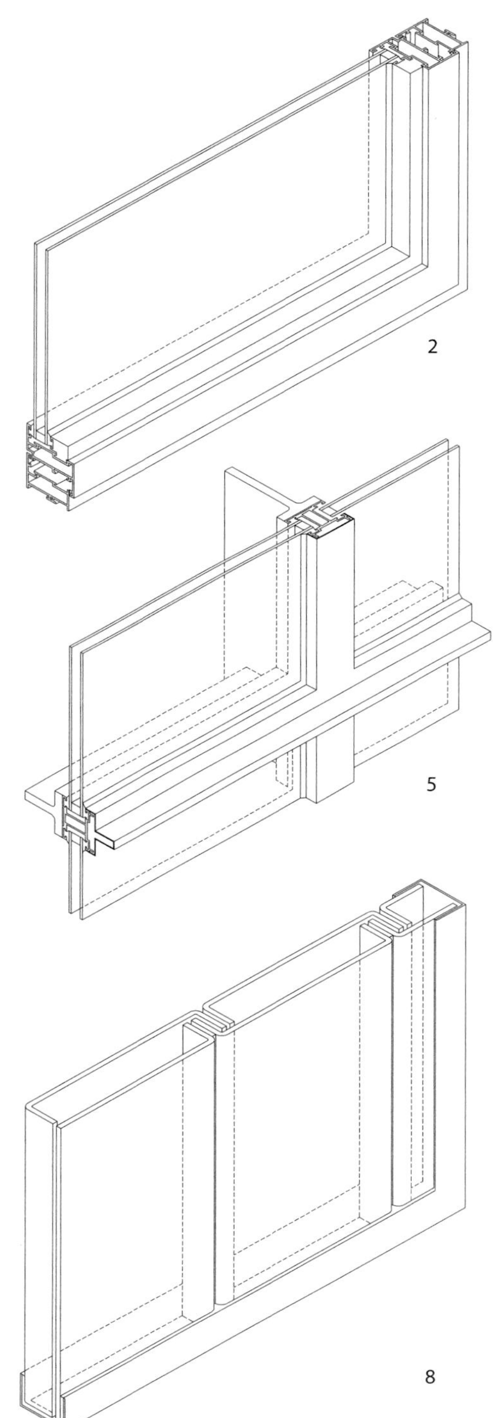

2
5
8

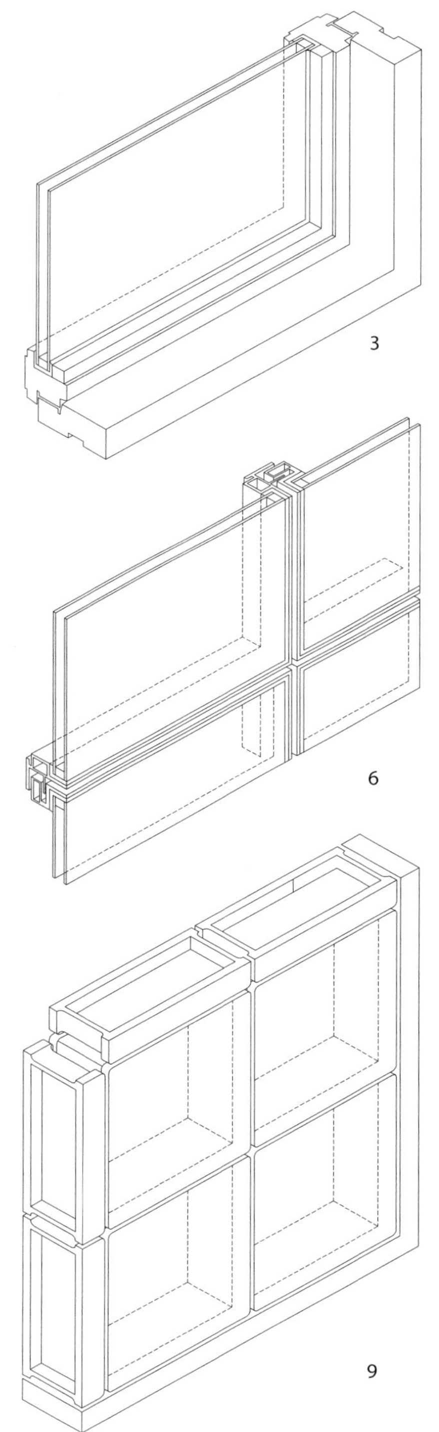

3
6
9

54 BALCONY AND BALUSTRADE

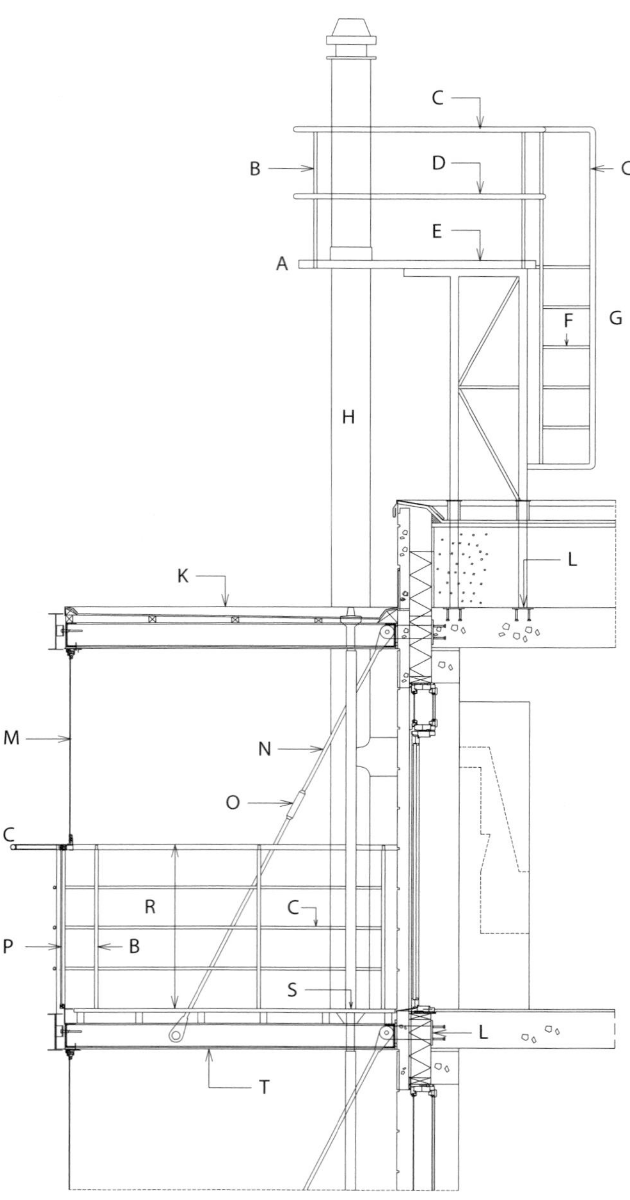

ACCESS PLATFORM AND LADDER

A access platform, gantry
B standard, upright, baluster
C handrail
D rail, intermediate rail
E gantry, access platform
F rung, step iron, step
G ladder – chimney ladder, access ladder
H chimney, flue
K canopy
L anchorage
M balcony glazing
N tie rod, hanger, tension rod
O turnbuckle
P glazing infill
R balustrade height
S balcony drain, balcony outlet
T balcony deck, balcony slab

BALCONY TYPES

1 cantilevered balcony
2 suspended balcony, hung balcony
3 self-supporting balcony, freestanding balcony

BALUSTRADE TYPES

4 solid balustrade
5 all-glass balustrade
6 wire-mesh balustrade
7 railed balustrade, rail balustrade
8 wire-rope balustrade, cable balustrade
9 railing, open balustrade
10 glazed balustrade, glass balustrade
11 banister, open stile balustrade
12 parapet

balcony
an accessible outdoor or glazed and balustraded platform projecting from the external face of a building, often for recreational use

balustrade
any waist-high barrier, open or closed, designed to provide protection from falling at the edge of a change in level

gantry, access platform, walkway
a lightweight platform used to give access to high levels for maintenance, and often to provide support for service installations, often with a railing

ladder
a freestanding or fixed frame to provide temporary or permanent vertical access, consisting of two vertical side rails with horizontal rungs or steps in between

1
4
7
10
2
5
8
11
3
6
9
12

55 SOLID-FUEL STOVES AND FLUE SYSTEMS

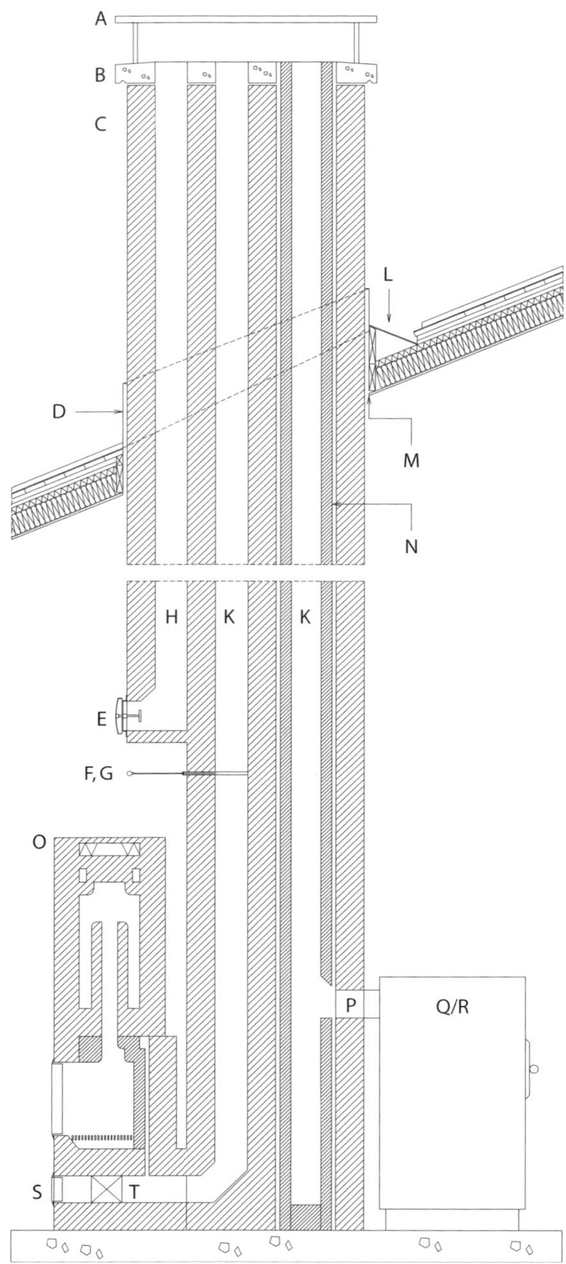

FLUE SYSTEM

A flue cap, chimney cap, rain cap
B chimney crown
C chimney, chimney stack
D upstand – abutment flashing, apron flashing
E air vent – disc vent
F smoke damper, throat restrictor – sliding damper
G draught diverter, barometric damper, (Am.) draught stabilizer
H ventilating duct, vent stack
K flue, flueway, chimney
L back gutter, chimney gutter
M roof penetration
N flue lining, fireproof lining
O masonry stove
P flue adaptor
Q cast-iron stove, solid fuel appliance
R central heating boiler
S soot door
T flue connector

TYPES OF STOVE

1 masonry counterflow heating stove
2 convective fireplace, storage heater
3 freestanding cast-iron stove

PARTS OF A STOVE

4 combustion chamber, firebox
5 grate, bottomgrate
6 firebox door
7 ash pan door
8 firebrick, refractory brick
9 fire tube, flue tube, smoke tube
10 smoke chamber
11 upper combustion chamber
12 hot air circulation duct
13 ash pan
14 hearth apron
15 smoke damper – sliding damper
16 smoke distributor – rotating damper
17 upper flue connector
18 lower flue connector
19 flue pipe, flueway – insulated metal flue

stove
a closed appliance for heating a space, often freestanding and connected to a flue if solid-fuel, gas or oil-fired, ventilated if operated by electricity

solid-fuel stove
a freestanding heater which burns coal and wood as fuel; usually a patented product of metal plate or cast-iron construction connected to a flue

flue, smoke pipe
a vertical pipe or duct to remove smoke, combustion gases and other gaseous products from a fireplace, boiler or other heating device to the outside of a building; a chimney

flue gas
any gas produced as a result of combustion within an appliance or installation, including soot and particles in suspension, which passes up through a flue

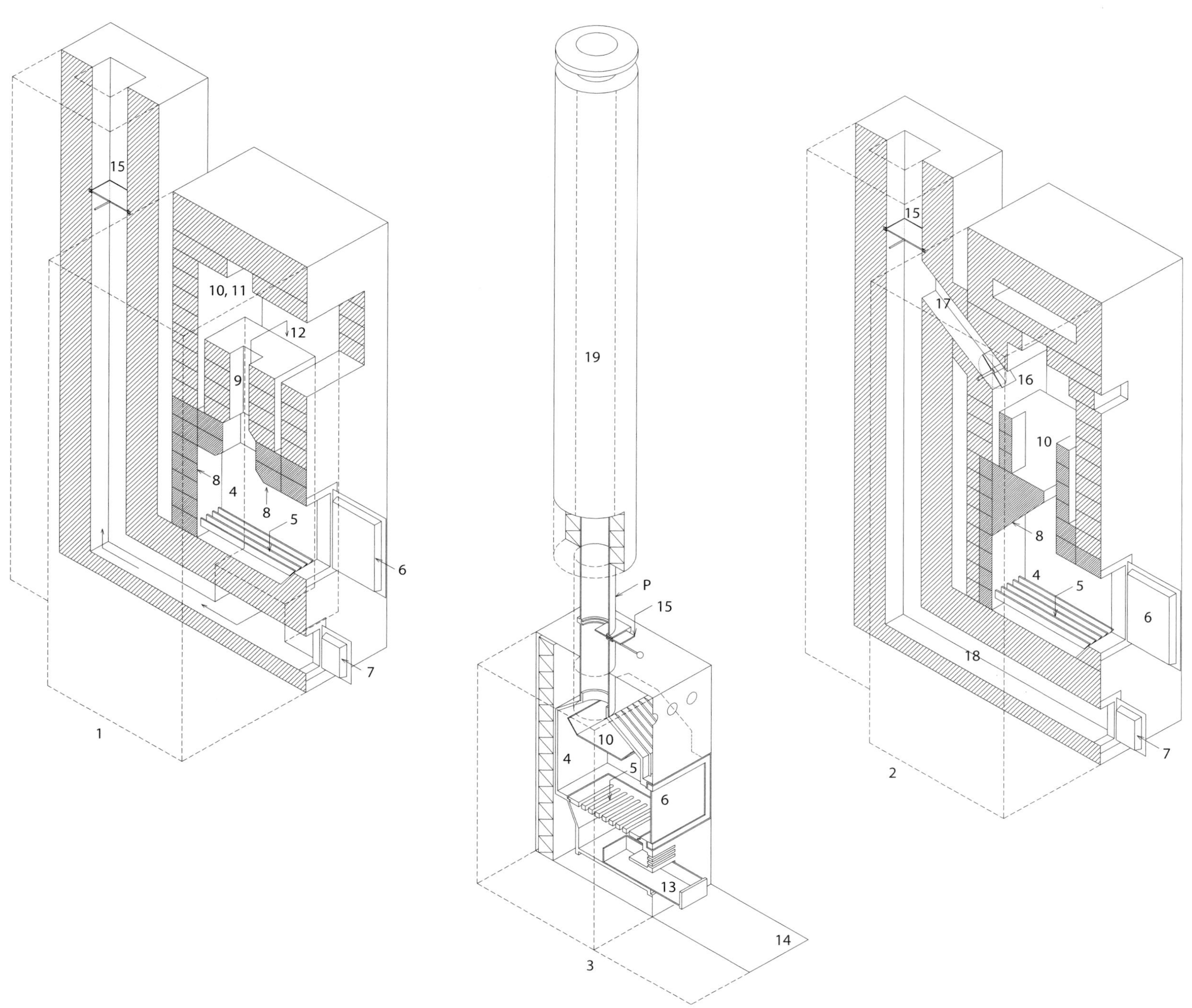
15
10, 11
12
9
8
4
8
5
6
7
1
19
P
15
10
4
5
6
13
14
3
15
17
16
10
8
4
5
6
18
7
2

56 MASONRY FIREPLACES

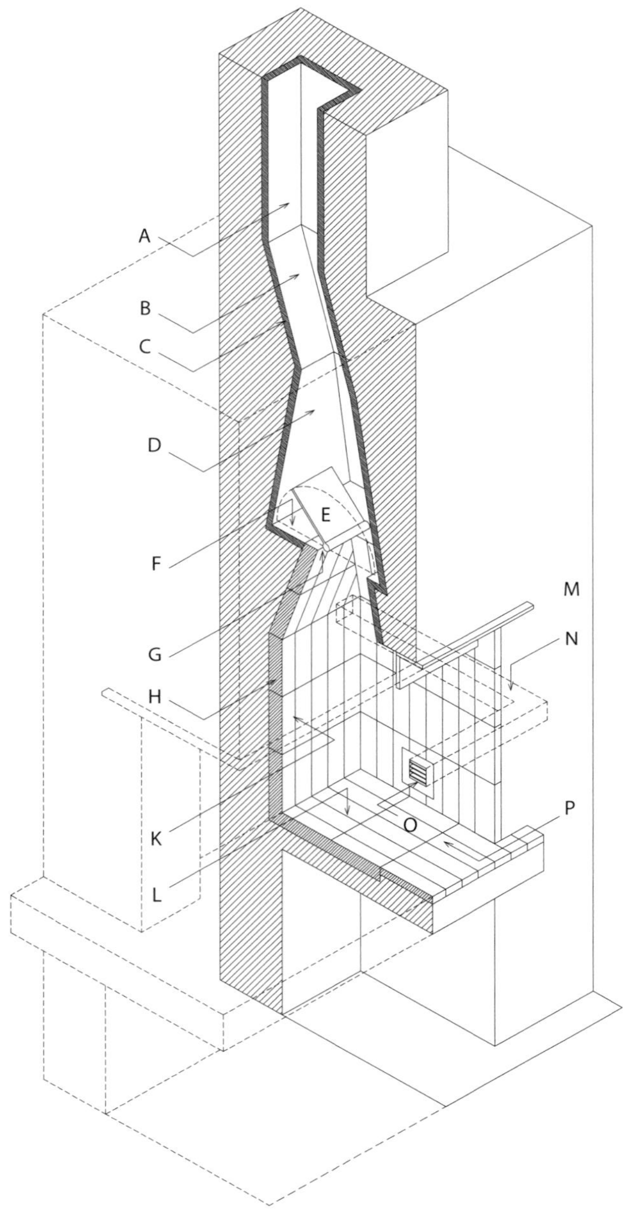

PARTS OF A FIREPLACE

A flue
B flue connector
C parge, flue lining
D smoke chamber
E smoke damper – pivot damper
F smoke shelf
G throat, gather, gathering – damper opening
H firebrick lining
K fireback
L hearth, back hearth
M canopy, hood
N combustion air inlet/intake
O grille
P firefront, fret

SINGLE-FACED FIREPLACE,
OPEN FRONT FIREPLACE

1 floor hearth fireplace
2 flush fireplace
3 raised-hearth fireplace
4 metal-hood fireplace

TWO-FACED FIREPLACE,
CORNER FIREPLACE

5 internal corner fireplace
6 external corner fireplace
7 through fireplace, see-through fireplace
8 three-faced fireplace
9 freestanding fireplace, central hearth
10 fireplace surround, mantlepiece
11 stool bottomgrate
12 fireplace recess

fireplace
a domestic masonry construction, recess or proprietary metal appliance, usually open or with glazed doors at the front and fitted to a flue, in which solid fuel is burnt to provide heating and atmosphere to a room

chimney
a vertical structure which contains one or more flues to extract waste gases and smoke from a building, boiler or other apparatus

chimney breast
a thickening or recess in a masonry wall containing space for a fireplace and flue constructions

hearth
the base or floor of a fireplace, on which combustion takes place

firebrick, refractory brick
a brick of special composition capable of withstanding high temperatures without melting or fusion, used for masonry chimneys, flue linings, kilns and fireboxes

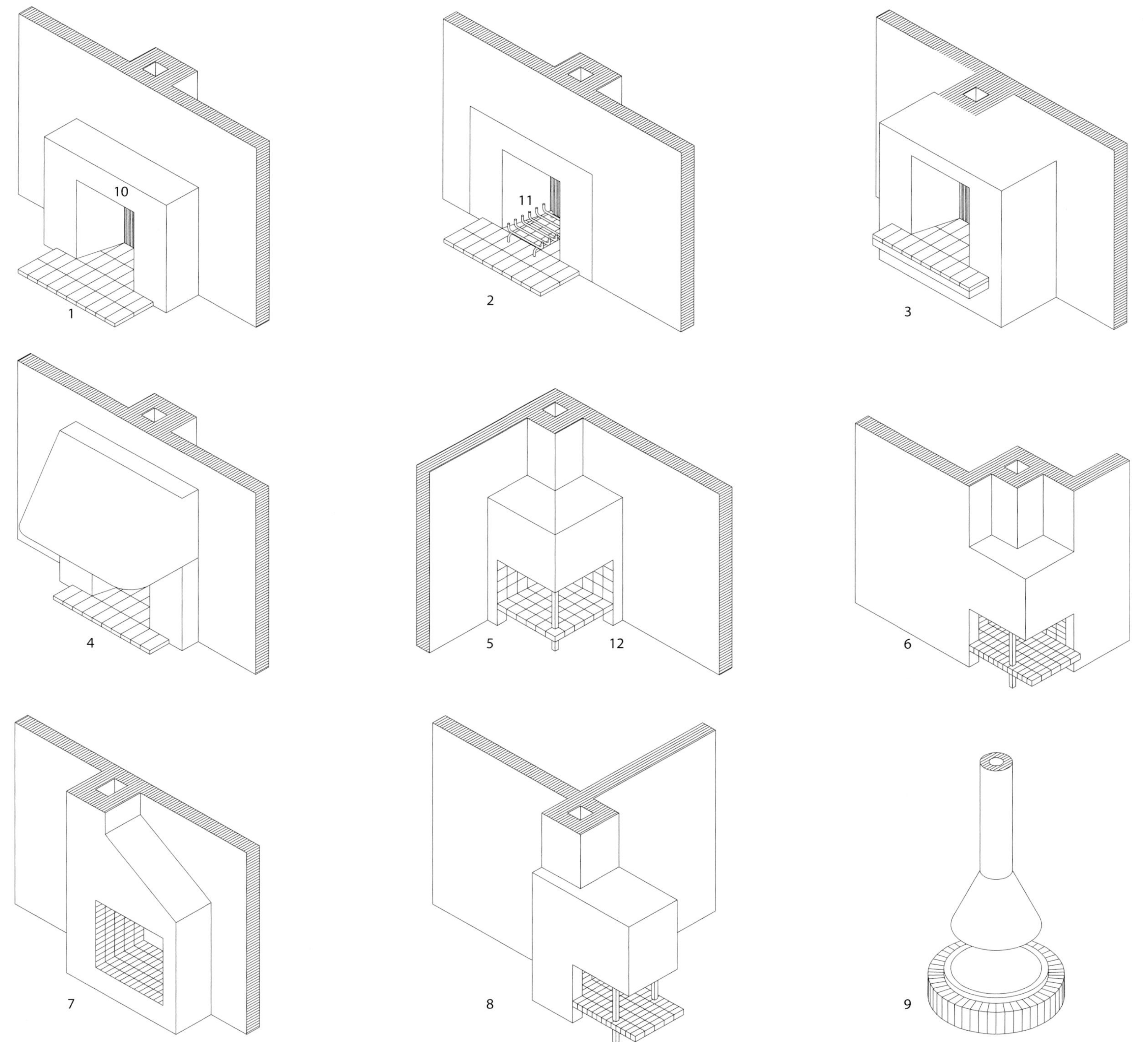
10
1
11
2
3
4
5
12
6
7
8
9

57 BALLOON-FRAMED TIMBER HOUSE

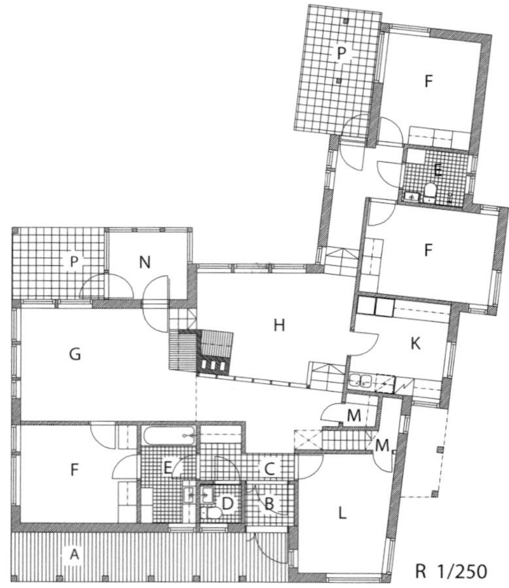

A porch, verandah
B draught lobby
C entrance hall, vestibule
D WC, toilet
E bathroom
F habitable room, bedroom
G living room, sitting room, lounge
H dining room, dining hall
K kitchen
L study
M built-in closet
N conservatory, winter garden
P patio

TYPES OF TIMBER CARCASS

R, S, U
balloon frame, box frame

T western frame, platform frame

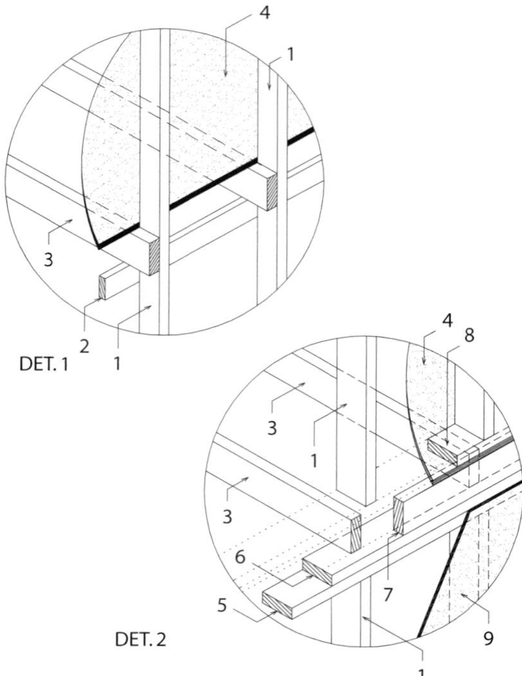

R, U) Risku House, Pello, Finland, 1986, Erkki Jokiniemi

timber-framed building
any building whose structural frame is of timber members clad and lined with sheet material

balloon frame
a form of timber frame construction in which vertical studs rise from sole plate to header plate through two or more stories; intermediate floors are carried on wall plates nailed to the inside face of the studs

platform frame, western framing
a form of multistorey timber frame construction in which single-storey stud walls bear on the floor or platform constructed at the level below

studwork
1 timber or pressed metal sections laid vertically as a framework for lightweight partitions

2 studding; the verticals in a timber frame wall

1 stud
2 wall plate, binder, runner
3 floor joist, floor beam
4 sub-floor decking, sheathing
5 head plate
6 head binder, binder
7 header
8 sole plate
9 bracing panel
10 diagonal brace, brace
11 gypsum board lining
12 battening, grounds, groundwork
13 concrete ground slab
14 footing, foundation
15 longitudinal reinforcement
16 block foundation
17 drainage membrane, cavity drainage membrane, air-gap membrane
18 base wall, wall base
19 sill plate, cill plate
20 lintel, lintol
21 eaves
22 verge
23 roof sheathing, roof boarding
24 close boarding
25 spaced boarding, open boarding, gapped boarding
26 underlay – roofing felt
27 supported sheet metal roofing, flexible metal roofing
28 ceiling boarding, soffit boarding
29 upstand, roofing upstand
30 upstand flashing, abutment flashing, apron flashing
31 board-on-board cladding, staggered siding
32 top edge, upper eaves

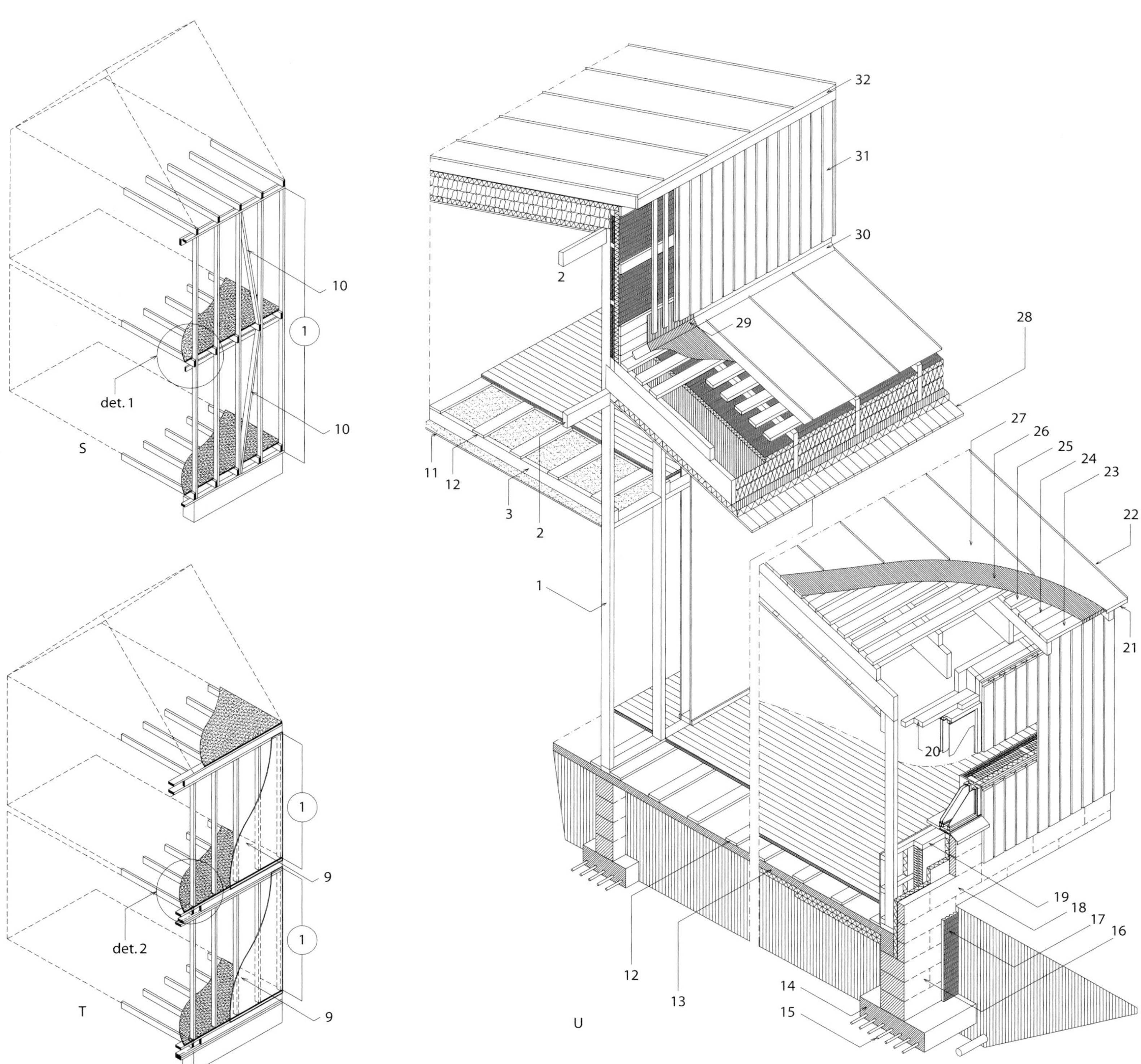

10
1
det. 1
10
S
1
9
det. 2
1
9
T
32
31
30
2
29
28
11
12
3
2
27
26
25
24
23
22
1
21
20
19
18
17
16
12
13
14
15
U

58 HOLIDAY HOME AND SAUNA

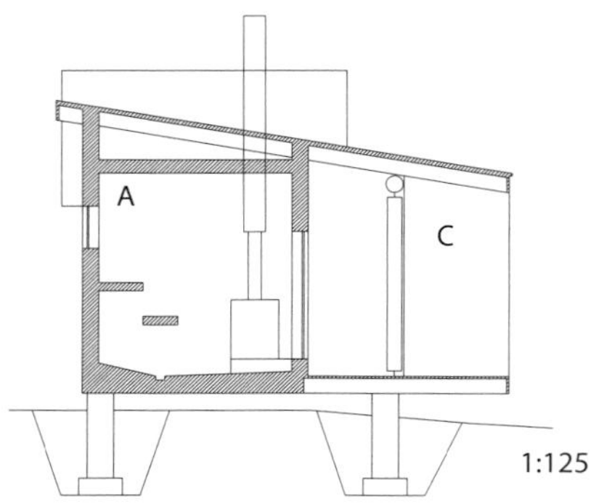

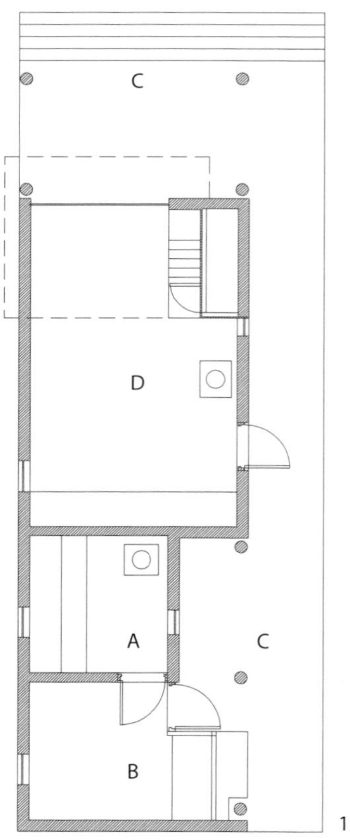

Suoperä cabin, Pudasjärvi, Finland, 1995, Nikolas Davies

A sauna, steam room
B changing room
C veranda, verandah
D living room, lounge

sauna
a building, room or series of spaces with wooden benches and a stove for bathing in steam

drainage
the use of drain systems to remove excess water from building surfaces and use

ventilation
1 the maintenance of the air quality of spaces in a building by continual provision of fresh air from the outside, either by natural or mechanical means

2 the natural passage of air into rooms to provide fresh air, and through gaps or cavities within roof, wall and floor construction to convey excess moisture out thus inhibiting mould and fungal attack

DRAINAGE

1 soakaway
2 drain
3 drainage pipe, discharge pipe
4 floor gully, floor drain, floor outlet
5 floor channel, drainage channel

HEATING AND INTERIOR

6 sauna benches, platforms
7 sauna heater, stove, stone heater
8 flue adaptor
9 insulated flue, flue
10 chimney flashing
11 rain cap, flue cap, cowl

VENTILATION

12 fresh-air inlet
13 fresh-air vent
14 exhaust outlet
15 exhaust vent

FOUNDATION

16 footing block, foundation block
17 concrete block foundation

STRUCTURE

18 floor joist
19 timber stud
20 sole plate, sole piece, base plate
21 head plate, header
22 ceiling joist – timber joist

ROOF STRUCTURE

23 roof joist
24 roof batten
25 ribbed-sheet roofing, profiled sheeting
26 fascia board

CLADDING

27 timber lining
28 floorboarding
29 weatherboarding, siding
30 decking – spaced boarding, open boarding, gapped boarding

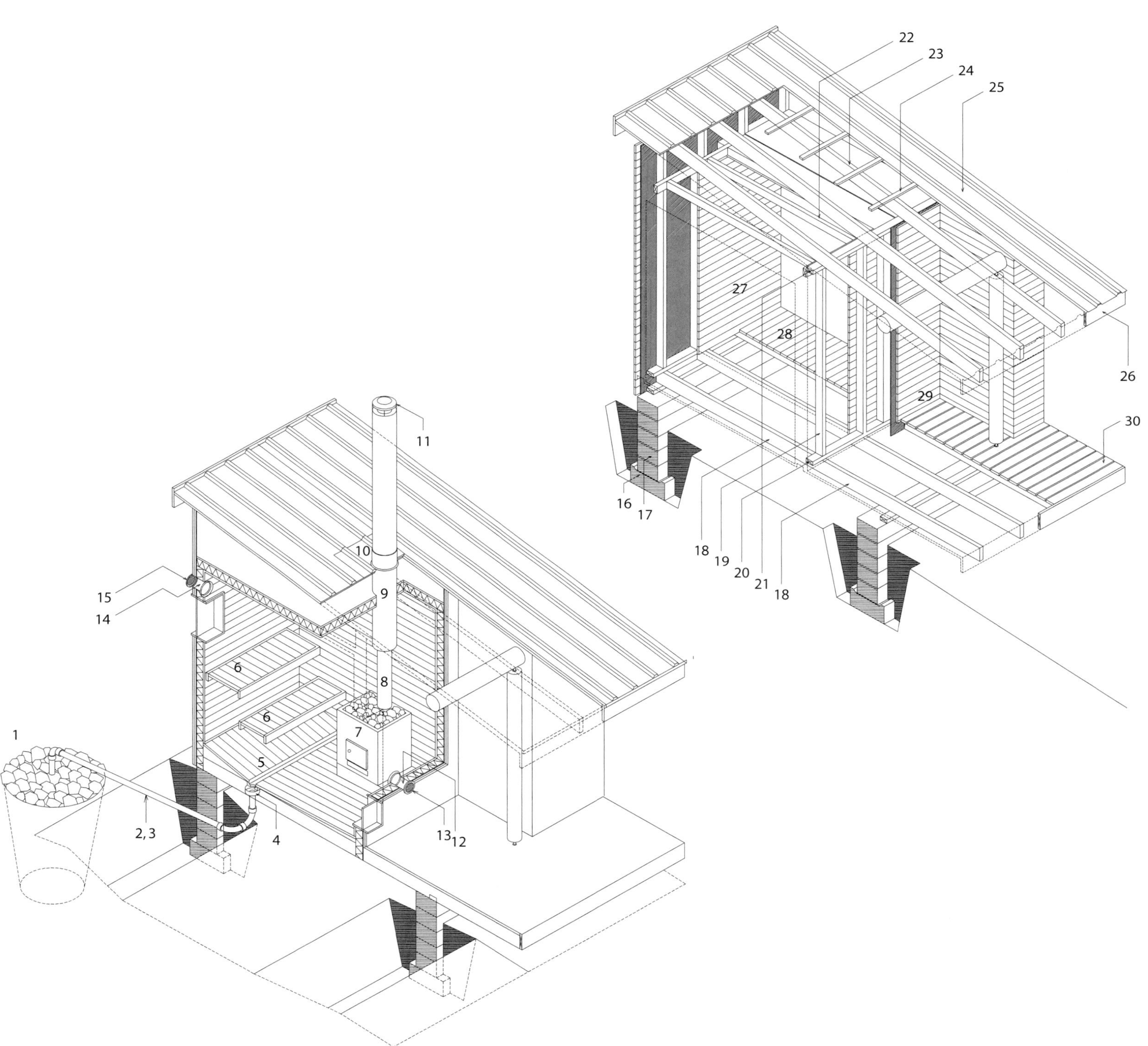
22
23
24
25
27
28
26
29
30
16
17
18
19
20
21
18
11
10
9
15
14
6
8
6
7
1
5
2, 3
4
13
12

59 BRICK HOUSE

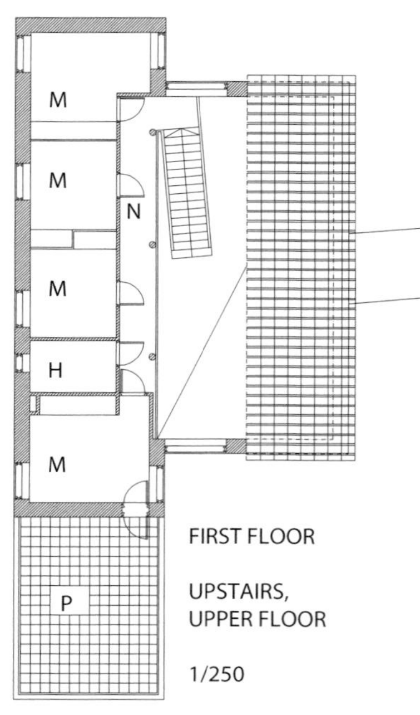

FIRST FLOOR

UPSTAIRS, UPPER FLOOR

1/250

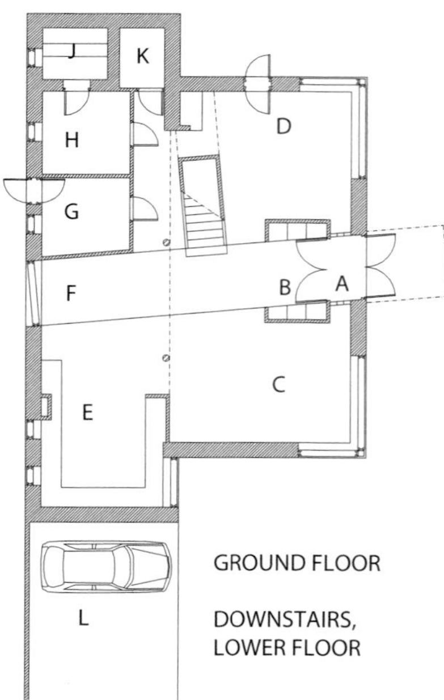

GROUND FLOOR

DOWNSTAIRS, LOWER FLOOR

Lähdesuonkatu House, Naantali, Finland, 1992, Vesa Huttunen

ROOMS

A draught lobby
B entrance hall
C living room
D lounge/sitting room
E kitchen
F dining area
G utility room, laundry room
H bathroom
J sauna
K store – built-in closet, closet
L garage
M bedroom
N corridor
P roof terrace

ROOF CONSTRUCTION

1 tiled roofing, roof tiling, tile roof, tiled roof
2 roof tile, roofing tile, tile
3 tiling batten, counter batten
4 ventilation gap, air gap
5 roof sheathing, sheathing board
6 roof beam, principal rafter, rafter
7 thermal insulation, mineral wool bats
8 vapour barrier, vapour check
9 ceiling boarding, soffit boarding – gypsum plasterboarding, plasterboarding

UPPER FLOOR CONSTRUCTION

10 overlay flooring
11 veneered parquet, multilayer parquet, parquet composite, parquet strip
12 impact sound isolation – corrugated cardboard, cellular plastic or granulated cork matting
13 flooring sub-base, subfloor – building board – chipboard
14 floor joist

BASE FLOOR CONSTRUCTION, BOTTOM FLOOR CONSTRUCTION, GROUND FLOOR CONSTRUCTION

15 tile flooring, floor tiling
16 ceramic tile – flooring tile, floor tile
17 tiling mortar, bedding mortar, fixing mortar
18 ground supported floor, ground slab, (Am.) slab-on-grade, floor bed
19 thermal insulation – expanded polystyrene
20 gravel fill

FOUNDATION

21 concrete strip foundation
22 cavity and thermal insulation
23 subsurface drain, subsoil drain – drain pipe, land drainage pipe, perforated pipe
24 drainage membrane, cavity drainage membrane, air-gap membrane
25 frost insulation

CAVITY WALL, HOLLOW WALL

26 inner leaf – blockwork
27 wall tie, cavity tie
28 outer leaf, external leaf – brickwork

structural brickwork
brickwork which is designed to be loadbearing

cavity wall, hollow masonry wall, hollow wall
a common exterior wall construction, often of masonry, composed of two adjacent walls or leaves tied together at intervals with an air space between, often partially or wholly filled with ventilated insulation

inner leaf
the skin of brickwork, blockwork, stonework or concrete cavity wall construction which faces the interior of a building; in concrete construction it is usually loadbearing

outer leaf, external leaf
the outer skin of masonry in a brick cavity wall or other sandwich construction; the leaf of a cavity wall which is exposed to the elements

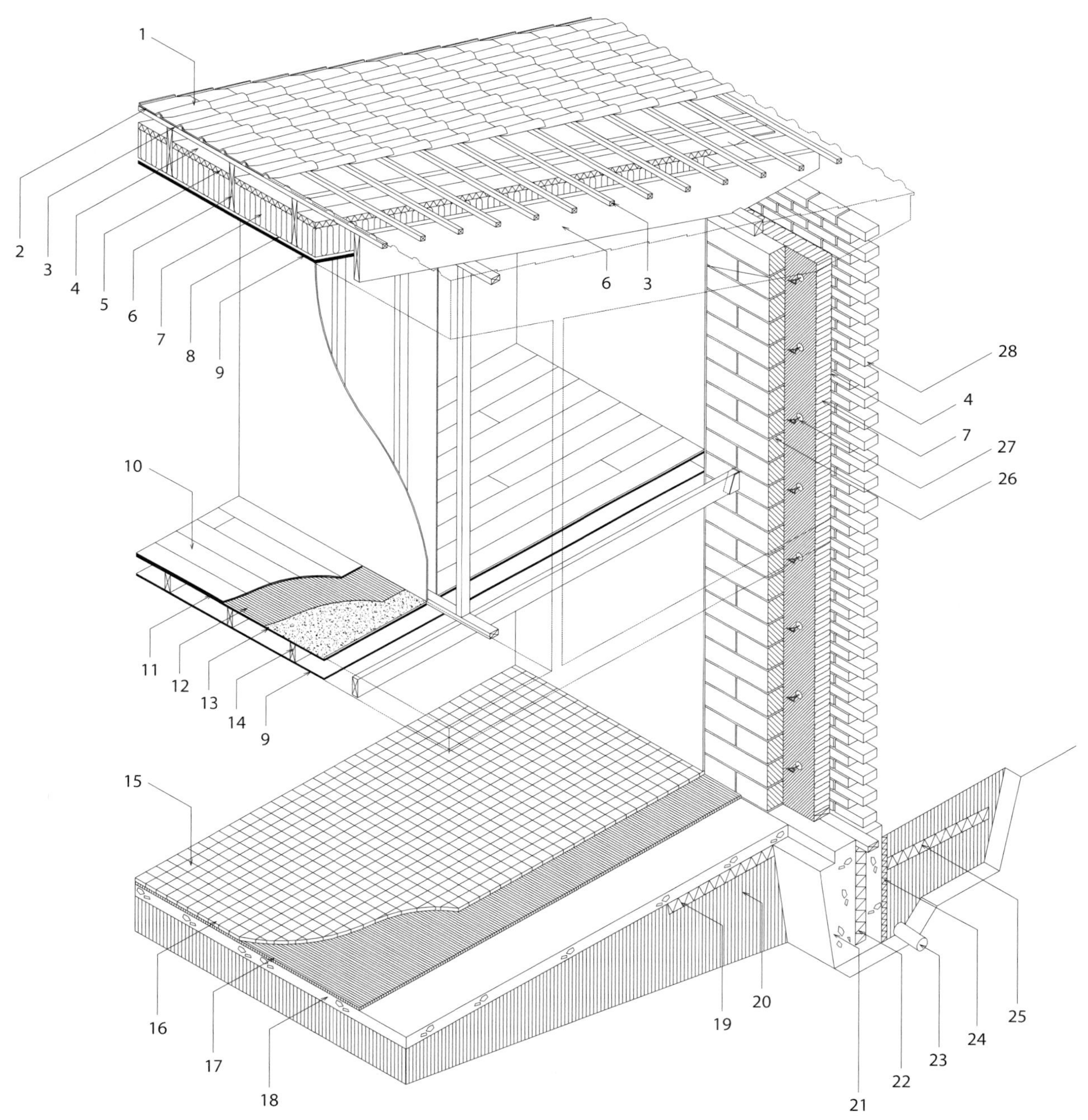

1
2
3
4
5
6
7
8
9
6
3
28
4
7
27
26
10
11
12
13
14
9
15
16
17
18
19
20
21
22
23
24
25

60 IN-SITU CONCRETE FRAMED OFFICE BUILDING

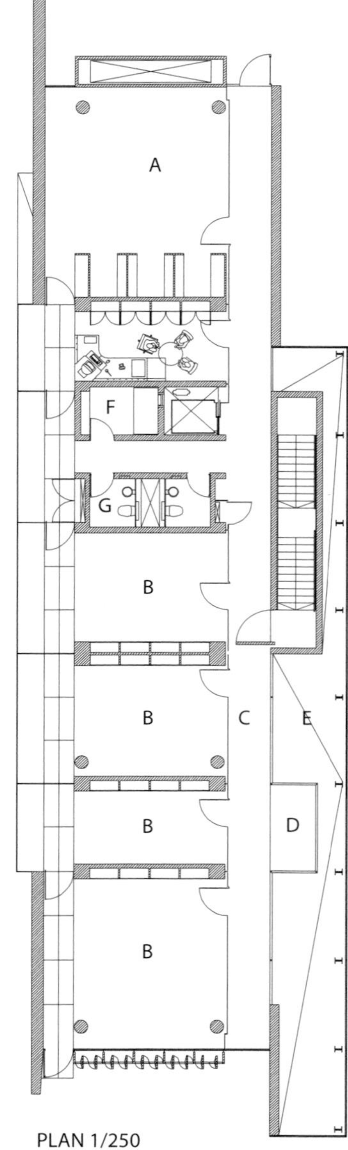

PLAN 1/250

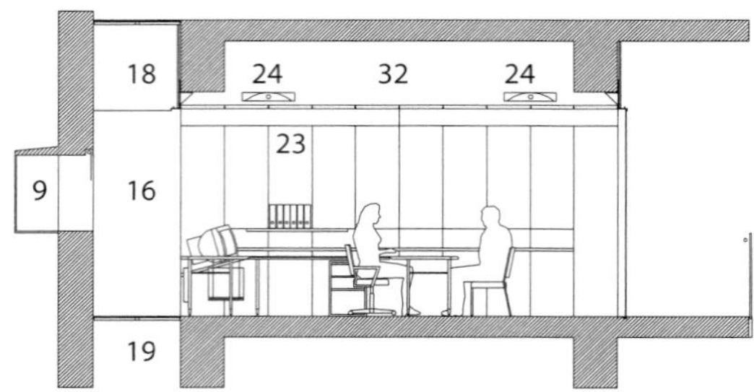

SECTION 1/125

A conference room, meeting room
B office space
C corridor
D cantilever balcony, internal balcony
E void
F store
G wc

concrete frame
any building frame of prefabricated or cast-in-situ concrete beams, columns, walls, slabs etc., onto which cladding components, flooring, roofing etc. are fixed

placing, placement
the laying, pouring or pumping of fresh concrete into formwork, moulds, excavations etc. to attain its final shape

in situ, cast-in-place (Am), cast-in-situ
referring to concrete and other similar materials which have been cast fresh on site as opposed to being prefabricated; written in-situ when used as an adjective

Office building, Darwin Avenue, Canberra, Australia, 2002, Vesa Huttunen

STRUCTURE

1 in-situ concrete floor
2 in-situ concrete beam
3 in-situ concrete wall
4 wall cladding
5 concrete slab, solid concrete slab
6 concrete beam
7 spine wall
8 sheetmetal cladding panel, pressed metal facing unit

EXTERNAL GLAZING

9 projecting window
10 rooflight, roof window, skylight – glazed roof, glass roof

ROOF

11 steel beam
12 steel purlin
13 profiled sheet roofing
14 roof channel
15 box gutter

INTERIOR

16 frameless glass partition
17 all-glass door
18 toplight, upper glazing
19 glazed floor
20 ventilation duct – air-conditioning duct
21 return-air terminal unit, air intake, extract unit – terminal unit
22 air duct, sheetmetal duct
23 fixed furnishing unit
24 light fitting, luminaire

CEILING SUSPENSION SYSTEM

25 perimeter trim
26 suspended ceiling, hung ceiling
27 ceiling panel
28 metal tray, metal pan
29 ceiling runner, runner
30 ceiling bearer, bearer
31 ceiling hanger, ceiling strap
32 ceiling void

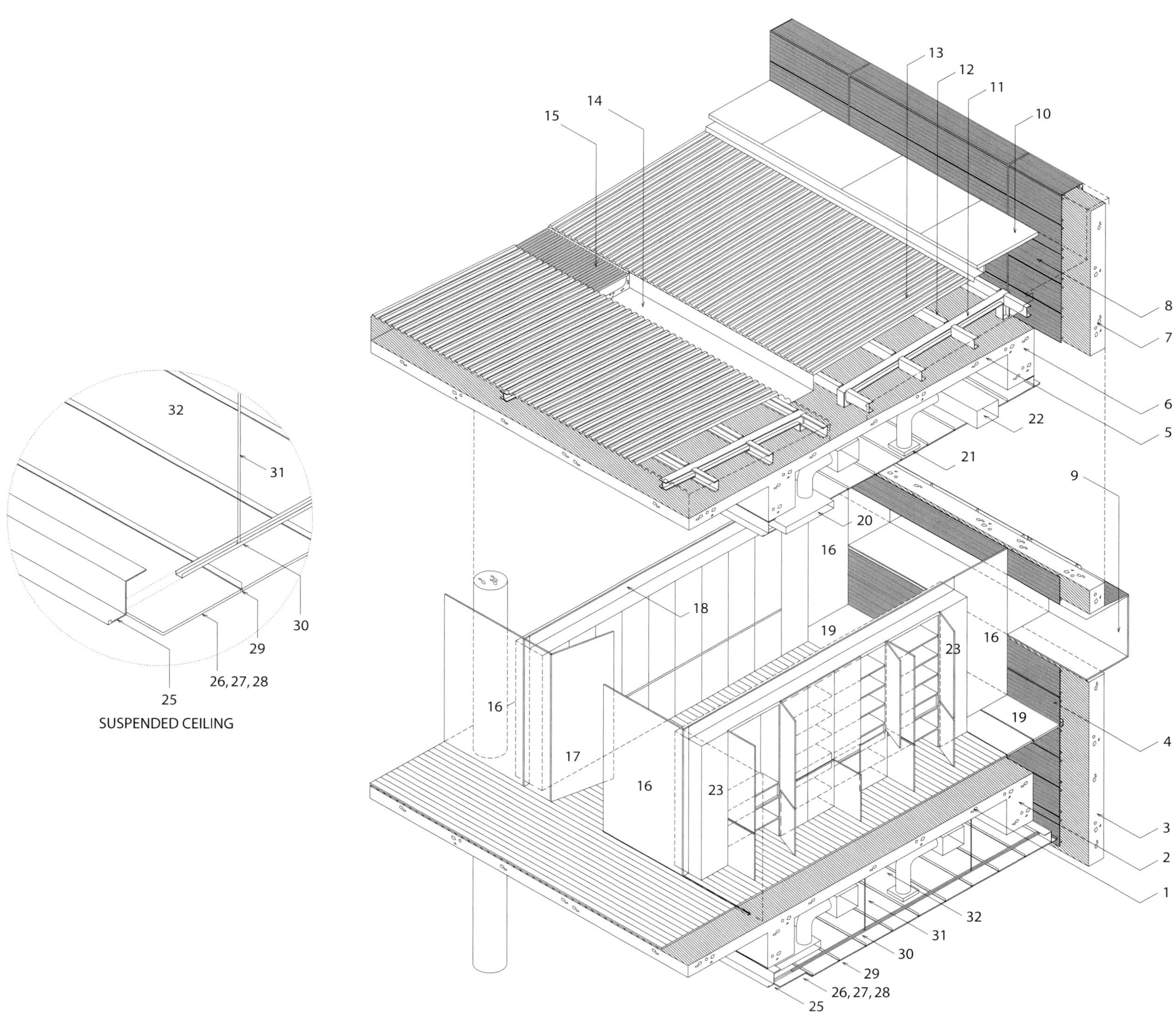

32
31
30
29
26, 27, 28
25
SUSPENDED CEILING
13
12
11
10
14
15
8
7
6
5
22
21
9
20
16
18
19
23
16
16
17
16
23
19
4
3
2
1
32
31
30
29
26, 27, 28
25

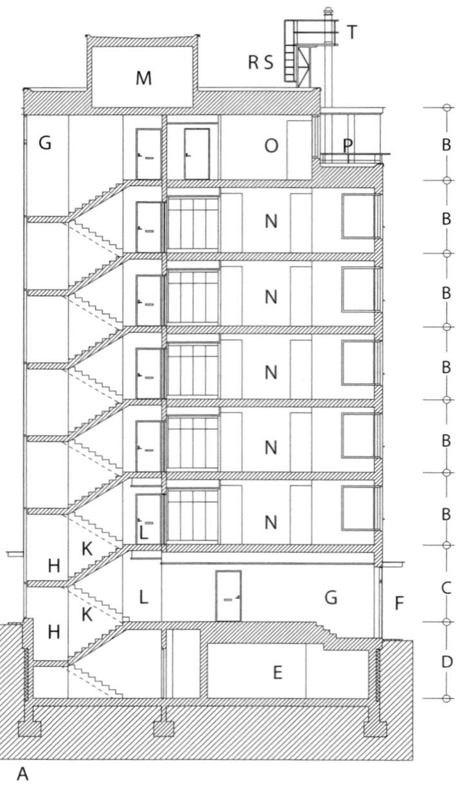

ORIENTATION OF DWELLING UNITS

- W double orientation unit, corner apartment
- X open ended unit, through apartment
- Y triple orientation unit, end apartment
- Z single orientation unit

DETACHED HOUSES

1 detached house, freestanding dwelling
2 bungalow, one-storey house
3 one-family house, single-family house
4 split-level house

LINKED DWELLINGS

5 semi-detached house, duplex house
6 two-family house
7 clustered apartments
8 row house, terraced house
9 link house, linked dwellings
10 stacked apartments
11 terraced house, town house, row house
12 back-to-back houses, (Am.) double row houses
13 atrium house, patio house
14 stepped block, terraced block

RESIDENTIAL BLOCKS, APARTMENT BLOCKS, BLOCKS OF FLATS

15 low-rise housing block
16 walk-up apartments, tenement
17 point-access block, single stair building, central core building
18 tower block, high-rise building, point-access block, single core block
19 corridor block
20 central or double-loaded corridor block
21 non-corridor block, point-access slab
22 slab block
23 balcony-access block of flats, gallery access slab, (Am.) gallery apartment house
24 single-loaded corridor block
25 garage
26 carport

- A apartment block, 1/300
- B storey, floor, level, (Am.) story
- C ground floor
- D basement storey, basement floor, basement level
- E civil defence shelter
- F entrance
- G stairway, staircase
- H intermediate landing
- K flight
- L landing
- M plant room, machine room, motor room
- N apartment, flat, dwelling unit
- O penthouse
- P roof terrace, balcony
- R chimney ladder, flue ladder
- S ladder
- T access platform, gantry

A) Apartment block, Helsinki, 2005, Gullichsen-Vormala Architects

residential building, dwelling house
a building which contains one or a number of dwellings, or one whose sole purpose is to serve as such

dwelling
a permanent residential unit containing sleeping, cooking and sanitary facilities; the collective name for a house, flat, home etc.

house
a freestanding dwelling with living space for one family unit; often also called a one-family house or single-family house

housing
1 policies, regulations, development and other matters relating to residential buildings, when viewed as a whole
2 a general term for a group of dwellings; when designed at any one time it is known as a housing development or housing scheme

storey, floor, story (Am.) level
one of the horizontal floor levels in a multistorey building

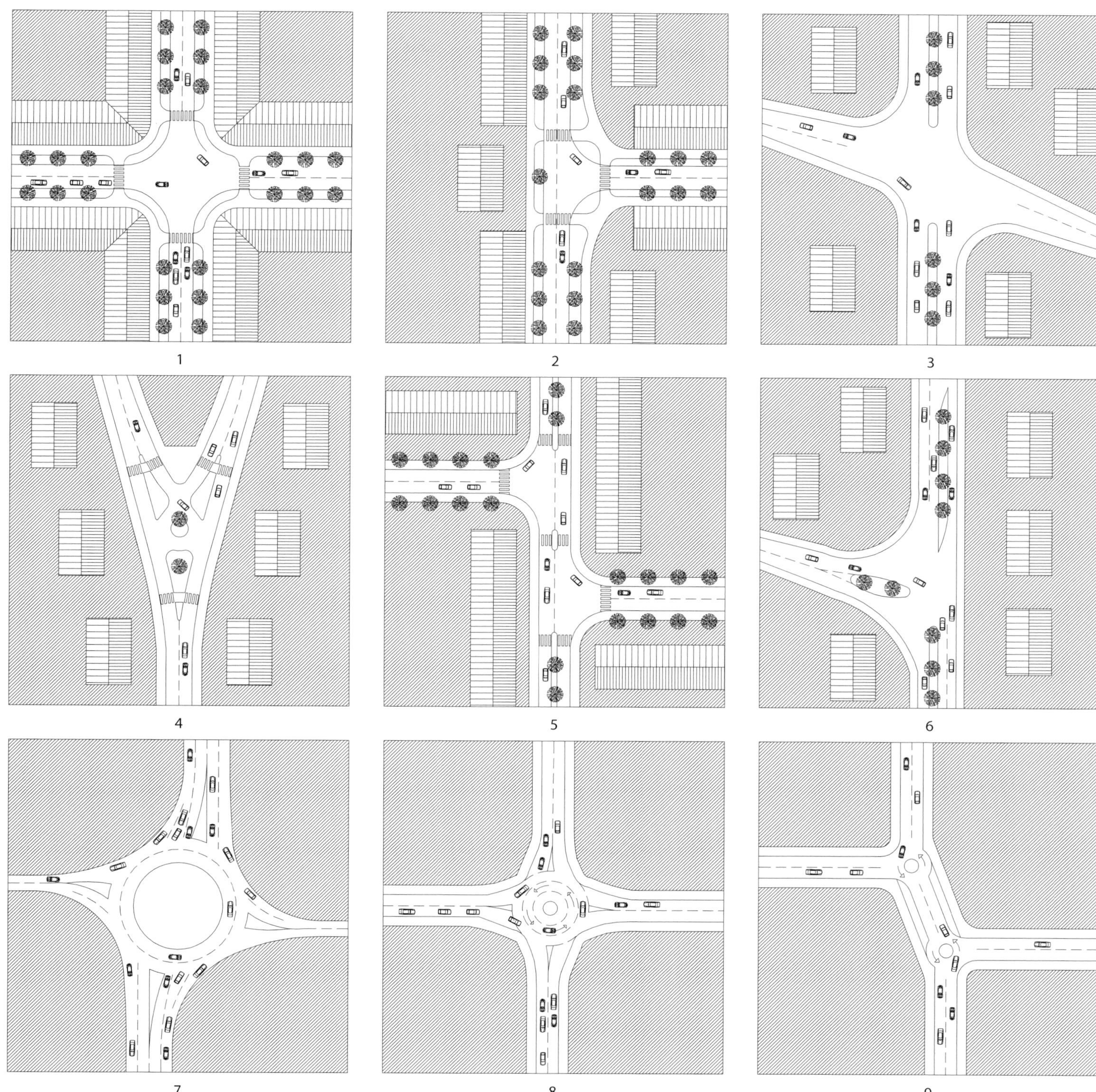
1
2
3
4
5
6
7
8
9

63 GRADE-SEPARATED JUNCTIONS, THROUGH TRAFFIC

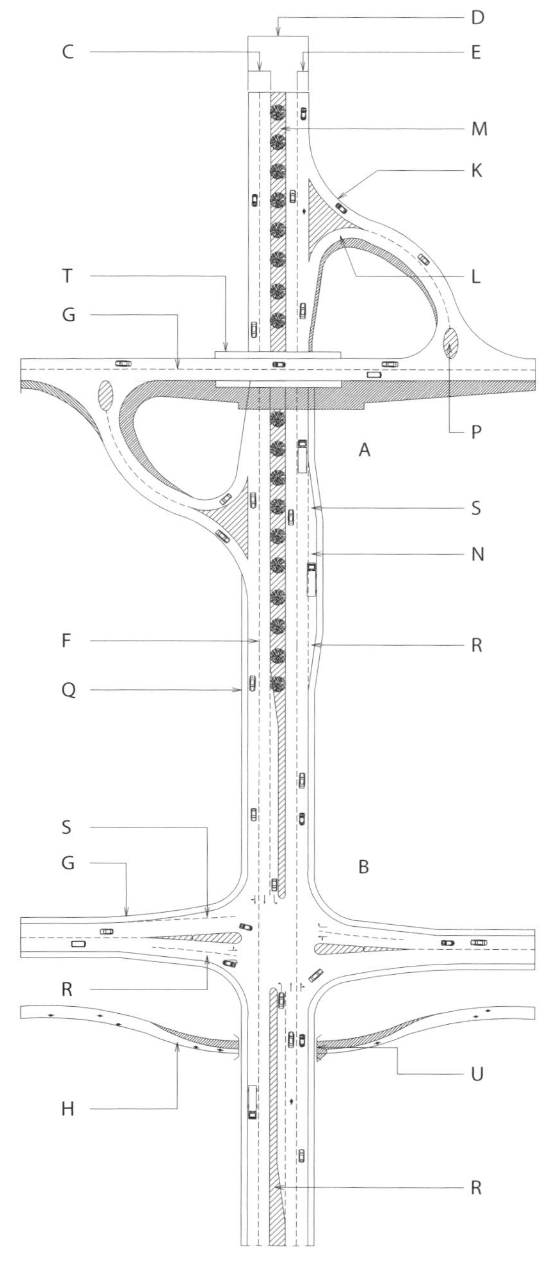

N.B. traffic driving on right

MOTORWAY JUNCTIONS

A grade-separated junction, interchange

B at-grade junction

ROUTES

C carriageway

D dual carriageway, divided carriageway

E lane

F major road

G minor road

H cycle path, cycle track or route

RAMPS AND OTHER

K slip road, ramp

L loop ramp

M central reservation, reserve, median

N bus bay, lay-by

P traffic island, refuge

Q hard shoulder, verge

R flare

S funnel

BRIDGES

T flyover

U underpass, pedestrian subway, subway

GRADE-SEPARATED JUNCTION & INTERCHANGE TYPES

1 trumpet junction, trumpet interchange

2 directional T junction

3 double trumpet junction

4 roundabout junction, roundabout interchange

5 full cloverleaf junction, cloverleaf interchange

6 grade-separated fork junction, fork interchange

7–9 partial cloverleaf junction, half cloverleaf interchange, parclo

10 diamond junction, diamond interchange

11 diamond interchange with carriageway separation

12 dumbell junction, dumb-bell interchange

grade-separated roundabout junction, graded interchange
a road junction or interchange with slip roads leading from a major road to a roundabout constructed above it, from which traffic is distributed to minor roads

interchange
a major road junction in which traffic can flow freely from one road or motorway to another without stopping or slowing down; most often a grade-separated junction with a number of ramps leading from carriageway to carriageway

carriageway, roadway
that part of a road used by vehicular traffic

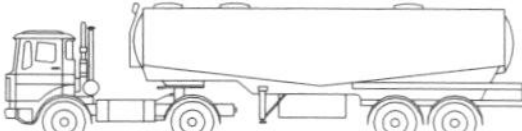

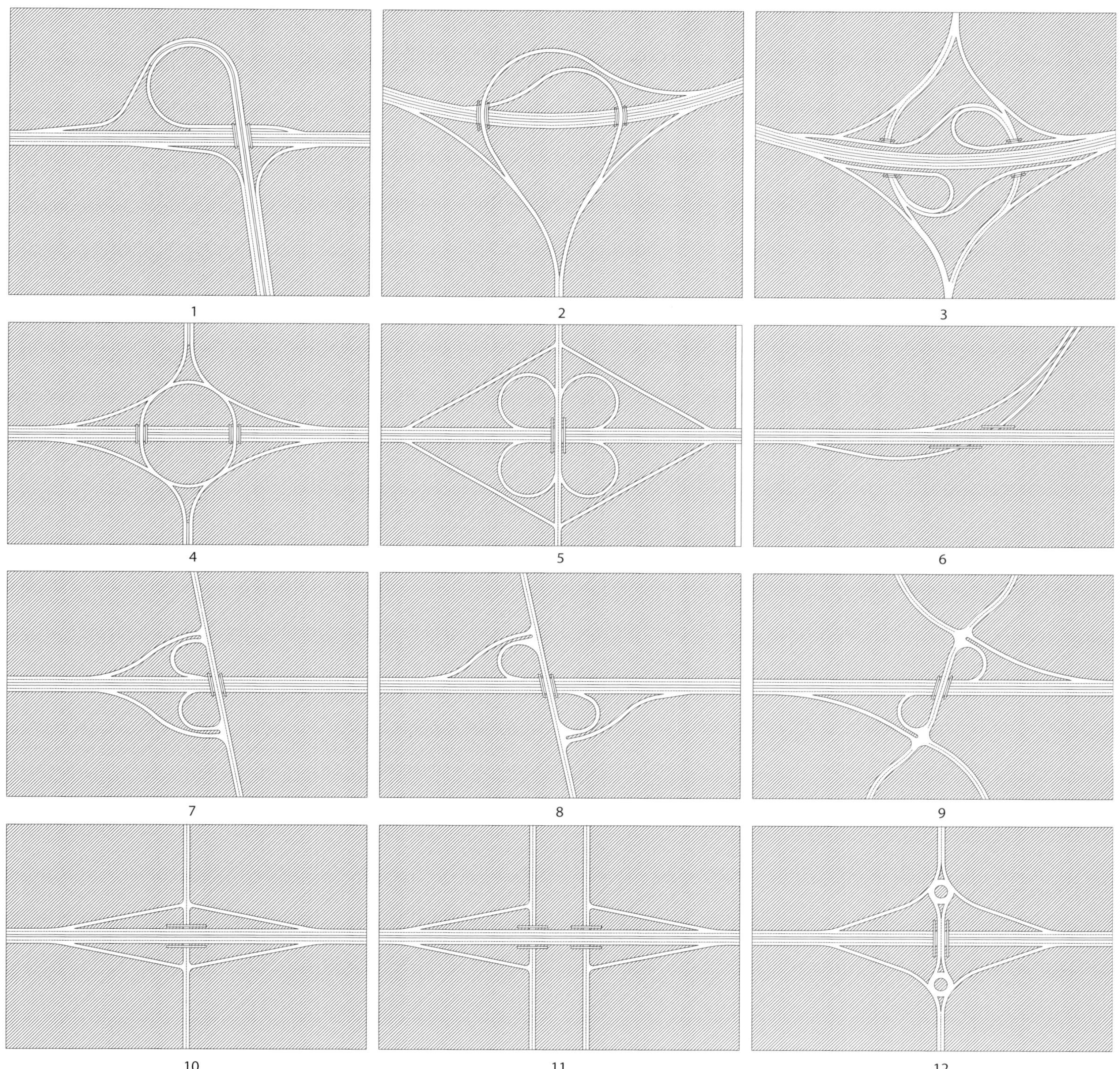

1
2
3
4
5
6
7
8
9
10
11
12

64 MOVABLE BRIDGES AND FLYOVERS

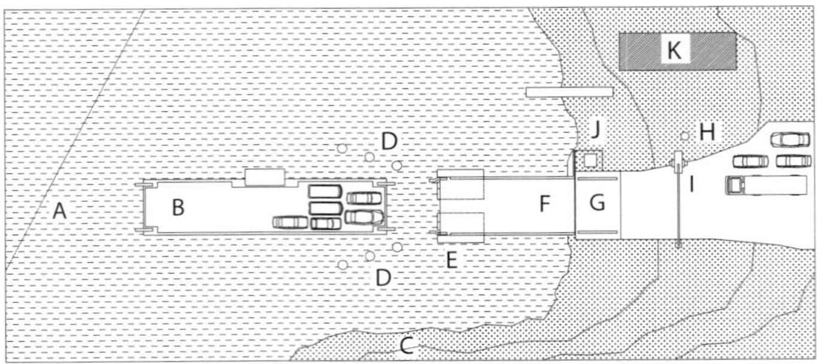

FLOATING BRIDGE

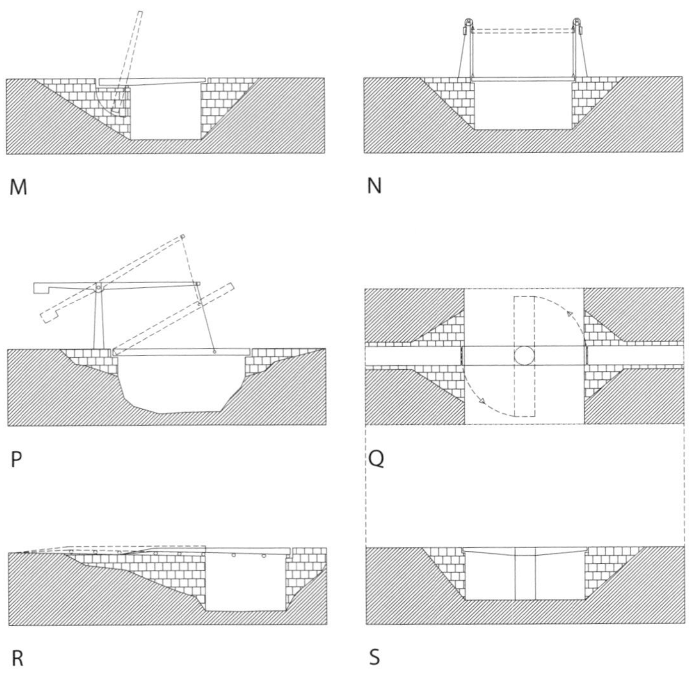

MOVING BRIDGES

FLOATING BRIDGE

A shipping route, sea lane
B floating bridge, cable ferry, chain ferry
C breakwater
D dolphins
E pontoon, float
F landing stage, wharf
G bridge abutment
H traffic light, light signal
I boom, barrier
J winch, hoist
K attendant's hut control room

MOVABLE BRIDGES

M bascule bridge, balance bridge, counterpoise bridge
N lift bridge
P crane bridge
Q pivot bridge, swing bridge turn bridge, swivel bridge (plan)
R rectractable bridge, traversing bridge
S pivot bridge, swing bridge, turn bridge

OVERPASSES

1 straight bridge: waterway bridge
2 skew bridge: waterway bridge
3 curved bridge: waterway bridge
4 underbridge: railway bridge
5 undercrossing, underpass: railway bridge
6 overpass, flyover: road bridge
7 crossover: road bridge
8 overpass: footbridge, walkway, pedestrian bridge
9 subway, underpass: pedestrian subway

movable bridge
a bridge which can be moved by raising, sliding or pivoting to allow larger vehicles or boats to pass by it

floating bridge, pontoon bridge
a bridge supported on floats or pontoons over water

flyover, overpass
a modern road bridge for an urban expressway etc. which passes over another road, railway or other obstacle

underpass
a road, passage or carriageway which passes beneath another road or obstruction in a short tunnel or shaft

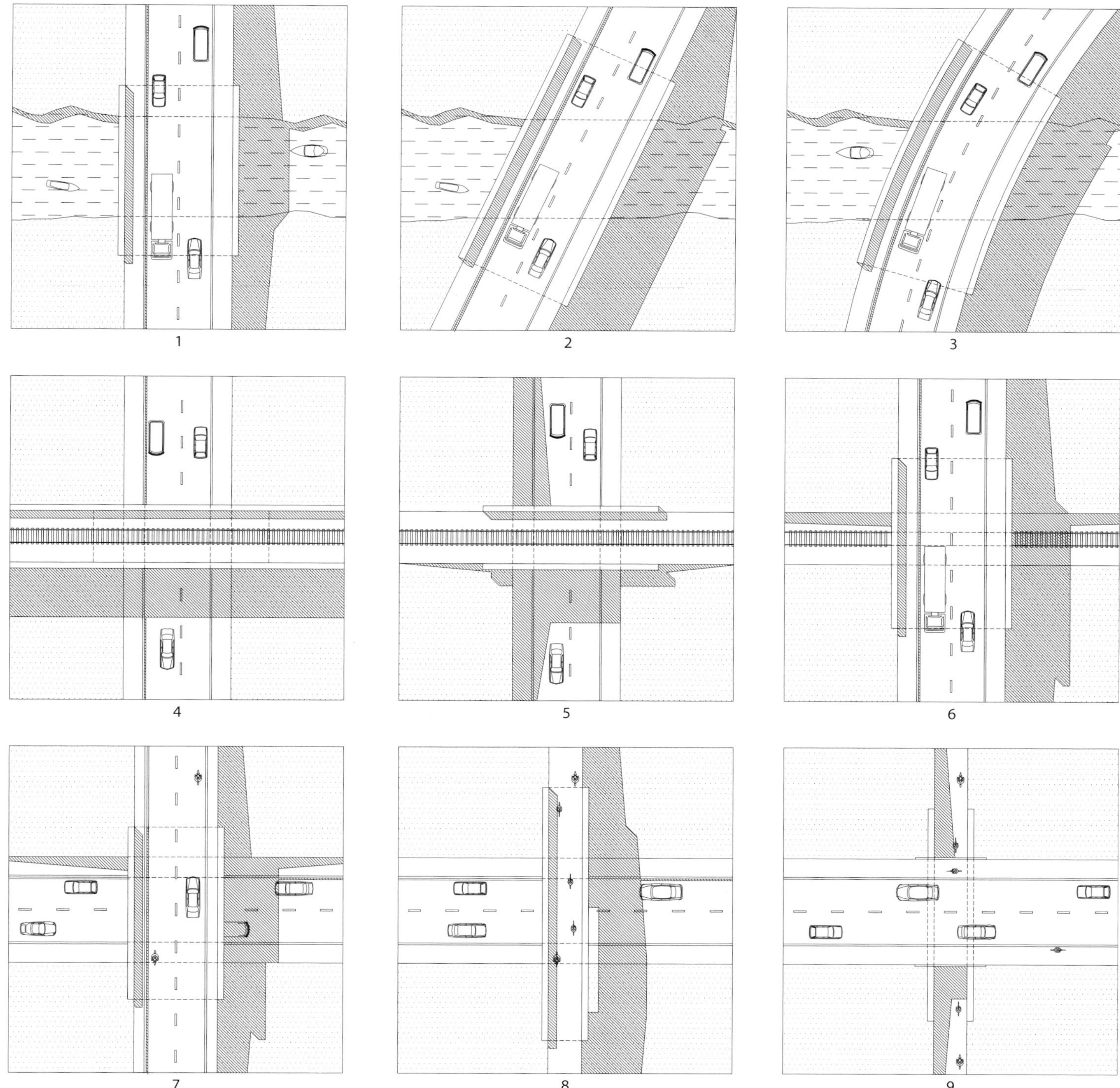

1
2
3
4
5
6
7
8
9

65 PREHISTORIC DWELLINGS, TEMPLES AND GRAVES

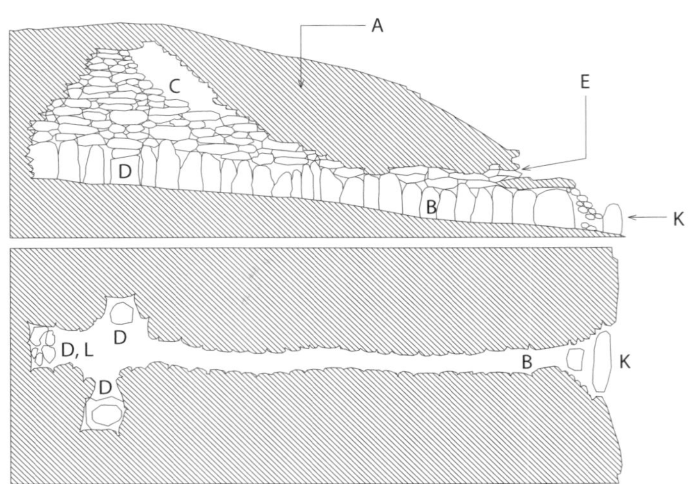

1 1/300

A burial mound, grave mound
B passage, passageway
C corbelled vault
D niche
E roof box
F dromos
G stomion
H tholos, tholus, beehive tomb
K entrance
L burial chamber
M chamber
N store
P courtyard, court, light well

1 passage grave, passage tomb, chambered cairn, chambered tomb
2 tholos tomb
3 wheelhouse, round house
4 longhouse, long building
5 oval house
6 megalithic temple
7 neolithic village
8 broch
9 megaron
10 hamlet of courtyard houses

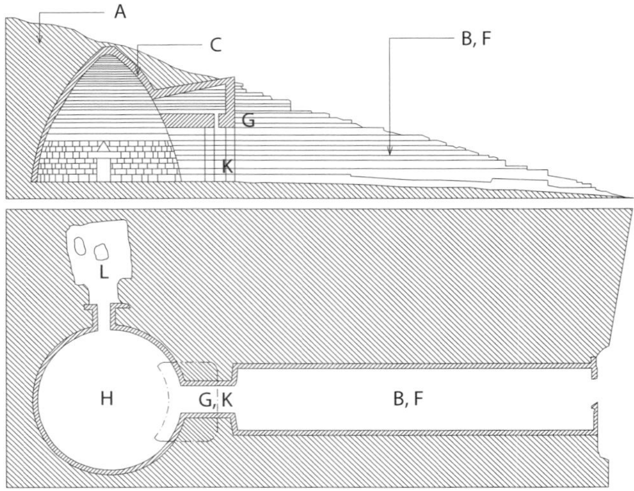

2 1/750

prehistoric
referring to an age which predates written historical records

Stone Age
a prehistoric period from about 600 000 BC–1200 BC during which the most important utensils were made from stone, usually divided into the Old, Middle and New Stone Age

palaeolithic period, (paleolithic), Old Stone Age
a prehistoric period from c.600 000–8000 BC, predating the mesolithic period and characterized by the rise to dominance of the human species, Homo sapiens, during which the first implements were struck from stone

mesolithic period, Middle Stone Age
a prehistoric period from c.8300–4000 BC, between the palaeolithic and neolithic, during which use of the axe became widespread and principal tools were struck from stone

neolithic period, New Stone Age
a prehistoric period in Europe from c.4000–2000 BC, after the mesolithic, during which the use of clay became widespread and the principal tools were finished by grinding

Iron Age
a prehistorical or historical period, running concurrent with the Bronze Age from c.1200 BC–1 AD, during which implements were forged from iron

1) Newgrange, Ireland, c.3250 BC; 2) Treasury of Atreus, 'Tomb of Agamemnon', Mycenae, Greece,1325–1250 BC; 3) Calf of Eday, Orkney Isles, Scotland, c.100 BC; 4) Köln-Lindenthal, neolithic period, c.5500–4900 BC; 5) Chamaizi (Khamazi), Crete, c.2000–1500 BC; 6) Hal Tarxien, Malta, 3000–2500 BC; 7) Skara Brae, Orkney Isles, Scotland, c.2000 BC; 8) Dun Troddan, Glen Elg, Scotland, c.100 BC; 9) Phylakopi, Mycenae, 3300–1100 BC; 10) Chysauster, Cornwall, England, c.50 BC

3 1/250

4 1/500

5 1/200

6 1/600

7 1/600

8 1/600

9 1/2000

10 1/1500

8 1/600

66 MESOPOTAMIAN TEMPLES

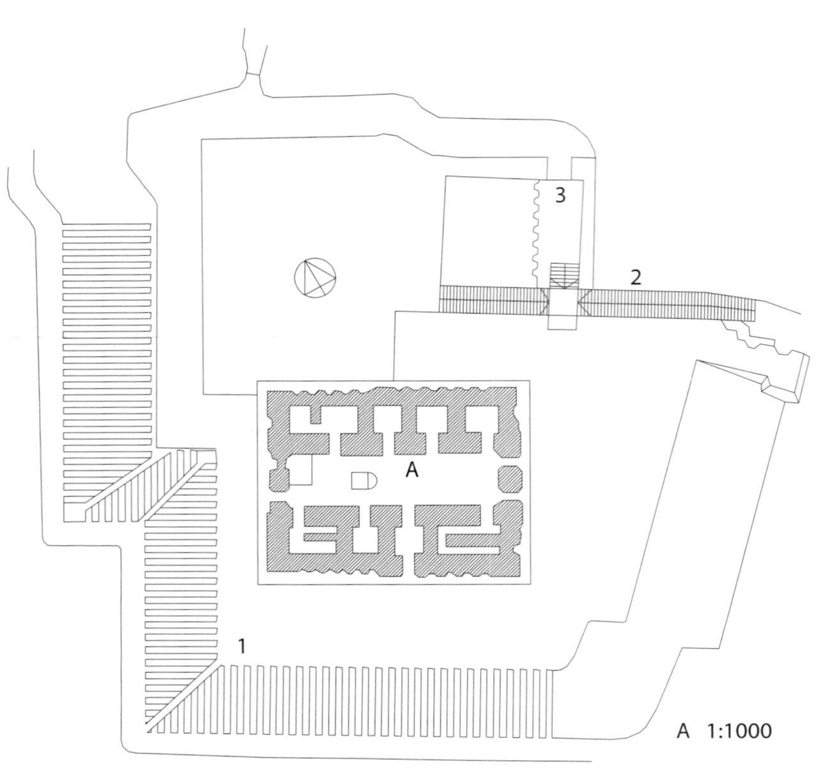

1 ziggurat
2 ceremonial stair
3 entrance ramp
4 entrance to palace chapel
5 chapel courtyard
6 antecella
7 cella
8 latrine
9 ablution
10 entrance to palace
11 palace courtyard
12 private suite
13 throne room
14 great hall
15 entrance to temple
16 forecourt
17 temple courtyard
18 cella
19 clergy
20 sacrificial altar
21 central hall
22 cult room

A pyramid temple
B palace chapel
C palace
D revelation temple
E hearth temple
F round temple, fort temple
G cult temple
H square temple
K square temple
L revelation temple

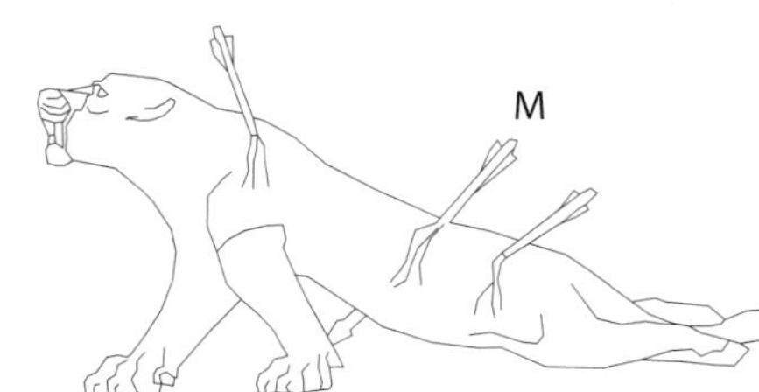

Mesopotamian architecture
architecture from 3000 BC to 600 BC originating in the valleys of the rivers Tigris and Euphrates in what is now Iraq; characterized by lavish palaces, tombs and ziggurats in massive masonry and mud bricks

Assyrian architecture
the Middle Eastern architecture of the organized society in the area now known as Iraq, at its height around 800 BC, characterized by single-storey dwellings in mud brick and expansive palaces and temples

temple, shrine
a building or consecrated space for the worship of a deity or effigy

A) 'White Temple' to the sky god Anu, Warka, Iraq, 3100–3000 BC; B–D) Palace and temple of Eshnunna, Tell Asmar, Iraq; c.2000 BC; E) First temple of Abu, god of vegetation, Tell Asmar, Iraq, 3100–3000 BC; F) round temple, 'fort temple', Tepe Gawra, Iraq, 4300–3100 BC; G) temple of Ishtar, Qalat Sharqat, Iraq, c.2300 BC; H) 'Square Temple', Tepe Gawra, Iraq, 4300–3100 BC; K) 'Square Temple' of the god Abu, Tell Asmar, Iraq, c.2750–2650 BC; L) Temple D, Eanna complex, Warka, Iraq, c.3000 BC; M) depiction of dying she-lion, Ninevah, Assyria, c.650 BC, British Museum, London

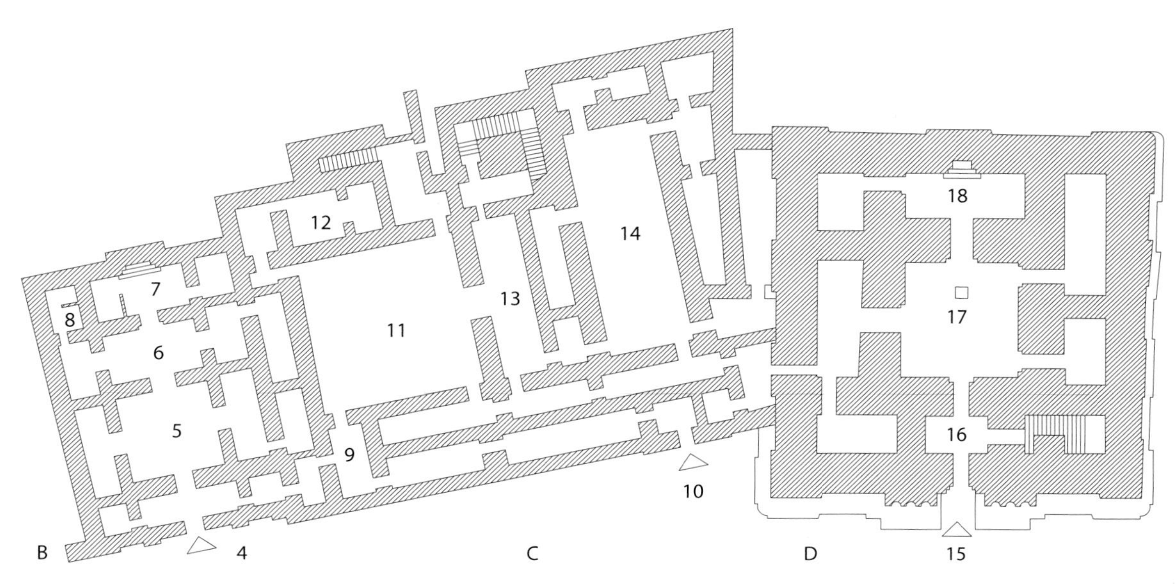

12
14
7
8
13
11
6
17
18
5
9
16
10
B
4
C
D
15

1/700

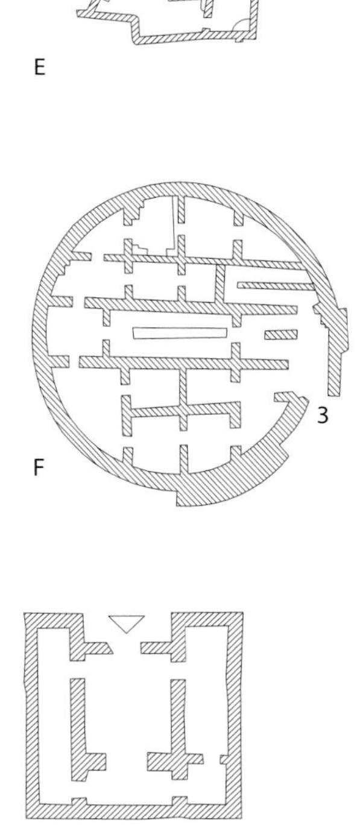

E
3
F
H

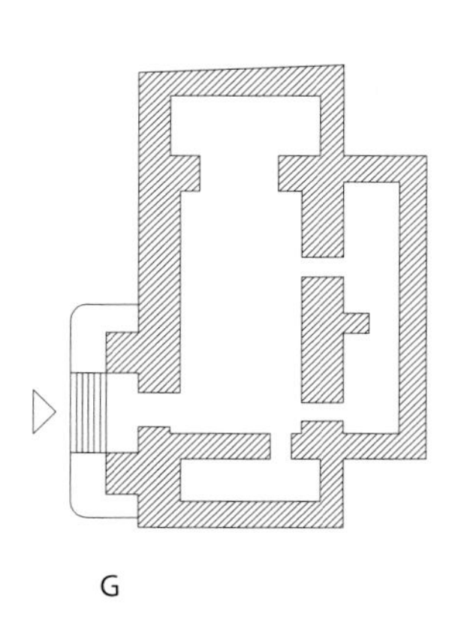

G

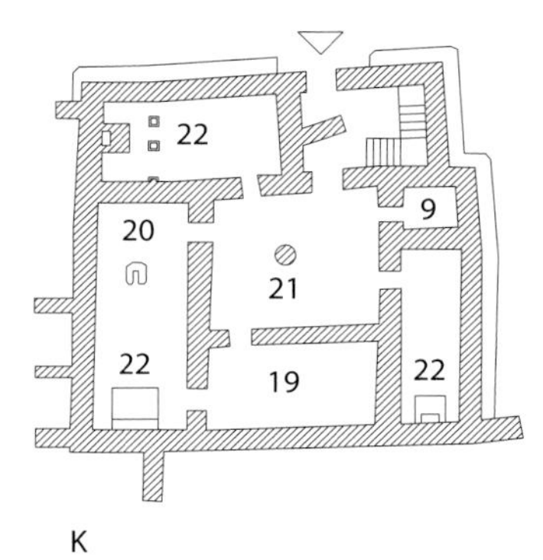

22
9
20
21
22
19
22
K

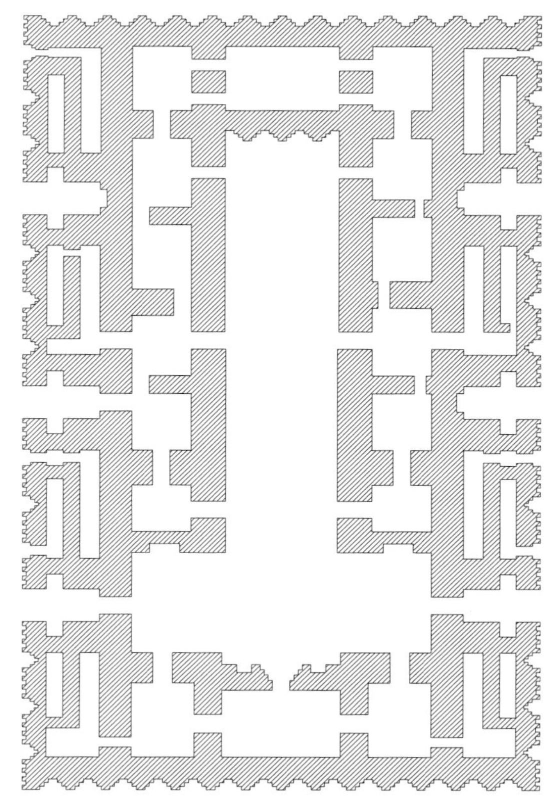

L

67 ZIGGURATS AND STEPPED PYRAMIDS

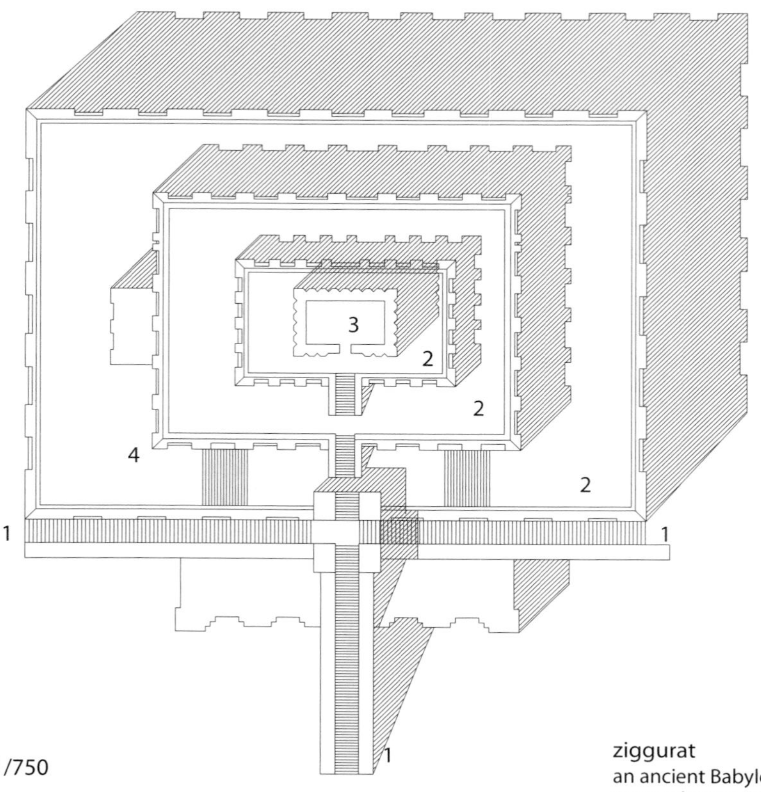

A 1/750

ZIGGURAT
1 great staircase
2 platform
3 temple
4 buttress

LEVELS OF PLANETARY DEITIES
5 sun
6 moon
7 Jupiter
8 Mercury
9 Mars
10 Venus
11 Saturn

TEOCALLI
12 grand stair
13 temple
14 roof comb

MINARET
15 spiral ramp, helical ramp

TEMPLE AND PYRAMID TYPES

A stepped pyramid, ziggurat (Mesopotamian)
B ramped temple, ziggurat or observatory (Assyrian)
C teocalli (Mayan stepped pyramid)
D teopan (Aztec pyramid temple, circular pyramid, round pyramid)
E spiral pyramid (Abbasid Moslem architecture)

ziggurat
an ancient Babylonian, Mesopotamian or Assyrian tiered structure of sun-baked bricks, similar to a stepped pyramid on a rectangular or ovoid plan, with straight or spiral ramped access to a summit temple, approached by a processional way; also similar structures in early Central and South American cultures

teocalli
'house of God'; an ancient Mexican or Central American temple on a truncated pyramid-shaped mound of earth and stone or brick

teopan
an Aztec teocalli, a stepped pyramid temple

minaret
a balconied tower in a mosque from which prayers and announcements are given, or the faithful are called to prayer

A) Ziggurat of Ur-Nammu, Ur (Tall al-Muqayyar), Iraq, 2113–2096 BC; B) Ziggurat or observatory, Khorsabad, Iraq 722–705 BC; C) Temple of the Giant Jaguar (Temple I), Tikal, Guatemala; c.500 AD; D) Temple of the God of the Winds, Calixtlahuaca, Mexico, 15th...16th century AD; E) Great Mosque, al Malwiyah minaret, Samarra, Iraq, 848–852 AD

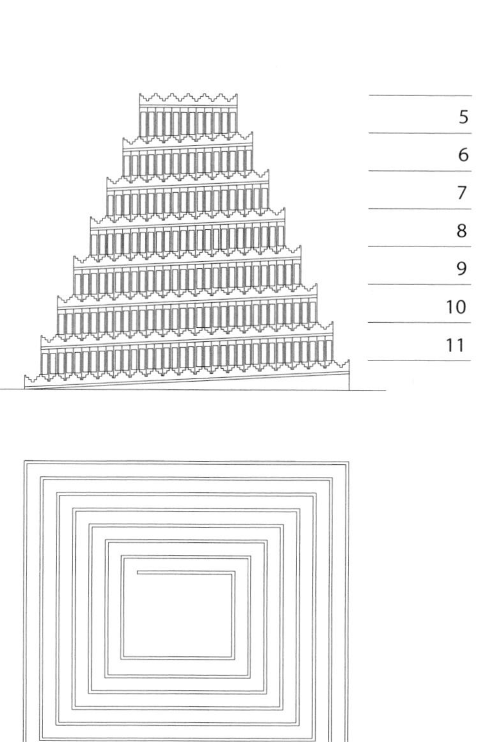

B 1/1000

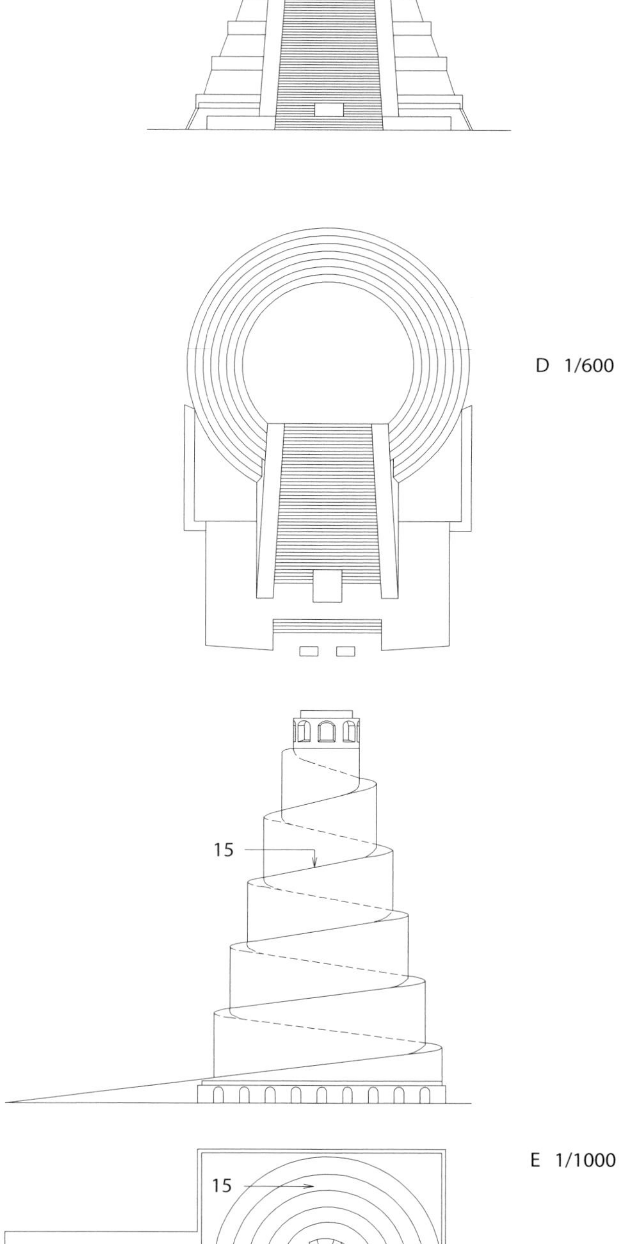

D 1/600

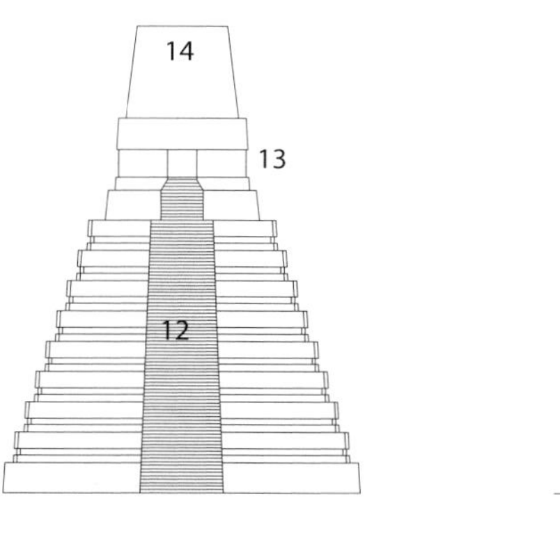

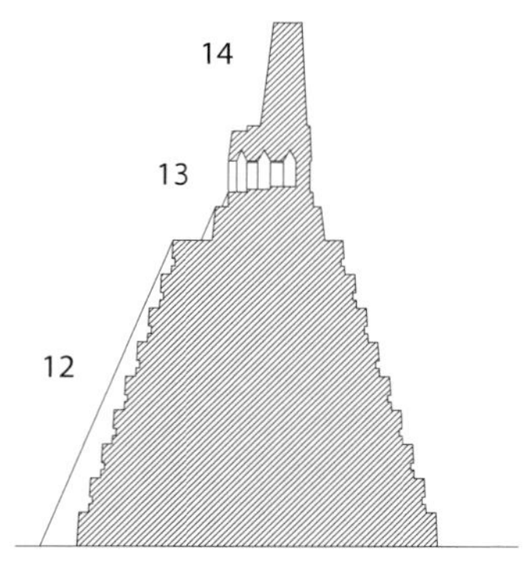

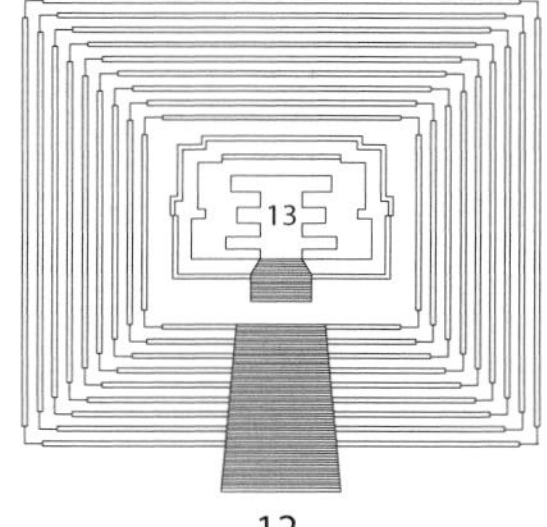

C 1/1000

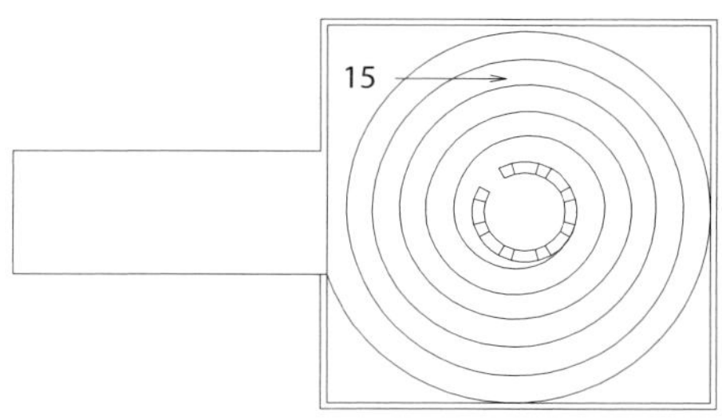

E 1/1000

68 ASIAN TEMPLES

A 1/50

A torii – gateway
B masugumi, kumimono/teou-kong – capital
C stupa, plan
D stupa, elevation
E rock-cut temple, section
F rock-cut temple, rock temple, cave temple
G pagoda

H BUDDHIST TEMPLE PRECINCT

K, L gateway
K sanmon – outer gate
L chumon – inner gate
M kondo, butsuden – golden hall
N kodo, hotto – assembly hall
O pavilion of the Sutras
P bell pavilion
R colonnade

STUPA – SACRAL BUILDING

1 torana – gateway
2 gopura, gopuram – gate tower
3 anda – dome, 'egg'
4 harmika – pavilion, railing
5 chattra – royal parasol
6 yasti – mast
7 vedika – fence, balustrade
8 ayaka – columned platform
9 vimana – temple precinct
10 pradakshinapatha – circumferential path

ROCK-CUT TEMPLE, ROCK TEMPLE

11 antarála – vestibule
12 garbha-griha – holy of holies
13 yoni & linga – cult statue

stupa
a dome-shaped sacred Buddhist building, often surrounded by a freestanding wall or railing and containing holy relics

rock-cut temple, cave temple, rock temple
a temple cut into a sheer rock face, a building-type found in the Indian architecture of the early Middle ages

pagoda
a multistorey Buddhist temple with projecting roofs at storey level, often replicated in Europe in the 1800s as an ornamental pavilion in gardens and parks

B

A) Vietnam; C, D) Great Stupa, Sanchi, India, Sunga period, 185–77 BC; E, F) Buddhist chaitya, Karli, India, 100–125; G, H) West temple precinct, Horyu-ji, Nara, Japan 700 AD

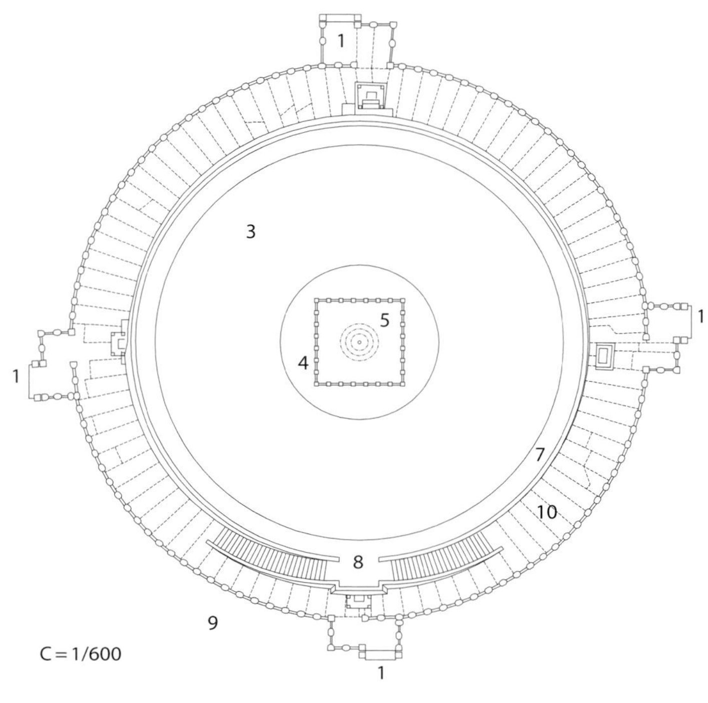

C = 1/600

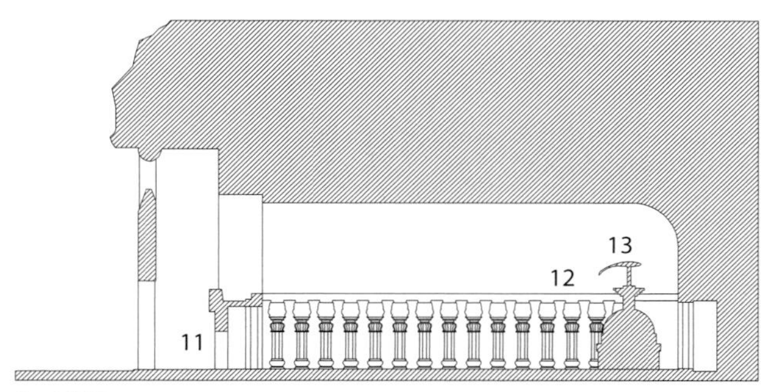

E = 1/700

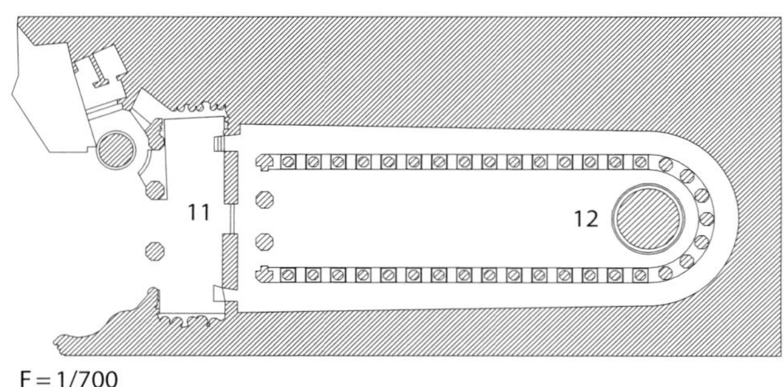

F = 1/700

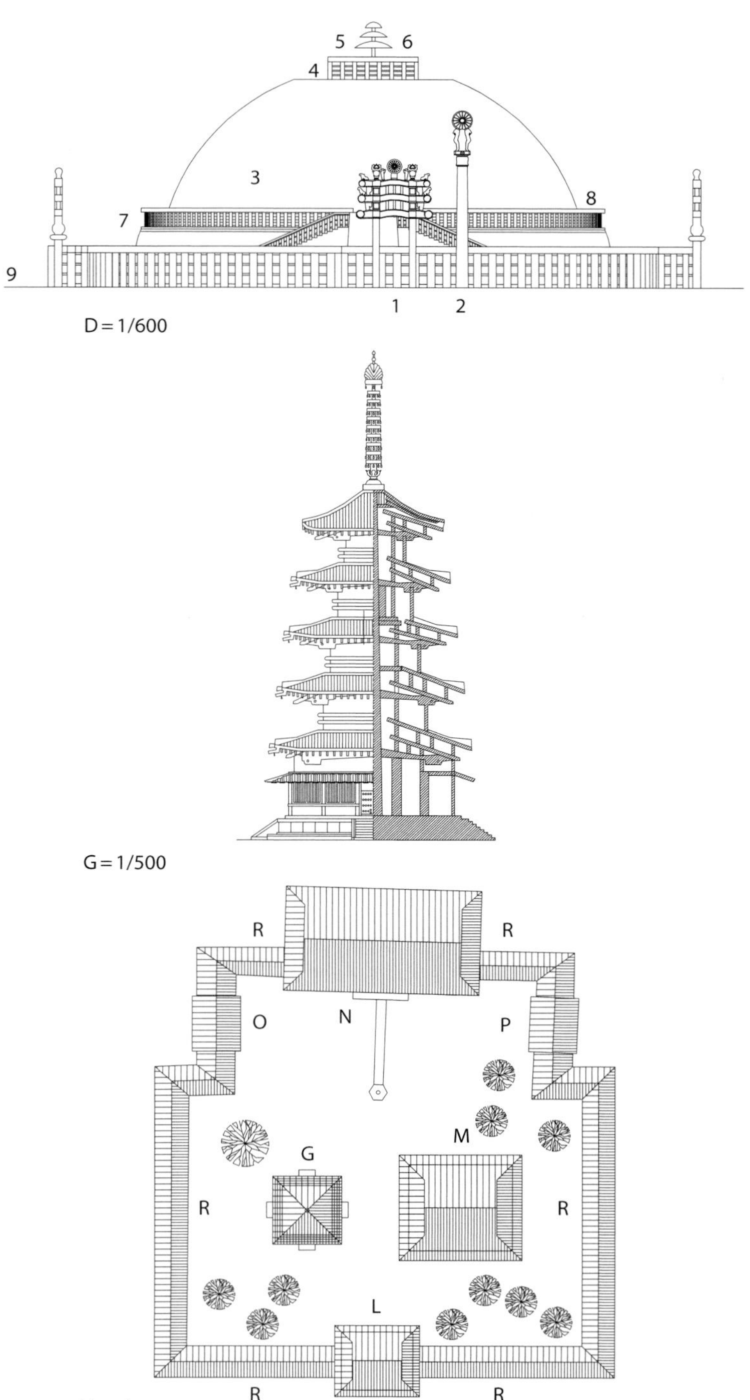

D = 1/600

G = 1/500

H = 1/2500

69 ASIAN AND MEDITERRANEAN COLUMNS AND CAPITALS

A cushion capital – Mycenaean
B Aeolic capital (volute capital)
C volute capital – Phoenician
D palm capital
E lion and lotus capital – Indian
F blossom capital
G bull capital
H Ephesian base, Asiatic base

1 Minoan column, Cretan column, Mycenaean column
2 reverse taper column
3 palm column – Greek with Phoenecian influence
4 rostral column, columna rostrata – Roman
5 serpent column, Aesculapian column, Asclepian column – Greek
6 baluster column – Assyrian
7 baluster column – Assyrian
8 edict pillar – Indian (Gupta period)
9 Indian column (Gupta period)
10 apadana column – Persian

column
a structural shaft of concrete, masonry, metal or timber which transfers applied vertical loads through its length to its base

capital
a separate block or a thickening at the top of a column or pilaster, used to spread the load of a beam, or as decoration

columna rostrata, rostral column
in classical Roman architecture, a freestanding pillar with maritime ornament, constructed in commemoration of naval success in battle

edict pillar
smooth-shafted freestanding ceremonial columns originally erected by the Indian ruler Asoka (273–232 BC); capped with lotus capitals carved with animal motifs, expounding Buddhist teachings; also called edict column

A) Treasury of Atreus, Mycenae, Greece, c.1325–1250 BC; B) Temple at Neandria, Turkey, c.600 BC; C) Cyprus; D) Khorsabad, Iraq, Assyrian period 850–500 BC; E) Lion capital of Ashoka column, Sarnath, India, c.250 BC; 1, 2) Great Palace of Knossos, Crete, c.1400 BC; 3) Treasury of Massalia (now Marseilles), Delphi, Greece, 6th cent. BC; 4) Rostral column of Gaius Duilius, Rome, Italy, c.260 BC; 5) Delphi, Greece; 6) Niniveh, Iraq, Assyrian period 850–500 BC; 7) Khorsabad, Iraq, Assyrian period 850–500 BC; 8, 9) India, classical Gupta period, c.400–700 AD; 10) Palace, Persepolis, Iran, 518–330 BC

F
H
G
1, 2
3
4
5
6
7
8
9
10

70 EGYPTIAN BURIAL MONUMENTS

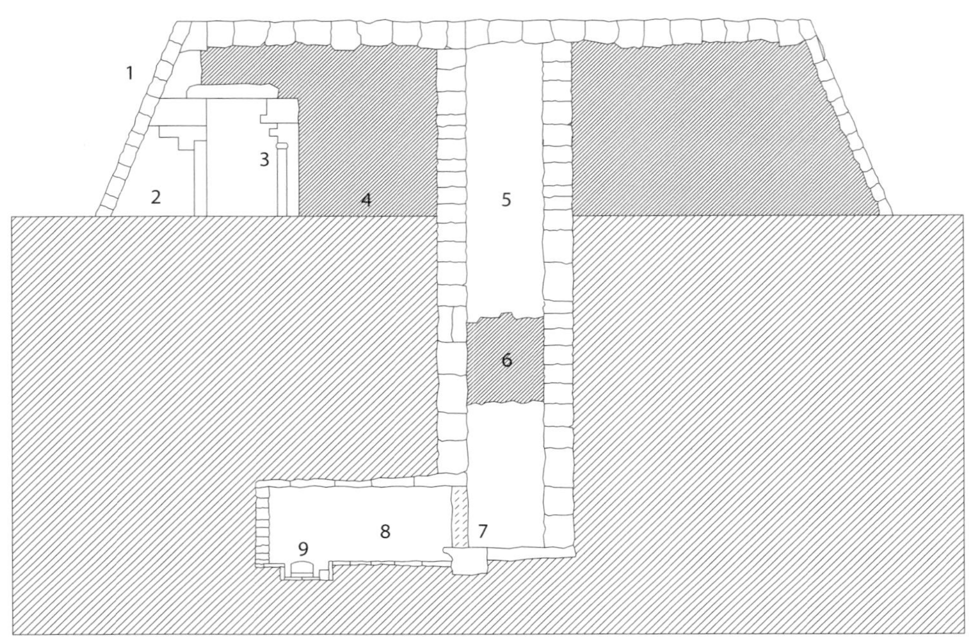

A 1/350

MASTABA
1 stone facing
2 sacrificial chapel
3 tombstone
4 fill
5 shaft
6 masonry seal
7 stone slab
8 burial chamber
9 sarcophagus

PYRAMID COMPLEX
11 sacrificial altar
12 mortuary temple, funerary temple
13 step pyramid, stepped pyramid
14 court
15 south tomb
16 north house
17 south house
18 cult chapel
19 ceremonial or Jubilee court
20 entrance hall, colonnaded hall
21 surrounding wall
22 western platform

FUNERARY BUILDINGS OF THE OLD KINGDOM (c.2650–2150 BC)

A mastaba
B step or stepped pyramid complex, plan
C step pyramid, cross section
D bent pyramid, rhomboid pyramid, cross section
E bent pyramid, plan
F Nubian pyramid tomb

mastaba, mastaba tomb

a large ancient Egyptian stone tomb with sloping stone sides and a flat top, built over a burial ground or chamber

step pyramid, stepped pyramid

a pyramid-type whose sides are stepped with tiers rather than smooth, in Egypt predating the true pyramids; the primary existing Egyptian example is that of King Zoser at Saqqara, south of Cairo

bent pyramid, rhomboid pyramid

an Egyptian pyramid-type in which each triangular planar surface changes direction as it approaches the top, as in a mansard roof; sometimes also called a blunt or false pyramid

A) mastaba, Saqqara, Egypt, Old Kingdom; B, C) Pyramid complex of Djoser (Zoser), Saqqara, Egypt, 667–2648 BC; architect Imhotep; D, E) pyramid of Snefru at Dahshur, 2613–2589 BC; F) Nubian royal pyramid tomb, Meroë, Sudan, c.300 BC–200 AD

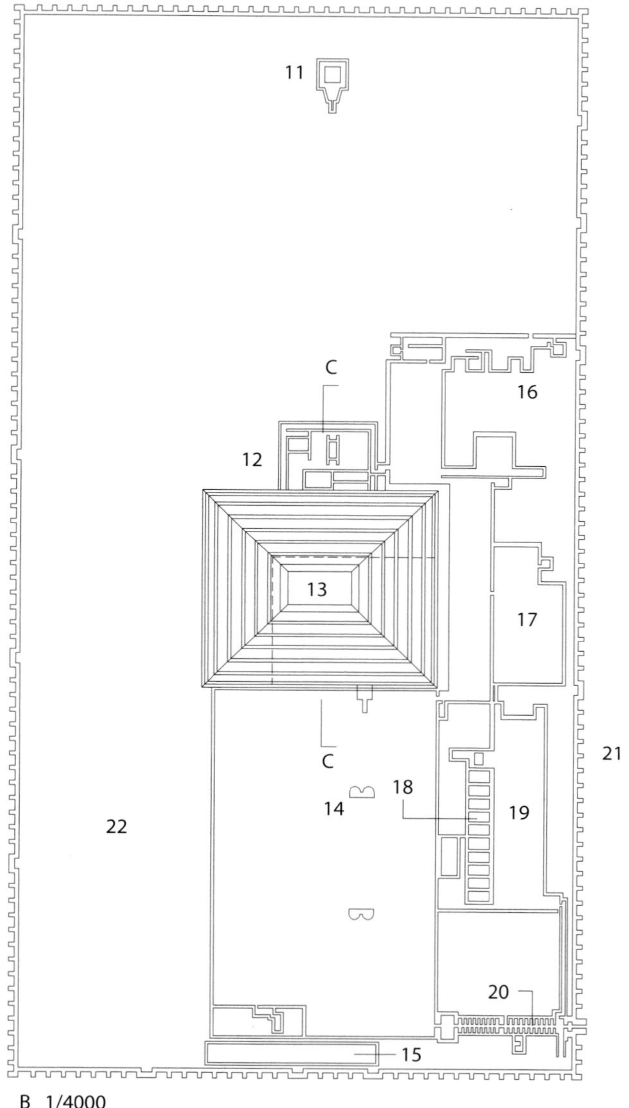

B 1/4000

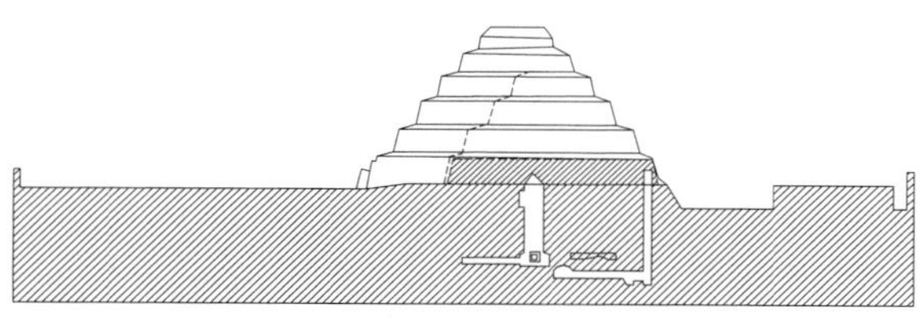

C 1/4000

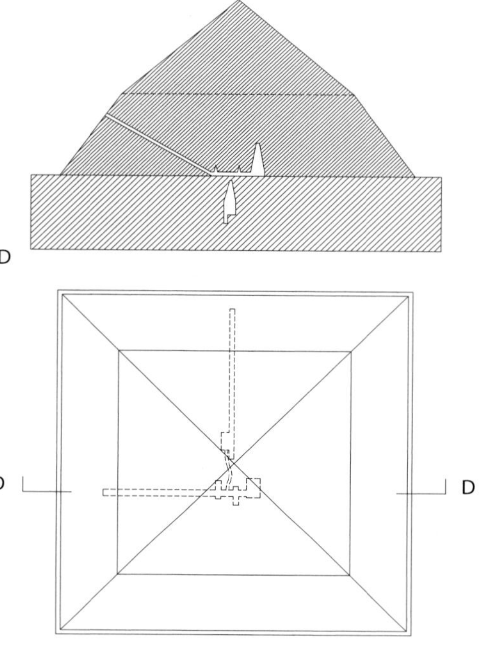

E 1/4000

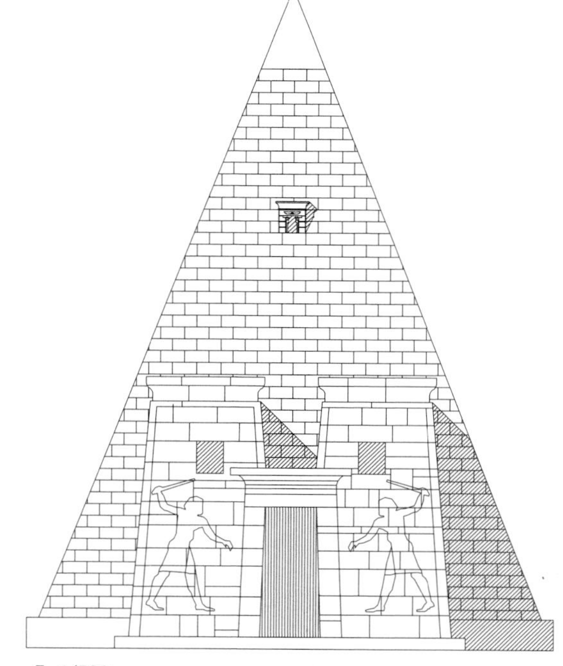

F 1/500

71 EGYPTIAN PYRAMID COMPLEX

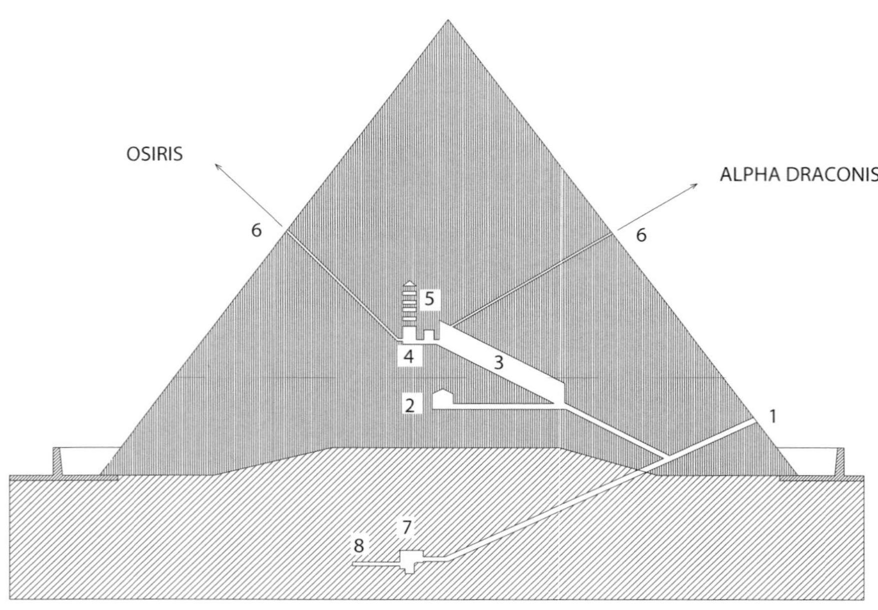

A 1/2000

GREAT PYRAMID

1 principal entrance
2 'Queen's Chamber'
3 great ascending corridor
4 King's Chamber
5 relieving vault
6 tunnel aligned with holy stars, or air shaft
7 false or unfinished burial chamber
8 dead-end or unfinished tunnel

PYRAMID COMPLEX

11 Western necropolis
12 boat grave, boat pit
13 Eastern necropolis
14 pyramid
15 mortuary temple, pyramid temple
16 pyramid causeway
17 valley temple
18 queen's pyramid
19 sphinx
20 sphinx temple

PYRAMIDS AND PYRAMID TEMPLES AT GIZA

A Great Pyramid of Khufu (Cheops)
B pyramid of Khafre (Chefren)
C pyramid of Menkaure (Mycerinus)
D pyramid temple of Khufu (Cheops)
E pyramid temple of Khafre (Chefren)
F pyramid temple of Menkaure (Mycerinus)
G valley temple of Khafre (Chefren)
H valley temple of Menkaure (Mycerinus)
J Great Sphinx
K sphinx temple of Amenhotep II
L 4th dynasty sphinx temple

pyramid complex
the ceremonial area of buildings and structures surrounding an ancient Egyptian pyramid

mortuary temple
in ancient Egyptian architecture, a place of worship of a deceased king or queen, especially one adjoining a pyramid or rock cut tomb, in which offerings of food and objects were made; also called a funerary temple

valley temple
a temple pavilion in an ancient Egyptian pyramid complex, connected via a covered causeway to a mortuary temple at the foot of a pyramid; used for preparing the Pharaoh for his final journey

pyramid temple
a mortuary temple connected specifically to a pyramid, or part of an Egyptian pyramid complex

pyramid causeway
a covered ceremonial route or corridor leading from a valley temple to a mortuary temple at the foot of a pyramid, notably at sites of the Nile valley pyramids

A) Great Pyramid of Khufu (Cheops), 2589–2566 BC; pyramid of Khafre (Chefren), 2558–2532 BC; pyramid of Menkaure (Mycerinus), after 2472 BC

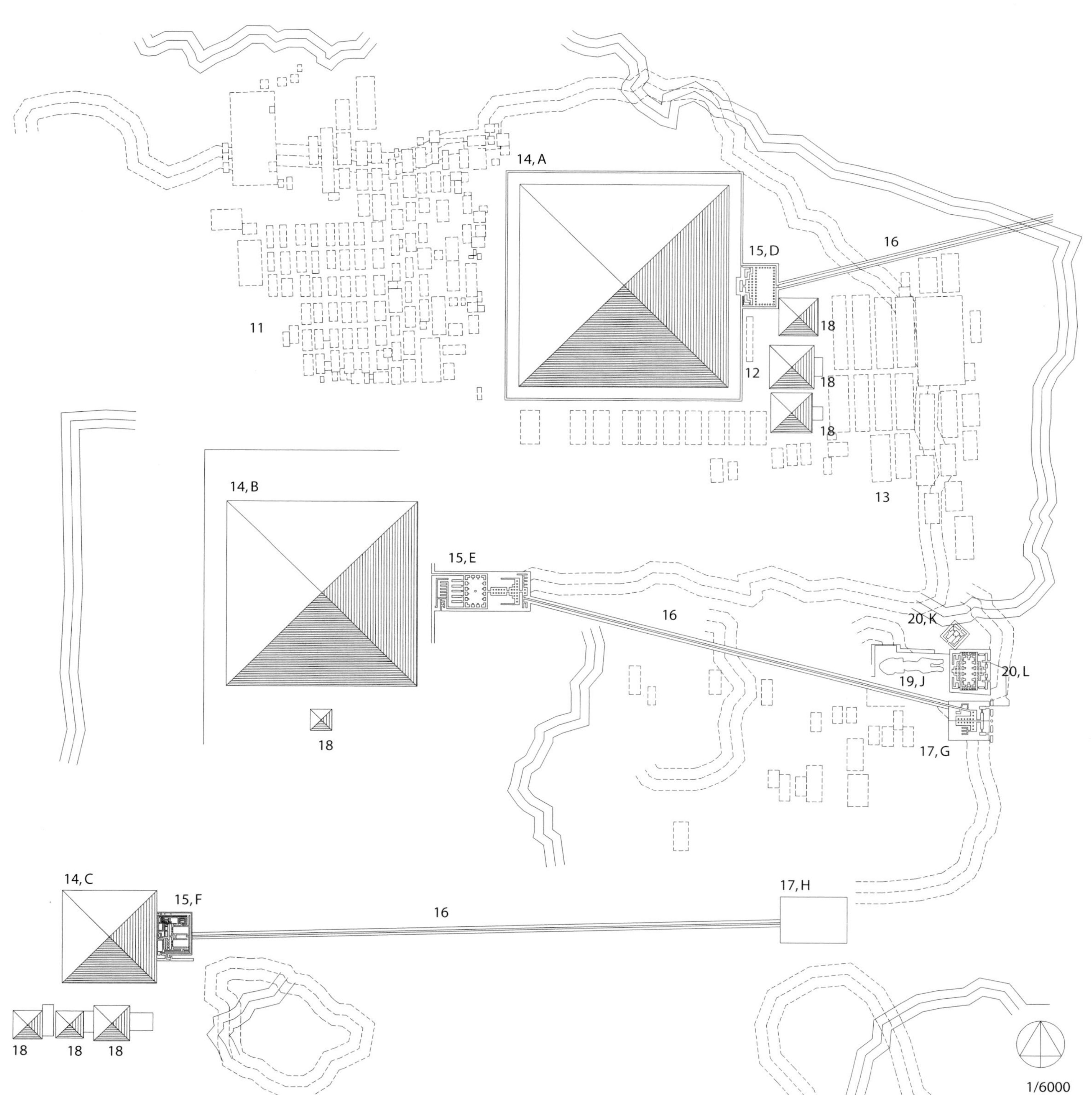
14, A
15, D
16
18
12
18
18
13
11
14, B
15, E
16
20, K
19, J
20, L
17, G
18
14, C
15, F
16
17, H
18
18
18
1/6000

72 EGYPTIAN TEMPLES

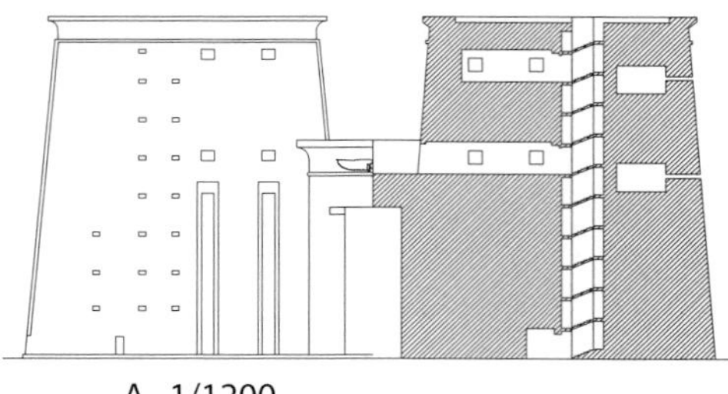

A 1/1200

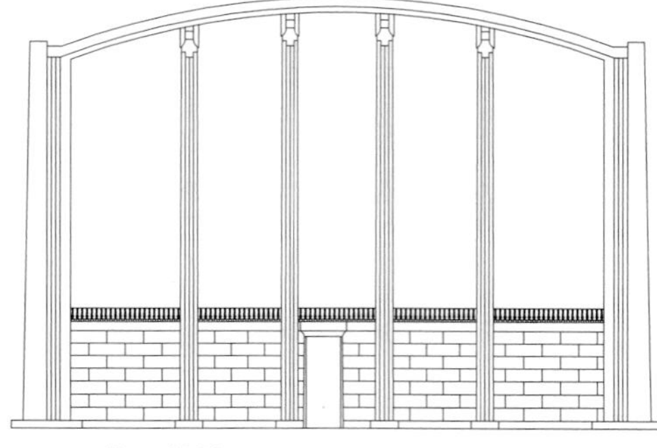

B 1/600

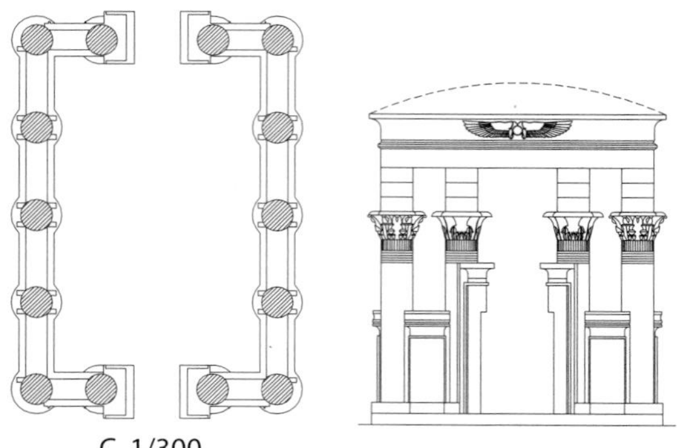

C 1/300

A pylon portal

B tent shrine imitation and false or blind door

C open-fronted tent shrine, mammisi

CULT TEMPLE, PYLON TEMPLE

1 1st pylons, c.320 BC
2 forecourt
3 birth house, mammisi
4 kiosk
5 pylon temple
6 2nd pylons, c.1320 BC
7 hypostyle hall, c.1290–1250 BC
8 3rd pylons
9 obelisks
10 4th pylons
12 5th pylons
13 6th pylons
14 barque temple
15 temple court (Middle Kingdom)
16 festival hall
17 holy of the holies
18 ambulatory `Botanical garden´

TERRACED TEMPLE

20 outer court
21 sphinxes
22 ramps
23 colonnades (lower)
24 terrace (lower)
25 ramp to shrine

ROCK TEMPLE – MORTUARY TEMPLE

26 shrine (of goddess Hathor)
27 colonnades (upper)
28 chapel (chapel of Anubis)
29 Osiris pillars
30 chapel (of Hatshepsut)
31 ceremonial court
32 sun temple
33 inner sanctuary

Egyptian architecture
architecture in ancient Egypt from c.2850 BC to the Roman conquest in 30 BC; it is characterized by stone burial tombs, massive pylons and geometrical structures, the use of beam and post construction, and elegantly carved and coloured religious and mythical motifs

Old Kingdom
the age of pyramid builders; the period of the 3rd to 6th dynasties of ancient Egyptian culture from 2778–2423 BC, characterized by monumental stone edifices, mastabas, pyramids, sphinxes and the first sun temples with obelisks and lotus, papyrus and palm columns

Middle Kingdom
the period of ancient Egyptian culture during the 11th and 12th dynasties from 2150–1785 BC, in architecture characterized by modest brick-filled pyramids, sun and mortuary temples, Hathor columns and the rock-tombs of private citizens

New Kingdom
the period of Egyptian culture during the time of the 18th to 20th dynasties, from 1580–1085 BC, characterized in architecture by the Amarna period and its temples, palaces, private dwellings and rock tombs

A) Great pylon of the Temple of Horus, Edfu; 237–57 BC; B) Djoser pyramid complex, Saqqara, c.2600 BC, architect Imhotep; C) Roman Kiosk of Trajan, Philae, c.100 AD; D) Temple of Amon (Amun), Karnak; 2000–300 BC; E) mortuary temple of Queen Hatshepsut and Shrine of Anubis, Deir el-Bahari; c.1470 BC, architect Senenmut

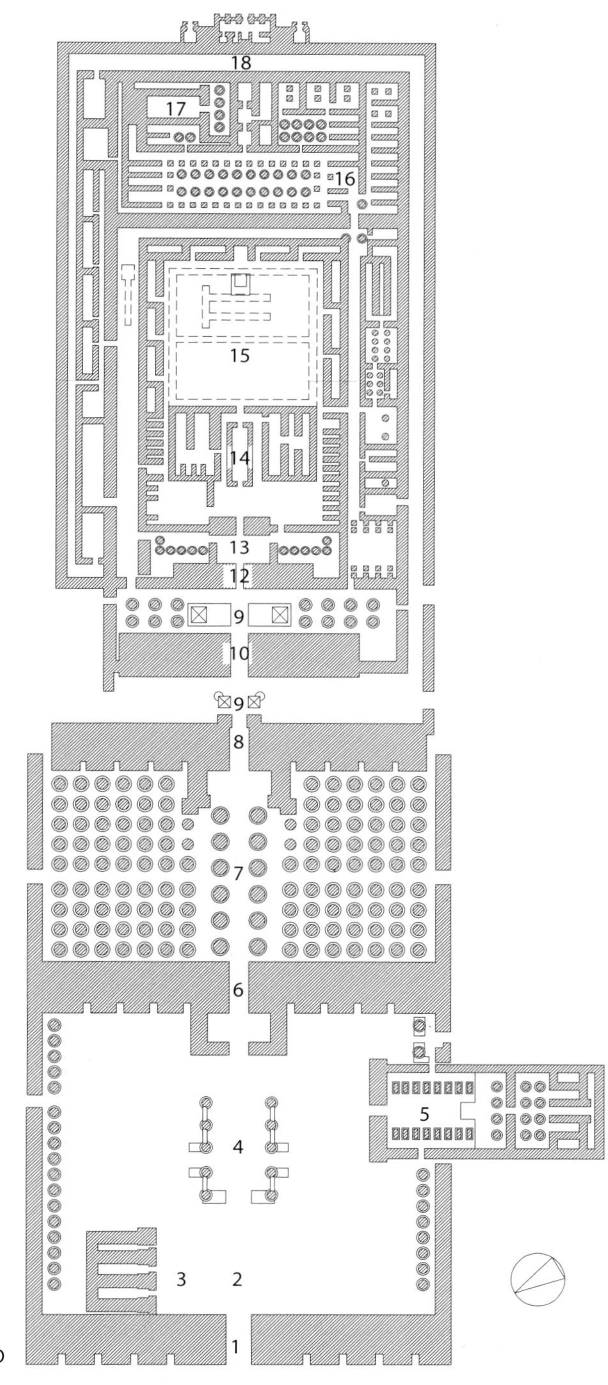
18
17
16
15
14
13
12
9
10
9
8
7
6
5
4
3
2
1
D

1/2000

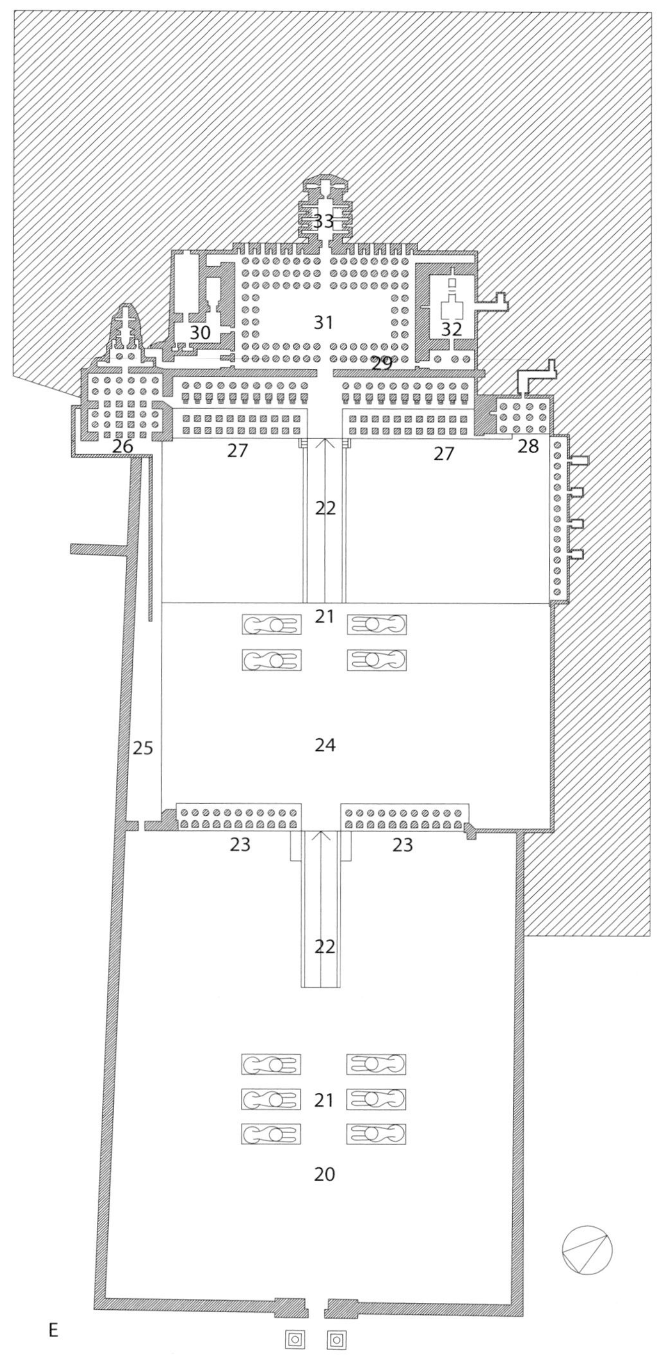
33
30
31
32
29
26
27
27
28
22
21
25
24
23
23
22
21
20
E

1/1500

73 EGYPTIAN COLUMNS AND CAPITALS

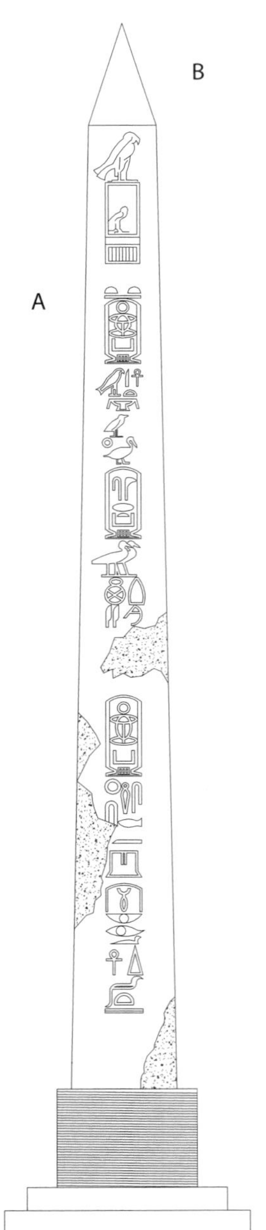

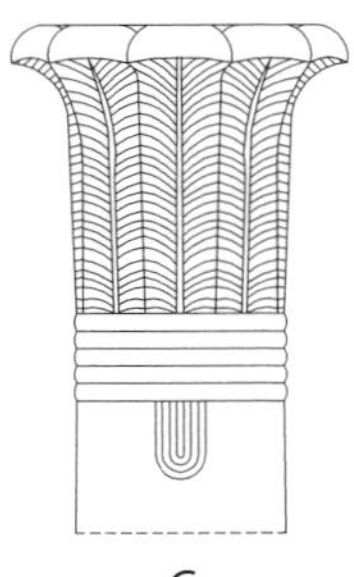

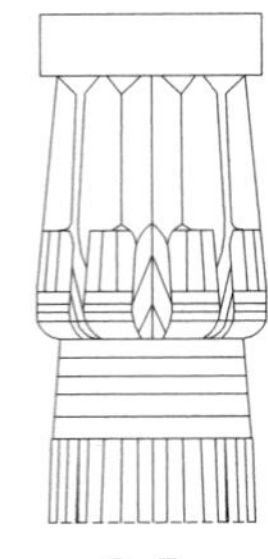

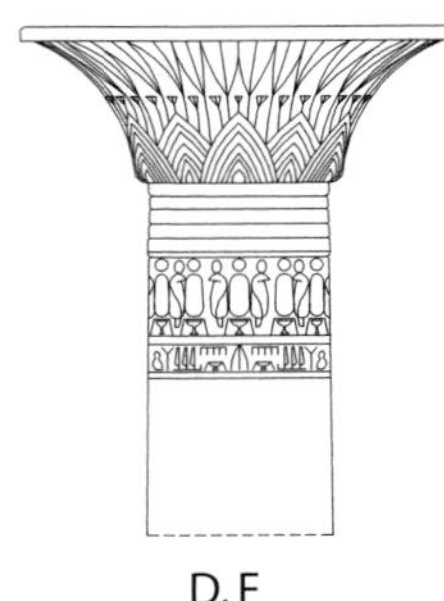

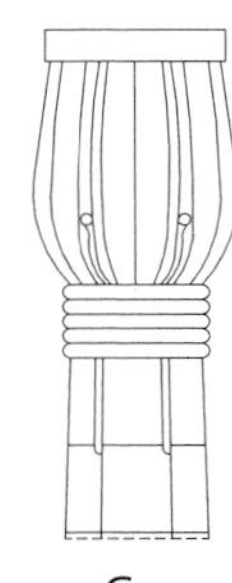

A obelisk
B pyramidion
C palm capital, palmiform (plume capital)
D papyrus capital, papyriform
E bud capital, closed bud capital, closed capital
F bell capital, blossom capital, campaniform, open capital
G lotus capital, lotiform, lily capital
H tent-pole capital
K composite capital
L palmette capital
M fruit capital, vegetable capital

1 proto-Doric column
2 fluted column
3 papyrus column, papyriform column
4 bundle column
5 bundle column
6 palm column, palmiform column
7 palm column, palmiform column
8 lotus column, lotiform column
9 composite column, complex column
10 composite column, complex column

11 heraldic column, Upper Egypt (lotus)
12 heraldic column, Lower Egypt (papyrus)
13 baldachin column, tent-pole column
14 composite column (Hathor capital)
15 Hathor column
16 sistrum
17 Hathor column
18 Osiris column, Osiris pillar
19 benben
20 benben

obelisk
an Egyptian monolithic four-sided standing stone, tapering to a pyramidical cap (a pyramidion), often inscribed with hieroglyphs and erected as a monument

benben
an ancient Egyptian short, slender obelisk with a polygonal cross section, symbolic of the rising sun and regeneration of life, often a cult object of sun-worship in a sun temple

lotus, lily
forms of flowering lily [*Nymphaea lotus* (white lotus), *Nymphaea caerulea* (blue lotus), *Nelumbo nucifera* etc.] sacred in ancient Egyptian, Buddhist and Hindu culture; the blue water lily (*Nymphaea caerulea*) was the heraldic plant of Upper Egypt (Nile Valley)

papyrus
an ornamental motif found in classical and Egyptian architecture consisting of a series of stylized leaves from the papyrus plant, *Cyperus papyrus*, of the genus *Cypereae*, an aquatic sedge found in tropical and sub-tropical regions, from which a form of paper was produced; heraldic plant of Lower Egypt (Nile Delta)

A) obelisk of Senuseret I, Heliopolis, 1965–1920 BC; 1,2) Beni–Hasan, 2040–1782 BC; 3) Havara; 4,7) Ramesseum, mortuary temple of Ramses II (Ramesses), Thebes, 1279–1213 BC; 5) mortuary temple of Ramses III (Ramesses), 1184–1153 BC; 6,C) pyramid complex of Sahure, Abusir, 2487–2475 BC; 7) see 4; 8,G) tomb of Prince Khety, Beni–Hasan, c.2000 BC; 9) temple of Amun, Karnak, 1479–1425 BC; 10) Temple of Isis, see 14; 11–12) Pillars of Tuthmosis III, temple of Amun, Karnak, c.1450; 13,H) temple of Amun, Karnak, Thutmosis III, (Tuthmosis) c.1450 BC; 14) Kiosk of Nectanebo I (Temple of Isis, Philae) c.380–343BC: 15) temple precinct of Mut at Karnak, 1500–343 BC; 17) temple of Hathor, Dendera, 54 BC – 60 AD: 18) see 4; 19) benben of Senuseret I, Abgig, Fayoum, 1965–1920 BC

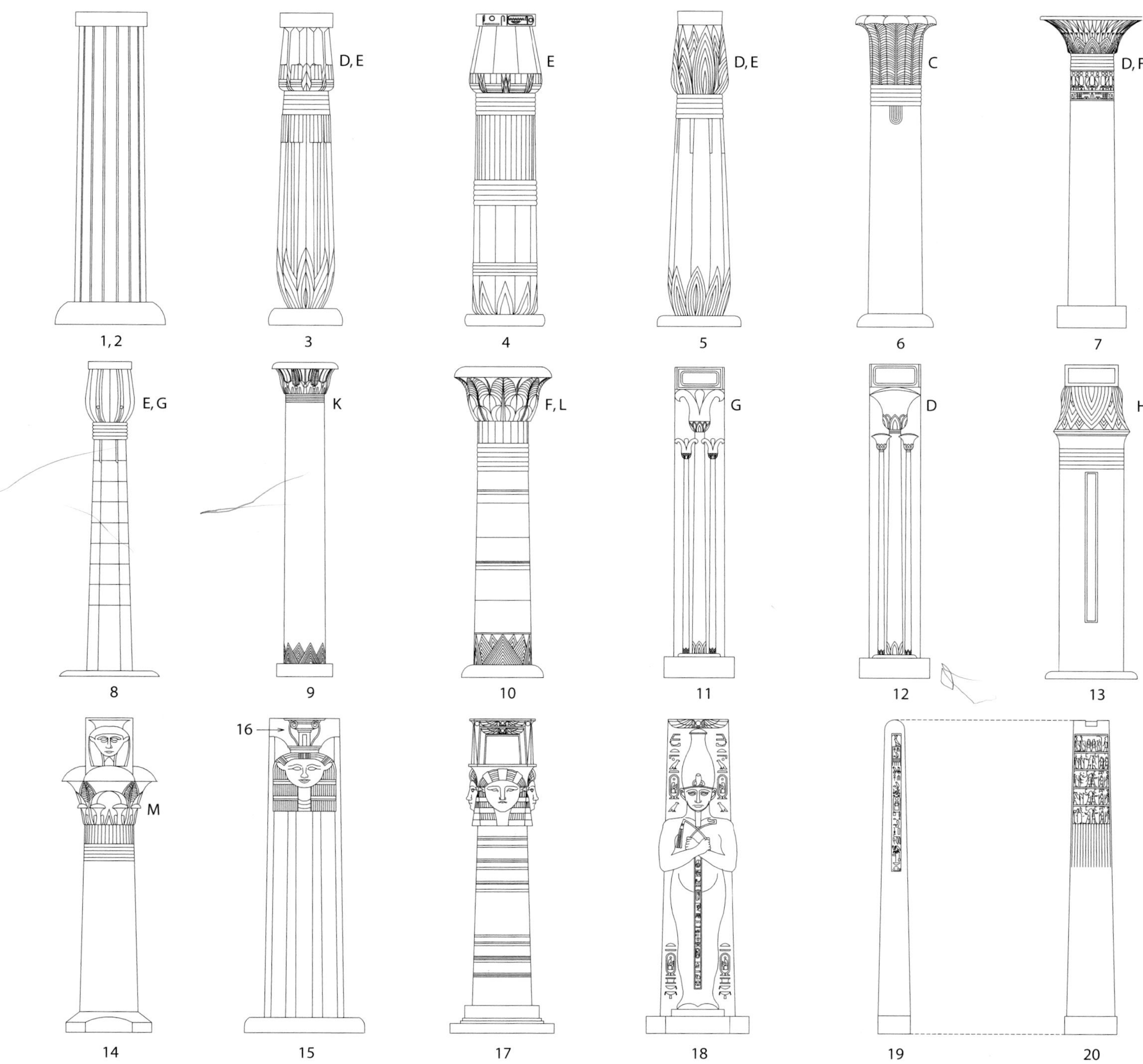

D, E
E
D, E
C
D, F
1, 2
3
4
5
6
7
E, G
K
F, L
G
D
H
8
9
10
11
12
13
M
16
14
15
17
18
19
20

74 EGYPTIAN MYTHOLOGY

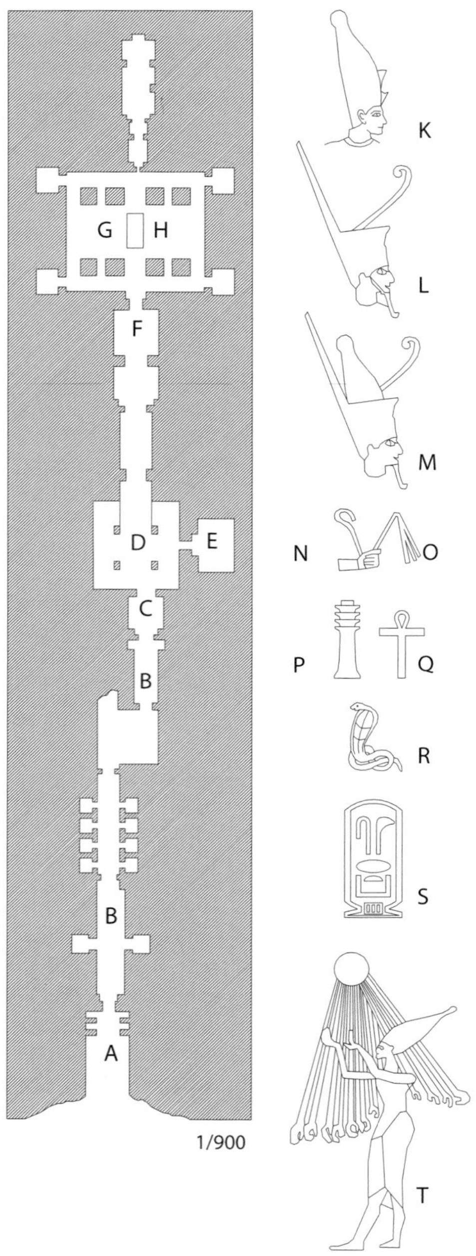

Tomb of Ramses III, Valley of the Kings, Thebes, Egypt, 1184–1153 BC

ROCK TOMB

- A entrance
- B passage
- C well room
- D pillared hall
- E side chamber
- F antechamber
- G burial chamber
- H sarcophagus

SYMBOLS

- K white crown (Upper Egypt)
- L red crown (Lower Egypt)
- M combined crown, double crown
- N crook, staff; regal administrative authority
- O flail, scourge; regal penal authority
- P Djet column – steadfastness
- Q ankh – key of life, key to the Nile
- R uraeus – guardian of the kings
- S cartouche – Pharaonic insignia
- T ATEN, ATON – sun disc

EGYPTIAN GODS

1. RA, RE – sun
2. OSIRIS – death, judgement
3. ISIS – motherhood, protection
4. HORUS – falcon, royalty
5. SETH, SET – storms, chaos, evil
6. ATUM, TUM – sun, creator of all things
7. MIN – fertility
8. MAAT – order
9. AMUN, AMEN, AMON – 'the unseen one'
10. MUT – mistress of heaven
11. KHONSU – moon 'the traveller'
12. HAPI – the Nile's fertility
13. NUT – the firmament
14. GEB – earth
15. SHU – air
16. PTAH – creation, craftsmanship

ANIMAL GODS

17. KHNUM – ram potter of mankind
18. HATHOR – cow love, dance
19. ANUBIS – jackal the underworld, embalming
20. THOTH – sacred ibis \`the divine scribe´, knowledge
21. BASTET – cat protrectress of cats
22. SOBEK – crocodile the Nile
23. WADJET – cobra king's protector (Lower Egypt)
24. SEKHMET – lion the destructive sun, war

Upper Egypt
one of the two ancient Egyptian kingdoms, that which grew along the banks of the river Nile (the other is Lower Egypt, the Nile Delta), its Pharaoh wore the white crown, and its heraldic plant was the lotus, a species of water lily

Lower Egypt
one of the two ancient Egyptian kingdoms, that which grew out of the Nile Delta (the other is Upper Egypt, the Nile valley), its Pharaoh wore the red crown, and its heraldic plant was the papyrus

1
2
3
4
5
6
7
8
15
9
10
11
12
13
14
16
17
18
19
20
21
22
23
24

75 SPHINXES AND APOTROPES

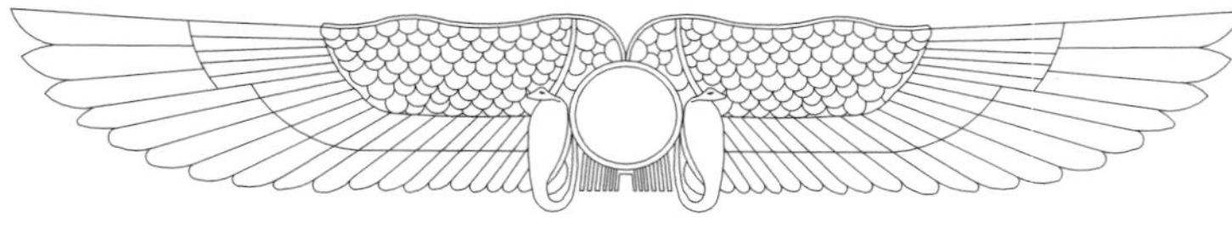

A

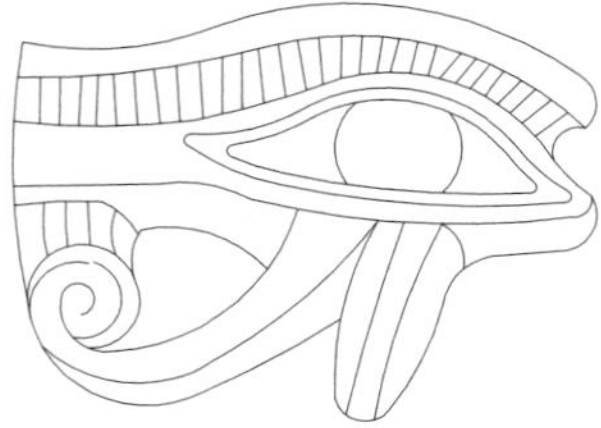

B

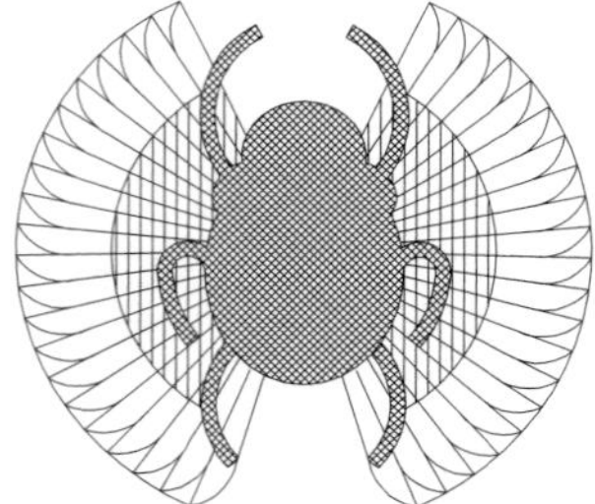

C

A winged sun disc, winged solar disc, feroher
B eye of Horus, Wadjet eye
C scarab, dung-beetle, sacred scarabeus, Khepri

1 lamassu (Mesopotamian),
Khorsabad, Iraq, 721–705 BC
2 sphinx (Phoenician),
Aleppo, Syyria c.900 BC
3 sphinx (Asia Minor),
Samaria, Israel, 8th cent. BC
4 sphinx (Asia Minor),
Asberg, Württemberg, Germany 500 BC
5 sphinx (Greek),
Priene, Greece, 7th cent. BC
6 hieracosphinx (Mycenaean),
Mediggo, Palestine, 13th cent. BC

EGYPTIAN SPHINXES

7 androsphinx: human-headed sphinx
Vatican Museum, Rome
8 androsphinx: human-headed sphinx
Amenemhet III, 12.dynasty, c.1800 BC
9 androsphinx: human-headed sphinx
Thutmosis III, 18th dynasty, Rek-minh-re, Thebes, Egypt
10 criosphinx: ram-headed sphinx
11 hieracosphinx: falcon-headed sphinx

apotrope
a symbolic statue, image or construction intended to provide protection against evil spirits

sphinx
a sculpted figure which has the prostrate body of a lion and the head of a human (androsphinx) or other animal such as a ram (criosphinx); especially prolific in an ancient Egyptian architecture

androsphinx
a sphinx with a human head or upper body, usually that of a male

criosphinx
a sphinx which has a ram's head

hieracosphinx
a sphinx which has the head of a hawk

1
2
3
4
5
6
7
8
9
10
11

CARYATID

A cornice
B frieze
C abacus
D echinus
E shaft
F column base, base
G cornice
H dado, die, tympanum
J base
K plinth
L entablature
M column
N pedestal

FIGURED COLUMNS

1 Hathor column: Egyptian
2 Osiris column, Osiris pillar: Egyptian
3 canephora, canephore (kore): Greek
4 caryatid (kore): Greek
5 herm, herma: Greek
6 herm, herma: Renaissance
7 atlas, telamon: Renaissance
8 atlas, telamon: Persian

figured column
any decorative column carved or shaped in the form of a human figure

caryatid
in classical architecture, a carved statue of a draped female figure which functions as a column

canephora, canephore, canephorum, kanephoros (Gk.)
`basket-carrying´ (Lat.); in classical architecture, a carved statuesque column of a draped female figure, a caryatid, carrying a basket, or with a basket on her head

kore
a classical statue of a young draped female figure, a canephora or caryatid

atlas, telamon (Gk.)
pl. atlantes; in classical architecture, a massive carved statuesque stooping male figure, often serving as a columnar support for a pediment

herm, herma
plural hermae; in classical architecture, a square tapered column capped with the carved head, bust or torso of a figure, usually Hermes; originally used by the Greeks as a boundary marker, later as decoration

1) Temple of Hathor, Dendera, Egypt, 54 BC–60 AD; 2) Ramesseum, Thebes, Egypt, 1279–1213 BC; 3) Treasury of Siphnos, Delphi, Greece, c.525 BC; 4) Erechtheion, Athens, Greece, 420–406 BC, Mnesikles; 6) Spain, 16th century, Juan de Arfe; 7) Palazzo Ducale, Venice, Italy, 1300–1400; 8) Palazzo Valmorana, Padua, Italy, 1566, Andrea Palladio

1
2
3
4
5
6
7
8

77 CLASSICAL COLUMNIATION

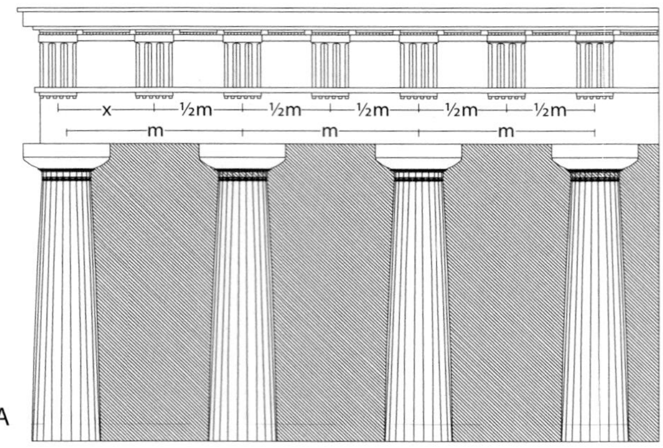

A

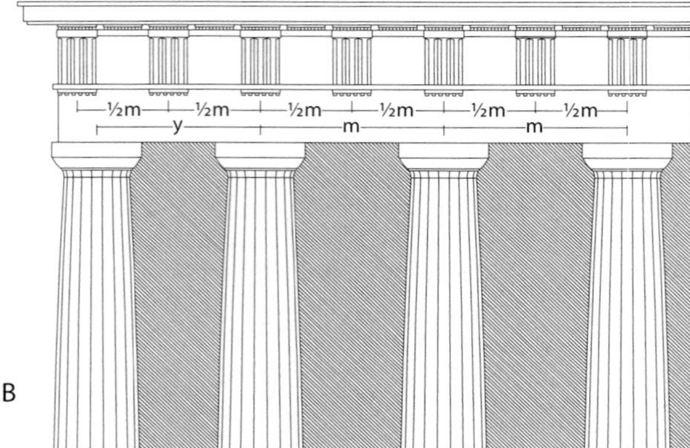

B

CORNER CONTRACTION (controversy of triglyphs)

A archaic solution
B classical solution
C module
D diameter of column
m mesostyle – columniation

TYPES ACCORDING TO NUMBER OF COLUMNS

1 henostyle, monostyle – one-columned
2 distyle – two-columned
3 tristyle – three-columned
4 tetrastyle – four-columned
5 pentastyle – five-columned
6 hexastyle – six-columned
7 heptastyle – seven-columned
8 octastyle – eight-columned
9 enneastyle – nine-columned
10 decastyle – ten-columned
12 dodecastyle – twelve-columned
21 araeostyle, barycephalae – lightly columned
22 diastyle – wide columned
23 eustyle – well columned
24 systyle – narrow columned
25 pycnostyle – close columned

STELA, STELE
Greek marble stele circa 207 AD

columniation
the proportioned lining up of or grouping of columns in classical architecture

intercolumniation
(Lat. intercolumnium); in classical architecture, the systematic spacing of columns expressed as multiples of column diameters; see araeostyle, diastyle, eustyle, pycnostyle and systyle; also written as intercolumnation

corner contraction
a visual refinement in the classical Doric frieze, as found in the Parthenon, in which the spacing of end columns in the row are reduced to maintain the impression that every other triglyph is centred over a column; this variation in spacing of triglyphs vs columns is called the controversy of triglyphs; see archaic solution, classical solution

archaic solution
the spacing of columns beneath an entablature evenly, so that, for each triglyph to be centrally above a column, the corner triglyphs are further apart than the others

classical solution
the spacing of triglyphs in an entablature evenly, so that, for each triglyph to be centrally above a column, the corner columns are nearer to one another than the others

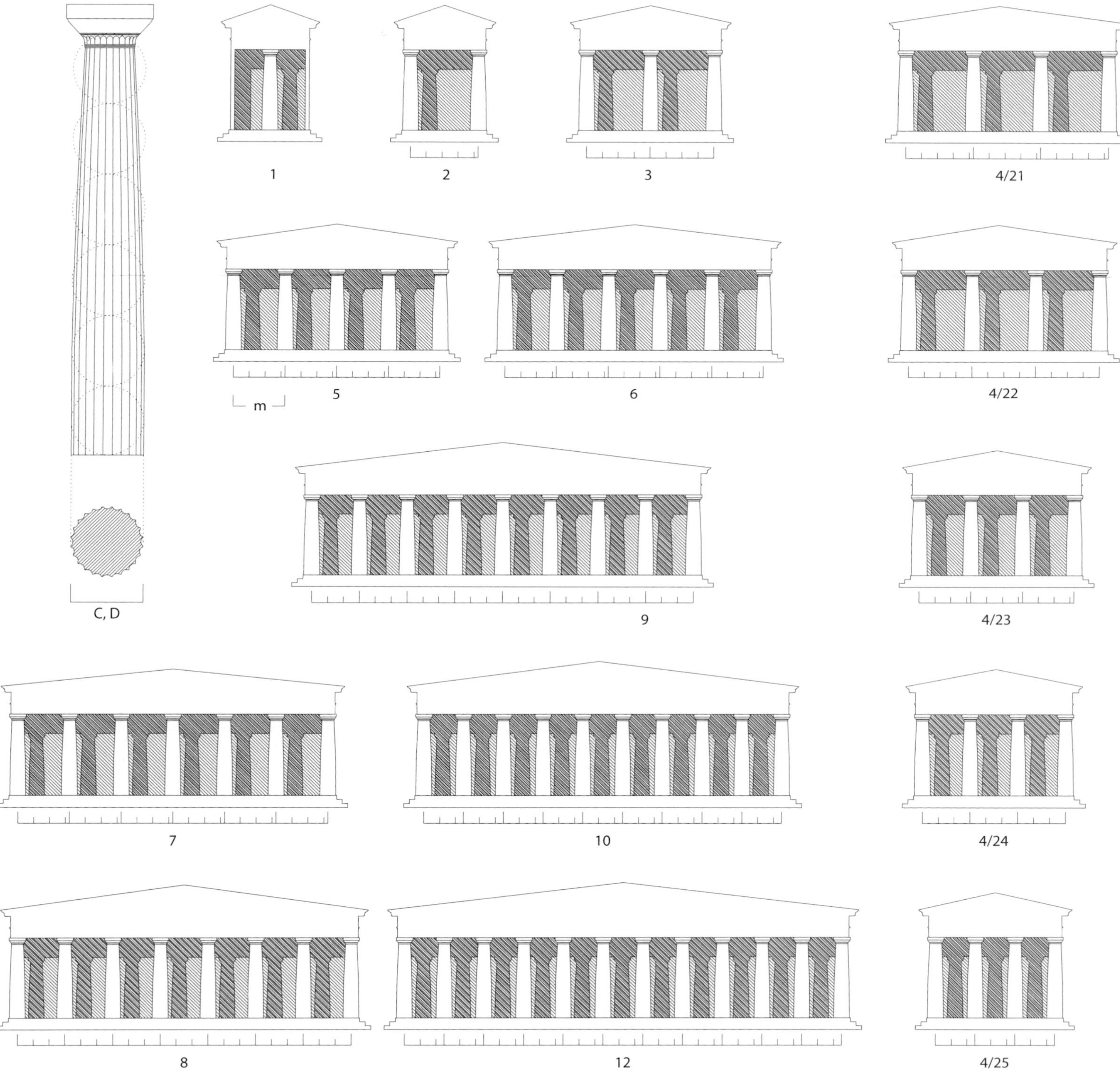
C, D
1
2
3
4/21
5
m
6
4/22
9
4/23
7
10
4/24
8
12
4/25

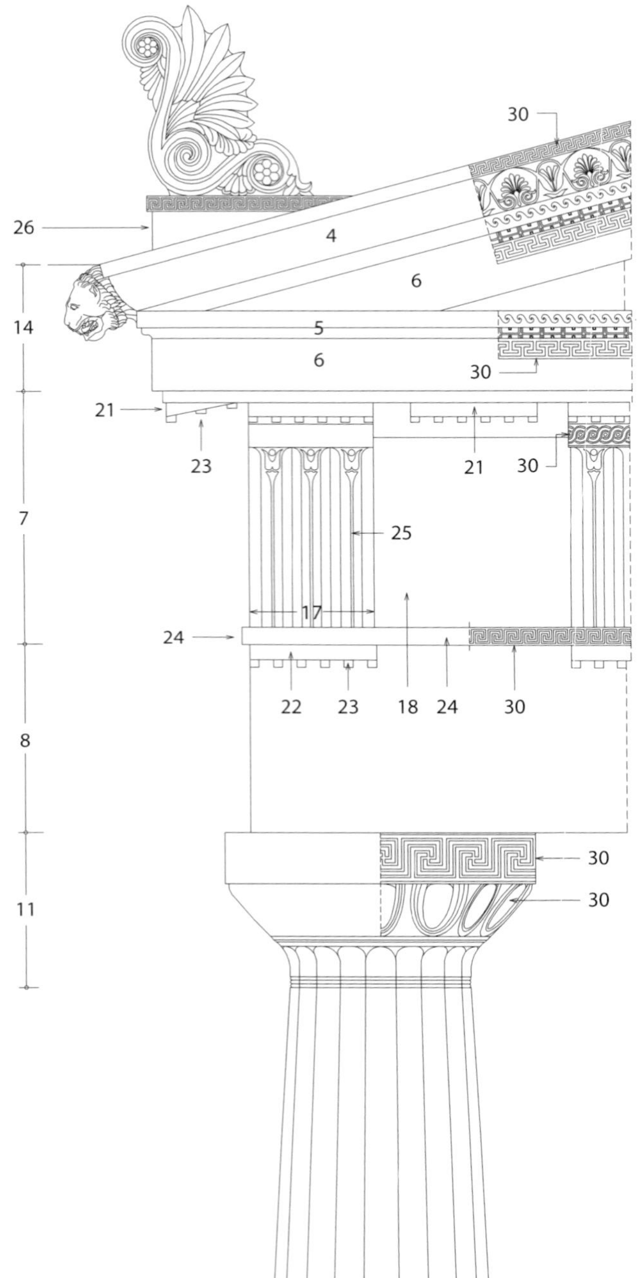

THE DORIC ENTABLATURE

21 mutule
22 regula, guttae band
23 gutta, drop
24 tenia, taenia
25 glyph
26 akroterion, acroter, acroterium
30 original surface–painted ornamentation

GREEK ORDERS

1 Doric order
2 Ionic order
3 Corinthian order
4 cymatium, sima
5 corona, geison
6 bed moulding (fascia)
7 frieze
8 architrave, epistyle
9 abacus
10 echinus
11 capital
12 column shaft
13 base, column base
14 cornice
15 entablature
16 column
17 triglyph
18 metope
19 entasis
20 zophorus, zoophorus

classical, Classical
referring to the architecture and art of ancient Greece and Rome, or any architecture which follows the same principles and ideas, such as Renaissance, neoclassical or revival styles

Greek architecture
the architecture of ancient Greece from c.3000 BC to the Roman period, characterized by temples, use of proportions and orders; roughly divided into the Geometrical, Archaic, Classic and Hellenistic periods

order
one of the predominating styles in classical architecture, the Doric, Ionic and Corinthian orders of ancient Greek classical architecture, and the Tuscan and Composite orders of Rome

entablature
in classical architecture, a thick horizontal band or beam member supported by columns in a portico, consisting typically of three sections, the architrave, frieze and cornice

1) Parthenon – Temple of Pallas Athena, 447–432 BC, Athens, architect Ictinos & Callicrates; 2) Temple on the River Illissus, Athens, 430 BC; 3) Temple of Zeus Olympios, Athens c.170 BC–130 AD

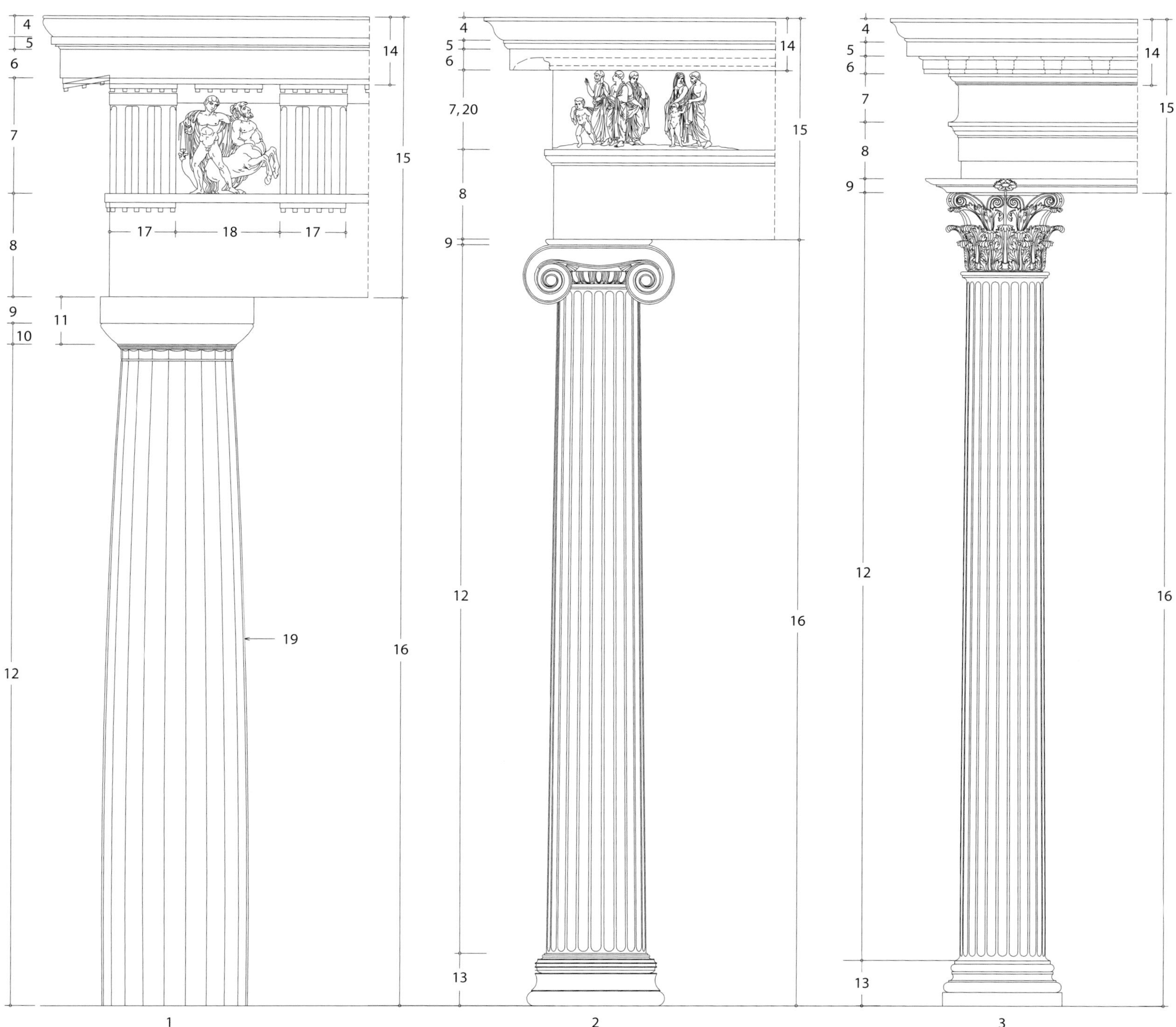
4
5
6
7
8
9
10
11
12
14
15
16
17
18
17
19
1
4
5
6
7, 20
8
9
12
13
14
15
16
2
4
5
6
7
8
9
12
13
14
15
16
3

79 CLASSICAL ROMAN ORDERS

ROMAN ORDERS

1 Tuscan order, Etruscan order
2 Roman Doric order, Doric Roman order
3 Composite order
4 cymatium, sima
5 corona, geison
6 bed moulding (fascia)
7 frieze
8 architrave, epistyle
9 abacus
10 echinus
11 capital
12 column shaft
13 base, column base
14 cornice
15 entablature
16 column
17 pedestal
18 triglyph
19 metope
20 entasis

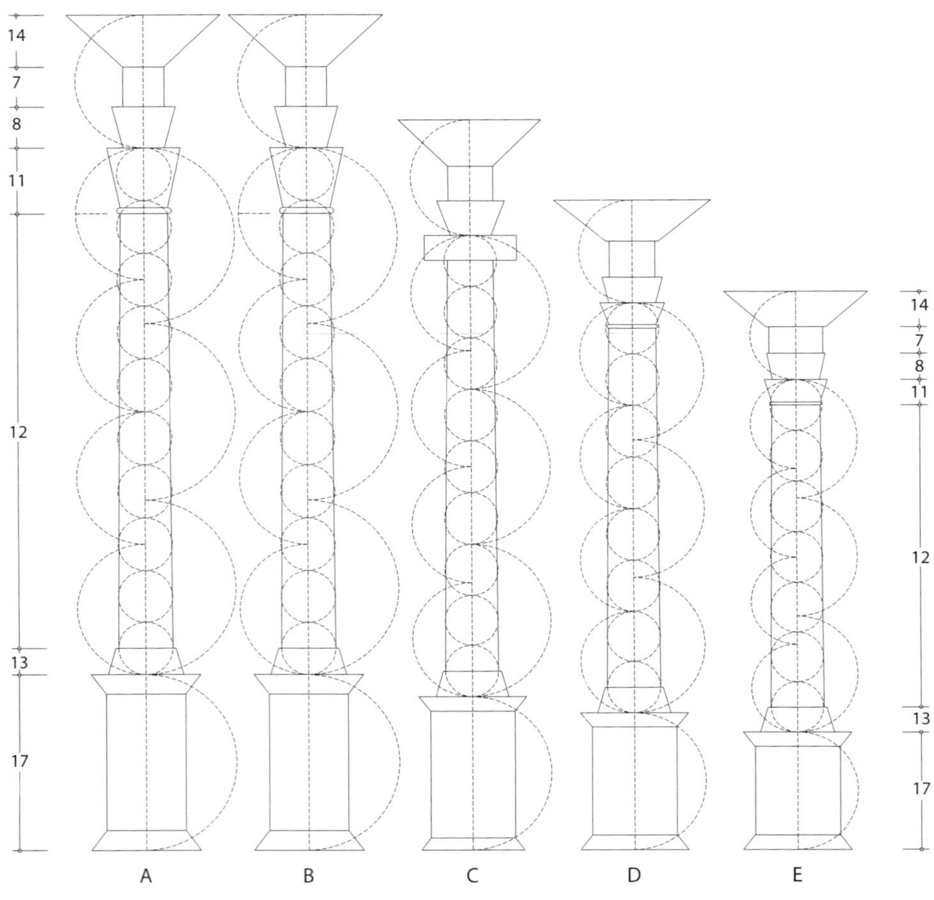

HARMONY OF PROPORTION IN NEOCLASSICAL ORDERS

A Composite column
B Corinthian column
C Ionic column
D Doric column
E Tuscan column

Roman architecture
the post-Etruscan classical architecture of the Romans from 750 BC–476 AD, characterized by Greek-influenced temples, theatres, baths and tenements, and by engineering ingenuity for structures such as roads, bridges and conduits

Tuscan order, Etruscan order
a simple classical Roman order, influenced by the old brick and timber temples of the Etruscans, and the Greek Doric, with smooth-shafted columns, a simple capital, base and entablature

Roman Doric order, Doric Roman order
a Roman and Renaissance version of the Doric order comprising columns with fluted shafts, simple capitals and bases, and an entablature with triglyphs and metopes

Composite order
a classical Roman order, a hybrid of Ionian and Corinthian, with fluted columns, a capital with both volutes and acanthus leaves, a base and an entablature with dentils

1) Andrea Palladio (1518–1580); 2) Praeneste (Palestrina), Albano, Italy; 3) triple arch of Septimius Severus, Rome, 203 AD; A–E) Bernardo Vittone: Instuzioni Elementari, 1760

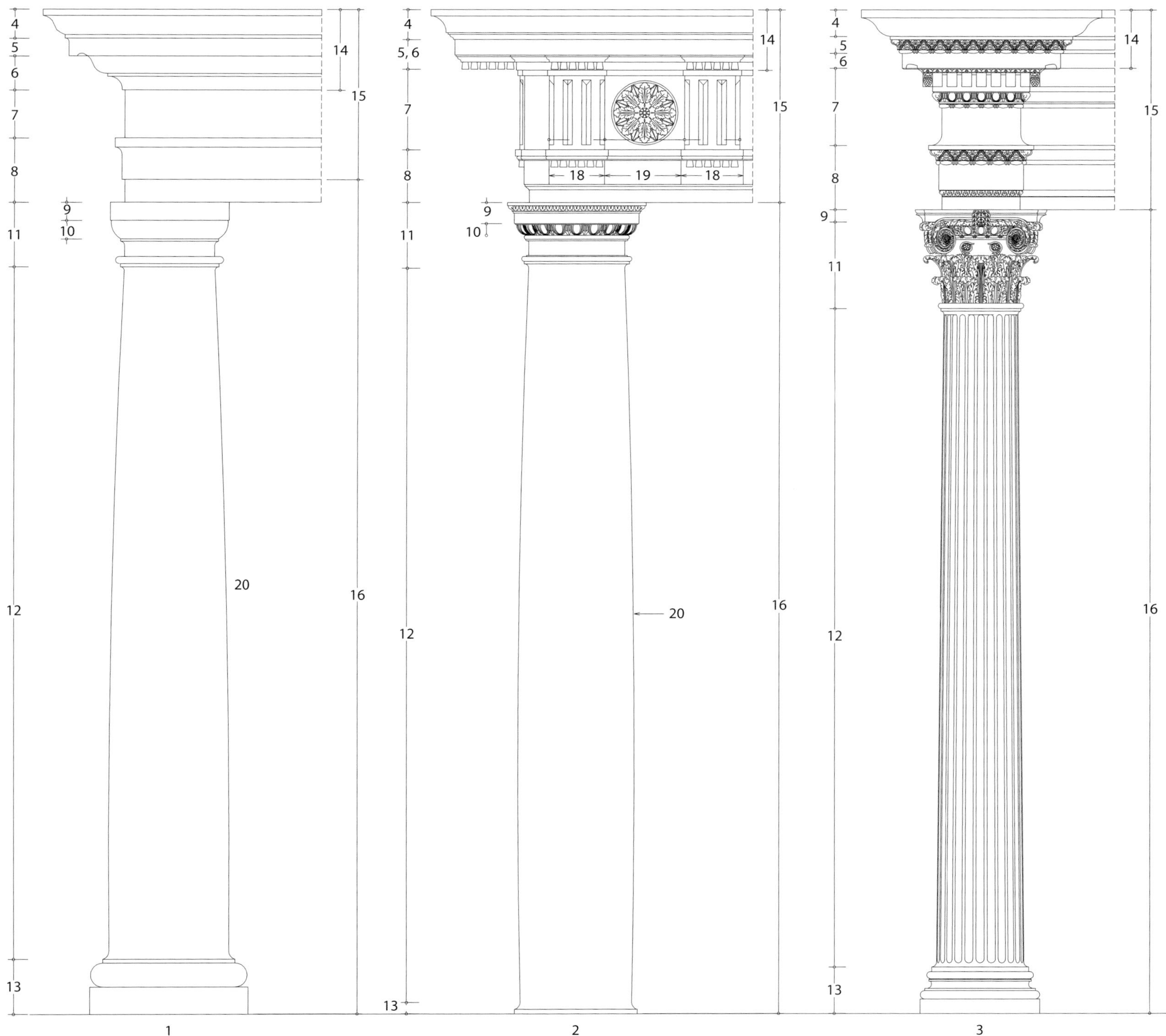
4
5
6
7
8
9
10
11
12
13
14
15
16
20
1
4
5, 6
7
8
9
10
11
12
13
14
15
16
18
19
18
20
2
4
5
6
7
8
9
11
12
13
14
15
16
3

80 THE IONIC ORDER

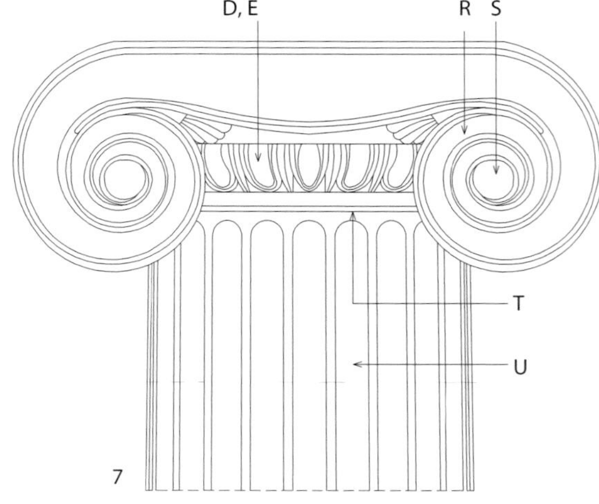

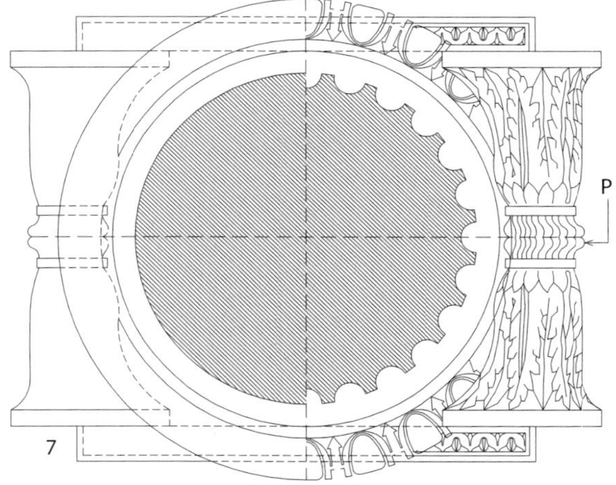

CLASSICAL MOULDINGS

A fascia, fillet
B cyma recta, ogee
C cyma reversa, reverse ogee
D egg and dart
E Ionic cyma
F dentils, dentilation
G Lesbian cyma
H bead and reel
K roll moulding, torus
L scotia, trochilus, cavetto
M base moulding (plinth)
N dado, die, tympanum
O plinth

CAPITAL

P balteus: 'belt'
R canalis: 'channel, hollow'
S volute
T apophyge
U flute, phyge

1 Ionic order
2 Roman Ionic order
3 edge column, corner column

ROMAN IONIC ORDER

4 entablature
5 column
6 pedestal
7 cornice
8 frieze
9 architrave, epistyle, epistylium
10 capital
11 shaft, column shaft
12 base, column base
13 plinth
14 dado, die, tympanum
15 base mouldings
16 cymatium, sima
17 corona, geison
18 bed mouldings
19 abacus
20 echinus
21 zophorus, zoophorus

Ionic order

a classical Greek order originating in Ionian Greece (now western Turkey), characterized by fluted columns, a voluted capital, a base and an entablature with dentils

capital

a separate block or a thickening at the top of a column or pilaster, used to spread the load of a beam, or as decoration

base

the lowest, thickened section of a column, pedestal etc. beneath its shaft, often decorated, which transfers loading onto a plinth or to a foundation; a classical column base is one on which a column of any of the classical Greek and Roman orders is placed, carved according to set patterns and proportions

1) Ionic capital: Temple at Ilissus, Athens, c.430 BC; 2–3) Roman Ionic entablature and column; Temple of Fortuna Virilis, Rome, c.40 BC

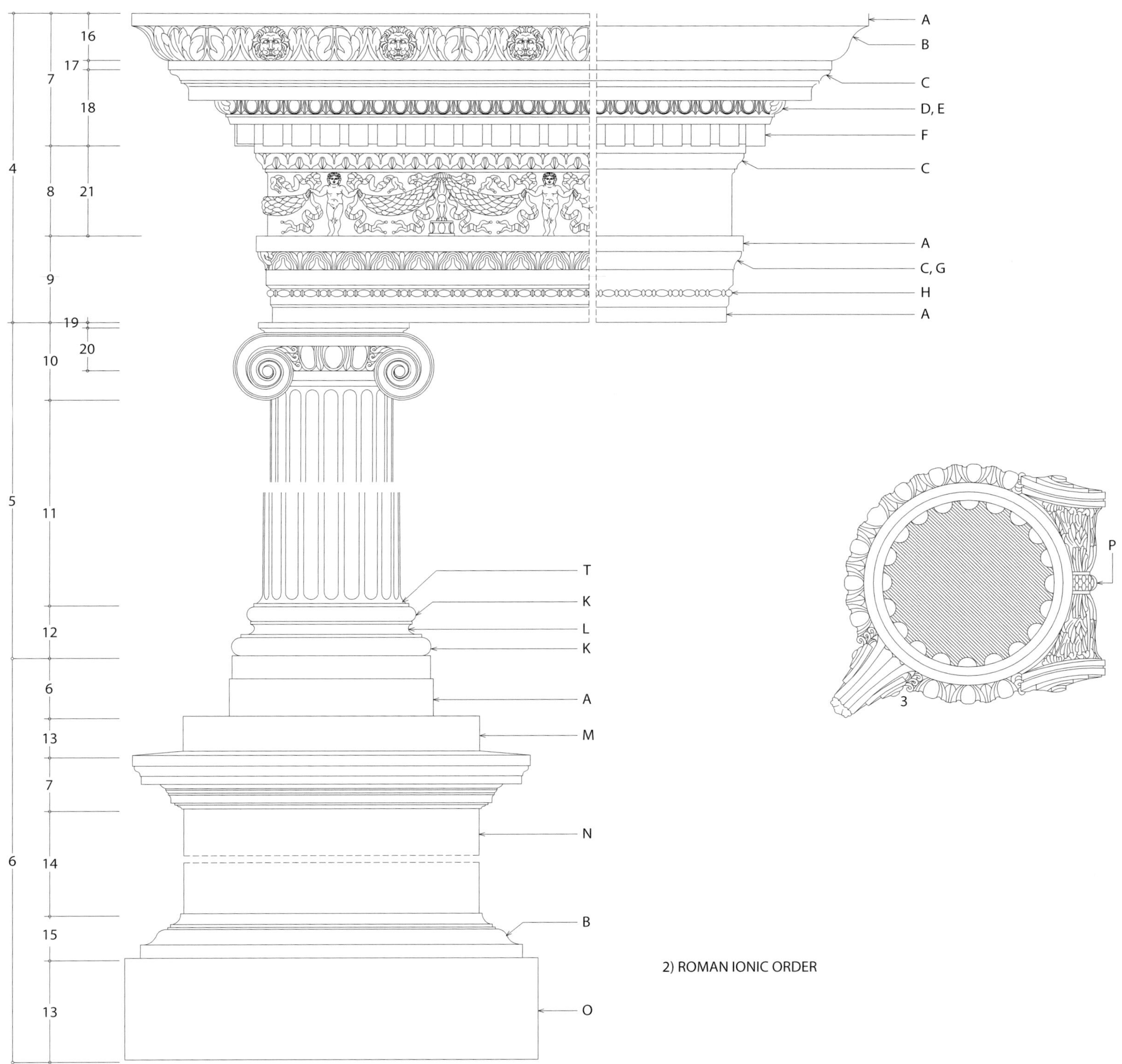

2) ROMAN IONIC ORDER

81 CLASSICAL CAPITALS AND BASES

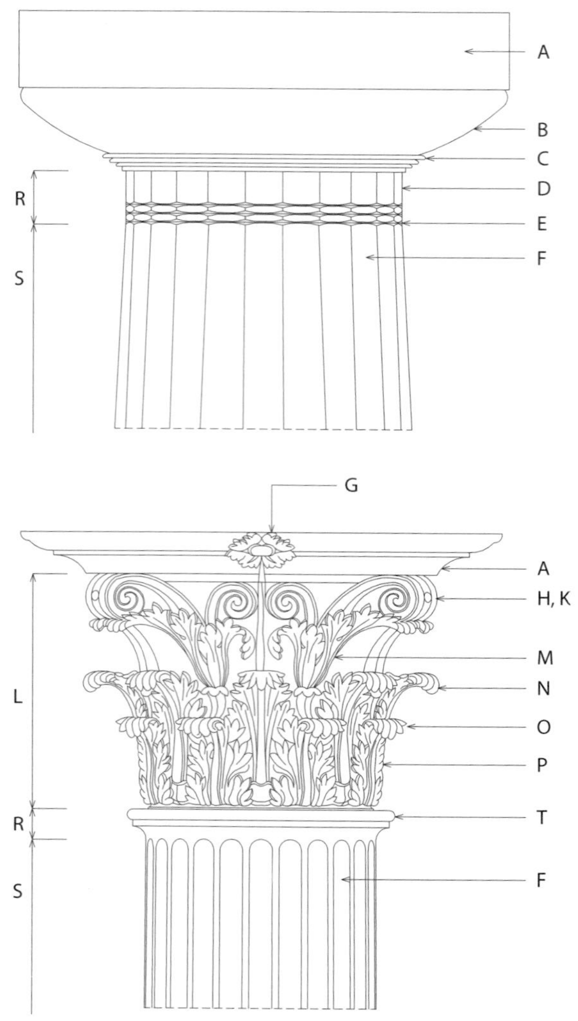

PARTS OF A CAPITAL

A abacus
B echinus
C annulet, shaft ring
D necking, trachelion, collarino
E hypotrachelion, hypotrachelium
F fluting
G fleuron
H helix
K volute
L calathus
M caulicole, cauliculus (calyx)
N secunda folia, second crown
O ima folia, first crown
P acanthus
R neck, necking
S shaft
T astragal

CAPITALS

1	Doric capital (archaic period)
2	Doric capital (classical period)
3–4	Tuscan capital
5–6	Roman Doric capital
7–8	Ionic capital
9–10	Corinthian capital
11–12	Composite capital

BASES

13–14	Attic base
15–16	Asiatic base, Ephesian base
17–18	Samian base
19	Naxian base
20	Ionic base
21	spira
22	fluted torus moulding

classical capital
a capital surmounting a column of any of the classical Greek and Roman orders, carved according to set patterns and proportions

classical base
the lowest, thickened section of a column, pedestal etc. beneath its shaft, often decorated, which transfers loading onto a plinth or to a foundation; a classical column base is one on which a column of any of the classical Greek and Roman orders is placed, carved according to set patterns and proportions

acanthus
Lat.; carved and decorative ornament found especially adorning classical Corinthian capitals, based on stylized leaves of the Mediterranean acanthus plant, Bear's breech or brank-ursine [*Acanthus molla*, *Acanthus spinosa*]; akanthos in Greek

1) Temple of Hera I or 'Basilica', Paestum, Italy, 550 BC; 2) Temple of Pallas Athena (Parthenon), 447–432 BC, Athens, Greece; architects Ictinos & Callicrates; 3) Volsinii (Bolsano), Italy; 4) Theatre of Marcellus, Rome, 17–11 BC; 5) Albano, Rome; 6) Andrea Palladio 1518–1580; 7) Temple of Apollo Epicurius, Bassai, Greece, c.430 BC, architect: Ictinos; 8) Temple by the Ilissus, Athens, Greece, 430 BC; 9) Temple of Zeus Olympios, Athens c.170 BC–130 AD; 10) Choragic monument of Lysicrates, Athens, Greece 334 BC; 11) Triumphal arch of Septimius Severus, Rome, 203 AD; 13) Temple by the Ilissus, Athens, Greece, 430 BC; 14) East portico of Erechtheum, Athens, c.415 BC; 15) Massalian (Marseille) treasury, Delphi, 6th cent. BC; 16) Artemisium, Ephesus c.550 BC; 17) First dipteros, Samos, c.560 BC; 18) Second dipteros, Samos, c.500 BC; 19) Delphi, c.570 BC; 20) Athenian stoa, Delphi, 478 BC

1
2
3
4
5
6
7
8
9
10
11
12
13
14
21
21
22
15
16
17
18
19
20

82 OGEES, FLORIATED AND FOLIATED ORNAMENTATION

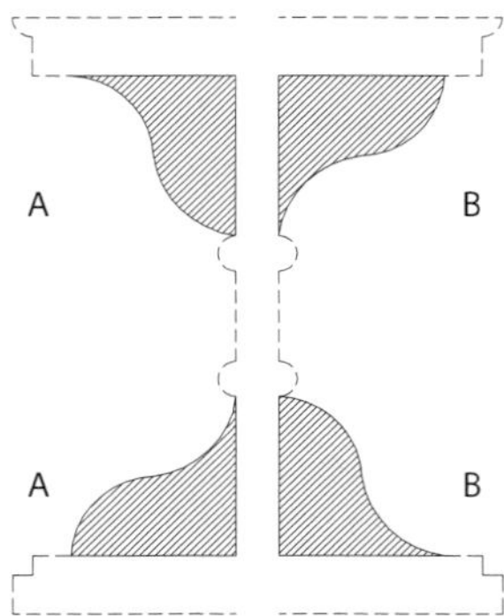

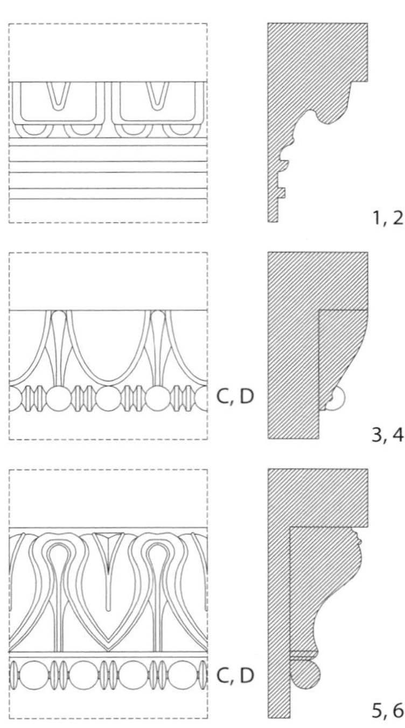

OGEE MOULDINGS

A cyma recta, ogee moulding
B cyma reversa, reverse ogee moulding
C bead and reel moulding, beaded moulding, reel and bead moulding
D astragal

GREEK CYMAE

1 Doric cyma
2 leaf scroll
3 Ionic cyma
4 egg and dart
5 Lesbian cyma
6 leaf and dart, waterleaf and dart, heart and dart, waterleaf and tongue, leaf and tongue

EGYPTIAN ANTHEMION MOTIFS

7 lotus anthemion
8 bud and blossom
9 bud and blossom, lotus and papyrus

MESOPOTAMIAN ANTHEMION MOTIFS

10 lotus anthemion
11 blossom and pine cone
12 hom-anthemion
13 hom blossom, bud and pine cone

GREEK ANTHEMION MOTIFS

14 acanthus anthemion
15 acanthus and lotus
16 acanthus and lily

OTHER LEAF MOTIFS AND GARLANDS

17 Egyptian kheker frieze
18 Greek palmette
19 rosette guilloche
20 bay-leaf garland
21 leaf scroll
22 leaf and rose scroll
23 vine, vignette, vinette, trayle
24 ivy leaf
25–27 Tudor flower

ogee moulding
a decorative moulding whose cross section is that of an ogee or S-shaped profile, the concave part uppermost; called a cyma recta in classical architecture

anthemion
an ornamental motif found in classical architecture consisting of stylized honeysuckle foliage; the word derives from the Greek for flower, anthos

floriated
carved or rendered with decorative flower motifs

foliated
carved or rendered with decorative leaf motifs

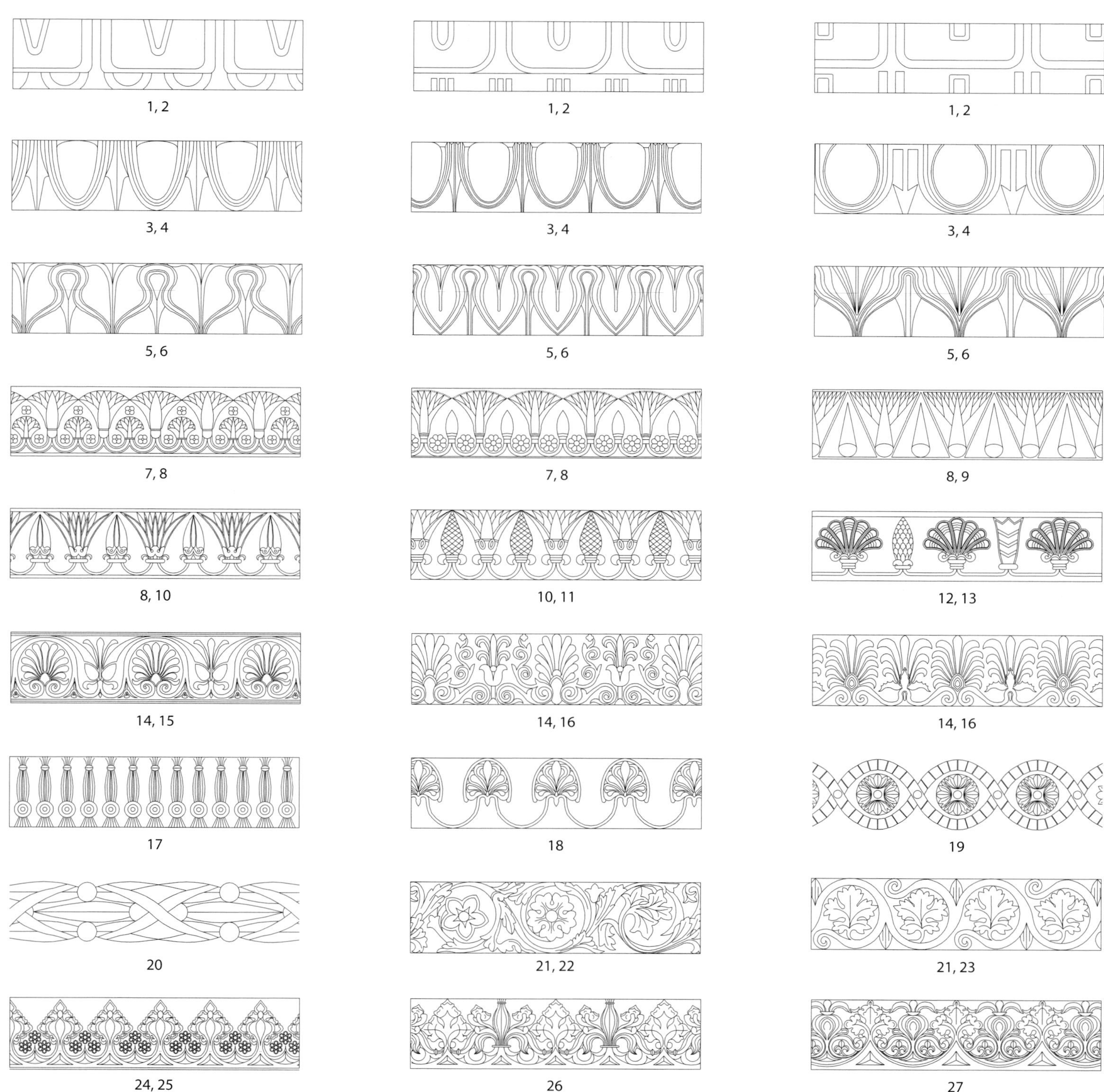
1, 2
1, 2
1, 2
3, 4
3, 4
3, 4
5, 6
5, 6
5, 6
7, 8
7, 8
8, 9
8, 10
10, 11
12, 13
14, 15
14, 16
14, 16
17
18
19
20
21, 22
21, 23
24, 25
26
27

83 GREEK AND ROMAN WALLING

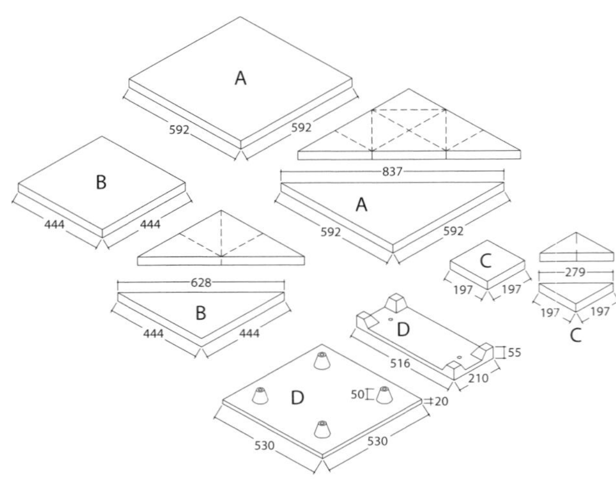

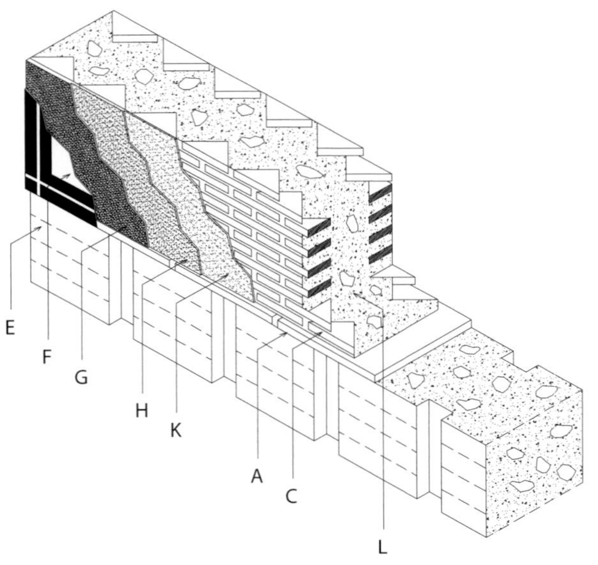

LATERES COCTI, TESTAE – ROMAN BRICKS

A bipedalis
B sesquipedalis
C bessalis
D tegula mammata

ROMAN CONCRETE WALL

E base wall cast in board formwork
F applied finish or mural painting: opus tectorium, marble veneer, marble stucco, fresco
G final plaster coat, face coat, finishing coat
H second plaster coat, floating coat, straightening coat
K first plaster coat, base coat, key coat
L concrete core

MASONRY AND CONCRETE WALLING

1 opus siliceum: polygonal masonry, cyclopean masonry, Pelasgic masonry
2 emplecton: coursed stone masonry
3 graecorum structura – 'Greek construction'
4 opus antiquum, opus incertum, opus intercentum, coursed stone masonry
5 opus gallicum, murus gallicus: 'Gallic wall'
6 opus testaceum, opus latericium, opus lateritium, brick-faced concrete

OPUS MIXTUM

7 opus vittatum mixtum, opus mixtum vittatum, banded brick and ashlar
8 opus listatum, banded brick and rubble
9 opus reticulatum mixtum
10 opus reticulatum – 'meshwork'
11 opus quasi reticulatum
12 opus africanum – 'African work'
13 opus isodomum, opus quadratum, coursed ashlar
14 opus pseudoisodomum
15 opus spicatum: herringbone brickwork
16 opus craticium: wattle and daub
17 opus signinum: rough render
18 opus caementicium, opus concretum, opus structile, structura caementica, concretework, concrete structure

opus
pl. opera, "work" (Lat.); an artistic composition or pattern, especially as used in relation to Roman stonework and walling construction

Roman concrete
Roman walling construction made from two skins of rubble with an infill of cement and small stones poured at intervals during construction

pozzolan, pozzolana, pozzuolana
a siliceous volcanic duct occurring naturally in Pozzuoli, Italy and used by the Romans in their concretework; nowadays a finely ground manufactured product, it sets in the presence of calcium hydroxide and water to form a hardwearing cement binder

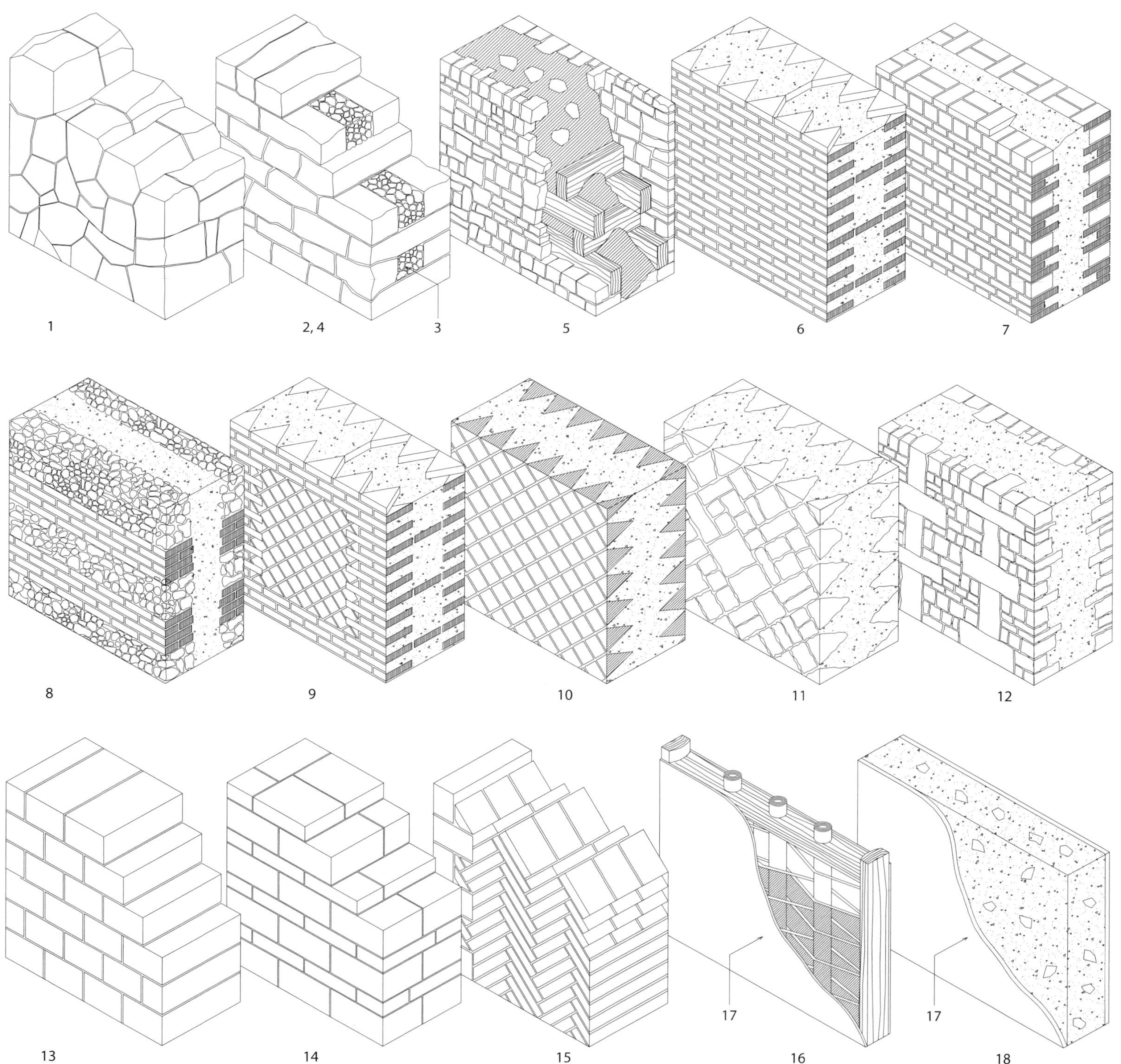
1
2, 4
3
5
6
7
8
9
10
11
12
13
14
15
17
16
17
18

84 CLASSICAL APTERAL TEMPLE

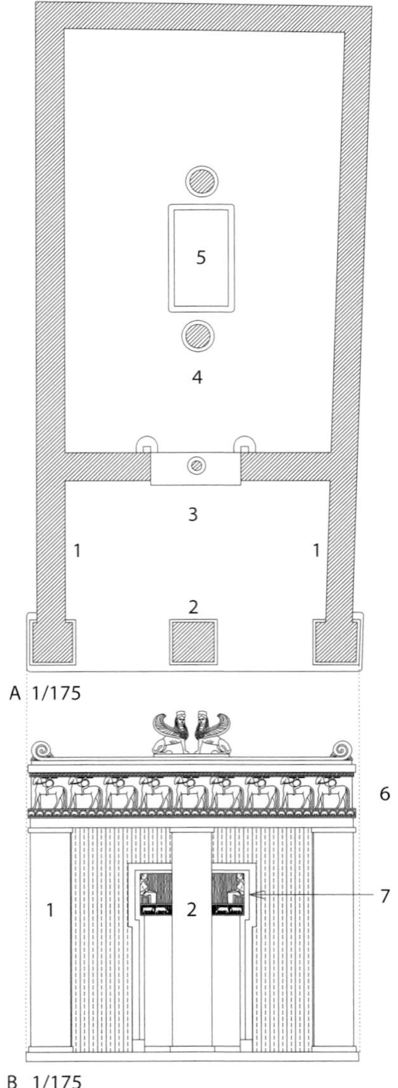

ANTIS OR ANTA TEMPLE – TEMPLUM IN ANTIS

- A monostyle in antis
- B pseudoprostyle
- C distyle in antis
- D double antis temple – amphidistyle (in antis)

PROSTYLE TEMPLE

- E diprostyle temple
- F tetraprostyle temple
- G amphiprostyle temple
- H hekatompedon – megaron temple

TUSCANICAE DISPOSITIONES – ETRUSCAN TEMPLES

- K prostyle temple
- L antis temple

PARTS

1 anta – side wall
2 henostyle
3 pronaos, antecella – porch
4 naos, cella – shrine
5 bomos – altar
6 frieze
7 antepagmentum – mouldings
8 opisthodomus, epinaos, posticum
9 agalma – image of god
10 thesauros – treasury

apteros, apteral temple
'wingless' (Gk.); a classical temple with a colonnade at one or both ends only, not lining its sides

anta, in antis
Lat.; in classical architecture, a corner pier or pilaster which is of a different classical order than those in the rest of the building, most often an extension of the side walls of the main body of a temple; plural, antae

prostyle
in classical architecture, referring to a temple or building which has a row of columns carrying a portico in front of the main entrance, but not along the sides

A, B) Temple at Prinias, Crete, c.650 BC; C) 'Treasury of Sikyon', Olympia, Greece, c.560 BC; D) Temple of Artemis and Poseidon, Eleusis, Greece, 100–200 AD; E) Temple of Apollo Delphinios, Dreros, Crete, c.700 BC; F) Temple of Tibertus, Tivoli, Italy, c.100 BC; G) Temple of Athena Nike Apteros, Acropolis, Athens, 437 BC; H) Heraion I, Samos, Greece, c.800–700 BC; K) Volsinii, Italy, c.350–300 BC; L) Capitolium of Cosa, Italy, c.150 BC

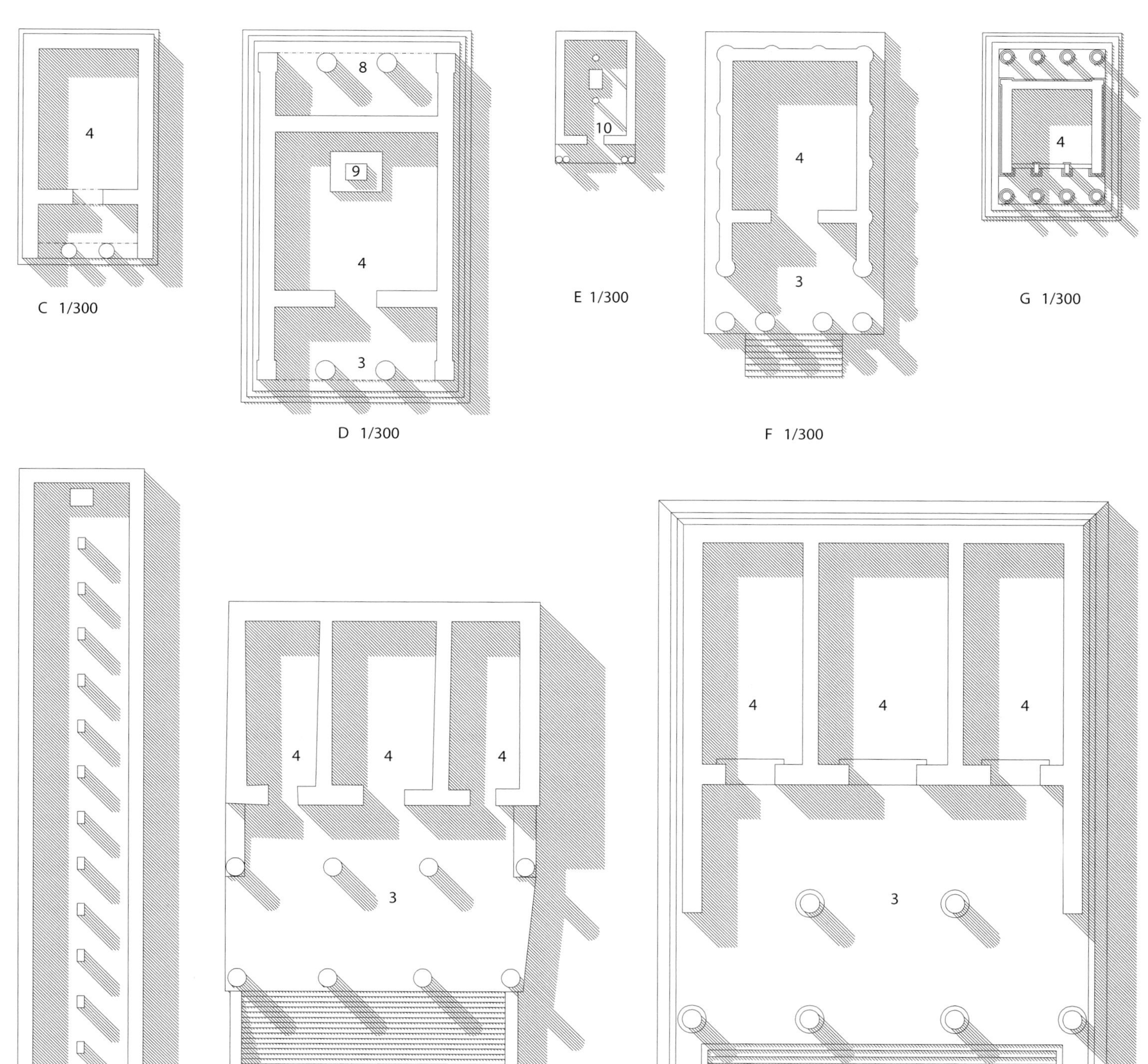
4
C 1/300
8
9
4
3
D 1/300
10
E 1/300
4
3
F 1/300
4
G 1/300
H 1/300
4
4
4
3
K 1/300
4
4
4
3
L 1/300

85 CLASSICAL PERISTYLE TEMPLES

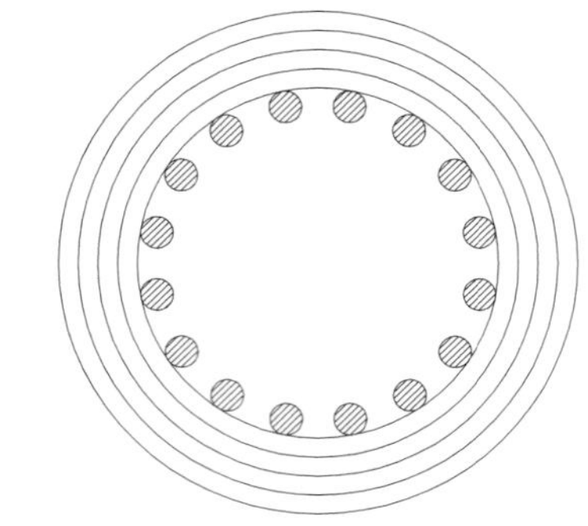

A 1/300

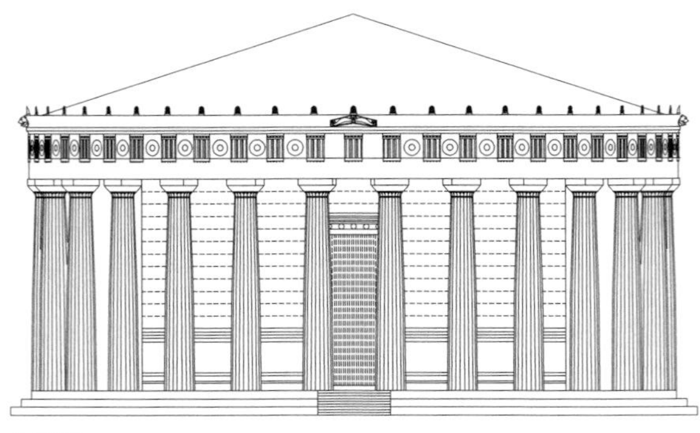

C 1/300

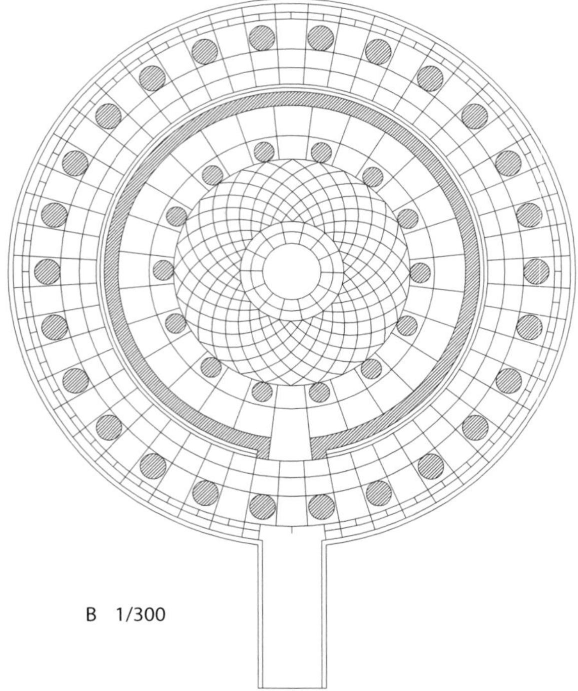

B 1/300

ROUND OR CIRCULAR TEMPLES

A heroon – tholos – monopteros

B tholos, thymele

C tholos, thymele

RECTANGULAR TEMPLES

D peripteros – peripteral temple

E Etruscan temple – tuscanicae dispositiones

F pseudoperipteros

G pseudodipteros

H double temple – pseudodipteros

K hypaethral temple – dipteros

1 pronaos – porch

2 naos – shrine

3 adyton – 'holy of holies'

4 antecella – porch

5 cella – sanctuary

6 dytum – 'holy of holies'

7 peribolos (–us) – temple surround

8 peridromos – colonnade

9 pteroma – temple colonnade

10 pteron, ptera – row of columns

11 peristasis – outer colonnade

12 sekos – temple court

13 naiskos – small sanctuary

14 ala, alae – side walls, 'wings'

peristylos (Gk.), peristyle temple, peristylar temple,
a classical temple-type which is surrounded by a colonnade on all sides

peripteros (Gk.), peripteral temple
a temple surrounded by a single row of columns

dipteros (Gk.), dipteral temple
a temple surrounded by a double row of columns

A) Heroon in Temple of Apollo Delphinios, Miletus, Late Antiquity; B) Epidauros, Argolis, Greece, 336–330 BC; C) Arsinoeion, Samothrake, Greece, 288–281 BC; D) 2nd temple of Zeus, Nemea, Argolis, Greece, 330 BC; E) Temple C (Temple of Feronia), Largo Argentina, Rome, c.290 BC; F) 'Maison Carrée', Nimes, France, 20–15 BC; G) Temple of Hera I or 'Basilica', Paestum, c.550 BC; H) Temple of Venus and Rome, Rome, 134–138 AD; K) Temple of Apollo, Didyma, Turkey, 250 BC

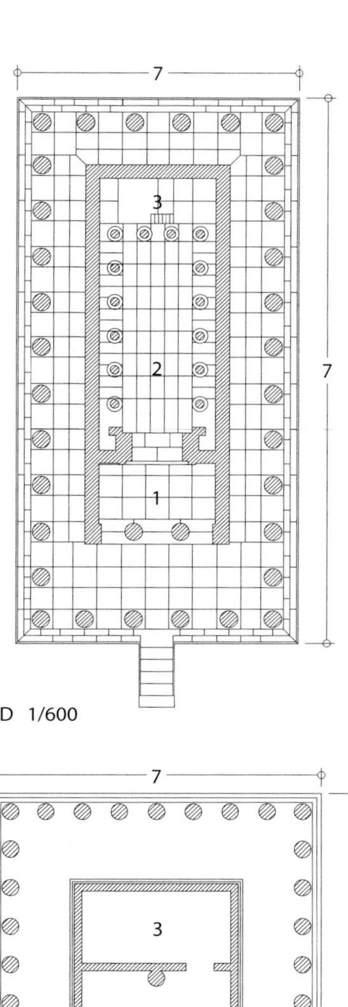

D 1/600

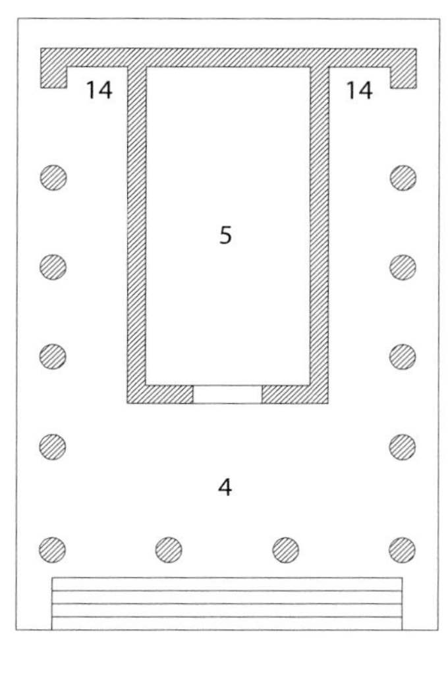

E 1/400

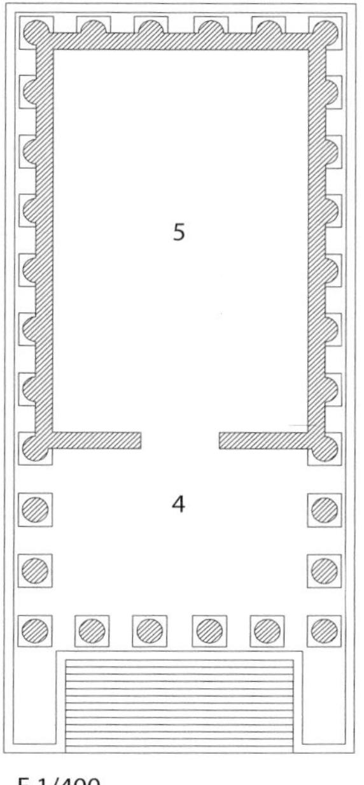

F 1/400

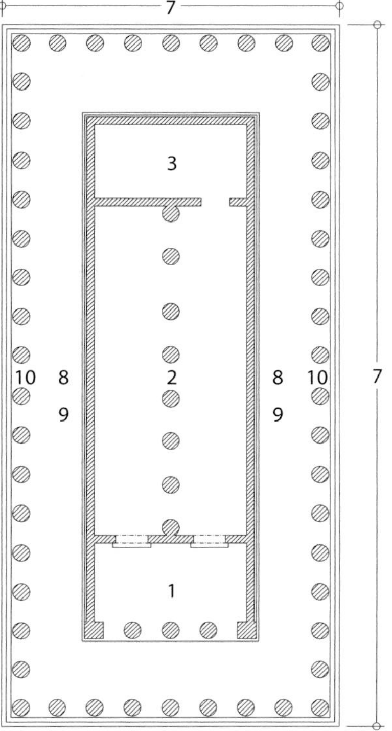

G 1/600

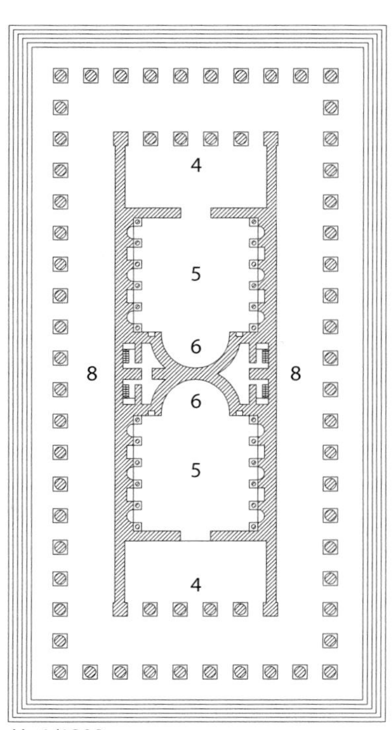

H 1/1200

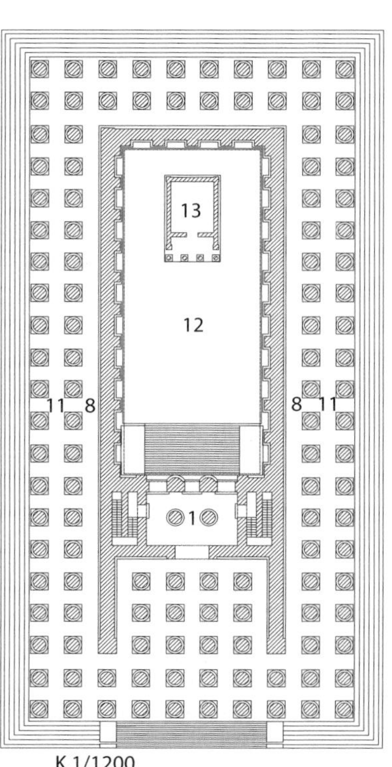

K 1/1200

86 TRABEATED GREEK AND ARCUATED ROMAN TEMPLE

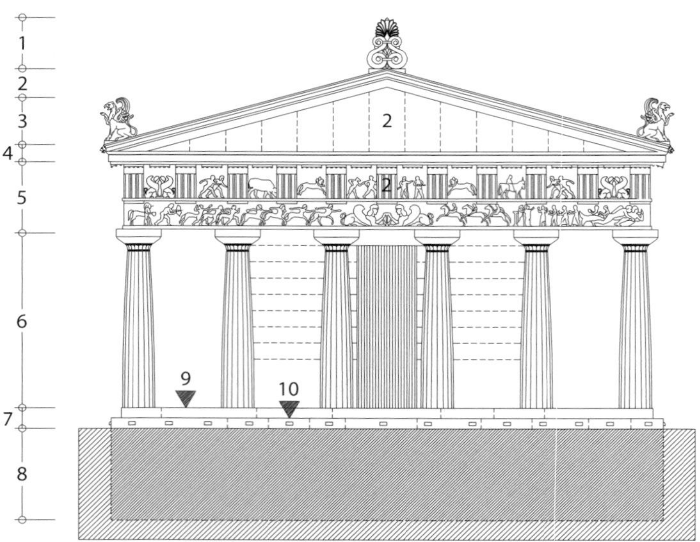

A 1/200

B 1/250

trabeated
describing a structural system based on the use of columns and beams

arcuated
of a construction or pattern which features arches as a main structural device or motif, or is bowed in shape

cupola
the central dome of an interior space; domed vaulting or a dome-shaped recess in a ceiling

acroterion, acroter
in classical architecture, a plinth or pedestal for statues, set at the apex or eaves of a temple; also often the statues or ornaments themselves; plural acroteria; Latin form is acroterium, Greek is akroterion

TRABEATED CONSTRUCTION

A frontage of peristyle temple
B section of hypaethral temple

ARCUATED CONSTRUCTION

C tholobate (ceiling plan)
D rotunda (plan)
E rotunda (section)

1 ridge acroterion
2 aetos, fastigium – tympanum
3 eaves acroterion
4 corona
5 entablature
6 portico, colonnade
7 crepidoma, podium
8 stereobate – foundation
9 stylobate – platform
10 euthynteria – base
11 agalma – god's image
12 exedra, exhedra – niche
13 lacunar, coffered ceiling
14 caisson, coffer
15 oculus, opaion – circular rooflight
16 dome

A) Temple of Athena, Assos, Turkey, c.530 BC; B) Parthenon, Athens, 447–432 BC, Ictinos and Callicrates; C–E) Pantheon, Rome, 118–126 AD

C 1/600

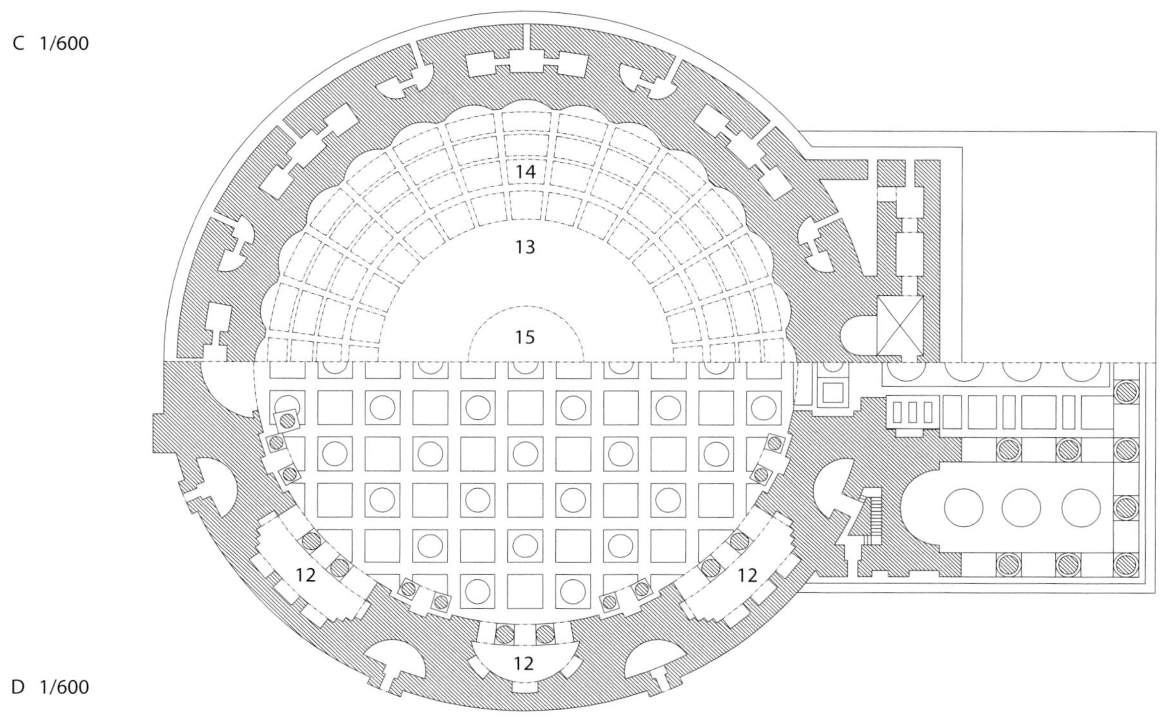

D 1/600

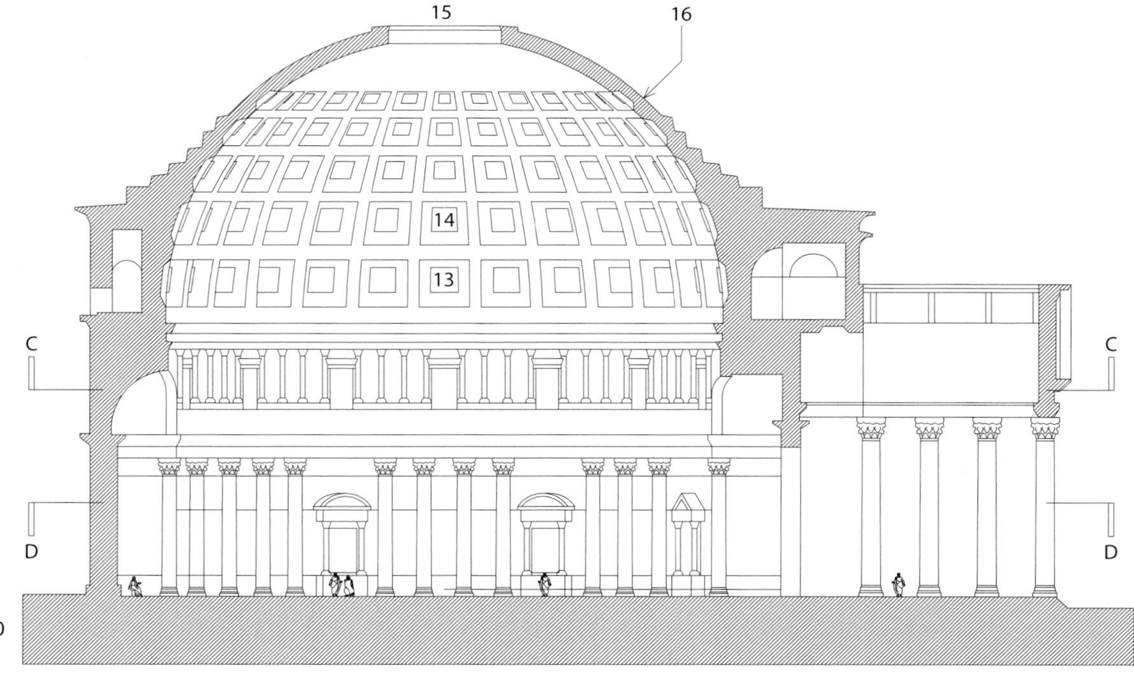

E 1/600

87 GREEK RESIDENTIAL BUILDINGS IN ANTIQUITY

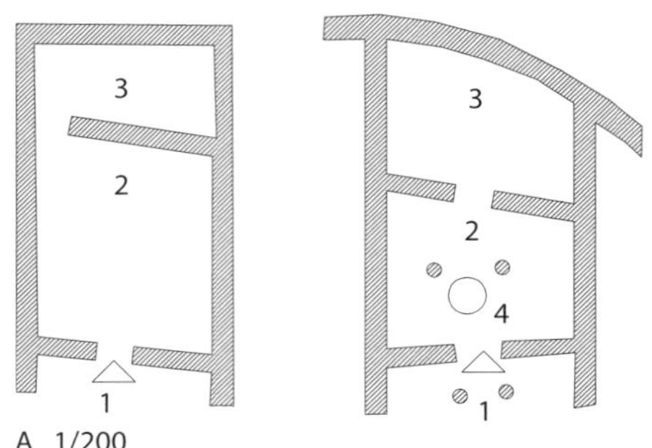

A 1/200

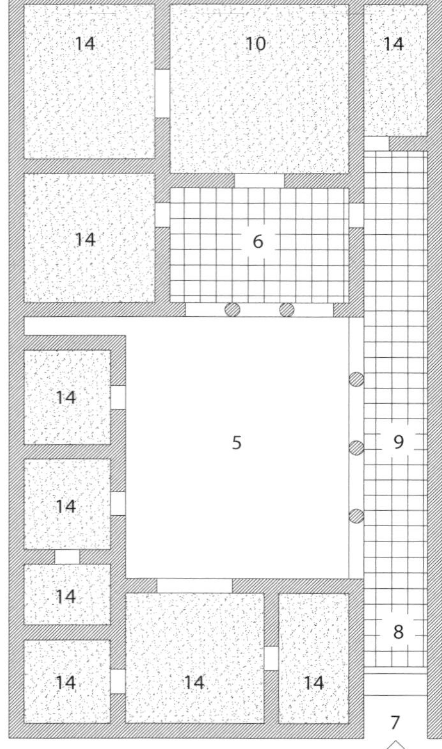

B 1/300

DWELLING TYPES

A megaron
B prostas house
C pastas houses
D peristyle house

SPACES

1 prodomos – porch
2 doma – main room
3 thalamos – rear chamber
4 hearth
5 court, courtyard
6 prostas – anteroom
7 prothyron – entrance
8 thyroreion – entrance passage
9 pastas – veranda
10 andron – mens' dining room
11 kitchen
12 peristylion – peristyle
13 hestia, eschara – altar
14 room's function uncertain; bed chamber, living room, store etc.

megaron

1 an early Greek or Mycenaean dwelling type
2 a long rectangular central hall in a Mycenaean dwelling or temple, with an entrance at one end; originally evolving from the Mycenaean dwelling type

prostas house

a Greek dwelling-type entered from the street via a passage to an open courtyard, around which all spaces are arranged; the principal rooms are accessed via a niche-like anteroom or prostas

pastas house

a dwelling-type from the classical period of northern Greece, 423–348 BC, with a courtyard in the centre of the south side and deep columned veranda or pastas affording access to rooms

peristyle house

a Greek dwelling-type whose open courtyard is surrounded by colonnades on all sides, often more luxurious than a prostas or pastas house

A) megaron, Dimini, Thessaly (Greece), neolithic period; B) prostas house, house 33, Priene, Ionia (modern Turkey), 200–100 BC; C) pastas houses, Olynthus (Greece), c.300 BC; D) peristyle house, Maison de la Colline, Delos (Greece), c.200 BC

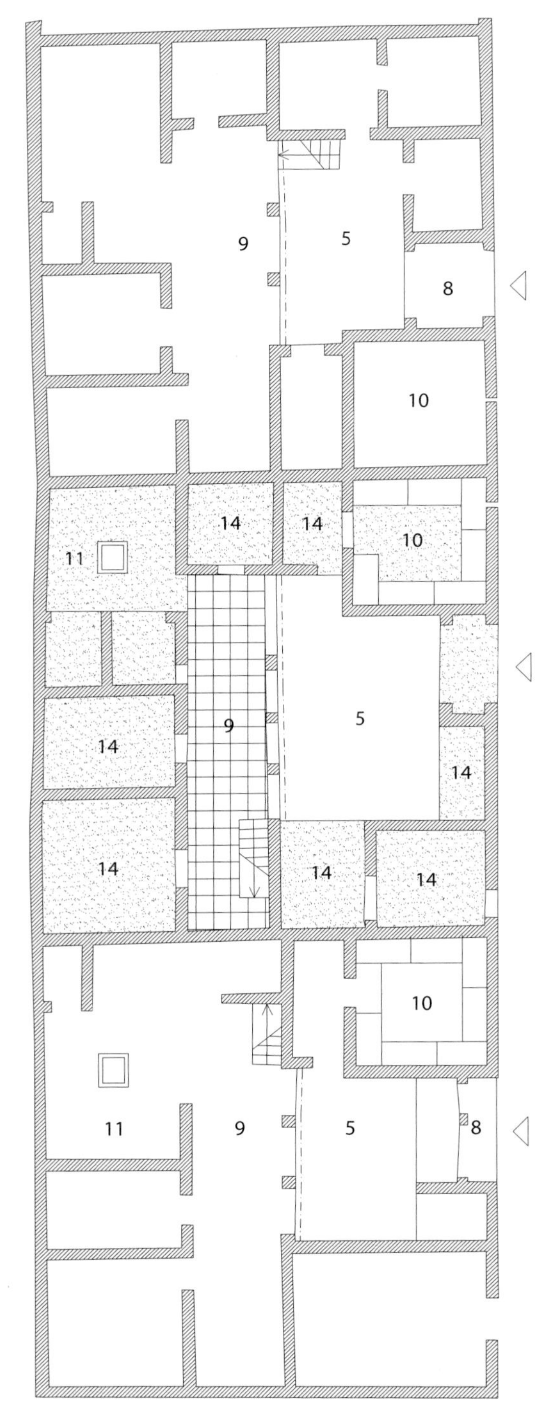

C 1/275

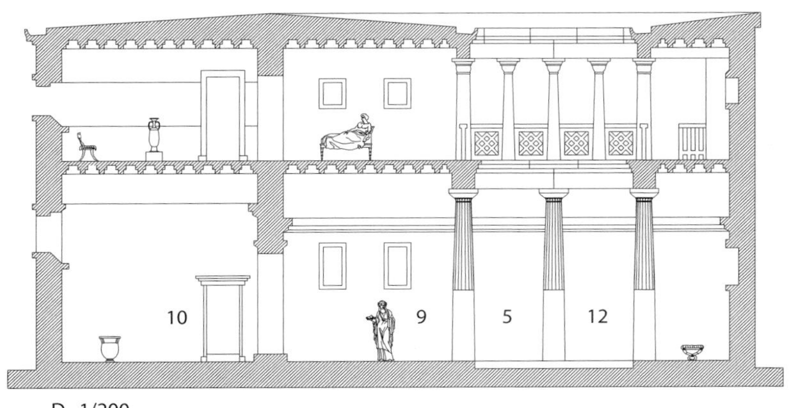

D 1/200

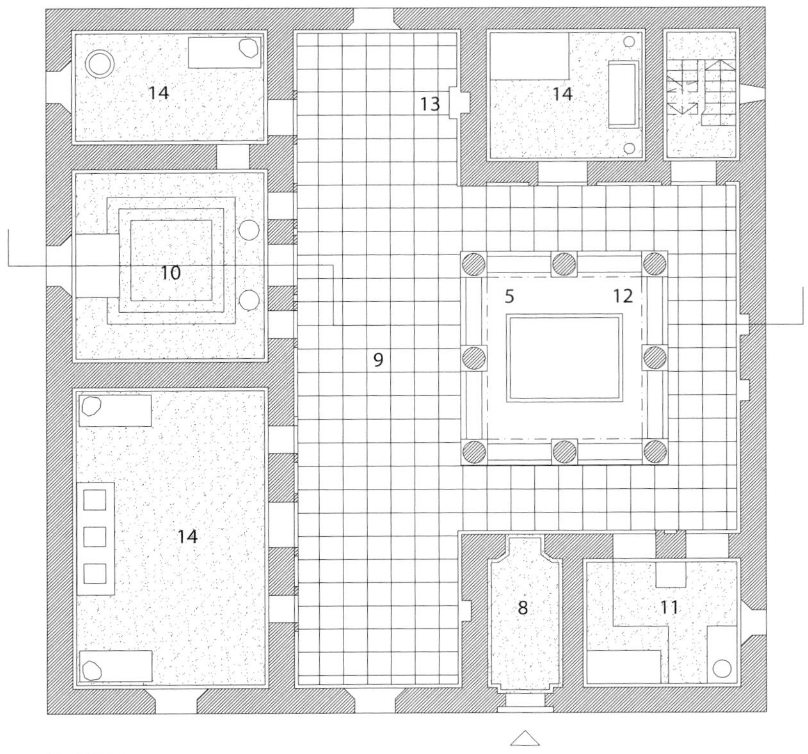

D 1/200

88 ROMAN RESIDENTIAL BUILDINGS

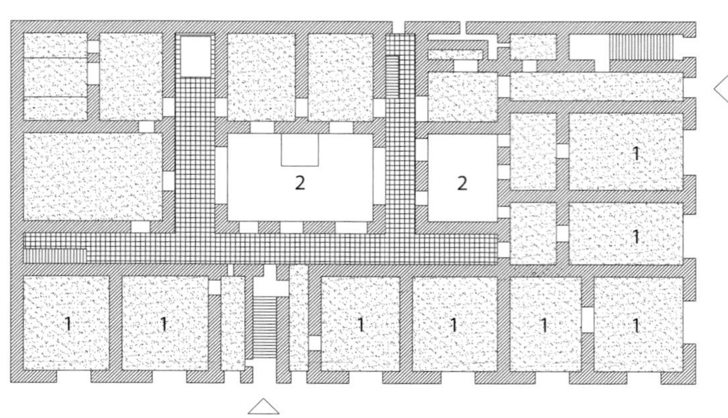

A 1/500

TYPES OF DWELLING

A insula, street level
B villa
C atrium house

SPACES

1 taberna – shop or workshop
2 courtyard, light well
3 vestibulum – entrance hall
4 atrium – court
5 impluvium – pool
6 lararium – altar
7 compluvium – opening
8 cubiculum – bed chamber
9 triclinium – dining room
10 ala – alcove
11 oecus, oikos – dining room
12 tablinum – reception room and archive
13 fauces – entrance passage
14 culina – kitchen
15 lavatrina – washroom
16 balneum, balineum – bathroom
17 porticus – veranda
18 exedra, exhedra – reception room
19 peristylium – colonnaded court
20 piscina, fons – pool
21 triclinium aestivum – outdoor dining area
22 coenatio, cenatio – dining room

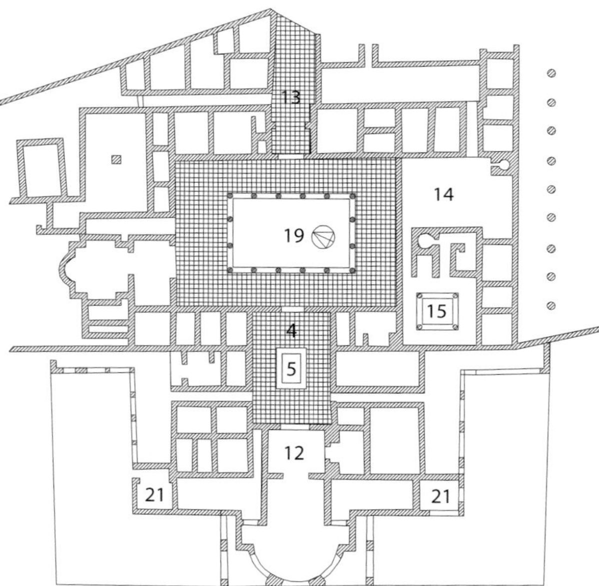

B 1/500

insula

Lat.; a Roman masonry and concrete tenement block for the labouring classes, often a multistorey structure with commercial premises and workshops (tabernae) at street level; originally the plot of land bounded by urban streets, on which one was built

villa

Lat.; a large classical Roman country house with an estate; originally divided into two parts, the pars urbana, or living area, and pars rustica or working area

atrium house

a Roman dwelling type in which the building mass surrounds a main central space, the atrium, open to the sky

A) Casa di Diana – Insula of Diana, Ostia, 130–40 BC; B) Villa dei Misteri – Villa of the Mysteries, Pompeii, c.200–100 BC; C) Casa di Trebius Valens – house of Trebius Valens, Pompeii

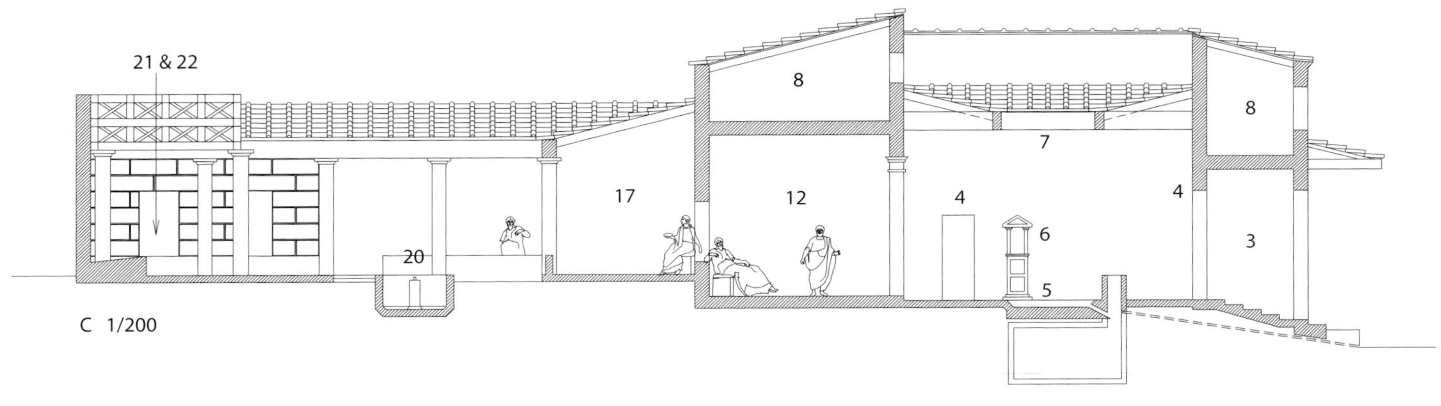
21 & 22
8
8
7
17
12
4
4
6
3
20
5

C 1/200

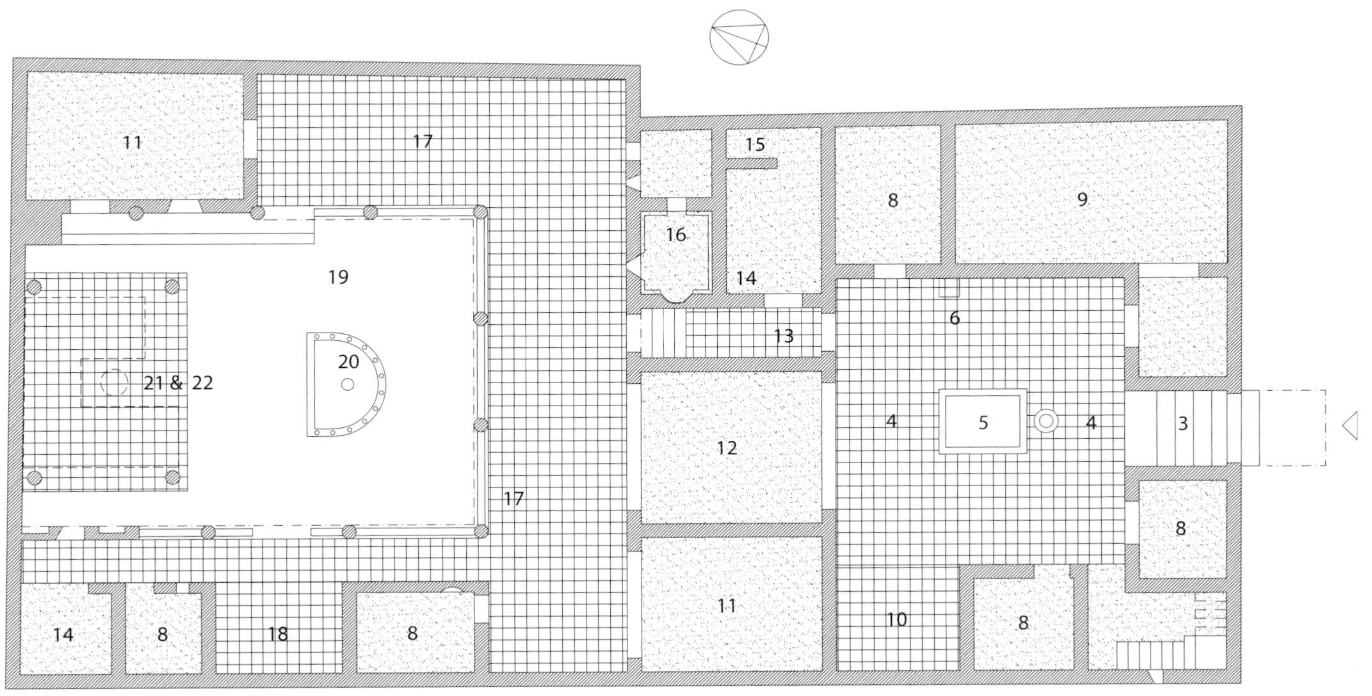
11
17
15
8
9
16
14
19
6
13
20
21 & 22
4
5
4
3
12
17
8
11
10
14
8
18
8
8

C 1/200

89 CLASSICAL STAGES AND SPECTATOR STRUCTURES

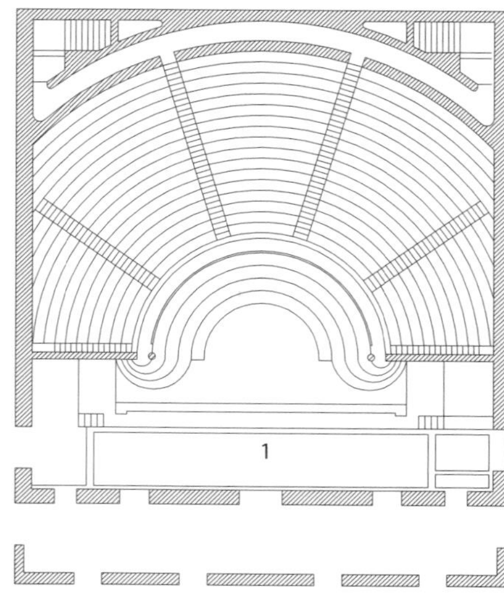

A 1/500

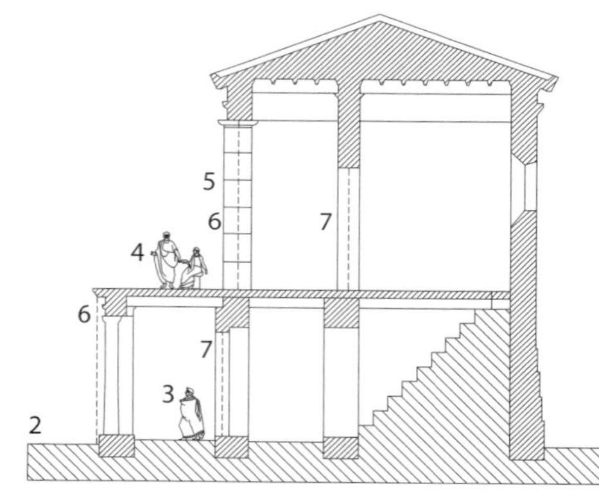

B 1/300

BUILDING TYPES

- A theatrum tectum, odeum, odeion – roofed theatre (Roman)
- B skene – stage building (Greek)
- C theatron – theatre, auditorium (Greek)
- D skene – stage building (Greek)
- E theatrum – theatre (Roman)
- F cavea – stands
- G scaena – stage building
- H stadium, stadion
- K hippodromos, hippodrome
- L circus

theatron
Gk.; the auditorium of a classical theatre, where the public were seated

theatrum
Lat.; a Roman theatre building or structure

stadion
an ancient Greek elongated sports venue with rounded ends, surrounded on all sides by banked spectator stands; a stadium

hippodrome, hippodromos
Gk.; an open or roofed track or arena for chariot and horse racing in ancient Greece and Rome; a Roman circus

circus
Lat.; in Roman architecture, a long U-shaped or enclosed arena for chariot racing; a hippodrome

1 logeion, pulpitum – platform
2 proskenion, okribas, proscaenium – front stage
3 hyposkenion – lower stage
4 episkenion – upper stage
5 skenotheke, scaena frons – stage wall
6 aulaeum – curtain
7 parapetasma, siparium – secondary curtain
8 orkhestra, orchestra – choir
9 thymele – altar
10 paraskenion, versurae – secondary stage
11 parados, itinera versurarum – side entrance
12 thyroma – stage door
13 porta regia – royal door
14 portae hospitales – guest doors
15 portus post scaenium – portico
21 prohedria – front seats
22 podium – diginitary seating
23 kerkis, kekrides, cuneus – seating block
24 diazoma, praecinctio – gangway
25 klimakes – steps
26 gradus – seating row
27 adit, aditus – entrance, passage
31 analemma, iskhegaon – retaining wall
32 balbides, carceres – starting gates
33 porta triumphalis
34 spina – dividing wall
35 meta prima
36 meta secunda
37 quadriga – four-horsed chariot

A) Pompeii, Italy, c.30 AD; B) Oropus, Greece, c.200 BC; C, D) Priene (principle), Turkey, c.350–300 BC; E, F, G) Sabrata, Libya, c.200 AD; H) Aphrodisias (Geyre) Turkey, 1st cent. AD; G) Leptis Magna (Lepcis Magna), Libya, c.200 AD

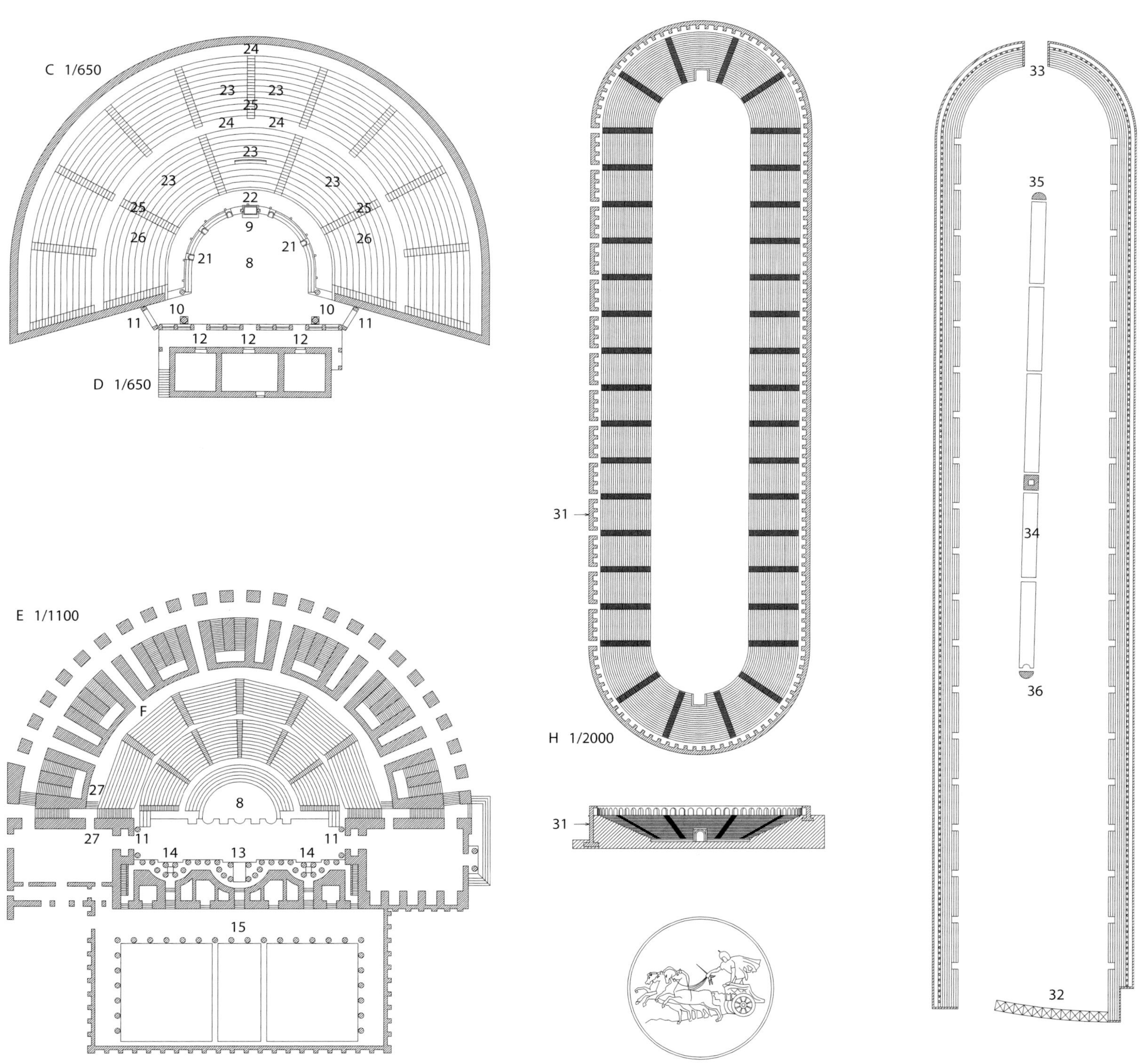
C 1/650
24
23 23
25
24 24
23
23 23
22
25 25
9
26 26
21 21
8
10 10
11 11
12 12 12
D 1/650
E 1/1100
F
27
8
27 11 11
14 13 14
15
G 1/1100
31
H 1/2000
31
37
33
35
34
36
32
K, L 1/2500

90 AMPHITHEATRE

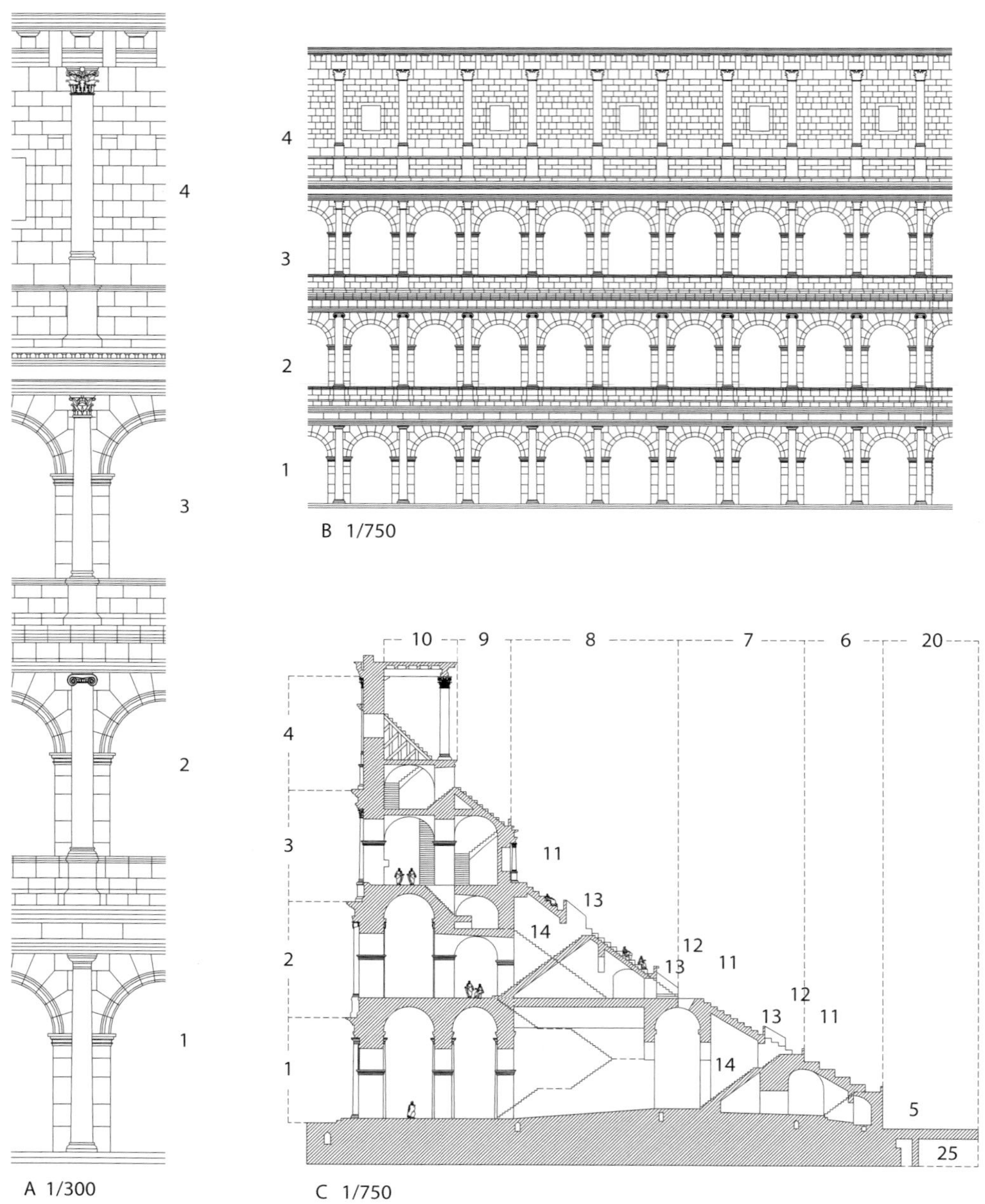

A superimposed orders
B elevation of amphitheatre
C cavea, visorium – section through seating
D plan of amphitheatre

Flavian Amphitheatre (The Colosseum), Rome, 72–80 AD

SPECTACULA – AMPHITHEATRE

1 Doric order, 1st storey
2 Ionic order, 2nd storey
3 Corinthian order, 3rd storey
4 Composite order, 4th storey

CAVEA, VISORIUM – SEATING

5 balteus, corona podii – parapet
6 podium – diginitaries' enclosure, 'ringside'
7 maenianum primum, ima cavea – first tier
8 maenianum media, media cavea – middle tier
9 maenianum summum, summa cavea – upper tier
10 maenianum summum in lignis – upper wooden tier, 'peanut gallery'
11 gradus – row of seats
12 praecinctio, precinctio, balteus – horizontal gangway
13 aditus – entrance to cavea
14 vomitorium (pl. vomitoria) – exit, escape route
15 pulvinar – box, loge
(a) emperor's, (b) consuls' and Vestal virgins'

20 ARENA

21 porta triumphalis – triumphal gate
22 porta pompae – ceremonial gate
23 porta libitinensis – funerary gate
24 porta sanavivaria – gate of life
25 hypogeum, hypogaeum – underground spaces

spectacula
Lat.; the original name for a Roman amphitheatre, as used by Roman citizens

amphitheatre, amphitheater (Am.)
a classical arena for gladiatorial contests and spectacles consisting of an oval or round space surrounded by tiered seating for spectators; amphitheatron in Greek

arena
the main central space of a Roman amphitheatre or circus, or of a bullring, often sanded

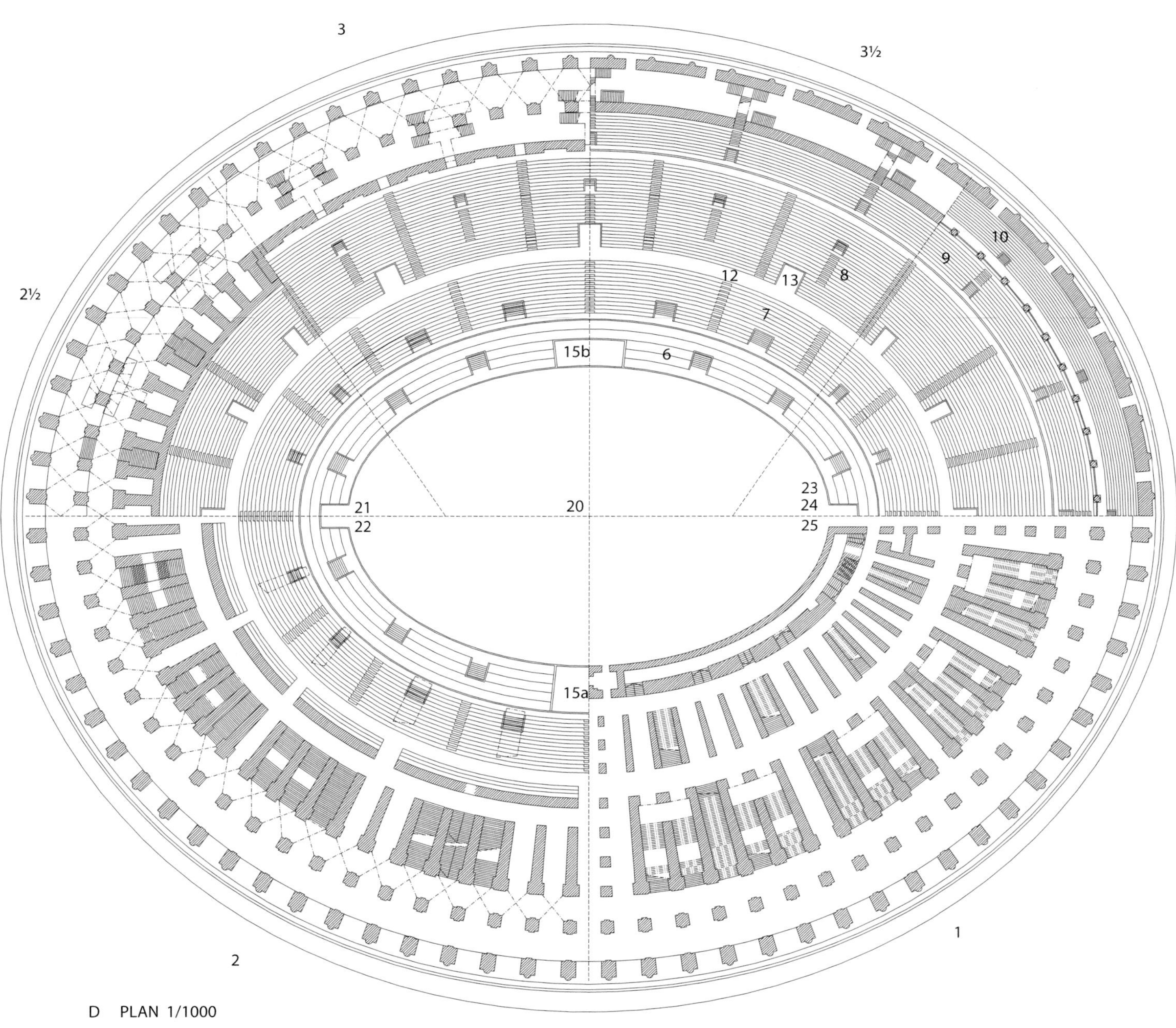

D PLAN 1/1000

91 CLASSICAL BUILDINGS OF RECREATION

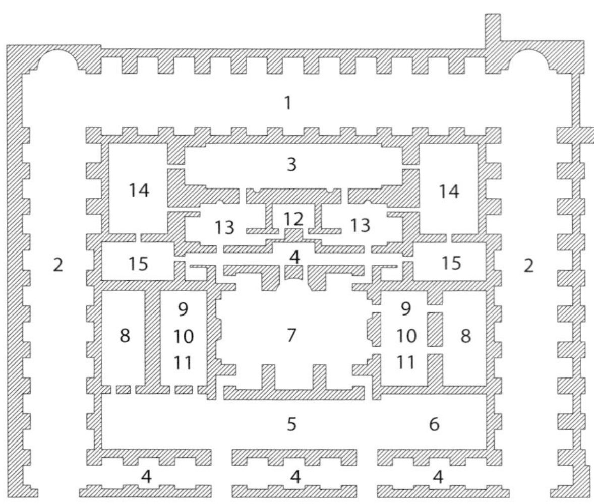

A 1/1400

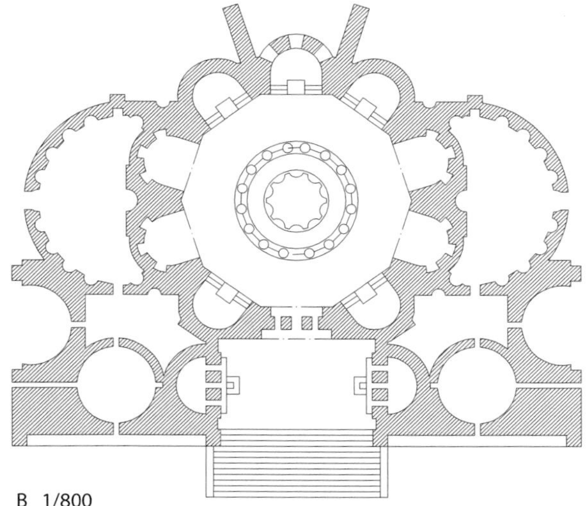

B 1/800

GYMNASION, GYMNASIUM

1 dromos – running track
2 xyst, xystus – passage, colonnade
3 sfairisterion, sphaeristerium – ball games
4 cryptoportico, cryptoporticus
5 palaestra – wrestling hall
6 korykeion, coryceum – boxing
7 ephebeion, ephebeum – main hall and classrooms
8 apodyterion – dressing room
9 elaiothesion, elaeothesium – oil and lotion store
10 alipterion, unctuarium – oiling and massage
11 konisterion, conisterium – sanding and powdering

LOUTRON, BALANEION – BATHS

12 lakonikon, pyriatherion, vaporarium – steam bath
13 caldarium, calidarium – hot baths
14 tepidarium – lukewarm baths
15 frigidarium – cold baths

THERMAE

20 vestibulum – entrance hall
21 main entrance
22 apodyterium – changing room
23 palaestra – wrestling area
24 ambulatio – exercise
25 balneum – bathing pool
26 destrictarium – massage
27 laconicum, sudatorium – steam baths
28 schola – conversation
29 caldarium – hot baths
30 heliocaminus
31 tepidarium – lukewarm baths
32 frigidarium – cold baths
33 natatio – swimming pool
34 exedrae – libraries and lecture halls
35 xystus – gardens, parks
36 stadium or waterfall
38 aqueduct
39 tabernae – shops, restaurants

gymnasium
Lat.; plural gymnasia; an ancient Greek centre for sports, with buildings, playing areas and baths; also written in Greek form as gymnasion

thermae
Lat.; ancient classical public baths with associated recreational facilities

balneum, balineum (Lat.), balneolum, balaneion (Gk.)
Lat., plural balneae; in Roman architecture, a small public or private bath house, suite of rooms etc.

nymphaeum
plural nymphaea; Lat.; in classical architecture, a temple, shrine or building dedicated to nymphs, mythological female water spirits; often built in proximity to a spring or water source; a fountain house

D

A gymnasium, gymnasion
B nymphaeum – fountain house or dining pavillion
C thermae – baths

A) Gymnasium of Hadrian, Ephesus, Turkey; B) Minerva Medica, Rome 260 AD; C) Thermae of Caracalla, Rome, 212–216 AD; D) Roman god of wine, Bacchus (Dionysus in Greece)

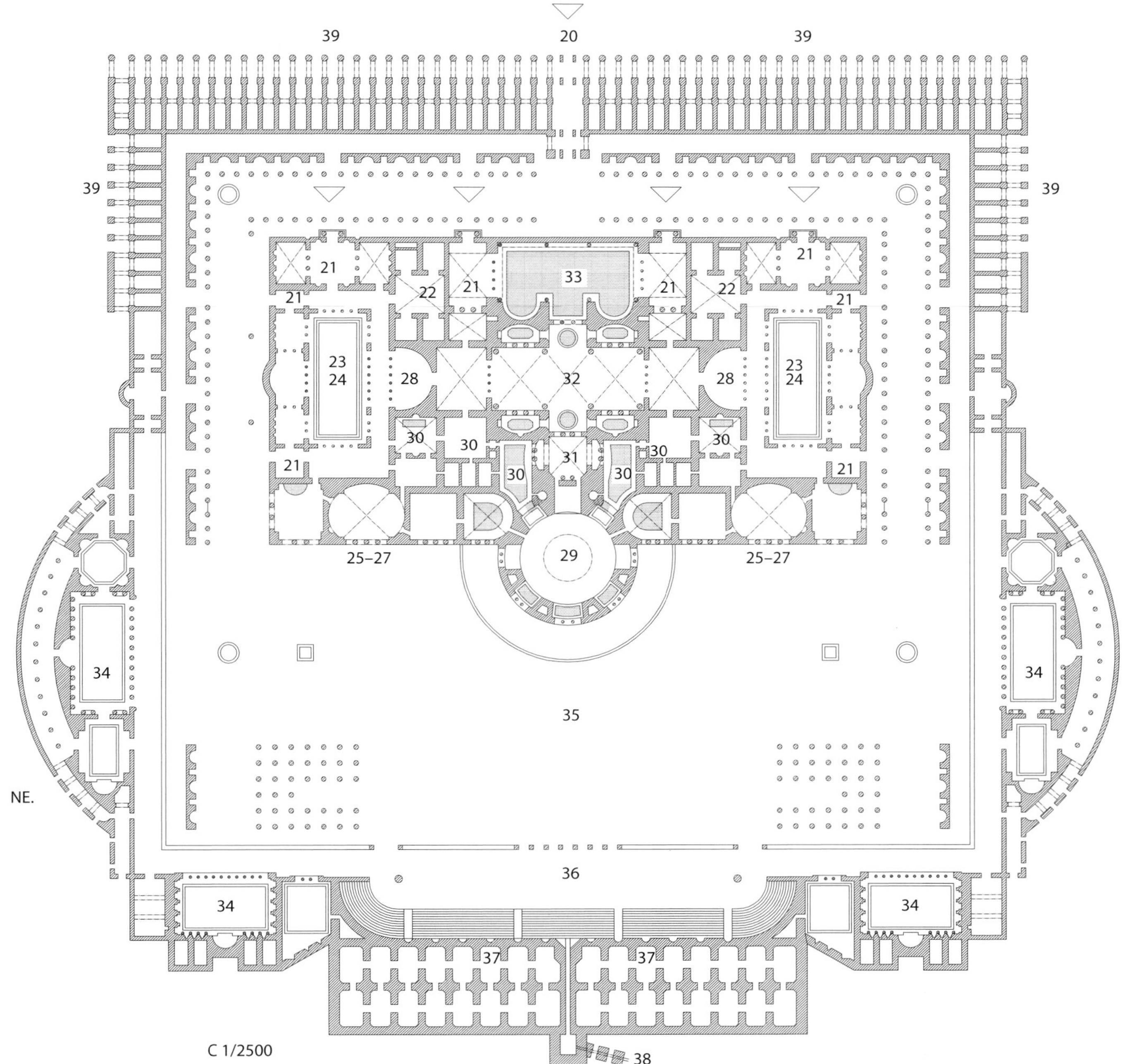
39
20
39
39
39
21
21
33
21
21
22
21
21
22
21
23
24
28
32
28
23
24
30
30
31
30
30
30
21
21
25–27
29
25–27
34
34
35
NE.
36
34
34
37
37
C 1/2500
38

92 CLASSICAL PUBLIC AND COMMERCIAL BUILDINGS

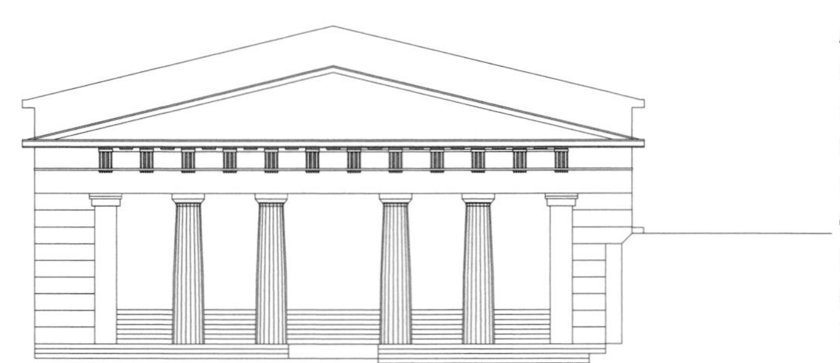

A 1/300

A propylaeum, propylon – gatehouse
B, C bouleuterion – council chamber
D estiatorion – banqueting hall
E xenodochium – guest house
F prytaneum – public town hall
G lesche – assembly hall
H ecclesiasterion – meeting room
K telesterion – mystery temple
L macellum – market court

1 propylaeum, propylon – gatehouse
2 stoa – colonnade
3 bomos – altar
4 bema, logeion, logeum – speaker's podium
5 anactoron, anaktoron – holy of holies
6 gatehouse
7 tholos – round building
8 well, fountain
9 macellum – market hall
10 lavatrina – public toilet
11 tabernae – shops, workshops

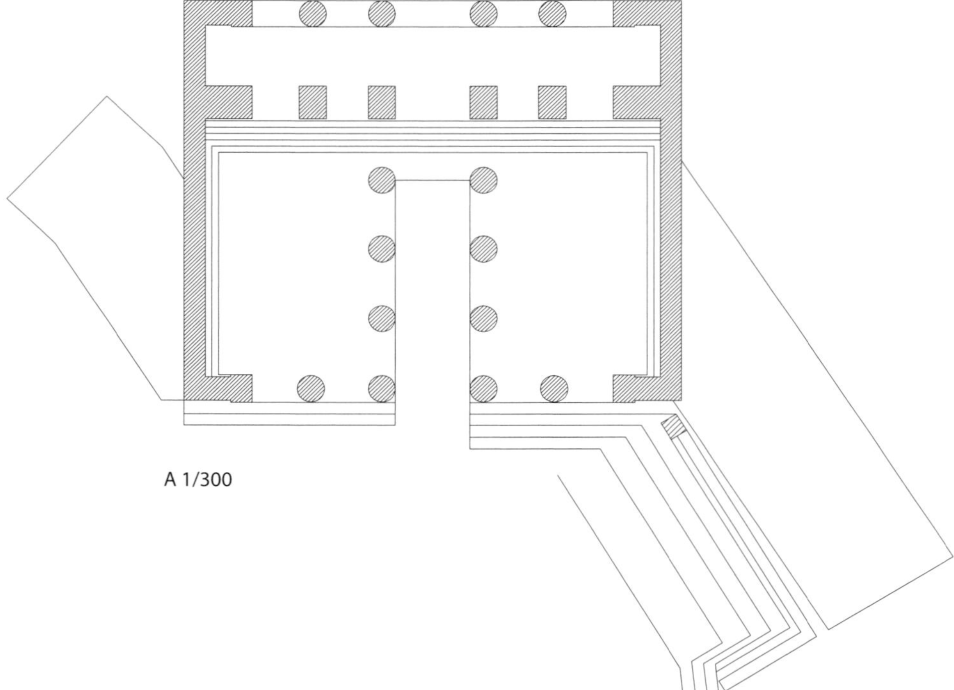

A 1/300

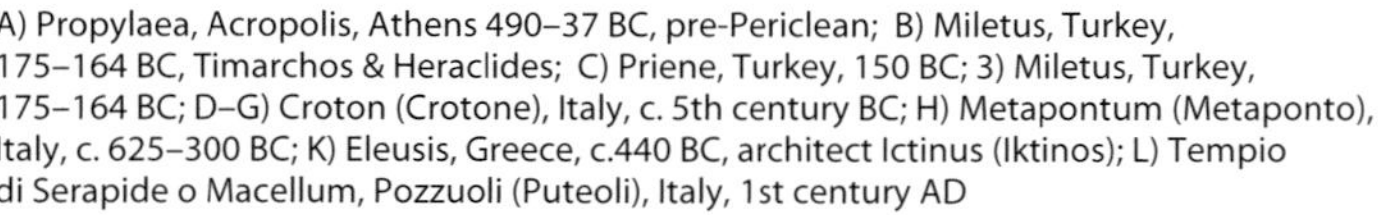

A) Propylaea, Acropolis, Athens 490–37 BC, pre-Periclean; B) Miletus, Turkey, 175–164 BC, Timarchos & Heraclides; C) Priene, Turkey, 150 BC; 3) Miletus, Turkey, 175–164 BC; D–G) Croton (Crotone), Italy, c. 5th century BC; H) Metapontum (Metaponto), Italy, c. 625–300 BC; K) Eleusis, Greece, c.440 BC, architect Ictinus (Iktinos); L) Tempio di Serapide o Macellum, Pozzuoli (Puteoli), Italy, 1st century AD

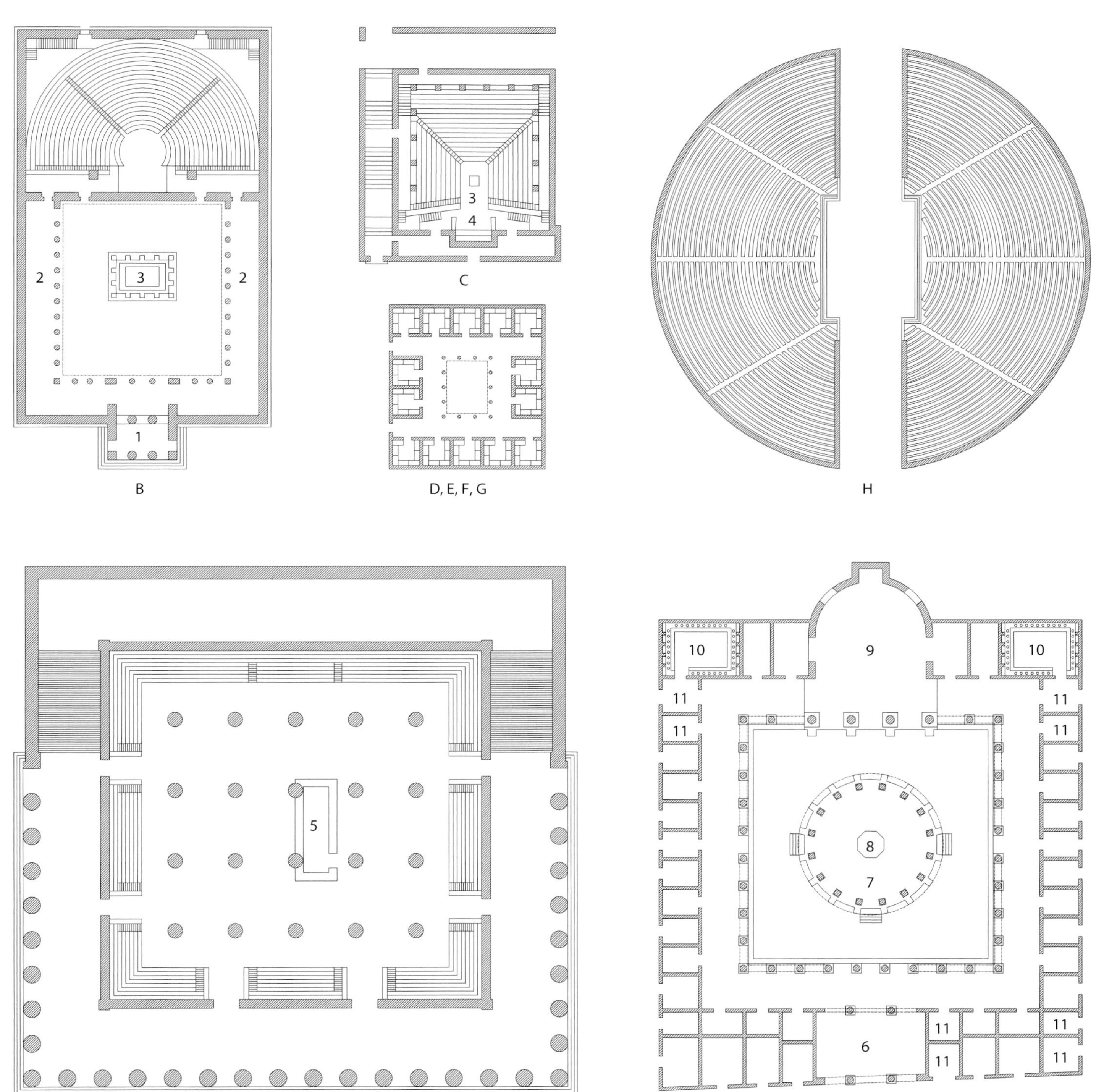

1/800

93 ROMAN STRUCTURES

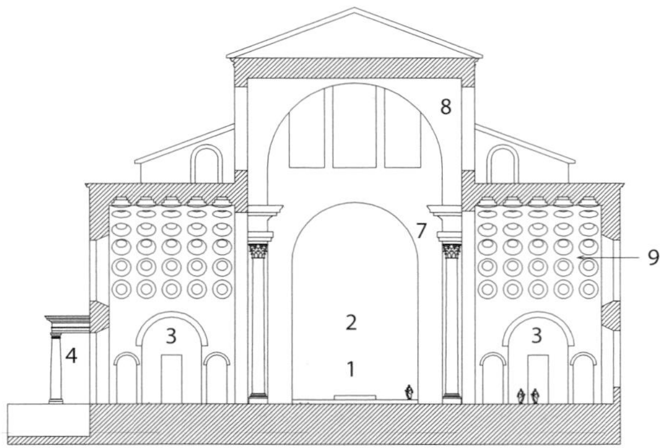

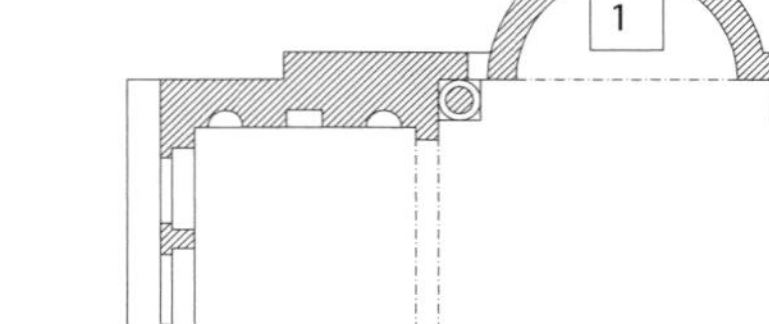

A 1/1000

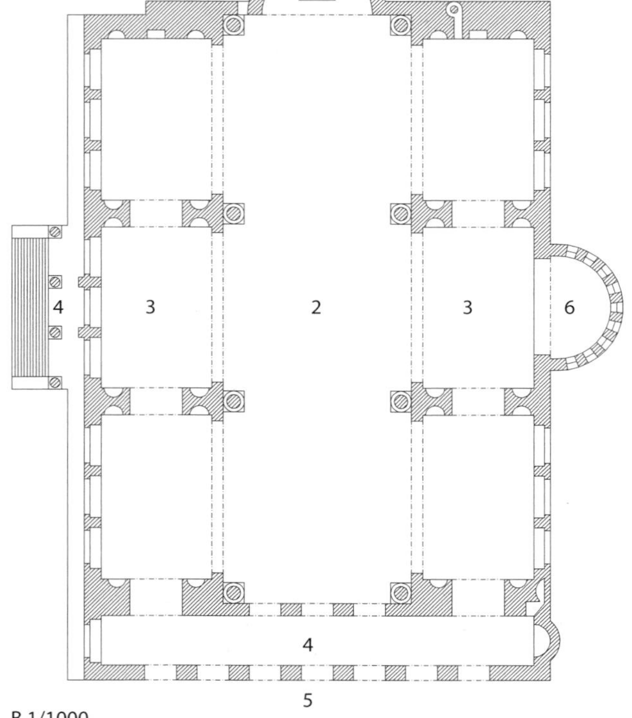

B 1/1000

A, B) Basilica of Maxentius (Basilica of Constantine, Basilica Maxentii), Rome, 306–312 AD; C) Basilica, Pompeii, Italy, c.120 BC; D) Tabularium, Rome, 83 BC, Lucius Cornelius; E) Arch of Marcus Aurelius, Tripoli, Libya, 163 AD; F) Triumphal arch of Septimius Severus, Rome, 203 AD; G) Iamblichus (Jamblique) tower tomb, Palmyra, Syria, 78–83 AD; H) Pont du Gard, Nîmes, France 15–14 BC; J) Augustus Caesar (63 BC–14 AD), known as Gaius Julius Caesar Octavianus (Octavian, in English)

1 tribune – apse, podium
2 navis media – nave
3 aisle
4 chalcidicum – porch
5 porticus, portico, colonnade
6 exedra, apse
7 epicranitis – moulding
8 clerestory window
9 coffered ceiling
10 loculus (pl.) loculi – burial chamber
11 columbarium

A basilica, section
B basilica, plan
C basilica, plan
D fornix (fornices)
E tetrapylon, tetrakionia, quadrifrontal arch
F arcus triumphalis, triumphal arch
G burial tower, tomb tower
H aqueduct

basilica
a Roman building-type, rectangular in shape with an apse at either end, used as a court of justice and an exchange

fornix
plural fornices; 'arch, vault' (Lat.); in classical architecture, originally a triumphal arch in the Roman republic, subsequently any arch supporting an entablature

quadrifrontal arch
(Lat. quadrifrons) a Roman urban monument situated at the meeting of two crossing streets, with four arches, one on each side, to allow passage through in all directions

aqueduct
a bridge or other structure designed to convey fresh water, usually a canal or river supported by piers and arches, or a tunnel; from the Latin, aquae ductus, 'conveyance of water'

J

3
6
4
5
2
1
3
6
C 1/750
D 1/400
E 1/400
F 1/400
10, 11
G 1/400
H 1/1250

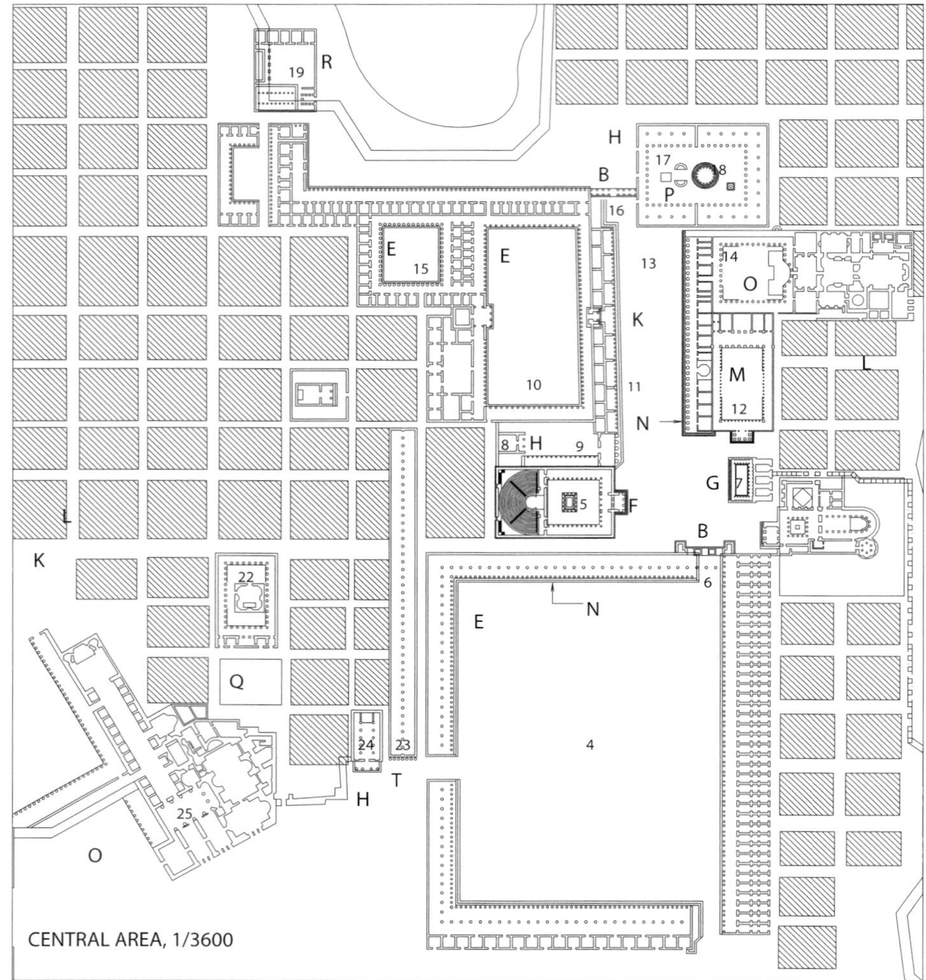

A acropolis: citadel
B gate
C via sacra, sacra via: sacred road
D city walls
E agora: main square
F bouleterion: council chamber
G nymphaeum: fountain house, nymph temple
H temple
K plateia (pl. plateiai): main street
L steponos (pl. steponoi): side street
M gymnasion: sports hall
N stoa: colonnaded court
O thermae: baths
P temenos: sacred enclosure
Q heroon (monopteros): heroic shrine
R synagogue (basilica)
S theatre
T warehouse
U stadion, stadium

grid plan

an urban plan type in which streets are laid out in an orthogonal network, forming a pattern of approximately rectangular blocks; also called a chequerboard plan, checkerboard plan, chessboard plan or gridiron plan

Hippodamian system

a rectilinear town layout in which blocks of dwellings are divided up by narrow side streets linked together by wider main roads, developed by the Ionian Hippodamus of Miletus in the 5th century BC

agora

a market or meeting place in a Greek city, the hub of public life where the most important public buildings were situated

MILETUS (MILETOS), Ionia, Ancient Greece (now modern Turkey); town plan probably by Hippodamus of Miletus c.450–400 BC: 1) acropolis (archaic period); 2) Holy gate; 3) city walls; 4) Southern agora; 5) bouleterion (175–164 BC); 6) Northern gate (150–200 AD); 7) nymphaeum (2nd cent. AD); 8) Temple of Asclepius; 9) shrine of the Caesar cult; 10) North agora (classical period); 11) ceremonial street; 12) gymnasion (2nd cent. AD); 13) Ionic stoa (classical period); 14) Thermae of Capito (41–54 AD); 15) Small agora (classical period); 16) Harbour gate (Roman period); 17) Delphinion, temple of Apollo: temenos (archaic period); 18) heroon: monopteros (Hellenistic and Roman); 19) synagogue basilica (Roman period); 20) Roman thermae (50–100 AD); 21) theatre (Hellenistic and Roman period); 22) heroon (Roman period); 23) warehouse (2nd cent. BC); 24) Temple of Serapis (3rd cent. AD); 25) thermae of Faustina (161–180 AD); 26) stadion, stadium (c.150 BC); 27) Western agora (late Hellenistic period); 28) Temple of Athene (450–400 BC)

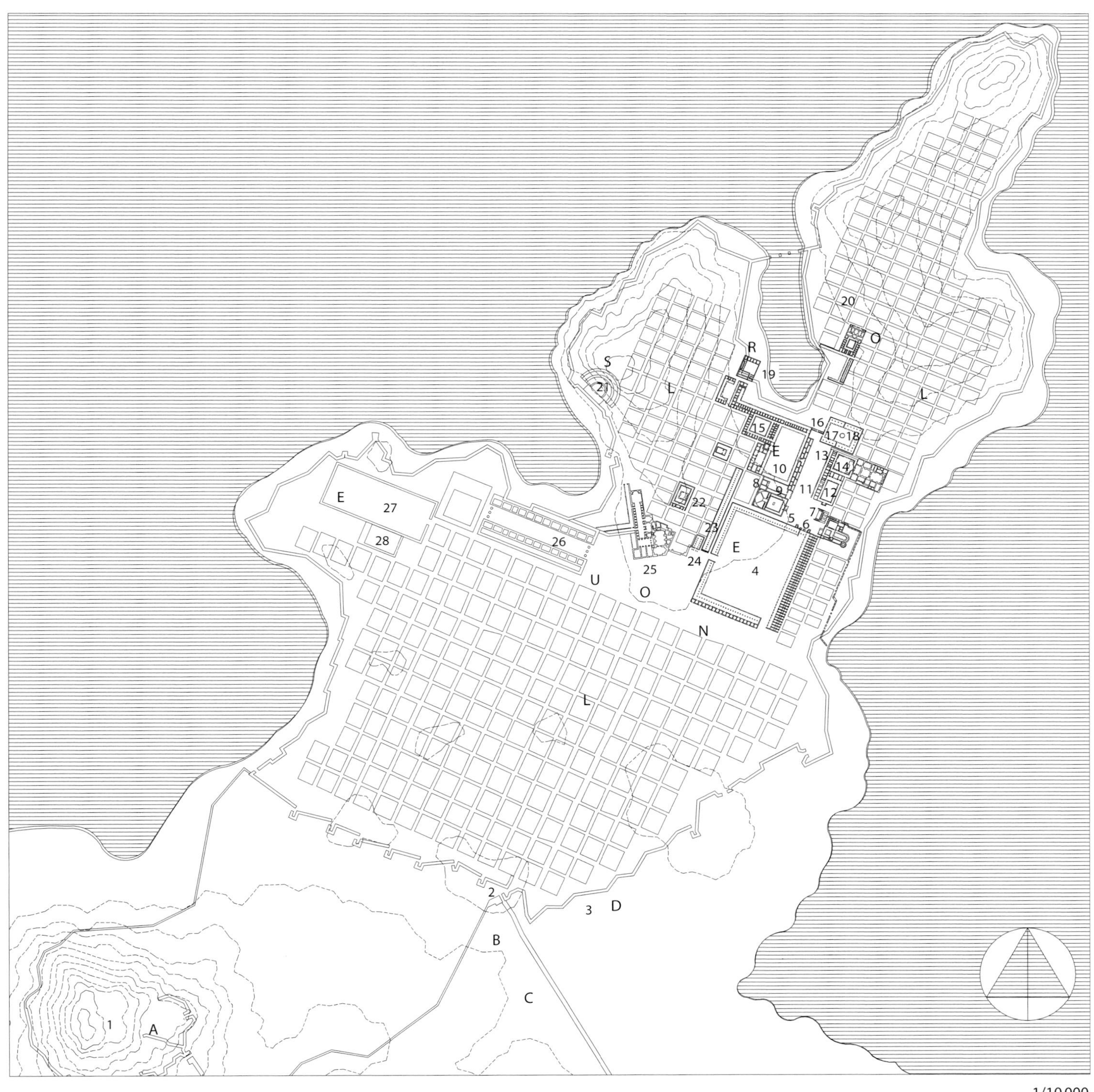

S
21
L
R
19
20
O
L
16
17
18
15
E
10
13
14
8
9
11
12
E
27
28
26
22
23
7
5
6
E
4
25
24
U
O
N
L
2
3
D
B
C
1
A

1/10 000

95 CHURCHES OF THE EARLY CHRISTIAN ERA AND LATE ANTIQUITY

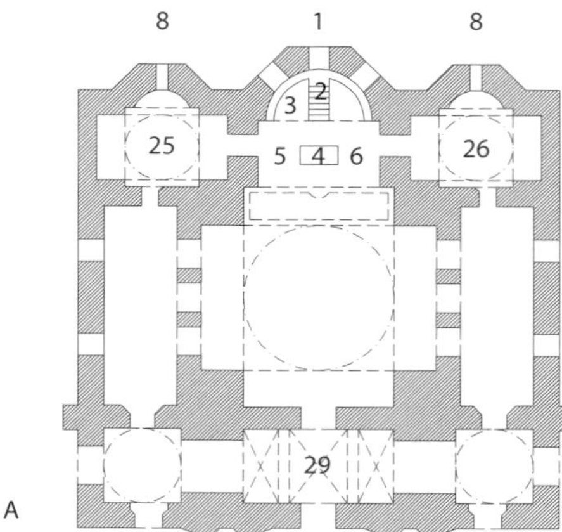

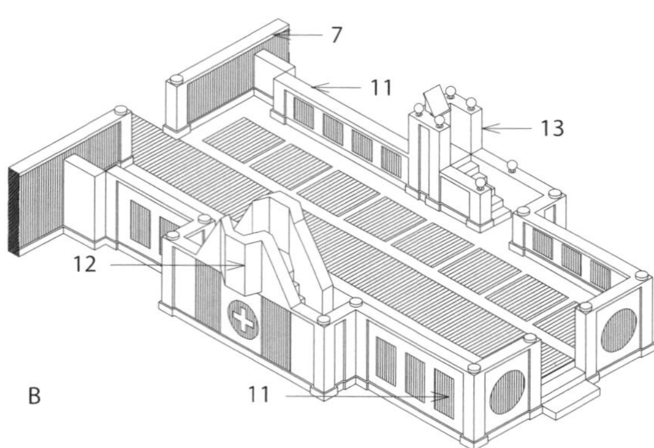

A cross-domed church, quincunx church, five-domed church
B cancelli and ambones
C orant (orans) figure
D ampulla, pilgrim's oil flask
E title church, titular church
F domical church of Late Antiquity

SANCTUARY, BEMA
1 apse
2 cathedra, bishop's throne
3 synthronos, synthronon
4 high altar
5 bema, altar platform

E EARLY CHRISTIAN BASILICA
6 solea
7 choir screen, rood screen, arcus toralis
8 apsidiole
9 by-altar, side altar
10 choir, schola cantorum
11 cancelli
12 gospel ambo
13 epistle ambo
14 nave
15 northern aisle, gospel side, women's side
16 southern aisle, epistle side, men's side
17 side chapel
18 sacristy, vestry, revestry, vestiary
19 stairs to undercroft
20 exonarthex
21 belltower
22 cloister
23 atrium, atrium paradisus, paradise
24 prothyron

F BYZANTINE CENTRALIZED CHURCH
25 prothesis, pastophorium
26 diaconicon, pastophorium
27 ambulatory (ground floor)
28 gallery (upper level)
29 narthex
30 galilee
31 parvis, gate of paradise

Early Christian architecture
church architecture from the first few centuries of Christianity in Europe during the late Roman period from 200 to 600 AD

Late Antiquity
the final period of Greek and Roman art and architecture from 250–600 AD, especially used in reference to the art of the Roman empire

basilica
a building type consisting of a clerestoried nave, side aisles and terminated with a rounded apse containing an altar; adopted by the Early Christian church from Greek and Roman precedents

cross-domed church, quincunx church, five-domed church
a common Byzantine church type with five domes arranged over the extremities and centre of its cross-shaped plan

A) Koimesis church, Nicaea (now Iznik, Turkey) 8th century; B, E) San Clemente, Rome; 4th century AD, additions from 1100s; C, D) Pilgrim's ampulla depicting St Menas, Louvre, Paris; c. 6th century AD; F) San Vitale, Ravenna, 526–547

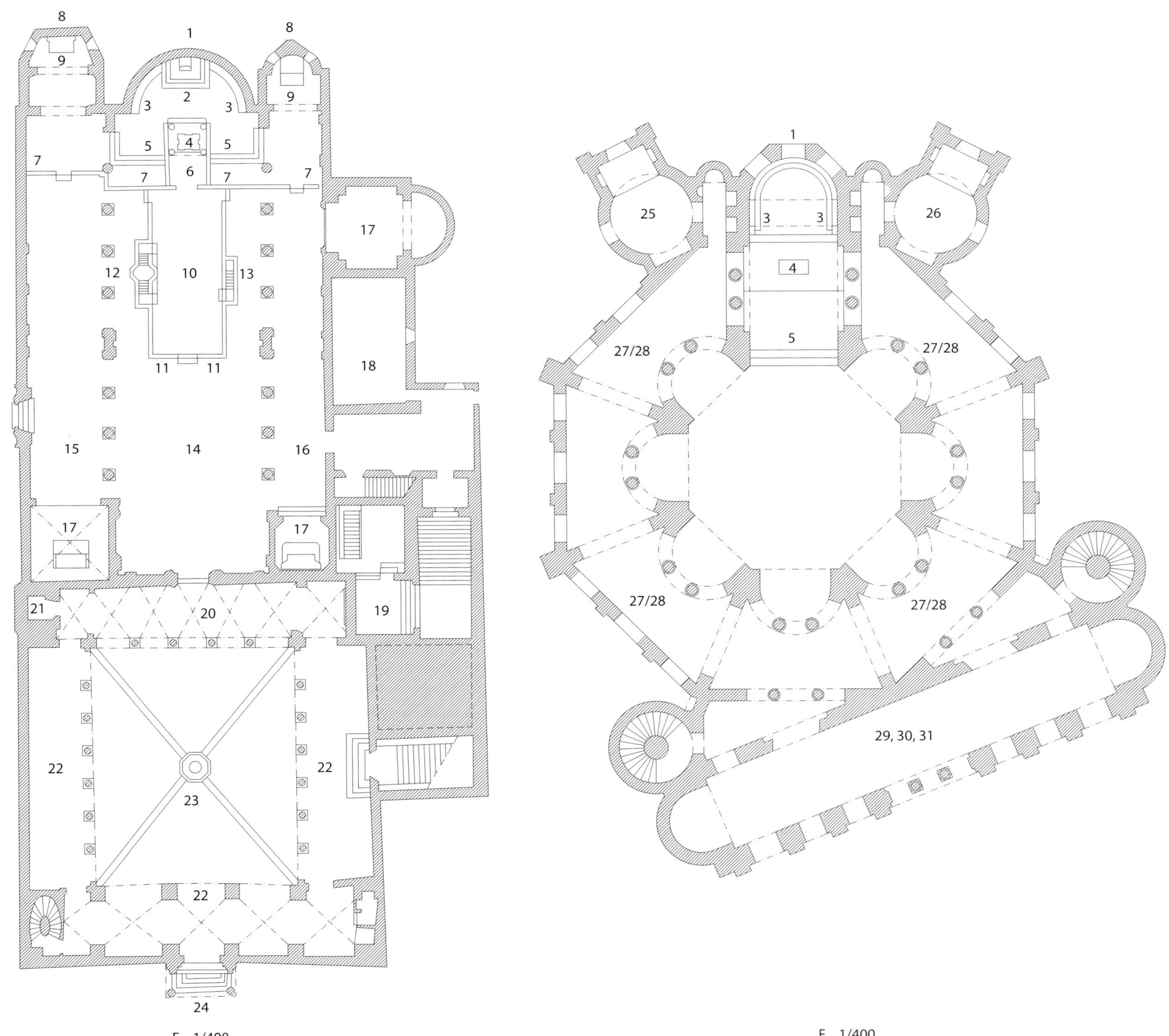
8
1
8
9
2
9
3
3
5
4
5
7
7
6
7
7
17
12
10
13
11
11
18
15
14
16
17
17
21
20
19
22
22
23
22
24
1
25
3
3
26
4
27/28
5
27/28
27/28
27/28
29, 30, 31

E 1/400

F 1/400

96 BYZANTINE DOMICAL CHURCH

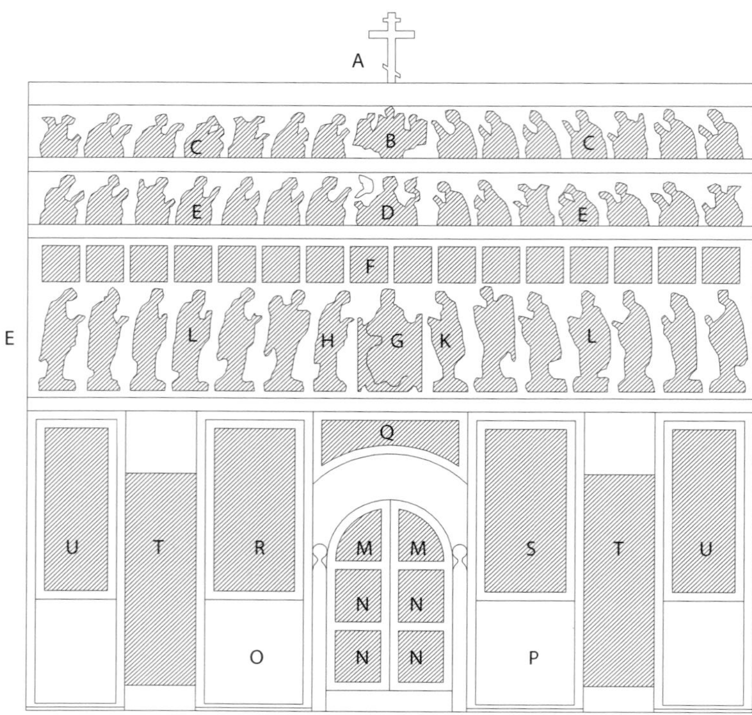

ALTAR SCREEN/REREDOS/TEMPLON

1 parvis, gate of paradise: colonnaded court
2 arcade, cloister
3 atrium paradisus: forecourt
4 cantharus, piscina: fountain, font
5 exonarthex: outer vestibule
6 esonarthex: inner vestibule
7 Imperial gate
8 tribelon: triple arch
9 trivela: curtain
10 navis media: nave
11 bema: altar platform
12 high altar
13 apse
14 side altar, by-altar
15 parecclesion: side chapel
16 pastophorium: clerical chamber
17 prothesis: table/niche
18 diaconicon: garments and vessels
19 aisle
20 Imperial chapel, capella imperialis, solarium
21 campanile: belltower
22 baptistery

FULL ICONOSTASIS

A holy cross
B icon of the Trinity or the Crucifixion
C forefathers, patriarchs
D icon of the Mary of the Sign
E prophets
F feasts of the ecclesiastical year
G Christ on throne
H the Virgin Mary
K John the Baptist
L group of intercessory prayers; angels, apostles, holy father liturgists, primary martyrs, and occasionally local saints or founders of monasteries

HOLY DOOR (main door)

M Annunciation
N evangelists
O St John Chrysostom and father liturgists
P St Basil and father liturgists

TRANSENNAE (perforated screens)

Q institution of Eucharist
R church icon or icon of the Christ, or iconostasis icon of the patron or festival to whom the church is dedicated
S Icon of Mary with Child
T side doors with images of archangels or deacons
U other icons

Byzantine architecture
architecture of Byzantium or the Eastern Roman Empire originating in c.400 AD, characterized by the round arch, the circle in plan, the dome and work in mosaic; sometimes referred to as Italian Romanesque

domical church
a centralized church-type capped by a dome, typical in Byzantine architecture

iconostasis
in Byzantine and Russian and Greek orthodox church architecture, an ornate painted screen containing icons, dividing the altar from the nave; a wall of icons

reredos, altar screen
a decorated screen hung behind the altar in a church

Facing page: Hagia Sophia (prior to addition of minarets), Constantinople (now Istanbul), Turkey, 532–537 AD, architect Anthemios of Tralles & Isidorus of Miletus

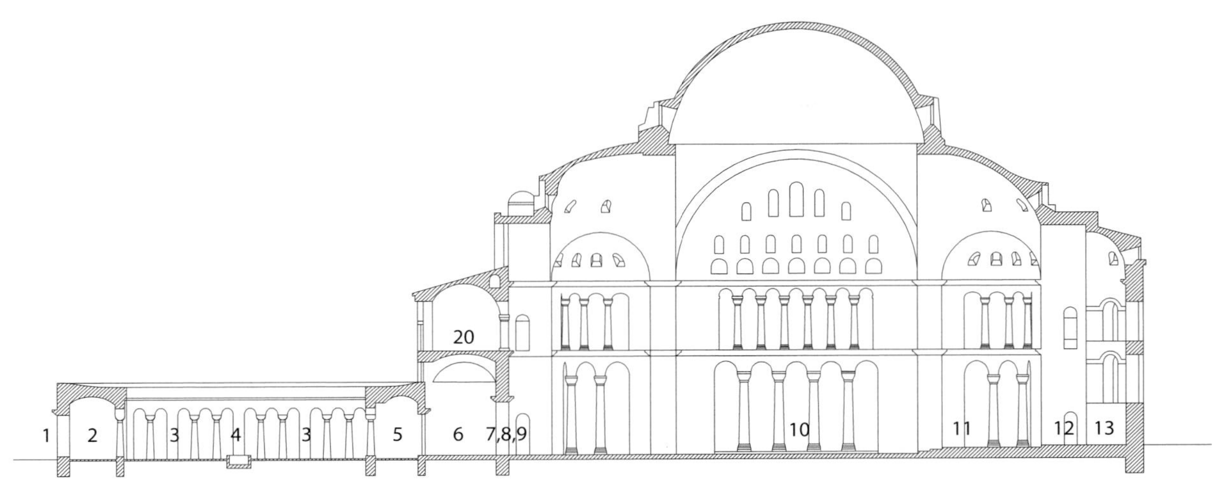

1
2
3
4
3
5
6
7,8,9
10
11
12
13
20

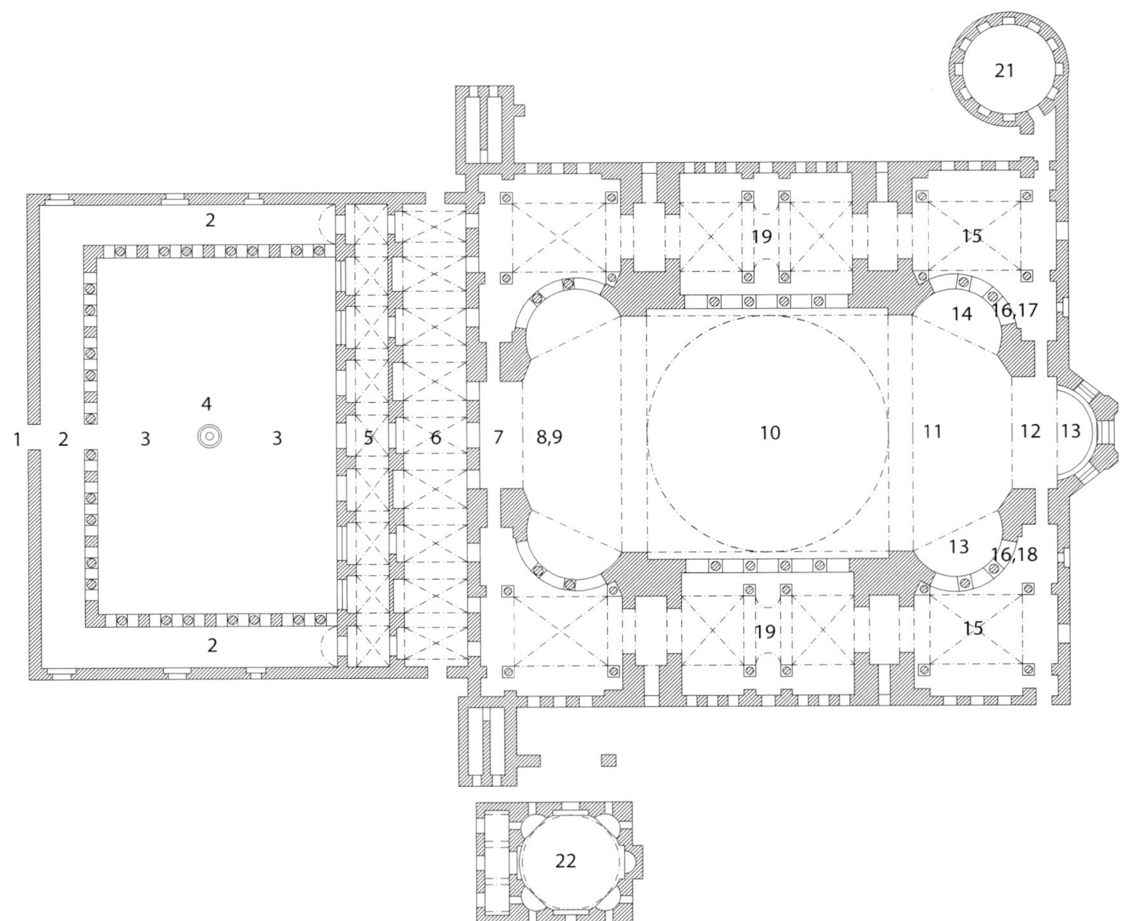

21
2
19
15
14
16,17
4
1
2
3
3
5
6
7
8,9
10
11
12
13
13
16,18
2
19
15
22

1/950

97 IDEAL PLAN FOR A CAROLINGIAN MONASTERY

INSULAR WORK
llumination from the Lindisfarne Gospels (St Matthew's gospel); c.700 AD

SPACES: 1) main entrance; 2) western paradise; 3) western altar, altar of St Peter; 4) western chancel, retro-choir; 5) baptismal font, piscina; 6) altar of St John; 7) rood altar, altar of the Holy Cross; 8) eastern chancel; 9) high altar, altar of the Virgin Mary and St Gall; 10) eastern paradise; 11a) sacristy [ground floor]; 11b) vestry [first floor]; 12) armarium; 13) side chapel; 14a) scriptorium [ground floor];14b) library [first floor]; 16) lodgings for visiting monks; 17) lodging of day school masters; 18) lodging of guest masters; 19) entrance to lodgings; 20) northern tower, St Michael's tower; 21) southern tower, St Gabriel's tower; 22) entrance to monastery; 23) hospice master; 24) pilgrims' hospice and almshouse; 25) hospital and kitchen; 26) reception room for monastery guests; 27) monastery with cloister; 28a) boiler room [ground floor]; 28b) dormitory [first floor]; 29a) refectory [ground floor]; 29b) vestiarium, wardrobe [first floor]; 30a) storage of wine and ale [ground floor]; 30b) pantry [first floor]; 31) kitchen; 32) lavatorium, lavabo; 33) latrine; 34) novitiate with cloister; 35) novitiate church; 36) patients' chapel, hospital chapel; 37) hospital with cloister; 38) garden for medical herbs; 39) medical quarters and chemist; 40) house for blood-letting; 41) abbot's kitchen, pantry and bath; 42) abbot's house; 43) day school; 44) house for visitors; 45) kitchen, bakery and brewery for visitors; 46) emperor's residence or coach house; 47) servants' lodging; 48) sheep pen and shepherd's lodging; 49) pigsty; 50) goat pen; 51) stable for mares in foal and unbroken colts; 52) stable for cows; 53) stable for horses and cattle; 54) coopery, joinery and malt granary; 55) lime kiln; 56) monks' bakery and brewery; 57) mortars; 58) mills; 59) workrooms for craftsmen; 60) stores; 61) barn; 62) poultry yard; 63) poultryman's lodging; 64) geese; 65) gardener's house; 66) monk's garden; 67) cementary and orchard

monastery
a religious community of monks with a church, accommodation, agricultural land and other buildings

monastic church
the main church of a monastery; an abbey or priory

minster
a church which was once governed by a monastery

double chancel church
a Carolingian and Romanesque church type which has a chancel at both east and west ends; also called a double-ended church

Insular art
the art and culture of the Celtic peoples of Ireland and Britain from 400–900 AD, especially illumination of scripts, lettering and calligraphy; characterized by the use of complex intertwined ornament and figures

ABBEY

- A monastic church, minster
- B double-chancel church
- C additive order
- D chancel, east chancel
- E west chancel
- F scriptorium
- G cloister, garth
- H almonry
- K refectory, frater, dining hall
- L dormitory, dorter (upstairs)
- M calefactory, heated room (downstairs)
- N reredorter, latrine
- P infirmarium and medicinal herb garden
- R slype, passageway
- S abbot's quarters
- T guests' quarters
- U livestock
- V workshops and stores
- W orchard and cemetery, vegetable plots, fowl

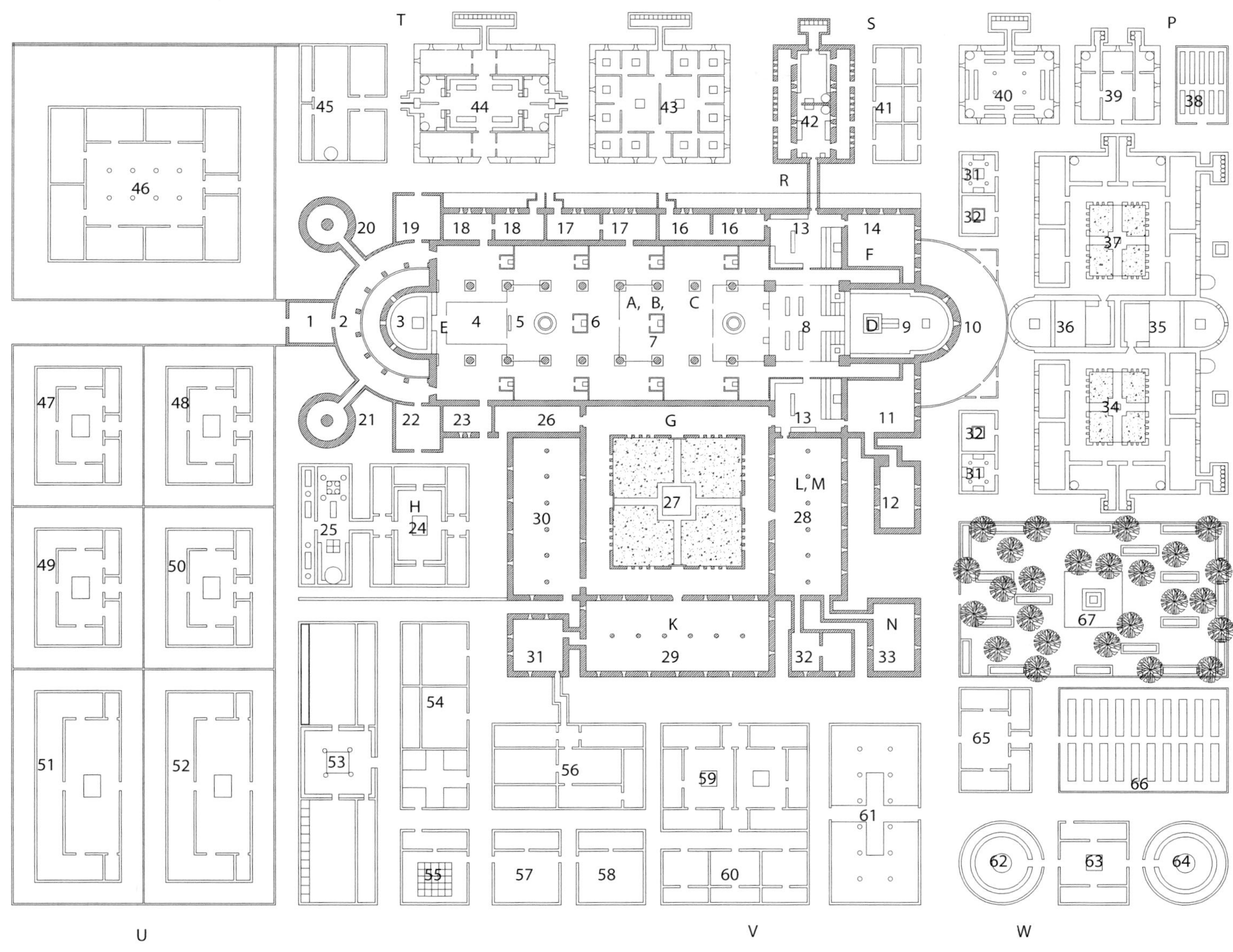

Plan of St Gall, monastery design from c.820 (based on the oldest surviving post-Roman architectural drawing), St Gall, Switzerland

98 CAROLINGIAN ABBEY CHURCH

NAVE-AND-CHANCEL CHURCH

- A westwork (as rebuilt 1596)
- B plan, ground floor
- C plan, first floor
- D plan, second floor
- E plan, third floor
- F transverse section to west
- G elevation, westwork (original)

CRUCIFORM CHURCH

1 apse
2 choir bay
3 presbytery
4 apsidiole
5 by-altar, side altar
6 crossing (crypt of Virgin Mary)
7 transept
8 monk choir
9 altar screen
10 altar of the Holy Cross
11 nave
12 aisle
13 narthex
14 westwork, crypt
15 porch
16 stair tower
17 atrium, atrium paradisus, paradise
18 cloister
19 gate of paradise
20 baptistery (chapel of John the Baptist)
21 singers' gallery, minstrel gallery
22 solarium
23 imperial choir, capella imperialis
24 empore, gallery

Carolingian
pertaining to the pre- and early Romanesque art and Byzantine-influenced architecture in France during the dynasty of the Frankish kings (768–843) founded by Charlemagne

abbey
a community of monks overseen by an abbot, or of nuns by an abbess; also the main buildings of this community

nave-and-chancel church
a church type emerging in the 800s, in which the nave extends up to the altar, beyond the transepts

A, 1/300

Benedictine Abbey of Corvey on the Weser (New Corbie), Westphalia, Germany; 822–885 (westwork after 1596)

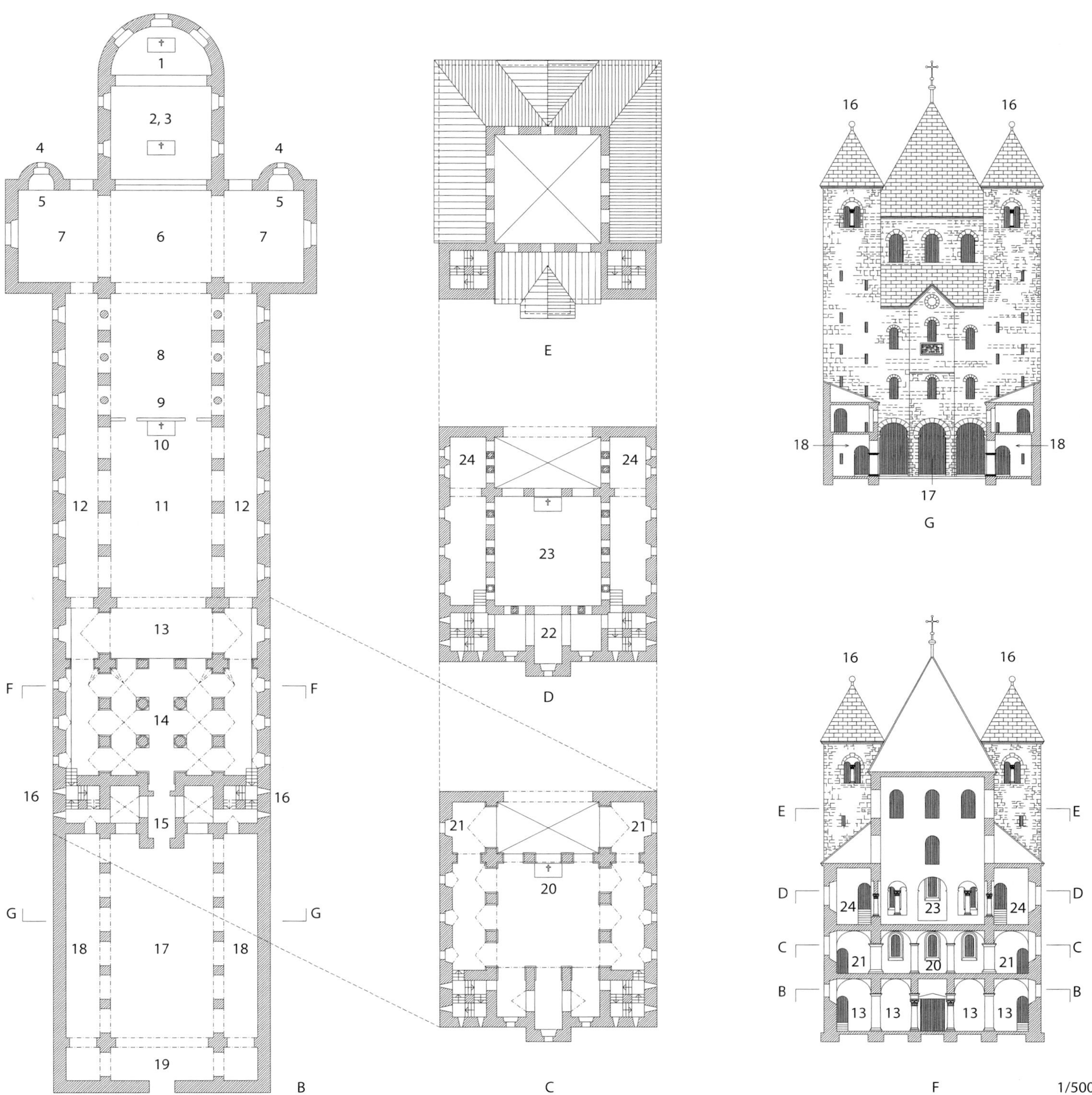

1
2, 3
4
4
5
5
7
6
7
8
9
10
12
11
12
13
F
F
14
16
16
15
G
G
18
17
18
19
B
E
24
24
23
22
D
21
21
20
C
16
16
18
18
17
G
16
16
E
E
D
D
24
23
24
C
C
21
20
21
B
B
13
13
13
13
F
1/500

99 MEDIEVAL CHURCH ARCHITECTURE

A

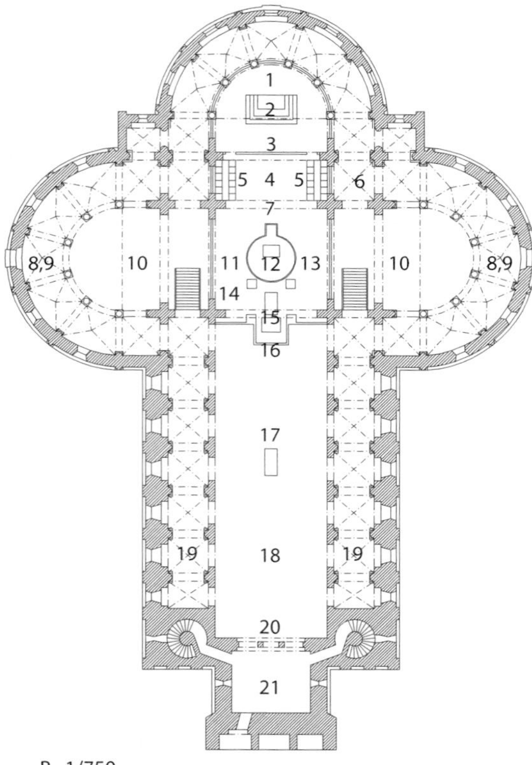

B 1/750

A Gothic gallery of kings
B Romanesque trefoil plan church, triconch church
C, D Romanesque abbey: westwork
E–G Salian cathedral, basilica

1 apse
2 cathedra
3 tribunal arch
4 presbytery
5 choir stalls
6 dossal, dorsal, dosser
7 triumphal arch, rood arch, trabs, arcus presbyterii
8 chancel aisle, choir aisle
9 ambulatory, deambulatory
10 sanctuary
11 crossing
12 high altar
13 chancel
14 north side-chapel, transept
15 chancel arch, arcus ecclesiae
16 choir screen, rood screen, arcus toralis
17 altar of the Holy Cross
18 nave, body of church
19 aisle
20 tribelon
21 antechurch, forechurch
22 westwork
23 porch, galilee, narthex
24 great paradise
25 parvis, parvise
26 pulpit
27 side chapel, chapel of St Afra
28 chantry
29 double chapel (a: baptistery)
31 sacristy
32 hall crypt, undercroft, crypt, croft, shroud
33 transept
34 by-altar, side altar
35 capella imperialis, solarium, King's choir
36 crossing tower, rood tower
37 dwarf gallery
38 colonnette

Medieval architecture
European architecture from the dissipation of the Roman Empire in 500 AD to the advent of the Renaissance in the 1500s, including Early Christian, Byzantine, Romanesque and Gothic architecture

Romanesque
religious architecture in Western Europe in the early 11th century, characterized by bulky massing, sparing use of detail and the round arch; known in England as Norman architecture

triconch church, three-apsed church
a form of long church whose choir terminates in three apses, arranged in a trefoil arrangement around the crossing

basilica church
a church-type based on a basilica antecedent, usually with a rectangular plan divided by colonnades into a nave and aisles, with an apse or apses at one end

A) Cathedral, Amiens, 1220–69; B) St Maria im Kapitol, 1150–1220, Cologne; C, D) Marmoutier Abbey, 1150–1160, Alsace; E–G) Speyer Cathedral, 1032–1090

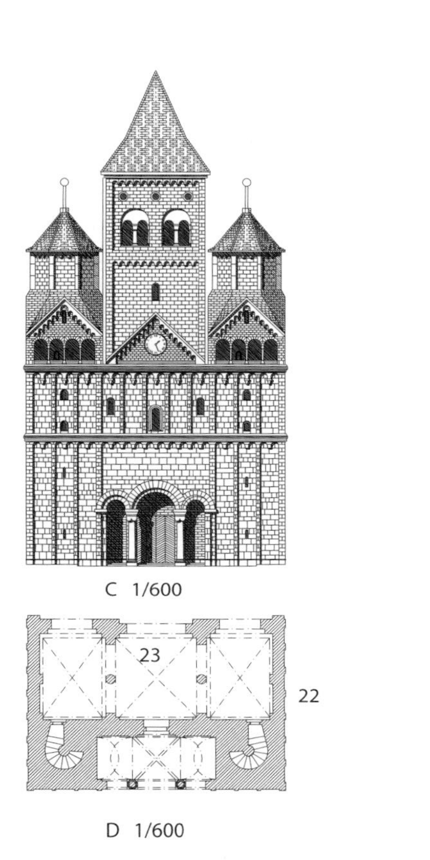

C 1/600

D 1/600

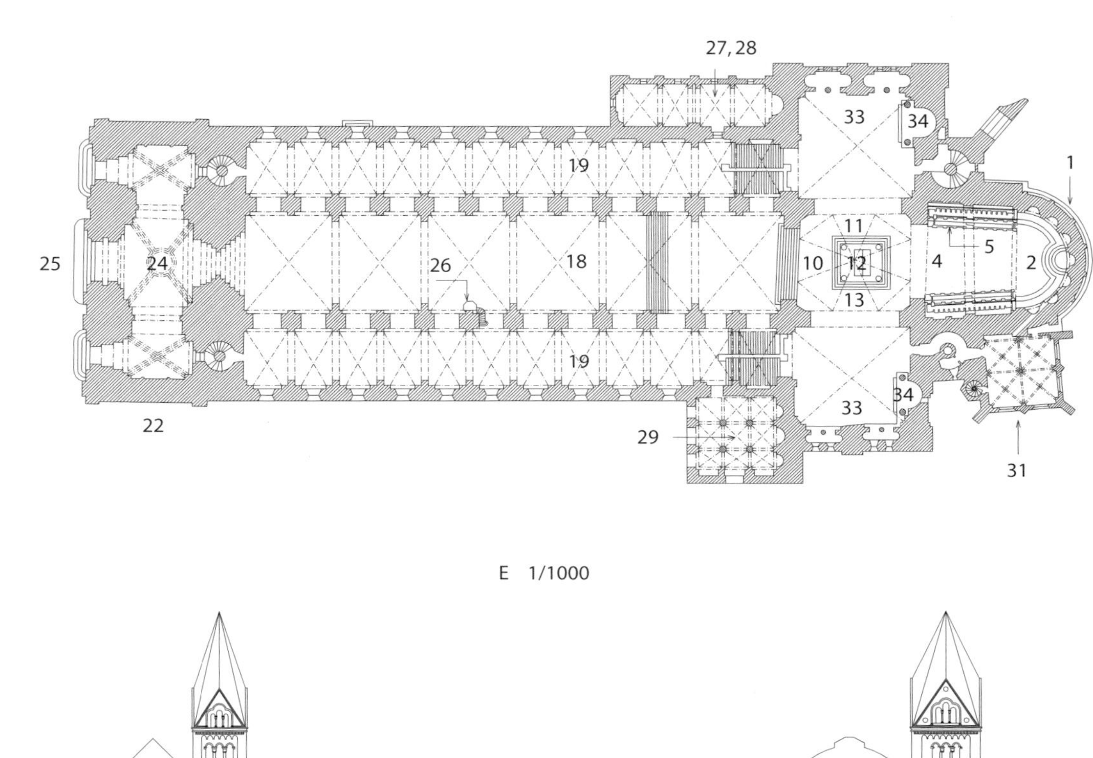

E 1/1000

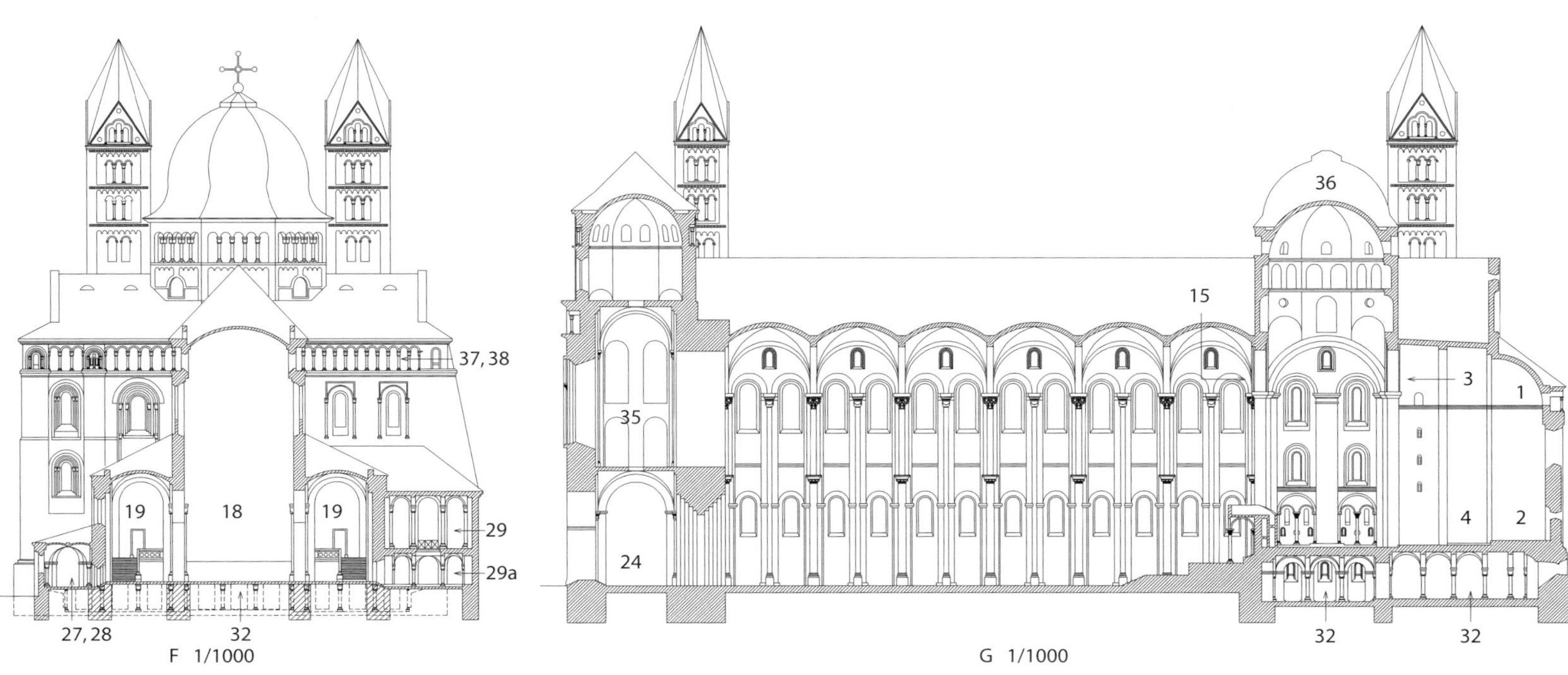

F 1/1000

G 1/1000

100 GOTHIC CATHEDRAL

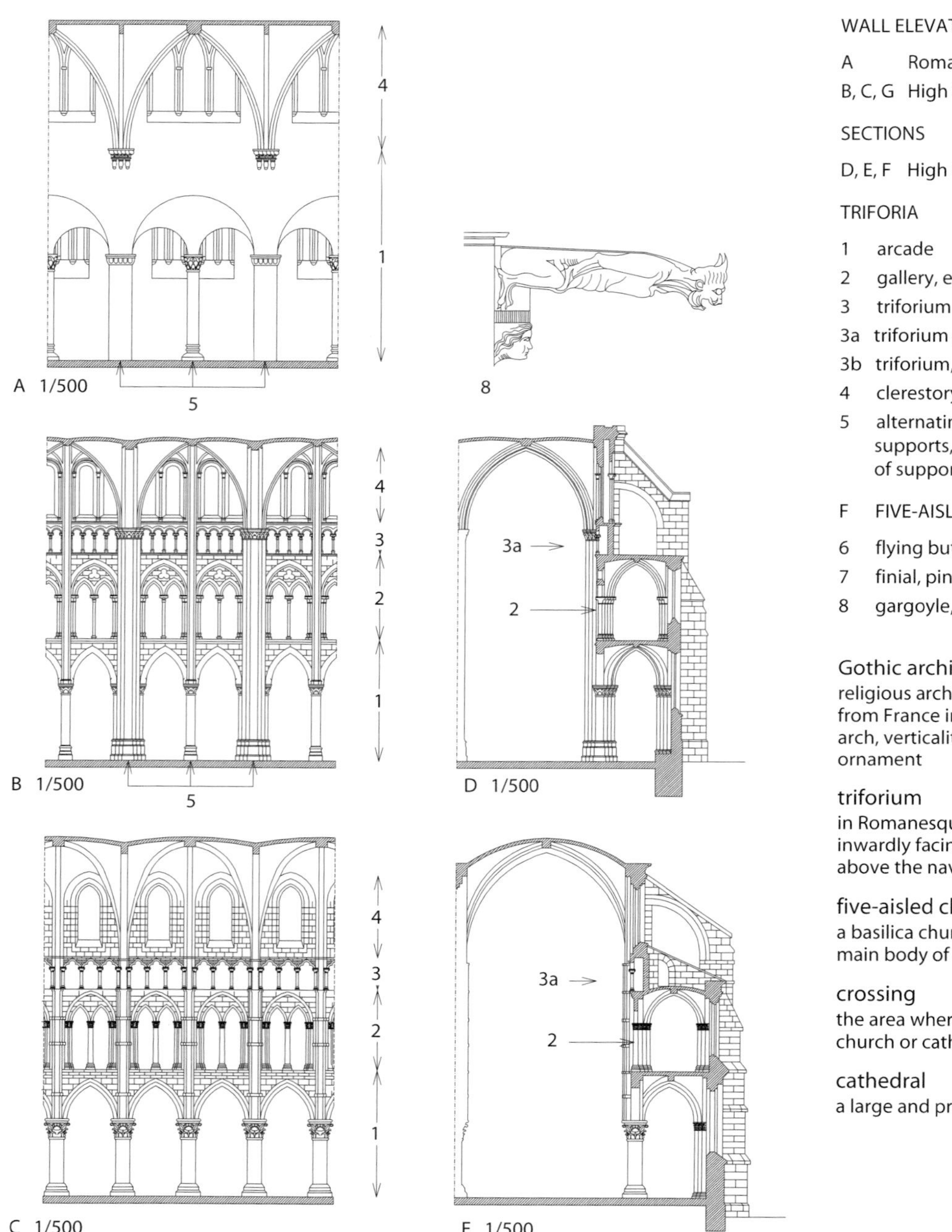

WALL ELEVATIONS

A Romanesque church
B, C, G High Gothic church

SECTIONS

D, E, F High Gothic church

TRIFORIA

1 arcade
2 gallery, empore
3 triforium
3a triforium gallery
3b triforium, blind arcade
4 clerestory, clearstory
5 alternating system of supports, alternation of supports

F FIVE-AISLED CHANCEL

6 flying buttress
7 finial, pinnacle
8 gargoyle, water spout
9 buttress, pier
10 aisle
11 nave

PLAN OF BASILICA

12 west end
13 body
14 transept
15 chancel
16 chevet, radiating chapels
17 arm, projecting transept
18 porch
19 crossing
20 choir screen, rood screen
21 choir stalls
22 chapel, radiating chapel
23 high altar
24 chancel aisle, apse aisle, ambulatory, deambulatory
25 parclose, perclose
26 Lady Chapel

Gothic architecture, pointed architecture
religious architecture in Europe in the Middle Ages, originating from France in the 1200s, characterized by use of the pointed arch, verticality of decoration, rib vaults and richly carved ornament

triforium
in Romanesque or Early Gothic religious architecture, an inwardly facing open wall passage, often arcaded, running above the nave arcade below clerestory level in a cathedral

five-aisled church
a basilica church type in which four colonnades divide the main body of the church into four aisles and a central nave

crossing
the area where the transepts, chancel and nave in a church or cathedral intersect, often surmounted by a tower

cathedral
a large and principal church of a diocese, the seat of a bishop

A) St Willibrord, Echternach, 1031, Luxembourg; B, D) Cathedral of Notre Dame in Noyon, France, c.1155–1205; C, E) Cathedral of Notre Dame in Laon, France, c.1157–1205; F–H) Cathedral of Notre Dame, Amiens, France, c.1220–69, Robert of Luzarches, Thomas and Renault of Cormont (prior to addition of chapels in 16th century); 8) Basilica of St Nazarius (St Nazaire), Carcassonne, France, 11th–14th century

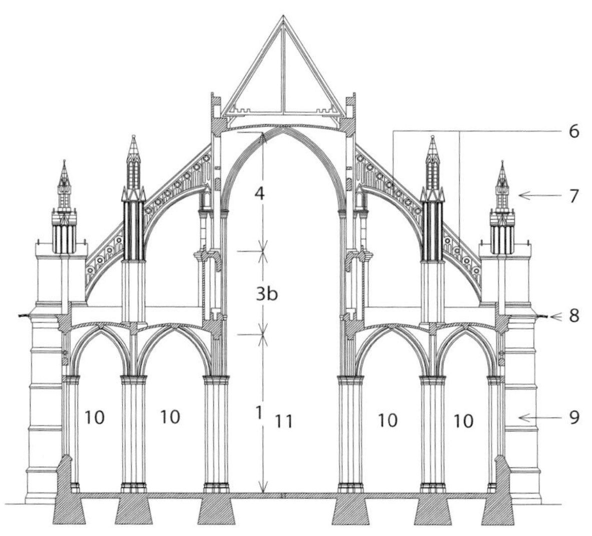

F 1/800

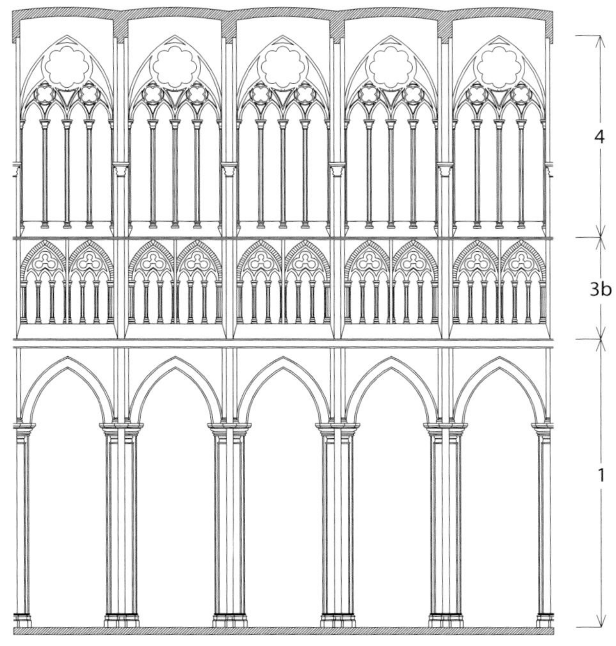

G 1/500

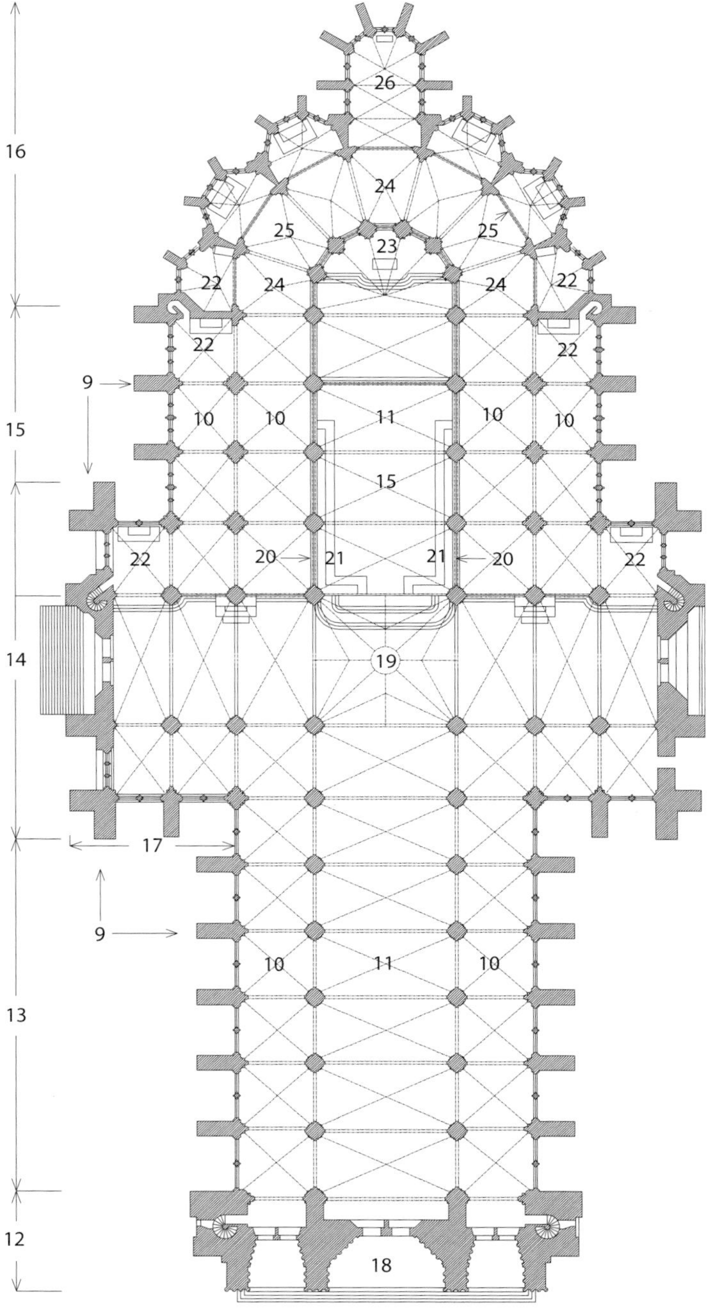

H 1/800

101 GOTHIC AND RENAISSANCE RIBBED VAULTS

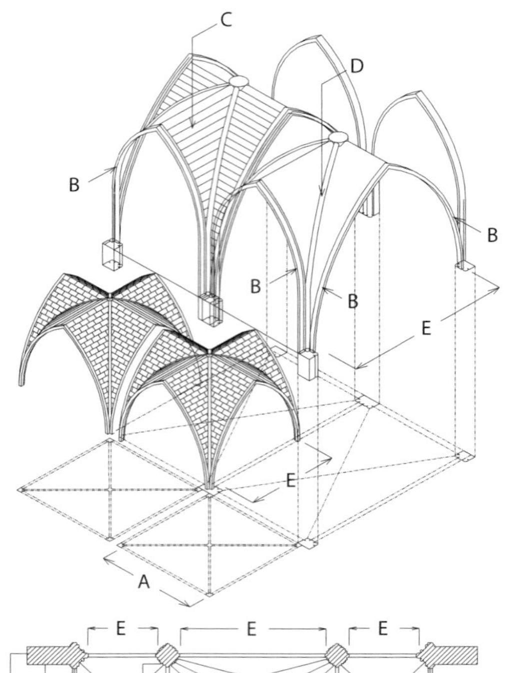

ANATOMY OF A RIBBED VAULT

A bay
B haunch, hanche, rib
C cell, web, severy
D groin
E transverse rib
F wall rib, forcement
G diagonal rib, groin rib, ogive
H tierceron, secondary rib
K lierne, tertiary rib
L transverve ridge-rib
M longitudinal ridge-rib, ridge rib
N boss, pendant
O compound pier

TYPES OF RIBBED VAULT

1, 2, 3	stellar vault, star vault, star-ribbed vault
4, 5	net vault
6	stellar and fan vault
7, 8	fan vault, palm vault
9	stellar and net vault
10	parasol vault
11	stellar and net vault
12	curved net vault, swung ribbed vault, loop vault
13	underpitched vault
14	loop stellar vault
15	branch and leaves work

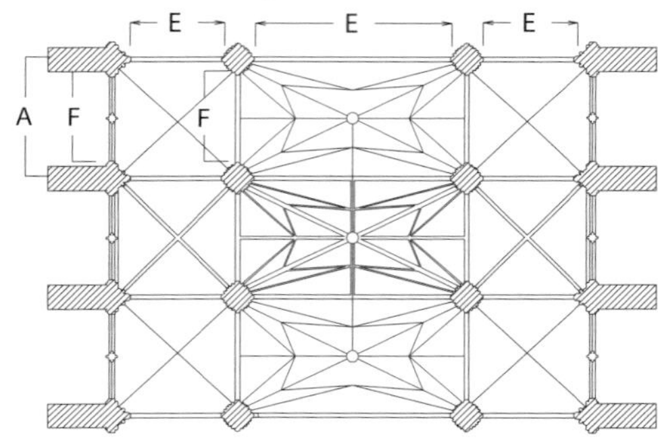

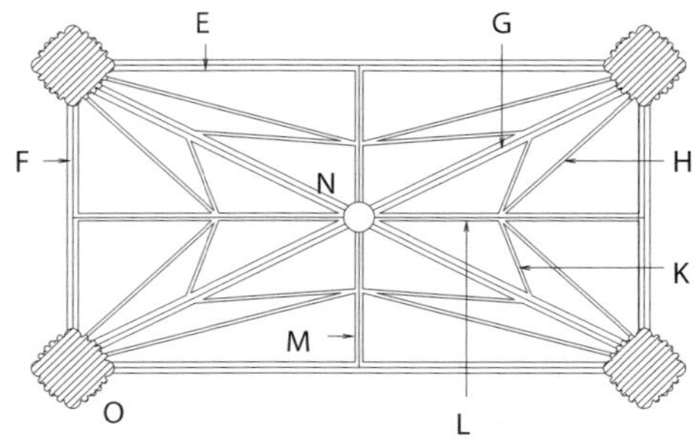

vault
a three-dimensional arched ceiling construction to support a floor or roof, often of masonry

rib vault, ribbed vault
a vault constructed of structural arched stone members or ribs with an infill of masonry; often with tiercerons or secondary ribs, and liernes or tertiary ribs

rib
the main structural member in a rib vault, or a line of stone which marks it

tierceron
a subsidiary rib which connects a point on the ridge rib or central boss with one of the main springers or supports

lierne
a tertiary rib in a vault, which connects a point on a rib with a tierceron or another lierne; often for decorative rather than structural purposes

2) Church of St Mary, Turku, Finland; 14th cent; 3) Trinity church, Regensburg, Germany, 1626, Johann Carl; 5) Minster of Holy Cross, Schwäbisch Gmünd, Germany, 1351, Heinrich Parler; 6) Lincoln cathedral, Lincoln, England, 1192; 8) King's College chapel, Cambridge, England, 1446–1515; 9) Minster of Holy Cross, Schwäbisch Gmünd, Germany, 1351, Heinrich Parler; 11) St Lorenz, Nuremberg, Germany, 1439–77; 12) Stadtptarrkirche, Freistadt, Austria, 1501–1508; 14) Vladislav hall, Prague castle, Czech Republic, 1493–1502, Benedikt Ried; 15) Czech chancellery, Prague castle, Czech Republic, 1505, Benedikt Ried

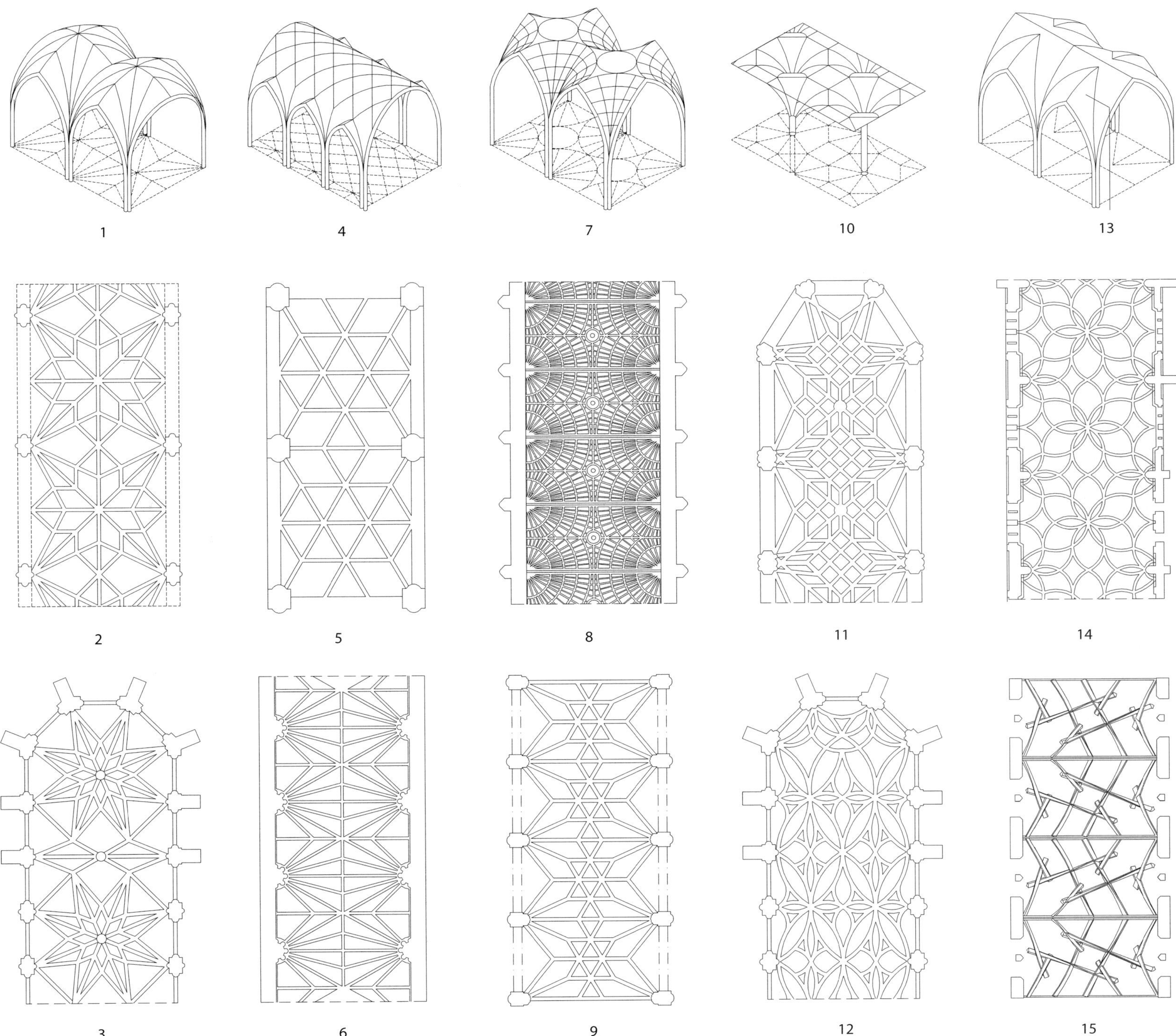
1
4
7
10
13
2
5
8
11
14
3
6
9
12
15

102 PARISH CHURCH

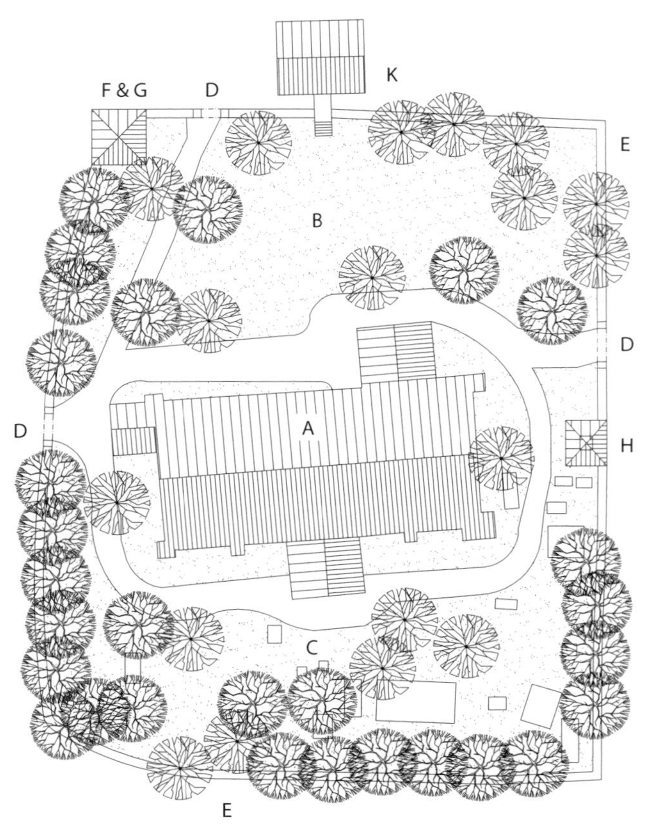

TYPES OF CHURCH
1 longitudinal church, axial church: end elevation
2 hall church: transverse section
3 three-aisled church: plan
4 log church, wooden church
5 block-pillar church
6 single nave church, aisleless church
7 pseudo-cruciform church
L funerary chapel

PARTS OF A CHURCH
8 sacristy, vestiary
9 north aisle
10 nave
11 south aisle
12 south porch, 'arms porch'
13 choir
14 sanctuary
15 belfry, belltower
16 buttress, pier, counterfort
17 louvre-window
18 block pillar
19 porch
20 organ loft
21 church tower, steeple
22 box pew
23 pew
24 pulpit
25 tester, sounding board
26 included transept
27 altar rail, communion rail
28 altar platform, suppedaneum
29 altar
30 spire
31 weathercock
32 weather-vane, vane
33 courtyard
34 pool
35 urn room
36 vestibule, foyer

SITE PLAN 1:800
A longitudinally planned church, axial church
B churchyard
C graveyard
D archway, postern
E perimeter wall, boundary wall
F mortuary
G lych gate, lich gate
H funerary chapel, burial chapel, cemetary chapel
K stable

church
a building or consecrated space for the practice of Christian worship

longitudinal church, nave-and-chancel church, axial church
a rectangular church-type in which the main spaces are laid out in a linear fashion along a central nave, rather than centralized

nave
the main longitudinal space of a church, cathedral, basilica etc.; the body of a church between the west end and crossing

chancel
the area to the east end of the crossing of a church, containing an altar, and often a choir and an apse

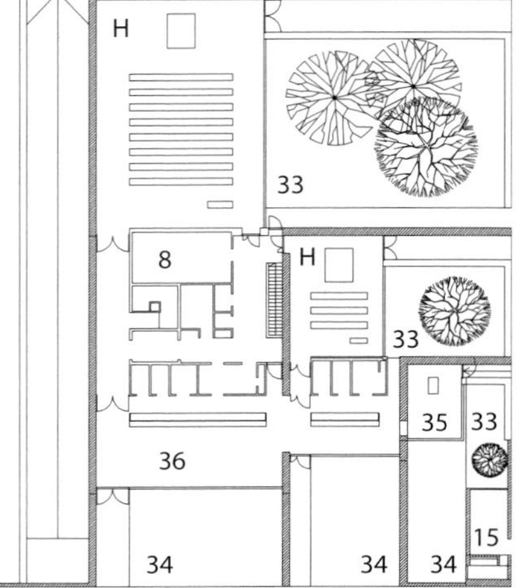

L) PLAN 1:700

1–3, A) Church of St Mary, Turku, Finland, 1300s; 4–5) Tornio church, Tornio, Finland, 1686, Matti Joosefinpoika Härmä; L) Funerary chapel of St Lawrence's Church, Vantaa, Finland, 2003– , Avanto Architects

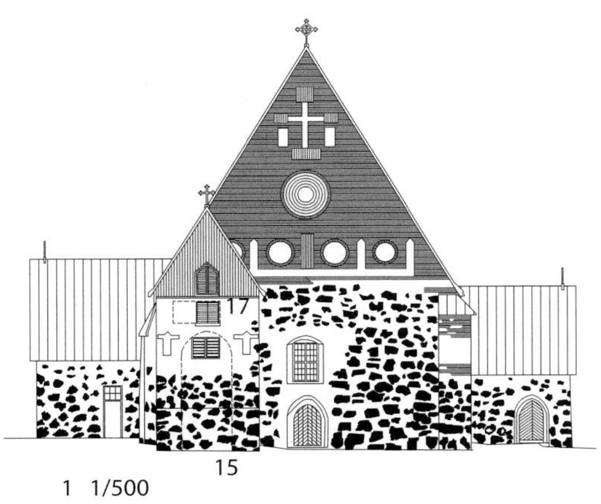

1 1/500

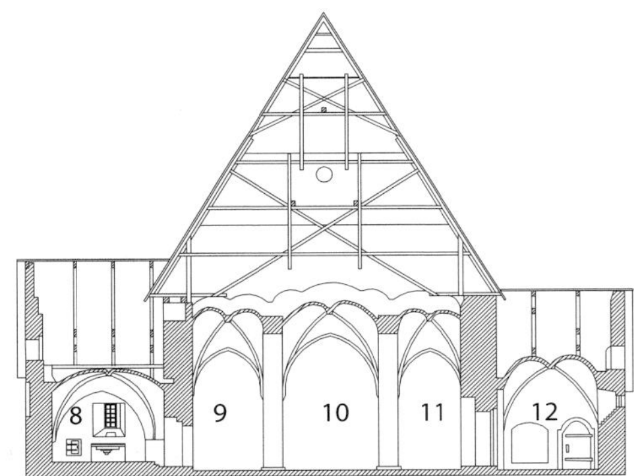

2 1/500

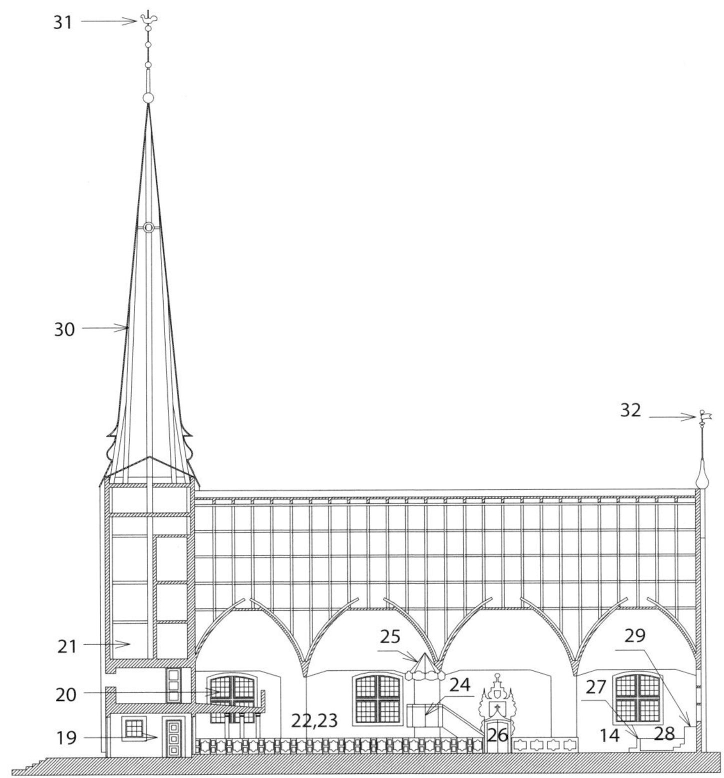

4, 5, 6, 7 1/400

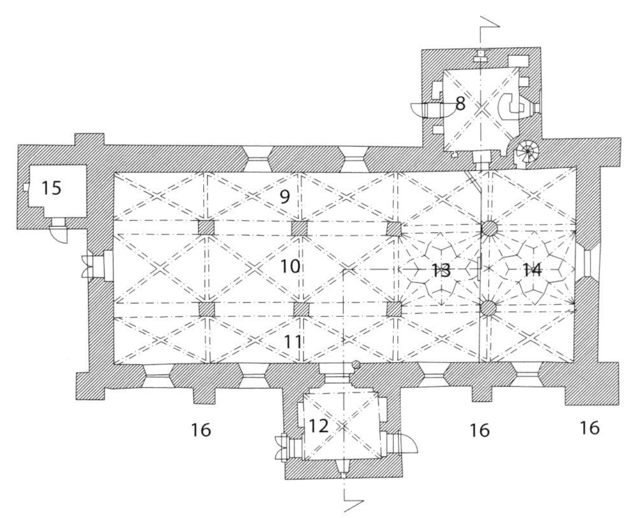

3 1/500

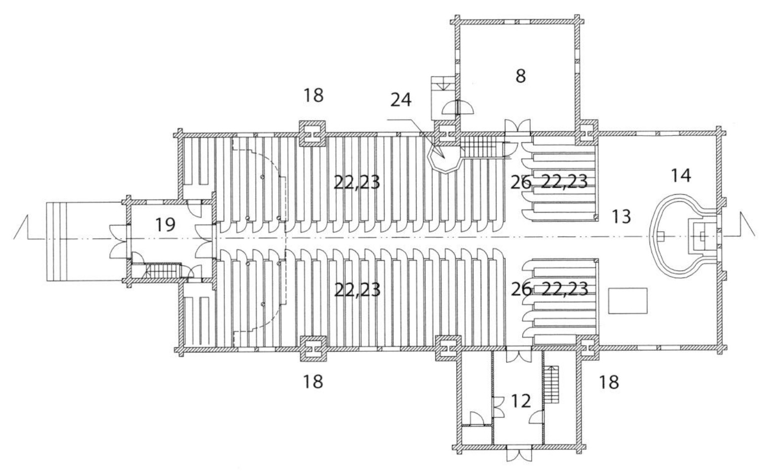

4, 5, 6, 7 1/400

103 MEDIEVAL CASTLE

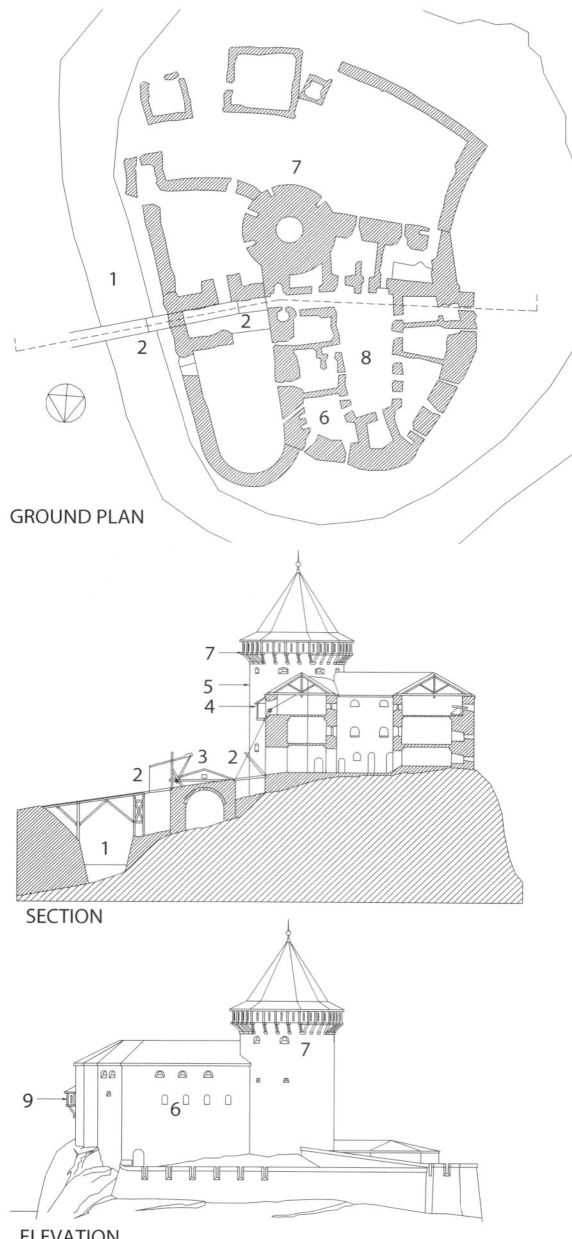

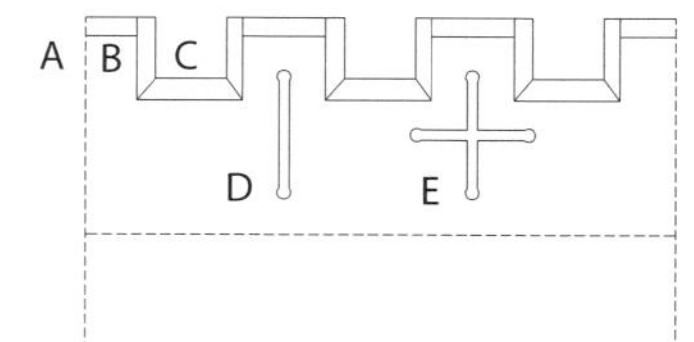

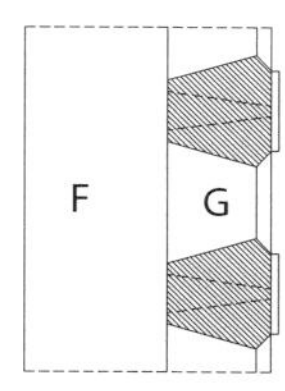

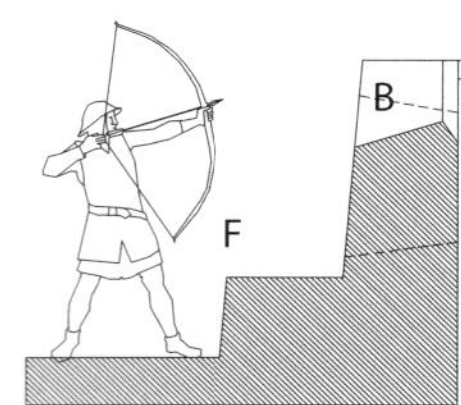

BATTLEMENT

A crenellation, castellation

B merlon

C crenelle, crenel, kernel

D arrow loop, loophole, oeillet

E balistraria, arbalestina

F banquette

G embrasure, embrazure

CASTELET, CASTLET

1 moat

2 drawbridge

3 gatehouse

4 machicolation, murder hole, meurtriere, drop box, fall trap, spy hole

5 observation tower, lookout tower, watch-tower

6 stronghold, shell keep

7 brattice, hoarding

8 inner courtyard, inner ward

9 garderobe, privy, necessarium, danske

KEEP AND BAILEY CASTLE

11 keep, stronghold, donjon, shell keep

12 bailey, ward

13 bailey (wall), curtain wall, enceinte

14 rampart

15 bastion

16 bulwark

17 alure, wall walk

18 casemate

19 batter, battering, talus

20 watergate

21 round tower, drum tower

22 battery, terreplein, emplacement, platform

23 wall stair

24 dungeon

25 oubliette

26 broken curtain

castle

a fortified military or residential building or group of buildings with defensive exterior walls to provide protection against attack

castelet, castlet

a small castle or fortification

battlement, embattlement

a crenellated parapet and walkway in a castle or fortified wall, used for the purposes of defence

bailey

1 bailey wall; the fortified outer wall of a castle, its first line of defence; often known as a curtain wall
2 ward; the open area of land, yard or court enclosed by a castle or fortification wall, between the keep and curtain wall bail and bayle (trad.) are synonymous with both meanings of bailey

Raseborg castle, Tammisaari, Finland, 1374–1550; reconstruction by architect M Schjerfbäck 1887 (not realized); 2) St Olaf's castle, Savonlinna, Finland 1475–1495 (as was in 1790)

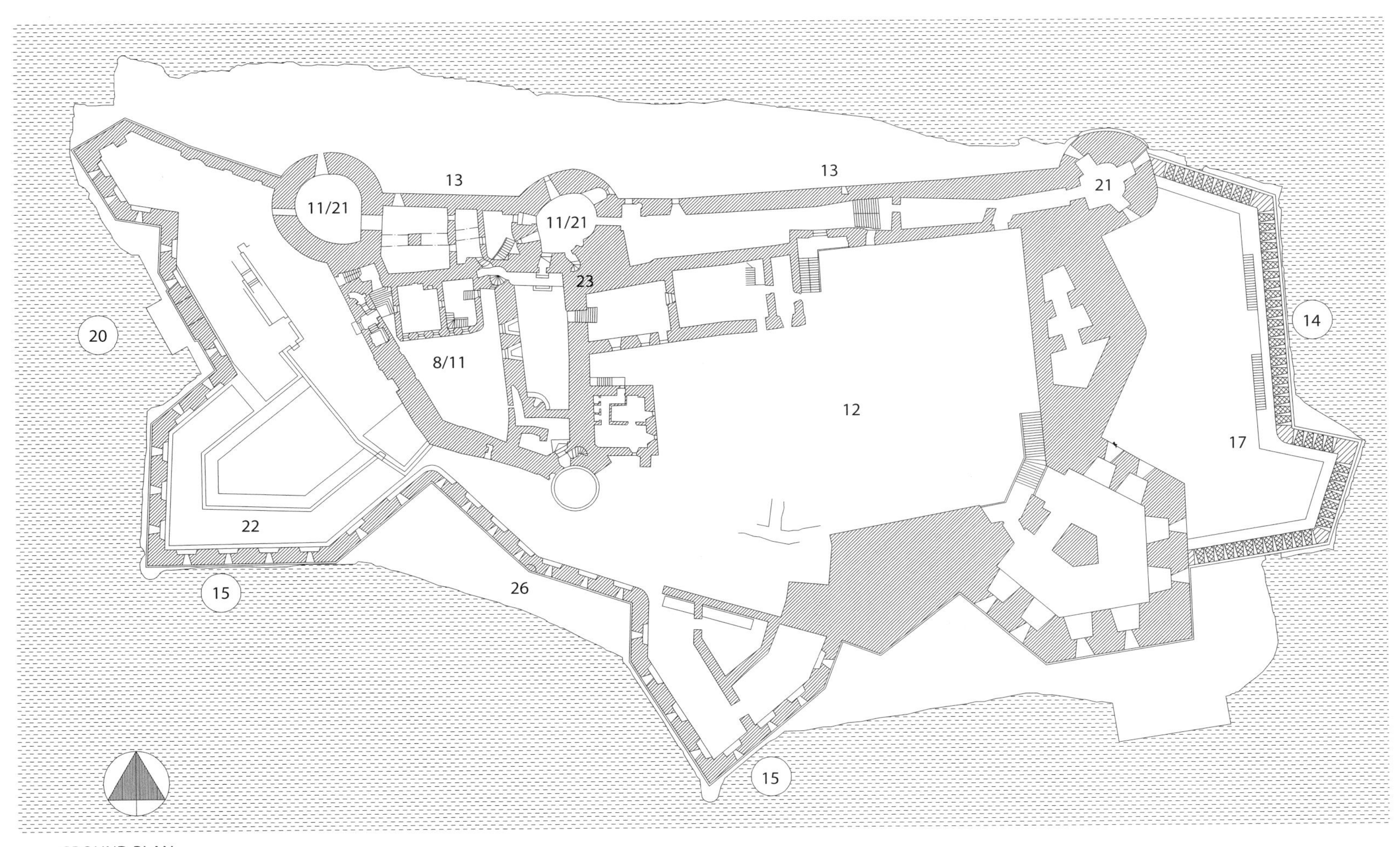

GROUND PLAN

SECTION 1/600

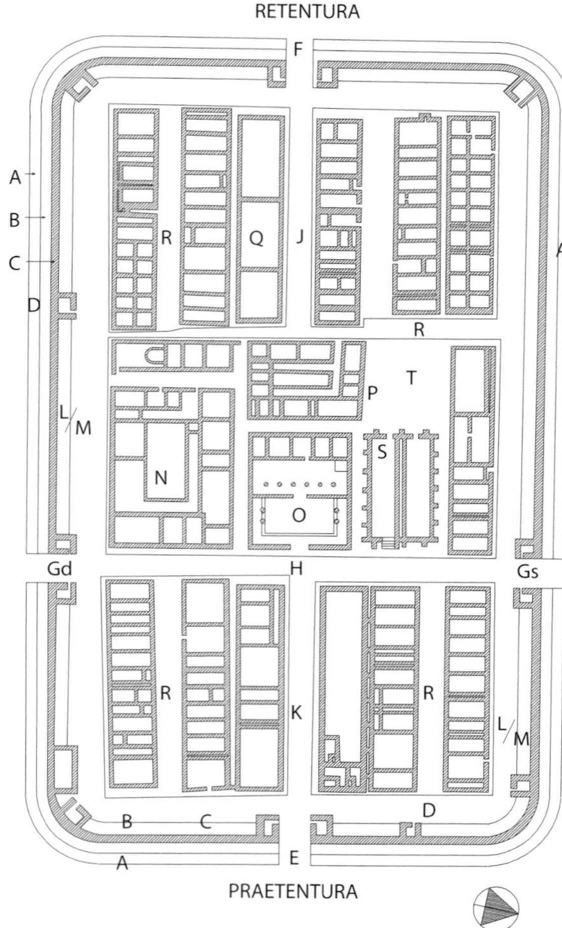

CASTRUM 1/1700
ROMAN MILITARY FORT

A FOSSA
fosse, ditch

B AGGER
earthwork

C VALLUM
rampart

D BURGUS
watchtower

E PORTA PRAETORIA
praetorian gate

F PORTA DECUMANA
rear gate

Gd PORTA PRINCIPALIS DEXTRA
right main gate

Gs PORTA PRINCIPALIS SINISTRA
left main gate

H VIA PRINCIPALIS, CARDO
principal road

J VIA DECUMANUS, DECUMANA
'way of the tenth'

K VIA PRAETORIA
praetorian way

L VIA SAGULARIS
'way of the cloak'– intervallum road

M POMERIUM, POSTMOERIUM
unbuilt land

N PRAETORIUM, PRETORIUM
commander's house

O PRINCIPIA
headquarters

P VALETUDINARUM
hospital

Q QUAESTORIUM
paymaster

R CONTUBERNIA
barracks

S HORREUM
granary

T FORUM
square

BASTIONED TRACE –
POLYGONAL FORTIFICATION

1 bastion
2 cavalier
3 bastion face
4 bastion flank
5 salient angle
6 shoulder angle
7 curtain, curtain wall
8 gorge
9 redoubt
10 half bastion
11 broken curtain
12 traverse
13 ravelin, redan
14 demilune, half moon
15 tambour
16 tenaille
17 counterguard
18 fleche, arrow
19 caponier
20 hornwork
21 crownwork
22 turret
23 main rampart, major work
24 middle bailey
25 advanced works, outwork
26 glacis, declivity
27 esplanade
28 main ditch, dry ditch
29 moat, ditch
30 covered way, covert way
31 abattis
32 caltrop
33 gun platform, battery, artillery terrace
34 banquette
35 parapet
36 scarp, escarp
37 counterscarp
38 batter
39 casemate

Roman military encampment: CASTRUM VERCOVICIUM ('the place of effective fighters'), Legionary fortress, Housesteads, Northumberland, England (on Hadrian's Wall), c.124 AD

105 PATTERNS FOR IDEAL CITIES IN THE 20th CENTURY

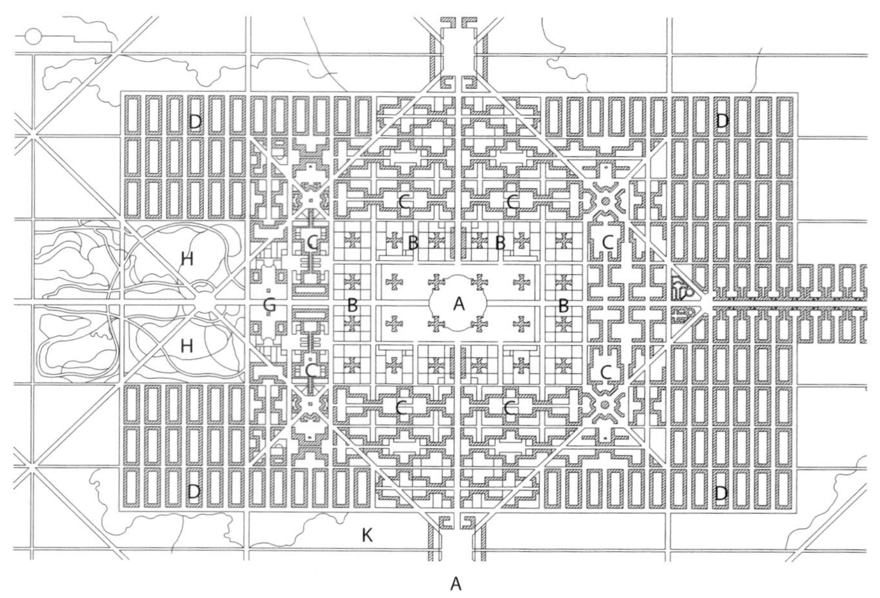

A

VARIETIES OF IDEAL CITY

- A metropolis, grid plan
- B linear city
- C garden city
- D residential suburb
- E woodland town

LAND-USE ZONES

1. central railway station
2. railway
3. motorway
4. residential buildings
5. green spaces, parks
6. agricultural land
7. public services
8. schools and educational buildings
9. sports
10. protected zone
11. industry

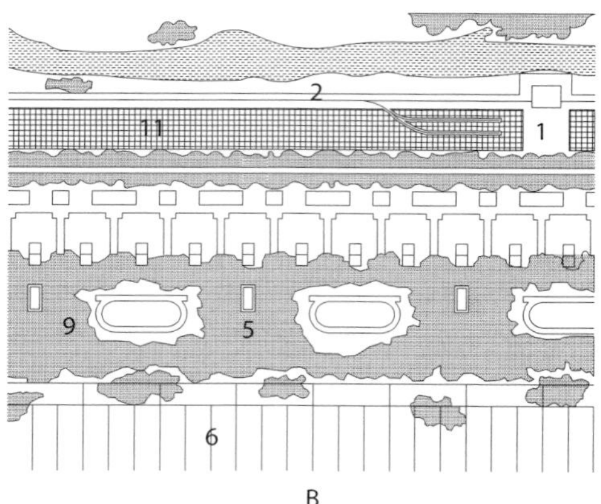

B

ideal city
a working city model based on utopian and ideal socio-political values, taking into account the zoning of industry, traffic, parks, workplaces and residential areas for the benefit of its inhabitants

city planning, town planning, urban planning
the legislative process of land-use planning, layouts etc. for an urban area, designed to regulate development and provide a healthy environment for its inhabitants, taking into account various socio-economic, aesthetic, industrial, and recreational factors

zoning
the division of a larger area of urban land into zones or districts, and the establishment of regulations within each zone to govern the scope of development with regard to land-use, height and volume of buildings etc. to form the basis of a local plan

A: UNE VILLE CONTEMPORAINE; A CONTEMPORARY CITY FOR THREE MILLION INHABITANTS,
Le Corbusier, 1922: A) central station: multi-level transport interchange, B) 60 storey skyscrapers in green belt, C) 12 storey luxury apartment blocks for the elite, D) housing blocks on the cellular system, G) public services, H) park, K) protected zone; B: URBANISTIC SCHEME FOR MAGNITOGORSK, Nikolai A. Miljutin, Sotsgorod, 1930; C: WARD AND CENTRE OF GARDEN CITY, Ebenezer Howard, England, 1902; D: PROJECT FOR A RESIDENTIAL AREA, Hilding Ekelund, Finland, 1932: 1) school, 2) sports pavillion, 3) sports field, 4) swimming pool, 5) diving pool, 6) swimming facility, beach, 7) paddling pool, 8) nursery, day care centre, 9) tennis court, 10) tram station, 11) residential block; E: AN AMERICAN TOWN IN FINLAND, Alvar Aalto 1940: a) residential buildings, b) administrative and commercial centre, c) educational buildings and sports ground, d) single family houses, detached houses, e) split-level dwellings, apartment blocks, f) row houses, stepped apartments

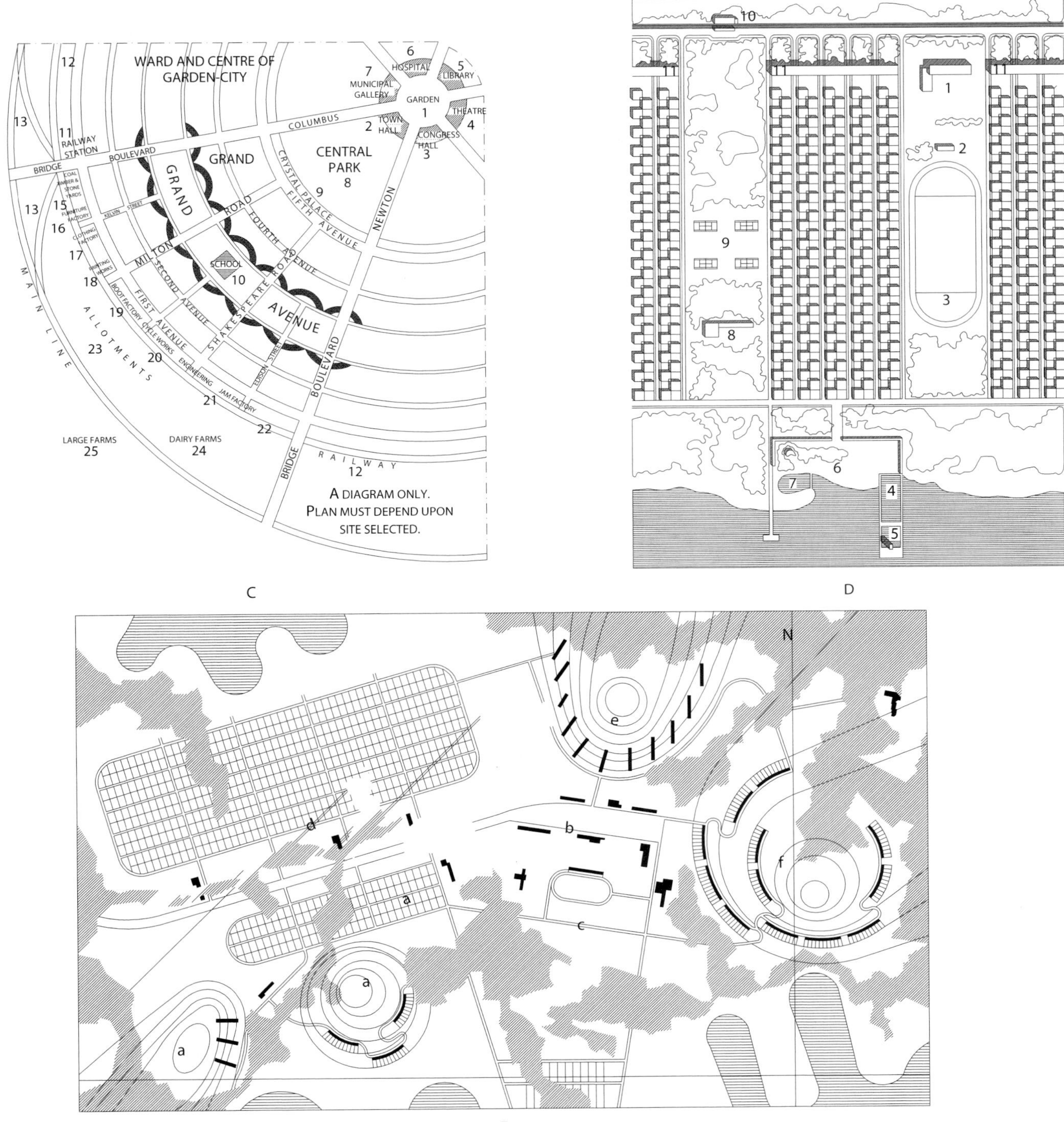

WARD AND CENTRE OF GARDEN-CITY
HOSPITAL
LIBRARY
MUNICIPAL GALLERY
GARDEN
TOWN HALL
THEATRE
CONGRESS HALL
COLUMBUS
RAILWAY STATION
BRIDGE
BOULEVARD
GRAND
GRAND
CENTRAL PARK
CRYSTAL PALACE
FIFTH AVENUE
FOURTH AVENUE
ROAD
NEWTON
KELVIN STREET
MILTON
SCHOOL
SECOND AVENUE
FIRST AVENUE
SHAKESPEARE ROAD
AVENUE
BOULEVARD
EDISON STREET
COAL TIMBER & STONE YARDS
FURNITURE FACTORY
CLOTHING FACTORY
PRINTING WORKS
BOOT FACTORY
CYCLE WORKS
ENGINEERING
JAM FACTORY
MAIN LINE
ALLOTMENTS
LARGE FARMS
DAIRY FARMS
RAILWAY
BRIDGE
A DIAGRAM ONLY.
PLAN MUST DEPEND UPON
SITE SELECTED.
N

C

D

E

106 EGYPTIAN AND RENAISSANCE STUDIES OF PROPORTION

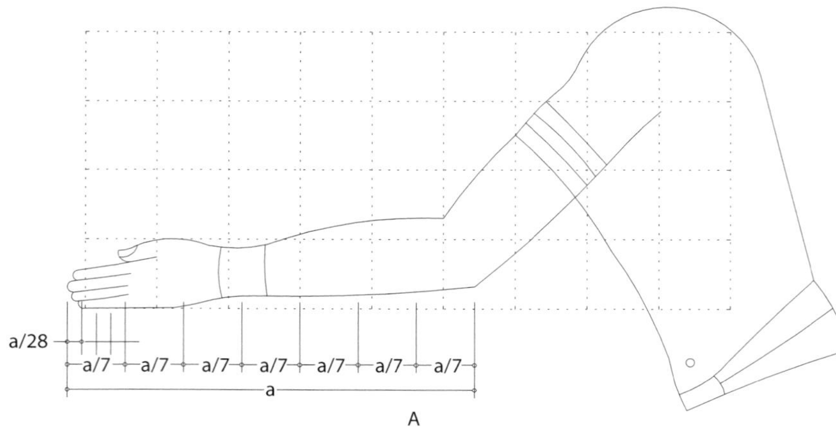

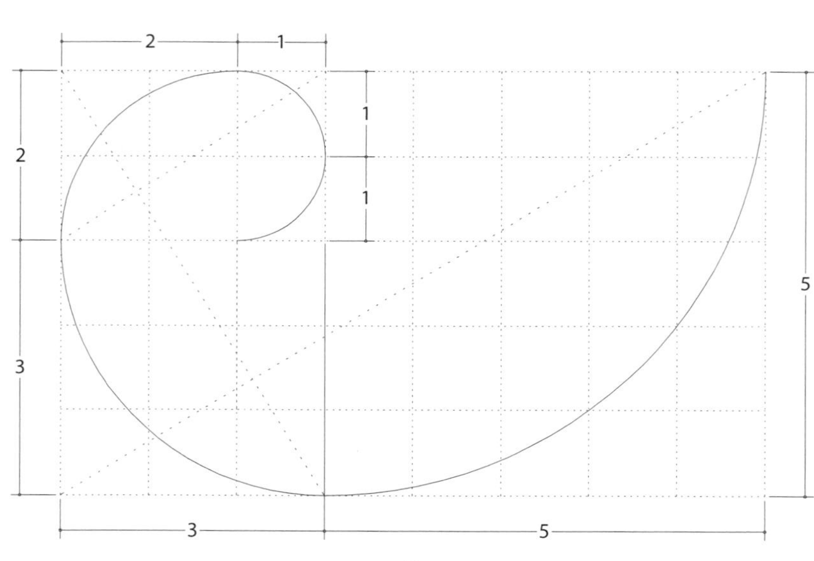

A EGYPTIAN SYSTEM OF PROPORTION

a meh nesut – royal cubit (approx. 52 cm)

a/7 shep, shesep – palm, palm-width

a/28 yeba – finger, finger-width, digit

B FIBONACCI SPIRAL

EGYPTIAN CANON OF PROPORTION

C canon, Old Kingdom

D canon, Middle Kingdom

E canon, New Kingdom

ANTHROPOMETRIC DESIGNS

F church facade

G town plan

H–K church plan

L–N entablature of classic order

O entablature of Tuscan order

proportion

1 an aesthetic quality relating to the massing and relative sizes of forms, lines etc.

2 the empirical or numerical comparison of one dimension or quantity with another

Fibonacci series

a number series in which each number is the sum of the previous two (2, 3, 5, 8, 13, 21 etc.), which bears the name of the Tuscan mathematician Leonardo Fibonacci (c.1170–1230), who observed that, as the series progresses, the ratio of each successive pair approaches the golden section (1:1.618)

anthropometric design

the design of buildings, rooms etc. according to the relative proportions of measurements taken from the ideal human body, a practice originating during the Renaissance period

B) Leonardo Fibonacci, 1170–1230; F, G, H, L) Francesco di Giorgio Martini, 1439–1501; K) Pietro Cataneo, 1510–1572; M) Diego de Sagredo, 1526; N) Jacques Francois Blondel, 1705–1774; O) Giacomo Barozzi Vignola 1507–1573

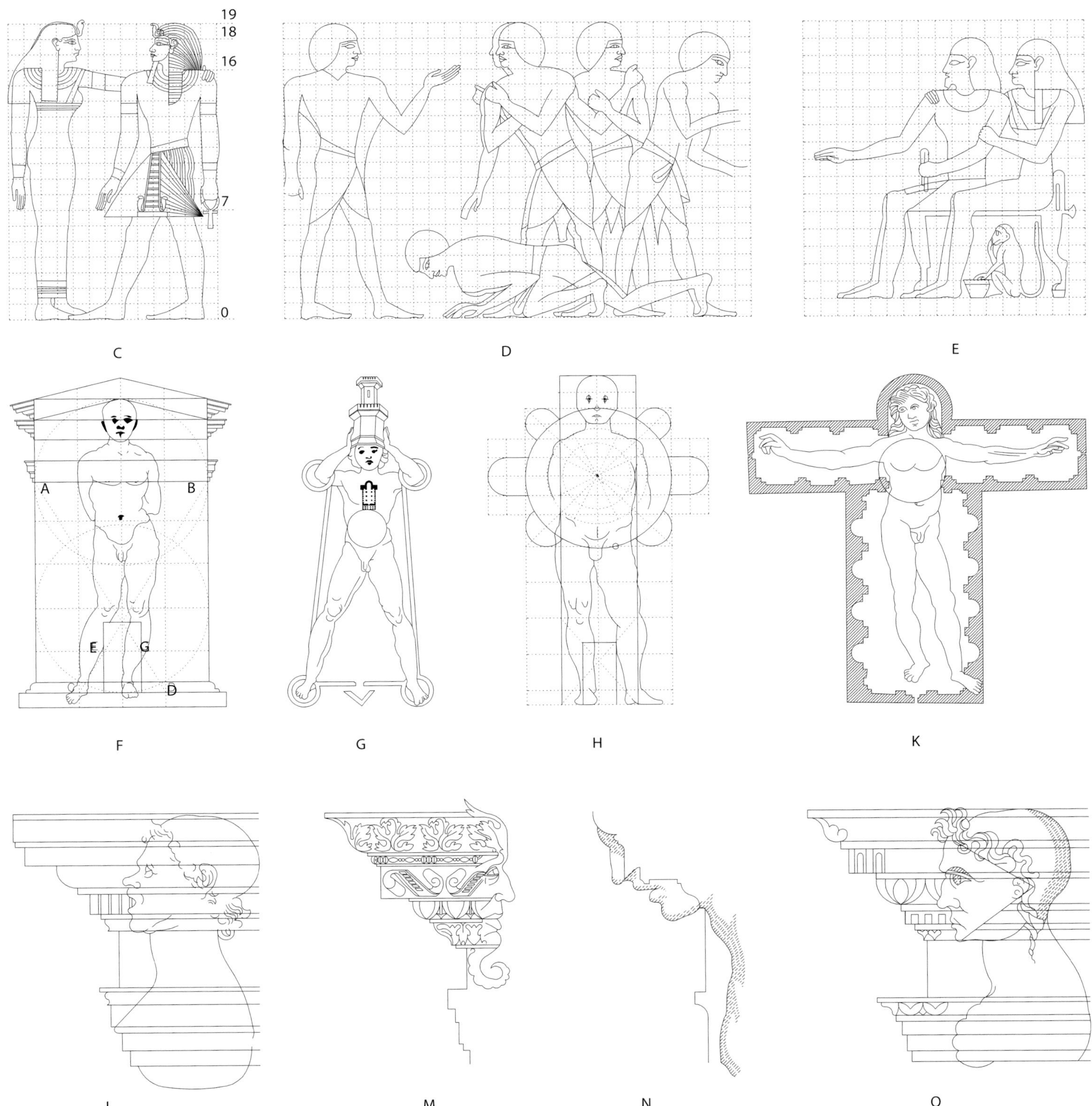
19
18
16
7
0
C
D
E
A
B
E
G
D
F
G
H
K
L
M
N
O

107 VITRUVIAN MAN AND THEORY OF PROPORTION

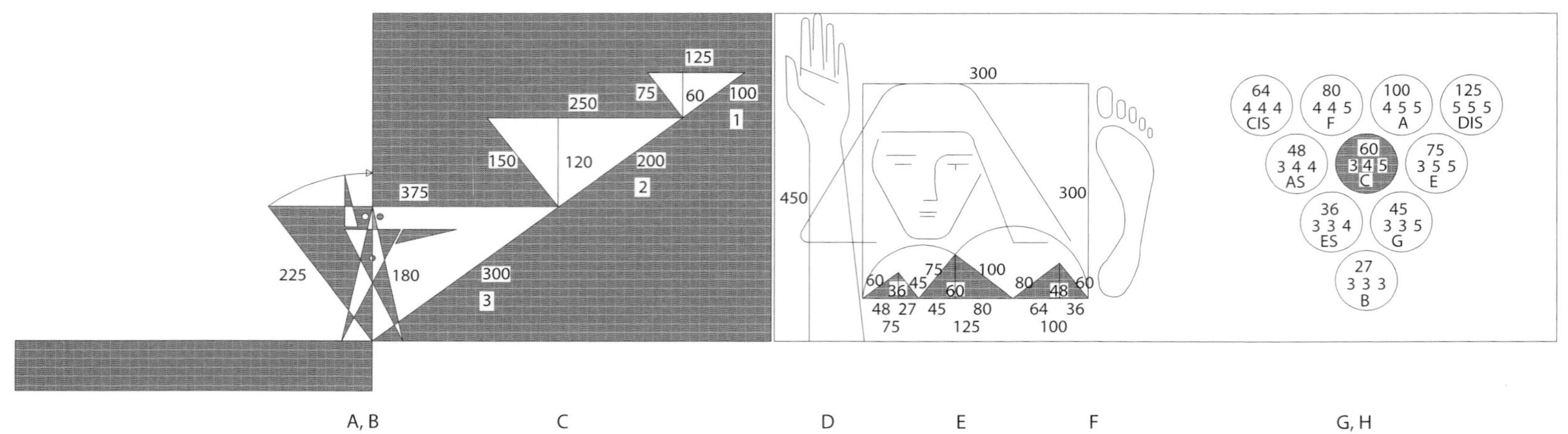

Canon 60 – Aulis Blomstedt (1906–1979)

A canonical man

B human scale

C right-angled triangles, Pythagorean triplet (3–4–5)

D cubit

E basic modules (75 mm, 100 mm, 125 mm)

F foot

G modular numbers

H harmony of proportion

1 Vitruvian man Francesco di Giorgio Martini (1439–1501)

2 Vitruvian man Leonardo da Vinci (1452–1519)

3 Vitruvian man Fra Giocondo (1445–1525)

4 Vitruvian man Giovanantonio Rusconi (n. 1520–1587)

5 Vitruvian man Vincenzo Scamozzi (1552–1616)

6 Octametric system (1936) Ernst Neufert (1900–1986)

7 golden section – sectio aurea Adolf Zeising (1810–1876)

8 Harmonical study Aulis Blomstedt (1906–1979)

9 Modulor II Le Corbusier (1887–1965)

Vitruvian man

a popular theme in theories of art and architecture from Renaissance times, depicting a man of ideal proportions with arms outstretched within a circle and square, thus proposing the proportions of the human body as a basis for aesthetic design in accordance with the canons of proportion suggested by Vitruvius

golden section, sectio aurea (Lat.)

a division of a line or value into two parts such that the ratio of the length of the longer part to the whole is equal to that of the length of the shorter part to the longer part (about 1:1.618); designs made on this basis are considered to have good composition

harmony

in architectural composition, the grouping of elements together in such a way so as to be in balance, well-proportioned and without contradiction

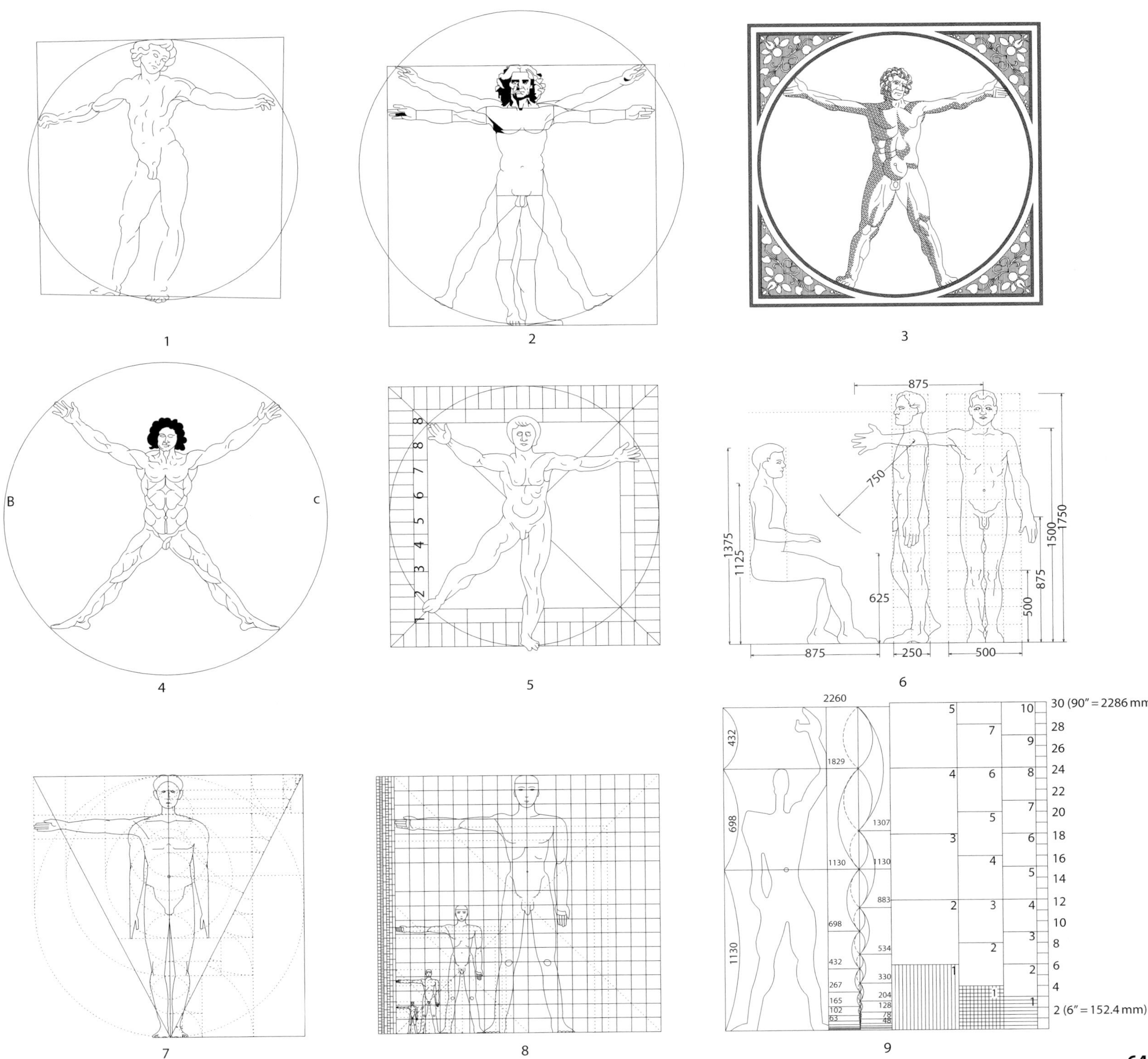

1
2
3
B
c
4
1 2 3 4 5 6 7 8 8
5
875
750
1375
1125
625
1500
1750
875
500
875
250
500
6
7
8
2260
432
698
1130
1829
1307
1130
1130
883
698
534
432
330
267
204
165
128
102
78
63
48
5 4 3 2 1
7 6 5 4 3 2 1
10 9 8 7 6 5 4 3 2 1
30 (90″ = 2286 mm)
28
26
24
22
20
18
16
14
12
10
8
6
4
2 (6″ = 152.4 mm)
9

A, B

A interlace, entrelace, knotwork
B Celtic love knot, Celtic circle

foil
a decorative design consisting of one of a number of stylized leaf motifs or lobes radiating outwards from a point, found especially in medieval architecture

regular polygon
a planar many-sided figure in which all sides are of equal length and all the interior angles are the same

knotwork, entrelace, interlace
in the early architecture and art of northern Europe, especially that of Christian Ireland, decorative ornamentation representing intertwined, overlapping and knotted bands

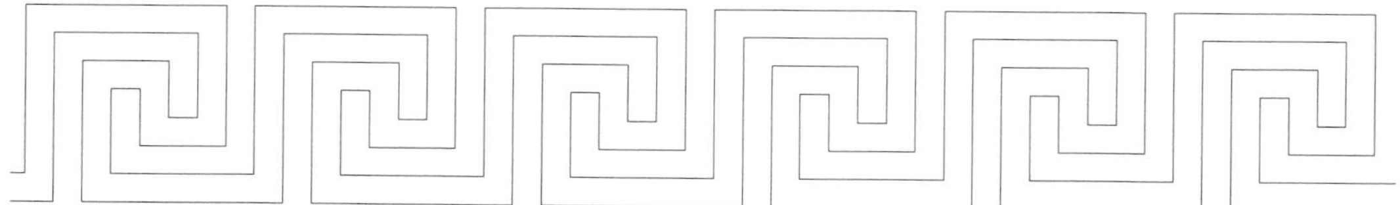

1 circle
2 parallelogram
3 rhombus

REGULAR POLYGONS
(EQUILATERAL AND EQUIANGULAR)

6 equilateral triangle
7 isosceles triangle
8 square
9 pentagon
10 hexagon
11 heptagon
12 octagon
13 nonagon
14 decagon
15 dodecagon

FOIL MOTIFS

16 trefoil
17 point, cusp
18 pointed trefoil
19 quatrefoil
20 pointed quatrefoil
21 cinquefoil
22 pointed cinquefoil
23 multifoil
24 curved triangle, reuleaux triangle
25 fish bladder, vesica piscis
26 ellipse
27 oval
28 double C-scroll

STAR MOTIFS

29 triquetra
30 triceps
31 three-pointed star
32 pentagram
33 hexagram
34 star of David, Solomon's seal, Solomon's shield, Magen David
35 six-pointed star
36 heptagram
37 octagram
38 enneagram

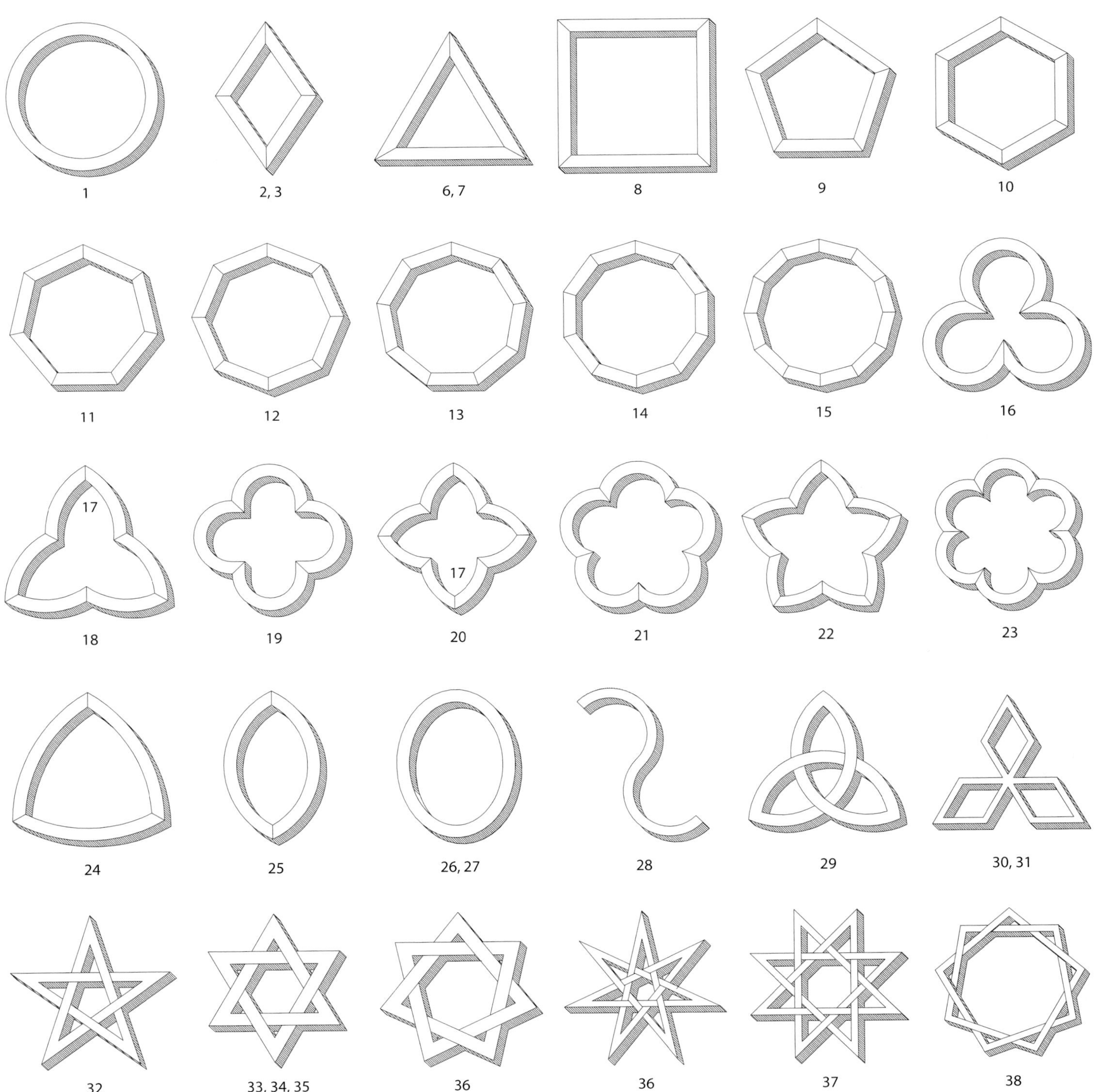
1
2, 3
6, 7
8
9
10
11
12
13
14
15
16
17
18
19
17
20
21
22
23
24
25
26, 27
28
29
30, 31
32
33, 34, 35
36
36
37
38

109 WHEEL AND ROSE WINDOWS

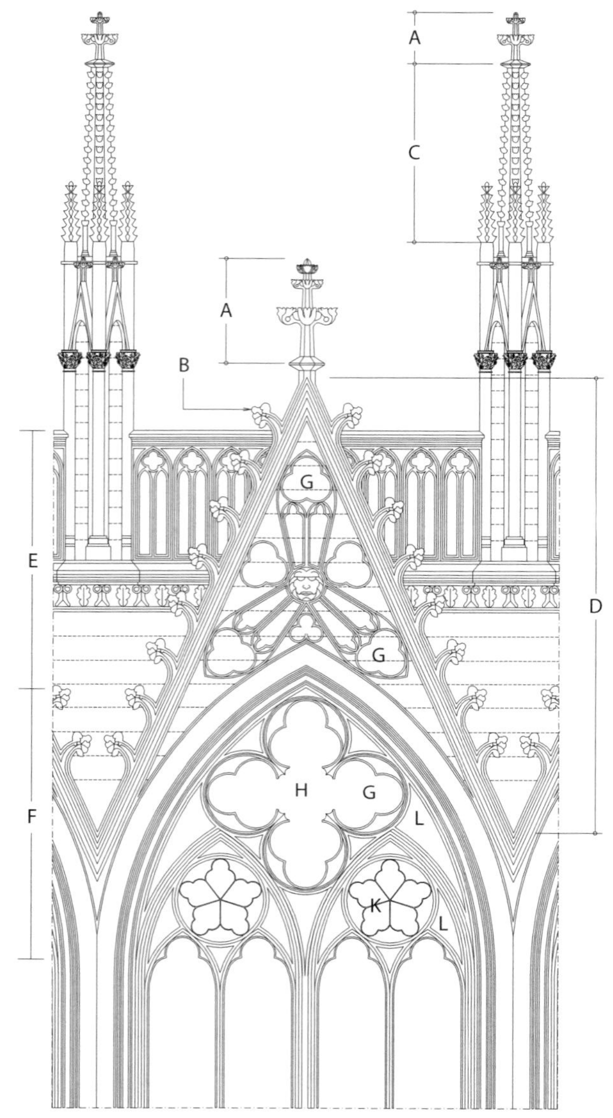

GOTHIC ORNAMENT

A finial
B crocket
C pinnacle
D Gothic ornate gable
E blind tracery, blank tracery
F geometric tracery
G trefoil
H quatrefoil
K cinquefoil
L angel light

STYLES OF ROUND WINDOW

1 wheel window, Catherine wheel window (Norman style, Anglo-Norman style)
2 wheel window, Catherine wheel window (Norman style, Anglo-Norman style)
3 wheel window, Catherine wheel window (Italian Gothic)
4 wheel window, Catherine wheel window (Early English)
5 rose window, marigold window (high Gothic, Rayonnant style)
6 rose window, marigold window (high Gothic, Geometric style)
7–9 rose window, marigold window (Curvilinear style, Flamboyant style)

rose window, marigold window
in medieval religious architecture, a large round ornamental window with tracery

Catherine wheel window, wheel window
a round window with a series of glazing bars radiating out from the centre

crocket
Gothic ornament based on a stylized florid motif, found adorning pinnacles, capitals and spires

finial
florid Gothic decoration for the top of a gable, spire or pinnacle

pinnacle
a small pointed or pyramidical turret in Gothic architecture, often adorning buttresses, doorways and roofs and ornamented with crockets and finials

A) Kölner Dom, Cologne, 1248–1880; 1) St Mary's church, Patrixbourne, Kent, 1170; 2) St Davids Cathedral, St. Davids, Pembrokeshire, Wales, 1181–, Peter de Laia, Giraldus de Barri; 3) Duomo, Orvieto, 1290–1330, Fra' Bevignate da Perugia, Arnolfo di Cambio, Lorenzo Maitani; 4) York Minster, York, 1220–1250; 5) Minoritenkirche, Vienna, 1276–1350; 6) Notre-Dame, Amiens, 1220–47; 7) Beauvais Cathedral, 1225–72; 8–9) St Ouen, Rouen, 14th Century, Alexander Berneval

1
2
3
4
5
6
7
8
9

110 GOTHIC TRACERY

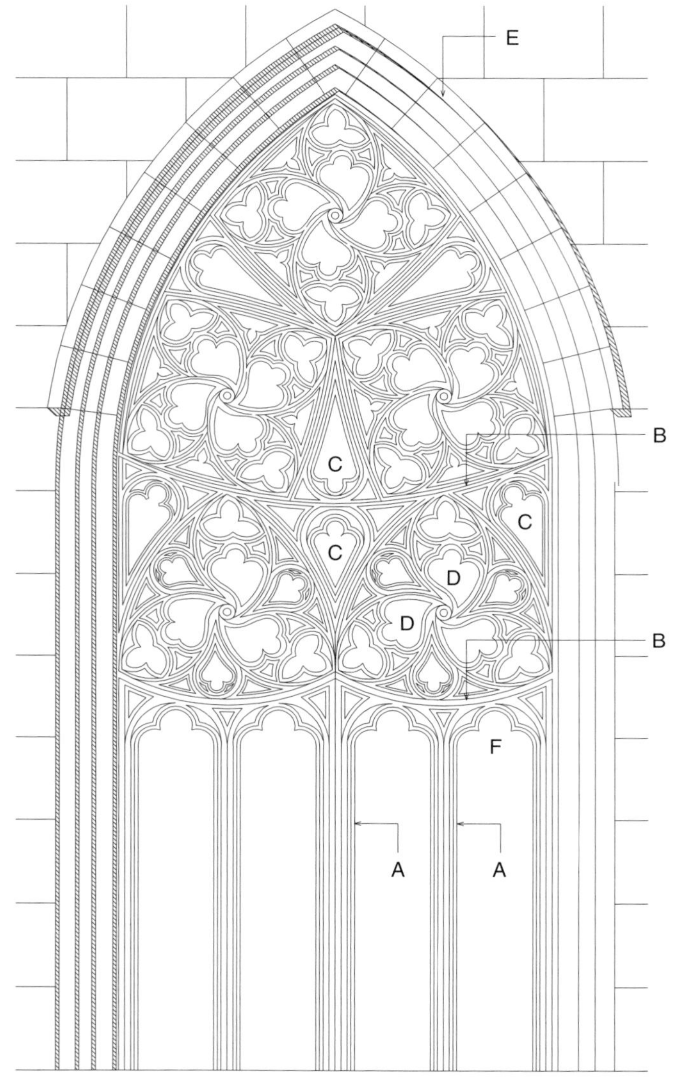

PARTS OF TRACERY

A mullion
B transom
C dagger
D mouchette
E hood-mould
F round trifoliated arch
G cinquefoil head

TRACERY

1 plate tracery
2 round window, roundel, oculus
3 quatrefoil
4 sexfoil, multifoil

BAR TRACERY

5 Y tracery
6 trifoliated arch
7 loop tracery
8 intersecting tracery, flowing tracery
9 geometric tracery, geometrical tracery
10 reticulated tracery
11 curvilinear tracery
12 flamboyant tracery
13 decorated tracery
14 panel tracery, panelled tracery
15 perpendicular tracery, rectilinear tracery

tracery
Gothic ornamental stone and woodwork decoration carved into an intricate vertical and interwoven framework of ribs for the upper parts of openings such as windows or perforated screens, or for the surface of vaults and walls

bar tracery
a range of types of Gothic tracery originating in the late 1200s, formed by vertical window mullions which interlink to form intricate patterns in the pointed window head

mullion, munnion, muntin (Am)
a vertical dividing or framing member in a window, tracery, proprietary glazing systems etc.

glazing bar, division bar, window bar
a framing member to which glazing is fixed

Above: Minoritenkirche, Vienna, 1276–1350; 1) S. Francesco, Assisi, Italy, 1228–53, Jacobus Meruan; 4) St Elisabeth, Marburg, Germany, 1235–83; 5) St Mary's church, Aldworth, Berkshire, England, 1340; 7) Exeter Cathedral, Exeter, c.1050–1350; 8) Blackfriars chapel, St Andrews, 1516; 9) Kölner Dom, Cologne, 1248–1880; 10) St Ouen, Rouen, France, 1318–1515; 11) Minoritenkirche, Vienna, 1276–1350; 12) Hone Church, Sutton, Kent; 14) Winchester Cathedral, Winchester, Hampshire, England, 1079–400; 15) King's College Chapel, Cambridge, England, 1446–1515

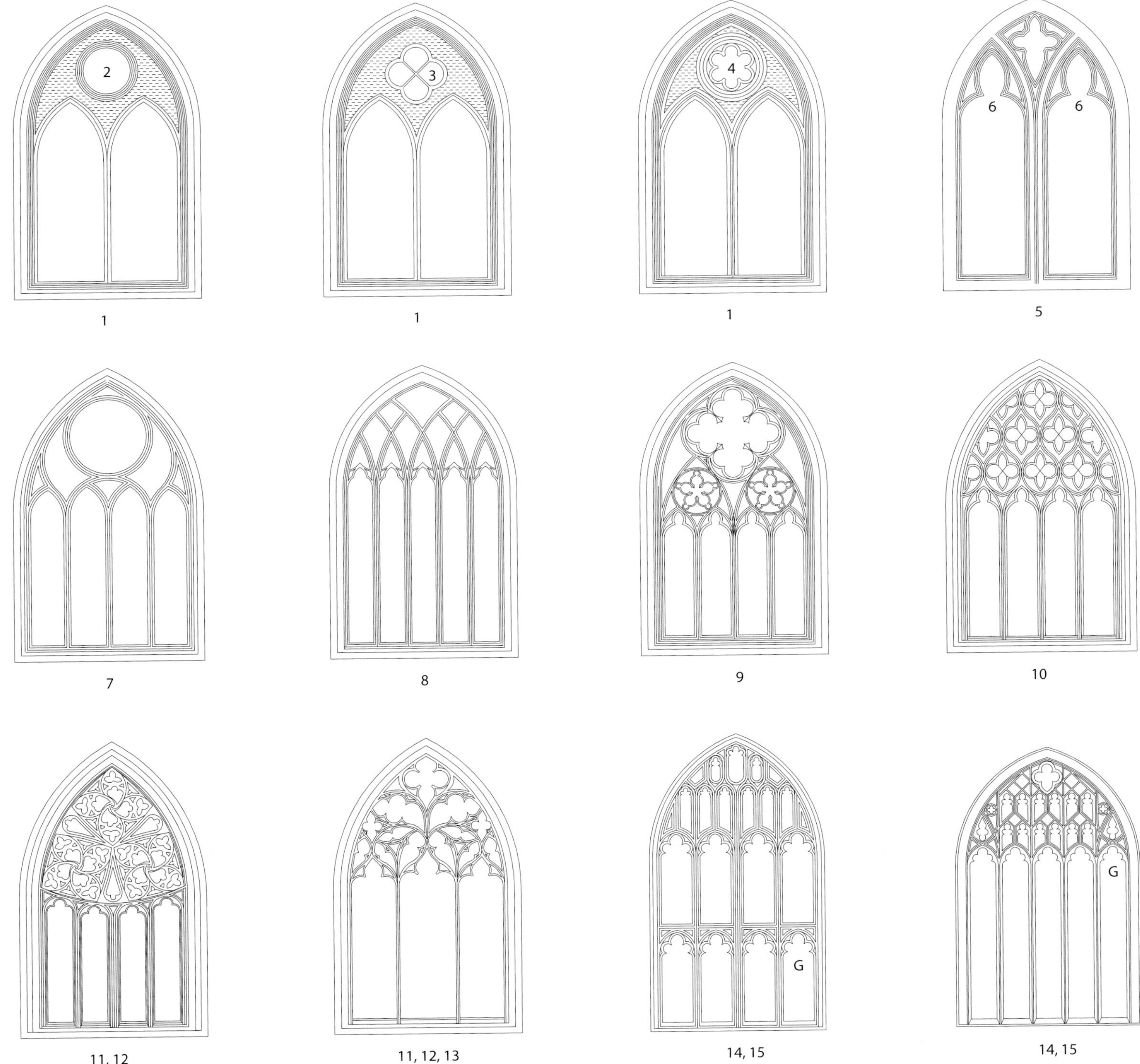
2
1
3
1
4
1
6
6
5
7
8
9
10
11, 12
11, 12, 13
G
14, 15
G
14, 15

111 WINDOWS OF DIFFERENT STYLES

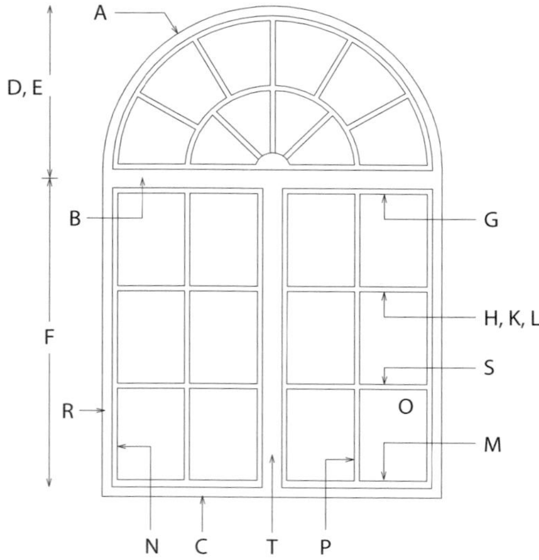

ARCH WINDOW

A arched head, arcuated head
B transom
C sill
D top light, upper window
E fanlight
F vertical sash
G top rail
H glazing bar, division bar, window bar
K horizontal glazing bar, lay bar
L astragal
M bottom rail
N stile
O pane, window pane
P vertical glazing bar
R jamb
S rail, horizontal glazing bar
T mullion; (Am.) munnion

STYLE PERIODS

X Manueline window
1, 2 transenna, late Antique, Early Christian
3 Greek window
4 Roman window
5 Romanesque window
6 Moorish window
7 Early Gothic window
8 High Gothic window
9 Late Gothic window
10 Early Renaissance window
11 High Renaissance window
12 Late Renaissance window
13 Baroque window
14 Rococo window
15 Neoclassical window

window
an opening in an external wall of a building for allowing light into a space; may be a simple opening or a glazed assembly of parts

light
an opening in a wall for a window; a small window or glazed unit

astragal
a small dividing glazing bar in a window

pane
a piece of glass or glazed unit fitted in a window frame or as glazing, a glazed panel

X) Chapter House, Tomar, Portugal, c.1520, Diego da Arrada; 1, 2) S.Lorenzo fuori le mura, Rooma, 570–590; 5) White Tower, London, 1078; 7) Great Abington church, c.1200; 8) Great Haseley church, c.1300; 9) St Mary-the-Virgin's church, Oxford, 1488; 10) Palazzo della Cancelleria, Rome, 1483–1517, Andrea Bregno; 12) Palazzo Pandolfini, Florence, 1514, Raphael (Raffaello Sanzio); 13) Michna palace, Prague, 1640–50; 14) Durchholzen–Walchsee, Germany

1
2
3
4
5
6
7
8
9
10
11
12
13
14
15

112 PEDIMENTS

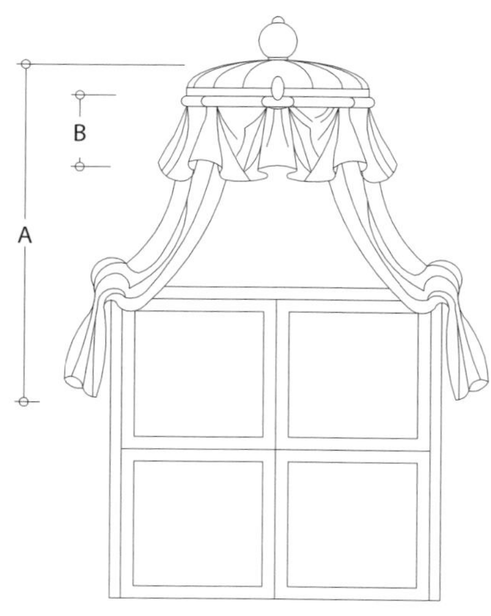

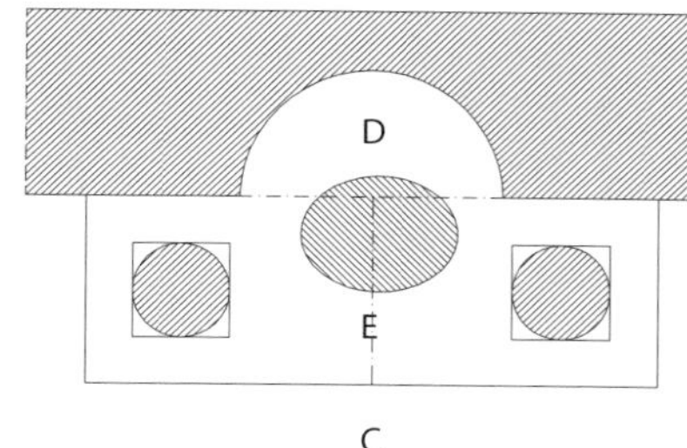

A baldachin, baldacchino, baldaquin
B lambrequin
C aedicula
D niche, recess
E sculpture, statue

PEDIMENTS

1	pediment, triangular pediment, fronton
2	broken-bed triangular pediment, broken-base triangular pediment, open bed triangular pediment
3	open-topped triangular pediment, broken-apex triangular pediment
4	stepped triangular pediment
5	segmental pediment
6	broken-bed segmental pediment
7	open-topped segmental pediment
8	stepped segmental pediment
9	open triangular pediment, broken triangular pediment
10–11	open segmental pediment, broken segmental pediment
12	scrolled pediment, bonnet-topped pediment
13–17	wavy pediment
13–14	pointed-top wavy pediment
15–17	round-top wavy pediment
18	winged pediment
19	broken-winged pediment
20	stepped pediment

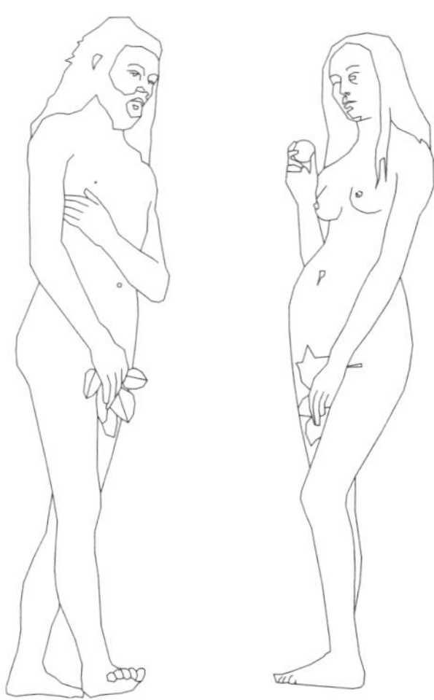

pediment
1 the triangular gabled portion of a classical portico or building; forerunners of this
2 fronton; in Renaissance, Baroque and Neoclassical architecture, a triangular or segmental ornamental device, panel or canopy above doorways, windows and panels

baldachin, baldacchino, baldaquin
an ornamental canopy of or representing fabric over an altar, throne, bed or doorway

ciborium
Lat.; in Early Christian and Byzantine churches, a canopy mounted on four posts over an altar, shrine, or the tomb of a martyr; a baldachin; the original Greek form is kiborion

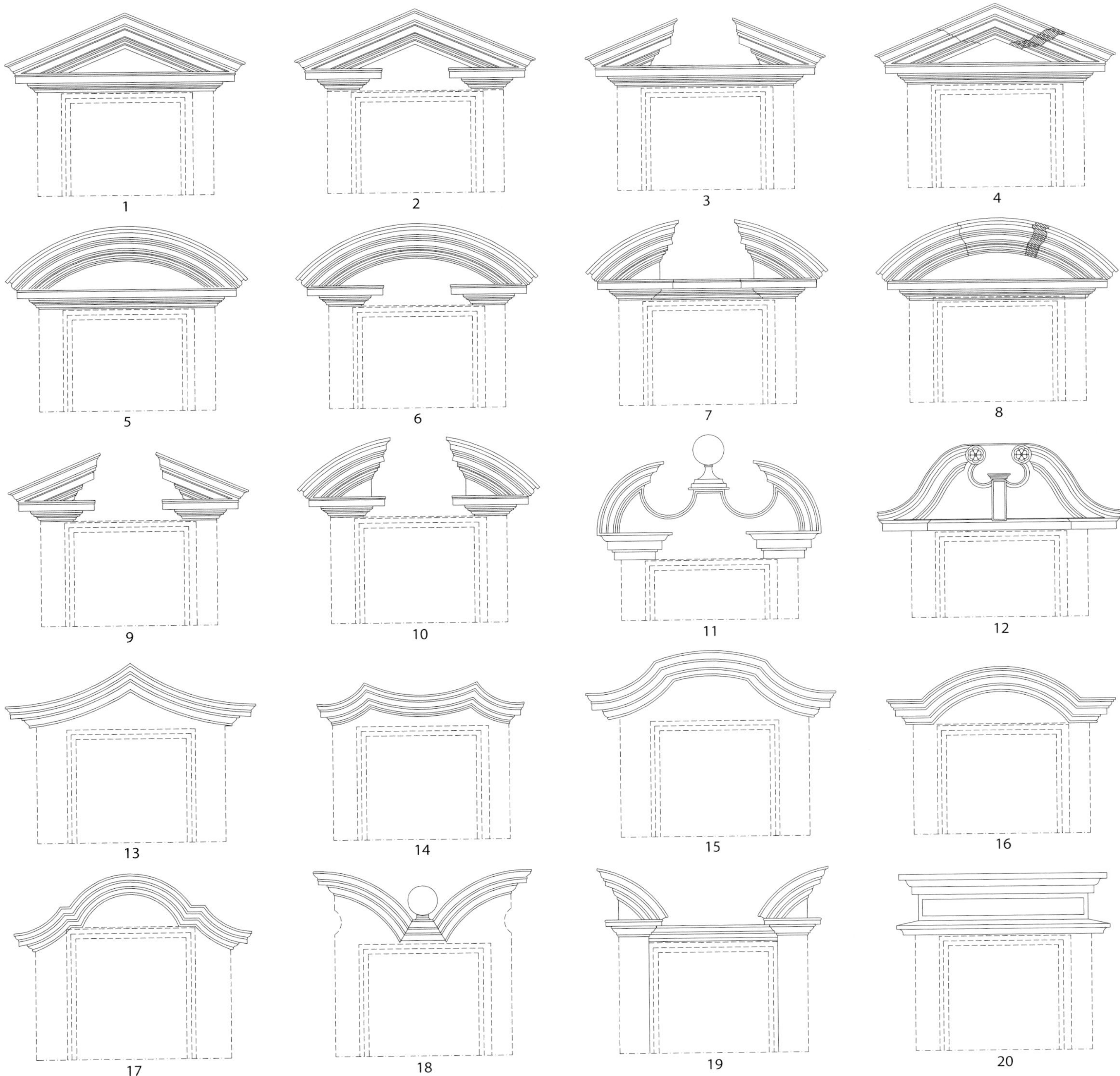
1
2
3
4
5
6
7
8
9
10
11
12
13
14
15
16
17
18
19
20

113 PORTALS AND DOORWAYS

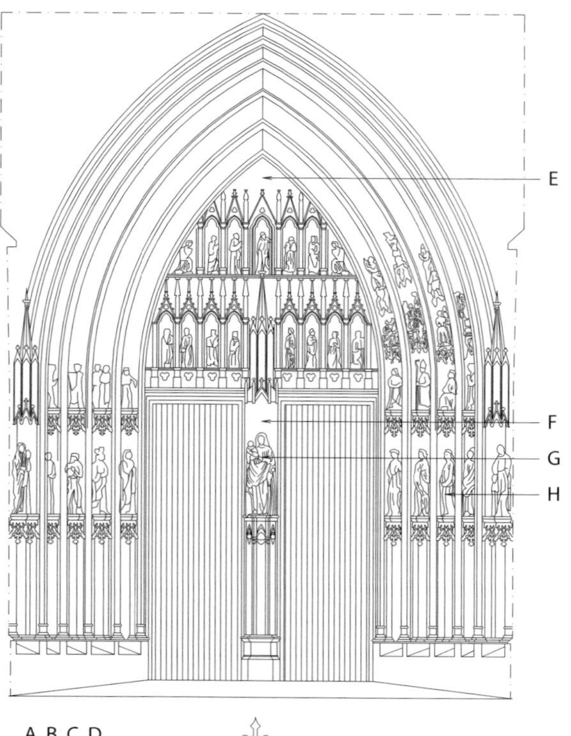

A, B, C, D

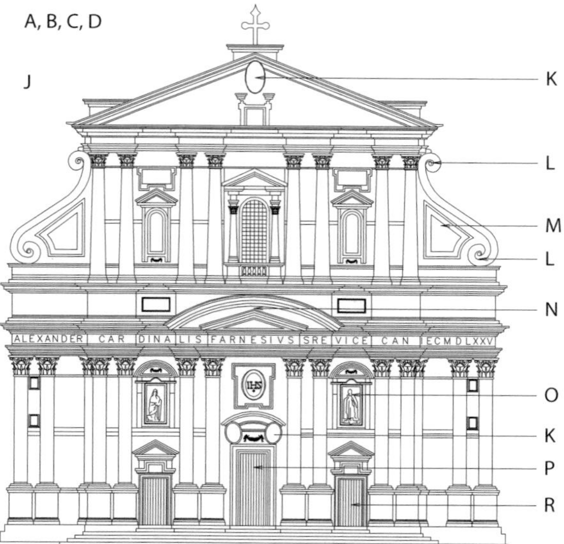

A GOTHIC RECESSED PORTAL
B jamb figure portal, sculptured portal
C royal portal
D Gate of Heaven
E tympanum
F trumeau
G trumeau figure
H jamb figure, column figure

J BAROQUE FRONTAGE OR FACADE
K medallion
L volute
M aileron
N double pediment
O niche
P main entrance, front door
R side door

1 Mycenaean portal
2 Egyptian portal
3 Doric portal
4 Ionic portal
5 Romanesque recessed portal
6 Renaissance portal
7 Baroque portal
8 Mannerist portal
9 Rococo portal
10 Art Nouveau portal jugendstil portal
11 Functionalist portal
12 post-modern portal

doorway, door opening
the opening formed by a door in a wall, into which a door frame is fitted

gateway, gate
the structural or ornate surround for an entrance opening in a wall or building; a portal

portal
a grand, often ornamental gateway, porch or main entrance for a castle, religious or large public building

trumeau
a masonry column, pillar or pier between two openings, often in religious buildings supporting the centre of the tympanum in an arched doorway or window

A) Cathedral, Cologne, 1248–1880; J) Il Gesù, Rome, 1568–1584, Giacomo Barozzi da Vignola (plan), Giacomo Della Porta (facade); 1) Treasury of Atreus, Mycenae, 1325–1250 BC; 2) Temple of Horus, Edfu 237–57 BC; 3) Belevi mausoleum (Ephesus), c.246 BC; 4) Erechtheion, Athens, 420–406 BC, Mnesicles; 5) Heilbronn; 6) Giuliano da Sangallo (1443–1516); 7) Palazzo Zuccari, Rome, Federico Zuccari (1540–1609); 8) Uffizi Gallery, Florence, 1580, Bernardo Buontalenti; 10) No. 6 Kauppakatu, Tampere, 1899–1900, Lars Sonck & Birger Federley; 11) Master House, Bauhaus, Dessau, 1925–26, Walter Gropius; 12) House Venturi, Chestnut Hill, Pennsylvania 1962, Robert Venturi

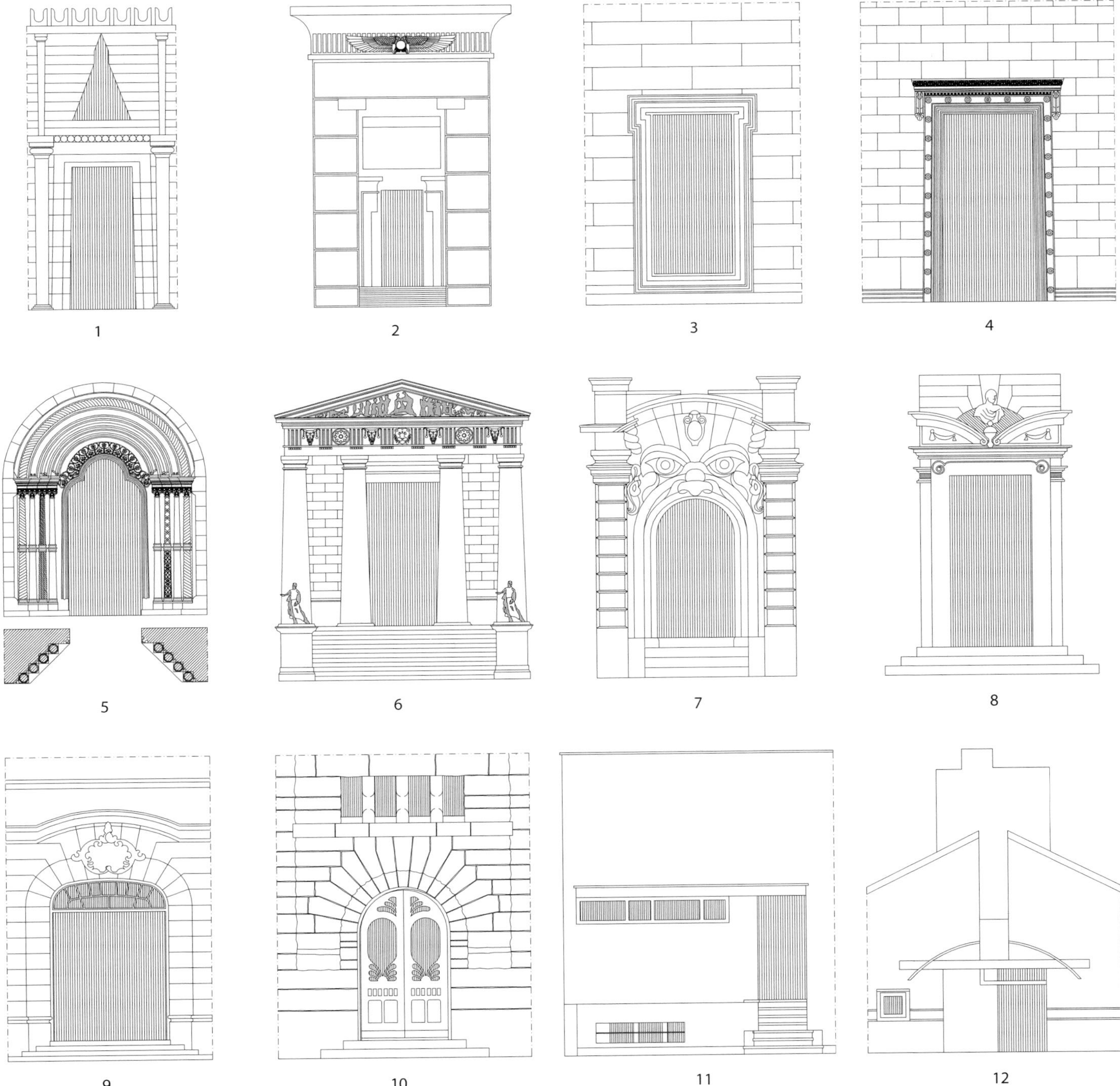
1
2
3
4
5
6
7
8
9
10
11
12

SUPERIMPOSED ORDERS

A Doric or Tuscan order
B Ionic order
C Corinthian order

COLUMN TYPES

1–2 banded column, annulet column – Romanesque
3–4 barley-sugar column, salomonica, Solomonic column, spiral column – Romanesque
5 barley-sugar column, salomonica, Solomonic column, spiral column – Gothic
6 coupled column – Romanesque
7 bundle column – Romanesque
8 bundle column – Renaissance
9 fluted column – Neo-Classicism
10–11 knotted column – Romanesque
12 knotted column, accouplement – Byzantism
13 coupled column, twinned column – Romanesque
14 animal column, beast column – Romanesque
15 rusticated column – Neo-Classicism
16–17 candelabrum column – Renaissance
18 barley-sugar column, salomonica, Solomonic column, spiral column – Baroque

superimposed orders
the stacking of classical orders as elevational devices in successive storeys of a classical building, by convention (from the bottom) Tuscan, Doric, Ionic, Corinthian and Composite

bundle column
a stone column-type in Gothic, Romanesque and Renaissance architecture with a shaft carved into a number of stems, as if of separate smaller columns, terminating at a capital; modern equivalents of this

spiral column
a column type with a shaft carved into a helical form, appearing in Late Gothic and Baroque architecture, and found in the legendary temple of King Solomon; variously called a barley-sugar column, salomonica, Solomonic column, torso, twisted column, wreathed column

knotted column
a Romanesque stone column or coupled columns whose compound shafts are carved as if knotted together in the middle; also known as a knotted pillar

A) St Maria della Carita, Venice, Italy, 1565, Andrea Palladio; 1) Abbey church of St Albans, Hertfordshire, England, 1080; 3) Canterbury Cathedral, Kent, England, 1070–77; 5) St Blasiu's Cathedral, Brunswick, Germany, 1173–95; 6) Dalby church, Skåne, Sweden, c.1060; 7) Cathedral, Regensburg, Germany, 1260; 12) St Mark's, Venice, Italy, 1050; 13) Cathedral, Limburg an der Lahn, Germany, 1235; 14) Abbey church of St Pierre, Moissac, France, 1115–20; 18) Val-de-Grace, Paris, France, 1654, Leduc

1
2
3
4
5
6
7
8
9
10
11
12
13
14
15
16
17
18

115 ROMANESQUE AND GOTHIC CAPITALS

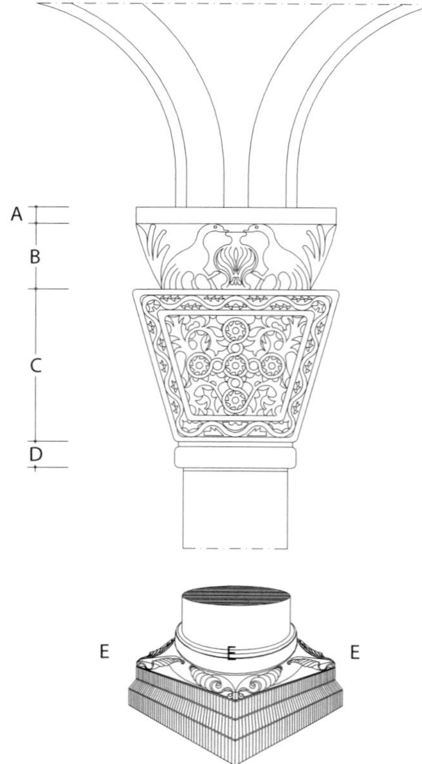

abacus
a flat squared slab at the very top of a column, making the transition between it and overlying structure

dosseret
an additional block of stone sometimes placed above the capital of Byzantine and Romanesque columns; also called a pulvin, impost block or supercapital

capital
a separate block or a thickening at the top of a column or pilaster, used to spread the load of a beam, or as decoration

torus
a thick decorative convex moulding, larger than an astragal

A abacus
B dosseret, impost block, super abacus, supercapital
C capital
D torus
E spur, griffe

TYPES OF CAPITAL

1 foliated capital – Roman
2 waterleaf capital – Byzantine
3 foliated capital – pre-Romanesque
4 foliated capital – Romanesque
5 stiff-leaf capital – Romanesque
6 vine leaf capital – Gothic
7 crocket capital – Romanesque
8 fold capital – Romanesque
9 bell capital – Romanesque
10 bell capital – Romanesque
11 trumpet capital –Romanesque
12 bell capital, moulded capital – Early Gothic
13 block capital, cushion capital – Romanesque
14 block capital, cushion capital – Romanesque
15 block capital, cushion capital – Romanesque
16 scallop capital, double scalloped capital – Romanesque
17, 18 scallop capital, scalloped capital, trumpet scalloped capital – Romanesque
19 basket capital – Byzantine
20 dosseret (super abacus, impost block) and basket capital – Byzantine
21 dosseret (super abacus, impost block) and trapezoidal capital – Byzantine
22 trapezoidal capital – brick Gothic, Backsteingotik
23 volute capital – Carolingian
24 volute capital – Anglo Norman
25 mushroom capital – Romanesque
26 figure and bestial capital – Romanesque
27 bestial capital, protome capital – Romanesque
28 foliate head capital – Romanesque
29 arabesque capital, Moresque capital
30 stalactite capital – Moorish

A–E) San Vitale, Ravenna, Italy, 526–547; 1) Capitoline Hill, Rome, c.180 AD; 2) Cathedral, As-Suwayda, Syria, 5th...6th cent.; 3) S. Maria del Naranco, Oviedo, Spain, 842–848; 4) Marienkirche, Würtzburg, Germany, 8th cent.; 5) St Mary the Virgin, West Walton, Norfolk, England, 1240; 6) Chapter House, Southwell Minster, England, c.1290; 7) Abbey of Lilienfeld, Austria, 1202; 9) Monastery of Comburg, Germany, 11th cent.; 12) St Mary, Uffington, Oxfordshire, England, c.1250; 13, 14) St Michael, Hildesheim, Niedersachsen, Germany, 1007–1033; 15) Collegiate church, Faurndau, Germany, c.1200; 16) St Michael, Bockleton, Worcestershire, England, 12th cent; 17) Fountains Abbey, Ripon, Yorkshire, England, c.1135–1147; 18) Schottenkirche, Regensburg, Germany, c.1150; 19) Hagia Sofia, Istanbul, Turkey, 532–537, Anthemion of Trallis & Isidoros of Miletus; 20, 21) San Vitale, Ravenna, Italy, 526; 22) Convent church, Arendsee, Germany, 1185–1240; 23) Cathedral, Fulda, Hessen, Germany, 819; 24) St John The Baptist church, Great Hale, Lincolnshire, England 11th cent.; 25) Crypt of St Wipert, Quedlinburg, Germany, c.950; 26) St Nikolai, Alpirsbach, Germany, 1125; 27) Cathedral, Speyer, Germany, 1032–90; 28) St Paul, Esslingen, Baden–Württemberg, Germany, 1233–68; 29) Alhambra, Granada, Spain, 1300

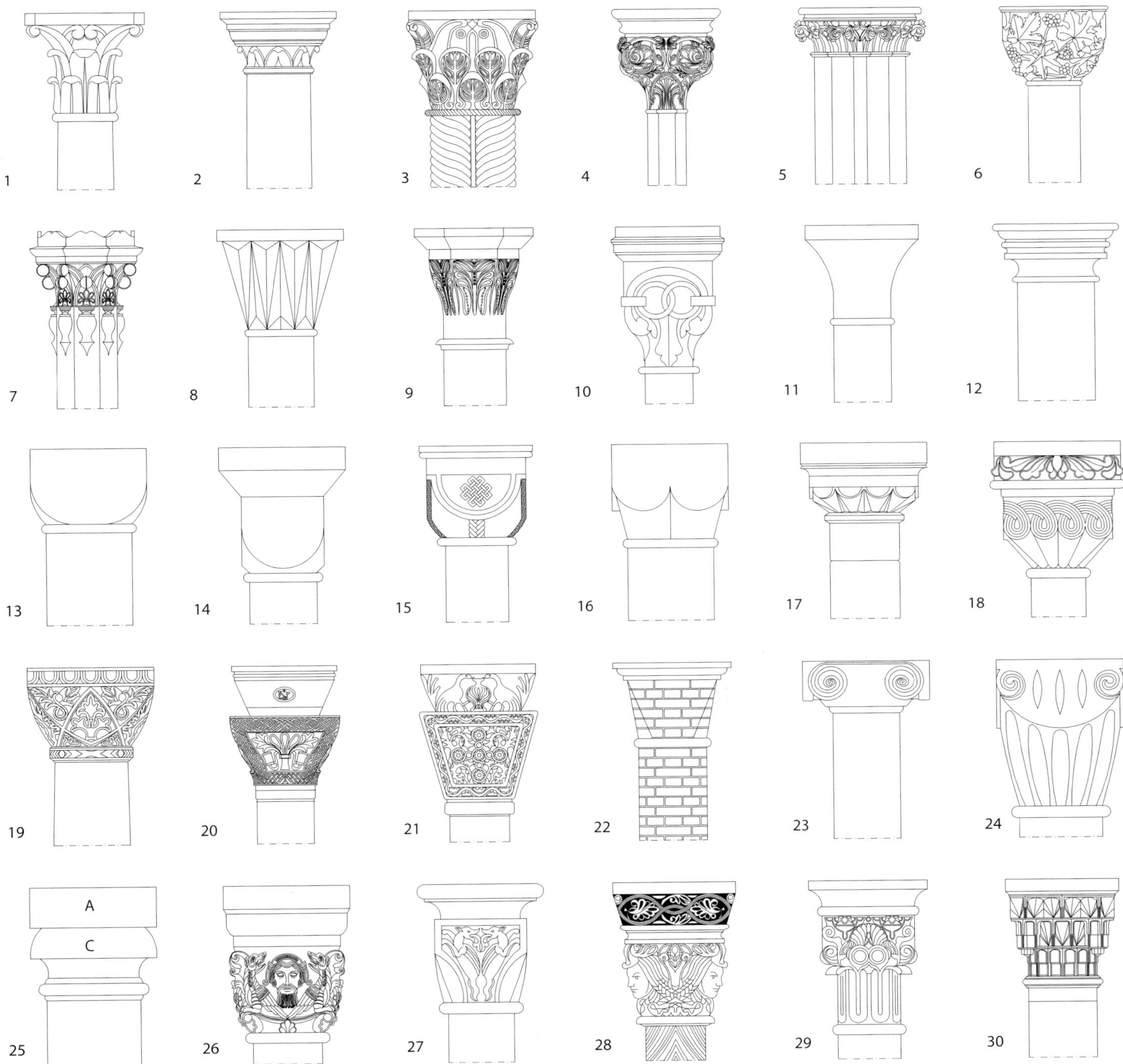

1
2
3
4
5
6
7
8
9
10
11
12
13
14
15
16
17
18
19
20
21
22
23
24
25
A
C
26
27
28
29
30

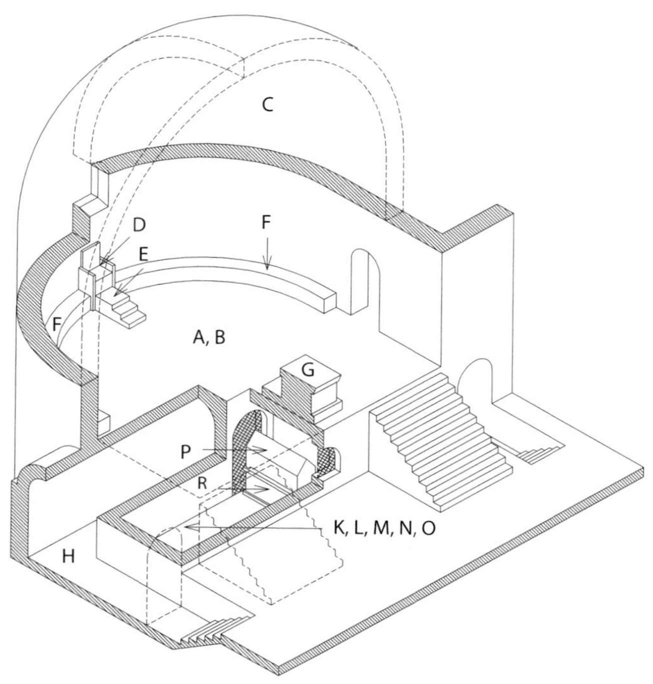

EAST END/CHOIR, CHANCEL/SANCTUARY

A apse
B retrochoir
C conch, concha
D cathedra, bishop's throne
E estrade
F synthronon
G altar tomb
H ambulatory
K crypt, croft, shroud
L confessio, confession
M burial chamber, funerary chamber
N grave
O catabasion
P sargophagus
R catafalque, catafalco

SACRIFICIAL ALTARS

1 sacrificial stone (Egyptian)
2 shewbread table, showbread table
3 cupstone
4 bomos (Greek)
5 thymele (Greek)
6 eskhara (Greek)
7 ara (Roman)
8 focus

COMMUNION TABLES

9 rood altar
10 communion bench
11 altar rail, communion rail
12 altar platform, suppedaneum
13 altar table, mensa
14 stipes: support
15 tabula
16 block altar
17 chest altar
18 sargophagal altar
19 ciborium altar
20 ciborium
21 altar canopy
22 retable altar, reverse altar
23 retable
24 altarpiece
25 ancona
26 winged altar
27 predella
28 corpus
29 wing (Lat. ala, pl. alae)
30 triptych
31 pulpit altar
32 pulpit

RELIQUARY ALTAR

33 portable altar, portatile
34 sepulchre, altar cavity
35 reliquary

PARAMENTS

41 altar frontal, antemensale
42 antependium, frontal
43 super frontal
44 pulpit scarf, pulvinarium
45 candlestick

altar
the focal point of worship in a church, temple or shrine

bomos
a stone altar situated at or near the entrance to a Greek temple, on which offerings were made to a deity

eschara, eskhara
an ancient Greek hearth altar for burnt offerings

thymele
in classical architecture, a sacrificial altar within the orchestra of a theatre, especially to Dionysus

ara
a classical Roman altar for a deity

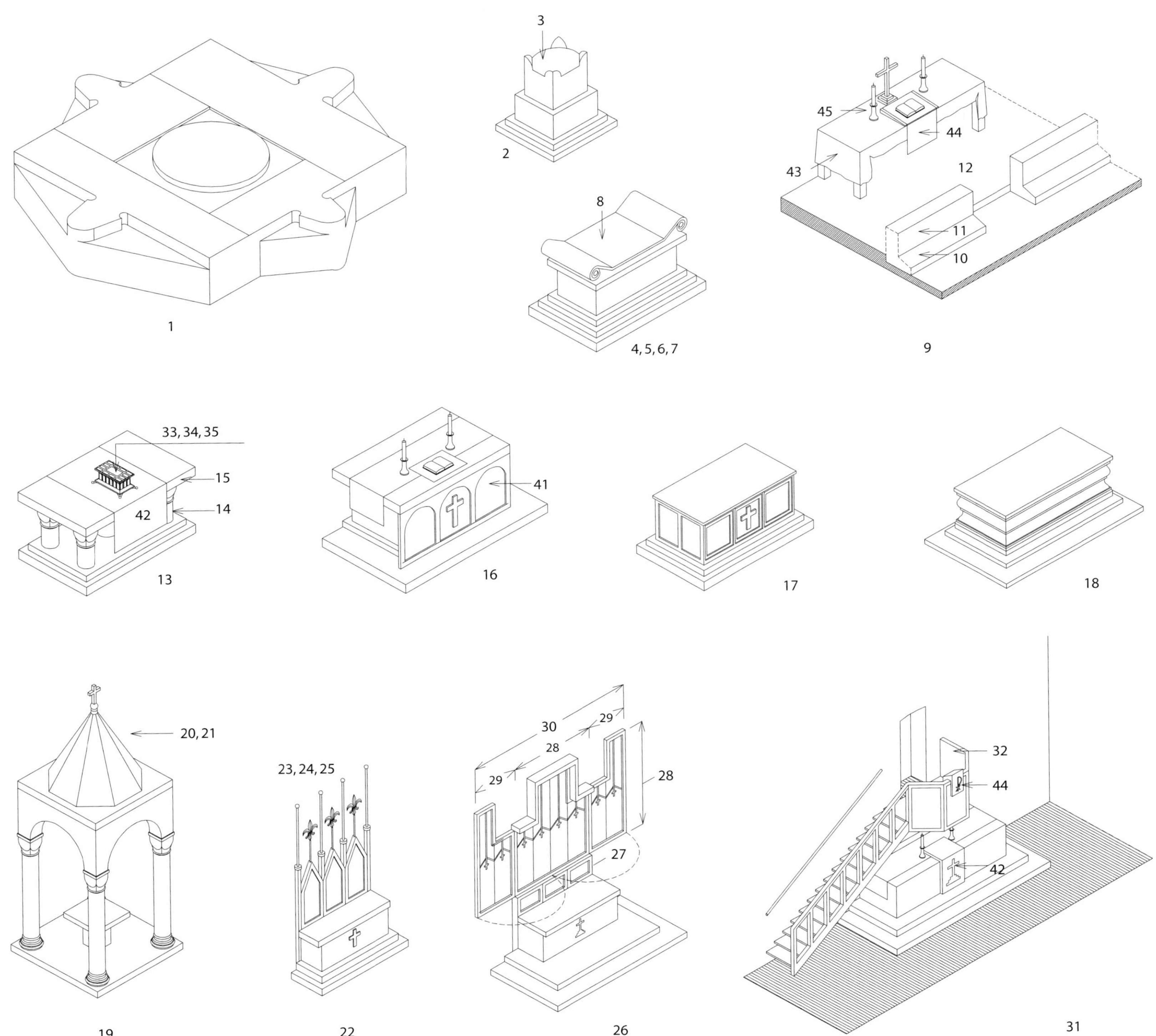

1
3
2
8
4, 5, 6, 7
45
44
43
12
11
10
9
33, 34, 35
15
42
14
13
41
16
17
18
20, 21
19
23, 24, 25
22
30
29
28
29
28
27
26
32
44
42
31

117 VARIATIONS OF THE LATIN CROSS

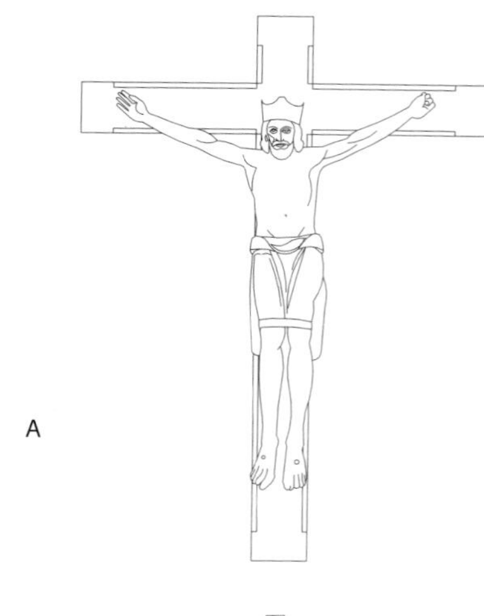
A

B

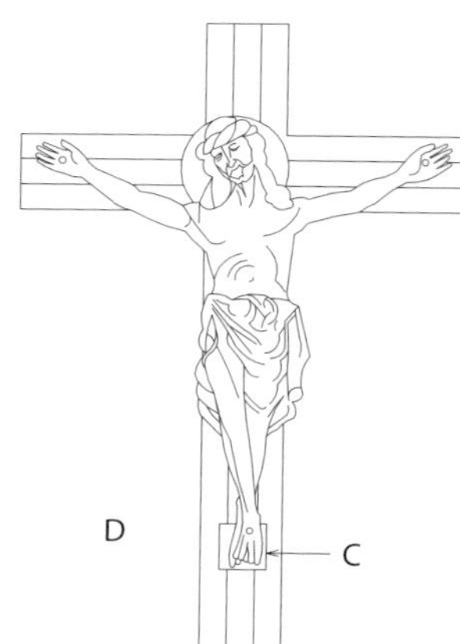

D

cross
an ancient symbolic figure consisting of two bars which cross each other, often at right angles; it appears as a religious motif and ornament in many different forms

Latin cross, crux immissa
a cross with four perpendicular limbs of which three are of equal length and the fourth, the lower, is longer; an ancient symbol of divinity found in China, Greece and Egypt, later the symbol of Christ's suffering and Christianity; variously known as the cross of life, cross of Christ, Passion cross, crux capitata (Lat.) or long cross

crucifix
a statue, carving or other effigy representing Christ on the cross

rood
a large crucifix in a church

A triumphal crucifix, rood (Romanesque)
B passion crucifix, rood (Gothic)
C suppedaneum
D passion crucifix, rood (Gothic)

A) Tryde church, Tomelilla, Sweden, c.1160; B) St Mary's church, Turku, Finland, 14th cent.; D) Sund Church, Åland, Finland, 13th cent.

1 Latin cross, crux immissa, crux capitata, long cross, Passion cross
2 pointed cross, cross fitchée, fitched cross
3 cross fitched at foot
4 pointed cross, cross urdee
5 cross barbée or barby, arrow cross
6 cross potent, cross billety, crutch cross
7 cross crosslet
8 tau cross, St Anthony's cross, crux commissa, Egyptian cross, robber's cross
9 ankh, ansated cross, crux ansata, cross of Horus, Egyptian cross, handlebar cross, key of life, key to the Nile
10 cross pommée (pommellé, pomy, pommy)
11 cross botonée or botony, cross of Lazarus, trefoil or threefoil cross
12 cross fleurettée, flory or fleury
13 cross fourchée, forked cross, fourchée cross, cleft foot cross, miller's cross
14 swallowtail cross, bifurcated cross
15 cross moline, cross sarcelly, cross resarcelly, crux dissimulata
16 anchor cross
17 Portuguese cross
18 cross capital, teutonic cross Templar cross
19 cross degraded
20 cross nowy circular, cross nowy
21 Celtic cross, Ionic cross, Irish cross
22 forked cross, ypsilon cross, Y-cross, furca, robber's or thief's cross
23 tree of life
24 shepherd's cross
25 patriarchal cross
26 Russian cross, orthodox cross, eastern cross,
27 Lotharingian cross
28 cross of Lorraine, double cross, passion cross
29 papal or pontifical cross, Roman cross, Western triple cross
30 triple cross
31 inverted cross, reversed cross, St Peter's cross
32 Calvary cross, cross of Calvary
33 Calvary cross, graded cross, holy cross
34 cross of the evangelists, four stepped Calvary cross
35 cross of St James, cross of Santiago, cruz espada

1
2
3
4
5
6
7
8
9
10
11
12
13
14
15
16
17
18
19
20
21
22
23
24
25
26
27
28
29
30
31
32
33
34
35

118 HERALDIC AND OTHER CROSSES

A stone cross, high cross, Celtic cross

A) Penally, Dyfed, Wales; 10th century

1 Greek cross, crux quadrata
2 cross couped, cross humetty
3 cross formée, cross formé, cross formy
4 Maltese cross, cross Maltese, cross of promise
5 cross patonce, cross griffee-de-loup
6 cross patée, cross paty, Mantuan cross
7 cross cotised, Iron cross
8 cross vidée, cross clechée
9 cross cramponée or barby, barbed cross
10 cross annuletty, annuletted cross
11 pierced cross
12 restoration cross
13 cross quadrate, cross nowy quadrate
14 crosslet cross quadrate, crossed square
15 cross avellane, Avillan cross
16 key cross, cross of Pisa
17 cross fimbriated, voided cross
18 cross of Toulouse
19 gammadion, gamma cross, crux gammata
20 hollow Greek cross
21 rose cross, Rosicrucian cross, rosy cross
22 St Bridget's cross, St Brigit's cross
23 Jerusalem cross, crusaders' cross, fivefold cross, cross of Palestine
24 saltire, St Andrew's cross, crux decussata, oblique cross
25 cross of St Julian, cross crosslet saltire
26 Coptic cross, Golgotha cross
27 consecration cross
28 cross wheel, wheel cross, sun cross, solar Cross, sun-wheel, Odin's cross, Woden's cross
29 St Bridget's cross, St Brigit's cross, St Bride's cross
30 cross invected, invected cross
31 cross engrailed, engrailed cross
32 cross indented, indented cross
33 cross raguly
34 cross of Burgundy, saltire raguly
35 Lutheran cross
36 Roman holy cross
37 fylfot, crux gammata, gammadion, swastika, tetraskelion
38 St Philip's cross
39 cross of suffering, broken cross, chevron cross, angled cross
40 four-pointed star, stellated cross, crux stellata
41 Bowen cross, cross of infinity, knotwork cross

cross
an ancient symbolic figure consisting of two bars which cross each other, often at right angles; it appears as a religious motif and ornament in many different forms

Greek cross, crux quadrata (Lat.), quadratic cross
a cross with four perpendicular limbs of equal length

formy, formée, paty, pattée
denoting a cross whose limbs are wedge shaped, getting wider towards their extremities

raguly
a cross whose limbs are ragged as if of sawn-off branches

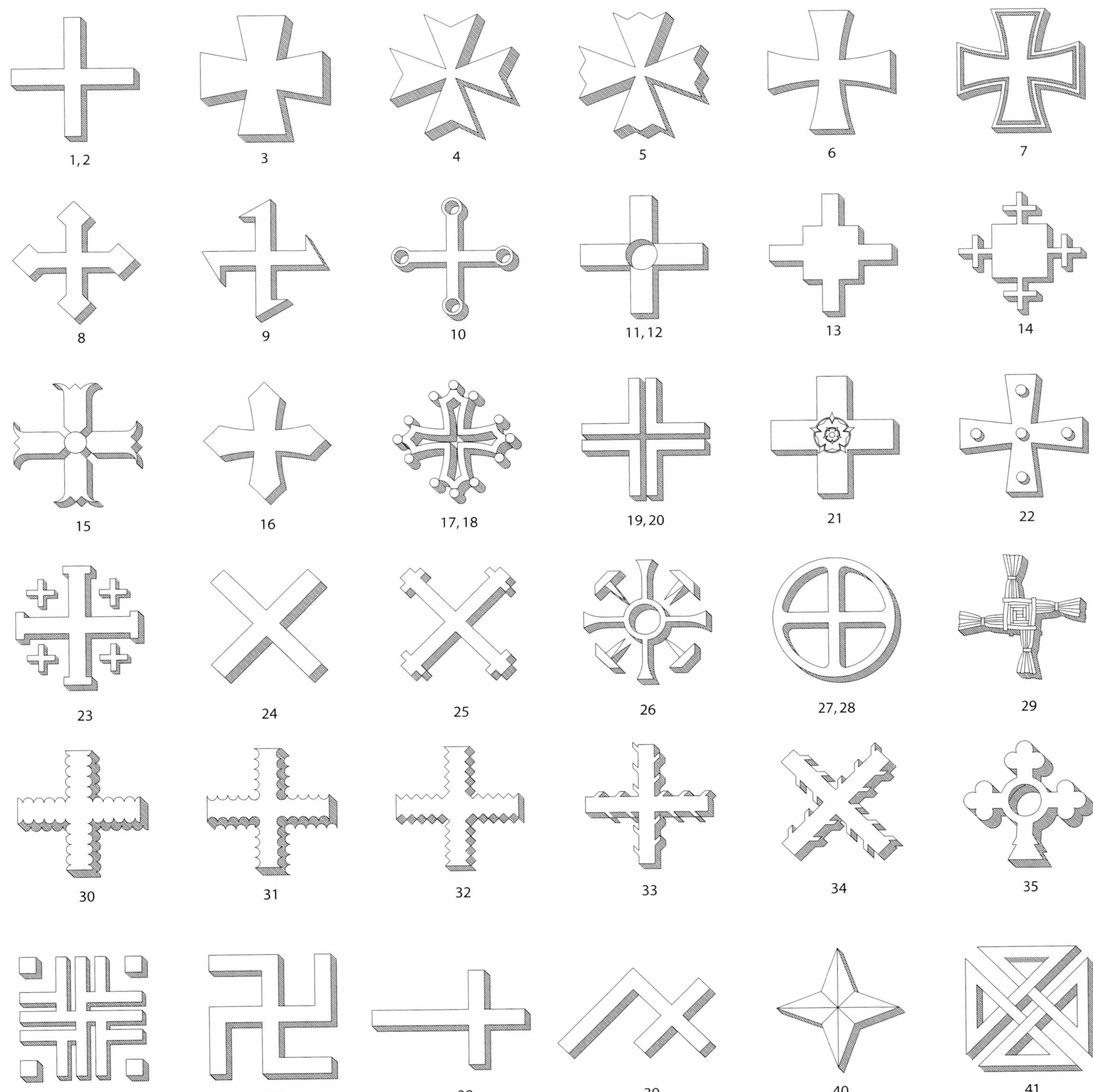
1, 2
3
4
5
6
7
8
9
10
11, 12
13
14
15
16
17, 18
19, 20
21
22
23
24
25
26
27, 28
29
30
31
32
33
34
35
36
37
38
39
40
41

119 CHRISTIAN SYMBOLS

A

B

C

MANDORLA, MYSTIC ALMOND

A mandorla, mystic almond, fish bladder, vesica piscis

B radiant mandorla, aureole, rays inwards

C radiant mandorla, aureole, rays upwards

Christian antiquity

referring to art and decoration from the early centuries of the Christian church that bears classical influences

mandorla, mystic almond

in Early Christian art, an oval halo given to depictions of Christ, the Virgin Mary and others in images of the crucifixion

aureole, glory, halo, nimbus

in painting and religious symbolism, light or radiance which surrounds a saint or sacred person; when limited to the head, it is called a nimbus, when surrounding the whole body, an aureole

monogram

a device, image or logo of intertwined letters, often initials; the stylized symbol of a person, event or word

1–5 trinity, Holy Trinity (trinitas)

5 triskelion, triskele

6 crown-of-thorns, thorny crown

7 eye of God, all-seeing eye

8 hand of God

9 alpha and omega, beginning and end

10 alpha and omega, crosses

11 labarum, flag of victory

12 Christ monogram, monogram of Christ, Christogram, Chi-Rho monogram, Chrismon

13 Constantine's cross, crux invicta, invincible cross

14 monogram of Jesus, ikthys, ichthus

15 fish, pisces

16 fish and anchor

17 anchor

18 dolphin

19 lamb, Agnus Dei

20 dove, Holy Spirit, Holy Ghost

21 phoenix

22 pelican

23 angel (St Matthew)

24 lion (St Mark)

25 ox, bull (St Luke)

26 eagle (St John)

HALO (aureole, glory, nimbus)

27 triradiant halo

28 circular halo

29 disc halo

30 radiant halo

31 square halo (living person)

32 triangular halo

1
2
3
4
5
6
7
8
9
10
12
13
11
14
15
16
17
18
19
20
21
22
23
24
25
26
27
28
29
30
31
32

A

B

C

A mandala, acroterium
B yantra, mandala
C cosmogram, mandala

symbol
a sign, mark or image whose purpose is to signify, represent or have associations with some ideal, message, institution etc.

ornament
two or three-dimensional decoration, sculpture, carving etc. for the surfaces or spaces of a building or other object

caduceus, staff of Hermes, staff of Mercury
a short rod entwined by two snakes and topped by a pair of wings, the magic wand of the Greek god Hermes, Roman Mercury, messenger of the gods; called a kerykeion in Greek

thyrsus
Lat.; architectural ornament depicting a staff tipped with a pine cone ornament and twined with ivy, as carried by the Roman god of wine, Bacchus (Dionysus in Greece), revellers and satyrs; thyrsos in Greek

arabesque
intricate decoration based on Moorish and Arabic antecedents, combining a complexity of flowing lines with geometrical and symmetrical patterns

Moresque
stylized Spanish Islamic and Moorish geometrical and foliated surface ornament and decorative art

1 Aaron's rod
2 herald's staff
3 kerykeion, rod of Hermes
4 caduceus, rod of Mercury
5 thursos, Dionysian staff
6 thyrsus, staff of Bacchus
7 thunderbolt
8 arrow of Jupiter, arrow of Zeus
9 trident
10 Neptune's trident, Poseidon's trident
11 staff of Aesculapius, serpent staff
12 sun
13 moon
14 crescent
15 increscent, increasing moon, waxing moon
16 star and crescent
17 decrescent, decreasing moon, waning moon
18 star of Ishtar, Venus star
19 Egyptian feather
20 Arabian feather
21 tarantula
22 hand of Fatima, khamsa, xomsa
23 Moresque (Alhambra)
24 arabesque
25 herati (Persian)
26 linga, lingam
27 yoni
28 torii
29 dharma chakra, wheel of law, dharma wheel
30 Japanese mon/cranes
31 omphalos, ovum mundi, Great Monad
32 tomoye
33 Buddha's navel
34 yin-yang, tai-chi, tai-qi
35 ovum mundi
36 Great Monad
37 cicada

1
2, 3, 4
5, 6
7, 8
7, 8
9, 10
11
12
13, 14, 15
16, 17
18
19
20
21
22
23, 24
25
26
27
28
29
30, 31
32, 33
34, 35, 36
37

121 PLANT AND LEAF DECORATIONS

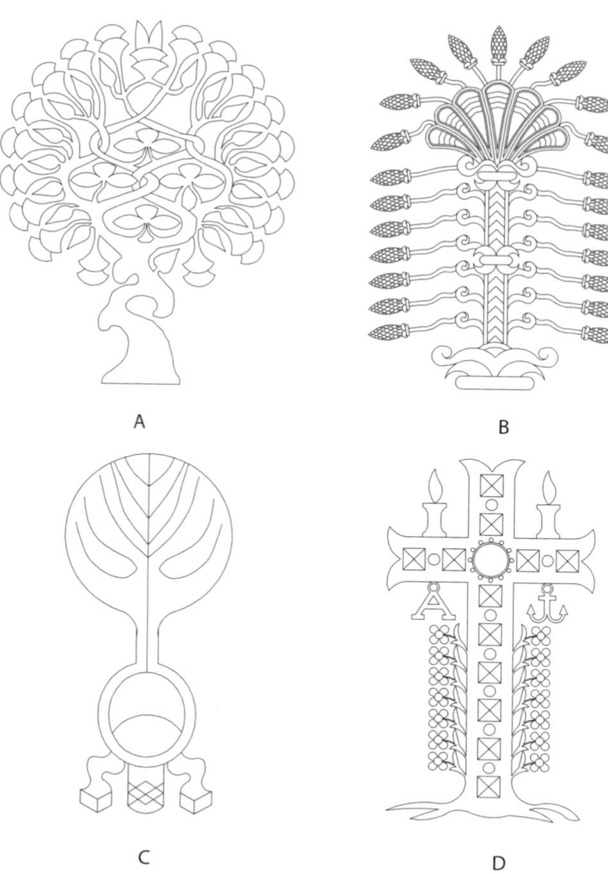

TREE OF LIFE

A Chinese tree of life
B Mesopotamian tree of life, hom
C tree of Buddha, bodhi tree, heaven's throne
D crux gemmata, Christian tree of life

tree of life
a symbolic figure appearing in many different forms in ornament and art, often a Y-shaped motif with an extra vertical limb, or an abstracted depiction of a real tree

palmette
a decorative motif found in the architecture of antiquity, consisting of a stylized fan-shaped palm leaf

lotus, lily
forms of flowering lily [*Nymphaea lotus* (white lotus), *Nymphaea caerulea* (blue lotus), *Nelumbo nucifera* etc.] sacred in ancient Egyptian, Buddhist and Hindu culture; the blue water lily (*Nymphaea caerulea*) was the heraldic plant of Upper Egypt (Nile Valley)

fleuron
decoration consisting of a carved flower or leaf motif

cloverleaf
a decorative motif derived from the leaves of some plant species of the pea family which have three lobes, *Trifolium spp*., symbolic of the Holy Trinity

shamrock
a decorative motif derived from the three-lobed leaf of various plants, principally that of the wood sorrel, *Oxalis acetosella*, but also white clover, *Trifolium repens* and black medic, *Medicago lupulina*; the symbol of St Patrick of Ireland

1 southern flower, bindweed (Upper Egypt)
2 southern flower, lotus (Upper Egypt)
3 southern flower, papyrus (Lower Egypt)
4 blue lotus
5 white lotus
6 sacred lotus
7 fleuron
8 fleuron
9 acanthus (Greek)
10 acanthus (Roman)
11 tablet flower, patera
12 patera, phiala
13 palmette (archaic, Greek)
14 palmette (early Classical, Greek)
15 palmette (Classical, Greek)
16 medusa palmette, gorgon palmette (Etruscan)
17 horn of plenty, cornucopia
18 pomegranate
19 lily (Greek, c.1500 BC)
20 lily
21 fleur-de-lis, French lily
22 heart-palmette, palmette heart
23 laurel wreath, wreath of triumph, victor's wreath
24 funeral wreath
25 Tudor rose
26 Tudor flower
27 Tudor flower
28 cloverleaf, shamrock
29 feston, festoon, encarpus, swag
30 pine cone, pineapple
31 acorn

1
2
3
4
5
6
7
8
9
10
11
12
13
14
15
16
17
18
19
20
21
22
23
24
25
26
27
28
29
30, 31

122 MYTHOLOGICAL ORNAMENTS

A trophy

1 crown (king's)
2 tiara
3 mitre
4 helmet (Greek)
5 great helmet, pot helmet, barrel helmet
6 tournament helmet
7 griffin
8 dragon
9 basilisk, cockatrice
10 sea lion
11 chimaira, chimera
12 centaur
13 unicorn
14 satyr, silenos, faun
15 double eagle, double-headed eagle
16 addorsed figure
17 octopus
18 fasces
19 labrys (Late Minoan), double axe, double headed axe
20 tondo, roundel
21 cupido, amoretto, amorino
22 gorgon
23 foliate head, green man
24 mask, mascaron
25 grotesque, grottesco
26 auricular ornament, lobate ornament
27 strapwork
28 bucrane
29 beakhead, beak moulding, bird's beak moulding
30 cat's head, catshead
31 bird's head moulding
32 dogtooth, tooth ornament
33 Catherine wheel, spiked wheel

gorgon

Gk.; an ornamental motif of a horrifying mythological female figure such as Medusa, with snakes for hair and grotesque teeth, whose gaze was reputed to turn an onlooker into stone

fasces

Lat.; a Roman emblem of magistrates' power and unity, characterized by a bundle of rods tied together with an axe, a common motif in Roman decoration

auricular ornament, lobate ornament

decorative ornament, foliage and volutes, resembling parts of the human ear, found in early Baroque architecture in northern Europe in the late 1500s and early 1600s

addorsed

a description of ornament or sculptured figures standing or situated back to back

affronted

a description of ornament or sculptured figures depicted facing towards the front or situated face to face

1
2
3
4
5
6
7
8
9
10
11
12
13
14
15, 16
17
18
19
20
21
22
23
24
25, 26
27
28
29
30
31
32
33

123 GENERAL ORNAMENTS

Cosmati work (Italy, 13th century)

Cosmati work

geometrical mosaic work in coloured marble, glass and stone, usually religious work for choir screens, pulpits, floors and walls, originating with a group of architects, sculptors and decorative artists who worked in the same style in marble and mosaic in the 1100s–1300s in Rome and Naples

ornamental motif, decorative motif

a design, pattern, sculpture, symbol etc. used as surface decoration for the surface of a building or other object; often with specific meaning, message or symbolic value

menorah

a Jewish candelabrum with seven branches, a symbol of divine wisdom representative of the seven days of creation, the sun, moon and planets and the seven stars of Ursa Major; also a candelabrum with nine branches, called a chanukiah

mullet

a heraldic star with five, six or eight points, also called a molet

1 Gordian knot
2 St Han's knot, Bowen's knot, true-lovers' knot, tristram
3 orb
4 dragon's eye
5 nine-branched candelabrum, menorah, chanukiah
6 seven-branched candelabrum, menorah
7 linenfold, linen scroll, drapery
8 cartouche
9 scroll ornament
10 ball and flower, ballflower
11 ball and flower, ballflower
12 Atlantis cross
13 three fish (pisces, ichthus)
14 three fish (pisces, ichthus)
15 labyrinth, road of Jerusalem
16 Cretan maze, classical maze, stone labyrinth, Troytown, Jericho
17 lyre
18 fer de moline, millrind
19 tondo
20 putto
21 scallop, scallop shell
22 conch, conch shell
23 cradle
24 banderole, bannerol
25 batswing, fan arch
26 escarbuncle
27 rose whorl
28 estoile, star
29 five-pointed star
30 mullet, molet
31 spur rowel, spur revel, pierced mullet
32 mullet of eight points voided

1
2
3
4
5
6
7
8
9
10
11
12
13
14
15
16
17
18
19
20
21
22
23
BANDEROLE
24
25
26
27
28
29, 30
30, 31
32

124 MOULDINGS WITH REPEATED MOTIFS, COAT OF ARMS

PARTS OF A PERFECT COAT OF ARMS

A crest
B wreath, torse
C helmet, helm
D dexter mantle, dexter mantling
E sinister mantle, sinister mantling
F medallion
G dexter supporter
H sinister supporter
K motto

SECTIONS OF A SHIELD

L honour point
M fess point, abyss, couer, heart point
N nombril, navel point
O dexter chief
P canton
Q sinister chief
R sinister canton
S dexter base
T sinister base
O–R chief
O–S dexter side
S–T base
Q–T sinister side

REPETITIVE MOULDINGS

1 dentils, dentil moulding
2 dovetail moulding, dovetail ornament
3 chevron moulding
4 indented moulding, dancetty, zigzag
5 rayonnée, rayonny moulding
6 rayonnée
7 billet moulding, square billet
8 Venetian dentils
9 Venetian dentils
10 wave moulding, undulating moulding,
11–12 nebuly, nebulé moulding, nebulé
13 nebuly, nebulé moulding, nebulé
14 chevron moulding
15 diamond fret, lozenge fret, lozenge moulding
16 scallop moulding, invected moulding
17 engrailed moulding
18 corbel table
19 interlacing arches, interlaced arches, laced arches
20 pellet moulding
21 nailhead, nailhead moulding
22 gadroon, godroon, knulled ornament, lobe ornament, nulled ornament, thumb moulding
23 calves'-tongue moulding, calf's-tongue moulding
24 double cone moulding
25 beaded moulding, bead moulding, pearl moulding, paternoster
26 bead and reel, reel and bead
27 bead and reel, reel and bead
28 dogtoothed ornament, houndstooth ornament, mousetooth ornament
29 crenellated moulding, embattled moulding
30 round billet

coat of arms
the official graphical emblem of a society, institution, family, district or company, usually a heraldic shield with various motifs

bead and reel, reel and bead
a decorative moulding consisting of a series of small round beads, elongated hemispheres or half-cylinders alternating with pairs of flattened discs

dexter
in heraldry, the part of a shield to the right of the wearer or bearer; to the left as viewed by the spectator

sinister
in heraldry, the part of a shield to the left of the wearer or bearer; to the right as viewed by the spectator

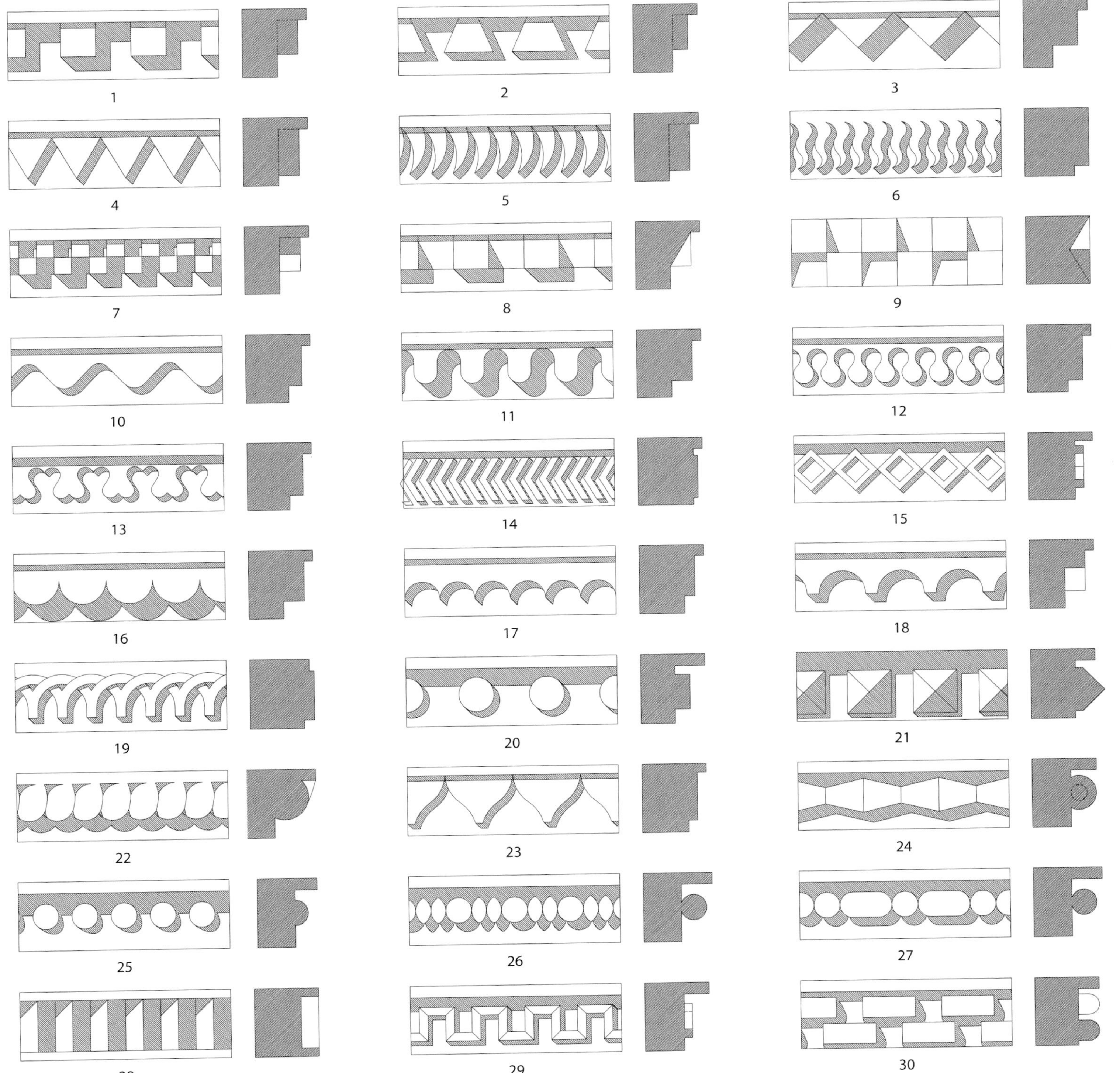
1
2
3
4
5
6
7
8
9
10
11
12
13
14
15
16
17
18
19
20
21
22
23
24
25
26
27
28
29
30

125 CONTINUOUS MOULDINGS AND HONORARY ORDINARIES

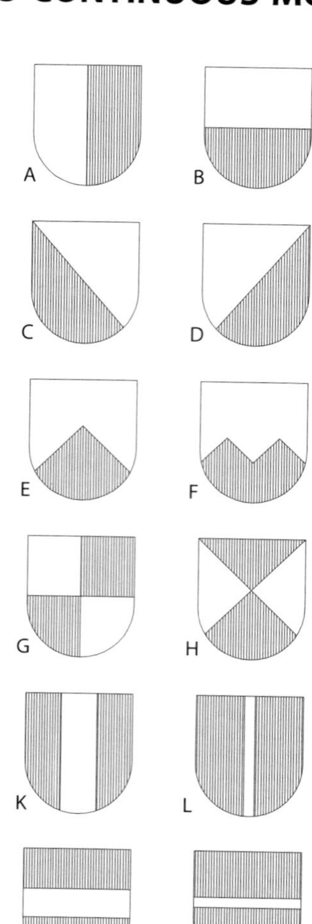

HERALDIC PARTITIONS

A parted per pale,
party per pale, per pale

B parted per fess,
party per fess, per fess

C parted per bend,
part per bend, per bend

D parted per bend sinister,
per bend sinister

E parted per chevron,
per chevron

F parted per fess dancetté,
per fess dancetté

G quarterly parted

H parted per saltire

HONORARY ORDINARIES

K pale

L pallet

M fesse, fess

N bar

O bend

P bend sinister

R bendlet

S bendlet sinister

heraldry
the study of historical coats of arms or shields

fret
banded running ornament of lines or fillets linked or interlinked to form a continuous motif; often called a key pattern, which always has orthogonal geometry

key pattern
classical banded running ornamentation made up of horizontal and vertical lines or fillets which interlink to form a geometrical pattern; often synonymous with fret

meander, labyrinth fret
a decorative pattern of intertwining perpendicular lines forming a band; a complex or intricate fret or key pattern, sometimes called an angular guilloche

MOULDINGS AND PARTITION LINES

1 crenellated moulding,
embattled moulding,
crenellation,
castellated moulding

2 indented embattled moulding

3, 4 fret, key pattern,
fretwork, running dog

5, 6 meander, potenty moulding

7 meander, labyrinth fret,
angular guilloche,
Greek key, running dog

8 continuous coil spiral, running dog
oundy or undy moulding
swelled chamfer

9 Vitruvian scroll, Vitruvian wave,
running dog

10 urdy moulding, vair moulding

11 urdy moulding, vallary moulding,
palisade moulding

12 urdy moulding, tower

13 raguly moulding

14 cable moulding, cabling, rope moulding

15 twining stem moulding

16 strigil moulding

17 fibula moulding

18 fibula moulding

19 cross moulding

20 fir twig moulding

21 fir tree moulding

22 fleury moulding

23 trefoil moulding, cloverleaf moulding

24 foil moulding, leaf moulding

25 grady embattled grady line,
battled embattled line

26 guilloche

27 interlace, entrelace, knotwork

28 ‘fingernail’ moulding

29 barbed moulding

30 chain moulding, chain

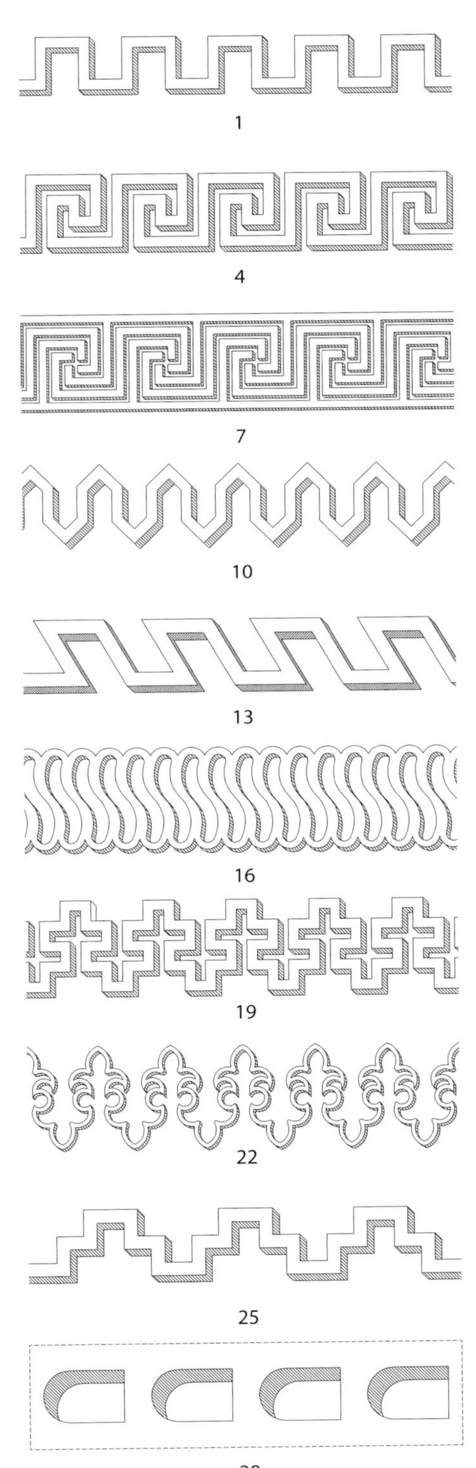
1
4
7
10
13
16
19
22
25
28

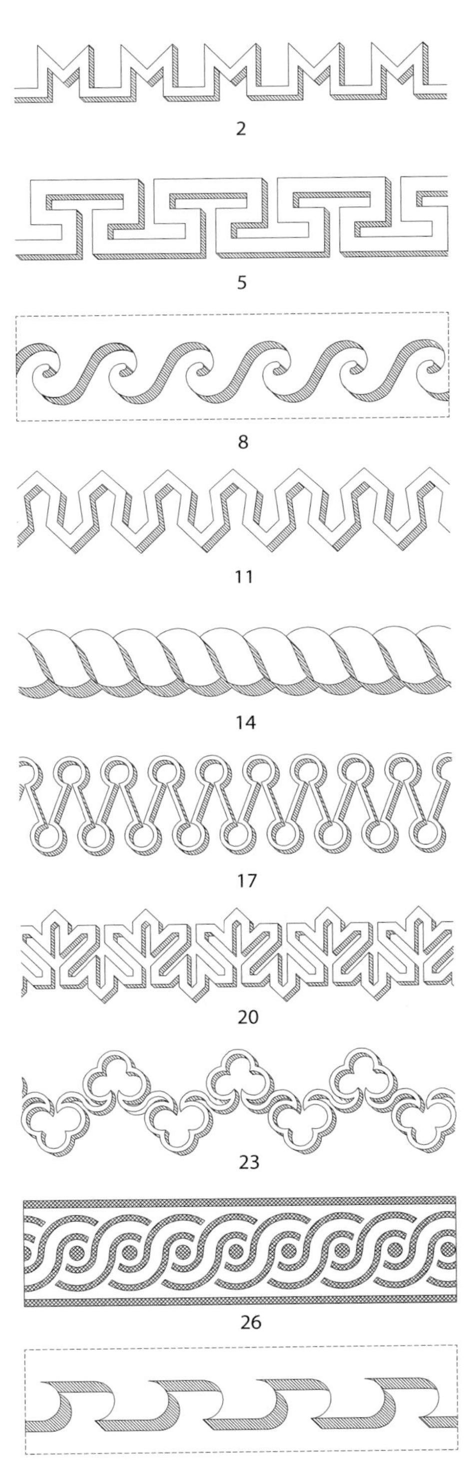
2
5
8
11
14
17
20
23
26
29

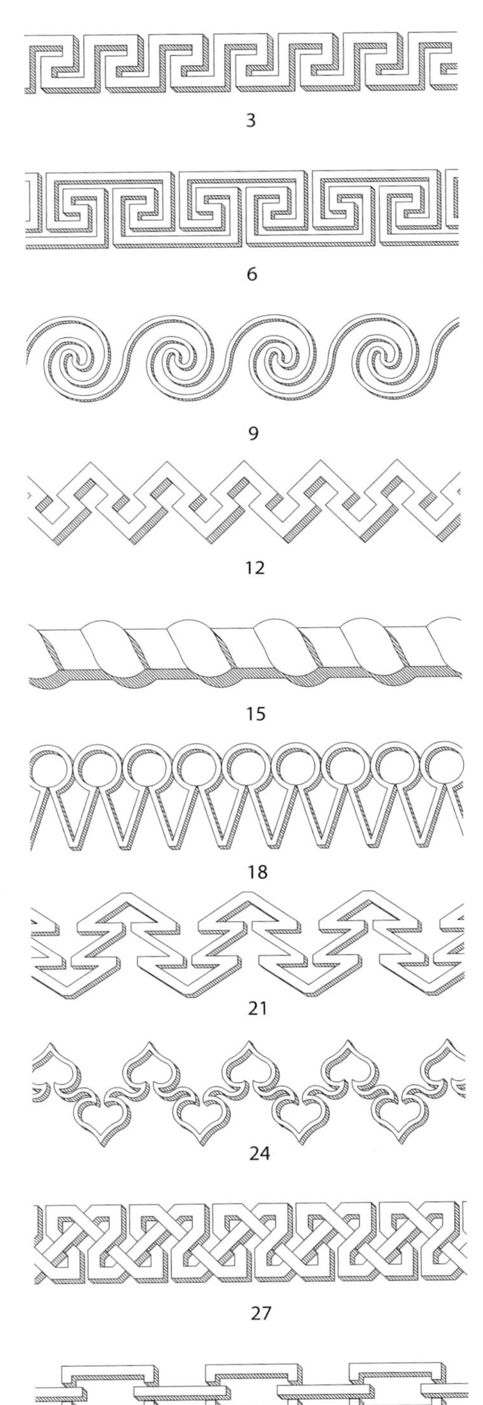
3
6
9
12
15
18
21
24
27
30

126 POMPEIAN STYLES

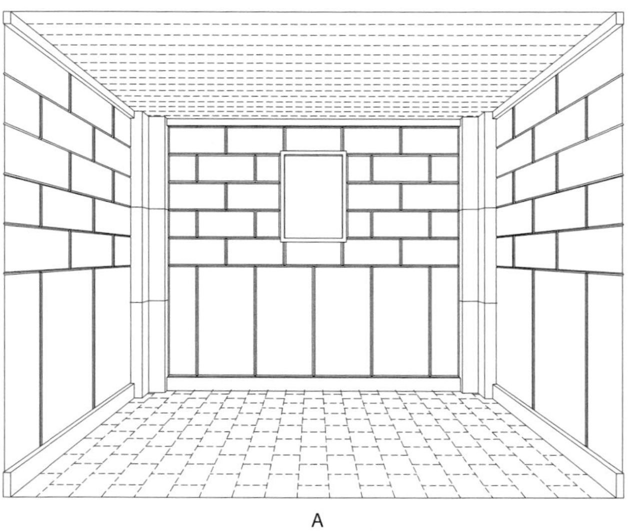

A

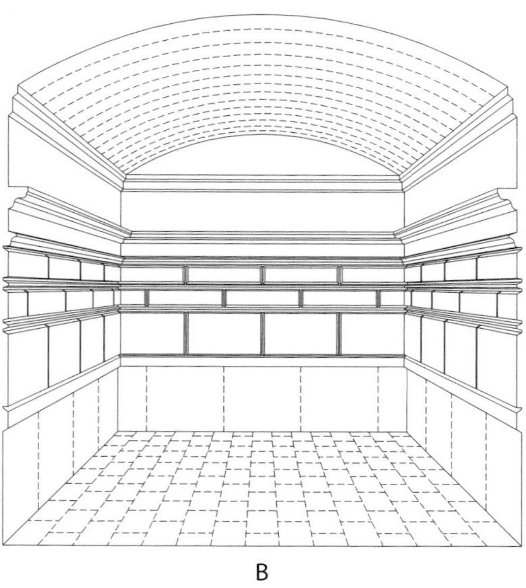

B

A Greek pattern
B Italian pattern, Roman pattern
C cornice
D dentilation, dentil frieze
E frieze
F bead moulding
G band course, string course
H isodomic course
K orthostat
L socle, dado

1 First Pompeian style, Incrustation style, Masonry style
2 opus quadratum
3 Second Pompeian style, Architectural style
4 Third Pompeian style, Ornamental style, Closed style
5 Fourth Pompeian style, Eclectic style, Fantastic style

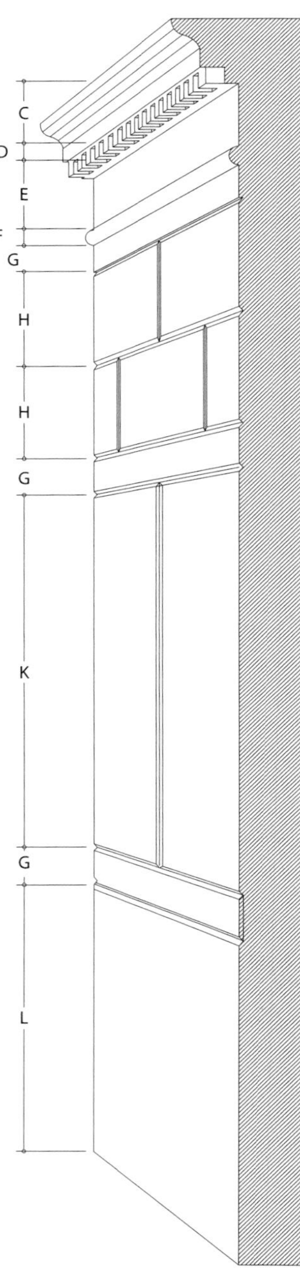

Pompeian style

forms of wall-painting and interior decoration typical of dwelling houses in Roman Pompeii from 200 BC to 100 AD; see also Incrustation, Architectural, Ornamental and Fantastic styles

fresco

mural painting in mineral or earth pigments applied to lime or gypsum plaster while it is still wet; otherwise known as buon fresco

fresco secco

decorating painting on dry plaster or subsequent touching up for true fresco, undertaken once the plaster surface has dried; also known as dry fresco or secco

A) Maison du trident – House of Trident. c.200BC, Delos; B) Casa Sannitica – Samnite house, c.200 BC, Herculaneum; C–L) Casa di M. Fabius Rufus – house of M. Fabius Rufus, Pompeii; 1, 2) Casa Sannitica – Samnite house, c.200 BC, Herculaneum; 3) Casa di Augusto – House of Augustus. c.30 BC, Rome; 4) Casa di M. Lucretius Fronto – House of M. Lucretius Fronto, AD 40–50, Pompeii; 5) Villa Negroni, 134 AD, Rome

1 & 2

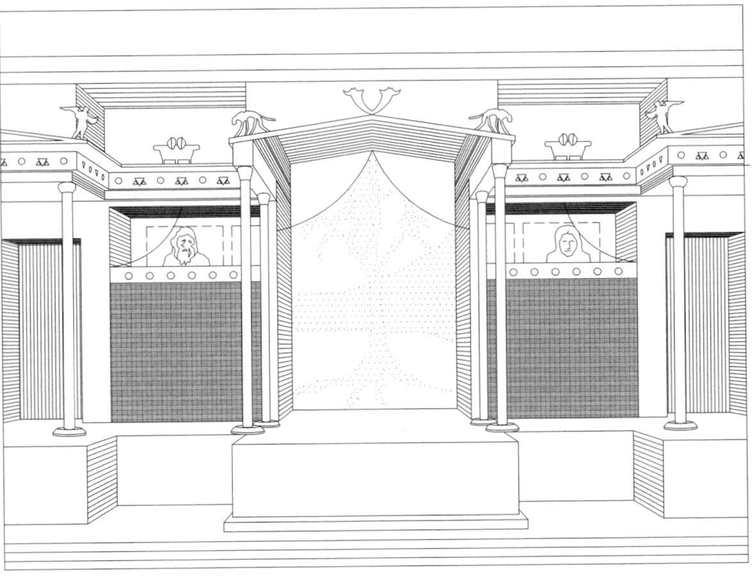

3

4

5

127 AXONOMETRY, PARALLEL PROJECTIONS

FIRST ANGLE PROJECTIONS, FIRST QUADRANT PROJECTIONS

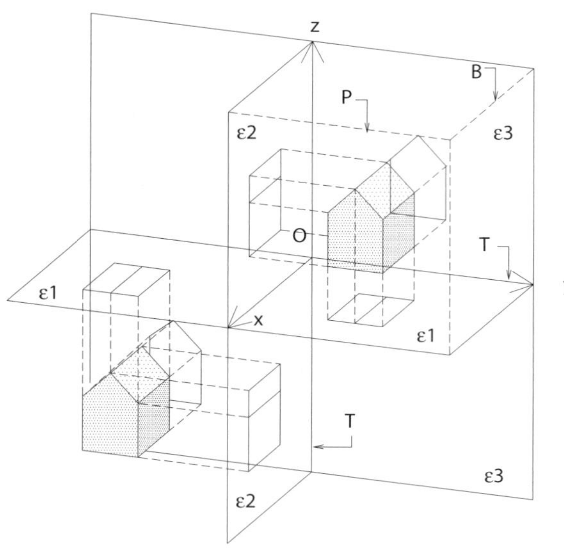

THIRD ANGLE PROJECTIONS, THIRD QUADRANT PROJECTIONS

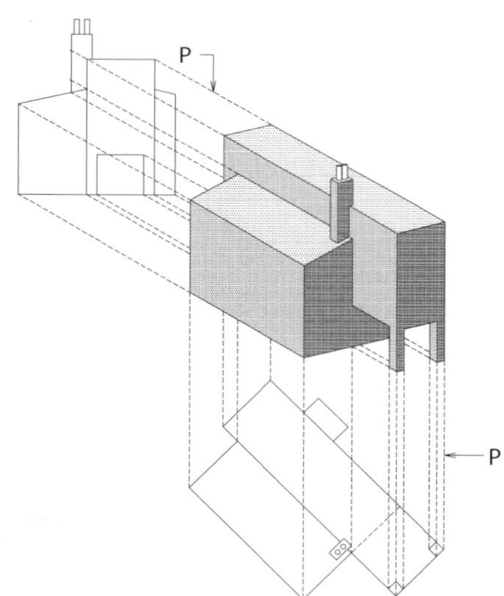

METHOD OF INTERSECTIONS, SCHMID-ECKHART METHOD

SPATIAL OR THREE-DIMENSIONAL COORDINATES

x, y, z coordinate system, system of coordinates

B coordinate cube, axonometric cube

O origin

P projector, projection line, sight line

T trace

COORDINATE PLANES

ε1 ground plane (horizontal plane)

ε2 front plane (vertical plane)

ε3 side plane, profile plane (vertical plane)

COORDINATE AXES

x x-axis, abscissa

y y-axis, ordinate

z z-axis, vertical axis

PARALLEL PROJECTIONS, ORTHOGRAPHIC PROJECTIONS

TRUE PROJECTIONS

1 top view, plan view

2 front view

3 side view, profile view, end view

AXONOMETRIC, ORTHOGRAPHIC PROJECTIONS

4 isometric projection

5 dimetric projection

6 trimetric projection

OBLIQUE PROJECTIONS

7 cabinet projection (dimetric oblique projection)

8 cavalier projection (isometric oblique projection)

9 military projection planometric projection

axonometry, parallel projection

a method of drawing in which the object is pictured in three dimensions such that all lines in each of the three major axes are parallel; especially pertaining to isometric, dimetric and trimetric projections, though usually used for all parallel projections depicting three dimensions on a flat plane

projection

the technical drawing of three-dimensional objects on a two-dimensional plane by extending imaginary lines, called projectors from a point or from infinity through the object to be visualized onto the plane

first angle projection

a standard draughtsman's method of arranging the six planar orthographic projection drawings of main views of a building or object in relation to one another, as if unfolding the hinged sides of an imaginary cube onto which the projections have been made; also called a first quadrant projection, it is widely favoured in Great Britain; third angle projections are arranged differently and are the norm in North America

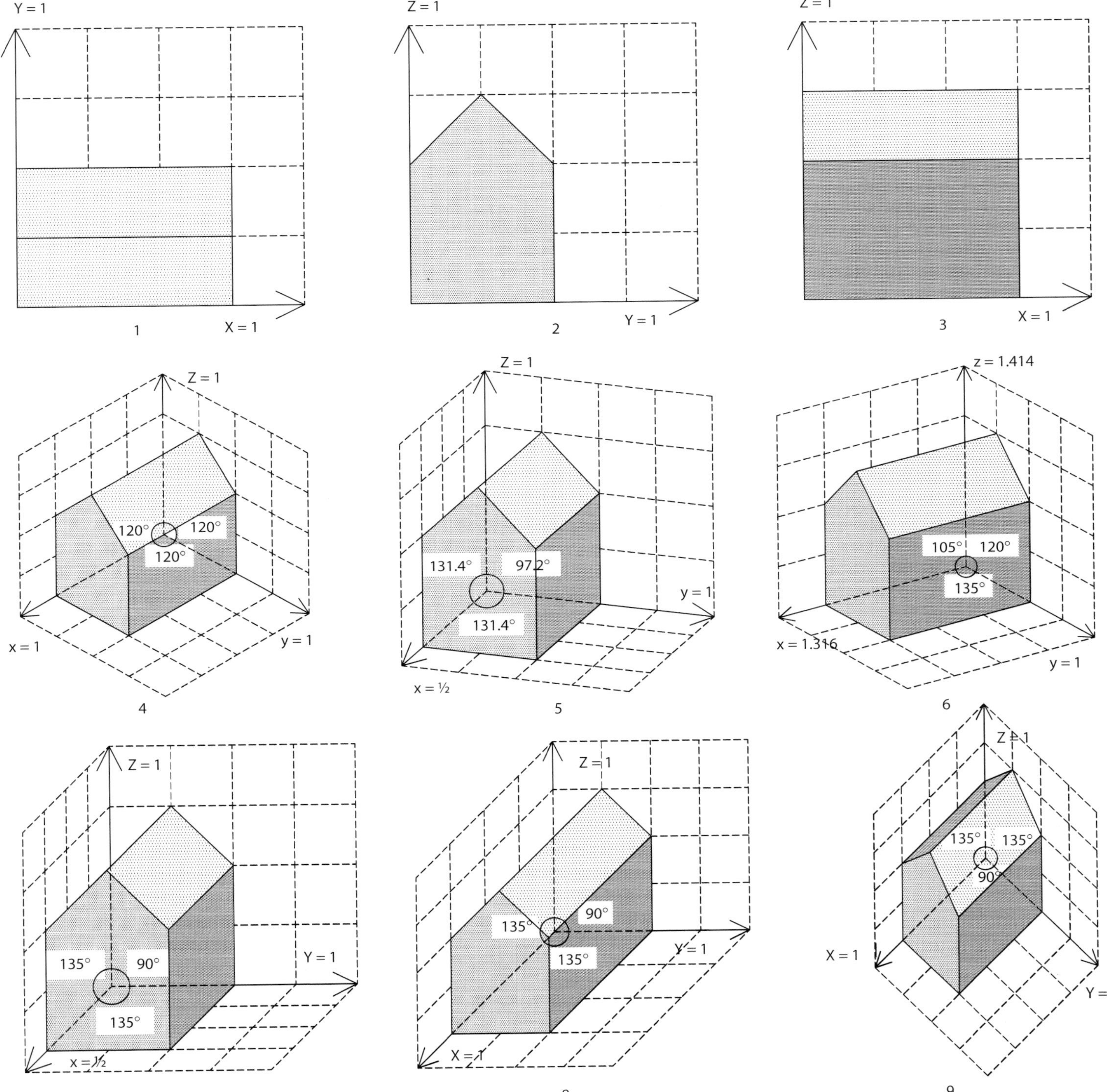
Y = 1
X = 1
1
Z = 1
Y = 1
2
Z = 1
X = 1
3
Z = 1
120°
120°
120°
x = 1
y = 1
4
Z = 1
131.4°
97.2°
131.4°
y = 1
x = ½
5
z = 1.414
105°
120°
135°
x = 1.316
y = 1
6
Z = 1
135°
90°
135°
Y = 1
x = ½
7
Z = 1
135°
90°
135°
Y = 1
X = 1
8
Z = 1
135°
135°
90°
X = 1
Y = 1
9

128 PERSPECTIVE PROJECTION, PARALLEL PERSPECTIVE

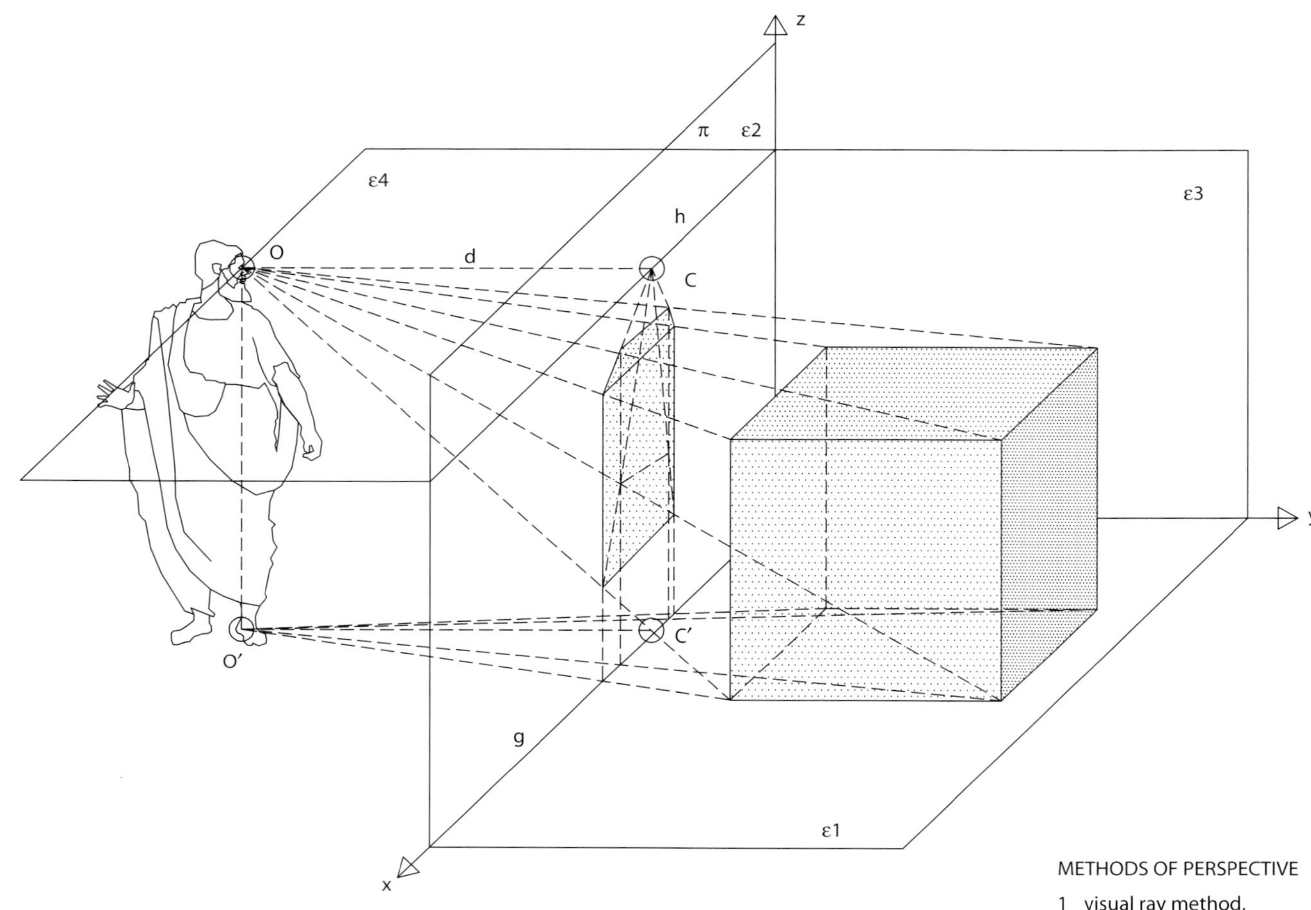

METHODS OF PERSPECTIVE

1 visual ray method, direct plan method
2 grid projection method
3 perspective plan method
4 method of diagonals

PRINCIPLES OF PERSPECTIVE

ε1 ground plane (horizontal plane)
ε2 front plane (vertical plane)
ε3 side plane, profile plane (vertical plane)
ε4 horizon plane (horizontal plane)
π picture plane, projection plane (vertical plane)
C centre of vision (projection of station point on picture plane,
C′ projection of centre of vision on ground plane
d distance (OC)
D distance point
F vanishing point
g ground line
h horizon line
M measuring point
O station point, viewpoint, eye point, centre of projection
OC central axis of vision
O′ projection of station point on ground plane

perspective
1 the optic phenomenon in which objects in the distance are perceived as smaller than objects in the foreground
2 a technique for rendering three-dimensional objects in a realistic way on a flat surface using converging projectors; sometimes called linear perspective to distinguish it from other forms of perspective rendering

one-point perspective
a method of perspective drawing using only one vanishing point, producing a view in which verticals are seen as vertical and horizontals parallel to the picture plane seen as horizontal; also known as central, Renaissance or parallel perspective

vanishing point
in perspective drawing, one of the points at which lines converge, constructed as if at infinity

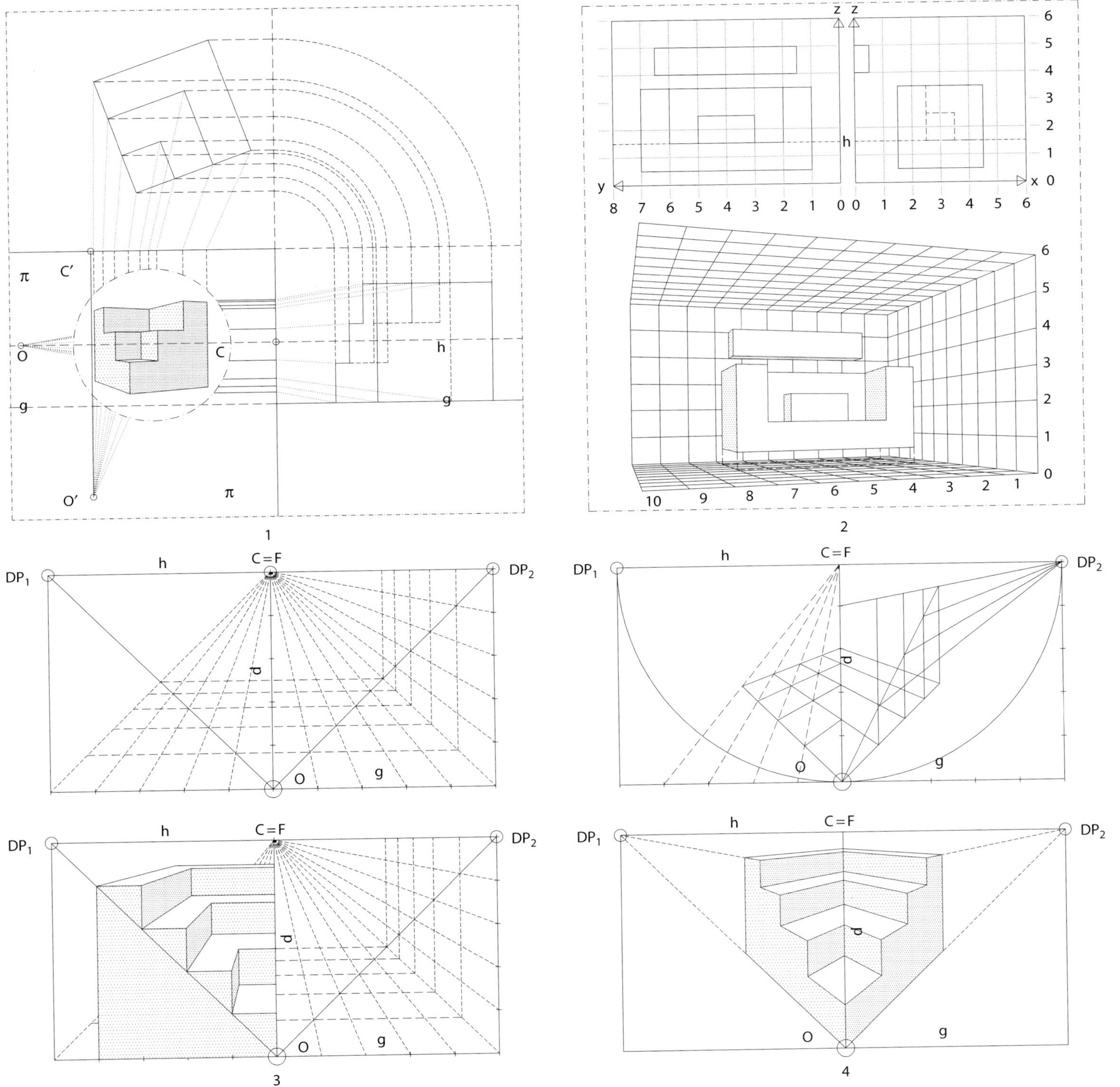
π
C′
O
C
h
g
O′
π
z z
6 5 4 3 2 1 0
h
y
x
8 7 6 5 4 3 2 1 0 0 1 2 3 4 5 6
10 9 8 7 6 5 4 3 2 1
DP1
h
C = F
DP2
d
O
g

1 2 3 4

129 TWO AND THREE-POINT PERSPECTIVES

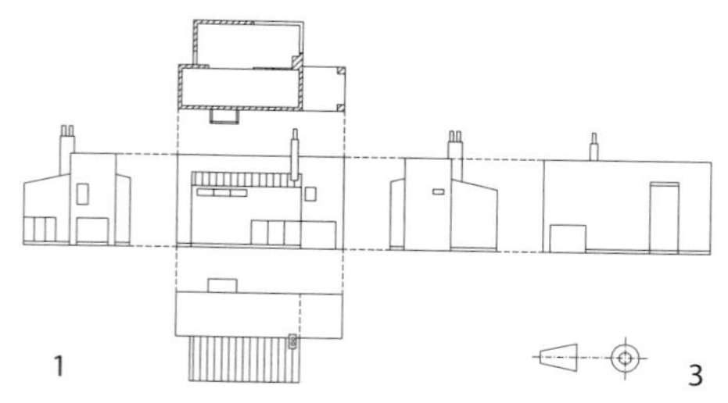

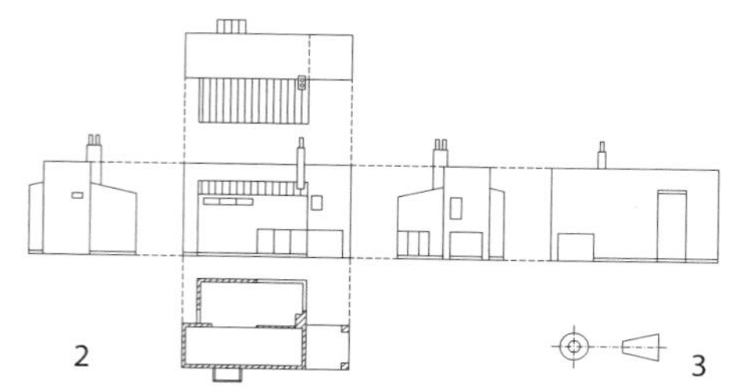

MULTIVIEW PROJECTIONS,
MULTIPLE-VIEW PROJECTIONS

1 first angle projection, first quadrant projection
2 third angle projection, third quadrant projection
3 identification of projection method

TYPES OF PERSPECTIVE

4 parallel perspective
5 bird's eye view – oblique perspective
6 worm's eye perspective – oblique perspective

CONSTRUCTION OF PERSPECTIVE DRAWING,
TWO-POINT PERSPECTIVE

7 common method, direct plan method
8 plan projection method
9 coordinate method

THREE-POINT PERSPECTIVE –
METHOD OF DIAGONALS

10a construction lines
10b measurement lines
10c bird's eye view

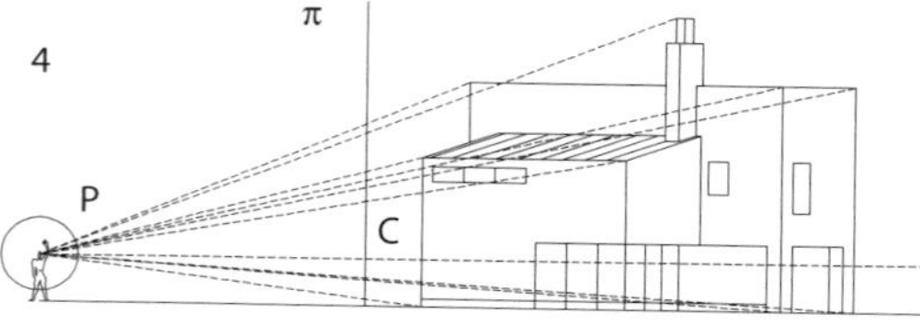

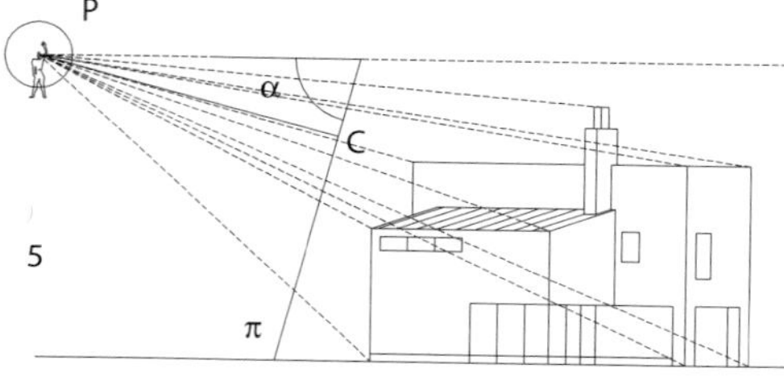

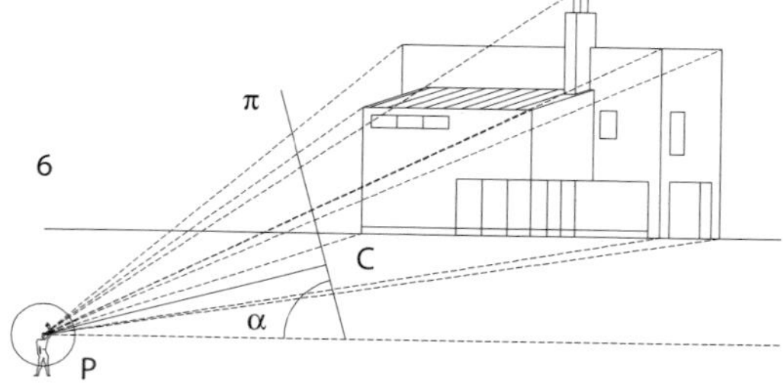

α angle of inclination
$\varepsilon 1$ ground plane
$\varepsilon 3$ side plane, profile plane
π picture plane
C centre of vision
d distance
DP distance point
F vanishing point
F′ projection of vanishing point on ground plane
g ground line
h horizon
O origin
P station point, viewpoint, eye point
P′ projection of station point on ground plane

two-point perspective

a perspective drawing constructed from two vanishing points, producing a view in which verticals are seen as vertical and lines on other axes seen as converging; also called angular perspective and, in Great Britain, sometimes called oblique perspective

three-point perspective

a perspective drawing constructed from three vanishing points, producing a view in which lines parallel to all three major axes are converging; sometimes also known as oblique perspective in North America

first angle projection

a standard draughtsman's method of arranging the six planar orthographic projection drawings of main views of a building or object in relation to one another, as if unfolding the hinged sides of an imaginary cube onto which the projections have been made; also called a first quadrant projection, it is widely favoured in Great Britain; a thrid angle projection, with views ordered differently, is favoured in North America

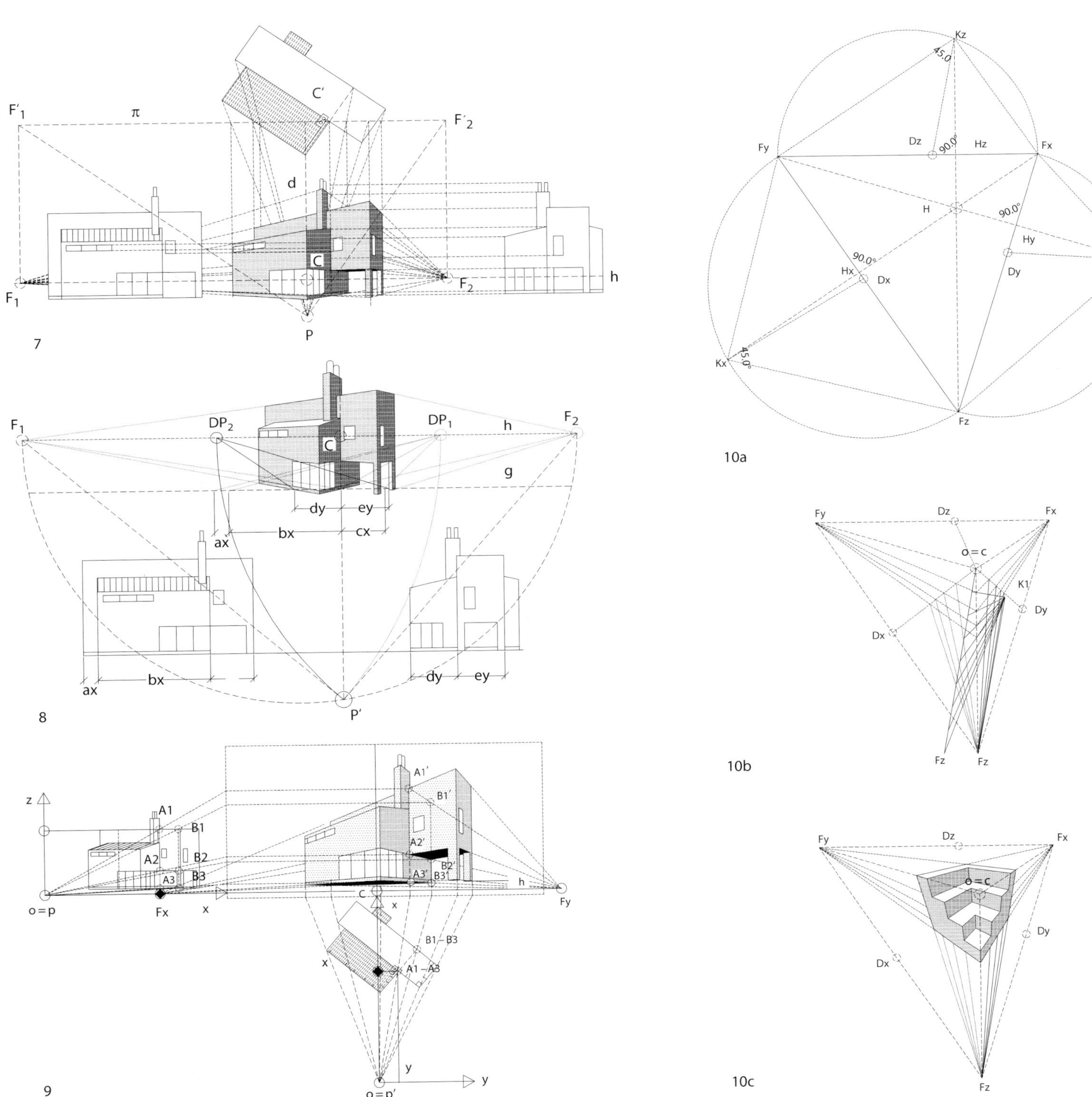

F'1
π
C'
F'2
d
C
F1
F2
h
P
7
F1
DP2
DP1
h
F2
C
g
dy
ey
ax
bx
cx
ax
bx
dy
ey
P'
8
z
A1
B1
A2
B2
A3
B3
o = p
Fx
x
A1'
B1'
A2'
A3'
B2'
B3'
h
C
Fy
x
B1 – B3
x
A1 – A3
y
y
o = p'
9
Kz
45.0
Fy
Dz
90.0°
Hz
Fx
H
90.0°
Hy
90.0°
Hx
Dx
Dy
45.0°
Kx
45.0°
Fz
10a
Fy
Dz
Fx
o = c
K1
Dy
Dx
Fz
Fz
10b
Fy
Dz
Fx
o = c
Dy
Dx
Fz
10c

130 DRAWING INSTRUMENTS AND TECHNICAL DRAWING

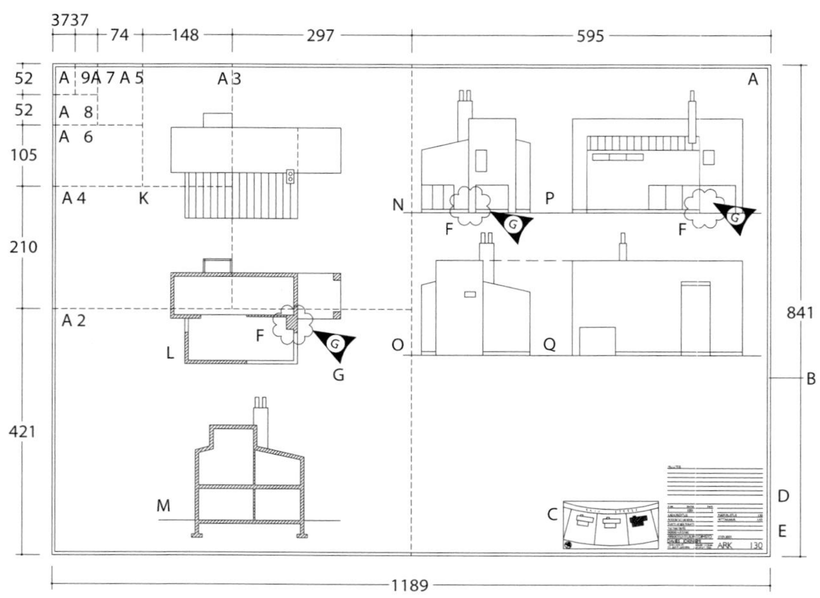

BUILDING PERMIT REVIEW PLAN

- A0 paper size 841 mm × 1189 mm
- B border
- C block plan
- D amendment block, revision panel
- E title block, title panel
- F revision cloud, amendment cloud
- G revision arrow, amendment arrow, arrowhead

PROJECTIONS

- K roof plan
- L plan
- M section
- N front elevation
- O rear elevation
- P court facade
- Q street facade

European paper sizes

A0	841 mm × 1189 mm
A1	595 mm × 841 mm
A2	421 mm × 595 mm
A3	297 mm × 421 mm
A4	210 mm × 297 mm
A5	148 mm × 210 mm
A6	105 mm × 148 mm
A7	74 mm × 105 mm
A8	52 mm × 74 mm
A9	37 mm × 52 mm
A10	26 mm × 37 mm

B0	1000 mm × 1414 mm
B1	707 mm × 1000 mm
B2	500 mm × 707 mm
B3	353 mm × 500 mm
B4	250 mm × 353 mm
B5	176 mm × 250 mm
B6	125 mm × 176 mm
B7	88 mm × 125 mm
B8	62 mm × 88 mm
B9	44 mm × 62 mm
B10	31 mm × 44 mm

C0	917 mm × 1297 mm
C1	648 mm × 917 mm
C2	458 mm × 648 mm
C3	324 mm × 458 mm
C4	229 mm × 324 mm
C5	162 mm × 229 mm
C6	114 mm × 162 mm
C7	81 mm × 114 mm
C8	57 mm × 81 mm
C9	40 mm × 57 mm
C10	28 mm × 40 mm

North American paper sizes

Letter	8,5" × 11"	(216 mm × 279 mm)
Legal	8,5" × 14"	(216 mm × 356 mm)
Executive	7,5" × 10"	(190 mm × 254 mm)
Ledger/Tabloid	11" × 17"	(279 mm × 432 mm)

DRAWING INSTRUMENTS

1. drawing board
2. T-square
3. parallel ruler
4. square, set square
5. adjustable set square
6. scale rule, scale
7. French curve
8. sharpener, pencil sharpener
9. circle template
10. eraser shield, erasing shield
11. eraser, rubber
12. eraser pencil
13. carpenter's pencil, builder's pencil
14. lead pencil
15. clutch pencil, lead holder
16. propelling pencil
17. felt pen, felt-tipped pen, marker pen
18. technical pen, stylo pen, drawing pen
19. drawing pen
20. ruling pen
21. spring compass, bow compass
22. precision compass
23. craft knife, scalpel
24. flexible curve
25. drafting machine, draughting machine
26. sketching paper, detail paper

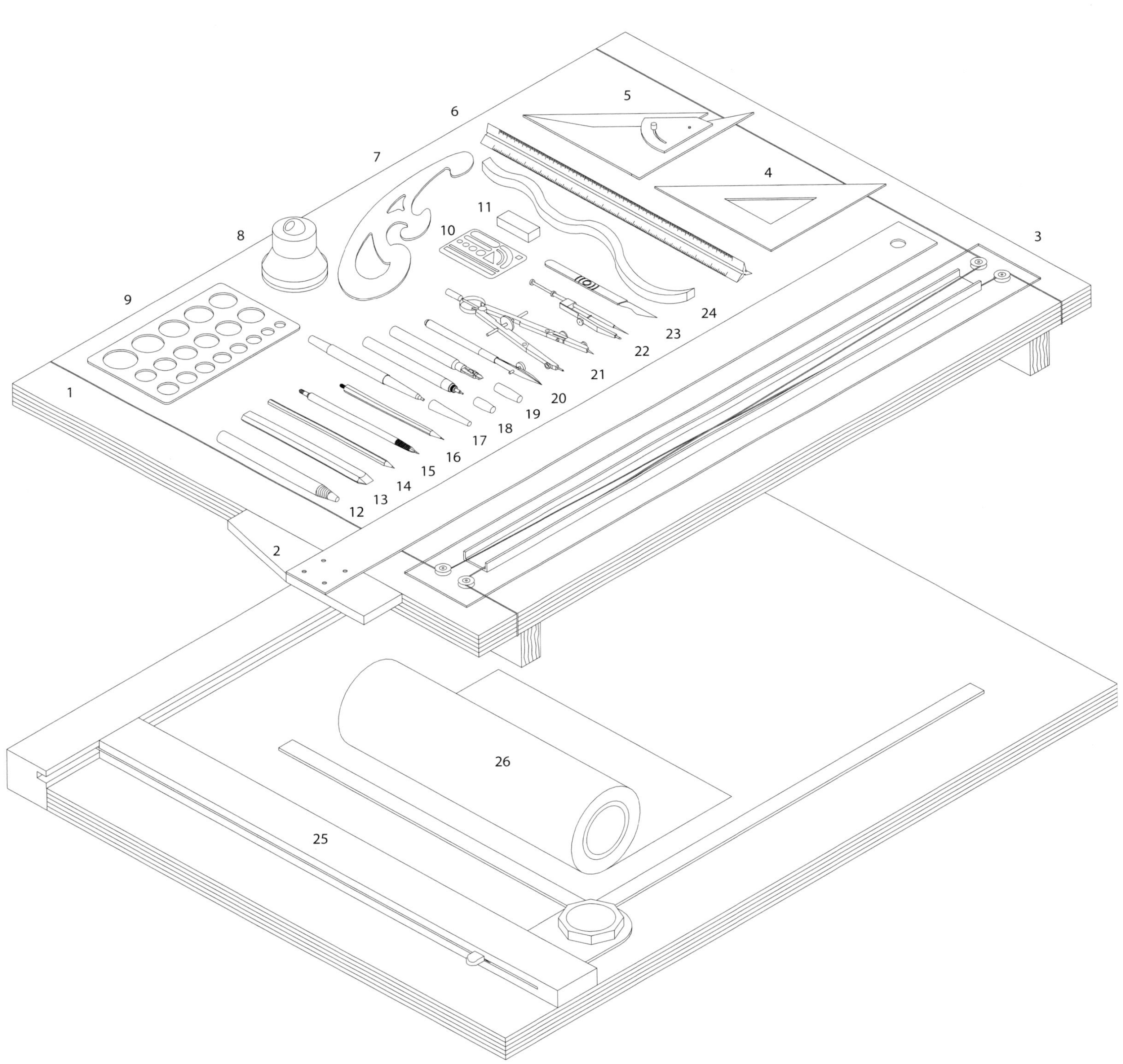
5
6
7
4
11
8
10
3
9
24
23
22
21
1
20
19
18
17
16
15
14
13
12
2
26
25

Part III

Tables

Table 1 SI prefixes

Prefix	Factor	Symbol
yotta	10^{24}	Y
zetta	10^{21}	Z
exa	10^{18}	E
peta	10^{15}	P
tera	10^{12}	T
giga	10^{9}	G
mega	10^{6}	M
kilo	10^{3}	k
hecto	10^{2}	h
deca	10^{1}	da
deci	10^{-1}	d
centi	10^{-2}	c
milli	10^{-3}	m
micro	10^{-6}	μ
nano	10^{-9}	n
pico	10^{-12}	p
femto	10^{-15}	f
atto	10^{-18}	a
zepto	10^{-21}	z
yocto	10^{-24}	y

Table 3 SI derived quantities and SI units

Quantity	Unit	Legend
frequency	hertz	$1\ Hz = 1\ s^{-1}$
force	newton	$1\ N = 1\ kg\ m/s^2$
pressure, stress	pascal	$1\ Pa = 1\ N/m^2$
energy, work	joule	1 J = 1 Nm
power	watt	1 W = 1 J/s
electric charge	coulomb	1 C = 1 As
voltage, potential difference	volt	1 V = 1 W/A
capacitance	farad	1 F = 1 As/V
resistance	ohm	1 W = 1 V/A
conductance	siemens	$1\ S = W^{-1}$
magnetic flux	weber	1 Wb = 1 Vs
magnetic flux density	tesla	$1\ T = 1\ Wb/m^2$
inductance	henry	1 H = 1 Vs/A
luminous flux	lumen	1 lm = 1 cd sr
illuminance	lux	$1\ lx = 1\ lm/m^2$
activity	becquerel	$1\ Bq = 1\ s^{-1}$
radiation dosage	gray	1 Gy = 1 J/kg

Table 2 SI basic quantities and SI units

Quantity	Symbol	Unit	Symbol
length	l	metre	m
mass	m	kilogram	kg
time	t	second	s
electric current	I	ampere, amp	A
temperature	T	kelvin	K
luminous intensity	I	candela	cd
quantity	n	mole	mol
plane angle	α	radian	rad
solid angle	ω	steradian	sr

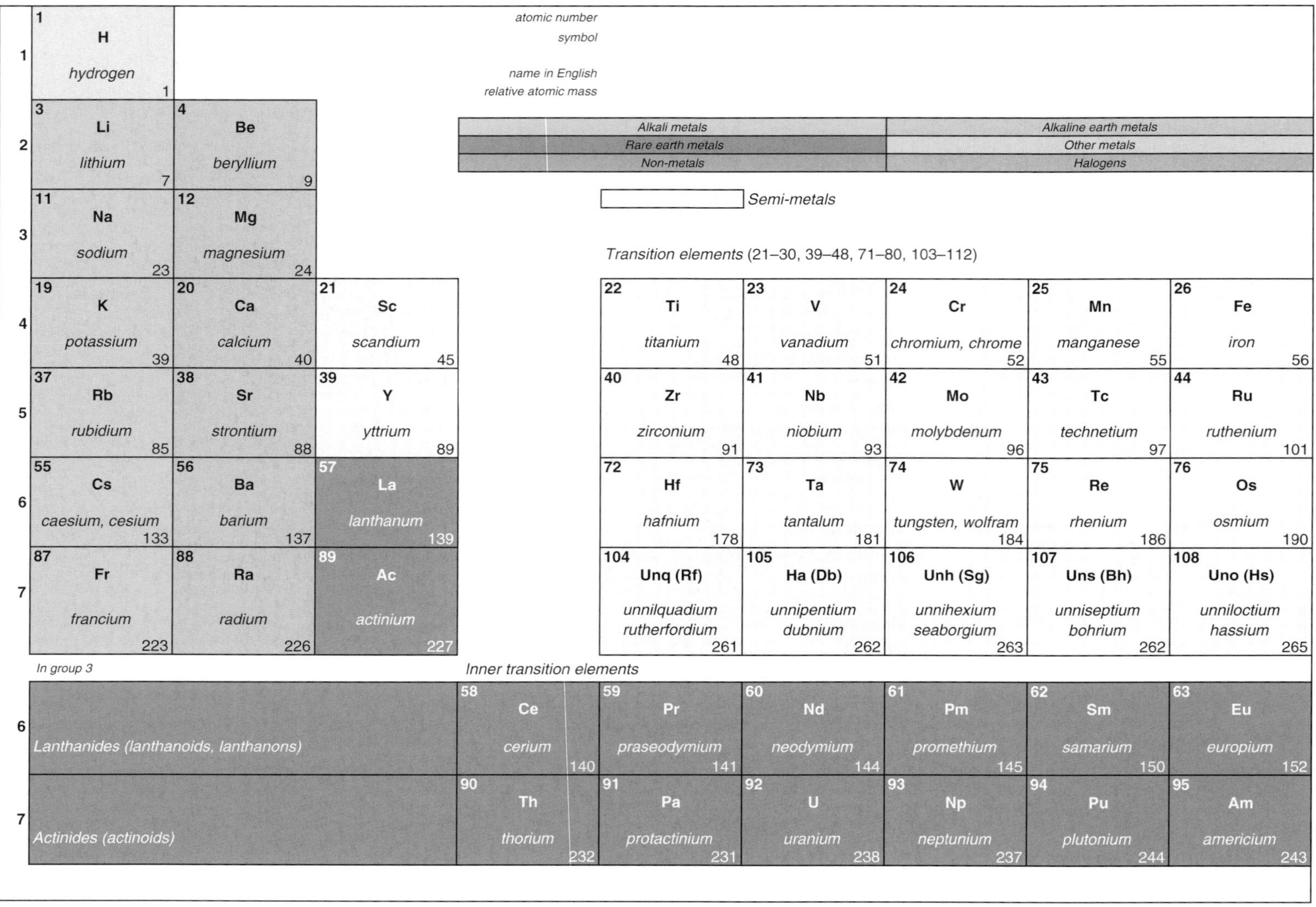
atomic number
symbol
name in English
relative atomic mass
Alkali metals
Alkaline earth metals
Rare earth metals
Other metals
Non-metals
Halogens
Semi-metals
Transition elements (21–30, 39–48, 71–80, 103–112)
1 H hydrogen 1
3 Li lithium 7
4 Be beryllium 9
11 Na sodium 23
12 Mg magnesium 24
19 K potassium 39
20 Ca calcium 40
21 Sc scandium 45
22 Ti titanium 48
23 V vanadium 51
24 Cr chromium, chrome 52
25 Mn manganese 55
26 Fe iron 56
37 Rb rubidium 85
38 Sr strontium 88
39 Y yttrium 89
40 Zr zirconium 91
41 Nb niobium 93
42 Mo molybdenum 96
43 Tc technetium 97
44 Ru ruthenium 101
55 Cs caesium, cesium 133
56 Ba barium 137
57 La lanthanum 139
72 Hf hafnium 178
73 Ta tantalum 181
74 W tungsten, wolfram 184
75 Re rhenium 186
76 Os osmium 190
87 Fr francium 223
88 Ra radium 226
89 Ac actinium 227
104 Unq (Rf) unnilquadium rutherfordium 261
105 Ha (Db) unnipentium dubnium 262
106 Unh (Sg) unnihexium seaborgium 263
107 Uns (Bh) unniseptium bohrium 262
108 Uno (Hs) unniloctium hassium 265
In group 3
Inner transition elements
6 Lanthanides (lanthanoids, lanthanons)
58 Ce cerium 140
59 Pr praseodymium 141
60 Nd neodymium 144
61 Pm promethium 145
62 Sm samarium 150
63 Eu europium 152
7 Actinides (actinoids)
90 Th thorium 232
91 Pa protactinium 231
92 U uranium 238
93 Np neptunium 237
94 Pu plutonium 244
95 Am americium 243

Table 4 Periodic table of elements

Legend
Metals
Semi-metals, metalloids
Noble gases

				boron group	carbon group	pnictogens	chalcogens		
									2 **He** *helium* 4
				5 **B** *boron* 11	6 **C** *carbon* 12	7 **N** *nitrogen* 14	8 **O** *oxygen* 16	9 **F** *fluorine* 19	10 **Ne** *neon* 20
				13 **Al** *aluminium, (Am) aluminum* 27	14 **Si** *silicon* 28	15 **P** *phosphorus* 31	16 **S** *sulphur, (Am) sulfur* 32	17 **Cl** *chlorine* 35	18 **Ar** *argon* 40
27 **Co** *cobalt* 59	28 **Ni** *nickel* 59	29 **Cu** *copper* 64	30 **Zn** *zinc* 65	31 **Ga** *gallium* 70	32 **Ge** *germanium* 73	33 **As** *arsenic* 75	34 **Se** *selenium* 79	35 **Br** *bromine* 80	36 **Kr** *krypton* 84
45 **Rh** *rhodium* 103	46 **Pd** *palladium* 106	47 **Ag** *silver* 108	48 **Cd** *cadmium* 112	49 **In** *indium* 115	50 **Sn** *tin* 119	51 **Sb** *antimony* 122	52 **Te** *tellurium* 128	53 **I** *iodine* 127	54 **Xe** *xenon* 131
77 **Ir** *iridium* 192	78 **Pt** *platinum* 195	79 **Au** *gold* 197	80 **Hg** *mercury* 201	81 **Tl** *thallium* 204	82 **Pb** *lead* 207	83 **Bi** *bismuth, vismuth* 209	84 **Po** *polonium* 209	85 **At** *astatine* 210	86 **Rn** *radon* 222
109 **Une (Mt)** *unnilennium meitnerium* 266	110 **Uun (Ds)** *ununnilium darmstadtium* 269	111 **Uuu (Rg)** *unununium roentgenium* 272	112 **Uub** *ununbium* 277	113 **Uut**	114 **Uuq**	115 **Uup**	116 **Uuh**	117 **Uus**	118 **Uuo**

64 **Gd** *gadolinium* 157	65 **Tb** *terbium* 159	66 **Dy** *dysprosium* 162	67 **Ho** *holmium* 165	68 **Er** *erbium* 167	69 **Tm** *thulium* 169	70 **Yb** *ytterbium* 173	71 **Lu** *lutecium, lutetium* 175
96 **Cm** *curium* 247	97 **Bk** berkelium 247	98 **Cf** californium 251	99 **Es** einsteinium 254	100 **Fm** fermium 257	101 **Md** mendelevium 258	102 **No** nobelium 259	103 **Lr** lawrencium 260

Table 5 Lime

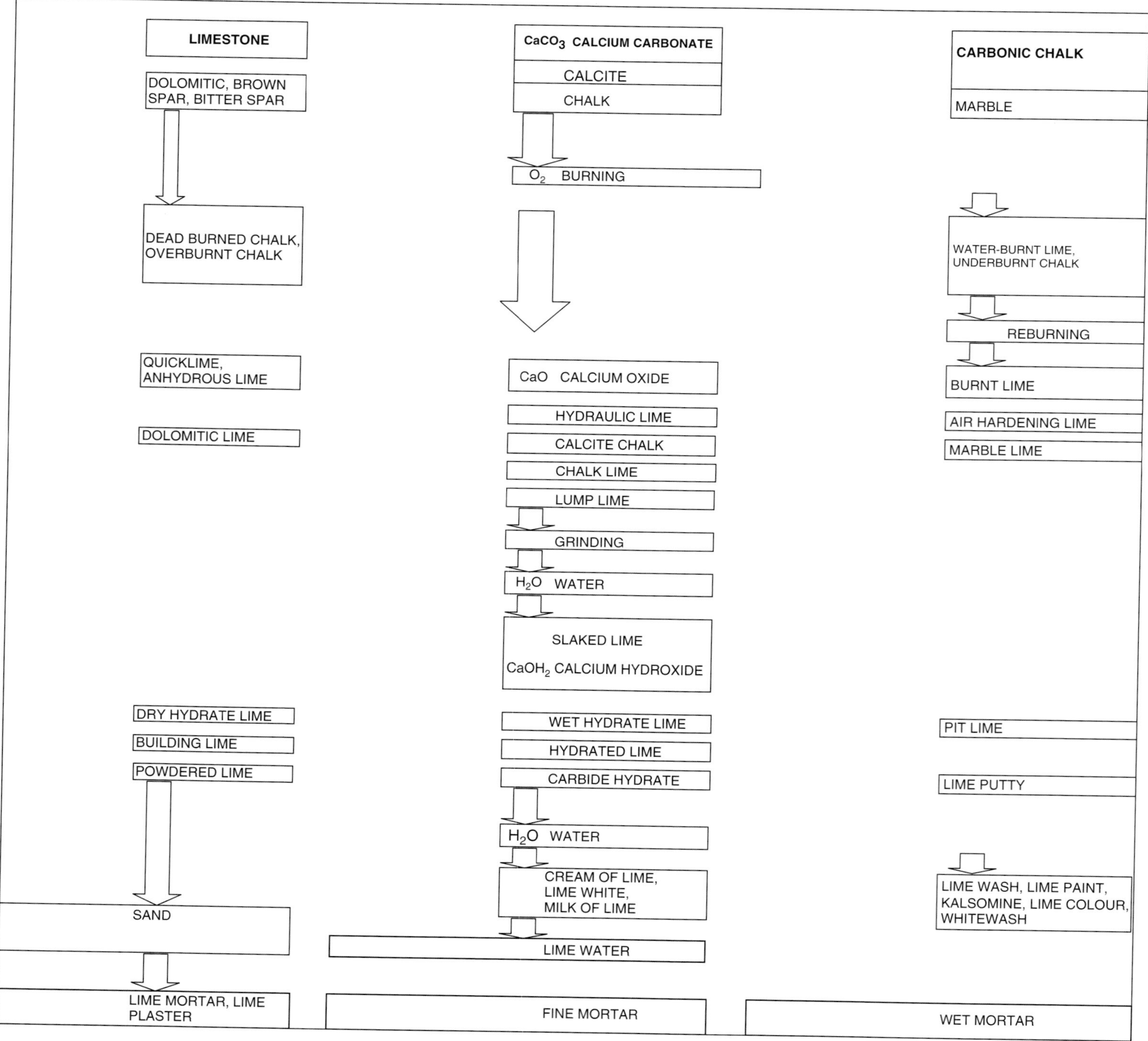

LIMESTONE
DOLOMITIC, BROWN SPAR, BITTER SPAR
DEAD BURNED CHALK, OVERBURNT CHALK
QUICKLIME, ANHYDROUS LIME
DOLOMITIC LIME
DRY HYDRATE LIME
BUILDING LIME
POWDERED LIME
SAND
LIME MORTAR, LIME PLASTER
CaCO3 CALCIUM CARBONATE
CALCITE
CHALK
O2 BURNING
CaO CALCIUM OXIDE
HYDRAULIC LIME
CALCITE CHALK
CHALK LIME
LUMP LIME
GRINDING
H2O WATER
SLAKED LIME
CaOH2 CALCIUM HYDROXIDE
WET HYDRATE LIME
HYDRATED LIME
CARBIDE HYDRATE
H2O WATER
CREAM OF LIME, LIME WHITE, MILK OF LIME
LIME WATER
FINE MORTAR
CARBONIC CHALK
MARBLE
WATER-BURNT LIME, UNDERBURNT CHALK
REBURNING
BURNT LIME
AIR HARDENING LIME
MARBLE LIME
PIT LIME
LIME PUTTY
LIME WASH, LIME PAINT, KALSOMINE, LIME COLOUR, WHITEWASH
WET MORTAR

Table 6

International paper sizes			**Imperial paper sizes**				
4A	3284 mm	4756 mm	Antiquarian	31"	51"	787 mm	1346 mm
3A	2378 mm	3284 mm	Atlas	26"	34"	660 mm	860 mm
2A	1642 mm	2378 mm	Cartridge	12"	26"	305 mm	660 mm
1A	1189 mm	1642 mm	Columbier	23½"	34½"	600 mm	880 mm
A0	841 mm	1189 mm	Crown	15"	20"	318 mm	508 mm
A1	595 mm	841 mm	Double Crown	20"	30"	508 mm	762 mm
A2	421 mm	595 mm	Quad Crown	30"	40"	762 mm	1016 mm
A3	297 mm	421 mm	Quad Double Crown	40"	60"	1016 mm	1524 mm
A4	210 mm	297 mm	Demy	17½"	22½"	450 mm	570 mm
A5	148 mm	210 mm	Double Demy	22½"	35"	570 mm	990 mm
A6	105 mm	148 mm	Quad Demy	35"	45"	990 mm	1040 mm
A7	74 mm	105 mm	Eagle	28¾"	42"	730 mm	1070 mm
A8	52 mm	74 mm	Elephant	20"	27"	510 mm	690 mm
A9	37 mm	52 mm	Double Elephant	27"	40"	686 mm	1016 mm
A10	26 mm	37 mm	Emperor	48"	72"	1220 mm	1840 mm
			Foolscap	13½"	17"	343 mm	432 mm
B0	1000 mm	1414 mm	Double Foolscap	17"	27"	432 mm	686 mm
B1	707 mm	1000 mm	Quad Foolscap	27"	34"	690 mm	870 mm
B2	500 mm	707 mm	Hand	16"	22"	410 mm	560 mm
B3	353 mm	500 mm	Royal Hand	20"	25"	510 mm	640 mm
B4	250 mm	353 mm	Imperial	22"	30"	560 mm	760 mm
B5	176 mm	250 mm	Half Imperial	15"	22"	380 mm	560 mm
B6	125 mm	176 mm	Double Imperial	30"	44"	760 mm	1120 mm
B7	88 mm	125 mm	Medium	18"	23"	460 mm	590 mm
B8	62 mm	88 mm	Double Medium	23"	36"	590 mm	820 mm
B9	44 mm	62 mm	Quad Medium	36"	46"	820 mm	1170 mm
B10	31 mm	44 mm	Post	15¼"	19¼"	390 mm	490 mm
			Large Post	16½"	21"	420 mm	530 mm
C0	917 mm	1297 mm	Double Post	21"	33"	590 mm	840 mm
C1	648 mm	917 mm	Pot	12½"	15½"	310 mm	400 mm
C2	458 mm	648 mm	Royal	20"	25"	508 mm	635 mm
C3	324 mm	458 mm	Double Royal	25"	40"	640 mm	1020 mm
C4	229 mm	324 mm	Super Royal	40"	50"	1020 mm	1280 mm
C5	162 mm	229 mm					
C6	114 mm	162 mm	**North American paper sizes**				
C7	81 mm	114 mm	Letter	8½"	11"	216 mm	279 mm
C8	57 mm	81 mm	Legal	8½"	14"	216 mm	356 mm
C9	40 mm	57 mm	Executive	7½"	10"	190 mm	254 mm
C10	28 mm	40 mm	Ledger/Tabloid	11"	17"	279 mm	432 mm

Bibliography

ENGLISH LANGUAGE:

Ackerman, James S.: *The Architecture of Michelangelo;* Penguin Books, London 1995

Adam, Jean-Pierre: *Roman Building – Materials and Techniques;* B.T. Batsford Ltd, London 1994

Adembri, Benedetta: *Hadrian's Villa;* Ministero per i Beni e le Attività Culturali, Soperintendenza Archelogica per il Lazio, Electa, Milan 2000

Adler, David (ed.): *Metric Handbook Planning and Design Data;* Architectural Press, Butterworth-Heinemann, Oxford 1999

Akurgal, Ekrem: *Ancient Civilizations and Ruins of Turkey;* Haset Kitabevi, Istanbul 1985

Alanne, V.S.: *Finnish-English Dictionary;* WSOY, Helsinki 1956

Allen, A.H.: *An Introduction to Prestressed Concrete;* Cement and Concrete Association, Slough 1984

Allen, Sam: *Finishing Basics;* Sterling Publishing Co., Inc., New York 1992

Allot – Azzarro – Vincent: *A Common Arrangement for Specifications and Quantities*

Amiert, Pierre: *Art of the Ancient New East;* Harry N. Abrams, Inc., Publishers, New York 1980

Amiet, Christian & Baratte, Francois & Desroches Noblecourt, Christiane & Metzger, Catherine & Pasquier, Alain: *Forms and Styles – Antiquity;* Benedikt Taschen Verlag GmbH, Köln 1994

Anderson, Stanford (ed.): *On Streets;* MIT Press, Cambridge, Mass. and London, England 1986

Approved documents: A – Structure (1992); B – Fire safety (2000); B – Fire safety (2002 amendments); C – Site preparation and resistance to moisture (1992); D – Toxic substances (1992); E – Resistance to the passage of sound (2003); E – Resistance to the passage of sound (1992); F – Ventilation (1995); G – Hygiene (1992); H – Drainage and waste disposal (2002); H – Drainage and waste disposal (1992); J – Combustion appliances and fuel storage systems (2002); K – Protection from falling, collision and impact (1998); L1 – Conservation of fuel and power in dwellings (2002); L2 – Conservation of fuel and power in buildings other than dwellings (2002); M – Access and facilities for disabled people (1999); N – Glazing (1998)

Arnold, Dieter: *Building in Egypt – Pharaonic Stone Masonry;* Oxford University Press, New York and Oxford

Ashurst, John & Dimes, Francis G.: *Stone in Building – its use and potential today;* The Architectural Press Ltd, London 1977

Atroshenko, A.T. & Collins, Judith: *The Origins of the Romanesque – Near Eastern Influences on European Art 4th-12th centuries;* Lund Humpries Publishers Ltd, London 1985

Atwell, David: *Cathedrals of the Movies – A History of British Cinemas and their Audiences;* The Architectural Press, London 1980

Auboyer, J. & Beurdeley, M. & Boisselier, J. & Massonaud, C. & Rousset, H.: *Asia – Forms and Styles;* Benedikt Taschen Verlag GmbH, Köln 1994

Baden-Powell, Charlotte: *Architect's Pocket Book;* Architectural Press, Butterworth-Heinemann, Oxford 2001

Banham, Reyner: *Guide to Modern Architecture;* Architectural Press, London 1962

Banister Fletcher, Sir: *A History of Architecture;* The Athlene Press, University of London 1975

Bannock, G., Baxter, R.E. & Rees, R.: *The Penguin Dictionary of Economics;* Penguin Books, Harmondsworth, Middlesex, England 1974

Barker, John A.: *Dictionary of Concrete;* Construction Press, London 1983

Barral i Altet, Xavier: *The Romanesque – Towns, Cathedrals and Monasteries;* Taschen GmBH, Köln 2001

Barry, R.: *The Construction of Buildings, vol. 1, Foundations, Walls, Floors, Roofs;* Granada Publishing Ltd, London-Toronto-Sydney-New York, Crosby Lockwood Staples, Bungay, Suffolk 1982

Barton, Ian M. (ed.): *Roman Domestic Buildings;* University of Exeter Press, 1996 Exeter

Battisti, Eugenio: *Brunelleschi – The Complete Work;* Thames and Hudson Ltd, London 1981

Beard, Geoffrey: *Craftsmen and Interior Decoration in England 1660-1820;* John Bartholomew and Son Ltd, Edinburgh 1981

Becker, Uno: *The Element Encyclopedia of Symbols;* Element Books Ltd, Shaftesbury, Dorset 1994

Benton, Janetta Rebold: *Art of the Middle Ages;* Thames and Hudson World of Art, Thames Hudson Ltd, London 2002

Berger, Horst: *Light Structures – Structures of Light – The Art and Engineering of Tensile Architecture;* Birkhäuser Verlag, Basel-Boston-Berlin 1996

Berlye, Milton K.: *The Encyclopedia of Working with Glass;* Everest House Publishers, New York 1983

Berve, Helmut & Gruben, Gottfried: *Greek Temples, Theatres and Shrines;* Thames and Hudson, London 1963

Betancourt, Philip P.: *The Aeolic Style in Architecture – A Survey of Its Development in Palestine, the Halikarnassos Peninsula, and Greece, 1000-500 BC;* Princeton University Press, Princeton, New Jersey 1977

Blackburn, Graham: *The Illustrated Encyclopedia of Woodworking Handtools, Instruments and Devices;* Simon and Schuster, New York 1974

Blanc, Alan: *Internal Components – Mitchell's Building Series;* Longman Scientific and Technical, Essex 1994

Boëthius, Axel & Ward-Perkins, John B.: *Etruscan and Roman Architecture;* Pelican History of Art, Penguin Books, Middlesex 1970

Boëthius, Axel: *Etruscan and Early Roman Architecture;* Penguin Books Ltd, Middlesex 1978

Bowman, Alan K.: *Egypt after the Pharaos – 332 BC-AD 642 from Alexander to the Arab Conquest;* Oxford University Press, Oxford 1990

Boyle, Godfrey: *Design Processes and Products – Block 5 – Communities – Planning and Participation*; The Open University Press, Walton Hall, Milton Keynes MK7 6AA, Great Britain 1986

Boyne, Colin & Wright, Lance: *Best of Architect's Working Details 1–2;* The Architectural Press, London and Nichols Publishing Company, New York 1982

Brick Development Association: *Bricks, Their Properties and Use;* The Construction Press Ltd, Lancaster, England 1974

British Standard Institution: *Glossary of Building and Civil Engineering Terms;* Blackwell Scientific Publications, Oxford 1993

Brooke, Christopher: *Die grosse Zeit der Klöster 1000-1300 – die Geschichte der Klöster und Orden und ihre religions-, kunst- und kulturgeschichtliche Bedeutung für das werdende Europa;* Verlag Herder GmbH and Co. KG, Freiburg im Breisgau 1976

Brooke, Christopher: *The Monastic World 1000–1300;* Paul Elek Ltd, London 1974

Brooks, Hugh: *Encyclopedia of Building and Construction Terms;* Englewood Cliffs, NJ, Prentice-Hall, London 1983

Brouskari, Maria: *The Monuments of the Acropolis;* Ministry of Culture, Archaeological Receipts Fund, Athens 1997

Brown, A.J. & Sherrard, H.M. & Shaw, J.H.: *An Introduction to Town and Country Planning;* Angus and Robertson, Sydney-Melbourne-London 1959

Brown, David J.: *Bridges – Three Thousand Years of Defying Nature;* Mitchell Beazley, Reed Consumer Books Ltd, London 1996

Brown, Leslie *et al.*: *The New Shorter Oxford English Dictionary on Historical Principles I–II;* Clarendon Press, Oxford 1993

Bruce-Mitford, Miranda: *The Illustrated Book of Signs and Symbols;* Dorling Kindersley Ltd, London 1996

Brunskill, R.W.: *Timber Building in Britain;* Victor Gollancz Ltd, London 1985; n. 450 kuvaa

Brunskill, R.W. & Clifton-Taylor, A.: *English Brickwork;* A Hyperion Book, Ward Lock Ltd, London 1978

Bugge, Gunnar & Norberg-Schulz, Christian: *Stav og laft i Norge – Early Wooden Architecture in Norway;* Byggekunst, Norske Arkitekters Landsforbund, Oslo 1969

Burberry, Peter: *Environment and Services, Mitchell's Building Series;* Longman Scientific and Technical, Essex 1994

Burke, Gerald: *Towns in the Making;* Edward Arnold Publishers Ltd, London 1971

Burtenshaw, D., Bateman M. & Ashworth, G.J.: *The City in West Europe;* John Wiley and Sons Ltd, Chichester-New York-Brisbane-Toronto 1984

Cannon-Brookes, P. & C.: *Baroque Churches – Great Buildings of the World;* The Hamlyn Publishing Group Ltd, Feltham, Middlesex 1969

Carlsson, Frans: *The Iconolgy of Tectonics in Romanesque Art;* Am-Tryck, Hässleholm 1976

Carpenter, T.H.: *Art and Myth in Ancient Greece;* Thames and Hudson Ltd, London 1991

Carr Rider, Bertha: *The Greek House – Its History and Development from the Neolithic Period to the Hellenistic Age;* Cambridge at the University Press, USA 1965

Carver, Norman F.: *Italian Hilltowns;* Documan Press Ltd, Kalamazoo, Michigan 1985

Casanaki, Maria & Mallochou, Fanny: *The Acropolis at Athens – Conservation, Restoration, and Research 1975-1983;* Ministry of Culture, Committee for the Preservation of the Acropolis Monuments, Athens 1985

Cassell: *Concise English Dictionary;* Cassell, London 1994

Cavan, H.J.: *Dictionary of Architectural Jargon;* Applied Suerie Publishers, 1973

Chambers: *Chambers Etymological Dictionary;* Chambers, London 1931

Charles-Charles: *Conservation of Timber Buildings;* Great Britain 1984

Chevalier, Jean & Gheerbrant, Alain: *The Penguin Dictionary of Symbols;* Penguin Books Ltd, London 1996

Chiara, Joseph de & Koppelman, Lee: *Urban Planning and Design Criteria;* Van Nostrand Reinhold Company, New York 1975

Child, Heather & Colles, Dorothy: *Christian Symbols, Ancient and Modern;* Bell and Hyman Ltd, London 1971

Chinery, Michael: *A Field Guide to the Insects of Britain and Northern Europe;* William Collins Sons and Co. Ltd, Glasgow 1973

Ching, Francis, D.K.: *A Visual Dictionary of Architecture;* Van Nostrand Reinhold, New York 1995

Ching, Francis, D.K. & Adams, C.: *Building Construction Illustrated;* Van Nostrand Reinhold Co., New York 1991

Ching, Francis, D.K.: *Drawing – A Creative Process;* John Wiley and Sons, Inc., New York 1990

Chudley, R.: *Construction Technology, Volume 2;* Longman, London 1979

Chudley, R. & Greeno, R.: *Building Construction Handbook;* Butterworth-Heinemann, Oxford 2001

Cipriani, Giovanni Battista: *Architecture of Rome – A Nineteenth-century Itinerary;* Rizzoli International Publications Inc., New York 1986

Cirlot, J.E.: *A Dictionary of Symbols;* Routledge and Kegan Paul Ltd, London 1962

Claridge, Amanda: *Rome – An Oxford Archaelogical Guide;* Oxford University Press Inc., New York 1998

Clifton-Taylor, Alec & Ireson, A.S.: *English Stone Building;* Victoria Gollancz Ltd, London 1983

Clifton-Taylor, Alec: *The Cathedrals of England;* Thames and Hudson, London 1967

Clifton-Taylor, Alec: *The Pattern of English Building;* B.T. Batsford Ltd, London 1965

Coarelli, Filippo & Gregori, Gian Luca & Lombardi, Leonardo & Orlandi, Silvia & Rea, Rossella & Vismara, Cinzia: *The Colosseum;* The J. Paul Getty Museum, Getty Publications, Los Angeles 2001

Collins Cobuild: *English Dictionary;* HarperCollins Publishers Ltd, London 1995

Collins Cobuild: *English Language Dictionary;* HarperCollins Publishers Ltd, London 1988

Collymore: *House Conversion and Renewal;* Great Britain 1975

Conant, Kenneth John: *Carolingian and Romanesque Architecture 800-1200;* Pelican History of Art, Penguin Books Ltd, Harmondsworth, Middlesex 1966

Construction Indexing Manual: RIBA, London

Construction Industry Thesaurus: Property Services Agency, Department of the Environment, London 1976

Construction Specification Institute: *Masterformat – Master List of Titles and Numbers for Construction Industry;* CSI, 601 Madison Str, Alexandria, VA 22314, USA

Cooper, J.C.: *An Illustrated Encyclopedia of Traditional Symbols;* Thames and Hudson, London 1978

Copplestone, Trewin (ed.): *World Architecture – An Illustrated History;* The Hamlyn Publishing Group Ltd, London-New York-Sydney-Toronto 1971

Cornell, Sara: *Art – A History of Changing Style;* Phaidon Press Ltd, Oxford 1983

Cotterell, Arthur: *The Encyclopedia of Ancient Civilizations;* Macmillan Publishers Ltd, London and Basingstoke 1983

Coulton, J.J.: *Greek Architects at Work – Problems of Structure and Design;* Elek Books Ltd, London 1977

Cowan, Henry J. & Smith, Peter R.: *Dictionary of Architectural and Building Technology;* Elsevier Applied Science Publishers, London and New York 1986

Craven, Roy C.: *Indian Art;* Thames and Hudson, London 1987

CRSI: *Reinforcing Bar Detailing;* CRSI Engineering Practice Committee, Concrete Reinforcing Steel Institute, Chicago 1980, Kingsport Press, Inc.

Cruickshank, Dan: *A Guide to the Georgian Buildings of Britain and Ireland;* George Weidenfeld and Nicolson Ltd, The Irish Georgian Society, London 1985

Crump, Derrick (& Rustin, Ronnie): *The Complete Guide to Wood Finishes;* HarperCollins Publishers, London 1993

Cullen, Gordon: *The Concise Townscape;* The Architectural Press, Great Britain 1985

Cullingworth, J. Barry & Nadin, Vincent: *Town and Country Planning in the UK;* Routledge, London 1997

Curl, James Stevens: *A Dictionary of Architecture;* Oxford University Press, Oxford 1999
Curl, James Stevens: *Classical Architecture – An Introduction to its Vocabulary and Essentials with a Select Glossary of Terms;* B.T. Batsford Ltd, London 2001
Curl, James Stevens: *English Architecture – An Illustrated Glossary;* David and Charles Ltd, Newton Abbot 1977
Curtis, William J.R.: *Le Corbusier – Ideas and Forms;* Phaidon Press Ltd, Oxford 1986
Curtis, William J.R.: *Modern Architecture since 1900;* Phaidon Press Ltd, London 1996
Dalley, Terence *et al.*: *The Complete Guide to Illustration and Design – Techniques and Materials;* Phaidon Press Ltd, Oxford 1988
Dalzell, J. Ralph & McKinney, James: *Architectural Drawing and Detailing;* American Technical Society, Chicago 1946
Danzig, George B. & Saaty, Thomas, L.: *Compact City – A Plan for a Liveable Urban Development;* W.H. Freeman and Co., San Francisco 1973
David, A. Rosalie: *Ancient Egypt;* Phaidon Press Ltd, Oxford 1988
Davies, J.G.: *Temples, Churches and Mosques – A Guide to the Appreciation of Religious Architecture;* Basil Blackwell, Oxford 1982
Davies, J.G.: *A Dictionary of Liturgy and Worship;* SCM Press Ltd, London 1972
Davis, Whitney: *The Canonical Tradition in Ancient Egyptian Art;* Cambridge University Press, Cambridge, USA 1989
Dean, Yvonne: *Finishes – Mitchell's Building Series;* Longman Scientific and Technical, Essex 1996
Dormes, Peter: *Illustrated Dictionary of 20th Century Designers;* Headline 1991
Doxiadis, Constantinos A.: *Architectural Space in Ancient Greece;* MIT Press, Massachusetts, and London, England 1972
Drew, Philip: *Tensile Architecture;* Granada Publishing Ltd in Crosby Lockwood Staples, London 1979
Duncan, Andrew (ed.): *The Woodworker's Handbook – A Complete Course for Craftsmen, Do-it-yourselfers and Hobbyists;* Pelham Books, London 1984
Durant, David N.: *The Handbook of British Architectural Styles;* Barrie and Jenkins, London 1992
Eberhard, Wolfram: *A Dictionary of Chinese Symbols – Hidden Symbols in Chinese Life and Thought;* Routledge and Kegan Paul Ltd, New York and London 1986
Eldridge, H.J.: *Properties of Building Materials;* MTP = Medical and Technical Publishing Co. Ltd, Lancaster 1974
Elsheikh, Ahmed: *An Introduction to Drawing for Civil Engineers;* McGraw-Hill Book Company Europe, University Press, Cambridge 1995
Etlin, Richard A.: *The Architecture of Death – The Transformation of the Cemetery in Eighteenth-Century Paris;* The MIT Press, Cambridge, Massachusetts and London, England 1984
Everett, Alan: *Materials, Mitchell's Building Series;* Longman Scientific and Technical, Essex 1994
Everett, Alan: *Mitchell's Building Construction – Environment and Services;* Batsford, London
Felden: *Conservation of Historical Buildings;* England 1982, **AOK**, sanasto englanti-saksa-ranska-espanja
Fleming, John & Honour, Hugh & Pevsner, Nikolaus: *The Penguin Dictionary of Architecture;* Penguin Books, Bungay, Suffolk 1977
Fleming, John & Honour, Hugh & Pevsner, Nikolaus: *The Penguin Dictionary of Architecture and Landscape Architecture;* Penguin Books, London 1999
Forbes, J.R.: *Dictionnaire d'architecture et de construction, Dictionary of architecture and construction, Eng-Fra-Eng;* Lavoisier, Paris 1984
Forbes, J.R.: *Dictionary of Architecture and Construction, English-French;* Lavoisies, France 1988, **HYK**
Foster, Jack Stroud: *Structure and Fabric, Part 2, Mitchell's Building Construction;* Batsford, London
Foster, Jack Stroud & Harington, Raymond: *Mitchell's Building Series – Structure and Fabric Part 2;* Longman House, Brunt Mill, Harlow, Essex 1994
Foster, Jack Stroud: *Structure and Fabric, Part 1, Mitchell's Building Series;* Longman Scientific and Technical, Essex 1994
Frampton, Kenneth: *Le Corbusier;* Thames and Hudson, London 2001
Frankfort, Henri: *The Art and Architecture of the Ancient Orient;* The Pelican History of Art, Penguin Books Ltd, Middlesex 1970
Frutiger, Adrian: *Signs and Symbols – Their Design and Meaning;* Studio Editions Ltd, London 1991
Furneaux Jordan, Robert: *A Concise History of Western Architecture;* Thames and Hudson Ltd, Norwich 1976
Gallion, Arthur B.: *The Urban Pattern – City Planning and Design;* D. Van Nostrand Co., New York 1950
Gardner Wilkinson, J.: *The Ancient Egyptians – Their Life and Customs;* Senate, Studio Editions, London 1994
Gee, Eric: *A Glossary of Building Terms used in England from the Conquest to c 1550;* Frome Historical Research Group, Frome 1984
Gibson, Clare: *Signs and Symbols – An Illustrated Guide to their Meaning and Origins;* Grange Books, London 1996
Glazier, Richard: *A Manual of Historic Ornament;* B.T. Batsford Ltd, London 1948
Gloag, John: *Guide to Western Architecture;* Spring Books, The Hamlyn Publishing Group Ltd, London 1969
Gowing, Sir Lawrence (ed.): *A History of Art – The Encyclopedia of Visual Art I-II;* Prentice-Hall, Inc., Eaglewood Cliffs, New Jersey 1985
Goy, Richard: *Venice – The City and its Architecture;* Phaidon Press Ltd, London 1997
Grant, Michael: *The World of Rome;* Weidenfeld and Nicholson, London 1960
Greater London City Council: *An Introduction to Housing Layout;* The Arcihtectural Press, London and Nichols Publishing Company, New York 1980
Gresswell, Peter: *Environment – An Alphabetical Handbook;* William Clowes and Sons Ltd, London, Beccles and Colchester 1971
Groenewegen-Frankfort, H.A. & Ashmole, Bernard: *The Art of the Ancient World – Painting, Pottery, Sculpture, Architecture – From Egypt, Mesopotamia, Crete, Greece, and Rome;* Harry N. Abrams, Inc., Publishers, New York
Gudmundson, Wayne & Winckler, Suzanne: *Testaments in Wood – Finnish Log Structures at Embarrass, Minnesota;* Minnesota Historical Society Press, St. Paul 1991
Guhl, E. & Koner, W.: *The Romans – Their Life and Customs;* Senate, Studio Editions Ltd, London 1994
Guhl, E. & Koner, W.: *The Greeks – Their Life and Customs;* Senate, Studio Editions Ltd, London 1994
Guidobaldi, F. & Lawlor, P. & Cosentino, V.: *The Basilica and the Archaeological Area of San Clemente in Rome;* Apud S. Clementem, Roma 1990
Guzzo, Pier Giovanni & d'Ambrosio, Alfredo: *Pompeii – Guide to the Site;* Ministero per i Beni e le Attività Culturali Soprintendenza Archeologica di Pompei, Electa, Napoli 2002
Gwilt, Joseph: *The Encyclopedia of Architecture – The Classic 1867 Edition;* Crown Publishers, Inc., New York 1982
Gympel, Jan: *The Story of Architecture from Antiquity to the Present;* Könemann VgmbH, Köln 1996 (Goodfellow and Egan, Cambridge)
Haggar, Reginald G.: *A Dictionary of Art Terms, Architecture, Sculpture, Painting and the Graphic Arts;* New Orchard Editions, Poole, Dorset 1984

Hall, F.: *Building Services and Equipment, vols 1–3;* Longman Group Ltd, Harlow 1982

Hall, James: *Dictionary of Subjects and Symbols in Art;* Icon Editions, Harper and Row Publishers, New York-Hagerstown-San Francisco-London 1979

Hall, James: *Illustrated Dictionary of Symbols in Eastern and Western Art;* John Murray Publishers Ltd, London 1994

Haneman, John Theodore: *Pictorial Encyclopedia of Historic Architectural Plans, Details and Elements;* Constable, London, NY, Dover 1984

Harris, Cyril M.: *Dictionary of Architecture and Construction;* McGraw-Hill Book Company 1975

Harris, John & Lever, Jill: *Illustrated Glossary of Architecture 850-1830;* Faber and Faber, London 1966

Hartt, Frederick: *History of Italian Renaissance Art – Painting – Sculpture – Architeture;* Harry N. Abrams, Inc., Publishers, New York

Hatje, Gerd: *Encyclopaedia of Modern Architecture;* Thames and Hudson, London 1971; 446 kuvaa

Hawkes, Jacquetta: *The Atlas of Early Man;* Dorling Kindersley Ltd, London 1976

Hayes, Baldwin & Cole: *History of Western Civilization;* The Macmillan Company, New York, London 1962

Henderson, John S.: *The World of the Ancient Maya;* Cornell University, John Murray Ltd, London 1998

Henig, Martin: *A Handbook of Roman Art – A Survey of the Visual Arts of the Roman World;* Phaidon Press Ltd, London 1992

Her Majesty's Stationery Office: *Development Plans – A Manual on Form and Content;* Ministry of Housing and Local Government Welsh Office, London 1970

Herzog, T. & Natterer, J. & Schweitzer, R. & Volz, M. & Winter, W.: *Timber Construction Manual;* Birkhäuser – Publishers for Architecture, Basel-Boston-Berlin, Edition Detail, Munich 2004

Hiekkanen, Markus: *The Stone Churches of the Medieval Diocese of Turku – A Systematic Classification and Chronology;* Suomen muinaismuistoyhdistyksen aikakauskirja 101, Helsinki 1994

Higgins, Raymond A.: *Materials for the Engineering Technician;* Arnold, London 1997

Higgins, Reynold: *Minoan and Mycenean Art;* Thames and Hudson Ltd, London 1971

Hilling, John B.: *The Historic Architecture of Wales;* University of Wales Press, Cardiff 1976

Hoadley, R. Bruce: *Understanding Wood;* The Taunton Press Inc 1980

Hohenberg, Paul M. & Hollen Lees, Lynn: *The Making of Modern Europe 1000-1994;* Harvard University Press, Cambridge, Massachusetts and London, England 1995

Holan, Jerri: *Norwegian Wood – A Tradition of Building;* Rizzoli International Publications, Inc., New York 1990

Honour, Hugh & Fleming, John: *A World History of Art;* Macmillan Reference Books, London 1985

Horden, Richard: *Light Tech – Towards a Light Architecture;* Birkhäuser Verlag, Basel-Boston-Berlin 1995

Hornby, A.S.: *Oxford Advanced Learner's Dictionary of Current English;* Oxford University Press 1977

Hölscher, Joost (ed.): *Mediaeval Design;* The Pepin Press, Amsterdam 2001

Infodoc Services: *Definitions of Construction Terms 1984;* Infodoc Services, London 1984

International Log Builders' Association: *2000 Log Building Standards;* The International Log Builders' Association formerly known as Canadian Log Builders' Association and International American Log Builders' Association, Lumby BC, Canada

Italian Institute for Foreign Trade: *Marmi Italiani – Italian Marble, Technical Guide;* F.lli Vallardi Editori, Milan 1982

Jackson, Albert & Day, David: *The Collins Complete Woodworker's Manual;* HarperCollins Publishers, 1993

Jackson, Albert & Day, David: *The Complete Book of Tools;* Dorling Kindersley Ltd, London 1978

James, M.R.: *Abbeys;* The Great Western Railway, Paddington Station, London 1926

Janson, H.W. & Janson, Anthony F.: *History of Art;* Harry N. Abrams, Inc., New York 1991

Jenner, Michael: *The Architectural Heritage of Britain and Ireland – An Illustrated A-Z of Terms and Styles;* Penguin Group, Michael Joseph Ltd, London 1993

Jokilehto, Jukka: *A History of Architectural Conservation;* Butterworth-Heinemann, Oxford 1999

Jones, Owen: *The Grammar of Ornament;* Dorling Kindersley, London 2001

Jones, Peter & Sidwell, Keith (ed.): *The World of Rome – An Introduction to Roman Culture;* Cambridge University Press, Cambridge 1997

Joyce, Ernest & Peters, Allan: *The Technique of Furniture Making;* B.T. Batsford Ltd, London 1987

Kawashima, Chuji: *Japan's Folk Architecture – Traditional Thatched Farmhouses;* Kodansha International Ltd, Tokyo-New York-London, 2000

Kemp, Barry J.: *Ancient Egypt – Anatomy of a Civilization;* Routledge, London and New York 1995

Kenyon, John R. & Avent, Richard: *Castles in Wales and Marches;* University of Wales Press, Cardiff

Khalili, Nader: *Ceramic Houses – How to Build Your Own;* Harper and Row Publishers, San Francisco 1986

Kinder, Hermann & Hilgemann, Werner: *The Penguin Atlas of World History, vols I-II;* Penguin Books Ltd, London 1974

King, Bruce: *Buildings of Earth and Straw – Structural Design for Rammed Earth and Straw-Bale Architecture;* Ekological Design Press, USA 1996

King H. & Everett, A.: *Components and Finishes;* B.T. Batsford Ltd, London 1975

King, Harold & Everett, A.: *Mitchell's Building Construction – Components and Finishes;* Batsford, London

Klose, Dietrich: *Multi-Storey Car Parks and Garages;* The Architectural Press, London 1965

Knapas, Marja Terttu & Ringbom, Åsa *et al.*: *Icon to Cartoon – A Tribute to Sixten Ringbom;* Studies in Art History 16 by the Society for Art History in Finland, Gummerrus Kirjapaino Oy, Jyväskylä 1995

Knight, Jeremy K.: *Caerleon – Roman Fortress;* Cadw: Welsh Historic Monuments (Crown Copywright), MWL Print Group Ltd, Great Britain 2003

Knight, T.L.: *Illustrated Introduction to Brickwork Design;* Brick Development Association, Windsor, XI

Kornerup, Andreas & Wanscher, Johan Henrik: *Methuen Handbook of Colour;* Methuen, London 1989

Kostof, Spiro: *A History of Architecture – Settings and Rituals;* Oxford University Press, Inc., New York 1985

Kostof, Spiro: *The City Assembled – The Elements of Urban Form through History;* Thames and Hudson, London 1992

Kostof, Spiro: *The City Shaped – Urban Patterns and Meanings through History;* Thames and Hudson, London 1991

Krautheimer, Richard: *Early Christian and Byzantine Architecture;* Pelican History of Art, Penguin Books Ltd, Harmondsworth, Middlesex 1975

Krautheimer, Richard: *Rome, Profile of a City 312–1308;* Princeton University Press, Princeton, New Jersey 2000

Kut, David: *Illustrated Encyclopedia of Building Services;* E and FN

Lawrence, A.W.: *Greek Architecture;* Pelican History of Art, Penguin Books Ltd, Great Britain 1973

Le Corbusier – Architect of the Century: Arts Council of Great Britain, Balding + Mansell UK

Limited, exhibition catalogue, Hayward Gallery, London 5 March-7 June 1987

Le Corbusier: *The Modulor;* Faber and Faber Ltd, London 1967

Le Corbusier: *The City of To-morrow and Its Planning;* Dover Publications, Inc., New York 1987

Leicht, Hermann: *History of the World's Art;* Spring Books, London 1963

Leick, Gwendolyn & Kirk, Francis J.: *A Dictionary of Ancient Near Eastern Architecture;* Routledge, London and New York, 1988

Lesser, George: *Gothic Cathedrals and Sacred Geometry I–III;* Alec Tiranti Ltd, London 1957

Lewis, Philippa & Darley, Gillian: *Dictionary of Ornament;* Macmillan London Ltd, London 1986

Lilius, Henrik: *Esplanadi – The Esplanade – Helsinki;* Anders Nyborg A/S International Publishers Ltd, Rungstedt Kyst, Denmark and Akateeminen Kirjakauppa, Helsinki 1984

Lilius, Henrik: *Suomalainen puukaupunki – The Finnish Wooden Town;* Anders Nyborg A/s International Publishers Ltd, Rungsted Kyst, Denmark and Akateeminen Kirjakauppa, Helsinki

Lisney, Adrian & Fieldhouse, Ken: *Landscape Design Guide 1-2;* Gower Publishing Company Ltd, Exeter 1990

Logie, G.: *Elsevier's Dictionary of Physical Planning;* Elsevier NL 1989

Loyer, Francois: *Paris, Nineteenth Century Architecture and Urbanism;* Abbeville Press Inc., New York 1988

Lucie-Smith, Edward: *The Thames and Hudson Dictionary of Art Terms;* Thames and Hudson Ltd, London 1995

Lukkarinen, Ville: *Classicism and History – Anachronistic Architectural Thinking in Finland at the Turn of the Century: Jac Ahrenberg and Gustaf Nyström;* Suomen Muinaismuistoyhdistyksen aikakauskirja nro 93, Helsinki 1989

Lynch, Kevin: *A Theory of Good City Form;* The MIT Press, Cambridge, Massachusetts and London, England, 1981

Lynch, Kevin: *City Sense and City Design – Writings and Projects of Kevin Lynch;* MIT Press, Cambridge, Massachusetts and London, England 1990

Lynch, Kevin: *Image of the City;* The MIT Press, Cambridge, Massachusetts

Lynch, Kevin: *Managing the Sense of Region;* The MIT Press, Cambridge, Massachusetts and London, England 1978

Lynch, Kevin: *Site Planning;* The MIT Press, Cambridge, Massachusetts 1962

Mackie, B. Allan: *Notches of All Kinds – A Book of Timber Joinery;* Firefly Books Ltd, Loghouse Publishing Company Ltd, Ontario, Canada 1998

Martin, Roland: *Greek Architecture;* History of World Architecture; Faber and Faber, London 1988

Mattila, Raija, (ed.): *Nineveh, 612 BC – The Glory and Fall of the Assyrian Empire;* Ninive, 612eKr – Assyrian imperiumin loisto ja tuho; Catalogue of the 10th Anniversary Exhibition of the Neo-Assyrian Text Corpus Project, Helsinki University Press, Helsinki 1995

McEvoy, Michael: *External Components, Mitchell's Building Series;* Longman Scientific and Technical, Essex 1994

McGraw-Hill Dictionary of Scientific and Technical Terms; 3rd Edition, McGraw-Hill, USA 1984

McKay, A.G.: *Houses, Villas and Palaces in the Roman World;* Thames and Hudson, Southampton

Meyer, Ralph: *Artist's Handbook of Materials Techniques;* Faber + Faber 1991

Micthell, William J.: *Computer-aided Architectural Design;* Van Nostrand Reinhold Co. Inc. 1977

Middleton, R. & Watkin, D.: *Architecture of the Nineteenth Century – History of World Architecture;* Electa Architecture, Milano 2003

Millon, Henry A. & Frazer, Alfred: *Key Monuments of the History of Architecture;* Harry N. Abrams, Inc. Publishers, New York 1968

Mills, John W.: *Encyclopedia of Sculpture Techniques;* B.T. Batsford Ltd, London 1990

Morris, A.E.J.: *History of Urban Form, before the Industrial Revolutions;* Longman Scientific and Technical, Harlow, Essex 1987

Morris, A.E.J.: *Precast Concrete in Architecture;* George Godwin Ltd, London 1978

Morwood, James (ed.): *The Pocket Oxford Latin Dictionary;* Oxford University Press 1995

Mumford, Lewis: *The Culture of Cities;* Harcourt Brace Jovanovich, Inc., New York 1938/1970

Murdock, L.J. & Brook, K.M.: *Concrete Materials and Practice;* Edward Arnold Publishers Ltd, London 1979

Neubecker, Ottfried: *Heraldry – Sources, Symbols and Meaning;* Macdonald and Jane's Publishers, McGraw-Hill Book Co., London 1977

Neufert, Ernst: *Architects' Data;* Granada Publishing Ltd, London 1984

Neville, A.M.: *Properties of Concrete;* Longman Scientific and Technical, Essex 1986

Nicolle, David: *The Hamlyn History of Medieval Life – A Guide to Life from 1000 to 1500 AD;* Hamlyn, London 1997

Norberg-Schulz, Christian: *Genius Loci – Towards a Phenomenology of Architecture;* Academy Editions, London 1980

Norberg-Schulz, Christian: *Meaning in Western Architecture;* Rizzoli International Publications, Inc., New York 1983

Norman, Edward: *The House of God – Church Architecture, Style and History;* Thames and Hudson, London 1990

Normand, Charles: *A Parallel of the Orders of Architecture – Greek and Roman;* John Tiranti and Company, London 1928

Nuttgens, Patrick: *The Story of Architecture;* Phaidon Press Ltd, Oxford 1983

Orchard, D.F.: *Concrete Technology, Volume 2 – Practice;* Applied Science Publishers Ltd, London 1964

Orchard, D.F.: *Concrete Technology, Volume 1 – Properties;* Applied Science Publishers Ltd, London 1979

Oresko, Robert: *The Works in Architecture of Robert and James Adams;* Academy Editions, London 1975

Osborn, Frederic J. & Whittick, Arnold: *New Towns – Their Origins, Achievements and Progress;* Leonard Hill, London – Routledge and Kegan Paul, Boston, Mass. 1977

Osbourn, Derek: *Introduction to Building;* Mitchell's Building Series, Longman Scientific and Technical, Essex 1995

Owens, E.J.: *The City in the Greek and Roman World;* Routledge, London and New York 1991

Oxford: *The Little Oxford Dictionary;* Oxford University Press 1989

Oxford: *The New Shorter Oxford English Dictionary on Historical Principles vols I-II;* Clarendon Press – Oxford, Oxford University Press 1993

Oxford: *The Oxford Colour Thesaurus;* Oxford University Press 1995

Oxford-Duden: *The Oxford-Duden Pictorial English Dictionary;* Oxford University Press 1987

Pakkanen, Jari: *The Temple of Athena Alea at Tegea – A Reconstruction of the Peristyle Column;* Publications by the Department of Art History at the University of Helsinki No. XVIII in Co-operation with the Finnish Institute at Athens, Helsinki 1998

Palladio, Andrea: *The Four Books of Architecture;* Dover Publications, Inc., New York 1965

Parker, John Henry: *Glossary of Arhitectural Terms;* Bracken Books, London 1896/1989

Parker, John Henry: *Glossary of Architecture vols 1-3;* Oxford University Press 1840

Patton, W.J.: *Construction Materials;* Prentice-Hall Inc., New Jersey 1976

PCI: *Architectural Precast Concrete Drafting Handbook;* PCI (Prestressed Concrete Institute) Commitee on Architectural Precast, Prentice-Hall, Inc., Englewood Cliffs, New Jersey 1975

Peters, Pam: *The Cambridge Guide to English Usage;* Cambridge University Press 2004

Petersen, Toni *et al.*: *Art and Architecture Thesaurus, I-III;* Oxford University Press, New York and Oxford 1990

Pettersson, Lars *et al.*: *Suomalainen puukirkko – Finnish Wooden Church;* Suomen Rakennustaiteen Museo, Martinpaino Oy, Helsinki 1989

Pettersson, Lars: *Kaksikymmentäneljäkulmaisen ristikirkon syntyongelmia – On Finnish Cruciformed Timber-Churches with Twenty-Four Corners;* Suomen Muinaismuistoyhdistyksen aikakauskirja (SMYL) 79, Helsinki 1978, Weilin+Göös, Espoo 1979

Pevsner, Nikolaus: *A History of Building Types;* Thames and Hudson, London 1979

Pevsner, Nikolaus: *An Outline of European Architecture;* Penguin Books Ltd, Middlesex 1963

Pfeiffer, Günther & Ramcke, Rolf & Achtziger, Joachim & Zilch, Konrad: *Masonry Construction Manual;* Birkhäuser – Publishers for Architecture (Basel-Boston-Berlin), Institut für internationale Architektur-Dokumentation GmbH, Edition Detail, München 2001

Phillips, Roger: *Trees in Britain, Europe and North America;* Pan Books, London 1978

Piranomonte, Marina: *The Baths of Caracalla;* Soprintendenza Archeologiga di Roma, Mondalori Electa S.p.A., Roma 2002

Pizzoni, Filippo: *The Garden – A History in Landscape and Art;* Aurum Press Ltd, London 1999

Powell Smith, Vincent: *Building Contract Dictionary;* Architectural Press, London 1985

Pugliese Carratelli, Giovanni (ed.): *Western Greeks;* Bompiani, RCS Libri and Grandi Opere S.p.A., 1996

Quiney, Anthony: *The Traditional Buildings of England;* Thames and Hudson Ltd, London 1990

Racinet, A.: *The Encyclopedia of Ornament;* Studio Editons, London 1988

Ramsey, Charles G. & Sleeper, Harold R.: *Architectural Graphic Standards;* John Wiley and Sons, Inc., New York-London-Sydney-Toronto 1970

Ramuz, Mark (ed.): *The Encyclopedia of Woodworking;* Grange Books, Quantum Publishing Ltd, Oceana Books, London 2001

Rasmussen, Steen Eiler: *Experiencing Architecture;* MIT Press, Cambridge 1964

Rasmussen, Steen Eiler: *London – The Unique City;* MIT Press, Cambridge 1991

Reed, David: *The Art and Craft of Stonecaping – Setting and Stacking Stone;* Lark Books, Asheville, North Carolina 1998

Reed, Peter (ed.): *Alvar Aalto – Between Humanism and Materialism;* The Museum of Modern Art, Harry N. Abrams, New York 1998

Renn, Derek: *Caerphilly Castle;* Cadw: Welsh Historic Monuments (Crown Copyright), Cardiff 1997

Rich, Jack C.: *The Materials and Methods of Sculpture;* Dover Publications, Inc., New York 1974

Richards, Ian: *Abbeys of Europe – Great Buildings of the World;* The Hamlyn Publishing Group Ltd, Feltham, Middlesex 1968

Richardson, Barry A.: *Wood in Construction;* The Construction Press Ltd, Lancaster 1976

Richardson, Barry Arthur: *Remedial Treatment of Buildings;* The Construction Press Ltd, Lancaster, London, New York 1980

Roberts, Marion & Greed, Clara (ed.): *Approaching Urban Design – The Design Process;* Longman, Pearson Education Ltd, London 2001

Robertson, D.S.: *A Handbook of Greek and Roman Architecture;* Cambridge University Press 1959

Rocco, Giorgio: *Introduzione allo studio degli ordini architettoni antichi;* Ediirice Librerie Dedalo, Roma 1995

Roget, Peter Mark: *Roget's Thesaurus;* Penguin Books, England 1980

Rohde, Elisabeth: *Pergamon, Burgberg und Altar;* Verlag C.H. Beck, München 1982

Roland, Conrad: *Frei Otto – Structures;* Longman Group Ltd, London 1972

Rosenberg, Jerome L. & Epstein, Lawrence M.: *Theory and Problems of College Chemistry;* Schaums's Outline of Theory and Problems of College Chemistry, McGraw-Hill, Inc., USA 1990

Roux, Georges: *Ancient Iraq;* Penguin Books Ltd, Middlesex 1980

Ruskin, John: *The Stones of Venice;* Little, Brown and Company, Bellew and Highton Publishers Ltd, London 1981

Saarikangas, Kirsi: *Model Houses for Model Families – Gender, Ideology and the Modern Dwelling, the Type-planned Houses of the 1940s in Finland;* Studia Historica 45, Suomen historiallinen seura, Vammalan kirjapaino Oy 1993

Salaman, R.A.: *Dictionary of Woodworking Tools c.1700-1970 and Tools of Allied Trades;* George Allen and Unwin Hyman Ltd, London 1982

Salvadori, Mario: *Why Buildings Stand up – The Strenght of Architecture;* W.W. Norton and Company, Inc., New York 1990

Saylor, Henry H.: *Dictionary of Architecture;* Science Editions, John Wiley and Sons Inc., New York 1963

Scarre, Chris: *Chronicle of the Roman Emperors;* Thames and Hudson, London 1995

Schilling, Terrence G. & Schilling, Patricia M.: *Intelligent Drawings – Managing CAD and Information Systems in the Design Office;* McGraw-Hill Book Company, R.R. Donnelley and Sons Company, USA 1987

Schumann, Walter: *Rocks, Minerals and Gemstones;* HarperCollins Publishers, Frome and London 1995

Schäfer, Heinrich: *Principles of Egyptian Art;* Oxford University Press, Clarendon Press, Oxford 1974

Scott, John S.: *The Penguin Dictionary of Building;* Penguin Books 1982

Scott, John S.: *The Penguin Dictionary of Civil Engineering;* Penguin Books 1982

Scott, Peter: *The Thames and Hudson Manual of Metalworking;* Thames and Hudson Ltd, London 1978

Scranton, Robert L.: *Greek Architecture – The Great Ages of World Architecture;* Studio Vista Ltd, London 1968

Scully, Vincent: *Architecture – The Natural and the Manmade;* St. Martin's Press, New York 1991

Sealey, Antony: *Bridges and Aquaducts;* Hugh Evelyn Ltd, London 1976

Sear, Frank: *Roman Architecture;* Batsford Academic and Educational Ltd, London 1982

Seike, Kiyosi: *The Art of Japanese Joinery;* Weatherhill/Tankosha, New York-Tokyo-Kyoto, 1978

Seymour, John: *The Forgotten Arts;* Dorling Kindersley Ltd, London

Speltz, Alexander: *The Styles of Ornament;* Dover Publications Inc., New York 1959

Spencer, A.J.: *Death in Ancient Egypt;* Penguin Books, London 1982

Spreiregen, Paul D.: *Urban Design – The Architecture of Towns and Cities;* McGraw-Hill Publishing Co. AIA, USA 1965

Stafford, Maureen & Ware, Dora: *An Illustrated Dictionary of Ornament;* St. Martin's Press, New York 1974

Stead, Ian: *Celtic Art in Britain before the Roman Conquest;* British Museum Press, London 1985

STEP 1 (Structural Timber Education Program): *Puurakenteet – suunnitteluperusteet, materiaaliominaisuudet, rakenneosat, liitokset;* Valtion teknillinen tutkimuskeskus ja Rakennustieto Oy, Tampere 1996

Stephens, John H.: *The Guinness Book of Structures – Bridges, Towers, Tunnels, Dams...* Guinness Superlatives Limited, Enfield, Middlesex 1976

Stephenson, John: *Building Regulations 1976 in Detail with Amendments 1, 2 and 3;* International Thomas Publishing Ltd, Aylesbury 1984

Stierlin, Hans: *Encyclopedia of World Architecture;* Benedikt Taschen Verlag GmbH, Köln 1994

Stierlin, Henri: *Greece – From Mycenae to the Parthenon;* Tashen GmBH, Köln 2001

Stierlin, Henri: *The Pharaohs' Master-builders;* Finest S.A./Éditions Pierre Terrail, Paris 1995

Stratton, Arthur: *Elements of Form and Design in Classic Architecture;* Studio Editions, Bestseller Publications Ltd, London 1987

Strefford, John & McMurdo, Guy: *Woodwork Technology for Schools and Golleges;* Schofield and Sims Ltd, Huddersfield 1978

Sturgis, Russel: *Architectural Sourcebook, Russel Sturgis 1836-1909;* Van Nostrand Reinhold, New York 1984

Summerson, John: *The Architecture of the Eighteenth Century;* Thames and Hudson, London 1994

Summerson, John: *The Classical Language of Architecture;* Thames and Hudson, London

Sunley, (eds) John & Bedding, B.: *Timber in Construction;* Batsford Ltd/TRADA, London 1985

Sutton, David: *Pocket Guide of Trees of Britain and Europe;* Larousse, London 1995

Sutton, Ian: *Western Architecture – A Survey from Ancient Greece to the Present;* Thames and Hudson Ltd, London and New York 1999

Suzuki, Kakichi: *Early Buddhist Architecture in Japan;* Kodansha International Ltd and Shibundo, Tokyo 1980

Szokolay, S.V.: *Environmental Science Handbook;* The Construction Press, Lancaster 1980

Tafuri, Manfred & Dal Co, Francesco: *Modern Architecture 1 and 2;* Faber and Faber Ltd, London 1986

Tafuri, Manfredo: *Architecture and Utopia – Design and Capitalist Development;* MIT Press, Cambridge, Massachusetts and London, England 1977

Taylor, Arnold: *Caernarfon Castle and Town Walls;* Cadw: Welsh Historic Monuments, Cardiff 1993

Thames and Hudson: *Thames and Hudson Encyclopedia of 20th Century Architecture;* Thames and Hudson, London 1986

Tomlinson, R.A.: *Greek and Roman Architecture;* British Museum Press, London 1995

Tuck, Allene (ed.): *Oxford Dictionary of Business English for Learners of English;* Oxford University Press, Oxford

Turner, Denis Philip: *Window Glass Design Guide;* The Architectural Press Ltd and Pilkington Brothers Ltd, London 1977

Turner, Jane (ed.): *The Dictionary of Art I-XXXIV;* Macmillan Publishers Ltd, London 1996

Turner, William Wirt: *Simplified Perspective – Its Theory and Practical Application;* The Ronald Press Company, New York 1947

Tutt, Patricia & Adler, David: *New Metric Handbook Planning and Design Data;* Reed Educational and Professional Publishing Ltd, Bodmin, Cornwall 1996

Tzonis, Alexander & Lefaivre, Liane: *Classical Architecture – The Poetics of Order;* MIT Press, Cambridge, Mass. and London, England 1989

van der Ree, Paul & Smienk, Gerrit & Steenbergen, Clemens: *Italian Villas and Gardens;* Prestel-Verlag Verlegerdienst München Gmbh and Co Kg, Amsterdam 1993

Vanderberghe, J-P: *Elsevier's Dictionary of Architecture;* 1988

Vastad, Kurt & Hallén, Lars & Visanti, Irmeli: *Takka ja uuni;* Tammi, Helsinki 1978

Vaughan, William: *Europäische Kunst im 19. Jahrhundert, Band 1: 1780-1850;* Verlag Herbert Freiburg im Breisgau 1990

Vignola, Giacomo Barozzi da: *Canon of the Five Orders of Architecture;* Acanthus Press, New York 1999

Vitruvius: *The Ten Books on Architecture;* Dover Publications, Inc., New York 1960

Walker, Derek & Addis, Bill: *Happold – The Confidence to Build;* Happold Trust Publications Ltd, P.J. Reproductions, London 1997

Walker, Peter M.B (ed.): *Chambers – Dictionary of Science and Technology;* Chambers Harrap Publishers Ltd, Edinburgh 1999

Walkes, J.A.: *Glossary of Architecture + Design since 1945;* Library Association Publications, UK 1992

Ward-Perkins, John B.: *Roman Architecture;* History of World Architecture; Faber and Faber, London 1988

Ward-Perkins, John B.: *Roman Imperial Architecture;* Pelican History of Art, Penguin Books, London 1990

Watkin, David: *A History of Western Architecture;* Barrie and Jenkins, London 1986

Webster: *Webster's Encyclopedic Unabridged Dictionary of the English Language;* Gramercy Books, New York – Avenel, New Jersey 1989

Weidhaas, Ernest R.: *Architectural Drafting and Construction – Third Edition;* Allyn and Bacon, Inc.; Boston-London-Sydney-Toronto 1985

West, T.W.: *Architecture in England;* The English Universities Press Ltd, Cox and Wyman Ltd, London 1966

White, Anthony & Robertson, Bruce: *Architecture and Ornament – A Visual Guide;* Studio Vista, Cassell, London 1990

White, Ron: *How Computers Work;* Ziff-Davis Press, Emeryville, California, USA 1993

Whittick, Arnold: *Encyclopedia of Urban Planning;* McGraw-Hill Book Company, New York 1974

Whittle, Elisabeth: *Glanmorgan and Gwent – A Guide to Ancient and Historic Wales;* HMSO, London 1992

Wickberg, Nils Erik: *Senaatintori – the Senate Square;* Anders Nyborg A/S International Publishers Ltd, Rungstedt Kyst 1981

Wigginton, Michael: *Glass in Architecture;* Phaidon Press Ltd, London 1996

Wildung, Dietrich: *Egypt – From Prehistory to the Romans;* Taschen GmBH, Köln 2001

Willis, A.J. & George, W.N.B.: *The Architect in Practice;* Granada Publishing Ltd, London 1982

Wilson Jones, Mark: *Principles of Roman Architecture;* Yale University Press, New Haven and London 2000

Windows – An Interior View: A Joint Student Project of Technische Hogeschool Delft Afdeling Bouwkunde – Vakgroep Interieur, Netherlands and City of Birmingham Polytechnics School of Interior Design, England 1979

Wittkower, Rudolf: *Art and Architecture in Italy 1600-1750;* The Pelican History of Art, Penguin Books Ltd, Harmondsworth, Middlesex 1980

Wright, Lawrence: *Perspective in Perspective;* Routledge and Kegan Paul, London-Boston-Melbourne-Henley 1983

Wycherley, R.E.: *How the Greeks Built Cities;* Anchor Books, Doubleday and Company Inc., Garden City, New York 1969

Yarwood, Doreen: *Encyclopedia of Architecture;* Batsford UK, London 1985

Yarwood, Doreen: *English Interiors: Pictorial Guide and Glossary;* Lutterworth, Guildford 1983

Yarwood, Doreen: *The Architecture of Europe – The Ancient Classical and Byzantine World, 3000 BC – AD 1453;* B.T. Batsford Ltd, London 1992

Zboinski, A.: *Dictionary of Architecture and Building Trades;* Pergamon 1963

Zwerger, Klaus: *Wood and Wood Joints – Building Traditions of Europe and Japan;* Birkhäuser – Verlag für Architektur, Basel-Berlin-Boston 2000

Önen, Ülgür: *Ephesus – The Way It Was – The City Viewed in Reconstructions;* Akademia Tanitma Merkezi, Izmir 1985

FOREIGN LANGUAGE:

Adam, Ernst: *Vorromanik und Romanik;* Umschau Verlag Breidenstein KG, Frankfurt am Main 1968

Afanassjewa, W. & Lukonin, W. & Pomeranzewa, N.: *Kunst in Altvorderasien und Ägypten;* VEB Verlag der Kunst, Dresden 1977

Ahoranta, Jukka & Ahoranta Jaakko: *Sähkötekniikka – WSOY – Kone- ja metallitekniikka;* WSOY, Porvoo-Helsinki-Juva, 1988

Ahstrand, Jan Torsten: *Arkitekturtermer;* Studentlitteratur 1969

Ahto, Sampo & Kilkki, Pentti & Knapas, Rainer: *Hämeen linna;* Sotasokeat ry:n kevätjulkaisu 1973, Oy Länsi-Savon Kirjapaino, Mikkeli 1973

Ahto, Sampo. (toim.): *Keski- ja Pohjois-Suomen rauniolinnat;* Sotasokeat ry:n kevätjulkaisu 1978, Kauppakirjapaino Oy, Helsinki 1978

Ahto, Sampo. (toim.): *Olavinlinna;* Sotasokeat ry:n kevätjulkaisu 1975, Kauppakirjapaino Oy, Helsinki 1975

Ahto, Sampo. (toim.): *Viipurin linna;* Sotasokeat ry:n kevätjulkaisu 1976, Kauppakirjapaino Oy, Helsinki 1976

Airola, Olli: *Kymenkartanon linnoitus – Kyminlinna;* Kymenlaakson Maakuntaliitto ry., WSOY, Porvoo 1970

Alén, Holger: *Maalit ja niiden käyttö;* Opetushallitus, Hakapaino Oy, Helsinki 1999

Allas, Anja: *Ympäristömielikuvat ja kaupunkisuunnittelu – ympäristökuvausten liittäminen osaksi kaupunkirakenteen ja kaupunkikuvan suunnittelua;* Arkkitehtuurin osasto, Oulun yliopisto, Acta Univ. Oul C 71, Oulu 1993

Anderson, Johan *et.al.*: *Teräs asuntorakentamisessa;* Teräsrakenneyhdistys, Rakennustieto Oy, Helsinki 1995

Andersson, John H.: *Lämpöoppi;* Oy Edita Ab, Espoo 1998

Andreae, Bernard: *Römische Kunst;* Verlag Herbert Freiburg im Breisgau 1982

Antikainen, P.J.: *Yleinen ja epäorgaaninen kemia;* WSOY, Porvoo-Helsinki-Juva 1980

Anttonen, Arto & Hytönen, L.: *Yhdyskuntatekniikka;* Rakentajain Kustannus Oy, Helsinki; Gummerrus Kirjapaino Oy, Jyväskylä 1988–1991

Ars – Suomen Taide 1–6: Otava, Helsinki-Keuruu 1987–1990

Ars Universitaria 1640–1990: *Arkkitehtuuripiirustuksia ja huonekaluja Helsingin yliopiston kokoelmista – näyttelyluettelo;* Helsingin yliopisto, Frenckellin Kirjapaino Oy, Espoo 1990

Asp, Gustaf Edvard: *Huonerakenteiden oppi: 1. vihko; Kivirakenteita (1900), 2. vihko; Puurakenteita (1903), 3. vihko; Rautarakenteet ja rautabetonirakenteet (1908), 4. ja 5. vihko; Portaita ja puusepäntöitä(1903) ja 6. vihko; Tulisijat ja yksinkertaiset ilmanvaihtolaitokset (1902);* Alkuperäiset teokset Turun Suomalainen Kirja- ja Sanomalehti paino Oy, faksimilejäljennös TKK:n monistamo, Arkkitehtuurin historian laitos, Otaniemi 1992

Aspelin, Heino: *Rakennustarvikkeita – rakennusalan hakemisto;* Suomen Rakennusteollisuusliitto ry, Helsinki 1955, Kirjapaino Sana Oy

Auboyer, Jeannine & Goepper, Roger: *Kaukoidän taiteet, Intia, Kaakkois-Aasia, Kiina, Korea, Japani – Maailmantaide 6;* Tammi, Helsinki 1968, ks. Maailmantaide

Bagge, John *et al.*: *Talo ja koti, LVIS-työt;* Rakentajain Kustannus Oy, Helsinki 1979

Bang, Asger: *Jokamiehen työkaluopas;* Otava, Helsinki 1972

Baroni, Costantino: *L'architettura Lombarda da Bramante al Richini – Questioni di metodo;* Centro nazionale di studi rinascimento sezzione Lombarda, Edizioni de 'L'Arte', Milano 1941

Bernabei, Giancarlo: *Otto Wagner;* Verlag für Architektur Artemis Zürich und München 1986

Berve, Helmut & Gruben, Gottfried: *Tempel und Heiligtümer der Griechen;* Hirmer Verlag, München 1978

Betonikeskus ry: *ITB – Itsetiivistyvbetoni;* Suomen Betonitieto Oy, Painoyhtymä Oy, Loviisa 2004

Betonikeskus ry: *Itsetiivistyvän betonin käyttö paikallavalurakenteissa;* Suomen Betonitieto Oy, Multiprint Oy, Helsinki 2004

Biedermann, Hans: *Suuri symbolisanakirja;* WSOY, Helsinki-Porvoo-Juva 1996

Biedermann, Hans: *Symbollexikonet;* Bokförlaget Forum, Stockholm 1991

Björk, Paul J.: *Ruotsalais-suomalainen rakennusteknillinen sanasto;* Rakentajain Kustannusosakeyhtiö, Helsinki 1916

Björkholz, Dick: *Lämpöja kosteus, rakennusfysiikka;* Rakennustieto Oy, Helsinki 1997

Blomberg, Timo: *Bitumit;* Neste Oy ja Rakentajain Kustannus Oy, Jyväskylä 1990

Boekhoff, Hermann & Winzer, Fritz: *Weltgeschichte der abendländischen Kultur;* Georg Westermann Verlag, Braunschweig 1963

Boëthius, Axel: *Hur Rom byggdes under antiken;* Albert Bonniers förlag, Stockholm 1938

Boëthius, Gerda: *Studier i den nordiska timmerbyggnadskonsten från vikingatiden till 1800-talet;* Fritzes hovbokhandel i distribution, Viktor Pettersons Bokindustri Ab, Stockholm 1927

Bonsdorff & Gardberg & Lindberg & Kruskopf & Nummelin & Ringbom & Ringbom & Schalin: *Suomen taiteen historia keskiajalta nykyaikaan;* Schildts Kustannus Oy, Helsinki 1998

Borelius, Aron: *Västerlandets konsthistoria – Egypten – Mesopotamien – Grekland;* P.A. Norstedt and Söners förlag, Stockholm, Centralryckeriet AB, Borås 1983

Borelius, Aron: *Västerlandets konsthistoria – Roma antiqua – Italien – Spanien;* P. A. Norstedt and Söners förlag, Stockholm, Centralryckeriet AB, Borås 1985

Boström, Ragnhild: *Sveriges Domkyrkor;* Forum, Victor Pettersons Bokindustriaktiebolag, Stockholm 1952

Bottineau, Yves: *Die Kunst des Barock;* Verlag Herbert Freiburg im Breisgau 1986

Brasholz, Anton: *Julkisivumaalaus;* Rakentajain Kustannus Oy, Helsinki 1985

Breymann, G.A.: *Muri – construzioni in mattoni ed di pietre artificiali e naturali (1885);* Edizioni Librerie Dedalo, Roma 1995

Broby-Johansen, R.: *Arkitaide – maailmantaide;* Euroopan taiteen tyylin kehitys; Tammi, Helsinki 1977

Broomé, Catarina & Cottin, Catherine: *I kyrkans mitt – kloster, ordnar och kongregationer;* Proprius förlag, Stockholm 1989

Bruun, Patrick: *Aasia kohtaa Euroopan 200eKr – 500jKr;* Suuri maailmanhistoria, osa 3, Bokförlaget Bra Böcker, Höganäs, Koko kansan kirjakerho Oy, Brepols 1983

Bucksch, Herbert: *Wörterbuch für Baurecht, Grundstücksrecht und Raumordnung – Dictionary of Construction Law, Land Law and Regional Policy – Deu-Eng-Ger;* Bauverlag, Wiesbaden 1986

Busch, Harald & Lohse, Bernd: *Baukunst der Romanik in Europa;* Umschau Verlag, Frankfurt am Main 1959

Cachin, Francoise: *Europäische Kunst im 19. Jahrhundert, Band 2: 1850–1905;* Verlag Herbert Freiburg im Breisgau 1991

Caluwé, Robert de: *Ikonografian sanasto;* Painomies Oy, Helsinki 1988

Castrén, Paavo (ed.): *Pompeiji – Venuksen kaupunki;* Näyttelyjulkaisu 5.3.-31.5.1998, Ulkomaisen taiteen museo, Helsinki 1998

Castrén, Paavo & Pietilä-Castrén, Leena: *Antiikin käsikirja;* Otava, Helsinki & Keuruu 2000

Charbonneaux, Jean & Martin, Roland & Villard, Francois: *Grèce hellénistique;* Éditions Gallimard, 1971

Charbonneaux, Jean & Martin, Roland & Villard, Francois: *Grèce archïque;* Éditions Gallimard, 1968

Charbonneaux, Jean & Martin, Roland & Villard, Francois: *Grèce classique;* Éditions Gallimard, 1970

Chastel, André & Guillaume, Jean: *Les traités d'architecture de la renaissance;* Picard éditeur, Paris 1988

Chinery, Michael: *Pohjois-Euroopan hyönteiset;* Tammi, Helsinki 1978

Christensen, Torben & Göransson, Sven: *Kirkkohistoria I-II;* Oy Gaudeamus Ab, Weilin+Göös, Tapiola 1974

Cichy, Bodo: *Baukunst der alten Hochkulturen – Anfänge und erste Blütezeit der Baukunst;* Burkhard – Verlag Ernst Heyer, Essen 1965

Clark, Kenneth: *Länsimainen perintömme;* Helsinki 1971, KK:n kirjapaino

Coche de la Ferté, Étienne: *Byzantische Kunst;* Verlag Herbert Freiburg im Breisgau 1982

Constantini, Otto: *Vom Tempel zum Hochhaus – Baustilkunde;* Tyroli Verlag, Innsbruck-Wien-München, 1953

Conti, Flavio: *Stilar i konsten – renässansen;* Wahlström and Widstrand, Rizzoli Editore 1978

Corbeil, Jean-Claude & Archambault, Ariane & Rekiaro, Ilkka: *Tammen suuri kuvasanakirja englanti/suomi;* Kustannusosakeyhtiö Tammi, Helsinki, Tammer-Linkki, Tampere 1990

Corboz, André: *Haut Moyen Age;* Office du Livre, Fribourg 1970

Cornell, Elias: *Arkitekturens historia;* Bokförlaget Natur och Kultur, Stockholm 1949

Cornell, Elias: *Arkitekturhistoria;* Almqvist and Wiksells Boktryckeri Ab, Uppsala 1968

Cornell, Elias: *Byggnadstekniken – metoder och idéer genom tiderna;* Stellan Ståls tryckerier 1983

Cornell, Elias: *Rummet i arkitekturen – historia och nutid;* Norstedts Förlag Ab, Stockholm 1996

Cornell, Henrik: *Gotiken;* Albert Bonniers Förlag, Stockholm 1968

Dagen, Philippe: *L'Art Francais I-VI;* Flammarion 1998

Dahlgren, Timo & Helakorpi, Seppo & Jalonen, Leena: *Ammattikoulujen teknillisten alojen kemia;* Insinööriteto Oy, 1984

Danska, Arja: *Alttarin uudistaminen;* Lisensiaatintyö Taideteollisen korkeakoulun sisustusarkkitehtuurin ja huonekalusuunnittelun osastolla, Tampere 22.7.1999

Dendrologian Seura; Hämet-Ahti, Palmen, Alanko, Tigerstedt, Koistinen: *Suomen puu- ja pensaskasvio;* Yliopistopaino, Helsinki 1989

Der Kunst-Brockhaus 1-2: F. A. Brockhaus, Wiesbaden 1983

Description de l Egypte – Edition complète – Publiée par les ordres de Napoléon Bonaparte: Benedikt Taschen Verlag Gmbh, Köln 1994

Det Bästa: *Pä jakt efter det förgångna;* Reader's Digest AB, Stockholm 1982

Doerner, Max: *Maaliaineet ja niiden käyttö taidemaalauksessa;* Tammi, Helsinki; Lounais-Suomen Kirjapaino Oy, Turku 1954

Drake, Knut: *Raaseporin rauniot;* Raseborgs Gille r.f., Ekenäs Tryckeri Ab 1983

Drot, Jean-Marie *et al.*: *Roma Antiqua – Forum, Colisée, Palatin – Envois de archite;* Académie de France à Rome, École francaise de Rome and École nationale supérieure des Beaux-Arts, 1985

Dué, Andrea & Laboa, Juan Maria: *Kristinusko 2000 vuotta;* Kirjapaja Oy, Helsinki 1998

Durant, Will: *Kreikan kulttuuri;* WSOY, Helsinki – Porvoo 1951

Durliat, Marcel: *Romanische Kunst;* Verlag Herbert Freiburg im Breisgau 1983

Dührkop, Henry & Saretok, Vitold & Sneck, Tenho & Svendsen, Sven D.: *Laasti, muuraus, rappaus;* Rakentajain Kustannus Oy, Helsinki 1966

Effman, Wilhelm: *Die Kirche der Abtei Corvey;* Druck und Verlag Bonifacius-Druckerei, Paderborn 1929

Ehrola, Esko: *Liikenneväylien rakennesuunnittelun perusteet;* Rakennustieto Oy, Helsinki 1996

Elisseeff, Danielle & Vadime: *Japan – Kunst und Kultur;* Verlag Herbert Freiburg im Breisgau 1987

Engel: *Carl Ludvig Engel 1778-1840, näyttely Helsingin tuomiokirkon kryptassa 7.8.-14.9.1990;* näyttelyluettelo, Helsinki 1990

Enkvist, Terje: *Johdatusta orgaaniseen kemiaan;* Otava, Keuruu 1973

Enlund, Urho: *Talonrakennusoppi 3;* Otava, Keuruu 1986

Enlund, Urho: *Talonrakennusoppi 1-2;* Otava, Keuruu 1991

Eramo, Hynynen & Kiiras: *Rakennustyö;* Rakentajain kustannus, 1978

Erat & Erkkilä & Löfgren & Nyman & Peltola & Suokivi: *Aurinko-opas – aurinkoenergiaa rakennuksiin;* Kustantajat Sarmala Oy, Rakennusalan Kustantajat RAK, Helsinki 2001

Eriksson, Eva: *Den moderna staden tar form – arkitektur och debatt 1910-1935;* Ordfronts Förlag, Stockholm 2001

Eriksson, Eva: *Den moderna stadens födelse – Svensk arkitektur 1890-1920;* Ordfronts Förlag, Stockholm 1990

Erlande-Brandenburg, Alain: *Gotische Kunst;* Verlag Herbert Freiburg im Breisgau 1984

Eskola, Meri & Eskola, Tapani (ed.): *Helsingin helmi – Helsingin tuomiokirkko 1852–2002;* Kustannus Oy Projektilehti, Helsinki 2002

Eskola, Reijo & Pelkonen, Heikki: *Puutarharakentaja;* Ilves-paino Ky, Hämeenlinna 1991

Eskola, Reijo: *Ympäristön kivikirja;* Hämeen ammattikorkeakoulu, Julkaisu C:23, Hämeenlinna 2000

Eskola, Tapani: *Rakennuttajan käsikirja;* WSOY, Porvoo-Helsinki 1970

Etelä-Savon seutukaavaliitto: *Etelä-Savon rakennusperintö- kulttuurihistoriallisesti merkittävät kohteet;* Etelä-Savon seutukaavaliiton julkaisu 114, Mikkeli 1984

Fagerstedt, Kurt & Pellinen, Kerttu & Saranpaä, Pekka & Timonen, Tuuli: *Mikäpuu – mistäpuusta;* Yliopistopaino, Helsinki 1996

Fahr-Becker, Gabriele: *Jugendtyyli;* Könemann Verlagsgesellschaft mbH, Köln 2000

Fanelli, Giovanni & Trivisonno, Francesco: *Città antica in Toscana;* G. C. Sansoni Editore Nuova S.p.A., Firenze 1982

Ferrari, Silvia: *1900-luvun taide;* Tammi, Helsinki 2000

Ficacci, Luigi: *Giovanni Battista Piranesi – Selected Etchings;* Taschen GmbH, Köln 2001

Fokus-tietosanakirja Taide, osa 2, aakkoselliset osat; Otava, Helsinki 1972

Fokus-tietosanakirja Taide, osa 1, taidehistoria: Otava, Helsinki 1971

Fält, Nieminen, Tuovinen, Vesterinen: *Japanin kulttuuri;* Otava, Helsinki-Keuruu 1994

Försti, Elina & Järvi, Outi & Leinonen, Sari & Ruokangas, Sirpa: *Englanti-suomi, tekniikan ja kaupan sanakirja;* Gummerrus Kustannus Oy, Jyväskylä, Helsinki 1996

Garbini, Giovanni: *Muinainen maailma – Mesopotamian, Egyptin ja muiden Lähi-idän maiden taide – Maailmantaide 2;* Tammi, Helsinki 1968, ks. Maailmantaide

Gardberg, C.J.: *Kivestäja puusta – Suomen linnoja, kartanoita ja kirkkoja;* Otava, Keuruu 2002

Genewein, Anton: *Vom Romanischen bis zum Empire – eine Wanderung durch die Kunstformen dieser Stile;* Ferdinand Hirt and Sohn, Leipzig 1905

Gerlach, Christoph: *Vorzeichnungen auf gotischen Planrissen;* Böhlau Verlag GmbH, Köln-Wien 1986

Giedion, Siegfried: *Ewige Gegenwart – der Beginn der Arcitehktur;* Verlag M.DuMont Schauberg, Köln 1964

Gradmann, Erwin: *Baustilkunde;* Verlag Hallwag, Bern

Gradow, G.A.: *Stadt und Lebensweise;* VEB Verlag für Bauwesen, Berlin 1970

Graf, Ulrich & Nyström, E.J.: *Deskriptiivinen geometria;* Otava, Helsinki 1940

Grube, Ernst J.: *Islamin taide – Maailmantaide 5;* Tammi, Helsinki 1968, ks. Maailmantaide

Grönblom, Rolf: *Faaraoiden Egypti;* Schildts Kustannus Oy, Italia 2002

Gröndahl, Eeva (ed.): *Rakennustyön perusteet;* Oy Edita Ab, Helsinki 1997

Gunnes, Erik: *Paimentolaiskansat ja korkeakulttuurit 1000–1300;* Suuri maailmanhistoria, osa 4, Bokförlaget Bra Böcker, Höganäs, Koko kansan kirjakerho Oy, Brepols 1985

Gunnes, Erik: *Uskontojen marssi 500–1000;* Suuri maailmanhistoria, osa 4, Bokförlaget Bra Böcker, Höganäs, Koko kansan kirjakerho Oy, Brepols 1984

Götz K-H., Hoor D., Möhler K., Natterer J.: *Holzbau Atlas;* Institut für internationale Architektur-Dokumentation, München 1980

Haahtela, Y. & Kiiras, J.: *Talonrakennuksen kustannustieto 1990;* Raki 1990

Haapio, Markku (ed.): *Suomen kirkot ja kirkkotaide 1-2;* Etelä-Suomen Kustannus Oy, Lieto 1978

Haarala, Risto *et al.*: *Suomen kielen perussanakirja I-III;* Valtion painatuskeskus, Helsinki 1991, 1993, 1994

Haarni, Tuukka & Knuuti, Liisa (ed.): *Kaupunkikulttuuriin;* Yhdyskuntasuunnittelun täydennyskoulutuskeskus, TKK, Espoo 1993

Hahr, August: *Arkitekturen genom tiderna, del V, barock och klassicism, rokoko och nyantik;* Bokförlaget Natur och Kultur, Stockholm 1928

Haila, Sirpa: *Suomalaisuutta rakentamassa – arkkitehti Sebastian Gripenberg kulttuurifennomanian lipunkantajana;* Suomen Historiallinen Seura, Tutkimuksia 201, Hakapaino, Helsinki 1998

Hakalin, Pekka: *Hirsirakentaminen;* Rakentajain Kustannus Oy, Helsinki 1984

Hakalin, Pekka: *Rakennan hirrestä;* Rakentajain Kustannus Oy, Tammer-Paino Oy, Tampere 1987

Hallenberg, Riikka & Karppinen, Veli-Matti & Määttä, Jyrki: *Liike-elämän sanakirja englanti-suomi;* Taloustieto Oy 1996, Tammer-Paino Oy, Tampere

Hallström, Björn: *Måleriets material;* Wahlström and Widstrand, Borås 1986

Halme, Alpo: *Rakennus- ja huoneakustiikka, meluntorjunta;* Otakustantamo nro 378, Kuriiri, Helsinki 1987

Halminen, Esa & Kuvaja, Osmo & Köttö, Reijo: *Ilmastointitekniikka;* Opetushallitus ja Rakennusalan Kustantajat RAK, Helsinki 1994

Hanka, Heikki & Kotkavaara, Kari & Lehtonen, Timo: *Ortodoksinen kirkko ja akateemisen taiteen ihanteet;* Suomen ortodoksinen kirkkomuseo, Kuopion Liikekirjapaino, Kuopio 1994

Hantverkets bok: *Mureri;* Lindfors Bokförlag, Stockholm 1943

Hantverkets bok: *Snickeri;* Bokförlaget Natur och Kultur, Stockholm 1943

Harju, Pentti & Matilainen, Veijo: *LVI-tekniikka – korjausrakentaminen;* Opetushallitus ja Suomen LVI-liitto, Vantaa 2001

Harju, Pentti: *LVI-tekniikan perusteet;* Otava, Helsinki-Keuruu 1994

Hartikainen, Olli-Pekka: *Maarakennustekniikka;* Otatieto Oy, 435, Tammer-Paino Oy, Tampere 1994

Hartikainen, Olli-Pekka: *Tietekniikan perusteet;* Otatieto 467, Oy Yliopistokustannus/Otatieto, Helsinki 2001

Hauser, Alois: *Styl-lehre der architektonischen Formen des Mittelalters;* Alfred Hölder, K. und K. Hof- und Universitäts-Buchhändler, Wien 1899

Hautala, Mikko: Insinöörin (AMK) fysiikka; Lahden teho-opetus Oy, Lahti 1997

Hautecœr, Louis: *Histoire de l'architecture classique en France;* Auguste Picard, Paris 1943

Hawkes, Jacquetta: *Människans väg, allmän kulturhistoria från 35000 år f Kr till år 500 e Kr;* Generalstabens Litografiska Anstalt, Stockholm 1978

Hecht, Konrad: *Der St.Galler Klosterplan;* VMA-Verlag, Wiesbaden 1997

Heikkilä, J., Kangas, M. & Kettunen, R.: *Hirsirakennuksen veistotyöt.;* Ammattikasvatushallitus, VAPK, Helsinki 1987

Heikkilä, J. & Kangas, M. & Kettunen, R.: *Hirsirakennuksen kokoamis- ja sisustustyöt;* Ammattikasvatushallitus, VAPK, Helsinki 1987

Heikkilä, Matti: *Tekninen piirustus ja suunnittelu;* WSOY, Porvoo 1996

Heikkilä, Matti: *Tekniset piirustukset;* WSOY, Porvoo 1997

Heikkilä, Mikko & Santasalo, Tuomas & Karppinen, Seppo: *Suomalaisia kävelykeskustoja;* Ympäristöministeriö, Oy Edita Ab, Helsinki 1996

Heikkinen, Heinämies, Jaatinen, Kaila & Pietarila: *Talo kautta aikojen – kiinteän sisustuksen historia;* Rakentajain Kustannus Oy, Helsinki 1989

Heino, Erja & Sundholm, Pirjo: *Ekotalon rakennusaineet;* Rakennusalan kustantajat, Jyväskylä 1995

Heinonen & Kolm: *Yhdyskuntasuunnittelun sanasto;* Rakennuskirja, Helsinki 1984, 1700 sanaa

Heinonen, Joki, & Kononen: *Puutyöalan rakenneoppi ja ammattipiirustus;* Kirjayhtymä

Helamaa, Erkki: *Rakennuksen rungon suunnittelu;* Tampereen teknillinen korkeakoulu, opintomoniste nro 16, Tampere 1976

Helamaa, Erkki: *Rakennuksen rungon materiaalit;* Tampereen teknillinen korkeakoulu, opintomoniste nro 46, Tampere 1979

Helamaa, Erkki: *Vanhan rakentajan sanakirja – rakentamisesta, rakennuksista, rakenteista;* Suomalaisen Kirjallisuuden Seuran Toimituksia 988, Helsinki 2004

Helander, Vilhelm & Henttonen, Sauvo & Simons, Tom & Ahlqvist, Richard: *Suomenlinnan maisema – kunnostussuunnitelma;* Suomenlinnan hoitokunta, Art-Print Oy, Helsinki 1987

Helander, Vilhelm & Freese, Simo *et al.*: *Hokos warma voloi – taloja ja kyliäsaaristosta, Karjalasta ja Inkeristä – mittauspiirustuksia Teknillisen korkeakoulun arkkitehtiosastolta arkkitehtuurin historian kokoelmista vuosilta 1990 – 1996;* Pohjoinen, Helsinki 1997

Helin, Pekka & Turtiainen, Jukka & Vesikansa, Matti: *Kaupunkikuva ja rakentaminen;* Kaupunkimaisten yhdyskuntien kehittämiskampanja, julkaisu 5/1982, Valtion Painatuskeskus, Helsinki 1983

Hellström, B. Harald: *Vaakunatietoutta I – kilpi;* Suomen Taidepiirtäjäliiton julkaisuja I, Helsinki 1951

Hemilä, Simo & Utriainen, Juha: *Lämpöoppi;* Suomen fyysikkoseuran julkaisuja nro 3, Jyväskylä 1989

Herrmann, Ferdinand & Sauser, Ekkart: *Symbolik der katolischen Kirche, Tafelband;* Anton Hiersemann, Stuttgart 1966

Hidemark, Ove & Stavenow-Hidemark, Elisabet & Söderström, Göran & Unnerbäck, Axel: *Sårenoveras torp och gårdar;* ICA bokförlag, Västerås 1982

Hintzen-Bohlen, Brigitte: *Andalusia – taide ja arkkitehtuuri;* Könemann, Köln 2001

Hirvensalo, Lauri: *Saksa-suomi suursanakirja – Grosswörterbuch Deutsch-Finnisch;* WSOY, Porvoo-Helsinki-Juva 1993

Hissimääräykset: *Sähkötarkastuskeskuksen julkaisu A 8-89;* Gummerrus kirjapaino Oy, Jyväskylä 1990

Hollo, Erkki J. & Kuusiniemi, Kari: *Rakennuslaki ja oikeuskäytäntö;* Lakimiesliiton Kustannus, Helsinki 1989

Holthoer, Rostislav: *Muinaisen Egyptin kulttuuri;* Otava, Helsinki-Keuruu 1994

Honour, Hugh & Fleming, John: *Maailman taiteen historia;* Otava, Helsinki 1994

Horn, Paridon von & Bergentz, Torsten: *Portar;* Byggförlaget Stockholm, Stellan Ståls Tryckerier Ab, Stockholm 1982

Huhtiniemi, Seppo & Knuuttila, Ilkka: *Muuraus-, laatoitus- ja rappaustyöt;* Rakennusalan Kustantajat RAK, Kustantajat Sarmala Oy, Jyväskylä 1993

Huhtiniemi, Seppo & Kiviniemi, Jukka: *Elementtityöt BY 208;* Rakennustieto Oy, Tammer-Paino Oy, Tampere 1992

Huldt, Bo: *Ennen liennytystä 1945–1965;* Suuri maailmanhistoria, osa 14, Bokförlaget Bra Böcker, Höganäs, Koko kansan kirjakerho Oy, Brepols 1983

Huovinen, Lauri: *Italian renessanssikulttuuri;* Turun yliopiston historian laitoksen julkaisuja nro 17, Turun yliopiston offset-paino, Turku 1987

Hurme, Raija & Pesonen, Maritta: *Englantilais-suomalainen suursanakirja;* WSOY, Porvoo 1982

Hurme, Raija & Malin, Riitta-Leena & Syväoja, Olli: *Uusi suomi-englanti suursanakirja;* WSOY, Porvoo-Helsinki-Juva 1988

Hurme, Riitta: *Suomalainen lähiö Tapiolasta Pihlajamäkeen;* Suomen Tiedeseura, julkaisu 142, Ekenäs Tryckeri Ab, Tammisaari 1991

Hyttinen, Rainer: *Puuelementtirakentaminen;* Rakentajain Kustannus Oy, Helsinki 1984

Hyvärinen, Jari: *Hirsilinnojen aika;* Otava, Keuruu 1998

Häkkinen, Tarja & Saari Mikko & Vares Sirje & Vesikari Erkki & Leinonen Jarkko: *Ekotehokkaan rakennuksen suunnittelu;* VTT Rakennustekniikka ja Rakennustieto Oy, Tampere 1999

Häkkinen, Tarja & Kaipiainen, Maarit: *Ekologiset kriteerit rakennussuunnittelussa;* Rakennustieto Oy, Helsinki 1996

Häkli, Markku: *Ruiskumaalaus;* VAPK-kustannus, Opetushallitus, Helsinki 1992

Håland, Randi & Gunnar: *Alussa oli... ensimmäiset ihmiset ja ensimmäiset sivilisaatiot;* Suuri maailmanhistoria, osa 1, Bokförlaget Bra Böcker Höganäs, Koko kansan kirjakerho Oy, Brepols 1983

Hällström, Olof af: *Sveaborg – Viapori – Suomenlinna – The Island Fortress off Helsinki, an Architectural History;* Anders Nyborg A/S International Publishers Ltd, Rungstedt Kyst 1986

Härö, Elias & Kaila, Panu: *Pohjalainen talo – rakentajan opas;* Etelä-Pohjanmaan Maakuntaliitto, Keski-Pohjanmaan Maakuntaliitto, Svenska Österbottens Lanskapsförbund, Kyriiri Oy, Helsinki 1976

Häyrynen, Maunu: *Maisemapuistosta reformipuistoon, Helsingin kaupunginpuistot ja puistopolitiikka 1880-luvulta 1930-luvulle;* Helsinki-seura – Helsingfors-Samfundet ry, Serieoffset, Turku 1994

Höner, Heinrich: *Puuntyöstötekniikka;* WSOY, Porvoo 1957

Höyhtyä, Matti & Vänttinen Yrjö: *Muuratut rakenteet 1, talonrakennus;* Rakentajain Kustannus Oy, Gummeruksen kirjapaino, Jyväskylä 1989

Ihalainen, Aaltonen, Aromäki & Sihvonen: *Valmistustekniikka;* Otatieto 487, Karisto Oy, Hämeenlinna 1991

Iisakkila, Leena: *Perustietoa maisemaan vaikuttavista luonnontekijöistä;* Otakustantamo nro 410, Otapaino, Espoo 1978

Ikola, Osmo: *Nykysuomen käsikirja;* Weilin+Göös, Gummerus Kirjapaino Oy, Jyväskylä 1991

Ikonen, Leander: *Ruotsalais-suomalais-saksalais-englantilainen rakennussanojen luettelo;* Suomen Teknillinen yhdistys, Kuopion Uusi Kirjapaino, Kuopio 1889

Ikävalko, Elina: *Painotuotteen tekijän käsikirja;* Tietopaketti Oy, Tampere 1995

Immonen, Kari & Råman, Tuula: *Maalatun julkisivun kesto;* SITRA:n julkaisusarja B: 108, Helsinki 1990

Insko: *Liikennetekniikka 14–72;* Insinöörijärjestöjen koulutuskeskus, Helsinki 1972

Jackson, Albert & Day, David: *Työkalukirja;* Otava, Keuruu 1982; (original: The Complete Book of Tools)

Jalava, Matti: *Puun rakenne ja ominaisuudet;* WSOY, Porvoo-Helsinki 1952

Jalkanen, R., Kajaste, T., Kauppinen, T. & Pakkala, P. & Rosengren, C.: *Asuinaluesuunnittelu;* Rakennustieto Oy, Tammer-Paino, Tampere 1997

Janson, H.W.: *Suuri taidehistoria;* WSOY, Porvoo 1965

Jantzen, Hans: *Die Gotik des Abendlandes – Idee und Wandel;* Verlag M.DuMont Scahuberg, Köln 1963

Jarle, P-O.: Rakenteiden yksikkökustannuksia 1990, RKOY 1990

Jaxtheimer, Bodo W.: *Suuri piirustus- ja maalauskirja;* WSOY, Porvoo-Helsinki 1964

Jeskanen, Timo: *Kansanomaisuus ja rationalismi – näkökohtia Suomen puuarkkitehtuuriin 1900–1925 esimerkkinä Oiva Kallion kesähuvila Villa Oivala;* Lisensiaatintyö Teknillisen korkeakoulun arkkitehtiosastolla 2.6.1998 valvojana professori Vilhelm Helander

Jestaz, Bernard: *Die Kunst der Renaissance;* Verlag Herbert Freiburg im Breisgau 1985

Johansson, Hans: *Kodin käsikirja- rakenna, maalaa, korjaa itse;* Kirjayhtymä Oy, Helsinki 1992

Johnsson, Lars: *Jokamiehen puutyökirja;* Tammi, Helsinki 1977

Johnsson, Raul & Lappalainen, Lea & Varjoranta, Kimmo & Virtanen, Pekka: *Puusepänverstaan tuotanto;* Käsi- ja taideteollisuusliitto ry, Helsinki

Jormalainen, Pentti & Matilainen, Ari: *Korjausrakennustyöt;* Kustantajat Sarmala Oy, Jyväskylä 1999

Jørnæs, Bjarne: *Stilar i konsten;* Almqvist and Wiksell Förlag AB, Stockholm 1977

Jungmann, Josef Andreas: *Symbolik der katholischen Kirche;* Anton Hiersemann, Stuttgart 1960

Junttila, Ulla-Kirsti: *Muuttuvat kadunkalusteet;* Rakennuskirja Oy, Jyväskylä 1986

Jutikkala, Eino & Kaukiainen, Yrjö & Åström, Sven-Erik: *Suomen taloushistoria 1-3;* Tammi, Helsinki 1980

Juvonen, Risto & Johanson, P.E.: *Sahateollisuus – mekaaninen metsäteollisuus 2;* Ammattikasvatushallitus, VAPK, Helsinki 1986

Jylhä-Vuorio, Heikki: *Keramiikan materiaalit;* VAPK-kustannus, Opetushallitus, Helsinki 1992

Jäppinen, Harri: *Synonyymisanakirja;* WSOY, Porvoo-Helsinki-Juva 1989

Järvelä, J.: *Maalarin aine- ja ammattioppi;* WSOY, Porvoo-Helsinki 1952

Järventaus, Esko: *Rakennustaide, Tiedon portaat, osa 6;* WSOY, Porvoo, 1969

Järvi, Petteri & Segersven, Anders: *Heraldiikka ja historia – heraldisten tnnusten ymmärtäminen sekäniiden käyttöhistoriantutkimuksessa;* Partioheraldikot ry., Kirjapaino Grafia, Turku 2000

Järvinen, Kalevi: *Puurakennusten ulkomaalaus;* Rakennustieto Oy, Helsinki 1999

Järvinen, Pasi (ed.): *Muovin suomalainen käsikirja;* Muovifakta Oy, Porvoo 2000

Jääskeläinen, Lauri & Syrjänen, Olavi: *Maankäyttö- ja rakennuslaki selityksineen – käytännön käsikirja:* Rakennustieto Oy, Helsinki 2000

Jääskeläinen, Raino: *Pohjarakennuksen perusteet;* Tammertekniikka, Tampere 2003

Kahri, Esko & Pyykönen, Hannu: *Asuntoarkkitehtuuri ja -suunnittelu;* Rakennuskirja Oy, Helsinki 1984

Kaila, Panu (ed.): *Antiikin rakennustekniikka – Rooma;* Julkaisu C74, Oulun yliopisto, Arkkitehtuurin osasto, Oulun yliopistopaino 2002

Kaila, Panu: *Kevät toi maalarin – perinteinen ulkomaalaus;* Rakennusalan kustantajat RAK, Kustantajat Sarmala Oy, Helsinki 2000

Kaila, Panu: *Mittajärjestelmät Suomessa;* Museoviraston moniste 25.4.1979

Kaila, Panu: *Talotohtori – rakentajan pikkujättiläinen;* WSOY, Porvoo 1997

Kaila, Pietarila & Tomminen: *Talo kautta aikojen – julkisivujen historia;* Rakentajain Kustannus Oy, Helsinki 1987

Kaitera, Heikki: *Työpaikat ja asuinympäristö;* Otakustantamo nro 399, Otapaino, Espoo 1982

Kaittola, Keijo *et al.*: *Rakennustyön järjestysohjeet selityksineen;* Rakentajain Kustannus Oy, Jyväskylä 1989

Kaivonen, Juha-Antti (ed.): *Rakennusten korjaustekniikka ja talous;* Tampereen teknillinen korkeakoulu ja Rakennustieto Oy, Helsinki 1994

Kalff, Ir.L.C.: *Kunstlicht und Architektur;* N.V.Philips' Gloeilampenfabriekien Eindhoven, Niederlande 1943

Kallioinen, Sarvimäki, Takala & Ådahl: *Maalialan materiaalioppi – käsikirja;* Ammattikasvatushallitus, Valtion painatuskeskus, Helsinki 1990

Kanerva, Liisa (ed.): *Rooma: Antiikin arkkitehtuuri ja sen jälkivaikutus – seminaariesitelmiä 1992–1993* Teknillisen korkeakoulun arkkitehtiosaston julkaisuja 1994/14, Espoo 1995

Kangasaho, J. & Mäkinen, J. & Oikkonen, J. & Paasonen, J. & Salmela, M.: *Geometria – pitkä matematiikka;* WSOY, Porvoo-Helsinki-Juva 1995

Kankainen, Jouko & Junnonen, Juha-Matti: *Rakennuttaminen;* Rakennustieto Oy, Tammer-Paino Oy, Tampere 2001

Kapanen, Jaakko: *Kiinteistön lämmitys- ja vesiputkistojen kunnossapito;* Kiinteistöalan kustannus Oy – REP Ltd, Suomen Kiinteistöliitto, Helsinki 1995

Kara, Kimmo (ed.): *Heraldiikan opas;* Suomen Heraldinen Seura ry., Julkaisusarja No. 25, WSOY:n kirjapaino, Porvoo 1998

Kara, Kimmo: Vaakunaselitys – opastusta vaakunaselityksen laadintaan; Suomen Heraldinen Seura, Painomies Oy, Helsinki 1989

Karamäki, E.M.: *Epäorgaaniset kemikaalit;* Kustannusliike Tietoteos, Gummerruksen kirjapaino, Jyväskylä 1983

Karhunen, Lassila, Pyy, Ranta, Räsänen, Saikkonen & Suosara: *Lujuusoppi;* Otatieto nro 543, Oy Yliopistokustannus/Otatieto, Hakapaino Oy, Helsinki 2004

Karjalainen, Markku & Koiso-Kanttila, Jouni: *Moderni puukaupunki – puu ja arkkitehtuuri;* Woodfocus Oy, Rakennustieto Oy, Tampere 2002

Kasso, Matti: *Asunto- ja kiinteistölainsäädäntö;* Rakentajain Kustannus Oy, Jyväskylä 1990

Kauppi, Ulla-Riitta & Miltšik, Mihail: *Viipuri – Vanhan Suomen pääkaupunki;* Suomalaisen Kirjallisuuden Seura, Helsinki 1993

Kauppinen, Heta & Multimäki, Leila: *Perspektiivioppi;* Kirjayhtymä, Oy Länsi-Suomi, Rauma 1978

Kaupunkiliitto: *Kaupunkiliikenteen suunnittelu;* Kaupunkiliiton käsikirjoja ja tutkimuksia C 7, Helsinki 1972

Kause, Kari: *Keskiasteen kemia;* Kustannus Ky Teknikus, Kirjapaino Grafia Oy, Turku 1981

Kavaja, Reino: *Muuraustyöt;* Rakennustieto Oy/ Rakentajain Kustannus, Jyväskylä 1992

Kavaja, Reino: *Rakennuksen puutyöt;* Rakentajain Kustannus Oy, Tampere 1991

Kavaja-Mentu-Jormalainen: *Muuraustyöt;* Rakentajain Kustannus Oy, Helsinki 1981, Gummerrus Oy:n kirjapaino, Jyväskylä 1981

Keinänen, W.: *Rakennusopin tietokirja ammattikouluja ja itseopiskelua varten;* WSOY, Porvoo 1943

Kekkonen, Mauri: *Suuri sorvauskirja;* Kustannus Oy Ajatus, Hämeenlinna 1997

Keppo, Juhani: *Omakotitalo rakennushankkeena – Talonrakentajan käsikirja 5:* Rakentajan tietokirjat, Gummerrus Kirjapaino Oy, Saarijärvi 2003

Keppo, Juhani: *Pientalon vesikatto- ja ulkoverhoustyöt – Talonrakentajan käsikirja 4;* Rakentajan tietokirjat, Gummerrus Kirjapaino Oy, Saarijärvi 2002

Keppo, Juhani: *Puutalon runkotyöt – Talonrakentajan käsikirja;* Rakentajan tietokirjat, Gummerrus Kirjapaino Oy, Jyväskylä 1993

Keronen, Asko: *Talonrakennusoppi;* Tampereen teknillinen korkeakoulu, opintomoniste 178, Tampere 1994

Kervanto Nevanlinna, Anja & Kolbe, Laura (ed.): *Suomen kulttuurihistoria 3 – Oma maa ja maailma;* Tammi, Helsinki 2003

Ketvel, Lauri & Toivonen, Matti: *Pisara 8, kemia;* Weilin+Göös, Tampere 1988

Kidson, Peter: *Keskiajan taide – Maailmantaide 7;* Tammi, Helsinki 1968, ks. Maailmantaide

Kihlström, Bengt Ingmar: *Kyrkorummet – kult och konst genom tiderna;* Proprius förlag, Stockholm 1989

Kiljunen, Veikko: *Taidemaalarin materiaalioppi;* Otava, Helsinki-Keuruu 1981

Kilkki, Seppo (toim.): *Hämeen linna;* Sotasokeat ry:n kevätjulkaisu 1973, Oy Länsi-Savon kirjapaino, Mikkeli 1973

Killer, W.K.: *Illustrerad byggnadsteknisk engelska och tyska;* Bauverlag Gmbh, Wiesbaden und Berlin, 1984

Kilpeläinen, Mikko & Ukonmaanaho, Antti & Kivimäki, Marko: *Avoin puurakennusjärjestelmäelementtirakenteet;* Wood Focus Oy, Vammalan Kirjapaino Oy, 2001

Kilström, Bengt Ingmar: *Kyrkorummet – kult och konst genom tiderna;* Proprius förlag, Stockholm 1989

Kinnunen, Jukka: *Muuratut rakenteet 2 – rakennesuunnittelu;* Rakentajain Kustannus Oy, Vaasa Oy:n kirjapaino, Vaasa 1988

Kinnunen, Saarinen, Tiira, Ulvinen, Väänänen: *Teräsrakenteiden suunnittelu;* Rakentajain Kustannus Oy, Vammalan Kirjapaino, Vammala 1989

Kitson, Michael: *Barokin aikakausi, barokki, rokokoo ja uusklassismi – Maailmantaide 9;* Tammi, Helsinki 1968, ks. Maailmantaide

Kivelä, Simo K.: *Perpektiivioppi ja aksonometria;* Otakustantamo 355, TKY Otapaino, Espoo 1976

Kivelä, Simo K.: *Algebra ja geometria;* Otatieto Oy 523, Karisto Oy, Hämeenlinna 1990

Kivijärvi, Harri: *Miten pyramidit rakennettiin – muinaisten kansojen kivityö;* Otava, Keuruu 1990

Kivimäki, Jaana & Immonen, Kari: *Ikkunoiden kunnossapito ja uusiminen;* Energiataloudellisten rakennusten ja rakennusosien tutkimusohjelma, ETRR raportti 19, Painatuskeskus Oy, Helsinki 1993

Kivinen, Antti & Mäkitie, Osmo: *Kemia;* Otava, Helsinki-Keuruu 1988

Kivinen, Olli: *Haminan keskustan asemakaava 1964;* Suomalaisen kirjallisuuden kirjapaino Oy, Helsinki 1965

Kivinen, Paula: *Tampereen jugend – arkkitehtuuri – taideteollisuus;* Otava, Keuruu 1982

Kiviniemi, Arto & Penttilä, Hannu: *RakennusCAD;* Rakennustieto Oy, Tammer-Paino, Tampere 1995

Kjellberg, Ernst & Säflund, Gösta: *Kreikan ja Rooman taide;* Otava, Helsinki 1961

Klimm, Franz: *Der Kaisedom zu Speyer;* Verlag Jaeger, Speyer am Rhein 1953

Knapas, Rainer & Forsgård, Nils Erik (ed.): *Suomen kulttuurihistoria 2 – Tunne ja tieto;* Tammi, Helsinki 2002

Koch, Rudolf: *Merkkien kirja;* Otava, Keuruu 1984

Koch, Wilfried: *Arkitektur, stilhistoriskt bildlexikon;* Esselte Kartor AB, Stockholm 1985

Koch, Wilfried: *Baustilkunde – das Standardwerk zur europäischen Baukunst von der Antike bis zur Gegenwart;* Bertelsmann Lexikon Verlag, Wissen Media Verlag GmbH, Gütersloh/München 2003

Koch, Wilfried: *Style w architekturze – arcydziela budownictwa europejskiego od antyku po czasy wspólczesne;* Bertelsmann Publishing, Warszawa 1996

Kodin korjauskirja: *Tuhat ohjetta pitää koti ja sen tavarat kunnossa;* Oy Valitut Palat – Reader's Digest Ab, Helsinki 1976

Koepf, Hans & Binding, Günther: *Bildwörterbuch der Architektur;* Alfred Kröner Verlag, Stuttgart 1999

Koepf, Hans: *Deutsche Baukunst von der Römerzeit bis zur Gegenwart;* Deutscher Fachzeitschriften- und Fachbuch-Verlag GmBH., Die Bauzeitung – Deutsche Bauzeitung Stuttgart 1956

Kolehmainen, Alfred & Laine, Veijo A.: *Suomalainen talonpoikaistalo;* Otava, Helsinki-Keuruu 1979

Kolehmainen, Alfred: *Hirsirakentamisperinne;* Rakentajain Kustannus, Rakennustieto Oy, Tammer-Paino 1996

Kolehmainen, Alfred: *Kämppiä ja pihapiirejä (Rural Building Styles in Finland);* Koliprint Oy, Eno 1992

Kolehmainen, Alfred: *Puurakentamisperinne;* Rakennustieto Oy, Helsinki 1998

Kolehmainen, Alfred: *Uunit;* Rakennusalan Kustantajat RAK, Kustantajat Sarmala Oy, Sulkava 1999

Konttinen, Riitta & Laajoki, Liisa: *Taiteen sanakirja;* Otava, Helsinki and Keuruu 2000

Koponen, Anu: *Antiikin seinämaalaukset tilasarjoissa – asunnon arkkitehtoniset koristeet, Pompeiji, Herculaneum ja Ostia;* Diplomityö Teknillisen korkeakoulun Arkkitehtiosasto, 01.12.1997

Koponen, Hannu: *Puusepänteollisuuden tuotteet;* Otakustantamo, Karisto Oy, Hämeenlinna 1989

Koponen, Hannu: *Puutuotteiden jalostus ja kehitys;* Otatieto 538, Otatieto Oy, Helsinki 1991

Koponen, Hannu: *Puutuotteiden pinnoitus;* Otatieto 511, Otakustantamo, Karisto Oy, Hämeenlinna 1988

Korhonen, Ahti: *Lähiympäristön suunnittelu;* Yhdyskuntasuunnittelun laitos, TKK, Otapaino, Otaniemi 1974

Korhonen, Ahti: *Maiseman merkitys suomalaisessa rakenetussa ympäristössä;* Armas-tutkimus, loppuraportti, Otakustannus 424, Otapaino, Espoo 1978

Korhonen, Aulikki: *Rakennussuojelun käsitteistö;* Opinnäyte Helsingin yliopiston taidehistoriaa laitoksella, Tta 72.1, moniste 31.05.1993

Korhonen, Teppo: *Kuisti – kansantieteellinen tutkimus (The Porch – An Ethnological Study);* Kansantieellinen arkisto 73, Suomen Muinaismuistoyhdistys, Helsinki 1991

Korjausrakentamisen perusteet: Teknillinen korkeakoulu, Täydennyskoulutuskeskus, Otaniemi 1986

Korkala, Tapio & Salminen, Markku: *Kiinteistön ilmastoinnin hoito ja huolto;* Suomen Kiinteistöliitto, Kiinteistöalan kustannus Oy-REP Ltd, Joutsa 1993

Korkala, Tapio & Luostarinen, Markku: *Rakennusvauriot kiinteistönpidossa;* Kiinteistöalan kustannus Oy-REP Ltd, Nettopaino Oy, Kouvola 1994

Kornerup, Andreas & Wanscher, Johan Henrik: *Värien kirja;* WSOY, Porvoo-Helsinki 1961

Koskenvesa, Anssi & Pussinen, Tarja: *Pientalon rakentaminen;* Rakennustieto Oy, Tampere 1999

Koski, Mikko & Mäkelä, Mikko & Soinne, Martti: *Teknillisen alan fysiikka 1;* Tammertekniikka, Gummerrus Kirjapaino Oy, Jyväskylä 1996

Kotinikkarin niksikirja: *Parhaat neuvot, ohjeet ja niksit;* Oy Valitut Palat – Reader's Digest Ab, 1996

Kottmann, Albrecht: *Das Geheimnis romanischer Bauten – Massverhältnisse in vorromanischen und romanischen Bauwerken;* Julius Hoffmann Verlag, Stuttgart 1971

Krannila, Matti: *Termodynamiikka;* Oy Sonator Ab, Tampereen Pikakopio Oy, Tampere 1980

Kraus, Theodor: *Das römische Weltreich;* Propyläen Verlag Berlin 1984

Kruft, Hanno-Walter: *Geschichte der Architekturtheorie – von der Antike bis zur Gegenwart;* Verlag C.H. Beck, München 1986

KTM-AK: *Rakennustyöt;* Kauppa- ja teollisuusministeriön ammattikasvatusosaston julkaisema ammattioppikirja, Erikoispaino Oy, Helsinki 1946

Kubach, Hans Erich: *Romanesque Architecture;* Harry N. Abrams Inc., New York 1975

Kuikka, Kalervo & Kunelius, Kauko: *Puutekniikka 2 – materiaalit;* Otava, Keuruu 1993

Kuntsi, Sauli: *Katon korjaus ja huolto;* Rakennustieto Oy/Rakentajain Kustannus, Tammer-Paino Oy 1993

Kuntsi, Sauli: *Katot kuntoon;* Rakentajain Kustannus Oy, Gummerrus Oy, Jyväskylä 1983

Kuntsi, Sauli: *Katot ja vedeneristys;* Opetushallitus, Rakennusalan Kustantajat RAK, Helsinki 1998

Kuokkanen, Esko: *Toivekoti vanhasta talosta;* Rakennustieto Oy/Rakentajain Kustannus Oy, Tammer-Paino Oy, Tampere 1992

Kyyrönen, Keijo: *Talonrakennus 1;* Otava, Keuruu 2004

Kürth, Herbert & Kutschmar, Aribert: *Baustilfibel – Bauwerke und Baustile von der Antik bis zur Gegenwart;* Volk und Wisswn Volkseigener Verlag Berlin, 1976

Kärkkäinen, Matti: *Puutiede;* Sallisen Kustannus Oy, Sotkamo; Arvi A. Karisto Oy:n kirjapaino, Hämeenlinna 1985

Käsityön kirja: *Puurakennustaito;* Oy Suomen Kirja, Tilgmannin kirjapaino, Helsinki 1946

Käsityön kirja: *Puusepän työt;* Oy Suomen Kirja, Tilgmannin kirjapaino, Helsinki 1942

Laakkonen, Pekka: *Puutekniikka 1 – muoto, rakenne ja tekninen piirustus;* Otava, Keuruu 1993

Lahontorjuntayhdistys ry: *Puunsuojaus;* Rakennuskirja Oy, Hangon Kirjapaino Oy, Hanko 1988

Lahti, Leena: *Sähköoppi;* Oy Gaudeamus Ab, Helsinki 1976

Laine, M. & Ylä-Mattila, R.: *Tiilirakenteet;* Rakennuskirja Oy, Jyväskylä 1980

Laine, Matti J.: *Kuinka Helsinkiäon rakennettu;* Rakentajain Kustannus Oy, Vammala 1960

Laitinen, Eero (ed.): *Teollinen betonirakentaminen;* Tampereen teknillinen korkeakoulu ja Rakennustieto Oy, Helsinki 1996

Laitinen, Eero (ed.): *Teollinen puurakentaminen;* Tampereen teknillinen korkeakoulu ja Rakennustieto Oy, Vammala 1995

Laitinen, Risto & Toivonen, Jukka: *Yleinen ja epäorgaaninen kemia;* Otatieto Oy, Nro 477, Hämeenlinna 1991

Lakikokoelma: *Rakennuslainsäädäntö;* Valtion Painatuskeskus, Helsinki 1992

Lakikokoelma: *Sähköturvallisuus;* Oy Edita Ab, Helsinki 1996

Laloux, V.: *L'Architecture Grecque;* Maison Quantin, Paris 1888

Lampén, Lea: *Ruotsalais-suomalainen suursanakirja – Svensk-finsk storordbok;* WSOY, Porvoo 1989

Lampinen, Lasse & Honkavuori, Raimo: *Betonitekniikan oppikirja, materiaalit, työnsuoritus, laatutekniikka 1991 – by 201;* Suomen Betonitieto Oy ja Suomen Betoniyhdistys, Jyväskylä 1991

Lamprecht, Heinz-Otto: *Opus caementitium – Bautechnik der Römer;* Beton-Verlag GmbH, Düsseldorf 1987

Lampugnani, Vittorio Magnano: *Hatje-Lexicon der Architektur des 20 Jahrhunderts;* Hatje, Stuttgart 1983

Landels, J.G.: *Antiikin insinööritaito;* Insinööritieto Oy, 1985

Lapinleimu & Moilanen: *Puusepänteollisuus 1;* Otava, Helsinki 1965

Larma, Otto & Hallberg, Pekka & Jatkola, Tapani & Wirilander, Juhani: *Rakennuslaki ja -asetus;* Suomen lakimiesliiton kirjasarja N:o 82, Vammalan kirjapaino Oy, Vammala 1983

Larma, Otto & Hallberg, Pekka & Jatkola, Tapani & Wirilander, Juhani: *Rakennuslaki ja -asetus;* Lakimiesliiton Kustannus, Helsinki 1992

Lassus, Jean: *Varhaiskristillinen ja bysantin taide – Maailmantaide 4;* Tammi, Helsinki 1968, ks. Maailmantaide

Laukkonen, Veikko: *Jälleenrakennusvuosien pientalo Suomessa;* Transkustannus Ky, Helsinki

Laurila, Pekka: *Rakennusuojelun perusteet;* TTKK, Arkkitehtuurin osasto, Arkkitehtuurin historia opintomoniste, kurssi 1461, Raportti 67, UDK 72.025.3, Tampere 1978

Lavonen, Jari & Kurki-Suonio, Kaarle & Hakulinen, Harri: *Lämpö ja energia – Galilei 2;* Weilin+Göös, WSOY, Porvoo 1994

Le Corbusier: *Ausblick auf eine Architektur (Vers une architecture);* Verlag Ullstein Gmbh, Berlin – Frankfurt am Main – Wien, Berlin West 1963

Lehtinen, Reijo: *Asuntojen hoito ja takuukorjaukset;* Rakentajain Kustannus Oy, Jyväskylä 1991

Lehtipuu, Eero: *Asfalttipäällysteet – suunnittelu – rakentaminen – kunnossapito;* Rakentajain Kustannus Oy, Helsinki 1983

Lehtipuu, Irma: *Englantilais-suomalainen asunto- ja rakennusalan sanasto;* Otava, Keuruu 1979

Lehtonen, Tuomas M.S. & Joutsivuo, Timo (ed.): *Suomen kulttuurihistoria 1 – Taivas ja maa;* Tammi, Helsinki 2002

Lehtovuori, Olli: *Suomalaisen asuntoarkkitehtuurin tarina;* Rakennustieto Oy and Ympäristöministeriö, Karisto Oy, Hämeenlinna 1999

Leinos, Markku: *Oviopas;* Rakennuspuusepänteollisuus ry. and Rakennuskirja Oy, Helsinki 1988

Lepola, Pertti & Makkonen, Matti: *Hitsaus ja teräsrakenteet;* WSOY, Konetekniikka, Porvoo 1998

Leppävuori, Erkki K.M. & Prokki, Helena & Kanerva, Pekka & Vähäkallio, Pentti: *Rakennusaineet;* Otatieto 453, Otakustantamo, Espoo 1981, Otapaino

Leroi-Gourham, André: *Prähistorische Kunst – die Ursprünge der Kunst in Europa;* Verlag Herbert Freiburg im Breisgau 1982

Levon, Martti *et. al*: *Puu, sen käyttöja jalostus, osat I–II;* Keksintöjen kirja; WSOY, Porvoo – Helsinki, 1933, 1934

Levón, Martti *et al*: *Puurakennustaito – käsityön kirja;* Oy Suomen Kirja, Helsinki 1946

Lexicon forestale: *Metsäsanakirja – Skogsordbok – Forest Dictionary – Forstwörterbuch – Lesnoi slovarj;* Suomen Metsätieteellinen Seura and WSOY, Porvoo 1979

Lexikon der Kunst I–VII – Architektur, Bildende Kunst, Angewandte Kunst, Industrieformgestaltung, Kunsttheorie: E.A. Seeman Verlag, Leipzig 1987–1994

Liberläromedel: *Teknisk Bilbordbok;* Stockholm 1981

Lilius, Henrik & Lilja, Saara & Thesleff, Holger & Setälä, Päivi & Suolahti, Jaakko & Kämäräinen, Eija: *Antiikin kulttuurihistoria;* WSOY, Porvoo-Helsinki-Juva 1981

Lilius, Henrik: *Joensuu 1848-1890, erään suomalaisen puukaupungin vaiheita;* Pohjois-Karjalan museo, Pohjois-Karjalan Kirjapaino Oy, Joensuu 1984

Lilius, Henrik: *Suomalaisen koulutalon arkkitehtuurihistoriaa – kehityslinjojen tarkastelua keskiajalta itsenäisyyden ajan alkuun;* Suomen Muinaismuistoyhdistyksen aikakauskirja nro 83, Helsinki 1982

Lilja, Raimo & Hyttinen-Lilja, Marianne: *Kompostikäymälän rakentaminen ja käyttö;* Suomen luonnonsuojeluliitto ry, Painoduo Oy, Vantaa 1991

Lindberg, Carolus & Hautala, Jouko: *Aunuksen asunnoilla – Itä-Karjalan kansanomaista rakennuskulttuuria;* WSOY, Porvoo – Helsinki 1943

Lindberg, Carolus *et al.*: *Rakennustaide ja rakennustekniikka – keksintöjen kirja;* WSOY, Porvoo – Helsinki 1938

Lindberg, Carolus: *Koristetaide;* WSOY, Porvoo 1927

Lindberg, Carolus: *Om teglets användning i finska medeltida gråstenskyrkor;* Holger Schildts tryckeri, Helsingfors 1919

Lindberg, Carolus: *Pohjolan rakennustaide;* WSOY, Porvoo 1931

Lindberg, Carolus: *Rakennustaide;* WSOY, Porvoo 1940

Lindberg, Carolus: *Suomen kirkot – maamme kirkkorakennuksia käsittelevä tietoteos;* Kustantaja Kuvataide, F.Tilgmannin kirjapaino Oy, Helsinki 1934

Lindell, Oy: *Toimisto- ja piirustustarvikkeet;* Tuoteluettelo, Helsinki 1992

Lindén, Haakon: *De heliga symbolerna och Egyptens byggnadskonst;* F. Tilgmanns Tryckeri, Helsingfors 1931

Lindén, Teuvo & Pesonen, Aaro: *Raudoitus- ja betonityöt;* Otava, Helsinki Keuruu 1989

Lindgren, Armas: *Rakennus- ja koristetyylit;* Otava, Helsinki 1930

Lindgren, Jack & Moeschlin, Jan: *Tegel – tillverkning, konstruktion, gestaltning;* Svensk Byggtjänst, Bodoni Tryck, Sundbyberg 1985

Lindqvist, Sven E.: *Työkalut – rautakaupan käsikirja 2;* Tammi, Helsinki 1968

Lindroos, Veikko, Sulonen, Matti & Veistinen, Mauri: *Uudistettu Miekk-ojan metallioppi;* Otava, Helsinki Keuruu 1986

Lindström, Kauko: *Vesi- ja viemäritekniikka;* Opetushallitus, Oy Edita Ab, Helsinki 1999

Linko, Jukka: *Teatteritila monikäyttöisissä rakennuksissa;* Taiteen keskustoimikunta ja Suomen Teatterijärjestöjen Keskusliitto ry, VAPK, Helsinki 1985

Linkoaho, Matti & Valjakka, Jukka: *Valo-oppi;* Otakustantamo 454, Otapaino, Espoo 1982

Litzen, Veikko: *Keskiajan kulttuurihistoria;* Gaudeamus, Helsinki 1994

Liungman, Carl G.: *Symboler – västerländska ideogram;* Aldebaran Förlag AB, Sverige 1990

Luckenbach, H.: *Kunst und Geschichte, Teil 1, Altertum;* Druck und Verlag von R.Oldenbourg, München und Berlin 1938

Lundberg, Erik: *Arkitekturen formspråk I–VIII;* Nordisk Rotogravyr, Stockholm 1945

Lunden, Kåre: *Euroopan ahdinko marssi 1300-1500;* Suuri maailmanhistoria, osa 6, Bokförlaget Bra Böcker, Höganäs, Koko kansan kirjakerho Oy, Brepols 1985

Luostarinen, Kaarlo: *Käsiteollinen puutyötaito;* Otava, Helsinki – Keuruu 1976

Luostarinen, Kaarlo: *Maalaustaito;* WSOY, Porvoo-Helsinki 1969

Lyly, Sulevi & Rytilä, Pekka: *Liikennetekniikan perusteet 389;* Otakustantamo, Otapaino, Espoo 1981

Lynton, Norbert: *Moderni maailma – 19. ja 20. vuosisadan maalaustaide, kuvanveisto, arkkitehtuuri ja muotoilu – Maailmantaide 10;* Tammi, Helsinki 1968, ks. Maailmantaide

Lübke, Wilhelm: *Taiteen historia pääpiirteissään I-III;* Suomalaisen kirjallisuuden seuran kirjapaino, Helsinki 1893

Maailmantaide 1-10: *Bernard S. Myers and Trewin Copplestone, toimittajat;* Tammi, Helsinki 1967 (Alkuperäisteos Landmarks of the World's Art I-X, Paul Hamlyn, London and McGraw-Hill Book Company, New York 1967)

Maankäyttö- ja rakennusasetus: 895/1999, 1.1.2000

Maankäyttö- ja rakennuslaki: 132/1999, 1.1.2000

Macauley, D. & Ardley, N.: *Kuinka kaikki toimii (The Way Things Work;* Dorling, London 1988; Otava, Helsinki 1990

Maczeński, Zdzislaw: *Elementy i detale architektoniczne w rozwoju historycznym;* Budownictwo i Architektura, Warszawa 1956

Major, Máté: *Geschichte der Architektur 1-3;* Henschelverlag Berlin and Akadémiai Kiadó, Budapest, Hungary 1976–1984

Makkonen – Malinen – Ovaska: *Konepuuseppä-Ammattityö I–II;* Ammattikasvatushallitus, VAPK, Helsinki 1986

Mallwitz, Alfred: *Olympia und seine Bauten;* Prestel-Verlag, München 1972

Mandelin, Walter: *Jokamiehen rakennusopas omakoti- ja talkoorakentajille;* WSOY, Porvoo – Helsinki, 1946

Mandelin, Walter: *Jokamies rakentajana – huvila- ja omakotirakentajan opas;* WSOY, Porvoo 1953

Manninen, Juhani: *Puu ja puutuotteet rakennustarvikkeina;* Rakentajain Kustannus Oy, Helsinki 1987

Manninen, Pekka: *Ammattikorkeakoulun deskriptiivinen geometria;* Tammertekniikka, Gummerrus Kirjapaino Oy, Jyväskylä 1992

Manninen, Pekka: *Teknillisen oppilaitoksen deskriptiivinen geometria;* Tammertekniikka, Jyväskylä 1988

Mantere, Heikki (ed.); Hirviluoto, A.-L., Lehtosalo-Hilander, P.-L., Maunuksela, M., Riska, T. & Sinisalo, A.: *Hollolan kirkko – asutuksen, kirkon ja seurakunnan historiaa;* Hollolan seurakunta, Arvi A. Karisto Oy, Hämeenlinna 1985

Martikainen, Matti & Santala, Jaakko: *Rakennusmittaus;* Suomen Stadardisoimisliitto ry ja Rakennuskirja Oy, Hangon Kirjapaino Oy 1990

Massimi, Giuseppe: *La chiesa di S.Maria in Cosmedin (in schoela Graeca);* Roma 1989

Maula, Jere: *Kapunkisuunnittelun kolme aarretta;* Tampereen teknillinen korkeakoulu, Arkkitehtuurin osasto, raportti 96, Tampere 1991

Mayeur, Jean-Marie & Pietri, Charles & Pietri, Luce & Vauchez, André & Venard, Marc: *Die Geschichte des Christentums – Religion, Politik – Kultur;* Machtfülle des Papsttums 1054-1274; Verlag Herder, Freiburg-Basel-Wien, 1994

Melkko, Tauno: *Kattosepän ammattitekniikka;* Ammattikasvatushallitus, Valtion painatuskeskus, Helsinki 1984

Melkko, Tauno: *Projektio- ja levitysoppi;* Otava, Keuruu 1978

Meriluoto, E. & Korander, O. & Lehtinen, E. & Ratvio, J.: *Betonipientalorakentajan opas;* Rakennuskirja Oy, Helsinki 1982

Mesimäki, Pekka & Harmaajärvi, Reijo: *Luonnonkivet ja julkisivut;* Rakennuskirja Oy, Helsinki 1989

Mesimäki, Pekka (ed.): *Kiviteknologia 1, luonnonkiven ominaisuudet;* Opetushallitus, Helsinki 1998

Mesimäki, Pekka (ed.): *Kiviteknologia 2, tarvekiven louhinta;* Opetushallitus, Helsinki 1999

Mesimäki, Pekka (ed.): *Kiviteknologia 3, kivituotteiden valmistus;* Opetushallitus, Jyväskylä 2001

Mesimäki, Pekka (ed.): *Luonnonkivirakenteiden suunnitteluohje;* Kiviteollisuusliitto ry, Karprint Ky, 1994

Mesimäki, Pekka (ed.): *Luonnonkivikäsikirja;* Kiviteollisuusliitto ry, Karprint Ky, Helsinki 1997

Methuen, John: *Englantilais-suomalainen arkkitehtuuri- ja rakennussanasto;* SAFA

Methuen, John: *Suomalais-englantilainen arkkitehtuuri- ja rakennussanasto;* SAFA

Metsäliiton, Kinderdey Ltd, Myyntikonttorit: *Kovapuuopas;* Helsinki 1983

Metsälä, Harri: *Puukirja;* Rakennusalan Kustantajat RAK, Kustantajat Sarmala Oy, Helsinki 1997

Meurman, Otto-I.: *Asemakaavaoppi;* Otava, Helsinki 1947

Michalowski, Kazimiere: Ägypten, *Kunst und Kultur;* Verlag Herbert Freiburg im Breisgau 1983

Miettinen, Jukka O.: *Intia – kaupunkeja, kulttuuria, historiaa;* Otava, Helsinki-Keuruu 1999

Mikkola, Kirmo: *Eliel Saarinen aikansa kaupunkisuunnittelunäkemysten tulkkina – Suomen aika;* YJK:n julkaisuja A 14, Yhdyskuntasuunnittelun jatkokoulutuskeskus, Espoo 1984

Mirsky, Jeannette: *Jumalan asunnot;* (Houses of God) K.J. Gummerrus Oy, Jyväskylä 1966

Moley, Christian: *Les Structures de la Maison – Exemple d'un habitat traditionnel finlandais;* Publication Orientalistes de France, 1984

Moorhouse, Jonathan & Carapetian, Michael & Ahtola-Moorhouse, Leena: *Helsingin jugendarkkitehtuuri 1895-1915;* Otava, Helsinki 1987

Mrusek, Hans-Joachim: *Romanik (Baukunst in Deutschland);* VEB E.A. Seemann, Buch- und Kunstverlag, Leipzig 1972

Mumford, Lewis: *Kaupunkikulttuuri;* WSOY, Porvoo-Helsinki 1949

Muoviyhdistys ry: *Muovitermit;* Gummerus Kirjapaino Oy, Jyväskylä 1992

Museovirasto: *Ensimmäisen maailmansodan aikaiset linnoitukset Helsingissä, suojeluluettelo;* Museovirasto, Rakennushistorian osasto, Julkaisu 9, Helsinki 1980

Museovirasto: *Hamina – Fredrikshamn*

Museovirasto: *Kotkan linnoitusten korjaus- ja restaurointityöt;* Museovirasto, Rakennushistorian osasto, Raportti 1/1989, Helsinki

Museovirasto: *Kuusiston linna -tutkimuksia;* Museoviraston Rakennushistorian osaston Raportteja 8, Turku 1994

Museovirasto: *Linnat ja linnoitukset;* Museovirasto, Rakennushistorian osasto, 1/1975, Helsinki

Museovirasto: *Maiseman muisti – valtakunnallisesti merkittävät muinaisjäännökset;* Museovirasto, Vammalan kirjapaino, Helsinki 2001

Museovirasto: *Suomenlinnan rakennusten historia;* Museoviraston rakennushistorian osaston julkaisuja 17, Suomenlinnan hoitokunta, Gummerrus kirjapaino Oy, Jyväskylä 1997

Mustonen, Vesa: *Perspektiivioppi;* Oulun yliopiston ylioppilaskunnan monistuskeskus, Oulu 1973

Muzik, Hugo & Perschinka, Franz: *Kunst und Leben im Altertum;* F. Tempsky, Wien and G. Freiteg GmbH, Leipzig, Wien 1909

Müller, W. & Vogel, G.: *dtv-Atlas zur Baukunst, Tafeln und Texte;* Deutscher Taschenbuch Verlag, München 1990; **KT**, 2 osaa, 264 kuvaa

Müller, Werner: *Grundlagen gotischer Bautechnik - 'ars sine scientia nihil';* Deutscher Kunstverlag, München 1990

Müller-Wiener, Wolfgang: *Griechisches Bauwesen in der Antike;* Verlag C.H. Beck, München 1988

Müther, Hans: *Baukunst in Brandenburg bis zum beginnenden 19. Jahrhundert;* Deutsche Bauakatemie, Sachsenverlag Dresden 1955

Mårtensson, Hans & Korhonen, Teppo: *Kuistit ja verannat;* Rakennusalan kustantajat RAK, Gummerrus Kirjapaino Oy, Jyväskylä 1995

Mårtensson, Hans: *Sorvauskirja;* Tammi, Helsinki 1987

Mäkelä, Harri & Hoikkala, Simo: *Pihojen pohja- ja päällysrakenteet;* Viatek Tapiola Oy ja Rakennustieto Oy, Tampere 1994

Mäkelä, Kari: *Kodin tulisijat;* Rakenustieto Oy Rakentajain Kustannus, Tammer-Paino Oy 1994

Mäkelä, Mikko & Mäkelä, Riitta & Siltanen, Olavi: *Insinöörikoulutuksen fysiikka 1;* Tammertekniikka, Jyväskylä 1997

Mäkeläinen, Pentti: *Muovirakenteet;* Otakustantamo, Nro 456, Otapaino, Espoo 1980

Mäkinen, Vesa: *Suomen vanhat linnat – The Castles of Finland;* WSOY, Porvoo-Helsinki 1975

Mäkiö, Erkki *et al.*: *Kerrostalot 1960-1975;* Rakennustieto Oy, Helsinki 1994

Mäkiö, Erkki *et al.*: *Kerrostalot 1880-1940;* Rakennustieto Oy, Helsinki 2002

Mäkiö, Erkki *et al.*: *Kerrostalot 1940-1960;* Rakennuskirja Oy, Porvoo 1990

Mälkönen, Pentti: *Orgaaninen kemia;* Otava, Helsinki 1989

NEKASU: *Luonnonolosuhteiden huomioonottaminen asuinalueiden suunnittelussa, symposiumi 21.-26.5.1979;* YJK:n julkaisusarja B23, Otaniemi 1979

Neuvonen, Petri (ed.): *Rakentajan ekotieto – uudisrakentaminen;* Rakennustietosäätiö ja Rakennustieto Oy, Tampere 2000

Neuvonen, Petri: *Viipurin historiallinen keskusta – rakennusperinnön nykytila;* Suomen Historiallinen Seura, Helsinki 1994

Niinikoski, Miikka: *Iäkkäiden autoilijoiden tarpeet liikenneympäristön suunnittelussa;* Tiehallinnon selvityksiä 56/2001, S12 Pääteiden parantamisratkaisut, Tiehallinto, Helsinki 2001

Niiranen, Timo: *Miten ennen asuttiin, vanhat rakennukset ja sisustukset;* Otava, Keuruu 1981

Nikula, Riitta (ed.): *Sankaruus ja arki – Suomen 50-luvun miljöö;* Suomen Rakennustaiteen museo, näyttelyluettelo, Vantaa 1994

Nikula, Svante: *Pyöröhirsirakentamisen oppikirja;* Oy Ylä-Vuoksi, Imatra 1986

Nilsson, Sten Åke: *Om den nordiska arkitekturens historia;* Utbildningsradion Stockholm and Danmarks Radion Undervisningsafdelningen 1985, P.J. Schmidt A/S, Danmark

Niskala, Eino: *Puutalon korjaus;* VTT and Rakennustie Oy/Rakentajain Kustannus, Tammer-Paino Oy, Tampere 1993

Norborg, Lars-Arne: *Vahva Eurooppa 1815-1870;* Suuri maailmanhistoria, osa 11, Bokförlaget Bra Böcker, Höganäs, Koko kansan kirjakerho Oy, Brepols 1986

Nordman, C.A. & Cleve, Nils: *Suomen kirkot-Turun arkkihiippakunta III osa (Tove Riska: Turun tuomirovastikunta I);* Suomen muinaismuistoyhdistys, Helsinki 1964, K.F. Puromiehen kirjapaino Oy

Norsk kunstnerleksikon: *Norsk kunstnerleksikon – bildende kunstnere, arkitektur, kunsthandverkere;* Univeritetsförlaget: Oslo 1982

Norwich, John Julius (ed.): *Byggnadskonst – världens arkitektur genom tiderna;* Wahström and Widstrand, Stockholm 1976

Nurmi, Timo & Rekiaro, Ilkka & Rekiaro, Päivi: *Suomalaisen sivistyssanakirja;* Gummerrus, Jyväskylä ja Helsinki 1995

Nurminen, Veli & Parvio, Martti: *Herran huoneen sanoma – kirkollisen taiteen kuvakieli ja tarkoitus;* Art-Print Oy, Helsinki 1987

Nykysuomen sanakirja Osat I-VIII

Oijala, Matti: *Rakennusaineet – ekologinen käsikirja;* Rakennusalan Kustantajat RAK, Helsinki 1998

Okkonen, Onni: *Antiikin taide;* WSOY, Porvoo 1936

Okkonen, Onni: *Suomen taiteen historia;* WSOY, Porvoo 1955

Oksman, Pekka: *Talonmiehen työt;* Weilin + Göös, 1985

Omura, George: *Autocad viiteteos;* Vammalan kirjapaino, Vammala 1990

Orola, Urho: *Rakennusten korjaus ja kunnossapito;* Pellervon kirja, Pellervo-seura ry, Yhteiskirjapaino Oy, Helsinki 1946

Osram: *Kodin lamppuopas '95;* Oy Osram Ab, Helsinki, Tenprint/Incognito 1994

Otavan Iso Tietosanakirja: Osat I-X

Outinen, Hannu & Koski, Jorma & Salmi, Tapio: *Lujuusopin perusteet;* Pressus Oy, Tampere 1998

Paananen, Eero & Talvitie, Juha: *Seutusuunnittelu;* Rakennuskirja Oy 1983

Paatela, Jussi: *Rakennusopin luentojen kuvamonisteet;* Teknillinen korkeakoulu, Helsinki 1947

Paavola, H. & Loikkanen, P. & Jutila, A.: *Sillanrakennustekniikan perusteet;* Otakustantamo, nro 423, Otapaino, Espoo 1984

Pajula, Pirkko: *Puuarkkitehtuuri;* Rakentajain kustannus Oy, Helsinki 1983

Pakarinen, Kari & Virtanen, Pekka V.: *Seutu- ja valtakunnansuunnittelu;* Otakustantamo, Nro 482, Otapaino, Espoo 1984

Paloheimo, Eero (toim.): *Ympäristösuunnittelun kysymyksiä;* Otava, Keuruu 1973

Palva, Heikki & Perho, Irmeli (ed.): *Islamilainen kulttuuri;* Otava, Keuruu 1998

Papadopoulos, Alexandre: *Islamische Kunst;* Verlag Herbert Freiburg im Breisgau 1982

Papaiannou, Kostas: *Griechische Kunst;* Verlag Herbert Freiburg im Breisgau 1980

Parrot, André: *Sumer und Akkad;* Verlag C.H. Beck, München 1983

Partek: *Äänikirja 1991;* Oy Partek Ab, Helsinki 1991

Pasanen, Sari: *Aidat ja portit;* Viherympäristöliitto ry., julkaisu nro 24, Helsinki 2002

Paulaharju, Samuli: *Asuinrakennuksista Uudellakirkolla Viipurin läänissä;* Kansantieteellisiä kertomuksia VI, Suomalaisen kirjallisuuden seura, Helsinki 1906

Paulaharju, Samuli: *Karjalainen talo;* Kansanelämän kuvauksia 22, Suomalaisen kirjallisuuden seura, Helsinki 1983

Paulsson, Gregor & Paulsson, Thomas: *Tie taiteen maailmaan oppitunteja maalaustaiteesta kaupunkisuunnitteluun;* WSOY, Porvoo-Helsinki-Juva 1972

Peesch, Reinhard: *Ornamentik der Volkkunst in Europa;* Karl Robert Langewiesche Nachfolger, Hans Köster Königstein im Taunus, Leipzig 1981

Peltonen, Hannu & Perkkiö, Juha & Vierinen, Kari: *Insinöörin (AMK) fysiikka I-II;* Lahden Theoopetus, Lahti 1998

Pennala, Erkki: *Lujuusopin perusteet;* Oy Yliopistokustannus/Otatieto 1994, Helsinki 2000

Penttilä, Hannu & Koskenvesa, Anssi: *Pientalon suunnittelu;* Rakennustieto Oy, Tampere 2000

Pere, Aimo: *Deskripitiivistä geometriaa koneensuunnittelua varten;* Offsetpiste Ky, Helsinki

Pere, Aimo: *Koneenpiirustus 1-2;* Cosmoprint Oy, Helsinki 1993

Pere, Aimo: *Teknisen piirustuksen perusteet – oppi- ja harjoituskirja ammattiopetukseen;* Kirpe Oy, Espoo 1998

Pero, Paavo: *Mekaaninen teknologia;* Otava, Helsinki 1926

Pero, Paavo: *Metallien ja puun mekaaninen teknologia;* Otava, Helsinki 1943

Pesonen, Hannu & Laine, Tomi: *Liikennejärjestelmän tekninen kehitys;* Liikenneministeriö, julkaisuja 37/99, Oy Edita Ab, Helsinki 1999

Peterson, Bengt & George, Beate: *Egyptens tempel;* Pyramidförlaget i samarbete med Medelhavsmuseet, Ab Grafisk Press, Stockholm 1988

Pettersson, Lars: *Templum Saloense – Pohjalaisen tukipilarikirkon arvoitus;* Suomen Muinaismuistoyhdistyksen aikakauskirja (SMYL) 90, Helsinki 1987, Vammalan kirjapaino 1987

Pettersson, Lars: *Tornion kirkko ja kellotapuli;* Pohjoinen, Oulu 1986

Pevsner, Nikolaus: *Euroopan arkkitehtuurin historia;* Otava, Helsinki 1963

Pietarinen, Ilmari: *Tietotekniikan perussanasto suomi-englanti-ruotsi;* Suomen ATK-kustannus Oy, Kouvolan Kirjapaino Oy, Kouvola 1991

Piha, Pentti & Mäkiö, Erkki: *Teatteritilan perusteita;* Opetusmoniste, Helsinki 1972

Piirainen, Heikki: *Älykäs rakennus – tarvelähtöinen rakentamistapa;* Sitra 117, Helsinki 1991

Pikku, jättiläinen: WSOY, Porvoo-Helsinki-Juva, 1986

Pinder, Wilhelm: *Deutsche Dome des Mittelalters;* Karl Robert Langewiesche Verlag, Düsseldorf and Leipzig 1910

Pirinen, Auli & Salminen, Markku: *Käytössäolevan asuintalon huoltokirja;* Suomen ympäristö nro 319, Ympäristöministeriö ja Rakennustieto Oy, Tampere 1999

Pirinen, Auli & Salminen, Markku & Speeti, Leo: *Asuintalon huoltokirja esimerkkikohteeseen;* Suomen ympäristö nro 31, Ympäristöministeriö ja Rakennustieto Oy, Tampere 1996

Pirinen, Auli & Salminen, Markku & Speeti, Leo: *Asuintalon huoltokirjan laadinta;* Suomen ympäristö nro 32, Ympäristöministeriö ja Rakennustieto Oy, Tampere 1996

Pitkäranta, Reijo: *Suomi-latina-suomi-sanakirja;* WSOY, Helsinki 2001

Pohto, Olavi: *Hitsauskurssilaisen metallioppia;* Oy Aga Ab, Painotekniikka Oy

Pothorn, Herbert: *Baustile – die Anfänge, die grossen Epoche, die Gegenwart;* Südwest Verlag Gmbh and Co., München 1968

Poulsen, Henning: *Sodasta toiseen 1914-1945;* Suuri maailmanhistoria, osa 13, Bokförlaget Bra Böcker, Höganäs, Koko kansan kirjakerho Oy, Brepols 1987

Puurakennukset – historia, tutkimus ja suojelu: Seurasaarisäätiön toimitteita, Rakennuskirja Oy, Vammala 1977

Päällystealan neuvottelukunta PANK: *Asfalttialan sanasto;* Rakentajain Kustannus Oy, Jyväskylä 1982

Pöykkö, Kalevi: *C.L. Engel 1778-1840;* Helsingin kaupunginmuseo, Memoria 6, Helsinki 1990

Rakennusalan Tutkimuskeskus Oy: *Talon sisustustyöt puusta – talonrakentajan käsikirja 2;* Rakentajan tietokirjat RATK and Gummerruksen kirjapaino Oy, Jyväskylä 1994

Rakennusalan Tutkimuskeskus Oy: *Lattianpäällysteet ja päällystystyöt;* Rakennusalan kustantajat, Gummerrus Kirjapaino Oy, Jyväskylä 1992

Rakennusalan Tutkimuskeskus Oy: *Talon runkotyöt puusta – talonrakentajan käsikirja 1;* Gummerruksen kirjapaino Oy, Jyväskylä 1993

Rakennusalan Tutkimuskeskus Oy: *Hirsitalon rakentaminen – talonrakentajan käsikirja 3;* Gummerrus Kirjapaino Oy, Jyväskylä 1994

Rakennuskirja: *Englantia rakentajille;* Rakennuskirja Oy

Rakennuskonepäälliköt: *Rakennuskoneet – käyttöturvallisuus;* Rakentajain kustannus Oy, Tammer-Paino Oy, Tampere 1991

Rakennuslaki: 370/1958, 16.8.1958

Rakennuspäivät '82: *Rakennusten pohjatyöt – 27. rakennuspäivien esitelmät;* Rakentajain Kustannus Oy, Helsinki 1982

Rakennussuunnittelun perusteet: *RAK 43.103;* Teknillisen korkeakoulun opetusmoniste S-93, Otatieto Oy, Espoo 1993

Rakennustekniikan käsikirja 1-8: Tammi, Helsinki 1973

Rakennustietosäätiö: *MaaRYL 2000, Talonrakennuksen maatyöt;* Rakennustieto Oy, Karisto Oy, Hämeenlinna 1997

Rakennustietosäätiö: *Rakennustarvikkeet 1993, RT-kortiston hakemistot;* Rakennustietosäätiö, Rakennustieto Oy, Karisto Oy, Hämeenlinna 1993

Rakennustietosäätiö: *RATU-kortistot;* Talonrakennuksen rakennustuotantokortit, Rakennustieto Oy, Helsinki

Rakennustietosäätiö: RT-kortit

Rakennustietosäätiö: *RYL 81; Rakennustöiden yleiset laatuvaatimukset 1981;* Rakennuskirja, Helsinki 1981

Rakennustuoteteollisuus RTT: *Julkisivu 2000 – Uudet betonijulkisivurakenteet;* Suomen Betonitieto Oy, Gummerrus Kirjapaino Oy, Jyväskylä 1998

Rakennustuoteteollisuus RTT: *Julkisivu 2000 – Yhdistelmäjulkisivut;* Suomen Betonitieto Oy, Gummerus Kirjapaino Oy, Jyväskylä 1998

Rakennustuoteteollisuus RTT: *Julkisivu 2000 – Betonijulkisivujen materiaali- ja valmistustekniikka;* Suomen Betonitieto Oy, Lahtiprint, Lahti 1998

Ramstad, Knut: *Kolmiulotteinen mallinnus ja visualisointi arkkitehteja varten;* Autodesk

Ranke, Hermann: *Meisterwerke der ägyptischen Kunst;* Holbein-Verlag, Basel 1948

Rantamo, Esa ym: *Väellä, voimalla, taidolla – Suomen maa- ja vesirakentamisen historia;* Suomen Maarakentajien Keskusliitto ry., Forssan Kirjapaino Oy 1997

Rantamäki – Jääskeläinen – Tammirinne: *Geotekniikka;* Otakustantamo, 464, Vaasa 1986

Rantamäki, Martti & Tammirinne, Markku: *Pohjarakennus;* Otatieto Oy, 465, Hämeenlinna 1993

Ratia, Aatto & Gehör, Seppo: *Jokamiehen kiviopas;* Weilin+Göös, Espoo 1987

RATU: *Rakennustöiden laatu 2000;* Rakennustuotantokirjasarja, Rakennusteollisuuden Keskusliitto ry and Rakennustietosäätiö, Juva 1998

Rautaruukki: *RR-paalutusohjekirja;* 21.08.2002 Rautaruukki Oy

Recht, Roland & Geyer, Marie-Jeanne, (ed.): *Les batisseurs des cathedrales gothiques;* Edition les musees de la ville Strasbourg, Strasbourg 1989

Reclam: *Kleines Wörterbuch der Architektur;* Philipp Reclam jun. GmbH and Co., Stuttgart/Ditzingen 2003

Reeves, Nicholas: *Muinaisen Egyptin aarteet;* Otava, Helsinki 2002

Reinikainen, Pertti & Kallioinen, Harri & Petrow, Seppo: *Märkälaastit – valinta ja käyttö;* Hyvinkään Betoni Oy, Hyvinkää 2001

Rettelbusch, Ernst: *Tyylikäsikirja – ornamentiikka, huonekalut, sisustus;* Lehtikirjakauppa, Turun Uusi Kirjapaino Oy, Turku 1996

Reznikoff, S.C.: *Interior Graphic and Design Standards;* The Architectural Press Ltd, London 1986

Rihlama, Seppo: *Värioppi;* Rakennuskirja Oy, Helsinki, Hangon Kirjapaino Oy 1985

Ringbom, Anette: *Rakennusapteekin käsikirja;* Rakennusapteekin tuoteluettelo ja käsikirja nro 1, Oy Ringbom Consulting and Rakennusapteekki, Helsinki 2002

Rinne, Juhani: *Suomen keskiaikaiset mäkilinnat;* K.F. Puromiehen kirjapaino Oy, Helsinki 1914

Rissanen Niilo ym: *Rakennustarvikkeet – rautakaupan käsikirja 1;* Tammi, Helsinki 1964

RKK-yhtiöt Rakennuskustannuskortisto: Pikkupaino Oy, Järvenpää 1992

Rohde, Tuula *et al.*: *Puru – puuteollisuuden sanasto;* Suomen Kehityskeskus Oy, Gummerus Kirjapaino Oy, Jyväskylä 1997

Roininen, R.H.: *Kirvestyöt;* Rakentajain Kustannus Oy, Hämeenlinna 1971, Arvi A. Karisto Oy:n kirjapaino

Roininen, R.H.: *Muuraustyön ammattitekniikka;* Otava, Helsinki 1965

Rosenberg, Erkki: *Geometria;* Limes ry, Helsinki 1984

Routio, Pentti: *Asuntotutkimus ja suunnittelun teoria;* Suomen Rakennusinsinöörien liitto (RIL), Helsinki 1987

Rowley, Keith: *Puunsorvaus – peruskurssi;* Oy Faktapro Ab, Lahti 1996

Ruohomäki, Jormalainen, Pärssinen, Saarikivi, Söderholm: *Raudoitustyöt;* BY 206, Rakentajain Kustannus Oy, Jyväskylä 1990

Rushforth, Keith: *Lehti- ja havupuut;* Weilin + Göös, 1982

Rytilä, Pekka: *Yhdyskuntatekniikka;* Otakustantamo, Nro 508, Hämeenlinna 1988

Rönkä, K., Rauhala, K., Harmaajärvi, I., Lahti, P.: *Ekologinen lähiöuudistus – Kestävän kehityksen periaatteen mukainen korjaus- ja lisärakentaminen suomalaisilla asuntoalueilla;* VTT yhdyskuntatekniikka, Yhdyskuntasuunnittelu, Helsinki 1995

Saarelainen, Urho: *Puurakenteet 1 – puu materiaalina;* Puuinformaatio and Rakentajain Kustannus Oy, Jyväskylä 1981

Saarelma, Hannu & Oittinen, Pirkko: *Graafisen tekniikan perusteet;* Otatieto 513, Otakustantamo Oy, Hämeenlinna 1988

Saarikangas, Kirsi: *Asunnon muodonmuutoksia – puhtauden estetiikka ja sukupuoli modernissa arkkitehtuurissa;* Suomalaisen kirjallisuuden Seura, Helsinki 2002

Saarinen, Eero & Kähkönen, Leo: *Betonirakenteiden suunnittelun oppikirja 1-3, by 202;* Suomen Betoniyhdistys, Gummerrus Oy, Jyväskylä 1983

Saarisalo, Aapeli: *Raamatun sanakirja;* Kirjaneliö, Helsinki 1980

Saarivuo, Johanna: *Ekologinen rakennuttaminen – malli ja soveltaminen rakennushankkeissa;* Suomen toimitila- ja rakennuttajaliitto RAKLI and Rakennustieto Oy, Tampere 1999

Saarni, Risto: *Ikkunan valintaopas;* Rakennustieto Oy, Tammerpaino Oy, 1992

Saarni, Risto: *Teräsjulkisivut – ulkoseinät – vesikatot – parvekkeet;* Tampereen teknillinen korkeakoulu and Rakennustieto Oy, Vammalan Kirjapaino Oy, Vammala 1993

Saarni, Risto (toim.): *Teräsrakentaminen;* Tampereen teknillinen korkeakoulu, Rakennustieto Oy, Tammer-Paino Oy 1994

Saartio, Rafael: *Kristilliset vertauskuvat ja tunnukset – johdatusta kristilliseen symboliikkaan;* WSOY, Porvoo-Helsinki 1963

Sainio, Olli & Honkavuori, Raimo & Kallberg, Eero & Lampinen, Lasse: *Betonirakenteiden perusteiden oppikirja – by 203;* Suomen Betoniyhdistys, Jyväskylä 1985

Salmi, J.W. & Linkomies, Edwin: *Latinalais-suomalainen sanakirja;* Otava, Helsinki 1964

Salmi, Tapio: *Statiikka;* Pressus Oy, Klingendahl Paino Oy, Tampere 2001

Salminen, Jarmo *et al.*: *Tulisija- ja erikoismuuraustyöt;* VAPK-kustannus, Opetushallitus, Helsinki 1992

Salminen, Jarmo ym: *Puurunkotyöt;* Ammattikasvatushallitus, VAPK, Helsinki 1988

Salokangas, Raimo & Hyrskyluoto, Jorma: *Rakennusalan yritystalous – Rakentamistalous 1;* Rakentajain Kustannus Oy, Vammala 1991

Salokorpi, Asko: *Suomen arkkitehtuuri 1900-luvulla;* Tammi, Helsinki 1971

Salokorpi, Sinikka (toim.): *Uima-altaat;* Weilin+Göös, Helsinki 1970

Salomies, Ilmari: *Suomen kirkon historia I – Suomen kirkko keskiaikana;* Otava, Helsinki 1944

Salonen, Armas: *Kaksoisvirranmaa eli kuvauksia ja kuvia Babylonian ja Assyrian kulttuurista nuolenpäätekstien ja kaivaustulosten perusteella;* WSOY, Porvoo-Helsinki 1945

Salonen, Eero-Matti: *Statiikka;* Otatieto Oy, Hakapaino Oy, Helsinki 1995

Sandström, Gösta: *Byggarna – teknik och kultur från vasshgus och pyramid till järnväg och högdamm;* Bokförlaget Forum, Stockholm 1968

Sandved, Kjell B. *et al.*: *Konstlexikon 1-2;* AB Kulturhistoriska Förlagen, Göteborg 1982

Sandved, Kjell B. *et al.*: *Konstens värld;* Ab Kulturhistoriska Förlagen, Göteborg 1974

Santakari, Esa: *Keskiajan kivikirkot – Medieval Stone Churches of Finland;* Otava, Keuruu 1979

Santavuori, Matti & Kilkki, Pertti: *Kastelholma, Kuusisto, Raasepori;* Sotasokeat ry:n kevätjulkaisu 1972, Kauppakirjapaino Oy, Helsinki 1972

Sarjakoski, Helena: *Rationalismi ja runollisuus – Aulis Blomstedt ja suhteiden taide;* Rakennustieto Oy, Tammer-Paino Oy, Tampere 2003

Sauser, Ekkart: *Symbolik der katholischen Kirche – Tafelband;* Anton Hiersemann, Jungmann, Stuttgart 1966

Schefold, Karl: *Die Griechen und ihre Nachbarn;* Propyläen Verlag Berlin 1984

Schmidt, Clara (ed.): *Architecture – Architektur – Arquitectura;* L'Aventurine, Paris 2001

Schneider, Kim & Gavrieliedes, Eleftherios: *äKreikkalais-suomalainen sanakirja (ΕΛΛΗΝΟΦΙΝΛΑΝΔΙΚΟ ΛΕΞΙΚΟ);* Kreikan kirja Oy, Jyväskylä 1992

Schneider, Kim & Gavrieliedes, Eleftherios: *Suomalais-kreikkalainen sanakirja (ΦΙΝΛΑΝΔΟ-ΕΛΛΗΝΙΚΟ-ΛΕΞΙΚΟ);* Kreikan kirja Oy, Helsinki 1985

Schoder, Raymond V.: *Mästerverk i grekisk konst – ett panorama i text och bild;* Natur och Kultur, Stockholm 1961

Schulitz, Helmut C. & Sobek, Werner & Habermann, Karl J.: *Stahlbau Atlas;* Institut für internationale Architektur-Dokumentation GmbH, München 1999

Schulz, Regine & Seidel, Matthias *et al.*: *Egypten – Faraorernas värld;* Könemann Verlagsgesellschaft mbH, Köln 1998

Schumann, Walter: *Jalokivet ja korukivet värikuvina;* Otava, Keuruu 1979

Schumann, Walter: *Kivet ja mineraalit värikuvina;* Otava, Keuruu 1989

Schütz, Bernhard & Müller, Wolfgang: *Deutsche Romanik – die Kirchenbauten der Kaiser, Bischöfe und Klöster;* Verlag Herder, Freiburg im Breisgau 1989

Scott, Ernest: *Suuri puutyökirja – suunnittelu, työkalut, työtavat, puumateriaali;* Kustannus Oy Tammi, Helsinki 1992

Seibert, Jutta u.a.: *Lexikon christlicher Kunst – Themen, Gestalten, Symbole;* Verlag Herder, Freiburg-Basel-Wien, 1980

Selberg, Knut: *Kaupunkimuotoilun historia – nykyaikaisen tie- ja liikennesuunnittelun historiallinen tausta;* Tielaitoksen selvitys 56/1992, Tiehallitus, Helsinki 1992

Seppälä, Jukka: *Polymeeriteknologian perusteet;* Otatieto 580, Otatieto Oy, Helsinki 1997

Seppänen, Olli & Seppänen, Matti: *Rakennusten sisäilmasto ja LVI-tekniikka;* Sisäilmayhdistys ry, Helsinki – Gummerrus Kirjapaino Oy, Jyväskylä 1996

Seppänen, Olli: *Rakennusten lämmitys;* Suomen LVI-yhdistysten liitto ry, Gummerrus kirjapaino Oy, Jyväskylä 1995

Setälä, Vilho: *Oman kodin rakentaja – rakennusohjeita jokamiehelle;* Otava, Keuruu 1959

Setälä, Vilho: *Taitokirja;* Otava, Helsinki 1957

Seuri, Markku & Reiman, Marjut: *Rakennusten kosteusvauriot, home ja terveys;* Rakennustieto Oy, Helsinki 1996

SFS-käsikirja 103: *Ilmastointitekniikka;* Suomen Standardisoimisliitto SFS ry., Hangon Kirjapaino Oy, Hanko 1988

SFS-käsikirja 121: *Kiinnittimet, osa 1: Ruuvit ja mutterit* Suomen Standardisoimisliitto SFS ry., Kyriiri Oy, Helsinki 1993

Siikanen, Unto: *Puurakennusten suunnittelu – tarvikkeet ja rakenteet;* Rakentajain Kustannus Oy, Jyväskylä 1990

Siikanen, Unto: *Rakennusaineoppi;* Rakennuskirja Oy, Helsinki; Gummerrus Kirjapaino Oy, Jyväskylä 1986

Siikanen, Unto: *Rakennusfysiikka;* Rakennustieto Oy, Helsinki; Tammer-Paino Oy 1996

Siikonen, Heikki: *Millaiseksi rakennan taloni;* WSOY, Porvoo 1929

Siikonen, Heikki: *Pienviljelijän rakennusoppi;* Maatalousseurojen keskusliiton julkaisu nro 236, Helsingin Uusi Kirjapaino Oy, Helsinki 1941

Silvenoinen, Tapio: *Sähköpientalossa;* Rakentajain Kustannus Oy, Jyväskylä 1989

Simensen, Jarle: *Länsi valtaa maailman 1870-1914;* Suuri maailmanhistoria, osa 12, Bokförlaget Bra Böcker, Höganäs, Koko kansan kirjakerho Oy, Brepols 1986

Simons, Tom *et al.*: *1900-luvun maisema-arkkitehtuuri ja sen taustoja;* Maisema-arkkitehtuurin aineryhmä, Arkkitehtiosasto, TKK, Otaniemi 1992

Sinisalo, Antero: *Olavinlinna 1475-1975;* Museovirasto, Valtion painatuskeskus, Helsinki 1976

Sinisalo, Antero: *Olavinlinnan rakentamisen vaiheet suuresta Pohjan sodasta nykypäivään;* Pyhän Olavin Kilta ry, Savonlinnan Kirjapaino Oy 1986

Sinisalo, Antero: *Puutarhataiteen historian perusteet – luennot 1966-1986;* Viherympäristöliiton julkaisu 6/1997, (ed.) Maunu Väyrynen, Viherympäristöliitto and Teknillinen korkeakoulu, arkkitehtiosasto, maisema-arkkitehtuuri, Helsinki 1997

Sipi, Marketta: *Sahatavaratuotanto;* Opetushallitus, Hakapaino Oy, Helsinki 1998

Sirelius, U.T.: *Suomen hirsirakennusten salvainmuodot ja -nimistö;* Sanastaja – aikakauslehti sanatietoja ja -tiedusteluja varten, 3/1927

Sirviö, Matti & Loponen, Leo: *Peruskoulun puutyöt 7-9;* Otava, Keuruu 1985

Sitte, Camillo: *Kaupunkirakentamisen taide;* Kustantajat Sarmala Oy/Rakennusalan Kustantajat RAK, Karisto Kirjapaino Oy, Hämeenlinna 2001

Sivaramamurti, C.: *Indien – Kunst und Kultur;* Verlag Herbert Freiburg im Breisgau 1987

Sjöström, Ingrid (ed.) & Knapas, Marja-Terttu & Strorsletten, Ola: *Kyrka af träd – kyrkobyggande under 1600- och 1700-talen i Finland, Norge och Sverige;* Museiverket, Helsingfors and Norsk institut for kulturminneforskning (NIKU) and Riksantikvarieämbetet, Sverige, Västervik 2000

Smith, Ray: *Taiteilijan käsikirja;* Otava, Helsinki 1990 (*The Artist's Handbook*, Dorling Kindersley, London 1987)

Smith, Wilbur & Polvinen, Tuomo: *Helsingin kaupunkiseudun liikennetutkimus;* Yhteispaino Oy, Helsinki 1968

Sotasokeat ry: *Turun linna;* Kauppakirjapaino Oy, Helsinki 1970

Sproccati, Sandro *et al.*: *Opas taiteen maailmaan – länsimainen taide varhaisrenessanssista nykypäivään;* WSOY, Porvoo – Helsinki – Juva, 1992

ST-käsikirja: *Sähköalan säännökset;* Sähköinfo Oy, Espoo, Tammer-Paino Oy 1996

Steenberg, Jan: *Levende barok – Romerske motiver påvandring;* G.E.C.Gads forlag, København 1971

Steensgaard, Niels: *Löytöretkien aika 1350-1500;* Suuri maailmanhistoria, osa 7, Bokförlaget Bra Böcker, Höganäs, Koko kansan kirjakerho Oy, Brepols 1985

Steensgaard, Niels: *Maailmankauppa ja kulttuurien kohtaaminen 1500-1750;* Suuri maailmanhistoria, osa 9, Bokförlaget Bra Böcker, Höganäs, Koko kansan kirjakerho Oy, Brepols 1986

STEP 1 and 2 (Structural Timber Education Program): *Timber Engineering – Basis of Design, Material Properties, Structural Components and Joints;* Centrum Hout, Salland De Lange, Deventer 1995

Streng, Adolf V.: *Latinalais-suomalainen sanakirja;* Suomalaisen kirjallisuuden seuran toimituksia 196, Gummerrus Kirjapaino Oy, Jyväskylä 1992

Strengell, Gustaf: *Kaupunki taideluomana;* Otava, Helsinki 1923

Strengell, Gustaf: *Rakennus taideluomana;* Otava, Helsinki 1929

Strobel, Richard: *Romanische Architektur in Regensburg – Kapitell -Säule – Raum;* Verlag Hans Carl, Nürnberg 1965

Strong, Donald E.: *Kreikan ja Rooman taide – Maailmantaide 3;* Tammi, Helsinki 1967, ks. Maailmantaide

Strömbom, Sixten: *Egyptens konst;* Albert Bonniers Förlag, Stockholm 1928

Sundelin, Seppo; Ranska – suomi, opiskelusanakirja: WSOY, Porvoo – Helsinki – Juva 1993

Sundman, Mikael (ed.): *Nils Erik Wikberg 90 – 10.9.1999;* juhlakirja N.E.Wikbergin kunniaksi, Yliopistopaino, Helsinki 1999

Suomen betoniteollisuuden keskusjärjestö: *Tehdään betonista – betoni suomalaisessa arkkitehtuurissa;* Näyttelyluettelo, Suomen betoniteollisuuden keskusjärjestö and Suomen rakennustaiteen museo, Helsinki 1989

Suomen Betoniyhdistys & Teräsrakenneyhdistys: *Liittorakenteet, suunnitteluohjeet 1988, by 26;* Suomen Betonitieto Oy, Helsinki 1988

Suomen Betoniyhdistys: *Betoninormit 2000 by 15;* Suomen Betonitieto Oy, Gummerrus Kirjapaino Oy, Jyväskylä 2000

Suomen Betoniyhdistys: *Betonipinnat – by 40;* Suomen Betoniyhdistys ry, Gummerus Kirjapaino Oy, Jyväskylä 1995

Suomen Betoniyhdistys: *Betonipinnat, luokitusohjeet – by 13;* Suomen Betoniyhdistys ry, Yleisjäljennös Oy 1985

Suomen Betoniyhdistys: *Betonirakenteiden perusteiden oppikirja – by 203;* Suomen Betoniyhdistys ry, Gummerus Kirjapaino Oy, Jyväskylä 1995

Suomen Betoniyhdistys: *Betonitekniikan oppikirja – by 201;* Suomen Betoniyhdistys ry, Gummerus Kirjapaino Oy, Jyväskylä 1998

Suomen Betoniyhdistys: *Rappauskirja – by 46;* Suomen Betoniyhdistys ry and Suomen Betonititeto Oy, Lahden Kirjapaino ja Sanomalehti Oy, Lahti 1999

Suomen geoteknillinen yhdistys: *Geotekniikan sanasto;* Rakentajain Kustannus Oy, Jyväskylä 1990

Suomen kaupunkiliitto: *Suomen kaupunkilaitoksen historia 1-3;* Kunnallispaino Oy, Vantaa 1981-1984

Suomen Kiinteistöarviointiyhdistys ry: *Kiinteistöarviointisanasto;* Rakentajain Kustannus Oy, Helsinki 1986

Suomen Kiinteistöliitto: *Asuinkiinteistön hoito-opas;* Kiinteistöalan kustannus Oy – REP Ltd, Suomen Kiinteistöliitto, Gummerrus kirjapaino, Jyväskylä 1997

Suomen kunnallistekninen yhdistys: *Rakennusten vesijohdot ja viemärit;* SKTY:n julkaisu N:o 7, Helsinki 1987

Suomen Kuntatekniikan Yhdistys: *Betoni- ja luonnonkivituotteet päällysterakenteena, SKTY julkaisu 14;* Suomen Betonitieto Oy, Forssan Kirjapaino Oy, Forssa 1997

Suomen Liimapuuyhdistys ry: *Liimapuukäsikirja;* Wood Focus Oy/Suomen Liimapuuyhdistys ry, Helsinki, Print and Media Center i Sundsvall AB 2003

Suomen Liimapuuyhdistys ry: *Monitoimihallit – liimapuun käyttösuurten hallien kantavissa rakenteissa;* Rakentajain Kustannus Oy, Vammalan Kirjapaino Oy, Vammala 1988

Suomen Rakennushallinto 1811-1961: Rakennushallitus, Valtion Painatuskeskus, Helsinki 1967

Suomen Rakennusinsinoörien liitto RIL: *Betonielementtirakenteet, RIL 115;* Suomen Rakennusinsinöörien liitto, Helsinki 1977, K.J. Gummerrus Oy, Jyväskylä

Suomen Rakennusinsinoörien liitto RIL: *Betonityöohjeet RIL 149 – 1995;* Suomen Rakennusinsinöörien liitto, Helsinki 1995

Suomen Rakennusinsinoörien liitto RIL: *Geomekaniikka I-II, RIL 157;* Suomen Rakennusinsinöörien liitto, Helsinki 1990

Suomen Rakennusinsinoörien liitto RIL: *Korjausrakentaminen I-IV, RIL 174-1–174-4;* Suomen Rakennusinsinöörien liitto, Helsinki 1988

Suomen Rakennusinsinoörien liitto RIL: *Korjausrakentaminen V, RIL 174-5;* Suomen Rakennusinsinöörien liitto, Helsinki 1991

Suomen Rakennusinsinoörien liitto RIL: *Liikenne ja väylät I, RIL 165-1;* Suomen Rakennusinsinöörien liitto, Helsinki 1987

Suomen Rakennusinsinoörien liitto RIL: *Liikenne ja väylät II, RIL 165-2;* Suomen Rakennusinsinöörien liitto, Helsinki 1988

Suomen Rakennusinsinoörien liitto RIL: *Maarakennus, RIL 156;* Suomen Rakennusinsinöörien liitto, Helsinki 1995

Suomen Rakennusinsinoörien liitto RIL: *Muuratut rakenteet, RIL 99;* Suomen Rakennusinsinöörien liitto, Helsinki 1975, K.J. Gummerrus Oy, Jyväskylä

Suomen Rakennusinsinoörien liitto RIL: *Pohjarakennusohjeet RIL 121-1988;* Suomen Rakennusinsinöörien Liitto RIL ry, Helsinki 1988

Suomen Rakennusinsinoörien liitto RIL: *Puurakenteet I RIL 162-1;* Suomen Rakennusinsinöörien Liitto RIL ry, Helsinki 1987

Suomen Rakennusinsinoörien liitto RIL: *Puurakenteet II RIL 162-2;* Suomen Rakennusinsinöörien Liitto RIL ry, Helsinki 1987

Suomen Rakennusinsinoörien liitto RIL: *Rakenteellinen palontorjunta, RIL 135;* Suomen Rakennusinsinöörien liitto, Helsinki 1981

Suomen Rakennusinsinoörien liitto RIL: *Sillat, RIL 179;* Suomen Rakennusinsinöörien liitto, Helsinki 1989

Suomen Rakennusinsinoörien liitto RIL: *Talonrakennuksen maatöiden työselitys, RIL 132-1987;* Suomen Rakennusinsinöörien liitto, Helsinki 1987

Suomen Rakennusinsinoörien liitto RIL: *Tunneli- ja kalliorakennus I; RIL 154-1;* Suomen Rakennusinsinöörien liitto, Helsinki 1987

Suomen Rakennusinsinoörien liitto RIL: *Urheilulaitokset, RIL 118;* Suomen Rakennusinsinöörien liitto, Helsinki 1988

Suomen Rakennusinsinoörien liitto RIL: *Vesihuolto, RIL 124;* Suomen Rakennusinsinöörien liitto, Helsinki 1981

Suomen Rakennusinsinoörien liitto RIL: *Yleinen vesitekniikka, RIL 141;* Suomen Rakennusinsinöörien liitto, Helsinki 1982

Suomen Rakennusinsinoörien liitto RIL: *Ääneneristyksen toteuttaminen RIL 129; Suomen Rakennusinsinöörien Liitto RIL ry, Helsinki 2003*

Suomen rakennusinsinoöriliitto RIL: *Lämmön- ja kosteudeneristys, RIL 155;* Suomen Rakennusinsinööriliitto, Helsinki 1984

Suomen Rakennusinsinoöriliitto RIL: *Rakennusalan sanakirja suomi-englanti-viro, RIL 188;* Suomen Rakennusinsinööriliitto, Helsinki 1994

Suomen rakennusinsinoöriliitto RIL: *Rakennusalan sanakirja venäjä-englanti-suomi, RIL 199;* Suomen Rakennusinsinööriliitto, Helsinki 1994

Suomen Rakennusteollisuusliitto: *Muottityöt – rakennusalan ammattioppi;* WSOY, Porvoo-Helsinki 1976

Suomen Rakennuttajaliitto: *Rakennusten vastaan- ja käyttöönotto – yleiset periaatteet;* Rakennuskirja Oy, Kauppa- ja teollisuusministeriö ja Suomen Rakennuttajaliitto ry, Helsinki 1988

Suomen rakentamismääräyskokoelma: *A-yleinen osa; B-rakenteiden lujuus; C-eristykset; D- LVI- ja energiatalous; E-rakenteellinen paloturvallisuus; F-yleinen rakennussuunnittelu; G-asuntorakentaminen;* Helsinki 1976–2003

Suomen Sähköurakoitsijaliitto: *Sähköasennukset 1-2;* Sähköurakoitsijaliiton Koulutus ja Kustannus Oy, Espoo, Forssan kirjapaino 1991

Suomen Sähköurakoitsijaliitto: *Sähköasennusopas;* Sähköinfo Oy, Espoo, Tammer-Paino Oy 1996

Suomen Sähköurakoitsijaliitto: *Sähköasennusten käsikirja I-II;* Sähköurakoitsijaliiton Koulutus ja Kustannus Oy, Espoo, Gummerrus kirjapaino Oy 1992

Suomen tieyhdistys: *Auto ja tie 1995 – Automobiles and Highways in Finland;* Tieyhdistyksen vuosijulkaisu, Nordmanin Kirjapaino Oy, Forssa 1995

Suomen tieyhdistys: *Tie- ja liikennesanasto;* Suomen tieyhdistys

Suomen tiiliteollisuusliitto ry & Teräsrakenneyhdistys ry: *Tiili ja teräs – tiiliverhouksen käyttöteräsrakenteiden yhteydessä;* Rakentajain kustannus Oy, Tammer-Paino Oy, Tampere 1991

Suomen vaneriyhdistys: *Sanasto – vocabulary – nomenklatur – vocabulaire;* SFS 2290 (ISO Recommendation n:o 2074), moniste

Suortti-Suominen, Tuula: *Pientalon perustusopas;* Rakentajain Kustannus, Rakennustieto Oy, Tampere 1995

Suuri maailmanhistoria 1-15: *Bokförlaget Bra Böcker, Höganäs, Koko kansan kirjakerho Oy, Brepols 1983-1987*

Suvanto, Kylliki: *Ikoni – erilainen kuva;* Ortodoksisten nuorten liitto – ONL ry., 1990

Swaan, Wim: *Die Grossen Kathedralen;* Verlag M.DuMont Schauberg, Köln 1969

Sähkötarkastuskeskus: *Rakennusten sähköasennukset;* Sähkötarkastuskeskus, julkaisu A2-94, Helsinki 1994

Särkinen, Åke W.: *Jälleenrakennusajan pientalo;* Rakennustieto Oy, Helsinki 2005

Taidehistoriallisia tutkimuksia: *Motiivi ja metodi;* Taidehistoriallisia tutkimuksia – Konsthistoriska studier 20, Gummerrus Kirjapaino Oy, Jyväskylä 1999

Taipale, Kalle: *Kivet – etsijän ja keräilijän opas;* WSOY, Porvoo 1995

Taiteen pikkujättiläinen: *WSOY, Porvoo 1989*

Taloustieto, Oy: *Taloussanasto – yritys- ja kansantaloutta suomeksi, ruotsiksi, englanniksi, saksaksi ja ranskaksi;* Taloustieto Oy 1994, Tammer-Paino Oy

Talvitie – Hytönen – Palovuori – Talvitie: *Englanti-suomi tekniikan ja kaupan sanakirja;* WSOY, Porvoo Helsinki Juva 1995

Talvitie, Jyrki K. & Hiltunen, Juha: *Mayamaa – muinaisten mayojen maailmaa tämän päivän ihmiselle;* Tietoteos Ky, Espoo 1993

Talvitie, Jyrki K. & Hytönen, Ahti: *Suomi-englanti tekniikan ja kaupan sanakirja;* WSOY, Porvoo Helsinki Juva 1995

Tammela, Viljo: *Polymeeritiede ja muoviteknologia, osa 3;* Otatieto 519, Otakustantamo, Hakapaino Oy, Helsinki 1990

Tampereen taidemuseo: *Muinainen Egypti – hetki ikuisuudesta;* Näyttelyluettelo 30.8.1993 – 2.1.1994, Tampereen taidemuseon julkaisuja nr. 51, Tampere 1993

Tattari, Juho: *Puusepän oppikirja;* Käsiteollisuuskirjasto nro 27, Otava, Helsinki 1951

Tee se itse, käsikirja: *Osa 1: työohjeet, osa 2: työkohteet;* Oy Valitut Palat -Reader's Digest Ab, Sanomapaino, Helsinki 1979

Tekes: *Asiakaslähtöinen teollinen rakentaminen – teollisen rakentamisen teknologiaohjelma;* Tekes, Helsinki 1992; Tammer-Paino Oy, Tampere 1992

Tekniikan käsikirja: *Liikennetekniikka, osa 6;* K.J.Gummerrus Oy, Jyväskylä 1975

Tekniikan käsikirja: *Lämpö- ja talonrakennustekniikka, osa 5;* K.J.Gummerrus Oy, Jyväskylä 1970

Tekniikan sanastokeskus: *Energiasanasto;* LVI-kustannus Oy, Helsinki 1989

Tekniikan sanastokeskus: *Kiinteistösanasto;* Rakennuskirja Oy, Jyväskylä 1984

Tekniikan sanastokeskus: *Palontorjuntasanasto;* Rakennuskirja Oy, Suomen Palontorjuntaliitto, Jyväskylä 1984

Tekniikan sanastokeskus: *Rikosilmoitusssanasto;* Rakennuskirja Oy, Jyväskylä 1984

Temporini, Hildergard & Haase, Wolfgang: *Aufstieg und Niedergang der römischen Welt – Principat II – Geschichte und Kultur Roms in Spiegel der neueren Forschung;* Walter de Gruyter, Berlin – New York, 1977

Thompson, Jan: *Matematiikan käsikirja;* Tammi, Helsinki 1994

Thomsen, Rudi: *Kulttuurien synty 1200eKr – 200eKr;* Suuri maailmanhistoria, osa 2, Bokförlaget Bra Böcker, Höganäs, Koko kansan kirjakerho Oy, Brepols 1983

Thurell, Sören: *Vård av trähus – en handbok i vård och upprustning av gammal träbyggelse;* LTs förlag, Stockholm 1975

Tiehallinto: *Perustamis- ja vahvistamistyöt – tienrakennustöiden yleiset laatuvaatimukset ja työselitykset;* Tielaitos, Edita Oyj, Helsinki 2001

Tiehallinto: *Porapaalutusohje – suunnittelu ja toteututtamisvaiheen ohjaus;* Tielaitos, Edita Oyj, Helsinki 2001

Tiehallinto: *Sillanrakentamisen laaduntarkastusohje – SILTO – Toteuttamisvaiheen ohjaus;* Tielaitos, Edita Prima Oy, Helsinki 2003

Tiehallinto: *Tasoliittymät – suunnitteluvaiheen ohjaus;* Tielaitos, Oy Edita Ab, Helsinki 2001

Tielaitos: *Yleiset tiet kaava-alueilla – Kaavojen vaikutus tienpitoon, kaavoitus yleisten teiden kannalta, yhteistyö;* Tiehallitus, Helsinki 1992

Tietotekniikan sanasto: Kustantaja Tietosanoma Oy, Probe Ky, Helsinki, WSOY:n graafiset laitokset, Juva 1990

Tietz, Jürgen: *1900-luvun arkkitehtuuri;* Könemann Verlagsgesellschaft, Köln 2000

Tiilikeskus: *Tiilirakenteiden pinnat:* Tiilikeskus Oy, Helsinki, 1979

Tiira, Seppo: *Vuolukivi rakennuskivenä;* Suomen Vuolukivi Oy, Kirjapaino Oy Maakunta, Joensuu 1986

Tikka, Martti: *Käytännön geodesia II – mittauskojeet;* Otakustantamo Nro 439, Otapaino, Espoo 1980

Tikka, Martti: *Käytännön geodesia I – mittaustekniikan perusteet ja rakennusteknilliset sovellukset;* Otakustantamo Nro 495, Kyriiri Oy, Helsinki 1989

Tiula, Martti: *Asunnon remonttiopas;* Rakennustieto Oy Rakentajain Kustannus, Tammer-Paino, Tampere 1993

Tiula, Martti: *Rakennuspiirustus – määräykset, standardit, ohjeet;* Rakennuskirja Oy, Jyväskylä 1982

TNC 59: *Geoteknisk ordlista – Glossary of Geotechnics;* Tekniska nomenklaturentralens publikationer nr. 59, Stockholm 1975

Tobolczyk, Marta: *Narodziny architektury- Wstep do ontogenecy architektury;* Wydawnictwo Naukowe PWN, Warszawa 2000

Tolvanen, Jouko: *Taidesanakirja;* Otava, Helsinki 1967

Tommila, Päiviö, Reitala, Aimo & Kallio, Veikko: *Suomen kulttuurihistoria I-III;* WSOY, Porvoo-Helsinki-Juva, 1980-1982

Tønnesson, Kåre: *Kaksi vallankumousta 1750-1815;* Suuri maailmanhistoria, osa 10, Bokförlaget Bra Böcker, Höganäs, Koko kansan kirjakerho Oy, Brepols 1986

Turun maakuntamuseo: *Riitmotti ja sapluuna – rakentaminen ja asuminen isomummun aikaan;* Näytttelyesite 30, Turun maakuntamuseo, Uusikaupunki 2002

Tägil, Sven: *Tulevaisuutta kohti 1965;* Suuri maailmanhistoria, osa 15, Bokförlaget Bra Böcker, Höganäs, Koko kansan kirjakerho Oy, Brepols 1987

Uusitalo, Jukka – Ihanamäki, Jouko – Rajala, Raimo – Vallin, Olavi: *Betonityöt, by 205;* Rakennustieto Oy, Jyväskylä 1994

Vainio, Martti & Niemi, Markku J.: *LVI-tekniikka;* WSOY, Porvoo-Helsinki-Juva, 1993

Valmet Oy: *Raaka-ainekäsikirja 4, muovit ja kumit;* Valmet Oy, Rautpohja , Tampere 1984

Valonen, Niilo & Vuoristo, Osmo: *Suomen kansanrakennukset;* Museovirasto, Vammalan Kirjapaino Oy 1994

Vanamo, Pekka: *Puusepän aineoppi;* Arvi A. Karisto Oy, Hämeenlinna 1960

Vehniä, Ari: *Kiinteistöjen valvontajärjestelmät;* Suomen Rakennuttajaliitto, Rakennustieto Oy, Helsinki 1995

Viherjuuri, H.J.: *Saunaopas;* Otava, Helsinki 1944

Viitala, H. (ed.): *Kirkkojen kunnostus ja pappilakulttuuri;* Snellman-instituutin B-sarja 16, Kuopio 1990

Viljakainen, Mikko: *Platform pientalo-opas – suunnittelu ja rakentaminen;* Puuinfo Oy, Vammala 1999

Viljakainen, Mikko: *Puukerrostalo;* Tampereen teknillinen korkeakoulu, Puuinfo Oy, Rakennustieto Oy, Tampere 1997

Virkkunen, Marjatta & Partanen, Seppo J.: *Suomen kivet;* Suomen Matkailuliitto, Gummerrus Kirjapaino Oy, Jyväskylä 1995

Visanti, Irmeli & Markus: *Takkapiirustuksia;* Tammi, Helsinki 1977

Watson, William: *China – Kunst und Kultur;* Verlag Herbert Freiburg im Breisgau 1982

Weber, Max: *Kaupunki;* Vastapaino, Sivilisaatiohistoria-sarja, Tampere 1992

Weck, Tor-Ulf: *Rakennustekniikan perusteet – Statiikka ja lujuusoppi;* TKK, Arkkitehtiosasto, Rakennussuunnittelun laitoksen julkaisu B 27/88, Otaniemi 1988

Weck, Tor-Ulf: *Talonrakennustekniikka;* TKK, Arkkitehtiosasto, Rakennussuunnittelun laitoksen julkaisu B 28/88, Otaniemi 1988

Wegelius – Lippa – Ruso: *Talonrakennustekniikan käsikirja 1-2;* Kirjamies, Helsinki 1953

Westermarck, Mikael & Heuru, Eeva-Riitta & Lundsten, Bengt: *Luonnonmukaiset rakennusaineet;* Teknillinen korkeakoulu, Arkkitehtiosaston julkaisuja 1998/46, Rakennuskirja Oy, Helsinki 1998

Weyres, Willy & Bartning, Otto: *Kirchen- Handbuch für den Kirchenbau;* Verlag Georg D.W. Callwey, München 1959

Wickberg, Nils Erik: *Städer, byggnader...;* Söderström and C:o Förlagsaktiebolag, Helsingfors, Ekenäs Tryckeri Ab, Ekenäs 1989

Winckelmann, Johann Joachim: *Jalosta yksinkertaisuudesta – kirjoituksia antiikin taiteesta ja arkkitehtuurista;* VAPK-kustannus, Kuvataideakatemia, Helsinki 1992

Winterhalter, Katri: *Kaksi työmaadokumentointia – kaksi näkökulmaa 1800-luvun rapatun julkisivun ornamentiikkaan ja materiaaleihin;* diplomityö Teknillisen korkeakoulun arkkitehtiosastolla 1999

Wrangel, E.: *Konststilarna – en kort framställning af arkitekturens och ornamentikens utveckling;* C.W.K. Gleerups förlag, Berlingska boktryckeriet, Lund 1905

Würth: *Tekniikan käsikirja;* Adolf Würth GmbH and Co. KG, Frohne Druck, Bad Salzuflen, 1990

Wäre, Ritva & Pakkanen, Jari & Saarikoski, Antero: *Taidehistorian opintomoniste, osa 3: Terminologia* Helsingin yliopiston taidehistorian laitos, Helsinki 1992

YJK: *Mitäyhdyskuntasuunnittelu on 1980-luvulla;* Harjoitustyö lukuvuonna 1982-1983, Yhdyskuntasuunnittelun jatkokoulutuskeskuksen julkaisu B 45, TKK, Espoo 1983

Ylilammi, Markku: *Sähkömateriaalifysiikka;* Otakustantamo nro 868, Helsinki 1989

Yrjölä, Pekka (toim.): *Stala-350 – Suunnittelijan putkipalkkikäsikirja;* Stala Oy, Kirjapaino Markprint, Lahti 1995

YTV Pääkaupunkiseudun yhteistyövaltuuskunta: *Maankäytön ja liikenteen suunnittelun keinoja ilmansuojelun ja meluntorjunnan edistämiseksi;* Pääkaupunkiseudun julkaisusarja B 2002:9, Helsinki 2002

Zechlin, Ruth & Olki, Mary: *Veistotöitä- nuoriso askartelee 2;* WSOY, Porvoo-Helsinki, 1956

Zevi, Bruno: *Storia e controstoria dell'architettura in Italia;* Grandi Tascabili Economici Newton, Roma 1997

Ågren, Kurt: *Uusi Eurooppa 1500-1750;* Suuri maailmanhistoria, osa 8, Bokförlaget Bra Böcker, Höganäs, Koko kansan kirjakerho Oy, Brepols 1986

Östergaard, Troels V. & Jensen, Gregers: *Kivet ja lohkareet;* Tammi, Helsinki 1979

Architects and locations referred to in the illustrations